The SAGE Handbook *of*
Social Science
Methodology

The SAGE Handbook *of*
Social Science
Methodology

Edited by

William Outhwaite and
Stephen P. Turner

Los Angeles • London • New Delhi • Singapore

Introductions and editorial arrangement © William Outhwaite and
Stephen P. Turner 2007
Chapters 1–32 © SAGE Publications Ltd 2007

First published 2007

SAGE Publications Ltd
1 Oliver's Yard
55 City Road
London EC1Y 1SP

SAGE Publications Inc.
2455 Teller Road
Thousand Oaks, California 91320

SAGE Publications India Pvt Ltd
B 1/I 1 Mohan Cooperative Industrial Area
Mathura Road
New Delhi 110 044

SAGE Publications Asia-Pacific Pte Ltd
33 Pekin Street #02-01
Far East Square
Singapore 048763

Library of Congress Control Number: 2006934307

British Library Cataloguing in Publication data

A catalogue record for this book is available from
the British Library

ISBN 0 978-1-4129-0119-2

Typeset by C&M Digitals (P) Ltd., Chennai, India
Printed in Great Britain by The Cromwell Press, Trowbridge
Printed on paper from sustainable resources

Contents

Notes on Contributors

Ben Agger is Professor of Sociology and Humanities at the University of Texas at Arlington. He also directs the Center for Theory there. He edits the electronic journal *Fast Capitalism* (www.fastcapitalism.com). Among his recent books are *Speeding Up Fast Capitalism* and the forthcoming *Fast Families, Virtual Children* (with Beth Anne Shelton), both with Paradigm Publishers. He is working on a book about the 1960s, *The Sixties at 40: Radicals Remember and Look Forward*.

Margo Anderson is Professor of History and Urban Studies at the University of Wisconsin, Milwaukee. She received her Ph.D. in History from Rutgers University in 1978. Her research and teaching interests have focused on the history of the social sciences and the development of official data systems, particularly censuses and surveys. She has published several books on the history of the American census, most notably *The American Census: A Social History* (Yale University Press, 1988); and with Stephen E. Fienberg, *Who Counts? The Politics of Census Taking in Contemporary America* (Russell Sage Foundation, revised edition, 2001). She teaches American labor, urban and women's history, and has taught quantitative history since the late 1970s. She taught Quantitative Historical Analysis in the ICPSR Summer Program from 1991 to 1995 and from 1996 to 2001, and she also served as a member (1998–2003) and chair (2000–2002) of the ICPSR Council. In 2006 she served as the president of the Social Science History Association. Her current research focuses on the use of population data in time of war and the ethical issues surrounding public data use.

Adele E. Clarke is Professor of Sociology and History of Health Sciences at U.C. San Francisco. Her research areas include the historical sociology of biomedical sciences and technologies, qualitative research methodologies, women's health and 'things medical' and globalization. Dr. Clarke's book, *Disciplining Reproduction: Modernity, American Life Sciences and the 'Problems of Sex'* (University of California Press, 1998) won the Eileen Basker Memorial Prize given by the Society for Medical Anthropology, and the Ludwig Fleck Award of the Society for Social Studies of Science. Her latest book, *Situational Analysis: Grounded Theory After the Postmodern Turn* (Sage, 2005), won the Charles Horton Cooley Award of the Society for the Study of Symbolic Interaction.

Norman K. Denzin Distinguished Professor of Communications at University of Illinois at Urbana Champaign; Research Professor of Communications, Cinema Studies, Sociology, Criticism and Interpretive Theory; received his Ph.D. from the University of Iowa in 1966. He joined the Sociology Department at Illinois in 1966. Professor Denzin's academic interests include interpretive theory, performance studies, qualitative research methodology, and the study of media, culture and society. He is the author, co-author or co-editor of over 50 books and 200 professional articles and chapters. He is the past president of The Midwest Sociological Society, and the Society for the Study of Symbolic Interaction. He is founding president of the International Association of Qualitative Inquiry (2005–), and director of the International Center of Qualitative Inquiry (2005–). He is past editor of *The Sociological Quarterly*, founding co-editor of *Qualitative Inquiry*, and founding editor of *Cultural Studies-Critical Methodologies*, and *Studies in Symbolic Interaction: A Research Annual.*

Thad Dunning is Assistant Professor of Political Science at Yale University and a research fellow at Yale's MacMillan Center for International and Area Studies. His recent research focuses on the influence of natural resource wealth on the development of political institutions. He has also written on a range of methodological topics, including the use of natural experiments in the social sciences. Dunning's previous work has appeared in *International Organization*, *The Journal of Conflict Resolution*, *Studies in Comparative International Development*, and *Geopolitics*. He received a Ph.D. degree in political science and an M.A. degree in economics from the University of California, Berkeley.

Ricca Edmondson is senior lecturer in political science and sociology at the National University of Ireland, Galway. Her training and subsequent work in Lancaster, Oxford and Berlin allowed her to combine philosophy, politics, sociology and ethnography, in the belief that argumentation, in the social sciences and elsewhere, cannot be understood except interdisciplinarily. Previous books have dealt with rhetoric, organizations and culture; she has also published on social capital, time, ageing, health and interculturality. She co-edits two book series on interdisciplinary approaches to the problems of modernity, and co-convenes the network on Ageing in the European Sociological Association. Recent research fellowships have come from the Irish Research Council for the Humanities and the Institute for Advanced Studies in the Humanities at the University of Edinburgh. She is now working on an international project on the idea of wisdom and its application to fields such as argumentation and ageing.

Justin Fox is Assistant Professor of Political Science, Yale University. His research interests include political economy and American political institutions. His current research addresses the impact that fundraising considerations have on the policies pursued by lawmakers. He has published in the *Journal of Theoretical Politics* and *Public Choice.*

David A. Freedman is professor of statistics at U.C. Berkeley, and a former chairman of the department. He has been Sloan Professor and Miller Professor, and is a member of the American Academy of Arts and Sciences. He has written several books, including a widely used elementary text, as well as many papers in probability and statistics. He has worked on martingale inequalities, Markov processes, de Finetti's theorem, consistency of Bayes estimates, sampling, the bootstrap, procedures for testing and evaluating models, census adjustment, epidemiology, statistics and the law. In 2003, he received the John J. Carty Award for the Advancement of Science from the National Academy of Sciences. He has worked as a consultant for the Carnegie Commission, the City of San Francisco, and the Federal Reserve, as well as several departments of the US Government—Energy, Treasury, Justice, and Commerce. He has testified as an expert witness on statistics in a number of law cases, including *Piva v. Xerox* (employment discrimination), *Garza v. County of Los Angeles* (voting rights), and *New York v. Department of Commerce* (census adjustment).

Kenneth J. Gergen is Research Professor of Psychology at Swarthmore College, and the President of the Board of the Taos Institute. He is also the Associate Editor of *Theory and Psychology*, a position in which he has also served for the *American Psychologist*. Among his most notable books are *Realities and Relationships, The Saturated Self,* and *An Invitation to Social Construction*. He is a co-editor of *Horizons in Buddhist Psychology*. Most recently he has been exploring issues in relational theory, representation as performance, cultural psychology, and dialogic practice. He is a fellow in several divisions of the American Psychological Association.

Mary M. Gergen, Professor Emerita, Psychology and Women's Studies, Penn State University, Delaware County, is a scholar at the intersection of feminist theory and social constructionism. Her most recent book is *Feminist Reconstructions in Psychology: Narrative, Gender and Performance*. With Kenneth Gergen, she has edited *Social Construction, A Reader*, and co-authored *Social Constructionism, Entering the Dialogue*. She is also a founder and board member of the Taos Institute, and has been active in promoting alternative methodologies and presentational forms for many years. She is a fellow of the Society for the Psychology of Women, American Psychological Association.

Donald P. Green is A. Whitney Griswold Professor of Political Science at Yale University, where he has taught since 1989. Since 1996, he has served as director of Yale's Institution for Social and Policy Studies, an interdisciplinary research center that emphasizes field experimentation. His research interests span a wide array of topics: voting behavior, partisanship, campaign finance, rationality, research methodology and hate crime. His recent books include *Partisan Hearts and Minds: Political Parties and the Social Identities of Voters* (Yale University Press, 2002) and *Get Out the Vote!: How to Increase Voter Turnout* (Brookings Institution Press, 2004). In 2003, he was elected Fellow of the American Academy of Arts and Sciences.

John R. Hall, Professor of Sociology at the University of California, Davis, has also served as Director of the UC Davis Center for History, Society, and Culture, and Director of the University of California Edinburgh Study Centre. His scholarly research spans epistemology, social theory, economy and society, the sociology of religion, and the sociology of culture. His published books include an edited volume, *Reworking Class* (Cornell University Press, 1997), *Cultures of Inquiry: From Epistemology to Discourse in Sociohistorical Research* (Cambridge University Press, 1999), *Apocalypse Observed: Religious Movements and Violence in North America, Europe, and Japan*, co-authored by Philip D. Schuyler and Sylvaine Trinh (Routledge, 2000), *Sociology on Culture*, co-authored by Mary Jo Neitz and Marshall Battani (Routledge, 2003), and *Visual Worlds*, co-edited by Blake Stimson and Lisa Tamiris Becker (Routledge, 2005). His current research focuses on apocalyptic terrorism and modernity.

Leslie A. Hayduk is Professor of Sociology at the University of Alberta. He has published several articles and two books on structural equation modeling, and is a co-author of two books on the sociology of education. He has been an active participant on the SEMNET web discussion group for the past several years. His research interests span the physiological/biological foundations of sociology, social psychology, and structural equation modeling. His recent publications have addressed issues like an improved definition of R^2 (the blocked-error-R^2), the development of a new class of indicators (reactive indicators), and a demonstration that cancer-fighting T-cell activity (with or without interferon-γ) is better measured at low effector/target cell ratios. He introduced the saying: A picture is worth a thousand words, but is only worth a thousandth of an equation, Picture = 1000Word = .001Equation.

Susan Hekman is a Professor of Political Science and the Director of Graduate Humanities at the University of Texas at Arlington. Her most recent books are *The Future of Differences: Truth and Method in Feminist Theory* and *Private Selves, Public Identities: Toward a Theory of Identity Politics*.

David Henderson is Professor of Philosophy at the University of Memphis. He received his Ph.D. from Washington University in St Louis. He has published numerous articles in the philosophy of the social sciences, many focusing on questions concerning the role of rationality in the social and psychological sciences. Some of this work coalesced in *Interpretation and Explanation in the Human Sciences* (1993). He has produced related work on conceptual schemes, and on the respective roles in interpretive understanding of empirical results and of capacities for simulating others. Recent publications have also addressed central issues in epistemology. These include an account of objectively justified belief (one that makes principled room for both coherentist and foundationalist themes), discussions of the implications of recent work in cognitive science for contemporary epistemology, and a revisionist account of *a priori* knowledge. Much of his work in epistemology has been undertaken jointly with Terrence Horgan of the University of Arizona.

David C. Howell is Emeritus Professor at the University of Vermont. After gaining his Ph.D. from Tulane University in 1967, he was on the faculty of the Department of Psychology at the University of Vermont. He retired as chair of the department in 2002. He also spent two separate years as Visiting Professor at the Universities of Durham and Bristol in the United Kingdom. Professor Howell is the author of several books and many journal papers, and he continues to write and serve on editorial boards even after retiring. His latest project was the *Encyclopedia of Statistics in Behavioral Science*, of which he and Brian Everitt were editors-in-chief. Professor Howell now lives in Colorado, where he has all of the outdoor recreational opportunities anyone could want, as well as the time to remain professionally active.

Douglas Kellner is George F. Kneller Chair in the Philosophy of Education at UCLA and is the author of many books on social theory, politics, history and culture, including works in cultural studies such as *Media Culture* and *Media Spectacle*; a trilogy of books on postmodern theory with Steve Best; a trilogy of books on the Bush administration, including *Grand Theft 2000*, *From 9/11 to Terror War*, and his latest text *Media Spectacle and the Crisis of Democracy*. His website is at http://www.gseis.ucla.edu/faculty/kellner/kellner.html.

Julie Thompson Klein is Professor of Humanities in the Department of Interdisciplinary Studies at Wayne State University. She has also held visiting posts in Japan, Nepal and New Zealand; was a Senior Fellow at the Association of American Colleges and Universities; and received the final prize in the Eesteren-Fluck & Van Lohuizen Foundation's international competition for new research models and the Kenneth Boulding Award for outstanding scholarship on interdisciplinarity. Klein has served on numerous national and international task forces and advisory groups on interdiscipinary and transdisciplinary approaches to research, education and problem-solving. Her authored and edited books include *Interdisciplinarity: History, Theory, and Practice* (1990), *Interdisciplinary Studies Today* (1994), *Crossing Boundaries: Knowledge, Disciplinarities, and Interdisciplinarities* (1996), *Transdisciplinarity: Joint Problem Solving among Science, Technology, and Society* (2001), *Interdisciplinary Education in K-12 and College* (2002), the monograph *Mapping Interdisciplinary Studies* (1999), and *Humanities, Culture, and Interdisciplinarity: The Changing American Academy* (2005).

Hans-Herbert Kögler is Chair Professor of Philosophy at the University of North Florida, Jacksonville. He received his Dr. Phil. at the Goethe University of Frankfurt (advisor J. Habermas) after graduate studies at Northwestern, the New School, and the University of California at Berkeley. His research centers on the methodological grounds of understanding and criticism in the human and social sciences, a hermeneutic theory of cultural self-identity and the normative implications of interpretation. Major publications include *The Power of*

Dialogue: Critical Hermeneutics after Gadamer and Foucault, (1999); *Michel Foucault* (2nd edition, 2004) and the co-edited volume *Empathy and Agency: The Problem of Understanding in the Human Sciences* (2000). In 1997, the journal *Social Epistemology* dedicated a special issue to Kögler's article 'Alienation as Epistemological Source: Reflexivity and Social Background after Mannheim and Bourdieu'. His further work includes many journal articles and book chapters in English and German as well as translations into Czech, Russian, and French. He has been invited to serve as guest professor at the University of Klagenfurt, Austria, and the Czech Academy of Social Sciences, Prague. Since 2005 Kögler has coordinated the newly inaugurated graduate program M.A. in Practical Philosophy & Applied Ethics at UNF.

John Law is a Professor at Lancaster University in Sociology and the Centre for Science Studies. With a background in both sociology and Science, Technology and Society (STS), he is interested in disorder, multiple orderings and materialities. He works primarily on nature and culture, agriculture, spatiality, and catastrophes, and he is currently exploring the 2001 UK foot and mouth epizootic. His most recent book, *After Method* (Routledge, 2004), is on methodologies for knowing disorderly phenomena, and it brings together humanities and social science insights to propose a much more generous and inclusive understanding of research method that is able to deal with 'mess'. His website is at http://www.lancs.ac.uk/fss/sociology/staff/law/law.htm.

Tyson Lewis received his Ph.D. in educational philosophy from UCLA in 2006 and is currently an assistant professor of education at Montclair State University. His work in the fields of educational theory and cultural studies has appeared in such journals as *Educational Theory*, *Educational Philosophy and Theory*, *The Philosophy of Education Society's Yearbook*, *Utopian Studies* (with Richard Kahn), and *Cultural Critique* (with Daniel Cho). Currently his research focuses on the relation between critical theory, critical pedagogy and the emerging field of biopolitics.

Michael Lynch is a Professor and Director of Graduate Studies in the Department of Science & Technology Studies, Cornell University. As a student and collaborator of Harold Garfinkel, he took an ethnomethodological approach to natural science practices during doctoral and post-doctoral studies at UC, Irvine and UCLA. His book, *Art and Artifact in Laboratory Science* (1985) was part of the first wave of ethnographic studies of laboratories in social studies of science. His book, *Scientific Practice and Ordinary Action* (1993), critically reviewed research in ethnomethodology and social studies of science, and recommended non-foundational empirical investigations of the topics of epistemology: practices of measurement, observation and representation in specific settings of ordinary and scientific inquiry. The book won the 1995 Robert K. Merton Professional Award from the American Sociological Association. His current research examines the interplay between law and science in criminal cases involving DNA evidence. He is currently editor of *Social Studies of Science*, and was recently elected president of the Society for Social Studies of Science (4S).

Peter T. Manicas is currently Director of Interdisciplinary Studies at the University of Hawai'i at Mānoa. He has published widely in the philosophy of social science, and social and political philosophy. In addition to many articles published in range of academic disciplines, his books include: *A History and Philosophy of the Social Sciences* (1987), *War and Democracy* (1989), *Social Process in Hawai'i: A Reader* (2004), *Globalization and Higher Education* (with Jaishree K. Odin, 2004) and, most recently, *A Realist Philosophy of Social Science* (2006).

Jon P. Mitchell is Reader in Anthropology at the University of Sussex. He has written on the anthropology of politics and identity, religion and ritual, performance, memory and modernity, primarily in the Mediterranean context of Malta. His books include *Ambivalent Europeans:*

Ritual, memory and the public sphere in Malta (Routledge, 2002), *Powers of Good and Evil: Social transformation and popular belief* (ed., with Paul Clough, Berghahn, 2002), *Human Rights in Global Perspective* (ed., with Richard Ashby Wilson, Routledge, 2003), and a special issue of *Journal of Mediterranean Studies,* 'Modernity in the Mediterranean' (2002). He is currently working with Helena Wulff (Stockholm) and Marit Melhuus (Oslo) on an edited volume on the current state of ethnography in anthropological research, entitled *Present Ethnography.*

Nancy A. Naples is Professor of Sociology and Women's Studies at the University of Connecticut where she teaches courses on qualitative methodology; contemporary social theory; feminist theory; feminist methodology; sexual citizenship; gender, politics and the state; and women's activism and globalization, She is author of *Feminism and Method: Ethnography, Discourse Analysis, and Feminist Research* (Routledge, 2003) and *Grassroots Warriors: Activist Mothering, Community Work, and the War on Poverty* (Routledge, 1998). She is also editor of *Community Activism and Feminist Politics: Organizing Across Race, Class, and Gender* (Routledge, 1998) and co-editor of *Women's Activism and Globalization: Linking Local Struggles with Transnational Politics* (with Manisha Desai) and *Teaching Feminist Activism* (with Karen Bojar), both published by Routledge in 2002. Her next book, *Restructuring the Heartland: Racialization and the Social Regulation of Citizenship*, reports on a long-term ethnographic study of economic and social restructuring in two small towns in Iowa. She is currently working on a comparative intersectional analysis of sexual citizenship and immigration policies.

Maureen A. O'Malley is currently a Research Fellow at Egenis, University of Exeter, where she examines philosophical and sociological issues in microbiology and systems biology. This work builds on her years in Ford Doolittle's lab at Dalhousie University in Halifax, Nova Scotia, where she studied evolutionary microbiology and was part of the university's interdisciplinary Evolutionary Study Group (http://evolutionstudygroup.biology.dal.ca/contents.html). The chapter she wrote for this anthology was greatly informed by involvement in that group's discussions and also draws on her earlier Ph.D. work, which compared a variety of evolutionary approaches in the social sciences and humanities with evolutionary biology.

William Outhwaite studied at the Universities of Oxford and Sussex, where he taught for over thirty years, and is now Professor of Sociology at Newcastle University. He is the author of *Understanding Social life: The Method Called Verstehen* (Allen & Unwin, 1975, second edition Jean Stroud, 1986); *Concept Formation in Social Science* (Routledge, 1983); *New Philosophies of Social Science: Realism, Hermeneutics and Critical Theory* (Macmillan, 1987); *Habermas. A Critical Introduction* (Polity Press, 1994), *The Future of Society* (Blackwell, 2006), and (with Larry Ray) *Social Theory and Postcommunism* (Blackwell, 2005). He edited *The Habermas Reader* (Polity Press, 1996); (with Tom Bottomore) *The Blackwell Dictionary of Twentieth-Century Social Thought* (Blackwell, 1993); *The Blackwell Dictionary of Modern Social Thought* (Blackwell, 1993); (with Luke Martell) *The Sociology of Politics* (Edward Elgar, 1998), and (with Margaret Archer) *Defending Objectivity* (Routledge, 2004). He is currently working on a book on Europe in society.

Piya Pangsapa is Assistant Professor in Women's Studies, University of Buffalo (SUNY) and researches gender, work and civic engagement in South East Asia. She is the author of *Textures of Struggle* (2007) as well as articles and papers on migration, women's rights and labor standards, ethnographic research methods and the cultural inclusivity of American universities. Her current work considers the impact of corporate responsibility on the global supply chain, the changing nature of factory production, and the status and citizenship rights of migrant workers. Her collaborative work with Mark J. Smith focuses on the construction of activist networks between NGOs, policy-making communities, state authorities, community groups, and local and regional campaigns on gender, labor and environmental issues, highlighting the importance of advocacy and leadership in the implementation and sustained monitoring of codes of responsible conduct in both developed and developing societies.

Hannah Pazderka-Robinson received her Ph.D. in Neuroscience from the University of Alberta. In 2004, she was awarded a one-month fellowship to study the human frontal lobes from the International Neuropsychological Society. She is interested in a number of different methodologies, including structural equation modeling, neuropsychological assessment, and electrophysiology. Her research interests are primarily in the area of mental health, particularly addictions and impulse control disorders. She is currently employed with the Alberta Mental Health Board as their Science and Academic Lead, and is affiliated with the University of Alberta as a sessional lecturer in psychology and a clinical lecturer in psychiatry. Her work has appeared in a number of journals including *Structural Equation Modeling*, the *International Journal of Psychophysiology*, *Psychopharmacology*, *BMC Medical Research Methodology*, and the *Canadian Journal of Public Health*.

Jennifer Platt is emeritus Professor of Sociology at the University of Sussex. Her research interests are in the history and sociology of sociology, and in aspects of research methods, including their history. Her relevant publications include 'Cases of cases ... of cases?' (1992), '"Case study" in American methodological thought' (1992), *A History of Sociological Research Methods in America, 1920–1960* (1996), and 'The history of the interview' (2002). She has been president of the British Sociological Association and of the ISA Research Committee on the History of Sociology, and is now Chair-Elect of the American Sociological Association Section on the History of Sociology.

Charles C. Ragin holds a joint appointment as Professor of Sociology and Political Science at the University of Arizona. In 2000/1 he was a Fellow at the Center for Advanced Study in the Behavioral Sciences at Stanford University, and before that he was Professor of Sociology and Political Science at Northwestern University. His main interests are methodology, political sociology and comparative-historical research, with a special focus on such topics as the welfare state, ethnic political mobilization and international political economy. His books include *Fuzzy-Set Social Science* (University of Chicago Press), *The Comparative Method: Moving Beyond Qualitative and Quantitative Strategies* (University of California Press), *Issues and Alternatives in Comparative Social Research* (E.J. Brill), *What is a Case? Exploring the Foundations of Social Research* (Cambridge University Press, with Howard S. Becker), and *Constructing Social Research: The Unity and Diversity of Method* (Pine Forge Press). He is also the author of more than a hundred articles in research journals and edited books, and he has developed two software packages for set-theoretic analysis of social data: *Qualitative Comparative Analysis* (QCA) and *Fuzzy-Set/Qualitative Comparative Analysis* (fsQCA). He has been awarded the Stein Rokkan Prize of the International Social Science Council, the Donald Campbell Award for Methodological Innovation by the Policy Studies Organization, and received honorable mention for the Barrington Moore, Jr. Award of the American Sociological Association. He has conducted academic workshops on methodology in Belgium, France, Germany, Italy, Japan, the Netherlands, Norway, South Korea, Taiwan, the United Kingdom, and for diverse audiences in the United States.

Michael Root is an Associate Professor of Philosophy at the University of Minnesota. He is the author of *Philosophy of Social Science: The Methods, Ideals and Politics of Social Inquiry* (Blackwell, 1993) and a number of articles on the use of racial classification in the social and biomedical sciences, including 'Race in the Social Sciences' (2007) and 'The Number of Black

Widows in the National Academy of Sciences' (2006). Besides his writing on issues in the philosophy of the social sciences, Root has written on the role of testimony in the transmission and confirmation of theories in the natural sciences.

Katherine E. Ryan is an Associate Professor in Educational Psychology at the University of Illinois. Her research interests include examining how democratic evaluation approaches might address educational accountability issues and high stakes assessment.

R. Keith Sawyer is Associate Professor of Education at Washington University in St. Louis. He studies creativity, collaboration, and learning. Dr. Sawyer's research focuses on the common elements to all three: improvisation and emergence. He has published over fifty articles and nine books, including *Social Emergence: Societies as Complex Systems* (2005, Cambridge) and *Explaining Creativity: The Science of Human Innovation* (2006, Oxford).

Sandra L. Schneider is Professor of Cognitive & Neural Sciences (CNS), Department of Psychology, University of South Florida. She recently transitioned from her position as Associate Dean for Research and Scholarship at the University of South Florida to her current assignment as Division Director, Behavioral and Cognitive Sciences, National Science Foundation. Her research focuses on cognitive and motivational processes in decision making. She edited, with J. Shanteau (2003), *Emerging Perspectives on Judgment and Decision Research*, and has most recently published in the *American Psychologist, Organizational Behavior and Human Decision Processes*, the *Journal of Behavioral Decision Making*, the *Journal of Interpersonal Violence*, and *Behavioral and Brain Sciences* among others.

Thomas Schwinn is Professor of Sociology at the University of Eichstaett-Ingolstadt. He received his doctorate from the University of Heidelberg in theoretical sociology comparing Max Weber, Alfred Schütz and Talcott Parsons. His research interests include differentiation and integration theory, micro-macro-links, systems and action theories, social inequality. Recently his research has focused on multiple modernities in the process of globalization. His most recent articles and books are on *Premises and Forms of World Culture* and *Diversity and Unity of Modernity*.

Michael Scriven is currently Director of the Interdisciplinary Evaluation Program, Associate Director of the Evaluation Center, and Professor of Philosophy at Western Michigan University. Prior to that he was Professor of Evaluation at Auckland University, New Zealand, and Professor of Psychology at Claremont Graduate University. Recent and current research, in press or in print, includes: 'Causation without Experimentation', 'Ex Ante vs. Ex Post Evaluation of Researchers', 'Hard-Core Qualitative Research Methods', 'Program Evaluation: An Introduction and an Extension', 'The Problem of Free Will in Program Evaluation', and 'The Philosophy of Informal Logic and Critical Thinking'.

Jane Sell is Professor of Sociology at Texas A&M University, College Station. She was a deputy editor of *Social Psychology Quarterly*, has served on the editorial board of the *American Sociological Review*, and is past chair of the Social Psychology Section of the American Sociological Association. Her research focuses upon cooperation within public and resource good contexts, and different factors that affect the generation or decay of inequality in group settings. With Murray Webster, Jr., she has edited *Laboratory Experiments in the Social Sciences*, published by Elsevier Press.

Mark J. Smith is Senior Lecturer in Politics & International Studies at the Open University and researches environmental responsibility, transnational corporations, civic engagement and the role of ethics in politics and the environment. An advocate of transdisciplinary and participatory research, he argues that issues of social and environmental justice are best understood in the context of application. He is author or editor of thirteen books including *Ecologism: Towards Ecological Citizenship* (1998), *Social Science in Question* (1998), *Thinking through the Environment* (1999), *Rethinking State Theory* (2000) and *Culture: Reinventing the Social Sciences* (2000) as well as many chapters and articles on environmental politics, global relations and corporate responsibility, including 'Social movements in Europe' (2002), 'Transforming international order' (2004), 'Taking part in politics' (2004), 'Territories of knowledge' (2005), and 'Obligation and ecological citizenship' (2006). His work is translated in Europe and Asia, including *Manual de Ecologismo* (Instituto Piaget, 2002) and *La Cultura* (Cittá Aperta, 2005). Formerly at Sussex University, his visiting professorships include the University of Oslo and Norwegian Business School. His current work considers environmental citizenship and civic engagement in Asia, America and Europe, and he collaborates with Dr. Piya Pangsapa on the impact of the global supply chain and the UN Global Compact on corporate obligations to human rights, labor standards and environmental sustainability in Southeast Asia.

Stephen P. Turner is Graduate Research Professor in Philosophy at the University of South Florida, where he is also appointed in the Department of Management. His writings on methodology have ranged from issues in explanation, in such books as *Sociological Explanation as Translation* (1980) to issues of theory construction and issues with statistical approaches to causality, including *Causality in Crisis? Statistical Methods and Causal Knowledge in the Social Sciences* (1997, co-edited with Vaughn McKim). He has dealt with methodological issues in such fields as organization studies and international relations. He has also written extensively on the history of methodology, especially of statistics and probabilistic thinking, including writings on Comte, Mill, Quetelet and Durkheim, and on the origins of quantitative sociology in the United States. He was co-editor of the *Blackwell Guide to the Philosophy of Social Science* (2003, with Paul Roth) and *Philosophy of Anthropology and Sociology* (2007, with Mark Risjord) in the *Handbook of Philosophy of Science* series.

Murray Webster, Jr. is professor of sociology at UNC Charlotte. He is a member of the editorial boards of *Social Science Research* and *Sociological Methodology,* and past chair of the Social Psychology and the Theory Sections of the American Sociological Association. He has served as Program Director for Sociology at the National Science Foundation, and has been a member of the Sociology Advisory Panel at NSF. With Jane Sell, he edited a book, *Laboratory Experiments in the Social Sciences,* published by Elsevier Press in 2007. Other recent work includes a book chapter on status processes with Joseph Berger, papers on gender status beliefs with Lisa Rashotte, and papers on philosophy and operations in experimental methods.

Kenneth W. Wachter is Professor of Demography and Statistics and Chair of the Department of Demography at the University of California, Berkeley. He holds a Ph.D. in Statistics from Cambridge University (Trinity). He is a member of the National Academy of Science and a fellow of the American Academy of Arts and Sciences. He chairs the Committee on Population of the National Research Council. Among other volumes, he is the author with R. Floud and A. Gregory of *Height, Health,and History* (1990) and editor with C. Finch of *Between Zeus and the Salmon* (1997). His research interests include mathematical demography, the biodemography of aging, federal statistical policy, kinship and microsimulation. He served on the Special Advisory Panel to the Secretary of Commerce on (1990) Census Adjustment, as a consultant to the Secretary of Commerce on 2000 Census Adjustment, and as an expert witness in litigation over possible adjustment of the censuses of 1980 and 1990.

General Introduction

William Outhwaite and Stephen P. Turner

This handbook is designed to meet the needs of disciplinary and non-disciplinary, problem-oriented social inquirers for a comprehensive overview of the critical issues in the methodology of the social sciences and its various and often extremely complex and controversial literatures. In the social sciences the term 'methodology' tends to indicate two increasingly differentiated areas of work—first, methodological issues arising from and related to theoretical perspectives, as in Marxist, functionalist or feminist methodology; and, second, issues of specific research techniques, concepts and methods. A glance at the contents of this book will show that we aim to cover both these fields. Our understanding of the needs of the reader, and thus of the content of the volume, however, requires some explanation.

The world cannot be said to suffer a shortage of works on either of the two kinds of methodology mentioned above. Books explaining techniques and even handbooks on various methods or kinds of methods are common. Nevertheless, there is a daunting problem for the student or practitioner, as well as for the senior scholar. The problems and disputes over methods are usually not readily accessible. A person trained in a psychology department program in behavioral science methods will, for example, be told that there are 'assumptions' in the kinds of experimental designs that are taught in these programs. But the same person may never be aware of the large and important technical literature on 'selection bias', a specific problem with the assumptions that routinely undermines the applications of these methods—for example, to such standard problems as evaluating the effectiveness of a social service program. Similarly, the readers of published research reports on such topics as the effectiveness of particular social interventions, even if they are reasonably sophisticated, will find it difficult to know what questions an appropriately skeptical reader should ask about the research design.

This volume is an attempt to make these kinds of issues accessible. One way of doing this is by providing technical chapters on a range of interrelated problems that plague causal inference. The approach is not to provide 'solutions', though solutions to many of the problems are discussed. The approach is to explain the kinds of problems that routinely arise in these settings, and the tradeoffs that researchers are routinely compelled to make in order to come up with the results that are presented as fact. At this level of methodological detail, matters are seldom as simple as textbooks make them appear. Things that we think we know—for example, that minorities are greatly under-reported by the US Census, turn out to depend on reasoning that is more problematic than the original enumeration. Knowing why is crucial to reading in a sophisticated way.

A second daunting problem is the sheer variety of methodological approaches, especially qualitative approaches. These present some different problems of explication. What is 'cultural studies'? What are the distinctive background ideas and theories that motivate it? Why do its practitioners not just do surveys? What is 'grounded theory'? Answering these questions often requires a bit of historical background, and typically requires an introduction to the motivating theoretical ideas.

In each case, however, we have tried to ensure that contributors keep an eye on broader perspectives as well as on the specific topic with which they are dealing. Thus, as Adele Clarke (Chapter 23) notes in her chapter in this book, the relatively delimited approach of 'grounded theory' raises central questions about the overall orientation of the social sciences. In Denzin and Ryan's discussion (see Chapter 32) of the focused interview, they explain the way in which this familiar method has become a means of recognizing and accounting for the 'postmodernist' recognition of 'different voices'. In discussing the idea of feminist methodology, we have been concerned both to have the theoretical background of such ideas as standpoint theory explained (see Chapter 29), and also, in a second chapter, to discuss the kinds of problems that arise in actual attempts at collaborative action research in the face of different voices (see Chapter 30).

One of the authors we recruited for the volume, after having its purpose explained, replied: 'I see what you are doing: you are surveying the new geography of knowledge.' This volume *is* an attempt to cover a much wider range of approaches and problems than methodology books have traditionally included. One innovative feature of the volume is the extensive discussion of the new situation in which the knowledge of the subjects of the research is incorporated into the research and in which scholars are engaged researchers collaborating with their subjects. We have tried to cover the main problems on which a developed literature exists. But the sheer variety of topics that the omnivorous reader is likely to encounter extends beyond this volume, and will continue to expand. Methodological controversy has gone far beyond the simple conflicts over 'positivism' of the sixties. This volume is an introduction to that transformation.

SECTION I
Overviews

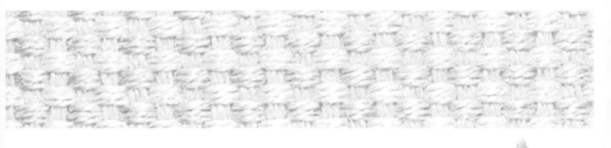

Introduction

William Outhwaite

The second half of the twentieth century saw the institutionalization of the social sciences and the rise and fall of the view that the methodologies for the social sciences had to be modeled on those of the natural sciences. This view favored econometrics, behaviorism in psychology, behavioralism in political science, empirical survey research in sociology and, in an extended, rather weaker, form of the doctrine, functionalism and structuralism in anthropology, sociology and political science and certain varieties of Marxism. By the mid-seventies, it was generally recognized, except in economics, that this was just one conception of social science and that more qualitatively oriented approaches also had something to offer, especially to feminist social science. The last decade of the century was marked by the continuing rise of rational choice theory and the revival of evolutionary theory at the 'hard' end of the spectrum, and by deconstruction, anti-foundationalism and postmodern relativism at the 'softer' end.

Peter Manicas, author of the magisterial *A History and Philosophy of the Social Sciences* (1987), traces in his chapter the intellectual and institutional contours of 'western' social science since 1945. What he calls a scientistic approach went along with disciplinary specialization and professionalization, most strikingly in North America but to an extent also in the UK and Western Europe, for all the differences between these sites. (In the present century, when social science has become substantially globalized, it is important to remember how high national barriers used to be as late as the 1980s: not just across the Iron Curtain, but even within a small space like that of Western Europe.)

Manicas traces the 'rise and fall' of scientism but, as he notes at the end of his essay, the future remains open, with some social scientists, especially in economics and psychology but not only there, looking to a revival of scientistic programs, others questioning the very idea of social science, and a third group, including such figures as Pierre Bourdieu and Anthony Giddens, pursuing the idea of social science in non-scientistic ways which recall in some respects the social theory of the late nineteenth and early twentieth centuries. One of the most influential attempts to reinstate the scientificity of the social sciences while recognizing the force of hermeneutic and historically based critiques of positivism has been, especially in the UK, a realist approach derived from the work of Mary Hesse and Rom Harré on models in natural science and extended to the social sciences by Harré himself and by Roy

Bhaskar. On this view, theories are seen as offering fallible models of the real relations between structures and mechanisms in the natural and/or social worlds. A supporter of this approach, Manicas closes with the suggestion that this may offer a way forward for social science.

The disciplinary specialization of the twentieth century was also accompanied by the growth of what came to be called inter-disciplinary social science. This is the subject of the second chapter in this section, by Julie Klein, author of *Interdisciplinarity: History,* *Theory, and Practice* (1990) and *Crossing Boundaries: Knowledge, Disciplinarities, and Interdisciplinarities* (1996). Klein traces the theory and practice of interdisciplinarity across the century. Like Manicas, she sees an ambiguous situation at the beginning of the twenty-first century: '...talk of interdisciplinarity becoming more the "norm" begs the question of how well prepared researchers are for this kind of work.' Together, these two chapters set the scene for the rest of the volume and demonstrate the need for it.

1

The Social Sciences Since World War II: The Rise and Fall of Scientism

Peter Manicas

INTRODUCTION

It is well to keep in mind that the disciplines of the social sciences are not 'natural kinds' and that, accordingly, they have a history, intellectual and institutional. While this is not the place to review this aspect, we should note that the disciplinary divisions and the view of science generally taken for granted among most social scientists are both fairly recent, dating only from the immediate post-World War I period. As I have noted elsewhere (Manicas, 1987), were we as social scientists to transport ourselves to Oxford, the Sorbonne, Harvard or Berlin in, say, 1890, we would find practices unfamiliar. There were no 'departments' of sociology or psychology; the research practices would be for us a hodgepodge of philosophy, social theory, history and hard science methods. But if we were to make a similar visit to any prominent American university in 1925, we would find very little which is not familiar.

'American university' is critical in the foregoing statement. As Peter Wagner has argued, the 'modernization' of the social sciences, including the tendencies toward 'scientization' and 'professionalization', was globally an uneven development. While 'it occurred almost across the board in the United States,' the trajectory was different in Europe, and, indeed, different in England, France, Italy, Germany and Scandinavia (Wagner et al., 1991: 350). No doubt these differences resulted from larger differences in the intellectual legacies of these states, in the particular nature and configurations of the state and civil society, and, more specifically, in differences in the policies and institutions available to meet problems of industrializing mass society. These differences will be pertinent, as I shall try to suggest, in the developments following World War II.

'Professionalization' could be achieved with disciplinary specialization, but the authority to be derived from this required 'scientization' is that social scientists be *scientists*. But one cannot simply assume that this idea is perfectly clear or that prevailing views are not contestable—and may be mistaken. It is of considerable importance to notice that during the period of the institutionalization of the social sciences, beginning at the turn of the last century, there was a dominating conception of what a science was. This view was profoundly propelled in the 1930s by Vienna 'logical positivism' and became by the 1950s the dominating conception among both philosophers and social scientists.[1]

In this view, the sciences were not metaphysical: they did not import into their explanations assumptions which could not be tested in experience. In this sense, then, the sciences were 'empirical'. This meant that the referents of terms in use had to be experimentally available. 'Hypotheses', understood as potential explanations, linked 'variables' that required evidence which had to be 'theory neutral'. A theory was simply a premise, a set of hypotheses for which there were deducible empirical consequences. Finally, if metaphysical assumptions were not to be allowed, then explanation had to be in the form of 'laws', which, following Hume's expunging of metaphysics from causality, were 'regularities' between associated 'variables'—'whenever this, then that'. Explanation, accordingly, proceeded by subsumption under law.

Here is an example from *Research Methods in the Social Sciences* by Frankfort-Nachmias and Nachmias, a textbook in wide use today. They write:

> Often the empirical attributes or events that are represented by concepts cannot be observed directly . . . In such cases, the empirical existence of a concept [*sic*] has to be inferred. Inferences of this kind are made with operational definitions (Frankfort-Nachmias and Nachmias, 1992: 31).

The structure of operational definitions is straightforward:

> If a given stimulus (S) is applied to an object, consistently producing a certain reaction (R), the object has the property (P) (Frankfort-Nachmias and Nachmias, 1992: 32).

Similarly:

> Ever since David Hume (1711–1776) … an application of the term explanation has been considered a matter of relating the phenomenon to be explained with other phenomena by means of general laws (Frankfort-Nachmias and Nachmias, 1992: 10).

Modeled on the assumption that there were no critical differences between the natural and social sciences, the approach eschewed subjectivity, theorized society as an objective functioning system, and employed objective methods to identify objective 'social facts'. This view favored econometrics; behaviorism in psychology; behavioralism in political science; and empirical survey research and quantitative methods and functionalism and structuralism in anthropology, sociology, political science and, perhaps paradoxically, in textbook versions of Marxism. Social science would be science—with a vengeance.

But just as this view of science began to be taken for granted in social science departments in the US, it was coming under attack from philosophers, including its most important expositors. W.V. Quine's remarkable 'Two Dogmas of Empiricism' (1950) and C.G. Hempel's criticism of his own previous work on explanation (e.g., 'The Theoretician's Dilemma', 1950) led the criticism from within. New directions were taken by Stephen Toulmin's *Foresight and Understanding* (1961), Thomas S. Kuhn's incredibly influential *The Structure of Scientific Revolutions* (1962), Rom Harré's generally ignored *Principles of Scientific Thinking* (1970), and Mary Hesse's *Models and Analogies in Science* (1970). By the mid-70s, *not one of the defining planks of positivism remained*.[2] Most critical was the idea that a theory of science could be epistemologically 'foundationalist' and metaphysically neutral. Thus, neither sense data nor appeals to putative theory-neutral 'basic sentences' could warrant truth-claims, for indeed there could be no 'God's eye view of the world'. Deductivism was replaced by an ontological realism which made sense of the role of theory in explanation. While there had been decisive criticisms of the covering law model of explanation since at least the 1950s, once Humean causality was replaced by a robust notion of causes as productive powers, the covering law model also finally had to be rejected.[3]

It is probably true that a good deal of mainstream thinking in the social sciences is still uncritically beholden to these views. Social scientists, like all others, are not comfortable with fundamental challenges to their ways of doing things. On the other hand, there were always challenges to this dominating view, beginning in a clear way with the work of Max Weber and extending in the recent past to a wide range of alternatives usually termed 'hermeneutic' or 'interpretative' sociologies. These critics sometimes argued that positivism and logical empiricism, or simply empiricism, may well be appropriate for the natural sciences, but that this is a fatally mistaken 'scientistic' approach to the social sciences. Or, more radically, these critics abandoned altogether the idea of a social or human *science*. Critically, neither party challenged the idea of science that was being assumed. But the undermining of the dominating theory of science has opened the way for a deep reconsideration of the nature and methods of social science, including resolution of the older dispute between 'naturalistic' and hermeneutical views of social scientific inquiry.[4]

POST-WORLD WAR II AMERICAN SOCIAL SCIENCE

The work of Talcott Parsons (1937, 1951, 1968) was central insofar as he offered a theory which could claim scientific status and could, even more importantly, easily accommodate the idea that quantitative social science provided the tools for applying a natural science model to the social sciences. Dismissing Marx, Parsons ingeniously absorbed and synthesized interpretations of Durkheim, Weber, Marshall and Pareto into his structural–functionalism. The result was not merely a sociology but a general theory of action, pertinent for all the human sciences. Here indeed, was a general theory reminiscent of Comte's early vision.[5] Parsons's work captured social scientific

theorizing on the American side of the Atlantic (e.g., Almond and Verba, 1965; Rostow, 1960; Smelser, 1964). But as Hans Joas (1987: 82) has remarked: 'When American sociology set on its triumphal march around the world after the end of the Second World War, it had passed its own historical turning point only a short time before.' Joas's reference is to the pragmatist theory of John Dewey and George Herbert Mead, 'the pioneering methodological achievements of the Chicago School of sociology and the theoretical implications of their large-scale empirical investigations' (Joas, 1987: 82). And Parsons, as Joas notes, 'literally did not devote a single word' to this tradition.

Anti-Scientism in Pragmatic Social Theory

In the academy, two pragmatist strands, both marginal, remained. The first, always acknowledged in anthologies of social theory, is 'symbolic interactionism' (SI), named in 1937 by Herbert Blumer. It drew directly on Mead. The other was the work of C. Wright Mills, whose dissertation (written in 1942 and retitled for publication (1966) *Sociology and Pragmatism: The Higher Learning in America*), omitted discussion of Mead and focused on Dewey (Mills later noted that the omission was a big mistake). But it now seems clear that even where there were no explicit references, much of his work was profoundly indebted to both Mead and Dewey.

Mills's best-known book, highly pertinent for present purposes, is *The Sociological Imagination* (1959). In it, Mills offered a savage criticism of both 'Grand Theory' and 'abstracted empiricism'. The attack on Grand Theory was aimed squarely at Talcott Parsons. 'Abstracted empiricism' referred, of course, to the quantitative hard science approach then being powerfully propelled by Mills's Vienna-influenced colleague at Columbia University, Paul Lazarsfeld (1955).

For Mills, echoing a version of Weber[6] which had been submerged by Parsons,[6]

Grand Theory was ahistorical and operated at such levels of abstraction that it could not get down to the real concrete. The 'findings' of abstracted empiricists were, by contrast, uninteresting except for the scientistic–bureaucratic and ideological uses to which they were so easily put. Mills called for a different *kind* of social science. It would, in Deweyan fashion, serve concrete human concerns by cultivating the 'sociological imagination', a linking of biography and history. It would be emancipating because it would enable persons to connect their domestic and local situation to the historical and global causes which explained their immediate milieux. Deweyan concerns with eclipse of 'the public' (1927) are evident in Mills's *Power Elite* (1956), an excellent example of how Mills put 'science' to work.

While 'the sociological imagination' is a term that has found its way into all the textbooks, and while Mills's work was important in the 60s and 70s among New Left writers and activists, he had little influence on the direction of inquiry in the social sciences. But at the margins, there is a continuing tradition of writers who, like Mills, draw on their understanding of Weber and Marx, even while they are explicitly non-Marxist. In this tradition, Barrington Moore Jr, a close friend of Herbert Marcuse, is perhaps the most outstanding example. Aspects of this approach find expression today among a range of 'institutionalists' and others working in historical and economic sociology, both of which seem to be having a renaissance in American social science (Theda Skocpol, 1984; Smelser and Swedberg, 1994; Margaret Somers, 1998; Stinchcombe, 1983; Charles Tilly, 1982, 1984).

Blumer similarly made an assault on the presumed science of prevailing social science. Perhaps the most persistent theme in this attack was rejection of the covering law idea—that behavior can be explained by appeal to regularities between 'causative' factors and 'the behavior they are supposed to produce'. 'Thus, the typical sociological scheme ascribes behavior to factors such as status position, cultural prescriptions, norms, values, sanctions, role demands, and social system requirements … Similarly, in the typical psychological scheme such factors as motives, attitudes, hidden complexes, elements of psychological organization, and psychological processes are used to account for behavior…' (Blumer, 1969: 7). The fallacy was obvious to him. In both cases, 'the meanings of things for the human beings who are acting are either bypassed or swallowed up in the factors used to account for behavior'. Moreover, they fail to see that 'the use of meanings by a person in his action involves an interpretative process.' Closely following Mead, the actor, in 'communication with himself', 'selects, checks, suspends, regroups, and transforms meanings in the light of the situation in which he is placed and the direction of his action' (ibid.: 5).

Blumer incorporated the powerful theory of meaning of Mead and Dewey: meanings are not 'psychical accretions' but are instead 'creations that are formed in and through the defining activities of people as they interact' (ibid.: 5). Indeed, for Blumer, 'social interaction is a process that forms human conduct instead of being merely a means or setting for the expression or release of human conduct'.[7] The rejection of empiricist assumptions regarding explanation demanded a rejection of

the mythical belief that to be scientific it is necessary to shape one's study to fit a pre-established protocol of empirical inquiry, such as adopting the working procedure of advanced physical science, or devising in advance a fixed logical or mathematical model, or forcing the study into the mould of laboratory experimentation, or imposing a statistical or mathematical framework on the study, or organizing it in terms of preset variables, restricting it to a particular standardized procedure such as survey research (ibid.: 48).

Following the Chicago tradition of W.I. Thomas and Robert Park, this reconceptualization of sociology entailed what Blumer termed 'a naturalistic approach' to inquiry, a deep immersion into the life-worlds of transacting actors. As part of this, agency was restored to inquiry. Indeed, this approach took the 'revolutionary' posture of what Rom

Harré and Paul Secord (1973: 6) later referred to as 'the anthropomorphic model of man': for scientific purposes, it would treat people as if they were human beings.

But, writing in 1964, Anselm Strauss noticed that the dominating structural-functional theories found a way to de-radicalize Mead by incorporating some of his seminal ideas into their programs. Thus, 'the generalized other became just another way of talking about reference group affiliation and Mead's notion of role tended to be reinterpreted to fit with the structural concept of status and its associated role-playing' (Kurtz, 1984: 40, quoting Strauss). Meanwhile debate as to whether Mead was behaviorist or phenomenological led to an 'Iowa school' and an 'Illinois school', splitting from the 'Chicago School'. Lingering in the background was the important question of whether Symbolic Interactionism was essentially a *social psychology* which had to be supplemented with a macro orientation or whether, as the founders had suggested, it was an entirely different way to carry on sociology.

There remain in the academy card-carrying symbolic interactionists of various stripes, and many others who do qualitative work but may not explicitly acknowledge the genesis of their approach (see Denzin and Lincoln, 1994). Indeed, many of these seem to have adopted a methodological eclecticism or pluralism which owes in part, perhaps, to Clifford Geertz's (1973, 1983) idea of 'thick description'. Current inquirers would seem to have absorbed a range of interpretive modes, including symbolic interactionism, ethnomethodology, hermeneutics, structuralism and poststructuralism. And many would seem to be comfortable with the idea that their concerns are descriptive and that, in what is seen to be a useful division of labor, macro concerns may be left to others.

Alfred Schütz and Phenomenology

At approximately the same time that Parsons was becoming dominant, the ideas of Alfred Schütz were becoming known in the United States. Schütz had been a member of a remarkable seminar which regularly met in Vienna in the 1920s, 'the *Mises-Kreis*'. In addition to Ludwig von Mises, it included among its distinguished regulars Friedrich von Hayek, Fritz Machlup, Felix Kaufmann (a member also of Moritz Schlick's more famous Vienna seminar), Oskar Morgenstern and Eric Voegelin. Mises reported that 'in these meetings we informally discussed all the important problems of economics, social philosophy, sociology, logic, and the epistemology of the sciences of human action' (Augier, 1999: 154). Weber and the earlier debates of the *Methodenstreit* were central. Critical here was the question, introduced by Weber, of 'subjective understanding'. But, and this cannot be overlooked, the group accepted Weber's view that *Verstehen* was but the first step in the effort to provide causal explanations in the human sciences. More generally, for the *Mises-Kreis*, there was the question of whether there was necessarily a distinct science of human action that would incorporate economics, sociology and politics. Mises had originally titled this 'sociology,' but by then the discipline was sufficiently well entrenched, and he therefore renamed his project 'praxeology'. A convincing case has been made that it was in this context, rather than the context of Husserlian phenomenology, that Schütz initially formed his ideas (Augier, 1999; Prendergast, 1986).

The Nazis would force the *Mises-Kreis* (as with the *Wiener Kreis*) to immigrate to the US (or to Britain). Schütz moved to New York in 1939. Von Hayek, then in London, suggested to Schütz that he review for *Economica* a new book by Talcott Parsons, *The Structure of Social Action* (1937). This initiated a correspondence between Parsons and Schütz which led to Schütz's decision not to publish his review. As the editor of this material notes: 'The reader will find himself engaged in an intense, sometimes stormy, and, at places, embittered exchange of notes and letters, which leads into a rather poignant debate on the differences between phenomenological and structural–functional analyses' (Grathoff, 1978: xvii). These texts allow us to get clearer on some of the central issues in social science, and especially the genesis of the important work of Goffman and Garfinkel. But unfortunately, some still hotly contested issues remain.

Since both Schütz and Parsons had taken Weber as a point of departure, one might have supposed that they could easily achieve a meeting of minds. Such was not the case, and, as now seems clear, they disagreed fundamentally on the nature and status of subjective meaning as regards the theory of action. Schütz insisted that inquiry needed to investigate the meaning *actually meant* by actors and thus had to address the taken-for-granted problem of intersubjectivity—a problem missed also by the Austrian economists. Parsons, by contrast, 'made subjective meaning a theoretical concept and, consequently, was largely substituting socially pre-given norms and values for individual motivations' (Wagner, 1983: 77). It was just this move, of course, which allowed for Parsons's 'macro' solution to 'the voluntaristic theory of action' and which, from the point of view of Schütz (and Blumer(!) as well as Goffman and Garfinkel) led them to the conclusion that agents had effectively disappeared. Thus Schütz writes:

> Professor Parsons has the right insight that a theory of action would be meaningless without the application of the subjective point of view. But he does not follow this principle to its roots. He replaces subjective events in the mind of the actor by a scheme of interpretation of such events, accessible only to the observer, thus confusing objective schemes for interpreting subjective phenomena with these subjective phenomena themselves (Grathoff, 1978: 36).

But,

> the answering of our question, 'What does the social world mean for me, the observer?' has as a prerequisite the answering of the quite different questions, 'What does this social world mean for observed actors within this world, and what did he mean by his acting within it?' With these questions, we no longer naively accept the world and its current idealizations and formalizations as ready-made and meaningful beyond all doubt, but undertake to study the process of idealizing and formalizing as such, the genesis of the meaning which social phenomena have for us as well as for

the actors, the mechanism of the activity by which human beings understand one another and themselves (Wagner, 1983: 48).

It was but a short step from this to the projects of Goffman and Garfinkel and more generally to the key 'social constructionist' idea, shared with Symbolic Interactionism, that social phenomena are the outcome of practical activities by skilled actors engaged in a taken-for-granted world and that any valid inquiry in social science must begin with an effort to grasp the meaning of an action actually held by them.[8]

But Schütz seems to have assumed—or assumed away—the problem of intersubjectivity. Augier (1999: 159) argues that 'Schütz wanted the concept of intersubjectivity to be unquestionable' and did not, for this reason, want to enter into question about 'the transcendental constitution of the "natural attitude"'. But as Schütz later admitted, 'it is "a scandal of philosophy" that so far the problem of our knowledge of other minds and, in connection therewith, of the intersubjectivity of our experience of the natural as well as the socio-cultural world, has not found a satisfactory solution …' (Schütz, 1954: 265). Here one might insist that Mead's social behaviorism and Dewey's account of experience is the far better response just because it disavows at the outset a Cartesian ego (Manicas, 1992).

The foregoing discussion also responds to the question of the relation of Schütz and Parsons to a 'positivist' theory of science. Schütz, like Weber, was very often explicitly anti-positivist, but it is critical to see why. In the well-known essay of 1954, 'Concept and Theory Formation in the Social Sciences', Schütz directly engaged Ernest Nagel and C.G. Hempel, leading empiricist participants in an APA symposium of the same title. First, there was no argument that for both the natural and social sciences, 'the principles of controlled inference and verification by fellow-scientists and the theoretical ideals of unity, simplicity, universality, and precision prevail.' This seems fundamental and sufficiently neutral between possible alternative conceptions of science. But the second point at issue is a different matter.

Schütz agreed that '"theory" means in all empirical sciences the explicit formulation of determinant relations between a set of variables in terms of which a fairly extensive class of empirical regularities can be explained' (Schütz, 1954: 260). This 'deductivist' idea was, of course, a pillar of the positivist theory of science, fully shared by Parsons and by many contemporary writers like Jonathan H. Turner (1987). Parsons, as noted, 'hoped that the theory of action would ... eventually "be stated as system of simultaneous equations"—a system whose several variables were duly allocated to the different social sciences' (Camic, 1987: 431, quoting Parsons).

Schütz's encounter with Weber was mediated by Mises, who had offered a powerful critique of Weber's ideal-type reading of neo-classical theory. The concepts of economics were not, in Mises's view, 'one-sided intensification of one or several aspects' of a concrete, but were, as Schütz put the matter, 'derived by abstraction from aspects of each of the individual phenomena taken into consideration' (Augier, 1999: 158). But Schütz's sympathy with Mises's conception of economic theory worked against his more fundamental Weberianism. Thus, it is easy to show that Schütz should not have been so polite and should have rejected the conception of theory as a deductive system whose entailments were 'laws' or events to be explained by subsumption under laws. For Schütz, once having established the subjective meaning shared by the actors, theory involved the construction of models of 'typical' behavior by 'personal types'. These are constructed 'homunculi' or 'puppets' to which we ascribe in-order-to and because motives. Implicit here is the idea that reasons are causes. And in contrast to the positivist dream, nothing would be deduced. Rather, theory would yield *understanding* by giving us 'the mechanism of the activity by which human beings understand one another and themselves'.

Neo-classical economic theory had provided a model which provided an account of the mechanisms which produced prices, and these were, as Schütz agreed, derived from postulates regarding the motivation and beliefs of individuals. But as was acknowledged, these postulations could not be said to be true of *actual* economic behavior—a problem for economics and, more generally, as we shall see, till today for what is called 'rational choice theory'.

What then was the objection to Nagel's and Hempel's naturalism? For Schütz, both had misunderstood Weber's 'postulate of subjective understanding. *Verstehen* has nothing to do with introspection, but 'is the result of processes of learning and acculturation ...'. It is not a private affair and it can be controlled through the use of evidence. Finally, and paradoxically, given the emphasis on prediction in the empiricist theory of science, predictions based on *Verstehen* are continuously and with high success made in common-sense thinking (Schütz, 1954: 264). The consequence was a redefinition of the tasks of an empirical human science. As already noted in his criticism of Parsons,

> all forms of naturalism and logical empiricism simply take for granted ... social reality ... Intersubjectivity, interaction, intercommunication, and language are simply presupposed as the unclarified foundation of these theories. They assume, as it were, that the social scientist has already solved his fundamental problem, before scientific inquiry starts (Schütz, 1954: 261).

Erving Goffman

As is well known, both Parsons and Schütz were important with regard to the work of Goffman and Garfinkel, both of whom also acknowledged debts to William James and Ludwig Wittgenstein. But getting clear on where they stand with respect to these writers—or to SI theory—remains contested. A big part of the problem regards their respective understanding of phenomenology and whether, unlike SI theory, what they offered was a challenge to the way of doing sociology or, rather, a supplement to this. In what must be taken as a provocative disclaimer, Goffman remarked that in *Frame Analysis* (1974), his most self-consciously theoretical book, he was making no claim whatsoever to be talking about the core matters of sociology—social organization and social structure ... I am not addressing the structure of social life but the structure of experience individuals have at any moment of their social lives. I personally hold society to be first in every way and any individual's current involvement to be second; this report deals only with matters that are second ... The analysis developed does not catch at the differences between the advantaged and the disadvantaged classes and can be said to direct attention away from such matters. I think that this is true. I can only suggest that he who would combat false consciousness and awaken people to their true interests has much to do, because the sleep is very deep. And I do not intend here to provide a lullaby but merely to sneak in and watch the way people snore (Goffman, 1974: 13–14).

Indeed, with its emphasis on 'the structure of experience', the posture taken in *Frame Analysis* seems more phenomenological than anything offered by Schütz. On the other hand, much of the substantive work of Goffman looks very much like a Schützian construction of a model of typical types—and indeed, as the foregoing hints, with critical, even emancipatory, implications.

Consider here *Asylums* (1961). Goffman establishes two typical sorts of actors standing in a well-defined social relation: 'the managers' and 'the managed' ('professionals vs. clients', 'staff vs. inmates'). They jointly participate in the construction of their identities and roles. Thus, the managed get constructed as something less than full persons, while managers are constructed as competent to 'treat' the managed. Each of the two parties has goals (which 'provide a key to meaning') and each has a system of beliefs (for the managers, an 'interpretative scheme' which includes 'a theory of human nature'). Typically, the 'managed' undergo 'mortification', the construction of a different self. The managed also have resources. Resistance by them takes on a number of forms, including contesting the meaning of rules, 'fraternization', and 'playing it cool' (Goffman 1961: 61–65). 'Institutional ceremonies'—including, for example, a newsletter produced by inmates, an annual party and an open house—are regular events in the life of the institution. These are intended to produce a

joint commitment to the official goals, even if, to be sure, everyone 'on the inside' knows better. Goffman very convincingly shows how the beliefs of actors, true *and* false, function in sustaining an institution in which there is a manifest disjunction between the official goals of the institution and the actual outcomes, and how even the inmates, contrary to their intentions, contribute to the outcomes.

In this marvelous account, one can easily discern key elements of both SI and Schützian perspectives. Moreover, it is distinctly antagonistic—and not complementary—to a Parsonian account.

Harold Garfinkel

Similarly Garfinkel, after distinguishing 'Formal Analytic (FA) technology' (mainstream sociology) and Ethnomethodology (EM), insisted that 'FA's achievements are well known and pointless to dispute.' 'Ethnomethodology (EM) is proposing and working out 'What More' there is to the unquestionable corpus status of formal analytic investigations', namely,

to find, collect, specify, and make instructably observable the local endogenous production and natural accountability of immortal familiar society's most ordinary organizational things in the world, *and to provide for them both and simultaneously as objects and procedurally, as alternative methodologies.* (Garfinkel, 1996: 6)

FA and EM are, he insists, 'incommensurably different. Nevertheless, they are inextricably related' (ibid., 1996: 10). What is their relation? Garfinkel offers, enigmatically, that 'it is a social fact in its own right' that 'they are asymmetrically alternate' (ibid., 1996: 10). Maynard and Clayman (1991: 387) argue that ethnomethodology is 'neither a critique, reaction, or rebellion against other forms of social theory, but rather a positive respecification of how investigators might approach sociology's most awesome phenomenon—the objective, immortal reality of social facts.'

But it would surely seem that ethnomethodology, like SI theory, is a distinctly different way *to do* sociology. It is even less clear, but probably true, that neither Schütz nor Garfinkel were much indebted to Husserl's introspective and cognitive version of phenomenonology, even while they adopt a Husserlian *Epoché* as regards 'reality'. Methodologically at least, they would seem to share with Blumer a distinctly sociological perspective which demands a commitment to naturalistic observation and participation.

Ethnomethodology has spawned a wide variety of empirical work, including efforts to discern generalizable properties of practical common-sense reasoning, and more particular instantiations of these procedures in a wide variety of contexts, including the criminal justice and health systems and, importantly, in the sociology of scientific knowledge.[9] Conversation analysis is an offshoot which was eagerly adopted but seems not to have been sustained. But indeed ethnomethodology, like the work of Goffman, has been integrated into the impressive meta-theories of Giddens and Bourdieu. Before turning to them, one last distinctly American development, rational choice theory, needs some attention.

Rational Choice Theory

There was one response to structural functionalism which aimed 'to bring people back in', but fully endorsed a positivist theory of science. Rational Choice Theory (RCT) has, to be sure, a long lineage in social theory, going back at least to Hobbes, who clearly articulated several of its main premises, for example, that we must look at individuals acting 'rationally' if we are to understand society, and that 'rationality' can be unpacked in terms of maximizing 'utility'. These ideas were systematically extended in the development of political economy, but especially in neo-classical economic theory. But until the 1950s, sociologists and political scientists remained unaffected by this fundamental orientation.

Homans was explicit in his view that action can be explained by appeal to fairly straightforward principles of behavioral psychology and that this proceeded by appeal to the covering law model of explanation. Homans insisted, with some credibility, that 'many social scientists who in fact use behaviorism do not realize that they are doing so. They call it utilitarianism or rational-choice theory,' and indeed,

> one advantage that would accrue to all of us if we accepted and acted upon the covering law view of theory is that different schools would have to ask themselves what covering laws they would in fact use if they formalized their theories … I think that all the schools would find that they would use principles of behavioral psychology, either in what I have called the stripped down form or in one that embodies more fully the still-developing experimental findings (Homans, 1987: 79).

One might here be reminded of C.S. Peirce's observation that 'the yoking together of the scientific ox and speculative ass' remains a problem for too much of social science.

But Homans inspired what became 'exchange theory', perhaps initiated by Peter Blau (1964). Working explicitly within an economic framework, Blau argued that the 'costs' and 'rewards' of social exchange—e.g., a marriage—answered to the same principles as market exchanges for goods, even if, to be sure, assessing the 'values' was more difficult. Unlike Homans, Blau acknowledged that some outcomes of interactions by rational individuals were emergent, for instance that while RCT can explain, presumably, the behavior of bureaucrats, bureaucracies have features which are not reducible to the exchanges of the parties. James Coleman (1990) has made the latest effort to systematically build social theory on generously conceived RCT premises. While not without its critics (Green and Shapiro, 1996), RCT is vigorous in American political science. Indeed, RCT also defines what is called 'Analytic Marxism' (Roberts, 1996)!

No doubt much of the motivation for the development of RCT as a general theory of action came from dissatisfaction with Parsons's theory, with the notion that modern micro-economics was an eminently successful science and with the idea, encouraged by positivist conceptions of theory, that theory construction could now proceed in sociology and political science with the use of sophisticated mathematics and the new powerful computers.

But of course, one can reject the assumption that neo-classical theory—including its most sophisticated mathematical and econometric forms—is a successful social science.[10] It is pertinent to notice that Mises and Hayek were already critics of general equilibrium theory exactly on the grounds that critical assumptions of the theory could not be met. They shared this line of criticism with Veblen in the US and the later institutionalists and economic sociologists who followed in this tradition. One might defend the mainstream view by taking the explicitly positivist posture well put by Milton Friedman (1953) that the assumptions of a theory need not be true—e.g., assumptions regarding rationality—if indeed, the theory provides 'good predictions'. But even if it could pass this test—which it does not—it is hard to see how one can *explain* an outcome on the basis of assumptions known to be false?

Marxism and the American Academy

Marxism, in both scientistic and non-scientistic forms, was a challenge to mainstream scientism. The scientistic form (Second International variety) never made much headway in American academic social science, but, as Gintis has noted, 'Marxian economics has dwelt as an undercurrent in American academic thought for at least a century' (Ollman and Vernoff, 1982: 53). A historically oriented political economy became important in the 1960s in direct response to the anti-war, civil rights and feminist movements, which challenged the consensus of the dominating paradigms: neo-classical economics and Parsonian theory in sociology. As Bruce Cumings has more recently noted,

> Because of the ferment of the 1960s, there emerged in the 1970s a social science which met a high standard of quality and relevance. In political science, sociology, and even to some extent economics, political economy became a rubric under

which scholars produced a large body of work on the multinational corporation, the global monetary system, the world pool of labor, peripheral dependency, and American hegemony itself. (Cumings, 1998: 180)

But, writing in 1998, he also says that 'it was amazing to witness the alacrity with which social scientists abandoned this political economy program' (1998: 181). Times had indeed changed. Similar considerations apply to the work of Herbert Marcuse, a long-standing member of the exiled Institute for Social Research. Marcuse remained in the US after the institute returned to Frankfurt and was important to the development of radical social analysis, especially in the so-called 'New Left' in the 1960s. But while the critical theory of Horkheimer, Adorno and Benjamin remains pertinent to contemporary concerns, it never did take hold in the US, and has, along with the work of Marcuse, remained marginal in the US academy. But, as noted with reference to Barrington Moore, features of Marx's orientation filtered into a wide range of non-Marxist work.

One important possible exception is the work of Immanuel Wallerstein (1974). 'World Systems Theory' certainly entered the thinking and vocabulary of many social scientists, Marxist and non-Marxist alike. Wallerstein drew on Braudel, whose 'structuralism' was a part of the French structuralist movement. We say 'possible exception' here since, as Brenner (1977) has argued, Wallerstein is better described as 'a neo-Smithian Marxist' rather than as Marxist *tout court*. Put briefly, as with Braudel (Tilly, 1984), Wallerstein's concern is 'conditions of exchange' rather than the classical Marxist 'mode of production'.

MARXISM AND THE EUROPEAN RESPONSE TO SCIENTISM IN SOCIAL SCIENCE

It is misleading, of course, to write as if there were not continuous influences between Europeans and Americans over the contested terrain of the social sciences. Not only were many American and European social scientists reading texts being produced by colleagues across the Atlantic but, as already noted, Schütz and the *Mises-Kreis* were but part of a large exodus of intellectuals from Germany and Austria following the accession to power of Hitler. Others included members of the critically influential Vienna Circle, and at about the same time both the entire *Institut für Sozialforschung*—the so-called Frankfurt School—and the intellectually heterogeneous group which found a home at Alvin Johnson's New School for Social Research. These included Hannah Arendt, Leo Strauss, Aron Gurwitsch, Claude Lévi-Strauss, Roman Jakobson and Adolph Lowe. Many others scattered in the American academy should be mentioned, including Eric Voegelin, Norbert Elias and Franz von Neumann. Vienna positivism was not in the least alien to the American scene and quickly took hold. Schütz's influence has also been noted. But while the members of the Frankfurt School, along with almost all the others, were in the 1940s and 50s already arguing for styles of social science which were explicitly historical and anti-positivist, these European writers, both Marxist and non-Marxist, have had but marginal influence as regards the US academy.

The European scene was different. Mainstream American social science came late to European social science. In part, this was a consequence of the continuing tradition established by Weber of a historical sociology (or of sociology as a propaedeutic to historical inquiry) and, more critically, the continuing pertinence of Marx. This last stems, in part at least, from the presence in Europe of viable working-class and Marxist political parties—a feature entirely absent from the American experience. In what follows I concentrate on developments within Marxism and its role in redefining the nature and character of social science. It is not an overstatement to say that nearly all the interesting recent alternatives to US mainstream social science were European and also drew on Marx.[11] This includes the development of Critical Theory, the innovations owed to the

Italian Antonio Gramsci, the existential Marxism of Jean-Paul Sartre and Maurice Merleau-Ponty, the hermeneutics of Gadamer and Ricoeur, and both structuralism and post-structuralism.

Germany

The Institute for Social Research had been created in 1923 to promote Marxist studies. The first generation, Horkheimer, Adorno and Marcuse, prominently and with differences, reconsidered the debt of Hegel, incorporated Freud and the lately published writings of the young Marx, rejected the eschatology of the Second International reading of historical materialism and turned their attention to cultural concerns that were missing in the older Marxist tradition. After the Institute returned to Frankfurt in 1950, as Jay (1973: 292) notes, 'instead of developing in relative isolation' it would become 'one of the major currents of German sociological and philosophical thought'. Some critics, of course, have argued that the turn taken early on and reinforced by its exile in the US made it less and less convincingly Marxist (Anderson, 1976). But of course that depends to a considerable extent on what is to count as 'Marxist'.

While these issues cannot be pursued here, we can also note that the current dominant second-generation figure, Jürgen Habermas, has not adopted the pessimism which was the result of the first generation's analysis of the highly repressive forces of 'rationalization', a key legacy of the work of Weber. To avoid pessimism and to combat more recent attacks on 'reason' from 'postmodernist' quarters, Habermas has returned to a version of Kant which offers a novel way to defend an 'Enlightenment' concept of reason in the face of repressive 'rationalization' (Outhwaite, 1994). Habermas, whose Weber tends in the direction of Parsons, has made serious efforts to incorporate American traditions into his version of critical theory, and, perhaps as part consequence, his work appears in US mainstream contexts. Related currents in Germany include a revitalized Parsons in the work of Richard Münch (1987) and the systems theory approach of Niklas Luhmann (1997).

As noted, the tradition of Weber was also a key part of the German scene, including but not restricted to the radicalization of the idea of *Verstehen* with the work of Hans-Georg Gadamer. If it be granted that there is a necessary hermeneutic moment in any social science and that interpretation requires 'a fusing of horizons', was Habermas correct in claiming (versus Gadamer) that 'hermeneutic consciousness remains incomplete as long as it does not include a reflection upon the limits of hermeneutic understanding?' (quoted by Outhwaite, 1985: 190). This is also a theme confronted by Bourdieu, Giddens and Bhaskar.

France

There are similarities in the French tradition, where Marxism was also a vital intellectual force. The pre-World War II work of Henri Lefebvre (who offered, in 1937, the first French translations of the writings of the young Marx), and the work of Lucien Goldmann, a student of Lukács, established the presence of Marxism in France. The War assured its prominence. Mark Poster (Poster, 1975: 4) writes:

> The only moral force left in France, on the eve of Liberation, came from the resistance movement, which had been dominated by politically progressive groups ... With a combined socialist and Communist vote reaching a majority, intellectuals harbored the dream of an imminent and radical social transformation.

Alexandre Kojève and Jean Hyppolite had brought Hegel to the attention of French intellectuals.[12] Simone de Beauvoir summarized his pertinence to them: 'We had discovered the reality and weight of history; now we were wondering about its meaning' (quoted by Poster, 1975: 20). Coupled with the powerful new ideas on alienation, and the attending incorporation of phenomenology, the study of Hegel's *Phenomenology* became 'an intellectual source for the renewal of

Marxism, for Sartre's existentialism, and perhaps even for the structuralism of the 1960s' (Poster, 1975: 5). Indeed, as now seems clear, 'structuralism' was a specific response to this 'renewed Marx', especially as promoted by the 'existential Marxists', Sartre and Merleau-Ponty.

Existential Marxism drew on Hegel and phenomenology—making it dubiously 'scientific', at least as that was conceived by many. And the Second Internationalist idea of a 'scientific' Marxism was hardly dead. Indeed, perhaps, as Althusser (1969) was to insist, there were two Marxes, one 'romantic' and 'metaphysical', and the other 'scientific'. Worth noting, the official position of the French Communist Party favored a more 'scientist' Old Marx, 'shorn of the idea of alienation', and, indeed, of any 'humanist', non-scientific, 'philosophical' strands.[13]

Althusser's structuralism (developed between 1960 and 1965) was a response to this question. But there were a range of other theories—all French—which have been termed 'structuralist'. All these, despite differences, start with Marx and share in rejecting both phenomenology and the turn to a 'humanist' Marx. And all of them represent an anti-empiricist, alternative conception of social science. These include the linguistic structuralism of Roland Barthes, the work of Lacan, 'a psychoanalyst combining Freudian orthodoxy with Heideggarian overtones', Lévi-Strauss's Durkheimian structuralist anthropology, and the *Annales* historians whose work offered that 'the individual agent and the individual occurrence cease to be central elements in social explanation' (Clark, 1985: 180).[14] But Kurzweil rightly notes that 'traces, or influences of existentialism and/or Marxism continue to be found in the work of such diverse figures as Barthes, Foucault, Lacan, Lévi-Strauss, and others,' and, to add to the confusion, these figures very often share attitudes toward economic injustice with Marxists (Kurzweil, 1980: 3).

As regards Althusser's structuralism, Perry Anderson writes: 'For the first time, a major theoretical *system* was articulated within the organizational framework of French Communism, whose power and originality were conceded even by its most determined opponents' (1976: 38).[15] As is well-known, Althusser argued that there was 'an epistemological break' in the Marxian corpus.[16] His very influential structuralist alternative drew on all the structuralists, but especially on Saussure and Lacan. A key theme pertinent for present purposes is summarized by Poster (1984: 34): 'In Lacan's complex and often opaque formulations, the subject is constituted in the unconscious through a process mediated by language, which fixes the subject in decentered misrecognition of itself.' This idea could be enriched by the structuralist linguistics of Saussure. Reading Marx 'symptomatically', the 'objective text' could then be 'decoded'.

Althusser offered a host of new ideas that became familiar—if often unclear—coin. Thus, a society was an ensemble of *practices*: economic, political, ideological and theoretical, comprising a 'social formation' (Althusser 1969: 166f.). A practice, for Althusser, was 'any process of *transformation* of a determinant given raw material into a determinant product' (ibid.). Practices then include different kinds of 'parts'. For example, economic practice includes raw materials, tools and workers, all united in the production process. Theoretical practice includes (as raw materials) 'ideology', the pre-given concepts which are the ideas of the 'lived' common-sense world, and theory. With theory, then, these are transformed into scientific knowledge (ibid.: 182f.).

An enduring problem of historical materialism was the relation of the 'base' to the 'superstructure'. This was 'solved' with the idea of 'structure in dominance'. The elements of the 'totality' are asymmetrically related. But the base 'determines' which of the asymmetrical elements are dominant at any given time (1969: 213). This allowed Althusser to refocus the problem of revolution and more generally of historical change. Finally, with practices as the unit of analysis, Althusser was able explicitly to expunge agents from his explanatory framework, and

thus any reference to humanism or phenomenology. Thus,

> The structure of the relations of production determines the places and functions occupied and adopted by agents of production, who are never anything more than the occupants of these places, insofar as they are supports (*Träger*) of these functions. The true 'subjects' (in the sense of constitutive subjects of the process) are therefore not these occupants or functionaries, [who] are not, despite all appearances, the 'obviousness' of the 'given' of naïve anthropology, 'concrete individuals', 'real men'—*but the definition and distribution of these places and functions* (quoted from James, 1985: 151).
>
> History, accordingly, is 'a process without a subject'.

These ideas are powerfully in the background of arguments in British Marxism, and thence to the work of Roy Bhaskar and Anthony Giddens. But before leaving the French academy, we need to notice the responses of Foucault and then of Bourdieu. In the 1960s Foucault was in agreement with structuralist writers in rejecting Marxist humanism and phenomenology. He agreed also on the decisive role of language in constituting social reality. But he never quite succumbed to an agentless fatalism. The days of May 1968 are critical. As Poster argues, 'The events of May 1968 signified that an oppositional stance toward existing society was possible beyond the confines of contemporary Marxist orientations' (1984: 7). What came to be called 'the New Social Movements': the women's movement, gay rights, ecology, anti-nuclear, prison reform, patient's rights, etc., could not be fitted into the revolutionary class analysis of standard Marxism. Foucault and others, including Derrida, Deleuze, Guattari, Castoriadis, Lefort, Lyotard and Baudrillard struggled for answers for what they took to be an entirely new social and political condition.

Some of these writers—Derrida, for example—seemed to have despaired not merely of offering an emancipatory social science but of the possibility of knowledge and truth at all. Having already rejected humanism, Derrida abandoned completely the idea that reality could be 'represented'.

He opted for 'deconstruction'. As summarized by Hoy (1985: 4): 'Deconstruction shows the failure of a work's attempt at representation and by implication, the possibility of failure of any such work, or by any text whatsoever.' As Hoy sees it, 'grammatology' was a very radical hermeneutics: Instead of arguing that there was a problem to be solved in interpreting a text, 'Derrida would make us unable to read it.'

Dissidents in anthropology, especially sensitive to issues of neo-colonialism, sexism and racism, found the Derridian challenge liberating.[17] It was not difficult to show that the standard ethnographies offered representations which were in the interests of the colonizers and of elite males. But political critique would seem to require that there had to be *some* veridical representation.

Sometimes unnoticed, Foucault, despite sharing some key assumptions with Derrida, was one of his sharpest critics—exactly because the only politics which it seemed to allow was dubious. Instead of offering deconstruction, Foucault, drawing on Bachelard via Canguilhem and Althusser, offered first 'archaeology', a way to inquire into the groundwork of bodies of knowledge; and in the post 1968 writings, 'genealogy'—'a form of history which can account for the constitution of knowledges, discourses, domains of objects, etc., without having to make reference to a subject which is either transcendental in relation to the field of events or runs in its empty sameness throughout the course of history' (Foucault, in Calhoun et al., 2002: 204).[18]

Foucault, then, like the structuralists, is properly seen as providing a critique of the conventional wisdom as regards the sciences, but especially those sciences whose focus is 'life, labor and language'. While 'archaeology' and 'genealogy' parallel efforts in the sociology of knowledge,[19] his aim would also seem to be critical—without assuming that there is some system of thought which could be known to actually 'represent' 'reality' and, as part of this, without assuming any sort of 'autonomous' self.[20] We might say that this is social construction with a

vengeance; and indeed, it raises a host of questions and possible responses.

The power/knowledge couplet is a central and influential feature of Foucault's effort to rethink history and the constitution of subjects. For Foucault, power is an inherent feature of all social relations and functions where there are alternative possibilities of action to constrain or direct action. Moreover, power is an inherent component of the production of truth (knowledge). But, in contrast to liberal and Marxist thought, Foucault's anti-realism makes this insight epistemologically relevant. That is, a liberal or Marxist might assent that claims made by various 'disciplines' are secured as authoritative through the use of structured power, but still argue that some or all of these claims are false. Foucault would insist that this is not a helpful response. At the same time, he has provided important historical trajectories of the constitution of modern medicine, psychiatry, punishment, sexuality, and the attending construction of active subjects—active because they are participants in this construction. He has argued that these are forms of 'disciplinary technology' and are, as such, forms of domination. Indeed, for Foucault, aligned with Weber and Critical Theory, while disciplinary technologies were a precondition for capitalism, we are, for him, fast approaching a 'disciplinary society.'

That Foucault stands in opposition to this is plain. But his critics have often noted that he would seem to lack epistemological ground for this posture (Rainbow, 1985). While his pronouncements are often unclear, ambiguous and perhaps equivocal, he seems to offer a version of anarchism—a generalized resistance to power in all its forms (Schürmann, 1985: 546; Rabinow, 1984: 22).

In the US, Foucault's influence is considerable in Women's Studies. It commands some attention in political science and anthropology, but only recently does it seem to have made some inroads into sociology departments. Even so, his work is usually thought of as a strand of what is unhelpfully called 'postmodern' theory. Here, the emphasis seems more structuralist than

Foucauldian. As the editors of a recent American collection have noted, it is not clear 'whether Foucault should be considered a philosopher or a historian' (Calhoun et al., 2002: 188). But in the case of France, we need to compare his work to the work of Pierre Bourdieu, the successor to Foucault's chair in the *Collège de France*.

Like Foucault, Bourdieu absorbed the vigorous French debate between existential Marxism, phenomenonology, structuralism and poststructuralism, and, like Foucault, he made the effort to transcend the whole string of polarities and dichotomies which had characterized that debate. These included the antinomy between 'subjective' and 'objective' modes of knowledge, the separation of the cultural and symbolic from the material, the divorce of theory and practice, and, more familiar to American sociology, the 'micro–macro' gap and the dualism of agency and structure.

Typically European, his effort to re-vision social science begins, logically, with epistemology and ontology. Indeed, as with Foucault, Bhaskar and Giddens, it is probably best to call the work of these writers 'metatheory' insofar as they are philosophical theories about the nature and domain of a human science, and how this is to be studied. And the most direct way into his effort is to suggest a comparison to the work of Foucault.

Bourdieu agrees with Foucault (and Derrida) that the idea of scientific 'objectivity' must be deconstructed, that power always plays a role in sustaining scientific belief. He agrees also that 'reason' needs to be historicized and that there can be no appeal to a transcendental subject. But employing a version of Foucault's appropriation of Althusser, he 'partakes wholeheartedly of the Enlightenment project of reason' (Bourdieu and Wacquant, 1992: 47n.). Wacquant (Bourdieu and Wacquant, 1992: 47) quotes him:

Against this antiscientism which is the fashion of the day and which brings grist to the mill of new ideologists, I defend science and even theory when it has the effect of providing a better understanding of the social world. One does not have to choose between obscurantism and scientism. 'Of two ills,' Karl Kraus said, 'I refuse to choose the lesser.'

He hopes to manage this with two moves, with his concept of 'epistemic reflexivity' and with the Althusserian idea of 'scientific practice'.

Wacquant summarizes 'epistemic reflexivity' as 'the inclusion of a theory of intellectual practice as an integral component and necessary condition of a critical theory of society' (Bourdieu and Wacquant, 1992: 6). It differs from the usual notions of reflexivity in three ways: 'first, its primary target is not the individual analyst but the social and *intellectual unconsciousness* embedded in analytic tools and operations; second, it must be *a collective enterprise* rather than the burden of a lone academic; and third, it seeks not to assault but *to buttress the epistemological security of sociology* (1992: 6).[21]

As with Althusser, 'practices' are the key unit of analysis (Turner, 1994), and, as for him again, a form of realism is sustained by the theoretical practice of a proper social science. The task of sociology, he writes, is to 'uncover the most profoundly buried structures of the various social worlds [fields] which constitute the social universe, as well as the "mechanisms" which tend to ensure their reproduction or their transformation' (Bourdieu and Wacquant, 1992: 7). As the product of properly reflexive theoretical work, these are 'objectivities', but there is a 'constructivist' 'moment', identified but misconceived by 'subjectivist' approaches.[22] Thus, 'if it is good to recall, against certain mechanistic visions of action, that social agents construct social reality, individually and also collectively, we must be careful not to forget, as the interactionists and ethnomethodologists often so do, that they have not constructed the categories they put to work in this construction' (Bourdieu and Wacquant, 1992: 10).

Two central concepts in this proffered solution are 'habitus' and 'field'. 'Habitus' are 'systems of durable, transposable dispositions, structured structures predisposed to function as structuring structures, that is, as principles which generate and organize practices and representations that can be objectively adapted to their outcomes without presupposing a conscious aiming at ends or an express mastery of the operations necessary in order to obtain them' (in Calhoun et al., 2002: 277). They are 'embodied history', traits of character, attitudes and capacities acquired by individuals who have 'internalized' structure. They get played out in a 'field', which 'may be defined as a network, or a configuration, of objective relations between positions.' Paralleling Foucault's 'discourse/practices', one can speak of the field of the academy, or the economic, artistic, religious, or political field. And in an Althusserian mode, these are 'relatively autonomous', 'spaces of objective relations that are the site of a logic and a necessity that are *specific* and *irreducible* to those that regulate other fields' (Bourdieu and Wacquant, 1992: 97). Thus, what is called 'society' is not an integrated 'system' and thus it cannot be reduced to an overall logic, e.g., capitalism. Actions are neither autonomous nor mechanical products, but are the outcome of specific tendencies (constitutive of habitus) of agents located in a field which defines the possibilities of action. Finally, one can speak of 'fields of power.' Given this metatheory, specific theories pertinent to a specific time and place are then called for—e.g., as regarding a specific field of power.

> The field of power is a *field of forces* defined by the structure of the existing balance of forces between forms of power, or between different species of capital. It is also simultaneously a *field of struggles for power among the holders of different forms of power* ... The struggle for the imposition of the dominant principle of domination leads, at every moment ... to a *division of the work of domination*. It is also a struggle over the legitimate principle of legitimation ... (Bourdieu, 1996: 376 emphasis in the original).

Wacquant is probably correct in judging that Bourdieu's overall re-visioning of the social sciences has not much penetrated US academic social science. This includes not only Bourdieu's effort to reformulate an epistemology and ontology for the social sciences but also his attack on the very idea of disciplines in the human sciences.[23] Instead, pieces of his project have been appropriated—e.g., the idea of symbolic capital, his analysis of the field of cultural production, and his critical ethnographies.

Great Britain

One might hold that the divorce of social science from history was the most critical step in the empiricist effort to assure the 'scientific' character of social science. In part, at least because the tradition of Weber and Marx remained viable in Europe, there was never there a complete divorce of history and social science. But this was perhaps most pronounced in British social science, which, as in France and Germany, came late to a 'disciplinary' division of labor (Soffer, 1978; Tribe, 1981; Vout, 1991). But the particular character of British social science is especially shaped by the early genesis of capitalist society in England from the 17th century and by British imperialism. As regards the latter, in a story too complicated to even sketch here, we can think of the critical role of British anthropology (Gellner, in Evans-Pritchard, 1981). As regards the former, there is both the tradition of British political economy from Adam Smith to Alfred Marshall to John Maynard Keynes, and the important tradition of British Marxism, especially beginning with Christopher Hill's *The English Revolution* (1940). As in France, Marxism was comfortably part of the intellectual atmosphere of Britain, but among Marxists, especially in the generation of the post-World War II period to the 70s, historians dominated. As Tribe writes: 'The history of theoretical Marxism in Britain assumes the form of writings on history' (1981: 1). The most important writers here include Maurice Dobb, Rodney Hilton, E.J. Hobsbawm, G.E.M. de Ste. Croix, (the expatriated) M.I. Finley, E.P. Thompson, Raymond Williams and Perry Anderson. This history is not absent of either controversy or of consequences regarding thinking in Britain in the social sciences.

For our purposes the critical problem is the proper understanding of 'historical materialism' (a term never used by Marx).[24] Although it is clear enough that the key authors, beginning with Hill and certainly including E.P. Thompson, had long since departed from Second International orthodoxy, they proceeded in their historical work without much explicit theory. Structuralism and the French debates had filtered across the Channel in the 60s. At the same time, developments in the philosophy of science in both the US and France entered the argument. Out of this welter came the efforts of Roy Bhaskar (1978) and Anthony Giddens (1976) to resolve the 'agency/structure' bifurcation; Cultural Studies, initiated by Stuart Hall (1980), and the attending question of a 'structure/culture' bifurcation; the development in Edinburgh by David Bloor (1976) and Barry Barnes (1977) of the so-called 'Strong Programme in the Sociology of Science'; and, finally, the emergence of a 'realist' theory of science appropriate to the human sciences (Bhaskar, 1975/78).[25] Critical here was Bhaskar's effort to show that the long standing conflict between 'naturalist' and 'hermeneutic' views of social science depended on a spurious empiricist theory of science; and that once one adopted a realist theory of science, the insights of both naturalistic and hermeneutic approaches would find their place.

Bhaskar and Giddens seemed to have arrived at their social scientific metatheories at about the same time, and while they share much, there are differences. Bhaskar identified himself as a Marxist. At Oxford, he was powerfully influenced by the groundbreaking work in the philosophy of science of Rom Harré (1970). Bhaskar (1978) pressed these themes and added a novel philosophical argument in defense of his version of realism—'transcendental realism.' This includes a critique of the usually unnoticed ontology presumed by an empiricist theory of science, and a penetrating analysis of the nature and role of experiment in the natural sciences, an analysis with serious implications for the social sciences. He turned his attention to the social sciences in

his 1978 essay and then in a book, *The Possibility of Naturalism* (1979). Giddens has explicitly denied an identity as a Marxist, even though he has defended Marx's *Capital,* and has remarked that his project 'might accurately be described as an extended reflection upon a celebrated and oft-quoted phrase to be found in Marx …that "Men [let us immediately say human beings] make history, but not in circumstances of their own choosing"' (Giddens, 1984: xxi).

In what follows, I concentrate on what is broadly shared by Bhaskar, Giddens, Bloor and Barnes.[26] In contrast to the 'interpretativist skepticism' which characterizes 'post modern' epistemology, the point of departure for Bhaskar, Giddens and the Edinburgh group is a realism which posits *a knowable and causally efficacious independently existing nature*. But for all four, versus positivist epistemology, given the impossibility of standing outside of a historically constituted conceptual scheme, 'objectivity' is not absolute and requires a hermeneutic moment.[27]

Second, for all four, society is a social construction, the outcome of 'a skilled performance, sustained and 'made to happen' by human beings' (Giddens, 1976: 15). But, following Marx, actors work with 'materials at hand'—historically sedimented structured practices. For Giddens, 'structures' are constituted by indexically interpreted 'rules' which legitimate, define and sustain social relations. These relations in turn constitute 'resources' for actors. Resources are means of power, and as Mills, Foucault and Bourdieu insist, power is the central concept of social theory. But for Giddens, structure, as incarnate in activity, has but 'virtual existence'. Accordingly, for Giddens, agency/structure dualism is replaced by a 'duality' in which there are no agents without structured practices and no structured practices without agents. The central concept of his metatheory is 'structuration'—'the attempt to determine the conditions which govern the continuity and dissolution of structures or types of structure' (1976: 120). For Giddens, then, as for all four of these writers, since these conditions are historically various and contingent, social science is inevitably historical and concrete, and there can be no general theory of social change. Finally, Giddens is committed to the idea that apart from natural causes, *only* agents are causes.

Bhaskar refers to his theory as 'the transformational model of social activity' (TMSA). Since 'structures' pre-exist for any individual (but not for all), human activity does not create structure: agents reproduce and transform it (1979: 42). Parallel to Giddens, he writes of a duality of practice. Bhaskar provides a convincing dispositional analysis of reasons as causes, an elaborated theory of ideology, a critique of the hermeneutical circle, and an account of the critical consequences for confirmation of the absence of experiment in the social sciences. But he is less clear regarding the ontology of 'structure'. The question is not the non-observability of social structures (since on realist grounds, theoretized structures of the natural world need not be observable), but rather whether, as in natural science, they have a causal role and if so, in what sense? Thus, he offers that we can assume that 'there are structures producing social phenomena analogous to the causal mechanisms of nature' (1986: 8). As with Bourdieu's notion of 'fields', if social structures are 'like' magnetic fields, then, of course, they play a causal role, but they would then seem also to exist independently of action.[28]

Third, for all four, acknowledging the power of the tradition of interpretative sociology, there is a critical hermeneutic moment for all social science. But in contrast to Schütz, for example, actors' understandings of themselves and their social world are corrigible. Thus, getting a grasp of the actors' understanding is but a first step (albeit an essential one) for social science. For Bhaskar, staying within the tradition of Marx, there is always the possibility of ideology; for Giddens, 'the knowledgeability of human actors is always bounded on the one hand by the unconscious and on the other by unacknowledged conditions/unintended consequences of action' (1984: 282). Hence, as with C. Wright Mills and Bourdieu, but in contrast to the usual readings of Goffman and Garfinkel, social science is potentially emancipating.

CONCLUSION

Beginning in the 1950s, we have seen both a vigorous critique of the empiricist philosophy of science and a clear and defensible alternative in some form of realism. Attending this was an explosion of efforts to redefine social science in non-positivist terms: from pragmatism to hermeneutics to structuralism to poststructuralism to the synthetic efforts of Bourdieu, Bhaskar and Giddens. But it is not clear that positivism and its correlative scientism have been expunged, except perhaps among philosophers. On the other hand, dissidents in the academy seem more attracted to the view that the very idea of a human science is a mistake. But while Foucault, Bourdieu, Bhaskar and Giddens would agree that a *scientistic* social science is part of the problem, unlike many fashionable dissidents they would insist also that a proper human science is also a critical part of the solution.

REFERENCES

Achinstein, Peter ([1981] 1993) 'Can there be a model of explanation?' in David-Hillel Ruben (ed.), *Explanation*. Oxford: Oxford University Press.

Agger, Ben (1991) 'Critical Theory, Poststructuralism, Postmodernism: Their sociological relevance', *Annual Review of Sociology*, 17, 105–131.

Almond, Gabriel, and Verba, Sidney (1965) *The Civic Culture: Political Attitudes and Democracy in Five Nations, an Analytic Study*. Boston: Little Brown.

Althusser, Louis (1969) *For Marx*. Allen Lane: Penguin.

Anderson, Perry (1974) *Lineages of the Absolutist State*. London: NLB.

—— (1976) *Considerations on Western Marxism*. London: NLB.

—— (1980) *Arguments Within English Marxism*. London: Verso.

Archer, Margaret (1995) *Realist Social Theory: The Morphogenetic Approach*. Cambridge: Cambridge University Press.

Aronson, Gerald (1984) *A Realist Philosophy of Science*. New York: St. Martin's Press.

Ashley, Richard K. (1989) 'Living on Border Lines: Man, poststructuralism, and war', in James Der Derian and Michael Shapiro (eds.), *International/Intertextual Relations*. Lexington, MA: Heath.

Ashmore, Malcolm (1989) *The Reflexive Thesis: Wrighting Sociology of Knowledge*. Chicago: University of Chicago Press.

Augier, Mie (1999) 'Some Notes on Alfred Schütz and the Austrian School of Economics: Review of *Alfred Schütz's Collected Papers*, Vol. IV, ed. H. Wagner, G. Psatha and F. Kersten', *Review of Austrian Economics*, 11, 145–162.

Barnes, S.B. (1977) *Interests and the Growth of Knowledge*. London: Routledge and Kegan Paul.

Barthes, Roland (1957) *Mythologies*. Paris: Éditions du Seuil.

Bendix, Reinhard (1978) *Kings or People*. Berkeley: University of California Press.

Berger, Peter L. and Luckmann, Thomas (1967) *The Social Construction of Reality*. New York: Anchor Books.

Bhaskar, Roy ([1975] 1978) *A Realist Philosophy of Science*. 2nd Edn. Atlantic Highlands, NJ: Humanities Press.

———— (1978) 'On the Possibility of Social Scientific Knowledge and the Limits of Naturalism', *Journal for the Theory of Social Behavior*, 8(1), 1–28.

———— (1979) *The Possibility of Naturalism*. Atlantic Highlands, NJ: Humanities Press.

———— (1986) *Scientific Realism and Human Emancipation*. London: Verso.

Blau, Peter (1964) *Exchange and Power in Social Life*. New York: John Wiley.

Bloor, David (1976) *Knowledge and Social Imagery*. London: Routledge and Kegan Paul.

Blumer, Herbert (1969) *Symbolic Interactionism: Perspective and Method*. Englewood Cliffs, NJ: Prentice Hall.

Bohm, David ([1957] 1984) *Causality and Chance in Modern Physics*. London: Routledge and Kegan Paul.

Bourdieu, Pierre ([1989] 1996) *The State Nobility*. Cambridge: Polity.

Bourdieu, Pierre and Wacquant, Loïc J.D. (1992) *An Invitation to Reflexive Sociology*. Chicago: University of Chicago Press.

Brenner, Robert (1977) 'The Origins of Capitalist Development: A critique of neo-Smithian Marxism', *New Left Review*, 104, 25–92.

Bunge, Mario (1979) *Causality and Modern Science*. New York: Dover.

Burawoy, Michael (1998) 'The Extended Case Method', *Sociological Theory*, 16(1), 4–33.

Calhoun, Craig, Gerteis, Joseph, Moody, James, Pfaff, Steven and Virk, Indermohan (eds.) (2002) *Contemporary Sociological Theory*. Oxford: Basil Blackwell.

Camic, Charles (1987) 'The Making of Method: A historical reinterpretation of the early Parsons', *American Sociological Review*, 52 (August), 421–439.

Chisholm, Roderick (1946) 'The Contrary to Fact Conditional', *Mind*, 55, 289–307.

Clark, Stuart (1985) 'The *Annales* Historians', in Quentin Skinner (ed.), *The Return of Grand Theory*. Cambridge: Cambridge University Press.

Clifford, J. and Marcus, G.E. (1986) (eds.), *Writing Culture: The Poetics and Politics of Ethnography*. Berkeley: University of California Press.

Clough, P.T. (1992) *The Ends of Ethnography: From Realism to Social Criticism*. Newbury Park, CA: Sage.

Cohen, G.A. (1978) *Karl Marx's Theory of History: A Defense*. Princeton: Princeton University Press.

Coleman, James S. (1990) *Foundations of Social Theory*. Cambridge, MA: Harvard University Press.

Collins, H.M. (1985) *Changing Order: Replication and Induction in Scientific Practice*. Beverley Hills and London: Sage.

Cumings, Bruce (1998) 'Boundary Displacement: Area studies and international studies during and after the Cold War', in Christopher Simpson (ed.) *Universities and Empire: Money and Politics in the Social Sciences During the Cold War*. New York: The Free Press.

Denzin, Norman K. (1969) 'Symbolic Interactionism and Ethnomethodology: A proposed synthesis', *American Sociological Review*, 34(6), 922–934.

Denzin, Norman and Lincoln, Yvonne S. (eds.) (1994) *Handbook of Qualitative Research*. Thousand Oaks, CA: Sage.

Dewey, John (1927) *The Public and Its Problems*. Chicago: Swallow Press.

Dretske, Fred (1977) 'Laws of nature', *Philosophy of Science*, 44, 248–268.

Eisenstadt, S.N. (1961) *Essays on Sociological Aspects of Political and Economic Development*. The Hague: Mouton.

Elias, Norbert (1939) *The Civilizing Process*, Vol 1. New York: Pantheon.

———— (1982) *The Civilizing Process*, Vol 2. Oxford: Basil Blackwell.

Evans–Pritchard, Sir Edward (1981) *A History of Anthropological Thought* (ed. André Singer). New York: Basic Books.

Etzioni, A. and Etzioni, E. (eds.) (1964) *Social Change: Sources, Patterns and Consequences*. New York: Basic Books.

Foucault, Michel (2002) 'Truth and Power', in Craig Calhoun, Joseph Gerteis, James Moody, Steven Pfaff, and Indermohan Virk (eds.), *Contemporary Sociological Theory*. Oxford: Basil Blackwell.

Frankfort-Nachmias, Chava and Nachmias, David ([1976] 1992) *Research Methods in the Social Sciences*. New York: St. Martin's Press.

Friedman, Milton (1953) 'The Methodology of Positivist Economics', in Milton Friedman, *Essays in Positive Economics*. Chicago: University of Chicago Press.

Gamble, Andrew, Marsh, David and Tant, Tony (eds.) (1999) *Marxism and Social Science*. Urbana: University of Illinois Press.

Garfinkel, Harold (1996) 'Ethnomethodology's Program', *Social Psychological Quarterly*, 59 (1), 5–21.

Geertz, Clifford (1973) *Interpretation of Cultures*. New York: Basic Books.

———— (1983) *Local Knowledge: Further Essays in Interpretative Anthropology*. New York: Basic Books.

Giddens, Anthony (1976) *New Rules of Sociological Method*. London: Hutchinson.

———— (1981) *Contemporary Critique of Historical Materialism*. Berkeley: University of California Press.

———— (1984) *The Constitution of Society*. Berkeley: University of California Press.

Goffman, Erving (1961) *Asylums*. Garden City: Anchor Books.

———— (1974) *Frame Analysis*. Cambridge, MA: Harvard University Press.

Grathoff, Richard (ed.) (1978) *The Theory of Social Action*. Bloomington: Indiana University Press.

Green, Donald and Shapiro, Ian (eds.) (1996) *Pathologies of Rational Choice Theory: A Critique of Applications in Political Science*. New Haven: Yale University Press.

Guha, Ranajit and Chakravorty Spivak, Gayatri (eds.) (1988) *Selected Subaltern Studies*. New York: Oxford University Press.

Hacking, Ian (1979) 'Michel Foucault's Immature Science', *Noüs*, 13, 39–51.

Hall, Stuart ([1980] 1981) 'Cultural studies: Two paradigms', *Media, Culture and Society*, reprinted in Tony Bennett, John Municie and Richard Middleton (eds.) *Politics, Ideology and Popular Culture*. Milton Keynes: The Open University Press.

Harré, Rom (1970) *Principles of Scientific Thinking*. Chicago: University of Chicago Press.

———— (1986) *Varieties of Realism*. Oxford: Basil Blackwell.

Harré, Rom and Secord, Paul (1973) *The Explanation of Social Behavior*. Totowa, NJ: Littlefield, Adams.

Harré, Rom and Madden, Edward (1975) *Causal Powers*. Oxford: Basil Blackwell.

Hempel, C.G. (1950) 'The Theoretician's Dilemma', C.G. Hempel, *Aspects of Scientific Explanation*. New York: Free Press, 1965.

Hesse, Mary (1970) *Models and Analogies in Science*. Notre Dame: University of Notre Dame Press.

Hindess, B. and Hirst, P.Q (1975) *Precapitalist Modes of Production*. London: Routledge and Kegan Paul.

Homans, George (1987) 'Behaviorism and After', in A. Giddens and J. Turner (eds.), *Social Theory Today*. Oxford: Polity Press.

Hoy, David (1985) 'Jacques Derrida', in Quentin Skinner (ed.), *The Return of Grand Theory*. Cambridge: Cambridge University Press.

James, Susan (1985) 'Louis Althusser', in Quentin Skinner (ed.) *The Return of Grand Theory*. Cambridge: Cambridge University Press.

Jay, Martin (1973) *The Dialectical Imagination*. Boston: Little Brown.

Joas, Hans (1987) 'Symbolic Interactionism', in Jonathan Turner and Anthony Giddens (eds.), *Social Theory Today*. Oxford: Polity Press.

Kim, Jaegwon ([1987] 1993) 'Causal Realism and Explanatory Exclusion', in David-Hillel Ruben (ed.), *Explanation*. Oxford: Oxford University Press.

Knorr Cetina, Karin (1981) *The Manufacture of Knowledge: An Essay on the Constructivist and Contextual Nature of Science*. Oxford: Pergamon.

Kuhn, Thomas (1962) *The Structure of Scientific Revolutions*. Chicago: University of Chicago Press.

Kurtz, Lester R. (1984) *Evaluating Chicago Sociology*. Chicago: University of Chicago Press.

Kurzweil, Edith (1980) *The Age of Structuralism: Levi Strauss to Foucault*. New York: Columbia University Press.

Latour, Bruno (1987) *Science in Action*. Cambridge, MA: Harvard University Press.

Latour, Bruno and Woolgar, Steve (1979) *Laboratory Life: The Social Construction of Scientific Facts*. Beverly Hills: Sage.

Lawson, Tony (1997) *Economics and Reality*. London: Routledge.

Lazarsfeld, Paul F. and Rosenberg, Morris (eds.) (1955) *The Language of Social Research: A Reader in the Methodology of Social Research*. New York: The Free Press.

Leontief, Wassily (1982) Letter in *Science*, 217.

Lewis, David ([1987] 1993) 'Causal Explanation', in David-Hillel Ruben (ed.), *Explanation*. Oxford: Oxford University Press.

Livingston, E. (1986) *The Ethnomethodological Foundations of Mathematics*. Boston: Routledge and Kegan Paul.

Lynch, M., Livingston, E. and Garfinkel, H. (1983) 'Temporal Order in Laboratory Life', in C. Knorr and M. Mulkay (eds.), *Science Observed: Perspectives on the Social Study of Science*. Beverley Hills: Sage.

Lynch, M. (1985) *Art and Artifact in Laboratory Science*. London: Routledge and Kegan Paul.

Luhmann, Niklas (1997) 'Limits of Steering', *Theory, Culture and Society*, 14.1, 41–57.

Manicas, Peter T. (1987) *A History and Philosophy of the Social Sciences*. Oxford: Basil Blackwell.

———— (1991) 'The Social Science Disciplines: The American Model', in Peter Wagner, Bjφrn Wittrock and R. Whitley (eds.), *Discourses on Society. The*

Shaping of the Social Science Disciplines, Vol. XV. Dordrecht: Kluwer.

———— ([1992] 1994) 'Nature and Culture', *Proceedings and Addresses of the American Philosophical Association,* 66 (3); reprinted in John Ryder, *American Philosophical Naturalism.* Amherst, NY: Prometheus Books.

———— (2006) *A Realist Philosophy of Social Science.* Cambridge: Cambridge University Press.

Manicas, Peter T. and Rosenberg, Alan (1985) 'Naturalism, Epistemological Individualism and "The Strong Programme" in The Sociology of Knowledge', *Journal for the Theory of Social Behavior,* 15 (1), 76–101.

———— (1988) 'The Sociology of Scientific Knowledge: Can We Ever Get it Right?', *Journal for the Theory of Social Behavior,* 18 (1), 51–76.

Maynard, Douglas W. and Clayman, Steven E. (1991) 'The Diversity of Ethnomethodology', *Annual Review of Sociology,* 17, 385–418.

Mills, C. Wright (1956) *The Power Elite.* New York: Oxford University Press.

———— (1959) *The Sociological Imagination.* Middlesex: Penguin.

———— (1963) *Power, Politics and People: Collected Essays of C. Wright Mills* (ed. Louis Irving Horowitz). London: Oxford University Press.

———— (1966), *Sociology and Pragmatism: The Higher Learning in America.* New York: Oxford University Press.

Moore, Barrington (1966) *Social Origins of Dictatorship and Democracy.* Boston: Beacon Press.

Mulkay, Michael (1985) *The Word and the World: Explorations in the Form of Sociological Analysis.* London: Allen and Unwin.

Münch, Richard (1987) 'Parsonian Theory Today: In Search of New Synthesis', in Anthony Giddens and Jonathan H. Turner (eds.), *Social Theory Today.* Cambridge: Polity.

Natanson, Maurice (ed.) (1963) *Philosophy of the Social Sciences.* New York: Random House.

Nelson, Benjamin (1981) *On the Roads of Modernity,* T. Huff (ed.) Totowa, NJ: Rowman and Littlefield.

Oakes, Guy and Vidich, Arthur (1999). *Collaboration, Reputation, and Ethics in American Academic Life: Hans J. Gerth and C. Wright Mills.* Urbana: University of Illinois Press.

Ollman, Bertell and Vernoff, Edward (eds.) (1982) *The Left Academy.* New York: McGraw-Hill.

Outhwaite, William (1985) 'Hans-Georg Gadamer', in Quentin Skinner (ed.), *The Return of Grand Theory.* Cambridge: Cambridge University Press.

———— (1994) *Habermas: A Critical Introduction.* Oxford: Polity Press.

Parsons, Talcott (1937) *The Structure of Social Action.* New York: McGraw-Hill.

———— (1951) *The Social System.* Glencoe, IL: The Free Press.

———— (1968) *The Structure of Social Action.* New York: The Free Press.

Prendergast, Christopher (1986) 'Alfred Schütz and the Austrian School of Economics', *American Journal of Sociology,* 92 (1), 1–26.

Pettit, Philip (1977) *The Concept of Structuralism: A Critical Analysis.* Berkeley: University of California Press.

Pickering, Andrew (ed.) (1992) *Science as Practice and Culture.* Chicago: University of Chicago Press.

Porpora, Douglas (1989) 'Four Concepts of Social Structure', *Journal for the Theory of Social Behavior,* 19:2, 195–210.

Poster, Mark (1975) *Existential Marxism in Postwar France.* Princeton: Princeton University Press.

———— (1984) *Foucault, Marxism and History.* Cambridge: Polity.

Quine, W.V. (1950) 'Two Dogmas of Empiricism', in W.V. Quine, *From A Logical Point of View,* Cambridge, MA: Harvard University Press.

Rabinow, Paul (ed.) (1984) *The Foucault Reader.* New York: Pantheon.

Roberts, Marcus (1996) *Analytical Marxism: A Critique.* London: Verso.

Rosaldo, R. (1989) *Culture and Truth: The Remaking of Social Analysis.* Boston: Beacon Press.

Rostow, W.W. (1960) *The Stages of Economic Growth: A Non-Communist Manifesto.* Cambridge: Cambridge University Press.

Ruben, David-Hillel (ed.) (1993) *Explanation.* Oxford: Oxford University Press.

Salmon, Wesley (1978) 'Why Ask "Why?"' Presidential Address. American Philosophical Association, Vol. 51.

———— (1984) *Scientific Explanation and the Causal Structure of the World.* Princeton: Princeton University Press.

Sayer, Derek (1979) *Marx's Method: Ideology, Science and Critique in Capital.* Sussex: Harvester Press.

———— (1987) *The Violence of Abstraction.* Oxford: Basil Blackwell.

Schürmann, Reiner (1985) '"What Can I Do?" in an Archaeological-Genealogical History', *Journal of Philosophy,* 540–547.

Schütz, Alfred (1954) 'Concept and Theory Formation in the Social Sciences', *Journal of Philosophy,* LI (9), 257–273.

Scriven, Michael (1959) 'Truisms as Ground for Historical Explanations', in P. Gardiner (ed.), *Theories of History.* New York: Free Press.

———— (1962) 'Explanations, Predictions and Laws', in H. Feigl and G. Maxwell (eds.), *Minnesota Studies in the Philosophy of Science,* Vol. III. Minneapolis: University of Minnesota Press.

Sewell, William H., Jr. (1992) 'A Theory of Structure: Duality, Agency and Transformation', *American Journal of Sociology,* 98 (1) (July), 1–29.

Skinner Quentin (ed.) (1985) *The Return of Grand Theory in the Human Sciences*. Cambridge: Cambridge University Press.

Skocpol, Theda (ed.) (1984) *Vision and Method in Historical Sociology*. Cambridge, England: Cambridge University Press.

Smelser, Neil (1964) 'Towards a Theory of Modernization', in A. Etzioni and E. Etzioni, *Social Change: Sources, Patterns and Consequences*. New York: Basic Books.

Smelser, Neil and Swedberg, Richard (eds.) (1994). *The Handbook of Economic Sociology*. Princeton: Princeton University Press.

Soffer, Reba (1978) *Ethics and Society in England: The Revolution in the Social Sciences, 1870–1914*. Berkeley: University of California Press.

Somers, Margaret (1998) '"We're No Angels": Realism, Rational Choice, and Relationality in Social Science', *American Journal of Sociology*, 104 (3) (November), 722–784.

Stinchcome, Arthur (1983) *Economic Sociology*. New York: Academic Press.

Suppe, Frederick ([1974] 1977) *The Structure of Scientific Theories*. Urbana, IL: University of Illinois Press.

Thompson, E.P. (1978) *The Poverty of Theory and Other Essays*. London: Merlin Press.

Tiles, Mary (1984) *Bachelard: Science and Objectivity*. Cambridge: Cambridge University Press.

Tilly, Charles (1982) *As Sociology Meets History*. New York: Academic Press.

—— (1984) *Big Structures, Large Processes, Huge Comparisons*. New York: Russell Sage.

Toulmin, Stephen (1961) *Foresight and Understanding*. New York: Harper and Row.

Tribe, Keith (1981) *Genealogies of Capitalism*. Atlantic Highlands, NJ: Humanities Press.

—— (1991) 'Political Economy to Economics via Commerce: The Evolution of British Academic Economics 1860-1920', in Peter Wagner, Bjørn Wittrock, and Richard Whitley (eds.), *Discourses on Society: The Shaping of the Social Science Disciplines*. Dordrecht: Kluwer Academic Publishers.

Turner, Jonathan H. (1987) 'Analytical Theorizing', in Anthony Giddens and Jonathan Turner (eds.), *Social Theory Today*. Oxford: Polity Press.

Turner, Stephen (1994) *The Social Theory of Practices: Tradition, Tacit Knowledge, and Presuppositions*. Chicago: The University of Chicago Press.

Varela, Charles and Harré, Rom (1996) 'Conflicting Varieties of Realism: Causal Powers and the Problem of Social Structure', *Journal for the Theory of Social Behavior*, 26 (3), 313–325.

Vout, Malcolm (1991) 'Oxford and the Emergence of Political Science in England 1945–1960', in Peter

Wagner, Bjørn Wittrock, and Richard Whitley (eds.), *Discourses on Society: The Shaping of the Social Science Disciplines*. Dordrecht: Kluwer Academic Publishers.

Wagner, Helmut (1983) *Alfred Schütz: An Intellectual Biography*. Chicago: University of Chicago Press.

Wagner, Peter, Wittrock, Bjørn, and Whitley, Richard (eds.) (1991) *Discourses on Society: The Shaping of The Social Science Disciplines*. Dordrecht: Kluwer Academic Publishers.

Wallerstein, Immanuel (1974) *The Modern World System: Capitalist Agriculture and the Origins of the European World*. New York: Academic Press.

Woodward, James ([1984] 1993) 'A Theory of Singular Causal Explanation', in David-Hillel Ruben (ed.), *Explanation*. Oxford: Oxford University Press.

Woolgar, Steve (ed.) (1988) *Knowledge and Reflexivity: New Frontiers in the Sociology of Knowledge*. Beverly Hills: Sage.

NOTES

1 The foundations were laid in the US just after World War I when German-inspired historical social science was expunged and replaced by quantitative and behaviorally oriented programs. Symptomatic is Herbert Hoover's 1929 gathering of a distinguished group of social scientists 'to examine the feasibility of a national survey of social trends'. Funded by the Rockefeller Foundation with the full support of the Social Science Research Council and the Encyclopedia of the Social Sciences, four years of work by hundreds of inquirers resulted in 'The Ogburn Report', 1600 pages of quantitative research. Pitirim Sorokin, who had no objection to the appropriate use of statistics, was not impressed. He noted: 'In the future some thoughtful investigator will probably write a very illuminating study about these 'quantitative obsessions' … tell how such a belief became a vogue, how social investigators tried to 'measure' everything; how thousands of papers and research bulletins were filled with tables, figures, and coefficients; and how thousands of persons never intended for scientific investigation found in measurement and computation a substitute for real thought' (cited from Smelser, 1964: 27; see also Manicas, 1990).

2 Although the work of Harré is omitted therein, a useful one-volume review of this history is Suppe (1977).

3 The ground-breaking work on causality is Harré and Madden (1975). See also Bunge (1979) and Bohm (1984). One might argue that the covering law model is a *defining* attribute of 'empiricist' (positivist, neo-positivist) understandings of science. For a sample of some of the critical philosophical literature see Scriven (1959, 1962); Harré (1970, 1986); Dretske (1977);

Bhaskar (1975); Salmon (1978, 1984); Achinstein (1981); Aronson (1984); Woodward (1984); Lewis (1987); Kim (1987), Manicas (2006).

4 Most of the writers in a very influential 1963 text edited by Maurice Natanson assumed a positivist theory of science which was then polarized against a phenomenological alternative (see Natanson, 1963). An essay by Thelma Lavine offered that the problem was to 'naturalize' *Verstehen*, an idea roundly rejected by both Ernest Nagel and Natanson. Natanson offered: 'To reinvoke naturalistic criteria as correctives for a reconstructed naturalistic method is to take a step forward and follow with a step back.' For Natanson, since *Verstehen* was 'foundational', the 'way out' was 'the transcension of naturalism in favor of a phenomenological standpoint'. Indeed, after saying that W.I. Thomas, Cooley and Mead were 'all representatives of the phenomenological standpoint', Natanson offered that this '"transcension" could be achieved by adopting the phenomenological stance of Edmund Husserl.' But it is not clear that the Americans should be so identified, despite some similarities. Nor indeed, is it even clear what program Alfred Schütz was pursuing.

5 Already in 1937 Parsons had insisted that 'not only do theoretical propositions stand in logical interrelations to each other so that they may be said to constitute "systems" but it is in the nature of the case that theoretical systems should attempt to become "logically closed". That is, a system starts with a group of interrelated propositions which involve reference to empirical observations within the logical framework of the propositions in question.' And indeed, 'the simplest way to see the meaning of the concept of a closed system in this sense is to consider the example of a system of simultaneous equations. Such a system is determinate, i.e., closed, when there are as many independent equations as there are independent variables' (1937: 9–10) This was Pareto's dream, too often unacknowledged in the theoretical work of Parsons.

6 The relation of Mills to Hans Gerth, and their relation to Parsons's Weber makes for a good story in the sociology of the academy. See Oakes and Vidich (1999).

7 Explicitly drawing on Mead, in his 1940 'Situated Actions and Vocabularies of Motive', Mills had said much the same: 'As over against the inferential conception of motives as subjective "springs" of action, motives may be considered as typical vocabularies having ascertainable functions in delimited social situations ... Rather than fixed elements "in" an individual, motives are the terms with which interpretation of conduct by *social actors* proceeds. This imputation and avowal of motives are social phenomena to be explained' (Mills, 1963: 439). That is, for Mills, as for Blumer, the task is distinctly sociological and suggestive of the later work of Goffman and Garfinkel.

8 For Schütz: 'Summing up, we come to the conclusion that social things are understandable only if they can be reduced to human activities; and human activities can be made understandable only by showing in-order-to or because motives. This fact has its deeper reason in that I am able to understand other people's acts while living naively in the social world only if I can imagine that I myself would perform analogous acts if I were in the same situation as the Other, directed by the same motives or oriented by the same in-order-to motives—all these terms understood in the restricted sense of "typical" sameness...' (Grathoff, 1978: 53).

9 See especially, Lynch et al. (1983); Lynch (1985); and Livingston (1986). Ethnomethodology and strands from France have influenced Mulkay (1985), Woolgar (1988), and Ashmore (1989) in a more radical 'reflexive' (anti-realist) program.

10 Writing in 1982, Nobel Prize-winner Wassily Leontief had this to say: 'Page after page of professional economic journals are filled with mathematical formulas leading the reader from sets of more or less plausible but entirely arbitrary assumptions to precisely stated but irrelevant theoretical conclusions ... Year after year economic theorists continue to produce scores of mathematical models and to explore in great detail their formal properties; and the econometricians fit algebraic functions of all possible shapes to essentially the same sets of data without being able to advance, in any perceptible way, a systematic understanding of the structures and the operations of a real economic system'(Lawson, 1997, quoting Leontief, 1982: 104).

11 Two important non-European neo-Marxist developments must be noted here. 'Dependency theory' originated in Latin America with the early work of Paul Prebisch, Celso Furtado, Rudolfo Stavenhagen, Theotonio Dos Santos and Fernando Cardoso and Enzo Faletto. Appropriating key insights from the American Paul Baran, several variations, represented prominently by André Gunder Frank, Immanuel Wallerstein and Samir Amin, emerged. The central idea was the rejection of Marx's optimistic scenario, shared by mainstream modernization theory, in which the extension of capitalism globally would produce development globally. It was clear enough that this was not happening. 'Dependent development' produced pockets of development at the expense of continuing underdevelopment. Critical in the debate over the explanation of this was the question of the very idea of capitalism, whether it was defined in terms of the mode of production (as in Marx), or whether in terms of market relations (as in Wallerstein).

The other very important non-European development came from a group of Indian writers called 'the subaltern group'. As Edward Said remarked, these writers, 'fiercely theoretical and intellectually insurrectionary', sought an alternative to the problem that 'hitherto Indian history had been written from a colonist and elitist point of view, whereas a large part of Indian history had been made by the subaltern classes…' (Foreword to Guha and Chakravorty Spivak (eds.), 1988: v). Said notes that all these writers are critical students of Marx, and that they have drawn on a variety of sources, including structuralist and post-structuralism writers. See below.

12 Kojève's classes in Hegel included Raymond Aron, Maurice Merleau-Ponty, Albert Camus, Georges Bataille and Jacques Lacan. Hyppolite taught Hegel to Michel Foucault, Gilles Deleuze, Louis Althusser and Jacques Derrida.

13 In this context, 'humanism' includes the following elements: (a) the assumption of a human nature which defines a human essence, (b) a rejection of assumptions of existential freedom, and (c) a denial of the enlightenment vision of historical progress. See Hoy, 1985.

14 A very much shared set of assumptions and distinctions in use by structuralist writers derives from the early work of de Saussure, whose fragmented *Cours de Linguistique Générale* appeared posthumously in 1916. But it is not clear why his work became so important to the generation which followed World War II. Lévi-Strauss, often called the first structuralist, appropriated a host of distinctions, if not the de Saussurian linguistic model, to extra-linguistic materials. See his *Anthropologie Structurale* (1958) and *La Pensée Sauvage* (1962). For a very useful discussion of Lévi-Strauss, see James Boon, 'Claude Lévi-Strauss', in Skinner (1985). For discussion of the structuralist 'linguistic model', see Philip Pettit (1977). Barthes's *Mythologies* (1957) was also critical in this development. His view 'that language does not follow reality but signifies it' and that the analysis of structure offers 'not so much reality as intelligibility', is found also in the work of the *Annales* group. See Clark (1985).

15 His ideas quickly became *de rigueur* in France, and rapidly spread to Great Britain and to various parts of the Third World. They made little headway in the US, but then neither had existential Marxism. Régis Debray was his student, and it is said that Ché Guevara favored his views. He was, unlike most of the existential Marxists, a member of the French Communist Party. Indeed, when it did not join the students in the events of May 1968—a genuinely critical moment for French intellectuals—many were disillusioned regarding his posture as an independent intellectual interested only in promoting a truly 'scientific' Marx.

16 The term, *coupure épistémologique* was made popular by Althusser, who, however, put it to his own use. The term was introduced by the philosopher of science Gaston Bachelard in *La Formation de l'Esprit Scientifique* (1938) to refer to the necessary but discontinuous ruptures in conceptualization and framework from common sense to the scientific. Bachelard is ill-studied in the US, but his work was critical to a whole generation of French Marxists, including, importantly, via Canguilhem, the work of Foucault.

Preceding Kuhn, Bachelard sought to replace Cartesian foundationalist epistemology and to redefine 'objectivity' in historicist terms, similar in some ways to the effort of Weber. For an excellent account of Bachelard, see Mary Tiles (1984).

17 See J. Clifford and G.E. Marcus (1986), R. Rosaldo (1989), P.T. Clough (1992).

18 Commentators have noted a number of critical shifts following the events of 1968. In addition to an obviously overt political concern, these include the shift to genealogy, which, unlike archaeology, was understood in terms of power, a shift from systems of exclusion—e.g., the insane or criminal—to concern with how humans turn themselves into subjects; and, finally, a shift from language to 'discourse/practice', a shift which, it seems, was lost on some his American epigones.

19 Hacking speaks of 'systems of thought' as Foucault's domain and notes that these are not transparent and are studied 'by surveying a vast terrain of discourse that includes tentative starts, wordy prolegomena, brief flysheets and occasional journalism. We should think about institutional ordinances and the plans of zoological gardens, astrolabes or penitentiaries; we must read referees' reports and examine the botanical display cases of the dilettante' (Hacking, 1979: 42).

20 This is best seen in his rejection of the concept of ideology: 'The notion of ideology appears to me to be difficult to make use of, for three reasons. The first is that, like it or not, it always stands in virtual opposition to something else which is supposed to count as truth. Now I believe that the problem does not consist in drawing a line between that in a discourse which falls under category of scientificity or truth, and that which comes under some other category, but in seeing how effects of truth are produced within discourses which in themselves are neither true nor false. The second drawback is that the concept of ideology refers, I think necessarily, to something of the order of a subject. Thirdly, ideology stands in a secondary position relative to something which functions as its infrastructure, as its material, economic determinant, etc.' (Calhoun, et al., 2002: 204).

21 This is evidently different from both the 'interpretativist skepticism' which characterizes work influenced by Derrida, and it is also very different from what Wacquant terms 'textual reflexivity', a posture which appropriates a hermeneutic approach. Bourdieu comments: 'What [has] to be done [is] not magically to abolish [the distance between the observed and the observer] by a spurious primitivist participation but to objectivize this objectivizing distance and the social conditions which make it possible, such as the externality of the observer, the techniques of objectivation he uses, etc.' (Bourdieu and Wacquant, 1992: 42f.).

22 Comparison to Berger and Luckmann (1967) is apt here. There is a Hegelian tone to both, but it is not clear whether the form of 'dialectic' transcends

'subjective'/'objective' or whether it collapses into a Cartesian ontology in which 'subject' and 'object' are related causally, reminiscent of Engels's classic effort. Appeal to 'dialectics' is always troublesome. Compare also Giddens (1984) and Bhaskar (1978).

23 Once we adopt his re-visioning, we can see 'how artificial the ordinary oppositions between theory and research, between quantitative and qualitative methods, between statistical recording and ethnographic observation, between the grasping of structures and the constructing of individuals can be. These alternatives have no function other than to provide a justification for the vacuous and resounding abstractions of theoreticism and for the falsely rigorous observations of positivism, or, as the divisions between economists, anthropologists, historians and sociologists, to legitimate the limits of competency: that is to say that they function in the manner of a *social censorship* ...' (Bourdieu and Wacquant, 1992: 28).

24 Of significance, the successor to Isaiah Berlin's chair at Oxford was the Marxist philosopher G.A. Cohen, who, significantly, made his mark with an effort to 'defend' historical materialism. His 'defense' (1978) amounted to both a functionalism and a technological determinism. This generated a host of critical responses, including Derek Sayer's (1987) excellent work. See also Giddens (1981).

25 Derek Sayer (1979) makes a persuasive case that Marx's implicit theory of science was a powerful form of realism.

26 In addition to the work done by the Edinburgh group, other strands in Sociology of Scientific Knowledge (SSK) must be mentioned. All reject the Merton-defined American mainstream sociology of knowledge. Harry Collins (1985) inspired a group at Bath; and a 'Paris' group, led by Bruno Latour (1979, 1987) with Bachelard and Canguilhem in the background, emerged. Another 'continental independent'

is K. Knorr Cetina (1981). An extremely useful collection is Pickering (1992).

27 Compare Bourdieu (1992). There are also differences between the three on how to resolve the problem of relativism in epistemology. Bhaskar gives the most developed argument for his transcendental realism. Giddens has not pursued the problem in any detail, but see his remarks in his 1976 (Introduction, and pp. 144–154). Since indeed, the Edinburgh group is doing sociology of knowledge and since it is a key feature of it being a 'strong programme' that 'the same types of causes would explain true and false beliefs' (Bloor, 1976: 7), their work has generated a huge critical literature from philosophers who are profoundly offended by its 'relativism'. For a critical review of some of this, see Manicas and Rosenberg (1985, 1988).

28 In Aristotelian fashion, Bhaskar distinguishes efficient causes—agents—and material causes, as for Marx, the 'materials of action'. For a critical account, see Varela and Harré (1996). Paradoxically, Giddens has also been read as dissolving agency into structure. See Ashley (1989: 277).

For a defense of Bhaskar and criticism of Giddens see Porpora (1989) and Archer (1995). These writers insist that on Giddens's account (but not Bhaskar's), 'structure' is insufficiently 'objective.' Compare here Bourdieu. This has been the more typical response to Giddens. See also Michael Burawoy (1998), who, while valuing 'reflexivity' and ethnographic depth, holds that for Giddens 'in the end intuitive notions of structure evaporate and we are left with a voluntarist vision that emphasizes the control we exercise over our worlds.' See also Manicas (2006) and Sewell (1992), who argues that 'resources' must be theorized as having actual rather virtual existence. But this would seem to reinstate the bifurcations that Giddens was trying to transcend.

2

Interdisciplinary Approaches in Social Science Research[1]

Julie Thompson Klein

Claims for the origin of interdisciplinarity span the centuries. Its formal emergence, though, is linked with the institutionalization of disciplines as a system of *Wissenschaft* marked by both differentiation and cooperation (Vosskamp, 1986: 20–1). Interdisciplinarity assumes the existence as well as the relative resilience of disciplines as models of thought and institutional practices (Moran, 2002: 17). A clear set of categories for denoting domains of social inquiry crystallized during the period extending from 1850 to 1914 (Wallerstein, 1995: 840). Even at that early point, the interplay between movements for specialization and for integration was apparent. August Comte, for one, envisioned a unified social science from the outset (Miller, 1982: 1). Over the course of the 20th century, competing intellectual syntheses emerged, and the number and variety of interdisciplinary activities increased. As a result, interdisciplinarity is a now familiar part of the intellectual landscape in Europe and North America. Familiar as it is, however, individuals and teams are often uncertain about its definition and nature. This chapter answers their most common questions. It sorts out the plurality and historical patterns of activities in social sciences, core

terminology and differing practices, and key methodological issues.

PLURALITY AND HISTORICAL PATTERNS

The history of social sciences in Europe and North America differs. Influences and rates of development vary, as do national interests. However, Neil Smelser emphasizes that the ultimate outcome has been similar—the forming of separate academic departments or faculties in universities. The 'mainstream' disciplines are anthropology, economics, political science, psychology and sociology. Yet, Smelser cautions, describing social sciences solely with reference to the 'big five' disciplines distorts reality in two ways. First, under those headings, various subareas of investigation rely on variables and explanations outside the commonly understood scope of social sciences. Geopolitics, socio-biology, behavioral genetics and behavioral neuroscience all appeal to non-social and non-psychological explanatory variables and explanations. Second, another range of disciplines could be labeled behavioral and social–scientific, although not entirely so. Demography might be considered a separate social science, or part of sociology, economics and anthropology. Archaeology might be classed as part of anthropology or as an independent social science. Geography, history, psychiatry, law and linguistics present similar complications for taxonomy. So do relations with the 'intersecting fields' of genetics, behavior, and society; behavioral and cognitive neurosciences; psychiatry; health; gender studies; religious studies; expressive forms; environmental/ecological sciences and technology studies; area and international studies; and urban studies and planning public policy. Assignment to one category of inquiry or another would vary according to the criteria used (Smelser 2004: 44, 48, 60–1).

Intersecting fields, in particular, have attracted a great deal of attention in discussions of interdisciplinarity because they are linked closely with innovation and novel approaches. Observing the increased number of hybrid formations, Dogan and Pahre (1990) proposed a theory of hybridization. The first stage of this process is specialization, and the second stage is continuous re-integration of fragments of specialities across disciplines. There are two types of hybrids. The first kind becomes institutionalized as a sub-field of a discipline or as a permanent cross-disciplinary committee or program. The second kind remains informal. Hybrids often form in the gaps between sub-fields. Child development, for example, incorporates developmental psychology, developmental physiology, language acquisition, and socialization. Hybrids may also beget other hybrids. Genetic epistemology is a hybridization of epistemology and general psychology that has fostered new affiliations. Psychologists interested in child development, for instance, are less likely to study clinical psychology than to use developmental psychology or the linguistic literature on language acquisition. Likewise, a sociologist interested in urbanization will have more in common with a geographer doing research on the distribution of cities than a sociologist studying social stratification.

Dogan and Pahre (1990) reject the term 'interdisciplinary research' as a catch-all notion that lacks the specialist focus of intersecting sub-fields. They also tend to universalize the notions of core and frontier, when in fact the balance of conventional and innovative practices varies by discipline. Nonetheless, they document the growing presence of hybrid forms. They also acknowledge the varied trajectories and conflicting interests in the same domain. Social psychology, for example, is often touted as a major interdiscipline, but it exhibits divisions along sociological and psychological interests. In contrast to hybrid formations, other activities may be less visible on knowledge taxonomies. One of the most common is the borrowing of tools, methods, concepts, and theories, including such notable examples as the importation of rational-choice models from economics into political science and sociology. Depending on one's point of view, Smelser (2004: 53–4) advises, the business of importing and exporting may be viewed as 'borrowing' or as 'imperialism'. Borrowing is generally regarded as a lower-level utilitarian type of interdisciplinarity. It is an important indicator of change, though. Patterns of borrowing signal new networks of affiliation and some borrowings become so incorporated into daily practices that they are no longer regarded as 'foreign'.

Synoptic work is another activity that has fostered claims of 'inherently interdisciplinary' identity. Geography's broad scope is evident in a multitude of conceptual and analytical approaches, from earth sciences to humanities. Synoptic scope, though, is more a matter of multidisciplinary expanse than deliberate interdisciplinary integration. Synthetic work of a different kind occurs in efforts to combine basic research findings from a large number of sub-fields, to integrate results from cognate disciplines, and to merge existing and new knowledge about a particular place or a region into a cohesive portrayal of an area. At the same time, another kind of interdisciplinary activity occurs in applied research on societal problems (Association of American Geographers, 1995: 39).

Even economics, which patrols its boundaries more closely than other social sciences, has multiple affiliations. In a study of disciplinarity based on a literature review and interviews, Tony Becher (1989: 36) found economics portrayed as having 'one common frontier with mathematics and another with political science; some trade relations with history and sociology; and a lesser measure of shared ground with psychology, philosophy and law'.

Sociology too exhibits a plurality of activities. Craig Calhoun (1992) reports that it is in principle a synthetic discipline that aspires to be the most synthetically encompassing of all social sciences. Yet, beyond holistic and generalist claims, it is also an interstitial discipline that fills in gaps among other social sciences and works along their borders. Sociology, Hunter and Brewer (2003: 577) add, has drawn more eclectically from the methodologies of other disciplines, borrowing fieldwork from anthropology, experiments from psychology, voting and public opinion polls from political science, and archival research from history. Calhoun's study of citation patterns in major sociological journals between the late 1940s and late 1980s demonstrates why the principle of clear and principled disciplinary divisions of labor does not hold. Citations to economics and interdisciplinary fields of organizational, administrative, management, and labor studies became more prominent over the years. So did references to interdisciplinary social and behavioral science publications and the field of political economy, especially with the rise of Marxist journals and development studies. Population became more prominent too, and also political science in the later 1960s. Citations to 'non-disciplinary' statistics and measurement journals grew gradually, and public opinion and public affairs journals were frequently cited in the middle of the period (Calhoun 1992: 137–8, 140–5, 148, 170).

Anthropology too has multiple affiliations. Its relationship with sociology is particularly long-standing. The early Chicago School of social science stressed ethnographical methods, and anthropology was the discipline implicated most closely in the efforts of Talcott Parsons and others to develop a general theory of society. Anthropology also shared a broadly functionalist orientation with sociology for many years and a broadly evolutionary orientation before that (Calhoun, 1992: 148). Interdisciplinary activities pluralized as the discipline expanded beyond the 'sacred bundle' of four fields that Franz Boas defined, spanning biological history, linguistics, ethnology, and prehistoric archaeology. Since 1983, George Stocking Jr recounts, many 'adjectival anthropologies' have emerged, and the number of subsidiary societies, associations and councils have increased. Anthropology's boundaries have always been problematic, but even more so in the period of 'crisis' and 'reinvention'. Anthropologists were more open to poststructuralist and postmodernist thought than other social scientists, destabilizing and relativizing a broad range of intellectual categories at the same time that a general blurring of genres and disciplinary boundaries was underway (Stocking, 1995: 933–5, 954–5; Calhoun, 1992: 153).

Historical Patterns

As the introductory overview reveals, there are historical patterns to interdisciplinary activities. Roberta Frank speculated that the very idea might have been born in the 1920s at the corner of 42nd and Madison Avenue in New York City, where the Social Science Research Council (SSRC) was located. The term was shorthand for research that crossed more than one of the Council's seven societies. The SSRC was the first council of its kind in the world and became a model for councils in other countries. Even at this early point in the formation of modern disciplines, the SSRC aimed to accelerate the tendency toward breaking down boundaries by cross-fertilizing ideas and joining methods and techniques. It brought together representatives of anthropology, sociology, political science, economics, psychology, statistics and history, with the aim of producing purposive and empirical social problem-oriented applied research, including targeted programs in such problem fields as social security and public administration (Frank, 1988: 91; Fisher, 1993: 4, 6, 9, 205–6, 220–3, 229).

In characterizing the early history of interdisciplinary approaches in social sciences, Landau et al. (1962: 8, 12–17) distinguish two phases. The first phase, dating from the close of World War I to the 1930s, was embodied in the founding of the SSRC, the University of Chicago School of Social Science, and publications such as Ogburn and Goldenweiser's *The Social Sciences* (1927). The interactionist framework at Chicago fostered integration, and members of the Chicago school were active in the efforts of Otto Neurath and others to construct a unified philosophy of natural and social sciences. The impact of these efforts was widely felt, and the scope and data of disciplines altered as a result. On occasion disciplinary 'spillage' even led to the embryonic formation of hybrid disciplines such as social psychology, political sociology, physiological psychology, and social anthropology. Yet, traditional categories of knowledge, structures of fields, and the organization of academic work remained intact. There was also a distinct pattern of interactions. Social scientists tended to emulate natural sciences, heightening concern for objectivity, precision and quantification. In the interests of scientific analysis, techniques and instruments were borrowed to support testing and measurement. Hence, the first phase was empirical in nature and instrumental in character.

The second phase, dating from the close of World War II, was stimulated by developments in logic and in the philosophy and sociology of science. It was embodied in 'integrated' social science courses, a growing tendency for interdisciplinary programs to become 'integrated' departments, and the concept of behavioral science. The traditional categories that anchored the disciplines for over a half-century were questioned and lines between fields began to blur, paving the way toward a new theoretical coherence and

alternative divisions of labor and distribution of resources. The emergence of area studies in the late 1930s was a particularly prominent development. The concept of area differed from earlier and more limited forms of 'interdisciplinary' borrowing. It was a new 'integrative' conceptual category with greater analytic power, stimulating a degree of theoretical convergence that was also potential in the concepts of role, reference groups, mobility, status, self, decision-making, action, information, communication, and applications of game theory.

Landau et al. (1962) liken the early 'interdisciplinary' approach to the older Baconian belief that broad basic generalizations will almost automatically drop out of the mass accumulation of discrete facts. In contrast, the behavioral science movement did not aim to borrow, reify and tack methods and concepts onto traditional categories. It sought an alternative method of organizing social inquiry based on theories of behavior that fixed the field of focus in a different way. When a political scientist, for example, adopts decision-making explicitly as a frame of reference, the nature of the field of focus changes and the work is not just 'politics'. The alternative construct attempts to order behavioral events in a theoretical context that is also sociological or psychological, or both. Differentiation of fields of focus also becomes a matter of theoretical relevance and conceptual clarity, not simply a function of 'convention and treaty'.

The culture–personality movement was another example that focused on links between macro and micro levels. In addition, a spirit of reform in the post-World War II period encouraged integrative thinking in government and private agencies about societal problems such as war, labor relations, population shifts, housing shortages, crime and welfare (Landau et al., 1962: 12). Applied social science was further stimulated by technological advances during the war. New engineering and technological methods evolved from operational research, feedback systems and computer manipulation. New conceptual tools of communication theory, game theory and decision theory also promoted common ground, fostering a new 'cross-disciplinary intelligence' with conceptual power (Mahan, 1970: 104). The import and export of tools was evident in the rise of behavioral political science during the 1950s and 1960s. Researchers relied heavily on methodological tools (such as survey research), theoretical formulations (such as modernization) and general theoretical orientations (such as structural–functionalism) that were all established to some degree in sociology at the time (Smelser, 2004: 53).

In the latter half of the 20th century, new developments expanded the scope of interdisciplinary research. One set of developments looked to the sciences. From the mid-1800s onwards, the sciences have been influential in the formulation of social research methods associated with positivism, empiricism, and quantitative or numerical techniques. These approaches reflect a set of assumptions about the social world: that it can be observed and measured directly, that meaning is fixed and universal, and that the study of human behavior can produce general statements or laws. Survey research, for instance, aims to control the elements that are being examined through construction of a closed system of sampling, and experimental research is controlled by the design of the experiment. The focus has tended to be on individual units of a system, and research is driven by processes of hypothesis formation and concept operationalism (Yates, 2004: 5, 12–14).

With the growing sophistication of scientific tools and approaches, new biological explanations of human behavior became possible and new hybrids developed with affiliations to cognitive science and neurosciences. New quantitative methods and advanced computing power facilitate the sharing of large quantities of data across disciplinary boundaries. Technologies of brain imaging and magnetic resonance imaging also facilitate mapping brain functions with increasing precision, and a new 'postdisciplinary' community of interests is emerging in projects such as Thomas Spence Smith's

investigation of the neurosociological foundations of human interactions during the earliest years of life (2004: 200–1).

The other set of developments looked toward humanities, informed by postpositivist, poststructural, constructivist, interpretive, and critical paradigms (Tashakkori and Teddlie, 2003b: 23). Some new approaches such as feminism, neo-Marxism, and the expanding field of cultural studies were self-described 'interdisciplinary' interventions into traditional practices. In 1980, anthropologist Clifford Geertz also identified a broader shift that was occurring within intellectual life in general and social sciences in particular. The model of physical sciences and a laws-and-instances ideal of explanation was being supplanted by a case-and-interpretation model and symbolic form analogies. Social scientists were increasingly representing society as a game, a drama or a text, rather than as a machine or a quasi-organism. They were borrowing methods of speech-act analysis, discourse models and cognitive aesthetics, crossing the traditional boundary of explanation and interpretation. Former keywords of 'cause', 'variable', 'force' or 'function' were being replaced by a new vocabulary of 'rules', 'representation', 'attitude', and 'intention'. On the other side of the fence—as social scientists were talking of 'actors', 'scenes', 'plots', 'performance' and 'personae'— humanists were talking of 'motives', 'authority', 'persuasion', 'exchange' and 'hierarchy'. Geertz rejected 'interdisciplinary brotherhood' or 'highbrow eclecticism'. Yet, he acknowledged, the principles of mapping knowledge were changing—conventional rubrics remained, but they were often jerry-built to accommodate a situation that was increasingly 'fluid, plural, uncentered, and ineradicably untidy'.

Increasing frustration with methodological purism and naïve empiricism, coupled with critical debates on methodology, also encouraged a 'third methodological movement'. The mixed-methods movement is young, and not all combinations or techniques of 'triangulation' are interdisciplinary. Yet, mixed methods are generating more complex borrowings across disciplinary lines (Rallis and Rossman, 2003: 491; Tashakkori and Teddlie, 2003c: ix–xii; Tashakkori and Teddlie, 2003b: 24). Mixed methods draw from both quantitative and qualitative traditions, combining them in unique ways to solve practical research problems and to answer research questions. Quantitative and numerical methods are more strongly associated with areas of sociology, psychology and politics. Qualitative and textual methods are more strongly associated with sociology, social anthropology, social psychology and cultural studies. Yet, alignment of quantitative work with the nomothetic goal of constructing general laws and alignment of qualitative work with the ideographic goal of detailed description of particular circumstances is not an absolute split. Researchers from all these disciplines, Simeon Yates (2004: 133, 135) reports, use one or more of these methods.

TERMINOLOGY AND TYPOLOGY

In early books that presented the entire field of social science as a unit, the word 'interdisciplinary' was not prominent. The term 'cooperative', Frank reports, was more customary. Books published between 1925 and 1930 also stressed 'interrelation', 'mutual interdependence', 'interpenetration', 'interactions' of disciplines, and the need to explore 'twilight zones' and 'border areas' in order to fill 'unoccupied spaces' and to encourage 'active cultivations of borderlands between the several disciplines'. The word 'interdisciplinary' also did not appear in the 15–volume *Encyclopaedia of the Social Sciences* (1930–1935). By the early 1930s, though, 'inter-discipline' and 'interdisciplinary' were appearing more widely. The first citation for the term in *Webster's Ninth New Collegiate Dictionary* and *A Supplement to the Oxford English Dictionary* came from a December 1937 issue of the *Journal of Educational Sociology*, in a subsequent notice about SSRC postdoctoral fellowships. By mid-century, Frank (1988: 92–6) surmised, it was common coin in social sciences

and grew during the late 1960s and 1970s into a 'kind of weather'.

The new 'weather' was stirred by worldwide demands for reform of universities. Heightened interest led to the first international conference on problems of interdisciplinary research and teaching in member countries of the Organization for Economic Cooperation and Development (OECD). Held in 1970 in France, the meeting produced the most widely influential set of terminology (OECD, 1972). The OECD typology presented four descriptors for teaching and research beyond disciplinary approaches. Over the next three decades, 'multidisciplinary' and 'interdisciplinary' became widely known; 'pluridisciplinary', while used, is cited less widely. 'Transdisciplinarity' had a restricted application at first, though by the start of the 21st century it had attained a new currency. The three words that gained the widest usage provide a framework for thinking about different types of practice. The differences represent points on a continuum of integration rather than absolute states. A program, a project or a field may move across points of the continuum over time and in sub-units. The distinction between the first two terms—*multidisciplinarity* and *interdisciplinarity*—is a matter of fairly wide consensus, based on the following characteristics.

Multidisciplinary approaches juxtapose separate disciplinary perspectives, adding breadth of knowledge, information and methods. Individuals and groups work independently or sequentially in an encyclopedic alignment or ad hoc mix. They retain their separate perspectives, and disciplinary elements remain intact. The OECD definition of 'interdisciplinary' was quite broad, ranging from simple communication of ideas to mutual integration of organizing concepts, methodology, procedures, epistemology, terminology, data, and organization of research and education (OECD, 1972: 25). Interdisciplinarity, though, is conventionally defined as a more conscious and explicitly focused integration that creates a holistic view or common understanding of a complex issue, question or problem. Seminar participants also introduced finer distinctions and, as the idea of interdisciplinarity proliferated, other terms emerged that signify differing practices and claims of what constitutes 'genuine' or 'true' interdisciplinarity. Some distinctions refer to scope. 'Narrow interdisciplinarity' occurs between disciplines with compatible methods, paradigms and epistemologies, such as history and literature. It has a different dynamic than 'broad' or 'wide' interdisciplinarity between disciplines with little or no compatibility, such as sciences and humanities (Van Dusseldorp and Wigboldus, 1994; Kelly, 1996). The Nuffield Foundation also proposed a macro distinction premised on two basic metaphors: bridge-building and restructuring. Bridge-building occurs between complete and firm disciplines. Restructuring detaches parts of several disciplines to form a new coherent whole, often with an implicit criticism of the state of those disciplines (The Nuffield, 1975: 43–4).

Ten years after the pioneer OECD seminar, Raymond Miller presented a more detailed typology for social sciences based on seven categories of 'cross-disciplinary' efforts: topical focus, professional preparation, life experience perspective, shared components, cross-cutting organizing principles, hybrids, and grand synthesis. *Topics* are associated with problem areas. 'Crime', for instance, is a social concern that appears in multiple social science disciplines and in criminal justice and criminology programs. Likewise, the topics of 'area', 'labor', 'urban' and 'environment' led to new academic programs. So did 'gerontology'. *Professional Preparation* led to new fields with a vocational focus, such as social work and nursing and, Smelser (2004: 61) adds, fields of application to problem areas such as organization and management studies, media studies and commercial applications, and planning public policy. The category of *Life Experience* became prominent in the late 1960s and 1970s with the development of ethnic studies and women's studies. And, the category at the

heart of Dogan and Pahre's theory, *Hybrids* formed 'interstitial crossdisciplines' such as social psychology, economic anthropology, political sociology, biogeography, culture and personality, and economic history (Miller, 1982: 11–15, 19).

Miller's category of *Shared Components* is particularly relevant to a volume on methodology. It has a 'longer and quieter history' than the other classifications. *Components* refers both to shared methods, such as techniques of statistical inference, and to conceptual vehicles, such as the mathematics of probability, or game theory, and information. Smelser adds the examples of computer sciences; methodological issues associated with design, execution, and assessment of empirical research; and logic of inquiry and research design including non-statistical examples such as comparative analysis, experimental methods and ethnography (2004: 60). Some methodologies, Tony Becher observed, even form the basis of recognized specialties, such as statistics, oral history, and econometrics (1989: 49). Miller's fifth category of *Cross-Cutting Organizing Principles* is similar. A focal concept or a fundamental social process such as 'role' or 'exchange' may cut across disciplines. Comparably, Ursula Hübenthal labeled the adoption of a model from another science *Concept Interdisciplinarity*, citing the examples of system theory, cybernetics, information theory, synergetics, game theory, semiotics and structuralism (1994: 66).

Wilhelm Vosskamp (1986: 25) grouped method-interdisciplinarity and concept-interdisciplinarity together as aspects of methodology. So did Jack Mahan when he linked common-ground methods, concepts, languages, logics, techniques, and strategies that facilitate communication across disciplines. In addition to statistical design, experimental design, mathematical models, and computer models, Mahan (1970: 114–15) cited procedures of data acquisition, surveying, interviewing, sampling, polling, case studies, and cross-cultural analysis.

The Academy of Finland Integrative Research (AFIR) team shed light on the core action in *Methodological Interdisciplinarity*. In a study of research proposals submitted to the country's key national funding agency for basic research, the team found the typical activity was combining methods from different disciplines or fields in order to test a hypothesis, to answer a research question or to develop a theory. The typical motivation is to improve the quality of results, not to generate a new theoretical construct (Bruun et al., 2005: 51). Hence, Methodological Interdisciplinarity is also regarded as a lower form of interaction. Heinz Heckhausen (1972: 86) labeled the borrowing of analytical tools such as mathematical models and computer simulation 'pseudo' and 'auxiliary' interdisciplinarity. The distinction depends on whether need for the method is transitory or enduring.

Another difference of type emerged as well. Empirical and methodological forms are strongly apparent in 'strategic', 'pragmatic', 'opportunistic', and 'instrumental' research that focuses on technologies of information and application for economic and technological problem-solving. In the 1980s and 1990s, interdisciplinarity gained heightened international visibility in science-based areas of economic competition such as computers, manufacturing, biotechnology and biomedicine. Strategic forms integrate disciplinary, professional and/or interdisciplinary approaches without regard for questions of epistemology or institutional structure. In contrast, 'critical' and 'reflexive' approaches interrogate the existing structure of knowledge and education with the aim of transforming them, raising questions of value and purpose that are silent in strategic forms.

New fields in Miller's Life Experience category were often imbued with a critical imperative, and many poststructuralist and postmodern practices constructed interdisciplinarity as an inherently political project. In a collection of research stories from the Canadian academy, Salter and Hearn (1996) called interdisciplinarity the necessary 'churn in the system', aligning the concept with a dynamic striving for change. Interdisciplinary work is most successful, Steve Fuller contends,

when borders are constantly engaged and when boundaries are being moved around as the result of constructive border engagements, not when there are rigid boundaries or no boundaries at all. Disciplines begin to see each other involved in a common enterprise and their boundaries are renegotiated (Fuller, 1993: 185). The distinction between *Instrumental* and *Critical* forms is not absolute. Research on problems of the environment and health often combine critique and problem-solving. Yet, critique is a major fault line in the debate over what constitutes 'genuine' interdisciplinarity.

Theoretical Interdisciplinarity and Transdisciplinarity

Theoretical Interdisciplinarity lies at a further point along the continuum of integration. The AFIR team found that the primary focus is developing, applying or combining conceptual tools with the aim of building a comprehensive general view, a theoretical synthesis or an integrative framework. To illustrate the difference, researchers in one project sought to develop a theoretical model of mechanisms that mediate mental stress experiences into physiological reactions and eventually the somatic illness of coronary heart disease. Previous studies emphasized correlation of single stress factors or separate personal features with the disease. In contrast, the project aimed to develop an interdisciplinary theory based on integration of psychological and medical elements and testing the conceptual tool of inherited 'temperament' (Bruun et al., 2005: 52). The outcomes of theoretical interdisciplinarity may also include conceptual frameworks for analysis of particular problems, integration of propositions across disciplines, and frameworks based on continuities between models, analogies or metatheory.

Macro social theory is a form of Theoretical Interdisciplinarity that has long been pursued in social science, including the work of Emile Durkheim, Georg Simmel, Max Weber, Robert Park and Talcott Parsons. Camic's and Joas's review of recent efforts documents the continuing quest in North America and Europe. British theorist Anthony Giddens has sought a new synthesis geared toward the contemporary world that is based on conceptual innovation and combines the strengths of multiple perspectives and approaches that would yield a new structuration theory. In the US, Randall Collins called for a comprehensive theory of every area of society that would arise from comparing, synthesizing and cumulating findings of specialized areas. He aims to link micro-level social interactional processes to macro-level social structures. Jeffrey Alexander has worked toward a convergence of all major classical and contemporary sociological theories, promoting multi-dimensional synthesis of normative and instrumental conceptions of action, material and ideal conceptions of order: a micro–macro synthesis that integrates actions and structure as well as subjectivity and objectivity, a new synthetic social theory along the model of culture-as-language, and an emerging neo-functionalism that might re-link theorizing about action and order, conflict and stability, and structure and culture. In France, Alain Touraine has urged reunification based on a general representation of society, a general vision of change, and an analysis of how actors are shaped and how humans can create a new society. In Germany, Jürgen Habermas has worked to preserve ties between system and lifeworld in an encompassing theory of communicative action. Niklas Luhmann has also drawn on biology and cybernetics to create a synthetic framework for analysis of autopoetic, or self-referential, social systems that might inform a comprehensive theory of everything that is 'social' (Camic and Joas, 2004: 1, 3–4).

Synthetic theoretical activity, Smelser (2004: 54) and the Nuffield Foundation observed, overlaps with the OECD notion of transdisciplinarity. The Nuffield Foundation noted a third possibility beyond bridge-building and reconstruction that occurs when a new overarching concept of theory subsumes theories and concepts of several existing disciplines, comparable to Miller's notion of *Grand Synthesis* (The Nuffield, 1975: 47). In the OECD typology, transdisciplinarity was defined as a 'common system of axioms for a set of disciplines', such as anthropology construed as the science of humans and their accomplishments. Transdisciplinary approaches transcend the narrow scope of disciplinary worldviews through a comprehensive and overarching synthesis (OECD, 1972: 25–6). Characteristic of the time, the organizing languages of general systems theory, structuralism, and cybernetics were prominent among OECD seminar participants. Today, the word has a new heightened currency evident in three trendlines of meaning.

One trendline is the contemporary version of the ancient quest for systematic integration of knowledge, not in the name of a single totalizing theory but new paradigms that recognize complexity and difference. This effort is being advanced by several groups, including the International University Reforms Observatory (ORUS) network of European and Latin American academics (http://www.orus-int.org/) and the Centre International de Recherches et Études Transdisciplinaire (http://perso.club-internet.fr/nicol/ciret). The second trendline is an extension of the OECD connotation of new synthetic frameworks. General systems, structuralism, Marxism, policy sciences, feminism, ecology and sociobiology became leading examples. The notion of 'transdisciplinary science' has also emerged in broad areas such as cancer research. This usage labels 'transcendent interdisciplinary research' that creates theoretical frameworks for defining and analyzing social, economic, political, environmental, and institutional factors in human health and well-being (Rosenfield, 1992).

The third trendline is the heightened imperative of problem-solving. This mandate is not new in social sciences. The pressing weight of social problems, though, prompted the OECD to declare in 1982 that interdisciplinarity *exogenous* to the university now takes priority over *endogenous university interdisciplinarity*. The exogenous originates in the continuous momentum generated by 'real' problems of the community and the demand that universities perform their pragmatic social mission (OECD, 1972: 130).

The momentum continued to grow. Eight years later, Robert Costanza proposed making transdisciplinary problem-solving the primary function of academics, requiring the creation of colleges, departments or programs of integrated transdisciplinary studies and fields (1990: 100–1). Gibbons et al. (1994) took a step further, proposing that a new mode of knowledge production has emerged that is fostering synthetic reconfiguration and recontextualization of knowledge. The older Mode 1 was hierarchical and homogeneous, with emphasis on disciplinary boundary work and certification. The new Mode 2 is characterized by complexity, hybridity, non-linearity, reflexivity, heterogeneity and transdisciplinarity. New configurations of research work are being generated continuously; the number of places where research is performed has increased; and a new social distribution of knowledge is occurring as a wider range of organizations and stakeholders brings heterogeneous skills and expertise to problem-solving.

Gibbons et al. (1994) initially highlighted contexts of application and use, such as aircraft design, pharmaceutics, electronics, and other industrial and private-sector research. In 2001, Nowotny et al. extended the Mode 2 theory to argue that contextualization of problems requires moving from the strict realm of application to the *agora* of public debate. When lay perspective and alternative knowledges are recognized, a shift occurs from solely 'reliable' scientific knowledge to inclusion of 'socially robust knowledge'. The emergence of a new discourse of transdisciplinarity was evident in the late 1980s and early 1990s in contexts of environmental research. At the 2000 International Transdisciplinarity Conference in Switzerland, results were reported in all fields of human interaction with natural systems and technical innovations as well as the development context (Klein et al., 2001). Problem domains vary. Some collaborations involve consumers in the process of innovative technology and product development. Other projects focus on controversial social issues involving members of communities that are affected by planning and decision-making. The common link, though, is the externality of a complex problem and the participation of a wider range of stakeholders.

Labels can be deceptive, so it is always important to ask exactly what is being described. It is a mistake, Richard Lambert (1991) suggests, to think of area studies as predominantly an 'interdisciplinary' enterprise. He describes the field as a 'highly variegated, fragmented phenomenon, not a relatively homogeneous intellectual tradition' (Lambert 1991: 176). Much of what would be described as 'genuinely interdisciplinary' work occurred at the juncture of the four disciplines that provided the bulk of area specialists: history, literature and language, anthropology, and political science. In that hybrid intellectual space, a kind of historically informed political anthropology developed using material in local languages. History operated as a swing discipline. Blending of disciplinary perspectives occurred most often at professional meetings and in research by individual specialists. In the first instance, broadly defined themes have been the dominant pattern in scholarly papers, creating a collective 'multidisciplinary' perspective. The topic of any particular gathering 'drives the disciplinary mix.' In the second case, topics regarded as substantively important to understanding a particular country frequently 'do not respect disciplinary boundaries.' Area studies and other interdisciplinary fields are also 'transdisciplinary' due to the broad scope of 'nonenclaved endeavors' and breadth of disciplines. They are 'subdisciplinary' in the sense that research by individuals, especially in social sciences, has tended to concentrate on particular sub-domains (Lambert, 1991: 175, 189–92).

METHODOLOGICAL ISSUES IN INTERDISCIPLINARY PRACTICES

Hübenthal (1994: 57, 59, 61) contends that the task of interdisciplinary research is not to be solved with a global interdisciplinary theory. Instead, it must be pursued within individual sciences in daily usage and in elements rather than wholes. Hübenthal's admonition shifts attention to the how-to of practices. There is no universal interdisciplinary methodology. Methodology is influenced by the purpose and goals of a particular project or program, the problems and questions that are addressed, the actors who are involved, their allegiances to particular research traditions and methodological preferences, the institutional setting, the balance of depth and breadth, and the type of interdisciplinarity that is being practiced. Even so, common issues arise. Two issues loom large: integrative process and collaboration.

Integrative Process

Integration is widely regarded as the crux of interdisciplinarity. In fields of critical interdisciplinarity, this premise is disputed. Suspicion of holism, synthesis, and integration runs high in fields and postmodern practices that critique meta-narratives which ignore differences, conflicts, or contradictions (Lattuca, 2001: 246). Nonetheless, all interdisciplinary activities integrate to some degree different disciplinary insights. The most frequently reported shortfall is the tendency to stay at the level of multidisciplinarity. Disciplinary defaulting is also common. Even as they appear across disciplines, Miller advises, cross-cutting principles are often embedded within a particular discipline's thought model. 'Role,' for example, is a prominent cross-cutting conceptual category. Yet, it is alternatively framed as the consumer role in the market model, an individual's role-playing in social structure seen through the lens of sociology's structural–functional model, a person's role in history, and a role model in one conceptual model used in sociology (Miller, 1982: 17–18).

Popular metaphors are misleading. Disciplinarity is usually signified as depth along a vertical axis, and interdisciplinarity as breadth along a horizontal axis. Breadth connotes multiple variables and perspectives. Depth connotes competence in pertinent disciplinary, professional, and interdisciplinary approaches. The depth/breadth dichotomy,

however, fails to acknowledge the role of integrative actions that move across the vertical and horizontal planes. Synthesis is not reserved for a final step. The possibilities are tested throughout, moving in zigzags and fits and starts as new knowledge becomes available, new insights are generated, disciplinary relationships are redefined, and integrative constructs are built (Klein, 1996: 212, 222–3). In an ideal model of decision-making by individuals that is informed by complexity theory, William H. Newell (2007) argues that interdisciplinary study entails a two-step process.

Part A draws critically on disciplinary perspectives in an iterative process. Tentative syntheses are reformed as the insights of additional disciplines are incorporated. Decisions in Part A are predominantly disciplinary: focusing on what concepts, theories, and methods to use; what information to collect; what research strategies are feasible given the constraints; and how much breadth and depth of knowledge in each discipline are required given the problem at hand, the goals and the collaborators. Yet, Part A also involves distinctively interdisciplinary decisions: going back and forth between disciplinary part and complex whole, comparative evaluation of the various disciplines' strengths and weaknesses, and the narrowing and skewing that results from their respective redefinitions of the problem.

In Part B, the insights of different disciplines are integrated into a more comprehensive understanding that replaces either/or thinking with both/and thinking. The fundamental decisions address conflicts that exist among disciplinary insights. Latent commonalties need to be identified, either directly by modifying the concepts through which they are expressed or indirectly by modifying the assumptions on which they are based. Once common ground has been constructed, modified insights can be integrated into a more comprehensive understanding. The goal is not to remove the tension between insights, but to reduce their conflict. To illustrate, Newell (2007) examined how Kenneth Boulding, Robert Frank and Amitai

Etzioni created common ground in works that brought together economics and sociology. The technique of *redefinition* reveals commonalties in concepts or assumptions obscured by discipline-specific terminology. *Extension* addresses differences or oppositions by extending the meaning of an idea beyond a single domain. *Organization* identifies a latent commonalty in the meaning of different disciplinary concepts or assumptions, redefines them accordingly, and then organizes, arranges or arrays redefined insights or assumptions to bring out their relationship. *Transformation* is used where concepts or assumptions are not merely different (e.g., love, fear, selfishness) but opposite (e.g., rational, irrational).

Joel L. Fleishman (1991: 235–8) provides a description of the process from a problem-oriented field. Policy analysis is a framework for integrating knowledge about many problems that lend themselves to purposive individual or social action. It starts where economics and political science leave off, building on disciplinary descriptions and inferences to formulate alternative solutions and projecting likely consequences. In the process, policy analysis incorporates only a fraction of the contents of participating disciplines, choosing portions that appear relevant to solving a specific problem and adding useful elements from statistics, operations research, history and ethics. Policy analysts are not bound by the substantive knowledge and perspective of the problem areas to which they are applying their skills. They construct an integrative lens and analytic framework that fits around the problem.

Micro-level interviews of over sixty researchers in five exemplary organizations yielded further insights into the dynamics of integration in five exemplary organizations. The centers and researchers' projects varied in goal, scope and type. Some were geared toward producing explanatory theories and descriptive accounts. Others were geared toward practical solution of medical and social problems. On the basis of the interviews, Veronica Boix-Mansilla and Howard Gardner (2003) identified three

core epistemic considerations in evaluating the content/substance of interdisciplinary work: consistency with disciplinary antecedents, balance and effectiveness. The second epistemic criterion of balance highlights the integrative leverage afforded by weaving together perspectives into a generative and coherent whole. Achieving 'reflective balance' does not imply equal representation of participating disciplines. Options must be weighed in a 'balancing act' that maintains generative tensions and reaches legitimate compromises in selecting and combining disciplinary insights and standards.

Mieke Bal's (2002) study of the methodological role of concepts in interdisciplinary study of culture contributes added insights. The metaphor of 'borrowing' suggests that concepts and methods occupy a designated place in the knowledge system. Yet, concepts exhibit both specificity and intersubjectivity. Concepts such as 'image', 'tradition', and 'performance' do not mean the same thing for everyone. However, they foster common discussion as they travel between disciplines, between individuals, between periods, and between academic communities. In the process of travel, their meanings and uses change. Concepts have an analytical and theoretical force with the potential to go beyond multidisciplinary diffusion. They stimulate productive propagation and prompt a new articulation with an emphasis on and ordering of phenomena within the cultural field that does not impose transdisciplinary universalism. The basis of interdisciplinary work, Bal maintains, is selecting one path while bracketing others. Interdisciplinary analysis has a specificity that is not lost in superficial generalisms. 'Surfing' and 'zapping', Bal cautions, only produce 'muddled multidisciplinarity'.

As these descriptions and illustrations suggest, interdisciplinary research has a highly generative nature. A priori unifying principles, theories, frameworks, and sets of questions provide coherence. Proven techniques for mediating different perspectives also help, such as Delphi method, scenario-building, general systems theory, brainstorming, and computer analysis of multiple perspectives. However, context-related adaptations, deletions and additions may be expected. Reconsideration, reformulation and restating are vital activities for constructing higher-order comprehensive meanings. Creating an integrated product, solution, or perspective, Steve Fuller suggests, requires moving from lower-level translation of disciplinary perspectives by bootstrapping up to higher levels of conceptual synthesis. Linguistic models are not imported intact from meta-mathematics, set theory, symbolic logic, or any paradigm. They evolve in the creation of a trade language that may develop into a pidgin, an interim tongue or a creole, a new first language among a hybrid community of knowers (Fuller, 1993: 42). Bilingualism is a popular metaphor of interdisciplinary work. However, mastery of two complete languages rarely occurs. Interdisciplinary language typically evolves through development of interlanguage (Klein, 1996: 220).

Collaboration

Many consider interdisciplinarity to be synonymous with teamwork. It is not. Heightened interest in teamwork to solve complex intellectual and social problems, though, has reinforced the connection. Every collaboration creates a unique dynamic and organizational structure. Teams differ by duration, size and physical proximity of members; their age, gender, and racial and cultural composition; and participating disciplines, professions and functions. All teams, however, need a results-driven structure, clear roles, strong leadership, an effective communication system, methods of monitoring performance and giving feedback, and a means of recording and making fact-based judgments (Davis, 1995: 92). Social and cognitive factors are tightly interwoven (O'Donnell and Derry, 2005: 60). Interdisciplinary teams are status systems that reflect external hierarchies of power. A prestigious person or discipline may dominate, inhibiting others from speaking, impeding role negotiation, delaying communal work, and

creating social and cognitive dependence. In her pioneering study of working relationships among psychologists, psychiatrists, and sociologists in mental-health projects, Margaret Barron Luszki (1958) also found that disciplines imported to help with a project often tended to be in subordinate power positions.

Simon and Goode's (1989: 220–1) account of a policy research project illustrates four models of collaboration that occur. The project focused on the efforts of laid-off employees and union leaders to save jobs in the supermarket industry. The dominance of an economic perspective and quantitative model restricted the anthropologists' role to supplying background context from interviews in a contracting mode rather than a full partnership:

1. *Background or context information*, an additive step that can be supplied separately from contributions of other researchers and may only appear as an appendix or separate case study;
2. *Elaboration or explanation of findings* from quantitative components; still limited to an additive role that typically produces a concluding chapter valued as descriptive detail, not findings;
3. *Definition of important variables or categories* for quantitative study, a step that sometimes occurs at the outset or prior to finalization of research design, structured instruments, or analytic approaches;
4. *Creative combination of ethnographic and multivariate approaches in research, analysis, and interpretation*, a rare occurrence in which fundamental questions are refined using participants' approaches on a mutually illuminating basis.

Shortfalls of integration in teamwork also occur for other reasons. Progress may be deterred by lack of incentives and an inadequate reward system, constraints of time and access to equipment, rigid budgetary and administrative categories, and restrictive legal mandates and policies. Social and psychological impediments block progress as well, including resistance to innovation and risk, mistrust, insecurity and marginality. Lack of integrative skills, systems thinking and familiarity with interdisciplinarity are added factors, along with the 'boundaries of reticence' that disciplinary socialization creates. Individuals must avoid the tendency to make a 'regressive return to categorization' (Caudill and Roberts, 1951: 14). Conflict must also be addressed surrounding both technical issues (definition of problem, research methodologies and scheduling) and interpersonal issues (leadership style and disciplinary ethnocentrism).

Krauss and Fussell emphasize the importance of mutual knowledge-building (1990). Joint definition of a project is required, along with the core research problem, questions and goals. Team members need to clarify differences in disciplinary language, methods, tools, concepts and professional worldviews. Role clarification and negotiation help members to assess what they need and expect from each other. Ongoing communication and interaction foster mutual learning and a sense of 'teamness' and interdependence. The organizational framework should also provide for progressive sharing and interactive cross-testing of empirical and theoretical work with coordinated inputs from the beginning. If individuals hold back during the early phase, the prospect of arriving at a shared or interfacing cognitive framework is foreshortened. Certain contextual factors, Daniel Stokols (2006) advises, influence the 'collaborative readiness' of team members and their prospects for success. They include the presence or absence of institutional supports for interdepartmental and crossdisciplinary collaboration; the breadth of disciplines, departments and institutions encompassed by a particular center; the degree to which team members have worked together on prior projects; the extent to which their offices and laboratories are spatially proximal or distant from each other; and the availability or absence of electronic linkages. The more contextual factors aligned at the outset, Stokols admonishes, the greater the prospects for achieving and sustaining effective collaboration across fields.

The challenge of collaboration is magnified when trans-sector stakeholders are involved. Ideally, cooperation of academic and non-academic partners should occur at all stages, from planning through implementation.

All aspects of a program or project should be included as well: from organization and management to consensus-building among stakeholders and knowledge production. Continuous evaluation provides feedback loops that improve the research process and the conceptual framework. Ultimately, Jack Spaapen et al. (pers. comm., 2003) advise, 'Quality' is a relative concept that is determined by relations within the environment of a research group and the goals of its members. Research must 'attune a pluralism of interests and values' within a dynamic set of programs and contexts where the interests of a variegated group of stakeholders may conflict but new opportunities arise. An empirical mode of evaluation and simplistic algorithmic models fail to capture the complexity, contingency, and emergent discovery and novelty that characterizes much of interdisciplinary research.

Maurice DeWachter's (1982) model of an interdisciplinary approach to bioethics bridges the gap between ideal models and the realities of practice. In bioethical decision-making, a particular problem forms the basis of a global question for all team members. The ideal model of integration and collaboration starts with the assumption that individuals will suspend their disciplinary/professional worldviews from the beginning, in favor of a global question based on the problem to be solved. Realistically, though, participants are usually unwilling to abstain from approaching a topic in terms of their own worldviews. The best chance of succeeding, DeWachter counsels, lies in starting by translating a global question into the specific language of each participating discipline, then working back and forth in iterative fashion, constantly checking the relevance of each answer to the task at hand. That way, no single answer is privileged.

Vosskamp (1994) and Klein (1996) treat interdisciplinarity as communicative action. Vosskamp proposes that the agreement/disagreement structure necessary for all communication shapes the possibility of interdisciplinary dialogue. Consent/dissent (*Alteritaet*) requires accepting the unforeseeable and productive role of misunderstanding from the outset. Després et al. (2004) also invoked Habermas's (1987) notion of 'communicative rationality' in a study of a collaborative urban planning project to redefine suburban neighborhoods built between 1950 and 1975 on the outskirts of Quebec City. Scientific and academic knowledge alone, they explain, cannot deal adequately with the complexity of subjects and problem domains such as revitalization of residential neighborhoods. Following Habermas, instrumental, ethical and aesthetic forms of knowledge are needed as well. Rational knowledge comes out of not only 'what we know' but 'how we communicate' it. Stakeholders enter into a process of negotiation, confronting the four kinds of knowledge in a series of encounters that allow representatives of each type to express their views and proposals. In the process, a fifth type of knowledge progressively emerges. It is a kind of hybrid product, the result of 'making sense together'. 'Intersubjectivity' requires an ongoing effort to achieve mutual understanding. Simply bringing people together and coordinating conversations is not enough, Després et al. (2004) stress. Mediation is required to collectively define what could and should be done. Each stakeholder expresses individual interests or views that are discussed and criticized by others. The role of the mediator is to extract this knowledge. As progressively shared meanings, diagnoses and objectives emerge, individual interests and views are seen in different perspectives.

There is no interdisciplinary Esperanto that may be universally applied. Studies of interdisciplinary communication in practice settings reveal that everyday language is usually combined with specialist terms. 'Interdisciplinary discussions', Gerhard Frey (1973) found, 'normally take place on a level very similar to that of the popular scientific presentation.' They become more precise as individuals acquire knowledge of other disciplines. At a higher level of conceptual synthesis, new and redeployed terminology form the basis of a working meta-language. The quality of outcomes cannot be separated from development

of a shared language culture and its richness. 'Most misunderstandings', Frey found, 'are caused by the fact that the same words are used with different meaning.' Luszki (1958) reported that members of mental-health teams paid a price for congeniality. By not dealing with conflicts in disciplinary definitions of such core terms as 'aggression', for instance, they reduced the number of creative problem-solving conflicts that would have promoted high-level, shared concepts. Difference, tension and conflict are not barriers that must be eliminated. They are part of the character of knowledge negotiation.

POSTSCRIPT

Talk of a 'postdisciplinary' age is premature. Disciplines have not disappeared; yet, Johan Heilbron (2004: 38) observes, they now stand alongside other modes of organization at a time when the significance of the classical disciplines is decreasing, practical fields have a growing importance in the knowledge system, and the heteronomy of academic institutions is increasing. Few doubt that change is occurring. Talk of increasing interdisciplinarity, though, begs the question of how well prepared researchers are for this kind of work. Many still learn on the job. As disciplines continue to respond to new needs and interests, and as interdisciplinary communities and hybrid fields secure a greater role in knowledge production, it is imperative that researchers become more self-conscious about the dynamics of integration and collaboration and more aware of cognate disciplines and intersecting interdisciplinary fields. These are becoming 'basic' to the conduct of research and education. Modern systems of higher education, Burton Clark (1995: 154–5) exhorted, are confronted by a gap between older, simple expectations and complex realities that outrun those expectations. Definitions that depict one part or function of the university as its 'essence' or 'essential mission' only underscore the gap between simplified views and new operational realities that are transforming the way we think about knowledge and education.

REFERENCES AND SELECT BIBLIOGRAPHY

Association of American Geographers (1995) 'Toward a reconsideration of faculty roles and rewards in geography', in Robert M. Diamond and Bronwyn E. Adams (eds), *The Disciplines Speak: Rewarding the Scholarly, Professional, and Creative Work of Faculty.* Washington, DC: American Association for Higher Education, pp. 35–47.

Bal, Mieke (2002) *Traveling Concepts in Humanities.* Toronto: University of Toronto Press.

Becher, Tony (1989) *Academic Tribes and Territories. Intellectual Enquiry and the Cultures of Disciplines.* Buckingham and Bristol: The Society for Research into Higher Education and Open University Press.

Boix-Mansilla, Veronica and Gardner, Howard (2003) 'Assessing interdisciplinary work at the frontier', *Rethinking Interdisciplinarity Conference.* Available at http://www.interdisciplines.org.

Bruun, H., Hukkinen, J., Huutoniemi, K. and Klein, J.T. (2005) *Promoting Interdisciplinary Research: The Case of the Academy of Finland.* Helsinki: Academy of Finland.

Calhoun, Craig (1992) 'Sociology, other disciplines, and the project of a general understanding of social life', in T.C. Halliday and M. Janowitz (eds), *Sociology and Its Publics: The Forms and Fates of Disciplinary Organization.* Chicago: University of Chicago Press, pp. 137–95.

Camic, Charles and Joas, Hans (2004) 'The Dialogical Turn', in C. Camic and H. Joas (eds), *The Dialogical Turn: New Roles for Sociology in the Postdisciplinary Age.* Lanham, MD: Rowman and Littlefield, pp. 1–19.

Caudill, W. and Roberts, B.H. (1951) 'Pitfalls in the organization of interdisciplinary research', *Human Organization*, 10 (4): 12–15.

Clark, Burton R. (1995) *Places of Inquiry: Research and Advanced Education in Modern Universities.* Berkeley: University of California Press.

Costanza, Robert (1990) 'Escaping the overspecialization trap', in Mary E. Clark and Sandra A. Wawrytko (eds), *Rethinking the Curriculum: Toward an Integrated Interdisciplinary College Education.* New York: Greenwood, pp. 95–106.

Davis, James R. (1995) *Interdisciplinary Courses and Team Teaching: New Arrangements for Learning.* Phoenix, AZ: American Council on Education, Oryx.

Després, Carole, Brais, Nicole and Avellan, Sergio (2004) 'Collaborative planning for retrofitting suburbs: Transdisciplinarity and intersubjectivity in action', *FUTURES*, 36(4): 471–86.

DeWachter, Maurice (1982) 'Interdisciplinary bioethics: But where do we start? A reflection on epochè as method', *Journal of Medicine and Philosophy*, 7(3): 275–87.

Dogan, Mattei and Pahre, Robert (1990) *Creative Marginality: Innovation at the Intersections of Social Sciences.* Boulder, CO: Westview Press.

Fisher, Donald (1993) *Fundamental Development of the Social Sciences: Rockefeller Philanthropy and the United States Social Science Research Council.* Ann Arbor: University of Michigan Press.

Fleishman, Joel L. (1991) 'A new framework for integration: Policy analysis and public management', in D. Easton and C. Schelling (eds), *Divided Knowledge: Across Disciplines, across Cultures.* Newbury Park, CA: Sage, pp. 219–43.

Frank, Roberta (1988) '"Interdisciplinary": The first half-century', in E.G. Stanley and T.F. Hoad (eds), *WORDS: For Robert Burchfield's Sixty-Fifth Birthday*, Cambridge: D.S. Brewer, pp. 91–101.

Frey, Gerhard (1973) 'Methodological problems of interdisciplinary discussions', *RATIO*, 1 (2): 161–82.

Fuller, Steve (1993) *Philosophy, Rhetoric, and the End of Knowledge.* Madison: University of Wisconsin Press.

Geertz, Clifford (1980) 'Blurred genres: The refiguration of social thought', *American Scholar*, 42 (2): l65–79.

Gibbons, Michael, Nowotny, Helga, Limoges, Camille, Trow, Martin, Schwartzman, Simon and Scott, Peter (1994) *The New Production of Knowledge: The Dynamics of Science and Research in Contemporary Societies.* London: Sage.

Habermas, Jürgen (1987) *The Theory of Communicative Action*, vol. 2. Trans. T. McCarthy. Boston: Beacon.

Heckhausen, Heinz (1972) 'Disciplines and interdisciplinarity', in OECD, *Interdisciplinarity: Problems of Teaching and Research in Universities.* Paris: Organization for Economic Cooperation and Development, pp. 83–90.

Heilbron, Johan (2004) 'A regime of disciplines: Toward a historical sociology of disciplinary knowledge', in C. Camic and H. Joas (eds), *The Dialogical Turn: New Roles for Sociology in the Postdisciplinary Age.* Lanham, MD: Rowman and Littlefield, pp. 23–42.

Hübenthal, Ursula (1994) 'Interdisciplinary thought', *Issues in Integrative Studies*, 12: 55–75.

Hunter, Albert and Brewer, John (2003) 'Multimethod Research in Sociology', in A. Tashakkori and C. Teddlie (eds), *Handbook of Mixed Methods in Social Behavioral Research.* Thousand Oaks: Sage, pp. 577–94.

Kelly, James (1996) 'Wide and narrow interdisciplinarity', *Journal of General Education*, 45 (2): 95–113.

Klein, Julie Thompson (1996) *Crossing Boundaries: Knowledge, Disciplinarities, and Interdisciplinarities*. Charlottesville: University of Virginia Press.

Klein, J.T., Grossenbacher-Mansuy, W., Häberli, R., Bill, A., Scholz, R. and Welti, M. (eds) (2001) *Transdisciplinarity: Joint Problem Solving among Science, Technology, and Society*. Basel: Birkhäuser.

Krauss, R.M. and Fussell, S.R. (1990) 'Mutual knowledge and communicative effectiveness', in J. Galegher, R.E. Kraut, and C. Egido (eds), *Intellectual Teamwork: Social and Technological Foundations of Cooperative Work*. Hillsdale, NJ: Lawrence Erlbaum Associates, pp. 111–45.

Lambert, R. (1919) 'Blurring the Disciplinary Boundaries' in D. Easton and C. Schelling, *Divided Knoweldge: Across Disciplines. Across Cultures*. Newbury Park: Sage, pp.171–94.

Landau, M., Proshansky, H., and Ittelson, W. (1962) 'The interdisciplinary approach and the concept of behavioral sciences', in N.F. Washburne (ed.), *Decisions: Values and Groups, II*. New York: Pergamon, pp. 7–25.

Lattuca, Lisa (2001). *Creating Interdisciplinarity: Interdisciplinary Research and Teaching among College and University Faculty*. Nashville: Vanderbilt University Press.

Luszki, Margaret B. (1958) *Interdisciplinary Team Research Methods and Problems*. Washington, DC: National Training Laboratories.

Mahan, Jack L. (1970) 'Toward transdisciplinary inquiry in the humane sciences', Ph.D. Dissertation, United States International University, San Diego, CA.

Miller, Raymond (1982) 'Varieties of Interdisciplinary Approaches in the Social Sciences', *Issues in Integrative Studies*, 1: 1–37.

Moran, Joe (2002) *Interdisciplinarity*. London and New York: Routledge.

Newell, William H. (2007) 'Decision making in interdisciplinary studies', in G. Morçöl (ed.), *Handbook of Decision Making*. New York: Marcel-Dekker, pp. 245–64.

Nowotny, H., Scott, P. and Gibbons, M. (2001). *Re-Thinking Science. Knowledge and the Public in an Age of Uncertainty*. Cambridge: Polity Press.

O'Donnell, A. and Derry, S.J. (2005) 'Cognitive processes in interdisciplinary groups: Problems and possibilities', in S.J. Derry, C.D. Schunn, and M.A. Gernsbacher (eds), *Interdisciplinary Collaboration: An Emerging Cognitive Science*. Mahwah, NJ: Erlbaum, pp. 51–82.

OECD (Organization for Economic Cooperation and Development) (1972) *Interdisciplinarity: Problems of Teaching and Research in Universities*. Paris: OECD.

Ogburn, William Fielding and Goldenweiser, Alexander (eds) (1927) *The Social Sciences and Their Interrelations*. Boston: Houghton Mifflin.

Organization for Economic Cooperation and Development (1972) *The University and the Community: The Problems of Changing Relationships*. Paris: Organization for Economic Cooperation and Development.

Rallis, S.F. and Rossman, G.G. (2003) 'Mixed methods in evaluation contexts: A paradigmatic framework', in A. Tashakkori and C. Teddlie (eds), *Handbook of Mixed Methods in Social Behavioral Research*. Thousand Oaks: Sage, pp. 491–512.

Rosenfield, Patricia L. (1992) 'The potential of transdisciplinary research for sustaining and extending linkages between the health and social sciences', *Social Science and Medicine*, 35 (11): 1343–57.

Salter, Liora and Hearn, Alison (eds) (1996) *Outside the Lines: Issues in Interdisciplinary Research*. Montreal and Kingston: McGill-Queen's University Press.

Simon, E. and Goode, J.G. (1989) 'Constraints on the contribution of anthropology to interdisciplinary policy studies: Lessons from a study of saving jobs in the supermarket industry', *Urban Anthropology*, 18 (1): 219–39.

Smelser, Neil J. (2004) 'Interdisciplinarity in theory and practice', in C. Camic and H. Joas (eds), *The Dialogical Turn: New Roles for Sociology in the Postdisciplinary Age*. Lanham, MD: Rowman and Littlefield, pp. 43–64.

Smith, Thomas S. (2004) 'Where sociability comes from: Neurosociological foundations of social interaction', in C. Camic and H. Joas (eds), *The Dialogical Turn: New Roles for Sociology in the Postdisciplinary Age*. Lanham, MD: Rowman and Littlefield, pp. 199–220.

Spaapen, J.F., Wamelink, F. and Dijstelbloem, H. (2003) 'Towards the evaluation of transdisciplinary research', in B. Tress, G. Tress, A. Van der Valk, and G. Fry (eds), *Interdisciplinary and Transdisciplinary Landscape Studies: Potential and Limitations*. Wageningen, Netherlands: DELTA SERIES 2, pp.148–59.

Stocking, George W. Jr. (1995) 'Delimiting anthropology: Historical reflections on the boundaries of a boundless discipline', *Social Research*, 62 (4): 933–66.

Stokols, Daniel (2006) 'Toward a science of transdisciplinary action research', *American Journal of Community Psychology*, 38, 1–2, Sept., pp. 63–77.

Tashakkori, A. and Teddlie, C. (eds) (2003a) *Handbook of Mixed Methods in Social Behavioral Research*. Thousand Oaks: Sage.

——— (2003b) 'Major issues and controversies in the use of mixed methods in the social and behavioral sciences', in A. Tashakkori and C. Teddlie (eds),

Handbook of Mixed Methods in Social Behavioral Research. Thousand Oaks: Sage, pp. 3–50.

———— (2003c). 'Preface', in A. Tashakkori and C. Teddlie (eds), *Handbook of Mixed Methods in Social Behavioral Research.* Thousand Oaks: Sage, pp. ix–xv.

The Nuffield Foundation. (1975) *Interdisciplinarity: A Report by the Group for Research and Innovation in Higher Education.* London: The Nuffield Foundation.

Van Dusseldorp, Dirk and Wigboldus, Seerp (1994) 'Interdisciplinary research for integrated rural development in developing countries: The role of social sciences', *Issues in Integrative Studies,* 12: 93–138.

Vosskamp, Wilhelm (1986) 'From scientific specialization to the dialogue between the disciplines', *Issues in Integrative Studies,* 4: 17–36.

Vosskamp, Wilhelm (1994) 'Crossing of boundaries: Interdisciplinary as an opportunity for universities in the 1980's?' *Issues in Integrative Studies,* 12: 43–54.

Wallerstein, Immanuel (1995) 'What are we bounding, and who, when we bound social research', *Social Research,* 62 (4): 839–55.

Yates, Simeon J. (2004) *Doing Social Science Research.* London: Sage Publications.

NOTE

1 I thank William Outhwaite of Sussex University, Stuart Henry of San Diego State University, and William Newell of Miami University for suggestions on an earlier draft.

Cases, Comparisons, and Theory

Introduction

William Outhwaite

This section explores some of the most influential broad-spectrum methodological orientations in the social sciences: ethnographic, comparative, historical and case study methods. The four chapters in this section are of course closely interrelated, since what in sociology or political science would be called a case study or comparative approach is more or less automatic in social or cultural anthropology. Jon Mitchell's account of fieldwork practice illustrates this, and also points towards Ben Agger's discussion of postmodernism in Section V. Jennifer Platt's discussion of case study brings out the wide range of practices and self-understandings associated with the term.

Historical sociology, which has enjoyed a resurgence in the past decades (Smith, 1991), also operates substantially in terms of case studies and comparisons, such as Theda Skocpol's classic comparative study based on the French, Russian and Chinese Revolutions. Charles Ragin, who has published very substantially on comparative method, analyzes the underlying logic of comparison, while John Hall discusses the interface between the methodologies in use in history and the other social sciences and their relation to positions such as historicism and critical realism.

REFERENCE

Smith, Dennis (1991) *The Rise of Historical Sociology.* Cambridge: Polity.

3

Ethnography

Jon P. Mitchell

ETHNOGRAPHY AS QUALITATIVE METHOD

'Ethnography' has achieved considerable currency across the social sciences, so much so, in fact, that it has effectively become a catch-all term to describe any form of long-term qualitative research based on a triangulation of methods. Indeed, Hammersley (1992: 78), one of the more prolific students of ethnography as a research method, acknowledges that at times it is legitimate to use 'ethnography' interchangeably with 'qualitative method', 'case study method', etc. From its origins in anthropology, ethnography has now expanded out to be part of the overall methodological 'toolkit'; ethnographic work is done by human geographers, sociologists, some political scientists, and the entire range of interdisciplinary 'studies' in the social sciences—business studies, cultural studies, gender studies, media studies, migration studies, etc.

'Ethnography', of course, means, literally, 'writing culture'. It is therefore rooted in the notion of description of a particular society, culture, group or social context: 'The most common conception of the descriptive character of ethnographic accounts is that they

map the morphology of some area of the social world' (Hammersley, 1992: 23).

This description is, for Hammersley, based on three central features: *induction; context; and unfamiliarity* (ibid.: 22–23). The inductive process within ethnographic work sees general statements about human society and culture—what one might call 'theory'—emerging out of the description of particular events. Ethnography is for this reason—explicitly or implicitly—wedded to the notion of the case study, which describes in detail a particular event or series of events, to derive from it broader inferences about social process or the human condition (Gluckman, 1940). A major part of the legitimacy for this induction process is careful attention within ethnographic work to the context of events, since it is assumed that events seen out of context might be misunderstood. Indeed, so central is context that it is not merely a pre-condition for the development of general theory out of particular event; rather, context when well described *is* the development of theory: 'description *is* explanation' (Hammersley, 1992: 23; see also Dilley, 1999). The description of events in context is particularly poignant—indeed, necessary—when dealing with situations unfamiliar to the general readership. Such work allows us to see the world from 'the native's point of view' (Malinowski, 1922: 25) and to better understand motivation and meaning of social action.

The methodology that has developed alongside and which is used to deliver these descriptive goals is what Clammer (1984) has called the 'fieldwork concept'. This involves a long-term period of social immersion in a particular setting, from which is generated the totalizing and holistic descriptive account— the 'ethnography of ...' the group being researched. Within this fieldwork, the dominant method is 'participant observation', although like 'ethnography' this label is used to gloss over the variety of methods actually used by ethnographers—from simple observation to the collection of stories/life histories, interviewing, household surveys, archival research, and so on. Indeed, in practice, ethnographers tend to let context drive not only their descriptions but also their research questions and methodological practice.

According to Hammersley (1992: 11–12), social scientists turned to this rather open-ended methodology as part of a critique of the more scientistic quantitative methods of survey and experimentation. For him, these critiques were fivefold. First, quantitative methodologies were seen to impose *a priori* structure on social inquiry, thereby over-determining results and blinkering researchers to the possibility of interesting data emerging from unexpected arenas. Ethnography, by contrast, is often an exercise in serendipity (Okely, 2003), in which an openness to chance finds or unpredictable social and political developments generates new research orientations.[1] Second, they were criticized for attempting to derive an understanding of what happens in 'normal' social conditions from the decidedly abnormal contexts of the experiment or formal interview. Third, and consequently, they were seen as naive in their reliance on people's own accounts of what they do. The focus on participant observation within ethnographic research aims to enable researchers to view social action 'on the ground' as it unfolds in

a 'normal' and 'natural' fashion. As long-term participants, rather than mere observers, their effect on social life is minimized, and they are able to gauge the relationship between what people say about what they do and what they actually do. Indeed, this relationship is often central to ethnographic research.[2] Fourth, quantitative methods were seen to reify social phenomena by treating them as distinct and isolable from the social contexts in which they emerge, develop and change. Fifth, they were seen as overly behavioristic in their assumption that people's actions are mechanically determined, thereby neglecting to take account of human agency. These critiques add up to the ethnographic conviction:

> that the nature of the social world must be *discovered;* that this can only be achieved by first-hand observation and participation in 'natural' settings, guided by an exploratory orientation; that research reports must capture the social processes observed and the social meanings that generate them (Hammersley, 1992: 12).

Although this successfully explains the emergence of ethnography as a privileged qualitative method across the social sciences, there is a longer history of attachment to ethnography in anthropology; which stems from an overlapping but different set of considerations.

ANTHROPOLOGY AND THE 'INVENTION' OF ETHNOGRAPHY

Most undergraduates in social or cultural anthropology are told in an early lecture the apocryphal tale of the 'invention' of the ethnographic method. Bronislaw Malinowski, a Polish expatriate at the London School of Economics, was researching in Australia in 1914, when war broke out. As a Pole, he was technically an enemy citizen, but rather than being incarcerated, he was allowed to spend the war years in the Trobriand Islands conducting first-hand empirical fieldwork among the people of the islands, and through that developing the classical method of ethnographic fieldwork, and with it the theoretical framework of functionalism.

From his work in the Trobriands, Malinowski produced a number of influential monographs that were the first works of anthropology to emerge from the long-term personal engagement of a scholar with the people being studied. Until then, anthropology had been a synthetic discipline, generating general theories of humankind based on the relatively thin and certainly partial evidence of missionaries, travelers and colonial officials. This 'armchair' anthropology was mainly geared towards the post-hoc justification ('proving') of existing theories of human social evolution, which placed different societies on a hierarchical axis of development, from the 'primitive' societies of aboriginal groups to the 'civilized' nation-states of Enlightenment Europe.

Malinowski's ethnographic method—and with it his functional school of anthropology—emerged as a critique of this evolutionary perspective. It offered a humanistic redemption of peoples previously condemned as 'primitive' and an empirical method for explaining the inherent logic of their apparently backward and base social practices. At the heart of this was a focus on social function, which democratized social analysis by demonstrating that even the most apparently irrational activities nevertheless 'made sense' from a functional point of view. The demonstration of function was dependent on an approach to holism that the new field methodology enabled, and also on an attention to context.

Malinowski railed against the often implicit but sometimes explicit racism of 19th-century evolutionism. For example, in his account of the Trobriand economy in *Argonauts of the Western Pacific* (1922), Malinowski set out to critique the prevalent argument that the backwardness of 'primitive society' was the consequence of a lack of organized and passionate striving for economic gain. What he showed in his account of *kula* was that Trobrianders were every bit

as rigorous and devoted as the most go-get-'em entrepreneur in the planning and execution of *kula* exchanges:

> After reading *Argonauts*, some commentators might impugn Trobrianders for putting their faith in bangles, but they could not fault them on their work ethic to get those bangles. A tacit criticism was that natives would labour for themselves, not their colonizers (Reyna, 2001: 17).

His relativizing argument about economy struck directly against the staged evolutionary model. The key components of Malinowski's approach were the pursuit of context (that sociocultural phenomena, no matter how apparently backward, strange or irrational, could be explained if seen from within their own context), of function, and of the social whole. Holism was permitted by the new methodological discipline of ethnographic fieldwork, which enabled the anthropologist to view different aspects of social life in relation to one another and as they operated in practice:

> the so-called functional method in modern anthropology consists in the parallel study of mutually dependent phenomena or aspects of tribal life. The functional principle teaches that if you want to understand magic, you must go outside magic, and study economic ritual within the context of those practical activities in which it is really embedded (Malinowski, 1922: 324).

The focus on practice heralded a new empiricism that favored an inductive process in which theoretical models and classificatory schemas were derived from direct, on-the-ground observations rather than pre-ordained evolutionary models. Malinowski's central preconception was of function. By definition, society was seen to serve the interests of its constituent members. Social organization and social institutions were developed by populations to deliver basic human needs, and could be classified as such: kinship provides for reproduction; protection for safety; training for growth, etc. (Malinowski, 1944). However, he was chary of attempts to generate social laws concerning how they might do this. In this respect, Malinowski's functionalism differed from that of his contemporary—and intellectual adversary—Radcliffe-Brown.

Radcliffe-Brown favored a more deeply structural account of social function, attempting from observation to establish general laws of society. He imported into anthropology Durkheim's metaphor of society as a social organism, which attracted ridicule from Malinowski. Whatever their short-run usefulness, Malinowski argued, 'no science can live permanently on analogies'; for Malinowski, anthropology should always return to fieldwork, to 'bedrock reality' (Stocking, 1984: 174). In this respect, Malinowski's functionalism was characterized by its insistence on the primacy of the person in any theory of society: 'The most important thing for the student … is never to forget the living, palpitating flesh and blood organism of man which remains somewhere in the heart of every institution' (Malinowski, 1934: xxxi).

BEING AN ANTHROPOLOGIST IN THE 1960s

This 'bedrock reality' was met during fieldwork, involving three interlocking techniques (Young, 1979: 8–9). First came 'the statistical documentation of concrete evidence' (Malinowski, 1922: 24) to generate an overall picture of the culture or society as a whole; through spatial mapping, drawing up genealogies and consulting censuses, documenting legal and normative frameworks, etc; second, documenting 'the imponderabilia of everyday life' (ibid.), to account for the ways in which the structural frameworks are inhabited; and, third, collecting a corpus of characteristic narratives, common phrases and sayings, folk tales and mythologies, seen as 'documents of native mentality' (ibid.), with which to build up a picture of life as seen through the eyes of the 'native'.

This is less a methodology than a set of guidelines to progress, and the generations of ethnographers who succeeded Malinowski were given little by way of practical guidance on ethnographic method. As an eager pre-fieldwork graduate student in the 1920s, before embarking on fieldwork in Sudan, Evans-Pritchard was famously told little more than 'Take ten grams of quinine every night and keep off the women.' Malinowski himself told him 'not to be a bloody fool' (Eriksen, 1995: 16).

Yet despite this lack of explicit technical guidance—or perhaps because of it—the notion of ethnographic fieldwork (Clammer's 'fieldwork concept') persisted as the central, even defining, method of anthropological research. By the 1960s, however, there was a recognition that ethnographers should be rather more explicit about what happens during fieldwork, partly to instruct neophyte ethnographers, and partly in acknowledgement of the place of the ethnographers themselves in the constitution of ethnographic knowledge. Evans-Pritchard himself had written in 1950 that anthropology—and the work of the ethnographer—should be seen as an active process of knowledge construction, more akin to the construction of historical narrative, rather than the more impassive or neutral 'discovery' of facts:

> we have … to observe what the anthropologist does. He goes to live for some months or years among a primitive people. He lives among them as intimately as he can, and learns to speak their language, to think in their concepts and to feel in their values. He then lives the experiences over again critically and interpretatively in the conceptual categories and values of his own culture and in terms of the general body of knowledge of his discipline. In other words, he translates from one culture into another. At this level social anthropology remains a literary and impressionistic art. (Evans-Pritchard, 1962: 22)

In 1973 the *Journal of the Anthropological Society of Oxford* published Evans-Pritchard's 'Some Reminiscences and Reflections on Fieldwork', which was later added as an appendix to the abridged edition of his ethnographic classic *Witchcraft, Oracles and Magic Among the Azande* (1976); thus emulating William Foote Whyte, whose appendix to *Street Corner Society* (1955)— itself a classic of the Chicago School of sociology—was, and is, regarded as an exemplary account of the ethnographic fieldwork process.

This spirit of reflection led in 1970 to the publication of *Being an Anthropologist* (Spindler, 1970), a collection of reflective essays on ethnographic fieldwork by contributors to the Holt, Rinehart and Winston series *Case Studies in Cultural Anthropology*. This series had been created to provide ethnographic case study material for anthropology students, but in a slightly different format from the usual ethnographic text. As Spindler (1970: xiii), one of the editors of the series, explained, 'the term "case study" was originally selected rather than "ethnography" to avoid the connotations of formality and completeness usually evoked by the latter term.' This signals an awareness of the literary conventions and structures that shaped the writing of ethnographic work—a theme that was to emerge more strongly in the 1980s.

More than anything, the contributions to *Being an Anthropologist* testify to the particularity of different pieces of ethnographic fieldwork. Each 'field' is different, presenting unique problems and challenges; and each 'fieldworker' is different, responding to those problems and challenges in different ways. Rather than a set methodological framework for identikit research, transferable from one context to another, the fieldwork concept describes a flexibility of approach and a willingness to respond to the constraints and possibilities of the field, rather than impose a version of fieldwork upon it. It therefore demonstrates the range of activities that the 'fieldwork concept' includes.

Jeremy Boissevain conducted fieldwork in Malta from 1960 to 1961, which contributed to his ethnography of Maltese village politics (1965). His chapter for *Being an Anthropologist* (Boissevain, 1970) traces the development of this fieldwork, and the various methods it involved. His interest in politics at a time of political tension determined that direct questioning of informants was problematic (ibid.: 78). Like many ethnographers, the inquisitive Boissevain was assumed to be a spy by at least one

intrigued informant (ibid.: 72). Participant observation was necessary both to establish rapport and to ensure invitations to key events in the village. He reports long hours of what he terms 'informant servicing' (ibid.: 71) to establish trust, and rounds of visits to church, coffee shop, grocery store to catch up on village gossip. Boissevain was accompanied during fieldwork by his wife and young family, and emphasizes that just as he saw his informants 'in the round'—in the variety of different social roles they adopted—so too they saw him in his various social roles. To this extent he was 'participating' in village life as much as 'observing' it, and much of that participation involved what one might term 'social learning'—learning and adopting local expectations of correct social behavior in order both to 'fit in' and to better understand how those expectations operate. He describes what he calls a 'typical day' of participant observing:

> Monday, September 19, 1960, started as usual. On the way to pick up the car I learned from Pietru that a number of Requiem Masses were to be held that day in memory of a nineteen-year-old boy electrocuted a year before in one the quarries surrounding the village … [later] I went first to the little bazar of Pietru's sister, where I spent forty-five minutes talking to Pietru's two sisters, his mother, and three customers who came to the shop. I then crossed the street to talk to a farmer, who had come to get a drink in Pietru's cousin's bar. We spent the best part of an hour discussing his farming problems and, of particular importance to me, his reactions to the discussion of the parish priest in church the day before about the financial situation of the Saint Rocco Confraternity … [I then] worked intensively with the parish priest on my household card system …
>
> After lunch, I reviewed the household cards I had prepared with Dun Gorg in the morning, and wrote up the case histories and other information he had provided. (Much later I compared his data to the door-to-door census of my own, and found his to be amazingly accurate.) After my wife and daughter returned home at 3:45 I took the car to the garage to wash it. Carmelo Abela came home at about 4:30. After his tea he came and gave me a hand with the car. When he started to tell me how he had met his fiancée, I began to wax the car to have an excuse to stay with him. As soon as Carmelo left me for his fiancée, I returned home and wrote up the story of his courtship while the details were still fresh …

That evening at 8:00, I met Pietru accidentally in front of the parish priest's house. We decided to go for a walk outside the village to find some cool air. At about 9:00 we returned and sat in front of the school chatting. Pietru told me the story of his own courtship and the difficult time he had deciding to break his engagement. We also discussed at great length the evil eye; it had given him a fever the day before. At about 10:30 Pietru went home, and I stopped by his aunt's wine shop … I left after fifteen minutes. Although I intended to write up my notes fully, when I got home I found that I was too tired. I simply filled in my diary for the day and outlined the topics to write up the following day. I went to bed at about midnight (ibid.: 75).

This lengthy excerpt gives a sense of the rhythm of fieldwork, and its dependence on chance encounter. It also demonstrates the extent to which much of the data gained during ethnographic fieldwork is determined by the concerns of the informants rather than those of the researcher. The stories of courtship did not form part of Boissevain's initial (1965) ethnography, but did feature in subsequent work, which not only described courtship as an important aspect of village life (Boissevain, 1969), but also contributed towards the development of a theory of social networks and connectedness (Boissevain, 1974). Many of these chance snippets of ethnographic data are furnished by key informants with whom the ethnographer establishes a particularly strong rapport. These are sometimes deliberately chosen, as official or unofficial research assistants, sometimes delivered to the ethnographer by a higher local authority—chief, administrator, priest— and sometimes self-selected, presenting themselves to the ethnographer in ways that are impossible to refuse.

Details of ethnography were recorded 'on the move' in a field notebook—sometimes in note form, and sometimes in more detail— and were later written up and indexed as fieldnotes *proper*. During more formal interviews, he might have his notebook open, when a contemporary ethnographer might use a tape or digital recorder. He also recorded ethnographic data using photography, subsequently asking informants to explain what was going on in particular photographs,

or to name those shown on a photograph (Boissevain, 1970: 77). His system of keeping household record cards with key demographic information contributed to the collection of genealogies, and was supplemented by Boissevain's own survey. What emerged, as with all ethnographic projects, was a huge corpus of fieldnotes—un-digested or semi-digested 'data'—that fed into the production of his ethnographic texts.

'THICK DESCRIPTION'

The 1980s saw the emergence of interest in ethnography as a kind of writing. This was due in no small part to the influence of Clifford Geertz, who effectively re-branded anthropology as an interpretive discipline and with it qualitative research methods as a whole and ethnography in particular across the social sciences. Although working within the American sub-discipline of cultural anthropology, and not without his critics (e.g. Roseberry, 1989), Geertz's influence has spread far and wide, particularly through the concept of 'thick description'.

Geertz's first step was to redefine 'culture'. He was critical of what he saw as the overly essentialist—even materialist— conceptions of culture which held sway in American cultural anthropology, which primarily saw culture as a collection of 'stuff', or 'stuff-like' phenomena. He replaced it with an idealist conception of culture, which focused not on the 'stuff' itself, but on what the 'stuff' *means*:

Culture is best seen not as complexes of concrete behaviour patterns—customs, usages, traditions, habit clusters—as has, by and large, been the case up to now, but as a set of control mechanisms— plans, recipes, rules, instructions (what computer engineers call 'programs')—for the governing of behavior (Geertz, 1973a: 44).

These plans, recipes, rules, and instructions consist of systems of meaning:

Believing, with Max Weber, that man is an animal suspended in webs of significance he himself has spun, I take culture to be those webs, and the analysis of it to be therefore not an experimental science in search of law but an interpretive one in search of meaning (Geertz, 1973b: 5).

The job of the ethnographer, then, becomes the description and interpretation of the meanings particular groups of people (cultures) make from their interaction with the world around them: how they understand the world. If culture is a system of meanings, and ethnography is writing culture, then ethnography consists of finding out what the system of meanings is, and writing it down. This is done through what Geertz calls 'thick description', which is effectively description-plus-interpretation. In identifying 'thick description', Geertz is partly proposing a manifesto for ethnographic work and partly himself describing what he considered ethnographers to always have done. He explains thick description by borrowing from Gilbert Ryle the example of a wink:

Consider … two boys rapidly contracting the eye-lids of the right eyes. In one, this is an involuntary twitch; in the other, a conspiratorial signal to a friend. The two movements are, as movements, identical … Yet … the difference between a wink and a twitch is vast; as anyone unfortunate enough to have had the first taken for the second knows. The winker is communicating, and indeed communicating in a quite precise and special way: (1) deliberately (2) to someone in particular (3) to impart a particular message (4) according to a socially established code (5) with the knowledge of others around him … the winker has done two things: contracted eyelids and winked; the twitcher has done only one (Geertz, 1973b: 6–7).

But, Geertz continues, how do we know which is which? He goes on to elaborate other forms of eyelid contraction—as a parody of a meaningful wink, as a false wink to mislead the others, etc. His point is one about description. First, that as soon as we say that the eye contraction is a 'wink', we have already made an interpretation of what the event was. We have combined straightforward description of the 'eyelid contraction' variety with an interpretation of what it means to produce thick description of a 'wink'. Second, that if this is what ethnographers do, then they need to be

careful to know that the interpretation they are making is the right one. It calls for a sensitivity to the processes of interpretation, and an awareness among ethnographers that their description *is* thick.

If ethnographic description is thick then it sits at an interpretive remove from the observations made by ethnographers in the field. Between an ethnographic event and its description in ethnography lies a process of inscription, which is also a process of sorting, selection and interpretation. Pelto and Pelto draw our attention to this in their discussion of fieldnotes, in which they distinguish 'vague notes'—which for them are problematic because not sufficiently attuned to the detail of events *as they happen*—from 'concrete notes'. They take the example of an argument observed during fieldwork, suggesting that the ethnographer might record it in (at least) two different ways—vague or concrete, thereby generating different types of notes (Pelto and Pelto, 1978: 70):

Vague Notes	Concrete Notes
A showed hostility toward B	A scowled and spoke harshly to B, saying a number of negative things, including 'Get the hell out of here, Mr B.' He then shook his fist in B's face and walked out of the room.

The concrete notes described here give much more detail of the events observed by the ethnographer, while the vague notes cut a descriptive corner to immediately offer up an interpretation of A's behavior as 'hostility'. To this extent, the vague notes correspond to Geertz's notion of 'thick description', in that they include not only description, but also interpretation.

Pelto and Pelto (ibid.) signal the danger of too hastily formulating a thick description, in the form of a vague note, but arguably oversimplify the process of fieldnote-taking and its relationship to the final ethnographic text. They rather assume that the concrete fieldnote is all that is available to the ethnographer when it comes to writing up, whilst

Simon Ottenberg (1990: 144ff.), helpfully coining the term 'headnotes', demonstrates the extent to which writing up is more often dependent on the ethnographer's memory, with fieldnotes acting as *aides mémoires* rather than neutral data to be analyzed on return from the field.

WRITING CULTURE

Thick description, with its focus on the active process of interpretation inherent in ethnographic writing, paved the way for the 1980s concern with ethnography as a genre of writing. The resulting critique of the form centered partly on the validity of ethnographic writing as a mode of representing the reality of other people's lives and partly on the ideological implications of the very project of ethnographic description.

As early as 1975, Wagner had argued that ethnographers are better described as inventors of culture than its describers, since they demarcate bounded, homogeneous units with a distinctive *ethos* (see Benedict, 1934), and call these 'cultures'. This criticism was aimed at, though not limited to, American cultural anthropology. British social anthropology, dominated by functionalist theories, also came under fire for over-emphasizing the functional integration and discreteness of social systems—conceived as 'societies' (Gluckman, 1964). By and large, these criticisms led in the 1970s to a theoretical shift away from cultural and social unity—the bounded description of 'cultures' and 'societies'—towards an analysis of conflict, power and process within and beyond these units: a 'political' critique (Ortner, 1984). By the 1980s, though, it provoked a 'literary' critique.

Clifford (1986: 6) argued that inasmuch as it is actively *produced*, ethnography should be considered fiction: of a particular and distinctive genre, characterized by particular rhetorical conventions born of its particular institutional, political and historical roots. With institutional backing in universities and research institutes, and with either covert or overt backing from colonial office or state department (see Asad, 1973), ethnographers were inevitably seen as the holders of power in an unequal relationship with those they described. Influenced by critical literary theory, itself influenced by Althusserian Marxism, this critique saw the ethnographer's remit as generating, or interpolating, 'others' and thereby creating the intellectual terms upon which they were dominated. This part of the argument followed Said's critique of Orientalism (1978) to forge a general account of ethnographers' production of 'others' (see also Fabian, 1983).

The Althusserian critique focused on the authors, and their role in the generation of authoritative 'truth' (Clifford, 1983) through falsehood: 'All constructed truths are made possible by the powerful "lies" of exclusion and rhetoric' (Clifford, 1986: 7). By selecting certain observations or events to write about—either consciously or unconsciously by lapse of memory—ethnographic authors effectively become the editors of the culture or society they describe. This is considered a position of power.

The focus on authorial voice led to calls for reflexivity in ethnographic writing, foregrounding the author's role in the writing of ethnography—and indeed the ethnographer's role in the research process—to weave ethnographic description with description of the process leading to ethnographic description. Clifford (1986: 13) praises a number of such 'experimental' ethnographic works that seek to reveal within the text the relations of its production, producing reflexive texts that acknowledge they are partial—in both senses of the word—and derive 'representational tact' (1986: 7) from that acknowledgement.

With this came a strong moral imperative to reconfigure the relationship between the ethnographer and their informants as one of co-authors, with the ethnographer acting as 'scribe and archivist' (1986: 17) as well as advocate of the cultures and societies researched. From this point of view, the writing of ethnography becomes not a scientific activity but a political one; doubly so when writing in highly politicized contexts, such as those surrounding indigenous peoples.

These politics came to the fore in the 'Darkness in El Dorado' controversy, which saw Napoleon Chagnon, a 1960s ethnographer of the Yanomami—an Amazonian hunter-forager society—accused in the year 2000 of deliberate manipulation of the ethnographic process to generate a representation of them as temperamentally violent, 'fierce people' (Borofsky, 2005; Chagnon, 1968; Gregor and Gross, 2004; Tierney, 2000). Journalist Patrick Tierney claimed to have discovered evidence that Chagnon had falsified data, irresponsibly encouraging the Yanomami to make war, which was then represented as their 'natural' behavior. The resulting furor provoked a thorough inquiry by the American Anthropological Association, which in 2002 published a report that effectively condemned Chagnon, along with co-fieldworker geneticist James Neel:

> The *Report* concluded that Neel and Chagnon misused their subjects in the course of ethnographic and biological research, they failed to obtain adequate informed consent for their work, and that their research left the Yanomami psychologically damaged. Chagnon was also found guilty of depicting the Yanomami in a harmful way in his publications and of consorting with corrupt politicians in Venezuela, thereby violating the association's code of professional ethics (Gregor and Gross, 2004: 687).

The report reveals the current concern with the morality of ethnographic practice and ethnographic writing; and with the politics of ethnography. The falsified evidence for and representation of endemic Yanomami violence, it argued, lent credence to the opinion that they were a backward, savage people who neither required nor deserved special protection or reservation from the Venezuelan state (ibid.: 689). Their representation, then, had direct political consequence, quite apart from the more subtle political implications of their being represented in essentialist terms. For Clifford, such essentialisation of 'cultures' or 'societies' is not only politically problematic, it is also empirically incorrect, generating an appearance of static and homogeneous units where in fact they are historically more contingent and differentiated.

> 'Cultures' do not hold still for their portraits. Attempts to make them do so always involve simplification and exclusion, selection of a temporal focus, the construction of a particular self-other relationship, and the imposition or negotiation of a power relationship (Clifford, 1986: 10).

BEYOND THE FIELD

The critique of ethnography as a kind of writing went alongside a critique of the notion of 'the field' as a location for ethnographic research (Amit, 2000; Coleman and Collins, 2006; Gupta and Ferguson, 1997; Marcus, 1998). The representation of cultures and societies as bounded, homogeneous and static units was bound up with the assumption that 'the field' was a particular kind of place: local, often isolated, spatially demarcated. This view contributed to the other part of the 'fieldwork concept'— the 'village study'. Gupta and Ferguson (1997: 2–5) argue that this notion of the field had been fetishized by ethnographers, both intellectually and institutionally, creating expectations about ethnographic fieldwork and ethnographic careers that reinforced the essentialist 'othering' of the cultures and societies that ethnographers researched. They point towards the emergence of newer fields, which 'decenter and defetishize the concept of "the field"' (ibid.: 5), incorporating a reflexive focus on 'own' rather than 'other' society, and breaking down the spatialized metaphor of the field.

The most influential argument in favor of a reconfigured 'field' is George Marcus's call for a 'multi-sited ethnography'. This ethnography:

> moves out from the single sites and local situations of conventional ethnographic research designs to examine the circulation of cultural meanings, objects, and identities in diffuse time-space. This mode defines for itself an object of study that

cannot be accounted for ethnographically by remaining focused on a single site of intensive investigation (Marcus, 1998: 79–80).

Rather, it involves a more fragmented and comparative approach to examining varied instantiations of a particular phenomenon, brought together in unity by the creative constructivism of the ethnographer, who establishes links and commonalities, often through extended metaphor (ibid.: 1998: 89–90). In more practical terms, multi-sited ethnography involves following processes in motion, rather than units *in situ*. It also involves a reconsideration of the politics of ethnography, away from an investigation of 'subaltern' peoples, seen in the context of an exploitative world system, towards an investigation of the system itself. This is achieved through 'following' various processes in motion. Marcus thus suggests we 'follow the person' in pilgrimage, migration, or even lifecycle; 'follow the thing' through commodity and exchange chains; 'follow the metaphor' as key concepts of contemporary life—'immunity' (Martin, 1994) 'performance' (Rapport, 1997) 'participation' (Stirrat and Henkel, 2001)—emerge and circulate in public culture; 'follow the plot, story or allegory' in mythology, popular history or social memory; 'follow the life or biography' of particular individual research subjects; or 'follow the conflict' as it links adversaries, combatants, observers and conciliators (Marcus, 1998: 90–95).

With this more fragmented and plural approach to ethnography, the stock-in-trade of more 'traditional' ethnographic research—long-term ethnographic immersion by participant observation—is substituted by shorter-term research methods: interviews, focus groups, life histories etc. Marcus (1998: 84) acknowledges the potential loss of quality of ethnography inherent in this move, but argues that the key feature of ethnographic work that is preserved in multi-sited fieldwork is that of 'translation' of meaning from one culture to another. Indeed the key components of ethnography as outlined by Hammersley—*induction, context* and

unfamiliarity—are—at least potentially—maintained in multi-sited fieldwork, but what disappears is the ambition of holism.

For Marcus, this is a virtue, as the older commitment to holism is revealed in contemporary critical ethnography to be a fiction (ibid.: 33–34). However, it does raise questions about the distinctive character of ethnography in relation to other qualitative methodologies. If ethnography abandons its commitment to long-term participant observation and holistic description, then what makes it different from any other qualitative method?

This question has recently been raised by Stirrat and Rajak (2007) who compare multi-sited fieldwork to international development practitioners' 'field trips', arguing that whilst the latter's highly staged brevity undermines the authority derived from direct contact with 'local people', the former risks doing exactly the same. It is best done, they argue, through situated participant observation research in two or three sites at most, thus maintaining the benefits of long-term, situated research:

> One of the chief qualities of [ethnographic] fieldwork, as opposed to, say, its evil twin—the [development] field trip—is held up to be the length and depth of the researcher's engagement with the field. Multi-sited fieldwork if taken in its literal sense is seen by some to reduce this to little more than a series of vignettes drawn from brief sojourns in multiple sites and awkwardly strung together (Stirrat and Rajak, forthcoming: 15).

Such an approach would undermine the value of ethnography over other, less intensive, qualitative methods.

REFERENCES

Amit, V. (2000) *Constructing the Field*. London: Routledge.

Asad, T. (ed.) (1973) *Anthropology and the Colonial Encounter*. New York: Humanities Press.

Benedict, R. (1934) *Patterns of Culture*. London: Routledge.

Boissevain, J. (1965) *Saints and Fireworks*. London: Athlone.

——— (1969) *Hal-Farrug: A Village in Malta.* New York: Holt, Rinehart and Winston.

——— (1970) 'Fieldwork in Malta', in G.D. Spindler (ed.) *Being an Anthropologist.* New York: Holt, Rinehart and Winston. pp. 58–84.

——— (1974) *Friends of Friends: Networks, Manipulators and Coalitions.* Oxford: Blackwell.

Borofsky, R. (2005) *Yanomami: The Fierce Controversy and What We Can Learn From It.* Berkeley: University of California Press.

Bourdieu, P. (1977) *Outline of a Theory of Practice.* Cambridge: Cambridge University Press.

Chagnon, N. (1968) *The Yanomamo.* New York: Holt, Rinehart and Winston.

Clammer, J. (1984) 'Approaches to ethnographic research', in R. Ellen (ed.), *Ethnographic Research.* London: Academic Press. pp. 63-85.

Clifford, J. (1983) 'On ethnographic authority', *Representations* 1:2: 118–146.

——— (1986) 'Partial truths', in G. Marcus and J. Clifford (eds.), *Writing Culture.* Berkeley: University of California Press. pp. 1–26.

Coleman, S. and Collins, P. (eds.) (2006) *Locating the Field: Space, Place and Context in Anthropology.* Oxford: Berg.

Dilley, R. (ed.) (1999) *The Problem of Context.* Oxford: Berghahn.

Eriksen, T.H. (1995) *Small Places, Large Issues.* London: Pluto.

Evans-Pritchard, E.E. (1962) *Essays in Social Anthropology.* London: Faber.

——— (1976) *Witchcraft, Oracles and Magic Among the Azande.* Oxford: Clarendon Press.

Fabian, J. (1983) *Time and the Other.* New York: Columbia University Press.

Geertz, C. (1973a) 'The impact of the concept of culture on the concept of man', in C. Geertz, *The Interpretation of Cultures.* New York: Basic Books. pp. 33–54.

——— (1973b) Thick description: Toward an interpretive theory of culture', in C. Geertz, *The Interpretation of Cultures.* New York: Basic Books. pp. 3–30.

Gluckman, M. (1940) 'Analysis of a social situation in modern Zululand', *Bantu Studies,* 14:1–30.

——— (ed.) (1964) *Closed Systems and Open Minds: The Limits of Naivety in Social Anthropology.* London: Oliver and Boyd.

Gregor, T.A. and Gross, D.R. (2004) 'Guilt by association: The culture of accusation and the American Anthropological Association's investigation of *Darkness in El Dorado'*, *American Anthropologist* 106 (4): 687–98.

Gupta, A. and Ferguson, J. (1997) 'Discipline and practice: "The field" as site, method and location in anthropology', in A. Gupta and J. Ferguson (eds.), *Anthropological Locations.* Berkeley: University of California Press. pp. 1–46

Hammersley, M. (1992) *What's Wrong With Ethnography?* London: Routledge.

Malinowski, B. (1922) *Argonauts of the Western Pacific.* London: Routledge and Kegan Paul.

——— (1934) *Coral Gardens and Their Magic.* London: Allen and Unwin.

——— (1944) *A Scientific Theory of Culture and Other Essays.* Oxford: Oxford University Press.

Marcus, G. (1998) *Ethnography Through Thick and Thin.* Princeton: Princeton University Press.

Martin, E. (1994) *Flexible Bodies: The Role of Immunity in American Culture from the Days of Polio to the Age of AIDS.* Boston: Beacon Press.

Okely, J. (2003) 'Anthropological fieldwork as serendipity and science', Paper presented at Association of Social Antropologists' Decennial Conference, Manchester, UK.

Ortner, S.B. (1984) 'Theory in anthropology since the sixties', *Comparative Studies in Society and History* 26: 126–66.

Ottenberg, S. (1990) 'Thirty years of fieldnotes: Changing relationships to the text', in R. Sanjek (ed.), *Fieldnotes: The Makings of Anthropology.* Ithaca: Cornell University Press. pp. 139–160.

Pelto, J. and Pelto, G.H. (1978) *Anthropological Research: The Structure of Inquiry.* Cambridge: Cambridge University Press.

Rapport, N. (1997) 'Hard sell: Commercial performance and the narration of the self', in F. Hughes-Freeland (ed.), *Ritual, Performance, Media.* London: Routledge.

Reyna, S. (2001) 'Theory counts: (Discounting) discourse to the contrary by adopting a confrontational stance', *Anthropological Theory,* 1: 9–31.

Roseberry, W. (1989) *Anthropologies and Histories.* New Brunswick: Rutgers University Press.

Said, E. (1978) *Orientalism.* London: Routledge.

Spencer, J. (1990) *A Sinhala Village in a Time of Trouble.* Oxford: Oxford University Press.

Spindler, G.D (ed.) (1970) *Being an Anthropologist: Fieldwork in Eleven Cultures.* New York: Holt, Rinehart and Winston.

Stirrat, R.L. and Henkel, H. (2001) 'Participation as spiritual duty; empowerment as secular subjection', in B. Cooke and U. Kothari (eds.), *Participation: The New Tyranny?* London: Zed Books.

Stirrat, R.L. and Rajak, D. (2007) 'The Romance of the Field?', in H.L. Seneviratne (ed.), *The Anthropologist and the Native.* Florence: Florence University Press and Delhi: Munshiram Manoharla.

Stocking, G. (1984) Functionalism Historicized: essays on British social anthropology. Madison: University of Winsconsin Press.

Tierney, P. (2000) *Darkness in El Dorado.* New York: Norton.

Wagner, R. (1975) *The Invention of Culture.* Chicago: University of Chicago Press.

Whyte, W. F. (1955) *Street Corner Society.* Chicago: University of Chicago Press.

Young, M. (1979) *The Ethnography of Malinowski: the Trobriand Islands 1915–1918.* London: Routledge.

ENDNOTES

1 Spencer's (1990) fieldwork in Sri Lanka, for example, coincided with the outbreak of civil war, demanding a re-orientation of research around questions of nationalism and conflict.

2 Numerous anthropological studies of kinship, for example, hinge on the relationship between 'official' and 'practical' kinship (Bourdieu, 1977); between stated prescriptions on the one hand and actual strategic behavior on the other.

4

Comparative Methods

Charles C. Ragin

INTRODUCTION

Unfortunately, it is still common to present comparative methodology as an inferior version of conventional variable-oriented analysis (e.g., King et al., 1994). The goals of comparative analysis are assumed to be the same as those of variable-oriented analysis: to assess the relative merits of theories, operationalized as the net effects of competing independent variables (see Ragin, 2005). In the conventional view, the 'problem' with comparative research is that comparativists usually study small Ns and the typical comparative study has too few cases to permit the proper use of techniques of statistical control (Smelser, 1976). When explanatory variables outnumber cases, it is impossible to assess their relative merit in the competition to account for variation in a dependent variable.

What is missing from this view is appreciation of the distinctiveness of comparative analysis, namely, that it is simultaneously case-oriented and set-theoretic in nature. The fact that comparative research is case-oriented is more widely recognized today than it was 10 or 15 years ago. In part, this recognition has followed from the greater legitimacy of 'the case' as an object of study

(Ragin and Becker, 1992). Even though there is little formalized methodology of case study research as a generic form of inquiry, most social scientists recognize that understanding a case is a legitimate social scientific goal and that conventional variable-oriented techniques are at best only indirectly relevant to this task (Achen, 2005). Less recognized is the fact that the mathematical basis of much comparative analysis, and of qualitative analysis more generally, is different from that of conventional quantitative analysis. The former is based in set theory (i.e., Boolean algebra); the latter is based in linear algebra. After addressing the case-oriented nature of comparative research, this chapter sketches several key features that follow from its set-theoretic nature. These features range from the simple mechanics of making empirical connections, to more complex procedures central to the discovery process.

Only by recognizing the distinctiveness of comparative analysis is it possible to use comparative methods effectively. Furthermore, understanding the set-theoretic nature of comparative analysis is central to understanding the nature of the gap between case-oriented and variable-oriented research and to efforts to bridge this gap (Rihoux, 2003).

THE CASE-ORIENTED NATURE OF COMPARATIVE RESEARCH

An important lesson in every course in quantitative research methods is that having more cases is better. More is better in three main ways. First, researchers must meet a threshold number of cases in order even to apply quantitative methods, usually cited as an N of 30 to 50. Second, the smaller the N, the more the researcher's data must satisfy the difficult assumptions of statistical methods, for example, the assumption that variables are normally distributed or the assumption that sub-group variances are roughly equal. (In point of fact, however, having a small N almost guarantees that such assumptions will be violated, especially when the cases are macro-level units such as organizations or countries. Thus, the motivation to use large Ns is considerable.) Third, the greater the number of cases, the easier it is to produce statistically significant results. The only practical problem, in this light, is whether the researcher is willing and able to gather data on as many cases as possible, preferably hundreds if not thousands.

By contrast, case-oriented research is often defined by its focus on phenomena that are of interest because they are infrequent—i.e, precisely because the N of cases is small. Typically, in comparative research these phenomena are large-scale and historically delimited, not generic 'observations' or 'units' in any sense. This key contrast with variable-oriented research derives from the simple fact that many of the phenomena that interest social scientists and their audiences are historically or culturally significant. To argue that social scientists should study only cases that are generic and abundant or that can be studied only in isolation from their historical and cultural contexts would severely limit both the scope and value of social science. One of the key lessons of case-oriented research is that having fewer cases is often better. After all, with large Ns in-depth knowledge of cases must be sacrificed.

The bias of variable-oriented research toward large Ns dovetails with the implicit assumption that 'cases' are empirically given, not constructed by the researcher, and that they are naturally abundant. Variable-oriented researchers rarely devote much intellectual energy to the problem of constituting cases and populations. The ideal—typical case in variable-oriented research is the individual survey respondent, found in a taken-for-granted population, which in turn is demarcated by geographic, temporal and demographic boundaries. The key problematic is how to derive a representative sample from the very large natural population of observations that is presumed to be at the researcher's ready disposal. When dealing with macro-level units (e.g., organizations, countries, etc.), variable-oriented researchers usually try to force these units into the survey research template, viewing their cases as generic observations drawn at random from an empirically given population.

Comparative researchers, by contrast, treat cases as singular, whole entities purposefully selected and constituted as instances of theoretically, culturally or historically significant phenomena, not as homogeneous observations drawn from a pool of equally plausible selections. Cases are typically selected for study because of the qualitatively distinct features or outcomes they exhibit. Often, the focus is on a qualitative change that the cases under investigation share—historically emergent phenomena or patterns that constitute a break of some sort with what existed before. Thus, in comparative research the key concern is not to account for variation in the levels of an outcome (the 'dependent variable') across cases ('observations') drawn from a generic population, but to account for qualitative changes in a meaningfully constituted set of cases in order to comprehend their distinctive outcomes. More generally, the objective of case-oriented research is to explain the 'how' of historically or culturally situated phenomena, as in 'how did this qualitative aspect or change come about.' Theory is central to this task because it provides important leads and guiding concepts for empirical research, not because it offers explicit hypotheses to be tested.

These case–oriented features of comparative research have important implications for how it is conducted (Ragin, 2004). Specifically, they favor research strategies that are 'set-theoretic' as opposed to 'correlational' in nature. Before addressing the set-theoretic character of comparative analysis, I first review basic features of set relations and their use in social research.

SET RELATIONS IN SOCIAL RESEARCH

The simplest and most basic set relation is the subset, which is easiest to grasp when it involves nested categories. Dogs are a subset of the set of mammals; Protestants are a subset of the set of humans. These subset relations are straightforward and easy to grasp because they are definitional in nature: dogs have all the characteristics of mammals; the set of humans is partially constituted by the set of Protestants. These examples also involve conventional, presence/absence sets and thus are simple to represent using Venn diagrams. The circle representing the set of dogs, for example, is entirely contained within a larger circle representing the set of mammals.

The subset relation also can be used to describe social phenomena that are connected causally or in some other integral manner. For example, when researchers note that 'religious fundamentalists are politically conservative,' they are stating, in effect, that religious fundamentalists form a rough subset of the set of political conservatives. In fact, almost all social science theory is formulated in terms of set relations. Subset relations are central to theorizing for the simple reason that most theory is verbal in nature, and most verbal statements employ set relations in some way. An important feature of set-theoretic statements is that they are *asymmetric*. For example, the fact that there are many political conservatives who are not religious fundamentalists does not challenge the claim that religious fundamentalists are politically conservative.

When set relations reflect integral social or causal connections and are not merely definitional in nature, they require explication—i.e., they are theory-and knowledge-dependent. Assume, for example, that among third-wave democracies, all those that adopted parliamentary governments soon failed. Thus, third-wave democracies with parliamentary governments form a subset of failed third-wave democracies. Was it just bad luck, a coincidence? Or is there a causal or some other kind of integral connection between adopting a parliamentary form of government and subsequent failure among third-wave democracies? The set-theoretic connection in this example is not definitional; it must be explicated or theorized in some way. This type of set relation, the kind that is central to almost all social science theorizing, is the main focus of this paper.

Set-theoretic arguments in social science theory are often erroneously reformulated as correlational hypotheses. This error is, in fact, one of the most common in all of contemporary social science. For example, a theory may claim that because of the many external vagaries faced by newly formed democracies, third-wave democracies adopting parliamentary governments (which often take a long time to form, as the many political parties bargain and negotiate terms) are unlikely to endure. After reading this argument, the conventional social scientist would try to test it by examining the correlation between 'parliamentary government' and 'failure' using data on third-wave democracies. Suppose, again, that the set-theoretic evidence supports this theory—i.e., third-wave democracies adopting parliamentary governments are a subset of failed third-wave democracies. Despite this explicit connection, the correlation between 'parliamentary form' and 'failure' might still be relatively weak, due to the fact that there are many other paths to failure and thus many failed democracies with presidential or other forms of non-parliamentary government. The set-theoretic claim that 'third-wave democracies with parliamentary governments fail' is not refuted in any way by these cases. However, these non-parliamentary paths to failure seriously undermine the correlation between 'parliamentary form' and 'failure'. Thus, it is important to evaluate set-theoretic claims with set-theoretic methods, not correlational methods.

To summarize: set relations in social research: (1) are the basic building blocks of social science theories, (2) involve causal or other integral connections between social phenomena, (3) require explication and therefore are theory- and knowledge-dependent, (4) are usually asymmetric, (5) are often erroneously reformulated as correlational hypotheses, and (6) can be strong despite relatively weak correlations.

THE SET-THEORETIC CHARACTER OF COMPARATIVE ANALYSIS

The set-theoretic character of comparative analysis follows from its case-oriented nature. To grasp this essential connection it is useful first to consider the nature of social scientific explanation in case study research. Suppose a researcher argues that Peru experienced waves of protest against austerity programs mandated by the International Monetary Fund (IMF) because of (1) the severity of IMF-mandated measures, (2) the high concentration of the poor in urban slums, (3) the perceived corruption of government officials, and (4) the substantial prior level of political mobilization and contention. This explanation of austerity protest cites a specific combination of four conditions—some long-standing (e.g., the concentration of the poor in urban slums) and some temporally proximate (e.g., the severity of the austerity measures mandated by the IMF). The explanation has the character of a recipe—all four conditions are simultaneously met in the case of Peru, and together they explain the explosion of protest following the imposition of stiff austerity measures.

Like almost all arguments based on the study of a single case, the argument that this combination of causal conditions accounts for austerity protest in Peru is an *asymmetric* argument—i.e., it is an explanation of a positive instance of austerity protest, and is not intended as an explanation of the absence of austerity protest. As a *symmetric* argument, the expectation would be that in order to avoid austerity protest, it is necessary simply to avoid satisfying this recipe. But there may be many recipes for austerity protest; avoiding the observed recipe may not offer any protection. In the language of set theory, the recipe for austerity protest observed in Peru is a member of the larger set of recipes for austerity protest. Viewing all instances of austerity protest as a set of cases, there may be cases displaying the same recipe as Peru, but there may be many other cases displaying alternative recipes. The fact that there are alternative recipes (and thus many instances of the outcome—austerity protest—which fail to display the causal conditions displayed by Peru) does not invalidate Peru's recipe. This fact also indicates that the absence of the satisfied recipe does not ensure that austerity protest will not occur. The reasoning here parallels that offered for the connection between religious fundamentalism and political conservatism: The fact that there are political conservatives who are not religious fundamentalists does *not* challenge or invalidate the statement that religious fundamentalists are politically conservative, nor does the absence of religious fundamentalism guarantee the absence of political conservatism.

Using the analysis of Peru as a springboard, the comparativist could move in either of two main research directions. The first possible direction would be to find other instances of austerity protest and examine whether they agree in displaying the same four causal ingredients found in Peru—i.e., do all instances of austerity protest display these antecedent conditions? This strategy employs the common qualitative research device of 'selecting on the dependent variable', an approach that is almost universally, but mistakenly, condemned by quantitative researchers (see, e.g., King et al., 1994). The second direction would be to try to find other instances of Peru's recipe and examine whether these cases also experienced austerity protest. In essence, the researcher would select cases on the basis of their score on the independent variable. In this instance, however, the 'independent variable' is a recipe with the four main conditions all satisfied. The goal of the second strategy would be to assess the recipe: Does it invariably (or at least regularly) lead to austerity protest?

Both these strategies are set-theoretic in nature. The first is an examination of whether instances of the outcome (austerity protest) constitute a subset of instances of a combination of causal conditions (i.e., Peru's recipe). The second is an examination of whether instances of a specific combination of causal conditions (Peru's recipe) constitute a subset of instances of an outcome (austerity protest). Of course, both strategies could be used, and, if both subset relations are confirmed, then the two sets (the set of cases with Peru's recipe and the set of cases with austerity protest) would coincide. While it might appear that the two strategies together constitute a correlational analysis, recall that correlations are strong when there are many 'null–null' instances: cases that lack both the causal recipe and the outcome. Neither of the two research strategies just described uses 'null–null' cases in any way. (The issue of 'null–null' cases is discussed in greater detail below.)

Note that both these set-theoretic strategies are methods for establishing explicit connections. If it is found, for example, that all (or nearly all) instances of austerity protest exhibit the same causal recipe, then an explicit connection has been established between this recipe and austerity protest—assuming this connection dovetails with existing theoretical and substantive knowledge. Likewise, if it is found that all (or nearly all) cases sharing Peru's recipe experienced austerity protest, then an explicit connection has been established between this combination of conditions and austerity protest. Establishing explicit connections is not the same as establishing correlations. For example, assume that 60 percent of the cases with Peru's recipe experienced austerity protest, while only 30 percent of the cases without Peru's recipe experienced austerity protest. Clearly, there is a correlation between these two aspects conceived as variables ('recipe satisfied versus not satisfied'

and 'austerity protest versus no austerity protest'). However, the evidence does not come close to approximating a set-theoretic relation. Thus, there would be evidence of a correlational connection (i.e., a tendency in the data), but not of an explicit connection between Peru's recipe and austerity protest.

It is important to recognize that the two subset relations described here as explicit connections entail different kinds of causal connections. As explained in Ragin (2000), the first analytic strategy—identifying causal conditions shared by cases with the same outcome—is appropriate for the assessment of *necessary* conditions. The second—examining cases with the same causal conditions to see if they also share the same outcome—is suitable for the assessment of *sufficient* conditions, especially sufficient combinations of conditions. Establishing conditions that are necessary or sufficient is a long-standing interest of comparative researchers (see, e.g., Goertz and Starr, 2002). However, it is important to note that the use of set-theoretic methods to establish explicit connections does not necessarily entail the use of the concepts or the language of necessity and sufficiency, or any other language of causation. A researcher might observe, for example, that instances of austerity protest are all ex-colonies without drawing any causal connection from this observation. A simpler example: colleagues might 'act out' only in faculty meetings, but that does not mean that analysts must therefore interpret faculty meetings as a necessary condition for acting out. Demonstrating explicit connections is important to social scientists, whether or not they are interested in demonstrating causation. In fact, qualitative analysis in the social sciences is centrally concerned with establishing explicit connections.

SET-THEORETIC VERSUS CORRELATIONAL ANALYSIS

As Ragin (2000) demonstrates, correlational methods are not well suited for studying

Table 4.1   Cross-tabulation of Cause and Outcome

	Cause Absent	*Cause Present*
Outcome Present	Cell #1: key cell for assessing necessary conditions	Cell #2: cases here confirm connection between cause and outcome
Outcome Absent	Cell #3: the null-null cell	Cell #4: key cell for assessing sufficient conditions

explicit connections. This mismatch is clearly visible in the simplest form of variable-oriented analysis, the 2 x 2 cross tabulation of the presence/absence of an outcome against the presence/absence of an hypothesized cause, as illustrated in Table 4.1.

The correlation focuses simultaneously and equivalently on the degree to which instances of the cause produce instances of the outcome (the number of cases in cell 2 relative to the sum of cells 2 and 4) and on the degree to which instances of the absence of the cause are linked to the absence of the outcome (the number of cases in cell 3 relative to the sum of cells 1 and 3). In short, it is an omnibus statistic that rewards researchers equally for producing an abundance of cases in cell 2 or cell 3, and penalizes them, again equally, for depositing cases in cell 1 or cell 4. Thus, it is a good tool for studying tendencies in the given set of data (i.e., in a defined population or in a sample drawn from a defined population).

A researcher interested in explicit connections, however, is interested in only specific components of the information that is pooled and conflated in a correlation. For example, comparative researchers interested in causally relevant conditions shared by instances of an outcome would focus on cells 1 and 2 of Table 4.1. Their goal would be to identify causal conditions that deposit as few cases as possible in cell 1. Likewise, researchers interested in whether cases that are similar with respect to causal conditions experience the same outcome would focus on cells 2 and 4. Their goal would be to identify combinations of causal conditions that deposit as few cases as possible in cell 4. It is clear from these examples that the correlation has major shortcomings when viewed from the perspective of explicit connections: (1) it attends only to relative differences

(e.g., relative rates of austerity protest); (2) it attaches equal importance and weight to the null–null cell, a cell which does not play a direct role in the assessment of either necessity or sufficiency; (3) it conflates different kinds of set-theoretic assessment; and (4) it conflates the assessment of necessity and sufficiency.

It is important to point out that the bivariate correlation is the foundation of most forms of conventional quantitative social research, including some of the most sophisticated forms of variable-oriented analysis practiced today. A matrix of bivariate correlations, along with the means and standard deviations of the variables included in the correlation matrix, is all that is needed to compute complex regression analyses, factor analyses and even structural equation models. In essence, these varied techniques offer diverse ways of representing the bivariate correlations in a matrix and the various partial relations (e.g., the net effect of an independent variable in a multiple regression) that can be constructed using formulas based on three or more bivariate correlations. Because they rely on the bivariate correlation as the cornerstone of empirical analysis, these sophisticated quantitative techniques eschew the study of explicit connections and the different kinds of causation linked to different set relations, as described here. Comparative analysis is, by contrast, centrally concerned with explicit connections and is grounded in set relations.

THE LOGIC OF COMPARATIVE ANALYSIS

An especially useful feature of comparative analysis is its attention to complex causation, defined as a situation where a given outcome may follow from several different combinations of causal conditions—different causal 'paths' or 'recipes'. For example, a researcher may have good reason to suspect that there are several distinct recipes for austerity protests. By examining the fate of cases with different combinations of causally relevant conditions, it is possible to identify the decisive recipes and thereby unravel causal complexity (see Mackie, 1965).

As Ragin (1987, 2000) demonstrates, the key tool for systematic analysis of causal complexity is the 'truth table', a tool that allows structured, focused comparisons (George, 1979). Truth tables list the logically possible combinations of causal conditions (e.g., presence/absence of severe IMF mandated austerity measures, presence/absence of high concentrations of the poor in urban slums, presence/absence of perceived corruption of government officials, and presence/absence of substantial prior level of political mobilization and contention) along with the outcome exhibited by the cases conforming to each combination of causal conditions (e.g., whether austerity protest is consistently present among the cases displaying each combination of conditions). A truth table using Peru's recipe to specific causal conditions would have 16 rows, one for each logically possible combination of causal conditions. In more complex truth tables the rows (combinations of causal conditions) may be quite numerous, for the number of causal combinations is an exponential function of the number of causal conditions (number of combinations = 2^k, where k is the number of causal conditions).

Truth tables are especially useful for assessing causal recipes (Ragin, 1987; Ragin, 2000; De Meur and Rihoux, 2002). They elaborate and formalize one of the key analytic strategies of comparative research—examining cases sharing specific combinations of causal conditions to see if they share the same outcome (i.e., assessing whether they constitute a subset of the cases with the outcome). The goal of truth table analysis is to identify explicit connections between combinations of causal conditions and outcomes. By listing the different logically possible combinations of conditions, it is possible to assess not only the sufficiency of a specific recipe (e.g., Peru's recipe, with all four causal conditions present), but also the other logically possible combinations of conditions that can be constructed from these four causal conditions. For example, if the cases with all four conditions present all experience austerity protest and the cases with three of four of the conditions present (and one absent) also all experience protest, then the researcher can conclude that the causal condition that varies across these two combinations is irrelevant. The key ingredients for the outcome are the remaining three conditions. Various techniques and procedures for logically simplifying patterns in truth tables, in addition to the simple one just described, are detailed in Ragin (1987; 2000) and De Meur and Rihoux (2002).

Often the move from recipe to truth table stimulates a reformulation or expansion of a recipe, based on a re-examination of relevant cases. For example, suppose the truth table revealed substantial inconsistency in Peru's row—that is, suppose there are several cases in the row that failed to exhibit austerity protest, in addition to the ones, like Peru, that did. This inconsistency in outcomes signals to the investigator that more in-depth study of cases is needed. For example, by comparing the cases in this row lacking austerity protest with those exhibiting protest, it would be possible to elaborate the recipe. Suppose this comparison revealed that the cases lacking austerity protest all had regimes with extensive repressive capacities and histories of severe political repression. This ingredient (absence of extensive repressive capacities) could then be added to the recipe and the truth table could then be reformulated accordingly with five causal conditions (yielding 32 rows). Notice that it would have been difficult to know, based on knowledge of only the Peruvian case, that this factor (absence of extensive repressive capacity) is an important part of the recipe, as it is absent in Peru and in cases like Peru. This point underscores the value of comparative analysis more generally, for it is often difficult to identify causal ingredients that must be absent when studying only positive instances of an outcome.

The task of truth table refinement is demanding, for it requires in-depth knowledge of cases and many iterations between theory, cases, and truth table construction. In effect, the truth table disciplines the investigative process, providing a framework for comparing cases as configurations of similarities and differences, and exploring patterns of consistency and inconsistency.

COMPARATIVE METHODS AND COUNTERFACTUAL ANALYSIS

One of the most interesting and powerful features of comparative analysis is its explicit consideration of unobserved combinations of causal conditions.[1] A central characteristic of comparative research, and qualitative research in general, is the simple fact that researchers work with relatively small *N*s. Investigators often confront more causal conditions than cases, a situation that is greatly complicated by the fact that comparativists typically focus on combinations of case aspects—how aspects of cases fit together configurationally. For example, a researcher interested in a causal argument specifying an intersection of five conditions should ideally consider all 32 logically possible combinations of these five conditions in order to provide a thorough assessment of the argument. Naturally occurring social phenomena are, however, profoundly limited in their diversity. The empirical world almost never presents social scientists all the logically possible combinations of causal conditions relevant to their arguments. While limited diversity is central to the constitution of social and political phenomena, it also severely complicates empirical analysis.

As a substitute for empirically absent combinations of causal conditions, comparative researchers often engage in 'thought experiments' (Weber, [1905] 1949). That is, they imagine counterfactual cases and hypothesize their outcomes, using their theoretical and substantive knowledge to guide their assessments (see, e.g., Hicks et al., 1995). With truth tables, the process of considering counterfactual cases (i.e., combinations of causal conditions lacking empirical instances) is explicit and systematic. In fact, this feature of truth table analysis is one of its key strengths.

Comparative researchers resort to counterfactual case analysis when they must contend with empirical cases that are 'limited' in their diversity. A very simple example of limited diversity is shown in Table 4.2. In this truth table (which uses hypothetical data) there are only two causal conditions (presence/absence of strong left parties and presence/absence of strong unions) and thus only four combinations of conditions. (The outcome is generous welfare states; the cases are advanced industrial societies.) However, one of the four combinations of causal conditions (presence of strong left parties combined with the absence of strong unions) lacks empirical instances—such cases do not exist.

The specific conclusion that is drawn from the evidence in Table 4.2 depends on how the last row is treated. The most conservative strategy is to treat it as false when assessing the conditions for the emergence of generous welfare states. Here, the thought experiment (counterfactual analysis) leads to the assumption that if such cases existed, they would not exhibit generous welfare states. The 'results' for the presence of generous welfare states can be expressed as follows:

$$L*U \rightarrow G$$

where upper–case letters indicate the presence of a condition, lower–case letters indicate its absence, L = strong left party, U = strong unions; G = generous welfare state; multiplication (*) indicates combined conditions (set intersection—logical *and*); addition (+) indicates the existence of alternate combinations of conditions (set union—logical *or*); and '→' indicates a causal connection. This equation simply summarizes the first row of Table 4.2 and states that the combination of strong left parties and strong unions explains the emergence of generous welfare states.

Table 4.2 Simple Example of the Impact of Limited Diversity

Strong Unions (U)	Strong Left Parties (L)	Generous Welfare State (G)	N of Cases
Yes	Yes	Yes	6
Yes	No	No	8
No	No	No	5
No	Yes	?	0

The alternative conclusion of the counterfactual analysis is that the fourth causal combination should lead to generous welfare states. This treatment of the fourth row leads to different results. The combinations linked to the presence of generous welfare state are now:

$$L*U + L*u \rightarrow G$$

which can be simplified as follows:

$$L*(U + u) \rightarrow G$$
$$L \rightarrow G$$

It is clear from these results that drawing a different conclusion from the counterfactual analysis leads to a logically simpler solution—that having strong left parties by itself causes generous welfare states. Thus, a researcher interested in deriving a more parsimonious solution might prefer the second counterfactual analysis. Notice that the second counterfactual analysis offers the same parsimonious result (L) as a conventional statistical analysis of these same data (L and G are perfectly correlated).

In comparative research it is incumbent upon the researcher to conduct counterfactual analyses when confronted with limited diversity, especially when decisions about the missing causal combinations have such a decisive impact on conclusions. Assume that the researcher in this example chose the more parsimonious solution for the presence of generous welfare states—concluding that this outcome is due entirely to the presence of strong left parties. It would then be necessary for the researcher to evaluate the plausibility of the counterfactual analysis that this solution incorporates—namely, that if instances of the presence of strong left parties combined with the absence of strong

unions did in fact exist, then these cases would display generous welfare states.

This is a very strong assumption. Many researchers would find it implausible in light of existing substantive and theoretical knowledge. That 'existing knowledge' in part would be the simple fact that all known instances of generous welfare states (as shown in Table 4.2) occur in countries that combine strong unions and strong left parties. Existing knowledge could also include in-depth case-level analyses of the emergence of generous welfare states. This knowledge might indicate, for example, that strong unions are centrally involved in the process of establishing generous welfare states. The important point here is not the specific conclusion of the study or whether or not having a strong left party is sufficient by itself for the establishment of generous welfare states. Rather, the issue is the status of assumptions about combinations of conditions that lack empirical cases and the role of counterfactual analysis in social research. In conventional quantitative research the issue of limited diversity is obscured because researchers use techniques and models that embody very strong assumptions about the nature of causation—e.g., that causes operate as 'independent' variables, that their effects are linear and additive, that parsimonious models are best, and so on.

Counterfactual analysis must be based on theoretical and substantive knowledge. 'Conclusions' do not follow completely and automatically from 'data', but are instead knowledge- and theory-dependent. This dependence can be seen clearly in the fact that some conclusions from counterfactual analysis are more plausible than others. On the basis of their theoretical and substantive knowledge, researchers define some counterfactuals as

Table 4.3 Truth Table with Four Causal Conditions (A, B, C, and D) and one Outcome (Y)

A	B	C	D	Y
No	No	No	No	No
No	No	No	Yes	?
No	No	Yes	No	?
No	No	Yes	Yes	?
No	Yes	No	No	No
No	Yes	No	Yes	No
No	Yes	Yes	No	?
No	Yes	Yes	Yes	No
Yes	No	No	No	?
Yes	No	No	Yes	?
Yes	No	Yes	No	?
Yes	No	Yes	Yes	?
Yes	Yes	No	No	Yes
Yes	Yes	No	Yes	Yes
Yes	Yes	Yes	No	?
Yes	Yes	Yes	Yes	?

plausible or 'easy' and others as implausible or 'difficult'. These evaluations are made explicit when truth tables are used to structure comparative analysis. For illustration, consider the evidence shown in Table 4.3, which shows a truth table with four causal conditions (labeled simply A, B, C, and D) and one outcome (labeled Y).

Limited diversity can be seen in the rows of the truth table shown in Table 4.3 that lack cases. As with Table 4.2, the solution to the truth table depends on how these causal combinations (rows without cases) are treated. The most conservative strategy is to treat combinations without cases as instances of the absence of the outcome when assessing the conditions for the presence of the outcome. Doing so yields the following solution to the truth table:

$$A*B*c \rightarrow Y$$

Again, upper–case letters indicate the presence of a condition; lower-case letters indicate its absence; A, B, C and D are causal conditions; Y is the outcome; multiplication (*) indicates combined conditions (logical 'and'—set intersection); addition (+)

indicates alternative combinations of conditions (logical 'or'—set union), and '→' indicates a causal connection. The equation for the presence of the outcome states simply that there is a single combination of conditions explicitly linked to Y, the presence of A and B combined with the absence of C (i.e. A*B*c).

A more liberal strategy would be to treat any row that lacks cases as an instance of the outcome, *if doing so produces a more parsimonious solution.*[2] This assessment is easy to conduct for the evidence in Table 4.3 because all rows with the outcome exhibit condition A, and all instances of absence of the outcome exhibit a (i.e., the absence of A). Thus, it is possible to generate the parsimonious solution,

$$A \rightarrow Y$$

by assuming that the six causal combinations that lack cases and include the presence of A would result in the outcome (Y) if they existed. In essence, the conclusion that A is the sole cause of Y assumes that if any of the following six combinations of conditions could be found, A*b*c*d, A*b*c*D,

A*b*C*d, A*b*C*D, A*B*C*d, and A*B*C*D, they would also display the outcome (Y). The analysis of these six counterfactual cases underpins the conclusion that A by itself causes Y, which is a dramatic use of simplifying assumptions.

Obviously, the solution incorporating six counterfactual combinations is remarkably parsimonious, but is it plausible? Before addressing this question, it is important to point out that given the evidence in Table 4.3, a conventional quantitative analysis of these data would quickly lead to the identification of condition A as the proper explanation of outcome Y. After all, as the table shows, whenever A is present, Y is present; whenever A is absent, Y is absent. None of the other causal conditions displays this simple relationship. Thus, the solution incorporating counterfactual combinations dovetails with the results of a conventional quantitative analysis of the same data.

The plausibility of this solution, however, depends upon the results of the plausibility of the counterfactual analysis. Too often researchers bypass counterfactual analyses because these assessments are demanding and time-consuming. Instead, they embrace parsimony and automatically use all the simplifying assumptions incorporated into the most parsimonious solution they can produce. This unfortunate practice duplicates many of the foibles of conventional quantitative analysis. At first glance, the task of evaluating counterfactual cases may seem daunting. However, once it is recognized that theoretical and substantive knowledge makes some counterfactuals 'easy', this task is greatly simplified. Further, the incorporation of 'easy' counterfactuals into a solution is straightforward and follows from the examination of the most complex solution (e.g., A*B*c) and the most parsimonious (e.g., A).

Imagine a researcher who postulates, based on existing theory and substantive knowledge, that causal conditions A, B, C and D are all linked in a positive way to outcome Y. That is, it is the *presence* of these conditions, not their *absence*, which should be linked to the occurrence of the outcome.

Suppose, however, the empirical evidence revealed that many instances of Y are coupled with the presence of causal conditions A, B and D, along with the absence of condition C (i.e., the researcher has found cases of A*B*c*D → Y). The researcher suspects, however, that all that really matters is having the three causes present, A, B and D. In other words, for A*B*D to generate Y, it is not necessary for C to be absent; C could be present or absent. However, there are no observable instances of A, B and D combined with the presence of C (i.e., there are no empirical instances of A*B*C*D). Thus, the decisive empirical comparison for determining whether the absence of C is an integral part of the causal mix (with A*B*D) simply does not exist.

Through counterfactual analysis (i.e., a thought experiment), the researcher could declare this hypothetical combination (A*B*C*D) to be a very likely instance of the outcome (Y). That is, the researcher might assert that A*B*C*D, if it existed, would lead to Y. This counterfactual analysis would allow the following logical simplification:

$$A*B*c*D + A*B*C*D \rightarrow Y$$
$$A*B*D*(c + C) \rightarrow Y$$
$$A*B*D \rightarrow Y$$

How plausible is this simplification? The answer to this question depends on the state of the relevant theoretical and substantive knowledge concerning the connection between C and Y in the presence of the other three causal conditions (A*B*D). If the researcher can establish, on the basis of existing knowledge, that there is every reason to expect that the presence of C should contribute to outcome Y under these conditions (or, conversely, that the absence of C does not make sense as a necessary contributing factor), then the counterfactual analysis just presented is plausible. In other words, existing knowledge makes the assertion A*B*C*D → Y an 'easy' counterfactual, because it involves the addition of a redundant contributing condition (C) to a configuration which is believed to be linked to the outcome (A*B*D).

It is important to point out that what has been accomplished in this simple example using set-theory is routine, though often implicit, in much case-oriented research. If conventional case-oriented researchers were to examine the empirical instance just listed (A*B*c*D → Y), they would likely develop their causal argument or narrative based on factors thought to be linked to the outcome (i.e., the presence of A, B and D). Along the way, they might consider the possibility that the absence of C observed in these cases might be connected in some way to the production of Y by A*B*D. They would be quite likely to conclude otherwise, given the presumed state of existing knowledge about the four causal conditions relevant to outcome Y—namely that it is the presence of these causal factors, not their absence, that is linked to the outcome. Thus, they would quickly arrive at the conclusion, A*B*D → Y. The point is that counterfactual analysis is not always explicit or elaborate in case-oriented research, especially when the counterfactuals are 'easy'. Such analyses are routinely conducted by case-oriented researchers 'on the fly'—in the process of constructing explanations of specific cases or categories of cases.

As a set-theoretic procedure, the incorporation of easy counterfactuals is straightforward. As just demonstrated, it is usually possible to derive two extreme solutions to a given truth table: (1) a solution that avoids incorporating any counterfactual causal combinations, and (2) a solution that permits the incorporation of as many as possible, with an eye toward producing the most parsimonious solution possible. The first solution bars counterfactual cases altogether from the solution for the presence of the outcome; the second permits the inclusion of both easy and difficult counterfactuals, without any evaluation of their plausibility. At first glance, neither of these options seems attractive. The first is likely to lead to results that are needlessly complex; the second may lead to results that are unrealistically parsimonious due to the incorporation of 'difficult' counterfactuals. It is useful, however, to view these two solutions as the two endpoints of a single continuum of possible results. One end of the continuum privileges complexity; the other end privileges parsimony. Both endpoints are rooted in evidence, but they differ in their tolerance for the incorporation of counterfactual cases.

The key is to use theoretical and substantive knowledge to derive a solution that is intermediate between these two extremes. Consider again the truth table presented in Table 4.3, which uses A, B, C and D as causal conditions and Y as the outcome. Assume, as before, that existing theoretical and substantive knowledge maintains that it is the presence of these causal conditions, not their absence, that is linked to the outcome. The results of the analysis barring counterfactuals reveal that combination A*B*c explains Y. The analysis of this same evidence permitting any counterfactual that will yield a more parsimonious result is that A by itself accounts for the presence of Y. Conceive of these two results as the two endpoints of the complexity/parsimony continuum, as follows:

A. B. c	A
complexity	parsimony

Observe that the solution privileging complexity (A*B*c) is a subset of the solution privileging parsimony (A). This follows logically from the fact that both solutions must cover the rows of the truth table with Y present; the parsimonious solution also incorporates six of the combinations lacking cases as counterfactual cases and thus embraces additional rows (i.e., a superset of the rows covered by the complex solution). Along the complexity/parsimony continuum are other possible solutions to this same truth table, e.g., the combination A*B. These intermediate solutions are produced when different subsets of the counterfactual combinations used to produce the parsimonious solution are incorporated into the results. These intermediate solutions constitute subsets of the most parsimonious solution (A in this example) and supersets of the solution allowing maximum complexity (A*B*c). The subset relation between solutions is maintained along the complexity/parsimony continuum. The implication is that any causal combination that uses at least some of the causal conditions specified in the complex solution (A*B*c) is a valid solution of the truth table as long as it also contains all the causal conditions specified in the parsimonious solution (A). It follows that there are two valid intermediate solutions to the truth table:

	A*B	
A*B*c	A*c	A
complexity		parsimony

Both intermediate solutions (A*B) and (A*c) are subsets of the solution privileging parsimony and supersets of the solution privileging complexity. The first (A*B) permits counterfactuals A*B*C*D and A*B*C*d as combinations linked to outcome Y. The second permits counterfactuals A*b*c*D and A*b*c*d.

The relative viability of these intermediate solutions depends on the plausibility of the counterfactuals that have been incorporated into them. The counterfactuals incorporated into the first intermediate solution are 'easy' because they are used to eliminate c from the combination A*B*c, and, in this example, existing knowledge supports the idea that it is the presence of C, not its absence, that is linked to outcome Y. The counterfactuals incorporated into the second intermediate solution are, however, 'difficult' because they are used to eliminate B from A*B*c. According to existing knowledge, the presence of B should be linked to the presence of outcome Y. The principle that only easy counterfactuals should be incorporated supports the selection of A*B as the optimal intermediate solution. This solution is the same as the one that a conventional case-oriented researcher would derive from this evidence, based on a straightforward interest in combinations of causal conditions that are (1) shared by the positive cases, (2) believed to be linked to the outcome, and (3) not displayed by negative cases.

As the example illustrates, incorporating different counterfactuals yields different solutions. However, these different solutions are all supersets of the solution privileging complexity and subsets of the solution privileging parsimony. Furthermore, it is possible to derive an optimal intermediate solution permitting only 'easy' counterfactuals. This solution is relatively simple to specify. The researcher removes causal conditions from the complex solution that are inconsistent with existing theoretical and substantive knowledge, while upholding the subset principle that underlies the complexity/parsimony continuum. Again, any intermediate solution constructed by the researcher must be a subset of the most parsimonious solution. The counterfactuals that are incorporated into this optimal solution would be relatively routine in a conventional case-oriented investigation of the same evidence. One of the great strengths of using truth tables is that all counterfactuals, both easy and difficult, are made explicit, as is the process of incorporating them into results. Truth tables make this process transparent and thus open to evaluation by the producers and consumers of social research.

CONCLUSION

When viewed from the perspective of conventional quantitative research, comparative methods seem dubious. Quantitative researchers know well that statistical analysis works best only when Ns are large. Not only is statistical significance easier to attain, but large Ns also can save researchers the trouble of meeting many of the assumptions of the techniques they use. Violations of these underlying assumptions are all too common when Ns are small or even moderate in size, as they must be in case-oriented research. On top of the small-N problem, there is the additional difficulty that when researchers know their cases well, they tend to construct combinatorial causal arguments from their evidence. From the perspective of conventional quantitative research, this interest in how causes combine places even more difficult demands on skimpy cross-case evidence. It also runs counter to the central logic of the most used and most popular quantitative techniques, which are geared primarily toward assessing the net independent effects of causal variables, not their multiple combined effects.

Comparative methods, however, have their own logic and rigor. They are explicitly case-oriented and set-theoretic in nature. Further, they are geared toward assessing combinations of conditions (causal 'recipes'). Because the comparative approach to causation is explicitly intersectional, the examination of different combinations of conditions is essential to this type of research. Truth tables, even very simple ones, greatly facilitate this type of analysis. The rigor of truth table analysis is lacking in most forms of quantitative research, where matching cases undermines degrees of freedom and statistical power.

As I show in this paper, the study of combinations of causes must very often involve counterfactual analysis because naturally occurring social data are profoundly limited in their diversity and researchers must engage in thought experiments using hypothetical cases. This practice may seem suspect, again especially to conventional quantitative researchers, because it runs counter to the norms of 'empirical' social research. However, many counterfactual analyses can be considered routine because they involve 'easy' hypothetical cases. The demonstration of counterfactual analysis offered in this contribution highlights a very important feature of social research—namely, that it is built upon a foundation of substantive and theoretical knowledge. It is this knowledge that makes it possible to distinguish between easy and difficult counterfactuals and to craft representations of evidence that reflect the necessary role of theoretical and substantive knowledge.

REFERENCES

Achen, Christopher H. (2005) 'Two cheers for Charles Ragin', *Studies in Comparative International Development,* 40 (1): 27–32.

De Meur, Gisèle and Rihoux, Benoît (2002) *L'Analyse Quali-Quantitative Comparée: Approche, techniques et applications en sciences humaines.* Louvain-la-Neuve: Bruylant-Academia.

George, Alexander (1979) 'Case studies and theory development: The method of structured, focussed comparison', in Paul G. Lauren (ed.), *Diplomacy: New Approaches in History, Theory and Policy.* New York: Free Press, pp. 43–68.

Goertz, Gary and Starr, Harvey (eds) (2002) *Necessary Conditions: Theory, Methodology, and Applications.* New York: Rowman and Littlefield.

Hicks, Alexander, Misra, Joya and Ng, Tang Nah (1995) 'The programmatic emergence of the social security state', *American Sociological Review,* 60: 329–49.

King, Gary, Keohane, Robert and Verba, Sidney (1994) *Designing Social Inquiry: Scientific Inference in Qualitative Research.* Princeton, NJ: Princeton University.

Mackie, John L. (1965) 'Causes and conditionals', *American Philosophical Quarterly,* 2: 245–65.

Markoff, John (1990) 'A comparative method: Reflections on Charles Ragin's innovations in comparative analysis', *Historical Methods,* 23 (4): 177–181.

Ragin, Charles C. (1987) *The Comparative Method.* Berkeley: University of California Press.

——— (2000) *Fuzzy-Set Social Science.* Chicago: University of Chicago Press.

——— (2004) 'La spécificité de la recherche configurationnelle', *Revue Internationale de Politique Comparée (RIPC),* 11 (1): 138–144.

——— (2005) 'From fuzzy sets to crisp truth tables', Working paper, available at: http://www.compasss.org/wp.htm.

Ragin, Charles C. and Becker, Howard S. (1992) *What Is a Case? Exploring the Foundations of Social Inquiry.* New York: Cambridge University.

Ragin, Charles C., Davey, Sean and Drass, Kriss A. (2005) *Fuzzy-Set/Qualitative Comparative Analysis,* Version 1.5. Available at : http://www.fsqca.com.

Ragin, Charles C. and Sonnett, John. (2004) 'Between complexity and parsimony: Limited diversity, counterfactual case and comparative analysis', in Sabine Kropp and Michael Minkenberg (eds), *Vergleichen in der Politikwissenschaft.* Wiesbaden: VS Verlag für Sozialwissenschaften, pp. 180–197.

Rihoux, Benoît. (2003) 'Bridging the gap between the qualitative and quantitative worlds? A retrospective and prospective view on qualitative comparative analysis', *Field Methods,* 15 (4): 351–65.

Romme, A.G.L. (1995) 'Boolean comparative analysis of qualitative data: A methodological note', *Quality and Quantity*, 29 (4): 317–29.

Smelser, Neil J. (1976) *Comparative Methods in the Social Sciences*. Englewood Cliffs, NJ: Prentice Hall

Weber, Max. ([1905] 1949) 'Objective possibility and adequate causation in historical explanation', in Edward A. Shils and Henry A. Finch (eds), *The Methodology of the Social Sciences*. Glencoe, IL: The Free Press, pp. 164–188.

ENDNOTES

1 This aspect of the truth table approach to comparative analysis is also subject to some (mostly misplaced) critiques (Markoff, 1990; Romme, 1995; see De Meur and Rihoux, 2002). Thus, a detailed discussion of this counterfactual analysis is warranted.

2 For more complex truth tables, researchers should use software designed for truth table analysis in order to find the most 'parsimonious' solution; see Ragin and Sonnett (2004); Ragin et al. (2005).

5

Historicity and Sociohistorical Research

John R. Hall

History and the social sciences converge in a broad domain defined in its origins through works by notables such as Ibn Khaldun, Alexis de Tocqueville, Karl Marx, Max Weber and Marc Bloch. By the 1960s the efflorescence of the historical social sciences began to give rise to various sub-, trans- and inter-disciplinary projects: historical–comparative sociology, social-science history, economic history, historical social science, social history, world-systems analysis, historical anthropology, historical geography, cultural history, and so on (Adams et al., 2005; Burke, 1993; Hall, 2003; Iggers, 1997; Smith, 1991). For all these projects, grouped here under the umbrella of 'sociohistorical inquiry', the high modernist methodological complacency of the 1960s has been undermined by devils that haunt the corridors of the human sciences—the crisis of positivism and the quest for a postpostivist epistemology, the postmodern linguistic turn, and the broader cultural turn. These conditions frame the present chapter, which is concerned with methodologies that pivot on historicity—the temporal structurations of social actions and processes.

On the one hand, the epistemological and methodological responses to the intellectual crisis that beset the human sciences nearly a half-century ago have been highly productive. Even if some among the old guard continue as if nothing has changed, the rising generation—of diverse methodological persuasions—now widely recognizes that all social phenomena involve historicity; that all practices of writing history are infused with theory; and that the social, the historical, and inquiry itself are culturally saturated. Historical scholarship, itself too often conventionally divided by region and time period, stands to benefit by transgressing those boundaries, and social scientists can cast new and revealing light on issues that time- or region-bound historians may have missed. Conventional lines that have divided disciplines do not divide methodologies. 'Local' practices of research thus can now be better grounded both in specific techniques and in relation to broader ontological and epistemological issues. Sociohistorical inquiry therefore has a future far more promising than it had 50 years ago.

On the other hand, the scholarly engagements with crisis are hardly all of a piece, and honest acknowledgment of the epistemological and methodological challenges to research makes formulating and conducting research a sometimes daunting prospect. The historian can no longer presume to fulfill Leopold von Ranke's dictum of the early 19th century—to tell what actually happened—any more than the social scientist can hope to engage in measurement without coming to terms with the historicity of theoretical constructs. Historians, of course, have always borrowed from other disciplines—a little psychoanalysis here, a dash of demography there. But they have nevertheless held to the steady conviction that history could not be subordinated to any external discourse or critique. For their part, social scientists, now that they seek to engage historicity, puzzle over what their distinctive contributions are, beyond those of historians. They thus wrestle over how to reconcile historical particularity with the quest for generalization, and they more often provide social–scientific studies of particular phenomena in the past than they offer historical accounts or models of social change. A fully historicized social science remains elusive.

Under these conditions, conducting sociohistorical inquiry is something of a heroic act, akin to the practice of science as a vocation that Weber described a century ago. Researchers must formulate a topic and choose an analytic strategy amidst a panoply of viable alternatives, bringing practices of inquiry to bear on a body of data in ways that will stand up to methodological critique by those who share their own research program, and will communicate to others who have an interest in the substantive topic, hopefully even those of radically different methodological persuasions. At the intersection of history and the social sciences, no single methodology, no reigning philosophy of science, can claim legitimate domination. The devils continue to lurk among the methodological choices of our practices, and we are honor-bound to wrestle with them,

hoping to hold them at bay and even harness them to our purposes.

How to deal with historicity is one of the devils, or perhaps a hydra-devil. Leopold von Ranke's nineteenth-century agenda of 'scientific' history was countered long ago by Marc Bloch's famous prospectus for history as a craft (1953). The subsequent collapse of the vaunted scientific 'view from nowhere' in the latter 20th century ushered in more ironic styles of narrative (White, 1973), along with anthropological histories of 'the times' that offer up tableaux of social worlds rather than explanations of event sequences (e.g., Ginzburg, 1980; Walkowitz, 1992). Yet despite a new modesty about the potential to uncover the truth of history, historians as diverse as Himmelfarb (1987), Iggers (1997) and Appleby et al. (1994) are reluctant to take a full cultural turn that they fear undermines efforts to discuss the past in as analytically rigorous terms as possible. In short, historians themselves sharply disagree about how to study history.

Thus social scientists who embrace historicity cannot simply adopt a ready-made ontology, for the construct of historicity defines rather than resolves a field of contestation. Historicity is a puzzle to be solved, not a solution to a puzzle. The present chapter therefore surveys the methodological problems, debates and strategies of historicizing social science by: (1) considering how inquiries can be framed in relation to issues concerning values, relativism and realism; (2) addressing questions about narrative, social theory and their relationships in the analysis of historicity; (3) addressing the long-standing debate about explanation versus understanding as alternative ways of offering accounts; and (4) describing a relational field of alternative methodological practices that resolve the tensions of values, narrative, theory and explanation/interpretation in different ways. Given the overwhelming number of empirical studies that could be cited in relation to these issues, I mostly leave it to readers to draw in relevant examples (for discussions and reviews, see especially Adams et al., 2005;

Hall, 1999; Iggers, 1997; Skocpol, 1984; Tilly, 1984).

VALUES, REALISM, PERSPECTIVE AND THE FRAMING OF INQUIRY

The challenge facing sociohistorical inquiry today continues to center on how to transcend the late-19th-century *Methodenstreit*: the neo-Kantian methodological conflict that arose in Germany concerning whether to distinguish between the natural and the human sciences, and if so, how (Köhnke, 1991). Answering these questions hinges on addressing issues about the ultimate nature of sociohistorical reality—ontology—and problems of epistemology—the philosophical challenge of how to obtain knowledge about the sociohistorical world.

If the ontological nature of sociohistorical reality could be affirmed in general, those who conduct inquiry would have a clear basis for deciding how to represent it, and thus avert the crisis to which Immanuel Kant (1963: 24) once alluded, of dealing with a 'planless agglomeration of human actions'. Researchers would thus like to have a strong idea of what constitutes an (historical) event (Sewell, 2005: chap. 8), and they would hope that clear ontological referents exist both for theoretical concepts (such as 'network' and 'class') and for what are called 'historical individuals' that 'colligate' or draw together a multitude of events under a single rubric (for example, the Renaissance, the Tai Ping rebellion and the Cold War).

The sturdy faith of historians from Leopold von Ranke to Paul Veyne (1984) and Gertrude Himmelfarb (1987) is what Appleby et al. (1994: 250) have called a 'pragmatic realism': though the challenges to finding out about the past are enormous, the basic facticity of the past is beyond question, and historians therefore can seek to discover what happened.

The prospectus for pragmatic historical realism runs parallel with another realism, a critical one advanced by Bhaskar and

embraced by some historical sociologists (e.g., Gorski 2004). Bhaskar (1986, 1989) adopts a metaphysical presupposition about the existence of sociohistorical reality external to any observer. Sociohistorical reality is 'constructed', and there is necessarily a gap between reality and any conceptualization of it. But, he affirms, even the knowledge yielded by the most interpretive hermeneutics depends on positing this reality. A more scientific approach, which Bhaskar supports, seeks to identify real structures and mechanisms. These, even if unobservable in and of themselves, can be demonstrated to exist and parsed as to their character by the study of their effects. Perhaps the most nuanced account of critical realism relevant to sociohistorical research is that of George Steinmetz (2004, 2005), who distances it from any single research program and aligns it with social constructivism and hermeneutics.

Doubtless few historians or social scientists are solipsists. However, even a realist position that acknowledges the socially constructed and meaningful character of social reality may not yield significant analytic benefits, for positing sociohistorical reality offers no ready road to its description or conceptualization. Indeed, radically different ontologies—Marxist and rational-choice, to name two—base their accounts in critical realist philosophy (Hall, 1999: 47–9). To add to the difficulties, sociohistorical constructions of reality are not simply external to social actors; rather, actors are themselves reflexively making meanings about situations in ways that construct, reconstruct and deconstruct reality. There are, as phenomenologist Alfred Schütz put it, 'multiple realities' (on phenomenology, see Chapter 21, this volume).

The problem of interpretive layering is compounded for the past, which is only accessible through the artifacts and texts and memories that survive. The difficulty is brought into focus by Ferguson (1997), who demonstrates for the run-up to World War I that historical actors themselves endeavored to construct 'what is happening' with an eye to how the history of their actions would *later* be understood. After the event, these and other actors 'edit' and thereby construct archives. Overall, the constructions of 'events' by participants and witnesses will vary according to their points of view, the passage of time, and other 'events' that have followed. Historical memories, both primary and secondary, are polyvalent and emergent (D. Cohen, 1994; Fentress and Wickham, 1992; Giesen and Junge, 2003; Henige, 1974; Kammen, 1991; Olick, 1999). Moreover, even non-archival artifacts will have differential prospects of survival. These phenomenological conditions pose inherent limitations to gaining knowledge about the past (Shiner, 1969). Thus, any realist precept must be tempered by epistemological humility.

The realist prospectus offers the most promise for researchers who agree about criteria for settling arguments concerning diverse issues ranging from measurement to the weighing of evidence and the logic of inference. They must value science as an objective enterprise untainted by other, contaminating value considerations. To admit even to Weber's ([1919] 1946) ethic of value neutrality would undermine the hopes of realism. Science under this ethic acknowledges that values, or matters of cultural significance, shape the *questions* posed, while excluding, as far as possible, the influence of values other than science from the procedures for formulating research projects, carrying them out and analyzing evidence. Researchers thus produce knowledge about sociohistorical reality, but that knowledge is necessarily kaleidoscopic. They see (possibly) meaningful patterns that are generated by real conditions, but rotating the kaleidoscope toward a different axis of cultural significance will array the elements in new configurations that (may) make sense in different terms (Weber [1904] 1949). History takes its own toll here, for the cultural significance of any given phenomenon—say, the French Revolution—will depend on historical vantage point (Furet, 1981).

The prospects for realism, undermined in value-neutral science, suffer further under regimes of inquiry where issues of cultural significance themselves dictate criteria of project formulation, measurement and adjudication of evidence. Such circumstances obviously arise in humanistic studies that acknowledge the particularistic hermeneutic circles of interpretation by both actors and analysts—psychoanalysis and the new historicism as two bases for art-historical investigation, for example. But much the same condition holds for critical theorists. Thus, Jürgen Habermas (1987) values human freedom and seeks to produce emancipatory knowledge that counters versions of science oriented toward technical control over phenomena.

The debate over realism is far from settled, and it is not simply 'philosophical'. Currently, given the variety of value presuppositions operative in sociohistorical inquiry, realist ontological assumptions fail to provide the 'big tent' under which a unified field of inquiry might be consolidated. Instead, despite the merits of a general assumption that (socially constructed) realities exist external to any particular observer, as the essays in Adams, Clemens, and Orloff's (2005) collection on the history and future directions of historical sociology in the US evidence, the diversity of actual research transcends any unifying ontology or epistemology, yielding a variety of kinds of knowledge, nevertheless of potential interest beyond the philosophical boundaries of their production. Under these circumstances, an alternative postpositivist account acknowledges a pluralism of ontologies and shifts from epistemology to discourse as a basis on which to identify alternative, mutually related forms of 'impure reason' (Hall, 1999).

This survey of sociohistorical methodology cannot resolve ontological and epistemological controversies. Yet they do impinge on methodology, and, implicitly or explicitly, researchers will take a stand. Whatever their positions, a central methodological concern in recent years has centered on the relation between narrative and social theory.

HISTORICITY, VIA NARRATIVE AND SOCIAL THEORY

Many historians hold formal method—much less philosophy—as anathema, preferring to engage in historiography as the history of historical treatments of a subject, and agreeing with Veyne (1984: 12) that 'there is no method of history because history makes no demands; so long as one relates true things, it is satisfied'. Not surprisingly then, history privileges narrative over theory, for theories tend to favor generalization over detailed exactitude. But narrative and theory are not so easily disentangled, and theory necessarily shapes any path to the study of historicity.

Narrative

With the cultural turn of the latter 20th century, narration became subject to deconstructions that revealed the disjunctures between events and their representation. Already in the 1930s, Kenneth Burke ([1937] 1984) elaborated connections between drama and history. Subsequently, Hayden White (1973) argued that textual principles of coherence in alternative narrative genres—i.e., comedy, tragedy, satire, romance, or some mixed type—infuse historical accounts with meanings not inherent in events themselves. Thus conflicts between historical accounts cannot always be resolved by 'facts' because alternative emplotments of the same events can emphasize different facts and give divergent meanings to the same facts. More fundamentally, rhetorical stratagems give narrative an 'aboutness' not available in unfolding events themselves (S. Cohen, 1986). Under these conditions, values shape the structuration of plot, often implicitly, to yield diverse stories—Whiggish histories of progress, conservative histories of irredeemable loss, Marxist histories of workers' collective struggles, and so on.

A different way of cutting into the problem of narrative derives from structuralist and phenomenological considerations of temporality. *Annales* historian Fernand Braudel suggested the inadequacy of locating history on a single scale of objective time, for some phenomena occur in unfolding moment-to-moment events, while others come into focus only on longer time-scales of structural, institutional and ecological history. But Braudel affirmed the coherence of history, proposing that all scales of time can be mapped on one objective line of clock and calendrical time.

Criticizing Braudel, Louis Althusser and Etienne Balibar ([1968] 1970) argued that there is no necessary single historical 'present' of simultaneous clock time and no continuous historical time. Their radically anti-historicist structuralism rejects objective temporality as an ideological and atheoretical construction that obstructs the possibility of scientific inquiry. Instead, they theorize a 'totality' comprised of diverse 'levels' (economic, political, scientific, etc.), each with its own time, its own historical 'punctuations' (transitions, breaks, revolutions), intersecting unevenly with other spheres, each thus developing on a relatively autonomous basis. In turn, this structuralist approach is open to phenomenological critique concerning the relation of temporality to social action. In this line of analysis, social temporalities (of bureaucracy, work, charisma and shopping, for example) are constructed through the meaningful *durée* of social action—in the vivid present, in anticipations of the future, and in meaningful remembrances of past events. Taken together, the structuralist and phenomenological deconstructions of what might naively be thought of as 'real' time shift the analysis from the study of events and processes 'in' continuously unfolding time towards theorizing sometimes intersecting, sometimes relatively autonomous *social* temporalities (Hall, 1980). 'History' is no longer a web of events linked on an objective temporal grid; it is an array of phenomena that have to be considered in their temporally textured historicities (see also Sewell, 2005: Chapter 3).

It is especially in narration that the multiple temporalities of historicity—objective and social—become manifest. Conventionally, in both fiction and history, narrative drapes its account on the framework of a plot that connects events, actions, and sub-plots to one another, organizing textual sequences through such devices as flashbacks and cuts from one scene or event to another. With Hayden White (1973) and Sande Cohen (1986), narration can no longer be assumed to tell 'what happened'. With deconstructions of historical time, narrative embodies representation of events and processes in their temporal structurations (Carr, 1986; Ricoeur, 1984, 1985, 1988).

Yet deconstruction has heralded not an avoidance of narrative, but its revival (cf. Stone 1979), and, indeed, self-conscious experimentation with its manifold possibilities. Most famously, in his study of madness, Althusser's student, Michel Foucault (1965), eschewed developmental history in favor of describing collages of events that might overlap in objective time but belonged to different regimes of organizing madness— totalities in Althusser's sense. On a different front, in *Dead Certainties* (1991) Simon Schama narrated the 1759 battle of Quebec from the point of view of one of the soldiers who was there. These two examples show that narrative is a resilient vehicle for representing the agency of social actors, meanings of events, and theorized social processes. Narration, then, itself has theoretical stakes.

Analytically, two alternative but interpenetrating principles of narrative construction can be distinguished. On the one hand, *intrinsic narrative* investigates the meanings that social actors themselves gave to events, and how these meanings structured their actions and interactions with others (Hall, 1999: 86-94). Here, meanings are to be found *in* history. Thus, Somers (1992) has pointed to the 'ontological' narrativities of social actors themselves—the self-narrations that they employ to make sense of their experiences, while Hall et al. (2000: Chapter 2) have explored how social actors' narratives during the course of events structure subsequent events.

A range of possibilities oriented toward construction of intrinsic narratives contrasts with *extrinsic narrative*, in which the researcher structures the plot on the basis of some organizing principle *external* to the social actors involved. To be sure, there is no hard line dividing extrinsic from intrinsic narrative, since 'the same' events can be treated within either approach. However, extrinsic narrative tends to tip the balance away from meanings of events for actors themselves toward their 'larger significance'. What might be the basis of this significance? In an approach that predominates among historical sociologists, the researcher may pose a theoretical or analytic question—concerning, for example, the dynamics of state bureaucracy in Prussia, or the class bases of revolutionary mobilization. Such possibilities include, but are considerably broader than, the rational-choice project of 'analytic narrative' (Bates, 1998). Alternatively, the conventional historicist organizing principle centers on some particular 'mosaic' of history, what Weber ([1904] 1949: 84–5) termed an 'historical individual'—such as 'Japanese feudalism', the 'industrial revolution', the rise of modernity, or World War II—that comes into view as more than a mere multitude of events on the basis of their collective meaning and cultural significance. Of course, historical individuals are themselves social constructions, either of historians or in broader discourse, or both. Thus, it would be naive to assume any facticity to 'early modern Europe' as an epoch. Instead, periodization is best problematized in relation to research, both on turning points and the temporal and spatial coherence of phenomena (Abbott, 2001: Chapter 8; Hall, 1994).

The issue of extrinsic coherence raises a basic challenge, that of doing justice to variation across a set of events, phenomena, and processes that the researcher groups under a single historical or theoretical construct. It is easy to invoke 'the French aristocracy in the early 18th century' or 'the technique of hog slaughtering used in pioneer Missouri'. But any such reference beyond a single instance inevitably elides sociohistorical variations that might be important. And as Pierre Bourdieu (1977) famously showed, even in the single instance, 'structure', when explored in relation to the historicity of practice, appears as a hypostatization of the social (either as an accomplishment of the social practitioners themselves or of the researcher) rather than as some obdurate or tangible thing.

The problem of describing and analyzing historical variation is especially the province of quantitative history (see Chapter 14 in this volume). But the same problem arises in discursive history as well. Given an array of instances (political attitudes, economic practices, forms of feudal contract, etc.), discursive historians may follow models of quantitative description, describing average cases, ranges of variation, sub-categories of similar cases, and the like. But as Jack Goldstone (2003) has observed, sociohistorical researchers may rightly want to 'fill in a map' by describing the lay of the land, rather than dealing solely with averages or correlations. One way to capture a range of variations discursively is the approach made famous by Max Weber, defining 'ideal types' or 'sociohistorical models' that clarify a particular logic of action or structure of organization by striving, as Weber ([1922] 1978: 20) put it, for 'the highest possible degree of adequacy on the level of meaning'. Once defined, such models and types can serve as theoretical benchmarks by which to chart empirical variation, as Weber did when he compared various theologies of asceticism in *The Protestant Ethic and the Spirit of Capitalism* ([1905] 1958).

Because ideal types are intended to be meaningfully adequate, if they are properly constructed they describe social action and interaction and thus have socially temporal historicity embedded in them. In these terms, bureaucracy as an ideal type, for example, reflects one temporal construction of a social world, and tradition reflects another. Nor need these models describe 'frozen' temporalities. Rather, Weber's model of the routinization of charisma

sketches alternative meaningful trajectories by which charisma may unfold. In effect, such ideal types amount to generic narratives of social process—a principle that has been elaborated in such methodologies as event–history analysis, Larry Griffin's (1993) narrative/causal event-structure analysis, and Andrew Abbott's (2001) explorations of temporality and event–sequence analysis.

Here, narration connects ever more directly with social theory, specifically with substantive models that theorize distinctive processes in time. The 15th-century North African historian Ibn Khaldun is famous for his theory of dynastic generational succession, from vigor to cultivation to corruption. At the dawn of the 20th century Max Weber theorized 'rationalization' as a model of social organizational transformation, though not in the unidirectional and inexorable way often assumed (Roth, 1987). And recently, Goldstone (2002: 333) has suggested that analysts of world history need to theorize not only 'crisis' (a 'relatively sharp, unexpected downturn in significant demographic and economic indices'), but also the possibility of 'efflorescence', a relatively sharp upturn in those indices. Goldstone locates these constructs within a broader panoply of models of change, including growth and stagnation. Bureaucracy, charisma, routinization, rationalization and efflorescence are only suggestive of the possibilities for theorizing historicity. The point for sociohistorical researchers is that both the character of temporal flux and change over historical time can be theoretically narrated, not only in general but also in the specifics of particular phenomena.

Theory

Any claim that narrative can provide a theory-free way of describing sociohistorical phenomena is highly suspect. Conversely, theory, if it engages historicity, will inevitably have narrative features. Beyond historicity, social theory is a topic in its own right that lies beyond our purview here. However, sociohistorical researchers have long debated the kinds of social theory and their relationships to the conduct of research.

For sociohistorical inquiry, the most important theoretical development over the past half-century has been the widespread rejection of efforts to construct holistic theories seeking to describe general 'laws' of societal development that could subsume history *in toto*. Both totalizing Parsonian-style systems theory and dialectical Marxian theories of development based on emergent contradictions in modes of production have become *passé*. The one 'grand' theory of history that remains salient is world-systems theory, but its totalistic variant was the subject of concerted critique from the beginning, and, as a result, contemporary practitioners often adopt a less holist approach to explaining long-term sociohistorical change. World-systems theory thus now connects to a wider debate concerning the prospects of 'general theory' in sociohistorical research.

The catalyst for recent iterations of the debate was an essay by Edgar Kiser and Michael Hechter (1991), who lamented what they discerned to be a particularistic and inductive turn in historical sociology, and proposed that researchers should use general theory—in their example, rational-choice theory—under realist ontological assumptions to identify causal processes and mechanisms. James Mahoney (2004) answered critics of Kiser and Hechter's program by further specifying general theory in a post-positivist way, as one or another postulate about foundational causes that entails both a causal agent and a causal mechanism that operates through the agent to produce outcomes. As examples of general theories that would be particularly relevant to sociohistorical analysis, Mahoney included—in addition to rational-choice theory—functionalist, power, neo-Darwinian, and cultural theories.

A number of scholars argue that the project of using general theory in sociohistorical research is grandiose, at variance with the classic agenda of understanding history, and fundamentally flawed in its ontological and epistemological assumptions. Margaret Somers

(1998, 1995) has challenged Kiser and Hechter's agenda, and she has demonstrated the historicity of social theoretical and public constructs such as (bourgeois) citizenship, which she argues are profoundly shaped by the often invisible ideologies in play in their construction. On a related front, Alan Sica (2004) criticizes Mahoney's and other rational-choice proposals for general theory as scientism—quests to make human studies into 'real' sciences, thereby running roughshod over the very nuances and complexities of historical social life that often turn out to be important. As alternatives to general theory, Calhoun (1998) emphasizes the possibility of 'historically specific' theory, and Paige (1999) proposes that the emerging generation of sociohistorical researchers is increasingly oriented toward the use of 'historically conditional' social theory.

Given these debates, how might the diversity of social theories be theorized? Elsewhere (Hall, 1999: Chapter 4), I have defined social theories more broadly than general theories as construed by Kiser and Hechter, as sets of mutually coordinated concepts intended to account for fundamental social phenomena. My description of the property space of theoretical discourse builds on a long-standing social theoretical distinction between case-oriented and variable-oriented concepts that, as Ragin and Zaret (1983) noted, is especially salient for sociohistorical research, where analysis is often centered on case histories (the French Revolution) and case comparisons (industrialization in Japan versus Germany). I further distinguish (1) whether concepts theorize *structures* that are relatively self-contained versus *systems* that are interactive; and (2) whether or not concepts are oriented toward taking into account subjectively meaningful action. These distinctions frame four modern approaches to theoretical discourse, each with its associated case-oriented concepts and variable-oriented concepts: (1) a functional/dialectical system approach exemplified in different ways by Marx and Parsons, (2) a formal approach of the sort classically employed by Simmel and Durkheim, (3) a hermeneutic approach given substance by Weber, and (4) an interchange approach centered on a 'market system' that includes less holistic variants of world-systems theory as well as network and market-exchange theories and theories of cultural capital (Hall, 1999: 127).

As Mahoney (2004) recognizes, the uses of general theory in sociohistorical research encompass the synthesis of existing research and the derivation of hypotheses, as well as causal explanation. Moreover, as Calhoun and Paige point out, not all theoretical approaches are 'general'. Some theories define research orientations or provide concepts for analysis, but eschew the project of searching for causal mechanisms. For example, in the hermeneutic, or interpretive, approach, ideal-type concepts can be compared to descriptions of cases to tease out the degree to which those cases approximate the meaningful constructions of action modeled by the ideal types. Analysts interested in a given state's bureaucracy, for example, may want to examine the degree to which the state approximates a 'patrimonial' versus a 'legal-rational' form. Given the alternative kinds of theory and their alternative uses, the sociohistorical researcher needs to clarify the kinds of concepts employed, and the logics of how they figure in research.

In thinking through such connections between theory and research, scholars have moved considerably beyond the modern positivist expectation that a general theory would explain a phenomenon in all its relevant aspects. Early in the renaissance of historical sociology, Arthur Stinchcombe pointed to the complexity of sociohistorical phenomena, and the likelihood that multiple processes are embedded in a given set of events, e.g., the Russian revolution. The task, he argued, is not to develop a single theory that explains all aspects of a phenomenon, but to proceed by 'deepening analogies' between various aspects of an overall phenomenon and relevant theoretical models, and other comparable instances (Stinchcombe, 1978: 21). Thus, a study of the Russian revolution might be concerned both with political party structures and with demographic aspects of class formations, topics that ought to bring to bear different theoretical models and empirical analogies. In a related vein, contributors to Ragin and Becker's (1992) collection, *What is a Case?*, have shown that basic units of analysis need to be problematized, in part by asking what a case as a whole is a case *of*, and in part by looking, as it were, at the cases within a case.

These considerations about theory bring us to a critical juncture defined by two points. First, researchers of a variety of persuasions—Stinchcombe, the contributors to Ragin and Becker's collection, and Steinmetz (2004)—hold that sociohistorical research is almost inevitably both theoretical and comparative, and that the one implies the other. The most anti-theoretical historians will resist such claims. But their resistance should be taken with a grain of salt, for historians almost routinely engage in comparisons that depend on theory. Sometimes the comparisons are explicit, internal to the topic at hand, and seemingly purely empirical, as when a historian considers the differential tendencies of members of various tribes to join an anti-colonial rebellion. Even here, where comparison may seem prima facie non-theoretical, an implicit theoretical sub-structure of assumptions about mobilization is likely to undergird the analysis. At other junctures, historians may be completely implicit or largely incidental in their comparisons, e.g., when discussing the problem of a state consolidating territorial control at its borders, or asking whether a particular person exhibits 'charismatic' leadership, in both cases without considering the problem either theoretically or comparatively, even though there is considerable basis on which to do so. These examples suggest that sociohistorical research is almost inevitably theoretical and comparative, even when its practitioners deny this. Indeed, the various strategies of comparison are fundamental to sociohistorical research, and a topic in their own right (see Chapter 4 in this volume).

Second, arguments in favor of using theory, general or otherwise, in relatively formal ways are countered by approaches to sociohistorical research that are not strongly centered on theory at all, but on the more particularistic analysis of sociohistorical phenomena. Research framed along these lines can contribute to theoretical discussions, but not necessarily in the ways that proponents of general theory want. The possibility that social theory (or narrative, for that matter) may not dominate sociohistorical analysis brings us to a final issue to consider before describing methodological strategies of inquiry.

EXPLANATION VERSUS UNDERSTANDING IN ACCOUNTS OF SOCIOHISTORICAL PHENOMENA

Why did the Soviet Union collapse in the late 1980s and early 90s? How does *samurai* culture find its way into 19th-century Japanese life? Even though values, narration, and theory in different ways shape answers to such questions, how to *account* for these and diverse other sociohistorical phenomena is also a topic in its own right. At its core, this activity concerns how the play of contingent events and processes yields specific outcomes in concrete circumstances (Hall, 1999: 151). The difference between two divergent approaches to offering accounts—explanation and understanding—frames a classic and continuing debate within the social sciences.

This debate addresses the question of whether there can only be one adequate explanation of a phenomenon or whether multiple meaningful interpretations inevitably co-exist. A related issue concerns whether the *purposes* of sociohistorical accounts (often focused on specific phenomena like the fall of the Soviet Union or the persistence of *samurai* culture) and the *possibilities* of interpreting meaningful action differentiate such accounts from those in the natural sciences, and, if so, how. Despite such controversies, explanation and interpretation share a core enterprise that tends to blur the boundary between them: they both draw on the most diverse evidence to marshal

arguments about how to make sense of phenomena. The account itself is the thing. Thus, in 'traditions of inquiry' such as that over the English civil war, scholars range across narrative styles, value commitments and theories, bound together by the debates that engage them (Hall, 1999:152-56).

Issues of explanation and interpretive understanding are topics in their own right, and they are considered elsewhere in this volume (see Chapter 20). Here, the most salient issue concerns how research methodologies—either interpretive or explanatory—come to terms with historicity. There are several possibilities beyond the theoretically modeled historicities discussed above. First, in the most anti-theoretical approaches to narrative, the narrative amounts to a representation of historicity, and a full narrative description—one that accords with all available evidence—is taken to be an adequate account.

An alternative approach, which historians sometimes use in lieu of narrative, is the 'explanatory-factor framework'. Lawrence Stone, for example, discussed the English civil war in terms of pre-conditions (necessary but hardly sufficient), precipitants (which begin to increase the likelihood of an outcome), and triggers (decisive events that bring events to a resolution, one way or another). Describing explanatory factors can provide a useful orienting basis for explanation or interpretation, so long as the researcher resists the temptation to reify the factors—especially those that are analytically general or remote in time from a particular outcome. After all, factors are simply colligations, and the phenomena that they draw together (a tax crisis, an epidemic, status-group mobilization, the personality of an individual) are not inalterable 'structures' but rather themselves subject to the interplay of forces, events and actions that might alter both their character and subsequent events (Hall, 1999: 156–59; Katznelson, 2003).

Recently, analysts have sought to build on the idea of contingency implicit in explanatory-factor approaches. To study contingency does not entail grouping causes into categories, but rather exploring the consequences of any particular phenomenon for other developments. Of course the array of contingencies that can affect social life is enormous, ranging from weather and disease, through forms of social organization, accidents, and subterfuge, to personality traits and ambitions. Without attempting a catalogue, it is possible to identify certain 'tropes' that structure sociohistorical accounts of contingencies. For example, world-systems theorists have focused on 'conjuncture', arguing that the co-occurrence of events will sometimes have consequences quite different from any event on its own. This insight has since been formalized in Charles Ragin's (2000; see also Chapter 4 in this volume) set-theoretic approach to comparative analysis.

A trope related to conjuncture that has gained wide interest over the past two decades is 'path dependence', i.e., events at one point in time establishing circumstances that make future events more (or less) likely. Typically, path dependence details causal mechanisms that reinforce early predominance. Although originally developed to account for the supremacy of seemingly less than optimal technologies (for example, VHS-format videocasette players over Sony's Betamax format), path dependency can be useful in accounting for how industries get located, or why one nation-state rather than another takes a position at the core of the world-economy. In a related way, Gladwell (2000) has popularized the 'tipping point'—a moment when other factors have arrayed to create particular circumstances, at which a small change or seemingly extraneous event can suddenly and precipitously yield a dramatic social shift, epidemic or contagion, most obviously of disease, but also of fashion, social practices, political commitments and so on.

Invoking path dependence or a tipping point has to be based upon recognizing that, as with explanatory factors more generally, asserting an argument does not affirm causal force, for the mechanisms, processes and actions that yield a path-dependent outcome or produce a tipping point may be more or less strong, and the degree to which it is possible to return to prior conditions may vary.

Researchers using path dependence will find that it sometimes produces a compelling analysis, but only if used carefully (Beyer, 2005; Crouch and Farrell, 2004; Mahoney, 2000). Much the same caution also applies to comparative analysis, where measurement across cases is a challenge (Ragin 2000; Steinmetz, 2004: 384–90), and the examination of whether factors are contingent, emergent, or relatively enduring often depends on a turn to narrative analysis. To ask such questions is, in effect, to inquire whether a particular development is what Jack Goldstone (1991: chap. 1) has called a 'robust process'—i.e., one that is relatively likely to occur, even when other relevant circumstances vary.

The ways that tropes such as conjuncture and path dependence are constructed demonstrate how intermingled narrative, theory and comparison are, certainly for the social scientist but even for the most resolute narrative historian. This convergence is signaled by a set of analytic strategies that typically undergird arguments based on such tropes, namely, the use of 'mental experiments' and counterfactuals to ask 'what would happen if?' Suppose a different path had been followed early on, would there have been a different outcome? What events, if they had unfolded differently, might have derailed even a robust process or forestalled a tipping point? If the British had stood aside in the run-up to the Great War, would the long-term history of Europe have been substantially different (Ferguson, 1997)? Such questions are inherently comparative, and can sometimes be addressed directly through empirical analysis. Failing that, however, the researcher can theorize or postulate what might have happened under alternative scenarios, compared to the events under consideration.

Conducting mental experiments is a delicate matter. But as Geoffrey Hawthorn (1991) has argued, the consideration of alternative scenarios can deepen an analysis if the counterfactual hypotheses are neither so distant from the course of events as to be irrelevant, nor so unstable in their dynamics as to make prediction unreliable. In undertaking such analyses, however, it is wise to recall the remarks of

Casaubon, the Templar scholar and narrator in Umberto Eco's (1989: 132) novel *Foucault's Pendulum*: 'Counterfactual conditionals are always true, because the premise is false'.

Older arguments about explanation and interpretation painted a sharp contrast between the two, a contrast that echoes binaries of value-structured and value-free inquiry, relativism and objectivity, narrative and theory. Drawing out other distinctions—between inductive and deductive historical social science, and between historical social science methodologies that are explicitly comparative and histories using comparison only implicitly—similarly threatens to divide practices of inquiry that share substantive interests, and that may share more common ground methodologically than the distinctions would suggest. One way to assess the validity of such binaries is to consider the overall domain of sociohistorical research and the relations of methodological practices to one another.

METHODOLOGICAL PRACTICES

To ask how to construe the overall domain of sociohistorical research suggests a theoretical formalization of methodology. Historians have rightly avoided any sterile formalization. Yet a general historiography reveals distinct phases and shifts in styles of historical inquiry, from Leopold von Ranke's early-nineteenth-century prospectus for a 'scientific' history that would tell 'what really happened', through *Annales* macrohistory, social history, the study of everyday life or 'microhistoria', and, with the linguistic turn in the late 20th century, to the flowering of cultural history. Despite the supposed suspicion with which historians regard social science, over the past century or more they have increasingly oriented their research by using social–scientific conceptualizations of classes, social movements, family structure, and so on; and they have become more reflexively critical of both the history of events and grand narratives, and, of course, of 'universal history'. Thus, while history has not become more formal in its methodologies, historians have become more

methodologically sophisticated in the practice of their craft, and historians stand to benefit from efforts to make sense of the methodologies that inform their research.

For their part, during the 1960s and 70s, historically oriented social scientists began pointing to exemplars as templates for research strategy. Then, in the 1980s, Theda Skocpol and Margaret Somers (1980) and Theda Skocpol (1984) invoked such exemplars to describe three alternative methodological research designs: theory application, contrast-oriented comparison, and analytic generalization. Around the same time, Charles Tilly (1984) identified four alternative methodologies: individualizing, encompassing, universalizing, and variation-finding. Seeking to account for the difference between the accounts of Skocpol and Somers on the one hand and Tilly on the other, I later argued that one of Skocpol and Somers's strategies—the application of theory—contained two somewhat different practices, and on this basis identified equivalences between the two schema (Hall, 1999: 278–79, note 8).

Yet as I pointed out, the debates among historical social scientists about methodology centered primarily on research oriented toward generalization. Meanwhile, on other fronts, scholars such as Abbott (2001) and Sewell (2005) were underscoring the limitations of comparative and other generalizing historical methods in dealing with issues of historicity, and historically oriented social scientists were increasingly engaged in research that focused on the specifics of discrete historical phenomena. I therefore differentiated four *particularizing* practices from the four *generalizing* practices of research, arguing that each of the eight alternative ideal–typical 'practices of inquiry' brings together four 'forms of discourse'–value discourse, narrative, social theory, and explanation/interpretation—in a distinctive way. This analysis suggests that any methodology is inevitably a hybrid exercise in 'impure reason' located within a broader relational domain encompassing diverse interconnected ways of conducting inquiry. Under these conditions, various alternative practical methodological strategies are appropriate to addressing different kinds of questions, and the challenge for the researcher is to structure a research project in a way that aligns methodology, research problems and data that can be brought to bear on the issue, in order to produce new and relevant knowledge. 'Particularizing' methodological practices arguably confront the representation of historicity more directly than 'generalizing' ones, and I will sketch them first, and in somewhat greater detail.

Four Particularizing Research Practices

Despite the diverse genres and topics of particularizing historical research—from political and national history, intellectual history, structural history, and social history, to microhistoria and cultural history—the actual research logics involved can be parsimoniously described by four ideal–typical practices (Hall, 1999: Chapter 8). These include the classic methodology of historicism, and three practices employed by Max Weber, who reacted against historicism in his own work (see Roth, 1976).

Historicism

Conventionally, history denies methodology beyond Ranke's commitment to 'scientific' use of the archives. A narrative is constructed to tell 'what really happened' by treating the origins, genesis, and unique character of events in empiricist, self-contained and seemingly anti-theoretical terms. The problem of colligation—selection of events drawn together to yield 'history'—is typically resolved by connecting events to a larger 'story'. Leopold von Ranke used the history of elites: the church, the state. But the basis of colligation is in principle open—for example, to the self-understanding of a community or nation, or to a resolutely historical Marxism. By some such device, historicism investigates a historical reality deemed to have an existence independent of the practice of research, while linking that investigation

with larger 'moral' stakes. Because of the explicit commitment to factual history and the implicit commitment to a value-based ordering principle, historicist arguments often center on which story is told, not which story is true. Historicism, then, is subject to ever new constructions of 'history'.

Specific history

When *intrinsic* narrative predominates, it frames 'specific history', a *verstehende* project of analyzing events in relation to the meanings given to them by historical social actors—in anticipation, in unfolding action, and in memory. However, because the 'plots' of actual life are manifold and overlapping, any actual colligation of intrinsic narrative is not determined solely by events but involves choices of the researcher, who could follow myriad alternative streams of specific history in relation to any given moment, whether trade in the 14th century, the French Revolution, or household life among Chinese peasants. Colligation in specific history thus varies widely in focus, from biography to the study of self-conscious social movements. Across this range, analysis centers on interwoven plots, clarified through narrative concerned with what happened and how, given the goals, motives, drives, interactions, meanings and misunderstandings of the people involved. Diverse theories and contingent explanations and interpretations are deployed in relation to intrinsic narrative to yield an analytically rigorous account ordered not by the implicit value colligation of historicism but by social actors' meanings as they are asserted *in* history.

Configurational history

This methodology, by contrast with specific history, depends on the researcher constructing a (typically analytic) narrative that is *extrinsic* to events. It operates theoretically by first identifying the elements, conditions and developments necessary for a particular ('configurational') social phenomenon to occur, e.g., modern capitalism or a particular technology of power. This theoretically defined configuration is first used as a basis for generating questions of focused historical analysis, and then for seeking to identify 'break points' at which the fulfillment of conditions and creation of elements that comprise the phenomenon are in play—for example, by engaging in what Goldstone (2003) calls 'process tracing'. This strategy is not inherently comparative in the conventional sense, but it involves a strong use of social theory in relation to historical analysis, and is thus favored by historical sociologists (e.g., Max Weber, Michael Mann) who develop sociologically informed explanations of distinctive historical developments.

Situational history

Historicism tends to submerge value commitments, and specific and configurational histories typically invoke value neutrality. By contrast, situational history pursues research questions that are designed explicitly to address moral or political issues, and knowledge produced is useful to those with particular social interests—members of a social movement seeking change, or a community buffeted by unwanted social forces. Such research addresses the questions of 'where we stand and are likely to go' (Roth, 1976: 310). Lenin's revolutionary tract, *What is to be Done?*, stands as a classic. But contemporary research often similarly combines resolute political commitment and hard- hitting inquiry. 'Situation', however defined, structures a distinctive set of questions, and although analytic rigor is paramount if the knowledge produced is to be of any use, narrative gives special attention to theories, interpretations and explanations that have contemporary implications for one course of action over another. Inquiry thus potentially empowers individuals, groups and even societies by puzzling out the context, the motives and intentions of protagonists and other actors, and the social processes, conjunctures and contingencies that shape current situation and future possibilities.

The four particularizing methodologies are all centrally concerned with the study of a single relatively bounded sociohistorical phenomenon. They all thematize historicity, but the specific kind of historicity differs according to the methodology. Situational history connects the past to a present framed in value-relevant ways, whereas historicism frames a narrative in relation to a self-referential story that typically has a *telos* and moral stakes. In turn, working the narrative–theory relation, specific history emphasizes the historicity of events meaningful to participants, while configurational history focuses on the theorization of events and processes in their causal significance relative to subsequent developments over historical time. Historicity thus cannot be reduced to a single structure to be 'represented'; rather, particularizing methodologies offer protean ways of exploring the manifold temporalities of social life.

Four Generalizing Practices

No matter how well particularizing research succeeds on its own terms, insofar as it makes an argument or offers an explanation or interpretation, it often begs basic methodological questions—for example, whether the explanation would hold up for other similar cases, and whether different conditions might yield the same outcome. Comparisons may be methodologically challenging to carry out, but they offer opportunities to test the validity of a particularizing argument, and sometimes to advance more general knowledge.

One way or another, particularizing practices of inquiry undergird generalizing practices. Because the latter typically involve comparison, they require less comment here (see Chapter 4 in this volume). The one exception—'universal history'—like particularizing methodologies, treats a single phenomenon, but uses a 'general theory' to theorize that phenomenon as an encompassing totality or system. The other three generalizing practices directly compare relatively bounded cases by employing one or another of alternative logics that connect value discourse, narrative, theory and explanation/interpretation (Hall, 1999: Chapter 7).

Universal history

To theorize 'history' in its totality requires specifying an exhaustive general conceptual framework (such as systems theory) or a temporally dynamic totality (for example, via Marxism or world-systems theory, or, possibly, a reconstructed evolutionary Darwinism). Systemic conditions marked by periodization and conjuncture give shape, significance, and developmental import to historical events. Though totalizing theories are widely criticized, world-systems analysts rightly observe that an increasingly interconnected world may involve encompassing processes that are rightful objects of inquiry. The warrant for generalization approximates that of astronomy, which similarly studies only one observable universe, but one that entails coherent and predictable phenomena. As with astronomy, universal history employs a paradigmatic theoretical framework, rarely modifying its fundamental concepts or theorizations, instead focusing on how particular phenomena advance or fail to advance the theorized *telos* of the totality. However, only interconnections constituting the totality are universal. Thus, like other researchers, those committed to a holistic universal history can study many phenomena within the totality through particularizing inquiry or by use of another generalizing methodology.

Theory Application

In this practice, the analyst seeks to bring parallel phenomena into view via narratives that apply a particular theoretical lens to the analysis of cases. Typically, a historically 'specific' (Calhoun, 1998) or 'conditional' (Paige, 1999) social theory dictates the central issues of comparative plot analysis for narratives, and explanation or interpretation centers on differentiating theoretically derived versus non-theoretical accounts, and on determining whether the non-theoretical accounts require modification or disconfirmation of the theory or are simply matters that lie outside the theory's domain. The emphasis on close and careful comparison of a small number of cases offers bases for deepening theorization of explanatory accounts and inductively refining theory, but generalization is typically undermined by the small number of cases studied.

Analytic generalization

This practice encompasses the formal methods formulated by Mill and elaborated and refined by Ragin (2000). Here, the researcher empirically tests or develops hypotheses deduced from theories—as Kiser and Hechter (1991) would want—or induced from observations. Narrative is structured to offer the basis for considering hypotheses relevant to theories, and the evaluation of alternative explanations and interpretations mediates the process of theoretical adjudication. The rigor of this practice approximates the intent of positivism, but problems of measurement equivalence and sample size can threaten validity, for, as Lieberson (1992) argues, small numbers of cases preclude probabilistic arguments, and the number of variables of interest may overwhelm the cases analyzed, thus making deterministic causal relationships difficult to infer. However, others have suggested that a different logic can be deployed. Goldstone (2003) points to the value of 'congruence testing' that yields general knowledge about patterns shared but only by a small number of cases. Steinmetz (2004) and Hall (2005) both point to the potential for close analysis of a small number of cases to yield causal and interpretive knowledge about social processes in themselves and *in situ*. And Emigh (1997) describes the methodological use of even a single-case study as a basis for revising a theory.

Contrast-oriented comparison

Many researchers invoke historicity, culture and contingency as circumstances that cast suspicion both upon any 'overly theorized' account of the social world, and upon any effort to seek analytic generalization by comparing cases that are not really causally independent of one another. Contrast-oriented comparison offers an alternative. Here, explanation and interpretation are the central discursive concerns that order inquiry oriented to the production of relatively modest 'bounded' generalizations and 'rules of experience' through contingent and idiographic analysis of sociohistorical phenomena deemed kindred in relation to a theoretical theme. The focus is on how a particular social phenomenon (e.g., proletarianization, nationalism or fundamentalism) plays out in different (but often historically connected or contemporaneously interacting) sociohistorical contexts. Narrative is used to trace the relations between contexts, processes and outcomes. Because causal independence of cases is not assumed, analysis of genealogies, diffusion, and mutual influence is readily incorporated into contrast-oriented comparative analysis.

CONCLUSION

The four particularizing and four generalizing methodological practices just described cannot formalize methodologies relevant to analysis involving historicity. Instead, they amount to alternative ideal–typical templates that can serve as benchmarks in strategizing methodologies within a relational methodological field characterized by 'integrated disparity'. Actual research will often adjust, build upon, bridge, combine or improvise beyond conventional methodologies. Thus, a study of workers and industrialization might incorporate elements of both specific and configurational history, or build contrast-oriented comparisons on the basis of case studies that are configurational histories, or theorize a new narrativity that, when applied, revises conventional interpretations. Whatever the research strategy, it will mediate diverse desiderata —structuring a study to answer questions, locating and using appropriate data, maximizing the validity of the analysis, and so on. Basically, the researcher needs to calibrate actual practice in relation to such desiderata. Though this chapter has focused on methodology, the practical questions cannot be underestimated.

Research concerned with historicity often makes use of archives, and simply getting to them and getting access can pose formidable challenges. Beyond access, the researcher faces problems of interpretation at multiple levels ranging from illegible handwriting to equivocal meanings. Given the inherently patchwork quality of information, whatever the methodological practice, the researcher may become engaged in triangulating information or constructing an analysis that attempts to do justice to contradictory accounts. Beyond research itself, sociohistorical inquiry has reached a point where, whatever their own approaches, researchers' communications with other researchers who share their substantive interests will often require 'translation' across both divides of methodology and cross-cutting conceptualizations of the things they study (Hall, 1999: 245–52). In turn, any analysis, any interpretation, becomes an historical artifact, subject to further conversations, potentially across generations. Yet for all the challenges, increasing reflexive self-consciousness about methodologies has created circumstances under which sociohistorical research has every prospect of flourishing in the decades ahead.

REFERENCES

Abbott, Andrew (2001) *Time Matters: On Theory and Method*. Chicago: University of Chicago Press.

Adams, Julia, Clemens, Elisabeth and Orloff, Ann (eds.) (2005) *Remaking Modernity: Politics, History, and Sociology*. Durham, N.C.: Duke University Press.

Althusser, Louis, and Balibar, Etienne ([1968] 1970) *Reading Capital*. London: NLB.

Appleby, Joyce, Hunt, Lynn and Jacob, Margaret (1994) *Telling the Truth about History*. New York: Norton.

Bates, Robert H. (1998) *Analytic Narratives*. Princeton, NJ: Princeton University Press.

Beyer, Jurgen (2005) 'Not all path dependence is alike— A critique of the "implicit conservatism" of a common concept', *Zeitschrift für Soziologie*, 34: 5–21.

Bhaskar, Roy (1986) *Scientific Realism and Human Emancipation*. London: Verso.

——— (1989) *Reclaiming Reality*. London: Verso.

Bloch, Marc (1953) *The Historian's Craft*. New York: Random House.

Bourdieu, Pierre ([1972] 1977) *Outline of a Theory of Practice*. New York: Cambridge University Press.

Burke, Kenneth ([1937] 1984) *Attitudes toward History*. Berkeley: University of California Press.

Burke, Peter (1993) *History and Social Theory*. Ithaca, N.Y.: Cornell University Press.

Calhoun, Craig (1998) 'Explanation in historical sociology: narrative, general theory, and historically specific theory', *American Journal of Sociology*, 104: 846–71.

Carr, David (1986) *Time, Narrative, and History*. Bloomington: Indiana University Press.

Cohen, David William (1994) *The Combing of History*. Chicago: University of Chicago Press.

Cohen, Sande (1986) *Historical Culture*. Berkeley: University of California Press.

Crouch, Colin and Farrell, Henry (2004) 'Breaking the path of institutional development? Alternatives to the new determinism', *Rationality and Society*, 16: 5–43.

Eco, Umberto (1989) *Foucault's Pendulum*. New York: Harcourt Brace Jovanovich.

Emigh, Rebecca (1997) 'The power of negative thinking: The use of negative case methodology in the development of sociological theory', *Theory and Society*, 26: 649–84.

Fentress, James and Wickham, Chris (1992) *Social Memory*. Cambridge, MA: Blackwell.

Ferguson, Niall (1997) 'The Kaiser's European Union: What if Britain had "stood aside" in August 1914?', in Niall Ferguson (ed.), *Virtual History*. London: Picador, pp. 228–81.

Foucault, Michel ([1961] 1965) *Madness and Civilization*. New York: Random House.

Furet, François ([1978] 1981) *Interpreting the French Revolution*. Cambridge: Cambridge University Press.

Giesen, Bernard and Junge, Kay (2003) 'Historical memory', in Gerard Delanty and Engin Isin (eds.), *Handbook of Historical Sociology*. Thousand Oaks, CA: Sage, pp. 326–36.

Ginzburg, Carlo ([1976] 1980) *The Cheese and the Worms: The Cosmos of a Sixteenth-Century Miller*. Baltimore, MD: Johns Hopkins University Press.

Gladwell, Malcolm (2000) *The Tipping Point: How Little Things Can Make a Big Difference*. Boston: Little, Brown.

Goldstone, Jack A. (1991) *Revolution and Rebellion in the Early Modern World*. Berkeley: University of California Press.

——— (2002) 'Efflorescences and economic growth in world history: rethinking the 'rise of the West' and the British industrial revolution', *Journal of World History*, 13: 323–89.

——— (2003) 'Comparative historical analysis and knowledge accumulation in the study of revolutions', in James Mahoney and Dietrich Rueschemeyer

(eds.), *Comparative Historical Analysis*. Cambridge: Cambridge University Press, pp. 41–90.

Gorski, Philip S. (2004) 'The poverty of deductivism: A constructive realist model of sociological explanation', *Sociological Methodology*, 34: 1–33.

Griffin, Larry J. (1993) 'Narrative, event-structure analysis, and causal interpretation in historical sociology', *American Journal of Sociology*, 98: 1094–1133.

Habermas, Jürgen ([1981] 1987) *The Theory of Communicative Action, Vol. 2: Lifeworld and System*. Boston: Beacon Press.

Hall, John R. (1980) 'The time of history and the history of times', *History and Theory*, 19: 113–131.

——— (1994) 'Periodization and sequences', in Peter N. Sterns (ed.), *Encyclopedia of Social History*. New York: Garland, pp. 558–61.

——— (1999) *Cultures of Inquiry: From Epistemology to Discourse in Sociohistorical Research*. Cambridge: Cambridge University Press.

——— (2003) 'Cultural history is dead (long live the Hydra)', in Gerard Delanty and Engin Isin (eds.), *Handbook for Historical Sociology*. Beverly Hills, CA: Sage, pp. 151–67.

——— (2005) 'Comparative sociology', in Kimberly Kempf-Leonard (ed.), *Encyclopedia of Social Measurement*. New York: Elsevier, pp. 391–97.

Hall, John R., with Philip Schuyler and Sylvaine Trinh (2000) *Apocalypse Observed: Religion and Violence in North America, Europe, and Japan*. London: Routledge.

Hawthorn, Geoffrey (1991) *Plausible Worlds: Possibility and Understanding in History and the Social Sciences*. New York: Cambridge University Press.

Henige, David P. (1974) *The Chronology of Oral Tradition: Quest for a Chimera*. Oxford: Clarendon Press.

Himmelfarb, Gertrude (1987) *The New History and the Old*. Cambridge, MA: Harvard University Press.

Iggers, Georg G. (1997) *Historiography in the Twentieth Century*. Hanover, NH: Wesleyan University Press.

Kammen, Michael (1991) *Mystic Chords of Memory*. New York: Knopf.

Kant, Immanuel ([1784] 1963) 'Idea for a universal history from a cosmopolitan point of view', in Lews W. Beck (ed.), *On History*. Indianapolis: Bobbs-Merrill, pp. 11–26.

Katznelson, Ira (2003) 'Periodization and preferences: Reflections on purposive action in comparative historical social science', in James Mahoney and Dietrich Rueschemeyer (eds.), *Comparative Historical Analysis*. Cambridge: Cambridge University Press, pp. 270–301.

Kiser, Edgar and Hechter, Michael (1991) 'The role of general theory in comparative-historical sociology', *American Journal of Sociology*, 97: 1–30.

Köhnke, Klaus Christian (1991) *The Rise of Neo-Kantianism: German Academic Philosophy between Idealism and Positivism*. New York: Cambridge University Press.

Lieberson, Stanley (1992) 'Small *N*s and big conclusions: An examination of the reasoning in comparative studies based on a small number of cases', in Charles C. Ragin and Howard S. Becker (eds.), *What is a Case?* New York: Cambridge University Press, pp. 105–118

Mahoney, James (2000) 'Path dependence in historical sociology', *Theory and Society*, 29: 507–48.

—— (2004) 'Revisiting general theory in historical sociology', *Social Forces*, 83: 459–89.

Mahoney, James and Rueschemeyer, Dietrich (eds.) (2003) *Comparative Historical Analysis*. Cambridge: Cambridge University Press.

Olick, Jeffrey K. (1999) 'Collective memory: The two cultures', *Sociological Theory*, 17: 333–48.

Paige, Jeffrey (1999) 'Conjuncture, comparison, and conditional theory in macrosocial inquiry', *American Journal of Sociology*, 105: 781–800.

Ragin, Charles C. (2000) *Fuzzy-Set Social Science*. Chicago: University of Chicago Press.

Ragin, Charles C. and Becker, Howard S. (eds.) (1992) *What is a Case?* New York: Cambridge University Press.

Ragin, Charles C. and Zaret, David (1983) 'Theory and method in comparative research: Two strategies', *Social Forces*, 61: 731–54.

Ricoeur, Paul (1984, 1985, 1988) *Time and Narrative*. 3 vols. Chicago: University of Chicago Press.

Roth, Guenther (1976) 'History and sociology in the work of Max Weber', *British Journal of Sociology*, 27: 306–18.

—— (1987) 'Rationalization in Max Weber's developmental history', in Scott Lash and Sam Whimster (eds.), *Max Weber, Rationality, and Modernity*. London: Allen & Unwin, pp. 75–91.

Schama, Simon (1991) *Dead Certainties (Unwarranted Speculations)*. New York: Knopf.

Sewell, William H., Jr. (2005) *Logics of History: Social Theory and Social Transformation*. Chicago: University of Chicago Press.

Shiner, Larry (1969) 'A phenomenological approach to historical knowledge', *History and Theory*, 8: 260–74.

Sica, Alan (2004) 'Why "unobservables" cannot save general theory: A reply to Mahoney', *Social Forces*, 83: 491–501.

Skocpol, Theda (1984) 'Emerging agendas and recurrent strategies in historical sociology', in Theda Skocpol (ed.), *Vision and Method in Historical Sociology*. Cambridge: Cambridge University Press, pp. 356–91.

Skocpol, Theda, and Somers, Margaret (1980) 'The uses of comparative history in macrosocial inquiry', *Comparative Studies in Society and History*, 22: 174–97.

Smith, Dennis (1991) *The Rise of Historical Sociology*. Philadelphia: Temple University Press.

Somers, Margaret R. (1992) 'Narrativity, narrative identity, and social action: Rethinking English working-class formation', *Social Science History*, 16: 591–630.

—— (1995) 'Narrating and naturalizing civil society and citizenship theory: the place of political culture and the public sphere', *Sociological Theory*, 13: 229–74.

—— (1998) '"We're no angels": Realism, rational choice, and relationality in social science', *American Journal of Sociology*, 104: 722–84.

Steinmetz, George (2004) 'Odious comparisons: Incommensurability, the case study, and "small Ns" in sociology', *Sociological Theory*, 22: 371–400.

—— (2005) 'The epistemological unconscious of US sociology and the transition to post-Fordism: The case of historical sociology', in Julia Adams, Elisabeth Clemens and Ann Orloff (eds.) *Remaking Modernity: Politics, History, and Sociology*. Durham, NC: Duke University Press, pp. 109–57.

Stinchcombe, Arthur L. (1978) *Theoretical Methods in Social History*. New York: Academic Press.

Stone, Lawrence (1979) 'The revival of narrative: Reflections on a new old history', *Past and Present*, 85 (November): 3–24.

Tilly, Charles (1984) *Big Structures, Large Processes, Huge Comparisons*. New York: Russell Sage.

Veyne, Paul ([1971] 1984) *Writing History*. Middletown, CT: Wesleyan University Press.

Walkowitz, Judith R. (1992) *City of Dreadful Delight*. London: Virago Press.

Weber, Max ([1919] 1946) 'Science as a vocation', in H. H. Gerth and C. Wright Mills (eds.), *From Max Weber: Essays in Sociology*. New York: Oxford University Press, pp. 129–56.

—— ([1904] 1949) 'Objectivity in social science', in, Max Weber *The Methodology of the Social Sciences*, Edward A. Shils and Henry A. Finch (eds.). New York: Free Press, pp. 49–112.

—— ([1905] 1958) *The Protestant Ethic and the Spirit of Capitalism*, trans. Talcott Parsons. New York: Scribners.

—— ([1922] 1978) *Economy and Society*, Guenther Roth and Claus Wittich (eds.), Berkeley: University of California Press.

White, Hayden (1973) *Metahistory: The Historical Imagination in Nineteenth-Century Europe*. Baltimore, MD: Johns Hopkins University Press.

6

Case Study

Jennifer Platt

'Case study' is a term that has been used in a variety of different ways, not all of them clear, and some of them mutually inconsistent. It has been both a major category distinguishing complete alternative research styles, and a passing description meaning no more than that the study is of a single case. Its salience in the methodological literature has fluctuated over time, somewhat following the ebb and flow of quantitative versus qualitative emphases, though empirical research practice has not necessarily corresponded to that. Some relevant discussion has appeared under other banners, while 'case study' figures in the titles of some work which is not consciously working within a developed methodological tradition that distinguishes a case-study approach from alternatives. On the other hand, some studies which seem very plausible candidates to call themselves case studies, such as Erikson (1976) on the effects of a devastating flood, or Vaughan (1996) on the Challenger launch, do not do so, although each has a (very different) sophisticated discussion of the rationale for studying a single episode; some studies always discussed in other terms (e.g., Katz and Lazarsfeld, 1955) have in fact been based on limited local areas,[1] and could be treated as case studies. Here, the focus is on the general methodological discussion of 'case-study method' and on the issues it raises (whether or not the discussion has used that name), and not on what is 'really' a case study.

The idea has been used in a range of disciplines within the social sciences, not always in the same way or following the same historical course, and the associated literatures have been to some extent distinct; in the following discussion, therefore, the material is initially arranged in terms of the relatively coherent and distinct literatures which touch on relevant issues, though boundaries between them are sometimes crossed. The aim has been not to do full justice to the details of every position, but to bring out broad alternative arguments wherever they have appeared. The conclusion brings together key themes to summarize the issues raised.

SOCIOLOGY

It was in inter-war US sociology that 'case study' was particularly salient as a key category of mainstream methodological discussion. In this first phase, 'case study' represented the qualitative side of the quantitative/qualitative antithesis, and was opposed to 'statistical method'. But the term had connotations which were not limited to the absence of statistics. Special emphasis was given to the case study's superior access to personal meanings, though other themes included the collection of data on many factors for each case and the placing of data on individual cases in a rich context. The case study was particularly associated with the life history and the 'personal document'. Shaw's *The Jack Roller* (1930), a lengthy autobiographical account mostly written by its subject, could be taken as the key exemplar; few other empirical publications fitted the abstract conception so well, though ones of rather different character were also sometimes treated as examples. It was assumed, to degrees varying among authors, that case studies could in some way offer a basis for generalization.

The boundaries between these traditional methodological categories were eroded by attempts such as Angell's (1936) to systematize case method (using analytical induction), and by the development of richer and more meaningful quantitative techniques. By the 1950s, the idea of access to meanings was becoming more associated with the new category of 'participant observation', and the category 'case study' ceased to be of significance in the methodological literature. This was the period of hegemony of the modern sample survey which had emerged in the war, and case study, when mentioned, was seen in the mainstream texts as unimportant and suited only to preliminary stages of research, when it might suggest hypotheses but certainly provided no basis for prediction or generalization.[2]

The hypothetico-deductive model of scientific method, with a covering law model of explanation, became dominant in sociology and other disciplines. Social psychologist Donald Campbell's important work on experimental design (Campbell, 1957; Campbell and Stanley, 1966) was widely invoked in textbooks. In this, case study

appeared only as the 'one-shot case-study' design, seen as unsatisfactory because it does not contain the before/after comparison which would justify the imputation of a cause. It also followed that case studies must show a bias towards confirmation of the researcher's hypotheses.

However, in the normal swing of reaction against dominant positions, the idea was to undergo a revival in Anglophone social science, and much of the later writing elaborates a critique of that orthodoxy. By the mid-1960s an increasing literature was developing which favored and elaborated new versions of qualitative method. This soon came to include fresh work on 'case study', not necessarily closely similar to the earlier work, and often apparently unaware of it. This is represented in works such as Eckstein (1975), Feagin et al. (1991), Gomm et al. (2000), Ragin and Becker (1992), Simons (1980), Stake (1995) and Yin (1984). (Hamel, 1992 and Hamel et al., 1993 show some parallel Francophone interest, though here Le Play is invoked as a key ancestor, and 'monograph' in his sense is equally salient as a category.)

This work, especially in the extremely influential 'grounded theory' of Glaser and Strauss (1967), moved away from the hypothetico-deductive model.[3] Moreover, Campbell shifted his earlier view, proposing now that it was not true that interpretations of case studies must be inadequately tested, since the richness of data in them means that a theory is in effect tested with the degrees of freedom represented by its multiple implications.[4] (Rosenblatt (1981: 195) points out that this represented a move from treating all case studies as analogous to experiments towards considering the specific characteristics of ethnographic studies. He also raises the question of whether it makes sense to apply to all those, as Campbell continued to do, epistemological criteria appropriate for work aiming to explain, when many of them have descriptive rather than explanatory goals.) It was also suggested that, in social-science case studies of one setting in one time period, the measurement of many variables at what could be seen as the post-test stage, combined with the existence of rich contextual knowledge and the possibility of making 'intelligent presumptions about what this group would have been like without X', could serve as logical equivalents of pre-test measures and control groups (Cook and Campbell, 1979: 96). Some attention was given to this within sociology, sometimes as legitimation for positions held primarily on other grounds. The growth of feminism, often associated with the belief that only qualitative method was adequate to the experience of women (Oakley, 2000), supported the trend, as did the prevalence of versions of left-wing politics which saw statistical method as associated with capitalist rationality, though neither took positions specifically on case-study method as such. Despite such changes, mainstream textbook orthodoxy has continued to be that case studies are of very limited use for central social-scientific goals, while their proponents have continued active in advocacy and defense of alternative orthodoxies.

'PRACTITIONER' LITERATURE

Some of the discussion of case studies has come from authors who, if not themselves non-academic practitioners (in education, business, nursing, planning, social work, etc., or drawn from those fields), train them, may offer them consultancy services, and are oriented to the audiences they provide; this tends to be associated with some distinctive approaches, represented in this section.

Stake is a prominent recent author on the case study who places himself at one end of the qualitative–quantitative spectrum, with a strong commitment to 'qualitative' research. He sees his ideas as drawing on 'naturalistic, holistic, ethnographic, phenomenological and biographic research methods' (Stake, 1995: xi). He distinguishes between 'intrinsic' and 'instrumental' case studies, with the former undertaken because that case in particular is of interest, while the latter are carried

out to throw light on matters beyond the case(s) studied; his rhetorical style suggests that his heart is with the former, less conventionally social-scientific style. With a background in educational psychology, his major work has been in educational evaluation, and his book (Stake, 1995), which is structured as a textbook, focuses on case studies in educational settings planned for use by practitioners. Stake was also a contributor to a volume on the use of case studies in educational evaluation (Simons, 1980), which has been treated as representing a controversial position within that field. There he introduces the concept of 'naturalistic generalization' (for which critics might find a less polite term!), arising as tacit knowledge based on personal experience, as contrasted with such alternatives as 'scientific' or 'rationalistic' generalization.

Case studies by researchers are seen as contributing to such generalization by practitioners (in this context, teachers), and the model is a 'democratic' one in which the research results are not systematically analysed and are negotiated with the subjects. This conception of how to proceed clearly invokes ideological preferences which are not specific to research method, and would only be applicable to a limited range of research topics or settings.[5] These authors take it for granted that case studies are carried out as a basis for practical action. But Atkinson and Delamont (1985), also committed to ethnographic research methods and with experience in educational evaluation, have strongly criticized such methodological proposals, both because they abandon the possibility of a cumulative and theorized research tradition and because as method it is not clear what is proposed, only what is rejected.

Sociologists Feagin, Orum and Sjoberg (1991) present a manifesto for case-study method, with a collection of chapters on empirical work to exemplify its use. For them too this is primarily a qualitative method, and one suited to a political commitment to research to promote social betterment and

'... to render social action in a manner that comes closest to the action as it is understood by the actors themselves' (Feagin et al., 1991: 8) so that it may facilitate public political participation. They also emphasize the importance of its holistic approach, allowing social wholes to be grasped as such. They argue (Feagin et al., 1991: 273–4) that case studies, as opposed to survey-based statistical research, avoid the methodological individualism of probability sampling, which misleadingly treats individuals as independent and equal and so conceals the realities of power in stratified societies.

Williams's chapter in Feagin et al. (1991) offers an interesting example which adds to the reasons for choosing a specific case-study approach. As a feminist especially concerned to retain the theoretical distinction between sex and gender, she felt that the usual quantitative methods' use of biological sex as an isolated variable was not adequate. Her wish to study 'the processes involved in maintaining and reproducing gender differences' (Williams, 1991: 232) led her to undertake case studies of male nurses and female Marines, on the assumption that in gender-deviant occupations such processes would be more evident. (She indeed found that much effort went into creating conventional gender differences which participants did not spontaneously display.) Thus a deliberate choice of atypical cases was made, on the assumption that what was found there would represent processes typical of the wider society. How could this be checked? 'The test of this, of course, is whether the findings strike a chord of recognition with those in other contexts' (Williams, 1991: 239), but it is not proposed to undertake further research to find that out, so this could be seen as again invoking 'naturalistic generalization'.

Robert K. Yin has also made leading contributions, of a somewhat different character, to practitioners' case study method. His *Case Study Research: Design and Methods* ([1984] 2003a) has gone through 38 printings in various editions; he has also published a book on its applications (Yin, [1993] 2003b) and an anthology of examples (Yin, 2004), as well as a number of chapters in other volumes. It is clear that his work is of interest to a wide audience. An experimental psychologist by training, he has made a later career in commercial consultancy. His firm describes its remit on its web site as 'provides applied research and evaluation, technical support, and management assistance aimed at improving public policy, private enterprise, and collaborative ventures' (COSMOS, 2005), and he often draws his examples from evaluation research done for clients. Within academia, it appears that his work is of special interest to departments such as business, education, planning and public administration; it does not articulate clearly with the mainstream of methodological discussion in less practice-oriented social-science fields, although Donald Campbell provided a foreword for the 2003 edition of *Case Study Research: Design and Methods*.

Yin hardly addresses the older literature on the subject; his emphasis is on advice to potential new practitioners. He defines a case study for his purposes as an empirical inquiry that 'investigates a contemporary phenomenon within its real-life context'. He then adds that this is 'especially when the boundaries between phenomenon and context are not clearly evident', and that the difficulty of distinguishing between phenomenon and context means that the technical definition needs to include that 'there will be many more variables of interest than data points'—which means that multiple data sources to give triangulation will be required, and that guidance from prior development of theoretical propositions will be advantageous (Yin, 2003a: 13–14). The total research strategy thus defined is distinguished from four other possibilities—experiment, survey, archival analysis and history—seen as applicable to different research questions and under different practical circumstances. In this typology 'case study' is distinguished from 'history' only by the fact that it focuses on contemporary events, and so has access to some additional sources of data (Yin, 2003a: 5).[6]

Basic definitions apart, a number of other points are made to elaborate the idea. The quantitative/qualitative distinction is not seen as relevant, and the style is much more quantitative. It is held that the goals of case-study research may be exploratory, descriptive or explanatory. The 'problem' of generalizability is boldly circumvented by saying that case studies may or may not set out to generalize, but that where generalization is attempted it should be to theory (which may later be tested) rather than to other particular cases (Yin, 2003a: 16, 38), so that it is neither necessary nor realistic to attempt to locate 'representative' cases.[7] Studies using multiple as well as single cases are seen as applying case-study method, and there is useful discussion of types of design. The distinction is made between 'holistic' studies which focus on the case as a whole, and 'embedded' ones where sub-units within the larger case are treated as cases.[8] For multiple case designs, it is held that a comparative or replicative rather than a sampling logic is appropriate, not a simple accumulation of more cases. These ideas are elaborated in discussion of modes of analysis of case data, which include 'pattern matching' of observations with one or more theoretical models, and time series analyses.

Yin frequently compares case studies with experiments, a comparison that is not salient to many other authors writing in this area, and the logic he follows has more in common with traditional discussions of 'scientific method' than do many of theirs—in Ragin's terms (see below), it is also more variable-oriented. His distinctive contribution may perhaps be understood as the interesting by-product of confrontation between psychological training and the contingencies of consultancy work where clients want to know about what applies to *their* organization, not about general theory. Although his work has been widely used, it does not seem to have been subject to critical commentary, despite its departure from some of the positions taken by other writers; perhaps this is because it serves another constituency, as well as being welcomed as the nearest approximation to a practical textbook on areas where there has been an unmet need.

PSYCHOLOGY

It is not surprising that most academic psychologists have discussed case studies against the background of their discipline's distinctive methodological traditions, of which both the experimental and the clinical are relevant. Writing on the clinical tradition, Bolgar (1965) sketches a history in which clinical psychologists (such as Freud) followed the medical tradition of case histories and, since their prime concern was with understanding the uniqueness of the particular individual under treatment, were less concerned with the potential generalizability of what they found.[9] She suggests, however, that in the somewhat separate field of human development psychologists (such as Piaget) commonly worked by intensive observation of very few children, often their own. The third area in which case histories of individuals have been used is the study of individuals chosen because they belong to special groups such as eminent scientists (e.g., Gruber, 1974), or are of unique historical importance such as Martin Luther (e.g., Erikson, 1959). She takes the line, conventional in other areas of the social sciences, that, while experimentation may be especially suitable to the testing of hypotheses, case histories are a valuable source for their discovery.[10]

Kazdin (1982) goes further, arguing that 'single-case designs' have many uses, even in experimentation. He thinks of experimentation as evaluating the effects of an intervention—in this case, a treatment intervention. Study of the single case is appropriate because 'The results of the average amount of change that serves as the basis for drawing conclusions in between-group research does not address the clinician's need to make decisions about treatments that will alter the individual client' (Kazdin, 1982: 14). He suggests that the well-known weaknesses of some studies of single cases follow not from their study of only a single case but from the use on it of informal procedures, the lack of systematic observation and measurement, and the absence of steps to rule out the impact of extraneous factors; his book sets out to elaborate the logic and the procedures that are required to overcome these weaknesses.

In the experimental tradition, dominant in modern academic psychology, Danziger (1990) has sketched the emergence over the period up to the end of World War II of what he calls 'the triumph of the aggregate'. He shows how in the reporting of psychological findings subjects were less and less often mentioned by name; group rather than individual data became dominant; and subjects' extra-experimental social identities were less often mentioned when abstract knowledge (rather than application) was the aim (Danziger, 1990: 74, 82–3, 98–9), as psychologists became increasingly concerned to make universalistic knowledge claims which could be presented as the attributes of collective subjects.[11] He suggests that one reason for the increasing dominance of statistical regularities as the basis of generalization was that individual behavior could vary markedly from one occasion to another, while if individual data were pooled regularities might emerge and be used for generalizing even if they corresponded to the behavior of no single person. In parallel with this, the nature of the subjects' experience—and of the specific characteristics of the experimental situation—was increasingly defined as irrelevant, which he sees as necessary to the support of the political claim to societal expertise (Danziger, 1990: 153, 183–7). The result is the dominance of a statistical tradition which he regards as an inadequate scientific basis for psychological theory. Whether or not this critical analysis is agreed or fully applicable to present-day psychology, it brings out some important general points of methodology. In both clinical and experimental traditions the influence of biological and medical models is evident, and there has been disagreement about the utility of small-N methods with

some of the characteristics of case study, though this has largely depended on the particular topics studied.

ANTHROPOLOGY

Anthropologists have also traditionally dealt with single cases, though these are societies rather than individuals. They have made intensive general studies of what became 'their' society, where 'the unit of investigation had to be small enough for the researcher to get to know every individual, which was hardly feasible in a community larger than 500 people,' and most 'had an area or a tribe to study, not a problem' (Barrett, 1996: 76). Given the linguistic and cultural problems that had to be overcome in carrying out fieldwork, there were strong practical as well as intellectual reasons for that. While this tradition held, it was so taken for granted as part of the defining character of the discipline that the issues were hardly discussed, and the ethnographies were not considered as case studies.

In the 1970s, however, what had become the standard social-science conception of scientific method started to be expounded by US anthropologists, in works such as Brim and Spain (1974), which assumed that hypothesis-testing and the use of representative samples and statistical tests were needed. In addition, the assumption that small isolated societies could be found (which it made sense to treat as independent units) was increasingly undermined by world developments (Barrett, 1996: 111). The felt need for comparative material led to suggestions that internal variation be sought within limited areas, or that a collective enterprise should be established to create comparative data (Levine, 1973: 187–8), and the advantages of team ethnography in more complex societies were discussed. More recently, the idea of 'multi-site ethnography' has been developed (Marcus, 1995). This is concerned to go beyond the traditional boundaries of the anthropological village study, especially under the circumstances of globalization which make it increasingly unhelpful to confine what is taken into account within narrow local geographical units. But the further 'sites' to be taken into account are not necessarily geographically defined, even if geographically separate. They are whatever is needed to locate the starting point within its global context:

> Multi-sited research is designed around chains, paths, threads, conjunctions or juxtapositions of locations in which the ethnographer establishes some form of literal, physical presence, with an explicit, posited logic of association or connection among sites that in fact defines the argument of the ethnography ... (Marcus, 1995: 105)

It should be noted that this is not an approach associated with comparative method; it is concerned rather to understand the case studied fully by placing it in its wider context, and thereby also to understand the wider context, which may be as wide as the capitalist world system—which is by definition unique, and so not open to (contemporary) comparative study. Insofar as Yin's approach is one which emphasizes the need to take seriously the setting of the case which is the central focus of study, that has something in common with this discussion. Both are concerned with how boundaries can appropriately be drawn around the cases studied, although they start from totally different assumptions about the nature of the conventional pattern of research with which the approaches they propose contrast.

The problems raised by globalization have also been recognized beyond anthropology. Urry maintains that '... the development of various global "networks and flows" undermines endogenous social structures which have generally been taken within sociological discourse to possess the powers to reproduce themselves ...' (Urry, 2000: 1), so that the separate units required no longer exist—or, indeed, perhaps seldom have, even in the past:

> The construction of the discourse of sociology around the concept of society in part stemmed from the relative autonomy of American society throughout the twentieth century. It thus represents

a universalization of the American societal experience ... self-sufficient societies are of course empirically rare and generally rely upon their domination of their physical and social environments ... (Urry, 2000: 6)

Such arguments have, however, probably been less acted on in practice than proposed in principle, except in fields such as migration or trade, where the value of following a flow is most easily evident.

A somewhat different line of discussion has been followed in some contributions from British anthropologists of the Manchester school led by Gluckman. He developed the idea of the 'extended case study' (Gluckman, 1961), suggesting that what is needed to improve on general statements about ritual and custom in a social system is study of specific cases of the way in which people behave in practice and, in particular, of the pattern of events in incidents involving the same people over time: this can show how social relations develop and change historically.[12] Mitchell (1983), in an important article, goes beyond Gluckman's discussion to raise issues in epistemological terms. His key point is to distinguish between statistical inference and logical or scientific inference. The former is concerned with inferring the distribution of characteristics in a population from observation of a sample, which only provides a plausible basis for inference if it can claim to be a representative sample; the relationships between variables which it provides are correlational, showing which characteristics go together, but not why. For plausible imputation of causal relationships, it must be shown that there is a logical nexus between the factors considered, and for Mitchell case studies aim to explore just that.

> A case study is essentially heuristic; it reflects in the events portrayed features which may be construed as a manifestation of some general abstract theoretical principle ... The inference about the *logical* relationship between the two characteristics is not based upon the representativeness of the sample and therefore upon its typicality, but rather upon the plausibility or upon the logicality of the nexus between the two characteristics ... (Mitchell, 1983: 192, 198)

It follows that the issue of whether one can generalize from a case study is an issue not of the number of cases studied but of the adequacy of the theory in relation to which it is interpreted, and the cogency of its theoretical interpretation against a background of knowledge of other cases.[13]

COMPARATIVE USE OF CASES

Authors advocating case study method have not always confined themselves to the use of a single case (which might be the case of a large group such as a tribe, town or organization), and some have seen the use of more than one case as in general an improvement. Complex designs in which the number of cases varies with the level considered are quite common in practice. Probably commonest is the type of study where one town, organization or country is the 'case' within which data are collected on a sample of members or social units; this is not usually regarded as constituting a case study, though it can be used as such. The individuals' characteristics may be used to characterize the group,[14] or the group's to characterize the individuals, and the meaning of either procedure will depend on what the other cases are from which they are distinguished. Types of case-study research design which include the possibilities of comparison between cases have been distinguished, and these begin to approach some of the problems that have been more consistently and systematically considered under the rubric of comparative method; we shall now move on to consider some of the work and ideas more associated with that.

There is a long-standing tradition of publishing books which collect papers by authors, often from different countries, who have studied cases of the same kind. Their chapters are then presented as case studies from which comparative conclusions can be drawn, or are given an editorial framework which attempts to draw such conclusions, despite the lack of advance coordination to ensure close comparability in the questions raised and the data collected. That pattern leaves research 'design' as retrospective, but there have also been more prospective designs which bring together work by different authors, and these demonstrate some interesting possibilities.

Shavit and Blossfeld (1993) provide an impressive example of work, coordinated among members of a research committee of the International Sociological Association (ISA), which brings together comparable data from 13 countries on class and gender differences over time in educational attainment. Burawoy (2000) has edited a book where the substantive chapters are provided by research students working on topics individually chosen before they came together, but developed in collective work. It takes the theme of globalization, and uses their data— on groups which range from breast-cancer activists in San Francisco to Irish software developers—both to understand and theorize those groups in terms of the way in which globalization enters into them, and also to throw light on understandings of globalization. (Burawoy invokes Gluckman, and defines the method as that of the extended case, both extending out from micro processes to macro forces, and extending theory by improving existing theory in the light of fresh cases.) Lamont and Thévenot (2000) present an enterprise designed to create comparisons between French and American cultural differences in principles of evaluation. The authors worked on their own topics, in this case ranging from the rhetorics of working-class racism and anti-racism to styles of literary theory, but compared French and American data and worked in ways informed by the group discussions. The editors state the logic thus:

> By making our case studies as diverse as possible, we aim to tap the full range of principles of evaluation used in each national context. Hence, each case study was chosen because it could teach us something particular about how different principles of evaluation coexist ... By juxtaposing results from a range of cases, we are able to identify repeated taken-for-granted cultural differences

across societies and to produce an understanding that is more qualitatively nuanced than is generally achieved from comparative survey research ... by bringing together several integrated case studies ... we can submit specific cross-national similarities and differences noted in the literature to empirically rigorous exploration across many contexts and subject areas. (Lamont and Thévenot, 2000: 2–3)

We may note that the argument, both here and in Burawoy (2000), is that a large phenomenon may be usefully approached by using a set of case studies chosen not as a random sample (which would scarcely be conceivable, since how could one list the population of possible case studies?) but arbitrarily, *except* in the crucial sense that they are sufficiently different from each other for common features nonetheless found to be treated as more widely generalizable. The chances of finding common features in such superficially different contexts are low enough, unless those features are more widely present within the social unit, for their detection to be seen as evidence of such wider presence.[15]

The more conventional 'comparative method' literature relates to bodies of empirical work which are most often on topics related to national politics, such as elections, welfare policies or revolutions. These are macro-social topics in which the whole society ('society' here usually meaning a nation-state) is the normal unit (though the problems of logic are the same when smaller units are used). They have in this sense been mainly the concern of political scientists and sociologists. Ragin (2000: 25) points out that the empirical distribution of comparative studies in sociology and politics shows a dip in the range of numbers of cases used between one or two and more than 50. He suggests that this is the range where comparative method applies. That is the main territory of this literature relevant to case-study issues. A strong reason for the use of limited numbers of cases is that few of the units of interest exist. That problem is exacerbated by the varying levels of data available on the existing cases and their uneven distribution across types; there are intrinsic difficulties

for a quantitative approach here.[16] There are also other practical issues with intellectual consequences. Where the unit for comparison is the whole society, considerable depth of expert knowledge (for which length of study and foreign-language acquisition are needed) is often required to give an adequate account of each case. (Those with the expertise are as likely to work within an 'area studies' paradigm as a comparative one.) This means that no single individual is likely to have expertise on many cases, while those who attempt to make secondary use of others' data may be open to criticism for the shallowness of their knowledge of the cases, as by Goldthorpe (2000: 28–44).

Among those identifying themselves as comparativists, Ragin (1987: 70) distinguishes usefully between the more case-oriented area specialists and the more variable-oriented generalists.[17] (The classic argument in favor of the variable-oriented approach was put by Przeworski and Teune (1970), who rejected the claim that national societies were unique and so could not meaningfully be compared; they proposed that, since comparability depends upon the availability of higher-level concepts which subsume historical particularities, the goal should be to replace the names of nations with the names of variables.) The case-oriented approach is strong in its access to complexity and historical specificity, and in its holistic grasp of the ways in which different factors are interrelated, but weak in its scope for plausible generalization because of the limits set by the small number of (commonly unrepresentative) cases that it draws on. The variable-oriented approach does not have the same problem of number of cases (though the cases it has may still be in practice an unrepresentative or narrow selection), and so can make use of sophisticated quantitative techniques, but it risks doing so at the cost of attention to the specific characteristics of individual societies, which may be concealed behind theoretical variable labels at such a high level of abstraction that they have little practical meaning. The case-oriented approach can address issues specific to relatively small numbers of societies, which the variable-oriented approach is compelled to ignore. Ragin develops a strategy that aims to overcome this distinction by providing methods which formalize qualitative comparison and can deal with configurations, not just separate variables, so that the strengths of the case-oriented approach are retained while some of the criticisms made of it are met. Such ideas are developed further in his later work on 'fuzzy sets' (Ragin, 2000).

Lieberson (1992), on the other hand, offers a critique of 'the reasoning used in comparative studies based on a small number of cases' by Ragin and others, which he sees as becoming increasingly common in macro-historical work. His arguments against it are that small-N studies are compelled to work deterministically rather than probabilistically, and that the use of Mill's methods of agreement and difference implies the assumption that multiple causes or interaction effects are absent, although measurement problems and the complexity of causation mean that often only probabilistic theories are appropriate.[18] He is obviously thinking of the establishment of general theoretical explanations.

Goldthorpe (2000: 49–53) argues that the key difficulty underlying the small-N problem is in fact one of data rather than method: insufficient information is available. But the information can be increased by adding more cases, either societal or of periods within the same societies, especially more diverse ones. Other issues he raises which proponents of case-study approaches have used against large-N work are the difficulty of identifying cases which are independent of each other, and the 'black-box' problem of establishing *why* it should be that certain inputs are associated with certain outputs. For each of these, he suggests that they are real, but as relevant to case-oriented as to variable-oriented research. Ebbinghaus (2005) reaches a similar conclusion, but treats it as implying more criticism of large-N research. He sees the critics of small-N work as tending to make the inappropriate assumption that comparative method can be reduced to the analysis of logical truth tables, though pointing out that Lieberson's criticism about the difficulties of dealing with probabilistic theories does not hold for conditions *necessary* to the outcome even if not sufficient, since those must be present whatever the intervention of chance events. He also points out that the cases used in large-N studies are in practice often far from a representative sample of the cases that exist, because of the difficulty of finding ones where the data required are actually available. In addition, where cases in large-N studies are relatively diverse, the extent to which they are effectively stratified violates the homogeneity assumptions of the inferential statistics used, while the path-dependency of some current historical situations means that the difficulty of introducing change when circumstances have changed (his examples are drawn from state welfare provision) produces an apparent lack of correlation with causal factors which is misleading.[19]

These authors generally take it for granted that the object of comparison is to reach general causal propositions, but that is not the only possibility. Harper (1992), in the same volume as Lieberson, argues for the value of small-N studies to ethnographic work, which necessarily starts in an inductive style, and where an initial problem may be to discover the socially meaningful boundaries of a case, and the aim may be descriptive understanding as much as or before explanation of the observed patterns or relating them to a wider theory. Holy (1987: 1, 15) says that

> Nowadays [within anthropology], the main question is whether description of particular societies is merely the means to generalization, or whether description itself is the key task and need not lead to generalizations ... the main object of the comparative method is no longer that of testing hypotheses but rather that of identifying or highlighting cultural specificity ... [20]

This approach follows from the shift to regarding social facts as constructions rather than as things, so that comparisons are seen as creating similarities and differences through the observer's constructs rather than as identifying features of the empirical phenomena. Thus the new paradigm becomes descriptive rather than explanatory, though what is done can still be described as comparative research—even if it might also be described as in some senses producing case studies, whether or not anthropologists have called them that.

But case studies on macro-social topics need not be taken only as cases to be used in comparative method. Eckstein (1975) focuses on the strengths of single-case studies in the testing of theory, as *contrasted with* those of what is generally seen in political science as comparative method. His conception is one in which theory aims to be explanatory in a strong sense, where predictions with a specific empirical meaning should follow logically from theory, and it is tested on cases different from any which may initially have led to its formulation. Then a real-life case which falls (or does not fall) on a curve where it should in terms of the theory provides strong evidence, and appropriately chosen cases may be crucial in that their confirmation or disconfirmation of a theory is sufficiently surprising to provide strong support for a theoretical argument. A crucial case is one that '… *must closely fit* a theory if one is to have confidence in the theory's validity, or, conversely, *must not fit* equally well any rule contrary to that proposed' (Eckstein 1975: 118). He argues that many of the weaknesses imputed to case studies have been equally present in comparative work, where the lack of precision in theoretical argument and of rigor in measurement often undermine the validity of conclusions, while the many practical difficulties of collecting adequate and comparable data on a set of suitable cases threaten the logic of abstract methodological principles.

CONCLUSIONS

It is clear that there is no single understanding of 'case study' or 'case-study method'. Different disciplines and sub-fields have commonly proposed and discussed it in ways which take for granted different empirical types of cases as those for study, and define the method by contrast to alternatives specific to their intellectual traditions. However, they have also responded to some shared historical developments in such matters as the philosophy of science, quantitative methods and the public availability of data. There are general themes which cut across the varying approaches, whether or not all writers have treated them as such. We conclude, therefore, by drawing out key themes and making a few comments.

What Is the 'Case' in Case Study?

The taken-for-granted typical 'case' ranges substantively from the single individual of psychology to the anthropologists' ethnographic study of a small local social unit or the national polity of political science. However, many writers have attempted to discuss the issues with a logic neutral to the substantive character of the cases concerned, which is obviously appropriate to general methodological consideration of such topics as the extent to which generalizations can be drawn from single cases. (Whether the results are or can be of equal value in relation to all types of case has not been an issue in the literature.) In addition some authors have distinguished between the case as substantive phenomenon, and as an analytical category used by the investigator. Thus Eckstein (1975: 85), after outlining the problem of defining what constitutes a single case, when, for instance, six British elections could be treated either as six cases of elections or as one case of British politics, decides that the way to deal with it is that '… a "case" can be defined technically as a phenomenon for which we report and interpret only a single measure on any pertinent variable.' If the case is defined analytically, the problem of where its boundaries should be drawn, or how much of its context should be taken into account to understand and/or explain it satisfactorily, will in effect have been conceptually decided. If it is defined substantively, the question remains relevant. (Can British politics be treated without taking into account European and American politics? Can politics be understood without the social stratification of its setting?) In practice the researcher must strike a balance between the need to limit work to a problem of viable scope and the need to take into account sufficient of the empirical realities.

No one other than the researcher (or the secondary user) can answer the question of what, if anything, a case employed is meant as a case *of*, and the choice of case cannot be evaluated without knowing that. A case that is excellent for one purpose may be feeble for another; once the intention is known, there is free scope for comment on its value for that purpose. But some users do not intend their cases as *of* anything beyond themselves; they are treated as historical individuals of intrinsic interest (though it may be that this leads to consideration of their historical role, or the social situation which created their interest).

What Is a Case Study?

A few examples of definitions or descriptions offered indicate the degree of variation in answers to this question:

1. 'The statistical method can be applied to many cases, the comparative method to relatively few ... and the case study method to one case ...' (Lijphart, 1971: 691).
2. As distinct from experiment or survey, 'It involves the investigation of a *relatively small* number of *naturally occurring*... cases' (Hammersley, 1992: 185).
3. '...we should reserve the term "case study" for those research projects which attempt to explain wholistically the dynamics of a certain historical period of a particular social unit' (Stoecker, 1991: 97–8).
4. 'A *case study* is here defined as an in-depth, multi-faceted investigation, using qualitative research methods, of a single social phenomenon. The study is conducted in great detail and often relies on the use of several data sources' (Feagin et al., 1991: 2).

The first definition above depends on the number of cases used; the second also uses number but allows more cases, and adds the character of the cases chosen. The third and fourth pay less attention to number: the third emphasizes how cases are treated in relation to the research purpose, while the fourth focuses on the type, depth and complexity of the data collected on the case. Given that for some writers the 'method' is only about the choice of cases to study, while for others that is just part of a larger package which includes the mode of data collection, the type of data collected and the way in which the data are analysed, the meaning of whatever general statements are made about the method is considerably affected. In the sense of case study as a package, it can become true by definition that the method is inherently associated with a qualitative approach. Sometimes, however, the connection made seems to be a more purely practical one: a commitment to rich, deep data is taken to mean that it is not possible to study many cases. That may indeed be so in practice, where money, time and opportunities are often limited, but is not so in principle.

It is useful when making methodological choices to consider how far the components of such packages are intrinsically connected rather than bundled together because each is chosen on independent grounds; there may be a wider range of possibilities than typologies of stereotypes imply. Several authors have pointed out that there is no evident reason why quantitative data should not be part of what makes up the richly detailed configurational picture of the case(s), or why some aspects of whole cases should not be quantified. But there is the argument that quantitative methods, at whatever level they are applied, cannot do justice to the complexity and configurational character of social reality. That is easier to maintain as a critique of the kinds of quantitative method which have sometimes been applied than as a reasoned reservation about all possible forms of quantification however they are used. An extreme position makes a principled rejection of the idea that any case can be satisfactorily categorized with another; the plausibility of that depends on how far the intellectual purpose in hand is affected by the differences between cases which also have something in common.

However, a real problem, to which such a position does not respond, remains in the area of conceptualization and theory: can abstract general concepts be created that make sense in relation to particular social situations which differ from each other? Hoffmeyer-Zlotnik and Wolf (2003) have shown how much work is required to create sufficient comparability without distorting local realities or risking inconsistency with local popular conceptualization, even when the data come from surveys, the units in question are all advanced industrial societies in modern Europe and the variables of interest are such standard face-sheet ones as education. A solution in principle is to create concepts at a sufficient level of abstraction to cut across local differences, whether at the level of individual variables or of higher-level types. But if that is attempted some of the locally relevant detail is necessarily wiped out, the sense of fit between theory and operational definition is threatened and the non-academic audience may no longer see connection with their lives. To some that loss will seem worth the gain, to others it will not. It is reasonable for the latter to favor strategies nearer the qualitative case-study end of the spectrum, even if their theorization will perforce be narrower in scope.

What Can Case Studies Be Used For?

Case studies have often been cast in the role of at best a preliminary to the main research: pilot studies, probes of the plausibility of theories to see whether they are worth more thorough exploration, or material which suggests hypotheses. (When the cases are to play such a preliminary role, they will need to be chosen in ways which correspond to the requirements of the particular project and the background state of knowledge in relation to it; this area has been little discussed.) The merely preliminary role has commonly been suggested by writers who treat those as low-level contributions to the real, hypothesis-testing research, and use this to dismiss the utility of case studies. But hypothesis-testing research cannot start without some sense of what the realities are that need to be accounted for, and it is certainly not obvious that this is best drawn from general knowledge derived from personal experience.

Some theory-related rationales for the choice of cases are listed in the next section, but cases which only fill a gap in our descriptive knowledge can also be of value for other social-scientific purposes (additional to those arising from practitioners' concerns with particular cases). The study of a novel type of case—political party, social movement, street gang, etc.—may open up a whole new field of work, as well as raising valuable questions about the applicability of general theories using terms such as 'organization' or 'group' to instances not drawn on in their initial formulation. It is evident that some famous works which have become regarded as successful case studies, such as Whyte's *Street Corner Society* (1943), were not planned as what they became (and, indeed, could not have been, given Whyte's level of knowledge at the start). However a study was planned, it may later be used by another author as a case of a theoretical category not employed by the original researcher, or brought together with other studies (as in Homans, 1951 or Frankenberg, 1966) to create an overarching interpretation. Perhaps it does not really matter how cases are chosen? Secondary use needs to be recognized as potentially valuable, and it might be suggested that the richer the data is the more the secondary uses that the case might serve. But it is difficult, if not impossible, to predict those in advance. Nobody remembers the case studies which were not found of use by later workers—but they exist.

It would be dangerous to assume that any arbitrarily chosen case could be as successful or useful intellectually as one chosen for specific reasons. But some cases which do constitute the main data of a research project have in practice been chosen at least in part for reasons not evidently relevant to their intrinsic intellectual value, such as convenience of access for the researcher, or the availability of existing data that can be used. This does not sound good, but such reasons are not all bad. The absence of data sources may mean that no research is practicable, and no one can research a situation to which they cannot get access; is it better to do no research? The fact that such cases may not be the optimal ones does not necessarily make their study worthless—though it may do so.

There are further uses of case studies to which other considerations are relevant. Various writers (e.g., Eckstein, 1975; Flyvbjerg, 2001; Gluckman, 1961; Lijphart, 1965; Platt, 1988; Stake, 1994; Strauss and Glaser, 1977) have listed ranges of different functions that they can perform. Some of these—illustration or exemplification, ostensive definition, the invocation of sympathy, the revelation of situations unfamiliar to the audience, or making findings more accessible to non-professional audiences—are presentational or rhetorical features of how the material is written up, rather than part of the method employed in doing the research.[21] It is probably safe to assert that nobody thinks that such functions, even if open to misuse, are illegitimate. But those could not be described as applications of 'case-study method', which gives the case(s) studied a more central role in arriving at theoretical or empirical conclusions.

HOW DO CASE STUDIES RELATE TO THEORY?

The major area of controversy is that over how case studies may contribute to empirical generalization or to general theory. But it is hard to disagree that cases appropriate to the research purpose should be chosen. If the research aim is to understand one particular case which is of interest in itself, or to predict outcomes in a clinical or consultancy setting where the uniqueness of the case one is dealing with is important to the adequacy of its treatment rather than a weakness to be conceptualized out, then it is arguable that not just is case study the only relevant method, but that the only relevant test of theory is fit

to the same case, or prediction as to its future. If, as Holy suggests in relation to modern cognitive anthropology, the aim is to describe differences carefully rather than to construct theory which overrides them, the issues again diverge from those more commonly discussed. However, it is not easy to avoid general ideas. If the goal is purely descriptive, that in itself gives no guidance on what features need to be described, so it is arguable that the theoretical task cannot be avoided. Equally, if the goal is to make predictions about, or to intervene effectively in, a single case, some explanatory ideas are required; one can be more sure of the causal relevance of particular features if they produce the same outcome in other cases.[22] It might be, though, that a theory is already sufficiently established for it to make sense merely to find out enough about the empirical character of the case for the theory to be applied.

The conventional critique of case study approaches assumes, often without finding it necessary to elaborate this explicitly, that the aim of all research is to test general theory, following the hypothetico-deductive paradigm as elaborated in the philosophy of social science. For psychology, that has been seen as entailing experimental design, which compares experimental and control groups on one variable at a time (a variable-oriented approach). In other disciplines that has sometimes been held out as an ideal, but the limited practical possibilities for *social* research on that model have meant that other methods of data collection, such as the survey, are the ones seen as appropriately scientific. In parallel, it is commonly assumed that the only useful sample is a random one, so that one may estimate from the sample the proportion that will be found to have a given characteristic in the population from which it is drawn. But statistical representativeness, important for descriptive purposes, is not a pre-requisite for the testing of theories. (The key feature of the classic logic of experimental design, structured specifically to test theory, requires cases randomly allocated to experimental and control groups, not a representative sample—even if some of the samples actually used have been convincingly criticized as sophomore psychology.) The same cases may be used in different ways. Too much of the literature, pro or con, attends only to the number of cases and the character of the data collected, without considering how the results may legitimately be used to reach a convincing conclusion of the kind desired.

Some proponents of case study have argued, as Mitchell (1983) and Danziger (1990) do, that the mode of generalization from case studies is theoretical, not empirical; it then depends on the adequacy of the perception of a logical nexus between effect and posited cause, which must surely be taken as tentative until further data have been collected. A theory of wider scope cannot be tested on the data from which it has been derived—though it can rule out potential theories which do not fit them—and, as Lieberson (1985: 70) has pointed out in relation to conventional quantitative data, individual cases bear causally relevant histories which mean that correlations may give a misleading impression of causation. Correlation between potential cause and effect is a necessary, but not a sufficient, criterion for causation, so the problem of getting from the studied to unstudied cases remains.

However, there are valuable theoretical roles for cases not chosen as representative:

- An apparently deviant case can refute a generalization or require its modification or, if found not really to be deviant, strengthen the theory. (Lieberson's (1992) objection on the ground that life is probabilistic, and thus no single deviant case is an adequate basis for refutation, is met at least in part by Ebbinghaus's (2005) above-mentioned distinction between necessary and sufficient conditions. It can also be suggested that insofar as the probabilistic features arise from the effects of factors not held constant, or from measurement problems, case-study method's holistic, deep and multi-method approach can get round that difficulty.)
- A case of a previously neglected kind can, if it does not turn out to be a deviant case, extend the known range of a theory or generalization
- An extreme case can provide the basis for an *a fortiori* or least/most likely argument, in which the case seeming most/least likely to support a

theory is examined and if it fails/succeeds the theory is disconfirmed/confirmed.
- Two extreme or contrasted cases can explore the *range* covered by a general proposition.
- A set of cases chosen as different kinds of example of the research topic can be used, as Burawoy (2000) or Lamont and Thévenot (2000) did, or analyzed sequentially as independent cases, with constant feedback to the initial theoretical ideas, using the data to modify, extend or specify more fully the theory in what Vaughan calls 'theory elaboration' (1992: 175).

It will be noted that each of these possible strategies rests on the availability of a framework of existing data and theorization, against which background the next project may add a brick to the wall. This is neither a weakness nor distinctive to the case-study approach. The development of theory and empirical generalizations is a collective enterprise, and no individual project has to cover all the possible ground in order to make a useful contribution to that process.

Central themes running through the discussion can be identified as the choices of depth and qualitative richness of data over breadth and statistical representativeness, of treating social units holistically rather than in terms of variables counted across individuals, and a rejection of the idea that all worthwhile research must itself test general explanatory hypotheses. There are strong arguments in favor of those (as well as good arguments against the ways in which they have sometimes been used). But that need not be at the expense of the alternatives. It makes sense to choose horses for courses, and there is more than one reasonable goal for a research project. Often, though, that goal may be best attained by drawing on more than one research style. Moreover, some of the sharp critical contrasts drawn between the merits of opposed stereotypes cannot be justified, and there are sophisticated methodological strategies which transcend the divide and offer the possibility of making use of some of the strengths of more than one position in the same project.

REFERENCES AND SELECT BIBLIOGRAPHY

Abbott, Andrew (2001) *Chaos of Disciplines*. Chicago: University of Chicago Press.

Angell, Robert C. ([1936], 1965) *The Family Encounters the Depression*. Gloucester, MA: Peter Smith.

Atkinson, Paul and Delamont, Sara (1985) 'Bread and dreams or bread and circuses? A critique of case study research in education', in Marten Shipman (ed.), *Educational Research: Principles, Policies and Practices*. London: Falmer Press, pp. 28–39.

Barrett, Stanley R. (1996) *Anthropology: A Student's Guide*. Toronto: University of Toronto Press.

Bolgar, Hedda (1965) 'The case study method', in B.B. Wolman (ed.), *Handbook of Clinical Psychology*. New York: McGraw Hill, pp. 28–39.

Brim, John A. and Spain, David H. (1974) *Research Design in Anthropology*. New York: Irvington.

Burawoy, Michael (ed.) (2000) *Global Ethnography*. Berkeley: University of California Press.

Campbell, Donald T. (1957) 'Factors relevant to the validity of experiments in social settings', *Psychological Bulletin*, 54: 297–312.

Campbell, Donald T. (1975) '"Degrees of freedom" and the case study', *Comparative Political Studies*, 8: 178–193.

Campbell, Donald T. and Stanley, J.C. (1966) *Experimental and Quasi-experimental Designs for Research*. Chicago: Rand McNally.

Cook, T.D. and Campbell, Donald T. (1979) *Quasi-Experimentation*. Chicago: Rand McNally.

COSMOS (2005) 'About *Cosmos* Corporation'. Available at: http://www.cosmoscorp.com/ about.html.

Danziger, Kurt (1990) *Constructing the Subject: Historical Origins of Psychological Research*. Cambridge: Cambridge University Press.

Diesing, Paul (1972) *Patterns of Discovery in the Social Sciences*. London: Routledge and Kegan Paul.

Dukes, W.F. (1965) 'N = 1', *Psychological Bulletin*, 64: 74–9.

Ebbinghaus, Bernhard (2005) 'When less is more: Selection problems in large-N and small-N cross-national comparisons', *International Sociology*, 20: 133–152.

Eckstein, Harry (1975) 'Case study and theory in political science', in Fred I. Greenstein and Nelson Polsby (eds), *Handbook of Political Science*. New York: Addison-Wesley, pp. 79–137.

Eggan, Fred (1961) 'Ethnographic data in social anthropology in the United States', *Sociological Review*, 5: 19–26.

Erikson, E.H. (1959) *Young Man Luther*. London: Faber and Faber.

Erikson, Kai T. (1976) *Everything in Its Path: Destruction of community in the Buffalo Creek flood*. New York: Simon and Schuster.

Feagin, Joe R., Orum, Anthony M. and Sjoberg, Gideon (eds) (1991) *A Case for the Case Study*. Chapel Hill: University of North Carolina Press.

Flyvbjerg, Bent (2001) *Making Social Science Matter*. Cambridge: Cambridge University Press.

Frankenberg, R. (1966) *Communities in Britain*. Harmondsworth: Penguin.

Geddes, Barbara (1991) 'How the cases you choose affect the answers you get: Selection bias in comparative politics', *Political Analysis*, 2: 131–50.

Glaser, Barney G. and Strauss, Anselm L. (1967) *The Discovery of Grounded Theory*. Chicago: Aldine.

Gluckman, Max (1961) 'Ethnographic data in British social anthropology', *Sociological Review*, 5–17.

Gluckman, Max (ed.) (1964) *Closed Systems and Open Minds*. Edinburgh: Oliver and Boyd.

Goldthorpe, John H. (2000) *On Sociology*. Oxford: Oxford University Press.

Gomm, Roger, Hammersley, Martyn and Foster, Peter (2000) *Case Study Method*. London: Sage.

Gruber, Howard (1974) 'A psychological study of scientific creativity', in H.E. Gruber and P.H. Barrett, *Darwin on Man*, New York: Dutton, pp. 1–243.

Hamel, Jacques (ed.) (1992) 'The case method in sociology', *Current Sociology*, 40:1.

Hamel, Jacques, Dufour, Stephane and Fortin, Dominic (1993) *Case Study Methods*. Thousand Oaks, CA: Sage.

Hammersley, Martyn (1992) 'So, what are case studies?', in Martyn Hammersley, *What's Wrong with Ethnography*. London: Routledge, pp. 183–200.

Harper, Douglas (1992) 'Small N's and community case studies', in Charles C. Ragin and Howard S. Becker (eds) *What is a Case?*. Cambridge: Cambridge University Press, pp. 139–158.

Hoffmeyer-Zlotnik, Jürgen H.P. and Wolf, Christof (eds) (2003) *Advances in Cross-National Comparison: A European Working Book for Demographic and Socio-Economic Variables*. New York: Kluwer Academic/Plenum Publishers.

Holy, Ladislav (1987) 'Description, generalization and comparison: Two paradigms', in Ladislav Holy (ed.), *Comparative Anthropology*. Oxford: Blackwell, pp. 1–21.

Homans, George C. (1951) *The Human Group*. London: Routledge and Kegan Paul.

Katz, Elihu and Lazarsfeld, Paul F. (1955) *Personal Influence*. Glencoe, IL: Free Press.

Kazdin, A. E. (1982) *Single-Case Research Design*. New York: Oxford University Press.

Lamont, Michèle and Thévenot, Laurent (eds) (2000) *Rethinking Comparative Cultural Sociology*. Cambridge: Cambridge University Press.

Levine, Robert A. (1973) 'Research design in anthropological fieldwork', in Raoul Naroll and Ronald Cohen (eds), *A Handbook of Method in Cultural Anthropology*. New York: Columbia University Press, pp. 183–195.

Leys, Ruth (1991) 'Types of one: Adolf Meyer's life chart and the representation of individuality', *Representations*, 34: 1–28.

Lieberson, Stanley (1985) *Making It Count*. Berkeley: University of California Press

Lieberson, Stanley (1992) 'Small Ns and big conclusions: An examination of the reasoning used in comparative studies based on a small number of cases', in Charles C. Ragin and Howard S. Becker (eds) *What is a Case?* Cambridge: Cambridge University Press, pp. 105–118.

Lijphart, Arend (1971) 'Comparative politics and the comparative method', *American Political Science Review*, 65: 682–93.

Lynd, Robert S. and Lynd, Helen M. (1929) *Middletown*. New York: Harcourt Brace.

Marcus, George E. (1995) 'Ethnography in/of the world system: The emergence of multi-sited ethnography', *Annual Review of Anthropology*, 24: 95–117.

McLaughlin, Neil (1998) 'How to become a forgotten intellectual: Intellectual movements and the case of Erich Fromm', *Sociological Forum*, 13: 215–46.

Mitchell, J. Clyde (1983) 'Case and situation analysis', *Sociological Review*, 31: 187–211.

Mochmann, Ekkehard (2002) *International Social Science Data Service*. Cologne: International Social Science Council

Noblit, George W. and Hare, R. Dwight (1988) *Meta-Ethnography: Synthesizing Qualitaitve Studies*. Newbury Park, CA: Sage.

Oakley, Ann (2000) *Experiments in Knowing: Gender and Method in the Social Sciences*. Cambridge: Polity.

Pelto, Pertti J. and Pelto, Gretel H. (1978) *Anthropological Research: The Structure of Inquiry*. Cambridge: Cambridge University Press.

Platt, Jennifer (1996) *A History of Sociological Research Methods in America, 1920–1960*. Cambridge: Cambridge University Press.

Platt, Jennifer (1988) 'What can case studies do?', in R. Burgess (ed.), *Studies in Qualitative Methodology*, vol. 1. London: JAI Press, pp. 1–24.

Price, John A. (1972) 'Holism through team ethnography', *Human Relations*, 26: 155–70.

Przeworski, A. and Teune, H. (1970) *The Logic of Comparative Social Inquiry*. New York: Wiley.

Ragin, Charles C. (1987) *The Comparative Method*. Berkeley: University of California Press.

Ragin, Charles C. (2000) *Fuzzy-Set Social Science*. Chicago: University of Chicago Press.

Ragin, Charles C. and Becker, Howard S. (eds) (1992) *What is a Case?* Cambridge: Cambridge University Press.

Rosenblatt, Paul C. (1981) 'Ethnographic case studies', in Marilynn B. Brewer and Barry E. Collins (eds), *Scientific Inquiry and the Social Sciences*. San Francisco: Jossey-Bass, pp. 194–225.

Rueschemeyer, Dietrich (2003) 'Can one or a few cases yield theoretical gains?' in James Mahoney and Dietrich Rueschemeyer (eds), *Comparative Historical Analysis in the Social Sciences*. Cambridge: Cambridge University Press, pp. 305–36.

Scholz, Roland W. and Tietje, Olaf (2002) *Embedded Case Study Methods: Integrating Quantitative and Qualitative Knowledge*. Thousand Oaks, CA: Sage.

Shavit, Yossi, and Blossfeld, H.P. (eds) (1993) *Persistent Inequality*. Boulder, CO: Westview Press.

Shaw, Clifford R. (1930) *The Jack Roller*. Chicago: University of Chicago Press.

Simons, Helen ed. (1980) *Towards a Science of the Singular*. Norwich: University of East Anglia.

Skocpol, Theda and Somers, Margaret (1980) 'The uses of comparative history in macrosocial inquiry', *Comparative Studies in Society and History*, 22: 174–97.

Stake, Robert E. (1994) 'Case studies', in Norman K. Denzin and Yvonna S. Lincoln (eds), *Handbook of Qualitative Research*. Thousand Oaks, CA: Sage, pp. 236–47.

Stake, Robert E. (1995) *The Art of Case Study Research*. Thousand Oaks, CA: Sage.

Stoecker, Randy (1991) 'Evaluating and rethinking the case study' *Sociological Review*, 39: 88–112.

Strauss, Anselm L. and Glaser, B.G. ([1970] 1977) *Anguish: A Case History of a Dying Trajectory*. London: Martin Robertson.

Urry, John (2000) *Sociology Beyond Societies*. London: Routledge.

Vaughan, Diane (1992) 'Theory elaboration: The heuristics of case analysis', in Charles C. Ragin and Howard S. Becker (eds), *What is a Case?* Cambridge: Cambridge University Press, pp. 173–202.

Vaughan, Diane (1996) *The Challenger Launch Decision*. Chicago: University of Chicago Press.

Warner, W. Lloyd and Lunt, Paul S. (1941) *The Social Life of a Modern Community*. New Haven: Yale University Press.

Whyte, William F. (1943) *Street Corner Society*. Chicago: University of Chicago Press.

Williams, Christine L. (1991) 'Case studies and the sociology of gender', in Joe R. Feagin, Anthony M. Orum and Gideon Sjoberg (eds), *A Case for the Case Study*. Chapel Hill: University of North Carolina Press, pp. 224–43.

Yin, Robert K. ([1984] 2003a) *Case Study Research: Design and Methods*. Thousand Oaks, CA: Sage.

Yin, Robert K. ([1993] 2003b) *Applications of Case Study Research*. Thousand Oaks, CA: Sage.

Yin, Robert K. (ed.) (2004) *The Case Study Anthology*. Thousand Oaks, CA: Sage

NOTES

1 But although this study was based wholly in Decatur, the town was chosen by a relatively elaborate—if nowadays unconvincing—procedure designed to identify one which could be regarded as representative.

2 For more detailed historical material on these issues, see Platt, 1996.

3. A less well-known way of moving away from that model, though with something in common, is offered by philosopher Diesing (1972: 158–63), who suggests that case studies use a different—'pattern'—model of explanation, in which the whole explains the parts, but no statement in the explanation needs to be generalized. Parts and whole are on the same level of generality, and any covering laws which could be stated would not explain the particular outcome but only specify the probability of alternative outcomes. A holistic model is developed which incorporates a network of propositions supported by evidence such that, even if it is weaker for some, 'the larger and more complex the pattern, the more difficult it is to imagine an alternative, and the time comes when no plausible alternative is imaginable' (Diesing, 1972: 58).

4 Rueschemeyer (2003), writing from within the comparative-historical tradition, points out that a single case studied over a long period of historical development may also provide many observations which can perform the same function.

5 Stoecker is another author with a commitment to what he calls 'advocacy research' (in the field of community development), and this leads him both to argue that '…the best validity check… comes from our subjects themselves' (1991: 106) and to see as a key goal the production of results which will enable effective intervention in the processes studied. However, he addresses the problems of logic raised by critics of case studies in terms which they would recognize, and suggests ways in which procedure could be improved to meet them.

6 It is not clear why the type he describes should be called 'case study' (indeed, it looks more like a description of the circumstances under which that type of study is felt to be appropriate than a specification of its defining characteristics) or why historical instances should be allocated to a separate category. The typology does not seem clearly to serve *logical* purposes, nor do the examples he uses of completed studies by others strictly follow his definition.

7 However, it may be noted that the same book offers as one of the possible rationales for choice of a single case that it is representative or typical (Yin, 2003a: 41), and that Yin (2004) chooses as two of its examples *Middletown* (Lynd and Lynd, 1929) and the Yankee City of *The Social Life of a Modern Community* (Warner and Lunt, 1941) where the towns studied were selected as 'average', even if with dubious plausibility.

8 Scholz and Tietje (2002), whose disciplinary setting is environmental science in Switzerland, start from Yin's work to develop an elaborate strategy for dealing with 'embedded' case studies for neuropsychology, education, business, law and environmental science. Their backgrounds in psychology and mathematics, coming together in interests in game theory and systems analysis, combined with ongoing concern with natural-science material relevant to environmental issues, make their approach rather different from that of most of the other authors in the field: they are serious users of sophisticated quantitative data, and their case studies find a place within that framework.

9 But Ruth Leys (1991) has shown how Adolf Meyer, who was very influential in the professionalization of American psychiatry, in his practice developed a visual tool, the 'life chart', which standardized the format of case histories, and summarized the individual's experience in such a way that its deviations from the normal could be seen.

10 Some of her examples, though, went well beyond this, treating arbitrarily chosen subjects as representative in ways which could only be justified on the assumption of the uniformity of nature.

11 However, Dukes (1965) found 246 N=1 studies in major psychological journals for 1939–63, of which about 70 percent were interested in generalizing rather than oriented to the particular individual as such. Among the justifications given, in addition to those where the author had more cases but had chosen to report only one example in depth, were that uniformity of the population could be assumed, that the case refuted a generalization (and so uniformity could not be assumed?), and that only one case was available or that it would be extremely difficult to obtain more, as with the home rearing of a chimpanzee.

12 Eggan (1961: 22), responding to Gluckman's paper in the light of developments in US anthropology, makes the very interesting point that US anthropologists have studied larger-scale societies than the British, and that these inevitably raise the issues of sampling and of the extent to which a random sample permits the rapport necessary for intensive study

13 Gluckman also had lead responsibility in developing an interesting discussion of how appropriately to draw boundaries, whether of discipline or of subject, around research topics to make the task manageable (Gluckman, 1964). Although this is not particularly focused on case studies, its relevance to the issue of bounding the case is evident.

14 Somewhat analogous is the 'barium meal' (Platt, 1988), where a case's trajectory in interaction with its setting is used to show the way in which a system operates in practice.

15 In addition to these possibilities, Yin (2003a: 47–50) suggests a 'multiple-case design'. However, it is not clear that this should be regarded as one design rather than a research programme, because what it consists of is replications, of either identical or purposefully varied conditions, in order to evaluate the propositions derived from the first case studied.

16 But there are some topics, such as elections and party systems, where data are easily available on a relatively large number of cases, and the wide diffusion of survey technique has opened up other topic areas, including attitudes. The creation of data archives has very much facilitated research in these areas, and in some fields there has been active cooperation among survey researchers to provide more closely comparable material (Mochmann, 2002). An archive logically similar to those with survey data is the Human Relations Area Files at Yale, which brings together a worldwide collection of the findings of anthropological studies more commonly treated as individual case studies, each coded on a number of standardized dimensions so that data is immediately available on a large number of examples. Valuable work has been done using these resources, which could be seen as collections of case studies, but work using them is normally classified as comparative rather than as itself being case-study research. Noblit and Hare (1988), whose field is education, propose a technique for synthesizing qualitative studies that they call 'meta-ethnography', in which multiple qualitative studies are translated into each others' terms. They start from a strong commitment to interpretive work and a hostility to 'positivism', which means that they have no interest in hypothetico-deductive uses of the material. They see this procedure as leading to a synthesis of understandings rather than of data,

and their orientation to practitioners means that they emphasize the need for audience-appropriate versions which enable the audience to compare their own perspectives with those of the studies and their synthesis, so that there is not one correct outcome.

17 Abbott (2001: 91–120) offers a detailed account of the complex divisions among historians and sociologists as they met at the borders of their disciplines in this area.

18 Rueschemeyer (2003) turns the argument against using a small number of cases the other way round, by suggesting that where only a small number of cases is available the historical-comparativist style can deal with them more effectively than variable-based quantitative approaches.

19 Geddes (1991) adds to the points about the *number* of cases a critique of the common practice in comparative politics of selecting the cases to be studied for the presence of the outcome variable of interest, and elaborates the biases that this can cause.

20 Note the similarity of idea to Skocpol and Somers' (1980) 'contrast-oriented comparative history', and the 'diversity-oriented research strategies' which Ragin (2000: 5) proposes to complement the assumptions of the dominant style of quantitative analysis.

21 Straddling the border between presentational and design uses is the 'embedded' case study design (Yin, 2003a: 42–3), where, within a larger sample, selected cases, typical or deviant, are studied more intensively to enhance insight and keep theorizing close to operational detail.

22 It has sometimes been suggested that a representative case would be the ideal, though that implies a population drawn sufficiently narrowly for such to exist; but how does one know that it is representative without studying others? Only if its representative character has already been established could it serve for deeper study of processes that can be assumed to operate more widely.

Quantification and Experiment

Introduction

Stephen P. Turner

Quantitative social research is sometimes descriptive, and is sometimes concerned with describing abstract structures (social networks, for example). Most of the time, however, it is concerned with cause—with questions about whether some intervention works, or whether some outcome would have occurred if some condition had been different. The data for doing this are abundant. Much of it is already collected for other purposes. More can be generated through experiments and surveys. When the results of social research appear in the press, causal claims are often made directly, or implied by the presentation of 'the facts'. As Ted Porter (1995) has pointed out, quantitative presentations have a special power—numbers seem more objective and therefore a better representation of reality. Yet, drawing causal conclusions from the quantitative data available to social researchers is fraught with difficulties. The chapters in this section examine these difficulties, show how some of them can be resolved, and explain the major areas of controversy.

The first two chapters here discuss the problems of causal models or structural equation models: the standard and best-developed methods for representing causal relationships in the social sciences. These models are designed to work where controlled experiments are not possible or are difficult to generalize from. These models work from regressions and correlations—relations that can be represented, in the case of two variables, as data points (or coordinates) on a plane. A regression line is a summary of the data: the line that best fits or is the closest to the data points taken as a whole. The correlation represents the degree to which the data spreads around the line, and indicates how good an approximation the regression line is. Multiple regression 'corrects' for the influence of other variables. The reasoning is simple, but deceptively so: we can calculate associations and use our knowledge of the values—such as 'age at menarche'—with respect to one kind of fact to predict the values of some other kind of fact—such as 'probability of completing 12 years of schooling'. But understanding such relationships in terms of cause is another matter.

Getting information about cause from these kinds of representations requires, as David Freedman points out in his chapter, a lot of additional information—information that we normally do not have, such as information about the relation of these variables to other variables which might be correlated with, and cause variations in, each of these variables. So we must assume a number of things. 'Assume' is, however, a deceptive term here. The assumptions are not, as we may remember this mathematical language from geometry, merely definitions or rules for deriving results. They are factual, typically cannot be known directly, and are in some cases quite esoteric and odd kinds of facts about the distributions of values in multi-dimensional space. What is or is not reasonable to believe about these facts is often far from clear. And since we must often choose which of these facts to take for granted, there is a degree of arbitrariness. Worse, the ordinary user of these methods is normally unaware of these 'assumptions'. Indeed, they are better understood as hidden implications of choices that the user of a technique is unaware of having made through the simple fact of the use of the technique itself.

The basic 'assumption' is that the choice of variables represents the actual causal processes. This may seem odd. Isn't this what the analysis is supposed to prove? Indeed it is. But the statistical procedures can come up with valid results only when the basic picture of the relevant causal processes is itself more or less correct in the first place. Things can go wrong when there are other variables, confounders, which are correlated with both the cause and the outcome and influence both. So the analyst needs to know a lot in advance about how the variables might relate to one another. One solution to this problem is to make these into factual questions, rather than matters of assumption, by including the questionable variable in the model. But in doing this one makes a new assumption that the way by which it is included represents the actual causal process, and this can also go wrong, and in several ways. Each addition to the model raises new questions. Could the influences go both ways? Are there other influences that have not been included? And these are the simple questions.

Among the more difficult questions is the one of whether, when we find a relationship between variables it was produced by the causal variables or was there already, a feature of the distribution of values in the population we are studying. Is the length of one's ear a cause of intelligence? Probably not! But one can imagine reasons why there might be a population in which long-eared people were more intelligent (e.g., as a compensatory virtue in sexual selection). We would not make the mistake of thinking that the fact that long-earedness predicts intelligence means that it *causes* intelligence. But we might very well make the same kind of mistake if we found a correlation that wasn't obviously non-causal. And even results that confirm a relation that we reasonably expected to be causal might in fact be a result of the pre-existing distribution of the properties in the population.

David Freedman's chapter deals with this group of problems, which, as we shall see, forms a template for understanding the problems of quantitative social research generally. Even such apparently different issues as missing data, drop-outs from studies, self-selection for participation in social interventions, citizens who cannot be found by census enumerators, and missing historical documents, turn out to pose similar issues. Moreover, as we shall see, parallel problems arise in experiments, with the same lesson: unless the causal processes are already accurately understood, we are prone to being misled by 'results' that are as much the product of our representations of the phenomenon as they are the result of the causal facts themselves.

Leslie Hayduk and Hannah Pazderka-Robinson consider three areas of current contestation within structural equation models that involve the problem of testing causal models. The controversies they consider come directly from discussions on the structural equation listserv, SEMNET. The first involves the crucial question of how to test models. In their introduction, they dismiss the problem of whether models represent real processes. More than one model is ordinarily consistent with the data. They suggest that one ask what facts about the world, as represented in quantitative data, are inescapably demanded by the equations that make up the model. The 'detection of model failure' often involves treating what are usually thought of as 'assumptions' as facts that can be checked, if only indirectly, by identifying empirical results—values—that indicate that the assumptions are wrong. This approach contrasts with a more liberal view of models that is based on the idea that all models have problems with fit. The defenders of this view reason that other considerations, such as simplicity, need to decide between various models, or that there is no point to refining models, especially in complex ways, to obtain modest increases in fit.

The second issue concerns using factor analysis to locate latent variables—i.e., variables that are not part of the model but influence the relationships in the model, and using the models themselves as detectors of these influences. The third issue involves selecting indicators. Should we throw lots of indicators into a model and let the data sort out which are most important? Or should we select a few good ones, relevant to our best theory, and stringently apply them with an eye to detecting the influence of latent variables? This turns on the same attitudinal question about fit: if your goal is to eliminate bad models, you will opt for fewer indicators; if you think that all models fit more or less badly, you will let the data show what many different indicators predict.

Is the alternative of experimental research the solution to these problems? To be sure, many of the problems do relate to the fact that the interpretation of correlations as evidence of cause depends on abstracting from complex situations whose pre-existing features are not known. Inventing a setting in which the features are determined by the researcher avoids this problem. But, as Sandra Schneider shows in her chapter on experiments, the same issue—of the quality of our understanding of the causal processes in question—arises in a different but related form. Experiments can show that a given

cause has a given effect. Applying this knowledge in the complex real world requires something more: an understanding of the casual mechanisms and how they relate to the other causes which will interfere with them or affect them. We may be able to find evidence that an intervention 'works', for example. But it may work because the mechanisms we think are operating are being substituted, with similar results, by other mechanisms. If so, not only will our casual analysis be wrong, it will not generalize to those situations in which the substitute mechanisms do not operate.

One solution to this problem of knowledge of causal processes is the use of other methods, such as qualitative methods. But there is a more general problem: experiments are themselves attempts to model recurrent casual situations, and implicity adopt ideas about what the relevant features of situations are and about what features are irrelevant, and what is 'general'. If behavior is largely a matter of adaptation to actual complex situations of experience and belief, the very fact that experiments are designed to radically reduce this complexity means that generalizing becomes problematic. The practical implications of this point for experiments themselves turn out to be significant. Seemingly minor differences in wording or the presentation of alternatives can produce drastically different results. There are many studies now which have enabled us to identify how the subjects of experiments may vary their responses in the face of different presentations of alternatives, for example, and these underscore the artificiality of the experimental setting itself.

The core problems with experiment, however, as with observational studies such as surveys, are the result of the complexity of the causal world. The primary value of experiment is that subjects can be randomly assigned to treatments, thus eliminating confounders without the need for additional theory. But the confounders come back the moment the results are generalized beyond the experimental setting itself. In some settings, such as epidemiology, we can use our knowledge of the relevant mechanisms to generalize with confidence. But the constructs we use to describe social and psychological causes (such as attitude, for example) tend to over-lap and correlate with one another, producing the same kind of problems that the correlational researcher has.

Murray Webster and Jane Sell discuss the use of experiment as part of the process of theory-building. They point out the advantages of experiment, such as the random assignment of subjects to treatment to minimize such problems as selection bias. But they emphasize the question of why researchers prefer or reject the experimenters' worldview, such as the focus on repeatable events. Webster and Sell contrast this attitude not only to those represented in other sections of this volume—such as postmodernism and social constructionism—but also to the kind of statistical study represented in this section, where the characteristics of actual populations are the main concern. They then explain how theories of a certain well-specified kind can produce predictions that can be meaningfully tested by experiments designed specifically to fit the scope conditions of the theory. This would be a case in which the causal processes are well understood. They illustrate this situation with work from a particularly well-developed tradition in the study of status information processing.

One of the most pervasive practical problems in social research is missing data. This is a problem, as David Howell points out in his chapter, both for experimenters and survey researchers, and, as Margo Anderson notes in her chapter, for historians. Howell distinguishes data missing at random and data not missing at random. The data not missing at random problem turns out to have a lot to do with issues of causality discussed by Thad Dunning and David Freedman in their chapter on selection bias. For data whose 'missingness' is random, however, there are a variety of technical solutions, useful for such common situations as those in which a number of participants drop out of a

study. Freedman and Dunning discuss a phenomenon called 'selection bias' that is central to understanding the commonplace situations in which results are treated as though individuals were randomly assigned to a treatment or randomly dropped out of the study, but where the relationships were in fact not random. If a study is done of the effectiveness of, for example, job training, and we ignore the fact that many people drop out of this 'treatment', we may wrongly attribute the success of those who stick it out to the training, rather than to such things as the character or desire of the participants. Those are properties that lead them to stay in the training, but they are also properties that would, in time, have led them to get jobs in the first place. Conclusions about the effectiveness of training need to account for this selection bias.

A different problem of missing data involves the census. It is a well-known fact that some people do not get counted in the census. But who are those people? We cannot assume that they are missing at random. So what can we do to correct the census or, for that matter, any survey with non-responses that we cannot assume to be randomly distributed? David Freedman and Kenneth Wachter discuss the methods used by the US census to adjust the census and explain the decision made in the 1990s to reject these adjustments. The fundamental difficulty is an extension of the issues discussed in these other chapters. 'Adjusting' for differential undercounts on the basis of estimates that correct for biases discovered by recounts is subject to new problems if the sample used in the recount is less representative than the original census. If it is, the 'correction' (using a model based on a set of correlations) based on the sample will have the effect of distorting results for a whole range of variables associated with the variable being corrected for. So there is a high likelihood of adding error in the course of correcting for error.

Historical data, as Margo Anderson points out in her chapter, represents a perfect storm for quantitative analysis. Missing data problems are ubiquitous, and unmeasured variables are commonplace. As she says, historians are at the mercy of their subjects' penchants for preserving data—which is almost never preserved in the machine-readable form that other quantitative researchers take for granted. Turning past records into this kind of usable data set presents novel problems. Issues of sampling, especially of understanding what kinds of data might be missing, are particularly important, for reasons made clear in previous chapters. But new kinds of non-randomness, involving the non-random survival of records, add to these familiar problems.

REFERENCES

Porter, Theodore (1995) *Trust in Numbers: The Pursuit of Objectivity in Science and Public Life.* Princeton, NJ: Princeton University Press.

7

Statistical Models for Causation

David A. Freedman

INTRODUCTION

Regression models are often used to infer causation from association. For instance, Yule (1899) showed – or tried to show – that welfare was a cause of poverty. Path models and structural equation models are later refinements of the technique. Besides Yule, examples discussed here include Blau and Duncan (1967) on stratification and Gibson (1988) on the causes of McCarthyism. Strong assumptions are required to infer causation from association by modeling. The assumptions are of two kinds: (i) causal, and (ii) statistical.

These assumptions will be formulated explicitly, with the help of response schedules in hypothetical experiments. In particular, parameters and error distributions must be stable under intervention. That will be hard to demonstrate in observational settings. Statistical conditions (like independence) are also problematic, and latent variables create further complexities.

Inferring causation by regression analysis will be the primary topic. Graphical models will be considered briefly. The issues are not simple, so examining them from several perspectives may be helpful. The article ends with a review of the literature and a summary.

REGRESSION MODELS IN SOCIAL SCIENCE

Legendre (1805) and Gauss (1809) developed regression to fit data on orbits of astronomical objects. The relevant variables were known from Newtonian mechanics, and so were the functional forms of the equations connecting them. Measurement could be done with great precision, and much was known about the nature of errors in the measurements and in the equations. Furthermore, there was ample opportunity for comparing predictions to reality.

Welfare and Poverty

By the turn of the century, investigators were using regression on social science data where such conditions did not hold, even to a rough approximation. Yule (1899) was a pioneer in this regard. At the time, paupers in England were supported either inside grim Victorian institutions called 'poor-houses' or outside, according to decisions made by local authorities. Did policy choices affect the number of paupers? To study this question, Yule proposed a regression equation,

$$\Delta Paup = a + b \times \Delta Out + c \times \Delta Old$$
$$+ d \times \Delta Pop + error. \qquad (1)$$

In this equation,

Δ is percentage change over time,

Paup is the number of paupers

Out is the out-relief ratio N/D,

  N = number on welfare outside the poor-house,

  D = number inside,

Old is the population over 65,

Pop is the population.

Data are from the English Censuses of 1871, 1881, and 1891. There are two Δ's, one each for 1871–81 and 1881–91.

Relief policy was determined separately in each 'union', a small geographical area like a parish. At the time, there were about 600 unions, and Yule divides them into four kinds: rural, mixed, urban, metropolitan. There are $4 \times 2 = 8$ equations, one for each type of union and time period. Yule fits each equation to data by least squares. That is, he determines a, b, c, and d by minimizing the sum of squared errors:

$$\sum (\Delta Paup - a - b \times \Delta Out$$
$$- c \times \Delta Old - d \times \Delta Pop)^2.$$

The sum is taken over all unions of a given type in a given time period, which assumes, in essence, that coefficients are constant within each combination of geography and time.

For example, consider the metropolitan unions. Fitting the equation to the data for 1871–81, Yule gets

$$\Delta Paup = 13.19 + 0.755\Delta Out$$
$$- 0.022\Delta Old - 0.322\Delta Pop + error. (2)$$

For 1881–91, his equation is

$$\Delta Paup = 1.36 + 0.324\Delta Out$$
$$+ 1.37\Delta Old - 0.369\Delta Pop + error. (3)$$

The coefficient of ΔOut being relatively large and positive, Yule concludes that outrelief causes poverty. Table 7.1 has the ratio of 1881 data to 1871 data for Pauperism, Out-relief ratio, Proportion of Old, and Population. If we subtract 100 from each entry, column 1 gives $\Delta Paup$ in equation (2). Columns 2, 3, and 4 give the other variables. For Kensington (the first union in the table),

$$\Delta Out = 5 - 100 = -95,$$
$$\Delta Old = 104 - 100 = 4,$$
$$\Delta Pop = 136 - 100 = 36.$$

The predicted value for $\Delta Paup$ from (2) is therefore

$$13.19 + 0.755 \times (-95) - 0.022 \times 4$$
$$- 0.322 \times 36 = -70.$$

The actual value for $\Delta Paup$ is –73, so the error is –3. Other lines in the table are handled in a similar way. As noted above, coefficients were chosen to minimize the sum of the squared errors.

Quetelet (1835) wanted to uncover 'social physics'—the laws of human behavior—by using statistical technique:

In giving my work the title of Social Physics, I have had no other aim than to collect, in a uniform order, the phenomena affecting man, nearly as physical science brings together the phenomena appertaining to the material world … in a given state of society, resting under the influence of certain causes, regular effects are produced, which oscillate, as it were, around a fixed mean point, without undergoing any sensible alterations …

This study … has too many attractions—it is connected on too many sides with every branch of science, and all the most interesting questions in philosophy—to be long without zealous observers, who will endeavor to carry it further and further, and bring it more and more to the appearance of a science.

Table 7.1 Pauperism, Out-relief ratio, Proportion of Old, Population. Ratio of 1881 data to 1871 data, times 100. Metropolitan Unions, England.

	Paup	Out	Old	Pop
Kensington	27	5	104	136
Paddington	47	12	115	111
Fulham	31	21	85	174
Chelsea	64	21	81	124
St. George's	46	18	113	96
Westminster	52	27	105	91
Marylebone	81	36	100	97
St. John, Hampstead	61	39	103	141
St. Pancras	61	35	101	107
Islington	59	35	101	132
Hackney	33	22	91	150
St. Giles'	76	30	103	85
Strand	64	27	97	81
Holborn	79	33	95	93
City	79	64	113	68
Shoreditch	52	21	108	100
Bethnal Green	46	19	102	106
Whitechapel	35	6	93	93
St. George's East	37	6	98	98
Stepney	34	10	87	101
Mile End	43	15	102	113
Poplar	37	20	102	135
St. Saviour's	52	22	100	111
St. Olave's	57	32	102	110
Lambeth	57	38	99	122
Wandsworth	23	18	91	168
Camberwell	30	14	83	168
Greenwich	55	37	94	131
Lewisham	41	24	100	142
Woolwich	76	20	119	110
Croydon	38	29	101	142
West Ham	38	49	86	203

Source: Yule (1899, Table XIX).

Yule is using regression to infer the social physics of poverty. But this is not so easily to be done. Confounding is one issue. According to Pigou (a leading welfare economist of Yule's era), parishes with more efficient administrations were building poorhouses and reducing poverty. Efficiency of administration is then a confounder, influencing both the presumed cause and its effect. Economics may be another confounder. Yule occasionally tries to control for this, using the rate of population change as a proxy for economic growth. Generally, however, he pays little attention to economics. The explanation: 'A good deal of time and labor was spent in making trial of this idea, but the results proved unsatisfactory, and finally the measure was abandoned altogether' (Yule, 1899: 253).

The form of Yule's equation is somewhat arbitrary, and the coefficients are not consistent over time and space. This is not necessarily fatal. However, unless the coefficients have some existence apart from the data, how can they predict the results of interventions that would change the data? The distinction between parameters and estimates runs throughout statistical theory; the discussion of response schedules (later in this paper) may sharpen the point.

There are other interpretive problems. At best, Yule has established association. Conditional on the covariates, there is a positive association between ΔPaup and ΔOut. Is this association causal? If so, which way do the causal arrows point? For instance, a parish may choose not to build poor-houses in response to a short-term increase in the number of paupers. Then pauperism is the cause and out-relief the effect. Likewise, the number of paupers in one area may well be affected by relief policy in neighboring areas. Such issues are not resolved by the data analysis. Instead, answers are assumed *a priori*. Although he was busily parceling out changes in pauperism—so much is due to changes in out-relief ratios, so much due to changes in other variables, so much due to random effects—Yule was aware of the difficulties. With one deft footnote (Yule, 1899 n. 25), he withdrew all causal claims: 'Strictly speaking, for "due to" read "associated with"'.

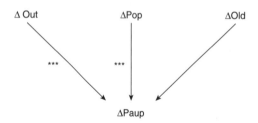

Figure 7.1   Yule's Model. Metropolitan Unions, 1871–81.

Yule's approach is strikingly modern, except that there is no causal diagram with stars indicating statistical significance. Figure 7.1 brings him up to date. The arrow from ΔOut to ΔPaup indicates that ΔOut is included in the regression equation that explains ΔPaup. Three asterisks mark a high degree of statistical significance. The idea is that a statistically significant coefficient must differ from zero. Thus, ΔOut has a causal influence on ΔPaup. By contrast, a

coefficient that lacks statistical significance is thought to be zero. If so, ΔOld would not exert a causal influence on ΔPaup.

The reasoning is seldom made explicit, and difficulties are frequently overlooked. Statistical assumptions are needed to determine significance from the data. Even if significance can be determined and the null hypothesis rejected or accepted, there is a deeper problem. To make causal inferences, it must be assumed that equations are stable under proposed interventions. Verifying such assumptions—without making the interventions—is problematic. On the other hand, if the coefficients and error terms change when variables are manipulated, the equation has only a limited utility for predicting the results of interventions.

Social Stratification

Blau and Duncan (1967) consider the stratification process in the US. According to Marxists of the time, the United States was a highly stratified society. Status was determined by family background, and transmitted through the school system. Blau and Duncan (1967: Chapter 2) present cross-tabulations to show that the system is far from deterministic, although family background variables do influence status. The United States has a permeable social structure, with many opportunities to succeed or fail. Blau and Duncan go on to develop the path model shown in Figure 7.2, in order to answer questions like these: 'How and to what degree do the circumstances of birth condition subsequent status? How does status attained (whether by ascription or achievement) at one stage of the life cycle affect the prospects for a subsequent stage?'

The five variables in the diagram are father's education, father's occupation, son's education, son's first job, and son's occupation. Data come from a special supplement to the March 1962 Current Population Survey. The respondents are the sons (age 20–64), who answer questions about current jobs, first jobs, and parents. There are

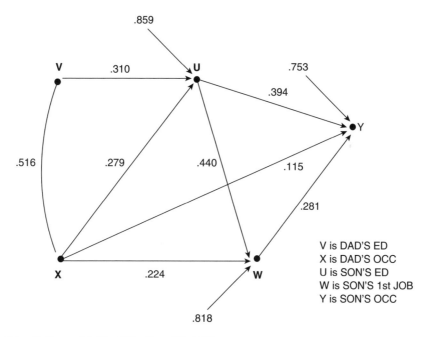

.859

V   .310   U   .753

.394

.516   .279   .440   .115

.281

X   .224   W

V is DAD'S ED
X is DAD'S OCC
U is SON'S ED
W is SON'S 1st JOB
Y is SON'S OCC

.818

Figure 7.2   Path model. Stratification, US, 1962.

Table 7.2. Correlation matrix for variables in Blau and Duncan's path model.

		Y Son's occ	W Son's 1st job	U Son's ed	X Dad's occ	V Dad's ed
Y	Son's occ	1.000	.541	.596	.405	.322
W	Son's 1st job	.541	1.000	.538	.417	.332
U	Son's ed	.596	.538	1.000	.438	.453
X	Dad's occ	.405	.417	.438	1.000	.516
V	Dad's ed	.322	.332	.453	.516	1.000

20,000 respondents. Education is measured on a scale from 0 to 8, where 0 means no schooling, 1 means 1–4 years of schooling, and so on; 8 means some post-graduate education. Occupation is measured on Duncan's prestige scale from 0 to 96. The scale takes into account income, education, and raters' opinions of job prestige. Hucksters are at the bottom of the ladder, with clergy in the middle, and judges at the top.

How is Figure 7.2 to be read? The diagram unpacks to three regression equations:

$$U = aV + bX + \delta, \qquad (4)$$
$$W = cU + dX + \epsilon, \qquad (5)$$
$$Y = eU + fX + gW + \eta. \qquad (6)$$

Parameters are estimated by least squares. Before regressions are run, variables are standardized to have mean 0 and variance 1. That is why no intercepts are needed, and why estimates can be computed from the correlations in Table 7.2.

In Figure 7.2, the arrow from V to U indicates a causal link, and V is entered on the right-hand side in the regression equation (4) that explains U. The path coefficient .310 next to the arrow is the estimated coefficient $\hat{a}$ of V. The number .859 on the 'free arrow' that points into U is the estimated standard deviation of the error term δ in (4). The other arrows are interpreted in a similar way. The curved line joining V and X indicates association rather than causation: V and X influence each other or are influenced by some common causes, not further analyzed in the diagram. The number on the curved line is just the correlation between V and X (see Table 7.2). There are three equations because three variables in the diagram (U, W, and Y) have arrows pointing into them.

The large standard deviations in Figure 7.2 show the permeability of the social structure. (Since variables are standardized, it is a little theorem that the standard deviations cannot exceed 1.) Even if father's education and occupation are given, as well as respondent's education and first job, the variation in status of current job is still large. As social physics, however, the diagram leaves something to be desired. Why linearity? Why are the coefficients the same for everybody? What about variables like intelligence or motivation? And where are the mothers?

The choice of variables and arrows is up to the analyst, as are the directions in which the arrows point. Of course, some choices may fit the data less well, and some may be illogical. If the graph is 'complete'—every pair of nodes joined by an arrow—the direction of the arrows is not constrained by the data (Freedman, 1997: 138, 142). Ordering the variables in time may reduce the number of options.

If we are trying to find laws of nature that are stable under intervention, standardizing may be a bad idea, because estimated parameters would depend on irrelevant details of the study design (see below). Generally, the intervention idea gets muddier with standardization. Are means and standard deviations held constant even though individual values are manipulated? On the other hand, standardizing might be sensible if units are meaningful only in comparative terms (e.g., prestige points). Standardizing may also be helpful if the meaning of units changes over time (e.g., years of education) while correlations are stable. With descriptive statistics for one data set, it is really a matter of taste: do you like pounds, kilograms, or standard units?

Moreover, all variables are on the same scale after standardization, which makes it easier to compare regression coefficients.

Hooke's Law

According to Hooke's law, stretch is proportional to weight. If weight x is hung on a spring, the length of the spring is $a + bx + \epsilon$, provided x is not too large. (Near the elastic limit of the spring, the physics will be more complicated.) In this equation, a and b are physical constants that depend on the spring not the weights. The parameter a is the length of the spring with no load. The parameter b is the length added to the spring by each additional unit of weight. The ϵ is random measurement error, with the usual assumptions. Experimental verification is a classroom staple.

If we were to standardize, the crucial slope parameter would depend on the weights and the accuracy of the measurements. Let v be the variance of the weights used in the experiment, let σ^2 be the variance of ϵ, and let s^2 be the mean square of the deviations from the fitted regression line. The standardized regression coefficient is

$$\sqrt{\frac{\hat{b}^2 v}{\hat{b}^2 v + s^2}} \approx \sqrt{\frac{b^2 v}{b^2 v + \sigma^2}}, \qquad (7)$$

as can be verified by examining the sample covariance matrix. Therefore, the standardized coefficient depends on v and σ^2, which are features of our measurement procedure, not the spring.

Hooke's law is an example where regression is a very useful tool. But the parameter to estimate is b, the unstandardized regression coefficient. It is the unstandardized coefficient that says how the spring will respond when the load is manipulated. If a regression coefficient is stable under interventions, standardizing it is probably not a good idea, because stability gets lost in the shuffle. That is what equation (7) shows. Also see Achen (1977) and Blalock (1989: 451).

Political Repression During the McCarthy Era

Gibson (1988) tries to determine the causes of McCarthyism in the United States. Was repression due to the masses or the elites? He argues that elite intolerance is the root cause, the chief piece of evidence being a path model (Figure 7.3, redrawn from the paper). The dependent variable is a measure of repressive legislation in each state. The independent variables are mean tolerance scores for each state, derived from the Stouffer (1955) survey of masses and elites. The 'masses' are just respondents in a probability sample of the population. 'Elites' include school board presidents, commanders of the American Legion, Bar Association presidents, and labor union leaders. Data on masses were available for 36 states; on elites for 26 states. The two straight arrows in Figure 7.3 represent causal links: mass and elite tolerance affect repression. The curved double-headed arrow in Figure 7.3 represents an association between mass and elite tolerance scores. Each can influence the other, or both can have some common cause. The association is not analyzed in the diagram.

Gibson computes correlations from the available data, then estimates a standardized regression equation,

$$\text{Repression} = \beta_1 \text{Mass tolerance} \\ + \beta_2 \text{Elite tolerance} + \delta$$

He says, 'Generally, it seems that elites, not masses, were responsible for the repression of the era … The beta for mass opinion is –.06; for elite opinion, it is –.35 (significant beyond .01).'

The paper asks an interesting question, and the data analysis has some charm too. However, as social physics, the path model is not convincing. What hypothetical intervention is contemplated? If none, how are regressions going to uncover causal relationships? Why are relationships among the variables supposed to be linear? Signs apart, for example, why does a unit increase in tolerance have the same effect

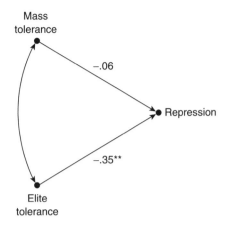

Figure 7.3   Path model. The causes of McCarthyism.

on repression as a unit decrease? Are there other variables in the system? Why are the states statistically independent? Such questions are not addressed in the paper.

McCarthy became a force in US national politics around 1950. The turning point came in 1954, with public humiliation in the Army–McCarthy hearings. Censure by the Senate followed in 1957. Gibson scores repressive legislation over the period 1945–65, long before McCarthy mattered, and long after. The Stouffer survey was done in 1954, when the McCarthy era was ending. The timetable is puzzling.

Even if such issues are set aside, and we grant the statistical model, the difference in path coefficients fails to achieve significance. Gibson finds that $\hat{\beta}_2$ is significant and $\hat{\beta}_1$ is insignificant, but that does not impose much of a constraint on $\hat{\beta}_1 - \hat{\beta}_2$ (The standard error for this difference can be computed from data generously provided in the paper.) Since $\beta_1 = \beta_2$ is a viable hypothesis, the data are not strong enough to distinguish masses from elites.

INFERRING CAUSATION BY REGRESSION

Path models are often thought to be rigorous statistical engines for inferring causation from association. Statistical techniques can be rigorous, given their assumptions. But the assumptions are usually imposed on the data by the analyst. This is not a rigorous process, and it is rarely made explicit. The assumptions have a causal component as well as a statistical component. It will be easier to proceed in terms of a specific example. In Figure 7.4, a hypothesized causal relationship between Y and Z is confounded by X. The free arrows leading into Y and Z are omitted.

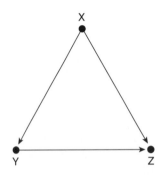

Figure 7.4 Path model. The relationship between Y and Z is confounded by X. Free arrows leading into Y and Z are not shown.

Figure 7.4 describes two hypothetical experiments and an observational study where the data are collected. The two experiments help to define the assumptions. Furthermore, the usual statistical analysis can be understood as an effort to determine what would happen under those assumptions *if* the experiments were done. Other interpretations of the analysis are not easily to be found. The experiments will now be described.

First hypothetical experiment

Treatment is applied to a subject, at level x. A response Y is observed, corresponding to the level of treatment. There are two parameters, a and b, that describe the response. With no treatment, the response level for each subject will be a, up to random error. All subjects are assumed to have the same value for a. Each additional unit of treatment adds b to the response. Again, b is the same for all subjects, at all levels of x, by assumption. Thus,

if treatment is applied at level x, the response Y is assumed to be

$$a + bx + \text{random error.} \qquad (8)$$

For Hooke's law, x is weight and Y is length of a spring under load x. For evaluation of job training programs, x might be hours spent in training and Y might be income during a follow-up period.

Second hypothetical experiment

In the second experiment, there are two treatments and a response variable Z. There are two treatments because there are two arrows leading into Z; the treatments are labeled X and Y (see Figure 7.4). Both treatments may be applied to a subject. There are three parameters, c, d and e. With no treatment, the response level for each subject is taken to be c, up to random error. Each additional unit of treatment #1 adds d to the response. Likewise, each additional unit of treatment #2 adds e to the response. The constancy of parameters across subjects and levels of treatment is an assumption. If the treatments are applied at levels x and y, the response Z is assumed to be

$$c + dx + ey + \text{random error.} \qquad (9)$$

Three parameters are needed because it takes three parameters to specify the linear relationship (9), namely, an intercept and two slopes. Random errors in (8) and (9) are assumed to be independent from subject to subject, with a distribution that is constant across subjects; expectations are zero and variances are finite. The errors in (9) are assumed to be independent of the errors in (8).

The observational study

When using the path model in Figure 7.4 to analyze data from an observational study, we assume that levels for the variable X are independent of the random errors in the two hypothetical experiments ('exogeneity'). In effect, we pretend that Nature randomized subjects to levels of X for us, which obviates the need for experimental manipulation. The exogeneity of X has a graphical representation: arrows come out of X, but no arrows lead into X.

We take the descriptions of the two experiments, including the assumptions about the response schedules and the random errors, as background information. In particular, we take it that Nature generates Y as if by substituting X into (8). Nature proceeds to generate Z as if by substituting X and Y (the same Y that has just been generated from X) into (9). In short, (8) and (9) are assumed to be the causal mechanisms that generate the observational data, namely, X, Y and Z for each subject. The system is 'recursive', in the sense that output from (8) is used as input to (9) but there is no feedback from (9) to (8).

Under these assumptions, the parameters a, b can be estimated by regression of Y on X. Likewise, c, d, e can be estimated by regression of Z on X and Y. Moreover, these regression estimates have legitimate causal interpretations. This is because causation is built into the background assumptions, via the response schedules (8) and (9). If causation were not assumed, causation would not be demonstrated by running the regressions.

One point of running the regressions is usually to separate out direct and indirect effects of X on Z. The direct effect is d in (9). If X is increased by one unit with Y held fast, then Z is expected to go up by d units. But this is shorthand for the assumed mechanism in the second experiment. Without the thought experiments described by (8) and (9), how can Y be held constant when X is manipulated? At a more basic level, how would manipulation get into the picture?

Another path-analytic objective is to determine the effect e of Y on Z. If Y is increased by one unit with X held fast, then Z is expected to go up by e units. (If $e = 0$, then manipulating Y would not affect Z, and Y does not cause Z after all.) Again, the interpretation depends on the thought experiments. Otherwise, how could Y be manipulated and X held fast?

To state the model more carefully, we would index the subjects by a subscript i in the range

from 1 to n, the number of subjects. In this notation, X_i is the value of X for subject i. Similarly, Y_i and Z_i are the values of Y and Z for subject i. The level of treatment #1 is denoted by x, and $Y_{i,x}$ is the response for variable Y if treatment at level x is applied to subject i. Similarly, $Z_{i,x,y}$ is the response for variable Z if treatment #1 at level x and treatment #2 at level y are applied to subject i. The response schedules are to be interpreted causally:

- $Y_{i,x}$ is what Y_i would be if X_i were set to x by intervention.
- $Z_{i,x,y}$ is what Z_i would be if X_i were set to x and Y_i were set to y by intervention.

Counterfactual statements are even licensed about the past: $Y_{i,x}$ is what Y_i would have been, if X_i had been set to x. Similar comments apply to $Z_{i,x,y}$.

The diagram unpacks into two equations, which are more precise versions of (8) and (9), with a subscript i for subjects. Greek letters are used for the random error terms.

$$Y_{i,x} = a + bx + \delta_i \tag{10}$$
$$Z_{i,x,y} = c + dx + ey + \epsilon_i \tag{11}$$

The parameters a, b, c, d, e and the error terms δ_i, ϵ_i are not observed. The parameters are assumed to be the same for all subjects.

Additional assumptions, which define the statistical component of the model, are imposed on the error terms:

(i) δ_i and ϵ_i are independent of each other within each subject i.
(ii) δ_i and ϵ_i are independent across subjects.
(iii) The distribution of δ_i is constant across subjects; so is the distribution of ϵ_i. (However, δ_i and ϵ_i need not have the same distribution.)
(iv) δ_i and ϵ_i have expectation zero and finite variance.
(v)   The δ's and ϵ's are independent of the X's.

The last is 'exogeneity'.

According to the model, Nature determines the response Y_i for subject i by substituting X_i into (10):

$$Y_i = Y_{i,X_i} = a + bX_i + \delta_i$$

Here, X_i is the value of X for subject i, chosen for us by Nature, as if by randomization. The rest of the response schedule—the $Y_{i,x}$ for other x—is not observed, and therefore stays in the realm of counterfactual hypotheticals. After all, even in an experiment, subject i would be assigned to one level of treatment, foreclosing the possibility of observing the response at other levels.

Similarly, we observe $Z_{i,x,y}$ only for $x = X_i$ and $y = Y_i$. The response for subject i is determined by Nature, as if by substituting X_i and Y_i into (11):

$$Z_i = Z_{i, X_i, Y_i} = c + dX_i + eY_i + \epsilon_i$$

The rest of the response schedule, $Z_{i,x,y}$ for other x and y, remains unobserved. Economists call the unobserved $Y_{i,x}$ and $Z_{i,x,y}$ 'potential outcomes'. The model specifies unobservable response schedules, not just regression equations. Notice too that a subject's responses are determined by levels of treatment for that subject only. Treatments applied to subject j are not relevant to subject i. The response schedules (10) and (11) represent the causal assumptions behind the path diagram.

The conditional expectation of Y given $X = x$ is the average of Y for subjects with $X = x$. The formalism connects two very different ideas of conditional expectation: (i) finding subjects with $X = x$, versus (ii) an intervention that sets X to x. The first is something you can actually do with observational data. The second would require manipulation. The model is a compact way of stating the assumptions that are needed to go from observational data to causal inferences.

In econometrics and cognate fields, 'structural' equations describe causal relationships. The model gives a clearer meaning to this idea, and to the idea of 'stability under intervention'. The parameters in Figure 7.4, for instance, are defined through the response schedules (8) and (9), separately from the data. These parameters are constant across subjects and levels of treatment (by assumption, of course). Parameters are the same in a

regime of passive observation and in a regime of active manipulation. Similar assumptions of stability are imposed on the error distributions. In summary, regression equations are structural, with parameters that are stable under intervention, when the equations derive from response schedules like (10) and (11).

Path models do not infer causation from association. Instead, path models *assume* causation through response schedules, and, using additional statistical assumptions, estimate causal effects from observational data. The statistical assumptions (independence, expectation zero, constant variance) justify estimation by ordinary least squares. With large samples, confidence intervals and significance tests would follow. With small samples, the errors would have to follow a normal distribution in order to justify t-tests.

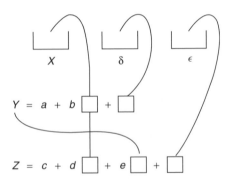

Figure 7.5   The path diagram as a box model

The box model in Figure 7.5 illustrates the statistical assumptions. Independent errors with constant distributions are represented as draws made at random with replacement from a box of potential errors (Freedman et al., 2007). Since the box remains the same from one draw to another, the probability distribution of one draw is the same as the distribution of any other. The distribution is constant. Furthermore, the outcome of one draw cannot affect the distribution of another, that is, they are independent. Verifying the causal assumptions (10) and (11), which are about potential outcomes, is a daunting task. The statistical assumptions present difficulties of their own. Assessing the degree to which the modeling assumptions hold is therefore problematic. The difficulties noted earlier—in Yule on poverty, Blau and Duncan on stratification, and Gibson on McCarthyism—are systemic.

Embedded in the formalism is the conditional distribution of Y, if we were to intervene and set the value of X. This conditional distribution is a counterfactual, at least when the study is observational. The conditional distribution answers the question of what would have happened if we had intervened and set X to x, rather than letting Nature take its course? The idea is best suited to experiments or hypothetical experiments.

There are also non-manipulationist ideas of causation: the moon causes the tides; earthquakes cause property values to go down; time heals all wounds. Time is not manipulable; neither are earthquakes and the moon. Investigators may hope that regression equations are like laws of motion in classical physics. (If position and momentum are given, you can determine the future of the system and discover what would happen with different initial conditions.) Some other formalism may be needed to make this non-manipulationist account more precise.

Latent Variables

There is yet another layer of complexity when the variables in the path model remain 'latent', i.e., unobserved. It is usually supposed that the manifest variables are related to the latent variables by a series of regression-like equations ('measurement models'). There are numerous assumptions about error terms, especially when likelihood techniques are used. In effect, latent variables are reconstructed by some version of factor analysis and the path model is fitted to the results. The scale of the latent variables is not usually identifiable, so variables are standardized to have mean 0 and variance 1. Some algorithms will infer the path diagram as well as the latents from the data, but there are

additional assumptions that come into play. Anderson (1984) provides a rigorous discussion of statistical inference for models with latent variables, given the requisite statistical assumptions. He does not address the connection between the models and the phenomena. Kline (1998) is a well-known text. Ullman and Bentler (2003) survey recent developments.

A possible conflict in terminology should be mentioned. In psychometrics and cognate fields, 'structural equation modeling' (typically, path modeling with latent variables) is sometimes used for causal inference and sometimes to get parsimonious descriptions of covariance matrices. For causal inference, questions of stability are central. If no causal inferences are made, stability under intervention is hardly relevant; nor are underlying equations 'structural' in the econometric sense described earlier. The statistical assumptions (independence, distributions of error terms constant across subjects, parametric models for error distributions) would remain on the table.

GRAPHICAL MODELS

Yule's equation (1) was linear: a unit increase in ΔOut is supposed to cause an increase of b units in ΔPaup, for any value of ΔOut and any values of the control variables ΔOld and ΔPop. Similarly, the Blau and Duncan equations (4), (5) and (6) were linear, as were equations (10) and (11). Linearity is a restrictive assumption. Graphical techniques have been suggested for relaxing this assumption and dealing with relationships that may be non-linear. Developments can only be sketched here.

In one set-up, the graph is known a priori, and the issue is to achieve control of unmeasured confounders. (Another set-up, where the graph is inferred from the data, will be considered below.) Figure 7.6 is an example used by Pearl (1995: 675–6; 2000: 81–3) to illustrate his methods. The graph is to be taken as given. The arrows are assumed by

Pearl to represent causation rather than mere association. The variables at the nodes are governed by a joint probability distribution. What features of this distribution can be read off the graph?

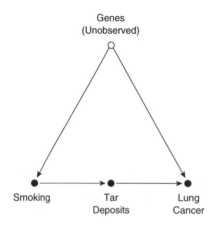

Genes
(Unobserved)

Smoking   Tar   Lung
               Deposits   Cancer

Figure 7.6   A graphical model for smoking and lung cancer. Genes are unobserved, confounding the relationship between smoking and lung cancer.

Notice that—by assumption—there is no arrow from genes to tar deposits, or from smoking to lung cancer. The first exclusion means that genes have no direct influence on tar deposits. In probabilistic terms, the implication is that

(Tar Deposits | Genes, Smoking)
$$= P(\text{Tar Deposits} \mid \text{Smoking})$$

The second exclusion—no arrow from smoking to lung cancer—means that smoking affects lung cancer risk only through the build-up of tar deposits, implying that

$P(\text{LC} \mid \text{Genes, Smoking, Tar Deposits})$
$$= P(\text{LC} \mid \text{Genes, Tar Deposits})$$

where LC stands for Lung cancer. The probabilistic conditions are said to make the graph 'Markovian'.

Another key point about the graph: genotype is unobserved, signaled by the open dot. The joint distribution of the observed variables—smoking, tar deposits and lung

cancer—is taken as given. However, the joint distribution of all four variables remains unknown, because genotype is unobserved.

Does smoking cause lung cancer? The relationship between smoking and lung cancer is confounded by an unobserved variable. But, given the assumptions behind Figure 7.6, the causal effect of smoking on lung cancer (averaged over the various possible genotypes in the population) can be determined from the data. This intriguing theorem is due to Robins (1986, 1987). It was rediscovered by Pearl (1995) as well as Spirtes et al. ([1993] 2000).

The implications for applied work are limited. To begin with, it is only by assumption that the arrows in Figure 7.6 represent causation. Moreover, there are three special assumptions:

(i)   Genes have no direct effect on tar deposits.
(ii) Smoking has no direct effect on lung cancer.
(iii) Smoking, tar deposits and lung cancer can be measured with good accuracy.

Pearl (2000: 83) acknowledges making these assumptions, but there is no support for them in the literature. (i) The lung has a mechanism—'the mucociliary escalator'— for eliminating foreign matter, including tar. This mechanism seems to be under genetic control. (Of course, clearance mechanisms can be overwhelmed by smoking.) The forbidden arrow from genes to tar deposits may have a more solid empirical basis than the permitted arrows from genes to smoking and lung cancer. Assumption (ii) is just that—an assumption. And (iii) is not plausible, especially for tar deposits in living subjects. If arrows are permitted from genes to tar deposits or from smoking to lung cancer, then the theory does not apply to Figure 7.6. If measurements are subject to large errors, the theory does not apply either. Other examples in Pearl (1995; 2000) are equally problematic. Graphical models cannot overcome the difficulties created by unmeasured confounders without introducing strong and artificial assumptions.

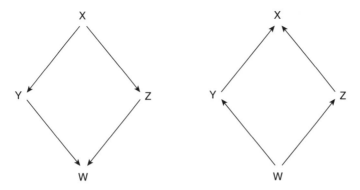

Figure 7.7   The faithfulness condition: No accidental independence

Figure 7.6 addresses a question with some intellectual history. Fisher's 'constitutional hypothesis' explained the association between smoking and disease on the basis of a gene that caused both. This idea is refuted not by making assumptions but by empirical work. For example, Kaprio and Koskenvuo (1989) present data from their twin study. The idea is to find pairs of identical twins where one smokes and one does not. That sets up a race: who will die first, the smoker or the non-smoker? The smokers win hands down, both for total mortality and death from heart disease. The genetic hypothesis is incompatible with these data. For lung cancer, the smokers win the two races that have been run. (Why only two? Smoking-discordant twin pairs are unusual, lung cancer is a rare disease, and the population of Scandinavia is small.)

Carmelli and Page (1996) have a similar analysis with a larger cohort of twins. Do not bet on Fisher. International Agency for Research on Cancer (1986: 179–98) reviews the health effects of smoking and indicates the difficulties in measuring tar deposits. Nakachi et al. (1993) and Shields et al. (1993) illustrate conflicts on the genetics of smoking and lung cancer. Also see Miller et al. (2003). Other examples in Pearl (1995, 2000) are equally unconvincing on substantive grounds. Finding the mathematical consequences of assumptions matters, but connecting assumptions to

reality matters even more. For additional detail, see Freedman (1997, 2004).

Inferring the Graph from the Data

Spirtes et al. ([1993] 2000) and Pearl (1988) have algorithms for inferring causal graphs from the data if the 'faithfulness' assumption is imposed. It will be easier to explain this idea by example. Let us assume that the graphs in Figure 7.7 are Markovian. In the left-hand panel, Y and Z will be independent given X; moreover, X and W will be independent given Y and Z. In the right hand panel, these independence relations will hold only for special values of the parameters governing the joint probability distribution of the variables X, Y, Z and W. The faithfulness condition precludes such 'accidents': the only independence relations that are permitted are independence relations that can be read off the graph. Given the faithfulness condition, there is some theory to determine which features of graphs can be recovered from the joint distributions of observables, and there are statistical algorithms to implement the theory.

Rather than exploring theoretical issues, it will be more helpful to consider applications. Spirtes et al. ([1993] 2000) (henceforth SGS) seem to give abundant examples to show the power of their algorithms. However, many of the examples turn out to

Table 7.3   Variables in the model.

ED	Respondent's education
	(Years of schooling completed at first marriage)
AGE	Respondent's age at first birth
DADSOCC	Respondent's father's occupation
RACE	Race of respondent (Black=1,other=0)
NOSIB	Respondent's number of siblings
FARM	Farm background
	(coded 1 if respondent grew up on a farm, else 0)
REGN	Region where respondent grew up (South=1, other=0)
ADOLF	Broken family
	(coded 0 if both parents present at age 14, else 1)
REL	Religion (Catholic = 1, other = 0)
YCIG	Smoking
	(coded 1 if respondent smoked before age 16, else coded 0)
FEC	Fecundability (coded 1 if respondent had a miscarriage before first birth;
	else coded 0)

be simulations, where the computer generates the data. Assumptions are satisfied by fiat, having been programmed into the computer; questions about the real world are finessed. Many other examples relate to the health effects of smoking. These causal diagrams are hypothetical too. No contact is made with data, and no substantive conclusions are drawn.

SGS do use their algorithms to analyze a number of real data sets, mainly from the social-science literature. What about those applications? Analyses were replicated for the most solid-looking cases (Freedman, 1997; Freedman and Humphreys, 1999). The examples all turned out to have the same texture; only one need be discussed here. Rindfuss et al. (1980) developed a model to explain the process by which a woman decides how much education to get, and when to have her first child. The variables in the model are defined in Table 7.3.

The statistical assumptions made by Rindfuss et al. (1980), let alone the conditions imposed by SGS, may seem rather implausible if examined at all closely. Here, we focus on results. According to SGS,

Given the prior information that ED and AGE are not causes of the other variables, the PC algorithm (using the .05 significance level for tests) directly finds the model [in the left-hand panel of Figure

7.8] where connections among the regressors are not pictured (Spirtes et al. [1993: 139] 2000: 103).

The main conclusion in Rindfuss et al. (1980) is that AGE does not influence ED. Apparently, the left-hand panel in Figure 7.8 confirms this finding, which allows SGS to claim a success for their algorithms. However, the graph in the left-hand panel is not the one actually produced by the algorithms. The unedited graph is shown in the right-hand panel. The unedited graph says, for instance, that race and religion cause region of residence. Other peculiarities need not detain us.

The SGS algorithms are successful only if one is very selective in reading the computer output. The difficulty seems to be that the algorithms depend on strong and artificial assumptions, which are unlikely to be satisfied in real applications. Graphical models are interesting, and may provide a natural mathematical language for discussing certain philosophical issues. But these models are unlikely to help applied workers in making valid causal inferences from observational data.

Directed Acyclic Graphs

The graphs in Figures 7.6, 7.7 and 7.8 are DAGs (Directed Acyclic Graphs)—directed

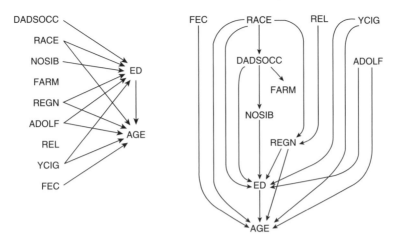

Figure 7.8   The left-hand panel shows the model reported by Spirtes et al. ([1993: 140] 2000: 104). The right-hand panel shows the whole graph produced by the SGS algorithms.

because each arrow points in a certain direction, acyclic because you cannot get from a node back to itself by following arrows. In particular, reciprocal causation is excluded by assumption. Interestingly, the SGS algorithms do sometimes produce graphs with cycles, showing that the algorithms are not internally consistent. For additional detail on DAGs and the SGS algorithms, see (Freedman, 1997, 2004; Freedman and Humphreys, 1996, 1999).

LITERATURE REVIEW

There is by now an extended critical literature on statistical models, starting perhaps with the exchange between Keynes (1939, 1940) and Tinbergen (1940). Other familiar citations in the economics literature include Liu (1960), Lucas (1976), and Sims (1980). Manski (1995) returns to the under-identification problem that was posed so sharply by Liu and Sims. In brief, a priori exclusion of variables from causal equations can seldom be justified, so there will typically be more parameters than data.

Manski (1995) suggests methods for bounding quantities that cannot be estimated. Sims' idea was to use simple, low-dimensional

models for policy analysis, instead of complex-high dimensional ones. Leamer (1978) discusses the issues created by specification searches, as does Hendry (1993). Heckman (2000) traces the development of econometric thought from Haavelmo and Frisch onwards, stressing the role of 'structural' or 'invariant' parameters, and 'potential outcomes'. Lucas too was concerned about parameters that changed under intervention. Engle et al. (1983) distinguish several kinds of exogeneity, with different implications for causal inference. Recently, some econometricians have turned to natural experiments for the evaluation of causal theories. These investigators stress the value of careful data collection and data analysis. Angrist and Krueger (2001) have a useful survey.

One of the drivers for modeling in economics and other fields is rational choice theory. Therefore, any discussion of empirical foundations must take into account a remarkable series of papers, initiated by Kahneman and Tversky (1974), that explores the limits of rational choice theory. These papers are collected in Kahneman et al. (1982), and in Kahneman and Tversky (2000). The heuristics and biases program has attracted its own critics (Gigerenzer, 1996). That critique is interesting and has some merit. But in the end, the experimental evidence demonstrates severe limits to the power of rational choice theory (Kahneman and Tversky, 1996). If people are trying to maximize expected utility, they generally do not do it very well. Errors are large and repetitive, go in predictable directions and fall into recognizable categories. Rather than making decisions by optimization—or bounded rationality, or satisficing—people seem to use plausible heuristics that can be identified. If so, rational choice theory is generally not a good basis for justifying empirical models of behavior. Drawing in part on the work of Kahneman and Tversky, Sen (2002) gives a far-reaching critique of rational choice theory. This theory has its place, but also leads to 'serious descriptive and predictive problems'.

Almost from the beginning, there were critiques of modeling in other social sciences too (Platt, 1996). Bernert (1983) reviews the historical development of causal ideas in sociology. Recently, modeling issues have been much canvassed in sociology. Abbott (1997) finds that variables like income and education are too abstract to have much explanatory power, with a broader examination of causal modeling in Abbott (1998). He finds that 'an unthinking causalism today pervades our journals'; he recommends more emphasis on descriptive work and on middle-range theories. Berk (2003) is skeptical about the possibility of inferring causation by modeling, absent a strong theoretical base. Clogg and Haritou (1997) review difficulties with regression, noting that you can too easily include endogenous variables as regressors.

Goldthorpe (1998, 2000, 2001) describes several ideas of causation and corresponding methods of statistical proof, with different strengths and weaknesses. Although skeptical of regression, he finds rational choice theory to be promising. He favors use of descriptive statistics to determine social regularities, and statistical models that reflect generative processes. In his view, the manipulationist account of causation is generally inadequate for the social sciences. Hedström and

Swedberg (1998) present a lively collection of essays by sociologists who are quite skeptical about regression models; rational choice theory also takes its share of criticism. There is an influential book by Lieberson (1985), with a follow-up by Lieberson and Lynn (2002). Ní Bhrolcháin (2001) has some particularly forceful examples to illustrate the limits of modeling. Sobel (1998) reviews the literature on social stratification, concluding that 'the usual modeling strategies are in need of serious change' (also see Sobel, 2000).

Meehl (1978) reports the views of an empirical psychologist. Also see Meehl (1954), with data showing the advantage of using regression to make predictions rather than experts. Meehl and Waller (2002) discuss the choice between two similar path models, viewed as reasonable approximations to some underlying causal structure, but do not reach the critical question – how to assess the adequacy of the approximation. Steiger (2001) has a critical review of structural equation models. Larzalere and Kuhn (2004) offer a more general discussion of difficulties in making causal inference by purely statistical methods. Abelson (1995) has an interesting viewpoint on the use of statistics in psychology.

There is a well-known book on the logic of causal inference by Cook and Campbell (1979). Also see Shadish et al. (2002), which has, among other things, a useful discussion of manipulationist vs. non-manipulationist ideas of causation. In political science, Duncan (1984) is far more skeptical about modeling than Blau and Duncan (1967). Achen (1982, 1986) provides a spirited and reasoned defense of the models. Brady and Collier (2004) compare regression methods with case studies; invariance is discussed under the rubric of causal homogeneity.

There is an extended literature on graphical models for causation. Greenland et al. (1999) give a clear account in the context of epidemiology. Lauritzen (1996, 2001) has a careful treatment of the mathematics. These authors do not recognize the difficulties in applying the methods to real problems. Strong claims are made for non-linear methods that elicit the model from the data and control for unobserved confounders (Pearl, 2000; Spirtes et al. [1993] 2000). However, the track record is not encouraging (Freedman, 1997, 2004; Freedman and Humphreys, 1996, 1999). Citations from other perspectives include Oakes (1990), Pearl (1995) and McKim and Turner (1997), as well as Freedman (1985, 1987, 1991, 1995, 1999, 2005a, 2005b, 2006).

The statistical model for causation was proposed by Neyman (1923). It has been rediscovered many times since: see, for instance, Hodges and Lehmann (1964, section 9.4). The set-up is often called 'Rubin's model', but that simply mistakes the history. See the comments by Dabrowska and Speed (1990) on their translation of Neyman (1923), with a response by Rubin; compare to Rubin (1974) and Holland (1986). Holland (1986, 1988) explains the set-up with a super-population model to account for the randomness, rather than individualized error terms.

Error terms are often described as the overall effects of factors omitted from the equation. But this description introduces difficulties of its own, as shown by Pratt and Schlaifer (1984, 1988). Stone (1993) presents a super-population model with some observed covariates and some unobserved. Formal extensions to observational studies—in effect, assuming these studies are experiments after suitable controls have been introduced—are discussed by Holland (1986) and Rubin (1974) among others.

CONCLUSION

Causal inferences can be drawn from non-experimental data. However, no mechanical rules can be laid down for the activity. Since Hume, that is almost a truism. Instead, causal inference seems to require an enormous investment of skill, intelligence and hard work. Many convergent lines of evidence must be developed. Natural variation needs to be identified and exploited. Data must be collected. Confounders need to be considered.

Alternative explanations have to be exhaustively tested. Before anything else, the right question needs to be framed. Naturally, there is a desire to substitute intellectual capital for labor. That is why investigators try to base causal inference on statistical models.

The technology is relatively easy to use, and promises to open a wide variety of questions to the research effort. However, the appearance of methodological rigor can be deceptive. The models themselves demand critical scrutiny. Mathematical equations are used to adjust for confounding and other sources of bias. These equations may appear formidably precise, but they typically derive from many somewhat arbitrary choices. Which variables to enter in the regression? What functional form to use? What assumptions to make about parameters and error terms? These choices are seldom dictated either by data or prior scientific knowledge. That is why judgment is so critical, the opportunity for error so large, and the number of successful applications so limited.

Author's Footnote

Richard Berk, Persi Diaconis, Michael Finkelstein, Paul Humphreys, Roger Purves and Philip Stark made useful comments. This paper draws on Freedman (1987, 1991, 1997, 1999, 2004, 2005a, 2005b). Figure 7.2 is redrawn from Blau and Duncan (1967); and Figure 7.3 from Gibson (1988), also see Freedman (1991).

REFERENCES AND SELECT BIBLIOGRAPHY

Abelson, R. (1995) *Statistics as Principled Argument*. Hillsdale, NJ: Lawrence Erlbaum Associates.

Abbott, A. (1997) 'Of time and space: The contemporary relevance of the Chicago School', *Social Forces*, 75: 1149–82.

———— (1998) 'The causal devolution', *Sociological Methods and Research*, 27: 148–81.

Achen, C. (1977) 'Measuring representation: Perils of the correlation coefficient', *American Journal of Political Science*, 21: 805–15.

———— (1982) *Interpreting and Using Regression.* Thousand Oaks, CA: Sage Publications.

———— (1986) *The Statistical Analysis of Quasi-Experiments.* Berkeley: University of California Press.

Anderson, T.W. (1984) 'Estimating linear statistical relationships', *Annals of Statistics,* 12: 1–45.

Angrist, J.D. and Krueger, A.K. (2001) 'Instrumental variables and the search for identification: From supply and demand to natural experiments', *Journal of Economic Perspectives,* 15: 69–85.

Berk, R.A. (2003) *Regression Analysis: A Constructive Critique.* Newbury Park, CA: Sage Publications.

Bernert, C. (1983) 'The career of causal analysis in American sociology', *British Journal of Sociology,* 34: 230–54.

Blalock, H.M. (1989) 'The real and unrealized contributions of quantitative sociology', *American Sociological Review,* 54: 447–60.

Blau, P.M. and Duncan O.D. ([1967, Wiley] 1978) *The American Occupational Structure.* New York: Free Press. [Data collection, p.13; coding of education, pp.165–6; coding of status, pp. 115–27; correlations and path diagram, pp. 169–70.]

Brady, H. and Collier, D. (eds) (2004) *Rethinking Social Inquiry: Diverse Tools, Shared Standards.* Lanham, MD: Rowman and Littlefield.

Carmelli, D. and Page, W.F. (1996) '24-year mortality in smoking-discordant World War II US male veteran twins', *International Journal of Epidemiology,* 25: 554–9.

Clogg, C.C. and Haritou, A. (1997) 'The regression method of causal inference and a dilemma confronting this method', in V. McKim and S.Turner (eds), *Causality in Crisis.* Notre Dame, IN: University of Notre Dame Press, pp. 83–112.

Cook T.D. and Campbell D.T. (1979) *Quasi-Experimentation: Design and Analysis Issues for Field Settings.* Boston: Houghton Mifflin.

Duncan, O.D. (1984) *Notes on Social Measurement.* New York: Russell Sage.

Engle, R.F., Hendry, D.F. and Richard, J.F. (1983) 'Exogeneity', *Econometrica,* 51: 277–304.

Freedman, D.A. (1985) 'Statistics and the scientific method', in W.M. Mason and S.E. Fienberg (eds), *Cohort Analysis in Social Research: Beyond the Identification Problem.* New York: Springer-Verlag, pp. 343–90 (with discussion).

———— (1987) 'As others see us: A case study in path analysis', *Journal of Educational Statistics,* 12: 101–223 (with discussion). Reprinted in J. Shaffer (ed.) (1992) *The Role of Models in Nonexperimental Social Science.* Washington, DC: American Educational Research Association/American Statistical Association, pp. 3–125.

———— (1991) 'Statistical models and shoe leather', in Peter Marsden (ed.), *Sociological Methodology 1991.* Washington, DC: American Sociological Association, Chapter 10 (with discussion).

———— (1995) 'Some issues in the foundation of statistics', *Foundations of Science,* 1: 19–83 (with discussion). Reprinted in van Fraassen, B.C. (ed.) (1997), *Some Issues in the Foundation of Statistics.* Dordrecht: Kluwer, pp. 19–83 (with discussion).

———— (1997) 'From association to causation via regression', in V. Mc Kim and S. Turner (eds), *Causality in Crisis?* South Bend, IN: University of Notre Dame Press, pp. 113–82 (with discussion). Reprinted in *Advances in Applied Mathematics,* 18: 59–110.

———— (1999) 'From association to causation: Some remarks on the history of statistics', *Statistical Science,* 14: 243–58. Reprinted (1999) in *Journal de la Société Française de Statistique,* 140: 5–32, and in J. Panaretos (ed.) (2003) *Stochastic Musings: Perspectives from the Pioneers of the Late 20th Century.* Mahwah, NJ, Lawrence Erlbaum, pp. 45–71.

———— (2004) 'On specifying graphical models for causation, and the identification problem', *Evaluation Review,* 28: 267–93. Reprinted in Andrews, D.W.K. and Stock, J. H. (eds) (2005), *Identification and Inference for Econometric Models: Essays in Honor of Thomas Rothenberg.* Cambridge: Cambridge University Press, pp. 56–79.

———— (2005a) 'Linear statistical models for causation: A critical review' in Everitt B. and Howell D. (eds), *Encyclopedia of Statistics in Behavioral Sciences.* Hoboken, NJ: John Wiley and Sons.

———— (2005b) *Statistical Models: Theory and Practice.* New York: Cambridge University Press.

———— (2006) 'Statistical models for causation: What inferential leverage do they provide?', *Evaluation Review* 30: 691–713.

Freedman, D.A. and Humphreys, P. (1996) 'The grand leap', *British Journal for the Philosophy of Science,* 47: 113–23.

———— (1999) 'Are there algorithms that discover causal structure?', *Synthese,* 121: 29–54.

Freedman, D.A., Pisani, R. and Purves, R.A. ([1978] 2007) *Statistics.* 4th edn. New York: W.W. Norton, Inc.

Gauss, C.F. (1809) *Theoria Motus Corporum Coelestium.* Hamburg: Perthes et Besser. Reprinted in 1963 (New York: Dover).

Gibson, J.L. (1988) 'Political intolerance and political repression during the McCarthy Red Scare', *American Political Science Review,* 82: 511–29.

Gigerenzer, G. (1996) 'On narrow norms and vague heuristics', *Psychological Review,* 103: 592–6.

Goldthorpe, J.H. (1998) 'Causation, Statistics and Sociology', Twenty-ninth Geary Lecture, Nuffield

College, Oxford. Dublin: Economic and Social Research Institute.

——— (2000) *On Sociology: Numbers, Narratives, and Integration of Research and Theory.* New York: Oxford University Press.

——— (2001) 'Causation, statistics, and sociology', *European Sociological Review,* 17: 1–20.

Greenland, S., Pearl, J. and Robins, J. (1999) 'Causal diagrams for epidemiologic research', *Epidemiology,* 10: 37–48.

Heckman, J.J. (2000) 'Causal parameters and policy analysis in economics: A twentieth century retrospective', *The Quarterly Journal of Economics,* CVX: 45–97.

Hedström, P. and Swedberg, R. (eds) (1998) *Social Mechanisms: An Analytical Approach to Social Theory.* Cambridge: Cambridge University Press.

Hendry, D.F. (1993) *Econometrics – Alchemy or Science?* Oxford: Blackwell.

Hodges, J.L. Jr. and Lehmann, E. (1964) *Basic Concepts of Probability and Statistics.* San Francisco: Holden-Day.

Holland, P. (1986) 'Statistics and causal inference', *Journal of the American Statistical Association,* 8: 945–60.

——— (1988) 'Causal inference, path analysis, and recursive structural equation models', in C. Clogg (ed.) *Sociological Methodology.* Washington, DC: American Sociological Association. Chapter 13.

International Agency for Research on Cancer (1986). 'Tobacco Smoking', Monograph 38. Lyon, France: IARC.

Kahneman, D., Slovic, P. and Tversky, A. (eds) (1982) *Judgment under Uncertainty: Heuristics and Biases.* Cambridge: Cambridge University Press.

Kahneman, D. and Tversky, A. (1974) 'Judgment under uncertainty: Heuristics and bias', *Science,* 185: 1124–31.

——— (1996) 'On the reality of cognitive illusions', *Psychological Review,* 103: 582–91.

——— (eds) (2000) *Choices, Values, and Frames.* Cambridge: Cambridge University Press.

Kaprio, J. and Koskenvuo, M. (1989) 'Twins, smoking and mortality: A 12-year prospective study of smoking-discordant twin pairs', *Social Science and Medicine,* 29: 1083–9.

Keynes, J.M. (1939) 'Professor Tinbergen's method', *The Economic Journal,* 49: 558–70.

——— (1940) 'Comment on Tinbergen's response', *The Economic Journal,* 50: 154–6.

Kline, R.B. (1998) *Principles and Practice of Structural Equation Modeling.* New York: Guilford.

Larzalere, R.E. and Kuhn, B.R. (2004) 'The intervention selection bias: An underrecognized confound in intervention research', *Psychological Bulletin,* 130: 289–303.

Lauritzen, S. (1996) *Graphical Models.* Oxford: Clarendon Press.

Lauritzen, S. (2001) 'Casual Inference in Graphic Models' in O.E. Barndorff-Nielson, D.R. Cox and C. Klüppelberg (eds) *Complex Stochastic Systems,* Boca Raton, FL: Chapman & Hall and CRC, pp. 63–108.

Leamer, E. (1978) *Specification Searches.* New York: John Wiley.

Legendre, A.M. (1805) *Nouvelles méthodes pour la détermination des orbites des comètes.* Paris: Courcier. Reprinted in 1959 (New York: Dover).

Lieberson, S. (1985) *Making it Count.* Berkeley: University of California Press.

Lieberson, S. and Lynn, F. B. (2002) 'Barking up the wrong branch: Alternative to the current model of sociological science', *Annual Review of Sociology,* 28: 1–19.

Liu, T.C. (1960) 'Under-Identification, structural estimation, and forecasting', *Econometrica,* 28: 855–65.

Lucas, R.E. Jr. (1976) 'Econometric policy evaluation: A critique', in K. Brunner and A. Meltzer (eds), *The Phillips Curve and Labor Markets.* Amsterdam: North-Holland Pub. Co., pp. 19–64 (with discussion).

Manski, C.F. (1995) *Identification Problems in the Social Sciences.* Cambridge, MA: Harvard University Press.

McKim, V. and Turner, S. (eds) (1997) *Causality in Crisis? Proceedings of the Notre Dame Conference on Causality.* South Bend, IN: University of Notre Dame Press.

Meehl, P.E. (1954) *Clinical Versus Statistical Prediction: A Theoretical Analysis and a Review of the Evidence.* Minneapolis: University of Minnesota Press.

——— (1978) 'Theoretical risks and tabular asterisks: Sir Karl, Sir Ronald, and the slow progress of soft psychology', *Journal of Consulting and Clinical Psychology,* 46: 806–34.

Meehl, P.E. and Waller N.G. (2002) 'The path analysis controversy: A new statistical approach to strong appraisal of verisimilitude', *Psychological Methods,* 7: 283–337 (with discussion).

Miller, D.P., Neuberg, D., De Vivo, I., Wain, J.C., Lynch T.J., Su, L. and Christiani D.C. (2003) 'Smoking and the risk of lung cancer: Susceptibility with GSTP1 polymorphisms', *Epidemiology,* 14: 545–51.

Nakachi, K., Ima, K., Hayashi, S.-I. and Kawajiri, K. (1993) 'Polymorphisms of the CYP1A1 and Glutathione S-transferase genes associated with susceptibility to lung cancer in relation to cigarette dose in a Japanese population', *Cancer Research,* 53: 2994–9.

Neyman, J. (1923) 'Sur les applications de la théorie des probabilités aux experiences agricoles: Essai des principes', *Roczniki Nauk Rolniczki,* 10: 1–51, in Polish. English translation by D. Dabrowska and T. Speed (1990), *Statistical Science,* 5: 463–80 (with discussion).

Ní Bhrolcháin, M. (2001) 'Divorce effects and causality in the social sciences', *European Sociological Review,* 17: 33–57.

Oakes, M.W. (1990) *Statistical Inference.* Chestnut Hill, MA: Epidemiology Resources Inc.

Pearl, J. (1988) *Probabilistic Reasoning in Intelligent Systems.* San Mateo: Morgan Kaufmann Publishers, Inc.

———— (1995) 'Causal diagrams for empirical research', *Biometrika,* 82: 669–710 (with discussion).

———— (2000) *Causality: Models, Reasoning, and Inference.* Cambridge: Cambridge University Press.

Platt, J. (1996) *A History of Sociological Research Methods in America.* Cambridge: Cambridge University Press.

Pratt, J. and Schlaifer, R. (1984) 'On the nature and discovery of structure', *Journal of the American Statistical Association,* 79: 9–21.

———— (1988) 'On the interpretation and observation of laws', *Journal of Econometrics,* 39: 23–52.

Quetelet, A. (1835) *Sur l'homme et le développement de ses facultés, ou Essai de physique sociale.* Paris: Bachelier.

Rindfuss, R.R., Bumpass, L. and St. John, C. (1980) 'Education and fertility: Implications for the roles women occupy', *American Sociological Review,* 45: 431–47.

Robins, J.M. (1987) 'A graphical approach to the identification and estimation of causal parameters in mortality studies with sustained exposure periods', *Journal of Chronic Diseases,* 40 (Supplement 2): 139S–161S.

Robins, J.M. (1986) 'A new approach to causal inference in mortality studies with a sustained exposure period – Application to control of the healthy worker survivor effect', *Mathematical Modelling,* 7: 1393–1512.

Rubin, D. (1974) 'Estimating causal effects of treatments in randomized and nonrandomized studies', *Journal of Educational Psychology,* 66: 688–701.

Sen, A.K. (2002) *Rationality and Freedom.* Cambridge, MA: Harvard University Press.

Shadish, W.R., Cook, T.D. and Campbell, D.T. (2002) *Experimental and Quasi-Experimental Designs for Generalized Causal Inference.* Boston: Houghton Mifflin.

Shields, P.G., Caporaso, N.E., Falk, K.T. , Sugimura, H., Trivers, G.E., Trump B.P., Hoover, R.N., Weston, A. and Harris, C.C. (1993) 'Lung cancer, race and a CYP1A1 genetic polymorphism', *Cancer Epidemiology, Biomarkers and Prevention,* 2: 481–5.

Sims, C.A. (1980) 'Macroeconomics and reality', *Econometrica,* 48: 1–47.

Sobel, M.E. (2000) 'Causal inference in the social sciences', *Journal of the American Statistical Association,* 95: 647–51.

Sobel, M.E. (1998) 'Causal inference in statistical models of the process of socioeconomic achievement – A case study', *Sociological Methods & Research,* 27: 318–348.

Spirtes, P., Glymour, C. and Scheines, R. ([1993] 2000) *Causation, Prediction, and Search.* Cambridge, MA: MIT Press.

Steiger, J.H. (2001) 'Driving fast in reverse', *Journal of the American Statistical Association,* 96: 331–8.

Stone, R. (1993) 'The assumptions on which causal inferences rest', *Journal of the Royal Statistical Society,* Series B, 55: 455–66.

Stouffer S.A. (1955) *Communism, Conformity, and Civil Liberties.* New York: Doubleday.

Tinbergen, J. (1940) 'Reply to Keynes', *The Economic Journal,* 50: 141–54.

Ullman, J.B. and Bentler, P.M. (2003) 'Structural equation modeling', in I.B. Weiner, J.A. Schinka and W.F. Velicer (eds) *Handbook of Psychology Volume 2: Research Methods in Psychology.* Hoboken, NJ: Wiley, pp. 607–34.

Yule, G.U. (1899) 'An investigation into the causes of changes in pauperism in England, chiefly during the last two intercensal decades', *Journal of the Royal Statistical Society,* 62: 249–95.

8

Fighting to Understand the World Causally: Three Battles Connected to the Causal Implications of Structural Equation Models

Leslie Hayduk and Hannah Pazderka-Robinson

INTRODUCTION

This chapter characterizes and attempts to resolve three debates currently confronting structural equation modeling. The first debate concerns testing structural equation models. Should a researcher test their model using a test hypothesis of exact-fit or close-fit? The second debate concerns whether or not researchers should employ the so-called 'four-step approach' of: (1) using an exploratory factor model (2) followed by a confirmatory factor model (3) before estimating a full structural equation model, and (4) adding restrictions into that model. The third debate is over how many indicators to use with latent variables. Is one indicator enough? Two indicators? Three? Four? More?

Structural equation models systematize *both* the representation of causal effects, and the unavoidable implications of those effects. A solid foundation in thinking causally, with, through, and via, structural equation models, resolves the debates in favor of using exact-fit testing, and opposing the four-step procedure. Systematic causal thinking confronts some traditional understandings of measurement, indicators, and validity, by recommending the adequacy of fewer indicators, but it does not dictate or forbid specific numbers of indicators.

THINKING CAUSALLY, ACTING ACCORDINGLY

You cannot be a researcher unless you believe there is an extant segment of the world whose structure could be better understood. If you believe, or imagine, that the structuring is causal (or contains influences, impacts or consequences) and if you don't have access to experimental manipulation of the putative causes, your thinking and your research will probably benefit from understanding structural equation models.

Structural equation models thrive in the context of an enigmatic tension: correlation is not causation but causal actions produce correlations. Some causal world underlies non-chance correlations or relationships between variables, though the existence of a stable correlation does not directly signal which specific causal actions produced the correlation. The correlation may result from direct or indirect effects between the variables, reciprocal effects, and/or through the actions of one or more common causes. Viewing correlations (relationships or associations) as artifacts produced through the actions of an underlying causal world was clear in structural equation modeling's infancy (Wright, 1921); it remained through structural equation modeling's youth (Blalock, 1964; Duncan, 1975) and persists today (Borsboom et al., 2004; Pearl, 2000; Shipley, 2001).

The natural and intuitive view that causal actions produce observed correlations has its detractors and even a few closet adversaries. Some philosophers would infinitely delay your examination of worldly causal structures with endless taunts of: 'But you can't precisely define cause!' And some statisticians propagate structural equation models as merely ways of fitting data, as opposed to striving to use structural equation models to understand how the world created the data. The gap between seeking to understand the world and fitting data provided by that world seems innocuous only until you encounter the bitter fighting required to maintain a research focus on learning about the world.

This chapter encourages you to retain and refine your causal thinking as a weapon to wield in defense of your efforts to *understand the world* that provided your data. We begin by reviewing several examples of simple causal worlds and the covariance (correlational) consequences resulting from those worlds. We follow this with some examples incorporating latent variables into causal thinking—the move that connects causation to measurement.

With this causal arsenal, we turn to three substantial debates: 1) testing structural equation models attentively, 2) doing measurement in conjunction *with* (*not before*) latent-level structural equation models, and 3) the adequacy of single-indicators. Warning: if current publications are a guide, we are likely to be fighting *against you* on at least one of these points.

IF THE WORLD IS THUSLY CAUSALLY STRUCTURED, THEN WE SHOULD OBSERVE...

At its core, each structural equation model is a hypothetical postulate having an if–then form. *If* some causal structural equations are specified, *then* some specific covariance or correlational features *must* be observed; and *if* the equations correspond to worldly causal forces *then* these covariance features **should** be observed in worldly covariances. There are statistical proofs that underwrite the preceding statement of 'must'; and 'should' could be replaced by 'must', were it not for the interference of 'random' sampling fluctuations in observed covariances. That is, the connection between a causal structural equation '*If*' and some specific '*Then*' is inescapable. What remains open is the veracity of the 'if' and the potential interference of sampling. (Measurement is part of the 'if', as we shall see below.) Researchers hope their structural equation models match the world's causal structure—but the veracity to the postulated structures remains suspect, or merely putative, in the absence of evidence. We as scientists seek the relevant evidence, and much of what constitutes evidence requires an understanding of how equations as causal claims (*ifs*) demand specific consequences (*thens*).

A Single Cause

Let us begin by imagining a simple causal world in which X causes Y, or equivalently

$$Y = a + bX \qquad (1)$$

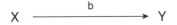

Figure 8.1 A single cause

or, also equivalently, see Figure 8.1.

For simplicity we presume that X and Y refer to variables having interval scales, and we presume that the above equation holds for some set of cases (where if necessary we could represent the values for an individual case as $y_i = a + bx_i$). The parameters a and b are hypothesized worldly features that have specific yet unknown numerical values— values we often attempt to estimate, but which might be asserted by more cogent theory. The linear form of Equation (1) postulates a progressive causal impact (on Y) resulting from hypothetical changes in an individual's value of X, or a difference in Y values for a hypothetical comparison of two individuals identical except for their differing X values. The scaling of the variables and linearity of the causal connection can be addressed as topics in their own right, but for our purposes we merely require these as part of the postulated *if*, and turn to a consideration of what this causal equation/world implies, and what follows unavoidably and undeniably from such an equation/world. What could not be escaped or avoided *if* the above-postulate (whether expressed as an equation, diagram, or equivalent verbal assertions) constituted the causal world?

The entities that cannot be escaped are specific features of, and coordinations between, the distributions of the X and Y variables. We confine our attention to the 'centers' (means, or expected values) of the X and Y distributions, the 'spreads' (variances) of these distributions, and the covariance between the X and Y variables (which becomes a correlation if the variables are standardized). If we designate the mean (or expected value) of X as E(X), the variance of X as Var(X), and the covariance between X and Y as Cov(X,Y), the Figure 8.1 (Equation (1)) model implies, requires, or demands that:

$$E(y) = a + bE(X) \qquad (2)$$

$$Var(Y) = b^2 Var(X) \qquad (3)$$

$$Cov(X,Y) = b Var(X) \qquad (4)$$

There are mathematical proofs that demand Equations (2), (3), and (4) once we are granted Equation (1). But rather than certifying the inescapability of these equations by forcing you through the proofs available in other texts (e.g. Hayduk, 1987: 14–17), we focus on the nature and uses of the features that become unavoidable.

Notice that Equation (2)'s structure is similar to that of Equation (1). One way—one causal way—to understand Equation (2) is to imagine a case/person whose value on the cause X happens to correspond to the mean (expected value) of X. What should happen to this person's score on Y if that person had an average (middling, or E(X)) value on the causal X variable, and that middling X value was put through the causal world postulated as Equation (1)? Would you anticipate *on the basis of this causal world* that such a person should have an extremely high Y value? An extremely low Y value perhaps? It seems intuitive that the Equation (1) (or Figure 8.1) causal world would result in a middling or average value of the dependent variable Y because the person was middling on the cause X. Only cases extreme on X (extremely high or low) should result in extreme scores on Y (high or low), because with X as the only cause in this postulated world, there would be nothing capable of pushing Y towards its extremes other than extreme X values being put through the b component of the causal process. As X's value gets progressively less extreme (closer to average), the Y value demanded by the postulated causal world also gets progressively closer to the center (or average) of the Y distribution. The Equation (1) causal world has no way to causally explain any score on Y other than the mean (middling, or expected value) of Y if the value of the causal variable X is the mean (middling or expected value) of X.

Does the demanded causal consequence of Equation (2) match with your intuitive causal thinking? That is, does the feature *inescapably demanded* by Equation (2)— namely, a middling value on effect Y if the case is middling on cause X—seem reasonable to you, according to your causal intuition? It is important that you have an 'intuition' corresponding to the unavoidable and inescapable Equation (2), and similar intuitions for Equations (3) and (4), even if you have to train yourself into having these 'intuitions'.

Now consider Equation (3). This equation should (but in our experience often does not) engender the same kind of intuitive certainty that accompanies Equation (2). Equation (3) demands that the variance or spread of cases on Y connect to the spread of scores on the causal variable X; but also that only the causal parameter b, and not parameter a, be involved in coordinating the variances of the two variables. You can intuitively see why a is inescapably unable to alter the variance of the dependent variable Y, if you imagine a scatterplot of X and Y values (which in this instance all fall on a line), and notice that the value a merely moves all the points a units up or down the Y axis but does not alter the *spread* of the Y values. The squaring of b in Equation (3) arises from the squaring in the formula defining variance, but we leave the details of this to introductory texts.

Now consider Equation (4) as an implication of the causal world. This equation says that the covariance between X and Y (or correlation if the variables are standardized) arises because of two features in the causal world: the magnitude of the causal impact of X (namely b) and the variability in the values of the causal variable X. Here we see the causal world producing covariance, and in this instance the covariance would correspond

to a perfect ±1.0 correlation (if the X and Y variables had been standardized) because all the cases would 'fall on a line'.

You should sense the causal world as unavoidably producing—not amorphously 'explaining', but explaining in a specific *demanded* causal way—the coordinations between the X and Y variables' means (Equation (2)), variances (Equation (3)), and their covariance (correlation) (Equation (4)). The observable features of the X and Y distributions, namely their means, variances and covariance, are linked in specific demanded ways if the variables are linked by the causal world postulated as Equation (1).

These implications provide a way to test this particular model. Notice that Equation (3) can be rearranged to:

$$b = \sqrt{\frac{Var(Y)}{Var(X)}} \qquad (5)$$

while Equation (4) can be arranged to:

$$b = \frac{Cov(X, Y)}{Var(X)} \qquad (6)$$

Thus this model's requirements create two different ways (using two different sets of observable variances and covariance) to calculate the magnitude of b.

These implications allow for a straightforward test of this model. If no single b value satisfied both Equations (5) and (6), we would have evidence speaking against this particular causal model, and the researcher would be prodded to seek some other causal model whose demanded covariance consequences were compatible with the observed evidence.

It is important to notice that parallel implications would have been demanded had we postulated that Y caused X, instead of X causing Y. The reverse causal ordering would switch the placement of the names X and Y in Equations (1) through (6), and the a and b values would differ but the test provided by comparing Equations (5) and (6) would be similarly passed (by both X causes Y, and Y

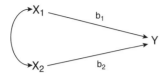

Figure 8.2   Two causes

causes X, models) or failed (by both models) irrespective of the true causal direction. These are two covariance equivalent models— where by covariance equivalent we mean that if one of the models is capable of matching the covariance data, the other model can also match the covariance data. If all the data values fell 'on a line' both models would pass the test, and if the data values did not fall on a line both models would fail the test.

The possibility of two different causal models being consistent with the observed covariance information means that confirming some, or even many, of a model's if–then covariance requirements *does not guarantee* that the model is correct. This should lead us to be attentive to every detectable sign of model failure. Given that we know that covariance-equivalent models will remain a challenge, it would be counterproductive to enlarge the set of 'still competing' models by failing to eliminate all the models that actually are inconsistent with the covariance data. It is our duty as researchers to certify our causal understandings by minimizing the number of 'still competing' models by eliminating as many data-inconsistent models as possible.

Two Causes

Let us now imagine a slightly more complex causal world in which variables X_1 and X_2 both cause Y, as in Figure 8.2 and the equation

$$Y = b_1 X_1 + b_2 X_2 \qquad (7)$$

We omit the 'intercept' (by imagining that nothing uniformly causes all the case's Y values to increase or decrease by an amount

like a), which permits us to focus on the causal actions of X_1 and X_2. This model acknowledges that causal forces can work simultaneously (for example, both gravity and electrostatic forces act on charged particles), and these forces may act in tandem or in opposition to one another (there may be different signs on the effects b_1 and b_2, or X_1 might increase while X_2 decreases). Here we discard the idea that a specific cause is necessary or sufficient for a specific outcome. For any specified values of b_1 and b_2, there will be several values of X_1 and X_2 that can provide that specific Y value, and a specific X_1 value does not guarantee a specific Y value because X_2's value can also alter Y.

We might ask ourselves again: what kind of Y value would you expect to observe for a case that had both an average value of X_1 and an average value of X_2 in this causal world? Would you expect an extreme Y value? A value a bit above average or below average? The model in Equation (7) (Figure 8.2) implies, and requires, that the mean (or expected value) of Y should be observed for a case possessing average values on both the causal variables.

$$E(Y) = b_1 E(X_1) + b_2 E(X_2) \qquad (8)$$

We trust that this demanded causal consequent seems intuitively reasonable to you.

Another instructive implication, or demand, of the Figure 8.2 (Equation (7)) model (see Hayduk, 1987: 20) is that

$$Var(Y) = b_1^2 Var(X_1) + b_2^2 Var(X_2) \\ + 2b_1 b_2 Cov(X_1, X_2) \qquad (9)$$

This instructs us that the variance in the dependent variable becomes 'partitioned' into various parts due to the partitioning of the causal world. The first term on the right of Equation (9) tells us that variations in X_1 (namely whatever makes some X_1 values higher or lower) causes variations in Y. Similarly, the second term on the right says that variations in X_2 (namely, whatever makes X_2 values higher or lower) also produces variations in Y.

The third term on the right demands that a covariance or correlation between the two causes also makes a separate contribution to the variance of the causally dependent variable Y. Think of this as something like a double-whammy or double-boost. Let us imagine that b_1, b_2, and $Cov(X_1, X_2)$ are all positive. The positive covariance between the causes means that high values on one cause tend to (or, more frequently) go along with high values on the other cause. Hence, when a case/person gets one causal boost in Y, they are also more likely to get an additional boost in Y due to the other cause. Or, if a case's Y value is lowered by a reduction in the value of one cause, that case's Y value is more likely (because of the covariance between the causes) to also be lowered by the action of the other cause (a double-whammy). The coordination between the values of the causal variables provides a coordination in the causal boosts or whammies, and this 'doubling up' of causal forces pushes cases towards the upper or lower extremes of the Y distribution, which increases the variance of Y.

Let us keep b_1 and b_2 positive but imagine that $Cov(X_1, X_2)$ is negative. Notice that this makes the third term on the right of Equation (9) negative. Here we have the causal world explaining a reduction in the variance of the dependent variable. How is one to imagine a causal world explaining a *reduction or decrement* in variance? This is merely a matter of countervailing effects. When one cause tries to push a case's Y value up, the negative covariance with the other cause means that the other cause is likely to be trying to push the Y value back down. The two causes' effects on Y tend to cancel out because they are tending (depending on the degree of covariance between X_1 and X_2) to act in opposition to one another. Hence the Y values are less likely to be pushed into extreme Y values.

Consider this in another light. Suppose X_2 in Equation (8) was to be thought of as an error variable—in that case Equation (9) would be reporting a demanded causal partitioning of the variance of Y into a part resulting from variations in X_1, a part resulting from error, and a part resulting from a coordination between X_1 and that error. We often assume that the error is independent of the predictors in an equation, but rather than thinking of this as a statistical assumption, you should think of it as a potentially fallible causal claim about the world's causal structure. If there really was a third term on the right of Equation (9) because X_1 and the error were correlated, and we erroneously assumed that it did not exist, our model would misrepresent the true variance in Y by having wrongly omitted the third term on the right of Equation (9). Statisticians will connect the incorrect assumption to biased estimates, because a value of b_1 that is somewhat different than the true b_1 would make the 'right side of Equation (9) minus the third term' more compatible with the other variances in the equation. You should see this bias as resulting from an incorrect representation of the causal world. The problematic statistical estimate would arise from having wrongly omitted the doubling-up of causal whammies and boosts.

It is often difficult to rectify a model that is misspecified by an erroneous assumption of error independence. Models typically contain many error variables, each having many assumedly-zero covariances, and the true covariances may be strong or weak, and positive or negative. If a model's variance and covariance implications fail to match with the observed variance/covariance data, the assumption of zero error-covariances should be reconsidered, but there are no available diagnostics that pinpoint specifically which of the multiple potential covariances are problematic. However, the difficulty in locating what is problematic should not detract from being attentive to inconsistencies in a model's demanded variance/covariance implications! Estimation biases of unknown sign, magnitude and location are not the kind of thing a researcher can safely ignore, no matter how difficult the diagnostic investigation.

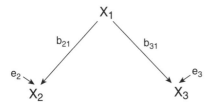

Figure 8.3   A common cause

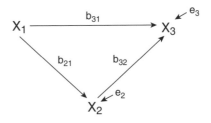

Figure 8.4   Indirect effects

A Common Cause

Next, consider a model in which X_1 acts as a common cause of X_2 and X_3 where the unspecified causal sources ('errors') e_2 and e_3 are independent of X_1 but cause X_2 and X_3 respectively (see Figure 8.3). The equations for this model are:

$$X_2 = b_{21}X_1 + e_2 \qquad (10)$$

$$X_3 = b_{31}X_1 + e_3 \qquad (11)$$

One unavoidable implication of this model (Hayduk, 1987: 31) is that

$$Cov(X_2, X_3) = b_{21}b_{31}Var(X_1) \qquad (12)$$

This model demands, and explains, a covariance (correlation, or coordination) between X_2 and X_3, not because X_2 causes X_3, or X_3 causes X_2, but because both X_2 and X_3 have X_1 as a common cause. If b_{21} and b_{31} are positive, and X_1's value is high, both X_2 and X_3 will take on relatively high values because of the causal impacts b_{21} and b_{31} carry that high X_1 value to both X_2 and X_3. When X_1 is low, the low value is similarly carried by b_{21} and b_{31} to low values of both X_2 and X_3. Thus X_2 and X_3 both tend to be high whenever X_1 is high, and they tend to be low whenever X_1 is low. Notice an important switch here. We are explaining covariance (between X_2 and X_3) with variance in X_1 and the causal world that connects X_1 to X_2 and X_3. That is, causal models are as much about explaining *covariance* as they are about explaining variance. A model's covariance implications are no less demanded, and no more avoidable, than are a model's variance implications and demands.

Indirect Effects

Another simple and instructive model is presented in Figure 8.4, and has the equations:

$$X_2 = b_{21}X_1 + e_2 \qquad (13)$$

$$X_3 = b_{31}X_1 + b_{32}X_2 + e_3 \qquad (14)$$

This model, with assumedly independent errors, requires (Duncan, 1975: 54) that

$$Cov(X_1, X_3) = b_{31}Var(X_1) + b_{32}b_{21}Var(X_1) \qquad (15)$$

and if the variables are standardized to have unit variances (Duncan, 1975: 31), this becomes

$$r_{13} = \beta_{31} + \beta_{32}\beta_{21} \qquad (16)$$

This re-emphasizes that causal structural equation models demandedly-explain correlations (or covariance), not just variance, and that a mistaken or unsatisfied correlation (or covariance) demand should be counted as speaking against the demand-making causal model.

But something new emerges if we consider that it is possible that the magnitudes of the effects might be such that the product $b_{32}b_{21}$ equals the negative of b_{31} (or in standardized form, that $\beta_{32}\beta_{21}$ equals the negative of β_{31}). That is, it is possible for the indirect effect of X_1 on X_3 (the product term) to be equal in magnitude but opposite in sign to the direct b_{31} effect. This would imply and demand that the correlation (covariance) between X_1 and X_3 should be zero despite the existence of both direct and indirect causal effects leading from X_1 to

X_3. This causal model would demand an absence of correlation—where that absence of a correlation is understood as the direct and indirect causal impacts acting in opposition to one another, and as canceling one another out. In this instance, observing a correlation (especially a substantial correlation) between X_1 and X_3 would constitute evidence against a causal model that claimed that the indirect effect given by the product $b_{32}b_{21}$ equals the negative of the direct effect b_{31}. Zero correlation between X_1 and X_3 would constitute evidence consistent with the model's causal demands. Causation does not demand correlation, it demands 'correlations whose magnitudes are consistent the model's causal structure'— where a correlation of magnitude of zero might be structurally demanded.

OVERCOMING A FEAR OF LATENT VARIABLES: INTRODUCING LATENT VARIABLES AS CAUSES

The Causal Foundations of Measurement

Let us imagine that X_1 in the Figure 8.3 common-cause model is a latent variable—it exists and its existence is made evident through its causal actions on observable variables X_2 and X_3. It is traditional to call X_2 and X_3 measures, or indicators, of the latent variable. We will change our notation to differentiate between which variables are latent (even if real) and which are observed (and also real). But do not be fooled into thinking that anything changes about the structure of a model's causal demands merely because the common cause is latent rather than observed. The primary objective of this section is to convince you of the consistency in the structure of the causally-demanded covariance implications—whether the common cause is called X_1 or ξ_1 (in a notation often employed with latent variables). By the end of this section we will have worked all the way back to Equation (12), merely using the Greek

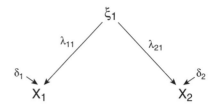

Figure 8.5   A latent common cause

characters employed by traditional LISREL notation (Jöreskog and Sörbom, 1996).

The causal structure of the Figure 8.5 model can be represented using only one of LISREL's three basic matrix equations (Jöreskog and Sörbom, 1996: 2; Hayduk 1987: 91), namely:

$$x = \Lambda\xi + \delta \tag{17}$$

The Figure 8.5 model has two observed X variables, one latent ξ variable, two error variables (designated δ_1 and δ_2), and the effects are designated as λs, whose first subscript keeps track of which X receives the effect and whose second subscript keeps track of which ξ variable sends the effect (namely $\lambda_{\text{(to this X)(from this }\xi)}$). Thus, the Figure 8.5 model in matrix form is

$$\begin{bmatrix} x_1 \\ x_2 \end{bmatrix} = \begin{bmatrix} \lambda_{11} \\ \lambda_{21} \end{bmatrix} [\xi_1] + \begin{bmatrix} \delta_1 \\ \delta_2 \end{bmatrix} \tag{18}$$

and this corresponds to the pair of equations

$$x_1 = \lambda_{11}\xi_1 + \delta_1 \tag{19}$$

$$x_2 = \lambda_{21}\xi_1 + \delta_2 \tag{20}$$

Note the similarity of these equations to Equations (10) and (11).

The proof detailing how models having the general form of Equation (17) demand a specific covariance matrix for the X variables is presented in Hayduk (1987: 106–110), where the error variances and covariances are contained in the θ_δ matrix, and the variances and covariances of the latent variable(s) are contained in the Φ matrix.

$$\begin{bmatrix} Covariance \\ Matrix\ of\ the \\ X\ variables \end{bmatrix}$$

$$= \begin{bmatrix} Var(x_1) & Cov(x_1x_2) \\ Cov(x_2x_1) & Var(x_2) \end{bmatrix} = \Lambda\Phi\Lambda' + \Theta_\delta$$
$$(21)$$

Equation (21) assumes the errors are independent of the latent ξ_1 cause, and we will assume the errors are also independent of one another. The Figure 8.5 model's demands can be found by expanding the right side of Equation (21) by inserting the lambda matrix (and its transpose) from Equations (17) and (18), the matrix containing the variances of the errors, and the matrix containing the variance of the latent variable.

$$\begin{bmatrix} Var(x_1) & Cov(x_1x_2) \\ Cov(x_2x_1) & Var(x_2) \end{bmatrix}$$

$$= \begin{bmatrix} \lambda_{11} \\ \lambda_{21} \end{bmatrix} [\phi_{11}][\lambda_{11} \ \ \lambda_{21}] + \begin{bmatrix} \theta_{\delta 11} & 0 \\ 0 & \theta_{\delta 22} \end{bmatrix} (22)$$

which equals

$$\begin{bmatrix} Var(x_1) & Cov(x_1x_2) \\ Cov(x_2x_1) & Var(x_2) \end{bmatrix}$$

$$= \begin{bmatrix} \lambda_{11}\phi_{11} \\ \lambda_{21}\phi_{11} \end{bmatrix} [\lambda_{11} \ \ \lambda_{21}] + \begin{bmatrix} \theta_{\delta 11} & 0 \\ 0 & \theta_{\delta 22} \end{bmatrix} (23)$$

and

$$\begin{bmatrix} Var(x_1) & Cov(x_1x_2) \\ Cov(x_2x_1) & Var(x_2) \end{bmatrix}$$

$$= \begin{bmatrix} \lambda_{11}^2\phi_{11} & \lambda_{11}\lambda_{21}\phi_{11} \\ \lambda_{21}\lambda_{11}\phi_{11} & \lambda_{21}^2\phi_{11} \end{bmatrix} + \begin{bmatrix} \theta_{\delta 11} & 0 \\ 0 & \theta_{\delta 22} \end{bmatrix}$$
$$(24)$$

and

$$\begin{bmatrix} Var(x_1) & Cov(x_1x_2) \\ Cov(x_2x_1) & Var(x_2) \end{bmatrix}$$

$$= \begin{bmatrix} \lambda_{11}^2\phi_{11} + \theta_{\delta 11} & \lambda_{11}\lambda_{21}\phi_{11} \\ \lambda_{21}\lambda_{11}\phi_{11} & \lambda_{21}^2\phi_{11} + \theta_{\delta 22} \end{bmatrix} (25)$$

The upper-right terms of this equation tell us that

$$Cov(x_1, x_2) = \lambda_{11}\lambda_{21}\phi_{11} \qquad (26)$$

where ϕ_{11} is the variance of the ξ_1 latent variable. Examine Equations (26) and (12) until you are convinced that they are making the same style of covariance demand about a pair of variables that share a common cause—where the notations differ merely because that common cause is observed in one instance and is latent in the other. You should see this consistency in causal understanding as a tool to tame students' fears of latent variables, and to overcome their doubts about what latent variables 'really are'. Latent structural equation variables can be thought of as real variables that really act causally in the same comfortable ways that observed variables act causally.

In case you had not recognized them, Equations (17) and (21) are the basic equations in factor analysis, and some people prefer to call the latent variable a latent factor. Factor models are a specific type of causal model, and they are as rigidly demanding in their required causal consequences as are other causal models. Some people prefer to not see, or even to hide, this, but before we stray into this contentious territory we will present two more relatively simple causal models containing latent variables.

Two Latents, One Indicator

The model in Figure 8.6 parallels the model in Figure 8.2, and we will again merely follow traditional LISREL notation to see how two latent causal variables end up demanding covariance consequences that parallel the demands made by causal connections between observed variables—in this instance a demand that parallels Equation (9).

For the Figure 8.6 model, the basic LISREL matrix Equation (17), namely

$$x = \Lambda\xi + \delta \qquad (27)$$

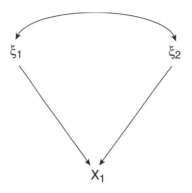

Figure 8.6: Two latent causes

takes the following form:

$$x_1 = [\lambda_{11} \ \lambda_{12}] \begin{bmatrix} \xi_1 \\ \xi_2 \end{bmatrix} + [\delta_1] \qquad (28)$$

This can be written as a single equation

$$x_1 = \lambda_{11}\xi_1 + \lambda_{12}\xi_2 + \delta_1 \qquad (29)$$

that parallels Equation (7), with the temporary inclusion of an error variable. The Figure 8.2 model does not contain an error variable, and we will remove this variable below, but we leave this in temporarily as a 'place holder' to help you see the parallel between the equations here and the equations in the preceding section.

This model's demanded covariance implications again come from Equation (21), but in this instance there is only one element in the covariance matrix for the X variables because there is only one X variable.

$$\begin{bmatrix} Covariance \\ Matrix\ of\ the \\ X variables \end{bmatrix} = [Var(x_1)] = \Lambda\Phi\Lambda' + \theta_\delta \qquad (30)$$

The Λ matrix of effects are as in Equation (28), and using the covariance matrices of the two latent ξ variables and the single error variable's variance provides:

$$[Var(x_1)] = [\lambda_{11} \ \lambda_{12}] \begin{bmatrix} \phi_{11} & \phi_{12} \\ \phi_{12} & \phi_{22} \end{bmatrix} \begin{bmatrix} \lambda_{11} \\ \lambda_{12} \end{bmatrix} + [\theta_{\delta 11}] \qquad (31)$$

Here we will add the assumption that there is no error causing the X_1 variable. It should be clear that all this does is set the final term of Equation (31) to zero. We then do the matrix multiplication of the two left matrices to obtain

$$Var(x_1) =$$

$$[(\lambda_{11}\phi_{11} + \lambda_{12}\phi_{12}) \ (\lambda_{11}\phi_{12} + \lambda_{12}\phi_{22})] \begin{bmatrix} \lambda_{11} \\ \lambda_{12} \end{bmatrix} \qquad (32)$$

and then multiply the two remaining matrices to obtain

$$Var(x_1) = \lambda_{11}^2\phi_{11} + \lambda_{12}\lambda_{11}\phi_{12} \\ + \lambda_{11}\lambda_{12}\phi_{12} + \lambda_{12}^2\phi_{22} \qquad (33)$$

In this form we notice that two of the terms are identical (they contain the same elements in a different order), so we can rearrange and rewrite this as

$$Var(x_1) = \lambda_{11}^2\phi_{11} + \lambda_{12}^2\phi_{22} + 2\lambda_{11}\lambda_{12}\phi_{12} \qquad (34)$$

Compare Equation (34) with Equation (9), and Figure 8.6 with Figure 8.2. These causal worlds are making the same style of causal demands regarding the variance of the dependent variable, whether the causal variables are latent or observed, and whether the notation is Greek or Latin. If you can convince yourself of the similar causal understandability of Equations (9) and (34), and the parallel demanded causal consequences expressed by Equations (9) and (34), you will be well on your way to resolving one of the big fights below. Is there anything that forbids, or renders inscrutable, the possibility of having one single indicator measure two different latent variables? We did not ask about estimation, nor about whether we would like to see such things frequently or infrequently. We are merely concerned with whether you can understand such an instance causally, and whether you can see that this requires the same kind of causal understanding as went along with Equation (9) with its partitionings and doubling of boosts and whammies. Now for our final style of preparatory model.

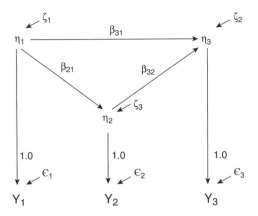

Figure 8.7   Latent variables with indirect effects

Latents Causing Both Indicators and Other Latents

Our final model (Figure 8.7) incorporates effects of some latent variables on other latent variables, as well as effects of the latents on observed indicators. LISREL notation designates latents that receive effects as η variables, and observed indicators of η's as Y variables. For ease of comparison to the 'indirect effects' model in Figure 8.4, we designate all the Figure 8.7 latents as η variables, even though we could have designated η_1 as an exogenous latent because its causal sources (the 'error' ζ_1) are entirely unknown.

LISREL uses the following equation (Jöreskog and Sörbom, 1996: 2) to express the effects among latent variables.

$$\eta = B\eta + \Gamma\xi + \zeta \qquad (35)$$

For the all-η model in Figure 8.7 (which has no ξ variables) this becomes

$$\begin{bmatrix} \eta_1 \\ \eta_2 \\ \eta_3 \end{bmatrix} = \begin{bmatrix} 0 & 0 & 0 \\ \beta_{21} & 0 & 0 \\ \beta_{31} & \beta_{32} & 0 \end{bmatrix} \begin{bmatrix} \eta_1 \\ \eta_2 \\ \eta_3 \end{bmatrix} + \begin{bmatrix} \zeta_1 \\ \zeta_2 \\ \zeta_3 \end{bmatrix} \qquad (36)$$

and corresponds to three equations:

$$\eta_1 = \zeta_1 \qquad (37)$$

$$\eta_2 = \beta_{21}\eta_1 + \zeta_2 \qquad (38)$$

$$\eta_3 = \beta_{31}\eta_1 + \beta_{32}\eta_2 + \zeta_3 \qquad (39)$$

Notice the parallel between the causal representation connecting these latents and the causal specification in Equations (13) and (14) for the Figure 8.4 model.

LISREL represents the effects leading from the η latents to the Y indicators as

$$y = \Lambda\eta + \varepsilon \qquad (40)$$

which for the Figure 8.7 model is

$$\begin{bmatrix} y_1 \\ y_2 \\ y_3 \end{bmatrix} = \begin{bmatrix} 1 & 0 & 0 \\ 0 & 1 & 0 \\ 0 & 0 & 1 \end{bmatrix} \begin{bmatrix} \eta_1 \\ \eta_2 \\ \eta_3 \end{bmatrix} + \begin{bmatrix} \varepsilon_1 \\ \varepsilon_2 \\ \varepsilon_3 \end{bmatrix} \qquad (41)$$

and corresponds to the equations

$$y_1 = 1.0\eta_1 + \varepsilon_1 \qquad (42)$$

$$y_2 = 1.0\eta_2 + \varepsilon_2 \qquad (43)$$

$$y_3 = 1.0\eta_3 + \varepsilon_3 \qquad (44)$$

The 1.0 values introduce the common convention of scaling the latent variables to have the same scale units as the corresponding Y indicators, by making each unit change in a latent's value causally produce precisely a unit change in the value of the corresponding indicator. The ε error variables constitute the errors in measuring the true values of the latent variables, in contrast to the ζ errors in Equation (36) which are substantive unknown causes of the latent variables' true values. The Figure 8.7 model's full set of equations can be thought of as either Equations (36) and (41), or as Equations (37), (38), (39) and (42), (43) and (44).

Hayduk (1987: 113) discusses the demanded covariance implications of any latent-level model following the form of Equation (35). With no ξ variables, and assuming independence of the error variables, the unavoidable latent-level covariance implications are

$$\begin{bmatrix} Covariance \\ Matrix \\ of\ the\ \eta's \end{bmatrix} = [(I - B)^{-1}\Psi(I - B)^{-1\prime} \qquad (45)$$

For the Figure 8.7 model the inverse of the $(I - B)$ matrix, in symbolic form, can be obtained as outlined in Endnote 1, so Figure 8.7 model's unavoidable latent-level covariance implications are given by

$$
\begin{bmatrix} Covariance \\ Matrix \\ of\ the\ \eta's \end{bmatrix} = \begin{bmatrix} 1 & 0 & 0 \\ \beta_{21} & 1 & 0 \\ \beta_{31} + \beta_{32}\beta_{21} & \beta_{32} & 1 \end{bmatrix} \begin{bmatrix} \psi_{11} & 0 & 0 \\ 0 & \psi_{22} & 0 \\ 0 & 0 & \psi_{33} \end{bmatrix} \begin{bmatrix} 1 & \beta_{21} & \beta_{31} + \beta_{32}\beta_{21} \\ 0 & 1 & \beta_{32} \\ 0 & 0 & 1 \end{bmatrix} \tag{46}
$$

Multiplying the two left-matrices provides

$$
\begin{bmatrix} Covariance \\ Matrix \\ of\ the\ \eta's \end{bmatrix} = \begin{bmatrix} \psi_{11} & 0 & 0 \\ \beta_{21}\psi_{11} & \psi_{22} & 0 \\ (\beta_{31} + \beta_{32}\beta_{21})\psi_{11} & \beta_{32}\psi_{22} & \psi_{33} \end{bmatrix} \begin{bmatrix} 1 & \beta_{21} & \beta_{31} + \beta_{32}\beta_{21} \\ 0 & 1 & \beta_{32} \\ 0 & 0 & 1 \end{bmatrix} \tag{47}
$$

And multiplying the remaining matrices provides

$$
\begin{bmatrix} Var(\eta_1) & Cov(\eta_1\eta_2) & Cov(\eta_1\eta_3) \\ Cov(\eta_1\eta_2) & Var(\eta_2) & Cov(\eta_2\eta_3) \\ Cov(\eta_1\eta_3) & Cov(\eta_2\eta_3) & Var(\eta_3) \end{bmatrix} \tag{48}
$$

$$
= \begin{bmatrix} \psi_{11} & \beta_{21}\psi_{11} & (\beta_{31} + \beta_{32}\beta_{21})\psi_{11} \\ \beta_{21}\psi_{11} & \beta_{21}^2\psi_{11} + \psi_{22} & (\beta_{31} + \beta_{32}\beta_{21})\beta_{21}\psi_{11} + \beta_{32}\psi_{22} \\ (\beta_{31} + \beta_{32}\beta_{21})\psi_{11} & (\beta_{31} + \beta_{32}\beta_{21})\beta_{21}\psi_{11} + \beta_{32}\psi_{22} & (\beta_{31} + \beta_{32}\beta_{21})^2\psi_{11} + \beta_{32}^2\psi_{22} + \psi_{33} \end{bmatrix}
$$

Fortunately we need not attend to all nine of these demanded causal implications of the Figure 8.7 latent-level model. Only the lower-left entries will concern us, so we extract this as a separate equation, namely

$$
Cov(\eta_1,\eta_3) = (\beta_{31} + \beta_{32}\beta_{21})\psi_{11} \tag{49}
$$

You should see this as nearly paralleling Equation (15). We can simplify this a bit by presuming we have scaled our latent variables to have unit variances (which for η_1 means that the corresponding error variable has unit variance because η_1 is entirely error). This standardization turns the covariance into a correlation, and permits rewriting the above equation as

$$
r_{\eta_1,\eta_3} = \beta_{31} + \beta_{32}\beta_{21} \tag{50}
$$

You should now be able to convince yourself that because Equations (38) and (39) are causally structured in parallel to Equations (13) and (14), parallel covariance implications are unavoidably demanded. That is, the causal structure that led to understanding how direct and indirect effects might cancel out and result in zero correlation despite real effects, leads to exactly the same kind of observation at the latent level. If the indirect effect $\beta_{32}\beta_{21}$ was equal in magnitude but opposite in sign to β_{31}, then zero correlation (and covariance) would appear between η_1 and η_3. The rigidity or unavoidability of the covariance implications of causal actions becomes a tool that permits understanding latent-level variables just as assuredly and just as confidently as one understands observed variables.

But we are not quite done with the Figure 8.7 model. The demanded covariance implications of this model do not just interconnect the latent variables in the model: they also connect to the observed Y indicators. The covariances among the indicators are primarily driven by the covariances among the underlying latent η variables, which subsequently get transferred down to the Ys by the causal impacts the ηs have on the Ys. The causally demanded covariance matrix for the Y indicators in any model having a form that can be expressed as Equations (35) and (40) (again assuming causally independent error variables) is discussed in Hayduk (1987: 114), and with no ξ variables, is

$$
\begin{bmatrix}
Covariance \\
Matrix \\
of\ the\ y's
\end{bmatrix}
= \Lambda_y (I - B)^{-1} \Psi (I - B)^{-1'} \Lambda'_y + \theta_\varepsilon
\tag{51}
$$

Notice that the middle portion of this formula is simply the matrix presented in Equation (45), and that this is unchanged if it is pre- and post-multiplied by the identity matrix that is the Λ matrix for the Figure 8.7 model (see Equation (41)). The θ_ε matrix for this model is a diagonal matrix of measurement error variances. Thus the $+$ sign in Equation (51) tells us that the covariance matrix of the Y variables in the Figure 8.7 model is 'the covariance matrix of the latent variables' with the appropriate measurement error variance added to the diagonal elements (variances) of Equation (48), namely.

$$
\begin{bmatrix}
Var(y_1) & Cov(y_1 y_2) & Cov(y_1 y_3) \\
Cov(y_1 y_2) & Var(y_2) & Cov(y_2 y_3) \\
Cov(y_1 y_3) & Cov(y_2 y_3) & Var(y_3)
\end{bmatrix}
$$

$$
=
\begin{bmatrix}
\psi_{11} + \theta_{\varepsilon 11} & \beta_{21}\psi_{11} & (\beta_{31} + \beta_{32}\beta_{21})\psi_{11} \\
\beta_{21}\psi_{11} & \beta_{21}^2\psi_{11} + \psi_{22} + \theta_{\varepsilon 22} & (\beta_{31} + \beta_{32}\beta_{21})\beta_{21}\psi_{11} + \beta_{32}\psi_{22} \\
(\beta_{31} + \beta_{32}\beta_{21})\psi_{11} & (\beta_{31} + \beta_{32}\beta_{21})\beta_{21}\psi_{11} + \beta_{32}\psi_{22} & (\beta_{31} + \beta_{32}\beta_{21})^2\psi_{11} + \beta_{32}^2\psi_{22} + \psi_{33} + \theta_{\varepsilon 33}
\end{bmatrix}
\tag{52}
$$

Notice that the lower-left entry again takes the same comfortable and understandable form as Equation (15). (Standardizing to get to a correlation comparable to Equation (16) or (50) would require standardizing the Y not η variables, but we need not pursue this for our current purposes.) That is, the observed covariance between indicator y_1 and y_3 would mirror the understandable causal behavior of the corresponding underlying latents. The causally demanded covariances of the indicators incorporates the causally demanded covariance behavior of the latent variables in the model.

Notice also that the entry in the lowest left corner ($Cov(y_3, y_1)$ which equals $Cov(y_1, y_3)$) arises despite no direct causal effect between y_1 and y_3. If this demanded covariance happened to be inconsistent with what was observed in the data as the covariance between y_1 and y_3, we should be led directly toward questioning the latent level of the model. Failure to fit with the covariances of the observed indicators should attract our attention to potential causal misspecification up at the latent level of the model, but failure to fit the covariance between y_3 and y_1 would not guarantee that the latent-level model was problematic. This is because a variety of other problems might also lead to ill-fit. Someone might have made a mistake in calculating the data covariances, or the latent model might be appropriate for some but not all the cases, or there might be some covariance between the measurement errors so that the θ_ε matrix contained an off-diagonal element that would change what is required/demanded for the ill-fit covariance, etc. But the possibility of misspecification at the latent level should be attended to whenever ill-fit is observed because this constitutes 'the theory of interest'. We would be using this set of indicators precisely because they connected to the latent-level theory of interest, and hence if the indicators misbehave according to what the theory demands, re-examination of the latent level theory would seem 'prudent'.

As a final observation, notice that we have incorporated measurement in this model by employing single indicators of the latent variables. There is no difficulty in understanding the demanded causal implications when using single indicators, so if anyone objects to the use of single indicators, the objections must be regarding something other than the causal clarity and implication-consistency of single indicators.

WHAT HAVE WE LEARNED FROM THE PRECEDING?

The most important message is that both a causal world and causal structural equation models have specifiable, understandable, and demanded (unavoidable, provable, inescapable) implications for the variances and covariances of the variables in the model. These inescapable consequences are detailed and precise, even if they are model-specific. Some of the inescapable consequences are intuitive in that we naturally recognize these as reasonable while others may have to be educated into our intuition. You should also have sensed that it can be both tricky and difficult to follow through the demanded and inescapable implications of structural equation models. This should lead you to consider that the literature is being written by researchers who vary greatly in their understanding of causally-demanded covariances. You might also notice corresponding variations in the more statistical presentations of structural equation modeling. These range from Hayduk (1987: 106–116) who attempted to provide an accessible introduction to causal models' covariance demands, through Bollen (1989: 324–325) who

provided a compacted version of the relevant mathematics, all the way to those who dispense with demanded causal consequences by merely saying the model equations and assumptions 'imply the following form for the covariance matrix of the observed variables' (Jöreskog and Sörbom, 1996: 3)—end of story. The statisticians do not intend to be unhelpful—they just have other statistical matters on their minds.

Second, these inescapable covariance consequences assist estimation of model parameters (e.g. Equation (5) or Equation (6)). A causal model's covariance demands make estimation possible by placing constraints on the permissible estimated values of the model's parameters.

Third, we have seen how causal rigidity or specificity can result in rigid covariance demands that make model testing possible. Again, recall Equations (5) and (6) where a specific (even though unspecified) effect magnitude in a model demands that a specific ratio should appear for two different sets of observable variances and covariances. The structural constraints in the causal model result in demanded constraints on the covariances, and model testability is founded on satisfying or failing to satisfy the required constraints.

Fourth, we learned that a model can be seriously causally wrong, even if there are no signs of covariance problems. Recall the covariance consistency of the Figure 8.1 model and its reversed causal direction, or see discussions of equivalent models (e.g., Hayduk, 1996: 79–120). Hence we must attend to all signs of covariance problems, lest these be the first detectable sign of multiple serious causal misspecification problems, like reversed effects.

And even though we have not demonstrated this, you should appreciate that there may be no clear statistical diagnostics that locate the specific problem(s) (recall the multiple potentially problematic assumptions of error independence). You should have a sense that, as a researcher using structural equation models, you will have to take charge and think through the covariance demands of your model so that you can see or intuit the kinds of covariance consequences attached to the model features you find most dubious on the basis of your informed understanding of the literature/theory and the methodology that provided the indicators.

CURRENT CONTROVERSIES AND THEIR CAUSAL RESOLUTIONS

The three controversies addressed below arose from discussions on SEMNET, a listserve set up by Carl Ferguson and Ed Rigdon. E-mail postings regarding structural equation models are distributed by the University of Alabama to about 1,900 researchers worldwide. SEMNET is free and instructions for joining are available at: http://www.gsu.edu/~mkteer/semnet.html. Many SEMNET postings are brief question-and-answer exchanges but some expand into prolonged discussions, where important substance tends to develop into a soap-opera-like mix of personalities, occasional heated words, hurt feelings, flare-ups, and a drama uncharacteristic of formal academic articles. The remainder of this chapter encapsulates the first author's (Leslie Hayduk's) perspective on the three major controversies he has been involved in since joining SEMNET in 1997.

The first major SEMNET controversy consisted primarily of exchanges between Leslie Hayduk and Stanley Mulaik, and came to be focused on whether or not researchers should use a multi-step (usually three-step, but occasionally four-step) procedure to develop and investigate structural equation models. Mulaik (on SEMNET) and others (Anderson and Gerbing, 1988, 1992; James et al., 1982) had proposed investigating a series of models—essentially an equivalent-to-exploratory factor model, a confirmatory factor model, and then the full structural equation model. This *seemed* to make intuitive sense because it placed

exploratory measurement prior to confirmatory measurement, and both these prior to investigating causal assertions connecting the measured latents. Hayduk and others thought this particular 'intuition' was in need of re-education (Hayduk 1996: Chapter 2; Fornell and Yi, 1992a, 1992b). Dale Glaser had reviewed Hayduk's 1996 book and brought the disagreement to SEMNET attention. The ensuing SEMNET discussion of the four-step lasted several years, and only abated when George Marcoulides, editor of *Structural Equation Modeling*, dedicated most of the first 2000 issue of this journal (volume 7, issue 1) to a 'target' article by Hayduk and Glaser (2000a), followed by commentaries by multiple parties (Bentler, 2000; Bollen, 2000; Herting and Costner, 2000; Mulaik and Millsap, 2000), and a rejoinder by Hayduk and Glaser (2000b). (Two additional commentaries appeared in the 7(2) issue but Hayduk and Glaser were given no opportunity to provide much-needed responses to these (Markus, 2000; Steiger, 2000).)

The exchanges in *Structural Equation Modeling* 7(1) quieted the SEMNET discussion of the four-step debate, but a 'new twist' introduced in the target article—asking 'Which Test: Chi-square or RMSEA?' was to be used in testing structural equation models (Hayduk and Glaser, 2000a: 25)—ignited a new and still-flaming SEMNET dispute over structural equation model testing.

The third major discussion—'How many indicators does one need to model a latent variable?'—also arose from a SEMNET discussion of Hayduk (1996: Chapter 1). The 'how many indicators' discussion has arisen repeatedly as a side disagreement connected to both the four-step and model-testing discussions, but this remains a flickering flame destined to turn into a roaring inferno as soon as the current 'structural equation model testing' flames have been brought under control (presumably by publication of a target article proposing careful structural equation model testing—with commentaries).

The following does not attempt to summarize all the points made in the SEMNET discussions of these debates. SEMNET has a searchable archive if you are interested in all the details. And the four-step debate is easily accessible because Lawrence Erlbaum Associates, the publisher of *Structural Equation Modeling* has generously made the relevant 2000 issue available online. (Just go to the publisher's web site at www.erlbaum.com to gain complementary access to the 7(1) issue.)

Instead, we attempt to show how the demanded and inescapable implications of causal models orient one's thinking about these big discussions. That is, we attempt to show how causally-demanded covariance implications provide an overarching structure that ties the three big controversies into a single resolvable package. An appreciation of the demanded and inescapable implications—or covariance consequences—of structural equation models provides a consistent foundation that we hope will protect you from taking a stance in the context of one debate that contradicts your stance in another debate. We have attempted to avoid a variety of technical details in order to help you see how a consistent mode of thinking connects these seemingly diverse debates. Naturally, our presentation of the structure of this big picture is our way of attempting to persuade you of our views—so you might pause a moment to consider your personal inclinations regarding 'measurement before latent structure', model testing, and numbers of indicators, and to reconsider the points presented above. We begin with the current flaming controversy.

Testing Structural Equation Models

It is clear that we as scientists must be committed to testing our causal models. We need to know whether our causal model is or is not consistent with the available evidence. Researchers usually hope the evidence is consistent with their model's claims, but the hope does not displace the need for test evidence. Unfortunately, no direct test of the correctness of a model's causal structure is currently available. The best we can do is test to see if the demanded, inescapable *consequences* of the model's causal structuring are consistent with the evidence. If a causal model's demanded covariance implications are inconsistent with the evidence, that constitutes a prima facie indication that something might be problematic about the model's causal specification. We would be observing something inconsistent with the model's causal demands.

It would be nice if we could estimate the effect parameters in the model (like the bs, βs, and λs above), and merely look to see if the parameter estimates were consistent with all the covariance data. For example, we might use Equation (5) to estimate b and then look to see whether this estimated b is also consistent with the covariances in Equation (6). A key obstacle to proceeding this way is that we typically do not have the population variance/covariance matrix—all we typically have is a variance/covariance matrix calculated for some sample of cases, and hence there is some sampling variability in the variances and covariances. This sampling variability means we cannot trust equations like (5) and (6) to give precise estimates or tests via inserting data-derived variances and covariances on the right-hand sides of these equations.

A superior iterative approach to estimation and testing begins with some initial estimates and then improves upon those estimates by progressively minimizing what must be ascribed to sampling fluctuations. The iterative process places a set of initial effect (parameter) estimates in the model equations, and then uses these to calculate the covariance matrix undeniably implied by the model with those initial estimates in place. This is like using numerical estimates for the effects (and variances of the errors) in Equation (17) to do the calculation in Equation (21), or using numerical estimates of the effects (and variances of the errors) in

Equations (35) and (40) to do the calculation in Equation (48). The covariance matrix implied by the model with the 'initial estimates' is compared to the data matrix by calculating the likelihood that the data covariance matrix could have arisen via mere sampling fluctuations around the 'model and initial-estimate implied' covariance matrix. Repeatedly adjusting (increasing or decreasing) the numerical estimates until they imply a covariance matrix that is as similar as possible to the observed covariance matrix results in the 'maximum likelihood estimates'. These are the estimates that maximize the likelihood that the observed data covariances could have been observed in a random sample from a population having the covariance matrix that would be demanded if 'the model containing these best estimates' constituted the world (population) from which the sample had been drawn (Bollen, 1989; Hayduk, 1987; Jöreskog and Sörbom, 1996).

The model-implied covariance matrix (usually called Σ, or sigma) contains the covariances that are as close as this model can come to matching up with the data covariance matrix through adjustment of the model's freely-estimable coefficient values. The repeated estimate adjustments give the model its 'best shot' at matching up with the data covariance matrix. But the researcher still confronts the issue of whether the remaining differences between the data and model-and-estimate-demanded (putative population) covariances are or are not larger than might be reasonably attributed to mere sampling fluctuations. If the model with its best estimates corresponds to the worldly causal forces, the model-and-estimate-demanded covariance matrix Σ would correspond to the worldly population covariance matrix. Hence it seems clear that the researcher should test whether the sample covariance data differs from the model-and-estimate-demanded covariance matrix (the putative population covariance matrix) by more than an amount that could reasonably be attributed to random sampling fluctuations. If the covariance

differences are small enough to be typical of mere chance sampling fluctuations, then the remaining differences would not stand as evidence speaking against the causal structuring of the model with its current estimates. But if the covariance differences were so large as to be unlikely to have resulted from chance sampling fluctuations, then these constitute evidence inconsistent with the model's causal demands.

Any beyond-chance inconsistency between the model-and-estimate-implied covariance matrix (the covariance matrix demanded by the model containing the optimal estimates) and the data covariance matrix should initiate a diagnostic investigation seeking what is wrong. Knowing that something is detectably problematic does not report on specifically what is problematic. The model might be wrong for any of a variety of reasons: improperly omitted effects, unmodeled non-linearity, incorrect assumptions of error independence, the cases failing to share a single causal structure, reversed causal effect directions, mistakes in calculating the data covariance matrix, and so on. Hence, the model should be tested to see if the data covariances differ significantly from the model-and-estimate-demanded covariances, and significant ill-fit should initiate a thorough diagnostic investigation of the possible reasons for ill-fit.

Why might anyone object to this? The people who object are the advocates of what has come to be called close-fit testing (or in SEMNET plain-speak, close-but-not-good-enough fit testing). This is model testing that 'permits', 'accepts' or 'overlooks' some degree of covariance ill-fit (between the model-demanded and observed-data covariance matrices) *in addition to* the ill-fit that might reasonably be attributed to sampling fluctuations (e.g.. Browne and Cudeck, 1993; Browne et al., 2002). This is usually presented as testing a hypothesized non-zero RMSEA (root mean square error of approximation) value. The idea of 'error of approximation' sounds harmless enough—until you notice that 'error of approximation' in this context is statistician-speak for evidence speaking against the model because the world that provided the data is inconsistent with the model under consideration (Browne and Cudeck, 1993: 141). Testing non-zero RMSEA values overlooks, or disregards, non-zero amounts of evidence speaking against the model by deviously including (hiding) the non-zero amount of ill-fit within the non-zero RMSEA value used as the statistical null hypothesis. Including larger non-zero RMSEA values within the model test null hypothesis merely increases the amount of evidence of covariance ill-fit that someone wants to hide, overlook or 'silence' by 'null-hypothesizing this out of sight', so that fewer people notice the evidence speaking against the model!

On what basis do the close-but-not-good-enough fit testers justify overlooking evidence speaking against their models? Their primary claim is that all models are wrong (in ways that *exceed* both measurement error and all the other features incorporated as components of the model) because models are mere approximations. As Browne and Cudeck put it: 'Since a null hypothesis that a model fits exactly in some population is known *a priori* to be false, it seems pointless even to try to test whether it is true' (1993: 137). This God-like assertion of knowing that all models are wrong disintegrates in the face of multiple cleanly-fitting models (Entwisle et al., 1982; Hayduk, 1996; Hayduk et al., 2005). For a compelling example arising from SEMNET discussions, contrast the model Browne et al. (2002) pass off as well-enough-fitting for them, with the substantively different causal model presented by Hayduk et al. (2005), which *cleanly* fits the very same data. God might know if all clean-fitting structural equation models are wrong, but until Browne or his co-authors become God, the multiple clean covariance-fitting models illustrate the utility of testing models right down to the limits of sampling fluctuations.

Another reason some people disregard ill-fit is that they have encountered models that stubbornly fail to fit, so they are inclined to call their model 'good enough to permit them to persist with their predetermined personal agenda'. It is no coincidence that the seriously causally-problematic model good enough for Browne et al. (2002) was a factor model. The context of significantly poor fit being called 'good enough for someone to resist having to change their modeling ideas' is often connected to factor analysis! Factor models are causal models (they extend the latent common cause model in Figure 8.5 to include more indicators and more latent common causes), where the researchers' agenda is to begin with as few factors as possible and use more factors 'only if they have to'. Unfortunately, what would make them 'have to' use more factors is *not* careful attention to the properness of their model's causal specification.

For any given set of indicators, each additional factor guarantees an improvement in fit between the model-demanded covariance matrix and the data matrix but this does *not* guarantee that the model is getting correspondingly closer to being properly causally-specified. For a demonstration of this see Hayduk and Glaser (2000a: 14), or see anyone discussing why following modification indices toward better fit cannot be trusted to lead to properly causally specified models (e.g., Herting and Costner, 2000). The disrespect for the causal importance of the remaining covariance ill-fit is endemic to factor analysis because the disrespect is founded in factor-analytic operating procedures. There the intent is often 'data reduction', whereby numerous indicators are to be 'reduced' to a few factors, so scales can be sold as measuring those factors—an exercise from which a dedication to seeking and respecting the world's causal structure is conspicuously absent. In factor analysis the 'next factor' is *supposedly* weaker and deficient because it does not account for much variance/covariance—where the *supposed* weakness is based on the presumption that the next smaller eigenvalue corresponds to the degree of model causal misspecification. The mistake being made is in thinking that the degree or seriousness of model causal misspecification can be trusted to correspond to the degree of the remaining covariance ill-fit. The 'next cause' might not be a common cause of many items, and it might seem less potent merely because the estimation of free effects from prior 'factors' erroneously glommed onto many of its rightful covariance consequences.

On SEMNET a series of exchanges between Leslie Hayduk and Roger Millsap investigated this, but the point can also be understood in the context of the simple causal model with which we began. Reversing the causal direction from X-causes-Y to Y-causes-X would surely constitute an important causal mistake, even though either of these models being true renders the reversed causal model also capable of perfectly fitting the covariance data. Covariance-equivalent models (Hayduk, 1996) and nearly-covariance-equivalent models (see the SEMNET archive attached to the web address provided previously) render it unreasonable to assume that a small degree of covariance ill-fit reports that there are only small or minimal causal specification problems. People calling significantly ill-fitting models 'good enough for them', are unlikely to locate properly causally specified models because their 'satisfaction' with the current model renders them unlikely to do the detailed diagnostic investigations that would be undertaken by researchers attentive to the implications of failed model tests.

Do Measurement With, Not Before, Latent Structure

The theme of model testing continues as we move to the next 'major disagreement', but the issue is not which test to use. We presume the test being used is the exact-covariance-fit test (χ^2 or RMSEA=0.0). Here the issue is implicitly about the hypotheses tested by a sequence of four model tests. The causal

models comprising the first three of the four steps are: an exploratory factor model, a confirmatory factor model, and a full structural equation model. (The fourth model step adds unspecified additional constraints so we focus on the first three of the four model steps.) The researcher is *supposed* to have obtained the three models by beginning with the full structural equation model, then converting this into the confirmatory factor model by replacing the latent-level causal claims with a saturated (full) set of correlations/covariances between the latents, and finally converting this into an equivalent-to-exploratory factor model by introducing as many effects from each latent to all the indicators as possible. This is suspiciously similar to the reverse sequence of starting with exploratory factor analysis to supposedly locate the number of latent variables, followed by confirmatory factor analysis to place selected items under specific latents (while leaving the latent factors oblique or correlated), and finally reaching a full structural equation model by replacing the latent factor covariances with directed causal effects. The endemic practice of developing (as opposed to just testing) the models in this reversed sequence, actually attacks the statistical foundations of model testing, but we circumvent this deficiency by presuming that the models actually had been developed appropriately: namely by beginning with the full model, and relaxing constraints (adding coefficients) to get to the confirmatory factor model, and relaxing more constraints (adding more coefficients) to get to a factor model that is fit-equivalent to an exploratory factor model.

The four-step procedure proposes *testing* these models in sequence. If the first-step exploratory (or fit-equivalent to exploratory) factor model fails, this is supposed to tell us that the number of latents is wrong. If the second-step model fails, this is supposed to tell us that something is problematic about which items are connected to which latents. And if the third-step model fails, this is supposed to tell us that something is wrong with the specified causal connections between the latents. To see the inadequacies of these suppositions, we will consider some models discussed on SEMNET and summarized in the volume 7 issue 1 of *Structural Equation Modeling*.

Imagine a first-step model in which three correlated latents ('factors') are modeled as causing 10 items. This would be somewhat like Figure 8.7 with loadings leading from each of the three latents to 10 indicators, and with the latents being correlated instead of engaging in effects. If this model failed to fit with the covariance data, that failure would provide evidence speaking against three underlying latents as causing the items. But what could we conclude if the covariance matrix demanded by the three-latent model was within sampling fluctuations of the data covariance matrix? Does this tell us the proper number of underlying latent variables is three? The answer is NO, it does not! What it tells us is that the proper number of latents may be three *or more*. This 'or more' is sufficient to severely wound exploratory factor analysis as 'measurement', and to kill the four-step procedure. If the true number of latents is 10—namely, if there really is one indicator per latent as in the SEMNET demonstration (Hayduk and Glaser, 2000a: 14)—and the first-step exploratory-factor model says the number is 'three or more', what would the exploratory-factor first-step model have told us about measurement of the 10 latents? The three-factor model that fit the data would not have even gotten to the proper number, let alone identity, of the latents, so it certainly could not tell us much about what, let alone how well, we are measuring anything!

How it is possible for the demanded covariance matrix for a model with three 'factors' to actually fit within sampling fluctuations of data arising from a world containing 10 latents? The key to understanding this is to notice that unnecessary but estimated coefficients in a model dilute, soften or weaken the stringency of the model's covariance demands. Consider what would happen

to the demanded covariances among the Ys in Equation (52) if the model had permitted covariances between the measurement errors of the Ys. The alterable values of these estimated error covariances would permit many more alternative covariance matrices for the Y variables to be 'demanded' (on the left-hand side of Equation (52)). That is, the model's covariance 'demands' would be weakened, diluted, and become less stringent, because adjustment of the free-but-unnecessary model coefficients would permit the estimation process to adjust these estimates to match up with a wider range of Y covariances. The loosening of the model's covariance demands by introduction of unneeded-but-free coefficients would permit the model to fit when it ought not fit. Similarly, a three-latent-factor model, with a multitude of *free-but-unnecessary loadings* can use the adjustment of those unnecessary-but-free coefficients during estimation, to *loosen* the model's covariance *demands* to the point where the model fits with three latent factors even if the model truly contained 10 latents (see Hayduk and Glaser, 2000a: 14 for an example of this).

Our point is to warn you of the danger of weakening a model's demanded covariances by entering free-but-unnecessary coefficients into that model. The four-step procedure explicitly enters free-but-unnecessary model coefficients in moving to (or starting from) the initial exploratory (or fit-equivalent to exploratory) model. That introduction of 'unnecessary-but-free' coefficients renders the exploratory factor model unspecific and unconvincing in its investigation of how many latents are being measured by the indicators. The minimum number of fitting 'factors' cannot be trusted to be the proper number of latents because any 'unnecessary-but-free loadings' in the factor model soften, weaken and dilute the covariance demands of the model to the point that the model becomes incapable of convincingly reporting on the number of latent variables (see Hayduk and Glaser 2000a: 8–18, Hayduk and Glaser, 2000b: 114–115).

When the researcher moves to the second-step or third-step models by adding more constraints into the model (by removing unnecessarily freed coefficients), the more rigid model covariance demands could make the second- or third-step models fail, and hence the researcher should seriously reconsider the number of latents in the model if later-step failure appears. But what use is the first step (the exploratory or fit-equivalent to exploratory step) if failure at the later steps ought to initiate a re-questioning of the number of latents in the model? We think the answer is: 'Not much'. And similarly what use is the second-step model if failure resulting from the even more rigid covariance demands (created by the elimination of additional unnecessary estimated coefficients) that get us to the most theoretically-appropriate third-step model should prod the researcher to reconsider the number of required latent variables? Again, the answer seems to be: 'Not much.'

Free estimates of unnecessary coefficients weaken a model's covariance demands by permitting the model to match up with a wider range of data covariances. Enough 'unnecessary but free' estimates can loosen a model's covariance demands to the point where even seriously wrongly causally specified models can fit practically any covariance data. In the extreme, if there is one freely estimated parameter for each data covariance, the model's demands will be so weakened by estimation of free coefficients that the model is guaranteed to fit. The model is said to be 'saturated' with estimates because the 'covariance demands' have been so eroded by the freeing (estimating) of coefficients that the model can contort itself into matching up with any observed covariance matrix. The model may be fitting the data not because it is properly causally specified, but because this model contains multiple estimated coefficients that have loosened the model's covariance demands to the point where it can morph to fit any covariance matrix whatsoever.

How can we most thoroughly investigate the proper number of latents? We can do this by demonstrating that the specific number and identity of the latents function as expected when placed in a maximally covariance-demanding and theoretically reasonable latent model—which is the step-three or full structural equation model. The most convincing examination of the number of latents arises from the full structural equation model because this model provides the strongest covariance demands while simultaneously corresponding to the clearest theoretical causal specification.

This seems straightforward, so why is it controversial? It is controversial because it questions the utility of factor models (whether exploratory or confirmatory) in the context of structural equation modeling. The researcher moves directly to the full structural equation model rather than dawdling in factor analysis. Factor models constituted a major part of the historical development of structural equation modeling, and many researchers are still taught factor analysis as a stepping-stone to learning structural equation modeling. Questioning the utility of factor analysis threatens to convert some people's active careers into history, and challenges other people by requiring that they rethink what they thought constituted an adequate factor-analytic foundation for structural equation modeling. Some people do not take kindly to having their careers relegated to past history, or to doing 'required rethinking'!

How Many Indicators Are Needed?

We should seek enough indicators to permit estimating and testing the theoretical understandings we place in our causal structural equation models. If we have a clear understanding of our latent variable and its postulated latent-level causes and effects, a single indicator should be sufficient to assert the meaning we wish to assign to that latent variable. We presume the researchers have a thorough grasp of the methodology that provided the indicator, which means that they should have a correspondingly clear understanding of how the desired latent differs from the available indicator.

It should be obvious that the fewer the indicators we use for any given latent variable, the better the quality of those indicators. If we use only a single indicator, we can choose the very best indicator. It has the clearest questionnaire wording, contains substantial variance, and most closely matches the latent concept our theory postulates as participating in specific latent-level causal actions. It should also be obvious that with fewer indicators per latent, the researcher can make the latent-theoretical segment of their model more realistic. This researcher can introduce, and hence control for, more and finer latent-level distinctions than can someone requiring multiple indicators per latent.

Procedurally, using the single best indicator usually requires a fixed 1.0 loading to provide the latent variable a scale, and a fixed measurement error variance to assert the extent of the difference between the intended latent and that best indicator. The self-conscious theory-assertive nature of this procedure strongly recommends that this same procedure be used for the first of multiple indicators, even if theory assertion could be avoided by error variance estimation with multiple indicators. Can you hear the unnecessary freeing of measurement error variances as 'inviting' a deficiency parallel to that introduced when the four-step procedure introduced unnecessary-but-free model coefficients? Here it is obvious the mere possibility of estimation (of an error variance) could be used to displace attentive theorizing and to avoid the testable covariance demands made by that theorizing. This evasion of theory can be contrasted with an assessment of the model's sensitivity to the specific theoretical demand as provided by halving and doubling the error variance specification. For procedural details regarding fixed measurement error variances, see Hayduk (1996: 28).

The covariances demanded by single-indicator models are largely dependent on the rigidity of the latent level of the model. If the latent level of the model contains few coefficients to estimate, the covariance demands can be sufficient to provide strong and theoretically oriented testing of the model. Adding a second indicator of any given latent typically adds two new coefficients to estimate (a 'loading' and an error variance) but substantially increases the model's covariance demands because these two estimates must (through the latent causal structure of the model) account for the covariances of this second indicator with all the other indicators in the model. If even half the latents in a model have two indicators each, and if the latent level of the model is reasonably sparse, this should provide sufficiently rigid covariance demands to be highly informative of the adequacy or inadequacies of the causal theory encapsulated in the latent level of the model. Even a model that fails to fit (because its demanded causal constraints are inconsistent with the data covariances) will 'speak to you' if it is structured this way. The simplicity provided by relatively few indicators, and the increased theoretical precision provided by the ability to include additional relevant latent variables, connects relatively specific model causal constraints to specific and rigid covariance demands. The diagnostics of ill-fit become more clearly focused.

Is this controversial? You bet! The single indicator (or few best indicators) approach encourages attention to up-front theorizing: via including more clearly cause/effect latents, via the statistical controlling permitted by more sophisticated latent-level models, and via clear measurement assertion of each theoretical latent. The model's demanded covariances become theoretically informed demands, and the model shouts out its theory via its rigid causal demands. Those lacking theory will object to having to shout their lack of theory!

Notice that it would be contradictory for anyone to propose using additional indicators to 'improve model testing' while simultaneously weakening testing by failing to attend to the χ^2 fit test. So the controversy over single indicators will reconnect to the model-testing controversy—and round and round we go.

CONCLUSION

Researchers are gradually becoming accustomed to thinking of structural equation models as causal representations having rigid covariance consequences. Enhanced understanding of the precision and utility of inescapable covariance consequences provides a foundation for thinking one's way through the major methodological controversies currently confronting structural equation models: exact-fit testing, use of single indicators, and saying no to factor analysis as first steps. When one appreciates the precision of causal consequences, one is more likely to see instances of significant ill-fit as potentially precisely correctable. One is more likely to engage in careful and attentive diagnostic investigations of ill-fit, knowing that there is hope of finding precise and unequivocal emendations. A failed model fit test becomes an invitation to conscientious diagnostic investigation and not 'bad news'. The world is handing the researcher structured evidence beyond what the model permitted or incorporated, and the structuring of the evidence can be heard as an invitation to investigate what is currently 'beyond'. The exact-fit (χ^2) test is making a clarion call to devote precise academic attention—with hair-splitting diagnostic detail and unflinching honesty—to the world that provided the data. One tests structural equation models not to be 'proven right'—we know that even fitting models do not prove a model is right—but to *learn*. The diagnostics of failed models require honest assessments of the multitude of causal details whose demands are noticed as demandingly-inconsistent with the world.

The steps of the four-step procedure are based on the good intention to attempt to specify what has gone wrong: *supposedly* the wrong number of indicators if the step-one factor model fails, and *supposedly* the connections of specific items to specific latents if the step-two confirmatory factor model fails. The attempt to locate the reasons for failure is laudable, but the certitude of the *supposedly*-located problems is lacking. Understanding models' covariance demands leads to understanding why one ought not trust these *supposed* identities of what has gone wrong at the various steps (Hayduk and Glaser, 2000a, 2000b).

Similarly, the issue of how many indicators one needs connects to the precision of causally demanded covariance consequences. The use of a fixed 1.0 'loading' and a fixed measurement error variance for the best indicator are not things that can be done in the absence of precise thinking-through of causal consequences. Gone is the imprecision of freeing all measurement error variances, and gone is the imprecision of uncritically saying that anything common to a set of items will be a latent capable of sending and receiving causal actions at the latent level of the model. Greater specificity and precision in one's understanding of the latents is possible, and is now being required of anyone claiming to have done sound research through structural equation modeling (e.g., Hayduk, 1996).

If you come to these structural equation model controversies from a perspective of having merely memorized procedural rules to follow (like scree rules telling you how many latent factors to use), you will likely be shocked at the vehemence of those you will end up confronting. You will be seen as, and responded to as, someone who has not dug deeply enough into the methodology you are using. Structural equation modeling is cutting itself loose from traditions that previously nourished it but now hamper it. The new way pays careful attention to model testing (it demands attention to the exact-fit χ^2 test even for factor models), focuses on the very best indicators (it demands attention to indicator methodology and the intended/asserted meanings of latents), and confronts lax investigative methodology (it demands recognition of the deficiencies of attaching *supposed* reasons for failure to the factor analytic steps of the four-step procedure). The three controversies we addressed are resolved by a deeper and more thorough understanding of causal models' covariance demands.

Research is not a data-fitting exercise. Research is a self-realignment introduced for consistency with previously unknown world structures. Paying careful attention to the precisely demanded covariance consequences (fit or fail) of causal structural equation models encourages self-realignment.

REFERENCES

Anderson, James C. and Gerbing, David W. (1988) 'Structural equation modeling in practice: A review and recommended two-step approach', *Psychological Bulletin*, 103: 411–23.

—— (1992) 'Assumptions and comparative strengths of the two-step approach: Comments on Fornell and Yi', *Sociological Methods and Research*, 20: 321–33.

Bentler, Peter M. (2000) 'Rites, wrongs, and gold in model testing', *Structural Equation Modeling*, 7(1): 82–91.

Blalock, Hubert. M. Jr. (1964) *Causal Inferences in Nonexperimental Research*. University of North Carolina Press: North Carolina State University Print Shop.

Bollen, Kenneth A. (1989) *Structural Equations with Latent Variables*. New York: John Wiley and Sons.

Bollen, Kenneth A. (2000) 'Modeling strategies: In search of the Holy Grail', *Structural Equation Modeling*, 7(1): 74–81.

Borsboom, Denny, Mellenbergh, Gideon J. and van Heerden, Jaap (2004) 'The concept of validity', *Psychological Review*, 111(4): 1061–1071.

Browne, Michael W. and Cudeck, Robert (1993) 'Alternative ways of assessing model fit', in Kenneth A. Bollen and J. Scott Long (eds.) *Testing Structural Equation Models*. Newbury Park: Sage Publications, pp. 136–62.

Browne, Michael W., MacCallum, Robert C., Kim, Cheong-Tag, Andersen, Barbara L. and Glaser, Ronald (2002) 'When fit indices and residuals are incompatible', *Psychological Methods*, 7(4): 403–21.

Duncan, Otis. D. (1975) *Introduction to Structural Equation Models*. New York: Academic Press.

Entwisle, Doris E., Hayduk, Leslie A. and Reilly, Thomas W. (1982) *Early Schooling: Cognitive and Affective Outcomes*. Baltimore: Johns Hopkins University Press.

Fornell, Claes and Yi, Youjae (1992a) 'Assumptions of the two-step approach to latent variable modeling', *Sociological Methods and Research*, 20: 291–320.

—— (1992b) 'Assumptions of the two-step approach: Reply to Anderson and Gerbing', *Sociological Methods and Research*, 20: 334–39.

Hayduk, Leslie. A. (1987) *Structural Equation Modeling with LISREL: Essentials and Advances*. Baltimore: Johns Hopkins University Press.

—— (1996) *LISREL Issues, Debates and Strategies*. Baltimore: Johns Hopkins University Press.

Hayduk, Leslie A. and Glaser, Dale N. (2000a) 'Jiving the four-step, waltzing around factor analysis, and other serious fun', *Structural Equation Modeling*, 7(1): 1–35. Freely available on the internet at the Lawrence Erlbaum Associates website— www.erlbaum.com—by clicking on the 7(1) issue of *Structural Equation Modeling*.

—— (2000b) 'Doing the four-step, right-2–3, wrong-2–3: A brief reply to Mulaik and Millsap; Bollen; Bentler; and Herting and Costner', *Structural Equation Modeling*, 7(1): 111–23.

Hayduk, Leslie A., Pazderka-Robinson, Hannah, Cummings, Greta G., Levers, Merry-Jo D. and Beres, Melanie A. (2005) 'Structural equation model testing and the quality of natural killer cell activity measurements', *BMC Medical Research Methodology* 5(1): 1–9. Available at: http://www.biomedcentral.com/1471–2288/5/1.

Herting, Jerald R. and Costner, Herbert L. (2000) 'Another perspective on "the proper number of factors" and the appropriate number of steps', *Structural Equation Modeling*, 7(1): 92–110.

James, Lawrence R., Mulaik, Stanley A. and Brett, Jeanne M. (1982) *Causal Analysis: Assumptions, Models and Data*. Beverly Hills: Sage.

Jöreskog, Karl G. and Sörbom, Dag (1996) *LISREL 8: User's Reference Guide*. Chicago: Scientific Software International.

Markus, Keith A. (2000) 'Conceptual shell games in the four-step debate', *Structural Equation Modeling*, 7(2): 163–73.

Mulaik, Stanley A. and Millsap, Roger E. (2000) 'Doing the four-step right', *Structural Equation Modeling*, 7(1): 36–73.

Pearl, Judea. (2000) *Causality: Models, Reasoning, and Inference*. Cambridge: Cambridge University Press.

Shipley, B. (2001) *Cause and Correlation in Biology: A User's Guide to Path Analysis, Structural Equations and Causal Inference*. Cambridge: Cambridge University Press.

Steiger, James H. (2000) 'Point estimation, hypothesis testing, and interval estimation using the RMSEA: Some comments and a reply to Hayduk and Glaser', *Structural Equation Modeling*, 7(2): 149–62.

Wright, S. (1921) 'Correlation and causation', *Journal of Agricultural Research*, 20, 557–85.

ENDNOTE 1

The $(I\text{–}B)$ matrix for this model

$$\begin{bmatrix} 1 & 0 & 0 \\ -\beta_{21} & 1 & 0 \\ -\beta_{31} & -\beta_{32} & 1 \end{bmatrix}$$

is transformed into the identity matrix by progressive pre-multiplications as explained by Hayduk (1987: 66):

$$\begin{bmatrix} 1 & 0 & 0 \\ \beta_{21} & 1 & 0 \\ 0 & 0 & 1 \end{bmatrix} \begin{bmatrix} 1 & 0 & 0 \\ -\beta_{21} & 1 & 0 \\ -\beta_{31} & -\beta_{32} & 1 \end{bmatrix}$$

$$= \begin{bmatrix} 1 & 0 & 0 \\ 0 & 1 & 0 \\ -\beta_{31} & -\beta_{32} & 1 \end{bmatrix}$$

$$\begin{bmatrix} 1 & 0 & 0 \\ 0 & 1 & 0 \\ \beta_{31} & 0 & 1 \end{bmatrix} \begin{bmatrix} 1 & 0 & 0 \\ 0 & 1 & 0 \\ -\beta_{31} & -\beta_{32} & 1 \end{bmatrix}$$

$$= \begin{bmatrix} 1 & 0 & 0 \\ 0 & 1 & 0 \\ 0 & -\beta_{32} & 1 \end{bmatrix}$$

$$\begin{bmatrix} 1 & 0 & 0 \\ 0 & 1 & 0 \\ 0 & \beta_{32} & 1 \end{bmatrix} \begin{bmatrix} 1 & 0 & 0 \\ 0 & 1 & 0 \\ 0 & -\beta_{32} & 1 \end{bmatrix}$$

$$= \begin{bmatrix} 1 & 0 & 0 \\ 0 & 1 & 0 \\ 0 & 0 & 1 \end{bmatrix}$$

The product of the three transformation matrices provides the inverse of $(I\text{–}B)$.

$$\begin{bmatrix} 1 & 0 & 0 \\ 0 & 1 & 0 \\ 0 & \beta_{32} & 1 \end{bmatrix} \begin{bmatrix} 1 & 0 & 0 \\ 0 & 1 & 0 \\ \beta_{31} & 0 & 1 \end{bmatrix} \begin{bmatrix} 1 & 0 & 0 \\ \beta_{21} & 1 & 0 \\ 0 & 0 & 1 \end{bmatrix}$$

$$= \begin{bmatrix} 1 & 0 & 0 \\ \beta_{21} & 1 & 0 \\ (\beta_{31} + \beta_{32}\beta_{21}) & \beta_{32} & 1 \end{bmatrix}$$

9

Experimental and Quasi-Experimental Designs in Behavioral Research: On Context, Crud, and Convergence

Sandra L. Schneider

Experimental designs are often exalted as the most powerful research designs because they are the only designs that can provide a straightforward test of causal relationships. In experimental designs, the variable that is thought to be essential to a process (i.e., the independent variable) is manipulated to see if it will bring about differences in the outcome measure of interest (i.e., the dependent variable). The idea is that if we change the level or amount of the independent variable, and we subsequently observe a change in the dependent variable, then it must be the change in the independent variable that caused the change in the dependent variable. Although the conceptual simplicity of the design makes it quite attractive, there are several reasons to be cautious in the use and application of experimental designs and their close associates, quasi-experimental designs.

Of course, many of the cautions in using experimental designs to study human behavior have been generated on philosophical or theoretical grounds and are alluded to in several of the chapters in this volume. Other reservations emanate from more practical considerations. In this chapter, the focus will be confined to specific cautions from both sources that provide guidance in improving the design of experiments and also of quasi-experiments. In particular, this chapter will be concerned with design issues that become evident as one considers how observed behavior is likely to be constrained by the natural and social surroundings in which the behavior occurs. In addition, the chapter will discuss some of the related issues that need to be considered when analyzing and interpreting findings from experimental and quasi-experimental studies.

FIRST THINGS FIRST: WHEN IS AN EXPERIMENTAL DESIGN A GOOD WAY TO GO?

Complex Causes

It is often tempting to try to develop an experimental design in order to isolate the cause of a particular phenomenon. This is especially so when there is pressure from publishers, editors and funding agencies to focus on highly controlled, quantitative and 'more objective' approaches to research. Often, however, experimental designs can be selected without sufficient thought about or understanding of the underlying processes or populations to be studied. How can a researcher develop a high quality experiment if it is not yet possible to isolate the critical variables likely to be the primary contributors to the phenomenon of interest? Methodologically, an experiment may seem sound, but without an overarching model of the process there is a substantial risk that the variables selected may not play a central role in the process. Even results that show 'a significant difference' cannot relieve this concern, as there are myriad variables that are likely to have at least some small effect on any phenomenon of interest at least among some groups. Studies have shown, for instance, that school performance is influenced by hundreds of factors ranging from the time of day that classes start to the availability of adult mentors. Both theoretically and practically speaking, these findings are hard to interpret or use without some overarching model or framework that will help guide—and then test—which of the variables are primary factors or priority areas for maximizing improvement in performance.

Explaining behavior is complex. There are often many causes that come together to bring about a given phenomenon and the set of causes may be different for different people or in different situations. So, conducting an experiment that examines one (or two) possible cause(s) in one setting and for one group of people may or may not contribute substantially to answering the larger questions about

what drives the phenomenon in general. Also, if one does not have a good representation of the process that brings about the phenomenon, an experiment can actually mislead, either because the independent variable only has an effect in combination with other factors or because the independent variable may not have the same effect under different conditions or for different groups of people. For this reason, the first step in evaluating experimental or quasi-experimental research is assessing whether enough is known about the phenomenon at issue to warrant such a highly specified design.

Stages of Research

Introductory methodology texts[1] typically point out that different types of research designs are more or less appropriate for answering different types of questions. Often, these questions are divided into the three major areas of description, prediction, and explanation or understanding. Descriptive studies are indicated when an area is rather new to study and relatively little is known about the phenomenon of interest. In this case, experiments are generally not a good idea because they are very expensive both in terms of time and resources. In addition, experiments limit the researcher to examining only one or two variables. If not much is known about the phenomenon, there is too much uncertainty about which variables might be the ones that are central in producing the phenomenon. Instead, more qualitative techniques such as interviews, focus groups, archival studies, examinations of media reports, etc., allow the investigator to more fully explore the various influences that might be related to the issue of interest. One of the most important tools in research design is the existing literature. There is an old saying that goes: 'Why spend an hour in the library when you can spend three months in the lab?' Almost always, exploring the literature can help inform whatever design is chosen, improving design efficiency and effectiveness. Learning about previous studies helps to provide a richer context for future investigations and helps to ensure that the investigator's efforts will fill a gap in our collective knowledge.

Until the investigator is in a position to develop an informed model or a framework for understanding how the process of interest works, experimental designs are premature. Even quasi-experimental (e.g., correlational) designs must be approached with caution, as it is too easy to gather together scales measuring a large variety of constructs, and to then let a statistical package produce a picture that may or may not have any substantial connection to the phenomenon of interest. Every time a scale or other measure is adopted for use, there is a critical responsibility to (a) make a well-reasoned case why the construct is expected to be of interest (e.g., why choose this construct over others?), (b) demonstrate that the measure provides a realistic representation of that construct (i.e., internal and external validity), and (c) provide evidence that the measure can routinely pick out meaningful differences in this construct (i.e., reliability, sensitivity and specificity). No serious researcher can afford to ignore the 'garbage in, garbage out' maxim.

Again, the selection of design comes down to the depth of understanding one has about the phenomenon of interest. If an investigator does not have access (even after exploring the literature) to sufficient information for the reasoned selection of variables, then designs other than the experiment or quasi-experiment must be considered. The importance of fitting the more qualitative designs into programs of research has not been emphasized, and has in many cases been ignored or even rejected. The current push in the social sciences to develop 'rigorous' designs such as experiments and quasi-experiments has made it especially difficult for researchers to recognize and develop a balanced approach to the different stages of research.

Despite the bias in support of quantitative techniques, the value of mixed methods (combining quantitative and qualitative approaches) is becoming more commonly recognized. For instance, the National Science Foundation supported an initiative

that resulted in the publication of the *User-Friendly Handbook for Mixed Method Evaluations* (Frechtling and Sharp, 1997). In this publication, the editors preface the volume by pointing out basic tradeoffs in quantitative and qualitative approaches to research:

> Quantitative and qualitative techniques provide a tradeoff between breadth and depth and between generalizability and targeting to specific (sometimes very limited) populations. For example, a sample survey of high school students who participated in a special science enrichment program (a quantitative technique) can yield representative and broadly generalizable information about the proportion of participants who plan to major in science when they get to college and how this proportion differs by gender. But at best, the survey can elicit only a few, often superficial reasons for this gender difference. On the other hand, separate focus groups (a qualitative technique) conducted with small groups of male and female students will provide many more clues about gender differences in the choice of science majors and the extent to which the special science program changed or reinforced attitudes. But this technique may be limited in the extent to which findings apply beyond the specific individuals included in the focus groups (Frechtling and Sharp, 1997: Chapter 1)

Using mixed methodologies allows investigators to develop a balance between detailed understandings of particular examples of a phenomenon and more generalized regularities that tend to exist across most examples of the phenomenon. Experiments and quasi-experiments are best reserved for situations that have already been subjected to more localized explorations, so that the most promising variables can be isolated and the possible constraints on the phenomenon can be tested directly.

ON DESIGNING STUDIES: WHAT KINDS OF QUESTIONS CAN BEHAVIORAL EXPERIMENTS ANSWER?

The Nomothetic–Idiographic Distinction

Even in situations that are fairly well understood, the use of experiments and quasi-experiments is often met with skepticism.

Typically, the skepticism involves what we can learn from experiments, and what we should expect to learn. In the social and behavioral sciences, there is always a tension between generalizable information and the specifics of unique instances, and this tension has a long-standing (and controversial) history.

In the mid-1900s, psychologists borrowed from the German philosopher Wilhelm Windelband the terms *nomothetic* and *idiographic* to describe and elaborate on the ongoing controversy between general and specific in the study of behavior. The terms were used (especially by personality psychologists) to try to distinguish those aspects of behavior that are guided by general rules or laws of behavior (nomothetic), and those aspects of behavior that are largely idiosyncratic and specific to an individual (idiographic). Arguments erupted as to whether the goal of behavioral sciences should be to understand these general rules or to understand the inner workings that make each individual unique.[2]

This controversy was especially important to the research enterprise, as it called into question the applicability of experiments for understanding behavior. Experimental research could only be expected to address questions that were nomothetic in nature, as experiments are most appropriate for elucidating commonalities in behavior across individuals (though there are exceptions, e.g., certain variations of repeated measures designs). However, many topics were deemed to require a completely different kind of research (e.g., case studies) because many phenomena can only be understood through an in-depth and less structured exploration of an individual and his or her experiences. Skepticism over the potential contribution of experimentation was frequently raised, with concerns that group averages as well as other categorical and statistical summaries were not likely to reflect the particular performance or experience of any individual (e.g., Brunswik, 1943; Jenkins, 1989; Lewin, 1935).

This view has also been central in the social construction literature (e.g., Radder, 1996). In its extreme form, the constructionist position suggests that any explanation of behavior is only understandable with reference to a particular situation, at a particular time, in a particular cultural context. That is, every instance of a behavior is a unique product of its surroundings, and can only be understood with respect to those surroundings. Despite these concerns, researchers in the behavioural sciences have amassed considerable evidence of any number of regularities in behavior that transcend a particular situation, time or person (see, e.g., Kazdin, 2000). Much is known, for instance, about the principles of sensory perception and basic emotions, learning and memory, stereotyping and impression formation. Moreover, studies have routinely been able to replicate these findings across a variety of contexts, suggesting that these regularities may be instantiations of nomothetic rules.

Although the larger theoretical arguments surrounding the nomothetic–idiographic debate are beyond the scope of this chapter, this brief introduction suggests that the investigator who wants to conduct experiments or quasi-experiments in the domain of behavior needs to be mindful that the results can, at best, shed light on possible generalized rules of behavior, but that the results of any single study will be constrained in interpretation to the particular context within which the study occurred. Furthermore, the debate serves as a constant reminder that our understanding and our ability to predict and explain phenomena will be limited by the many idiosyncrasies that exist within individuals, situations, time periods and cultures. The behavioral and social sciences require patience, replication and respect for the complex causes of human behavior.

CONTEXTUALISM

A theme that is closely associated with the theoretical tension between nomothetic and idiographic approaches involves the proper role of context in understanding behavior. As mentioned previously, social constructionists have argued that behavior can only be understood with reference to the context in which the behavior takes place. From an experimental perspective, this possibility has critical implications.

Although it has been several years now, James Jenkins (1974) eloquently summarized an important set of conceptual difficulties encountered within the experimental approach by drawing a distinction between *associationism* and *contextualism*. Jenkins argued that many theories of behavior assume that behavior and its causes can be broken down into discrete units that are connected by straightforward and identifiable relationships. If this were true, an experimental approach would be ideal for isolating what these units—or variables—are for any given behavior and for identifying the associations between these units. The goal would be to conduct a series of experiments, and the expectation would be that we can gradually learn more about which variables are important and how the variables are connected. This is the essence of the associationist approach, and it clearly embodies a reductionist philosophy in which we are searching for the essential elements of behavior. Although Jenkins was referring to theories espoused decades ago, the experimental tradition continues to implicitly encourage the adoption of an associationist approach, with the resulting expectations that there are a set of more-or-less fixed variables out there (or in our brains) and that with enough experiments, we can find them, map their associations, and move forward in a fairly linear fashion to explain why people behave the way they do.

Contextualism, on the other hand, is a perspective that is much more like the pragmatist position of William James (1890, 1907), which assumes that there are no essential units of behavior, but instead that behavior is understandable only in terms of the experiences of the individual and the environment to which the individual is trying to adapt. This position is also clearly related to the social constructionist view. On this account, behaviors mean different things in different circumstances, and presumably the causal factors involved change as well. Given this, the contextualist argues that the appropriate unit of

analysis is not a particular behavior but rather an *event*, which consists of the behavior embedded within its historical and situational context. Of course, defining an event can get complicated, as one could argue that there are essentially infinitely many contexts within which behaviors occur, and the contexts that are of importance will vary with the questions being asked.

Jenkins (1974) uses the example of an utterance to illustrate how behaviors are inextricably embedded within a context. Jenkins points out that the meaning of a sentence depends on the context in which it occurs, and so too do the words chosen to express the idea behind the utterance. These things in turn will depend on who is in the conversation, suppositions about the level of mutual understanding, and whatever biases and predispositions the speaker and listener may have with respect to the message. The utterance itself will essentially be at least two different events—the event experienced by the speaker, and the event experienced by the listener. When we experience simple misunderstandings in a conversation, it becomes obvious that the message that the speaker intends to convey may not be the same message that the listener ends up hearing.

Operationalizations (i.e., the way that constructs are measured) are especially subject to the perils of interpretation. Imagine, for instance, a study designed to explore how anxiety-provoking experiences are likely to affect one's confidence regarding future performance. Suppose anxiety is induced in the study by having college seniors complete a practice GRE test and then informing them that they have scored in a range that is likely to make them ineligible for most graduate school programs. There are issues with this manipulation, both in terms of the likelihood that students will believe the manipulation and also the likelihood that doing poorly on a practice GRE (if believed) will induce a feeling of anxiety. Moreover, one might reasonably be concerned that any reports of confidence (however that is measured) may result from *demand characteristics* or the tendency of participants to try to comply with the assumed purpose of the study. Participants might simply conclude that they 'ought to' report less confidence in their future GRE performance if they are told that they did not do well on a current practice test, independent of how they really might feel about the feedback. Regardless of whether the results seem to support a relationship between anxiety and confidence, it is not clear whether the evidence can inform us about the underlying question or whether the study's design is flawed.

With respect to the experimental process, the contextualist view suggests that researchers must pay attention to more than individual variables and their relationships. In particular, the researcher must take into consideration the relevant psychological and situational contexts of the phenomena that are the objects of study. In memory experiments, for instance, Jenkins (1974, 1976) argues that there are at least four critical influences on what participants will remember. These are: (a) the skills and knowledge of the participants, (b) the characteristics of the materials they are required to remember, (c) the setting in which the learning takes place, and (d) the type of tasks used to learn the information and then to report what is remembered. More broadly, the contextualist perspective suggests that researchers must know something about the characteristics of their participants, and they must be sensitive to the possibility that their choices of materials, tasks and setting are likely to influence their results in potentially unexpected ways. The contextualist perspective also points out the importance of creating experiments that are *ecologically valid*, or ones that can faithfully map onto the real-world problems and issues that the studies are designed to assess.

REFERENCE DEPENDENCE IN THE DEVELOPMENT OF EXPERIMENTS

Psychophysical Laws

Yet another line of research and theory points to the importance of context, but in a different way. Context may also play a fundamental role in defining what we as human beings actually experience psychologically. Throughout the 1800s into the early 1900s, the beginnings of psychological/behavioral science were dominated by the study of *psychophysics*, which attempted to measure how physical stimuli are represented in psychological experience. Ernst Weber became known for studying what he called the *just noticeable difference* or the smallest increase in physical stimulation that is needed for a person to detect that a change in the amount of stimulation has occurred. Thus, for instance, in his experiments, Weber might shine two different lights and ask a participant to decide if one light is brighter than the other. What Weber found (known as Weber's Law; and considered one of the best-known candidates for a nomothetic law) is that the size of the difference in physical stimulation needed to perceive a change in that stimulation depends on the size or strength of the original stimulus. The larger or brighter (or more whatever) the original stimulus, the bigger the change in stimulation needed in order to detect that a change has occurred.

Although Weber's Law has been refined (e.g., by Fechner and much later by Stevens) and even explored with respect to neural mechanisms (see, e.g., Johnson et al., 2002), its implications for research have not changed: human beings' psychological responses are *reference dependent*. Our psychological responses are physiologically tied to whatever the current situation (i.e., the original 'stimulation') is, and our experience of any change will depend on whatever that situation entails. Thus, predicting psychological responses is only possible when one knows the reference point for making those responses. If a person starts with only a little bit of whatever is of interest, their reactions will be quite different than if they start with a large amount.

In the late 1970s, Daniel Kahneman and Amos Tversky borrowed these ideas from psychophysics and combined them with other basic principles to create prospect theory, which was designed to describe how people make choices. One of the basic tenets of prospect theory is *decreasing sensitivity*, or the notion that we are less sensitive to changes in value the further we get from a value of zero. If we consider money, for instance, the idea is that people experience the difference between receiving $0 and $10 as psychologically much greater than the difference between receiving $1,000 and $1,010, even though both examples involve outcomes that differ by $10. Tversky and Kahneman (e.g., 1981) have created a number of telling demonstrations of this effect. For instance, many people report being willing to drive an extra few miles to go to a store to save $5 on a calculator, but they wouldn't do the same to save $5 on a jacket or a car. The car example seems almost silly—but the savings would be exactly the same in any case!

Tversky and Kahneman apply this basic psychophysical principle not only to objectively verifiable differences, but they also theorize that decision-making processes will depend fundamentally on the decision maker's subjective view of their current status, and that choice options will be interpreted as changes relative to that status. The reinterpretation of experiences in terms of perceived current status has been deemed *reference dependence* to highlight people's dependence on salient reference points for evaluating experiences. Reference dependence has been shown to have large and pervasive effects on how people respond to a wide variety of events. In designing experiments and quasi-experiments, it is important to be aware of these effects so that they can be taken into account in the development of study materials and in the interpretation of study results.

Framing and Contrast Effects

Probably the best known example of reference dependence has come to be known as the *framing effect*. The classic demonstration involves a risky decision that is described or 'framed' in two different ways, with remarkably different results. The 'Asian disease problem' (Tversky and Kahneman, 1981), as it is now commonly known, is described in Box 9.1.

Box 9.1   The 'Asian Disease Problem'

All the study participants read the following cover story:
   Imagine that the United States is preparing for the outbreak of an unusual Asian disease, which is expected to kill 600 people. Two alternative programs to combat the disease have been proposed. Assume that the exact scientific estimates of the consequences of the programs are as follows:

   Half the study participants, selected at random, were then given the following two options, Program A and Program B:

→   If Program A is adopted, 200 people will be saved.
→   If Program B is adopted, there is a one-third probability that 600 people will be saved and a two-thirds probability that no people will be saved.

Which of the two programs would you favor?

   The other half of the study participants were given a different description of the two options, Program A and Program B:

→   If Program A is adopted, 400 people will die.
→   If Program B is adopted, there is a one-third probability that nobody will die and a two-thirds probability that 600 people will die.

Which of the two programs would you favor?

In the 'saved' versions of the options, the majority of participants select Program A, whereas in the 'die' versions, the majority of participants select Program B. Kahneman and Tversky suggested that this outcome illustrates how sensitive we are to reference points, because only the superficial descriptions of Programs A and B are different. In reality, the outcomes are the same. In Program A for instance, if 200 people are the only ones saved then the other 400 must have died. Nevertheless, those superficial changes in wording were enough to cause people to reverse their preferences, opting for a sure outcome when thinking about saving lives, but opting for the risky option when focusing on those who would die.

Although some have questioned the generalizability of this example, given that it is simply a hypothetical case, there is substantial evidence that these effects are likely to hold up in a variety of real-world settings. Eric Johnson and his colleagues have shown that the accepted reference point or default option has profound effects on actual choices. In the purchase of car insurance, for instance, insurance companies have tried to reduce premiums by limiting the policy-holder's right to sue in the case of minor accidents. A study of the insurance choices of New Jersey versus Pennsylvania drivers showed that the framing of this reduction predicted consumer preferences (Johnson et al., 1993). When this reduction in the right to sue was presented as the default or standard option (in New Jersey), 80 percent of policy-holders chose to give up that right for the less expensive premium. In contrast, when retaining the full right to sue was presented as the default (in Pennsylvania), only 25 percent of policy holders chose to give up their right to sue. The authors estimate that this framing effect cost the Pennsylvanians an extra $200 million in insurance!

In a recent *Science* article, Johnson and Goldstein (2003) have provided evidence that the number of organ donors could be doubled in America simply by rephrasing the question on drivers' license applications so that organ donation becomes the default option. Given the current shortage in organ donors, this simple change in wording could save thousands of lives annually (and better match national approval ratings for organ donation).

The consequences of reference dependence have also been demonstrated in the form of contrast effects in consumer choice. Simonson and Tversky (1992), for instance, have shown that people's preferences for various consumer products such as cameras, personal computers and microwave ovens depend on the set of alternatives available for choice. *Extremeness aversion* is one form of reference dependence in which consumers tend to opt for items that seem to be the most typical or practical. However, the impression of what is typical or practical depends on the reference set of options. Thus, when a basic less expensive item and a costlier item with additional features are the only two options, preferences are usually about evenly split between the basic and the costlier item. However, when a third even more expensive option with lots of 'bells and whistles' is added to the set, the middle option now becomes overwhelmingly the most popular. Another type of contrast effect occurs when people are shown different kinds of tradeoffs, and these tradeoffs are used by consumers to infer which items are a 'good deal'. After participants saw a personal computer for which additional memory cost $4 per 1K of memory, a computer with additional memory that cost $2 per 1K of memory seemed very attractive. However, when the original option was instead a computer with extra memory for $1 per 1K, the $2 per 1K option seemed relatively unattractive. More to the point, people would pay more or less for the $2 per 1K memory option based on these context-driven differences in their judgments of attractiveness.

Context and Study Design

This kind of effect is important not only for those who are interested in marketing but also for any researcher who is planning to ask participants to respond to particular questions or to make comparisons of any kind. The wording of the questions and the selection of study topics, examples or alternatives will substantially impact how the participants respond. This, in turn, will of course influence what the researcher concludes about the phenomenon of interest. The goal here is to help researchers become sensitized to the importance of these contextual influences so that they can design experiments and quasi-experiments that are not likely to mistake these superficial influences for the more fundamental issues that their studies are trying to address.

One particularly common problem in studies using questionnaires are the context effects that come from providing response categories. Consider a study concerned with alcohol consumption, and a hypothetical investigator who designs response categories for an item that asks: How much alcohol do you drink on average per week? Imagine that the investigator decides to use the following categories:

(a)   0–1 drinks per week
(b)   2–3 drinks per week
(c)   4–5 drinks per week
(d)   more than 5 drinks per week

Now, imagine instead that the investigator decides to use a scale with these categories:

(a)   0–5 drinks per week
(b)   6–10 drinks per week
(c)   10–15 drinks per week
(d)   more than 15 drinks per week

Unless the respondents are teetotalers, they are likely to report much more drinking if the second scale is used, simply because the scale itself seems to suggest that more drinking is the 'norm' than in the first scale. People are not especially accurate in making these types of retrospective reports in general, and they commonly use the scale to help guesstimate the most reasonable answer. This reference dependence on the scale is especially problematic for topics in which social desirability

is likely to bias responses in a particular direction. In this case, respondents are especially apt to try to understate their alcohol consumption by avoiding the most extreme category—whatever it is. Perhaps the best way to deal with these scaling problems is to ask the questions in an open-ended fill-in-the-blank type format, so that participants cannot use the context to try to infer the most reasonable or favorable response.

One more especially important example of the effect of reference dependence in study design has to do with the selection of between-subjects versus within-subjects or repeated measures designs. In a *between-subjects design*, participants are asked to respond to only one condition or situation. In a *within-subjects* or *repeated measures design*, participants are asked to respond to several related situations or conditions. Michael Birnbaum (1999) recounted a particularly surprising effect related to the choice of study design. He asked two different groups of participants (in a between-subjects or BS design) to rate a single number on a scale from very, very small to very, very large. He asked one group to rate the number 9 and he asked the other group to rate the number 221. When he analyzed the data, he found that participants who evaluated the number 9 consistently gave it a rating that was higher than the rating given to the number 221 by the other group, ostensibly suggesting that people must judge the number 9 to be larger than the number 221. However, as Birnbaum concludes:

> If people had been asked to compare 9 and 221, they would have judged 9 < 221. If you agree that 9 is not greater than 221, you should be skeptical of studies that use methods that yield the silly conclusion that 9 is significantly 'bigger' than 221 … The key to the result is that when judges are 'free' to choose their own contexts, they choose different contexts for different stimuli. For this reason, it is important to beware of conclusions based on judgments obtained between groups of people who experienced different contexts. Even when there is 'no' context besides the stimulus itself, comparison of judgments between subjects can be misleading (Birnbaum, 1999: 248).

Birnbaum goes on to clarify that these potential problems in the interpretation of between-subjects designs can be alleviated by avoiding totally subjective judgment scales in favor of more objective dependent measures (e.g., use standardized measures of height, weight, volume, etc. to indicate sizes rather than ambiguous labels such as 'very large'). Birnbaum also cautions that within-subjects or repeated measures designs are not always the perfect solution, given the potential for order effects and other kinds of carryover effects (see also Keren, 1993). In addition, within-subjects designs may some-times produce unusual context effects of their own, such as contrast effects like the ones discussed above.

As we have seen, within-subjects studies in consumer choice have shown that the set of options available will influence how judg-ments are made. It is also well known that providing particular dimensions for comparing products causes the importance of those dimensions to be exaggerated. For example, if study participants were asked about their preferences for buying a car, and the possible cars were only described in terms of how they varied from one another on price and fuel efficiency (miles per gallon of gas), the results would overstate how much people would be willing to pay for fuel efficiency, as compared to a more realistic context in which all the other attributes of cars would also be included in the evaluation.

With respect to study design, these exam-ples illustrate how important it is to put sufficient care into the development of the design of an investigation. The absence of contextual information in between-subjects designs may make some questions ambigu-ous, particularly when the dependent mea-sure is a subjective scale. This ambiguity forces participants to guess about the rele-vant context, making it difficult to provide a meaningful interpretation of the results. On the other hand, the presence of comparative information in within-subjects or repeated measures designs almost always primes par-ticipants to become overly sensitized to that information and respond in ways that are tied directly to whatever stimuli or scales are presented. Although this may seem like a 'no-win' situation, the preferred design for obtaining meaningful answers is likely to be the one that most closely maps onto the situ-ations encountered in real-world settings (see, e.g., Hogarth, 1981, 2005). In addition, more than one study may be needed in order to vary how the critical information is pre-sented, and thus ensure that a participant's response is not simply an accident of how the question was asked.

ON ANALYZING STUDY RESULTS

The Crud Factor

Although a good design is always a prerequi-site to ensuring a reasonable interpretation of results, there are several implications of the social and contextual constraints on behavior that must also be taken into consideration during the analysis of results. It is commonly argued that research in the social sciences can be more difficult than in other sciences because the constructs that are of interest to social scientists are much harder to define and harder to measure than in other disci-plines. As mentioned earlier, this difficulty often arises in the form of questions about the reliability and validity of measures. However, there are other implications as well, particularly when one moves to the analysis of study results.

Paul Meehl (1990) argued that interpreting research results in the social sciences is especially difficult because social constructs inherently involve substantial overlap. Because of this, social constructs are natu-rally correlated with one another in ways that make interpretation of research results quite difficult. He called this typical interrelated-ness 'the crud factor'. Consider constructs such as attitudes, stereotypes, beliefs, impres-sions and expectations. These are undoubt-edly important constructs for understanding human behavior, yet there are any number of questions about how to define each, how to differentiate each from the others, and how to think about the relationships between these psychological entities and related behaviors.

As Meehl points out:

> There is nothing mysterious about the fact that in psychology and sociology, everything correlates with everything. Any measured trait or attribute is some function of a list of partly known and mostly unknown causal factors in the genes and life history of the individual, and both genetic and environmental factors are known from tons of empirical research to be themselves correlated ... Anybody familiar with large scale research data takes it as a matter of course that when the N gets big enough she will not be looking for the statistically significant correlations but rather looking at their patterns, since almost all of them will be significant. (Meehl, 1990: 204–05)

As a simple demonstration, Meehl described the analysis of a dataset representing questionnaire responses of 57,000 high-school seniors, with items from a wide variety of topics dealing with their families, attitudes, interests, plans and activities. Meehl and his colleague David Lykken computed tests of statistical significance on the entire matrix of the 990 potential relationships between each of the 45 variables and every other. They found that 92 percent of the relationships were significant, meaning that the median number of significant relationships for any given variable was 41 out of a possible 44. Meehl emphasizes that these findings are not due to statistical Type I errors, but that the vast majority of these relationships are real and quite stable given the input of 57,000 students. Instead, the results point out that, with enough data, social scientists will find that almost every variable they test *is* actually related to every other.

Given this, the challenge for social scientists resides in their ability to conduct studies that will go beyond identifying *which* variables are related (as this is likely to be almost all of them), to identifying which variables are the most strongly related or which are related in theoretically or practically important ways. This implies at least two things: (1) social scientists should have some sense of the likely size of variable relationships that would be meaningful for their topic of research, and (2) social scientists should be in a position to posit a well-reasoned model describing the likely kinds of relationships among possible variables. The former criterion allows social scientists to examine variable relationships not just for 'significance' (which suffers from a host of problems; see, e.g., Loftus, 1996, 2002) but also for *effect size*, which enables the kind of strong hypothesis testing that is the standard in the physical sciences. The second criterion helps to ensure that experiments or quasi-experiments do not suffer from being arbitrary in the selection of variables or from inviting the ever-popular 'fishing expedition', which typically contributes little to the existing knowledge base.

Effect Size and the Not-So-Magic .05

Over the last several decades, there has been growing concern that behavioral researchers often apply statistics in a mechanical fashion without an adequate understanding of what different statistics can tell them. In particular, critics have been concerned about the misuse of significance testing and the routine adherence to the .05 probability criterion as the indicator of worthwhile findings (see, e.g., Schmidt, 1996). Gerd Gigerenzer (e.g., 1993; Gigerenzer and Murray, 1987) provides an historical account of what he calls the *inference revolution* during which behavioral scientists came to adopt null hypothesis testing and the .05 significance criterion as the single acceptable method of scientific inference. Gigerenzer (1993: 314) argues that this approach to statistical inference is 'an incoherent mishmash of some of Fisher's ideas on one hand, and some of Neyman and E.S. Pearson on the other.'

Gigerenzer and others, such as Paul Meehl (see, e.g., Waller et al., 2006), Jacob Cohen (e.g., 1990, 1992) and Geoffrey Loftus (e.g., 1996, 2002), have worked throughout their careers to help inform behavioral scientists about how to improve their methods of statistical inference. In an invited address to the American Psychological Association's Division of Evaluation, Measurement, and Statistics, Jacob Cohen reminded behavioral researchers that the answers to their questions are not magically tied to a significance level:

> The prevailing yes—no decision at the magic .05 level from a single research is a far cry from the use of informed judgment. Science simply doesn't work that way. A successful piece of research doesn't conclusively settle an issue, it just makes some theoretical proposition some degree more likely. Only successful future replication in the same and different settings (as might be found through meta-analysis) provides an approach to settling the issue (Cohen, 1990:1311).

Cohen has become particularly well known for his efforts to train researchers in the use of various measures of effect size (e.g., Cohen, 1969, 1988, 1992). All too often researchers erroneously conclude that the level of significance is what communicates the importance or size of an effect. So a 'highly significant' finding (e.g., with $p < .001$) is frequently misinterpreted as especially strong, instead of the correct interpretation that the finding is highly reliable or likely to be found again with another comparable sample of the same size. As discussed earlier, with enough participants even very small effects can be reliably identified. What is needed is a mechanism to estimate effect size, which, unlike the p value, is largely independent of the number of participants. As Cohen (1990: 1309) informs us: 'Effect-size measures include mean differences (raw or standardized), correlations and squared correlation of all kinds, odds ratios, kappas—whatever conveys the magnitude of the phenomenon of interest appropriate to the research context.' He also reminds us that 'the primary product of a research inquiry is one or more measures of effect size, not p values' (ibid.). Bottom-line: No quality experiment or quasi-experiment can be interpreted without some

measurement and assessment of the size of the effects that have been found.

Although the many other tips for interpreting results go beyond the scope of what can be covered here,[3] the most common advice includes encouragement to (a) recognize that analysis should rely more heavily on patterns of data and informed judgment than on mechanical rules of applying statistics, (b) carefully look at the data (and not just statistical output) using a variety of graphing techniques to better understand the results, (c) use measures such as confidence intervals to help get a sense of the range of likely values of measures of interest, and (d) look to methods of combining information across studies, such as meta-analysis, in order to obtain a more accurate estimate of the effect size of the variable of interest and to develop a cumulative sense of outcomes across different contexts. (Of course, problems with single studies may sometimes be compounded within meta-analyses. For more on properly conducting and addressing issues in meta-analysis, see Cook, 1992; Hedges and Olkin, 1985; Konstantopouluos and Hedges, 2004; Rosenthal, [1984] 1991; Schmidt, 1996).

Differentiating Experimental and Quasi-Experimental Designs

In addition to statistical considerations, it is important to remember that the conclusions one can draw from a set of data will be highly dependent on the study's design. The most important issue in this regard is being aware of the conditions that will and will not support statements about the causes of the observed results. In almost any study, it is tempting to conclude that the chosen independent or predictor variables are responsible for the pattern of results observed in the dependent or criterion measures. However, most studies are not designed to isolate *only* cause-and-effect relationships. Even when a clear-cut pattern is observed between two variables, it may only be possible to conclude with confidence that a relationship exists, but not to be able to say whether the first variable is responsible for the observed pattern of results in the second variable, whether the second variable caused the pattern in the first, or perhaps some other unspecified variables were involved in producing the observed patterns.

Statistics are only designed to provide methods for assessing the likelihood that a pattern exists between variables, or to provide information about the direction, magnitude or observed characteristics of the relationship. Nothing about a simple statistical test can tell a researcher about whether any observed pattern is likely to be the result of a causal relationship as opposed to other possible kinds of relationships. Inferences regarding whether relationships are causal or not are determined by (a) the original *design* of the study, or (b) a systematic evaluation and comparison of possible causal models (e.g., in path analysis or structural equation modeling; see Kline, 2005; Schumacher and Lomax, 2004; Freedman, this volume).

With respect to study design, a researcher can only be confident about the cause of the results when employing experimentally manipulated independent variables in controlled settings. Of course, this brings us back to the critical distinction between experimental and quasi-experimental designs.[4] Experimental designs are attempts to control environmental factors to rule out competing causal explanations and to use true independent variables which are those that are *randomly assigned* to the participants in a study, so that each participant at the outset of the study is equally likely to end up being assigned into a particular level or condition of the given variable. For example, a researcher might manipulate whether participants are given a hard or an easy test. Test difficulty would be a true independent variable if the investigator flipped a coin for each participant to see which test he or she would complete. This ensures that the participants in each group are not likely to systematically share other characteristics besides test difficulty, so that the researcher can be confident that group differences in test results will be caused by the difference in test difficulty.

A quasi-experimental design often looks much like an experiment; however, it involves a less controlled environment and tends to use *grouping variables* or *predictor variables* rather than (randomly assigned) independent variables. Grouping and predictor variables are those that are not assigned randomly, but are assigned or selected on some other basis. For instance, test difficulty would be a grouping variable if the hard versus easy tests were assigned based on who volunteered to take the hard test or the results of an earlier IQ test or the order that participants walked in the door. Each of these methods of group assignment leaves open the possibility that something about the way the assignment was done might end up being the cause of any observed results. That is, volunteering or having a high IQ or being early to the study might have their own (direct or indirect) influences on how well a person is likely to do on the test, so that we cannot be confident that test difficulty will be the only systematic influence on test results. Some of the most common grouping variables are innate characteristics such as gender and age. Although we can describe observed differences, there is typically no straightforward rationale (without the help of causal modeling) for determining what the reasons for those differences might be.

One of the mantras that students learn early on about conducting research is that 'correlation does not imply causation'. What many may fail to realize is that this statement refers to the study's design and not to the selection of statistics for analysis. If a correlation coefficient is computed to assess the potential relationship within a well-controlled study between a randomly assigned independent variable and a dependent measure, then it may be reasonable to infer that the manipulation of the independent variable is responsible for the size and direction of the observed correlation with the dependent variable. The correlation as a statistic does not imply anything about whether a relationship between variables is or is not causal; it is the controlled nature of the design that may persuade us that we have isolated the only possible cause of the relationship within that setting. By the same token, if analysis of variance (a statistical technique that is typically applied to experimental data) is used to evaluate the likelihood of a relationship between a grouping or predictor variable and some criterion variable, the analysis does not confer causal status to the grouping or predictor variable. Even with a 'significant F', the most that can be concluded without random assignment is that there are reliable differences in the criterion for the different levels of the grouping variable (or different values of the predictor variable), but it is not clear from the investigation what might have caused those differences.

TOWARD CONVERGING PRINCIPLES AND DISCRIMINATING SPECIAL CASES

Issues such as reference dependence, the 'crud factor', and the complexities of statistical analysis and interpretation may make it seem that there are simply too many obstacles to worthwhile experimental and quasi-experimental research in the social and behavioral sciences. Although it is certain that serious research—in any field—requires a great deal of care and attention to detail, there are also tools and approaches available to help in ensuring high-quality research.

As we have seen, attention to methods of ensuring *ecological validity* can be especially helpful for creating reasonable experimental and quasi-experimental analogs of real-world situations. (For a detailed treatment of the construct and its development in the Brunswikian tradition, see Hammond and Stewart, 2001). *Convergence* and *discrimination* are also critically important tools for ensuring the contribution of experimental and quasi-experimental investigations in social science. The goal here is to measure critical constructs using a variety of approaches in a variety of situations to

distill out broad-based regularities from the more context-specific observations. In this way, studies over time should gradually converge on the essential elements of the phenomenon of interest, while discriminating special cases and context effects.

An Example of the Systematic Evolution of Research

Before closing this chapter, it may be worthwhile to highlight an example of how a research program can successfully evolve over time. Consider the classic four-card problem developed by Wason (1966) to examine people's ability to reason logically. Participants in the standard task are asked to consider the four cards in the box shown in Figure 9.1 and to use the cards to evaluate the rule, 'If a card has a vowel on one side, then it has an even number on the other side'. Participants must determine which of the four cards below they must turn over to see if the rule holds true for the entire set.

Figure 9.1   The four-card problem

Although almost everyone correctly turns over the 'A' card to see if there is an odd number on the other side, most participants do poorly on this task because they also erroneously turn over the '4' card which they do not need to (as it does not matter what is on the other side) and they tend to miss the '7' card which provides a critical test of the rule (because if there is a consonant on the other side, the rule has been broken). Participants are often hard-pressed to see why they needed to check the card that did not have an even number, and why they did not need to check the card that did have an even number.

Although the conclusion from the initial study was that this shows the difficulties people have in reasoning logically, the provocative finding created a flurry of follow-up studies in which researchers tried to zero in on the conditions under which people would demonstrate these kinds of errors in reasoning. (Variations of these studies are still being conducted today!) Early on, researchers hypothesized that participants might be doing poorly on this task because the content of the task was presented in an abstract form, and that if it were presented in a more realistic context, maybe participants would do better (e.g., Johnson-Laird et al., 1972).

In a clever variation, Griggs and Cox (1982) introduced what has come to be known by some as the 'Bartender problem', presenting the four-card problem in a context that ties directly to the social rules and experiences that are common to the participants. In this variation, participants are asked to assess the rule, 'If a person is drinking beer, then the person must be over 19 years of age'. Participants were shown the set of cards below and told that they should check the minimum number of people (i.e., cards) possible to be sure that the rule was being followed.

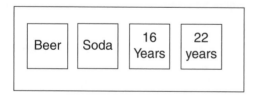

Figure 9.2   The Bartender Problem

This time participants were much more successful, recognizing immediately that it is important to check both the person who is drinking beer *and* to check the person who is *not* over 19. They were far less inclined to check the person who *was* over 19, recognizing that he or she can drink either beer or soda without threatening the status of the rule. Griggs and Cox concluded that studying this kind of familiar pragmatic context was key to demonstrating how people apply logical rules in practice. Since then, research programs have expanded on this paradigm to advance knowledge in the area of social contracts and cheater detection (e.g., Cosmides and Tooby, 1989), to address broader issues of confirmation bias in reasoning (including hypothesis testing, e.g., Klayman, 1995; Nickerson, 1998) and to explore the role of semantics in characterizing descriptive versus deontic (duty- or norm-related) rules (e.g., Stenning and van Lambalgen, 2004). The impact of the converging and discriminant findings in this area over the years can be seen in several scholarly volumes aimed at advancing perspectives on theories of reasoning (e.g., Manktelow and Chung, 2004; Newstead and Evans, 1995). As this work continues to evolve, there is a gradual push to expand these techniques to a broader range of research paradigms and applications in order to ascertain the generalizability and practical significance of these reasoning principles in a wide variety of contexts (e.g., Sperber and Girotto, 2002).

The Long and Short of Systematic Explorations

The example of the evolution of findings from the original Wason four-card selection task illustrates the gradual nature of elucidating evidence in the social and behavioral sciences. Experimental and quasi-experimental studies will rarely be able to exactly mirror a particular situation in practice. This does not by itself undermine the value of the work, provided that the conclusions of that research are confined to the set of situations that are sufficiently similar. This judgment cannot always be made at the conclusion of a particular study. Often additional research is necessary to determine the reasonable limits of findings from a study. In the years following Wason's introduction of the four-card selection task, he was careful to point out the need to limit the scope of conclusions about what the task in its original form could tell us about reasoning:

In its abstract form the four-card problem is almost certainly not a satisfactory technique for investigating how the conditional is construed in a natural language, but it may be a potential technique for investigating intuitive and ill-defined thought processes (Wason and Evans, 1972: 152).

As researchers, it is often difficult to have the patience—and perhaps humility—to provide a balanced assessment of both the limits and likely impacts of any individual study. Nevertheless, as tempting as it may be, it is a serious disservice to over-interpret the implications of any single study. Studies must be evaluated within larger systematic programs of knowledge generation. The real test is whether the results of a study can be combined with existing (and future) evidence to continue to advance our understanding, even as we acknowledge the context-specific nature of those results.

REFERENCES

Abelson, R.P. (1995) *Statistics as Principled Argument.* Hillsdale, NJ: Erlbaum.

Beins, B.C. (2004) *Research Methods: A Tool for Life.* Boston: Pearson Education.

Birnbaum, M.H. (1999) 'How to show that 9 > 221: Collect judgments in a between-subjects design', *Psychological Methods,* 4: 243–49.

Brunswik, E. (1943) 'Organismic achievement and environmental probability', *Psychological Review,* 50: 255–72.

———— (1955) 'Representative design and probabilistic theory in a functional psychology', *Psychological Review,* 62: 193–217.

Cohen, J. ([1969] 1988). *Statistical Power Analysis for the Behavioral Sciences.* Hillsdale, NJ: Erlbaum.

———— (1990) 'Things I have learned (so far)', *American Psychologist,* 45: 1304–312.

———— (1992) 'A power primer', *Psychological Bulletin,* 112:155–59.

Cook, T.D. (1992) *Meta-Analysis for Explanation—A Casebook.* New York: Russell Sage Foundation.

Cosmides, L. and Tooby, J. (1989) 'Evolutionary psychology and the generation of culture, Part II. Case study: A computational theory of social exchange', *Ethology and Sociobiology,* 10: 51–97.

Fischhoff, B. (1996) 'The real world: What good is it?', *Organizational Behavior and Human Decision Processes,* 65: 232–48.

Frechtling, J. and Sharp, L. (eds.) (1997) *User-Friendly Handbook for Mixed Method Evaluations.* Arlington, VA: National Science Foundation. (http://www.ehr.nsf.gov/EHR/REC/pubs/NSF97-153/start.htm)

Gigerenzer, G. (1993) 'The superego, the ego, and the id in statistical reasoning', in G. Keren and C. Lewis (eds.), *A Handbook for Data Analysis in the Behavioral Sciences.* Hillsdale, NJ: Erlbaum, pp. 311–39.

Gigerenzer, G. and Murray, D.J. (1987) *Cognition as Intuitive Statistics.* Hillsdale, NJ: Erlbaum.

Griggs, R.A. and Cox, J.R. (1982) 'The elusive thematic-materials effect in Wason's selection task', *British Journal of Psychology,* 73: 407–20.

Hammond, K.R. and Stewart, T.R. (eds.) (2001) *The Essential Brunswik: Beginnings, Explications, Applications.* New York: Oxford University Press.

Hedges, L.V. (2000) 'Meta-analysis', in A.E. Kazdin (ed.), *Encyclopedia of Psychology.* Washington, DC: American Psychological Association. Vol. 5. (pp. 202–204)

Hedges, L.V. and Olkin, I. (1985) *Statistical Methods for Meta-Analysis.* New York: Academic Press.

Hogarth, R.M. (1981) 'Beyond discrete biases: functional and dysfunctional consequences of judgment heuristics', *Psychological Bulletin,* 90: 197–217.

———— (2005) 'The challenge of representative design in psychology and economics', *Journal of Economic Methodology,* 12: 253–63.

James, W. (1890) *The Principles of Psychology.* New York: Dover.

———— (1907) *Pragmatism.* New York: Dover.

Jenkins, J.J. (1974) 'Remember that old theory of memory? Well, forget it', *American Psychologist,* 29: 785–95.

———— (1976) 'Four points to remember: A tetrahedral model of memory experiments', in L.S. Cermak and F.I.M. Craik (eds.), *Levels of Processing in Human Memory.* Hillsdale, NJ: Erlbaum, pp. 429–46.

———— (1989) 'The more things change, the more they stay the same: Comments from an historical perspective', in R. Kanfer, P.L. Ackerman and R. Cudeck (eds.), *Abilities, Motivation, and Methodology: The Minnesota Symposium on Learning and Individual Differences*. Hillsdale, NJ: Erlbaum.

Johnson, E.J. and Goldstein, D. (2003) 'Do defaults save lives?', *Science*, 302:1338–39.

Johnson, E.J., Hershey, J., Meszaros, J. and Kunreuther, H. (1993) 'Framing, probability distortions, and insurance decisions', *Journal of Risk and Uncertainty*, 7: 35–51.

Johnson, K.O., Hsiao, S.S. and Yoshioka, T. (2002) 'Neural coding and the basic law of psychophysics', *Neuroscientist*, 8: 111–21.

Johnson-Laird, P.N., Legrenzi, P. and Legrenzi, M. (1972) 'Reasoning and a sense of reality', *British Journal of Psychology*, 63: 395–400.

Kahneman, D. and Tversky, A. (1979) 'Prospect theory: An analysis of decisions under risk', *Econometrica*, 47: 313–27.

Kazdin, A.E. (2000) *Encyclopedia of Psychology*. New York: Oxford.

Keppel, G. and Zedeck, S. (1989) *Data Analysis for Research Designs*. New York: Freeman.

Keren, G. (1993) 'Between- or within-subjects design: A methodological dilemma', in G. Keren and C. Lewis (eds.), *A Handbook for Data Analysis in the Behavioral Sciences*. Hillsdale, NJ: Erlbaum, pp. 257–72.

Klayman, J. (1995) 'Varieties of confirmation bias', *Psychology of Learning and Motivation*, 32: 385–418.

Kline, R.B. ([1998] 2005) *Principles and Practice of Structural Equation Modeling*. New York: Guilford.

Konstantopoulos, S. and Hedges, L.V. (2004) 'Meta-analysis', in D. Kaplan (ed.), *Handbook of Quantitative Methodology for the Social Sciences*. Thousand Oaks, CA: Sage, pp. 281–97.

Lamiell, J.T. (1998) '"Nomothetic" and "idiographic": Contrasting Windelband's understanding with contemporary usage', *Theory and Psychology*, 8: 23–38.

Lewin, K. (1935) *A Dynamic Theory of Personality*. New York: McGraw-Hill, pp. 1–26.

Loftus, G.R. (1996) 'Psychology will be a much better science when we change the way we analyze data', *Current Directions in Psychological Science*, 5: 161–71.

———— (2002) 'Analysis, interpretation, and visual presentation of data', in H. Pashler and R. Gallistel (eds.), *Stevens' Handbook of Experimental Psychology*, Vol. 4. New York: Wiley, pp. 339–90.

Manktelow, K. and Chung, M.C. (2004) *Psychology of Reasoning: Theoretical and Historical Perspectives*. New York: Psychology Press.

Meehl, P. (1990) 'Why summaries on research on psychological theories are often uninterpretable', *Psychological Reports*, 66: 195–244.

Newstead, S. and Evans, J.St.B.T. (eds.) (1995) *Perspectives on Thinking and Reasoning: Essays in Honour of Peter Wason*. New York: Psychology Press.

Nickerson, R.S. (1998) 'Confirmation bias: A ubiquitous phenomenon in many guises', *Review of General Psychology*, 2: 175–220.

Radder, H. (1996) *In and About the World: Philosophical Studies of Science and Technology*. Albany: State University of New York Press.

Rosenthal, R. ([1984] 1991) *Meta-Analytic Procedures for Social Research*. Newbury Park, CA: Sage.

Schmidt, F.L. (1996) 'Statistical significance testing and cumulative knowledge in psychology: Implications for training or researchers', *Psychological Methods*, 1: 115–29.

Schumacher, R.E. and Lomax, R.G. ([1996] 2004) *A Beginner's Guide to Structural Equation Modeling*. Mahwah, NJ: Erlbaum.

Shaughnessy, J.J., Zechmeister, E.B. and Zechmeister, J.S. ([1963] 2002) *Research Methods in Psychology*. New York: McGraw Hill.

Simonson, I. and Tversky, A. (1992) 'Choice in context: Tradeoff contrast and extremeness aversion', *Journal of Marketing Research*, 29: 281–95.

Sperber, D. and Girotto, V. (2002) 'Use or misuse of the selection task? Rejoinder to Fiddick, Cosmides, and Tooby', *Cognition*, 85: 277–90.

Stenning, K. and van Lambalgen, M. (2004) 'A little logic goes a long way: Basing experiment on semantic theory in the cognitive science of conditional reasoning', *Cognitive Science*, 28: 481–530.

Stommel, M. and Wills, C.E. (2003) *Clinical Research: Concepts and Principles for Advanced Practice Nurses*. Philadelphia: Lippincott, Williams and Wilkins.

Tversky, A. and Kahneman, D. (1981) 'The framing of decisions and the psychology of choice', *Science*, 211: 453–58.

Waller, N.G., Yonce, L.J., Grove, W.M., Faust, D.A. and Lenzenweger, M.F. (2006) *A Paul Meehl Reader: Essays on the Practice of Scientific Psychology*. Mahwah, NJ: Erlbaum.

Wason, P.C. (1966) 'Reasoning', in B.M. Foss (ed.), *New Horizons in Psychology*. Harmondsworth: Penguin.

Wason, P.C., and Evans, J.St.B.T. (1972) Dual processes in reasoning? *Cognition*, 3 (2): 141–154.

Windelband, W. (1915) 'Geschichte und Naturwissenschaft', in *Praeludien,* Vol. 2. Tuebingen: Mohr (Siebeck), pp. 136–60. Cited in Nagel, E. (1961) *The Structure of Science: Problems in the Logic of Scientific Explanation.* London: Routledge, pp. 547–548.

NOTES

1 E.g., Beins (2004), Keppel and Zedeck (1989); Shaughnessy et al. (2002).

2 For an historical account, see Lamiell (1998).

3 See, e.g., Abelson (1995); Gigerenzer (1993); Loftus (1996).

4 For a detailed treatment of the distinction, with insightful examples from applied health settings, see Stommel and Wills (2003).

10

Theory and Experimentation in the Social Sciences

Murray Webster, Jr. and Jane Sell

INTRODUCTION: THE ONTOLOGY OF EXPERIMENTS

Experimental methods are one way to develop and assess knowledge claims in social science. While it is sensible to pick a research method on criteria such as suitability to the questions and convenience, other cognitive and emotional processes also come into play. Choosing experimental research— or refusing to consider ever doing experiments—derives from value systems and more general beliefs about what is important to know and how to know it. Experiments can be very useful, but they are not suited to all questions in social science, and they certainly do not fit the temperament of every social scientist. Understanding when experiments can be useful and what sorts of values and beliefs are congenial to experimental methods can be helpful as researchers contemplate different ways to develop social science knowledge.

A term like 'experimental sociology' can mislead by suggesting that the method is the primary focus of interest for those who use it. To the contrary, experiments are a method, a means to an end. That end is better understanding of social processes and social structures. Sociological knowledge is about processes and structures, not about experiments. In a quest for knowledge, a person might use experiments some of the time and other methods at other times. To say the same thing more precisely, the goal is to formulate, test and improve theories of social processes and social structures. Theory building is the goal of sociology; the empirical methods used are means to that end. The investigations sometimes termed 'experimental sociology' would better be labeled 'theoretical sociology'. The goal is theory creation and development, not the running of experiments.

In this chapter we investigate the links between theory and experiments in the context of the social sciences. The most general question is how experiments can be useful in improving knowledge of social structures and social processes. We also address opposition to experimentation—not to decry it as a form of prejudice, but rather to show its sources in different overarching worldviews that different social scientists have adopted, not always consciously or deliberately. Following that, we outline design elements and show their links to theory development, and illustrate those points with an analysis of a sensitive experiment in sociology. We begin with a definition of 'experiment' as we understand the term.

What Experiments are and How They are Useful

In the social sciences, experiments are social situations deliberately created for the purpose of better understanding some aspects of social structures and social processes. An experiment is a research design in which an investigator controls the level of independent variables before measuring the level of dependent variables. The time ordering is what makes an experiment. In other methods—surveys, content analyses, structured and unstructured observation—a researcher confronts the independent and dependent variables simultaneously. Then 'control' of independent and intervening variables is accomplished statistically to assess correlations with the dependent variables. This temporal ordering is associated, as we will show below, with different meanings of 'generalization'. At this point, it simply supplies us with a definition of the kinds of settings we are discussing.

The term 'experiment' is not appropriately applied to some other everyday usages. For instance, sometimes a treatment is called 'experimental' to indicate that the person doing the treatment has little idea how it will turn out. By contrast, in a scientific experiment an investigator has a clear idea precisely how it will turn out because the experiment is based on a theory. (Of course the theory could be wrong and the experiment should show that. However making a precise prediction and having it disconfirmed is different from saying 'I have no idea what will happen here.')

The sort of experiments we refer to in this chapter involve manipulation of independent variables, optimal conditions of observation, and measurement of dependent variables. The independent and dependent variables are interpretations of concepts in explicit theories and derivations from those theories. The specification of 'some aspects' is important because experiments are not created for mirroring or reproducing all of a particular social setting. If the interest is in describing the details of an event, experiments are not really well suited. Most of the time, experiments are instances of situations designed to be informative for particular theoretical purposes. An experiment may

- Create a situation that is hard to observe in natural settings (e.g., continuous disagreement between partners, cheating on a test);
- Isolate one or a few processes that normally are obscured by other processes (e.g., separating judgments about fair earnings from one's own payment level);
- Repeatedly create situations that occur rarely or unreliably in nature (e.g., confronting someone with a unanimous majority of others whose answers are wrong);
- Remove or minimize known confounding factors that normally cannot be separated from phenomena of interest (e.g., removing history by having strangers interact, or by asking people to work on tasks they have never seen before);
- Control unknown confounding by assigning participants to experimental conditions (e.g., randomly assigning participants in drug trials to groups receiving an older drug, a new drug or a placebo); and therefore they produce strong evidence directly or closely relevant to ideas under examination (i.e., experimental evidence usually is more convincing than evidence from other methods because alternative interpretations are harder to sustain—though alternatives always are possible).
- Create circumstances that do not yet exist or are known to exist in natural settings (e.g. testing implications of theories that may not have any observed instances to date).

The Experimenter's Worldview

Experimental designs developed first in the natural sciences, within a particular worldview. As we use the term, 'worldview' incorporates values, beliefs, background understandings and interpretations that are congenial to conducting experimental research. Good research of kinds other than experiments may be conducted under different worldviews; however we believe that the views we describe in this section certainly facilitate experimental research and may be essential for this kind of research.[1]

While the first experiment may be lost to history, an early example is Galileo (1564–1642) dropping balls of different weights (a cannonball and a musket-ball) to assess acceleration due to gravity. Galileo's experiment shows that, so long as air resistance is negligible, masses of every material and of every weight fall at the same rate. We see in this case many features of contemporary experiments in social science. These include scope conditions, independent and dependent variables, measurement operations, predictions and hypotheses, and interpretations of outcomes.

Moreover, Galileo and contemporary experimentalists share a distinctive view of the world, one that is far from universal but is particularly congenial to experimental research as a way to build knowledge. Later we consider elements of this view that are not shared by other perspectives, and see why those with a different view may see less value in experimental research. First, we consider elements of the experimenter's view. Its primary elements include:

1. *Significant phenomena repeat.* Features of a situation must recur in order for experimental research—or any research other than observational at the time a unique event occurs—to be conducted on it. While any case of a falling body may have unique features (e.g., color or shape of the object), the concept 'falling body' obviously recurs. This feature separates science from history.
2. *Abstraction from individual instances is crucial.* 'Falling body' abstracts similar properties from, for instance, a pen dropped on the floor and a boulder falling from a mountain. The essential quality here is that something is moving towards the earth; shape, time, color, even the year in which it exists are irrelevant. Abstraction is essential for developing general principles.
3. *The positive utility of observable evidence.* Evidence is significant for assessing the truth of some idea(s). In other words, empirical outcomes have relevance for whether investigators believe a set of ideas. In Galileo's case, his idea was that all bodies accelerate towards the earth at the same rate. Though we take Galileo's view for granted today, in his day the prevailing view was Aristotle's, namely, that rate of fall was proportional to the weight of an object, because of inherent properties of things.[2] The experimenter's view of evidence may be decomposed into two parts:

   a. Evidence disconfirming predictions from the underlying ideas reduces confidence in those ideas; and
   b. Evidence confirming predictions from the underlying ideas increases confidence in those ideas.

Evidence is essential for improving theories of sociological subject matter.

4. *The goal of prediction.* The most important relationship between theoretical ideas and our empirical world is successful prediction. In other words, we can never know whether our theories are true in an absolute sense of telling how the world really is. We are satisfied if our theories enable us to predict events regularly.[3] Stronger evidence is provided by outcomes that are more precise and thereby eliminate alternative reasons by which they might occur. So, for example, experiments with extremely precise controls help eliminate plausible alternative sources of outcomes. Taking prediction rather than absolute truth as a criterion allows experimenters to decide when their understanding of phenomena is adequate.
5. *Conditional knowledge.* Nothing we know about the social world is true under all circumstances and everywhere. Rather, things happen under certain conditions. Such conditions preserve the universality of the propositions being tested—that is, they specify the abstract conditions under which the theory being tested is presumed to operate. Those conditions are essential for designing experimental research. An experiment must create the conditions specified in a theoretical statement—which is another way of saying that theoretical statements stated unconditionally are not suited for experimental assessment. Explicitly stating conditions with general principles allows experimenters to know what sorts of situations to create to assess those principles.[4]
6. *Measurement and quantification.* Consequences or outcomes of interest are those that can be measured; immeasurable outcomes are not the

sorts of things experimental investigators study. This point does not rule out an interest in studying internal states such as attitudes or emotions. It does, however, insist that the relevant facts about such phenomena are their effects on something measurable, whether that is behavior, questionnaire responses or answers given in an interview. When measurable outcomes are predicted, it is possible to determine whether the predictions are or are not supported. In fact, experimenters more often seek disconfirmation than confirmation of theories, for disconfirmation is much more useful for improving theories.

7. *The independence of outcome and investigator.* Experimentalists (and many other researchers as well) maintain that results are reproducible independent of specific observers. This principle (usually labeled intersubjectivity or reliability) requires several commitments. First, the methodology of the study must be publicly available so that others can repeat the study (see tenet number 1). Second, there can be no restrictions upon *who* can replicate the study (only on *how* it is replicated—that is, the same procedures must be followed). This does not mean that experimentalists believe that interaction between an observer and the observed has no effect—quite the contrary! A rather large proportion of social psychology is devoted to the investigation of the general range of interaction effects—for example, the study of teacher expectations upon students, the study of doctors' expectations upon patients, etc. Knowing the potency of such effects allows the design of experiments to eliminate them.

These seven elements of a worldview underlie social science experimentation, in the sense that most experimenters accept them. Someone who does not accept one or more of those elements is likely to consider other kinds of research more useful than experiments; for instance, close observation of natural settings. Could someone do experiments without entirely buying that worldview? Perhaps so. However it is difficult to know how such an approach would begin. For example, if someone believed that unique features of social situations are more important than repeatable features (refuting tenet number 1), it is hard to imagine an experiment that would help understand those unique features.

ALTERNATIVE WORLDVIEWS THAT ARE NOT CONGENIAL TO EXPERIMENTAL RESEARCH

Some sociologists do not accept one or more elements of the experimenter's worldview. Under different worldviews, experiments may be either inappropriate or irrelevant. There are several other worldviews that have been important in sociology. We briefly describe those views and consider why they probably are incompatible with an experimental research agenda.

Social Constructivism and Postmodernism

Social constructivism is a worldview that emphasizes how knowledge arises. It is true that scientific knowledge is produced socially, and our best understandings of the world come from shared evidence and interpretations. However, some social constructivists have taken those facts to extreme conclusions, such as the idea that scientific knowledge is nothing more than what scientists believe or are able to force others to believe. If one views the world in that way, evidence has little additional meaning—because it is fully determined by what the investigator already believes. Thus, the third tenet listed above—the utility of observable evidence—is not fully accepted by constructivists. Confirmatory evidence is not needed to strengthen their confidence in their views, and disconfirmatory evidence does nothing to weaken them.

There are different variations of social constructivism and an extreme form can be found in the literature on the sociology of science. This line of thought maintains that science is no different from other forms of knowledge such as folklore. The emphasis is upon how scientists come to believe what they believe. In such expositions, the nature of reality or tests of empirical evidence are not viewed as consequential, or at least no more consequential than any other source of information.[5]

Related to social constructivism is the general approach of postmodernism.[6] Postmodernism is not a well-defined body of knowledge, but rather a set of sensitizing concepts and ideas. Part of the focus is upon authority and power structures and how preconceived views may shape what we can observe and how it is interpreted. Some postmodernists believe that changes in what we consider scientific knowledge come about through social means such as power relations, and that evidence cannot be independent of the language and the researcher using the language. This is a rejection of the seventh tenet of experimental views.

There are merits to less extreme versions of both the postmodern and the social constructivist arguments. Values and orienting approaches (which we discuss below) certainly affect decisions about what to study, what variables are worth investigating, what evidence is considered important, and what the evidence means. For instance, Haraway (1989) has shown how cultural factors can affect what is studied and how it is interpreted. Japanese anthropologists studying groups of primates in the wild may identify and describe every individual, while American anthropologists often identify and describe only the troupe leaders. Such studies demonstrate the importance of recognizing biases of all sorts in research design. Recognition necessitates measures to counteract and counterbalance biases in experimental design; it does not imply a need to surrender to them.

If one adopts an extreme relativist view and argues that all knowledge is local, there is no reason to do experiments; in fact, there is no reason to do empirical research of any sort. Experimentalists have to treat outcomes of experiments as consequential. Results have to affect our views of the way the world is, or else there is not much justification for going to the trouble of getting those results.

Ethnomethodological Investigations

Ethnomethodology (literally, the method of the people) aims to document the practices of individuals in their familiar, ordinary activities. Harold Garfinkel, whose theoretical and empirical writings contributed greatly to this perspective, described ethnomethodology as going beyond other types of research (that he called 'formal analysis') to study the social contexts in which formal analysis takes place.[7] The social 'whole' is more than the sum of its parts because of unstated understandings, individual histories, unique features of settings, and many other facts. The artificial simplicity of experiments that appeals to experimentalists for theoretical purposes is antithetical to the goals of ethnomethodology. Consequently, ethnomethodologists would strongly object to the second tenet listed above, i.e., abstraction from individual instances. Abstract concepts and principles are of little use to ethnomethodology because they are not the 'stuff' of life as experienced by its participants. 'Ethnomethodology is not in the business of interpreting signs. It is not an interpretive enterprise. Enacted local practices are not texts which symbolize "meanings" or events. They are in detail identical with themselves and not representative of something else' (Garfinkel, 1996: 8).

USING AND MISUSING EXPERIMENTS

Just as some philosophical views are not congenial to using experimental methods, some kinds of research questions are not well answered with experiments. Even for investigators who espouse the seven tenets listed above, experiments do not always provide useful information for certain kinds of questions. Such questions might be important; however, experiments can do little or nothing to help answer them.

Characterizing populations

Experiments isolate or create conditions to investigate predictions. The predictions derive from theories that have particular properties, the most important of which is that all of the concepts are abstract rather than specific or particular (see tenet number 2). So, such theories might, for example, address the abstract issue of conformity, but no theory would specifically focus upon particulars such as conformity in speech patterns of US presidential candidates in 2004. Because experiments are meant to test ideas expressed in abstract concepts and propositions, the populations that theories refer to are not defined in a particular time and space, but are rather defined in abstract terms.

It follows then that a superficially appealing but specious use of experiments is to characterize differences among naturally occurring groups, without any theoretical reason for anticipating such differences.[8] We give a couple of examples of such misuse of experiments; the first involves conformity, the second involves collectivism.

One of the best-known experimental designs was developed by Solomon Asch (1956) for studying behavioral conformity in the absence of private agreement. In that experiment, a single naïve participant is confronted by a unanimous majority of 3 or more who give deliberately wrong answers to a simple perceptual task, judging which lines are the same length. Overall, about a third of the time, participants' answers conform to what the majority says. Some investigators thought it would be interesting to see whether, by conducting Asch-type experiments in several countries, national differences in conformity rates appeared. Are Germans or Britishers more conformist?

The problem with this approach is that neither the Asch experiment nor any other experiment can answer that question or similar questions. There are two reasons why. First, the Asch experiments, as is the case with most experiments, are artificial realities. The experiment creates a very unusual situation, one in which most people will never find themselves. How people act in the experiment may be informative for some theory, if the experiment instantiates scope conditions and variables of that theory. However it reveals practically nothing directly generalizable about what those people do outside the laboratory in their ordinary lives because lives are lived in conditions very different from conditions that obtain inside the laboratory in an Asch-type experiment.

If we think about it, we can see that an investigator is not really interested in whether Germans act differently from English inside a laboratory in a contrived situation. An investigator is probably interested in knowing whether people in one country or another will be more susceptible to a demagogue politician who might appear, or which people are more receptive to advertising. The Asch experiment does not—and cannot—tell us such things.

The second reason an experiment is not appropriate to characterize populations is that the experimental generalization process is different from that of a study designed to address the different characteristics of a specific population such as Germans in 2010. There is an important distinction between *theoretical generalization* (for which experiments are useful) and *statistical generalization* (for which experiments are not useful). Statistical generalization is the process of generalizing from characteristics of one group to another, unobserved group, as in representative sampling of a finite population.[9] Examples of statistical generalization include generalizing from the attitudes of a sample of registered voters to the entire population of registered voters. Such statistical generalization involves meticulous attention to defining the time and place of the empirical population of interest (registered voters in 2004 for example) and then randomly sampling from such a population.

Theoretical generalization, by contrast, involves abstract concepts, such as 'discrimination' or 'conformity', and it applies to theoretically defined populations. Such populations are not defined based upon time and space, but by the definitions of the concepts and the scope conditions associated with the propositions. Here the purpose of empirical testing is to reflect upon whether the theoretical predictions (which involve theoretical populations) are or are not supported. This is the type of generalization for which experiments excel. On the other hand, experiments are not useful for statistical generalization.

Let us take a more recent example. Some investigators wondered what the effects of a country's joining the European Union were on citizens' orientations towards individualism or collectivism. They proposed to study it by choosing some participants from countries that had joined the Union and others from countries that had not. Participants would play a game in which they could choose to share part of their resources with others in hopes of getting returns from the others, or they could keep their resources for themselves.

This design has the same conceptual flaws as using the Asch experiment to study national differences in conformity. If we wished the study to represent a particular group of people at a certain point in time, in a specific environment, we would want to be meticulous about drawing random samples. But, this is most certainly not the case. We do not really care whether people in one country differ from those in another country in how they play some simple laboratory game. We may be interested in whether they are more willing to support taxes for social welfare or to welcome immigrants, but their laboratory behavior tells us nothing about those tendencies.

All that a laboratory can tell us is how people in a particular experiment respond to the limited social situation created. A laboratory is so far from a natural setting that anyone who thinks about it will realize no direct generalization is reasonable. In a laboratory, participants typically do not know or even see each other; they interact in limited ways; their decisions have no significance once the session ends; and they never have to see the other people again. If you believe those conditions make the laboratory different from life in a natural setting, you would not expect people to act the same way in the laboratory as outside it.

However, a laboratory can be very useful for assessing theoretically derived predictions. If an experimental subject population fits the abstract scope conditions of a theory, results provide an appropriate test of those predictions. Laboratory findings are not immediately generalizable to any finite sample, such as, for instance, college sophomores. At stake are the scope conditions which determine the theory's range of applicability outside the laboratory. If college sophomores fit the scope conditions, they are an appropriate population to test the theory's predictions. If the theory is supported, the burden of proof seems to be on someone else to demonstrate that the propositions of the theory *cannot* be applied to some subset of the population—that is, to demonstrate that the scope of the theory is not so great as was originally claimed, or that those college sophomores did not actually meet the scope conditions.

Fundamental Orienting Approaches

A second kind of question experiments cannot answer are those having to do with fundamental orientations to the ways we go about studying social structures and social processes. Examples of what we mean by fundamental orientations are whether behavior is guided by God or by individual choices; whether people are basically good or evil; and what are the fundamental human motivations—territoriality, resource maximization, identity verification, managing sexual and aggressive drives, or others.[10]

The main problem with trying to assess orienting approaches experimentally is that there is no way to construct testable hypotheses from them. Put another way, there is no way to imagine what *dis*confirmation would look like. What possible pattern of results from an experiment (or any other research design) would convince someone who believes that God directs all human action that some event was *not* God-directed?

Perhaps more relevant to contemporary social science, consider some versions of evolutionary psychology. Adherents believe that most patterns of behavior and cultural differences among groups result from inherited tendencies selected under conditions of early hunting and gathering societies. It is very difficult or impossible to imagine designing an experiment whose results conceivably could convince an adherent that evolution did not create inherited tendencies that do *not* govern behavior patterns. The reason is that evolutionary psychology is a fundamental orientation, not a theory of social behavior.[11]

The problem with trying to assess orienting approaches through experiments is that most elements of orienting approaches are not empirical. Orienting approaches do not directly make claims about empirical events. Rather, they identify important problems, describe ways to go about conducting research, tell how to interpret outcomes, and the like. Such views are closer to articles of faith than they are statements about what the world is like.

Orienting approaches are properly seen, we believe, as background elements against which the empirical world appears. Thus the outcomes of an experiment might be seen as evidence of God's love of humanity, of individuals' attempts to create understanding, of individuals' seeking material rewards, of the operation of natural selection for certain inherent behavior patterns—and many other things besides. None of those background views is directly confronted by experimental data. Instead, the background gives different contexts for the meanings of data.

Background interpretation is very different from assessing theoretical predictions where an investigator deliberately selects predictions that might be wrong and tests them. In other words, an experimental investigator routinely searches for derivations that might *dis*confirm part of the theory. By comparison, adherents to an orienting strategy do not look for disconfirmation of their orientation; they are much more likely to look for confirming instances. Experimental data can confirm or disconfirm hypotheses derived from a theory. That is a modest task, though an important one. Experimental data cannot tell whether our fundamental beliefs about moral values are correct, or how human action fits into larger schemes. Issues of orientation properly fall into spheres outside the ones experimenters investigate.

Design Elements of Experiments

The foundation of experimental research lies in certain elements that experimenters design into their studies. Here we are not discussing considerations that figure in a research proposal or a report, such as number of conditions, cell sizes and power analyses, or subject populations. Rather, we mean philosophical and practical foundations of experimental design. We also discuss some issues in theory construction as well as experimental design, for the two activities are closely related.

A theory attempts to represent abstract features of specified kinds of situations, and it has the potential to predict outcomes in such situations. An experiment attempts to create an instance of the kinds of situations represented in a theory, and it has the potential to measure certain outcomes in that instance. When the concrete experimental outcomes are close to the outcomes represented abstractly in the theory, they increase confidence in the theory.

Theorists and experimentalists must consider several issues in their work, including scope conditions, definitions, interrelated theoretical propositions, and logical derivations from the propositions. Here is what those terms mean for a theorist:

- *Scope conditions*: These tell the classes of situations a theory deals with. For instance, many exchange theories deal with situations where individuals are primarily concerned with maximizing rewards and minimizing costs. If some people do not share those concerns, their actions are outside the scope of such a theory. In other words, a theory does not claim to apply to a particular case or to an experiment unless its scope conditions are met. Scope conditions are not limited by time or place—that is, a theory does not claim to apply only to behavior in the 21st century or only to people in the US. Rather, it applies to social structures of certain general types, or to people who have had certain general kinds of motivations or experiences.
- *Initial or antecedent conditions*: These are specific historical elements describing the specific

situation in which theoretical processes can be observed. They describe instances of independent and dependent variables, scope conditions, situational definitions, structural facts, and constraints on interaction. In the Asch experiment, an initial condition is that the naïve participant believes that the confederates' reports represent their own views. If a participant guesses that the confederates are actually following a script, group pressure vanishes and that participant is not in the situation described by the initial conditions of the design. In the experiment described in the next section, participants are ranked on differing characteristics. Two initial conditions are that participants understand the differential ranks and believe they occupy the rank positions assigned to them. So, for example, participants realize that high school graduates occupy lower educational status than do college graduates. If someone does not believe that, or misunderstands some other aspect of the situational definitions provided by the experimenters, that person is not in the intended situation because one or more of the initial conditions of the experimental design has failed.

- *Definitions*: These tell what the important terms or concepts in a theory's propositions mean, so someone can understand exactly what the theorist intends when the terms appear. Definitions are of two types, *explicit* and *implicit*. Explicit definitions appear in sentences of the form 'X always means Y in this theory.' They are sometimes called replacement operators because every defined term could be replaced by its definition without changing the intended meaning. Implicit definitions are contained in the theory's propositions. For example, 'gravity' is not explicitly defined in Newton's laws, but its meaning becomes apparent through the laws of motion in which it figures. Defined terms, like scope conditions, are abstract.[12]
- *Theoretical propositions*: These are general statements of how two or more abstract concepts relate.[13] They are the heart of the theory for they contain its claims for predicting how the world operates. Propositions generally have the form 'If A then B', where 'A' and 'B' are abstract terms defined either explicitly or implicitly earlier.
- The propositions are *interrelated* in the sense that they deal with some common concepts, and it is possible to see a deductive structure in their statements. The deductive structure might be logical or mathematical, and both types have

several variants. The important thing is that there be some structure to the propositions. A very simple structure would be a theory of three propositions: 'If A, then B', 'If B, then C', and 'If C, then D'.

- *Derivations*: One could, by combining the propositions above, get a derivation: 'If A, then D'. In words, this theory claims that, for all cases meeting the scope conditions, when you find A you will also find D. If you do find them together, consider that as support for the theory. If you do not find D with A in a case meeting the scope conditions, consider that disconfirmation and examine the theory's propositions to find out why.

An Illustration: An Experiment Contrasting Four Theoretical Predictions

Philosophers and practitioners in various fields have attempted to describe the cognitive status of theories and relations between theory and evidence.[14] Here we offer a simple view of the relations that seems to us reasonable and that seems close to the views of most contemporary experimenters in social science. We organize our presentation around an ambitious experiment reported by Joseph Berger, Robert Z. Norman, James W. Balkwell and Roy F. Smith (1992) assessing predictions derived from four differing abstract theoretical perspectives.

The experiments were designed to compare predictions from four ideas on how people process inconsistent status information. Situations of interest are those in which two or more members work together at a task and the members possess three or more status characteristics allocated inconsistently, with one actor higher on at least one status and also lower on at least one other status. For example, with two people working together, one might be a college graduate (higher status on education) and the other a high-school graduate (lower on education), while the first person has a lower status job than the second. Presume for argument's sake that the first person is a woman (lower status in our culture) and the second is a man (higher status). The question is how people use such information to create an interaction hierarchy among themselves.

Table 10.1   Status relations in the experiment

Person	Education status	Occupation status	Gender status
#1	Advantage (high)	Disadvantage (low)	Disadvantage (low)
#2	Disadvantage (low)	Advantage (high)	Advantage (high)

Table 10.1 shows status relations in this simple situation.

The researchers identified four possible status-processing mechanisms in the literature:

1. Individuals might focus on the status giving them an advantage. Then the first person in the experiment would treat education as important and occupation and gender as irrelevant, and the second person would treat occupation or gender as important and education as irrelevant. Call this process 'simple balancing'.
2. Individuals might go with the majority of status information for each of them, ignoring inconsistent information. Person #1 has a disadvantage on gender and occupation, and Person #2 has comparable advantages; education would become irrelevant for both the individuals. In this mechanism, both actors treat Person #1 as low status and Person #2 as high status because of the majority of the status information. Call this 'majority balancing'.
3. Individuals might tally up status advantages and disadvantages. Person #1's advantage on education is cancelled by her disadvantage on occupation, leaving her with the single status disadvantage of gender. Person #2 similarly cancels the education disadvantage with the occupation advantage, putting him in the same status relation as someone with only the single characteristic of gender. Call this 'canceling'.
4. Individuals might process the status information according to a complicated function in which minority inconsistent information against a field of consistent information has greater effect than it would by itself. Person #1's advantage on education has more effect than it would by itself because it contrasts with her disadvantages on occupation and gender. Person #2's disadvantage on education also has greater effect than it would by itself for a complementary reason. Consistent status information is subject to diminishing effect for each additional item, rather like declining marginal utility in economic theories. Call this 'organized subset combining'.

Berger et al. (1992) constructed an experimental situation to compare predictions from the four principles described above. Individuals were given supposed rankings on one, two, three or four status characteristics, and they then worked in pairs at an additional task. The research question was how much of the earlier status information would transfer to the new task, which of course depends on how individuals process the information when they get it. The researchers were able to cast the four alternative processing mechanisms into precise quantitative predictions for their experimental design, and they found that predictions representing mechanism #4 were considerably closer to the data than predictions from the other three mechanisms.

What is the significance of this outcome?[15] First, results confirmed an explicit theory of status processing that contained the model for mechanism #4. Had results better supported one of the other mechanisms, that outcome would reduce confidence in the theory and perhaps impel the investigators to explore modifications of their status-processing model.

Second, results show that some intuitively plausible status processing mechanisms, such as the first two, do not do a good job representing how people actually act. It might seem obvious that we try to make relevant only status elements that advantage us (mechanism #1), but that is not what happened. The canceling mechanism (#2) also did not represent the data very well.

Third, we see that people use all available status information; none is ignored. The first three models all presume that people ignore some information, and those models did not represent the outcomes as well as #4. Thus when you hear someone say 'No matter what my accomplishments, once they learn that I am a person (with any low status characteristic), they stop listening to me,' you know that it does not really work that way. People use all the status information they have access to, and they process it in a fairly sophisticated manner.

Some relevant features of this case are worth noting. First, the researchers began with *explicit scope conditions*; in this case, that individuals were task-focused, collectively oriented, and that the only salient information participants had about each other was the three status characteristics. Task focus means that their primary motivation was to solve some problem or set of problems, as happens in a committee or on a team, as compared to meeting for the sake of the interaction itself, as at a party. Collective orientation means that individuals consider it legitimate and necessary to take everyone's contributions into account. Team members are not working alone—everyone must have a chance to participate, and the solution is a group product. The experimental situation allowed participants to know only the status characteristics under investigation, not other information such as family income or personality characteristics (for example). When a situation is within the scope conditions of a theory, predicted results support the theory and contrary results weaken confidence in it. When a situation is outside the scope conditions of a theory, any results are irrelevant to assessing the theory.

In designing experiments, scope conditions limit the kinds of situations that may be used. An experimenter would not intentionally design an experiment outside the scope of a theory, as its results then would be irrelevant to that theory. Creating a design that instantiates abstract scope conditions is not always straightforward, and it may take pretesting to develop a situation that participants see as incorporating the scope of a theory.

Second, key terms in the theory have *clear definitions*. For instance, *status characteristics* are explicitly defined as (1) socially significant characteristics; (2) having at least two states, differentially evaluated in a society as to their desirability, social worth and prestige; and (3) differential performance

expectations associated with each state of the characteristic. *Performance expectations* are defined implicitly, by a structure of propositions that tell conditions creating them, their components and some of their behavioral consequences.

Third, the experimenters worked with an *explicit set of theoretical propositions*. Those describe conditions under which status information becomes socially significant in situations meeting the scope conditions, how various items of status information get combined (the main concern of the experiment described here), relations linking a structure of status elements to performance expectations, and observable consequences of performance expectations that form through the status information.

Fourth, the propositions had an *interrelated structure*. While the structure of this theory is more complex than the simple example given earlier in this chapter, the consequence is the same. It was possible to combine the theoretical propositions logically to derive predictions for behavior in this situation. In fact, it was possible to derive four different predictions, depending on which of four information-processing principles one used. Experimental results help choose among the four predictions—the closer a prediction was to the observed data, the stronger its empirical confirmation from this experiment.

Fifth, the research team created a situation in which initial structural and interaction conditions *made the theoretical processes visible*. The experiment operationalizes independent and dependent variables of the theoretical predictions, and at the same time it permits variation in relevant information (e.g., how many status characteristics an individual possessed and of what valence) and clear observation.

It should be apparent that experimental design is challenging. Creating a situation that meets a theory's scope conditions and that also creates the needed initial conditions and independent variables that are a theory's guidelines is far from a simple task. The Berger et al. research team benefited from having access to a standardized experimental situation that had been used for many other investigations of status effects, and that has been adapted for many newer questions in more recent research. The design and modifications of it have been used since the early 1960s, first for investigations of how 'performance expectation states' organize a group hierarchy, and later for many other kinds of research including the status inconsistency study just described. For most investigations, there are substantial advantages to adapting an existing experimental design rather creating a new one for each new question.

How do Experimental Results Relate to Settings outside the Laboratory?

We have argued that experimental design is directly related to the theory being tested. The theory itself is composed of scope conditions, defined terms, propositions and a deductive interrelationship. By its very nature, this theory is artificial; it is not designed to capture the complexities or nuances that characterize actual settings. The theory is not time-space specific because the concepts are abstract and therefore not time-space specific.

An experiment should capture the important elements of a theory. Remembering that any theory is artificial, the experiment is necessarily artificial as well. This is an important property for theory testing and provides a significant advantage to experimental research.[16] Because of the control afforded in an experiment, plausible alternatives for experimental outcomes can be eliminated much more readily than they could be in actual settings. Consequently, if a theory is repeatedly supported, despite rigorous attempts to disconfirm or falsify it, we can be more confident of its predictive value.

But if a theory and the method used to test theory are both artificial, how do they relate to actual settings? The answer rests with characteristics of application as well as characteristics of theory. When theoretical principles are applied to particular problems, the most theoretically relevant characteristics of the theory must be paired with the most

theoretically relevant characteristics of the setting. One setting is different from any other setting in many ways; but important abstract properties may be the same. So, for example, a classroom setting can, at times, meet all the scope conditions associated with theory behind the status inconsistency experiment described above. That is, classrooms are situations of collective orientation and task orientation, where participants know their respective positions on external status characteristics. When a classroom meets the scope conditions, expectation states theories apply to that classroom. When scope conditions are not fulfilled, such as when children are not task-oriented and do not really care about solving problems, the theory would not apply.

An excellent example of how such application of theory might work appears in the applied research of Elizabeth G. Cohen and her colleagues.[17] Those studies developed intervention strategies to diminish participation differences between minority and majority children.

IDEAL AND ACTUAL EXPERIMENTS

Experiments are ideally suited to testing derivations that are logically linked to explicit theories. If an investigator starts with a set of abstract, logically interrelated statements, and is able to derive testable hypotheses whose confirmation or disconfirmation lends confidence to the theory and whose disconfirmation identifies statements in the theory that are unsound, then experimental methods can provide a strong foundation for increasing knowledge.

Yet we cannot always enjoy the experimental and other benefits of an ideal world. Theorizing in several fields in the social sciences is not always explicit, logical abstract theory—though there is more of that kind of theory than some may realize. Social scientists are often interested in phenomena that have not been conceptualized abstractly or theoretically. Many such phenomena are important on practical and other grounds, and we need to study them even without waiting for someone to develop acceptable theories of aspects of them. Because we live and work in an imperfect environment, our understanding is always provisional, subject to revision with new information and better methods. What theories we have are incomplete, and in many cases they are growing in scope of application and precision of predictions. Social science measurements include both systematic and random error, just as do measurements in natural sciences.

Given these facts, it is worthwhile to consider how departures from the ideal set of affairs affects experimental research and the knowledge gained from it.

First, what happens if *scope conditions* are not clearly defined, or if they are clearly defined but an experiment fails to realize them? It is unfortunately common that sociological theories are presented without explicit scope conditions. One interpretation of this is that the theorist is claiming implicitly that the theory applies everywhere to everything, which would be impossible. Things happen in the social world *under certain conditions*. Under other conditions, those things do not happen, and other things happen. For example, when two jurors disagree about how to proceed with deliberations, other jurors are more likely to side with the juror having an obvious status advantage. Of course, this is not always true. They are likely to side with the status-advantaged juror *if* their main goal is to get the best verdict—the theoretical scope condition of task-focus. They are likely to side with the status-advantaged juror *if* no competing influence, such as liking or disliking, interferes. And so on. We need scope conditions so that we know whether evidence from a particular setting is relevant to confidence in a theory.

Maybe, then, failure to state scope conditions means that a theorist has not thought about them. If so, it is a significant oversight, for this makes a theory vulnerable to disconfirmation from situations the theorist has not even thought about. If someone presents disconfirmatory evidence, the theorist cannot very well say, 'Well, I never intended my theory to apply to that type of situation,' if he

or she has not stated any scope conditions. (Actually, a theorist could say that, but it would not look good.)

The point is that it is always difficult to design a good experimental test of a theory, and that it is impossible until the theorist provides scope conditions. An experiment is a constructed reality, and an experimenter needs a theory's guidelines to constrain the type of reality he or she creates. If a theorist has not provided guidelines, an experimenter has to make guesses about the kinds of situations the theorist has in mind. Experimenters may not want to make those guesses because the danger is high that any disconfirming evidence will be dismissed by the theorist as being 'obviously' outside the unstated scope of the theory.

Even when a theory clearly states scope conditions, it is usually not simple to realize them in an experiment. For instance, many network exchange theories use a scope condition that individuals are primarily motivated to achieve as many points as possible. While an experimenter might try to so motivate individuals, he or she will not perfectly succeed with all of them. Imperfect operations and individual variance among participants affect the usefulness of experimental data for assessing theory, but they are universal problems. What is the effect of less-than-perfect operational creation of scope conditions?

There is no general answer. In network-exchange experiments, uneven motivation for points probably produces variance in behavior. If the variance is too high and an experimenter suspects failure to create necessary scope conditions, she might investigate other ways to induce the needed condition. Theories of status processes discussed above require task focus and collective orientation. It turns out that in many cases, status processes are quite robust across failure of collective orientation, but task focus seems to be crucial. Without theoretical guidance to decide when collective orientation will be crucial and when it does not matter much, an experimenter relies on experience and pre-testing measures to decide whether a situation must instantiate that condition. The behavioral measurement Berger et al. (1992) used for performance expectations does not work well unless participants are collectively oriented, but for other kinds of measurement such as questionnaires, the collective orientation condition seems to be less important (Balkwell et al., 1992).

Our next issue is what happens when explicit or implicit *definitions of key theoretical terms* are unavailable for the theoretical foundation of an experiment. In the experiment by Berger et al. described earlier, 'status characteristic' has an explicit definition that includes prestige, worthiness and honor; and it also carries differential notions of performance capacity, such as the ability to do some particular task or 'tasks in general'. The performance element of the definition is often omitted from informal conversation about status; one of the significant contributions of the theoretical perspective guiding the above experiment is to show that conceptions of skill always accompany status differences. Further, the idea of performance capacity is crucial for the measurement operation used in the experiment.

Given the explicit definition of the term 'status characteristic' in this theory, an argument that this is not 'really' status lacks force. Unless an explicit definition departs so greatly from common usage that it becomes confusing, theorists have fulfilled their obligation to specify what they are talking about, and an observer can decide whether she is interested in the phenomenon or not.

Suppose an experiment were conducted on a phenomenon not explicitly defined, we might expect great arguments over what the experiment 'really' shows. Recall the earlier description of the Asch experiment on conformity: a lone individual confronts a unanimous group giving answers that very obviously are wrong, and has to decide whether to conform (verbally) to them. Does that show conformity? Of course the experiment involves a type of social influence; the question is *what type*.

An older experiment also involves influence, though perhaps of a different sort.

Muzafer Sherif (1937) placed a lone individual in a very dark room with one or more confederates. The experimenter exposed a pinpoint light source and asked everyone to watch it for a few minutes and see how far it moved. Again a naïve individual answered after hearing others' reports, and again influence of their reports was evident. If the confederates reported a large movement, so did the naïve participant; and similarly for small movement. (The light actually does not move, but observers' eyes do, a phenomenon called *nystagmus,* a problem in optical astronomy and related fields.) What the Sherif experiment shows is that social influence affects what people believe in an unstructured situation.

But is that the same as what Asch found? Many textbooks treat both as instances of conformity, but that relies on a particular informal definition of that term—one equating conformity with influence. To the contrary, one might argue that those phenomena differ in an important way. In the Asch experiment, when a naïve participant says the same thing as the confederates, he or she knows he is saying something that is not true. In the Sherif experiment, naïve participants believe what they report. If we restrict the word 'conformity' to cases where someone is going against his beliefs, you might say only Asch studied conformity. Sherif studied influence or structuring, but not conformity.

Resolving the question whether these phenomena are the same thing is possible only if someone accepts certain definitions of the terms. As no universally accepted definitions have been imposed, and no theory explicitly defined the relevant terms, we may anticipate continued argument over whether Asch and Sherif studied the same thing. The point is, without shared definitions of important concepts, we are more likely to get arguments over meanings than a growing body of knowledge about social phenomena.

Third, suppose a theorist has not developed *propositions and derived hypotheses* before someone conducts an experiment. What can we learn in such cases?

For quite some time, little attention was given to race and gender issues, even in social psychology, a birthplace for studies of prejudice and discrimination. In the 1970s, however, many studies appeared that began to investigate the effects of sex and gender. Many of the experimental studies simply asked whether gender affected particular dependent variables, ranging from justice decisions or resource allocations to attitudes. Rarely were abstract, theoretical propositions developed to interpret the meaning of gender differences. Instead, hypotheses were often justified based upon results of past studies or conjectures of how women might differ from men.

This created a large literature, the results of which were difficult to reconcile. Sometimes, for example, it appeared that women were more cooperative than men while at other times men were more cooperative than women.[18] There was little systematic development of what gender meant to interactants under particular contexts. Instead, there seemed a default assumption that gender was a relatively static characteristic of the person himself or herself. The problem with that assumption is that there is no apparent way to reconcile contradictions or no way to interpret disconfirmations. Without a prior set of logically related propositions, a finding is simply a finding. It has no bearing upon a particular theoretical argument.

It is important to notice how very different this approach toward gender was from the expectation states approach mentioned previously, which conceptualized gender as one instance of a diffuse status characteristic. If gender is conceptualized as an instance of a diffuse status characteristic, then there exist an interrelated set of propositions that provide predictions about when it should or should not make a difference for some types of behaviors. So, for example, gender should not have an effect upon influence within groups when all group members are of the same gender. It should have an effect when there is variance in gender composition of a task group.[19]

To summarize these points, experiments may be designed and conducted without the strong theoretical development we advocate. We have considered results from three kinds of failures: to specify scope conditions, to present unambiguous definitions of key concepts, and to offer theoretical propositions predicting behavior in the experiment.

Unstated scope conditions frequently leads to claims by others that some results of theirs disconfirm a theory. Sometimes the claims have merit and sometimes they do not, but whenever they appear they distract attention from developing the theoretical ideas that led to the experiments.

Undefined and ill-defined concepts make it particularly difficult to know what experimental results mean. Do they confirm the experimenter's theory, or do they actually show something the experimenter had not considered? It is hard to tell unless we share understandings of what the experimenter is studying.

Implicit or unknown theoretical propositions may generate considerable more research in an attempt to find propositions that account for an experiment's results. While sometimes helpful, these efforts do little to build or extend theories; rather, they simply attempt to see if some existing theory can account for what was found in the early experiment.

SUMMARY

We have argued that experiments are particularly suited for theoretical investigations that specify scope conditions, utilize well-defined abstract concepts and develop deductively related propositions. As illustrated, such an approach rests on seven tenets of a distinctive worldview, with which we began our discussion. The worldview defines a particular approach toward knowledge that emphasizes the goal of prediction as assessed through data, the role of replication and the importance of exposing both ideas and data to many researchers who may have different biases.

Experimental methods and an experimental worldview are far from universal in the social sciences. Neither is essential for doing good work in social science. We do believe, however, that it is difficult to do good experiments without adopting a version of an experimental worldview. Differing worldviews may be behind many of the misunderstandings and occasionally the outright hostility towards experiments in social science. Recognizing different fundamental views of what is important and how to improve understandings is, we hope, a first step towards developing a tolerant approach to the different empirical methods used to develop knowledge.

The experimental worldview is compatible with developing and assessing a large number of questions in a variety of disciplines. While experiments are most often associated with small group dynamics, the 'size' of a social phenomenon is not the issue. Experiments can address small group phenomena, large organizational phenomena, and linkages between them. This does not mean that experiments can assess how a particular organization such as Halliburton is run or how uncertainty is handled within the Central Intelligence Agency. To investigate phenomena experimentally, we must refine questions so that they refer to theoretically relevant aspects of those phenomena. So, for example, rather than asking about Halliburton Oil and Petroleum Company, we might ask how organizational hierarchy can affect implementation of policy. Or, rather than asking about the CIA we might ask how decision making characterized by rigid hierarchy of command affects the coordination among organizations. The point is that researchers are obligated to specify the theoretically relevant aspects under consideration.[20]

Asking questions this way, researchers are forced to formulate their reasoning in ways that are not dependent upon any specific instance—such as Halliburton or the CIA. Such formulations constrain researchers in one way: the local setting at a particular point in time cannot be depended upon. But such formulations also liberate researchers; abstraction and deduction enable new and sometimes counter-intuitive theories. Consequently, such abstract approaches can do what description or investigation of a local setting can never do—formulate theories that address settings or contexts that might not have occurred naturally.[21]

As an example, it may be possible to design classroom settings in which the race and ethnic stratification are not 'imported in'. Rather than try to search for such classrooms (and perhaps never find them), theories can specify the conditions under which we would expect equality rather than inequality based on ethnicity. Elizabeth Cohen and her colleagues' research (Cohen and Lotan, 1997) mentioned earlier has demonstrated such possibilities. And such instances present one of the strongest arguments for experiments. A particular context is just that. However an abstract theory can explain the past and predict the future. For developing and improving theories, experiments are an ideal method.

REFERENCES

Achinstein, Peter and Barker, Stephen F. (eds) (1969) *The Legacy of Logical Positivism: Studies in the Philosophy of Science*. Baltimore, MD: Johns Hopkins University Press.

Asch, Solomon E. (1956) 'Studies of independence and conformity: I. A minority of one against a unanimous majority', *Psychological Monographs*, 1956, 70, No. 416, pp. 1–70.

Balkwell, J., Berger, J., Webster, M. Jr., Nelson-Kilger, M. and Cashen, J. (1992) 'Processing status information: Some tests of competing theoretical arguments', in E.J. Lawler, B. Markovsky, C.L. Ridgeway and H.A. Walker (eds), *Advances in Group Processes*, vol. 9. Greenwich, CT: JAI Press, pp. 1–20.

Berger, Joseph, Norman, Robert Z., Balkwell, James W. and Smith, Roy F. (1992) 'Status inconsistency in task situations: A test of four status processing principles', *American Sociological Review* 57: 843–55.

Berger, Joseph and Zelditch, Morris Jr. (1993) 'Orienting strategies and theory growth', in Joseph Berger and Morris Zelditch, Jr. (eds) *Theoretical Research Programs: Studies in the Growth of Theory*. Stanford, CA: Stanford University Press, pp. 3–19.

———— (1997) 'Theoretical research programs: A reformulation', in Szmatka Jacek, John Skvoretz and Joseph Berger (eds), *Status, Network, and Structure:*

Theory Development in Group Processes. Stanford, CA: Stanford University Press, pp. 29–46.

Bloor, David (1976) *Knowledge and Social Imagery.* London: Routledge & Kegan Paul.

Cohen, Bernard P. (2003) 'Creating, testing, and applying social psychological theories', *Social Psychology Quarterly,* 66: 5–16.

Cohen, Elizabeth G. and Lotan, Rachel A. (1997) *Working for Equity in Heterogeneous Classrooms: Sociological Theory in Practice.* New York: Teachers College Press.

Cosmides, Leda and Toobey, John, 'Evolutionary psychology primer'. Available at: http://www.psych. ucsb.edu/research/cep/primer.html. (Accessed on 19 July 2005).

Foschi, Martha (1980) 'Theory, experimentation, and cross-cultural comparisons in social psychology', *Canadian Journal of Sociology* 5: 91–102.

Freese, Lee (1980) 'The problem of cumulative knowledge', in Lee Freese (ed.), *Theoretical Methods in Sociology: Seven Essays.* Pittsburgh, PA: University of Pittsburgh Press, pp. 13–69.

Freese, Lee and Sell, Jane (1980) 'Constructing axiomatic theories in sociology: Part I', in Lee Freese (ed), *Theoretical Methods in Sociology: Seven Essays.* Pittsburgh, PA: University of Pittsburgh Press, pp. 263–309.

Garfinkel, Harold (1996) 'Ethnomethodology's Program', *Social Psychology Quarterly,* 59: 5–21.

Haraway, Donna (1989) *Primate Visions: Gender, Race and Nature in the World of Modern Science.* New York: Routledge.

Hempel, Carl G. (1965) *Aspects of Scientific Explanation.* New York: Macmillan.

Laudan, Larry (1990) *Science and Relativism.* Chicago: University of Chicago Press.

Lucas, Jeffrey (2003) 'Theory-testing, generalization, and the problem of external validity', *Sociological Theory* 21: 236–53.

Meeker, B.F. and Leik, Robert K. (1995) 'Experimentation in social psychology', in Karen S. Cook, G.A. Fine and J.S. House (eds), *Sociological Perspectives on Social Psychology,* Needham Heights, MA: Allyn and Bacon, pp. 629–49.

Moreland, Richard L. and Levine, John M. (1992) 'The composition of small groups', in Edward J. Lawler, Barry Markovsky, Cecilia L. Ridgeway and Henry A. Walker (eds), *Advances in Group Processes,* vol. 9. Greenwich, CT: JAI Press, pp. 237–80.

Nagel, Ernest ([1960] 1979) *The Structure of Science: Problems in the Logic of Scientific Explanation.* Indianapolis IN: Hackett Publishing Company.

Ridgeway, Cecilia L. and Smith-Lovin, Lynn (1999) 'The gender system and interaction', *Annual Review of Sociology* 25: 191–216.

Sell, Jane, Griffith, Wanda I. and Wilson, Rick K. (1993) 'Are women more cooperative than men in social dilemmas?', *Social Psychology Quarterly* 56: 211–22.

Sherif, Muzafer (1937) 'An experimental approach to the study of attitudes', *Sociometry* 1: 90–8.

Simpson, Brent T. (2003) 'Sex, fear and greed: A social dilemma analysis of gender and cooperation', *Social Forces* 82: 35–52.

Turner, Stephen (2002) *Brains/Practices/relativism: Social Theory after Cognitive Science.* Chicago: University of Chicago Press.

Turner, Stephen, and Turner, Jonathan (1990) *The Impossible Science: An Institutional Analysis of American Sociology.* Beverly Hills and London: Sage.

Walker, Henry A. and Cohen, Bernard P. (1985) 'Scope statements: Imperatives for evaluating theory', *American Sociological Review* 50: 288–301.

Webster, Murray, Jr. (2005) 'Laboratory experiments in social science', *Encyclopedia of Social Measurement,* vol. 2. New York: Elsevier Academic Press, pp. 423–33.

Webster, Murray Jr. and Kervin, John B. (1970) 'Artificiality in experimental sociology', *Canadian Review of Sociology and Anthropology,* 8: 263–73.

Willer, David and Walker, Henry A. (2007) *Building Experiments: Developing and Testing Social Theory.* Stanford, CA: Stanford University Press.

Willer, David and Murray Webster, Jr. 1970. 'Theoretical Concepts and Observables', *American Sociological Review* 35: 748–57.

Zelditch, Morris, Jr. (1969) 'Can you really study an army in the laboratory?', in Amitai Etzioni (ed.), *A Sociological Reader in Complex Organizations.* New York: Holt, Rinehart and Winston, pp. 528–39.

NOTES

1 The experimenter's worldview is congenial also to the development of social science through theoretical explanation, and, in fact, most scientists are experimenters. Some years ago, S.P. Turner and J.H. Turner (1990) showed how sociology had largely failed to develop scientific theory, for both historical and philosophical reasons. However, scientific theory has certainly developed in some areas of sociology. We believe that this is at least partly due to experimental methods. Later, we will argue the complementary view that experimental research needs a theoretical foundation in order to produce results useful to sociology.

2 Aristotle's view had been endorsed by the Church as not only empirically true, but also necessarily true. Given the inaccuracy of clocks at the time, nobody could measure speed accurately enough to

know whether one or the other view was correct. Galileo used dripping water as his measure of time, presuming that drips fall from a small hole in a bucket at approximately equal intervals. It is telling that this was more accurate than measuring time by a clock. We thank Willer and Walker (2007) for this example.

3 This might appear to be a subtle difference, but, as we will see below, others focus efforts more on understanding how things 'truly' are than upon predicting events.

4 Conditions also make experimental data relevant to natural settings. On the conditional nature of knowledge, see Cohen (2003); Foschi (1980); Walker and Cohen (1985); and Webster and Kervin (1970).

5 Perhaps the best-known explication of this social constructivist view is Bloor's (1976) book, *Knowledge and Social Imagery*.

6 We would not presume to attempt a full representation of postmodern views, and our use of the term may be seen as a convenience for assisting recognition. We are interested here in one common element: the view that evidence is largely irrelevant to theoretical assessment. Laudan (1990) outlines this view of social science, which he calls 'relativism'. Turner (2002) shows that the relativist view rests upon a questionable presumption that members of a scientific community share enough understandings that they can communicate without relying on evidence.

7 Garfinkel (1996: 16–20) notes that for a demonstration of gravity comparable to Galileo's, an ethnomethodologist would study how textbook instructions for the experiment differ from actual practices of someone conducting it. The difference between an instruction manual and actual practice is familiar to anyone who consults a manual to understand how to get software to perform a particular task!

8 We are here not referring to the desirability of including both women and men, or individuals drawn from different ethnic groups, in experimental research. Scope conditions of the theoretical foundation usually do not rule out demographic groups; thus, most theories claim they apply to all people. Therefore, experimental research must include all such groups in order to provide broad tests of those theories. Here we criticize using experiments to show (or to determine whether) men and women, or Americans and Japanese, differ in their behavior in an experiment just for the purpose of documenting such differences.

9 See Meeker and Leik (1995) and Lucas (2003) for discussions of different types of generalization.

10 Berger and Zelditch (1993; 1997) discuss orienting strategies and their relationships to theories and research.

11 Evolutionary psychologists Cosmides and Toobey (1997: 1) state that the approach is 'a way of thinking about psychology that can be applied to any topic within it.'

12 Some philosophical traditions treat explicit definitions as replacement operators: a defined term could, in principle, be replaced by its definition wherever the term appears. However abstract terms cannot ever be fully specified by replacements (Nagel, 1979: 97–105), and there are reasons from cognitive science to doubt that any two people can share exactly the same understanding of a concept (Turner, 2002: 1–22). We view definition pragmatically, as reducing uncertainty about meaning, not as definitively establishing meaning. Freese and Sell (1980) provide fuller discussion of uses of definition in sociological theory development.

13 Willer and Webster (1970) discuss the uses of abstraction for theory building, with examples.

14 The so-called 'Vienna School' has had a major impact on the thinking of social scientists since about the 1930s. Ernest Nagel (1960), Carl G. Hempel (1965) and Peter Achinstein and Stephen F. Barker (1969) present clear expositions of this viewpoint. As noted above, other perspectives have influenced theory and research in social sciences. Whatever the philosophical topic, practicing researchers often say that philosophers do not accurately describe what researchers do. For our purposes here, the various epistemological debates provide a language for describing theories and evidence and the relations between them, and we use terms from that discourse without always adopting all elements of the viewpoints that generated those terms.

15 Findings are always conditional upon situations meeting scope conditions of theories under assessment. Thus the three findings we discuss should all be prefaced with the words 'In situations meeting the theory's scope conditions ...'

16 For discussion see Webster (2005).

17 See Cohen and Lotan (1997).

18 For discussion see Moreland and Levine (1992), Sell et al. (1993), and Simpson (2003).

19 For a thorough discussion of gender effects in interaction, see Ridgeway and Smith-Lovin (1999)

20 A well-known article by Morris Zelditch, Jr. on the use of experiments is entitled, 'Can You Really Study an Army in the Laboratory?' (1969). A superficial answer is 'No, because they wouldn't fit.' Zelditch's more thoughtful answer is 'You can study abstract properties of armies, such as authority relations, status processes, obedience, and legitimacy in a laboratory. What you establish experimentally then can be applied to understand instances of those phenomena in armies, business organizations, schools, and many other settings.'

21 See discussion of this aspect of formal theories in Freese (1980).

11

The Treatment of Missing Data

David C. Howell

The treatment of missing data has been an issue in statistics for some time, but it has come to the fore in recent years. The current interest in missing data stems mostly from the problems caused in surveys and census data, but the topic is actually much broader than that. (For an excellent discussion of the problems encountered by the 2000 US Census, and the question of whether or not to adjust for missing data, see the contribution by Freedman and Wachter (Chapter 13) in this volume.) In this chapter I will discuss the treatment of missing data across a range of experimental designs, starting with those designs whose treatment is relatively straightforward (though not necessarily satisfactory) and moving to situations where the optimal solution is elusive. Fortunately we have come a long way since someone could say that the best treatment for missing data is not to have any. That may be the best treatment, but recent techniques have come far in narrowing the gap between the ideal and the practical.

The treatment of missing data is not an area that is particularly controversial, leaving aside the political issues involved in the US Census. There are a number of alternative approaches, but there is pretty much universal agreement about the strengths and weaknesses of each. Over time new procedures

replace older ones, but this, like many areas in statistical methods, is an area that changes slowly. So we often find that the older methods are still used, but that is mostly because in a specialized area like this, it takes a long time for newer methods to be understood and to replace the old.

My goal in this chapter is to give the reader an understanding of the issues involved in the treatment of missing data and the ability to be conversant with the approach that is adopted. When it comes to selecting an approach, it is not necessary to have an in-depth knowledge of the technical issues, but it is necessary to understand the alternatives and to have a grasp of what is involved in each method.

TYPES OF MISSINGNESS

Any discussion of missing data must begin with the question of why data are missing in the first place. They could be missing for perfectly simple and harmless reasons, such as a participant having an automobile accident and not being able to appear for testing. In such a case missingness is more of a nuisance than a problem to be overcome. On the other hand, data could be missing on the basis of either the participant's potential score on the dependent variable (Y) or any of the independent variables (X_i). The reasons for missing data play an important role in how those data will be treated.

Missing Completely at Random (MCAR)

Rubin (1976) defined a clear taxonomy of missingness that has become the standard for any discussion of this topic. This taxonomy depends on the reasons why data are missing. If the fact that data are missing does not depend upon any values, or potential values, for any of the variables, then data are said to be *missing completely at random (MCAR)*. The example of the careless motorist, who does not appear for testing because of an accident, having nothing to do with the study is a case in point. Pickles (2005) phrased the condition somewhat differently by saying that for MCAR the probability of missingness is a constant. Any observation on a variable is as likely to be missing as any other. If you are going to have missing data, this is the ideal case because treatment of the existing data does not lead to bias in the estimated parameters. It may lead to a loss in power—which is often not a serious problem in census work, though it certainly can be in experimental studies—but it will not lead to biased parameter estimates.

Little (1998) has provided a statistical test of the MCAR assumption. His MCAR test is a chi-square test. A significant value indicates that the data are not MCAR. This test is provided in the SPSS Missing Values Analysis (MVA), which is not part of the base system, and should be applied whenever there is some question about MCAR. SAS also includes this test in PROC MI.

Missing at Random (MAR)

Data are *missing at random (MAR)* if the probability of missing data on a variable (Y) is *not* a function of its own value after controlling for other variables in the design. Allison (2001) uses the example of 'missingness' for data on income being dependent on

marital status. Perhaps unmarried couples are less likely to report their income than married ones. Unmarried couples probably have lower incomes than married ones, and it would at first appear that missingness on income is related to the value of income itself. But the data would still be MAR if the conditional probability of missingness were unrelated to the value of income *within each marital category*. Here the real question is whether the value of the dependent variable determines the probability that it will be reported, or whether there is some other variable *(X)* where the probability of missingness on Y is conditional on the levels of X. To put it more formally, data are MAR if $p(Y$ missing $|Y,X) = p(Y$ missing $| X)$.

Missing Not at Random

Data are classed as *missing not at random (MNAR)* if either of the above two classifications are not met. Thus if the data are not at least MAR, then they are missing not at random. When data are MNAR there is presumably some model that lies behind missingness. If we knew that model we might be able to derive appropriate estimators of the parameters in the model underlying our data. For example, if people with low incomes are in fact more reluctant to report their income than people with higher incomes, we could presumably write an equation (a model) predicting missingness on the basis of income. Such an equation could then be incorporated into a more complex model for estimating missing values. Unfortunately we rarely know what the missingness model is, and so it is difficult to know how to proceed. In addition, incorporating a model of missingness is often a very difficult task and may be specialized for each application. See the article by Dunning and Freedman (2007) for a useful example of a model dealing with missingness. Notice also Dunning and Freedman's interesting example of a situation in which data are missing because of their score on the independent variable. That example illustrates that such data may seriously distort the correlation between the two variables, but may have little effect on the regression coefficient.

Ignorable and Nonignorable Missingness

As I have suggested, when we have data that are MNAR, life becomes very much more difficult. Here we say that the mechanism controlling missing data is *nonignorable*. That means that we cannot sensibly solve whatever model we have unless we are also able to write a model that governs missingness. Modeling missingness is a very difficult thing to do, and most discussions, including this one, do not discuss the treatment of data whose missingness is nonignorable. Freedman and Wachter's discussion in this volume (see Chapter 13) of what is involved in dealing with missing census data illustrates just how difficult, and perhaps unsuccessful, such efforts can be.

On the other hand, if data are at least MAR, the mechanism for missingness is *ignorable*. Thus we can proceed without worrying about the model for missingness. This is not to say that we can just ignore the problem of missing data. We still want to find better estimators of the parameters in our model, but we do not have to write a model that gets at missingness. We certainly have enough to do to improve estimation without also worrying about why the data are missing.

MISSING DATA AND ALTERNATIVE EXPERIMENTAL DESIGNS

How we deal with missing data depends in large part on the experimental design that we are employing. Consider the difference between a correlational study where data on many variables are collected and then subjected to an analysis of linear multiple regression and an experimental study where we have two independent variables, usually categorical in nature, and one dependent variable. In an analysis of variance setting we most often think in terms of 'unequal

sample sizes' rather than 'missing data', although unequal sample sizes very often are the direct result of data being missing rather than a planned inequality. With unequal sample sizes the techniques are quite well worked out. But in regression, we often want to substitute pseudo-values of a variable (referred to hereafter as 'imputing data') and then solve the regression with a complete dataset. The way we approach these two examples is quite different.

Traditional Experimental Designs

For those whose main focus is experimental studies of behavior, the idea of missing data usually means that a person did not show up to participate in a study, or that one classroom had more students than another, or that a piece of equipment did not record the data correctly. In these situations missing data create problems, but they are nothing like the problems involved in survey research, for example. In this section I am not taking a strict interpretation of 'experimental' by always requiring that observations be assigned to levels of the independent variable(s) at random. But I am distinguishing those studies which we loosely call 'experimental' from those that we think of as 'observational'.

In experimental studies we most often have data missing on the dependent variable, though there are times when it is the independent variable that is missing. The latter situation is most common when the level of the independent variable is defined by self-report on the part of the participant, though there can be other causes. We have somewhat different problems depending on whether it is the independent or dependent variable that is missing.

Missing data on the independent variable

We will begin with the situation in which we class observations into groups on the basis of self-report, and then try to compare those groups on some dependent variable. For example, Sethi and Seligman (1993) compared three religious groupings—'Liberal, Moderate, and Fundamentalist'—on their level of optimism. In their study they were able to identify religious groups on the basis of direct observation, though obviously random assignment was not an option. But what if they had identified groups on the basis of a separate item that they included on the questionnaire that they gave out to measure optimism? Certainly there are a number of people who would fail to disclose their religious affiliation, and it is unlikely that the probability of disclosure is constant across all religious groups. (Certainly if you consider your religious affiliation to be a local coven, you would probably be less likely to report it than if you went to the local Methodist church.)

In this situation the simplest approach is to form four groups instead of three. In other words we identify participants as Liberal, Moderate, Fundamentalist and Missing, and then run the analysis using those four groups. If contrasts show that the Missing group is not different from the other groups, we might be justified in dropping the missing data and proceeding normally with our analysis of the other three groups.

If we discover that the mean optimism score from those participants for whom group membership is unknown is significantly different from some other means (but perhaps not from all), we have a problem of interpretation, but at least we have learned something about missingness. A major interpretive problem here is that not only do we not know anything about the religious orientation of those for whom we have missing data, but we also have some concerns about those for whom we do have data. Suppose, for example, that religious liberals were far more likely to refuse to identify their religious preferences than the other two groups. What does that say about the data from those liberals who *do* self-identify? Do we actually have a distorted sample of liberals, or are the ones who didn't self-report just a random sample of liberals (for a more complete discussion of this issue, see Cohen et al., 2003).

Missing data on the dependent variable

We have somewhat different problems when data are missing on the dependent variable. When we have a design that reduces to a one-way analysis of variance or a *t* test, the treatment of missing data on the dependent variable is usually straightforward if we can assume that the data are at least MAR. Any software solution for an analysis of variance or *t* will provide a satisfactory result. The most serious problems we have are that our parameter estimates are better for large groups than for small ones. This assumes, of course, that our missingness is MAR and therefore ignorable. I don't mean to suggest that missing data are harmless in this situation, but the problem is more one of statistical power than interpretation.

But what about those situations where we would not be willing to assume that data are MAR, and therefore that the missingness mechanism is nonignorable? There are certainly situations where nonignorable missingness arises and creates problems. Imagine that we are running a treatment study for hypertension and people who are not receiving much benefit from the treatment start dropping out. Here missingness falls in the nonignorable category. We will probably see that average blood pressure falls for those remaining in our study, but that may simply mean that we no longer have those unsuccessfully treated patients remaining in the study and raising the mean. All we have are data from those who remain, which largely means from those who derive benefit. In this case means and standard errors are going to be decidedly biased with respect to the parameters in the population, and we will be hard pressed to draw meaningful conclusions.

When it comes to designs that lead to a factorial analysis of variance, missing data are more of a problem. But even here the solutions are at least well spelled out, even if there is not always complete agreement on which solution is best.

It is easy to illustrate the problem caused by missing data in a factorial design. When we have a factorial with equal number of

Table 11.1   Illustration of the contaminating effects of unequal sample sizes

	Non-Drinking	Drinking	Row Means
Michigan	13 15 14 16 12	18 20 22 19 21 23	
		17 18 22 20	$\bar{X}_{1.} = 18.0$
	$\bar{X}_{11} = 14$	$\bar{X}_{12} = 20$	
Arizona	13 15 18 14 10	24 25 17 16 18	
	12 16 17 15 10 14		$\bar{X}_{2.} = 15.9$
	$\bar{X}_{21} = 14$	$\bar{X}_{22} = 20$	
Column Means	$\bar{X}_{.1} = 14$	$\bar{X}_{.2} = 20$	

observations in each cell, then the main effects and interaction(s) are orthogonal to one another. Each effect is estimated independent of the others. We do not have to draw any conclusion conditional upon the level of another independent variable. When we have unequal sample sizes however, row, column and interaction effects are confounded. As a simple, though extreme, example, consider the following design. In this experiment with hypothetical data we recorded data on driving errors both from participants who had and had not been drinking. We further broke the data down into those collected in Michigan and Arizona.

The most obvious, and expected, result is that drivers who have been drinking make far more errors than drivers who have not been drinking. That will probably surprise no one. But notice also that drivers from Michigan appear to make more errors than drivers from Arizona. Is that really true? Are drivers from Michigan really that bad? If you look at the non-drinking drivers you see that Michigan and Arizona both have means of 14. And if you look at drinking drivers, the two states both have means of 20. So when we control for drinking—in other words, when the results are treated as conditional on drinking—there is no between-state effect. The higher score in Michigan actually came from the fact that there were proportionally more drinking drivers in that sample, and they made more errors because they had been drinking.

The example of drinking and driving errors was intended to point to the fact that missing data can cause important problems even in a simple factorial design. How we treat these data depends on why data are missing. Perhaps the data were collected by two different groups of researchers working in conjunction. The ones in Michigan decided that they would rather have twice as many drinking than non-drinking drivers. The researchers in Arizona made just the opposite choice for some reason. Then missingness does not depend in any way on the variables in the study, and is ignorable. In this case we would most likely want to partial all other effects out of the effect in question. Thus we look at states after partialling drinking and the state x drinking interaction (which would in this example be zero). Similarly for drinking and for the interaction. This is the solution which SPSS and SAS call the Type-III solution. It has been the default in that software through many versions and should be used unless there is a very specific reason to do something else.

However let us assume for the moment that there are just many more drinking drivers in Michigan than in Arizona (I have absolutely no reason to think this is really the case). Then it may be meaningful to say that Michigan drivers, on average, make more errors than Arizona drivers. The apparent cause is the higher percentage of drunken drivers in Michigan, but, whatever the cause, there are still more driving errors in that state. This points out the important fact that even with a nice neat tidy analysis of variance, determining why the data are missing is important both in selecting an appropriate analysis and in drawing meaningful conclusions. If I really did think that there were a higher percentage of drinking drivers in Michigan, I would not want to partial the Drinking variable in calculating a main effect for State.

Repeated measures designs

Within the category of experimental research designs we have repeated measures designs where participants are measured repeatedly over time or trials. The nice feature of these designs is that very often if you do not have data for one trial for a particular participant, you probably do not have data for other trials. The only thing you can do there is drop the participant from the analysis. Assuming that nonresponse is at least MAR, your parameter estimates will remain unbiased.

In some repeated measures (or time series) designs that take place over a period of time, there may be a different kind of problem with missing data. For example, if the study takes place over a year and participants move away, get sick, or just get tired of the experiment, you will have data for the first few trials but not for later trials. There is no simple solution to this problem. Simply dropping those individuals from the study is one possibility, and it may be an acceptable one if the data are MAR. If the data are not MAR, with the poorer-performing participants tending to drop out, then deleting whole cases will lead to bias in our estimates.

One solution that is sometimes employed, more often in medical research than in the social sciences, is called *Last Observation Carried Forward (LOCF)*. As the name implies, the last observation a participant gave is entered into the empty cells that follow (and hopefully the degrees of freedom are adjusted accordingly). In the past the FDA recommended this approach in clinical trials, but we now know that it leads to biased results and underestimates variability across trials. Similar strategies involve replacing missing observations with the participant's mean over the trials on which data are present, or basing imputed values on trends from past trials. All these approaches carry

with them assumptions about what the data would have looked like if the participant had not dropped out, and none of them is to be recommended. Methods discussed later in this chapter offer somewhat better solutions with less bias.

The intention-to-treat model

A common procedure in medical research, which is far less often used in the behavioral sciences, but which does have much to offer in many behavioral studies, is known as the intention-to-treat model. While it is not always thought of as a technique for missing data, that is exactly what it is since some number of participants in one condition are actually 'missing for that condition' because they were switched to a different treatment.[1]

Assume that we are doing a clinical study of two different treatments for angina. (I use a medical example because I have useful data for that, but you could just as easily think of this study as a comparison of cognitive behavior therapy and family therapy as treatments for anorexia.) Assume further that patients were randomly assigned to a surgical or a pharmacological treatment of angina. Two years later we record the number of patients who are still alive and who have died.

This sounds like a perfectly reasonable experimental design and we would expect a clear answer about which approach is best. But our patients are actual human beings, and the physicians who treat them have an ethical obligation to provide the best care possible. So although a patient is randomized to the pharmacological treatment group, his physician may decide part way through the study that he really needs surgery. So what do we do with this patient? One approach would be to drop him from the study on the grounds that the randomized treatment assignment was not followed. However, that would bias the remaining sample toward those who did well on medication. Another possibility would be to reassign that patient to the surgical group and analyze his data 'As-Treated'. The third way would be to continue to regard him as being in the pharmacological group regardless of what actually happened. This is the intention-to-treat model, and at first it sounds foolish. We know the guy had surgery, but we pretend that he received only medication.

The first thing to recognize is that under the intention-to-treat model a null difference between groups must *not* be taken to mean that the two therapies are equivalent. As originally proposed by Richard Peto in the early 1980s, that was clearly part of the model, though this often gets forgotten. This is especially troublesome as 'equivalence testing' is becoming more important in clinical settings. Suppose that we imagine that the pharmacological group was treated with a daily dose of castor oil. (I am of the generation that still remembers that wonderful stuff.) I would assume, though I am not a physician, that castor oil will not do anything for angina. (The only thing it does is taste awful.) After a short period the doctors of those in the castor oil group decide that it is a useless therapy and move most of their patients to the surgical group, which they have some ethical responsibility to do. So what has happened is that almost all of the patients were actually treated surgically, and, because they were treated alike, we would expect that they would respond alike. So when we run our statistical test at the end of treatment we would not be able to reject the null hypothesis. This certainly should not be taken to mean that castor oil is as good as surgery— we know that it clearly does not mean that. It simply says that if you assign some people to castor oil and some to surgery, they will all come out the same at the end. However, if the surgery group does come out with a significantly greater survival rate than the castor oil group, we have evidence that surgery is better than castor oil. So a statistically significant difference here means something, but a non-significant difference is largely uninterpretable. (Of course this was Fisher's model all along, but we often lose sight of that.)

In addition to analyzing the data as intent-to-treat, there is another analysis that we should be doing here. We should simply count the number of patients who ended up receiving each kind of treatment. When we

Table 11.2 Results from Hollis and Campbell (1999)

	As Assigned		As Treated	
	Drug	Surgical	Drug	Surgical
Survivors	344	373	316	401
Deaths	29	21	33	17
Total	373	394	349	418
Mortality (%)	7.8%	5.3%	9.5%	4.1%

discover that almost all patients were switched away from castor oil, this tells us a lot about what their physicians thought of the castor oil treatment. It may also be very profitable to also run an analysis on groups 'as-treated' and to present that result as well as the intent-to-treat result.

Table 11.2 shows the results of a study by the European Coronary Surgery Study Group, reported by Hollis and Campbell (1999), on surgical and pharmacological treatment for angina pectoris. In that study 767 men were randomized to the two groups, 373 to the pharmacological treatment and 394 to the surgical treatment.

We can see from the table that the As-Treated analysis would suggest that the surgery condition has a much lower mortality rate than the pharmacological condition. There were six patients who were *assigned* to surgery but died before that surgery could be performed, and so were actually only treated pharmacologically. In the Intent-to-Treat (As-Assigned) analysis those six deaths raise the death rate for the surgical group. In the As-Treated analysis we see that there are much larger, and significant, differences between groups.

Contingency tables

Missing data are also a problem when the data are collected in the form of contingency tables, as they were in the intent-to-treat example above. Here we often cross our fingers and hope that the data are at least MAR. If they are not MAR, the interpretation of the results is cloudy at best. Here again the problems are the same ones that we have been discussing. If there is systematic dropout from one or more cells, the missing

Table 11.3   Attitude about weight gain/loss in African-American and White high-school girls

Ethnic Group	Gain	Goal			
		Lose	Maintain	Missing	Total Non-missing
African–American	24(35.63)	47(63.60)	28(41.15)	30	99
White	31(40.12)	352(409.12)	152(194.38)	60	535
Missing	10	20	30		
Total Non-Missing	55	399	180		634

Source: Gross (1985) with hypothetical missing data added

data mechanism is confounded with the results of the data that are there.

We will take as an example a study by Gross (1985). She investigated attitude about weight in African-American and White high-school girls. She classified by ethnic group and recorded whether the girls wanted to gain weight, lose weight or maintain their current weight. The data in Table 11.3 are from her study, except for the fact that she did not have any missing data; I have added the missing data to create an example.

Cohen et al. (2003) discuss the analysis of categorical data in detail and describe an imputation method that assigns missing data to the non-missing cells of the table on the basis of a reasonable model of missingness. This is conceptually a very simple procedure. If we look at the African–American row in the above table we see that there are 30 missing observations—cases in which we know the ethnic group, but not their goals about weight gain or loss. But we also know that 24/99 = 24% of the African–American cases for which we *did* know the goal fell in the Gain column. So it seems reasonable to assume that 24 percent of the 30 missing cases would also have fallen in that column if we had been able to collect their data on Goal. Similarly, 24/55 = 44% of the group that wanted to gain weight were African–American, and so it is reasonable that 44 percent of the 10 missing cases in that column should be assigned to African–Americans. Therefore our new estimate of the count in the African–American/Gain cell should be 24 + (24/99)*30 + (24/55)*10 = 35.63. If we do the same for the rest of the cells we find the values indicated in parentheses in each cell.

At this point we have allocated a total of 140.38 cases to the first row. Of those, 35.63/140.38 = 25.38% are in the African–American/Gain cell (whereas we formerly had 24/99 = 24.24% in that cell. In other words we have slightly changed our estimate of the percentage of observations falling in $cell_{11}$. Cohen et al. (2003) suggest reallocating the 30 missing observations in row 1 on the basis of this revised estimate, and performing similar calculations on each cell. If you do this you will again change, slightly, the percentage of observations in each cell. So you again reassign missing observations on the basis of those revised estimates. Eventually this iterative process will stabilize, with no further changes as a result of reallocation. At that point we declare the process completed, and run a standard chi-square test of the revised contingency table. For these data it took eight iterations for this process to stabilize when I did the calculations, and the resulting observed frequencies are shown in Table 11.4.

The Pearson chi-square value for this table is 51.13 on 2 *df* which is clearly significant. For Gross's data (recall that she did not have the extra observations that I added as missing values), the chi-square was 37.23.

OBSERVATIONAL STUDIES

A high percentage of the research studies reported in the literature are non-experimental. Among others, these include standard regression studies, many studies of structural equation models, and survey studies. These studies do not use random assignment and are often limited to those who happen to fall within the

Table 11.4   Observed frequencies after iteratively reallocating missing observations to Table 11.3

	Goal			
Ethnic Group	Gain	Lose	Maintain	Total
African-American	36.49	63.01	42.30	141.80
White	39.96	407.38	194.86	642.20
Total	76.45	470.39	237.16	

sample at hand. Here there is even more opportunity for missing data, and perhaps even less chance of adequately modeling missingness. Moreover missing values are nearly as likely to occur with the independent variable (if there is one) as the dependent variable. Many methods have been developed to handle missingness in these situations, and the remainder of this chapter will focus on those. But keep in mind that these methods apply only when the data are at least missing at random.

Linear regression models

Many of our problems, as well as many of the solutions that have been suggested, refer to designs that can roughly be characterized as linear regression models. The problems—and the solutions—are certainly not restricted to linear regression: they apply to logistic regression, classification analyses and other methods that rely on the linear model. But I will discuss the problem under the heading of linear regression, because that is where it is most easily seen.

Suppose that we have collected data on several variables. One or more of those variables is likely to be considered a dependent variable, and the others are predictor, or independent, variables. We want to fit a model of the general form $\hat{Y}_{ij} = b_0 + b_1 X_{1i} + b_2 X_{2i} + e_{ij}$

In this model data could be missing on any variable, and we need to find some way of dealing with that situation. We will assume that the missing data are either MCAR or MAR. A number of approaches to missingness in this kind of situation have been used over the years.

Casewise deletion

Probably the most common approach to missing data in regression analyses is what is called casewise deletion (or 'listwise deletion', or 'available case analysis'). Using this approach we simply drop from the analysis all cases that include any missing observation. The analysis is then carried out on the data that remain. This is usually the default analysis for most statistical software.

There are definite advantages to casewise deletion. If the missing data are at least MAR, casewise deletion leads to parameter estimates that are unbiased. The only loss is to statistical power, and in many situations this is not a particularly important consideration because this type of study often has a high level of power to begin with.

If the data are MNAR, this approach produces biased estimates. The resulting model is difficult to interpret because of confounding with missingness. However, in many situations this approach has much to recommend it. It is certainly better than many of the alternatives.

Pairwise deletion

In pairwise deletion, data are kept or deleted on the basis of pairs of scores. In computing the overall covariance or correlation matrix, a pair of scores contributes to the correlation if both scores are present, but does not contribute if one or both of them are missing. Thus if a participant has data on Y, X_1, X_2, and X_5, but not on X_3 or X_4, that participant would be included in computing r_{YX_1}, r_{YX_2}, and r_{YX_5}, but not in computing r_{YX_3} or r_{YX_4} (and similarly for the rest of the pairs of observations). All available observations would be used in estimating means and standard deviations of the variables.

This method has one advantage, which is that it makes use of all available data and thus estimates parameters on the maximum sample size. But that is its only advantage. The major disadvantage is that each correlation,

Table 11.5 Salary and citations of members of university faculty

Analysis	N	r	b_1	Standard error (b_1)
Complete cases	62	.55	310.747	60.95
Mean substitution	69	.54	310.747	59.56
Mean substitution plus Missingness	69	.56	310.747	59.13

Source: Derived from Cohen et al. (2003)

mean and standard deviation is estimated on a somewhat different dataset. In addition, it is not only possible but also not uncommon that the covariance or correlation matrices resulting from this approach and needed for the analysis will not be positive definite. This means that it is impossible to calculate a normal inverse of either matrix, and solve the necessary equations.

Pairwise deletion is generally a bad idea and I can think of no situation in which I would recommend it. As someone once said of stepwise regression, I would characterize pairwise deletion as 'unwise' deletion.

Mean substitution

One approach that is sometimes taken when data on an independent variable are missing is to substitute for the missing scores the mean on that variable for all nonmissing cases. This approach has the dubious advantage of using all the cases, but it has several disadvantages.

The results in Table 11.5 were obtained using a data file from Cohen et al. (2003). In this situation he was predicting the salary of members of the university faculty solely on the basis of the number of times their publications were cited. There are 62 cases with complete data and another 7 cases with Salary but without Citation. The results for an analysis of complete cases ($N = 62$) and an analysis of all cases with mean substitution for missing data ($N = 69$) are shown in the first two rows of the above table. Ignore the last row of the table for a moment.

In this table you should notice that the regression coefficient for citations (b_1) is the same in the two analyses. However the standard error of the coefficient is smaller in the mean substitution analysis. This is because we have added seven cases where the deviation of the observation from the mean is 0, but we

have increased the sample size. Holding the numerator constant while increasing the denominator automatically reduces the result. Although we have added cases, we have added no new information, and any change is in some way spurious. What we have is a standard error that is biased downward, leading to an inappropriate test on b_1 and incorrect confidence limits. This is one of the reasons why mean substitution is not a particularly good way to proceed when you have missing data. It has been argued that if you have only a few missing cases, the use of mean substitution will lead to only minor bias. But if you have only a few missing cases, you also have very little to gain by finding a way to add those cases into the analysis. I suggest that you do not even consider mean substitution.

Missing data coding

One way to improve on the mean substitution approach is to make use of any information supplied by missingness. A good way to do this is to add a variable to the regression that is coded '1' if the observation is missing and '0' if the observation is present. We again use mean substitution for the missing data.

Jacob Cohen was once an advocate of this approach, but his enthusiasm seems to have cooled over the years. The result of using both mean substitution and coding for missingness is shown in the bottom row of the Table 11.5. There you can see that the coefficient for Citations remains the same, but the standard error is still underestimated. The one advantage is that the coefficient for the missingness variable of 4439 (not shown) represents the difference in mean income between those who do and those who do not have missing data on Citations. This is useful information, but we did not need a regression solution to find it.

Jones (1996) has shown that coding for missingness when we have multiple independent variables can lead to bias in both the regression coefficients and their standard errors. He examined a somewhat less biased approach, but still found that wanting. Coding for missingness in conjunction with mean substitution has not been particularly successful, and is no longer to be recommended.

Regression substitution (Imputation by least squares)

One additional fairly simple approach to the treatment of missing data is to regress the variable that has missing observations on the other independent variables (or even variables not used in the study), thus producing a model for estimating the value of a missing observation. We then use our regression equation to impute (substitute) a value for that variable whenever an observation is missing.

When there is a strong relationship between the variable that has missing observations and other independent variables, regression substitution is thought to work reasonably well. Lynch (2003) has characterized it as perhaps the best of the simple solutions to missing data. However regression imputation will increase the correlations among items because some of the items will have been explicitly calculated as a linear function of other items. This will affect the regression coefficients that result from the analysis. The imputed values would be expected to have less error than if the values were not missing. Thus regression imputation is likely to underestimate the standard error of the regression coefficients by underestimating the variance in the imputed variable. But this leads to an alternative solution, which will be discussed later, wherein we resolve this problem by deliberately adding random error to our imputed observation.

In computing regression imputations, a fairly new procedure in SPSS, known as missing value analysis, by default adds a bit of error to each observation. We will see this in more detail later, but it is an attempt to reduce the negative bias in the estimated

standard errors (see Acock, 2005) This additional error does not solve the problem, but it reduces it somewhat. Like most imputation procedures, regression imputation assumes missing values are MAR (but not necessarily MCAR). The regression method also assumes homogeneity of regression, meaning that the same model explains the data for the non-missing cases and for the missing cases. If this assumption is false, the imputed values may be quite different from what the values would be if we had been able to measure them.

Hot deck imputation

One of the earliest methods of imputing missing values is known as hot deck imputation. Scheuren (2005) provides an interesting glimpse of how hot deck procedures developed within the US Census Bureau. In the 1950s people generally felt that they had an obligation to respond to government surveys, and the non-response rate was low. In an effort to deal with unit non-response (the case where all data from a participant are missing), data cards (yes, they did use Hollerith cards in those days) for respondents were duplicated, and non-responders were replaced by a random draw from these duplicate cards. Thus if you were missing a respondent of a certain gender from a certain census track, a draw was made from the data of respondents of that gender residing in that census track. The method worked well when only a small amount of data were missing, and the variance properties of the method were understood (Hansen et al., 1953).

If it was acceptable to substitute 'pseudo-respondents' for missing respondents, it was not a big step to replace missing items (questions) with pseudo-items. Again, items were replaced by a random draw from records selected on the basis of values on appropriate covariates. As long as the amount of missing data was minimal, this procedure worked well and was well understood. Unfortunately, the response rate to any survey or census has fallen over the years, and as we replace more and more data, the properties of our estimators, particularly their standard errors, become a problem. Hot deck imputation is not common today, although it is apparently useful in some settings.

EXPECTATION–MAXIMIZATION (EM)

The two most important treatments of missing data in the recent literature are expectation/maximization (known as the EM algorithm) (Dempster et al., 1977) and multiple imputation (MI) (Rubin, 1987). These are not distinct models, and EM is often used as a starting point for MI. I will discuss the two in turn, though they tend to blend together.

EM is a maximum likelihood procedure that works with the relationship between the unknown parameters of the data model and the missing data. As Schafer and Olsen (1998) have noted, 'If we knew the missing values, then estimating the model parameters would be straightforward. Similarly, if we knew the parameters of the data model, then it would be possible to obtain unbiased predictions for the missing values.'(pp. 553-554) This suggests an approach in which we first estimate the parameters, then estimate the missing values, then use the filled-in dataset to re-estimate the parameters, then use the re-estimated parameters to estimate missing values, and so on. When the process finally converges on stable estimates, the iterative process ends.

For many, perhaps even most, situations in which we are likely to use EM, we will assume a multivariate normal model. Under that model it is relatively easy to explain in general terms what the EM algorithm does. Suppose that we have a dataset with five variables $(X_1 - X_5)$, with missing data on each variable. The algorithm first performs a straightforward regression imputation procedure where it imputes values of X_1, for example, from the other four variables, using the parameter estimates of means, variances, and covariances or correlations from the existing data. (It is not important whether it calculates those estimates using casewise or pairwise deletion, because we will ultimately come out in the same place in either event.) After

imputing data for every missing observation in the dataset, EM calculates a new set of parameter estimates. The estimated means are simply the means of the variables in the imputed dataset. But recall that when I discussed regression imputation, I pointed out that the data imputed with that procedure would underestimate the true variability in the data because there is no error associated with the imputed observations. EM corrects that problem by estimating variances and covariances that incorporate the residual variance from the regression. For example, assume that we impute values for missing data on X_1 from data on X_2, X_3 and X_4. To find the estimated mean of X_1 we simply take the mean of that variable. But when we estimate the variance of that variable we replace $\Sigma(X_i - \bar{X})^2$ with $\Sigma(X_i - \bar{X})^2 + s^2_{1.234}$. Similarly for the covariances. This counteracts the tendency to underestimate variances and covariances in regression imputation. Now that we have a new set of parameter estimates, we repeat the imputation process to produce another set of data. From that new set we re-estimate our parameters as above, and then impute yet another set of data. This process continues in an iterative fashion until estimates converge.

EM has the advantage that it produces unbiased—or nearly unbiased—estimates of means, variances and covariances. Another nice feature is that even if the assumption of a multivariate normal distribution of observations is in error, the algorithm seems to work remarkably well.

One of the original problems with EM was the lack of statistical software. That is no longer a problem. The statistical literature is filled with papers on the algorithm and a number of programs exist to do the calculations. A good source, particularly because it is free and easy to use, is a set of programs by Joseph Schafer. He has developed four packages, but only NORM is available to run as a stand-alone under the Windows operating system. The others—CAT, which handles categorical data; MIX, for mixed models; and PAN, for panel or cluster data—are available as S-Plus libraries. Unfortunately

Coefficients[a]

Model	Understandardized Coefficients		Standardized Coefficients		
	B	Std. Error	Beta	t	Sig.
1 (Constant)	−2.939	12.003		−.245	.809
SexP	−3.769	2.803	−.183	−1.344	.194
DeptP	.888	.202	.764	4.393	.000
AnxtP	−.064	.169	−.062	−.380	.708
DeptS	−.355	.155	−.460	−2.282	.034
AnxtS	.608	.166	.719	3.662	.002

a. Dependent Variable TotBpt

$N = 26$, $R^2 = .658$

Source: Derived from data at www.uvm.edu/~dhowell/StatPages/More_Stuff/Missing_Data/CancerDataRaw.sav

Figure 11.1 Casewise Deletion Using SPSS

S-Plus is not simple to use for those without experience with that programming environment. These programs are available from http://www.stat.psu.edu/~jls/misoftwa.html. I show printout from NORM below, and it is quite easy to use. The paper by Schafer and Olson (1998) listed in the references is an excellent introduction to the whole procedure. SPSS version 13 also includes a missing data procedure (as a separate add-on) that will do EM. The results of that procedure closely match that of NORM, but in my experience the standard errors in the resulting regression are smaller than those produced by data imputed using NORM.

An example

The following example is based on data from a study by Compas (1990, pers. comm.) on the effect of parental cancer on behavior problems in children. The dependent variable is the Total Behavior Problem T score from the Achenbach Child Behavior Checklist (Achenbach, 1991). One might expect that the gender of the parent with cancer (SexP) would be a relevant predictor (things fall apart at home faster if mom is sick than if dad is sick). Other likely predictors would be the anxiety and depression scores of the cancer patient (AnxtP and DeptP) and the spouse (AnxtS and DeptS). These five predictors were to be used in a multiple linear regression analysis of behavior problems.

Unfortunately, due to the timing of the first round of data collection, many of the observations were missing. Out of 89 cases, only 26 had complete data. The good thing is that it is reasonable to assume that missingness was due almost entirely to the timing of data collection (different families receive a diagnosis of cancer at different times) and not to the potential value of the missing values. So we can assume that the data are at least MAR without too much concern. The data for this example are available as an ASCII file and as an SPSS file at *www.uvm.edu/~dhowell/ StatPages/More_Stuff/Missing_Data/Cancer DataASCII.dat* and at *www.uvm.edu/~dhowell/StatPages/More_Stuff/Missing_Data/Can cerDataRaw.sav* , respectively.

Using only casewise deletion in SPSS (version 13.0), we obtain the results in Figure 11.1. In the variable names, 'P' stands for 'patient' and 'S' for 'spouse.'

Notice that the sex of the parent with cancer does not have an effect, which is somewhat surprising, but the patient's level of depression and the depression and anxiety levels of the spouse are all significant predictors. However, as noted above, complete data are available only for 26 of the 89 cases.

We can improve the situation using the EM algorithm as implemented by Schafer. An analysis of missingness on these variables is shown in Table 11.6.

Notice that for this analysis all the variables in the dataset are included. That will be

Table 11.6   Analysis of missing data from Figure 11.1

NUMBER OF OBSERVATIONS = 89

NUMBER OF VARIABLES = 9

	NUMBER MISSING	% MISSING
Sexp	7	7.87
deptp	10	11.24
anxtp	10	11.24
gsitp	10	11.24
depts	29	32.58
anxts	29	32.58
gsits	29	32.58
sexchild	48	53.93
totbpt	48	53.93

true with imputation as well. In other words we will use variables in the imputation process that we may not use in the subsequent analysis, because those variables might be useful in predicting a participant's score, even if they are not useful in subsequently predicting behavior problems. This is especially important if you have variables that may be predictive of missingness.

The SPSS analysis of the EM-imputed dataset is shown in Table 11.7. The data were imputed using Schafer's NORM program and then read into SPSS.

Notice that the regression coefficients are not drastically different from those in the previous analysis with casewise deletion, but the standard errors are considerably smaller. This is due mainly to the large increase in sample size with the imputed data. Interestingly the sex of the patient is much closer to significance at $\alpha = .05$. Notice also that the squared multiple correlation has increased dramatically, from .658 to .871. I

am much more comfortable with this model than I was with the earlier one which was based on only 26 cases.

MULTIPLE IMPUTATION

One additional method for imputing values for missing observations is known as multiple imputation (MI). The original work on this approach was due to Rubin (1987), and it and EM are now becoming the dominant approaches to the treatment of missing data. A discussion of this material can be found in Allison (2001), Schafer and Olsen (1998), and Little (2005). There are a number of ways of performing MI, though they all involve the use of random components to overcome the problem of underestimation of standard errors. The parameter estimates using this approach are nearly unbiased.

The interesting thing about MI is that the word 'multiple' refers not to the iterative nature of the process involved in imputation but to the fact that we impute multiple complete datasets and run whatever analysis is appropriate on each dataset in turn. We then combine the results of those multiple analyses using fairly simple rules put forth by Rubin (1987). In a way it is like running multiple replications of an experiment and then combining the results across the multiple analyses. But in the case of MI, the replications are repeated simulations of datasets based upon parameter estimates from the original study.

Table 11.7   SPSS analysis of the EM-inputed dataset

	Coeffecients[a]						
	Unstandardized Coefficients		Standardized Coefficients			95% Confidence Interval for B	
Model	B	Std. Error	Beta	t	Sig.	Lower Bound	Upper Bound
1 (Constant)	−11.591	6.215		−1.865	.066	−23.953	.771
SexP	−3.238	1.749	−.106	−1.851	.068	−6.717	.241
DeptP	.886	.094	.722	9.433	.000	.699	1.073
AnxtP	−.004	.099	−.003	−.039	.969	−.202	.194
DeptS	−.418	.097	−.357	−4.310	.000	−.610	−.225
AnxtS	.762	.099	.631	7.716	.000	.565	.958

a. Dependent Variable Totbpt

$N = 89$ $R^2 = .871$

For many years the implementation of MI was held back by the lack of good algorithms by which to carry it out and by the lack of software. In the last 10 years or so, both these problems have been largely overcome. The introduction of new simulation methods known as Markov Chain Monte Carlo (MCMC) has simplified the task considerably, and software is now available to carry out the calculations. Schafer has implemented a method of Markov Chain Monte Carlo called data augmentation, and this approach is available in his NORM program referred to earlier. MI is not yet available in SPSS, but it is available in SAS as PROC MI and PROC MIANALYZE.

The process of multiple imputation, at least as carried out through data augmentation, involves two random processes. First, the imputed value contains a random component from a standard normal distribution. (I mentioned this in conjunction with the SPSS implementation of regression imputation.) Second, the parameter estimates used in imputing data are a random draw from a posterior probability distribution of the parameters.

The process of multiple imputation via data augmentation with a multivariate normal model is relatively straightforward, although I would hate to be the one who had to write the software. The first step involves the imputation of a complete set of data from parameter estimates derived from the incomplete dataset. We could obtain these parameters directly from the incomplete data using casewise or pairwise deletion; or, as suggested by Schafer and Olsen (1998), we could first apply the EM algorithm and take our parameter estimates from the result of that procedure.

Under the multivariate normal model, the imputation of an observation is based on regressing a variable with missing data on the other variables in the dataset. Assume, for simplicity, that X was regressed on only one other variable (Z). Denote the standard error of the regression as s_{XZ}. (In other words, s_{XZ} is the square root of $MS_{residual}$.) In standard regression imputation the imputed value of X ($\hat{X}$) would be obtained as

$$\hat{X}_i = b_0 + b_1 Z_i$$

But for data augmentation we will add random error to our prediction by setting

$$\hat{X}_i = b_0 + b_1 Z_i + u_i s_{xz}$$

where u_i is a random draw from a standard normal distribution. This introduces the necessary level of uncertainty into the imputed value. Following the imputation procedure just described, the imputed value will contain a random error component. Each time we impute data we will obtain a slightly different result.

But there is another random step to be considered. The process above treats the regression coefficients and the standard error of regression as if they were parameters, when in fact they are sample estimates. But parameter estimates have their own distribution. (If you were to collect multiple datasets from the same population, the different analyses would produce different values of b_1, for example, and these estimates have a distribution.) So our second step will be to make a random draw of these estimates from their Bayesian posterior distributions—the distribution of the estimates given the data, or pseudo-data, at hand.

Having derived imputed values for the missing observations, MI now iterates the solution, imputing values, deriving revised parameter estimates, imputing new values, and so on until the process stabilizes. At that point we have our parameter estimates and can write out the final imputed data file.

But we do not stop yet. Having generated an imputed data file, the procedure continues and generates several more data files. We do not need to generate many datasets, because Rubin has shown that in many cases three to five datasets are sufficient. Because of the randomness inherent in the algorithm, these datasets will differ somewhat from one another. In turn, when some standard data analysis procedure (here we are using multiple regression) is applied to each set of data, the results will differ slightly from one analysis to another. At this point we will derive our final set of estimates (in our case our final regression equation) by averaging over these estimates following a set of rules provided by Rubin.

For a discussion and example of carrying out the necessary calculations, see the excellent paper by Schafer and Olsen (1998). Another example based on data used in this chapter is available from the author.

SUMMARY

This chapter has discussed many ways of dealing with missing data. In all cases, missing data is a problem, but as we learn more about how to handle it, the problems become somewhat less important.

I pointed out that with standard experimental studies the solutions are relatively straightforward and do not lead to significant bias. In those studies, missing data can lead to difficulty in interpretation, as shown in the example of driving performance under the influence of alcohol. But those problems are not going to be solved by any mathematical approach to missing data, because they are at heart problems of logic rather than problems of mathematics.

With observational studies there are many methods that have been identified for dealing with missing observations. Some of the earlier solutions, such as hot deck imputation, mean substitution and pairwise deletion are slowly tending to fall by the wayside because they lead to bias in parameter estimation. The most important techniques, now that the necessary software is available, are the expectation/maximization (EM) algorithm and multiple imputation (MI). Both these rely on iterative solutions in which the parameter estimates lead to imputed values, which in turn change the parameter estimates, and so on. MI is an interesting approach because it uses randomized techniques to do its imputation, and then relies on multiple imputed datasets for the analysis. It is likely that MI will be the solution of choice for the next few years until something even better comes along.

REFERENCES

Achenbach, T.M. (1991) *Manual for the Child Behavior Checklist/4–18 and 1991 Profile*. Burlington, VT: University of Vermont, Department of Psychiatry.

Acock, A.C. (2005) 'Working with missing values', *Journal of Marriage and the Family*, 67: 1012–28.

Allison, P.D. (2001). *Missing Data*. Thousand Oaks, CA: Sage Publications.

Cohen, J., Cohen, P., West, S.G. and Aiken, L.S. (2003) *Applied Multiple Regression/Correlation Analysis for the Behavioral Sciences*, 3rd edition. Mahwah, N.J.: Lawrence Erlbaum.

Dempster, A.P., Laird, N.M. and Rubin, D.B. (1977) 'Maximum likelihood from incomplete data via the EM algorithm (with discussion)', *Journal of the Royal Statistical Society*, Series B 39: 1–38.

Dunning, T., and Freedman, D.A. (2007) Modeling selection effects, in William Outhwaite and Stephen Turner (eds.) *The SAGE Handbook of Social Science Methodology*. London: Sage. pp. 225–31, in this volume.

Freedman, D.A. and Wachter, K.W. (2007) Methods for Census 2000 and statistical adjustments, in William Outhwaite and Stephen Turner (eds.) *The SAGE Handbook of Social Science Methodology*. London: Sage. pp. 232–45, in this volume.

Gross, J.S. (1985) 'Weight modification and eating disorders in adolescent boys and girls', Unpublished doctoral dissertation, University of Vermont.

Hansen, M.H., Hurwitz, W. and Madow, W. (1953) *Sample Survey Methods and Theory*. New York: Wiley.

Hollis, S. and Campbell, F. (1999) 'What is meant by intention to treat analysis? Survey of published randomized controlled trials', *British Journal of Medicine*, 319: 670–74.

Jones, M.P. (1996) 'Indicator and stratification methods for missing explanatory variables in multiple linear regression', *Journal of the American Statistical Association*, 91: 222–30.

Little, R.J.A. (1998) 'A test of missing completely at random for multivariate data with missing values', *Journal of the American Statistical Association*, 83: 1198–1202.

———— (2005) Missing data, in B.S. Everitt and D.C. Howell (eds.) *Encyclopedia of Statistics in Behavioral Science*. Chichester, England: Wiley, pp. 1234–1238

Little, R.J.A. and Rubin D.B. (1987) *Statistical Analysis with Missing Data*. New York: John Wiley & Sons.

Lynch, S.M. (2003) 'Missing data'. Available at: http://www.princeton.edu/~slynch/missingdata.pdf.

Pickles, Andrew (2005) 'Missing data, problems and solutions', in Kimberly Kempf-Leonard (ed.), *Encyclopedia of Social Measurement*. Amsterdam: Elsevier, pp. 689–94.

Rubin, D.B. (1976) 'Inference and missing data', *Biometrika*, 63: 581–92.

Rubin, D. B. (1987) *Multiple Imputation for Nonresponse in Surveys*. New York: John Wiley & Sons.

———— (1996) 'Multiple imputation after 18+ years', *Journal of the American Statistical Association* 91: 473–489.

Schafer, J.L. (1997) *Analysis of Incomplete Multivariate Data*. London: Chapman & Hall, London. (Book No. 72, Chapman & Hall series Monographs on Statistics and Applied Probability.)

———— (1999) 'Multiple imputation: A primer', *Statistical Methods in Medical Research*, 8: 3–15.

Schafer, J. L. and Olsen, M.K. (1998) 'Multiple imputation for multivariate missing-data problems: A data analyst's perspective', *Multivariate Behavioral Research*, 33: 545–571.

Scheuren, F. (2005) 'Multiple imputation: How it began and continues', *The American Statistician*, 59: 315–19.

Sethi, S. and Seligman, M.E.P. (1993) 'Optimism and fundamentalism', *Psychological Science*, 4: 256–59.

NOTE

1. Gerard Dallal has a good web page on this topic at http://www.tufts.edu/~gdallal/itt.htm.

12

Modeling Selection Effects

Thad Dunning and David A. Freedman

INTRODUCTION

Selection bias is a pervasive issue in social science. Three research topics illustrate the point:

(i) What are the returns to education? College graduates earn more than high-school graduates, but the difference could be due to factors like intelligence and family background that lead some persons to get a college degree while others stop after high school.

(ii) Are job training programs effective? If people who take the training are relatively ambitious and well organized, any direct comparison is likely to overestimate program effectiveness, because participants are more likely to find employment anyway.

(iii) Do boot camps for prisoners prevent recidivism? Possibly, but prisoners who want to go straight are more likely to participate and less likely to find themselves in jail again, even if boot camp has no effect.

These questions could be settled by experiment, but experimentation in such contexts is expensive at best, impractical or unethical at worst. Investigators rely, therefore, on observational (non-experimental) data, with attendant difficulties of confounding.

In brief, comparisons can be made between a treatment group and a control group that does not get the treatment. But there are likely to be differences between the groups other than the treatment. Such differences are called 'confounding factors'. Differences on the response variable of interest (income, employment, recidivism) may be due to treatment or confounding factors, or both. Confounding is especially troublesome when subjects select themselves into one group or another, rather than being assigned to different regimes by the investigator. Self-selection is the hallmark of an observational study; assignment by the investigator is the hallmark of an experiment.

This chapter will review one of the most popular models for selection bias. The model, due to Heckman, will be illustrated on the relationship between admissions tests and college grades. Causal inference will be mentioned. There will be some pointers to the literature on selection bias, including critiques and alternative models. The intention-to-treat principle for clinical trials will be discussed, by way of counterpoint.

Model-based corrections for selection bias turn out to depend strongly on the assumptions built into the model. Thus, caution is in order. Sensitivity analysis is highly recommended: try different models with different assumptions. Alternative research designs should also be considered: stronger designs may permit data analysis with weaker assumptions.

ADMISSIONS DATA

In the United States, many colleges and universities require applicants to take the SAT (Scholastic Achievement Test). Admission is based in part on SAT scores and in part on other evidence—high school GPA (grade point average), essays, recommendations and interviews by admissions officers. Figure 12.1 shows a somewhat hypothetical scatter diagram. Each student is represented by a dot. The response variable is first-year college GPA, plotted on the vertical axis. The explanatory variable is the SAT score, plotted on the horizontal axis. The correlation between the two variables is about 0.5, which is fairly realistic. The 'regression line', which slopes across the diagram from lower left to upper right, estimates the average GPA at each level of SAT. GPAs are between 0 and 4. If the college requires two SATs, the combined score will be between 400 and 1600, as in the diagram.

A dataset like in Figure 12.1 would be available only for a college that takes all comers. If the college rejects applicants with an SAT below 800, we get a truncated scatter diagram, as Figure 12.2. Truncation reduces the correlation coefficient. The reduction is called 'attenuation due to restriction of range'. The slope of the regression line is, however, largely unaffected. Selecting on values of the explanatory variable need not bias the slope of the regression line. Truncation has one impact on correlation and quite another on slope.

Suppose now that the admissions office selects students who will get good grades despite low SAT scores. (This is hypothetical;

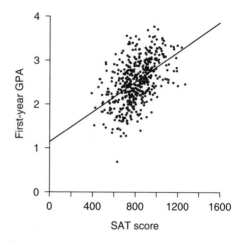

Figure 12.1   No selection

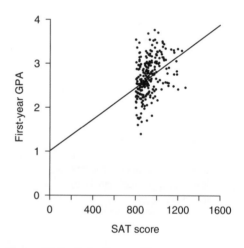

Figure 12.2   Selection on X

there is little empirical evidence to suggest that admissions offices have that ability, beyond using high school GPA—which, like the SAT, is a good predictor of college GPA—to help guide the decisions.) We might get a scatter diagram like the one shown in Figure 12.3. The correlation is much reduced. Correspondingly, the regression line is much shallower than the line in Figure 12.1. This kind of selection impacts correlation and slope in similar ways.

Selecting on the response variable—or more generally on variables correlated with the error term in the regression—is likely to bias the slope of the line. *If* we have a valid model for

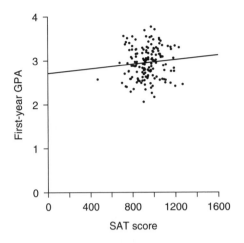

Figure 12.3   Selection on Y

the selection process—and that is a big if—the bias can be corrected; details are given below. For educational policy analysis, the scatter diagrams have a clear message. Highly selective institutions cannot expect to see any substantial correlation between variables that drive admissions decisions and measures of student performance—a point that often gets lost in debates over 'high-stakes testing'.

ASSOCIATION VERSUS CAUSATION

In the admissions example, there is no implication that SAT scores cause GPA. In many other examples, selection models are used to draw causal inferences from observational data. This raises additional questions; see, for instance, Heckman (1989, 2000), Briggs (2004), or Freedman (2005, 2007). Briggs discusses the effect of coaching programs on SAT scores. As the admissions example shows, however, selection bias is a problem even when causation is not in the picture.

SOME POINTERS TO THE LITERATURE

Heckman (1976, 1978, 1979) proposed formal statistical models for dealing with selection bias. However, the model—like other such models—is rather sensitive to specification error (Briggs, 2004; Breen, 1996; Copas and Li, 1997; Hartman, 1991; Lalonde,

1986; Nawata, 1993, 1994; Stolzenberg and Relles, 1990; Vella, 1998; Zuehlke and Zeman, 1991). Estimates may be more stable if the selection equation includes some explanatory variables that can be excluded a priori from the response equation.

Lalonde (1986) and Fraker and Maynard (1987) contrast the effects of job training programs, as estimated from observational data, with results from experiments. Heckman and Hotz (1989) try to reconcile the estimates. A more recent cite is *Review of Economics and Statistics*, 86 (February 2004) no. 1. Also see *Journal of Econometrics*, 125 (March–April 2005) no. 1–2.

Other methods for handling selection bias include weighting (Scharfstein et al., 1999), and modeling based on conditional independence assumptions (Little and Rubin, 2002). In the health sciences, selection effects are often handled using proportional-hazard models (Lawless, 2003).

Scharfstein et al. (1999) quantify the (substantial) extent to which inferences depend on unidentifiable parameters; also see Robins (1999) and Manski (1995). There is a lively discussion from various perspectives in Wainer (1989).

INTENTION-TO-TREAT

Randomized controlled experiments generally give the best evidence on causation, because they minimize problems created by confounding and self-selection. However, experiments on people cannot be immune from difficulty. By way of example, consider the first randomized controlled experiment on mammography—that is, screening for breast cancer by X-rays (Shapiro et al., 1988). This trial started in the 1960s, when mammography was very unusual. Some women were randomized to screening, and others (the controls) were randomized to usual medical care without screening. There was, however, 'crossover': many women assigned to screening declined to be screened. Subjects who cross over are very different from compliers, which raises the issue of selection bias—even in an experimental setting.

The mammography experiment was therefore analyzed according to the 'intention-to-treat' principle: deaths from breast cancer among those assigned to treatment—whether or not they accepted—were counted in the treatment arm. Similarly, deaths among women assigned to the control condition were charged to the control arm, even if these women sought out screening. Intention-to-treat gives an unbiased estimate for the effect of assignment, and (in many situations) a conservative estimate for the effect of treatment. Intention-to-treat is the standard analysis for clinical trials. Despite occasional bursts of controversy, the experiments gave solid evidence for the efficacy of mammography: screening cuts the death rate from breast cancer by a factor of about two (see International Agency for Research on Cancer (2002), Health Council of the Netherlands (2002), Freedman et al. (2004)).

When there is crossover from the treatment arm to the control arm, and little if any crossover in the other direction, there are robust estimates for the effect of treatment on the treated (Freedman et al., 2004: 73). When there is crossover in both directions, estimating the effect of treatment on the treated requires additional modeling assumptions. Under some circumstances, econometric techniques like instrumental-variables regression may be helpful.

Intention-to-treat and related analyses can be useful methods for handling selection effects, because they are relatively simple and depend on minimal assumptions about selection mechanisms. These techniques are readily applied to natural experiments, where assignment to the treatment and control conditions can be taken as random. Although data collection is likely to be expensive, causal inferences are often persuasive with this kind of strong research design. In a typical observational study, assignment to treatment or control cannot be viewed as random; modeling assumptions may then play an uncomfortably large role in determining conclusions. There is an informative survey in Angrist and Krueger (2001). Also see Freedman (2005, 2006).

A FORMAL MODEL

In the admissions study discussed earlier, GPA is observed only for subjects in the sample—the ones who go to the college where the study is done. We present Heckman's model in that context. Subjects are indexed by i. Let $C_i = 1$ if subject i is in the sample, else $C_i = 0$. Let X_i be the SAT score for subject i, and let Y_i be the GPA. Assume that X_i is observed for all subjects (e.g., all applicants) but Y_i is observed only if $C_i = 1$. The model has two equations:

$$Y_i = a + bX_i + \sigma U_i \qquad (1)$$

$$C_i = 1 \text{ if } c + dX_i + V_i > 0, \text{ else } C_i = 0 \quad (2)$$

The pairs (U_i, V_i) are assumed to be independent and identically distributed across subjects i, and independent of the Xs. The common distribution of (U_i, V_i) is assumed to be bivariate normal, with expected values equal to 0 and variances equal to 1; the correlation is ρ. The parameters in the model are a, b, c, d, σ, ρ. The U_i and V_i are 'latent' (unobserved) variables, which represent unmeasured characteristics of the subjects.

Equation (1) is the 'response equation': it explains how Y_i is related to X_i. The error term is σU_i, with expectation 0 and variance σ^2. Equation (2) is the 'selection equation': it explains how subjects come to be in the sample. This equation involves the latent variable V_i. The two equations are connected by the correlation ρ between U_i and V_i.

The response equation may look like an ordinary regression equation, but there is a crucial difference. The variable Y_i is observed only for i in the sample. If i is in the sample, then U_i has a non-zero conditional expectation: $E(U_i|C_i=1) \neq 0$ and

$E(U_i|C_i = 1)$ depends on i. Ordinary least squares therefore gives biased estimates for a and b.

Using the two equations together leads to unbiased—or nearly unbiased—estimates. This works because Equation (2) assumes a particular mechanism for selection into the sample: i is selected if $c + dX_i + V_i > 0$. Correspondingly, the expected value of U_i changes in a very special way, controlled by the correlation ρ between U_i and V_i. If $\rho = 0$, then selection bias is not an issue after all, and the second equation is unnecessary. Further details on the model and estimation procedures will be found in the next section.

Other explanatory variables could be entered into Equations (1) and (2): e.g., high school GPA, denoted by Z:

$$Y_i = a + bX_i + cZ_i + \sigma U_i \qquad (3)$$

$$C_i = 1 \text{ if } d + eX_i + fZ_i + V_i > 0,$$
$$\text{else } C_i = 0 \qquad (4)$$

In typical applications, the choice of explanatory variables may seem a little arbitrary. So is the functional form. Why linearity? Why are the coefficients the same for all subjects? The statistical assumptions might raise other questions. Why do the latent variables have the same distribution for all subjects? Why normality? Even the independence assumption may seem questionable in competitive situations like college admissions: if one applicant gets in, another must be excluded.

Mathematical Details

Our object here is to sketch Heckman's two-stage estimation procedure, illustrated on Equations (1) and (2). Recall that (U_i, V_i) were assumed to be bivariate normal with $E(U_i) = E(V_i) = 0$, $\text{var}(U_i) = \text{var}(V_i) = 1$, and the correlation is ρ; the Us and Vs were assumed to be independent of the Xs, and independent across subjects.

As a preliminary mathematical fact, there is a random variable W_i with the following properties:

(i) W_i is normal with expectation 0 and variance 1,
(ii) W_i is independent of V_i and the Xs,
(iii) $U_i = \rho V_i + \sqrt{1 - \rho^2}\, W_i$,

Indeed, we can set $W_i = (U_i - \rho V_i)/\sqrt{1 - \rho^2}$ and verify (i)–(ii)–(iii). In (ii), for instance, W_i is independent of the Xs because $W_i = (U_i - \rho V_i)/\sqrt{1 - \rho^2}$ and (U_i, V_i) is independent of the X's by assumption. Moreover, W_i is independent of V_i because the correlation between these two variables is 0, and they are jointly normal. That in turn is because (U_i, V_i) were assumed to be jointly normal.

We turn now to estimation. Equation (2) is a probit model, which can be estimated by maximum likelihood. Actually, Equations (1) and (2) could be estimated together using maximum likelihood. However, Heckman suggested estimating (1) on its own, after putting in a new variable M_i to mop up $\sigma E(U_i | C_i = 1)$:

$$Y_i = a + bX_i + qM_i + \text{error},$$
$$\text{error} = \sigma U_i - qM_i \qquad (5)$$

Besides the intercept, this equation has two explanatory variables, X_i and M_i. The equation can be estimated by ordinary least squares, although generalized least squares might be preferable.

The new explanatory variable needs to be put into a more explicit form. Condition on the Xs, which can then be treated as constant:

$$\sigma E(U_i|C_i = 1) = \sigma E(U_i|V_i > -c - dX_i)$$
$$= \sigma\rho\, E(V_i|V_i > -c - dX_i)$$
$$= \sigma\rho\, M(c + dX_i), \qquad (6)$$

where

$$M(v) = \phi(v)/\Phi(v), \qquad (7)$$

Φ being the standard normal distribution function, and $\phi = \Phi'$ its density. 'Mills' ratio' is $\Phi(x)/\phi(x)$, which is the inverse of M.

The normal distribution is relevant because, by assumption, U_i and V_i are standard normal variables: $P(U_i < x) = P(V_i < x) = \Phi(x)$. The first equality in (6) comes from the selection equation (2). To get the second equality, substitute $U_i = \rho V_i + \sqrt{1 - \rho^2} W_i$, then use properties (i)–(ii) of W_i: $E(W_i | V_i > -c - dX_i) = E(W_i)$ by independence, and $E(W_i) = 0$. To get the last equality, we must compute $E(V_i | V_i > -v)$. This is an exercise in calculus, though the signs are confusing. To begin with,

$$\phi(x) = \frac{1}{\sqrt{2\pi}} e^{-x^2/2}, \tag{8}$$

so $x\phi(x)$ is the derivative of $-\phi(x)$. Now

$$E(V_i | V_i > -v) = \frac{1}{P(V_i > -v)} \int_{-v}^{\infty} x\phi(x)dx$$

$$= \frac{\phi(-v)}{P(V_i > -v)}$$

$$= \frac{\phi(v)}{P(-V_i < v)}$$

$$= \frac{\phi(v)}{\Phi(v)} = M(v). \tag{9}$$

We cannot set $M_i = M(c + dX_i)$ in (5), because c and d are unknown. Heckman's estimation procedure begins by fitting the selection equation (2) to the data, using maximum likelihood. This gives estimated values $\tilde{c}$ for c and $\tilde{d}$ for d. Next, set $M_i = M(\tilde{c} + \tilde{d}X_i)$, and fit

$$Y_i = a + bX_i + qM_i + \text{error} \tag{10}$$

to the data using least squares. That gives $\hat{a}, \hat{b}, \hat{q}$. The estimates of main interest are usually $\hat{a}$ and $\hat{b}$, but $\hat{q}$ would estimate $\sigma\rho$. When Heckman published his papers, estimating two equations by maximum likelihood would have been a major-league enterprise: fitting one equation by maximum likelihood and the other by least squares was

a real simplification. Today, computers are much faster...

Heckman developed models to cover a variety of situations. Variables can be binary (yes/no), or continuous; the response variables might be observed for all subjects, or just for subjects in the sample. In a study that compares incomes for college and high school graduates, the key explanatory variable is binary, indicating whether the subject did or did not graduate from college. The response variable (income) is continuous. Both variables are observed for all subjects in the study. Other control variables could be added to the equations. In the admissions study, the explanatory variable (SAT) and the response variable (GPA) are continuous; GPA is observed only for subjects in the sample, as noted above. Other cases will not be discussed here.

REFERENCES

Angrist, J.D. and Krueger, A.K. (2001) 'Instrumental variables and the search for identification: From supply and demand to natural experiments', *Journal of Economic Perspectives*, 15: 69–85.

Breen, R. (1996) *Regression Models: Censored, Sample Selected, or Truncated Data*. Thousand Oaks, CA: Sage.

Briggs, D.C. (2004) 'Causal inference and the Heckman model', *Journal of Educational and Behavioral Statistics*, 29: 397–420.

Copas, J.B. and Li, H.G. (1997) 'Inference for non-random samples', *Journal of the Royal Statistical Society*, Series B, 59: 55–77.

Fraker, T. and Maynard, R. (1987) 'The adequacy of comparison group designs for evaluations of employment-related programs', *Journal of Human Resources* 22: 194–217.

Freedman, D.A. (2005). *Statistical Models: Theory and Practice*. New York: Cambridge University Press.

——— (2006). Statistical models for causation: What inferential leverage do they provides? *Evaluation Review* 30: 691–713.

——— (2007) 'Statistical models for causation', This volume.

Freedman, D.A., Petitti, D.M. and Robins, J.M. (2004) 'On the efficacy of screening for breast cancer', *International Journal of Epidemiology*, 33: 43–73. (correspondence, pp. 1404–6).

Hartman R.S. (1991) 'A Monte Carlo analysis of alternative estimators in models involving selectivity', *Journal of Business and Economic Statistics,* 9: 41–9.

Health Council of the Netherlands (2002) *The Benefit of Population Screening for Breast Cancer with Mammography.* The Hague: Health Council of the Netherlands.

Heckman, J.J. (1976) 'The common structure of statistical models of truncation, sample selection and limited dependent variables and a simple estimator for such models', *Annals of Economic and Social Measurement,* 5: 475–92.

——— (1978) 'Dummy endogenous variables in a simultaneous equation system', *Econometrica,* 46: 931–59.

——— (1979) 'Sample selection bias as a specification error', *Econometrica,* 47: 153–61.

——— (1989) 'Causal inference and nonrandom samples', *Journal of Educational Statistics* 14: 159–68. Reprinted in J. Shaffer (ed.), *The Role of Models in Nonexperimental Social Science.* Washington, DC: AERA/ASA.

——— (2000) 'Causal parameters and policy analysis in economics: A twentieth century retrospective', *The Quarterly Journal of Economics,* CVX: 45–97.

Heckman, J. and Hotz, V.J. (1989) 'Choosing among alternative nonexperimental methods for estimating the impact of social programs: The case of manpower training', *Journal of the American Statistical Association,* 84: 862–80 (with discussion).

International Agency for Research on Cancer (2002) *Breast Cancer Screening,* IARC Handbooks of Cancer Prevention, vol. 7. Lyon: IARC.

Lalonde, R.J. (1986) 'Evaluating the econometric evaluations of training programs with experimental data', *The American Economic Review,* 76: 604–20.

Lawless, J.F. ([1982] 2003) *Statistical Models and Methods for Lifetime Data.* New York: Wiley-Interscience.

Little, R.J.A. and Rubin, D.B. (2002) *Statistical Analysis with Missing Data.* Wiley.

Manski, C.F. (1995) *Identification Problems in the Social Sciences.* Cambridge, MA: Harvard University Press.

Nawata, K. (1993) 'A note on the estimation of models with sample selection biases', *Economics Letters,* 42: 15–24.

——— (1994) 'Estimation of sample selection bias models by the maximum likelihood estimator and Heckman's two-step estimator', *Economics Letters,* 45: 33–40.

Robins, J.M. (1999) 'Association, causation, and marginal structural models', *Synthese,* 121: 151–79.

Scharfstein, D.O., Rotnitzky, A. and Robins, J.M. (1999) 'Adjusting for non-ignorable drop-out using semiparametric non-response models', *Journal of the American Statistical Association,* 94: 1096–146.

Shapiro, S., Venet, W., Strax, P. and Venet, L. (1988) *Periodic Screening for Breast Cancer: The Health Insurance Plan Project and its Sequelae, 1963–1986.* Baltimore: Johns Hopkins.

Stolzenberg, R.M. and Relles, D.A. (1990) 'Theory testing in a world of constrained research design', *Sociological Methods & Research,* 18: 395–415.

Vella, F. (1998) 'Estimating models with sample selection bias: A survey', *The Journal of Human Resources,* 33: 127–69.

Wainer, H. (1989) 'Eelworms, bullet holes, and Geraldine Ferraro: Some problems with statistical adjustment and some solutions', *Journal of Educational Statistics,* 14: 121–99 (with discussion). Reprinted in J. Shaffer (ed.), *The Role of Models in Nonexperimental Social Science,* Washington, DC: American Educational Research Association/ American Statistical Association.

Zuehlke, T.W. and Zeman, A.R. (1991) 'A comparison of two-stage estimators of censored regression models', *Review of Economics and Statistics,* 73: 185–8.

13

Methods for Census 2000 and Statistical Adjustments

David A. Freedman and Kenneth W. Wachter

INTRODUCTION

The census in the US has been taken every ten years since 1790, and provides a wealth of demographic information for researchers and policy-makers. Beyond that, counts are used to apportion Congress and re-district states. Moreover, census data are the basis for allocating federal tax money to cities and other local governments. For such purposes, the geographical distribution of the population matters more than counts for the nation as a whole. Data from 1990 and previous censuses suggested there would be a net undercount in 2000. Furthermore, the undercount would depend on age, race, ethnicity, gender, and—most important—geography. This differential undercount, with its implications for sharing power and money, attracted considerable attention in the media and the courthouse.

There were proposals to adjust the census by statistical methods, but this is advisable only if the adjustment gives a truer picture of the population and its geographical distribution. The census turned out to be remarkably good, despite much critical commentary. Statistical adjustment was unlikely to improve the accuracy, because adjustment can easily put in more error than it takes out.

We will sketch procedures for taking the census, making adjustments and evaluating results. (Detailed descriptions cover thousands of pages; summaries are a necessity.) Data will be presented on errors in the census, in the adjustment, and on geographical variation in error rates. Alternative adjustments are discussed, as are methods for comparing the accuracy of the census and the adjustments. There are pointers to the literature, including citations to the main arguments for and against adjustment. The present chapter is based on Freedman and Wachter (2003), which may be consulted for additional detail and bibliographic information.

THE CENSUS

The census is a sophisticated enterprise whose scale is remarkable. In round numbers, there are 10,000 permanent staff at the Bureau of the Census. Between October 1999 and September 2000, the staff opened

500 field offices, where they hired and trained 500,000 temporary employees. In spring 2000, a media campaign encouraged people to cooperate with the census, and community outreach efforts were targeted at hard-to-count groups.

The population of the United States in 2000 was about 280 million persons in 120 million housing units, distributed across 7 million *blocks*, the smallest pieces of census geography. (In Boston or San Francisco, a block is usually a block; in rural Wyoming, a 'block' may cover a lot of rangeland.) Statistics for larger areas like cities, counties or states are obtained by adding up data for component blocks.

From the perspective of a census-taker, there are three types of areas to consider. In city delivery areas (high-density urban housing with good addresses), the Bureau develops a Master Address File. Questionnaires are mailed to each address in the file. About 70 percent of these questionnaires are filled out and returned by the respondents. Then 'Non-Response Followup' procedures go into effect: for instance, census enumerators go out several times and attempt to contact non-responding households, by knocking on doors and working the telephone. City delivery areas include roughly 100 million housing units.

Update/leave areas, comprising less than 20 million households, are mainly suburban and have lower population densities; address lists are more difficult to construct. In such areas, the Bureau leaves the census questionnaire with the household while updating the Master Address File. Beyond that, procedures are similar to those in the city delivery areas.

In update/enumerate areas, the Bureau tries to enumerate respondents—by interviewing them—as it updates the Master Address File. These areas are mainly rural, and post-office addresses are poorly defined, so address lists are problematic. (A typical address might be something like Smith, Rural Route #1, south of Willacoochee, GA.) Perhaps a million housing units fall into such areas. There are also special populations that need to be enumerated—institutional

(prisons and the military), as well as non-institutional 'group quarters'. (For instance, 12 nuns sharing a house in New Orleans are living in group quarters.) About 8 million persons fall into these special populations.

DEMOGRAPHIC ANALYSIS

DA (Demographic Analysis) estimates the population using birth certificates, death certificates and other administrative record systems. The estimates are made for national demographic groups defined by age, gender and race (Black and non-Black). Estimates for sub-national geographic areas like states are currently not available. According to DA, the undercount in 1970 was about 3 percent nationally. In 1980, it was 1–2 percent, and the result for 1990 was similar. DA reported the undercount for Blacks at about 5 percentage points above non-Blacks, in all three censuses.

DA starts from an accounting identity:

$$\text{Population} = \text{Births} - \text{Deaths} + \text{Immigration} - \text{Emigration}.$$

However, data on emigration are incomplete. And there is substantial illegal immigration, which cannot be measured directly. Thus, estimates need to be made for illegals, but these are (necessarily) somewhat speculative.

Evidence on differential undercounts depends on racial classifications, which may be problematic. Procedures vary widely from one data collection system to another. For the census, race of all household members is reported by the person who fills out the form. In Census 2000, respondents were allowed for the first time to classify themselves into multiple racial categories. This is a good idea from many perspectives, but creates a discontinuity with past data. On death certificates, race of decedent is often determined by the undertaker. Birth certificates show the race of the mother and (usually) the race of the father; procedures for ascertaining race differ from hospital to hospital. A computer algorithm is used to determine the race of an infant from the race of the parents.

Prior to 1935, many states did not collect birth certificate data at all; and the further back in time, the less complete is the system. This makes it harder to estimate the population aged 65 and over. In 2000, DA estimates the number of such persons starting from Medicare records. Despite its flaws, DA has generally been considered to be the best yardstick for measuring census undercounts. Recently, however, another procedure has come to the fore, the DSE ('Dual System Estimator').

DSE – DUAL SYSTEM ESTIMATOR

The DSE is based on a special sample survey done after the census—a PES ('Post-enumeration Survey'). The PES of 2000 was renamed ACE ('Accuracy and Coverage Evaluation Survey'). The ACE sample covers 25,000 blocks, containing 300,000 housing units and 700,000 people. An independent listing is made of the housing units in the sample blocks, and persons in these units are interviewed after the census is complete. This process yields the *P-sample*.

The *E-sample* comprises the census records in the same blocks, and the two samples are then matched up against each other. In most cases, a match validates both the census record and the PES record. A P-sample record that does not match to the census may be a gross omission—that is, a person who should have been counted in the census but was missed. Conversely, a census record that does not match to the P-sample may be an erroneous enumeration—in other words, a person who got into the census by mistake. For instance, a person can be counted twice in the census because he sent in two forms. Another person can be counted correctly but assigned to the wrong unit of geography: she is a gross omission in one place and an erroneous enumeration in the other.

Of course, an unmatched P-sample record may just reflect an error in ACE; likewise, an unmatched census record could just mean that the corresponding person was found by the census and missed by ACE. Fieldwork is done to resolve the status of some unmatched cases, deciding whether the error should be charged against the census or ACE. Other cases are resolved using computer algorithms. However, even after fieldwork is complete and the computer shuts down, some cases remain unresolved. Such cases are handled by statistical models that fill in the missing data. The number of unresolved cases is relatively small, but it is large enough to have an appreciable influence on the final results, as discussed in the context of the adjustment decision for Census 2000 below.

Movers—people who change their address between census day and ACE interview—represent another complication. Unless persons can be correctly identified as movers or non-movers, they cannot be correctly matched. Identification depends on getting accurate information from respondents as to where they were living at the time of the census. Again, the number of movers is relatively small, but they are a large factor in the adjustment equation. More generally, matching records between the ACE and the census becomes problematic if respondents give inaccurate information to the ACE or the census, or to both. Thus, even cases that are resolved though ACE fieldwork and computer operations may be resolved incorrectly. We refer to such errors as *processing error*.

The statistical power of the DSE comes from matching, not from counting better. In fact, the E-sample counts came out a bit higher than the P-sample counts, in 1990 and in 2000: the census found more people than the post-enumeration survey in the sample blocks. As the discussion of processing error shows, however, matching is easier said than done.

Some persons are missed both by the census and by ACE. Their number is estimated using a statistical model, assuming that ACE is as likely to find people missed by the census as people counted in the census— 'the independence assumption'. Following this assumption, a gross omission rate

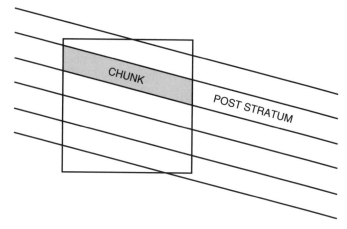

Figure 13.1   Area by Post Stratum Intersection

estimated from the people found by ACE can be extrapolated to people in the census who were missed by ACE, although the true gross omission rate for that group may well be different. Failures in the independence assumption lead to *correlation bias*. Data on processing error and correlation bias will be presented later.

SMALL-AREA ESTIMATION

The Bureau divides the population into *post strata* defined by demographic and geographic characteristics. For Census 2000, there were 448 post strata. One post stratum, for example, consisted of Asian male renters age 30–49, living anywhere in the United States. Another post stratum consisted of Blacks age 0–17 (male or female) living in owner-occupied housing in big or medium-size cities with high mail return rates, across the whole country. Persons in the P-sample are assigned to post strata on the basis of information collected during the ACE interview. (For the E-sample, assignment is based on the census return.)

Each sample person gets a *weight*. If 1 person in 500 were sampled, each person in the sample would stand for 500 in the population and be given a weight of 500. The actual sampling plan for ACE is more complex, so different people are given different weights. To estimate the total number of gross omissions in a post stratum, one simply adds the weights of all ACE respondents who were identified as (i) gross omissions and (ii) being in the relevant post stratum.

To a first approximation, the estimated undercount in a post stratum is the difference between the estimated numbers of gross omissions and erroneous enumerations. In more detail, ACE data are used to compute an *adjustment factor* for each post stratum. When multiplied by this factor, the census count for a post stratum equals the estimated true count from the DSE. About two-thirds of the adjustment factors exceed 1. These post strata are estimated to have undercounts. The remaining post strata are estimated to have been over counted by the census; their adjustment factors are less than 1.

How to adjust small areas like blocks, cities, or states? Take any particular area. As Figure 13.1 indicates, this area will be carved up into 'chunks' by post strata. Each chunk has some number of persons counted by the census in that area. (The number may be zero.) This census number is multiplied by the adjustment factor for the post stratum. The process is repeated for all post strata, and the adjusted count is obtained by adding the products; complications due to rounding are ignored here. The adjustment process makes the 'homogeneity assumption', that undercount rates are constant within each post stratum across all geographical units. This is not plausible, and was strongly contradicted by census data on variables related to the undercount. Failures in the homogeneity assumption are termed *heterogeneity*. Ordinarily, samples are used to extrapolate upwards, from the part to the whole. In census adjustment, samples are used to extrapolate sideways, from 25,000 sample blocks to each and every one of the 7 million blocks in the United States. That is where the homogeneity assumption comes into play.

Heterogeneity is endemic. Undercount rates differ from place to place within population groups treated as homogeneous by adjustment. Heterogeneity puts limits on the accuracy of adjustments for areas like states, counties, or legislative districts. Studies of the 1990 data, along with more recent work discussed below, show that heterogeneity is a serious concern.

The adjustment issue was often framed in terms of sampling: 'sampling is scientific'. However, from a technical perspective, sampling is not the point. The crucial questions are about the size of processing errors and the validity of statistical models for missing data, correlation bias and homogeneity—all in a context where the margin of allowable error is relatively small.

STATE SHARES

All states would gain population from adjustment. Some, however, gain more than others. In terms of population share, the gains and losses must balance. This point was often overlooked in the political debate. In 2000, even more so than in 1990, share changes were tiny. According to Census 2000, for example, Texas had 7.4094 percent of the population. Adjustment would have given it 7.4524 percent, an increase of 7.4524 – 7.4094 = .0430 percent, or 430 parts per million. The next biggest winner was California, at 409 parts per million; third was Georgia, at 88 parts per million.

Ohio would have been the biggest loser, at 241 parts per million, followed by Michigan,

at 162 parts per million. Minnesota came third in this sorry competition, at 152 parts per million. The median change (up or down) is about 28 parts per million. These changes are tiny, and most are easily explained as the result of sampling error in ACE. *Sampling error* means random error introduced by the luck of the draw in choosing blocks for the ACE sample: you get a few too many blocks of one kind or not quite enough of another. The contrast is with *systematic* or *non-sampling* error like processing error.

The map (Figure 13.2) shows share changes that exceed 50 parts per million. Share increases are marked '+'; share decreases as '– '. The size of the mark corresponds to the size of the change. As the map indicates, adjustment would have moved population share from the Northeast and Midwest to the South and West. This is paradoxical, given the heavy concentrations of minorities in the big cities of the Northeast and Midwest, and political rhetoric contending that the census shortchanges such areas ('statistical grand larceny', according to New York's ex-Mayor Dinkins). One explanation for the paradox is correlation bias. The older urban centers of the Northeast and Midwest may be harder to reach, both for census and for ACE.

THE 1990 ADJUSTMENT DECISION

A brief look at the 1990 adjustment decision provides some context for discussions of Census 2000. In July 1991, the Secretary of Commerce declined to adjust Census 1990. At the time, the undercount was estimated as 5.3 million persons. Of this, 1.7 million persons were thought by the Bureau to reflect processing errors in the post-enumeration survey, rather than census errors. Later research has shown the 1.7 million to be a serious underestimate. Current estimates range from 3.0 million to 4.2 million, with a central value of 3.6 million. (These figures are all nationwide, and net; given the data that are available, parceling the figures down to local areas would require heroic assumptions.)

Figure 13.2 ACE Adjustment: State Share Changes Exceeding 50 Parts Per Million

Table 13.1   Errors in the adjustment of 1990

The adjustment	+5.3	
Processing error	−3.6	
	———	
Corrected adjustment		+1.7
Correlation bias		+3.0
		———
Demographic Analysis		+4.7

The bulk of the 1990 adjustment resulted from errors not in the census but in the PES. Processing errors generally inflate estimated undercounts, and subtracting them leaves a corrected adjustment of 1.7 million. (There is an irritating numerical coincidence here, as 1.7 million enters the discussion with two different meanings.) Correlation bias, estimated at 3.0 million, works in the opposite direction, and brings the undercount estimate up to the Demographic Analysis figure of 4.7 million (Table 13.1). On the scale of interest, most of the estimated undercount is noise.

CENSUS 2000

Census 2000 succeeded in reducing differential undercounts from their 1990 levels. That sharpened questions about the accuracy of proposed statistical adjustments. Errors in statistical adjustments are not new. Studies of the 1980 and 1990 data have quantified, at least to some degree, the three main kinds of error: processing error, correlation bias and heterogeneity. In the face of these errors, it is hard for adjustment to improve on the accuracy of census numbers for states, counties, legislative districts and smaller areas.

Errors in the ACE statistical operations may from some perspectives have been under better control than they were in 1990. But error rates may have been worse in other respects. There is continuing research, both inside the Bureau and outside, on the nature of the difficulties. Troubles occurred with a new treatment of movers (discussed in the next section) and duplicates. Some 25 million duplicate persons were detected in various stages of the census process, and removed. But how many slipped through? And how many of those were missed by ACE?

Besides processing error, correlation bias is an endemic problem that makes it difficult for adjustment to improve on the census. Correlation bias is the tendency for people missed in the census to be missed by ACE as well. Correlation bias in 2000 probably amounted, as it did in 1990, to millions of persons. Surely these people are unevenly distributed across the country ('differential correlation bias'). The more uneven the distribution, the more distorted a picture of census undercounts is created by the DSE.

The Adjustment Decision for Census 2000

In March 2001, the Secretary of Commerce—on the advice of the Census Bureau—decided to certify the census counts rather than the adjusted counts for use in redistricting (drawing congressional districts within state). The principal reason was that, according to DA, the census had overcounted the population by perhaps 2 million people. Proposed adjustments would have added another 3 million people, making the over-counts even worse. Thus, DA and ACE pointed in opposite directions. The three population totals are shown in Table 13.2.

If DA is right, there is a census overcount of .7 percent. If ACE is right, there is a census undercount of 1.2 percent. DA is a particularly valuable benchmark, because it is independent (at least in principle) of both the census and the post-enumeration survey that underlies proposed adjustments. While DA is hardly perfect, it was a stretch to blame DA for the whole of the discrepancy with ACE. Instead, the discrepancy pointed to undiscovered error in ACE. When the

Table 13.2   The population of the United States

Demographic Analysis	279.6 million
Census 2000	281.4 million
ACE	284.7 million

Table 13.3   Missing data in ACE, and impact of movers

Non-interviews	
P-sample	3 million
E-sample	6 million
Imputed match status	
P-sample	3 million
E-sample	7 million
Inmovers and outmovers	
Imputed residence status	6 million
Outmovers	9 million
Inmovers	13 million
Mover gross omissions	3 million

Secretary made his decision, there was some information on missing data and on the influence of movers, summarized in Table 13.3.

These figures are weighted to national totals, and should be compared to (i) a total census population around 280 million, and (ii) errors in the census that may amount to a few million persons. For some 3 million P-sample persons, a usable interview could not be completed; for 6 million, a household roster as of census day could not be obtained (lines 1 and 2 in Table 13.3). Another 3 million persons in the P-sample and 7 million in the E-sample had unresolved match status after fieldwork: were they gross omissions, erroneous enumerations, or what? For 6 million, residence status was indeterminate—where *were* they living on census day? (National totals are obtained by adding up the weights for the corresponding sample people; non-interviews are weighted out of the sample and ignored in the DSE, but we use average weights.) If the idea is to correct an undercount of a few million in the census, these are serious gaps. Much of the statistical adjustment therefore depends on models used to fill in missing data. Efforts to validate such models remain unconvincing.

The 2000 adjustment tried to identify both inmovers and outmovers, a departure from past practice. Gross omission rates were computed for the outmovers and applied to the inmovers, although it is not clear why rates are equal within local areas.

For outmovers, information must have been obtained largely from neighbors. Such 'proxy responses' are usually thought to be of poor quality, inevitably creating false non-matches and inflating the estimated undercount. As the table shows, movers contribute about 3 million gross omissions (a significant number on the scale of interest) and ACE failed to detect a significant number of outmovers. That is why the number of outmovers is so much less than the number of inmovers. Again, the amount of missing data is small relative to the total population but large relative to errors that need fixing. The conflict between these two sorts of comparisons is the central difficulty of census adjustment. ACE may have been a great success by the ordinary standards of survey research, but not nearly good enough for adjusting the census.

Gross or Net?

Errors can be reported either gross or net, and there are many possible ways to refine the distinction. (Net error allows overcounts to balance undercounts; gross error does not.) Some commentary suggests that the argument for adjustment may be stronger if gross error is the yardstick. Certain places may have an excess number of census omissions while other places will have an excess number of erroneous enumerations. Such imbalances could be masked by net error rates, when errors of one kind in one place offset error of another kind in another place. In this section, we consider gross error rates.

Some persons were left out of Census 2000 and some were counted in error. There is no easy way to estimate the size of these two errors separately. Many people were counted a few blocks away from where they should have been counted: they are both gross omissions and erroneous enumerations. Many other people were classified as erroneous enumerations because they were counted with insufficient information for matching; they should also come back as gross omissions in the ACE fieldwork. With some rough-and-ready

allowances for this sort of double-counting, the Bureau estimated that 6–8 million people were left out of the census while 3–4 million were wrongly included, for a gross error in the census of 9–12 million; the Bureau's preferred values are 6.4 and 3.1, for a gross error of 9.5 million in Census 2000.

Before presenting comparable numbers for ACE, we mention some institutional history. The census is used as a base for post-censal population estimates. This may sound even drier than redistricting, but $200 billion a year of tax money are allocated using post-censal estimates. In October 2001, the Bureau revisited the adjustment issue: should the census be adjusted as a base for the post-censals? The decision against adjustment was made after further analysis of the data. Some 2.2 million persons were added to the Demographic Analysis. Estimates for processing error in ACE were sharply increased. Among other things, ACE had failed to detect large numbers of duplicate enumerations in the census, because interviewers did not get accurate census-day addresses from respondents. That is why ACE had overestimated the population. The Bureau's work confirmed that gross errors in ACE were well above 10 million, with another 15 million cases whose status remains to be resolved. Error rates in ACE are hard to determine with precision, but they are quite large relative to error rates in the census.

Heterogeneity in 2000

This section demonstrates that substantial heterogeneity remains in the data, despite elaborate post stratification. In fact, post stratification seems on the whole to be counterproductive. Heterogeneity is measured as in Freedman and Wachter (1994, 2003), with SUB ('whole-person substitutions') and LA ('late census adds') as proxies—surrogates— for the undercount: see the notes to Table 13.4. For example, .0210 of the census count (just over 2 percent) came from whole-person substitutions. This figure is in the first line of the table, under the column headed 'Level'.

Table 13.4   Measuring heterogeneity across Congressional Districts (CD).[1]

Proxy & Post Stratification[2]	Level	Standard Deviation		
		Across CD	Across P-S	Within P-S across CD
SUB 448	.0210	.0114	.0136	.0727
SUB 64	.0210	.0114	.0133	.0731
SUB 16	.0210	.0114	.0135	.0750
LA 448	.0085	.0054	.0070	.0360
LA 64	.0085	.0054	.0069	.0363
LA 16	.0085	.0054	.0056	.0341

Notes: 1 In the first column, post stratification is either (i) by 448 post strata, or (ii) by the 64 post-stratum groups, collapsing age and sex, or (iii) by the 16 evaluation post strata. 'SUB' means whole-person substitutions, and 'LA' is late census adds. In the last two columns, 'P-S' stands for post strata; there are three different kinds, labeled according to row.

2 The level of a proxy does not depend on the post stratification, and neither does the SD across CDs. These two statistics do depend on the proxy. A 'substitution' is a person counted in the census with no personal information, which is later imputed. A 'late add' is a person originally thought to be a duplicate, but later put back into the census production process. Substitutions include late adds that are not 'data defined', i.e., do not have enough information for matching. Substitutions and late adds have poor data quality, which is why they may be good proxies for undercount. Table 5 in Freedman and Wachter (2003) uses slightly different conventions and includes the District of Columbia.

Substitution rates are computed not only for the whole country but for each of the 435 congressional districts: the standard deviation of the 435 rates is .0114, in the 'Across CD' column. The rate is also computed for each post stratum: across the 448 post strata, the standard deviation of the substitution rates is .0136, in the 'Across P-S' column, the post strata exhibit more variation than the geographical districts, which is one hallmark of a successful post stratification.

To compute the last column of Table 13.4, we think of each post stratum as being divided into 'chunks' by the congressional districts. We compute the substitution rate for each chunk with a non-zero census count, then take the standard deviation across chunks within post stratum, and finally the root-mean-square over post strata. The result is .0727, in the last column of Table 13.4. If rates were constant across geography within post strata, as the homogeneity assumption requires, this standard deviation should be 0. Instead, it is much larger than the variability across congressional districts. This points to a serious failure in the post stratification. If the proxies are good, there is a lot of heterogeneity within post strata across geography.

Similar calculations can be made for two coarser post stratifications: (i) The Bureau considers its 448 post strata as coming from 64 PSGs. (Each PSG, or 'post-stratum group,' divides into 7 age-sex groups, giving back $64 \times 7 = 448$ post strata.) The 64 PSGs are used as post strata in the second line of Table 13.4. (ii) The Bureau groups PSGs into 16 EPS, or 'evaluation post strata'. These are the post strata in the third line of Table 13.4. Variability across post strata or within post strata across geography is not much affected by the coarseness of the post stratification, which is surprising. Results for late census adds (LA) are similar, in lines 4–6 of the table. Refining the post stratification is not productive. There are similar results for states in Freedman and Wachter (2003).

The Bureau computed 'direct DSEs' for the 16 evaluation post strata, by pooling the data in each. From these, an adjustment factor can be constructed, as the direct DSE divided by the census count. We adjusted the United States using these 16 factors rather

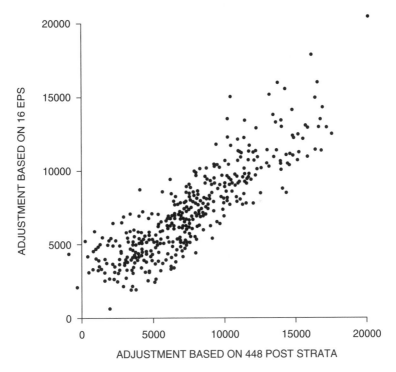

TWO ADJUSTMENTS COMPARED. 435 CONGRESSIONAL DISTRICTS
DIFFERENCE BETWEEN ADJUSTED COUNT AND CENSUS COUNT

Figure 13.3   Changes to congressional district populations
The production adjustment, with 448 post strata, is plotted on the horizontal. An
alternative, based only on the 16 evaluation post strata (EPS), is plotted on the vertical.

than the 448. For states and congressional districts, there is hardly any difference. The scatter diagram in Figure 13.3 shows results for congressional districts. There are 435 dots, one for each congressional district. The horizontal axis shows the change in population count that would have resulted from adjustment with 448 post strata; the vertical, from adjustment with 16 post strata.

For example, take CD 1 in Alabama, with a 2000 census population of 646,181. Adjustment with 448 post strata would have increased this figure by 7630; with 16 post strata, the increase would have been 7486. The corresponding point is (7630, 7486). The correlation between the 435 pairs of changes is .87, as shown in the third line of Table 13.5. For two out of the 435 districts, adjustment

by 448 post strata would have reduced the population count: their points are plotted just outside the axes, at the lower left. On this basis, and on the basis of Table 13.4, we suggest that 448 post strata are no better than 16. (For some geographical areas with populations below 100,000, however, the two adjustments are likely to be different.)

Tables 13.4 and 13.5 and Figure 13.3 show that an elaborate post stratification does not remove much heterogeneity. We doubt that heterogeneity can be removed by the sort of post stratification—no matter how elaborate—that can be constructed in real census conditions. The impact of heterogeneity on errors in adjustment is discussed by Freedman and Wachter (1994: 479–81). Heterogeneity is more of a problem than sampling error.

Table 13.5 Comparing the production adjustment based on 448 post strata to one based on 16 evaluation post strata. Correlation coefficients for changes due to adjustments

Changes in state population counts	.99
Changes in state population shares	.90
Changes in congressional district counts	.87
Changes in congressional district shares	.85

Within a state, districts are by case law almost exactly equal in size—when redistricting is done shortly after census counts are released. Over the decade, people move from one district to another. Variation in population sizes at the end of the decade is therefore of policy interest. In California, to take one example, 52 districts were drawn to have equal populations according to Census 1990. According to Census 2000, the range in their populations is 583,000 to 773,000. Exact equality at the beginning of the decade does not seem like a compelling goal.

Loss Function Analysis

A statistical technique called 'loss function analysis' has been used to justify adjustment. In effect, this technique attempts to make summary estimates of the error levels in the census and the adjustment. However, the apparent gains in accuracy—like the gains from adjustment—tend to be concentrated in a few geographical areas, and heavily influenced by the vagaries of chance. At a deeper level, loss function analysis turns out to depend more on assumptions than on data.

For example, loss function analysis depends on models for correlation bias, and the model used in 2000 assumes there is no correlation bias for women. The idea that only men are hard to reach—for the census and the post-enumeration survey—is prima facie unlikely. It is also at loggerheads with the data from 1990 (see Wachter and Freedman, 2000). A second example: loss function analysis depends on having precise estimates of error rates in ACE. But there is considerable uncertainty about these error rates, even at the

national level, as has already been described. A last example: adjustment makes the homogeneity assumption—census errors occur at a uniform rate within post strata across wide stretches of geography. Loss function analysis assumes that and more: error rates in the census are uniform, and so are error rates in ACE. That is how processing errors and correlation bias in ACE can be parceled out to local areas without creating unmanageably large variances. But these homogeneity assumptions are not tenable for reasons explained above, under the heading "Heterogeneity in 2000".

POINTERS TO THE LITERATURE

Reviews and discussions of the 1980 and 1990 adjustments can be found in *Survey Methodology*, 18 (1992): 1–74; *Journal of the American Statistical Association*, 88 (1993): 1044–1166; and *Statistical Science*, 9 (1994): 458–537. Other exchanges worth noting include *Jurimetrics*, 34 (1993): 59–115 and *Society*, 39 (2001): 3–53. These are easy to read and informative. Pro-adjustment arguments are made by Anderson and Fienberg (1999), but see Stark (2001) and Ylvisaker (2001). Prewitt (2000) may be a better source, and Zaslavsky (1993) is often cited. Cohen et al. (1999) try to answer arguments on the 1990 adjustment, but see Freedman and Wachter (2003). Skerry (2000) has an accessible summary of the issues. Darga (2000) is a critic. Freedman et al. (2001) have a probability model for census adjustment, which may help to clarify some of the issues.

The decision against adjustment for 1990 is explained in US Department of Commerce

(1991). On the 2000 adjustment decision, see US Bureau of the Census (2001a, 2001b, 2003). For another perspective on Census 2000, see Citro et al. (2004). Problems with the PES, especially with respect to detecting duplicates, are discussed in the same reference (Citro et al., 2004: 214ff and 240ff). However, there is residual enthusiasm for a PES in 2010 and a corresponding lack of enthusiasm for Demographic Analysis (ibid.: 8). Cork et al. reach different conclusions (2004: 11).

LITIGATION

The Commerce Department's decision not to adjust the 1980 census was upheld after trial in *Cuomo v. Baldrige* (674 F. Supp. 1089, SDNY, 1987). The Department's decision not to adjust the 1990 census was also upheld after trial and appeal to the Supreme Court (517 US 1 (1996)). Later in the decade, the Court found that use of adjustment for reapportionment, that is, allocating congressional seats among the states, violated the Census Act (525 US 316 (1999)). The administration had at the time planned to adjust, so the Court's decision necessitated a substantial revision to the design of ACE (Brown et al, 1999).

Efforts by Los Angeles and the Bronx among others to compel adjustment of Census 2000 were rejected by the courts (*City of Los Angeles et al. v. Evans et al., Central District, California*); the decision was upheld on appeal to the Ninth Circuit (307 F. 3d 859 (9th Cir. 2002)). There was a similar outcome in an unpublished case, *Cameron County et al. v. Evans et al.*, Southern District, Texas. Utah sued to preclude the use of imputations but the suit was denied by the Supreme Court (*Utah et al. v. Evans et al.*, 536 US 452 (2002)).

The Commerce Department did not wish to release block-level adjusted counts, but was compelled to do so as a result of several lawsuits. The lead case was *Carter v. US Dept. of Commerce* in Oregon. The decision was upheld on appeal to the Ninth Circuit (307 F. 3d 1084 (9th Cir. 2002)).

OTHER COUNTRIES

For context, this section gives a bird's-eye view of the census process in a few other countries. In Canada, the census is taken every five years (1996, 2001, 2006, etc.). Unadjusted census counts are published. Coverage errors are estimated, using variations on the PES (including a 'reverse record check') and other resources. A couple of years later, when the work is complete, post-censal population estimates are made for provinces and many subprovincial areas. These estimates are based on adjusted census counts. The process in Australia is similar; the PES there is like a scaled-down version of the one in the US.

In the UK, the census is taken every ten years (1991, 2001, 2011, etc.). Coverage errors are estimated using a PES. Only the adjusted census counts are published. The official acronym is ONC, for One-Number Census. Failure to release the original counts cannot enhance the possibility of informed discussion. Moreover, results dating back to 1982 are adjusted to agree with current estimates. 'Superseded' data sets seem to be withdrawn from the official UK web page (www.statistics.gov.uk). Anomalies are found in the demographic structure of the estimated population (not enough males age 20–24) (see Redfern, 2004; also pp. 17 and 48 in http://www.statistics.gov.uk/downloads/theme population/PT113.pdf).

In Scandinavian countries, the census is based on administrative records and population registries. In Sweden, for example, virtually every resident has a Personal Identification Number (PIN); the authorities try to track down movers—even persons who leave the country. Norway conducted a census by mail in 2001, to complete its registry of housing; but is switching to an administrative census in the future. The accuracy of a registry census is not so easy to determine.

SUMMARY AND CONCLUSION

The idea behind the census is simple: you try to count everybody in the population, once and only once, at their place of residence rather than somewhere else. The US Bureau of the Census does this sort of thing about as well as it can be done. Of course, the details are complicated, the expense is huge, compromises must be made, and mistakes are inevitable. The idea behind adjustment is to supplement imperfect data collection in the census with imperfect data collection in a post-enumeration survey, and with modeling. It turns out, however, that the imperfections in the adjustment process are substantial, relative to the imperfections in the census. Moreover, the arguments for adjustment turn out to be based on hopeful assumptions rather than on data.

The lesson extends beyond the census context. Models look objective and scientific. If they are complicated, they appear to take into account many factors of interest. Furthermore, complexity is by itself a good first line of defense against criticism. Finally, modelers can try to buttress their results with another layer of models, designed to show that outcomes are insensitive to assumptions or that different approaches lead to similar findings. Modeling has considerable appeal. Technique is seductive, and seems to offer badly needed answers. However, conclusions may be driven by assumptions rather than data. Indeed, that is likely to be so. Otherwise, a model with unsupported assumptions would hardly be needed in the first place.

Authors' footnote:

The authors testified against adjustment in *Cuomo v. Baldrige* (1980 census) and *New York v. Department of Commerce* (1990 census). They have consulted for the Department of Commerce on Census 2000.

REFERENCES

Anderson, M. and Fienberg, S.E. (1999) *Who Counts? The Politics of Census-Taking in Contemporary America*. New York: Russell Sage Foundation.

Brown, L.D., Eaton, M.L., Freedman, D.A., Klein, S.P., Olshen, R.A., Wachter, K.W., Wells, M.T. and

Ylvisaker, D. (1999) 'Statistical controversies in census 2000', *Jurimetrics,* 39: 347–75.

Citro, C.F., Cork, D.L. and Norwood, J.L. (eds.) (2001) *The 2000 Census: Interim Assessment*. Washington, D C: National Academy Press.

——— (eds.) (2004) *The 2000 Census: Counting under Adversity*. Washington, DC: National Academy Press.

Cohen, M.L., White, A.A. and Rust K.F. (eds.) (1999) *Measuring a Changing Nation: Modern Methods for the 2000 Census*. Washington, DC.: National Academy Press.

Cork, D.L., Cohen, M.L. and King, B.F. (eds.) (2004) *Reengineering the 2010 Census: Risks and Challenges*. Washington, DC: National Academy Press.

Darga, K. (2000) *Fixing the Census Until it Breaks*. Lansing: Michigan Information Center.

Freedman, D.A., Stark, P.B. and Wachter, K.W. (2001) 'A probability model for census adjustment', *Mathematical Population Studies,* 9:165–80.

Freedman, D.A. and Wachter, K.W. (1994) 'Heterogeneity and census adjustment for the intercensal base', *Statistical Science,* 9: 458–537 (with discussion).

——— (2003) 'On the likelihood of improving the accuracy of the census through statistical adjustment', in Darlene R. Goldstein (ed.) *Science and Statistics: A Festschrift for Terry Speed*. IMS Monograph 40, pp. 197–230.

Prewitt, K. (2000) 'Accuracy and coverage evaluation: Statement on the feasibility of using statistical methods to improve the accuracy of Census 2000', *Federal Register,* 65: 38373–398.

Redfern, P. (2004) 'An alternative view of the 2001 census and future census taking', *JRSS Ser. A,* 167: 209–48 (with discussion).

Skerry, P. (2000) *Counting on the Census? Race, Group Identity, and the Evasion of Politics*. Washington, DC: Brookings.

Stark, P.B. (2001) 'Review of *Who Counts?*', *Journal of Economic Literature,* 39: 592–5.

US Census Bureau (2001a) *Report of the Executive Steering Committee for Accuracy and Coverage Evaluation Policy*. With supporting documentation, Reports B1–24. Washington, DC: US Census Bureau. Available at: http://www.census.gov/dmd/www/EscapRep.html.

——— (2001b) 'Report of the Executive Steering Committee for Accuracy and Coverage Evaluation Policy on Adjustment for Non-Redistricting Uses', With supporting documentation, Reports 1–24. Washington, DC. Available at: http://www.census. gov/dmd/www/EscapRep2.html.

——— (2003) *Technical Assessment of A.C.E. Revision II*. Available at: http://www.census.gov/dmd/www/ace2.html

US Department of Commerce, Office of the Secretary (1991). *Decision on Whether or Not a Statistical Adjustment of the 1990 Decennial Census of Population Should Be Made for Coverage Deficiencies Resulting in an Overcount or Undercount of the Population, Explanation.* Three volumes, Washington, DC. Reprinted in part in *Federal Register* 56: 33582–33642 (July 22).

Wachter, K.W. and Freedman D.A. (2000) 'The fifth cell', *Evaluation Review,* 24: 191–211.

Ylvisaker, D. (2001) 'Review of "*Who Counts?*"', *Journal of the American Statistical Association,* 96: 340–41.

Zaslavsky, A.M. (1993) 'Combining census, dual system, and evaluation study data to estimate population shares', *Journal of the American Statistical Association,* 88: 1092–1105.

14

Quantitative History

Margo Anderson

WHAT IS QUANTITATIVE HISTORY?

Quantitative history is the term for an array
of skills and techniques used to apply the
methods of statistical data analysis to the
study of history. Sometimes also called cliometrics by economic historians, the term was
popularized in the 1950s and 1960s as social,
political and economic historians called for
the development of a 'social science history',
adopted methods from the social sciences,
and applied them to historical problems.
These historians also called for social scientists to historicize their research and consciously examine the temporal nature of the
social phenomena they explored. For both
types of questions, historians found that they
needed to develop new technical skills and
data sources. That effort led to an array of
activities to promote quantitative history.

Classical historical research methodology
relies upon textual records, archival research
and the narrative as a form of historical writing. The historian describes and explains particular phenomena and events, be they large
epic analyses of the rise and fall of empires
and nations, or the intimate biographical
detail of an individual life. Quantitative
history is animated by similar goals but takes
as its subject the aggregate historical patterns

of multiple events or phenomena. Such a
standpoint creates a different set of issues for
analysis. A classic historical analysis, for
example, may treat a presidential election as
a single event. Quantitative historians consider a particular presidential election as one
element in the universe of all presidential
elections and are interested in patterns which
characterize the universe or several units
within it. The life-course patterns of one
household or family may be conceived as
one element in the aggregate patterns of family history for a nation, region, social class or
ethnic group. Repeated phenomena from the
past that leave written records, which read
one at a time would be insignificant, are particularly useful if they can be aggregated,
organized, converted to an electronic database and analyzed for statistical patterns.
Thus records such as census schedules, vote
tallies, vital (e.g., birth, death and marriage)
records; or the ledgers of business sales, ship
crossings, or slave sales; or crime reports
permit the historian to retrieve the pattern of
social, political, and economic activity in the
past and reveal the aggregate context and
structures of history.

The standpoint of quantitative history also
required a new set of skills and techniques
for historians. Most importantly, they had to

incorporate the concept of the data set and data matrix into their practice. Floud (1972: 17) defined the data set as 'a coherent selection of data from the whole range of historical data available to the historian, and it is selected because it relates closely to the questions that the historian wishes to consider.' The myriad instances of a phenomenon—for example, all United States presidential elections—form the cases of the data set. The pieces of information collected about the cases—for example, the candidates running, the year of the election or the vote totals—become the variable characteristics of the data set, that is, the varying characteristics of any particular case. The historian arranges the data in tabular form, that is, in a matrix of rows and columns, 'consisting of a number of rows, which will normally represent cases, and a number of columns, which will normally represent variables' (Floud, 1972: 18). The creation of quantitative data sets thus required the historian to carefully compile consistent information about the phenomenon to be investigated, and prepare the data in tabular form. Historians then were prepared to apply the techniques of statistical data analysis to the data set to answer the research question posed.

In short, to make effective use of quantitative evidence and statistical techniques for historical analysis, practitioners had to integrate the rapidly developing skills of the social sciences, including sampling, statistical data analysis and data archiving into their historical work. That task led to the development of new training programs in quantitative methods for historians, to the creation of new academic journals and textbooks, and to the creation of data archives to support the research.

EARLY EFFORTS

Historians had made use of quantitative evidence prior to the 1950s, particularly in the fields of economic and social history. The *Annales* school in France pointed the way in the pre-World War II period. The rapid growth and expansion of the United States had long required American historians to consider quantitative issues in their study of the growth of the American economy, population and mass democracy. Thus, for example, Frederick Jackson Turner's classic 1893 essay on 'The Significance of the Frontier in American History' was largely based on a reading and interpretation of the results of the 1890 population census.

But true 'data analysis' in the current sense had to await the growth of the social and statistical sciences in the first half of the twentieth century, and the diffusion to universities in the 1950s of the capacity for machine tabulation of numerical records, and then of mainframe computing in the 1960s. One can see the emerging field exemplified in seminal studies in the late 1950s and early 1960s. In 1959, for example, Merle Curti and his colleagues at the University of Wisconsin published *The Making of an American Community: A Case Study of Democracy in a Frontier County*. Curti et al. (1959) explored Turner's thesis with an in-depth look at the mid-nineteenth century history of Trempeleau County, Wisconsin, including its records of newspapers, diaries, private papers and county histories. But they also added data analysis of the employment patterns derived from the individual-level federal census manuscripts for the censuses from 1850 through 1880.

Similarly, the 'new' economic historians of the 1950s challenged the conventional wisdom of the day on several key issues in economic history. One debate centered on the 'necessity' of the US Civil War. Historians at the time argued that the war had been 'unnecessary' since the institution of race-based slavery would collapse under the weight of its unprofitability. In contrast, economic historians employed economic theory and data on output of southern agriculture to argue that the southern agricultural economy could have survived profitably into the twentieth century using slave labor (Conrad and Meyer, 1958). Robert Fogel challenged the conventional wisdom on the centrality of railroads for the industrial development of the United States. Making use of economic theory, carefully compiled data series, and the logic of the counterfactual, Fogel argued that canals would have also succeeded as a transportation system underpinning nineteenth-century American industrial development (1964).

'New political historians' such as Lee Benson, Allan Bogue, Richard P. McCormick, and political scientists with historical interests, such as Warren Miller and Walter Dean Burnham, translated the emerging techniques of political scientists analyzing contemporary election results and voter surveys to historical questions, and opened up dramatic new insights into American political history.[1] The new political historians identified the parameters of party systems, developed the theory of the critical election, and argued that underlying structures of electoral politics were accessible through historical analysis of voter turnout and election results. In 1964 in England, demographers and historians founded the Cambridge Group for the History of Population and Social Structure and began a forty-year project to retrieve, assemble and reconstruct 400 years of the family history of Britain.[2]

The new possibilities of quantitative history fit well with other trends within the discipline of history, particularly with the growth of social history and calls for what Jesse Lemisch (1967) called 'history from the bottom up'—that is, for historians to treat the lives of ordinary people, to complement the study of elites. By the mid-1960s, the interest in the new techniques led the American Historical Association to recognize that 'quantification in history' would require new skills and institutions within the historical profession. The AHA created a Quantitative Data Committee to consider the issues. Summer institutes and classes in quantitative methods for historians were held in 1965, 1967 and 1973 at the University of Michigan, Cornell University and Harvard University respectively. In 1968, the Interuniversity Consortium for Political Research at the University of Michigan began offering a four-week course in quantitative historical

analysis as part of its summer program in quantitative methods. The course continues to be offered each summer. At the Newberry Library in Chicago, from 1971 to 1982 Richard Jensen spearheaded a summer program in quantitative methods for historians. By the early 1980s, about 40 percent of history graduate programs offered training in quantitative history as part of the graduate curriculum (Bogue, 1983: 220ff.).[3]

Additional institutional infrastructure of quantitative history can also be dated to the 1960s. New journals, textbooks, and edited collections also promoted the growth of quantitative history. The *Historical Methods Newsletter,* for example, began publishing in 1967, and was renamed *Historical Methods* in 1978. The *Journal of Interdisciplinary History* began publication in 1970. The Social Science History Association (SSHA) was founded in 1974 and the first issue of its journal, *Social Science History*, appeared in 1976. SSHA became the professional venue for bringing together historians who consciously adopted theory and methodology from the social sciences and social scientists doing historical work. The cross-fertilization has continued, and, as noted below, many of the innovations in quantitative history have been developed by scholars with formal training in the social sciences and appointments in departments of economics, demography, sociology, anthropology, geography and political science.

Textbooks in quantitative history began to appear in the early 1970s, and many have been published since.[4] Numerous edited volumes introduced the new field and techniques to professional and student audiences.[5] Finally, researchers created data archives. In the United States, the Interuniversity Consortium for Political Research (ICPR) was founded in 1962 primarily by political scientists. Renamed the Interuniversity Consortium for Political and Social Research (ICPSR) in 1975, the Consortium has also pioneered in the creation and preservation of historical data collections. The United States National Archives and Records Administration (NARA) created an electronic records preservation program in the early 1970s for federal government data that was 'born digital' (Ambacher, 2003; Adams, 1995, forthcoming; Fishbein, 1973). Similar work began in Britain with the founding of the UK Data Archive in 1967.[6]

Thus by 1980, historians had taken major steps to establish the institutional structures necessary to integrate quantitative history into larger historical practice. That infrastructure has, if you will, both matured and faced challenges in the generation of work since, and in many ways quantitative history is still a work in progress. Nevertheless, it is possible to identify the types of questions quantitative history was intended to and has been able to address; the major types of data sets that have developed and the key characteristics of historical data sets; and the most commonly used techniques within the field. That background in turn provides the framework for a review of a number of methodological issues historians uniquely face, for a review of the achievements of quantitative history, and for a discussion of emerging issues.

QUESTIONS, DATA AND ISSUES IN CREATING HISTORICAL DATA SETS

Quantitative history has been most successful in addressing big questions about long-term historical patterns of change. Practitioners have achieved important results by assembling substantial amounts of numeric or countable information, and organizing it into tabular data matrices for statistical analysis. The first generation of studies focused especially on the history of the family and social structure, trends in economic growth and change, patterns of electoral behavior and voter participation, or the record of inter-generational social mobility and living standards. More recently, the examples have proliferated. Historians of crime and the criminal justice system, for example, have retrieved court and newspaper records to examine the long-term patterns of crime and

violence in the past. Historians of the family have examined patterns of inheritance and the inter-generational transfer of wealth. The emerging work of 'anthropometric' history— the study of living standards and well-being in the past using measures of height, weight, stature and disease in the past—has cast an even wider net, aiming to evaluate comparative living standards over centuries and ultimately millennia.[7]

Making such studies possible was an explosive growth in the data sets informing quantitative history. Quantitative history, like other branches of the social sciences, requires what was once called 'machine-readable' (and are now known as 'electronic') data for analysis. Though there are some examples of large-scale data analysis undertaken by manual systems of tabulation and statistical analysis, most notably the nineteenth-century tabulations of census or vital registration records, social science data in the modern sense required the development of machine tabulation devices, counter sorters, and other mechanized calculators. The first system was the Hollerith system of punch-card tabulation used for the 1890 American population census; the social and statistical sciences grew with the new machinery. By the 1940s, social scientists had developed rules and procedures for collecting quantitative data to make best use of machine tabulation and analysis. These conventions included the fixed format data matrix, the classification of variables into nominal, ordinal, interval and ratio variables, the organization of questionnaires and survey forms to facilitate conversion to punch-cards for analysis, and coding systems such as the Likert scale. Quantitative historians inherited these practices and adapted this existing technology and set of conventions to their historical project. They soon recognized that they had to solve major new methodological and logistical problems before the potential for quantitative history could be achieved.

The first problem derives from the larger evidentiary issue faced by all historians, namely, that historical analysis must rely on the extant record of the past. Historians are at the mercy of their subjects' penchant and capacity for preservation. And before 1890, that is, for most of the historical record of human history, no preserved data were 'machine-readable'. Thus all potential historical data had to be created from surviving, usually text-based, records and converted to machine-readable or electronic format. Even records collected in the twentieth century and informed by the conventions of the emerging social sciences frequently no longer exist in machine-readable format. Thus, the United States Census Bureau, for example, preserved the original paper census questionnaires from the eighteenth century forward. But census officials did not retain the punchcards they used to tabulate the censuses from 1890 to 1960. These cards were destroyed once the results of the census appeared in published form. Thus historians interested in reanalyzing the microdata from past censuses faced creating, or recreating, the machine-readable records.

Quantitative historians faced additional major methodological problems resulting from the recalcitrance of the existing archival historical records. All historians face the problems of missing data, and the difficulties of interpreting illegible, damaged, incomplete or destroyed records. For quantitative historians, though, aiming to translate the archival record to a data matrix for statistical analysis, these questions of data quality are particularly difficult. Cases and variables for a data matrix require precise conceptual and operational definitions, as do the allowable entries for particular cell values within the matrix, since the goal of statistical analysis is to assess extent, central tendency and dispersion of any particular characteristic. What does one do if the records for a year or period of years are missing? How does one handle illegible entries in the records of a company's finances? How does one know if the probate records found in a county archive are complete? Historians have had to confront the requirements for case and variable definition, classification and coding in building a data set. The solutions to these problems emerged with the overall field. The journal, *Historical*

Methods, in particular, became the venue for identifying, debating and proposing methodological solutions to these issues.

A related issue is the set of rules for extracting the information from a text-based evidentiary source to create a data set. Historical archives frequently contain text-based records that lend themselves to data set construction, but require considerable conceptual work before they can be manipulated statistically. Historians have made use of sales invoices, wills, parish registers and case files of charity or social welfare agencies, for example, and have had to create the cases and variables from the extant texts.

Historians have had to solve these methodological questions as they select the evidence to be analyzed and create the code-book for the data set. Whether one is analyzing existing tabular data from the past—for example, the records of imports and exports of a nation over a period of years, or the published results of a census—or whether one is creating a data set from text-based sources, the historian needs to define the case or unit of analysis, define the characteristics or variables to be selected to characterize the cases within the data set, and define the coding system used to organize the source information for the data set. Several examples of the issues involved best illustrate the work of quantitative historians.

COMPILATION AND ANALYSIS OF PREVIOUSLY PUBLISHED DATA

The most accessible sources for quantitative historians were data that were already published in tabular format. The first generation of quantitative historians in particular compiled data sets from existing, usually aggregated, published data sources—for example, tabulated census results, election results, government reports of tax collections, imports and exports, and data from trade publications. Assembled into time series, such data permitted researchers to undertake basic analyses of historical trends and use regression models to correlate the determinants of change. For example, Walter Dean Burnham's 950+-page study of count-level presidential election results, published in 1955, included a compilation of results from state archives and newspaper sources, and a discussion of the methodological issues he faced in compiling the data. Combined with denominator data from census results that allowed the researchers to measure turnout, the new data set permitted Burnham and his colleagues to begin the analysis of historical election analysis (Burnham, 1955). In similar ways, economic historians made particularly good use of the data compiled in statistical abstracts, such as the *Statistical Abstract of the United States*, published annually since 1878.

CONVERTING TABULAR DATA IN MANUSCRIPT FORM TO ELECTRONIC FORMAT

A second source of quantitative data were archived tabular records in text-based format, probably best illustrated by individual-level census manuscript schedules. See Figures 14.1 and 14.2,[8] a facsimile of the 1950 US Census population schedule.

For the United States, such original census responses are available for all the federal censuses except 1890, and are available for public use through 1930.[9] The schedule is already in a matrix format, with rows of cases and columns of variables. The original difficulty with using these records is their volume. With one record per person for the censuses of 1850 and later, data set creation for a large portion of the population was beyond the capacities of an individual researcher. The first generation of quantitative historians resolved this problem by sampling, and usually by organizing a research project of a particular locale. The historical social mobility studies were designed as community studies to solve the problem of the volume of data.

Later generations of quantitative historians have by and large solved the problem of

volume through collaboration and by building historical public-use microdata samples, or PUMS files. Starting with the 1900 census, historians proposed to create historical PUMS files that would be similar to the contemporary PUMS files that the Census Bureau has created since 1970. In the late 1980s, researchers at the University of Minnesota, initially led by Russell Menard, Steven Ruggles and Robert McCaa, began systematic retrieval of the historical census data from the United States, and more recently from other nations. The Integrated Public Use Microdata Sample (IPUMS) Project and the International IPUMS project have created microdata samples for the United States from all the censuses from 1850 to 2000, and are now collecting such data for many nations of the world. The data are easily downloadable from the web. The researchers have also built the code-books, technical support materials, and research bibliography necessary for the user to understand the context of the questions and responses to the census.[10]

Creating Tabular Data from Text-Based Records

The most time-consuming type of data set creation is the conversion of text-based records to matrix format. For existing tabular data, whether in manuscript or published form, the basic framework of the matrix is given in the original source. For text-based records with no tabular structure, it is up to the researcher to create the code-book, and thus all the variable definitions and coding rules. Figure 14.3,[11] an illustration of a record of a slave sale in antebellum America, illustrates the issues.[12]

There are thousands of such records in newspapers, private collections and archives, and, if marshaled for analysis, provide detailed, if somewhat gruesome, evidence of this chapter in American economic history. Robert Fogel and Stanley Engerman compiled such records for their study, *Time on the Cross* (1974) from the New Orleans Slave

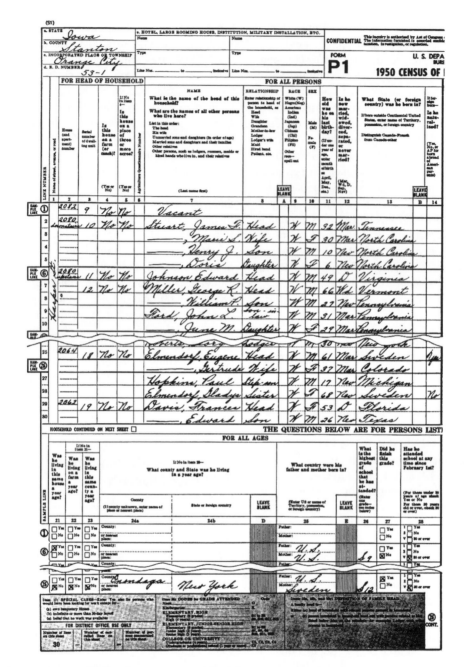

Figure 14.1   Facsimile of 1950 Census Schedule for Orange City, Iowa (left side of page)

Market. ICPSR Study 7423 contains the data and code-book for the New Orleans Slave Sale Sample.[13]

For their sample, Fogel and Engerman converted the text-based records into cases and variables and codes, making decisions on unit

of analysis (the slave), sampling (2.5 percent or 5 percent, depending on the year of sale), number of variables (46), and codes. Each decision extracted a piece of information from the original text-based records, and had implications for ultimate analysis. The final

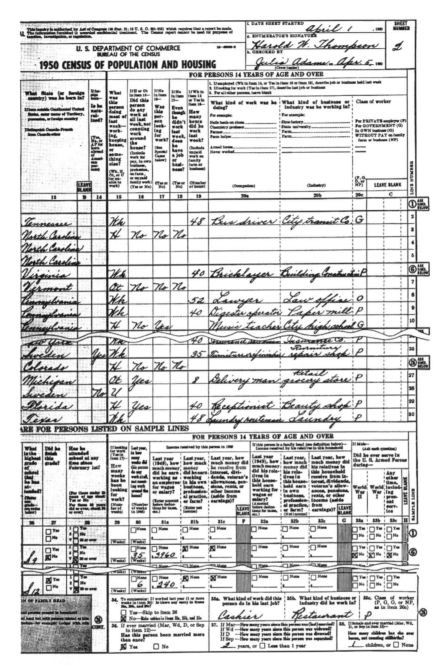

Figure 14.2   Facsimile of 1950 Census Schedule for Orange City, Iowa (right side of page)

data set contained 5009 records, and included information on the characteristics of the slave (e.g., age, sex, occupation, color), the terms of the sale (e.g., the date, price, whether paid in cash, the number of slaves sold together), and information on the buyer and seller.

Fogel and Engerman used the data to analyze the inter-state slave trade, and to address questions about the economic viability of the slave economy (Fogel and Engerman, 1974).

The work of building the corpus of machine-readable databases began in the

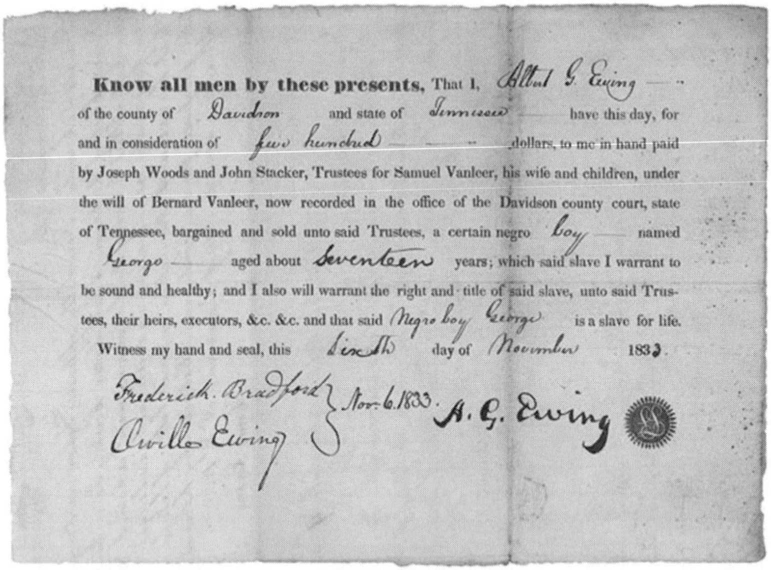
Know all men by these presents, That I, Albert G. Ewing — of the county of Davidson and state of Tennessee have this day, for and in consideration of five hundred — dollars, to me in hand paid by Joseph Woods and John Stacker, Trustees for Samuel Vanleer, his wife and children, under the will of Bernard Vanleer, now recorded in the office of the Davidson county court, state of Tennessee, bargained and sold unto said Trustees, a certain negro boy named George aged about seventeen years; which said slave I warrant to be sound and healthy; and I also will warrant the right and title of said slave, unto said Trustees, their heirs, executors, &c. &c. and that said Negro boy George is a slave for life.

Witness my hand and seal, this sixth day of November 1833.

Frederick Bradford
Orville Ewing
Nov. 6. 1833.
A. G. Ewing

Figure 14.3 Slave Bill of Sale, Davidson County, Tennessee, 1833

1960s, and continues both with small compilations and large collaborative data projects. In addition to the IPUMS project mentioned above, one can find large-scale historical data compilations of cost-of-living studies, election results, crime data, and the records of the heights and weights of people in the past. The creation and retrieval of historical data has also led to revision and improvement of data series compiled in earlier years and to the analysis of the history of data development. Most recently, for example, economic historians have produced a new 'millennial' edition of the *Historical Statistics of the United States* (Carter et al., 2006), which promises to provide opportunities for even more quantitative historical analysis.

ANALYZING HISTORICAL DATA SETS

Sampling and the Universe of Cases

As have data analysts in the other social sciences, historians have made use of the theory of probability sampling to reduce the volume of information for a particular study to a manageable level. Just as one does not need to survey the entire electorate to develop quite precise estimates of the ultimate election results, so historians studying family structure or economic activity or consumer behavior have not had to record all such behavior for study. As noted above, the process of creating historical data sets is sufficiently time-consuming to strongly recommend sampling strategies designed to reduce the volume of coding and data entry to the minimum necessary for robust analysis. Thus the original users and secondary users of the archived historical data sets need to attend to sampling strategy and introduce appropriate sample weights and measures of error into the analysis.

A more difficult issue is the one facing the historian who cannot be sure that she knows what the universe of cases actually is. Do the extant newspaper reports of lynchings, for example, encompass all lynchings (Griffin et al., 1997; Tolnay and Beck, 1995)? Are the records of wills filed with a particular county complete, or might some have been destroyed or lost over the centuries? These dilemmas have their analogues in non-quantitative research. But as with code-book creation, the research must provide best estimates of answers to such questions before analysis, and a substantial methodological literature has emerged to address the issues, often with specific reference to the kind of data set being compiled.

Techniques of Analysis

Statistical analysis of historical data has ranged from elementary data analysis of the patterns of central tendency and dispersion of the phenomena under study to elaborate explanatory models of events and behavior. Much historical quantitative analysis has been descriptive, simply excavating and documenting patterns of change and activity in quantitative form that cannot be revealed by traditional historical analysis. Thus much work—important work—is simple counting of a phenomenon, and describing trends over time.

Somewhat more elaborate analysis involves determining the correlates of the phenomenon under study, or building a model to explicate more complex patterns in the data. Here the standard bivariate and multivariate techniques of statistics provide the tools necessary for the analysis. Quantitative historians have borrowed heavily from sociology, political science, demography and economics, and made use of the classic linear regression model and its variants as the workhorse technique for more complex analysis. Statistical packages, such as SPSS, SAS, STATA and the like underpin the analysis of quantitative historical work, as they do for the social sciences.

There is some evidence that quantitative history has begun to have an impact on the larger methodological practice of the social sciences, as quantitative historians have brought their methodological expertise to the social sciences. Two brief examples should illustrate that impact.

The first is development of the field of ecological regression, particularly for analysis of electoral patterns. Political scientists can supplement analysis of election results with surveys of individual voters. Indeed the National Election Survey, conducted since 1948, has itself become an historical source of changing electoral behavior. But historians cannot go back and survey voters from the election of 1860, and thus must make use of the aggregate election results and the ecological characteristics of the voting units— e.g., precincts, districts or counties—that provided the vote. Ecological inference suffers from the threat of the ecological fallacy, that is, the danger of wrongly inferring individual level behavior from the patterns of aggregates. Practitioners of quantitative history have taken up new methods developed by political scientists and have devoted good effort to minimizing, if not completely solving, this dilemma. With historically minded political scientists, they have produced a methodological literature and new techniques that have produced rigorous results.[14]

The second contribution is serious attention to the development of statistical techniques to conceptualize and model time and temporal explanations. The methodological bread and butter for all historians is 'thinking in time' (Neustadt and May, 1986), and that standpoint has prompted historians and historically attuned social scientists to think about how to develop techniques of statistical analysis suitable for the goals of historical analysis.

Historians think about questions of what is an event, how is it bounded and measured; what is a turning point; what is a transition; what is a conjuncture or a rupture; and how is a period of time organized and bounded. Economists and other social and biological scientists have developed techniques to measure time series and temporal and cyclical events, for example, life cycles. The entry of quantitative historians into these discourses has been a useful clarification of the methodological issues involved. For example, the phrase, 'longitudinal analysis' that social scientists use does not necessarily privilege time as a central concern for analysis. Historians and social scientists who make temporal analysis such a central concern have thus argued for the need to add methods that will address 'thinking in time' to the standard repertoire of statistical techniques. Such techniques as sequence analysis, event history analysis and the methodological discussions surrounding autocorrelation in time series analysis have usefully been enriched by the growth of the field of quantitative history.[15]

THE COSTS OF DOING QUANTITATIVE HISTORY

The cost of scholarly work in quantitative history, like the cost of all scholarly work, can be measured in terms of both time and money required for the scholarship to flourish. The largest change in the working environment since the 1960s is that computing costs, which were quite expensive in the early years of the field, have dropped as the larger information revolution has developed. To my knowledge, there is no extant scholarly analysis of the costs of quantitative history versus traditional history, though I suspect that the underlying funding situation for quantitative historians has had an effect on the progress of the field.

In the early years of the development of quantitative history, in the United States the Social Science Research Council, the American Historical Association, the National Endowment for the Humanities, and the National Science Foundation, as well as research universities around the country, all provided sponsorship of the field by funding grants for data development, conference sponsorship and the institutional work required to promote the field. This early institutional support was aimed at jump-starting the field, not at providing sustained long-term support. Related to this, the National Endowment for the Humanities, the main federally sponsored grant agency for historians, has a much lower funding level than the federal funding agencies that support related social science research—for example, the National Science Foundation or the National Institutes of Health. The United States, unlike European nations, does not

include history in the main governmental foundation for funding academic research. Accordingly, quantitative history projects in the United States have had major difficulty in competing with both large-scale humanities grant projects, such as compilations of archival papers, and with large-scale long-term research projects in the social sciences such as the National Election Study or the Panel Study of Income Dynamics. Allan Bogue (1983) identified the chronic problems of funding faced by quantitative historians in the late 1970s. They remain unsolved as the concrete example which follows illustrates.

Robert Fogel, by any measure, represents one of the most successful and innovative quantitative history scholars in the field, yet even he has faced major funding obstacles. Fogel was awarded the Nobel Prize in Economics in 1993, and in his autobiographical statement prepared for the award, he described his career and acknowledged the problems of funding he faced, particularly, as he put it, for the 'current research projects on which I reported in the Prize Lecture'. The Center for Population Economics at the University of Chicago and the Walgreen Chair provided funding when federal grants would not. 'The data on health conditions', he wrote:

comes from a project called 'Early Indicators of Later Work Levels, Disease, & Death' which is tracing nearly 40,000 Union Army men from the cradle to the grave. It takes over 15,000 variables to describe the life-cycle history of one of these men. These life-cycle histories are created by linking about a score of data sets. It took more than half a decade of work to investigate the potential of these data sets, work out procedures for data retrieval and file management, and to establish the feasibility of the enterprise in our own minds.

The site committee of the National Institutes of Health which reviewed the original project proposal in 1986 agreed that such a project could in principle make a significant contribution to an understanding of the process of aging, but they were skeptical about the quality of some of the data, about whether the software and programming procedures we had developed by that time were adequate for the management of such a large data set, and about whether the project could be completed within the proposed budget.

To resolve these doubts it was necessary to draw a six percent subsample which linked together all of the separate sources and which demonstrated the effectiveness of the software by analyzing the information in the subsample. It took an additional four years to complete the second phase of the justification of the project. Thus nearly a decade of preliminary research, much of it funded by Walgreen and the CPE, was required before the project was accepted by the peer reviewers of NIH and NSF.[16] (Fogel, 1993)

Despite such barriers, quantitative historians have been able to take advantage of the technological developments in computing and data management to make major advances in the ease of analysis, in terms of both time and money. For example, historians of the 1960s through the 1980s who wished to have access to the archived data sets at ICPSR had to order tapes and paper codebooks which were delivered by mail. The tape was then mounted on a mainframe computer, to be accessed in a statistical package run in a mainframe environment (with computer usage often charged by the university in the same way that phones or paper were charged). By the early 1990s, users could access files using FTP (file transfer protocol), and micro-computers on university desktops were providing direct access to statistical packages, even if those programs were sometimes still lodged on a mainframe. By the mid-1990s, desktop computing had replaced mainframe computing for most applications, and by the early 2000s, ICPSR initiated ICPSR Direct, the application that permitted an authorized user to download data files and PDF code-books directly to a desktop.

CRITIQUES OF QUANTITATIVE HISTORY

From the outset of the development of the field of quantitative history, powerful critics have challenged practitioners on their work, and even challenged the usefulness of the field itself. In the early 1960s, Carl Bridenbaugh devoted a portion of his 1962 American Historical Association Presidential Address to a condemnation of quantitative history

(Bridenbaugh, 1962), memorably labeling it a 'bitch goddess' (Bogue, 1983). Even during the period of the rapid growth of quantitative history in the 1960s and 1970s, 'traditional' historians expressed doubts about the new methods, challenging them as reductionist, brittle and not pertinent to the main goal of the historical narrative. Critics were extremely dubious of the 'scientific' claims of quantitative historians, and resisted the challenge of the quantifiers that traditional historical writing was not theoretically rigorous or conceptually consistent.

In the 1980s, some of the original proponents of the field also renounced their earlier enthusiasm and suggested that quantitative methods had not fulfilled their promise. Most notable among these critics were Lee Benson and Lawrence Stone, early enthusiasts who had changed their minds (Benson, 1984; Stone, 1977, 1979). Such recantations gave support to the anti-quantifiers at a time when major new methodological challenges were facing historians, most notably from the postmodernists and what came to be called 'the cultural turn'. Through this welter of debate, quantitative practitioners continued their efforts, somewhat chastened by their fall from the heights of fashion of earlier years, but grounded sufficiently institutionally and intellectually to continue to work.[17]

Through some twenty years of debate, neither side of the traditional/quantitative divide 'won' their arguments. Rather, by the 1990s, the debate cooled into something of an uneasy truce, with practitioners acknowledging some of the points of their opponents, but agreeing to disagree on the larger validity of their enterprise.[18] In practical terms, quantitative techniques did not become a routine part of history graduate student training as they did in the social sciences, but have remained a specialty of some historians in some graduate training programs, considered more akin to language requirements for reading historical literature and texts of a non-English-speaking society than to a methodological necessity for all practicing historians. This compartmentalization of the skills of quantification for historians has in turn affected the practice of quantitative historians within the larger history profession.

History as a field has maintained its roots as a 'humanities' discipline and quantitative historians' connections to the social sciences seem to many to be a betrayal of the historical project. The methodological 'training gap' has meant that when quantitative historians research and write for other historians, as opposed to other social scientists, they cannot expect their readers to appreciate or even understand the technical issues involved in their work. The history profession has maintained its commitment to accessible writing as well, and thus when writing for the broader audience of historians, quantitative historians have had to avoid technical jargon—for example, by avoiding the use of variable names in the explication of a model—and be mindful to explicate their arguments clearly.

The critiques have also encouraged quantitative historians to attend to the limitations in statistical methodology for analyzing historical processes, as discussed above. Much of this new work on statistical techniques for analyzing temporal processes is still in development and has yet to provide enough empirical work to demonstrate the robust nature of the new techniques, and hence convince non-quantitative historians, as well as the larger social science community, of the need to integrate explicitly temporal analysis into basic methods. But the promise is there, and as noted below, there are encouraging signs on the horizon.

THE FUTURE OF THE FIELD

The intellectual achievements of quantitative history in conjunction with the larger information technology revolution make the prognosis for the future of the field better today than it has been for many years.[19] Almost a half-century on, one can look back at steady development, though not always in a satisfyingly linear pattern.[20] Perhaps the most interesting recent development is the impact of the information technology revolution on the larger practice of historians.

When quantitative history as a field was in its most rapid initial development, most traditional historians labored much as their nineteenth-century predecessors had with pen, pencil, typewriter and note-card as technological support. Bibliographic work entailed using library card catalogs or reading large indexed tomes of articles, books, compilations, and the like. 'Data management' meant developing a file of index cards, not an electronic spread sheet or database. Secretaries typed manuscripts for publication, and though some large research institutions had introduced line editors for manuscript production by the 1970s, these were machines for staff, not faculty or students. By the 1980s, the situation changed. Desktop computers proliferated and for most historians, word processing opened up the possibility of the electronic future. By the 1990s, email replaced typed letters. After 1995, the content on the internet exploded, and first bibliographical work, and then much actual archival work, shifted to a computerized format. In short, non-quantitative historians had come to operate in a technological environment that was very similar to their quantifying peers. Most recently, cheap computing has made multimedia evidence—visual and oral, video and audio—accessible to the practicing historian. One can see these developments in particularly acute form in the developing field of historical geographic information systems, or historical GIS. GIS, was until quite recently, a very expensive technology, and thus adding historical maps to geographic databases has only just begun. As with the digitizing projects of the 1960s and 1970s, the payoff for the large initial costs of first translating maps to a new medium to become 'data', and then the development of new theory, software programs and methods to make the best use of these new data, are just beginning (Knowles, 2006).

More broadly, the effect of these technological changes has been to produce a convergence of work of what one might call 'technologically enabled' history. Traditional historians and humanists in general—for example, in the work of Franco Moretti

(2005)—also now work with electronic databases, learn new computer programs to analyze the rapidly proliferating data, and explore new forms of presentation of the results of their analysis. Quantitative historians had to learn the skills necessary to prepare and present statistical results in print. Historians more generally are using visual images, audio and video in their presentations, not as 'illustration' to enhance or supplement an analysis but as core evidence for analysis.[21]

Richard Steckel (2007) recently proposed an agenda for what he called 'Big Social Science History', which would extend the capacities of quantitative history and translate some of its methods of work to non-quantitative projects.[22] Andrew Abbott (2005) has also proposed such possibilities. As with the first generation of quantitative history, these large agendas will require collaborative efforts to manage the enormously expanding data infrastructure and the myriad computer technologies required to make best use of the expanding corpus of digitized historical evidence, and to develop appropriate theoretical approaches to such historical work.

ACKNOWLEDGEMENTS

* This essay has been improved considerably by comments from colleagues, particularly Peggy Adams, Erik Austin, Morgan Kousser, Jim Oberly, Lex Renda, Jack Reynolds, Steve Ruggles, Carole Shammas and Dan Scott Smith, The overall interpretation and remaining errors are all mine.

REFERENCES AND SELECT BIBLIOGRAPHY

Abbott, Andrew (2001) *Time Matters: On History and Method*. Chicago: University of Chicago Press.
———— (2005) 'Looking backward and looking forward, social science history at 2000' in Harvey Graff, Leslie Page Moch and Philip McMichael with Julia Woesthoff (eds), *Looking Backward and Looking Forward: Perpspectives on Social Science History*. Madison: University of Wisconsin Press, pp. 69–72.

Abbott, Andrew and Tsay, A. (2000) 'Sequence analysis and optimal matching methods in sociology', *Sociological Methods and Research,* 29: 3–33.
Adams, Margaret (1995) 'Punch card records: Precursors of electronic records', *American Archivist,* 58 (Spring): 182–201.
———— (forthcoming) 'Analyzing archives and finding facts: Use and users of digital data records', *Archival Science.*
Alter, George (1988) *Family and the Female Life Course.* Madison: University of Wisconsin Press.
Alter, George and Gutmann, Myron (1999) 'Casting spells: Database concepts for event-history analysis', *Historical Methods,* 32 (4): 165–76.
Ambacher, Bruce I. (ed.) (2003) *Thirty Years of Electronic Records.* Lanhan, MD: The Scarecrow Press.
Annual Report of the American Historical Association (1893).
Aydelotte, William, Bogue, Allan and Fogel, Robert (eds) (1972) *The Dimensions of Quantitative Research in History.* Princeton: Princeton University Press.
Benson, Lee (1957) 'Research problems in American political historiography', in Mirra Komarovsky (ed.), *Common Frontiers of the Social Sciences.* Glencoe, IL: Free Press, pp. 113–83, 418–21.
———— (1961) *The Concept of Jacksonian Democracy: New York as a Test Case* Princeton: Princeton University Press.
———— (1984) 'The mistransference fallacy in explanations of human behavior', *Historical Methods,* 17 (3): 118–31.
Bogue, Allan G. (1983) *Clio and the Bitch Goddess: Quantification in American Political History.* Beverly Hills: Sage Publications.
———— (1986) 'Systematic revisionism and a generation of ferment in American history', *Journal of Contemporary History,* 21 (2): 135–62.
———— (1990) 'The quest for numeracy: Data and methods in American political history', *Journal of Interdisciplinary History,* 21 (1): 89–116.
Bourke, Paul, DeBats, Donald and Phelan, Thomas (2001) 'Comparing individual-level voting returns with aggregates: A historical appraisal of the King solution', *Historical Methods,* 34 (3): 127–34.
Bridenbaugh, Carl (1962) 'The Great Mutation', AHA Presidential Address. Available at: http://www.historians.org/info/AHA_History/cbridenbaugh.htm. (Accessed on May 15 2006.)
Burnham, Walter Dean (1955) *Presidential Ballots, 1836–1892.* Baltimore: Johns Hopkins University Press.
———— (1970) *Critical Elections and the Mainsprings of American Politics.* New York: W.W. Norton & Co.

Burton, Orville Vernon (2002) *Computing in the Social Sciences and Humanities.* Urbana: University of Illinois Press.

Cameron, Sonja and Richardson, Sara (2005) *Using Computers in History.* New York: Palgrave Macmillan.

Carter, Susan, Gartner, Scott, Haines, Michael R., Olmstead, Alan, Sutch, Richard and Wright, Gavin (2006) *Historical Statistics of the United States: Millennial Edition.* New York: Cambridge University Press.

Chambers, William Nisbet and Burnham, Walter Dean (eds) (1967) *The American Party Systems: Stages of Political Development.* New York: Oxford University Press.

Chopwhittle, Darcy and Taleglad, Lars Mooson (2001) 'Review of Philinda Blank's *When the Cows Come Home: Barn Architecture and Changes in Bovine Public Space,*' *Social Science History,* 25 (5): 609–14. (See note 18.)

Conrad, Alfred and Meyer, John (1958) 'The economics of slavery in the ante-bellum South', *Journal of Political Economy,* 66 (2): 95–130.

Curti, Merle, Curti, Margaret Wooster, Daniel, Robert, Livermore Jr., Shaw, and Van Hise, Joseph (1959) *The Making of an American Community: A Case Study of Democracy in a Frontier County.* Stanford: Stanford University Press.

Darcy, R. and Rohrs, Richard C. (1995) *A Guide to Quantitative History.* Westport, CT: Praeger.

Dollar, Charles M. and Jensen, Richard J. (1971) *Historian's Guide to Statistics: Quantitative Analysis and Historical Research.* New York: Holt, Rinehart and Winston, Inc.

Feinstein, Charles and Thomas, Mark (2002) *Making History Count: A Primer in Quantitative Methods for Historians.* New York: Cambridge University Press.

Fishbein, Meyer H. (ed.) (1973) *The National Archives and Statistical Research.* Athens, OH: Ohio University Press.

Fitch, Nancy (1986) 'Statistical fantasies and historical facts: History in crisis and its methodological implications', *Historical Methods,* 18 (4): 239–54.

Floud, Roderick (1972) *An Introduction to Quantitative Methods for Historians.* Princeton: Princeton University Press.

Floud, Roderick, Wachter, Kenneth and Gregory, Annabel (eds) (1990) *Height, Health and History: Nutritional Status in the United Kingdom, 1750–1980.* New York: Cambridge University Press.

Fogel, Robert W. (1964) *Railroads and American Economic Growth: Essays in Econometric History.* Baltimore: Johns Hopkins University Press.

——— (1993) Nobel Prize in Economics Autobiographical Statement. Available at: http://www.nobelprize.org/economics/laureates/1993/fogel-autobio.html. (Accessed on May 15, 2006.)

——— (2003) *The Slavery Debates: A Retrospective.* Baton Rouge: Louisiana State University Press.

——— (2004) *The Escape from Hunger and Premature Death, 1700–2100: Europe, America, and the Third World.* New York: Cambridge University Press.

Fogel, Robert and Costa, Dora L. (1997) 'A theory of technophysio-evolution, with some implications for forecasting population, health care costs, and pension costs', *Demography,* 34 (1): 49–66.

Fogel, Robert William and Elton, G.R. (1983) *Which Road to the Past?* New Haven: Yale University Press.

Fogel, Robert and Engerman, Stanley (1974) *Time on the Cross,* Vols. 1 & 2. Boston: Little, Brown.

Goldin, Claudia (1997) 'Exploring the "Present Through the Past": Career and family across the last century', *The American Economic Review,* 87 (2): 396–9.

Graff, Harvey, Moch, Leslie Page and McMichael, Philip with Woesthoff, Julia (eds) (2005) *Looking Backward and Looking Forward: Perspectives on Social Science History.* Madison: University of Wisconsin Press.

Greif, Avner (1997) 'Cliometrics after 40 Years', *The American Economic Review,* 87 (2): 400–3.

Griffin, Larry (1993) 'Narrative, event-structure analysis, and causal interpretation in historical sociology', *American Journal of Sociology* 98: 1094–133.

Griffin, Larry and Isaac, Larry W. (1992) 'Recursive regression and the historical use of "time" in time-series analysis of historical process', *Historical Methods,* 25: 166–79.

Griffin, Larry J., Clark, P. and Sandberg, J. (1997) 'Narrative and event: Historical sociology and lynching', in W. Fitzhugh Brundage (ed.), *Under Sentence of Death: Lynching in the New South.* Chapel Hill: University of North Carolina Press, pp. 24–47.

Gutmann, Myron and Alter, George (1993) 'Family reconstitution as event history analysis', in David Sven Reher and Roger S. Schofield (eds), *Old and New Methods in Historical Demography.* Oxford: Oxford University Press, pp. 159–77.

Hacker, David and Fitch, Catherine (eds) (2003a) 'Building Historical Data Infrastructure: New Projects of the Minnesota Population Center', *Historical Methods* 36 (1).

——— (eds) (2003b) 'Building Historical Data Infrastructure: New Projects of the Minnesota Population Center', *Historical Methods* 36 (2).

Harvey, Charles and Press, Jon (1996) *Databases in Historical Research: Theory, Methods and Applications.* London: Macmillan Press Ltd.

Haskins, Loren and Jeffrey, Kirk (1990) *Understanding Quantitative History.* New York: McGraw-Hill.

Heckman, James J. (1997) 'The value of quantitative evidence on the effect of the past on the present', *The American Economic Review,* 87 (2): 404–8.

Hudson, Pat (2000) *History by Numbers: An Introduction to Quantitative Approaches.* New York: Oxford University Press.

Isaac, Larry W. and Griffin, Larry (1989) 'Ahistoricism in time-series analyses of historical process: Critique, redirection, and illustrations from US labor history', *American Sociological Review,* 54: 873–90.

Jarausch, Konrad and Hardy, Kenneth (1991) *Quantitative Methods for Historians: A Guide to Research, Data, and Statistics.* Chapel Hill: University of North Carolina Press.

King, Gary (1997) *A Solution to the Ecological Inference Problem: Reconstructing Individual Behavior from Aggregate Data.* Princeton, NJ.: Princeton University Press.

Kousser, J. Morgan (1973) 'Ecological regression and the analysis of past politics', *The Journal of Interdisciplinary History,* 4 (2): 237–62.

———(1974) *The Shaping of Southern Politics: Suffrage Restriction and the Establishment of the One-party South, 1880–1910.* New Haven: Yale University Press.

——— (1984) 'The revivalism of narrative: A response to recent criticisms of quantitative history', *Social Science History,* 8 (2): 133–49.

——— (1986) 'Must historians regress?' *Historical Methods* 19 (2): 62–81.

———(1989) 'The state of social science history in the late 1980s', *Historical Methods,* 22: 13–20.

———(2001a) 'Evaluating ecological inference: An introduction', *Historical Methods,* 34 (3): 100.

——— (2001b) 'Ecological inference from Goodman to King', *Historical Methods,* 34 (3): 101–26.

Knowles, Anne Kelly (2006) 'GIS and history', Paper presented at the Annual Meeting of the American Historical Association, Philadelphia.

Lemisch, Jesse (1967) 'The American Revolution seen from the bottom up', in Barton Bernstein (ed.), *Towards a New Past: Dissenting Essays in American History.* New York: Vintage Books, pp. 3–45.

Lewis, Jeffrey B. (2001) 'Understanding King's ecological inference model: A method-of-moments approach', *Historical Methods* 34 (4): 170–88.

Lorwin, Val and Price, Jacob (1972) *The Dimensions of the Past: Materials, Problems, and Opportunities for Quantitative Work in History.* New Haven: Yale University Press.

McCormick, Richard P. (1966) *The Second American Party System; Party Formation in the Jacksonian Era.* Chapel Hill: University of North Carolina Press.

McDonald, Terrence (1986) *The Parameters of Urban Fiscal Policy: Socioeconomic Change and Political Culture in San Francisco, 1860–1906.* Berkeley: University of California Press.

Meyer, John R. (1997) 'Notes on cliometrics' fortieth', *The American Economic Review,* 87 (2): 409–11.

Monkkonen, Eric (2001) *Murder in New York City.* Berkeley: University of California Press.

Neustadt, Richard E. and May, Ernest R. (1986) *Thinking in Time: The Uses of History for Decision Makers.* New York: Free Press.

Moretti, Franco (2005) *Graphs, Maps, Trees: Abstract Models for a Literary History.* New York: Verso.

North, Douglass C. (1997) 'Cliometrics – 40 years later', *The American Economic Review,* 87 (2): 412–14.

Palmquist, Bradley (2001) 'Unlocking the aggregate data past – Which keys fit?' *Historical Methods,* 34 (4): 159–69.

Redding, Kent and James, David R. (2001) 'Estimating levels and modeling determinants of Black and White voter turnout in the South, 1880 to 1912', *Historical Methods* 34 (4): 141–58.

Reher, David Sven and Scholfield, Roger S. (eds) *Old and New Methods in Historical Demography.* Oxford: Oxford University Press.

Reiff, Janice (1991) *Structuring the Past: The Use of Computers in History.* Washington, DC: American Historical Association.

Reynolds, John F. (1998) 'Do historians count anymore', *Historical Methods,* 31 (4): 141–8.

Rowney, Don Karl and Graham, James Q. Jr. (eds) (1969) *Quantitative History: Selected Readings in the Quantitative Analysis of Historical Data.* Homewood, Ill.: Dorsey Press.

Shammas, Carole (1990) *The Pre-industrial Consumer in England and America.* Oxford: Clarendon Press.

Shammas, Carole, Salmon, Marylynn and Dahlin, Michel (1987) *Inheritance in America from Colonial Times to the Present.* New Brunswick, NJ: Rutgers University Press.

Shorter, Edward (1971) *The Historian and the Computer: A Practical Guide.* Englewood Cliffs, NJ: Prentice Hall.

Shreibman, Susan, Siemens, Ray and Unsworth, John (2004) *A Companion to Digital Humanities.* Malden, MA: Blackwell Publishing.

Silbey, Joel, Bogue, Allan and Flanigan, William (eds) (1978) *The History of American Electoral Behavior.* Princeton: Princeton University Press.

Smith, Dan Scott (1984) 'A mean and random past: The implications of variance for history', *Historical Methods,* 17: 14– 48.

——— (1992) 'Context, time, history', in Peter Karsten and John Modell (eds), *Theory, Method, and Practice in Social and Cultural History.* New York: New York University Press, pp. 13–32.

Steckel, Richard (2007) 'Big Social Science History', *Social Science History,* 31: 1–34.

Steckel, Richard H. and Floud, Roderick (eds) (1997) *Health and Welfare During Industrialization.* Chicago, IL: University of Chicago Press.

Steckel, Richard and Rose, Jerome (eds) (2002) *The Backbone of History: Health and Nutrition in the Western Hemisphere.* New York: Cambridge University Press.

Stone, Lawrence (1977) 'History and the social sciences in the twentieth century', in C. Delzell (ed.), *The Future of History.* Nashville: Vanderbilt University Press. pp. 3–42.

———— (1979) 'The revival of narrative: Reflections on a new old history', *Past and Present,* 89: 3–24.

Swierenga, Robert (ed.) (1970) *Quantification in American History: Theory and Research.* New York: Atheneum.

Tolnay, Stewart E. and Beck, E.M. (1995) *A Festival of Violence: An Analysis of the Lynching of African-Americans in the American South, 1882–1930.* Urbana: University of Illinois Press.

Turner, Frederick Jackson (1893) 'The Significance of the Frontier in American History', *Annual Report of the American Historical Association:* 199–227.

Whaples, Robert (1991) 'A quantitative history of the *Journal of Economic History* and the cliometric revolution', *Journal of Economic History,* 51 (2): 289–301.

NOTES

1 See, for example, Benson (1957; 1961); Burnham (1970); Chambers and Burnham (1967); Richard P. McCormick (1966).

2 For information on the Cambridge Group, see their website, http://www-hpss.geog.cam.ac.uk.

3 See also Kousser (1989) and Reynolds (1998).

4 See for example, Darcy and Rohrs (1995); Dollar and Jensen (1971); Feinstein and Thomas (2002); Floud (1972); Haskins and Jeffrey (1990); Hudson (2000); Jarausch and Hardy (1991); Shorter (1971).

5 See, for example, Aydelotte et al. (1972); Lorwin and Price (1972); Rowney and Graham (1969); Silbey et al. (1978); Swierenga (1970).

6 See the website for the UK Data Archive at http://www.data-archive.ac.uk for the background on the 40th anniversary in 2007.

7 See, for example, Floud et al. (1990); Monkkonen (2001); Shammas et al. (1987); Shammas (1990); Steckel and Floud (1997); Steckel and Rose (2002).

8 The schedule in Table 14.1 is available on the IPUMS website at http://www.ipums.umn.edu/usa/voliii/form1950.html.

9 The United States maintains census schedules as confidential records for 72 years. The 1890 Census manuscript schedules were destroyed by fire in 1921.

10 See the special issues of *Historical Methods* (Hacker and Fitch 2003a; 2003b) on 'Building Historical Data Infrastructure: New Projects of the Minnesota Population Center' and the website of IPUMS at www.ipums.org for details.

11 Nattional Archives and Records Administration, 'Inside the National Archives – Southeast Region, 1825-1863 Slave Sale Documents'. Available at: http://www.archives.gov/southeast/exhibit/2.php.

Transcription of Slave Sale Document in Figure 14.3

Know all men by these presents, That I, Albert G. Ewing, of the county of Davidson and state of Tennessee have this day for and in consideration of five hundred dollars, to me in hand paid by Joseph Woods and John Stacker, Trustees for Samuel Vanleer, his wife and chldren, under the will of Bernard Vanleer, now recorded in the office of the Davidson county court, state of Tennessee, bargained and sold unto said Trustees, a certain negro boy name George aged about seventeen years; which said slave I warrant to be sound and healthy; and I also will warrant the right and title of said slave, unto said Trustees, their heirs, executors, &c. &c. and that said negro boy George is a slave for life.

Witness my hand and seal, this Sixth day of November 1833.

A.G. Ewing

Frederick Bradford
Orville Erving
Nov. 6. 1833.

12 For other examples of slave sale documents, see the Slave Documents Collection from the Enoch Pratt Free Library, Baltimore, Maryland, available at http://www.pratt.lib.md.us/exhibits/slavery/

13 The data set and code-book are available at: http://www.icpsr.umich.edu/cocoon/ICPSR-STUDY/07423.xml.

14 See, for example, Kousser (1973, 1974). For recent methodological developments in the field and their impact in history, see King (1997), and the articles in the Summer and Fall 2001 (34 (3 & 4)) issues of *Historical Methods* on the time period by: Kousser (2001a, 2001b); Bourke et al. (2001); Redding and James (2001); Palmquist (2001); and Lewis (2001).

15 See Abbott (2001); Abbott and Tsay (2000); Alter and Gutmann (1999); Alter (1988), Gutmann and Alter (1993); Griffin (1993); Griffin and Isaac (1992); Isaac and Griffin (1989); Reher and Schofield (1993). On time series, see also McDonald (1986). On quantification and historical explanation, see Smith (1984; 1992).

16 For the results of this research, see Fogel (2004); Fogel and Costa (1997).

17 For discussion of Benson's change in position and critiques of the change, see Bogue (1986; 1990) and Kousser (1986). See also Fogel and Elton (1983); Kousser (1984); Fitch (1986); and Fogel (2003).

18 For a hilarious parody of the issues involved, see the Winter 2001 issue of *Social Science History.* Outgoing editors Paula Baker and Elizabeth Faue

published reviews by Darcy Chopwhittle and Lars Mooson Taleglad of Philinda Blank's (2001) *When the Cows Come Home: Barn Architecture and Changes in Bovine Public Space* (2001). (The reviewed book does not exist, though perhaps it might. Many people contributed to the review; Paula Baker and Elizabeth Faue take responsibility for it.)

19 On anthropometric history, for example, see the Summer 2004 Special Issue of *Social Science History*, Volume 28, no. 2, guest edited by John Komlos and Jorg Baten. For the impact of the IPUMS project, see the bibliography of work listed on the IPUMS website, http://www.ipums.org. For recent evaluations of 'social science history' as a field, see Graff et al. (2005).

20 For retrospectives on quantitative history, see Reynolds (1998). For retrospective analysis of 'cliometrics', see the special section of the 'Papers and Proceedings of the Hundred and Fourth Annual Meeting of the American Economic Association' in *The American Economic Review* (1997), 87 (2), on 'Cliometrics After 40 Years'. Papers in this section include Goldin (1997); Greif (1997); Heckman (1997); Meyer (1997); and North (1997). See also Whaples (1991).

21 See, for example, Burton (2002); Cameron and Richardson (2005); Harvey and Press (1996); Reiff (1991); Shreibman et al. (2004).

22 Steckel listed the large data projects social science historians have produced in the last generation and then added his own wish list: including an inventory of all archeological sites; an inventory of all artifacts at these sites; a database on natural disasters and human history; and an international catalogue of films and photos. He called for extending the digitization of all extant manuscript censuses in the past; a digitized and annotated collection of diaries; voting records at the precinct level; and probate records.

Rationality, Complexity, Collectivity

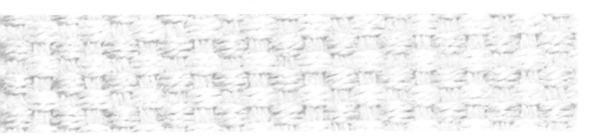

Introduction

William Outhwaite

Rational action and rational choice approaches are central to much economic theory, but they also have a long-standing and prominent place in the other social sciences. The beginnings of the social sciences in the seventeenth and eighteenth centuries coincide with rationalism in philosophy and politics, and critiques of political rationalism have also been linked to the rise of sociology in the late nineteenth century. Conceptions of the rationality or irrationality of human beings have been central to, for example, economics and mass society theory. Approaches of the former kind have come together with game theory and decision theory into a cluster of approaches generally known as rational choice or rational action theory, particularly well represented not just in economics and its extension to other areas of social life but also in the disciplines of politics and international relations.

As with many of the broader methodological approaches discussed in this volume, some advocates would suggest that they are all we need, while others see them as having a more limited role, along with other approaches to, say, the study of social movements. As Jürgen Habermas ([1981] 1984: xl) noted, rationality issues arise for sociology (and, he might have added, for the other social sciences) at a number of different levels,

notably 'the metatheoretical question of the rationality assumptions of its guiding concepts of action [and] the methodological question concerning the rationality implications of gaining access to its object through the understanding of meaning ...'

These interrelations are brought out here in the relation between the two complementary chapters explicitly devoted to rational action approaches, in which David Henderson surveys the philosophical bases and Donald Green and Justin Fox discuss a number of examples of its use in economics and the other social sciences. A further element of context is provided by the chapter by Thomas Schwinn; all three relate in turn to Bert Kögler's chapter on interpretation and understanding (in Section V).

Sociologies of action have long been opposed to sociologies of system or those making major use of the category of society. Alain Touraine and others in the last decades of the twentieth century have argued for a conception that moves from individual and collective practice to what Touraine (1973) calls the production of society. In Marxism too, praxis-oriented approaches conflict with more structural ones, and rational choice Marxism tries to restate classical themes in an individualistic frame of reference. Schwinn, the author of an influential book on action theory (Schwinn, 2001), compares the various ways in which the concept of agency has been handled in contemporary social science. As discussed by Keith Sawyer, theories of complexity and differentiation were central to early evolutionary sociology, and have remained so in modern evolutionary social science and in all the many varieties of system theory. Finally, Maureen O'Malley offers a comprehensive overview of evolutionary thought in the social sciences, from its beginnings in the nineteenth century to the current revival of selectionist approaches.

REFERENCES AND SELECT BIBLIOGRAPHY

Habermas, Jürgen (1981) *Theorie des kommunidativen Handelns*. Frankfurt: Suhrkamp.
——— (1984) *Theory of Communicative Action, vol 1: Reason and the Rationalization of Society*, trans. Thomas McCarthy. Boston: Beacon Press.
Schwinn, Thomas (2001) *Differenzierung ohne Gesellschaft. Umstellung eines soziologischen Konzepts*. Weilerswist: Velbrück Wissenschaft.
Touraine, Alan (1973) *Production de la société*. Paris: Seuil.

15

Rational Choice Theory

Donald P. Green and Justin Fox

Rational choice theories are predicated on the notion that individual actors pursue their goals efficiently. These individuals may have a great deal of information or none at all, but based on their understanding of the alternatives before them, they select the course of action that promises to deliver the greatest net benefits.

The nature of these benefits varies from one rational choice theory to the next. Sometimes individuals are said to seek money or re-election, but the ends that they pursue need not be self-serving in nature (cf. Becker, 1976; Downs, 1957; Olson, 1965; Schelling, 1960). Although rational choice theories tend to assume selfish goals, nothing in rational choice theory precludes the theorist from stipulating tastes for altruism or, for that matter, self-destruction (Margolis, 1982). If a man desires to hang himself, rationality merely dictates that he follow what he believes to be an efficient route to the nearest cord of rope. The defining characteristic of rational choice theory is not what it assumes about human objectives but rather the notion that individuals pursue their aims efficiently.

Although rational choice theories need not be confined to the domain of selfish motives, it is nevertheless true that many such theories assume that individuals seek money, power and (occasionally) prestige. In part, these assumptions about core motives reflect the intellectual origins of this type of scholarship. Microeconomists have played a dominant role in developing both the technical and substantive aspects of rational choice theory, and the most compelling accounts of strategic profit-minded behavior are those involving economic markets.

Another reason has to do with the broader theoretical objective of eliminating logical inconsistencies in accounts of human behavior. If a microeconomic theory of the firm assumes that business owners seek to maximize profits, it would be peculiar if theories about how business owners manage their home finances did not make similar assumptions. Some of the most arresting examples of rational choice theorizing attempt to model behaviors such as marriage proposals or street crime as though they were conventional market transactions (Becker, 1976; Posner, 1985). In recent decades, microeconomic perspectives have spread rapidly to neighboring disciplines as theorists have attempted to impute a consistent set of motives to individuals negotiating their economic, social and political environments (Radnitzky and Bernholz, 1987).

Just as rational choice theories vary widely in terms of what they assume about actors' goals, they also vary in what they assume about actors' cognitive capacities. At one end of the spectrum are models that assume actors can reason through a welter of differential equations. At the other end are evolutionary models that envision a process of natural selection whereby the actors who survive are those who happen to play a game in a particular way (Axelrod, 1984). The former requires enormous logical powers; the latter might characterize the behavior of a person or an invertebrate (McFarland and Bosser, 1993). Somewhere in between are models that merely assume that people have sufficient cognitive power to play intuitively 'as if' guided by mathematical calculations. For example, models of rational evaluations of political leaders sometimes assume that voters process information rationally, as if applying Bayes's rule when updating their prior beliefs in light of new information (Achen, 1992; Gerber and Green, 1998, 1999). Few voters are aware of the existence of Bayes's rule or the mathematics that one would use to apply it to current events, but voters' intuitions arguably enable them to arrive at the same conclusions as a formal Bayesian analysis.

A related issue concerns strategic foresight. Decision-theoretic models are those that assume actors consider only the immediate choice before them, without regard to the fact that other actors may be facing similar choices. In effect, the behavior of other actors is assumed. Game theoretic models, on the other hand, presuppose that actors contemplate the strategic behavior of all of the other actors in the system.

NASH EQUILIBRIA

The preceding discussion has emphasized the wide variety of models that fall under the umbrella of rational choice theory. Despite the heterogeneity of the substantive assumptions that go into these models, the analytic tools used in these theories are generally quite similar. Central to rational choice theory and foreign to many other forms of political theorizing is the concept of equilibrium. Many different kinds of equilibrium concepts have been proposed (see Myerson, 1991), but the most important among them is the idea of Nash equilibria. The strategic game presented by a marketplace or political institution is said to be in equilibrium if none of the individual actors has an incentive to change his or her behavior unilaterally. If, for example, the actors in question were political parties and their objective were to win elections, their political platforms would be in equilibrium if no political party could increase its chances of winning the election by altering its platform. An equilibrium result is an analytic fact proved formally based on a characterization of the options available to the actors and their preferences over these options.

Rational choice theory is in large part an attempt to discern the conditions under which equilibria exist in political, economic and social systems, and to describe the nature of such equilibria. These equilibrium results have both theoretical and conceptual implications. From a conceptual (and often normative) standpoint, equilibrium results often serve to illustrate interesting conundrums in human behavior. For example, the famous prisoners' dilemma involves a pair of actors who are each confronted with two options (cooperate or defect) and a schedule of rewards. If both players cooperate, they both receive some moderate-sized reward. If both players defect, they receive nothing. And if one defects while the other cooperates, the defector receives a large payoff while the cooperator suffers a loss. From the standpoint of each actor, defection is preferable to cooperation, regardless of what the opponent chooses to do. (If the opponent cooperates, one is better off defecting; if the opponent defects, one is still better off defecting than cooperating.) This logic impels both players to defect, resulting in a social outcome, mutual defection, which is worse for both players than mutual cooperation (Hardin, 1982).

This equilibrium result is one of several that call attention to the tension between individual rationality and social welfare, a prominent theme among rational choice theories. Analytic results of this kind have had enormous impact on the way in which social scientists think about 'public goods', that is, goods that one is entitled to consume regardless of whether one contributes to their upkeep. When a large number of individuals pursue common objectives (e.g., voters seeking to elect their preferred candidate) and any single individual's actions have little consequence for the aggregate outcome (one vote is unlikely to be decisive), these individuals will tend to 'free-ride' (Olson, 1965). Voters will stay home rather than incur the costs of voting because they can enjoy the benefits of the electoral outcome regardless of whether they participate. Only when these collective actors are offered 'selective incentives' (side payments to participate or punishments for non-participation) can collective action problems be overcome.

Collective action problems represent one of the most intensively investigated subjects of rational choice scholarship. The central contention is that wherever there are public goods—national security, an informed citizenry—there will be a tendency for individuals to fob the costs onto others while enjoying the benefits. In international affairs, for example, collective action problems are said to arise in the maintenance of multilateral agreements, the exploitation of natural resources, and balance of power between large numbers of diffuse actors and small numbers of actors with concentrated political and economic power. Rational choice theory sets itself the task of identifying these underlying problems and the institutional mechanisms by which they are or could be held in check.

Equilibrium results also serve to inspire empirical research by predicting the outcome of rational play. An extensive body of research, much of it conducted under laboratory conditions, examines whether various equilibrium predictions hold (Camerer, 2003; Roth, 1988). These studies typically confront players with a set of options and a schedule of financial payoffs that depend on how they and others behave. Some studies examine the frequency with which the equilibrium predictions suggested by a theoretical model occur in practice. Other studies examine the 'comparative statics' implied by the model, that is, the manner in which the equilibrium changes as the conditions of the game change. For example, to what extent do individuals increase their contributions to public goods when everyone is given the opportunity to sanction others for shirking? Some of the most interesting comparative statics predictions are those that lay out a null hypothesis. For example, to what extent do players become more likely to cooperate when they are given the opportunity to communicate informally with their anonymous opponents in advance of playing a prisoners' dilemma? So long as communication cannot result in binding commitments or side payments, communication is predicted to have no effect on players' propensity to cooperate in a one-shot prisoners' dilemma. Interestingly, communication between subjects generally increases rates of cooperation in experimental prisoners' dilemmas (Dawes and Thaler, 1988).

The disjuncture between theory and experimental data raises an interesting issue. Equilibrium results are analytic facts. In the same way that one cannot test the Pythagorean theorem by measuring the legs of triangles, one cannot disprove an equilibrium result by finding it wanting in a laboratory setting. If the deduction fails to predict an empirical result, one may infer either that the experiment did not approximate the preferences and choice options assumed by the deductive proof or that the players did not pursue optimal strategies due to some cognitive mistake. In the former case, the data are impeached; in the latter, the theory. In an effort to minimize the former interpretation, experimentalists strive mightily to confirm that their subjects understand the games that they are playing. But the level of understanding that they require is comprehension of the rules; experiments do not necessarily induce subjects to disregard extraneous considerations that are inconsistent with the preference schedule that the experimental payoffs attempt to induce. To some extent, these extraneous factors recede in significance as the financial stakes of a game increase, but even then one sees departures from putatively rational strategies. Are the players misunderstanding how best to play the games, or are they motivated by factors outside the purview of the model?

The scientific allure of rational choice theory is its capacity to accumulate equilibrium results within a unified deductive framework. Assumptions about individual preferences, information, institutional incentives, sequencing of decisions and the like may vary from model to model, but the explicit, formal character of these models makes it possible to retrace the steps of the theorist and examine the significance of any particular modeling assumption. Not all rational choice theories are formal in presentation, but it is generally presumed that a 'soft' rational choice theory's conjectures about equilibrium behavior are rooted in some underlying deductive exercise. After all, if the conjectures of a rational choice theory were discovered to be logically incoherent, they would no longer form the basis for a proper characterization of rational behavior.

SIGNALING, REPEATED PLAY AND COMPLEXITY

Evidence of this accumulation is apparent from models of rational behavior, which have grown increasingly sophisticated since their introduction into political science in the mid-twentieth century. One of the most important developments concerns the role of information. Recent decades have witnessed an explosive growth in the use of models in which the actors' behavior 'signals' something about their hidden preferences or resources (Harsanyi, 1986). Players in such games consider not only the immediate consequences of their actions but also what their actions reveal about their private attributes.

The literature on international crises, for example, has been influenced greatly by rational choice theories about signaling and decision making under conditions of uncertainty (Fearon, 1994). Each country has private information about its own capabilities and objectives. The actions they take in the international arena reveal something about their aims and resolve. In equilibrium, countries distill all the information they can from the murky signals given by other countries, placing special emphasis on signals that are costly for the sender to convey.

Among the most thought-provoking variants of signaling games are those in which an actor's hidden characteristic is his rationality. Consider, for example, a game that is sometimes characterized as a way to gauge social trust (Berg et al., 1995). Two players are asked, in effect, to hold a sum of money for one another. The sum of money triples (thanks to the experimenter's generosity) as long as it moves from the possession of one player to another. When it stops moving, the owning player gets it all, and the opposing player gets nothing. If the game is played a finite number of rounds (say 10), then backward induction suggests that the game should unravel. No rational player in round nine would conclude the game by passing the money to his opponent. Knowing that one's opponent would never pass in round nine, a player would never pass in round eight. And so on, suggesting that no rational player would pass in round one. But suppose that one's opponent *does* pass in round one. This unexpected behavior may signal that there is some probability that the opponent is irrational or confused. If so, there may be some basis for you to pass the growing sum of money back to your opponent, which in turn calls into question *your* rationality.

Another important line of theoretical development concerns repeated play. Imagine a prisoners' dilemma game in which the players are forced to repeat the game every day for the rest of their lives. Although a single game has a clear equilibrium—defection—repeated games such as this one open up an array of possible equilibria. The

Folk Theorem (so named because many theorists formulated it at about the same time) points out that mutual cooperation can be an equilibrium in prisoners' dilemma 'supergames', so long as one player is willing to punish the other for defection and patiently wait for her to come around to cooperative play (Fudenberg and Tirole, 1991). Unfortunately for those hoping to make precise predictions to this effect, a host of equilibria are possible in such games, which renders the empirical implications of this line of theoretical development unclear. (This indeterminacy has fueled scholarly interest in 'focal points'—shared understandings or rules of thumb that allow players to make educated guesses about what others will do amid multiple equilibria. See Harsanyi and Selten, 1988.) In contrast to the dour predictions of the one-shot prisoners' dilemma about the tendency for rational individuals to dig themselves into a hole, the repeated-play perspective leaves open the possibility that rational play might lead to cooperation and, more generally, the development of pro-social norms.

A rather different type of theoretical indeterminacy arises when strategic situations are so complex that they become analytically intractable. It is no accident that game theories have little to say about venerable games such as chess, go or backgammon; the equilibria for such games lie beyond the range of what can be derived from an analysis of the rules (cf. Berlekamp et al., 2001). Indeed, it is the very lack of knowledge about optimal strategies and the equilibria that flow from them that makes these games interesting to play. Theoretically intractable games present a number of fascinating challenges to rational choice theorizing. Even a casual observer of chess matches can see that some players routinely prevail over their opponents, regardless of whether they move first or second. Moving first or second is actually a rather poor predictor of chess outcomes; much more important are the relative ratings of the two players. In other words, given the extraordinary depth of the game of chess, its underlying equilibrium (white always wins?)

is of little empirical value. The larger point here is that asymmetries of skill among the players can wreak havoc with equilibrium predictions (Green and Shapiro, 1994: Chapter 6). Granted, players may be pursuing what they believe to be optimal strategies and thus behaving rationally, but rarely do rational choice models allow for the possibility that the players possess different degrees of foresight.

The problem of analytic intractability arises as theorists attempt to model complex institutional settings involving many different actors and rounds of strategic interaction. Although one of the hallmarks of rational choice theory is methodological individualism, for the sake of analytic simplicity, states, parties, and other corporate entities are often assumed to be unitary actors with a coherent schedule of preferences over a fairly limited set of available options. By making the game more tractable, these models sidestep the issue of asymmetries of skill as well as the broader question of whether one or more equilibria exist in the actual setting that inspires the model. It is one thing to make an analytic claim about a given model and quite another to contend that this claim applies to a real-world setting, the features of which may depart markedly from the model.

Although rational choice theories are often prefaced with spirited defenses of simplification, the trajectory of rational choice theories over time suggests some ambivalence about the merits of abstraction versus verisimilitude. Pulling against the tendency to simplify for the sake of analytic tractability is the constant drive to specify the underlying micro-foundations, that is, the strategic behavior of individuals who comprise corporate entities such as states, parties or firms. This concern with micro-foundations is especially pressing when individuals express their preferences through institutional mechanisms such as elections. Kenneth Arrow (1951) pointed out early on that even when individuals have well-ordered preferences over outcomes, majority rule may give rise to collective choices that are unstable and self-contradictory.

Subsequent scholars, notably William Riker, have argued that this problem is endemic to voting systems and that the inherent instability of legislative and popular decisions makes them susceptible to manipulation by clever agenda-setters (Riker, 1980, 1986). Many scholars focus their attention on the normative implications of 'preference aggregation' in democratic systems, an endeavor that lies at the heart of the field known as Public Choice (Mueller, 2003). Scholars working at this nexus of empirical and normative concerns often seek to identify voting rules, parliamentary procedures, and counterbalancing institutions that alleviate these perverse features of democracy.

ILLUSTRATIVE APPLICATIONS

In this section, we describe two recent modeling applications. The first demonstrates how formal models of rational choice have been employed to address empirical puzzles. The second illustrates how models have been employed to understand the systemic effects of alternative constitutional arrangements.

How do campaign contributions affect legislators' behavior? The conventional wisdom is that interest group campaign resources bias the decisions of lawmakers. Like most journalists, most scholars of campaign finance have assumed that these distortions were the result of quid pro quo exchanges between various interest groups and various politicians. However, two empirical regularities seem to contradict this assumption: First, in recent years, few United States federal office holders have been indicted on charges of corruption. Second, the overwhelming majority of empirical research (cf. Ansolabehere et al., 2003) examining the relationship between campaign donations and roll-call voting in Congress finds that those incumbents receiving interest group campaign donations are no more likely to support policies preferred by their campaign donors than those incumbents not receiving such donations.

A recent formal model of lawmaking and elections offers one resolution to this empirical puzzle (Fox, 2005). The model examines incumbent policy-making in the presence of a contributor. This interest group employs its resources solely to aid the electoral prospects of those politicians believed to share its policy commitments. (Examples of such contributors in the United States are the Club for Growth—an interest group committed to supply-side economic policies, and Emily's List—an interest group committed to backing pro-choice female candidates.) The main finding of the model is that an interest group that uses its resources solely to influence election outcomes can nonetheless influence incumbent policy choices.

The key assumption of the model is that the interest group is uncertain of the incumbent's policy preferences. Consequently, the interest group draws inferences about the incumbent's policy preferences based upon her policy choice, believing that those incumbents who select its preferred policy are more likely to share its goals than those who do not. As the interest group is more likely to bankroll the campaign of a challenger to the incumbent when the group believes that the incumbent does not share its policy aims, incumbents whose policy preferences diverge from the interest group's have a strong electoral incentive to mask this fact. The way they do this is by selecting the interest group's preferred policy. In other words, the fear that the interest group will finance a challenger more sympathetic to its policy aims leads those incumbents who do not share the group's policy ends to pursue policies which result in the interest group believing otherwise. Thus, even in a world in which incumbents are never bribed by interest groups, this application suggests that stricter campaign contribution limits could significantly affect incumbent policy choices.

These conclusions can be derived from a formal model that is mathematically rather sparse and therefore useful for illustrative purposes. As in all formal models, it includes three main ingredients: assumptions about timing, assumptions about the preferences of the model's actors, and assumptions about what each actor knows about the others' preferences. It is from these assumptions that one can deductively derive the above story about how an interest group motivated purely by influencing election outcomes can nonetheless influence the policy choice an incumbent makes. To get a sense of how the model is constructed, we describe below the mathematical formalization of each of the model's main features.

We begin with the model's timing. There are two periods. In each of the two periods, one of two policies is selected: either policy x or policy y. An existing incumbent (i) selects policy in the first period. In between periods an election is held between the incumbent and her challenger (c). An interest group (g) finances the campaign spending of each politician.

The incumbent's probability of re-election increases along with a rise in the size of the donation she receives from the interest group, and decreases along with a rise in the size of the donation her challenger receives. Formally, let d_i denote the interest group's donation to the incumbent, and let d_c denote the interest group's donation to the challenger. The incumbent's probability of re-election is given by a function $r (d_i, d_c)$, where r is increasing in d_i and decreasing in d_c. The interest group determines how much to give after the first-period policy is selected.

We now turn to specifying the payoffs of the model's actors. All actors in the model care about policy outcomes, receiving a payoff of zero whenever y is selected and receiving a payoff of t whenever x is selected. Thus, an agent for whom $t > 0$ prefers policy x to policy y. And, an agent for whom $t < 0$ prefers policy y to policy x. Consequently, t characterizes an agent's policy preferences, and is henceforth referred to as a politician's *type*.

In addition to caring about policy outcomes, the interest group cares about the cost of its campaign outlays. That is, for every dollar the interest group spends on influencing the election outcome, the interest group forgoes spending that dollar for some other purpose that could further the group's ends. To capture these preferences, the interest group's payoff to the game is specified as the sum of its policy payoffs minus the cost of its outlays. Thus, if policy x is chosen in each period, $d_i > 0$ and $d_c = 0$, the interest group's payoff to the game is $2t_g - d_i$, whereas if y is chosen in each period, $d_i = 0$ and $d_c > 0$, the interest group's payoff to the game is $- d_c$.

As for the incumbent, in addition to caring about policy outcomes, she also cares about holding on to power. Formally, in the event the incumbent is re-elected, she receives a benefit of $\rho > 0$. Thus, if policy x is chosen in each period and the incumbent is re-elected, her payoff to the game is $2t_g + \rho$, whereas if x is selected in each period and the incumbent is defeated, her payoff to the game is $2t_g$.

Finally, we address the assumptions made about what each actor knows about the other's policy preferences. The interest group's policy preference is known by both the incumbent and the challenger. For the purpose of this example, we assume that the interest group prefers policy x. However, as mentioned earlier, the interest group does not know either the incumbent's or the challenger's policy preference. This is formalized by assuming that the interest group does not know either the incumbent's or the challenger's type. In other words, the interest group places positive probability on the event that the incumbent's type is positive and positive probability on the event that the incumbent's type is negative.

The above model constitutes an extensive form game of incomplete information (the incomplete information being the interest group's uncertainty about the incumbent's policy preference). To solve it, a solution concept in the modeling literature known as Perfect Bayesian Equilibrium is applied. The essence of this solution concept is that at each point in time one of the model's actors selects the action that maximizes her expected payoff to the game.

As the game ends after the second period policy is chosen, the election winner maximizes her expected payoff by selecting her preferred policy (in the second period). Consequently, the interest group is better off when the election winner shares its policy preferences than when the election winner does not. As such, the intensity of the interest group's support for the incumbent (challenger) is increasing (decreasing) in its belief that the incumbent shares its preference for policy x. This implies that the incumbent's re-election prospects are increasing in the interest group's belief that the two share the same policy goals. Therefore, those incumbents who do not share the interest group's preference for policy x (that is, those incumbents for whom $t_i < 0$) have an incentive to lead the interest group to believe that they actually do. In an equilibrium, this is accomplished by selecting the interest group's preferred policy—policy x—in the first period. Consequently, those incumbents who prefer policy y, but place little weight on policy goals relative to re-election goals ($-t_i < \rho$), select x in period one, whereas in the absence of the interest group, they would select y.

We now turn to a second application, which illustrates how formal models have been employed to understand the benefits and costs of alternative democratic institutional arrangements. Specifically, Maskin and Tirole (2004) ask: Under what conditions should the public subject office-holders to elections? Alternatives to doing so include limiting office holders to a single term or providing office holders with lifetime appointments, as is the case for some judges.

Similar to the interest group in Fox's model, the electorate in Maskin and Tirole's model draws inferences regarding a politician's policy preferences based upon her policy choices. As such, elections provide the public with the opportunity to remove those office holders whose actions suggest that their preferences are divergent. Consequently, the threat of removal provided by elections generates incentives for those politicians who do not share the public's preferences to nonetheless act as if they did. Such incentives, which are absent when office holders are not held electorally accountable, would seem to make subjecting office holders to elections a more desirable institutional arrangement than not doing so.

However, Maskin and Tirole add an extra wrinkle to their framework: they assume that politicians have better information regarding the effects of policies than the public. Thus, the possibility arises that the policy that maximizes a politician's probability of re-election does not coincide with the policy which is in the public's interest. Thus, Maskin and Tirole's model, in addition to capturing the potential benefits of electoral accountability, also captures a potential cost: incumbents who share the public's policy preferences, and would therefore act in public's interest in the absence of such accountability, wind up instead pandering to public opinion to avoid having the electorate draw unfavorable inferences regarding their respective policy commitments.

Within this framework, subjecting office holders to elections dominates not doing so when the risk that office holders do not share the public's policy preferences is high (as might be the case in societies where corruption is rampant), and the likelihood that those policies which are politically popular are in fact in the electorate's interest is high (as might be the case on moral issues). Consequently, Maskin and Tirole's model provides a simple heuristic to guide one in carefully analyzing the types of collective decisions which should be delegated to unaccountable officials (such as judges and bureaucrats) as opposed to elected officials.

EMPIRICAL ADEQUACY

The scientific enterprise of rational choice theory is best described as a process of building from a sparse analytic foundation, adding embellishments and extensions in an effort to gauge how the equilibrium results change. Inevitably, however, even the most technically astute rational choice theorists are forced to simplify their representations of the world in order to make them analytically tractable. The empirical adequacy of the resulting theories is therefore an important concern.

Rational choice theories about particular subjects—auctions, legislators, social policies—are seldom advertised as providing a complete explanation of behavior within these realms. Instead, theories are typically defended on one or more of the following grounds. First, it is argued that all models simplify and that the function of simplification is to draw attention to the central causal mechanisms at work. For example, even if people do value public goods such as environmental protection, it could be argued that, consistent with theories about free-riding, the level of support falls far below what one would expect if people were forced to reveal their true tastes for environmentalism in a marketplace. Second, it is argued that rational choice models provide a baseline set of expectations about behavior; to the extent that people deviate from this baseline, the model has enabled us to discover new facets of the phenomenon in question. When elderly people are found to save their money at a vigorous rate, for example, the theorist who treats the lifetime income hypothesis as given discovers the bequest motive. Third, rational choice theories often make precise and therefore potentially instructive claims about specific causal parameters. These claims not only tell empirical researchers what to look for but theoretical results also help guide the way in which statistical models are specified. Some of the best examples of this type of interplay between theory and data occur in the realm of measurement, where spatial models have proven useful in gauging the ideological distances between parties and the legislators who comprise them. Fourth, rational choice models sometimes inspire proposals about how to structure institutions in order to produce certain types of outcomes. For example, a large literature has investigated the properties of various types of auctions in an effort to devise an institutional mechanism for encouraging participants to reveal the true value that they place on the good that is to be auctioned. Similarly, theorists have investigated a wide array of voting procedures in an

effort to come up with a system that both encourages voters to support their most-preferred candidate while at the same time diminishing the chances that a fringe candidate will win because candidates with more centrist policy positions divided each other's votes. To the extent that these ideas, when put into practice, affirm the empirical predictions of those who engineered them, rational choice theory may be credited with producing useful empirical insights.

Finally, and most controversially, comes the claim that rational choice theories have a strong record of predicting empirical regularities. However, both the record itself and the criterion of predictive accuracy are subject to dispute. With respect to the latter, predictive accuracy is a superficial and untrustworthy criterion by which to judge a model's success. Granted, no respectable theory would aspire to have a poor predictive record. But theorists are often inspired to propose models on the basis of known empirical regularities. That such models should comport with these regularities hardly counts as evidence for the strength of the deductive model. Indeed, it is difficult to imagine any outcome that could not be explained after the fact with reference to *some* set of strategic objectives. Although it is considered bad form among theorists to resort to explanations based on 'intrinsic' or 'expressive' goals, this move is often made for particularly knotty anomalies, such as mass participation in elections (Green and Shapiro, 1994: Chapters 4–5).

ROBUSTNESS

A more pertinent empirical criterion is whether the model stipulated for one application performs well when applied to an altogether different setting with similar strategic features. This logic, which is analogous to out-of-sample forecasting in statistics, helps explain why the successful development of new institutional arrangements is potentially so important; the novelty of these arrangements means that deduction, rather than observation, plays a crucial role. A second potential problem with predictive accuracy is that it often risks a version of the ecological fallacy. The typical prediction to flow from a rational choice theory is an aggregate outcome that follows from the micro-level assumptions of the model. For example, the aggregate prediction that a pair of competing political parties will converge to the median voter's ideal point rests on a micro-level model that specifies how voters arrayed along a one-dimensional ideological continuum vote for the most ideologically proximate party (Downs, 1957; Enelow and Hinich, 1990). Suppose it were true that in first-past-the-post electoral systems, political parties tended to converge to the center of the electorate. It is not clear whether this regularity is attributable to this particular mechanism. It may be that voters make decisions based on several dimensions, not one; or that the parties converge to the center for other reasons.

To take this example one step further, suppose one's theoretical model included two competing elements, a drive to the center in an effort to win over voters who sometimes vote based on non-ideological factors as well as a drive to the extremes in order to obtain the financial backing of ideologically driven campaign donors and the labor of ideologically motivated campaign volunteers. The model potentially predicts everything from convergence to the median voter to ideologically polarized parties, depending on the relative value of ideological appeal and money as means of generating votes. Now a wide array of potential outcomes is consistent with the model's logic, and with such a large target, a theory will scarcely fail to predict. Yet even in this situation the model's success in no way guarantees that it has identified the true causal mechanisms in play. The ideological location of the parties could conceivably reflect an altogether different mechanism, such as the policy convictions of the leading candidates.

The tendency for rational choice theories to become more nuanced over time often coincides with a more diffuse range of empirical predictions. Only a naïve or selective reading of the literature would lead one to infer that 'Rational Choice Theory predicts X' and that the theory's value hinges on whether X is empirically sustainable. A given rational choice theory might predict X today, but another may predict something else tomorrow. For good or ill, there may be nothing that some rational choice theory cannot predict. This point has special resonance for 'analytic narratives', which attempt to construct accounts of specific historical events in ways that are informed by rational choice models (Bates et al., 1998; Elster, 2000). It is difficult to think of an event that cannot be interpreted in a manner consistent with at least one rational choice model. This point holds not only for the handpicked examples that inspire analytic narratives but also for apparent anomalies. Miscalculations occur, and leaders embark on wars that devastate their own countries and result in their overthrow. Whether these miscalculations stem from the actors' rational reading of the available evidence, tastes for reckless action, or delusions of grandeur is a question that inevitably follows. A persistent methodological issue surrounds apparent disjunctures between theory and data: is the theoretical model wanting, or is the discrepancy between the theoretical prediction and actual observation the product of a momentary disequilibrium?

This point cuts both ways. Critics are often hasty in dismissing rational choice modeling on the grounds that specific rational choice models are empirically inadequate, and proponents are often selective in adducing what they take to be shining examples of successful modeling exercises. The latter point is of particular concern given the common scholarly motif, when advancing a rational choice model, of illustrating its operation by reference to a few supportive anecdotes. This type of casual empiricism runs afoul of basic methodological strictures regarding sampling and also creates the temptation to present the anecdotes in ways that exaggerate the support they lend to the model at hand.

ARE THE ASSUMPTIONS TRUE?

A more fundamental empirical critique of rational choice theory may be found in studies that call into question the micro-level assumptions on which rational choice models often rest. The field of behavioral economics, which draws on insights from social psychology, has generated a variety of interesting findings suggesting that people are quite sensitive to the manner in which choices are framed (Kahneman, 1984; 2003). It appears that the public's taste for risk varies depending on whether the prospect is one of loss or gain. The trail of findings inspired by Prospect Theory (Kahneman and Tversky, 1979) indicates that most people would rather receive $100 with certainty than receive a 50 percent chance of getting $200. On the other hand, most people would rather be confronted with a 50 percent chance of losing $200 than the certain loss of $100. This asymmetry exposes an intransitive preference schedule, since a given outcome can be described as a gain or loss. Rescue missions involving 1000 soldiers, 300 of which are likely to be killed, will be evaluated differently from rescue missions involving 1000 soldiers, 700 of which are likely to survive. Research in the area of behavioral economics emphasizes the contextual nature of preferences. People are much more likely to say they would drive across town in order to save $5 on a $50 consumer item than drive the same distance to save $5 on a $500 item. If one only intends to purchase one such item, the cost of driving across town should be worth either more or less than $5, regardless of the purchase price. In sum, research in behavioral economics cast doubt on the extent to which people make decisions in conformance with the axioms of probability, and possess stable, transitive preferences. The net effect is to undercut the notion, central to many rational choice theories, that individuals possess well-ordered utility functions that they maximize in logically coherent fashion.

The challenge posed by behavioral economics has met with a number of responses.

One is to dismiss the evidence of preference reversals and the like as measurement artifacts (Wittman, 1991). Most of the empirical results used to bolster Prospect Theory stem from questionnaires in which people are asked to express their preferences toward different options. Skeptics contend that these costless expressions of preference are not subject to the same caliber of reasoning that an actual economic decision would be. If preferences were in fact intransitive, why do we not see people exploited by repeated transactions in which they pay to undo their previous trades? A second type of response is that equilibrium results may still obtain even if only a portion of the individuals behave rationally. For example, consider two brands of soda. Suppose that half the consumers flip coins when deciding which brand to buy regardless of price, while the other half selects the lower priced option but flips coins when the prices are identical. Even though only the latter group is rational, its price-sensitive behavior nevertheless forces price competition between the two brands (but see Akerlof and Yellen, 1985).

Much the same arguments are advanced among students of politics. Few voters are inclined to learn about the policy positions of the competing candidates, but if the uninformed can take cues from the endorsements of the well informed, the electorate will behave as though it were ideologically astute (Lupia, 1994). A third reply is that however true the insights of behavioral economics may be, integrating them into the framework of traditional rational choice models makes them inelegant and analytically complex, as models strain to accommodate variations in the coherence of actors' aims and the sophistication with which they evaluate uncertain prospects in various situations. Prominent textbooks that attempt to teach the tools of game theory often say little about the challenges posed by behavioral approaches (see, for example, Myerson, 1991).

Quite apart from the specific empirical challenges it poses, behavioral economics invites scholars to reflect on some of the deeper questions posed by rational choice theory. Rational choice theory is simultaneously a normative and a predictive theory. It specifies how people should behave if they are to maximize their utility in a given choice situation. At the same time, it predicts that actors do behave as predicted. This dual role raises the question of whether the diffusion of the rational choice perspective creates something of a self-fulfilling prophesy. If enough people are taught that rational voters do not waste their time voting because election outcomes are public goods and that one's chances of swaying the election are negligible, one may create a collective action problem that did not formerly exist (Frank et al., 1993). Similarly, if society acts to eliminate public goods, such as open fisheries, on the grounds that rational actors will exploit and destroy them, one may extinguish the kinds of public-regarding norms and self-policing behavior that might otherwise substitute for these kinds of policy interventions.

At a more fundamental level, the inductive style of behavioral economics throws into relief the deductive structure of rational choice theory. In effect, the enterprise of developing rational choice theory is predicated on the view that deductive modeling is a more efficient path to knowledge than the accumulation of (possibly disjointed) empirical observations, be they descriptions of empirical regularities or estimates of causal parameters obtained through randomized experiments. Deductive modeling has the potential to direct inductive research toward interesting topics, assist the interpretation of the empirical results, and extrapolate these results to areas where only theory exists as a guide. On the other hand, deductive theorizing also has the potential to misdirect resources, encourage inaccurate interpretations of empirical findings, and generate mistaken extrapolations. It remains to be seen whether the intellectual resources that have been invested in this deductive theoretical project pay off. Although no competing social theories compare to rational choice theory in terms of range or sophistication, the question remains whether investments in theoretical advances, rather than improvements in measurement and estimation, will ultimately contribute more to the stock of knowledge about human behavior.

REFERENCES AND SELECT BIBLIOGRAPHY

Achen, Christopher (1992) 'Social psychology, demographic variables, and linear regression: Breaking the iron triangle in voting research', *Political Behavior*, 14: 195–211.

Akerlof, George and Yellen, Janet (1985) 'Can small deviations from rationality make significant differences to economic equilibria?', *American Economic Review*, 75 (4): 708–20.

Ansolabehere, Stephen, De Figueiredo, John M. and Snyder, James M. (2003) 'Why is there so little money in U.S. politics?', *Journal of Economic Perspectives*, 17 (1): 105–30.

Arrow, Kenneth J. (1951) *Social Choice and Individual Values*. New Haven, CT: Yale University Press.

Axelrod, Robert (1984) *The Evolution of Cooperation*. New York: Basic Books.

Bates, Robert H., Greif, Avner, Levi, Margaret, Rosenthal, Jean-Laurent and Weingast, Barry R. (1998) *Analytic Narratives*. Princeton, NJ: Princeton University Press.

Becker, Gary S. (1976) *The Economic Approach to Human Behavior*. Chicago: University of Chicago Press.

Berg, J., Dickhaut, J. and McCabe, K. (1995) 'Trust, reciprocity, and social history', *Games and Economic Behavior*, 10: 122–42.

Berlekamp, Elwyn R., Conway, John H. and Guy, Richard K. ([1982] 2001) *Winning Ways for Your Mathematical Plays*. Natick, MA: A.K. Peters.

Camerer, Colin F. (2003) *Behavioral Game Theory: Experiments on Strategic Interaction*. Princeton, NJ: Princeton University Press.

Dawes, Robyn M. and Thaler, Richard H. (1988) 'Anomalies: Cooperation', *Journal of Economic Perspectives*, 2 (3): 187–97.

Downs, Anthony (1957) *An Economic Theory of Democracy*. New York: Harper.

Elster, Jon (2000) 'Rational choice history: A case of excessive ambition', *American Political Science Review*, 94 (3): 685–95.

Enelow, James M. and Hinich, Melvin J. (eds) (1990) *Advances in the Spatial Theory of Voting*. Cambridge: Cambridge University Press.

Fearon, James D. (1994) 'Signaling versus the balance of power and interests – An empirical test of a crisis bargaining model', *Journal of Conflict Resolution*, 38 (2): 236–69.

Fox, Justin (2005) 'Electoral donations and interest group influence', Working Paper, Yale University.

Frank, Robert H., Gilovich, Thomas D. and Regan, Dennis T. (1993) 'Does studying economics inhibit cooperation?', *Journal of Economic Perspectives*, 7 (2): 159–71.

Fudenberg, Drew, and Tirole, Jean (1991) *Game Theory*. Cambridge, MA: MIT Press.

Gerber, Alan S. and Green, Donald P. (1998) 'Rational learning and partisan attitudes', *American Journal of Political Science*, 42: 794–818.

——— (1999) 'Misperceptions about perceptual bias', in Nelson W. Polsby (ed.), *Annual Review of Political Science*, 2: 189–210.

Green, Donald P. and Shapiro, Ian (1994) *Pathologies of Rational Choice Theory: A Critique of Applications in Political Science*. New Haven, CT: Yale University Press.

Hardin, Russel (1982) *Collective Action*. Baltimore, MD: John Hopkins University Press for Resources for the Future.

Harsanyi, John C. (1986) 'Advances in understanding rational behavior', in John Elster (ed.) *Rational Choice*, New York: New York University Press.

Harsanyi, John C. and Selten, Reinhard (1988) *A General Theory of Equilibrium Selection in Games*. Cambridge, MA: MIT Press.

Kahneman, Daniel (1984) 'Choices, values, and frames', *American Psychologist*, 39: 341–50.

——— (2003) 'A psychological perspective on economics', *American Economic Review*, 93 (2): 162–8.

Kahneman, Daniel and Tversky, Amos (1979) 'Prospect theory: An analysis of decision under risk', *Econometrica*, 47: 263–91.

Lupia, Arthur (1994) 'Shortcuts versus encyclopedias: Information and voting-behavior in California insurance reform elections', *American Political Science Review*, 88 (1): 63–76.

Margolis, Howard (1982) *Selfishness, Altruism, and Rationality: A Theory of Social Choice*. Chicago: The University of Chicago Press.

Maskin, Eric and Tirole, Jean (2004) 'The politician and the judge: Accountability in government', *American Economic Review*, 94 (4): 1034–54.

McFarland, David and Bosser, Thomas (1993) *Intelligent Behavior in Animals and Robots*. Cambridge, MA: MIT Press.

Mueller, Dennis C. (2003) *Public Choice III*. Cambridge: Cambridge University Press.

Myerson, Roger B. (1991) *Game Theory: Analysis of Conflict*. Cambridge, MA: Harvard University Press.

Olson, Mancur (1965) *The Logic of Collective Action*. Cambridge, MA: Harvard University Press.

Posner, Richard A. (1985) 'An economic theory of the criminal law', *Columbia Law Review*, 85: 1193–1231.

Radnitzky, Gerard and Bernholz, Peter (eds) (1987) *Economic Imperialism: The Economic Method Applied Outside the Field of Economics*. New York: Paragon House.

Riker, William H. (1980) 'Implications from the disequilibrium of majority rule for the study of institutions', *American Political Science Review*, 74: 432–47.

——— (1986) *The Art of Political Manipulation*. New Haven, CT: Yale University Press.

Roth, Alvin E. (1988) 'Laboratory experimentation in economics: A methodological overview', *Economical Journal*, 98:974.

Schelling, Thomas C. (1960) *The Strategy of Conflict*. Cambridge, MA: Harvard University Press.

Wittman, Donald (1991) 'Contrasting economic and psychological analyses of political choice: An economist's perspective on why cognitive psychology does not explain democratic politics', in Kristen Monroe (ed.), *The Economic Approach to Politics*. New York: Harper Collins.

16

Rationality and Rationalist Approaches in the Social Sciences

David Henderson

FRAMEWORK

Rationalism may be understood as the philosophical position asserting a certain distinctive epistemic status for certain classes of claims—that asserts or supposes that there are a priori knowable truths. On this understanding, one is a rationalist if one holds that there are certain necessary truths that can be justifiably believed (and that would then count as knowledge) independent of empirical evidence for their truth. This is a somewhat minimalist understanding of rationalism (although these days there are those who would count themselves as rationalist merely by virtue of embracing this much).

Rationalism has traditionally been understood as making a stronger claim. In the modern period, empiricist philosophers such as Locke and Hume sought to debunk what they believed to be the pretensions of rationalist thinkers such as Descartes and Leibniz. The empiricists would have granted there were some claims that satisfied the rather minimal characterization just now associated with rationalism (the claim that some truths were a priori knowable). But, they hastened to add that whatever was so knowable would be something on the order of definitional truths—claims that were necessarily true as a consequence of the character of, and relations between, the ideas or concepts employed in those claims. All unicorns are mammals—necessarily, since our idea of a unicorn is of a rather particular horsey thing, and our idea/concept of a horse is the idea of a particular sort of mammal (or so the rather plausible story goes). Nothing would count as a horse, and thus as a unicorn, were it not a mammal. But, they insisted, this of itself does not guarantee that there are any unicorns, or horses, in the world. For that, field work, or trips through the country with one's eyes open, would be needed.

While one might know by reflection the relations between our own ideas, said Hume, it is a wholly different question whether there is, in fact, anything in the world satisfying those ideas or concepts. Matters of fact could only be justifiably believed, could only be known, empirically. In opposition, the rationalists insisted that there were at least some things beyond the creations of our own idea-craft that could be known a priori—they insisted that one could know substantive truths about the world by reflection, without reliance on experiential evidence. Descartes, for example, thought that we could know that we were non-material souls, that God existed, and that material objects were (Euclidean) three-dimensional extended things. (Perhaps there should be a three-strikes rule applied to philosophies.)

In any case, were we to be fully faithful to the terms of this venerable debate, we would need to refine our characterization of rationalism: we would need to understand rationalism as the view that there are certain *substantive* claims that are both necessary and can justifiably be believed (and thus known) independent of empirical evidence for their truth—where a claim is substantive if it is not 'merely definitional', or 'analytic' or guaranteed by the content of its featured concepts.

I mention the traditional and more robust understanding of rationalism only to explicitly lay it to the side. There are multiple reasons for focusing on the minimal understanding in this contribution. Several reasons have to do with the state of play in contemporary philosophy.

First, the idea of a truth that is guaranteed by the semantics of its elements no longer seems to be what it used to be—and the changes have significantly complicated the philosophical landscape. A central development has come with the advent of what is termed 'externalist semantics'. Up until the 1970s, almost all thought about the meaning family (ideas, meanings, intensions, concepts, semantics) supposed that these things were settled by what went on inside a given individual. While such things as meanings or concepts might be abstract entities, whether a given individual entertained or deployed a given meaning or concept in a given stretch of thinking was thought to depend on what occurred within the skin (or perhaps head) of that individual.[1]

This picture was challenged by a line of thought developed by Kripke (1972), Putnam (1975a), and Burge (1979, 1992). They argued that what made for, or constituted, the concepts in play could include elements of the individual's social and physical environment—and was thus not wholly internal to the individual: thus the idea of an externalist semantics. On this view, at least some elements of the semantics of (at least some important) concepts are not (or need not be) accessible to agents employing those concepts. As a result, there could be claims whose truth are guaranteed by the semantics of the concepts featured in them, but which could not be appreciated by those individuals merely by their drawing on whatever makes for an individual's possession of the relevant concepts. Perhaps all a priori knowable truths are conceptual truths, it might then be said, but, if externalism is correct, not all conceptual truths are a priori knowable (even by those who count as conceptual adepts at a given time). Even more significantly, when concepts (semantic entities, meanings, and the like) come to be conceived as rather *more than* ideas in individual heads, the suggestion that a priori truths might turn out to be conceptual truths does not seem as threatening to their significance as was once readily supposed. The empiricist idea that a priori truths might be limited to conceptual truths no longer lends itself to the deflationary rephrasing, '*mere* conceptual truths'.

Second, perhaps influenced by such considerations, those with avowedly rationalist inclinations have come to think largely in terms of conceptual truths without feeling insignificant (for example, Bealer, 1987; Chalmers, 1996, 2002a, 2002b; Jackson, 1998; Peacocke, 1992). Conceptual truths pack some punch, at least if contemporary understandings are roughly correct.

Now that conceptual truths have come to be thought of as 'more muscular' or substantive as a class, the fan of a priori knowledge has come to face a new challenge: to explain how it can be that those who are relatively proficient with the concept have, by virtue of that conceptual competence, access to powerful elements of that semantics. This has been a matter of identifying a component of the semantics of the concept that is accessible at least to those who count as 'possessors' of the concepts involved.[2] But, we will not now detail the lines of the contemporary debate over the epistemology of the a priori.

These philosophical preliminaries do serve to indicate why it is that contemporary rationalists do not seem much concerned with what their modern ancestors would have thought crucial—why they commonly are not much concerned to show that there are a priori knowable truths that are not 'merely conceptual truths'. They also serve to explain to my readers why my discussion of 'rationalist approaches to the social sciences' will focus on positions regarding the subjects of social-scientific thought (on positions regarding beliefs, thought, actions, and the like) that might be thought to be conceptual in their foundation.

In connection with the social sciences, the central matter on which a priori truths have been sought or sensed by those with rationalist inclinations has been the role of rationality in the explanation of action. Put starkly and overly simply, it is said to be a priori that finding one's subjects to have beliefs and desires that make their actions rational explains their actions, while failing to do so leaves their actions unintelligible and unexplained. This is said to follow from the concept of an action—which is said to involve the idea of a behavior engendered by reasons. The concept of a reason is said to involve the idea of a contentful state that bears a (normatively approvable, i.e., rational) support relation to some other contentful state (that for which it is a reason). Putting these thoughts together, it is said to be a conceptual truth that actions are the sort of thing engendered by contentful states (prominently, beliefs and desires) that rationally support the decision to undertake that action.

Doubtless, such points would need to be sharpened and qualified in certain ways (I will try for more nuance below). At this juncture, it is useful to state the general thrust of the rationalist position. One then sees that the

putative a priori truth—that actions have rational antecedents and explanations, or something along this line—would both inform and constrain work in the social sciences. It would inform a kind of explanatory practice—and one apparently 'on the cheap'. After all, one would not have to develop well-evidenced generalizations or descriptive theories of cognition; one would not need empirical theories of human cognition that underwrite the explanatory practice in question. Instead, one's own normative principles of reasoning would supposedly turn the trick of informing and supporting explanations. One's own normative principles or reasoning competence, representing or tracking support relations between contents, would structure explanations underwritten by the very concepts of action and reasons. Such normative principles would also be constraining (again a priori constraining)—normative principles would need to figure in explanation, thereby limiting the kind and character of explanation one could employ in the human sciences. Such, in outline, is the central rationalist approach to the social sciences. In all variations of this generic approach, some significant degree of rationality in belief, desire and action is thought to be a priori conceptually guaranteed.

THE RATIONALIST BRIEF

Why embrace some variant on the basic line of thought sketched above? In surveying the rationalist case, one can begin by reflecting on the everyday practice of explaining an action by attributing reasons to the agent or agents. This is pretty pervasive. One encounters it in discussions of friends, enemies and acquaintances. One encounters it in histories, in newspapers, in meetings and just about anywhere that actions are up for explanation. It is reasonably taken to reflect some of our most fundamental understandings of what it is to act—and very central elements of this understanding might reasonably be taken to reflect our concept of an action,[3] and so to be grist for the rationalist mill. What then does the rationalist find when reflecting on the practice of explaining actions by citing reasons in the form of beliefs, desires, and the like?

When explaining an action by citing some of an agent's beliefs and desires, it seems important that the (typically small) constellation of the agent's contentful states mentioned be such as would count as a reason for so acting. If the cited beliefs and desires seem unrelated to the apparent action, then no explanation has yet been provided. To say that an agent had such and such a reason for some action seems to require that the beliefs and/or desires here mentioned *rationally favor* that action. This is *not* to say that they need make the action rational for the agent *all things considered* (that is, given the full range of the agent's beliefs and desires). It is to say that, considered just of themselves, they must rationally count in favor of doing such an action. This observation is crucial for rationalists, and is taken to reveal the most fundamental outlines of the coordinate concepts of an *action* and a *reason*. An action is the sort of thing undertaken for a reason. A reason for an action is a contentful state, or perhaps small constellation of such states, that presents that action, that undertaking, as rationally a good thing. Because this much only supposes that the reasons cited make the action narrowly rational, rather than all things considered rational, the commonsensical practice of explaining by citing reasons may be termed narrow rationalizing explanation.

Donald Davidson is perhaps the most influential of contemporary commentators on rationalizing explanation, and the rationalist brief here recounted is indebted to his writings. He argues that rationalizing explanation in terms of reasons turns on the idea of mental states as *rational causes*. Thus, it is taken to be central to our concept of an action, and to our most rudimentary explanatory practice with respect to actions, that actions are events with (in at least some minimal sense) a rational cause. To explain an action of an agent, the beliefs and desires attributed to the agent must 'make the act intelligible', must amount to rational reasons

for so acting. Indeed, Davidson (1982: 299) insists that such rationalizing explanation provides 'the only clear pattern of explanation that applies to action'. It is a pattern that has been elaborated in significant ways within economics, for example. But, whatever we ultimately want to make of these elaborations (and that is something to be considered below), the core rationalist idea seems to be that this 'only clear pattern'—this practice of narrow rationalizing explanation—represents a deep element of our concepts of *action* and *reason*. This is to say that *action* and *reason* are coordinate concepts—concepts made for each other—and that it is then a priori necessary that actions be rational at some significant level.

Suppose that an individual agent undertakes some action that can be given a relatively uncontroversial characterization. Commonly, there will be several constellations of the agent's beliefs and desires that could have prompted such an action. That is, within the agent's full array of beliefs and desires, there may be several small constellations that are each made up of beliefs and desires so related as to present that action (under the uncontroversial understanding) as a good thing. Understanding and explaining the action will then depend on identifying what—from among the various reasons that the agent might have had (even did have) for so acting—was *the reason* that the agent did the action. For example, the agent may have given a gift. Is that to be explained by a strong altruistic desire to meet a need of the receiver, or by a desire to be remembered in an upcoming decision process (or in a will), or by a nagging guilt over the giver's own role in a recent decision, or by some combination of these? Perhaps the agent had all these reasons for giving a gift.

To explain the action—the giving of a gift—one must appreciate which reasons were operative or dominant. To correctly explain the action, one must be able to say that the agent did the action *because* the agent desired such and such, and believed this and that, and sometimes this requires saying that the agent did the action for these reasons rather than because of certain other constellations of beliefs and desires that the agent might (even did) have. As Donald Davidson (1980a) argued, there is really no account to be given of the 'because' here, without invoking a causal relation. It will not do to say that the beliefs and desires *simply* 'make intelligible' the action—for any of various constellations would do that—and of only one (more or less sprawling) constellation of the agent's actual reasons will it be correct to say that the agent did the action because of those reasons. Only prominent members of this constellation will do as explanations (or will serve as the core of an explanation) of the action in question. So, the rationalist insists, it is a priori that actions are caused by constellations of beliefs and desires that together rationally indicate the desirability of the action. Not only must the agent have reasons for his or her action, but some constellation of such reasons must have been central to the processes that causally produced that undertaking.

Many a piece of behavior—say, the giving of a gift—might be motivated by various beliefs and desires. Indeed, the piece of behavior might then be understood as one of several actions. A given stretch of behavior might be understood as a selfless gift, an obsequious bit of pandering, a response to felt guilt, and so on. In important respects, the character of the action, as action, itself depends on the reasons that caused it. (This is so, even though we clearly allow some latitude for various descriptions of a given action, and some of these do not suppose that the agent was motivated to undertake an action so described. For example, we allow actions to be described in terms of their unintended consequences. So the present point would need to be understood in a fashion consistent with the possibility of such re-descriptions.) Insofar as the character of an action depends on the engendering reasons, insofar as this much is a deep element of the concept of an action, it is conceptually mandated that actions are caused by reasons—by contentful states that rationally (perhaps narrowly rationally) present them in a favorable light.

The upshot of these few quick paragraphs, focusing on the coordinate concepts of *beliefs* and *desires* as *reasons*, and of *actions* as caused by reasons, has been to present the most rudimentary prima facie case for the rationalist idea that it is a priori that actions and reasons must be understood in terms of processes that are preponderantly rational, at least narrowly so. Thus, subject to qualifications, we can announce a general, if crude, result:

Restricted Rationality Principle Concerning Actions (RRP–a)

Actions are behaviors with rational causes. To be an action is to be a bit of behavior which is (at least narrowly) rationalized by a constellation of beliefs and desires that cause it.

The parenthetical qualification is important. For the above paragraphs have not established or defended any sweeping rationality principle—no principle to the effect that actions are rational in virtue of the full set of the agent's beliefs and desires, or that the agent's beliefs and desires are themselves preponderantly rational. (The extent to which one might reasonably seek to extend these general lines of thought to provide for such a stronger rationalist principle will be the concern in much of the discussion below.) In its limited form, it is plausible that RRP represents something central to, something guaranteed by the concepts of *action, belief,* and *desire.*

RRP as depicted above focuses on *actions*—saying that they are behaviors with rational causes. (Thus, I designated it the Restricted Rationality Principle Concerning Actions.) But parallel lines of thought suggest a parallel limited rationality principle with application to beliefs and desires. The result would be conceptually grounded rationality principles that apply to any given belief (RRP–b) and to any given desire (RRP–d)—indicating that these must also be at least narrowly rational in their interrelations with generating and sustaining beliefs and desires. Of course, beliefs and desires are not undertakings, while actions are. So the arguments supporting these additional rationality principles will need to be somewhat different. Still, it seems central to beliefs and desires that they must be such as could be rendered intelligible in terms of certain of the agent's (narrowly) associated beliefs and desires. The cumulative effect is an understanding of the various items—beliefs and desires, as well as actions—according to which these are generated and sustained in a web of contentful supports that are (at least narrowly) rational.

The most parallel line of thought here would take the form of reflection on how one explains a person's having a belief that that person apparently holds (or a desire that an agent apparently possesses). A common explanatory move here is to show that the belief was (fairly obviously) rationally indicated by at least some set of the agent's (salient) other beliefs. Similarly, one commonly explains an agent's desire for some state or object by appeal to apparent antecedent desires salient to the agent, along with beliefs that seem rationally to jointly indicate that the state or object would facilitate the satisfaction of these antecedent desires. Here again, one explains by noticing the agent's reasons for so believing (or desiring). But, here, one need not suppose that the belief (or desire) so explained is rationally *chosen*, as this would involve an implausible voluntarism with respect to belief and desire. Nevertheless, reasons are readily in question when explaining beliefs and desires—and showing the belief (or desire) in question to be reasonable makes the agent and the belief (or desire) 'intelligible'. Here also, one only succeeds in explaining the agent's holding the belief (or desire) in question when the antecedent beliefs (and desires) alluded to are (or feature in) 'the reasons' that the agent believes (or desires) as he or she does. Again, causal dependencies are at issue.

Generalizing we arrive at a restricted rationality principle with respect to belief and desire:

RRP–b/d: Beliefs and desires are states that interact in significantly contentfully appropriate ways.

But, again, as with RRP–a, it is important to keep in mind that the rationality indicated in these lines of thought should be understood as narrow rationality: a matter of not particularly subtle rationality involving some limited range of beliefs and desires that are salient to the agent in those processes that issue in the beliefs, desires and actions being explained. There does not yet seem to be a *conceptual* demand for a subtle and far-reaching holistic rationality involving vast ranges of a given individual's beliefs and desires and turning on sophisticated support relations.

A related argument will begin to push one towards the stronger principles that most rationalists regarding rationality in the human and social sciences would also embrace. It comes into view when pursuing a question only touched upon above: how can one determine which of the possible beliefs and desires that might rationalize an action are 'the agent's reasons for' so acting? This is best thought of as a complex question, one that can be decomposed into at least two questions, each of which might motivate rationalist argument.

One question is: which of the beliefs and desires that might help to rationalize the action are possessed by the agent? Action is the joint product of interacting beliefs and desires, as already noted. In paradigmatic cases, one can take an action as reflecting a choice, and look for sets of beliefs and desires that might have (rationally) produced it. But which of these are possessed by the agent? Further, this way of putting the question obscures the magnitude of the interpretive task, for the action undertaken itself can only be appreciated or understood against an understanding of the beliefs and desires engendering it. Thus, as Davidson (1984c, 1980c) argued, there seem to be *three unknowns* that must be sorted out on the basis of the behaviors presented to an observer/interpreter: beliefs, desires and actions/intentions. Here we confront directly what has been termed *charity in interpretation. If we presuppose rationality* on the part of the agent, information about any two of the three (beliefs, desires, actions undertaken) will allow one to determine the third. Given any two of the three, and the presupposition of rationality, one can 'solve for the other'. For example, desires can be determined from actions undertaken and from beliefs. There seems to be no alternative but to suppose some measure of rationality, or so it is argued. But, says Davidson, one must presume more.

The rationality envisioned here as presupposed or imposed as a part of the interpretive endeavor seems to take one beyond the narrow rationality at issue in the above discussion. Significant light is shed on an agent's 'standing' beliefs and desires by looking at a wider set of actions undertaken by the agent in question. Of course, there might be various interpretations that one might plausibly put on these—but the idea is that one might constrain workable alternative interpretations by looking for plausible *coherence over the standing beliefs and desires* attributed against *the 'data points' provided by large sets of behaviors.* But, as one imposes a rationality assumption over wider sets of actions—and their precipitating reasons—one imposes a *more holistic* and less narrow sort of rationality in interpretation.

Focus on this issue: how can one get some principled grasp on any one pair—for example, beliefs and actions—within the triad of unknowns? Again, as Davidson would insist, there is in play a charitable presumption having to do specifically with beliefs—and beliefs provide a common entering wedge for interpretation. Davidson (1980c, 1984b) holds that we can and must charitably provide some determinacy to the belief element in the triad by assuming that most beliefs about any given subject are true. (For now, I am looking to Davidson's understanding of charity in interpretation for inspiration in developing a rationalist brief. Later, I will compare this understanding with a more cautious or limited charitable approach as suggested in Quine's writings.) Davidson's charitable policy with respect to the attribution of beliefs serves as a way of 'holding belief constant enough' to get on with the

business of interpretation—in order to solve for other factors in the interpretive trinity, where solving for the 'other factors' involves charitable presumptions regarding rationality. Rationalists, of course, insist that that charitable presumption of rationality is conceptually mandated—a conceptually mandated principle significantly stronger than RRP.

Thus, to tentatively summarize the rationalist response to the first question: to figure out what beliefs and desires a subject holds, we are instructed to make two charitable presumptions in interpretation. We are to presume some significant degree of correctness of belief on the part of the subject, at least with respect to some significant range of matters. Further, we are to presume some significant measure of rationality in the structure and interaction of beliefs and desires—so that the content of a belief or desire will be understood in terms of its patterned relation to other beliefs and desires, given their contents. To cut down on alternative sets of attributable beliefs and desires, we are to extend the range of observed choices/undertakings and speech to be accounted for.[4] This will allow one to rule out some alternative explanations for a given action, as the eliminated explanation would be inconsistent with the agent's pattern of actions and motivations. The crucial point is that in casting our interpretive and explanatory net more broadly, one must apparently presume *stronger and more holistic forms of rationality* in beliefs, desires and decisions.

Then there is the second question: which of the constellations of rationalizing reasons to be found in the agent represents 'the reason' that the agent so acted? Here, the rationalist idea is that, in keeping with what has been said to this point, the determination of an agent's reasons for acting in a certain fashion (that is, for determining what reasons were *the* reasons, for determining which were causally salient) is a matter to be settled by a kind of inference to the best explanation, constrained by the range of that agent's beliefs and desires (charitably determined) and by the kind of holistic rationality necessarily supposed in their determination.

The upshot of all this might now be formulated as an unrestricted (or much less restricted) Rationality Principle in two clauses.

Rationality Principle (RP)

RP–a: Actions or undertakings are behaviors with rational causes—beliefs and desires cause them, and do so by virtue of certain contents that make them reasonable, significantly holistically rational, and thus intelligible.

RP–b/d: Beliefs and desires (while not choices or voluntary in the same limited sense in which actions/undertakings might be) are caused products of each other, in a fashion that reflects contents and makes for their being reasonable, significantly holistically rational, and thus intelligible.

Much thought in economics and related disciplines is aptly understood as continuous with the common thought about beliefs, desires and actions that we have been considering. In various ways, economists have sought to develop precise mathematical ways of thinking about choice, ways that attempt to measure strength of desire and degree of belief in scales with understood properties. While such thought may be more articulate and more careful than everyday talk of beliefs, desires and actions, it must be recognized that something like RRP and RP plays a parallel role there. The central issue for our purposes is whether, or to what extent, something like RP has an a priori status there.

This will need to serve as the main brief for rationalist approaches to the social sciences—particularly with regard to the putative a priori role of rationality in understanding action. It reflects the considerable reasons that one might have for advancing several claims as a priori in character:

1. That actions are behaviors with rational causes—at least the agent must have certain belief states and desire states that make it narrowly rational for the agent to undertake that action (RRP–a).
2. That beliefs and desires are states which interact in the ways that are significantly rational—and

perhaps that they are states with the relevant content by virtue of this pattern of dependencies. Here, it seems, rationality is partially constitutive of beliefs and desires. Again, we have the idea of a cause that is also a reason (RRP–b/d).

3. To exhibit or reveal the narrow rationality of a choice or action is to explain it. To exhibit the significant rationality of an agent's beliefs or desires is to explain them. In both cases, one is exhibiting the choice or mental state to be caused by its rational antecedents in 'intelligible' or 'reasonable' ways.
4. Overall, to qualify as a belief, desire or action, a result requires more than the narrow rationality of choices or actions undertaken, or the narrow rationality of belief and action—as it requires that the choice and its belief and desire parameters themselves exhibit rationality of some significant holistic or extended sort (although certainly not perfect holistic rationality) (RP).

Alexander Rosenberg (1985, 1988) provides a particularly clear and striking way of advancing the rationalist points made here.[5] He takes note of the ways in which finding rationality is taken to be explanatory—by making intelligible a choice or undertaking by revealing the reasons that motivate it. He is led to give expression to RRP when he formulates an 'oversimplified general statement [that] seems to lie behind ordinary explanations of human action' (1988: 25):

[L] Given any person x, if x wants d and x believes that a is a means to attain d, under the circumstances, then x does a.

Taken as expressing a narrow form of rationality, the exhibition of which is central to intentional explanation, [L] serves to express the sort of thin putatively a priori claim—the RRP—envisioned by rationalists.

Then, reflecting on how beliefs and desires are thought to conspire holistically to produce a choice, Rosenberg is led to suggest a more full-bodied principle representing how rationality is putatively involved in the explanation of action and in the interpretation of agents' beliefs and desires. The suggestion is that something very like normative decision theory represents a (again fairly commonsensical) refinement on [L]—call it

[L^r]. It is worth noting that these refinements are developed and advanced largely 'from the armchair'. That is, the wrinkles associated with decision theory can certainly seem 'natural' when systematically reflecting on sorts of cases in which the antecedent of [L] would be satisfied and yet the agent not undertake the indicated action. One is likely to think: 'Now, x may want d and x believe that a is a means to attain d, under the circumstances. But what if x wants g more than d and believes that getting g is incompatible with doing a.' Just as [L] expresses a weak and thin rationality principle thought to be a priori hold action, so decision theory would constitute a highly substantive refinement— [L^r]—and is taken by Rosenberg to express a much more constraining and substantive, putatively a priori claim: in effect, RP.

According to Rosenberg (1988: 30–6), you should come to a striking realization: little testing and refinement of [L^r] is possible. The reason is again rooted in the principle of charity in interpretation: [L^r] is supposed in arriving at the interpretations that would be the necessary preliminaries to determining whether agents conform to [L^r]. Rosenberg concludes that a rationality principle along the lines of [L^r] functions as something like a 'definition', rather than providing an empirically testable or refineable description of cognitive tendencies or as a nomic generalization (1988: 33).

CRITICAL EVALUATION, STAGE ONE: REGARDING RRP

Let us begin by looking at the least demanding element of the position: the Restricted Rationality Principles. We can focus on RRP–a. We should keep in mind two respects in which RRP–a advances a very limited claim. The first has to do with the etiology of undertakings or actions; it holds only that, among the agent's vast set of beliefs and desires, there are or were some contextually salient beliefs and desires that both (a) featured in the near causal antecedents of the

choice or undertaking and (b) added up to a reason for so acting (jointly portraying the action as good to do). It does not claim that these causal antecedents, these contextually salient occurrent beliefs and desires, are themselves ultimately rational for the agent to hold—ones that makes rational sense in light of the agent's wider set of beliefs and desires, or ones that result from rational inquiry or deliberation. Second, it does not hold that the belief is presented in an overall favorable light by the *total set* of the agent's beliefs and desires—or even by a very extensive set. It does not suppose that the action is 'all things considered' rational, given the agent's full range of beliefs and desires.

This said, it becomes plausible that RRP–a (and Rosenberg's [L]) might indeed be a central element of the concept of an action. Paradigm cases of actions are intentional behaviors undertaken for certain reasons— such reasons jointly amount to a representation of that undertaking as a way of attaining certain of the agent's ends. This does not mean that every action is intentional—that (so described) it was intended by the agent. There are familiar ways of describing an action that do not turn on the agent's understandings or representation of that undertaking. For example, we sometimes describe an action in terms of consequences that were not intended. Descriptions in terms of institutional consequences can be a case in point. It is said that in 2000 a significant number of voters in Florida voted for the Republican candidate for president unintentionally. Yet such agents possessed reasons for their undertaking *as they understood it*. It is said that they understood themselves to be voting for the Democratic candidate or perhaps the Green Party candidate, but marked the ballot incorrectly. As they understood their action or undertaking, they had their reasons, and these made it out to be desirable in the sense envisioned in RRP–a.

Further, RRP–a should be understood to apply to less paradigmatic cases of actions or undertakings. In impulsive acts which were not conditioned by significant deliberation, one might 'just have felt that it would be nice to' do such-and-such (pinch the child, crack a joke, run to the top of the hill …). Yet, there is a sense in which the agent inarticulately 'chose' to engage in an action which 'seemed good at the time'. Here, 'the constellation of beliefs and desires that cause' the action may be rather thin, but they present it in a good (if feeble) light, and this conforms to RRP–a.

I do find it plausible that this much is conceptually guaranteed by the very concept of an action. Were we to give up on the notion that this holds for a wide range of those events that we have been thinking about as undertakings, we would thereby have compelling reason to give up on the idea that there are any undertakings and any actions at all.

RRP does not provide much guidance in settling the real substantive questions that concern social scientists, or even those that concern folk in everyday contexts. It does not, for example, give much direction for determining what are 'the agent's reasons' for a given stretch of behavior that might well be an action. For many episodes that one plausibly treats as some undertaking or action, there may be various constellations of beliefs and desires that the agent might hold, and that would put the undertaking (under some interpretations) in a favorable light, and it is a significant question which of these sets the agent had, which were the agent's reason for so acting, and what then is the intentional character of this undertaking. *If there is to be strong a priori guidance or constraint on the explanation of actions, there would need to be markedly stronger a priori principles.*

EVALUATION, STAGE TWO: REGARDING RP

Empirical Resources and the Revisability of Rationality Expectations

We need to understand how the range of an individual's beliefs and desires interact as considerations and compose themselves so as to yield a choice. We need to understand how various reasons or considerations resolve themselves into something that might be termed *the* reason—a causal vector of meaningful states in which some stand out as dominant or controlling of the subsequent course of action.

The central idea in the more robustly rationalist approach to the human sciences, and to the place of rationality in those sciences, turns on one simple idea that is said to be guaranteed by the coordinate concepts of *belief, desire* and *action/undertaking*: *that beliefs and desires as considerations interact according to holistic rational principles, and thereby compose themselves, all things considered, into rational choices—choices that are, from the point of view of such considerations, a rational resolution.* As reflected in Davidson's and Rosenberg's writings, the projected a priori rationality in action is of the sort represented by normative decision-theory (and logic, and epistemology). It is thought to be conceptually necessary that, in the preponderance of cases, actions undertaken are the rational product of the strengths of the agent's various desires and of the agent's beliefs concerning the propensity of various courses of action to produce or frustrate those desires. The rational course of action for an agent is that with the highest expected value among those courses of action open to the agent—where the expected value of an action is understood as the sum of the possible (positive and negative) outcomes of that course of action (as conceived against the agent's background beliefs), each weighted by the agent's understanding of the probability of that outcome given that course of action.

Such is the full-blooded conception of rationality *in action* that the proponent of RP commonly envisions. This understanding itself supposes an understanding of a corresponding holistic rationality in belief and desire. In keeping with the principle of charity, agents are understood as possessing a rich set of standing beliefs and desires. These may evolve over time, under prompting by experience and reflection. But, these standing states are understood to be 'reasonably' constant, and changes in them are thought to be of a largely rational character. Their inter-actions or interrelations are said to be such as to evince a preponderance of rationality. Rationalists seem less articulate on the pre-cise character of the rationality that is sup-posed to be guaranteed here—and they resort to general and hedged formulations. Davidson writes of a 'large degree of consis-tency' (1980b: 221), and of significant conformity with 'stipulated structures' of a normative character (1980c: 6–7), of 'impos-ing our logic' in interpretation. 'It is uncer-tain to what extent these principles can be made definite—it is a problem of rationaliz-ing and codifying our epistemology,' says Davidson (1980c: 7). It should now be clear that RP amounts to a rather significant ratio-nality claim regarding both cognition and action—a claim taken to hold a priori of all creatures with beliefs and desires, creatures who undertake actions. Compared to the first small rationalist step (RRP), this second step (RP) seems quite a stretch! In keeping with the conceptual status claimed for it, it is said to so constrain both the attribution and expla-nation of actions and cognitive states that it is neither at risk of significant empirical chal-lenge nor susceptible to significant empirical refinement. Call this the *strong rationalist position* regarding rationality in the human sciences.

Confronted with such sweeping claims derived from abstract philosophical reflec-tion, one does well to approach them with caution. If strong rationalism is correct here, then something along the lines of full norma-tive decision theory descriptively applied—[L^r]—must be correct. If strong rationalism is correct, then [L^r] should not be subject to empirical test or refinement. [L^r] could not be subjected to empirical refinement or test because [L^r] would play a conceptually grounded constraining role in the attribution of beliefs and desires; attributions involving significant violations of [L^r] would count as problematic (indeed as conceptually incoher-ent) interpretations.

However, there is reason to believe that [L^r]—in effect, decision theory deployed as a descriptive account of human cognition[6]—*is*

subject to empirical test, i.e., [L^r] can be empirically shown inadequate and refined. The best reason for thinking so is that there is reason to think that [L^r] *has been* tested and found inadequate—prompting empirical refinements. An apparently instructive exam-ple can be found in the well-known work of Tversky and Kahneman (1974). Tversky (1975) contrives experimental situations in which people's responses give us empirical reasons for revising our understanding of human cognitive tendencies—evidence indi-cating that [L^r] must be abandoned or, what amounts to the same thing, significantly revised. Consider a set of situations and results that Tversky discusses. The situations are of a common sort found in studies of decision-making under uncertainty: choices between gambles. (Using the standard notion, (X,P,Y) will represent a gamble where one will receive X with a probability of P, or Y with a probability of $1 - P$.) Tversky pre-sented subjects with a choice between gambles A and B:

A= ($1000, 1/2, 0), B= ($400)

Presented with this choice, almost all sub-jects prefer the 'sure thing', B. They do this despite the fact that A has a greater actuarial value: $500.

Such results are not themselves news within standard decision theory, and present no immediate threat to [L^r]. After all, it is common to distinguish between the amount of goods or money to be had and its 'utility'. The latter is conceived as a subjective, non-linear, function of the former. The common postulation of decreasing marginal utility—a concave positive utility curve—is clearly enough to accommodate the results obtained in connection with choice situa-tions of just this first sort. One need only claim that, commonly, $u($400)>1/2u($1000)$. This response is just what the strong ratio-nalist would anticipate: [L^r] is not impugned by the above results because we interpret our subjects on the basis of its charitable insistence on standard normative decision theory.

However, this is an overly simple description of our interpretive practice. At some point, and Tversky's work takes us to such a point, the [L^r]-informed identification of values held by subjects comes to clash with other constraints—and [L^r] can give way. This begins to be in evidence in connection with a second choice situation, one produced by multiplying the probabilities of gains by 1/5. That is, subjects are presented the choice between C and D:

C= ($1000, 1/10, 0), D= ($400, 1/5, 0)

If the explanation of the choices found in the first situation were really the concave shape of the subjects' preference curves, then we could expect a preference of D over C. However, that is not what is observed. Within the confines of standard decision theory, the overall pattern of choices is 'incompatible with any utility function' (Tversky, 1975: 166). Tversky's results suggest that there is a *'positive certainty effect* ... [in which] the utility of a positive outcome appears greater when it is certain than when it is embedded in a gamble' (1975: 166). He also provides evidence for a negative certainty effect. Such interactions of utility and probability violate aspects of standard normative decision theory, where it is supposed that there are utility functions (unique up to a certain transformation) associated with particular goods and that such utility functions interact simply with subjective probabilities according to the rule: $u(x)p(x)$.

One tempting response would be to insist that Tversky's subjects just did not understand the situations in the way he supposes. This would be to invoke the strong rationalist position regarding charity and [L^r]. However, and this is crucial, one can raise and address this issue in a principled fashion— one that itself seems empirically informed. Consider, just what was it about the situations that Tversky's subjects plausibly understood differently? They were American college students. Is it plausible that they did not understand talk of 'dollars'? Or that they did not understand the rudimentary

mathematical relations between 1000 and 400—or that whatever could be purchased with $400 can typically be purchased in a matched pair with $200 remaining from $1000? The reason that such differences in understanding are not plausible is that in addition to some expectations for certain forms of rationality, we also have expectations regarding roughly when people learn rudimentary matters of importance within their society. We expect such elementary math and monetary units to be learned much earlier than college. Such relatively mundane, but nevertheless empirical, expectations effectively block positing significantly different understandings of the relevant aspects of the situations Tversky presents to his subjects.

It is more plausible that Tversky's subjects understood the probabilities stipulated in ways differing from Tversky's (and ours). And it certainly is true that they may not have developed any sophisticated understanding of probability. But, Tversky's results do not require sophisticated understandings. It seems quite likely that his subjects could have applied talk of probabilities to matters such as coin tosses, urns with colored balls, and whether their car would start next time tried. That would be enough to make Tversky's results telling. (If it was lacking in most people's thoughts, normative decision theory is likely in trouble anyway.) Again, we find some relatively mundane and empirical expectations constraining interpretation— and these could be given further empirical development.

Thus, in addition to some [L]-like expectations serving as constraints on interpretation, we find various more or less mundane, more or less empirically developed, expectations also constraining interpretation—with the result that suggested refinements of [L] can be put under significant empirical test in ways reflected in Tversky and Kahneman's work (to name just one prominent example). Call these empirical constraints—*empirical expectations* (or EE). These EE are a diverse lot. Some are fairly general in character—for example, they may have to do with the power of human cognitive abilities, whether it is reasonable to expect that someone would 'put certain things together' and appreciate certain implications, with whether it is likely that certain learning or experiences would be recalled from memory, with certain commonality in human motivation, 'needs' and the like. They may have to do with various domains of human cultural phenomena: religion, group identity, political phenomena, the flow of information within various groups, economic phenomena and the like. They may have to do with particular cultures or groups, as in what things are learned when within a certain culture. The point is that such diverse EE provide a significant constraint on our understanding of people, and can make it empirically plausible that one has encountered a case where some proposed development on [L], such as [L^r], is violated. With systematic enough violation, one can have empirical basis for abandoning some proposed development on [L] in favor of others.[7]

The essential issue in evaluating strong rationalism is whether [L^r] plays such a decisive and dominant role in informing what beliefs and desires are attributable to agents that [L^r] is itself rendered immune to empirical pressure and revision. We have just considered a kind of empirical inquiry in which it seems that significant basis is provided for revising [L] in ways that amount to abandoning [L^r]. The suggestion has been that there are multiple empirical constraints on interpretation—EE—that can provide leverage for abandoning or deeply revising [L^r].

Tversky and Kahneman (1974) then advance an alternative to [L^r]—an alternative descriptive account of human choice behavior—which they term prospect theory (PT). It counts as an empirical refinement for several reasons. First, the motivation for abandoning [L^r] in favor of some alternative is empirical. Second, the particular alternative is judged promising and worthy of further empirical investigation because it accommodates the observations obtained in Tversky and Kahneman's work. Third, PT not only

accommodates Tversky and Kahneman's observations, but those observations are highly plausible; it seems, in fact, that they are most plausible, given the sorts of empirical constraints in question.

Those of a strong rationalist bent may have conceived of a rejoinder. They will note that the various above-mentioned concrete empirical constraints themselves turn on antecedent interpretations of human beings generally, and of those in more narrow populations such as those from which Tversky and Kahneman's subjects are drawn. After all, how do we know that most folk of college age were long ago exposed to information regarding certain topics? How do we know that humans are capable of learning what little math is needed to recognize the points of significance? These empirical constraints seem to be ploddingly obvious generalizations arrived at on the basis of everyday experience with those very populations, or presumably similar populations. As such, they depend on antecedent interpretation. The rationalist would insist that such interpretation must have been constrained and informed by something like [L^r] all along. It then seems that, in retaining these interpretations—and in making the revisions that constitute PT, or something on this order—one must be, or should be, seeking to diverge from [L^r] in the most minimal fashion. This is to say that [L^r] cannot be empirically revised *much*, and that [L^r] itself serves as an irrevisable constraint from which deviations under interpretation must be minimized. The strong rationalist point might be put in terms of the performance/competence distinction: one may need to attribute moments of irrationality, it is conceded, but these must always be isolated enough to count as mere performance errors against a background of rational competence.

There are reasons for doubting that the rationalist has things quite right here. The essential issue has now to do with the character of the ultimate constraints on interpretation. Is it really the case, a priori, that any empirical refinement of [L^r] would need to rely on interpretations that largely confirm [L']? The rationalist rejoinder requires that *some rather powerful normative model of rationality* (something like standard decision theory together with some parallel account of epistemic rationality) *serves as an invariant constraint on interpretation—that there is some such constraint on interpretation, which is invariant, does not evolve, being set a priori.* Again, in philosophy, this view is prominently associated with Donald Davidson's writings.

The Principle of Charity vs. The Principle of Explicability

The principle of charity in interpretation is roughly that one must so interpret as to find those interpreted to be preponderantly rational and believers of mostly truths. (This formulation reflects Davidson's influential development of the principle.) Let us focus on the idea that we must find rationality under interpretation. Here it is crucial to distinguish between two understandings of this supposed constraint on adequate or acceptable interpretation. One sees the first as absolutely fundamental, and the other as derivative and plastic in certain respects. The strong rationalist idea is not merely that we must find our subjects to be reasoning in certain ways, and that many of those ways happen to be rational ways to think, so that we need to find such rationality under interpretation. (That much is congenial to one who sees the constraints on interpretation as a matter of deploying expectations for human reasoning that are commonsensical but ultimately empirical in character.) Rather, the strong rationalist idea is that that the need to attribute rationality is fundamental, that rational ways of thinking (and acting) must— *because they are rational* ways of thinking and acting—be supposed in interpretation. It is the idea that it is by virtue of being rational that certain ways of thinking must be found under acceptable or adequate interpretation. Not all understandings of the principle of charity turn out to suppose this, but strong rationalist understandings (such as Davidson's) do.

The rationalist understanding of the principle of charity contrasts with Quine's understanding of that principle, according to which the charitable constraint is derived and plastic. Quine (who is writing somewhat narrowly of translation) says that we must translate others so as to preserve 'the obvious'—where what is obvious is a matter of empirical psychology. Before discussing attributions of rationality and irrationality, consider the implications of Quine's admonition for attributions of true and false beliefs. Some truths are (in context) relatively obvious—for example, given a context of good illumination where one's subject is at arms length, it should be obvious that one is faced with a rabbit (and not a grizzly bear). (Of course, there might be less frequent contexts involving good light and proximity where it would be at least equally obvious that one is faced with a grizzly bear, not a rabbit.) So, if one's scheme for translating some people has them regularly misidentifying instances of these two kinds—insisting (obviously mistakenly) that they have killed a grizzly bear, and warning of the rabbit protecting some winter kill— one would have reason to rethink one's translations. Such matters are perceptually obvious (and this is in large degree an empirical matter): people tend to get right such everyday matters about middle-sized physical and biological objects in plain sight, and with respect to which they have a significant practical interest in developing a competence. On the other hand, what is not perceptually obvious need not be treated as true under translation. The ill-glimpsed form in the brush might be misidentified, and this does not indicate a problem with translation. Similarly, translation that has us attributing glaring errors in reasoning of sorts that 'one would find obvious' should not be accepted, unless there are mitigating circumstances. (Factors that might count include the presence of drugs, alcohol, sleep deprivation, very strong personal interest in a conclusion other than that rationally indicated, and some kinds of defective training.) Empirical results regarding human foibles seem highly significant when determining what perceptual matters should be relatively obvious in context.

Empirical results also seem significant for determining what forms of reasoning are cognitively obvious and which are not. People seem rather better at working with conjunction and negation than with conditionals. They seem better at working with conditionals when these involve concrete matters with which they have significant experience. They can believe the damnedest things when gods or governments are involved. They may believe contradictory things when that contradiction is 'well hidden'—so that it might require subtle proofs or particularly agile minds to appreciate. To insist that we 'preserve the obvious' in our interpretation is to insist that there are certain ways of reasoning that should be found in those we interpret:— the ones that characterize reasoning in the relevant set of critters (say humans). Some of these ways happen to be rational. This is a fact about human beings about which we are getting a progressively better grasp as we investigate human inferential tendencies. Since there is arguably significant human rationality, the advice to interpret so as to 'save the obvious' would have us interpret so as to find significant rationality (the obvious rationality). Still, to put it mildly, humans turn out to be subject to non-negligible irrationality. The rational principles that would serve as a corrective to such tendencies are, emphatically, not generally obvious to folk in context. So, if we must preserve the obvious, then findings of such irrationality (cases of forms of irrationality to which folk are given, cases where the contrasting form of rationality is not obvious), are no strike against an interpretation.

What is crucial on Quine's understanding of the principle of charity is that while there are real substantive constraints on interpretation, the substantive constraints here do not constitute a kind of a priori constraint. What is obvious perceptually or cognitively is an empirical matter: it is a matter of psychological tendencies. It is a matter regarding which we have significant empirical access rooted

in everyday and common experience (of common perceptual capabilities and limits, and of common intellectual capabilities and foibles). It is a matter subject to systematic study (as in the empirical work on human inferential strategies and errors). On Quine's understanding, the charitable constraint that we preserve the obvious provides substantive constraints on interpretation only when conjoined with such empirical information—so that the substantive constraint here does not constitute an a priori constraint on interpretation to the effect that we must find rationality. Rather, if anything is a priori demanded here, it is that we should seek to find others reasoning in ways characteristic of the class of cognitive systems to which they belong (or characteristic of such critters in relevantly similar circumstances). The principle of charity is thus understood as an empirically informed constraint on interpretation, one that results from the application of our evolving empirical understanding of the relevant cognitive systems. 'The translator will depend early and late on psychological conjectures as to what the native is likely to believe' (Quine, 1987: 7). Since human beings are given to some significant forms of rationality (as well as to some significant forms of irrationality), the *derivative* demand that our interpretation be informed and conditioned by these expectations for some forms of rationality (and some irrationality) can be termed a principle of charity. We are to seek to find rationality of the common sorts—and failure to do so results in an account which is likely mistaken (for when the errors attributed to folk are highly unlikely, mistaken interpretation is relatively likely).

To be fair to the rationalists, one must notice that they would typically acknowledge a role for empirical information about human cognitive capacities and incapacities. Such information is acknowledged to be important in determining what interpretation is the best interpretation of an agent or people. Thus, Davidson (1984c, 1984d) insists that all attributions of error and irrationality count against an interpretation in some measure (this is the a priori part), but that some count more strongly than others (this is at least partly an empirical matter). So, in determining what is the best interpretation of an agent or community of agents, we seek to attribute no irrationality; but, as some attribution of irrationality will be unavoidable, we should settle for attributions of irrationality that violate our learned expectations the least—i.e., the empirical information contributes to the negative weighting of attributions of error. (Of course, one would also want to allow that expectations will continue to evolve over time.)

This seems reasonable, but it also seems to make for a more attenuated form of rationalism. It originally seemed as if the strong rationalist could insist that there are certain levels and forms of rationality that would need to be found under interpretation. If this much could be taken to be a priori, and if the levels and forms of rationality corresponded at least to [L'], then [L'] becomes unassailable (at least at the level of competence)— and an RP is vindicated. But once one allows that empirical expectations can modulate the putatively a priori demand for finding rationality under interpretation, it becomes less clear what is *a priori guaranteed*. As noted earlier, the rationalist tends to adopt somewhat hedged formulations at this point. Thus, Davidson writes of it being a priori that beliefs, desires and actions are *preponderantly rational*. Here it seems that RP/[L'] serves to characterize an a priori ideal to which all adequate interpretation must approximate, from which no acceptable interpretation can diverge *too much*. It is then acknowledged that what counts as 'too much' is at least partially an empirical matter. (If it were wholly an empirical matter, then again it seems that the a priori element here becomes vacuous.) So, as long as the 'too much' is not much, interpretations will need to conform largely to [L'], and background interpretations will not provide the basis for any but minor revisions of [L'].

The contrast boils down to this: On the Davidsonian understanding (the strong rationalist understanding) the principle of charity articulates a powerful a priori constraint on interpretation, an invariant a priori ideal to which all interpretation must approximate. What makes for the best approximation may be empirically informed, as expectations for human capabilities and limitations may inform what errors make for significant divergence and which do not, but the model of reasoning to which the interpretations must ultimately approximate is invariant. On the Quinean understanding, that model of reasoning to which our interpretations must find our subjects approximating is neither a priori nor invariant. It is rather our evolving empirical understanding of human reasoning. As our understanding of human reasoning tendencies evolves under work in cognitive psychology (for example), the resulting expectations for both rationality *and irrationality* form a composite model of human cognition, and this model is that to which interpretation should conform for now. An element of this model—say, the expectation for certain forms of valid deductive reasoning, or the expectation for certain (fallacious) overuse of some judgment heuristic—is a piece of the model because it is a piece of our present best understanding of humans, not because it is given a priori as rational.[8]

To illustrate the difference between the strong rationalist approach and the empiricist approach, we can contrive a cartoon history of our interpretive practice. So suppose some point in that practice that should surely be congenial to the rationalist. Suppose that there were a time in which interpreters had no empirical expectations regarding human reasoning—only a normative model that includes things like normative decision theory, statistical reasoning, basic logic and the like. (I doubt that there ever was such a point, but let us not pause over this point.) According to the strong rationalist, this is not too impoverished a position from which to begin, for they insist that interpreters yet have the a priori ideal to which all interpretations must approximate anyway. Admittedly, interpreters would have no nuanced way of weighting divergence from the ideal—no empirical weighting of errors. But, we may suppose that they might then count apparent divergences equally against an interpretation—and decide on an interpretive scheme for a people by choosing that scheme that minimizes divergence. But at this point there is a wrinkle to consider. On the one hand, interpreters could go on ever modifying their interpretations so as to 'explain away errors', adding ever more epicycles to their interpretive schemes, or they could have some sense of 'reasonable' or 'plausible' complexity. At some time, they may sense that an error in inference, an unacknowledged inconsistency or some other piece of irrationality is 'more likely' than yet another sense of the relevant terms in the subjects' lexicon, yet another epicycle. Perhaps, drawing on analogies with their own reasoning, they may sense that the avoidance of attributions of error is making for an unrealistically baroque interpretive scheme. It would be natural to think of such judgments as empirically informed, as drawing on courses of experience. But this is no problem for the strong rationalist who is ready to acknowledge that empirical information can help ascertain when an interpretation closely enough approximates to the a priori ideal. All that has been supposed here is that at some point interpreters do not feel a priori obliged to continue to complicate their interpretations to avoid yet another attribution of inconsistency.

So interpreters now find themselves attributing some irrationality to their subjects: the subjects are found to be marginally diverging from the ideal that was initially supposed. Significantly, they will find a pattern in the divergence; they will find that there seem to be systematic ways in which folk diverge from the normative model. Interpreters will also come to appreciate much about when folk in a given social context learn certain things, for example, and what patterns of motivation are prevalent within a society or within a profession within that society (recall the EE that seemed relevant when thinking about Tversky and Kahneman's work). As suggested earlier, such empirical expectations serve to constrain an interpretation, and can add to the confidence of researchers that their interpretations are reasonable and that the divergences from some rational ideal that they seem to find are indeed real and systematic. As a result, investigators will come to have empirical theories or expectations having to do with human rationality and irrationality.

To this point, the cartoon history has been developed in a way that is highly favorable to the strong rationalist. For purposes of illustration I have supposed that the sort of normative model that the strong rationalist envisioned as anchoring interpretation does indeed constrain interpretation, at least at a mythical beginning in which no empirical expectation regarding human reasoning is brought to the table. Now we can let the disagreement between rationalists and empiricists emerge.

Suppose that we now undertake to understand some new agent or people. According to the rationalist, the model that is presupposed—from which attributed deviations are to be counted against the interpretations that we will entertain—continues to be the same, invariant, normative model (logic, statistical methods, the rest of normative epistemology, and decision theory). What has changed over time is the empirical background understanding which may influence how we weight the seriousness of attributed divergence from this model (but any divergence counts in some measure against the interpretation). So, when we find agents to be reasoning in defective ways that we have come to expect, this counts against our interpretation, at least a little. According to the strong rationalist, there is always some 'tax' on any attributions of irrationality—so that an interpretation that proceeds smoothly and corresponds to our empirically informed expectations for certain forms of irrationality will have yet thereby incurred an 'error tax' on its acceptability. Further attributions of irrationality—even if they conflict with no empirical expectations, and even if these expectations conform to EE-like expectations—may then be difficult to sustain. The a priori normative model continues to anchor and constrain our interpretations—and error taxes on attributions of irrationality preclude interpretive findings that are too much in divergence from that model. Such is the strong rationalist picture.

In contrast, the empiricist need count little more than RRP as conceptually grounded. As expectations for ways of reasoning, including forms of irrationality and forms of rationality, emerge in the course of empirical work drawing on acceptable interpretive schemes, these constitute *an evolving model of human cognition—one that then serves for the empiricist as the model from which divergence is counted against an interpretation.* On this view, there is no 'tax' on attributions conforming to these expectations, this empirical model, even where these diverge from the normative model from which (for purposes of illustration we are supposing that) earlier interpretation took its departure.

Focus now on the issues left hanging at the close of our discussion of Kahneman and Tversky's challenge to RP/ [L^r]. The suggestion was that a range of empirically informed expectations of a diverse sort—EE— serve to provide support for an interpretation that has our subjects systematically violating [L^r]. It would seem that such results can accumulate so as to support an understanding of human cognition that is deeply at odds with [L^r]. The projected rationalist response was that such expectations were themselves dependent on interpretations and thus hostage to [L^r], so that deep challenges to [L^r] were foreclosed. In effect, while [L^r] might be given some 'tweaking', it remains an invariant a priori attractor to which all interpretive results remain tethered. The strength of the tether may vary somewhat with empirical results, but these themselves remain conditioned by interpretations tethered to [L^r].

The empiricists think differently of the fundamental constraints on interpretation. On their view there is no such a priori, invariant and substantive, model serving as an attractor for interpretation (nothing beyond something like RRP). As empirical understandings of human reasoning evolve, so does the 'attractor' to which interpretations must approximate—for those understandings constitute the model that informs interpretation

as an evolving attractor. Because the background empirical expectations—EE— are not tethered to an invariant model along the lines of [L^r], there is no a priori guarantee that these background interpretations, and the interpretations/inquiries that they support, cannot give rise to deep challenges to [L^r]; in fact they themselves could already reflect deep revisions of [L^r]. Thus, on the empiricist understanding, there can be adequate interpretations that attribute deep violations of [L^r], and that thus can occasion revision in [L^r] treated as an account of human cognition.

How can one decide between the two understandings of the principle of charity on offer—the strong rationalist understanding and the empiricist understanding (itself compatible with a weak a priori element such as RRP)? To settle the matter would require an extended reflection on the considerations adduced in a range of interpretive inquiries (such as those found in history and cultural anthropology) and on a range of investigations that suppose and sometimes reconsider interpretations (such as careful work in cognitive psychology). For my own part, I am convinced that the empiricist model provides the most adequate and best-motivated understanding of the relevant inquiries, but developing the support for this conclusion is beyond the scope of this article.

REFERENCES AND SELECT BIBLIOGRAPHY

Bealer, G. (1987) 'The philosophical limits of scientific essentialism', *Philosophical Perspectives* 1: 289–365.

Burge, T. (1979) 'Individualism and the mental', *Midwest Studies in Philosophy*, 4: 73–121.

—— (1992) 'Philosophy of mind and language: 1950–1990', *Philosophical Review*, 101: 3–51.

Chalmers, D. (1996) *The Conscious Mind*. Oxford: Oxford University Press.

—— (2002a) 'Sense and intension', in J. Tomberlin (ed.), *Philosophical Perspectives 16: Language and Mind*. Oxford: Blackwell, pp. 135–82.

—— 2002b. 'The Components of Content', in D. Chalmers (ed.), *Philosophy of Mind: Classical and*

Contemporary Readings. Oxford: Oxford University Press, pp. 608–33.

Davidson, D. (1980a) 'Actions, reasons, and causes', in *Essays on Actions and Events.* Oxford: Clarendon Press, pp. 1–19.

——— (1980b) 'Mental events', in *Essays on Actions and Events.* Oxford: Clarendon Press, pp. 207–25.

——— (1980c) 'Towards a unified theory of meaning and action', *Grazer Philosophical Studies,* 2: 1–12.

——— (1982) 'Paradoxes of irrationality', in R. Wollheim and J. Hopkins (eds), *Philosophical Essays on Freud.* Cambridge: Cambridge University Press, pp. 289–305.

——— (1984a) 'Radical interpretation', in *Inquiries into Truth and Interpretation.* Oxford: Clarendon Press, pp. 125–40.

——— (1984b) 'Belief and the basis of meaning', in *Inquiries into Truth and Interpretation.* Oxford: Clarendon Press, pp. 141–54.

——— (1984c) 'Thought and talk', in *Inquiries into Truth and Interpretation.* Oxford: Clarendon Press, pp. 155–70.

——— (1984d) 'On the very idea of a conceptual scheme', in *Inquiries into Truth and Interpretation.* Oxford: Clarendon Press, pp. 185–98.

Henderson, D. (1987) 'The principle of charity and the problem of irrationality', *Synthese,* 73: 225–52.

——— (1990) 'An empirical basis for charity in translation', *Erkenntnis* 32: 83–103.

——— (1993) *Interpretation and Explanation in the Human Sciences.* Binghamton: State University of New York Press.

——— (1994) 'Conceptual schemes after Davidson', in Gerhard Preyer, Frank Siebelt and Alexander Ulfig (eds), *Language, Mind, and Epistemology: On Donald Davidson's Philosophy.* Dordrecht: Kluwer Academic Publishers, pp. 171–97.

Jackson, P. (1998) *From Metaphysics to Ethics: A Defense of Conceptual Analysis.* Oxford: Clarendon Press.

Kripke, S. (1972) *Naming and Necessity.* Cambridge, MA: Harvard University Press.

Putnam, H. (1975a) 'The meaning of meaning,' in *Mind, Language, and Reality: Philosophical Papers,* vol. 2. Cambridge: Cambridge University Press, pp. 215–71.

——— (1975b) 'The analytic and the synthetic', in *Mind, Language and Reality.* Cambridge: Cambridge University Press, pp. 33–69.

Peacocke, C. (1992) *A Study of Concepts.* Cambridge, MA: MIT Press.

Risjord, M. (2000) *Woodcutters and Witchcraft.* Albany: State University of New York Press.

Quine, W. (1953) 'Two dogmas of empiricism', in *From a Logical Point of View.* Cambridge, MA: Harvard University Press.

——— (1960) *Word and Object.* Cambridge, MA: MIT Press.

——— (1970) 'Philosophical progress in language theory', *Metaphilosophy* 1: 2–19.

——— (1981) 'On the very Idea of a third dogma', *Theories and Things.* Cambridge, MA: Harvard University Press, pp. 38–42.

——— (1987) 'Indeterminacy of translation again', *Journal of Philosophy* 84: 5–10.

Rosenberg, A. (1985) 'Davidson's unintended attack on psychology', in E. LaPore and B. McLaughlin (eds), *Actions and Events: Perspectives of the Philosophy of Donald Davidson.* Worchester, MA: Blackwell, pp. 399–407.

——— (1988) *Philosophy of Social Science.* Boulder, CO: Westview Press.

Stich, S. (1990) *The Fragmentation of Reason.* Cambridge, MA: MIT Press.

Tversky, A. (1975) 'A critique of expected utility theory: Descriptive and normative considerations', *Erkenntnis,* 9: 163–73.

Tversky, A. and Kahneman, D. (1974) 'Judgments under uncertainty: Heuristics and biases', *Science* 185: 1124–31.

Whorf, B. (1956) 'The punctal and segmentative aspects of verbs in Hopi', in J.B. Carroll (ed.), *Language, Thought and Reality: Selected Writings of Benjamin Lee Whorf.* Cambridge, MA: The MIT Press, pp. 51–6.

NOTES

1 Putnam (1975a) provides a useful discussion of this tradition, which he then criticizes.

2 There is, of course, an obvious possibility which would take the air out of the neo-rationalist program: the element of the semantics of concepts that is accessible to one who is conceptually competent, merely by virtue of that person being conceptually competent, might turn out to be such a wimpy component of the conceptual semantics that traditional empiricist deflationary responses seem appropriate.

3 Although the transition just now suggested reflects a grounds for skepticism regarding whether there is *any* line to be drawn between conceptual truths (analytic claims) and truths that are central to empirically supported theories of some matter (which would be synthetic). Famously, Quine (1953, 1960) argued that central elements of our empirical theories or understandings may seem relatively safe from revision, but that this matter of degree should not be confused with the supposed status of being

'true by meaning' or being 'purely conceptually grounded'—or any status that would make for a prioricity.

4 And to cut down on alternative understandings of choices/undertakings, we are to progressively constrain our understanding of these in terms of wider sets of standing beliefs and desires attributable to the agent or agents.

5 Those familiar with Rosenberg's work will doubtless find it strange to read of him as advancing a 'rationalist' position. This is a function of the early choice to treat the claim that there are significant a priori principles as a mark of rationalism, even when these principles are understood as conceptually grounded. As explained, many contemporary self-labeled 'rationalists' fall into this camp—for example, Peacocke, Chalmers and Bealer. Using the designation 'rationalist' is so broad a fashion that one can be an empiricist and yet still be a rationalist. Rosenberg would be a case in point. He thinks that there are significant, conceptually mandated, a priori constraints on interpretation—ones that are 'almost definitional' of action and related concepts—and then he insists that this renders such concepts unworkable for any respectable science. The conceptual constraints certainly do not seem trivial, as they amount to the idea that actions, beliefs, and desires interact so as to largely conform to the rather elaborate dictates of decision theory. Since he thinks that the social sciences are so constrained, he thinks that these are not respectable sciences, and would have us change the subject of inquiry. The same verdict is applied to any intentional psychology. In effect, Rosenberg accommodates the rationalist brief presented here by insisting that such concepts and constraints have no place in any respectable empirical science. We do not study unicorns—for good empirical reasons. Neither should we study actions and reasons.

6 Of course, the rationalist would insist that [L'] serves as an a priori truth regarding all agents—all who act for reasons—not just humans. But, given that humans are supposedly such agents, it would need to serve as an a priori truth of human cognition: *if* humans have beliefs and desires, *if* they act, then [L'] must (on the rationalist account) hold true of human cognition.

7 For further development of these themes, see Henderson (1993) Chapter 7.

8 For a more sustained development of this contrast, see Henderson (1993), chapters 2–3.

17

Individual and Collective Agency

Thomas Schwinn

The relation between individual action and social structures is one of the central fundamental problems in sociology. It has accompanied it throughout its existence and has been the focus of repeated vigorous debates. One can distinguish three phases of particularly intensive discussion (Udehn, 2002: 479). The first was at the end of the nineteenth and the beginning of the twentieth centuries, when the subject was established as an independent discipline; the second was in the immediate post-World War II decades, in which a critical controversy developed over the range of Parsonian system theory. The third phase began in the 1980s (Alexander et al., 1987; Knorr-Cetina and Cicourel, 1981) and is still continuing, largely driven by the enormous spread of rational choice theory in the social sciences. The concepts used are multiple and changing: individual/society, action/order, system/action theory, micro/macro, methodological individualism/methodological holism. One can also, and independently, distinguish two types of explanatory question (Schimank, 2000): the explanation of action choices and the explanation of the structural effects of the interaction of many actors. The following observations focus on these two questions. For the explanation of action choices there are essentially four sociological models of the actor: homo sociologicus, homo economicus, dramaturgical action and emotionally determined action. Methodological individualists and methodological holists compete over the explanation of the micro/macro connection, i.e., over how a multiplicity of individual actions are arranged into structures or systems. There are different variants of both.

ACTOR MODELS

Let us turn first to the question of individual action. There is general agreement in the social sciences that human action is intentional or purposively directed. Max Weber provided the best known definition: '"action" denotes human behavior if and insofar as the actor or actors link it with a subjective meaning' (1978: 4). As a rule intentions are multifarious and the actor is confronted with the problem of selecting between possible alternative actions. The central question here is how actors choose from among the available alternatives those which they actually carry out. Sociology considers every concrete action first of all in the light of other possibilities. The situation in which an actor finds him or herself does not dictate a specific action; otherwise one would not need action theory. The actors must first make sense of the situation for themselves within the socially available possibilities. They must interpret and define it as a specific situation and derive from it their choice of action. The sociological analysis of an action situation always asks about other possibilities as well as those actually realized. Why does someone define their situation in this way and not otherwise, and why do they decide on the basis of this definition of the situation to do just this and not something else? Such questions are not only asked by social scientists: everyone does this again and again in everyday life, when confronted by the unexpected action of another, or when one asks oneself what one is really doing and why. What is involved in such thought experiments in which other possibilities are played out in the imagination is the search for a well-grounded explanation of why the actor chose just this possibility—for example, because other action alternatives played out in thought revealed themselves as unrealistic.

The analysis of alternative action choices does not mean that sociology attributes to the actor unlimited freedom of action. Every sociological explanation is based on the premise that the actor's range of alternatives is structurally limited. A sociological explanation of action can only work if actors are also led along by structures and if these structures are social ones. Biological, genetic, psychological, geographical or other conditions are only data or parameters of action (Schmid, 2004: 12). Thus theories of inborn behavioral programs, psychological theories of cognition and perception, the psychoanalytic theory of the unconscious or, say, genetics are not a central component of action theory but merely background theories (Weber, 1978: 7). If action were determined by the social structures in which it moves, a structural theory would be sufficient. So-called structuralism indeed believed that in our action we are channeled and led by prior conditions.

What can one oppose to such an assumption, other than that the thought that all our action is pre-determined is uncomfortable, because we like to conceive ourselves as freely acting individuals? The number and diversity of structures or conditions which impinge on an actor in a specific situation is very great, and they are mostly not determinate in their effect. All one needs to do is to recall in outline various types of social structures: structures of distribution, authority structures, organizational, legal, cultural, technical structures etc. Usually more than one of these structural aspects is involved in any situation in various forms. The effects of the different structural dimensions intersect and reinforce or weaken one another in many different ways. Some structures have more of a restrictive effect; others are more enabling. It is completely illusory to try to derive a determinate action choice from the multiplicity of structural components which influence any action. The various individual structural influences do not converge on a determinate outcome: they accumulate in an uncoordinated and fragmentary way. There may be situations where one has no other choice, where the structural context of action has such a strong effect in shaping it. This is however not the normal and typical situation and it therefore cannot serve as a standard model of sociological explanation.

How can we classify the various action theories? The student or teacher of sociology is indeed confronted by a confused mass of approaches and theories. I have already mentioned one criterion for classification: theories can be differentiated according to which type of action orientiation they emphasize: utility, norms, dramaturgical aspects or emotions. It is helpful to look at Max Weber's *Basic Concepts of Sociology* ([1962] 1980). There Weber presents various ways in which an actor can orient his or her action (Weber, [1962], 1980: 24f.): purposive-rational, value-rational, emotional and traditional. Apart from the traditional type, which is really concerned not with action but behavior, these various action types are at the center of various theories of action (see for example Habermas, 1981, I: 114ff.; tr. 75ff.).

In rational choice approaches the purposefully calculating actor predominates. The norm-oriented type is found in various theories, one of the most prominent of which is in Talcott Parsons's (1968) *The Structure of Social Action*. The dramaturgical model of action is not to be found in Weber but is introduced by Erving Goffman (1959; Habermas, 1981 I: 128, 135ff.; tr. 86, 90ff). Emotionally shaped action has been brought to prominence in the last decades by various authors (Collins, 1993; Flam, 1990; Gerhards, 1988; Hochschild, 1983).

But what about such well-known approaches as the pragmatism founded by George Herbert Mead (1959), which formed the basis of what came to be called symbolic interactionism (Blumer, 1986), or Alfred Schütz's phenomenological sociology (1974), which was developed in ethnomethodology (Garfinkel, 1989) and elsewhere? Here again a reference to Max Weber is useful. Before introducing various types of action in Paragraph 2 of his *Basic Concepts of Sociology* he discusses 'Methodological Foundations' in Paragraph 1. Independently of the types of action to be specified by their content there are prior general questions for any theory of action. How is action to be defined and distinguished from behavior? How do meaning and intersubjectivity come about? What is the role of the understanding of human action in relation to its explanation? How is the transition from action to social action possible? How is the relation of scientific observer to participants to be specified? Whatever action orientation predominates, for example, the actors must in all cases give meaning to a situation through processes of definition. Recourse to symbols and to shared stocks of meaning and knowledge is important here, but so are subjective expectations. And whatever the type of action there is the problem of role-taking, the ability to put oneself in the other's place so as to anticipate his or her standpoint and action and to react appropriately.

These problems are undoubtedly addressed and thematized in every action theory, but the different approaches can still be distinguished by whether they tend to set one of the differentiated types of action in the foreground of their analysis and also discuss the methodological issues in that context, or whether these issues are made central. Mead and Schütz, for example, do not thematize any particular type of action but rather the general questions of action theory. This is where the philosophical affiliations of sociology become relevant. Weber and Schütz, for example, attempt to ground sociology in the philosophy of consciousness, whereas Mead and Habermas rely on the philosophy of language (Habermas, 1981; Schwinn, 1993a; Schluchter, 2000). This differentiation between sociological theories of action which address foundational problems and those which pursue a specific type of action cannot admittedly be upheld in strict terms. Some representatives of a rational choice approach, for example, address basic theoretical issues (Coleman, 1990; Esser, 1993); Talcott Parsons derives the primacy of the normative approach from a discussion of problems in sociological theory (Parsons, 1968). Max Weber's continuing prominence over the past century is surely due to the fact that we find in his work both the important foundational problems and almost all the types of action. Later theories have concentrated more narrowly on individual types. In what follows I will confine myself to a presentation of the four basic types of action and leave aside foundational issues. This seems appropriate for a chapter on 'Individual and Collective Agency'; moreover, methodological questions arise again with the transition to collective action.

Homo Economicus

Sociology has developed a limited number of models of actors or types of action to deal with the question of how actors select from among the situationally available action alternatives those which they in fact carry out. I should like to begin with *homo economicus* (Schimank, 2000: 71ff.). This is a model, originally developed in economics, which has in recent years become very widely diffused in sociology and has been further developed to suit its purposes. Among its prominent representatives are James Coleman, Jon Elster, Hartmut Esser and Raymond Boudon. They all belong to the same theoretical family: 'rational choice'.

Homo economicus displays certain basic properties. 'He' orients his action choice according to *utility* and acts so as to maximize his own utility at the least possible cost. This is under the condition of the *limited resources* available to achieve his goal. *Homo economicus* lives in a world of scarcity. His needs and goals exceed his means and possibilities. In all our actions we encounter scarcities of the most diverse kind; hence the need to make choices. If I had enough of everything—money, time, power, knowledge etc.—I would not have to decide and could leave myself to follow my inclinations. So I must make a rational choice only because scarcity forces me to do so.

A further basic characteristic is *diminishing marginal utility*. When I am very thirsty, the first bottle of water I buy gives me the greatest utility, the second much less; I am not even ready to buy a third, because its marginal utility is close to zero. Our thirst is no more insatiable than our hunger, our need for knowledge, our pursuit of career, prestige and so on. *Diminishing marginal utility* ensures that we change our goals and do not remain fixed on a single one. Thus a human being's stream of action displays a sequence of always temporarily pursued, and mostly only partially fulfilled, goals. Thus the pursuit of every goal has *opportunity costs* in the form of the lost utility of pursuing other goals. Under conditions of scarcity we set everything we do in relation to what we could do instead—always calculating several utilities and need satisfactions.

Homo economicus weighs costs and benefits *subjectively*, not according to objective criteria and dimensions which are valid for all. It is not only the cost-benefit calculation which is subjective, but also the judgment of the likelihood of a particular action taking effect. The utility of an action depends not only on the volume of the positive effects resulting from the attainment of the goal, but also the likelihood of its attainment. This is for example subjectively overestimated in lottery gambling, although it is objectively infinitesimal. This actor model does not assume that the prospects of action in a particular situation are equally estimated by all concerned. Moreover, the subjective estimation of costs and benefits of an action choice vary with the *time horizon*. The effects of an action are estimated lower, the further off in the future they are expected to occur.

A final relevant element is the *size of the group* to whose collective utility I am to contribute and from which I as an individual am to profit. This is known as the collective goods dilemma which is typical of larger groups or collectives. An example is ecological goods such as clean water or air. Actors are less willing to incur costs for a collective benefit the less they can identify a direct connection between their individual contribution and the result or effect of their action. Even very small participation costs will here appear subjectively irrational. Thus larger groups encourage a free-rider mentality.

The *homo economicus* model has attracted a number of critical objections. Real actors do not behave in their action choices anything like as rationally as the theory assumes. They are mostly content with a satisfying action choice and do not work through all the elements in an optimally rational way. Rationality is expensive in terms of time, information and consensus, and these three conditions are rarely adequately given. The closest approximation is in so-called high-cost situations. These are decision situations in which a lot is at stake for the actor. Mistakes can be enormously costly and right decisions can provide great benefits. Here actors will take the necessary time to reflect thoroughly on what they are doing; they will carefully try to augment their information and they will be ready to work out conflicts with others in order to obtain the necessary consensus for what they consider right. Low-cost situations, on the other hand, are marked by routinized action schemes which drastically simplify the complexity of the action contexts and thus permit rapid action.

Finally there is a further fundamental problem: how do the actors arrive at their judgments of utility? As long as one cannot specify these, the utility-maximizing principle remains abstract and empty. This is where the rational choice approach hits its limits, since one cannot explain what people find useful in terms of utility. Max Weber emphasized this with his distinction between ideas and interests. Moreover it is questionable whether one can explain morally or ethically motivated action in terms of rational calculations of utility (Elster, 1991).

Homo Sociologicus

According to Weber action can be not only purposive–rational, but also *value-rationally* oriented. This was later developed into another actor model, the so-called *homo sociologicus* (Dahrendorf, 1973). This is an actor who makes action decisions on a primarily normative basis. Parsons's (1968) theory of action emphasized the normative dimension in explicit opposition to the utilitarian tradition discussed above. This model was primarily developed in role theory. Emile Durkheim was one of the first sociologists to identify the peculiar force of social norms. According to him it is norms which keep action on a particular path. Role theory later begins from this basic idea.

The concept of role derives from the theater world and describes how, like stage actors, actors in social institutions also perform according to a specific script. Here one does not need a theory of individual action, since this is anyway seen as determined 'from outside'. However we saw in the introduction to this chapter that structural determination cannot serve as a basic conception for a theory of action. Even the norms associated with social roles do not determine the

actor carrying them out, but merely demand decisions in the light of action alternatives. The degree to which the norms are binding varies, and so do the associated sanctions. One can distinguish between 'must', 'should' and 'can' expectations (Dahrendorf, 1973: 20ff.). Must-expectations are highly obligatory and often legally specified. Non-compliance is punished with massive negative sanctions. Should-expectations are less binding. Violations are also punished, but much more mildly. Arriving at work on time and sober is a must-expectation for a teacher, and sanctions are only negative. To take particular care in one's teaching is a should-expectation which can also result in positive sanctions if one complies with it. Finally can-expectations are least binding. Non-compliance entails no negative sanctions. A teacher who does a lot for his or her pupils outside immediate working hours may count on positive sanctions (rewards).

As well as their varying degrees of associated obligation, the multiplicity of norms raises decision problems for actors. Reference group theory (Merton, 1968: 279ff.) draws attention to this. Normative role expectations mostly come from different directions and they do not converge towards a common result but partially contradict one another. Conflicts within and between roles demand of the actor a substantial degree of competence in decision and action.

Two aspects of role behavior can be distinguished here (Schimank, 2000: 55ff.): role-taking and role-making. Role-taking is possible in situations in which norms unproblematically provide secure expectations. The normative expectations coming from various reference groups interact so as to reinforce one another and give the actor clear directions. Role-making by contrast refers to situations in which action confronts contradictions and normative gaps. As a rule, in modern societies the frequency of 'role-making' has tended to increase, and that of unproblematic 'role-taking' to decrease. This is due to growing role differentiation and the associated multiplicity of normative expectations. Standard solutions are harder to regulate and institutionalize, since one cannot find a generally valid rule for every situation and complication. Individuals must then find their own solutions to their problems. The complexity of modern social relations and the autonomy of the individual are two sides of the same coin. Actors must sustain social order through role-making. Detailed regulations and solutions have to be found. This demands the ability to understand the Other and to grasp long and complicated chains of interactions and role positions. Modern social orders are no longer brought about as a merely mechanical application of given norms, but require the active and creative *homo sociologicus*.[1] What is important in this model, however, is that these action decisions are not taken according to cost-benefit calculations but according to norms. Utility is the idea of an advantage which becomes the cause of my action. A norm is the idea of an inner duty which becomes the cause of my action. Normative orientation is, then, another mode of decision which is distinct from the utilitarian one previously presented.

Emotional Man

Although this type of action was already conceptualized by Max Weber as affectual action, it has only been developed more systematically in the last decades (Collins, 1993; Flam, 1990; Gerhards, 1988; Hochschild, 1983; Schimank, 2000: 107ff.). *Homo emotionalis* or emotional man (Flam, 1990) is a distinct model of the actor. We often act on the basis of emotions such as envy, rage, love or joy, and this cannot be adequately grasped by the two previously presented models.

In order to make clear the specificity of emotions, I shall distinguish them from instincts on the one hand and cognitions on the other. All three are basic modes of grasping the world. *Instincts* are inborn dispositions to particular forms of behavior. They largely determine motor processes, perception and the scope which is opened up to learning. Instinctual determination specifies a one-to-one relation between the organism and its environment. Specific initial conditions necessarily result in corresponding behavior. Emotions, by contrast, are not biologically programmed like instincts. Even very strongly emotional reaction patterns are socially shaped. This is shown, for example, by cultural comparisons which document the substantial variability in forms of expression of rage. Further, emotions unlike instincts, allow for the interruption of strong stimulus-response sequences. Stimuli do not lead automatically to specific emotional behavior. Between the stimulus and the reaction come emotions, which make it possible to evaluate the meaning of the environmental stimulus. This intermediate evaluation of stimuli leads to a more flexible and differentiated relation to the environment. If we had an instinct which linked injuries to our body with aggressive behavior, we would have to strike out every time someone stepped on our foot. Instead, the emotion of 'irritation' in response to such an event makes it possible to de-couple the reactive action from the immmediate reception of the stimulus. Once we are sure that it was not intentional, we make light of the event.

Now to the relation between emotions and *cognitions*. These are both modes of orientation which create order in our experience of our environment, but in two different ways. Emotions constitute a *simultaneous* form of construction of the world, and cognitions a *sequential* way of perceiving it. Simultaneous means grasping the world as a gestalt, in which the details are grasped, not in a differentiated way one after another, but simultaneously and figuratively. A cognitive grasp of reality, by contrast, is sequential. Here the central medium is language. The relation between word and object operates according to a building-block principle: one can select infinitely many aspects of the world and make varied combinations out of them.

There are differences not only in *content* but also in the *time dimension*. Thanks to their simultaneous character emotions permit a rapid grasp of a situation, whereas a cognitive assessment would take longer. On encountering a new person or situation certain emotions tend to arise very quickly. One feels comfortable, uncomfortable or insecure without yet having cognitively understood the person/situation. The strength of emotions in the time dimension becomes a weakness in the content dimension, since here only limited depth and precision is possible. This explains when we take action decisions more emotionally, and when on a more strongly cognitive basis. In surprising situations emotions come to the fore as impulses to action, because the sequential character of cognitions is too slow to handle the surprise. Massive interruptions in routine, negative as well as positive, generate emotional forms of behavior, not cognitive chains of conclusions. These only set in again when the surprise is over. One also takes action decisions on an emotional basis when one has carefully thought something through, say according to cost/benefit or normative criteria and still not arrived at a clear result. But only in very few situations do we act only cognitively or only emotionally: in most cases both components operate together.

Cognitions enable an analytical dissection of reality and hence enormous multiplicity and flexibility. The resultant complexity is limited and bound by emotions: they set limits to the analysis. Thus, for example, one can approach the analytical dissection and recombination of the human gene with mixed feelings and emotionally call for limits; one does not feel 'comfortable' with it. Furthermore, emotional and normative components interact. Norms specify what kind of emotions can be lived out and to what degree. Hochschild (1983) speaks here of 'feeling rules'—for example, for a nurse who should not let her distaste for a particular patient be noticed.

'Goff-Man'

The Canadian sociologist Erving Goffman (1959) developed a fourth, quite independent model of action, in which the identity of the actor is central. There are actions which we carry out only, or primarily, because we want to present to the outside world and to ourselves a particular self-image. Habermas (1981, I: 128, 135ff.) has well described this type as the *dramaturgical model of action.* What are decisive here for action decisions are not criteria of purposive–rational utility maximization or normative orientation, but rather the concern to adequately express our identity in our action. George Herbert Mead assumed that we attain our identity by taking on the perspective of the other. This however presupposes that the other is in a specifiable relation to me—something which cannot be assumed as a matter of principle. According to Goffman, actors' reciprocal approaches to one another in interactions are partial and limited. Hence taking on the perspective of the other does not provide any clear indication about how s/he will see me, what image s/he forms of me, so that I could derive from this my own self-image.

This fundamental incompleteness and uncertainty of our knowledge of others forms the starting-point for Goffman's basic idea that everyone tries to present their behavior in such a way as to lead others to form an image of them which corresponds to their own self-image. I use presentation and dramaturgy to control the situation in my interest and so as to ensure that others form the impression of me that I want them to form. Identity is not something which develops on the margins of our social interactions but rather demands ongoing impression management. Thus the formation of identity demands much more of our own input than Mead seemed to assume. The techniques of self-presentation operate precisely because we have an incomplete knowledge of others. If we had a far-reaching insight into other people, impression and identity management could be checked for their accuracy and could hardly be sustained.

In his book *Asylums* (1961), Goffman shows that even in total institutions, which attempt to impose on their inmates a corporate identity as their personal identity, one can observe attempts to evade these imposed identities. Individuals cannot be prevented from constructing an identity which escapes complete subordination to the institution. Goffman lays out a repertoire of ways of behaving in total institutions: forms of ritual disobedience, irony, parody or extreme self-control. From a utilitarian point of view such behavior is foolish, because it entails enormous costs and disadvantages. Nor can it be captured with the normative criteria of *homo sociologicus*. One must therefore include the dramaturgic model of the actor as an independent one that enables us to grasp important aspects of action which cannot be grasped or even seen in the other approaches.

This section ends with the question of the relation between these four types of action. Utilitarian, normative, emotional and dramaturgic orientations are normally present to different degrees in any single action. There may also be a change of type: capitalist action, initially based on normative religious motives, changes into something motivated by purposive rationality and utility; a commercial relationship can develop into a love relationship or acquire a normative dimension, and so on (Schwinn, 1993b). Can these transitions and the relations between the four models of action be integrated into an inclusive theory? Rational choice theory claims to do this. It aims to show that all forms of action are sub-types of a single primary type of action. All actions which do not belong to the core domain of the theory are redefined: a normative orientation is explained by the interests of rational egoists; a love relationship serves to provide the benefit of bodily comfort.

One must be skeptical about the explanatory power of such an inflated concept of utility. A 'theory' of this kind is universal, but empty. What is offered here is less an explanation than a mere redefinition. For the moment there is no theory in sight which could convincingly integrate all these models of action. A more promising strategy would seem to be to start by pursuing inductive insights into the predominance of particular action orientations and transitions from one to another, so as to derive general propositions about their inter-relation. We have, for example, identified a predominance of *homo economicus* in

high-cost situations and of *homo emotionalis* in situations of surprise. Changes in the situational context will lead to a change in orientation or a new combination of orientations. It is questionable whether there could ever be a theory capable of theoretically modeling these interrelations.

COLLECTIVE ACTION: METHODOLOGICAL INDIVIDUALISM VERSUS METHODOLOGICAL COLLECTIVISM

When we know the criteria according to which human beings act, we still do not know how their actions are arranged into structures and to what degree they depend on one another. Issues concerning collective action cannot be derived from the models of action previously presented. In scarcely any action is an actor independent of what others do. Cumulative effects, interferences and interactions between actors are normally present. This raises the second central explanatory problem for sociology. There are also theoretical models and traditions concerned with the problem of collective action: essentially the two explanatory strategies of methodological individualism and methodological collectivism. Both have a long tradition in their respective variants. Methodological collectivism assumes that the processes of collective action constitute an independent level which cannot, as methodological individualism assumes, be explained from the level of individual action. I shall first discuss the latter position and present different variants of it.

From Atomistic to Structural Individualism

A historical retrospective (Udehn, 2002) is interesting here. One of the oldest variants of this approach are so-called contract theories. With Greek predecessors, Thomas Hobbes and John Locke are the main representatives. The starting point for all these theories is a pre-social state of nature, in which, according to Hobbes, people live in violence, war and fear. In order to escape this situation, the individuals enter into contracts, in which they commit themselves to a generally binding system of law, protected and sanctioned by a state. This is an extremely individualistic perspective on the emergence of collective patterns of action, since the contract theories presuppose pre-social, isolated individuals who only subsequently discover forms of order. We can label this *atomistic individualism*.

In contrast to contract theories, economic thought assumes a spontaneous emergence of order. Social orders are not shaped consciously by human insight, but are the result of unintended consequences of the action of individuals. There are different versions of this. John Stuart Mill assumed that macro-social phenomena must be derived from psychological laws. This *psychological individualism* is further developed by Leon Walras and Kenneth Arrow (Udehn, 2002: 482ff.). Here, an economic explanation is only seen as satisfactory if the variables are derived from individual psychological factors and natural conditions. With Carl Menger, an important Austrian economic theorist, social institutions play a greater role, but they are still explained as the unintended result of the action of individuals. The methodological individualism of Austrian economic theory continues in the work of Ludwig von Mises and Friedrich von Hayek, and also with Max Weber and Alfred Schütz, who extend this methodology from economics to social science and support it with additional epistemological and ontological grounds. Weber furthermore emphasizes the social pre-conditions of action. Although social orders must *logically* always be explained interpretatively in terms of the action of individuals, *historically* they are always prior to the individuals. This is not an atomistic individualism, presupposing asocial actors who only later enter into relations with one another (Schluchter, 2000: 131; Schwinn, 1993a: 35f.).

Max Weber, like Karl Popper subsequently, also rejects the idea that macro-phenomena

can be explained by psychological laws. Primacy is given to a situational and institutional logic, not a psychological one. In this *structural individualism,* unlike the earlier atomistic and psychologistic individualism, social institutions appear not only in the explanandum but also in the explanans. Institutions form part of the pre-conditions of action and cannot be seen only as a result of it (Udehn, 2002: 489). The sociology of the last few decades has strengthened this insight, and it is now one of the inescapable basic premises of sociological thought. Anthony Giddens did not discover it, but his duality model gives it a precise expression: social structures are both consequences and pre-conditions of action. Even in the more recent rational choice theories (Coleman, 1990; Esser, 1993; Esser, 2000), we can observe a greater role given to structural components as an independent explanatory factor. Social structure takes the form of a set of interdependent positions that are prior to the interaction between the individuals occupying these positions. According to Coleman this means that to talk about 'aggregation' is misleading: 'for the phenomena to be explained involve interdependence of individuals' actions, not merely aggregated individual behavior' (Udehn, 2002: 494).

This short historical outline has shown that there are different versions of methodological individualism. The line of development has been roughly from an atomistic and psychologistic to a more structural individualism, in which institutions and orders are given a stronger weight as explanans and not only as explanandum. There are admittedly variants even in structural individualism which are more subjectivistic or more objectivistic. Within the rational choice theory family, Raymond Boudon and Jon Elster, for example, adopt a more subjectivistic emphasis, which takes into account a complex psychology. Coleman's approach, by contrast, is more objectivistic: he is more interested in structural conditions than in how subjects respond to them (Udehn, 2002: 496, 500).

In the history of methodological individualism, sociological explanations have given increasing importance to macro-phenomena of collective action. This does not resolve the issue of what status is given to structures or systems. For this it is necessary to expand the methodological investigation to ask about epistemological premises. Methodologies indicate to researchers *how* they should carry out the analysis of a problem. Epistemologies offer reasons *why* they should operate in that way. Every social theory contains such epistemological and ontological assumptions (Habermas, 1981, I: Chapter 1.3; Schluchter, 2000; Schwinn, 1993a). One can distinguish three basic positions on the micro/macro problem in sociology (Heintz, 2004): eliminative, reductionist and emergentist. The last of these is also described as methodological collectivism or as system theory.

Eliminative Theories

These approaches do not only reduce macro-phenomena to micro-processes but make the further claim that strictly speaking there are no macro-phenomena. Randall Collins is a representative of this theory family. For him, social macro-structures are not an independent level of reality but *aggregates* of a larger or smaller number of micro-events. 'A micro-translation strategy reveals the empirical realities of social structures as patterns of repetitive micro-interaction' (Collins, 1981: 985). For Collins (1981: 989, 995; 1988) there are only three real macro-variables: the distribution of individuals in space, the time taken by social processes, and the number of participating individuals. It is only these physical accompaniments of action which cannot be reduced to micro-events: all others are denied the status of reality:

What is 'empirical' meets us only in the form of micro encounters, and any macrostructure, no matter how large, consists only of the repeated experience of large numbers of persons in time and space. Our macroconcepts are only words we apply to these aggregations of microencounters ... The structures never *do* anything; it is only persons in real situations who act. (Collins, 1987: 195)

In a second variant of eliminative theories macro-phenomena are seen as *mental constructs* (Heintz, 2004: 16f.). According to Max Weber, a 'state' or an 'organization' does not exist as an independent ontological structure, but merely as a representation in the heads of human beings (Weber, [1962] 1980: 14; cf. also Schimank, 1988). Such conceptual constructs may have an enormous effect on people's action, but in this approach collective phenomena must not be reified.

Reductionist Theories

Unlike eliminative theories, reductionist approaches do not deny that social macro-phenomena display properties which are more than mere aggregates of individual actions or mental constructs (Heintz, 2004: 17ff.). Instead, social structures are attributed their own level of reality. The reductionist program is most clearly pursued by rational choice theories.

The assumption that society is *not* a mere *aggregate* of individual, isolated actors, but that it forms its own level which goes clearly beyond the properties of the individual actors, is one of the basic assumptions of sociology in the most general sense: *all* sociological conceptions of society—whatever their differences in other respects—share at least this common premise: society *is* in fact *more* than the mere sum of its parts; and it *is* a force which in reality is prior to the concrete individuals and strongly shapes their action. (Esser, quoted from Heintz, 2004: 17)

Coleman (1987) also explicitly opposes a merely aggregative conception of macro-phenomena. But unlike the emergence or system theoretical positions to be discussed later, for reductionist theories all collective phenomena must be derivable from individual action (Coleman, 1987; Esser, 2000: 44, 59; Esser, 1993: 93ff.). The micro–macro connection is established by means of bridging hypotheses and transformation rules. The bridging hypotheses track the effect of the structural conditions on the action situation, thus putting together the macro-social context with the micro-sociological analysis of the subjective definition of the situation, while the transformation rules show how the individual actions build up into macro-phenomena. These in turn then determine the action situation in which the actor takes a decision. This body of theories assume 'downward causation'. The system is a level 'which arises and imposes itself *independently* of the particular motives and relations of the individual actors and often even *against* their intentions and interests, as it were anonymously and behind their backs' (Esser, 2000: 270).

The difficulty here is how to reconcile the assumption of an 'objective force' of the macro-level with the reductionist explanatory strategy:

> As soon as one assumes that macro-phenomena are not mere fictions, which are only relevant to action as 'representations', one is no longer far from the assumption of the ontological irreducibility of the social, thus coming close to what the reductionists see as the cardinal sin of the 'collectivists'. (Heintz, 2004: 19)

This contradiction can only be resolved if the reductionist program is consistently followed through, and macro-structures are analyzed in terms of the actors and their relations. Reductionism can only mean that there is no difference in the system properties without differences in the properties of the components of the system or their arrangement (Stephan, 2000: 37). Macro-phenomena then cannot be given an ontological status or an empirical correlate. This also follows implicitly from the reductionists' rejection of 'same-level-causation' on the macro-level: a macro-phenomenon at time t_1 does not produce by macro-determination the subsequent macro-phenomenon at t_2.[2] Sociology has recently abandoned macro-laws and a strongly deductive–nomological explanatory strategy (Hedström and Swedberg, 1998; Mayntz, 2002).

Emergence and System Theories

Whereas in the reductionist perspective the reduction of macro-phenomena to micro-processes must be possible in principle, for system theorists emergent properties are not caused by micro-processes. This does not mean that this type of theory is concerned only with macro-phenomena. System theory is a comprehensive social theory which claims validity for all levels, from simple interactions to organizations and right up to the world society. 'System' is not a specific domain but a particular method of analysis. In much social science the conception of system is based on size or complexity: it is claimed that beyond certain levels of complexity, indicated by the number of actors, action theory fails and another, system theoretical approach is necessary. This is however a misunderstanding. The concept of system is not dependent on size but is a fundamental theoretical concept (Schwinn, 2004). The subject of action is replaced by the system.

The action theories previously discussed, and eliminative and reductionist theories, have one thing in common: the subject is the central bearer of meaningful conduct and thereby the basic unit of analysis. In system theory, by contrast, these entities are constituted 'from above'. Elements are elements only for the system that employs them as units and they are such only through this system (Luhmann, 1984: 43; tr.: 22). Parsons's unit act is conceived from the beginning as an elementary building block of a system in which the subject of action is just a component (Schwinn, 1993a). For Luhmann it is communications which are irreducible social elements. The relation between the subject and the social is specified by the system-environment model. Subjects merely are part of the environment of the social; they do not construct it. This is just like the relation of brain to consciousness. Without a brain there is no consciousness, but consciousness is emergent in relation to its organic basis in the brain. They reciprocally constitute environments for one another which cannot be derived from one another. The same is true of the relation between the subject and the social. Without consciousnesses there would be no communications, but the latter are emergent in relation to the former. Both reciprocally provide environments for one another. According to Luhmann, even a simple interaction or communication between two people is something emergent, whose course cannot be derived from the intentions of the actors taking part. For Luhmann there are further social levels, such as organizations—functional systems—society or world society. Each is emergent in relation to the previous one and not, as in reductionist theories, derivable from them. The relations between these social levels are explained by the system–environment model: they reciprocally constitute environments for one another. If, for example, societal structures change, this may have consequences for organizations, but the way in which the latter react to changes in their social environment is determined only by system–immanent (i.e., organizational) criteria. The social in general, like its various levels, displays independent properties which cannot be epistemically reduced to others.

One can essentially distinguish three stages or models of the development of system theory (Luhmann, 1982: 229ff.). The first was the model of the *whole and parts*, which makes substantial use of biological analogies and can be found in Emile Durkheim's account of the division of labor. The second is the *system–environment* model as developed by Parsons. Whereas in the earlier model the emphasis was on the parts and their relations, but it was often not clear where the external borders were, this second model is concerned also with strategies by which a system maintains itself in confrontation with an unpredictable environment. Parsons, for example, thematizes this through the evolutionary universals. The internal processes of the system are however again analyzed according to the part-whole model and specified in the AGIL formula. This is the starting point for Luhmann's elaboration, in which the system–environment model is also used for processes internal to the system. The partial systems and societal sub-systems arising from differentiation constitute environments for one another. The overall system of society is not separated into

parts whose relations, as with Parsons, could be understood as an exchange precisely modeled in the AGIL scheme. Overall this exacerbates the integration problem, since according to the system–environment model the reaction to changes in the environment can take place only according to mechanisms internal to the system. Hence Luhmann rejects the AGIL scheme and the cybernetic hierarchy it presupposes between the partial systems. There are no longer fixed relations between them which could be represented in a formula.

CONCLUSION

The two concepts forming the title of this chapter describe the basic question for sociology. All sociological investigations are concerned with two issues. First, the explanation of people's action: why does a particular actor act in this way and not otherwise? Second, the explanation of the collective effects of interaction. For the first issue we presented the four central models of the actor. Action can be utility-oriented, norm-oriented, or emotionally or dramaturgically directed. This gives us four sets of motives for action decisions and impulses to action. Although there are attempts to reduce them to a fundamental type, in relation to which the others would be merely sub-types, this has not so far been successful or convincing. Rational choice theory in particular claims primacy here. A more promising strategy is that of Max Weber, working with various types of action and choosing the appropriate one for each object of analysis.

For the second explanatory problem—how a number of individual actions are arranged into structures or systems—we presented various versions of methodological individualism. What is common to all of them is the premise that macro-phenomena should be explained by the micro-activity of the actors' action. If one pursues the historical development of this explanatory strategy, the question of the reciprocal constitution of action and structures becomes central. Whereas the early contract or market theories still assumed atomistic and asocial individuals, and perceived structures as merely the result of their decisions and action, it was subsequently realized that structures are equally among the pre-conditions, as well as the consequences, of action. Giddens expressed this neatly as the duality of structure and action.

There remain different conceptions of the nature of macro-phenomena. For eliminative theories they do not have an independent reality. They exist only as aggregates of actions or as representations in people's heads. Reductive theories, by contrast, start from emergent properties but insist that, as the name suggests, these must be derived from the micro-process of action. Here there is an unexplained tension between the affirmation of the existence of an independent level of reality and the reductive explanatory strategy. It remains unclear what is the basis of the emergent 'more'.

For emergence and system theories the macro-level has explanatory priority. What counts as a basic unit of social processes is determined by the macro or system level. Explanation cannot therefore be from below. There are also different versions of this position, often described as methodological collectivism: these range from the part and whole model and the system/environment model to the application of this distinction to processes within society itself. The transition from one model to the other is accompanied by a more complex approach to the integration of modern social systems.

In Luhmann's autopoietic[3] system theory the various partial systems are no longer centrally ordered through a comprehensive set of values (Parsons) or an overall system. It is also ruled out that actors could direct and plan social processes, since this would presuppose constitution 'from below'. Here the more recent version of system theory delimits itself strictly from action theory and claims methodological priority. There are corresponding claims to primacy on the side of action theory, and a number of authors attempt instead to combine both. For them,

micro and macro, action and system, is not a question of ontology but an analytical distinction which can be applied and combined according to the question and object of analysis (Alexander, 1987; Archer, 1995; Heintz, 2004).[4]

REFERENCES AND SELECT BIBLIOGRAPHY

Alexander, Jeffrey C. (1987) 'Action and its environments', in Jeffrey Alexander, Bernhard Giesen, Richard Münch and Neil Smelser (eds), *The Micro-Macro-Link*, Berkeley: University of California Press, pp. 289–318.

Alexander, Jeffrey C.; Giesen, Bernhard; Münch, Richard and Smelser, Neil (eds) (1987) *The Micro-Macro-Link*. Berkeley: University of California Press.

Archer, Margaret S. (1995) *Realist Social Theory: The Morphogenetic Approach*. Cambridge: Cambridge University Press.

Blumer, Herbert ([1969] 1986) *Symbolic Interactionism*. Berkeley: University of California Press.

Coleman, James S. (1987) 'Microfoundations and Macrosocial Behavior', in Jeffrey Alexander, Bernhard Giesen, Richard Münch, Neil Smelser (eds), *The Micro-Macro-Link*, Berkeley: University of California Press, pp. 153–73.

Coleman, James (1990) *Foundations of Social Theory*. Cambridge, MA/London: Belknap Press.

Collins, Randall (1981) 'On the microfoundations of macro-sociology', *American Journal of Sociology*, 86: 984–1014.

——— (1987) 'Interaction ritual chains, power and property: The micro-macro connection as an empirically based theoretical problem', in Jeffrey Alexander, Bernhard Giesen, Richard Münch, Neil Smelser (eds), *The Micro-Macro-Link*. Berkeley: University of California Press, pp. 193–206.

——— (1988) 'The micro contribution to macro sociology', *Sociological Theory*, 6: 242–53.

——— (1993) 'Emotional energy as the common denominator of rational choice?', *Rationality and Society*, 5: 203–30.

Dahrendorf, Ralf ([1958] 1973) *Homo Sociologicus*. London: Routledge.

Elster, Jon (1991) 'Rationality and social norms', *European Journal of Sociology*, 32: 109–29.

Esser, Hartmut (1993) *Soziologie. Allgemeine Grundlagen*. Frankfurt am Main/New York: Campus.

——— (2000) *Soziologie. Die Konstruktion der Gesellschaft*. Frankfurt am Main/New York: Campus.

Flam, Helena (1990) 'Emotional man I: The emotional man and the problem of collective action', *International Sociology,* 5: 39–56.

Garfinkel, Harold ([1967] 1989) *Studies in Ethnomethodology.* Cambridge: Polity Press.

Gerhards, Jürgen (1988) *Soziologie der Emotionen.* Weinheim and München: Juventa.

Goffman, Erving (1959) *The Presentation of Self in Everyday Life.* New York: Doubleday & Company.

——— (1961) *Asylums.* New York : Doubleday.

Habermas, Jürgen (1981) *Theorie des kommunikativen Handelns.* 2 vols. Frankfurt am Main: Suhrkamp. Tr. *Theory of Communicative Action.* Cambridge: Polity,

Hedström, Peter and Swedberg, Richard (eds) (1998) *Social Mechanisms. An Analytical Approach to Social Theory.* Cambridge: Cambridge University Press.

Heintz, Bettina (2004) 'Emergenz und Reduktion. Neue Perspektiven auf das Mikro-Makro-Problem', *Kölner Zeitschrift für Soziologie und Sozialpsychologie* 56 (1): 1–31.

Hochschild, Arlie R. (1983) *The Managed Heart. Commercialization of Human Feelings.* Berkeley: University of California Press.

Knorr-Cetina, Karin and Cicourel, Aaron V. (1981) *Advances in Social Theory and Methodology. Toward an Integration of Micro- and Macro-Sociologies.* London: Routledge.

Luhmann, Niklas (1982) *The Differentiation of Society.* New York: Columbia University Press.

——— (1984) *Soziale Systeme. Grundriß einer allgemeinen Theorie.* Frankfurt: Suhrkamp. Tr. *Social Systems.* Stanford University Press, 1995.

Mayntz, Renate (2002) 'Zur Theoriefähigkeit makrosozialer Analysen', in Renate Mayntz (Hg.), *Akteure – Mechanismen – Modelle.* Frankfurt/New York: Campus, pp. 7–43.

Mead, George Herbert ([1934] 1959) *Mind, Self & Society.* 11th edn. Chicago: University of Chicago Press.

Merton, Robert K. (1968) *Social Theory and Social Structure.* New York/London: The Free Press.

Parsons, Talcott ([1937] 1968) *The Structure of Social Action.* New York: Free Press.

Schimank, Uwe (1988) 'Gesellschaftliche Teilsysteme als Akteursfiktionen', *Kölner Zeitschrift für Soziologie and Sozialpsychologie,* 40: 619–39.

——— (2000) *Handeln und Strukturen.* Weinheim and München: Juventa.

Schluchter, Wolfgang (2000) 'Handlungs- und Strukturtheorie nach Max Weber', *Berliner Journal für Soziologie,* 10 (1): 125–36.

Schmid, Michael (2004) *Rationales Handeln und soziale Prozesse.* Wiesbaden: VS Verlag.

Schütz, Alfred ([1932] 1974) *Der sinnhafte Aufbau der sozialen Welt.* Frankfurt am Main: Suhrkamp. Tr. *The Phenomenology of the Social World.* London: Heinemann, 1972.

Schwinn, Thomas (1993a) *Jenseits von Subjektivismus und Objektivismus. Max Weber, Alfred Schütz und Talcott Parsons.* Berlin: Dunker & Humblot.

——— (1993b) 'Max Webers Konzeption des Mikro-Makro-Problems', *Kölner Zeitschrift für Soziologie und Sozialpsychologie* 45: 220–37.

——— (1998) 'False connections: Systems and action theories in neofunctionalism and in Jürgen Habermas', *Sociological Theory,* 16 (1): 75–95.

——— (2004), Unterscheidungskriterien für akteur- und systemtheoretische Paradigmen in der Soziologie. Überlegungen im Anschluss an Max Weber und Talcott Parsons', in Manfred Gabriel (ed.), *Paradigmen der akteurszentrierten Soziologie.* Wiesbaden: VS Verlag, pp. 69–89.

Stephan, Achim (2000) 'Eine kurze Einführung in die Vielfalt und Geschichte emergentistischen Denkens', in Thomas Wagenbaur (Hg.), *Blinde Emergenz?* Heidelberg: Synchron, pp. 33–47.

Udehn, Lars (2002) 'The changing face of methodological individualism', *Annual Review of Sociology,* 28: 479–507.

Weber, Max ([1922] 1978) *Economy and Society.* Berkeley: University of California Press.

——— ([1962] 1980) *Basic Concepts of Sociology,* trans.H. P. Secher. Seacaucus, NJ: Citadel Press.

NOTES

1 Here there are connections to Jean Piaget's and Lawrence Kohlberg's theories of socialization and child development, which differentiate stages of moral autonomy and capacity for action.

2 Esser (2000: 71, 351) is inconsistent here, since he pursues a reductionist program but at the same time assumes 'self-regulation' by systems.

3 The concept of autopoiesis is drawn from biology and denotes the self-production and self-organisaton of a system, which responds to and processes influences from the environment not directly but only via its own structures.

4 I have shown in relation to so-called neofunctionalism and the theories of Jürgen Habermas that this combination is at the price of logical inconsistencies (Schwinn, 1998).

18

Simulating Complexity

R. Keith Sawyer

Sociologists are deeply interested in social processes and mechanisms; they know that descriptions of static structures are always incomplete because they fail to capture the reality of how structure is lived, created, and reproduced (Abbott, 1995; Archer, 1995; Giddens, 1984; Hedström and Swedberg, 1998). Unfortunately, sociologists have found it difficult to develop good theories of social processes, and they have found it even more difficult to empirically study social processes. As a result, much of modern sociology neglects process (cf. Cederman, 2002; Gilbert, 1997, para. 3.3).

The modern science of complexity can provide both theoretical and methodological tools to explore social processes. The interdisciplinary field of complexity science is foundationally concerned with processes of change over time. The systems studied by complexity researchers are usually called *complex dynamical systems*. 'Dynamical' means that although the system maintains itself with a relatively stable structure, top-level stability is the result of continuously changing and interacting components. These systems are sometimes referred to as complex *adaptive* systems, indicating that the changes are towards ever-increasing improvements in functionality of the system

in response to feedback from the environment. All social systems are complex, dynamical and adaptive in these senses.

Societies have often been compared to other complex systems. Inspired by the rise of science and technology, in the eighteenth century societies were compared to complex artificial mechanisms like clocks; such metaphors are now broadly known as *mechanistic*. Inspired by Darwin's influential theory of evolution, nineteenth-century *organicists* such as Lilienfeld, Schäffle, and Spencer compared the various institutions of society to the organs of the human body. Just after World War II, Talcott Parsons's influential structural–functional theory was inspired by cybernetics, the study of 'control and communication in the animal and the machine', the sub-title of a seminal book published by mathematician Norbert Wiener in 1948. Cybernetics was centrally concerned with developing models of the computational and communication technologies that were emerging in the post-World War II period, but many cyberneticians applied these models to biology, anthropology and sociology. In the 1960s and 1970s, General Systems Theory continued in this interdisciplinary fashion; it was grounded in the premise that complex systems at all levels of analysis—from the smallest unicellular organisms up to modern industrial societies—could be understood using the same set of theories and methodologies (Bertalanffy, 1968; Miller, 1978). Common to all of these approaches is the basic insight that societies are complex configurations of many people, engaged in overlapping and interlocking patterns of relationship with one another.

Beginning in the mid-1990s, several methodological developments converged to create a qualitatively more advanced methodology for studying complex systems, and these developments have significant implications for social scientists. Following Sawyer (2005), I refer to these recent developments as a *third wave* of systems theory. The latest work in complex dynamical systems theory is particularly well-suited to sociological explanation. Methodologies that allow the simulation of complexity have the potential to contribute to resolutions of long-standing unresolved issues in sociology.

The development of third-wave systems theory is closely related to new simulation methodologies based in computer technology. In the 1990s, computer power advanced to the point where societies could be simulated using a distinct computational agent for every individual in the society, using a computational technique known as *multi agent systems*. A multi agent system contains hundreds or thousands of agents, each engaged in communication with the others. The researcher can use these simulations to create *artificial societies* and to run 'virtual experiments'—in which properties of agents and of the communication language are varied, and the subsequent changes in the overall macro behavior of the system are observed. Multi agent systems have been used by complexity researchers to simulate a wide range of natural systems, including sand piles, industrial processes, and neuronal connections in the human brain; in the late 1990s, this methodology was increasingly used to simulate social systems.

The term 'complexity' has been used somewhat loosely in the last decade. In the most general sense, complex phenomena are

those that reside between simplicity and randomness: at 'the edge of chaos', in Kauffman's (1993) terms. When the laws governing a system are relatively simple, the system's behavior is easy to understand, explain and predict. At the other extreme, some systems seem to behave randomly: there may be laws governing its behavior, but the system is highly non-linear—small variations in the state of the system at one time could result in very large changes to the later state of the system. Such systems are often said to be *chaotic*. Complex systems are somewhere in between these two extremes: the system is not easy to explain, but it is not so chaotic that understanding is completely impossible.

In complex systems so conceived, relatively simple higher-level order 'emerges' from relatively complex lower-level processes. Canonical examples of emergence include traffic jams, the colonies of social insects, and bird flocks. For example, the 'V' shape of the bird flock does not result from one bird being selected as the leader, and the other birds lining up behind the leader. Instead, each bird's behavior is based on its position relative to nearby birds. The 'V' shape is not planned or centrally determined; it emerges out of simple pair-interaction rules. The bird flock demonstrates one of the most striking features of emergent phenomena: higher-level regularities are often the result of simple rules and local interactions at the lower level.

In the social sciences, a comparable example of an emergent phenomenon is language shift. Historians of language have documented that languages have changed frequently throughout history, with vocabulary and even grammar changing radically over the centuries. Yet until the rise of the modern nation-state, such changes were not consciously selected by any official body, nor were they imposed by force on a population. Rather, language shift is an emergent phenomenon, arising out of uncountable everyday conversations in small groups scattered throughout the society (Sawyer, 2001). In this social system, the 'lower level' are the individual speakers; their interactions are the individual conversations; and the 'higher level' is the collective social fact of language as a group property.

This new methodology has led complexity theorists to become increasingly concerned with *emergence*—the processes whereby the global behavior of a system results from the actions and interactions of agents. In psychology, sociology and economics, the relation between lower- and higher-level properties has often been theorized in terms of emergence.

In emergence, patterns, structures or properties emerge at the global system level that are difficult to explain in terms of the system's components and their interactions. Whether or not a global system property is emergent, and what this means both theoretically and methodologically, has been defined in many different ways. For example, in some accounts system properties are said to be emergent when they are *unpredictable* even given a complete knowledge of the lower-level description of the system—a complete knowledge of the state of each component and of their interactions. In other accounts, system properties are said to be emergent when they are *irreducible*, in any lawful and regular fashion, to properties of the system components. In yet other accounts, system properties are said to be emergent when they are *novel*, when they are not held by any of the components of the system. Social scientists have applied widely different definitions of emergence, resulting in conceptual confusion (Sawyer, 2005).

Emerging from all of these debates is a consensus that complex systems may have autonomous laws and properties at the global level that cannot be easily reduced to lower-level, more basic sciences. Thus the paradigm of complexity is often opposed to the paradigm of reductionism. For example, philosophers of mind generally agree that mental properties may not be easily reduced to neurobiological properties, due to the complex dynamical nature of the brain. In an analogous fashion, several sociological theorists have used complex dynamical systems theory to argue against methodological individualism, the attempt to explain groups in terms of individuals (Archer, 1995; Sawyer, 2005).

Complexity theorists have discovered that emergence is more likely to be found in systems (1) which have many components interacting in densely connected networks; (2) in which global system functions cannot be localized to any one subset of components, but rather are distributed throughout the entire system; (3) in which the overall system cannot be decomposed into sub-systems, and those into smaller sub-sub-systems, in any meaningful fashion; and (4) in which the components interact using a complex and sophisticated language. Not all complex systems have all these features—for example, interaction between birds in a flock involves very simple rules, but it manifests emergence because of the large number of birds. Conversely, the complex musical communication among the four musicians in a jazz group leads to emergent properties, even though there are only four participants (Sawyer, 2003). All four of these properties are found in social systems, perhaps to an even greater extent than in natural systems (Sawyer, 2005).

These properties are interrelated in most complex systems. For example, social systems with a densely connected network are less likely to be decomposable or localizable. In modern societies, network density has become progressively greater as communication and transportation technology has increased the number and frequency of network connections among people; some complexity theorists suggest that this results in *swarm intelligence* (Kennedy and Eberhart, 2001).

THREE WAVES OF SYSTEMS THEORY

The first wave of social systems theory is Parsons's structural functionalism; the second wave is derived from the general systems theory of the 1960s through the 1980s; and the third wave is based on complex dynamical systems theory that developed in the 1990s. Like the first two waves, the third wave conceives of societies as systems, and draws on a range of interdisciplinary work from outside social science. Third-wave systems theory has more potential relevance to sociology than the first two, and offers theoretical concepts and methodological tools that have the potential to speak to core unresolved sociological issues. This third wave emerged from recent methodological developments in computer science and the interdisciplinary field of complex dynamical systems. As my paradigm case of simulating complexity, I focus on *multi agent system* technologies that emerged only in the late 1990s, but have already begun to be applied to social simulation.

Most social-scientific applications of these complexity methodologies have been undertaken by neoclassical microeconomists, and they have considered complexity science to provide a new methodology with which to accomplish a reductionist, methodologically individualist program. Using complexity methods—non-linear dynamical modeling and multiagent systems—microeconomists have attempted to reproduce empirically observed macro phenomena by modeling micro events and interactions—individuals' calculations of optimal outcomes, and their rational decisions to pursue those outcomes. In economics, 'emergence' is considered to be consistent with the program of methodological individualism.

The reductionist, individualist challenge posed by economics has not been successfully answered by sociology, and the relation between the disciplines remains unstable. Economists have been the social scientists most enamored with complex-systems thinking; for example, economists associated with the Santa Fe Institute have been applying complex dynamical systems theory to social systems since the late 1980s (Waldrop, 1992). Methodological individualism has increased in influence in the second half of the twentieth century, with the growth and success of microeconomics, rational choice theory and game theory. Some sociologists

have responded by embracing the reductionist system approaches of economics; Coleman's 1990 *Foundations of Social Theory* outlined how sociologists could proceed using rational choice methods, and such methods have become increasingly widespread in sociology since that time.

Although both economists and sociologists are concerned with emergence, they maintain distinct versions of emergence. Economists tend to believe that because social phenomena emerge from collective individual action, the best way to study those phenomena is to study the lower level of individual action from whence they emerge. This is the reading of complex dynamical systems theory that one often finds in the writings of economists: a reductionist, atomistic version, as perhaps most explicitly demonstrated in multi agent system computer models of societies. Yet this version of systems thinking is not acceptable to many sociologists, because it seems to deny the reality of social phenomena like networks, symbolic interactions and institutions. In contrast, many sociological theories of emergence argue that emergent social properties cannot be analyzed in terms of their constituting individuals because, once emergent, they take on autonomous properties, and seem to exert causal force over the participating individuals.

The problem is that neither economists nor sociologists have prepared a sustained analysis of the concept of emergence. The third-wave focus on social emergence provides an opportunity for sociologists and economists to find common ground.

A METHODOLOGY FOR SIMULATING COMPLEXITY: MULTI-AGENT SYSTEMS

Until the development of *multi agent systems (MAS)* in the 1990s, computer simulations of social phenomena primarily used analytics, or *equation-based modeling (EBM)*. Examples include the utility functions of rational choice theory (e.g., Coleman, 1990) and the system dynamics of macrosociological and organizational models (e.g., Forrester, 1968). In EBM, the model is a set of equations (typically differential or difference equations) and the execution of the simulation consists of evaluating the equations (Halpin, 1999; Parunak et al., 1998).

Social simulations using MAS technology are known as *artificial societies*. An artificial society contains a set of autonomous agents that operate in parallel, and that communicate with each other. The earliest implementation of an artificial society was the famous checkerboard simulation of racial segregation of Schelling (1971). Like Schelling's early simulation, artificial societies allow researchers to run *virtual experiments*, setting up a series of simulations to address a specific research question. The simulation consists of activating all the agents and observing the macro behavior that emerges as the agents interact. In the 1990s, computer modeling techniques and computational power evolved to the point where MAS became a viable simulation tool for sociologists and economists. This approach to social simulation has rapidly gathered momentum among computer scientists; several edited collections have appeared (Conte et al., 1997; Gilbert and Conte, 1995; Gilbert and Doran, 1994; Moss, 2001; Sallach and Macal, 2001; Sichman et al., 1998), and a journal was founded in 1998, the *Journal of Artificial Societies and Social Simulation* (http://jasss.soc.surrey.ac.uk/, accessed 24 September 2004).

By allowing a rigorous exploration of the mechanisms of social emergence, artificial societies provide new perspectives on contemporary discussions of social emergence, focusing on three of its aspects: micro-to-macro emergence, macro-to-micro social causation, and the dialectic between social emergence and social causation (cf. Alexander et al., 1987; Archer, 1995; Knorr-Cetina and Cicourel, 1981; Wiley, 1988).

MAS are computer systems that contain more than one computational agent. The agents are *autonomous:* they have control over their own behavior, and can act without the intervention of humans or other systems. Interest in MAS among computer scientists was first driven by the development of multiprocessor computers in the 1980s, and then by the rapid expansion of the Internet in the 1990s. The Internet is a type of MAS, because it is constituted by thousands of independent computers, each running autonomous software programs, and each capable of communicating with a program running on any other node in the network. Other contributing factors are the proliferation of powerful desktop computers resulting from the declining costs of computation, and the research field of *ubiquitous computing,* which attempts to embed very small autonomous agents in many household objects, such as a shirt or a carton of milk, and to network them using wireless technology. As these technologies have evolved, there is an increasing need for more sophisticated formalisms that can better understand, manage and predict the performance of complex systems that are composed of many computational agents.

The term 'agent' does not carry the same connotations as it does in sociological theory. To understand the term's connotations, a brief history of MAS is helpful. MAS emerged in the mid-1990s, and grew out of precursor systems with multiple interacting processes but in which the processes were not autonomous. The earliest precursor of MAS was *object-oriented programming* (OOP). In OOP, an object is a single computational process—an operating program—maintaining its own data structures and its own procedures. Objects communicate with each other using *message passing*. Each object has a defined set of messages that it is capable of receiving and responding to. When a message arrives at an object, the corresponding procedure, called a 'method', is executed.

By 1990, artificial intelligence researchers had begun to use OOP to build *distributed artificial intelligence* (DAI) systems (O'Hare and Jennings, 1996). Whereas objects had typically been rather simple programs, DAI objects each contained sophisticated software to represent intelligent behavior. Unlike the AI systems of the 1970s and 1980s—which focused on isolated agents— the interaction of the group of agents was an essential aspect of each agent's intelligence, and of the overall behavior of the system. In most DAI systems, the individual processing units were not autonomous; instead, the units were hierarchically organized around a single centralized controller (Connah and Wavish, 1990: 197; Conte et al., 1998: 1). Gradually, researchers began to experiment with decentralization, designing distributed systems without any centralized controller, with each object having autonomy.

This shift to autonomy was foundational, and led to the use of the term 'agent.' An agent is situated in an environment, and is capable of autonomous action in that environment (Wooldridge, 1999: 29). The notion of action in an environment is critical, and in part developed out of research in situated robotics (Agre, 1995). Because real-world environments are non-deterministic (constantly changing and not fully known by the agent), agents that interact directly with the environment must be capable of autonomous action. Because agents do not have complete knowledge of the environment, the same action performed twice—in two environments that seem identical to the agent—may have different results, due to unperceived yet important features of that environment. In particular, an agent's action may fail to have the desired effect.

Autonomous agents have control over their behavior and their internal state. Agents, unlike objects, can decline to execute the request of another agent, or can respond by proposing to negotiate the parameters of the task. Thus, MAS raise a wide range of issues related to coordination and cooperation. The introduction of agents with autonomy has forced computer scientists to consider what sociologists have long called the *problem of order*—why, and under what conditions, do individuals yield autonomy to social groups? How do social groups emerge and reproduce over time?

Developers of artificial societies have increasingly realized that one of the key issues facing them is to develop effective theories of social emergence. Because MAS have no central control, they are complex systems in which the combination of all of the agents' autonomous actions results in the global behavior of the system. MAS developers have discovered that the global behavior of these systems cannot always be predicted or derived from the properties of the component agents; the behavior can only be known by running the simulation (Gilbert, 1995: 150). The global behavior can then be observed as it emerges from the agents and their interactions.

MAS developers begin by modeling individual agents and their interactions. The simulation is then run to see what macro patterns and processes emerge as the agents interact with one another. These emergent macro patterns are then compared to the empirically observed patterns of the society. Thus, artificial societies are *microsimulations*, simulations based on the properties of lower-level units such as individuals, in contrast to 'macrosimulation' of the system dynamics variety, which attempts to directly model emergent macro phenomena. As such, MAS allow the exploration of what Coleman (1990) referred to as the foundations of sociology: the micro-to-macro relation.

Emergence has been widely discussed by artificial society developers (Axtell, 2002; Conte et al., 2001; Gilbert, 2002; Moss, 2001: 10). Most of these developers are methodological individualists (Axelrod, 1997: esp. 4; Conte et al., 2001; Epstein and Axtell, 1996: esp. 6–20; see Macy and Willer, 2002). In complexity theory in general, emergence is often used in an implicitly reductionist fashion: 'the laws at the higher level derive from the laws of the lower-level building blocks' (Holland, 1995: 36; also see Bedau, 2002), although non-linear interactions can make this derivation difficult to discover (Holland, 1995: 15). Although the artificial-society community often speaks of emergence, they use the term in the reductionist and individualist sense associated with economics, rational choice and game-theoretic frameworks. Consistent with these paradigms, many agent modelers believe that group properties are best explained by first modeling the participating individuals, then modeling their interactions, and then running the simulation to examine the processes whereby collective properties emerge from this micro simulation (Conte et al., 2001).

Computer scientists have explored the possibility of using MAS for a wide range of applications, including industrial process control, combinatorial auctions and electronic marketplaces, channel-allocation schemes for cellular phone networks, and network routing (for examples, see *International Foundation for MultiAgent Systems*, 2000). As the MAS community expanded rapidly in the 1990s, several computer scientists and economists realized the potential of using MAS to model social systems. This line of work has been given various names, including *agent based social simulation (ABSS)*, *multi-agent based simulation (MABS)*, and *artificial societies*, the term used here.

MAS and EBM differ in several ways, and each technique has a different scope of applicability. Several of these contrasts were first noted by economists, who have used MAS to allow them to relax some of the assumptions built into neoclassical theory (Epstein and Axtell, 1996; Moss, 1998); others have been noted by computer scientists interested in modeling social phenomena (Gilbert, 1999; Parunak et al., 1998).

- In an artificial society, the model consists of a set of agents that simulate the behaviors of the various entities that make up the social system, and execution of the model involves emulating those behaviors. In EBM, the model is a set of equations, and execution of the model involves evaluating the equations.
- System dynamics makes extensive use of macro-level observable variables (macrosimulation), whereas artificial societies define agent behaviors in terms of micro-level individual factors (microsimulation). Thus, artificial societies are better suited to domains where the natural unit of decomposition is the individual; system

dynamics may be better suited where the natural unit of decomposition is the macro-level observable variable, rather than the individual.
- Economic models of utility functions assume the rational actor of economic theory. Economists have long realized that such an actor is not very realistic, but the mathematical methods of EBM make it difficult to relax this assumption. MAS, by drawing on cognitive science, allow the representation of actors that use a wide range of decision strategies, both rational and non-rational. For example, MAS allow consideration of the internal representations of agents and their processes of plan construction and implementation, thus avoiding the behaviorist tinge of most rational choice theory. The role of an agent's internal models of social obligations, commitments and responsibilities can be simulated, thus allowing an exploration of different theories of the sociological actor.
- In most EBM methods, agents are represented as homogeneous, and agent behavior does not change during the simulation. In theory, a representative actor is modeled; in system dynamics simulations, highly aggregate models of individuals are used to model social processes. (Some simulations allow highly constrained forms of agent variation, such as assigning a distribution of trait values to agents.) MAS, in contrast, allow the modeling of populations of radically heterogeneous actors, and these actors may modify their behavior during the simulation.
- Much of sociology (structural functionalism, network theory) has been concerned with static equilibria and has neglected social dynamics. After the structural–functional consensus faded in American sociology, sociological theories—most notably, conflict theory—became more concerned with social dynamics. System-dynamics EBM also support the exploration of social dynamics (Hanneman, 1988); but MAS provides a methodology to study the mechanics of the micro-macro relations underlying social dynamics.

EXAMPLES OF SIMULATING SOCIAL EMERGENCE USING ARTIFICIAL SOCIETIES

The ability to simulate the processes of social emergence is perhaps the most distinctive feature of artificial societies. In the artificial societies that I describe below, structural phenomena emerge, attain equilibrium, and remain stable over time. Thus, artificial societies provide sociologists with a tool to explore social processes and mechanisms. In the following, I provide examples of artificial societies that represent two types of social emergence: the emergence of social structure, and the emergence of norms.

The Emergence of Social Structure

Several artificial societies have been created which begin with no social structure, and in which differentiated and hierarchically structured groups emerge during the simulation. An early example of such a simulation is Schelling's (1971) checkerboard simulation of residential segregation, which showed that almost total segregation can result from even rather small tendencies towards like neighbors. In the following, I give examples of simulations of the emergence of opinion clusters, the emergence of clusters of commitment surrounding supranational states, and the emergence of hierarchically structured and differentiated groups.

The emergence of opinion clusters has been observed in a simulation by Nowak and Latané (1994), in which agents behave according to Latané's theory of social impact. In this theory, the impact of a group of people on an individual's opinion is a multiplicative function of the persuasiveness of the members of the group, their social distance from the individual, and the number of the group members. At any moment during the simulation, each agent's opinion is determined by a multiplicative rule that derives its opinion from those of its neighbors. The outcome of this simulation is that opinion clusters emerge and remain in dynamic equilibrium, over a wide range of assumptions and parameters. The emergent equilibrium states contain multiple opinion clusters, and minority views remain active.

Axelrod (1995) used an artificial society to explore the emergence of new political actors: supranational entities that can regulate resource use at the global level. In his model, each agent represents a national state,

and, in repeat runs of the model, clusters of commitment emerge surrounding strong states. Thus, higher-level actors emerge from interactions among lower-level actors. This is a simpler version of Coleman's theory of how corporate actors emerge from the rational action of component members (Coleman, 1990). Yet the simulation, despite its simplicity, allows an examination of the unexpected effects of microtheoretical assumptions. For example, Axelrod's simulation reproduced historically observed patterns, such as *imperial overstretch*, when powerful empires are weakened by being dragged into fights involving weaker actors to whom they have developed commitments.

The purpose of the *Emergence of Organized Society (EOS)* project (Doran and Palmer, 1995) was to investigate the growth in complexity of social institutions in southwestern France during the Upper Paleolithic period, when the archeological record indicates a transition from a relatively simple hunter-gatherer society to a more complex society with centralized decision making and several forms of differentiation, including division of labor, roles and ethnicity. The EOS simulation was developed to explore various theories about the causes of this transition. For example, Mellars (1985) hypothesized that environmental change—resource deterioration as a result of the glacial maximum—led to the emergence of hierarchical, centralized decision-making. The EOS researchers began by creating a virtual environment, drawing on the environmental historical data from the known archeological record, such as the extent of glaciation in each year and the corresponding resource deterioration. They then created an artificial society composed of agents that operated within this environment.

When the simulation begins, agents do not have any knowledge of groups or of other agents. Each agent has the goal to acquire a continuing supply of resources, and some of those resources can only be acquired through the cooperation of other agents. Thus, agents attempt to recruit each other to support their own plan of action. Based on these purely local rules of interaction, hierarchically structured groups emerge as the simulation is run. EOS supported Mellars's theory of this transition: decreasing resources led to the emergence of more complex social structure.

The Emergence of Norms

A perennial issue for sociological theory has been what Parsons called the *problem of order*: Why do autonomous, rational individuals come together to form groups? Why and under what conditions do individuals yield autonomy and power to macrosocial entities? MAS developers, by introducing autonomy into their computational agents, have been faced with a similar problem: how to design systems of autonomous agents in which cooperation and coordination occur. MAS developers have often solved this problem by imposing norms on their agents. (I use the term 'norm' quite loosely, to also refer to what sociologists call 'values', 'conventions' and 'laws'; the methodological points are the same in each case.) An active area of theoretical work in MAS has been the study of *deontic logic*, extensions to predicate calculus that provide operators for conventions, responsibility, social commitment, and social laws (e.g., Dignum et al., 2000). Because many MAS are designed with a specific engineering goal in mind, designers often explicitly design agents that are predisposed to coordinate with other agents (e.g., Fitoussi and Tennenholtz, 2000). Because there is no centralization in MAS, such norms must be programmed individually into each agent.

In Parsons's structural–functional theory, the 'problem of order' is also resolved by shared norms. The integration function of social systems is served by the propagation of shared norms and conventions, via socialization of individuals into an existing social structure. Much of subsequent sociological theorizing about norms occurred within a functionalist framework, in which norms were hypothesized to serve various systemic functions like integration and cohesion. Many sociologists have criticized the functionalist assumptions of this normative

approach to the question of order. A commonly noted problem with structural–functional approaches is their inability to explain the dynamics of systems: how do norms emerge in the first place? For example, network theorists reject the functionalist view of norms, arguing instead that analysts should look for integration in the network of connections linking individuals (Burt, 1982). This is a more objectivist approach, because it focuses on observable behavior rather than subjective belief (Wellman, 1983: 162). A range of artificial societies are relevant to these sociological debates, including both simulations that impose norms in structural–functional fashion and simulations in which norms emerge during the simulation.

Many artificial societies impose norms and examine the resulting changes in the macro phenomena that emerge, contrasting the behavior with utilitarian rational actor systems in which there are no norms. For example, an artificial society by Conte and Castelfranchi (1995) explored how the introduction of norms affected macro emergence in a simple society of food-eater agents. The agents were placed in an environment with randomly scattered food. Eating food increased an agent's energy, whereas fighting with another agent to take their food reduced both agents' energies. First, they ran the simulation with no norms, in which all agents acted according to personal utility. Agents frequently attacked other agents to take their food. After the simulation reached equilibrium, the researchers calculated the average strength of all agents. In a second simulation, they introduced a norm designed to reduce the overall amount of aggression—'finders keepers'—specifying that the first agent to find food has rights to that food and will not be attacked. The introduction of this norm dramatically reduced aggression among agents, and resulted in a correspondingly higher average agent strength once the society had reached equilibrium. They also found that the normative society was more equitable, with a smaller variance in strength of agents.

This simulation shows how artificial society methods can be used to explore the macro implications of the introduction of norms. However, in this simulation the norms were imposed by the designers rather than emerging from the agents themselves. Such normative agents are not truly autonomous, because they do not create or choose their own norms. Note the similarities between these artificial societies and variants of sociological functionalism in which cooperation and common interest always result due to the functional requirements of the system (cf. Castelfranchi and Conte, 1996).

Although designer-imposed norms can be an efficient solution to many engineering problems, such systems do not address some fundamental theoretical problems raised by autonomous agents. How do norms emerge in the first place? Why does an agent agree to adopt the goal requested by another agent? Why yield autonomy to a group? In addition to these theoretical concerns, engineering considerations have also led MAS designers to explore how norms might emerge during the simulation. In some applications, not all system requirements are known at design time, the goals of agents might be constantly changing in response to environmental changes, and in very complex systems, designers may find it quite difficult to design effective social laws.

Thus for both theoretical and practical reasons, MAS developers became interested in exploring how norms might spontaneously emerge from the local interactions of individual autonomous agents. If autonomous agents seek to maximize personal utility, then under what conditions will agents cooperate with other agents? In game theory terms, this is a prisoner's dilemma problem (Lomborg, 1996: 278, 284). Purely self-interested agents have no desire to invest the resources in collaboration, because they don't know if the other agent will also cooperate. Many studies of cooperation in MAS have been implementations of the *iterated prisoner's dilemma* (IPD), where agents interact in repeated trials of the game, and agents can remember what other agents have done in the past (Axelrod, 1984, 1997). Many MAS have been developed to simulate variations of the IPD,

including the introduction of noise and of bounded rationality (Cox et al., 1999; Lomborg, 1992, 1996; Macy and Skvoretz, 1998; Sullivan et al., 2000).

In IPD-based artificial societies, norms of cooperation emerge even though they are not pre-programmed. These emergent norms of cooperation are not propositionally represented anywhere in the system; rather, cooperation is a component of the utility function. Thus, IPD agents are not normative in the sociological sense of the term because norms are not internalized and shared by all agents. In the late 1990s, artificial societies were developed in which explicit, internal norms emerged during the simulation. One of the first attempts was by Walker and Wooldridge (1995), who extended Conte and Castelfranchi's (1995) system of food eaters described above. In their extension, a group of autonomous agents reached a global consensus on the use of social conventions, with each agent deciding which convention to adopt based solely on its own local experiences. They found that global norms emerged in each of 16 different simulations, each using a different *strategy update function*. Once the global norm emerged, the system remained at equilibrium. For example, one strategy update function was a *simple majority* function: agents change to an alternative norm if so far they have observed more instances of it in other agents than their present norm. They found that each of the 16 functions resulted in a different amount of time before all the agents converged on a single norm. Each of the functions also resulted in a different average number of norm changes—because changes in norm can be costly for an agent, and can lead to overall inefficiencies in the system, it is preferable for designers to choose an update function that results in the fewest norm changes while attaining norm convergence as quickly as possible.

Steels (1996) implemented a series of simulations in which agents have the task of learning how to communicate with each other about objects in their environment. They begin without any shared names for these objects. Steels explored a range of artificial societies in which all agents attain global agreement on a lexicon for these objects by playing successive rounds of the *naming game*. In the naming game, a speaker attempts to identify an object to a hearer, based on pointing and using a name. The game succeeds if the hearer correctly guesses the object chosen. If a speaker does not yet have a name for the object, the speaker may create a new name. A hearer may adopt a name used by a speaker. Both players monitor use and success, and in future games they prefer names that succeed the most. In Steels's artificial societies, all agents gradually attain global coherence: they all use the same name for any given object. The resulting lexicon is an emergent property of the system. Each agent engages only in local dyadic interactions and no agent has any awareness of the overall state of the system.

Steels and Kaplan (1998) then extended the simulation to allow for changes in the agent population. After global coherence is attained, one agent (out of 20 in all) is allowed to change in every N games. When $N = 100$, the language remains stable (although the global coherence measure drops slightly), with new agents acquiring the language of the other agents in the group. These new agents occasionally create a new word for an object, but this word quickly gets rejected, dominated by the preferred word of the rest of the group. When $N = 10$, however, the language disintegrates, and coherence cannot be maintained.

In the above examples, structures and norms emerge from the interactions of autonomous agents. These simulations provide support for methodologically individualist accounts of social emergence, and allow rigorous examination of theories concerning social emergence in the micro-to-macro transition. They also provide a perspective on a related problem in sociological theory: once a macro pattern has emerged, how is it maintained over time? Some sociological theorists have suggested that emergence and maintenance are similar processes (Giddens, 1984), others that they are analytically distinct (Archer, 1995). The above artificial societies show that emergence and reproduction of

structure are not necessarily distinct mechanisms and may not require distinct theories. In these simulations, macro patterns emerge, and are then reproduced through the same dynamic processes. These macro patterns are similar to the equilibrium states of economics—which emerge from independent rational action—and they are dynamically maintained; thus, they are demonstrations of the functionalist concept of dynamic equilibrium.

Artificial societies suggest how sociological theory and methodology can be extended to model social change. Parsons's structural–functional theory was widely perceived to be only capable of modeling societies which remained in homeostasis. Contemporary structural theories, such as network analysis, are criticized on the same grounds. Artificial societies model both stability over time (the 'problem of order') *and* social change. In this sense, artificial societies suggest a form of structural theory which can potentially explain processes of emergence, conflict, and change: stability emerges from dynamic processes, and those same dynamic processes can result in future change in response to change in environmental conditions (as in EOS). The Comtean distinction between static and dynamic sociology is blurred.

THE EMERGENCE PARADIGM

The simulation of complexity and emergence has been most advanced in the natural sciences. As a result, the unique features of complex social systems have been neglected. And most critically, complexity science has neglected the unique nature of symbolic interaction among human agents using natural language and non-verbal interaction. In Sawyer (2005), I argued that social simulations should introduce two additional levels of social reality: *stable emergents* and *ephemeral emergents*. In any social situation, there is a continuing dialectic: social emergence, where individuals are co-creating and co-maintaining ephemeral and stable emergents; and downward causation from those emergents. The new, modified versions of ephemeral emergents and stable emergents continually constrain the flow of the interaction. During conversational encounters, interactional frames emerge, and these are collective social facts that can be characterized independently of individuals' interpretations of them. Once a frame has emerged, it constrains the possibilities for action. Although the frame is created by participating individuals through their collective action, it is analytically independent of those individuals, and it has causal power over those individuals. I refer to this process as *collaborative emergence* (Sawyer, 2003), to distinguish it from models of emergence that fail to adequately theorize interactional processes and emergence mechanisms. Simulations can help social scientists to identify the mechanisms of collaborative emergence that lead to ephemeral and stable emergents.

Ephemeral emergents include the interactional frames of conversation analysis. In conversation, an interactional frame emerges from collective action and then constrains and enables collective action. These two processes are always simultaneous and inseparable. They are not distinct stages of a sequential process—emergence at one moment and then constraint in the next; rather, each action contributes to a continuing process of collaborative emergence, at the same time that it is constrained by the shared emergent frame that exists at that moment. The emergent frame is a dynamic structure that changes with each action. No one can stop the encounter at any one point and identify with certainty what the frame's structure is. It is always subject to continuing negotiation, and because of its irreducible ambiguity there will always be intersubjectivity issues, with different participants having different interpretations of the frame's constraints and affordances.

The collaborative emergence of frames has been studied by several researchers in interactional sociolinguistics and conversation analysis, including Deborah Tannen, Alessandro Duranti and Charles Goodwin (Duranti and Goodwin, 1992; Tannen, 1993). These researchers shifted the focus to how participants collectively create their context.

However, due to the interpretivist theoretical foundations of most of these researchers, they have been resistant to arguing that the emergent frame is a real social phenomenon with autonomous social properties. Rather, the frame is considered to exist only to the extent that it is 'demonstrably relevant' (Schegloff, 1992) to participants, a classic interpretivist stance. Due to these interpretivist assumptions, interactionist sociology generally fails to explain social emergence.

The second form of collaborative emergence is that of stable emergents, with a complicated mediation through ephemeral emergents. Stable emergents are the shared, collective history of a group. Stable emergents of small groups include group learning (Hertz-Lazarowitz et al., 1992), group development (Frey, 1994), peer culture (Corsaro, 1985), and collective memory (Wertsch, 2002). Stable emergents of an entire society include its culture and its language; their collaborative emergence has been studied by cultural and linguistic anthropology.

The line between stable and ephemeral emergents is a fine one; for purposes of definition, I consider an emergent to be stable if it lasts across more than one encounter. Stable emergents have different degrees of stability; some are stable over generations, and others are stable only for weeks or months. From most to least stable, examples of stable emergents include language, catchphrases, trends and tastes, cohort private jokes and stories, and the ensemble feel of a theater group during a month-long run of a play. The issue of how stable emergents are related to ephemeral emergents is still unresolved within social science. In different ways, the issue is central to folkloristics, ethnomusicology, popular culture studies, the study of peer cultures and sub-cultures, and collective behavior studies of rumors and fads.

Ephemeral emergence occurs within a single encounter. Most sociological discussions of emergence have focused on the broader macrostructures that emerge and how those emergent patterns constrain future interaction. Yet, these studies have not had much success in tracing the exact details of the moment-to-moment emergence processes whereby macrostructures are collectively created. In contrast, interactionism has focused exactly on the moment-to-moment details of how ephemeral emergents result from interaction. However, in shifting their focus to interactional processes, interactionists have tended to neglect the nature of what emerges, and of what endures across repeated encounters.

The collaborative emergence of stable emergents is the concern of the field known as *collective behavior*, the study of phenomena such as mob actions, riots, mass delusions, crazes, fads, and fashions (Lang and Lang, 1961; Park and Burgess, 1921). But these classic theories of collective behavior went from the individual to the emergents directly, without an examination of the mechanisms of interaction. These theorists used extremely simplistic notions of interaction such as 'social contagion' (Blumer, 1939) or 'milling' (Park and Burgess, 1921); historically, this is because these writings on collective behavior predated the development of sophisticated methodologies for analyzing interaction. The sociology of collective behavior never made connections to the study of how stable emergents are created over time— oral culture, ritual change, and related subjects from linguistic anthropology. Today we have an opportunity to revisit these phenomena of collective behavior, using the additional sophistication provided by the methodologies available to simulate complexity.

Several social theorists have recognized the theoretical benefits of introducing stable emergents as a mediator between individual and macrostructure. These include Collins's *repetitive patterns of behavior* (1981), Giddens's *situated social practices* (1984), and Lawler, Ridgeway, and Markovsky's *microstructures* (1993). For Lawler et al., microstructures 'emerge from and organize particular encounters' (1993: 272). Stable emergents are symbolic phenomena that have a degree of intersubjective sharing among some (more or less stable) group of individuals.

Some network analysts have argued that in many cases, institutions are crystallizations of emergent activity patterns and personal networks. Granovetter (1990) cited two historical examples of such institutional emergence: the development of the electrical utility industry in the United States between 1880 and 1930, and the professionalization of psychiatric practice. In both cases, the original institutions were 'accretions of activity patterns around personal networks' (Granovetter, 1990: 105). Empirical and historical study suggests that these economic institutions emerged from the same processes as other social institutions. This sort of historical analysis of institutional emergence demonstrates that institutions are contingent and are socially constructed; the processes of their emergence must be studied empirically; and they cannot be predicted from neoclassical economic theory. As Granovetter (1990: 106) concluded, explanations of institutions that do not incorporate the contingencies of social emergence 'fail to identify causal mechanisms; they do not make an adequate connection between micro and macro levels, and so explain poorly when historical circumstances vary from the ones under which they were formulated.'

CONCLUSION: IMPLICATIONS OF ARTIFICIAL SOCIETIES FOR SOCIOLOGICAL THEORY

Artificial societies provide sociologists with a new tool for the simulation of complexity. Artificial societies do not strongly support either methodological individualism or social realism, and they can be used as tools for theory development by advocates of both positions. As such, artificial societies can be viewed as implementations of hybrid sociological theories: theories that attempt to reconcile individual autonomy on the one hand, and structural and network phenomena on the other. Artificial societies allow an exploration of the role of the individual, and of how different theories of the individual relate to different hypotheses about the micro-macro relation (Alexander and Giesen, 1987: 14; Cook and Whitmeyer, 1992: 116–18).

Current artificial societies have several features that limit their relevance to sociological theory. To realize its full potential as a tool for sociological simulation, artificial societies may need to be extended by including explicit modeling of emergent macro features of the system. This would require a simulation that could dynamically create models during the run of the simulation, so that the macro phenomena represented would have emerged from the micro interactions of the agents. The emergence of a macro pattern would automatically result in the generation of a computational structure to be added to the model, which would then be perceived and internally represented by social agents (cf. Servat et al., 1998).

The macro-level phenomena would themselves emerge from micro interaction, rather than being explicitly designed into the simulation. This would allow simulation of a new consensus in sociological theory (Alexander and Giesen, 1987; Archer, 1995): that macro structures emerge from the actions and interactions of individuals, and that once they have emerged, those structures then constrain and influence the future actions and interactions of those same individuals.

Many sociologists argue against explicit theories or models of emergent macro phenomena, claiming that this would be a reification or hypostatization of such structures (Giddens, 1984; King, 1999). Yet in the artificial societies described here, structural phenomena have effects even when only local knowledge is explicitly modeled. And it may be necessary to explicitly model macrosocial properties in those cases where social properties are real, and their ontological autonomy results in causal powers (Sawyer, 2005).

Such simulations could contain complex social agents which are capable of examining the entire structure of the simulation and internalizing representations of it (cf. Castelfranchi, 1998, 2001). For example, agents could form and break network links and make decisions about whether or not to join groups, after becoming consciously aware of what groups exist, and what their missions and compositions are. However, in complex modern societies, it is impossible for each individual to directly perceive the entire social order. Instead, individuals' perceptions of macrosocial phenomena are typically mediated by institutions, such as the mass media, government agencies and educational institutions. To adequately simulate complex modern societies, artificial societies may need to explore the roles of such institutions.

Artificial societies provide a novel perspective on social emergence. They partially support both individualist and collectivist extremes of sociological theory. Artificial society methodologies can be used to rigorously implement and test hybrid micro–macro theories. More complex sociological theories can be developed, and unexpected consequences and internal conflicts can be identified. In this way, artificial societies have the potential to substantively contribute to the study of social processes and mechanisms.

REFERENCES

Abbott, Andrew (1995) 'Things of boundaries', *Social Research*, 62: 857–82.

Agre, Philip E. (1995) 'Computational research on interaction and agency', in P.E. Agre and S.J. Rosenschein (eds), *Computational Theories of Interaction and Agency*. Cambridge, MA: MIT Press, pp. 1–52.

Alexander, Jeffrey C. and Giesen, Bernhard (1987) 'From reduction to linkage: The long view of the micro-macro link', in J.C. Alexander, B. Giesen, R. Münch and N.J..Smelser (eds), *The Micro-Macro Link*. Berkeley, CA: University of California Press, pp. 1–42.

Alexander, Jeffrey C., Giesen, Bernhard, Münch, Richard and Smelser, Neil J. (eds) (1987) *The Micro-Macro Link*. Berkeley, CA: University of California Press.

Archer, Margaret S. (1995) *Realist Social Theory: The Morphogenetic Approach*. New York: Cambridge University Press.

Axelrod, Robert (1984) *The Evolution of Cooperation*. New York: Basic Books.

——— (1995) 'A model of the emergence of new political actors', in N. Gilbert and R. Conte (eds),

Artificial Societies: The Computer Simulation of Social Life. London: University College London Press Ltd., pp. 19–39.

————— (1997) *The Complexity of Cooperation: Agent-Based Models of Competition and Collaboration*. Princeton, NJ: Princeton University Press.

Axtell, Robert L. (2002) 'A positive theory of emergence for multi-agent systems', UCLA Computational Social Sciences Conference, Lake Arrowhead, CA.

Bedau, Mark (2002) 'Downward causation and the autonomy of weak emergence', *Principia*, 6: 5–50

Bertalanffy, Ludwig von (1968) *General System Theory: Foundations, Development, Applications*. New York: G. Braziller.

Blumer, Herbert (1939) 'Collective behavior', in R.E. Park (ed.), *An Outline of the Principles of Sociology*. New York: Barnes and Noble, pp. 219–80.

Burt, Ronald S. (1982) *Toward a Structural Theory of Action: Network Models of Social Structure, Perception, and Action*. New York: Academic Press.

Castelfranchi, Cristiano (1998) 'Simulating with cognitive agents: The importance of cognitive emergence' in J.S. Sichman, R. Conte, and N. Gilbert (eds), *Multi-Agent Systems and Agent-Based Simulation*. Berlin: Springer, pp. 26–44.

————— (2001) 'The theory of social functions: Challenges for computational social science and multi-agent learning', *Cognitive Systems Research*, 2: 5–38.

Castelfranchi, Cristiano and Conte, Rosaria (1996) 'Distributed artificial intelligence and social science: Critical issues', in G.M.P. O'Hare and N.R. Jennings (eds), *Foundations of Distributed Artificial Intelligence*. New York: Wiley, pp. 527–42.

Cederman, Lars-Erik (2002) 'Computational models of social forms: Advancing generative macro theory', in C. Macal and D. Sallach (eds), *Proceedings of the Agent 2002 on Social Agents: Ecology, Exchange, and Evolution*. Chicago, IL: University of Chicago Press.

Coleman, James S. (1990) *Foundations of Social Theory*. Cambridge, MA: Harvard University Press.

Collins, Randall (1981) 'On the microfoundations of macrosociology', *American Journal of Sociology*, 86: 984–1014.

Connah, David and Wavish, Peter (1990) 'An experiment in cooperation', in Y. Demazeau and J.P. Müller (eds) *Decentralized AI: Proceedings of the First European Workshop on Modelling Autonomous Agents in a Multi-Agent World*. New York: Elsevier, pp. 197–212.

Conte, Rosaria and Castelfranchi, Cristiano (1995) 'Understanding the functions of norms in social

groups through simulation', in N. Gilbert and R. Conte (eds), *Artificial Societies: The Computer Simulation of Social Life*. London: University College London Press Ltd., pp. 252–67.

Conte, Rosaria, Edmonds, Bruce, Moss, Scott and Sawyer, R. Keith (2001) 'Sociology and social theory in agent based social simulation: A symposium', *Computational and Mathematical Organization Theory*, 7: 183–205.

Conte, Rosaria, Gilbert, Nigel and Simão Sichman, Jaime (1998) 'MAS and social simulation: A suitable commitment', in J.S. Sichman, R. Conte, and N. Gilbert (eds) *Multi-Agent Systems and Agent-Based Simulation*. Berlin: Springer, pp. 1–9.

Conte, Rosaria, Hegselmann, Rainer and Terna, Pietro (1997) *Simulating Social Phenomena*. New York: Springer

Cook, K.S. and Whitmeyer, J.M. (1992) 'Two approaches to social structure: Exchange theory and network analysis', *Annual Review of Sociology*, 18: 109–27.

Corsaro, William A. (1985) *Friendship and Peer Culture in the Early Years*. Norwood, NJ: Ablex Publishing Corp.

Cox, S.J., Sluckin, T.J. and Steele, J. (1999) 'Group size, memory, and interaction rate in the evolution of cooperation', *Current Anthropology*, 40: 369–76.

Dignum, F., Morley, D., Sonenberg, E.A.and Cavedon, L. (2000) 'Towards socially sophisticated BDI agents', in *Proceedings of the Fourth International Conference on Multiagent Systems* (ICMAS 2000). Boston, MA: IEEE Computer Society, pp. 111–18.

Doran, Jim and Palmer, Mike (1995) 'The EOS project: Integrating two models of Palaeolithic social change', in N. Gilbert and R. Conte (eds), *Artificial Societies: The Computer Simulation of Social Life*. London: University College London Press Ltd., pp. 103–25.

Duranti, Alessandro and Goodwin, Charles (1992) *Rethinking Context: Language as an Interactive Phenomenon*. New York: Cambridge University Press.

Epstein, Joshua M. and Axtell, Robert (1996) *Growing Artificial Societies: Social Science from the Bottom Up*. Cambridge, MA: MIT Press.

Fitoussi, David and Tennenholtz, Moshe (2000) 'Choosing social laws for multi-agent systems: Minimality and simplicity', *Artificial Intelligence*, 119: 61–101.

Forrester, Jay W. (1968) *Principles of Systems*. Cambridge, MA: MIT Press

Frey, Lawrence R. (1994) *Group Communication in Context: Studies of Natural Groups*. Hillsdale, NJ: Lawrence Erlbaum Associates.

Giddens, Anthony (1984) *The Constitution of Society: Outline of the Theory of Structuration*. Berkeley: University of California Press.

Gilbert, Nigel (1995) 'Emergence in social simulations', in N. Gilbert and R. Conte (eds), *Artificial Societies: The Computer Simulation of Social Life*. London: University College London Press Ltd., pp. 144–56.

——— (1997) 'A simulation of the structure of academic science', *Sociological Research Online 2*. Available at: http://www.socresonline.org.uk/socresonline/2/2/3.html.

——— (1999) 'Simulation: A new way of doing social science', *American Behavioral Scientist*, 42: 1485–7.

——— (2002) 'Varieties of emergence in social simulation' in C. Macal and D. Sallach (eds), *Proceedings of the Agent 2002 on Social Agents: Ecology, Exchange, and Evolution*. Chicago, IL: University of Chicago Press.

Gilbert, Nigel and Conte, Rosaria (1995) *Artificial Societies: The Computer Simulation of Social Life*. London: University College London Press.

Gilbert, Nigel and Doran, Jim (1994) *Artificial Societies: The Computer Simulation of Social Phenomena*. London: University College London Press.

Granovetter, Mark (1990) 'The old and the new economic sociology: A history and an agenda', in R. Friedland and A.F. Robertson (eds), *Beyond the Marketplace: Rethinking Economy and Society*. New York: Aldine de Gruyter, pp. 89–112.

Halpin, Brendan (1999) 'Simulation in sociology', *American Behavioral Scientist*, 42: 1488–1508.

Hanneman, Robert A. (1988) *Computer-Assisted Theory Building: Modeling Dynamic Social Systems*. Newbury Park, CA: Sage.

Hedström, Peter and Swedberg, Richard (1998) *Social Mechanisms: An Analytical Approach to Social Theory*. New York: Cambridge University Press.

Hertz-Lazarowitz, R., Benvinisti Kirkus, V. and Miller, N. (1992) *Interaction in Cooperative Groups: The Theoretical Anatomy of Group Learning*. New York: Cambridge University Press.

Holland, John H. (1995) *Hidden Order: How Adaptation Builds Complexity*. Reading, MA: Addison-Wesley.

International Foundation for MultiAgent Systems (2000) *Proceedings of the Fourth International Conference on Multiagent Systems*. Los Alamitos, CA: IEEE Computer Society.

Kauffman, Stuart A. (1993) *The Origins of Order: Self-Organization and Selection in Evolution*. New York: Oxford University Press.

Kennedy, James and Eberhart, Russell C. (2001) *Swarm Intelligence*. San Francisco, CA: Morgan Kaufmann Publishers.

King, Anthony (1999) 'Against structure: A critique of morphogenetic social theory', *The Sociological Review*, 47: 199–227.

Knorr-Cetina, Karin D. and Cicourel, Aaron V. (1981) *Advances in Social Theory and Methodology: Toward an Integration of Micro- and Macro-Sociologies*. Boston: Routledge and Kegan Paul.

Lang, Kurt and Lang, Gladys Engel (1961) *Collective Dynamics*. New York: Thomas Y. Crowell Company.

Lawler, Edward J., Ridgeway, Cecilia and Markovsky, Barry (1993) 'Structural social psychology and the micro-macro problem', *Sociological Theory*, 11: 268–90.

Lomborg, Bjorn (1992) 'Game theory versus multiple agents: The iterated prisoner's dilemma', in C. Castelfranchi and E. Werner (eds), *Artificial Social Systems*. Berlin: Springer-Verlag, pp. 69–93.

——— (1996) 'Nucleus and shield: The evolution of social structure in the iterated prisoner's dilemma', *American Sociological Review*, 61: 278–307.

Macy, Michael W. and Skvoretz, John (1998) 'The evolution of trust and cooperation between strangers: A computational model', *American Sociological Review*, 63: 638–60.

Macy, Michael W. and Willer, Robert (2002) 'From factors to actors: Computational sociology and agent-based modeling', *Annual Review of Sociology*, 28: 143–66.

Mellars, Paul A. (1985) 'The ecological basis of social complexity in the Upper Paleolithic of southwestern France', in T.D. Price and J.A. Brown (eds), *Prehistoric Hunter-Gatherers: The Emergence of Cultural Complexity*. New York: Academic Press, pp. 271–97.

Miller, James G. (1978) *Living Systems*. New York: McGraw Hill.

Moss, Scott (1998) 'Social simulation models and reality: Three approaches', in J.S. Sichman, R. Conte, and N. Gilbert (eds) *Multi-Agent Systems and Agent-Based Simulation*. Berlin: Springer, pp. 45–78.

——— (2001) 'Messy systems: The target for multi agent based simulation', in S. Moss and P. Davidsson (eds), *Multi-Agent-Based Simulation*. Berlin: Springer, pp. 1–14.

Nowak, Andrzej and Latané, Bibb (1994) 'Simulating the emergence of social order from individual behavior', in N. Gilbert and J. Doran (eds), *Simulating Societies: The Computer Simulation of Social Phenomena*. London: University College London Press, pp. 63–84.

O'Hare, G.M.P. and Jennings, N.R. (1996) *Foundations of Distributed Artificial Intelligence*. New York: Wiley.

Park, Robert E. and Burgess, Ernest W. (1921) *Introduction to the Science of Sociology*. Chicago: University of Chicago Press.

Parunak, H. Van Dyke, Savit, Robert and Riolo, Rick L. (1998) 'Agent-based modeling vs. equation-based modeling: A case study and user's guide', in J.S. Sichman, R. Conte, and N. Gilbert (eds) *Multi-Agent Systems and Agent-Based Simulation*. Berlin: Springer, pp. 10–25.

Sallach, David L. and Macal, Charles N. (2001) *Social Science Computer Review: The Simulation of Social Agents*. Thousand Oaks, CA: Sage.

Sawyer, R. Keith (2001) *Creating Conversations: Improvisation in Everyday Discourse*. Cresskill, NJ: Hampton Press.

———— (2003) *Group Creativity: Music, Theater, Collaboration*. Mahwah, NJ: Erlbaum.

———— (2005) *Social Emergence: Societies as Complex Systems*. New York: Cambridge University Press.

Schegloff, Emanuel A. (1992) 'In another context', in A. Duranti and C. Goodwin (eds), *Rethinking Context: Language as an Interactive Phenomenon*. New York: Cambridge University Press, pp. 191–227.

Schelling, Thomas C. (1971) 'Dynamic models of segregation', *Journal of Mathematical Sociology*, 1: 143–86.

Servat, David, Perrier, Edith, Treuil, Jean-Pierre and Drogoul, Alexis (1998) 'When agents emerge from agents: Introducing multi-scale viewpoints in multi-agent simulations', in J.S. Sichman, R. Conte, and N. Gilbert (eds), *Multi-Agent Systems and Agent-Based Simulation*. Berlin: Springer, pp. 183–98.

Sichman, Jaime S, Conte, Rosaria and Gilbert, Nigel (eds) (1998) *Multi-Agent Systems and Agent-Based Simulation*. Berlin: Springer.

Steels, Luc (1996) 'Self-organizing vocabularies', in C.G. Langton and K. Shimohara (eds), *Artificial Life V: Proceedings of the Fifth International Workshop on the Synthesis and Simulation of Living Systems*. Cambridge, MA: MIT Press, pp. 179–84.

Steels, Luc and Kaplan, Frederic (1998) 'Stochasticity as a source of innovation in language games', in C. Adami, R.K. Belew, H. Kitano and C. Taylor (eds), *Artificial Life VI*. Cambridge, MA: MIT Press, pp. 368–76.

Sullivan, David G., Grosz, Barbara J. and Kraus, Sarit (2000) 'Intention reconciliation by collaborative agents', in *Proceedings of the Fourth International Conference on Multiagent Systems* (ICMAS 2000). Boston, MA: IEEE Computer Society, pp. 293–300.

Tannen, Deborah (1993) *Framing in Discourse*. New York: Oxford University Press.

Waldrop, M. Mitchell (1992) *Complexity: The Emerging Science at the Edge of Order and Chaos*. New York: Simon and Schuster.

Walker, Adam and Wooldridge, Michael (1995) 'Understanding the emergence of conventions in multi-agent systems', in V. Lesser (ed.), *Proceedings of the International Conference on Multiagent Systems* (ICMAS-95). Cambridge, MA: MIT Press, pp. 384–9.

Wellman, Barry (1983) 'Network analysis: Some basic principles', in R. Collins (ed.), *Sociological Theory*. San Francisco: Jossey-Bass, pp. 155–200.

Wertsch, James V. (2002) *Voices of Collective Remembering*. New York: Cambridge University Press.

Wiley, Norbert (1988) 'The micro-macro problem in social theory', *Sociological Theory*, 6: 254–61.

Wooldridge, Michael (1999) 'Intelligent agents', in G. Weiss (ed.), *Multiagent Systems: A Modern Approach to Distributed Artificial Intelligence*. Cambridge, MA: MIT Press, pp. 27–77.

19

Evolutionary Approaches in the Social Sciences

Maureen A. O'Malley

The contemporary resurgence of evolutionary thinking across the social sciences is hailed by some participants as a revolutionary and unifying paradigm (e.g., Machalek and Martin, 2004; Runciman, 1998; Sanderson, 1997). This movement draws from the conceptual framework provided by Darwinian evolutionary theory and attempts to explain and predict multiple levels of social phenomena. These explanations are sometimes offered in the light of evolutionary biology, but are more often framed within a general evolutionary framework that does not privilege biology. There are considerable differences between these evolutionary approaches, and the following overview will describe the forms they take, the relationships between them, and their problems and future directions. We will then look again at the claims that a paradigm has formed or is forming.

HISTORICAL ROOTS OF EVOLUTIONARY THINKING

Although there are numerous histories of ideas which outline a much older lineage of evolutionism (e.g., Bock, 1964; Nisbet, 1969),

the starting place for modern evolutionary ideas is Lamarck, whose notions of transformation from one class of entity to another began to displace earlier developmental histories and typologies of unchanging natural kinds (Mayr, 1982). He is more famous for his notion of the inheritance of acquired characteristics, which is the basis for popular interpretations of Lamarckian processes. Despite downplaying the roles of variation and chance, Lamarck paved the way for a warmer reception of Darwin than might otherwise have been the case—although even Darwin's key idea of selection did not fall on fertile ground in biology until the 1930s (Bowler, 1988).

Darwin's definition of natural selection was 'the preservation of favourable variations and the rejection of injurious variations' (1964: 81). The 'Modern Synthesis' of evolutionary biology combined Darwin's concept of selection with population statistics and genetics (as well as natural history and palaeobiology), to establish selection as a three-step process involving variation, fitness differences and heritability (Gould, 1983; Mayr, 1980). Although evolutionary biology has had to accommodate a variety of other processes and outcomes (such as neutral evolution), selection is still its lynchpin.

EVOLUTIONARY SOCIAL SCIENCE

There is a long history of evolutionary social science that will barely be touched on here, except to say that it did not enjoy anything like the eventual success of evolutionary biology. Waves of evolutionary attempts, failures and revivals led to a general skepticism that had hardened into almost mandatory anti-evolutionism in the 1970s (Sanderson, 1990; 1997). Evolutionary social science was often seen as synonymous with simple stories of social progress (Nisbet, 1969) or even more suspect ones of social Darwinism— generally conceived of as a laissez-faire political philosophy promulgating the benefits of raw competition between differently advantaged individuals (e.g., Dickens, 2000; Hofstadter, 1955). From there, it was a simple step to eugenics for critics and some promoters of social Darwinism. The contemporary phase of evolutionary social science is, however, not so much linked to these problematic frameworks, as it is to another—that of sociobiology (Wilson 1975; 1978). The relationship between the social sciences and sociobiology is a curious one, because even though sociobiology attracted a great deal of hostility from the social sciences and humanities (e.g., Archer, 1991; Kitcher, 1985; Montagu, 1980; Rose, Kamin, and Lewontin, 1984; Ruse, 1985; Sahlins, 1976), it also apparently opened the floodgates to a new wave of evolutionary social science.

This chapter will characterize a variety of these new evolutionary projects by disciplinary affiliation and analyze the ways in which they deal with different levels of evolutionary phenomena. Some evolutionary social sciences or aspects of them will have to be neglected for reasons of space. The main field left out is evolutionary psychology, about which a great deal of commentary

has already been written (see, for example, Buller, 2005; Dupré, 2001; Stotz and Griffiths, 2002). Others are evolutionary studies of politics, law, ethics and religion— all of which show similar patterns of diversity to the evolutionary fields analyzed below.[1]

EVOLUTIONARY ANTHROPOLOGY

Anthropology epitomizes the fraught relationship of the social sciences with evolutionary theory. Early evolutionary anthropology took social evolution as its object, for which it was roundly denounced by Franz Boas and his followers (Lieberman, 1989; Sanderson, 1990). Evolutionism was then cast aside by several subsequent generations of anthropologists as too general, too ethnocentric, and potentially too biologistic to serve anthropology's aims—especially in the cultural studies form that rose to prominence in anthropology in the 1970s. Some of the most strident denunciations of sociobiology came from these cultural anthropologists.

Although large-scale accounts of cultural evolution have mostly been abandoned, there are still some anthropologists who do provide grand historical analyses of cultural change (e.g., Harris, 1977; Johnson and Earle, 1987).[2] More noticeable now in number and popularization, however, is a rapidly growing group of anthropologists who study cultural units and their evolution, sometimes in conjunction with biological evolution. All of them develop theories about the selection of cultural variations, but not all presume that social or cultural fitness contributes to genetic fitness. They often explicitly distance themselves from social evolution in both form and focus (Durham, 1990: 192), and some distance themselves from presuppositions inherent in sociobiology and evolutionary psychology (e.g., Richerson and Boyd, 2001). This section will review only two categories from this range of approaches and positions: memetics (or the meme-based analysis of cultural evolution) and one form of gene-culture coevolution.[3]

Meme-Based Cultural Evolution

Memetics is a widely known approach that takes *memes*, or units of cultural information, to be the object of cultural transmission and evolutionary selection. Anthropological understanding is not crucial to propound this form of cultural evolution, and its key proponents have been from disciplines as different as cognitive science (Dennett, 1995), evolutionary biology/zoology (Dawkins, 1976) and psychology (Blackmore, 1999). The analogy between genes and memes is often drawn very tightly, and memes are argued to exhibit all the necessary qualities of *replicators*, which are entities (like genes) able to make copies of themselves. They need *interactors* or entities (like organisms) that can interact with the environment in a way that affects replication success (Hull, 1988b; Wilkins, 1998b). Meme interactors are brains, and the means of propagation are social learning or imitation. Memes compete for reproductive dominance through qualities such as memorability or catchiness, and those with the greatest fitness are selected. Meme fitness is not biological fitness (Wilkins, 1998b), although occasionally memeticists suggest there may be inadvertent biological advantages from hosting certain memes (e.g., Blackmore, 1999).

Memes are also often compared to viruses (parcels of genetic material that require proper cells to replicate) because of the way they choose and manipulate humans. This notion runs counter to the conventional idea of humans choosing and adjusting their beliefs and ideas (Brodie, 1996; Dawkins, 1976). In fact, consciousness and a sense of self are often suggested as the *creation* of memes for their effective survival and spread, following the logic that genes help construct niches that allow organisms to survive and reproduce their genes (Dennett, 1995; 1991). In other words, memes are thinking us, not we them. From this perspective, then, culture

is a by-product of meme propagation. This supposed quality of memes and the delight memeticists take in inverting standard assumptions about consciousness, identity and agency have not endeared the field to humanists, notes one memeticist (Dennett, 1995: 361), and nor has its treatment of religion (e.g., Blackmore, 1999).

Criticisms

Although memetics has a journal and something of a sub-sub-disciplinary status, the study of memes has not been taken up to the same extent that the word (used casually) has. A key problem for the field is that of defining the units of selection, the memes. Definitions range from simple information concepts to ones that involve complex neural structures and social institutions (Laland and Brown, 2002; Rose, 1998; Wilkins, 1998b). The structure of memes and meme complexes has been much debated, since the analogy to genes is often argued to depend on how true the copying is. However, as several commentators have pointed out, only outdated concepts of the gene and biological evolution insist on genes as natural kinds involved in purely vertical transmission. Consequently, this class of objections becomes largely irrelevant (Blute, 2005).

Numerous critics still persist, however, in setting out the more subtle problems of the meme–gene analogy and all the associated concepts (such as how transmission or selection do or do not occur) even though they are not opposed to evolutionary theories of culture in general (e.g., Sperber, 2000; Wimsatt, 1999). Even though meme stories certainly suggest avenues of investigation, most claims about memes are made without empirical evidence or substantive proposals for how data could be collected and evaluated (Atran, 2001). Memes are posited primarily to fill a theoretical gap that would otherwise prevent theoretical translations from biology to anthropology, argues Bryant (2004). They were not discovered by investigation and are not the objects of appropriately meticulous empirical studies.

Because many versions of meme theory downplay the role of choice and cognitive evaluation, and take account of too few of the processes involved in the transmission of information (Wimsatt, 1999), several critics conclude that memetics provides only a very thin theory of human cultural evolution. The exclusive focus on meme fitness ignores the likely interactions between memes, cognitive architecture, biology and social environment (Laland and Brown, 2002: 231–2; Gil-White, 2004a), the investigation of which would look very much like gene–culture co-evolution.

Boyd and Richerson's Dual-Inheritance Theory

Robert Boyd and Peter J. Richerson propose an interactive account of genetic and cultural evolution in which each inheritance system can and does influence the other.[4] They argue that cultural adaptation has allowed humans to adapt to a vast range of circumstances because of information stored in brains, not genes. Rather than expensively investigating the world by trial and error, social learning and cultural transmission allow us to gain information 'cheaply' and rapidly in response to changing natural and social environments. Boyd and Richerson's approach builds on Cavalli-Sforza and Feldman's (1981) quantitative modeling of cultural traits in populations. It foregrounds population dynamics and proximate mechanisms rather than the evolution of underlying mechanisms (the focus of one form of evolutionary psychology)[5] that bring about those population-level characteristics.

Boyd and Richerson (1985; Richerson and Boyd, 2005) argue that because culture is behavior-affecting information that can be acquired from other people through teaching, social learning or imitation, the study of cultural evolution requires careful attention to the *effects* of different psychological and social processes of transmission. A population approach is necessary for a causal understanding of cultural evolution, say Boyd and Richerson (1985), because it will explain the net effect of cultural transmission processes on the distribution of beliefs and values across an evolving population. Selection does not explain everything in cultural evolution, they agree, but it occurs wherever there is heritable variation that affects the survival or transmission of cultural information (Henrich et al., 2002). In other words, phenomena such as beliefs will increase in frequency if they cause people to behave in ways that makes transmission of those beliefs more likely.

Boyd and Richerson believe that although cultural traits are often not analogous to genes, the dynamics and final distribution of cultural variants show patterns that approximate the dynamics and distribution of discrete gene-like entities (Heinrich et al., 2002). However, the strict requirements of replicators (fidelity, fecundity and longevity) are not necessary for processes of cultural evolution, because there are other evolved cognitive factors involved (such as bias towards prestige and conformity) that can correct errors and improve social learning strategies (Henrich and Gil-White, 2001; Henrich and McElreath, 2003). Even though cultural evolutionists do not understand the exact nature of these cultural units, they think they can still proceed with models based on observable features of transmission because the unknown entity of the gene was once modeled with exactly the same level of ignorance (Richerson and Boyd, 2005). Boyd and Richerson's models recognize the human capacity for horizontal transfer (within generations) of cultural information as well as 'oblique' or cross-generational transmission (Boyd and Richerson, 1985). They thus avoid the problems of solely vertical transmission that trouble strict meme–gene analogies. Competition is not the same as for genes either. It is generally looser and more diffuse (Boyd and Richerson, 2005). Overall, however, these cultural evolutionists believe that they have to construct their theory from the actual properties of culture, not from the imposition of analogies.

Boyd and Richerson's dual-inheritance or coevolution model calculates fitness from the interactions of psychological, social and ecological processes (Richerson and Boyd,

2005). Cultural processes can lead to very different results than those predicted from purely genetic analyses, and the interaction of cultural and natural selection can illuminate why biologically maladaptive cultural traditions can evolve (Laland and Brown, 2002). Boyd and Richerson hold that cultural evolution can have effects (positive and negative) on biological adaptation by changing the environment and opening up new evolutionary pathways. The biology which culture has shaped includes cognition, digestive processes,[6] disease resistance and human body hair distribution (Henrich et al., forthcoming). In particular, gene-culture coevolution can explain the evolution of cooperation among non-relatives and, ultimately (via group selection), of social institutions (Gil-White and Richerson, 2003; Henrich and Boyd, 2001; Paciotti et al., 2006). Boyd and Richerson (2005: 195) argue that we should see complex cooperative societies as the product of an 'obligate mutualism' between genes and culture that leads to group selection on cultural variation and overwhelms selection on individual and kin-related groups. Once a cultural inheritance system leads to group selection, genetically selfish selection is usually unable to reverse that shift (Richerson and Boyd, 2001).

The differences and interactions between culture-based and gene-based evolution have to be carefully modeled, and coevolutionists borrow their tools from population genetics in order to do a 'painstaking quantitative microhistory' that can measure small cultural changes in a sample of individuals and then extend it to populations and long-term change (Richerson and Boyd, 2005). Understanding the micro-foundations of cultural evolution needs the incorporation and development of social-psychological experimentation to illuminate the proximate mechanisms and transmission processes underlying cultural evolution (Paciotti et al., 2006). While Boyd and Richerson admit that their models contain many simplifications, they argue that they do allow different hypotheses and intuitions to be tested and either abandoned or

modified in light of simulation results (e.g., Whitehead, Richerson and Boyd, 2002).

Criticisms

Boyd and Richerson's work is well read but not extensively emulated (outside a prolific group of colleagues) or even criticized. The low level of application may be due to the technical nature of the models (Laland and Brown, 2002), but the small amount of criticism is perhaps because Boyd and Richerson have anticipated standard objections (such as the lack of fidelity in the replication of cultural variants) and shown how their dual-inheritance account does not rely on such properties (although it can encompass them). When critics complain that humans need cognitive capacities to transmit information units and do not mindlessly make perfect copies of the variant, or that because cultural change happens more quickly than genetic change the two cannot be so easily linked, then Boyd and Richerson are able to reply that such differences are exactly what they are investigating with their models. They claim, nonetheless, that their models do not dichotomize or fully separate nature and culture.

Some commentators, however, do find that Boyd and Richerson are guilty of such separation. Oyama (2000), for example, perceives the dual-inheritance approach as dualistic, but Gil-White (2004b) defends it by arguing that in order to model interaction, population theorists need to theoretically separate interacting elements (whereas the developmental approach Oyama wants would have to study the unseparated outcomes of these interactions). Ereshefsky (2004) also finds Boyd and Richerson's approach dichotomous and restricted but from a more substantive perspective. He argues that the units of cultural transmission can be artefacts, not just information in brains, and that primates can also demonstrate observational learning and cumulative cultural evolution.[7] Boyd and Richerson (1996; Henrich and McElreath, 2003) restrict this level of culture to humans, unlike cultural variation and social learning, which they agree that many species exhibit. Against

Ereshefsky, they argue that information about tool manufacture and use is what is transmitted between human brains (Boyd and Richerson, 1996). They have already considered and disposed of the examples Ereshefsky uses, such as potato washing in macaques, which is too simple and thus easily learned anew by individuals. In addition, experimental evidence is not able to demonstrate observational learning in macaques. Even if Ereshefsky is right, his argument is not a real problem for Boyd and Richerson's approach: it would merely require a slight extension.

Sober (1991) argues that population approaches to cultural change are about outcomes, not causes, and are therefore not interesting. Boyd and Richerson (2005) reply that a focus on mechanisms can be misleading (as many commentators claim is the case for evolutionary psychology) and that there is still a huge knowledge gap between the evolved mechanism (if it is known) and its population-level outcome. Sterelny (2006) argues that Boyd and Richerson's models do not explain the transmission of rare cultural variants, and nor do they give a sufficient role to cultural group selection in the evolution of social learning. He suggests that human learning is a hybrid process that combines socially enhanced direct individual exploration of the world with social learning about it, as well as modification or engineering of the epistemic environment. Since the flow of cultural transmission is likely to vary according to group composition and size, information type, in-built psychological constraints and environment, the development of accurate models of cultural transmission will be very difficult.

The models offered by Boyd and Richerson and their colleagues are indeed highly simplified and make many assumptions. Their modeling methods employ abstract mathematical techniques and there is little corroborating experimental data yet (Laland and Brown, 2002: 279–81). Boyd and Richerson (2005) find such criticisms weak, however, because their simple models are designed to bring some clarity to otherwise overwhelmingly complex and diverse processes. The models

allow the identification of errors and can be modified in response to their failures. 'We look for the simplest real cases we can find to develop some confidence that our models and experiments are at least sometimes true,' they claim (Boyd and Richerson, 2005: 98). It certainly seems that even their 'unsophisticated' models can give better interpretations of data than can wholly genetic or cultural models (Laland and Brown, 2002). Social psychological experimentation is gradually augmenting the modeling (Henrich and Gil-White, 2001; McElreath et al., 2005), and model predictions provide valuable lines of research for future experimentation. At the moment, however, even strong advocates of the dual-inheritance approach can conclude only that 'there is considerable potential for an empirical science of gene-culture coevolution' (Laland and Brown, 2002: 281).

The debates amongst anthropologists over the units of cultural selection and how to study them echoes those in another discipline with similar divisions over what is selected and what evolves: evolutionary epistemology. One of its forms is widely believed to take the investigation of meme theory further, into the realm of science and the evolution of theories.

EVOLUTIONARY EPISTEMOLOGY

Evolutionary epistemology (EE) covers two kinds of knowledge processes: human cognition (the investigation of which is probably best categorized as a variant form of evolutionary psychology),[8] and theoretical change and the collective construction of theory as determined by processes of variation and selection. We will call the latter EE (see Bradie, 1986)[9] and make it the focus of this section so that we can make some of the links to the evolution of institutions promised by theories of cultural evolution.

The most well-known new-wave evolutionary epistemologists were Karl Popper (1979; 1987) and Donald Campbell (1987),[10] both of whom proposed a unified model of cognitive and theoretical selection. They emphasized a trial-and-error process of 'blind variation and retentive selection' that allowed 'hypotheses to die in our stead' (Popper, 1979: 244–5). For them, science's success could be explained by the adaptation of its method to its objects of inquiry, with the consequent increase of fit between theory and evidence (Campbell, 1987).[11] After Popper and Campbell, evolutionary epistemology was taken up by a number of philosophers of science (e.g., Hahlweg and Hooker, 1989;[12] Toulmin, 1972; Wuketits, 1990). The version with the most conceptual development and empirical application, however, is David Hull's (1988b) selectionist account of scientific processes. It also emphasizes the social processes intrinsic to socially institutionalized selection, although few social scientists have yet paid any attention to Hull's work on science.

David Hull's Evolutionary Epistemology

Hull devised his selectionist account of science (1988a; 1988b) in order to understand how science works and why it is so successful. If science really is best understood as an ongoing process of selection, he believes it would have to exhibit features of replication, variation, heritability, transmission and continuity over time. Hull argues that an account of science couched in these concepts is not a mere invocation of biological metaphors but a dynamic explanation of scientific change and diversification that is achieved via a set of abstract concepts applicable to many different domains of phenomena.

His clarification of the units and levels involved in any kind of selection process has had a huge impact not just on EE but on the entire philosophy of evolution. We have already met his most important redefinitions of replicator and interactor in the sub-section on mimetics, but will elaborate a little more on them here (since the following sections also rely on them). Hull defines *replicators* as the unit of heredity. They are information structures that are able to copy and reproduce

themselves, albeit with some variation. *Interactors* are the means by which replicators interact with the environment, since replicators themselves never refer directly to anything outside themselves. As cohesive wholes, interactors adapt to specific environmental conditions with varying degrees of success, whereby replication becomes differential. Selection can then be described as 'a process in which the differential extinction and proliferation of interactors *cause* the differential replication of the relevant replicators' (Hull, 1988b: 408–9).

Replicators in science, which Hull sometimes calls memes, include research results in the form of data, the identification of problems and their possible solutions, beliefs about science itself, the aims and goals of scientific practice, and understandings about methods to achieve results. Their structures of transmission are human brains, journals, books, computers and any other material able to embody information. The interactors are scientists who function as vehicles for the transmission and interaction of the replicator. Interaction is what happens when testing is carried out to ascertain the fit of idea-entity to nature. Selection occurs when the differential success of the interactors leads to the differential success of the replicators. Competition takes place when theories are trying to explain the same phenomenon. Different explanations cannot fit identical conceptual niches and so competition for niches eventually results in either the extinction of weaker competitors or their diversification (in order to utilize resources not used by others).

Hull then links the selection process with some pivotal social factors and proposes that science is a function of *conceptual inclusive fitness* (1988b: 283, 304–5; 1988a: 129). For any scientist, an increase in conceptual fitness means that his or her work has been replicated in subsequent 'generations' of other scientists' work. Conceptual inclusive fitness is an explanation for why a scientist would propagate other scientists' ideas. It relies on the crucial mechanism of credit, which Hull perceives as the driving force of science

(1988b: 376, 393). Credit means 'use', in the sense of scientists having to mutually rely on one another's work. Like it or not, scientists are usually neither able to claim credit entirely for themselves nor achieve support without exchanging some credit for it. No single scientist possesses the conceptual resources necessary to deal adequately with even very specific research problems, let alone broader programs of inquiry. It is this reliance that compels cooperation, with the success of the cited work being indirectly tied to the success of the individual's work.

It is in every scientist's self-interest that the scientific findings he or she uses hold up under examination because otherwise, as his or her own work is subjected to the scrutiny of allies and competitors, it is more likely to fail. Consequently, rigorous examination is institutionalized in science and the whole enterprise becomes cumulative and self-correcting in a manner quite beyond the aims and actions of its individual practitioners. 'Scientists cheat so rarely,' reasons Hull, 'because they suspect they are very likely to be caught' (1988b: 312, 367; 1988a: 131).

Hull applies his selectionist framework to a long case study of biological systematics (classification) to show how competition in a community of systematists produced a clear diversification of scientific lineage. Although he is primarily interested in descent relationships rather than the distributions across populations of replicators that enable interactor advantages, he does not construct lineage trees of theoretical relationships (as has been done by one very interesting application of his theory)[13] but relies solely on a narrative interpretation of a large amount of historical data.

Criticisms

Most of the reaction to Hull's selectionist theory of science has come from philosophers of biology, not sociologists of science. The majority of criticisms are, therefore, about the basic concepts of his account rather than the social mechanism. Quite a number of critics find the interactor–replicator distinctions in science or any form of culture problematic

(Cain and Darden, 1988; Griesmer, 1988; Rosenberg, 1992; Sterelny, 1994). The core problem is that while genes 'encode' organisms, elements of scientific theory or memes do not 'encode' scientists. Hull admits the salience of the disanalogy but believes it does not do serious damage to his theory.

Critics contrast the blindness of natural evolutionary processes and their lack of goal-directedness with the goals and their achievements so apparently characteristic of science. Genetic novelty cannot be generated by an organism's intentions but conceptual innovation can. In fact, argues Sterelny (1994), the intrinsic motivation of scientists is as crucial to the success of scientific activity as are the extrinsic motivations provided by the social mechanism. Hull does not think these complaints have much purchase because the same process of selection occurs in nature both 'naturally' and 'artificially' (the latter as directed by animal breeders, for example). Variation is the key, whether it is 'random' or intentional variation.

A related difficulty for other critics is the transmission process. The evolution of science requires the transmission of acquired characteristics (things scientists learn), and is therefore a Lamarckian process, not a Darwinian one (e.g., Bechtel, 1988). As such, Hull's EE is really a theory of socially inherited learning, rather than a strictly selectionist account of science, says Hussey (1999). Hull's response is that this metaphorical use of Lamarck's idea is unnecessary and these criticisms are really more about the apparently goal-directed nature of scientific activity (1988b: 452–7).

Where Hull does give ground to EE critics is in relation to the disanalogy criticism that 'science progresses but biology doesn't' (e.g., Ruse, 1995: 140–1; Sterelny, 1994). Hull tries to argue for the global progressiveness of science (on top of local progress), but this position catches him in a number of inconsistencies and question-begging problems (Gatens-Robinson, 1993; Grantham, 1994). For both conceptual and biological evolution, localized problem-solving is an adequate description of evolutionary change.

The primary issue that needs solving in regard to this criticism is not that of progress but the issue of adaptive *fit*, or the relation between interactor and environment that contributes to the degree of *fitness* (reproductive success) of the interactor. Hull believes there are 'eternal regularities' in nature and that scientific theories move increasingly closer to nature in their degree of fit (1988b: 467). Because, however, scientists are social interactors, a theory for which they are the vehicle may decline or increase in adaptive fitness due to socio-cultural environmental changes, while the theory's 'empirical fitness' or degree of fit to nature remains the same (Wilkins, 1998a). The complex relationship between fit and fitness has to be worked out very carefully for a coherent evolutionary epistemology, and Hull's reliance on 'eternal regularities' oversimplifies the social nature of the environment and any selection process that may be happening.

In most of the criticisms above, what is actually being contested is whether there are any significant differences of entity, mechanism or environment between natural and cultural evolution processes. The real problem, of course, is not the closeness of analogy but the explanatory power of any selectionist account of scientific success and failure. How successful is Hull's explanation? His method of detailed historical study of a particular field is certainly made more interesting with a selectionist framework, but the observations of competition, cooperation and divergence are not more compellingly explained by adding an overarching account of a selectionist process. Can his model discriminate between conceptual change (or lineage diversification) due to selection and conceptual change due to other processes? No, it cannot. Is the selectionist part of his theory necessary or is he proposing what could be two separate accounts of conceptual change (Grantham, 2000; Kitcher, 1988)? It is possible, in fact, to rewrite Hull's explanation of why science works, as a purely sociological account that says just as much about scientific process but avoids the problems of the selectionist

account (see Grantham, 2000). This very general problem of conceptual redundancy in applying Darwinian logic to non-biological change is an inescapable one for any evolutionary social science.

Because evolutionary epistemology is concerned with the institutionalization of successful innovation, it has conceptual parallels with the next evolutionary discipline of economics. There, innovation and institutionalization occur in organized systems that, although socially different from those of science, are nevertheless conceived under a selectionist rubric.

EVOLUTIONARY ECONOMICS

Evolutionary economics has been hailed by some of its practitioners as a 'Copernican turn' of perspective that overthrows neoclassical assumptions of undifferentiated rational individuals and stable equilibria (e.g., Andersen, 1994: 1).[14] Although still a minority theme in economics, evolutionary approaches have spawned a sizable literature about economic change and revived a variety of older evolutionary perspectives in economics.[15] The 'landmark' theorists in the contemporary revival are Nelson and Winter (1974; 1982; 2002), who posit organizational routines as analogous to genes, and firms to organisms, with profit the selection criterion in economic competition. Their principal concern, however, is to incorporate long-term change and effective understandings of innovation into economics rather than to develop Darwinian analogues.

Other evolutionary economists focus on markets, industries, information flows, and cultural norms of economic activity.[16] The evolution of technology is a related field of inquiry, oriented primarily towards explaining why certain innovations are selected and others not (e.g., Basalla, 1988; McKelvey, 1996; Ziman, 2000). Another level of evolutionary economics theorizes the economic motivation and behavior of individual actors, thereby constituting something akin to an evolutionary psychology of economic behavior (e.g.: Gandolfi et al., 2002; Paquet, 1994; Twomey, 1998). Some versions use game theory to understand the dynamics and outcomes of real-world individual choices in social interactions that involve learning (see Vromen, 2004c, for an outline). This section will continue this chapter's trend towards higher social levels and focus on *institutional* evolutionary economics as represented by Geoffrey Hodgson's work.

Hodgson's Evolutionary Economics

Amongst the multiple forms of contemporary evolutionary economics, Geoffrey Hodgson's work is amongst the most prolific, well-known and accessible. It is not, however, of the same intellectual lineage as the neo-Schumpeterian evolutionary economics of Nelson and Winter,[17] but owes its insights to Veblen's Darwinian framework. Following Hull, Hodgson (2002a; 1999) uses a set of general Darwinian principles[18] that can be filled in by specific investigations and other causal explanations. He employs Hull's definitions of interactor and replicator and agrees with Nelson and Winter that habits and routines (as dispositions, however, and not behaviors) are the replicators, and firms the interactors in evolutionary selection processes in economics (Hodgson and Knudsen, 2004).[19] Habits are individual dispositions that 'energize' routines at the organizational level (Hodgson, 2001; Hodgson and Knudsen, 2004: 295).

Hodgson focuses on what he calls generative or replicative selection (the differential generation of variation in a population) as opposed to subset selection in which variation is removed and not replaced (Hodgson and Knudsen, 2004, 2005). He now includes Lamarckian inheritance in this generally Darwinian process, because acquired behavior can modify the replicator-habit (Hodgson, 2001). Structured interactions between individuals in firms leads to the 'differential profitability' of firms in competitive environments, and thus the differential selection of replicators.

At present, Hodgson's main activity is theoretical refinement, which he justifies

with the claim that neoclassical economics has become obsessed with mathematical puzzles and description and has forgotten that its real aim is to *explain* economic phenomena (Hodgson, 1999). Much of his work, in fact, appears to consist of introducing economists to the philosophy of biology, translating it into economic equivalents, and doing some conceptual re-jigging (for example, showing how selection can incorporate choice). As he notes, the task of identifying specific social and economic mechanisms underlying selection has barely begun (Hodgson and Knudsen, 2005). However, some of his work does include statistical analyses and simulations that generally corroborate aspects of the evolutionary framework (e.g., Hodgson, 1996; Hodgson and Knudsen, 2004).[20] A new aim is to develop a general mathematical definition of selection and other Darwinian concepts to eventually build a multi-level theory of social evolution. Currently, this involves translating equations from biology[21] into economics (Hodgson and Knudsen, 2005; Knudsen, 2004).

Criticisms

Many commentators, even if they are sympathetic to some form of evolutionary theorizing, have problems with Hodgson's (or any evolutionary economist's) close adherence to Darwinian concepts, because of the important differences they see between cultural and biological evolution and the range of other processes and mechanisms at work (e.g., Witt, 2004). The differences are at least as interesting as the similarities from this viewpoint (Nelson, 2004). Even though Hodgson's general definitions try to remove domain-specific content, these critics believe the general theory is still shaped and informed by its biological starting place (Cordes, 2004; Nelson, 2004).

These criticisms are more than just disanalogy arguments. They are empirical as well as theoretical critiques of the application of general Darwinian concepts to economic change. For some (e.g., Buenstorf, 2005), replication is too thin a concept for how economically important information is reproduced and shared, and selection misses out several important dimensions of economic processes (e.g., customers, prices, market regulations, market feedback). Variation is generated by very different processes from those found in biological evolution (Cordes, 2004). The problems of fitness as the frequency of replicated routines means that success would be the result of all firms copying one firm's routines, which would remove the competitive advantage of the originating firm (Buenstorf, 2005). The populational analyses that are becoming the popular way to calculate fitness (e.g., Andersen, 2004; Hodgson and Knudsen, 2005) mean evolutionary economics pays little attention to descent and speciation.[22] If painstakingly translating Darwin is the key task, asks Witt (2004), why are these key concepts neglected? Moreover, advances in molecular and developmental biology and ecology should surely be considered if non-simplistic accounts of evolution are to be generated in economics (Vromen, 2004b). Cordes (2004) goes on to produce a systematic overview of how general Darwinian concepts derived from biology are insufficient for economics and other forms of cultural evolution, and, in fact, obscure the real mechanisms of non-biological evolution.

Hodgson's response to most of these criticisms is that either they are mistaken in how they conceive of Darwinian concepts, or that the points are valid and can be incorporated into Darwinian accounts of economic evolution (e.g., choice and purpose) without altering the metatheory. However, dealing with dis-analogy or inadequacy arguments does mean that making room for or removing extra-Darwinian elements forms a large part of his work. Rather than a conceptual checklist, asks Jack Vromen, can evolutionary economics supply *explanations* with these general Darwinian principles and produce a fruitful research program (2004a)? One common answer is that 'as compelling as [evolutionary] analyses may seem, they do not provide the rigour to develop evolutionary economics into a science and cannot be substitutes for measurements and models'

(Ruth, 1996: 140). Evolutionary economists recognize that their field has a long way to go yet before it is able to analyze evolutionary processes in economics and 'saturate' its theoretical work with quantitative and historical analyses (Andersen, 2004).

One potential inhibitor of research is the fact that routines are non-observable because they are dispositions. Their substantive vagueness makes them very problematic for economic research and the falsification of evolutionary theory (Buenstorf, 2005). It is likely that Hodgson's reply to this criticism would be that this was once the case for genes and that lack didn't stop evolutionary biology from becoming a successful science.

The bigger problem with evolutionary economics of the universalist scope, argues Buenstorf (2005), is that it is a top-down approach imposing an overarching theory on economics, whereas Darwin himself started from the bottom up with detailed evidence. Evolutionary economics might be better served by translating this approach into economics if it insists on strict adherence to Darwinian thinking. Nelson (2004: 30) echoes this argument, and says that the progress of evolutionary economics is more likely if general evolutionary concepts were to arise out of empirically driven work, rather than the presumption that analogies should exist. Across all forms of evolutionary economics, however, there is at least a recognition of the need for methodological depth and scope, and effort is being made to develop appropriate analyses. In this regard, therefore, evolutionary economics is no worse off than most other evolutionary social sciences.

Given that evolutionary economics is a form of institutional economics, it might be expected that it would have many connections with evolutionary sociology, but so far there is little sign of this. This disconnection between economics and sociology may be because of the historical antipathy between sociology and economics, or another indication that evolutionary frameworks have no necessarily unifying capacities for the social sciences. Evolutionary economist Richard Nelson (2002) argues very strongly that sociology and economics have to reconnect and that economists have to become general social scientists again. The problem with this aspiration, says Hodgson (2002b), is that sociology itself is in a mess, though for very different reasons than economics (fragmentation versus formalization). Is it possible that evolutionary theory can solve both disciplines' problems?

EVOLUTIONARY SOCIOLOGY

As in evolutionary economics, sociology can either try to unite biology and society in an evolutionary framework, or it can focus on generating an evolutionary account of the chosen social phenomena and leave the biology implicit (at a different level). The first option is taken by evolutionary sociologists who investigate the evolved biological bases of human social behavior (e.g., Freese et al., 2003; Lopreato and Crippen, 1999). Other evolutionary sociology perspectives set up a very different problematic for the field. Maryanski and Turner (1992: Chapter 8), for example, believe that sociological processes lead to the evolution of institutions that constrain and even violate biological propensities, to the extent of socially 'caging' instinctively individualistic humans. This position inverts the more common idea of biology 'holding culture on a leash' (Lumsden and Wilson, 1981: 13; Wilson, 1978: 167), which most sociologists think would somehow prevent the full realization of human creativity and freedom. Some evolutionary work uses game theory to understand how social norms and institutions can eventually result from individual learning strategies (e.g., Young, 1998), but despite using notions of variation and adaptation, this sort of evolution simply means cumulative formation. In this section we will focus on work that deals with the evolution of social institutions and uses Darwinian concepts.[23]

The first thing any evolutionary sociologist working at this level of analysis has to do is overcome the legacy of Spencer's and Parsons's evolutionary ideas, which—for

good and bad reasons—are seen as paradigm cases of both bad sociology and the problems of evolutionary thinking in the social sciences.[24] Most attempts to leave this inheritance behind are couched in Darwinian language,[25] and argue that a better Darwinian understanding is the key to success (as did Parsons, of course). The most rigorously Darwinian of these evolutionary sociologies is W.G. Runciman's, which we will contrast with the much more hybridized Darwinism of Jonathan Turner.

Runciman's Evolutionary Sociology

Runciman follows the route Hull and others have established of seeing social evolution as just one of the evolutionary processes that operates under strict Darwinian abstractions. He argues for three 'levels' of selection (2001), only one of which is biological. The other two are cultural and social, and Runciman's concern is the latter (although it has a close relationship with cultural evolution). Using the example of a baseball game, Runciman (1998) illustrates how the three levels are entwined into the evolution of the game. The *evoked* behavior of hitting the ball is a biological inheritance; the behaviors associated with the game and its audience are *acquired* by imitation or learning, and the institutional structure of ownership of teams is an *imposed* behavior. It is at the institutional level that he situates most of his evolutionary analysis, although biological and cultural phenomena are brought in to supplement the social analysis.

Runciman makes close social analogies with neo-Darwinian concepts in biology (and devotes some effort to ruling out or incorporating dis-analogies). He identifies practices as the unit of social selection and defines them as 'functionally defined units of reciprocal action informed by the mutually recognized intentions and beliefs of designated persons about their respective capacity to influence each other's behavior by virtue of their roles' (1989a: 41). Roles are interactors, and institutions are the 'underwriters' of practices as well as their outcomes. Certain practices confer adaptive advantages on their carriers in particular conditions of power distribution.[26]

Runciman conceives of advantages within a threefold theory of power as economic, ideological or coercive (or any combination of these). These advantages or disadvantages enable practice carriers to adapt with varying degrees of success to their power environments, the result of which can be changes in the dominance of roles and institutions (1989a: 42–3, 1989b: 30–6). Through this process, carriers of advantageous practices can modify the niche they occupy and transform that environment (the structure and culture of the society) to the extent that it too evolves into something qualitatively different (1989a: 45). Any analysis of social evolution, therefore, depends on an analysis of selected practices and their functions, which will involve the disentanglement of the relative importance of multiple practices involved in particular episodes of social change. In the end, says Runciman (1989b: 31), evolutionary explanation stands or falls upon making a correct assessment of the power held by competing carriers in a given social niche.

The way in which Runciman initially elected to demonstrate his theory was by constructing a typology (actually an identification key) of possible forms of society (1989a). Its weaknesses (see Anderson, 1989; Wickham, 1991) and limited explanatory value forced him to focus on the provision of numerous historical narratives (employing ethnographic and archaeological findings, as well as primary historical analyses), which he re-interprets with selectionist concepts and occasional uses of evolutionary game theory (e.g., Runciman, 2004). These narratives stress the importance of understanding social evolution in order to understand biological and cultural contributions to behavior in different social contexts. One example is his explanation of the persistence of lethal violence in a variety of cultures (originally analyzed at the cultural level by Boyd and Richerson, 2005). He argues that the persistence of such violence is insufficiently explained by biological or cultural selection, and that it therefore requires an institutional-level account as well (1998). He thereby adds substance to Boyd and Richerson's openness to the incorporation of the social dimension, but unlike them has no modeling process to describe it. Even if he is providing 'just so' stories, says Runciman (2002: 21), at least they are plausible and superior to the atheoretical narratives that string together vast numbers of historical facts in the work of non-evolutionary social science.

Criticisms

Although Runciman's interpretation of evolutionary concepts has been criticized (e.g., Benton, 2000; Fracchia and Lewontin, 2005), it is their explanatory efficacy in regard to his historical material that is more strongly questioned. As in evolutionary economics, the whole practice of importing biologically derived terminology (no matter how generalized it has become) is deemed invalid and obfuscatory by some critics, and to consist of redescription rather than appropriate social analysis (e.g., Bryant, 2004). Jonathan Turner's (1992: 522) conclusion is that 'what emerges [from Runciman's work] is a long series of descriptions of scattered historical examples with allusions to Darwinian selection processes.' Even Wickham, a far more favorable reviewer, notes that Runciman's plethora of examples is sometimes so sketchily presented as to decorate rather than really illuminate the evolutionary theme (1991: 194). While the comparative historical method may give us a great deal of insight into particular societies, that evidence is not strong enough from many critics' perspectives to support evolutionary explanations, which are deemed to require far more specific causal mechanisms in order to be convincing (Collins, 1990: 88).

For these critics, the real problem in Runciman's approach is his 'selectionist hindsight' (Fracchia and Lewontin, 2005), which means that Runciman *begins* with the supposedly selected outcome and then— naturally enough—finds the variation and chain of subsequent processes that produced the selection effect. The only obvious selection that is happening occurs in Runciman's approach to the historical material, argue Fracchia and Lewontin (2005). Runciman, of course, argues vigorously against this criticism (which he thinks must have ideological roots) and says it is up to his critics to show him compelling non-selectionist stories that fit the evidence better (Runciman, 2005). Since, however, explanatory weakness is a perennial charge against evolutionary history (even in biology), it is incumbent on the evolutionist to develop methods that are less vulnerable to such criticisms and to generate historical accounts that show how it is possible to discriminate between selected outcomes and the outcomes of other processes.[27] Imitating biology (simply by saying there is 'cultural drift', for example) is unlikely to prove satisfactory.

Evolutionary sociology has serious problems working at this level of social change (institutions and, ultimately, the structure of whole societies), no matter how well the units of selection are theorized. Although Runciman has done as much historical work as conceptual fine-tuning, it is unlikely—despite his protestations to the contrary—that any historical narrative will provide an adequate test of an evolutionary explanation (Chattoe, 2002). Historical narratives certainly provide suggestive hypotheses about what may have happened, but are not able in themselves to adjudicate between plausible stories that roughly encompass the data.

Where does this methodological shortfall leave Runciman's evolutionary sociology? In a conceptual limbo, it would appear. His framework has not yet been applied by other sociologists or social historians, even if the scope of his historical knowledge has been much admired, alongside the conceptual sophistication of his three-tiered evolutionary theory. Runciman is convincing that a selectionist framework can guide an interesting interpretation of a set of historical events. However, he does not achieve his self-stated aim of making his account the *best* explanation for many sociologists—a failure

that undermines the 'paradigm shift' he advocates for the social sciences. As we saw in evolutionary economics, conceptual sophistication and refutation of Darwinian analogies are insufficient for an evolutionary research program. Would a theory of social evolution that used Darwin more loosely in conjunction with other theories of social change be more successful? Jonathan Turner offers such an alternative.

Jonathan Turner's Societal Evolution

Turner (2003; 2004) wants to develop a macro-level account of social organization and how it is constituted by macro-dynamic forces of population, power, production, distribution and reproduction,[28] all of which work separately and together in a manner similar to that of natural selection. He constructs a three-dimensional definition of selection that is *Darwinian* (about the selection and retention of social units with greater fitness than others in periods of adversity and competition), *Durkheimian* (employing selection processes in which the less fit are not extinguished but instead diversify and move into new unexploited niches), and *Spencerian* (involving the creation of new structures in social units in order to cope with selection pressures). Most generally, selection means 'the process of creating and recreating social structures', and it is more likely to be Durkheimian or Spencerian than Darwinian (Turner, 2004: 231).

Turner sets up some basic 'quasi-mathematical' equations (non-conventional for the sake of his readership) to represent these insights and explain the effect of forces on one another and social organization. He then provides a long history of core institutions (economy, kinship, religion, law, polity and education) and their increasing differentiation through 'the most visible stages of societal evolution' (hunting and gathering, horticultural, agrarianism, industrialism, and post-industrialism). The ongoing differentiation of these institutions has led to different patterns of integration and institutional inter-relationships, which Turner describes historically. Institutional analysis cannot be done in isolation, he argues: each institution must be understood within a larger complex connected by dynamic inter-relationships so that regularities and irregularities over time can be investigated. Although his evidence currently consists of historical narrative, the theory does allow him to modestly and broadly extrapolate into the future ('we may see' trend A or trend B given a set of conditions).

Criticisms

So far, Turner's account has been little noticed or challenged in either sociological or anthropological literature.[29] Anyone seeking a purely Darwinian form of evolutionary theory will no doubt be disappointed by what he has to offer (his model is much more about the 'push' of forces than about selection of differently adapted units), but it does appear as if Turner has furnished sociology with both a roster of the interacting forces that it is necessary to consider if social evolution is to be investigated and a more precise means of investigating and disconfirming claims that social evolution has occurred. It is probable that his equations are too simple and imprecise for the task devolved upon them, and there is a big question about how non-quantified socio-historical variables (the forces) would be computed. Crude generalizations (e.g., institutional evolution is more likely to be Spencerian and Durkheimian than Darwinian') are a weak basis, however, for the generation of more precise hypotheses and further research.

An immediate target of complaints is Turner's functionalism. His language does sometimes lend itself to Parsonian interpretations of functional requisites, but these are remedied by going back to the causal propositions embedded in the equations (Sanderson, 2004; Vaisey, 2004). Another potential problem is that his history leads to a typology of increasingly complex societies as a consequence of his macro-perspective and emphasis on differentiation.[30] Although Turner frequently claims he is providing a multi-causal explanation of social stages (as opposed to

either description or mono-causal explanation), it is easy to see how critics could perceive just an interpretation of historical material that is guided by a general narrative theme (i.e.: another 'just so' story). To really convince sceptics, Turner would have to find more compelling methods and to develop a history that is more culturally diverse and less a linear timeline of increasing differentiation (something quite uninteresting even if it is mostly true). Unlike Runciman, Turner does not outline how other levels of evolutionary analysis might be integrated with the macro-institutional.

Boyd and Richerson, whose work could be thought of as complementary to Turner's, acknowledge the importance of Turner's formulation of Spencerian evolution and attempt to investigate it within a natural and cultural selectionist perspective (Richerson and Boyd, 2000). Although they do not directly criticize Turner, they argue that any complete theory of social change will have to bring in dynamic processes at multiple levels and that a Darwinian framework can do this more effectively and comprehensively than any other. They think that there are strong limits on the predictability of evolutionary trajectories, and that an understanding of underlying cultural dynamics is essential to recognize the 'uncontrolled' processes on which social evolution rests. Working in the other direction from Turner, they find a multilinear pattern for the evolution of institutional complexity, with varying paces (including stagnation and regression) that call out for explanation (2000). Their findings are not necessarily incompatible with Turner's broader historical framework, but they do draw attention to the problems of working at the level that Turner does, where culture is just another environmental factor.

The problem of doing history at this macro-level is the same as for Runciman: it results in a general picture of trends (i.e., increasing social differentiation or complexity) that is not surprising to any audience and surely indicates that either the focus is wrong or the methods inadequate. It remains to be seen whether Turner will develop his formulation of social evolution in more nuanced ways. Runciman is telling interesting historical stories that can more immediately incorporate cultural analyses, but his interpretive method is still insufficient to convince many readers that there is a scientific theory being tested by his accounts. Social evolution lies at the tough end of the spectrum in evolutionary social science (not that there is really an 'easy' end), and its investigation may raise similar issues to those associated with providing an account of the major transitions in biological history (e.g., Maynard Smith and Szathmáry, 1995). This kind of macro-macro-evolutionary overview requires a further range of approaches than those sufficient to establish the role of natural selection in evolutionary biology, but it is highly questionable whether there are enough parallels between social change and biological change to warrant the import of further abstractions from biology.

GENERAL CRITICISM OF EVOLUTIONARY APPROACHES

There are several general problems persistently identified with evolutionary approaches in the social sciences, mostly to do with the mode of explanation it offers and the empirical difficulties it faces in substantiating those explanations.[31] Many complaints have been made of the metaphorical and inferential nature of evolutionary explanations in these various forms. Its adaptationist[32] hypotheses are often no more than dubious and unsubstantiated assertions, say some critics (e.g., Dickens, 2001: 97–8; Gould, 2000). They believe that adequate evolutionary analysis would demand more solid evidence and precise analytical tools than provided by the historical narratives—sometimes circular—currently on offer.

The only really interesting question to ask about social-scientific theories cut to a Darwinian pattern is how well confirmed they are—not how well the conceptual matching can be done (Rosenberg, 1994). Serious skeptics of evolutionary social science, such as anthropologist Tim Ingold

(2000: 2), say they have 'yet to read any interpretation of social or cultural phenomena by a selectionist that has added anything to what we already know by other means.' The evolutionists' claim to be setting out testable hypotheses is just a logical device to conceal superficial conversions of descriptions into pseudo-explanations. The only thing added is a metaphor, says Ingold, and it is spurious to call such rhetorical tricks science. Runciman's comment that evolutionary sociology is about 'what happened to happen' recast within an evolutionary framework might seem to confirm this view, although many pro-evolutionary social scientists would argue that this very framing makes social history scientific (Blute, 1997).

However, since a lot of social science (sociology in particular) is more about interpretation than explanation, and since many social scientists think 'science' is definitely not what social disciplines are or should be doing, any failure to explain should not be considered much of a problem. The fact is that evolutionary social science is read and thought about only by those wanting good explanatory science, and hence social evolutionism pleases nobody. Non-explanatory social interpreters ignore or denounce evolutionary efforts; explanatory social scientists find them inadequate.

AN EVOLUTIONARY PARADIGM?

Most of the claims that a new evolutionary paradigm is emerging are predicated on the mere existence of a large number of approaches in different disciplines that describe themselves as evolutionary. As the outline above makes clear, however, there is no unitary evolutionary social science. There are a wide range of currently disconnected approaches concerned with a plurality of topics, mechanisms and processes. There are major methodological differences between most of these evolutionary approaches, and they posit different units of selection, hold different understandings of evolutionary processes, and are investigated within very different disciplinary contexts. They share only a very general problematic, and their strongest common feature appears to be the problems they face in generating the research necessary to test their propositions and convince their opponents.

Despite these different agendas (and the background of increasing specialization), the idea of an emergent paradigm in which different levels of explanation and phenomena are unified is tremendously appealing to many social scientists. Some of them hope evolutionary theory can connect *all* the life sciences, both social and biological (Barkow, 2001; Boyd and Richerson, 2005; Hodgson, 1999; Sheets-Johnstone, 1994: 63–4). The aspired-for parallel is, of course, the successful synthesis of similarly different lines of inquiry in modern evolutionary biology, which brought together the methods and theories of approaches as different as population genetics, palaeobiology, ecology, evolutionary theory, and comparative physiology and anatomy.

As we have seen, many discipline-specific approaches to evolution argue for a much more general logic of selection and evolution. This logic, often called 'Universal Darwinism',[33] sees organic evolution as just one instance of a much broader model of replication, variation and selection processes (Cziko, 1995; Darden and Cain, 1989; Durham, 1991: 200). The scientist's (natural and social) task is to reveal the details and domains of specific instances, although connecting levels together is not generally advocated. Perhaps these aims will be realized if a wealth of successful research programs is eventually generated around the different objects of explanation claimed by the social sciences.

For the present at least, universal Darwinism appears to obscure or neglect at least as much as it reveals, relying on a 'plausibility by analogy' appeal (Darden and Cain, 1989), and it is certainly not advocated by most evolutionists in social science or biology. Evolutionary biologist Jerry Coyne (2000) calls the extreme application of this logic 'the Darwinization of Everything',

and sees it as part of an urge for a totalistic and inevitabilist explanation of human life, whereas Richard Lewontin (2005) sees only an epistemological rationale for all these Darwinian efforts ('they serve an intellectual interest but cannot be said to accord better with the phenomena they are meant to explain'). Evolutionary economist Richard Nelson (2004) takes a similar view that different spheres of culture will involve quite different mechanisms and processes of evolution (e.g., arts versus sciences), and a universal Darwinist framework will not connect these together in a meaningful way.

Darwinian frameworks seemed to be seized on for different reasons by different disciplines: sometimes for the scientific credibility they confer; at other times for the general oppositional force Darwinian thinking has against mainstream thinking in the discipline; and yet others for the potential sense of unity and positive reorientation it can provide a whole discipline or range of disciplines.[34] As we have seen from the overview above, these benefits are at best only partially realized, except for the negative function of serving as a thorn in the side of the majority approach in the discipline.

Even evolutionary biology faces some of the problems that evolutionary social science does. Evolutionary biology is not the solid indisputable science that many evolutionary critics and sympathizers seem to believe it is. Because it is a historical discipline, it has a lowly status amongst other sciences and struggles to find hard evidence for many assumptions of adaptation (Coyne, 2000). This does not mean evolutionary explanations in biology are not science, but that they require rigor and strong evidence to be accepted as good science. Strong evolutionary explanations are more likely to be the exception than the rule and even the best ones will not explain a lot of what we want to know about organisms and environments (Dupré, 2003). If a great deal more than evolutionary theory is required to make sense of biological phenomena, then social phenomena are also likely to need at least as many other forms of explanation. Social scientists who think Darwin has an easy-to-fit unifying framework that will solve their disciplines' problems, elevate their status and bring coherence to all the social sciences are, sadly, misguided.

THE FUTURE OF EVOLUTIONARY SOCIAL SCIENCE

While the inferential nature of some evolutionary arguments may disturb hard-minded observers, it is also undeniable that every evolutionary specialism in the social sciences is committed to collecting more and better evidence, with the aim of reducing the evidence-to-conclusion leaps that have to be made at present. As with Darwinian biology a century ago, much still depends on the capacity of the research programs that are driven by evolutionary interests and the tools that they are able to develop. Some disciplines will do better than others, especially if their problems are amenable to solutions that allow fitness calculations and other quantifiable analyses or the modeling of qualitative data (see Chattoe, 2002). Gene-culture coevolution will probably do the best in developing these methods. The farther evolutionary accounts are from biology, the more difficult it is for evolutionary explanations to offer more than interesting analogies and contestable historical narratives. Evolutionary economics may be the exception because of its capacity to generate models and simulations, but methodological progress will probably lead to the 'debasement' of purely Darwinian abstractions.

Evolutionary social science is unlikely ever to be totally extinguished in any of the disciplines it has colonized, but it is just as unlikely to break down barriers between specialized social sciences. Any conceivable unification of evolutionary approaches would happen because of the nature of the research problem or topic being addressed. If such collaborations did begin to occur and the overlaps between different disciplinary approaches were exploited for deeper insight, then we might see the development of evolutionary approaches that were truly problem-solving rather than discipline-defining.

ACKNOWLEDGEMENTS

Many thanks to Jim Byrne and Francesco Guala for sharing useful material and discussion.

REFERENCES AND SELECT BIBLIOGRAPHY

Andersen, E.S. (1994) *Evolutionary economics: post-Schumpeterian contributions*. London: Pinter.
——— (2004) 'Evometrics: Quantitative evolutionary analysis from Schumpeter to Price and beyond', Paper presented at the Conference of the Japan Association of Evolutionary Economics, Fukui, Japan, March 27–28.
Anderson, P. (1989) 'Societies', *London Review of Books*, 11: 6–9.
Archer, J. (1991) 'Human sociobiology: Basic concepts and limitations', *Journal of Social Issues*, 47 (3): 11–26.
Aoki, K. (2001) 'Theoretical and empirical aspects of gene-culture coevolution', *Theoretical Population Biology*, 59: 253–61.
Atran, S. (2001) 'The trouble with memes: Inference versus imitation in cultural creation', *Human Nature*, 12: 351–81.
Aunger, R. (2000) 'Introduction', in R. Aunger (ed.), *Darwinizing Culture: The Status of Memetics as a Science*. Oxford: Oxford University Press, pp. 1–23.
Barkow, J.H. (2001) 'Universals and evolutionary psychology', in P.M. Hejl (ed.), *Universalien und Konstruktivismus*. Frankfurt: Suhrkamp Verlag, pp. 126–38.
Basalla, G. (1988) *The Evolution of Technology*. Cambridge: Cambridge University Press.
Bechtel, W. (1988) 'New insights into the nature of science: What does Hull's evolutionary epistemology tell us?', *Biology and Philosophy*, 3: 157–64.
Benton, T. (2000) 'Social causes and natural relations', in H. Rose and S. Rose (eds), *Alas, Poor Darwin: Arguments against Evolutionary Psychology*. London: Jonathan Cape, pp. 206–24.
Blackmore, S. (1999) *The Meme Machine*. Oxford: Oxford University Press.

Blute, M. (1997) 'History versus science: The evolutionary solution', *Canadian Journal of Sociology*, 22: 345–64.

——— (2002) 'The evolutionary ecology of science', *Journal of Mimetics*, 7. Available at: http://www.jom-emit.cfpm.org/2003/vol7/blute_m.html.

——— (2005) 'Memetics and evolutionary social science', *Journal of Mimetics*, 9. Available at: http://jom-emit.cfpm.org/2005/vol9/blute_m.html.

Bock, K.E. (1964) 'Theories of progress and evolution', in W.J. Cahnman and A. Boskoff (eds) *Sociology and History: Theory and Research*. Glencoe, NY: Free Press, pp. 21–41.

Bowler, P.J. (1988) *The Non-Darwinian Revolution: Reinterpreting a Historical Myth*. Baltimore: Johns Hopkins University Press.

Boyd, R. and Richerson, P.J. (1985) *Culture and the Evolutionary Process*. Chicago: University of Chicago Press.

——— (1996) 'Why culture is common, but cultural evolution is rare', *Proceedings of the Royal British Academy*, 88: 73–93.

——— (2006) 'Culture, adaptation and innateness', in P. Carruthers, S. Stich and S. Laurence (eds), *The Innate Mind: Culture and Cognition*. Oxford: Oxford University Press, pp. 23–38.

Bradie, M. (1986) 'Assessing evolutionary epistemology', *Biology and Philosophy*, 1: 401–59.

Brodie, R. (1996) *Virus of the Mind: The New Science of the Meme*. Seattle: Integral Press.

Bryant, J.M. (2004) 'An evolutionary social science? A sceptic's brief, theoretical and substantive', *Philosophy of the Social Sciences*, 34: 451–92.

Buenstorf, G. (2005) 'How useful is Universal Darwinism as a framework to study competition and industrial evolution?', *Papers on Economics and Evolution*. Max Planck Institute for Research into Economic Systems, MPI Jena (#0502).

Buller, D.J. (2005) *Adapting Minds: Evolutionary Psychology and the Persistent Quest for Human Nature*. Cambridge, MA: MIT Press.

Cain, J.A. and Darden, L. (1988) 'Hull and selection', *Biology and Philosophy*, 3: 165–71.

Campbell, D.T. (1987) 'Blind variation and selective retention in creative thought as in other knowledge processes', in G. Radnitzky and W.W. Bartley, (eds), *Evolutionary Epistemology, Rationality, and the Sociology of Knowledge*. La Salle, Illinois: Open Court, pp. 91–114.

——— (1965) 'Variation, selection and retention in sociocultural evolution', in H.R. Barringer, G.I. Blanksten and R.W. Mack, (eds), *Social Change in Developing Areas: A Reinterpretation of Evolutionary Theory*. Cambridge, MA: Schenkman, pp. 19–49.

Cavalli-Sforza, L.L. and Feldman, M.W. (1981) *Cultural Transmission and Evolution: A Quantitative Approach*. Princeton, NJ: Princeton University Press.

Chase-Dunn, C. and Hall, J.D. (1994) 'The historical evolution of world-systems', *Sociological Inquiry*, 64 (3): 257–80.

Chattoe, E. (2002) 'Developing the selectionist paradigm in sociology', *Sociology*, 36: 817–33.

Collective authors. (1925) *Evolution in the Light of Modern Knowledge: A Collective Work*. London: Blackie and Son.

Coleman, M. (2002) 'Taking Simmel seriously in evolutionary epistemology', *Studies in the History and Philosophy of Science*, 33: 59–78.

Collins, R. (1990) 'Review of W.G. Runciman's *A Treatise on Social Theory: Volume Two*', *European Sociological Review*, 6: 87–9.

Cordes, C. (2004) 'Darwinism in economics: from analogy to continuity', *Papers on Economics and Evolution*. Max Planck Institute for Research into Economic Systems, MPI Jena (#0415).

Coyne, J.A. (2000) 'The fairy tales of evolutionary psychology: Of vice and men', *New Republic*, April 3.

Cronk, L., Chagnon, N. and Irons, W. (eds) (2000) *Adaptation and Human Behavior: An Anthropological Perspective*. NY: De Gruyter.

Csányi, V. (1989) *Evolutionary Systems and Society: A General Theory of Life, Mind, and Culture*. Durham, NC: Duke University Press.

Cziko, G. (1995) *Without Miracles: Universal Selection Theory and the Second Darwinian Revolution*. Cambridge, MA: MIT Press/Bradford.

Darden, L. and Cain, J.A. (1989) 'Selection type theories', *Philosophy of Science*, 56: 106–29.

Darwin, C. ([1859] 1964) *On the Origin of Species* (facsimile edition). Cambridge, MA: Harvard University Press.

Dawkins, R. (1976) *The Selfish Gene*. Oxford: Oxford University Press.

——— (1983) 'Universal Darwinism', in D.S. Bendall (ed.), *Evolution from Molecules to Men*. Cambridge: Cambridge University Press, pp. 403–28.

Dennett, D.C. (1991) *Consciousness Explained*. Boston, MA: Little, Brown and Co.

——— (1995) *Darwin's Dangerous Idea: Evolution and the Meanings of Life*. NY: Simon and Schuster.

Dickens, P. (2000) *Social Darwinism: Linking Evolutionary Thought to Social Theory*. Buckingham: Open University Press.

——— (2001) 'Linking the social and natural sciences: Is capital modifying human biology in its own image?', *Sociology*, 35 (1): 93–110.

Dodgshon, R.A. (1987) *The European Past: Social Evolution and Spatial Order*. London: Macmillan.

Dopfer, K. and Potts, J. (2004) 'Evolutionary realism: A new ontology for economics', *Journal of Economic Methodology*, 11: 195–212.

Dupré, J. (2001) *Human Nature and the Limits of Science*. Oxford: Oxford University Press.

——— (2003) *Darwin's Legacy: What Evolution Means Today*. Oxford: Oxford University Press.

Durham, W.H. (1990) 'Advances in evolutionary culture theory', *Annual Review of Anthropology*, 19: 187–210.

——— (1991) *Coevolution: Genes, Culture, and Human Diversity*. Stanford, CA: Stanford University Press.

Endler, J.A. (1986) *Natural Selection in the Wild*. Princeton, NJ: Princeton University Press.

Ereshefsky, M. (2004) 'Bridging the gap between human kinds and biological kinds', *Philosophy of Science*, 71: 912–21.

Fagerberg, J. (2003) 'Schumpeter and the revival of evolutionary economics: An appraisal of the literature', *Journal of Evolutionary Economics*, 13: 125–59.

Fracchia, J. and Lewontin, R.C. (2005) 'The price of metaphor', *History and Theory*, 44: 14–29.

Freese, J., Li, J.-C.A. and Wade, L.D. (2003) 'The potential relevances of biology to social inquiry', *Annual Review of Sociology*, 29: 233–56.

Gandolfi, A.E., Gandolfi, A.S. and Barash, D.P. (2002) *Economics as an Evolutionary Science: From Utility to Fitness*. New Brunswick, NJ: Transaction Press.

Gatens-Robinson, E. (1993) 'Why falsificationism is the wrong paradigm for evolutionary epistemology: An analysis of Hull's selection theory', *Philosophy of Science*, 60: 535–57.

Gil-White, F. (2004a) 'Common misunderstandings of memes (and genes): The promise and the limits of the genetic analogy to cultural transmission processes', in S. Hurley and N. Chater, (eds), *Perspectives on Imitation: From Mirror Neurons to Memes*. Cambridge, MA: MIT Press, pp. 317–38.

——— (2004b) 'The postmodern biologist (cum psychologist)', *Theory and Psychology*, 14: 134–7.

Gil-White, F.J. and Richerson, P.J. (2003) 'Large-scale human cooperation and conflict', in L. Nadel (ed.), *Encyclopaedia of Cognitive Science*. London: Nature/Macmillan, pp. 828–37.

Gould, S.J. (1983) 'The hardening of the modern synthesis', in M. Grene (ed.), *Dimensions of Darwinism: Themes and Counterthemes in Twentieth-Century Evolutionary Theory*. Cambridge: Cambridge University Press, pp. 71–93.

——— (2000) 'More things in heaven and earth', in H. Rose and S. Rose (eds), *Alas, Poor Darwin: Arguments Against Evolutionary Psychology*. London: Jonathan Cape, pp. 85–105.

Gould, S.J. and Lewontin, R.C. (1979) 'The spandrels of San Marco and the Panglossian paradigm: A critique of the adaptationist programme', *Proceedings of the Royal Society*, B, 205: 581–98.

Grantham, T.A. (1994) 'Does science have a 'global goal'?: A critique of Hull's view of conceptual progress', *Biology and Philosophy*, 9: 85–97.

——— (2000) 'Evolutionary epistemology, social epistemology, and the demic structure of science', *Biology and Philosophy*, 15: 443–63.

Griesmer, J.R. (1988) 'Genes, memes and demes', *Biology and Philosophy*, 3: 179–84.

Hahlweg, K. and Hooker, C.A. (1989) 'Historical and theoretical context', in K. Hahlweg and C.A. Hooker (eds), *Issues in evolutionary epistemology*. Albany, NY: SUNY, pp. 23–44.

Hallpike, C.R. (1987). *The Principles of Social Evolution*. Oxford: Clarendon.

Hardcastle, V.G. (1993) 'Evolutionary epistemology as an overlapping, interlevel theory', *Biology and Philosophy*, 8: 173–92.

Harris, M. (1977) *Cannibals and Kings: The Origins of Cultures*. NY: Random House.

Hayek, F.A. (1978) *New Studies in Philosophy, Politics, Economics and the History of Ideas*. London: Routledge and Kegan Paul.

Henrich, J. and Boyd, R. (2001) 'Why people punish defectors: Weak conformist transmission can stabilize costly enforcement of norms in cooperative endeavours', *Journal of Theoretical Biology*, 208: 79–89.

Henrich, J., Boyd, R. and Richerson, P.J. (forthcoming) 'Five misunderstandings about cultural evolution'. Available at www.des.ucdavis.edu/faculty/richerson/five%20 misunderstandings.pdf

Henrich, J. and Gil-White, F.J. (2001) 'The evolution of prestige: Freely conferred deference as a mechanism for enhancing the benefits of cultural transmission', *Evolution and Human Behavior*, 22: 165–96.

Henrich, J. and McElreath, R. (2003) 'The evolution of cultural evolution', *Evolutionary Anthropology*, 12: 123–35.

Hodgson, G.M. (1996) 'An evolutionary theory of long-term economic growth', *International Studies Quarterly*, 40: 391–410.

——— (1997) 'The evolutionary and non-Darwinian economics of Joseph Schumpeter', *Journal of Evolutionary Economics*, 7: 131–45.

——— (1999) *Evolution and Institutions: On Evolutionary Economics and the Evolution of Economics*. Cheltenham, Gloucester: Edward Elgar.

——— (2001) 'Is social evolution Lamarckian or Darwinian?', in J. Laurent and J. Nightingale (eds), *Darwinism and Evolutionary Economics*. Cheltenham: Edward Elgar, pp. 87–118.

——— (2002a) 'Darwinism in economics: From analogy to ontology', *Journal of Evolutionary Economics*, 12: 259–81.

———— (2002b) 'Visions of mainstream economics: A response to Richard Nelson and Jack Vromen', *Review of Social Economy*, LX: 125–33.

Hodgson, G.M. and Knudsen, T. (2004) 'The firm as an interactor: Firms as vehicles for habits and routines', *Journal of Evolutionary Economics*, 14: 281–307.

Hodgson, G.M. and Knudsen, T. (2005) 'The nature and units of social selection', *Papers on Economics and Evolution*. Max Planck Institute for Research into Economic Systems, MPI Jena (#0424).

Hofstadter, R. ([1944] 1955) *Social Darwinism in American Thought*. Boston: Beacon Press.

Holmwood, J. and O'Malley, M.A. (2003) 'Evolutionist and functionalist historical sociology', in G. Delanty and E.F. Isin (eds), *Handbook of Historical Sociology*. London: Sage.

Hull, D.L. (1988a) 'A mechanism and its metaphysics: An evolutionary account of the social and conceptual development of science', *Biology and Philosophy*, 3: 123–55.

———— (1988b) *Science as a Process: An Evolutionary Account of the Social and Conceptual Development of Science*. Chicago: University of Chicago Press.

Hussey, T. (1999) 'Evolutionary change and epistemology', *Biology and Philosophy*, 14: 561–84.

Ingold, T. (2000) 'The poverty of selectionism', *Anthropology Today*, 16 (3): 1–2.

Jantsch, E. (1981) *The Evolutionary Vision: Toward a Unifying Paradigm of Physical, Biological, and Sociocultural Evolution*. Boulder, CO: Westview Press.

Johnson, A.W. and Earle, T. (1987) *The Evolution of Human Societies: From Foraging Group to Agrarian State*. Stanford, CA: Stanford University Press.

Kastelle, T. (2005) 'A classification method for evolutionary economics', Paper presented at the 4th European Meeting on Applied Evolutionary Economics, May 19–21.

Kitcher, P. (1985) *Vaulting Ambition: Sociobiology and the Quest for Human Nature*. Cambridge, MA: MIT Press.

Kitcher, P. (1988) 'Selection among the systematists', *Nature*, 336 (6196) pp. 277–78.

Knudsen, T. (2002) 'Economic selection theory', *Journal of Evolutionary Economics*, 12: 443–70.

———— (2004) 'General selection theory and economic evolution: The Price equation and the replicator/interactor distinction', *Journal of Economic Methodology*, 11: 147–73.

Laland, K.N. (2003) 'Gene-culture coevolution', in L. Nadel (ed.), *Encyclopedia of Cognitive Science*. London: NPG/Macmillan, pp. 268–74.

Laland, K.N. and Brown, G.R. (2002) *Sense and Nonsense: Evolutionary Perspectives on Human Behavior*. Oxford: Oxford University Press.

Laszlo, E. (1987) *Evolution: the grand synthesis*. Boston: Shambala New Science Library

Laszlo, E. (1991) *The New Evolutionary Paradigm*. NY: Gordon and Breach Science Publishers.

Lenski, G. (1966) *Power and Privilege: A Theory of Social Stratification*. NY: McGraw-Hill.

———— (1970) *Human Societies: A Macrolevel Introduction to Sociology*. NY: McGraw-Hill.

———— (2005) *Ecological-Evolutionary Theory: Principles and Applications*. NY: Paradigm Publishers.

Lewontin, R.C. (2005) 'The wars over evolution', *New York Review of Books*, 52 (16). Available at: www.nybooks.com/articles/18363. (accessed on May 30 2006).

Lieberman, L. (1989) 'A discipline divided: Acceptance of human sociobiological concepts in anthropology', *Current Anthropology*, 30 (5): 677–81.

Lopreato, J. and Crippen, T. (1999) *Crisis in Sociology: The Need for Darwin*. New Brunswick, NJ: Transaction Publishers.

Lumsden, C.J. and Wilson, E.O. (1981) *Genes, Mind and Culture: The Coevolutionary Process*. Cambridge, MA: Harvard University Press.

Mace, R. and Holden, C.J. (2005) 'A phylogenetic approach to cultural evolution', *TREE*, 20: 116–21.

Machalek, R. and Martin, M.W. (2004) 'Sociology and the second Darwinian revolution: A metatheoretical analysis', *Sociological Theory*, 22 (3): 455–76.

Maryanski, A. and Turner, J.H. (1992) *The Social Cage: Human Nature and the Evolution of Society*. Stanford, CA: Stanford University Press.

Maynard Smith, J. and Szathmáry, E. (1995) *The Major Transitions in Evolution*. Oxford: W.H. Freeman.

Mayr, E. (1980) 'Prologue: Some thoughts of the history of the evolutionary synthesis', in E. Mayr and W.B. Provine (eds), *The Evolutionary Synthesis: Perspectives on the Unification of Biology*. Cambridge, MA: Harvard University Press, pp. 1–48.

———— (1982) *The Growth of Biological Thought: Diversity, Evolution and Inheritance*. Cambridge, MA: Harvard University Press/Belknap.

McElreath, R., Lubell, M., Richerson, P.J., Waring, T.M., Baum, W., Edsten, E., Efferson, C. and Paciotti, B. (2005) 'Applying evolutionary models to the laboratory study of social learning', *Evolution and Human Behavior*, 26: 483–508.

McKelvey, M.D. (1996) *Evolutionary Innovations: The Business of Biotechnology*. Oxford: Oxford University Press.

Montagu, A. (ed.) (1980) *Sociobiology Examined*. Oxford: Oxford University Press.

Nelson, R.R. (2002) 'Thoughts stimulated by reading Geoffrey Hodgson's *Economics and Utopia*', *Review of Social Economy*, LX: 109–113.

———— (2004) 'Evolutionary theories of cultural change: An empirical perspective', *Papers on Economics and Evolution*. Max Planck Institute for Research into Economic Systems, MPI Jena (#0422).

Nelson, R.R. and Winter, S.G. (1974) 'Neoclassical versus evolutionary theories of economic growth: critique and prospectus', *Economic Journal*, 84: 886–905.

——— (1982) *An Evolutionary Theory of Economic Change*. Cambridge, MA: Harvard University Press.

——— (2002) 'Evolutionary theorizing in economics', *Journal of Economic Perspectives*, 16: 23–46.

Nisbet, R.A. (1969) *Social Change and History: Aspects of the Western Theory of Development*. NY: Oxford University Press.

Oyama, S. (2000) *Evolution's Eye*. Durham, NC: Duke University Press.

Paciotti, B., Richerson, P.J. and Boyd, R. (2006) 'Cultural evolutionary theory: A synthetic theory for fragmented disciplines', in P. Van Lange (ed.), *Bridging Social Psychology: Benefits of Transdisciplinarity*. Mahwah, NJ: Erlbaum. Available at: www.des.ucdavis.edu/faculty/richerson/Bridging%20final.pdf.

Paquet, G. (1994) 'From the information economy to evolutionary cognitive economics', in R.E. Babe (ed.), *Information and Communication in Economics*. Boston: Kluwer, pp. 34–40.

Plotkin, H.C. (1987) 'Evolutionary epistemology as science', *Biology and Philosophy*, 2: 295–313.

——— (1994) *Darwin Machines and the Nature of Knowledge: Concerning Adaptations, Instinct and the Evolution of Intelligence*. Harmondsworth, Middlesex: Penguin.

Popper, K.R. ([1977] 1987) 'Natural selection and the emergence of mind', in G. Radnitzky and W.W. Bartley (eds), *Evolutionary Epistemology, Rationality, and the Sociology of Knowledge*. La Salle, Illinois: Open Court, pp. 139–53.

——— (1979) *Objective Knowledge: An Evolutionary Approach*. Oxford: Clarendon.

Rendell, L. and Whitehead, H. (2001) 'Culture in whales and dolphins', *Behavioral and Brain Sciences*, 24: 309–82.

Richerson, P.J. and Boyd, R. (2000) 'Evolution: The Darwinian theory of social change, an homage to Donald T. Campbell', in W. Schelkle, W.-H. Krauth, M. Kohli and G. Elwert (eds), *Paradigms of Social Change*. Frankfurt: Campus, pp. 257–82.

——— (2001) 'Built for speed, not for comfort', *History and Philosophy of the Life Sciences*, 23: 423–63.

——— (2005) *Not by Genes Alone: How Culture Transformed Human Evolution*. Chicago: The University of Chicago Press.

Rose, N. (1998) 'Controversies in meme theory', *Journal of Memetics*, 2. Available at: http://jom-emit.cfpm.org/1998/vol2/rose_n.html (accessed on 30 May 2006).

Rose, S., Kamin, L.J. and Lewontin, R.C. (1984) *Not in Our Genes: Biology, Ideology and Human Nature*. Harmondsworth, Middlesex: Penguin.

Rosenberg, A. (1992) 'Selection and science: Critical notice of David Hull's *Science as a Process*', *Biology and Philosophy*, 7: 217–28.

——— (1994) 'Does evolutionary theory give comfort or inspiration to evolutionary economics?', in P. Mirowski (ed.), *Natural images in Economic Thought: 'Markets read in tooth and claw'*. Cambridge: Cambridge University Press, pp. 384–407.

Runciman, W.G. (1989a) *A Treatise on Social Theory, vol. 2: Substantive Social Theory*. Cambridge: Cambridge University Press.

——— (1989b) *Confessions of a Reluctant Social Theorist: Selected Essays of W.G. Runciman*. Hemel Hempstead: Harvester Wheatsheaf.

——— (1998) 'The selectionist paradigm and its implications for sociology', *Sociology*, 32 (1): 163–88.

——— (2001) 'From nature to culture, from culture to society', *Proceedings of the British Academy*, 110: 235–54.

——— (2002) 'Heritable variation and competitive selection as the mechanism of sociocultural evolution', *Proceedings of the British Academy*, 112: 9–25.

——— (2004) 'The diffusion of Christianity in the third century AD as a case-study in the theory of cultural selection', *European Journal of Sociology*, 45: 3–21.

——— (2005) 'Rejoinder to Fracchia and Lewontin', *History and Theory*, 44: 30–41.

Ruse, M. (1985) *Sociobiology: Sense or Nonsense?* Dordrecht: D. Reidel Publishing.

——— (1995) *Evolutionary Naturalism: Selected Essays*. London: Routledge.

Ruth, M. (1996) 'Evolutionary economics at the crossroads of biology and physics', *Journal of social and evolutionary systems*, 19 (2): 125–44.

Sahlins, M. (1976) *The Use and Abuse of Biology: An Anthropological Critique of Sociobiology*. Ann Arbor: University of Michigan Press.

Sanderson, S.K. (1990) *Social Evolutionism: A Critical History*. Cambridge, MA: Blackwell.

——— (1995) *Social Transformations: A General Theory of Historical Development*. Oxford: Blackwell.

——— (1997) 'Evolutionism and its critics', *Journal of World Systems Research*, 3 (1): 94–110.

——— (2004) 'Review of Jonathan H. Turner's *Human Institutions: A Theory of Societal Evolution*', *American Journal of Sociology*, 110: 806–8.

Saviotti, P.P. and Metcalfe, J.S. (1991) *Evolutionary Theories of Economic and Technological Change: Present Status and Future Prospects*. Chur, Switzerland: Harwood Academic Publishers.

Sheets-Johnstone, M. (1994) *Roots of Power: Animate Form and Gendered Bodies*. Chicago: Open Court Press.

Skagestad, P. (1981) 'Hypothetical realism', in M.B. Brewer and B.E. Collins (eds), *Scientific Inquiry and the Social Sciences.* San Francisco: Jossey-Bass, pp. 77–97.

Sober, E. (1991) 'Models of cultural evolution', in P.E. Griffiths (ed.), *Trees of Life: Essays in Philosophy of Biology.* Dordrecht: Kluwer, pp. 17–38.

Sperber, D. (2000) 'An objection to the mimetic approach to culture', in R. Aunger (ed.), *Darwinizing Culture: The Status of Mimetics as a Science.* Oxford: Oxford University Press, pp. 163–73.

Sterelny, K. (1994) 'Science and selection', *Biology and Philosophy*, 9: 45–62.

———— (2006) 'The evolution and evolvability of culture', *Mind and Language*, 21(2), 137–65.

Stone, J.R. (1996) 'The evolution of ideas: A phylogeny of shell models', *American Naturalist*, 148: 904–29.

Stotz, K.C. and Griffiths, P.E. (2002) 'Dancing in the dark: Evolutionary psychology and the argument from design', in S.J. Scher and F. Rauscher (eds), *Evolutionary Psychology: Alternative Approaches.* Dordrecht: Kluwer, pp. 135–60.

Toulmin, S. (1972) *Human Understanding.* Oxford: Clarendon Press.

Turner, J.H. (1992) 'Review of W.G. Runciman's *A Treatise on Social Theory, Volume Two*', *Social Forces*, 71: 521–2.

———— (2004) 'Toward a general sociological theory of the economy', *Sociological Theory*, 22: 229–46.

———— (2003) *Human Institutions: A Theory of Societal Evolution.* Lanham, MD: Rowman and Littlefield.

Twomey, P. (1998) 'Reviving Veblenian economic psychology', *Cambridge Journal of Economics*, 22: 433–48.

Vaisey, S. (2004) 'Review of Jonathan H. Turner's *Human Institutions*', *Social Forces*, 83: 432–3.

Vromen, J. (2004a) 'Conjectural revisionary economic ontology: Outline of an ambitious research agenda for evolutionary economics', *Journal of Economic Methodology*, 11: 213–47.

———— (2004b) 'Routines, genes and programme-based behaviour', *Papers on Economics and Evolution.* Max Planck Institute for Research into Economic Systems, MPI Jena (#0420).

———— (2004c) 'Taking evolution seriously: What difference does it make for economics?', in J.B. Davis, A. Marciano and J. Runde (eds), *The Elgar Companion to Economics and Philosophy.* Cheltenham: Edward Elgar, pp. 102–31.

Watkins, J.P. (1998) 'Towards a reconsideration of social evolution: Symbiosis and its implications for economics', *Journal of Economic Issues*, 32 (1): 87–105.

Whitehead, H., Richerson, P.J. and Boyd, R. (2002) 'Cultural selection and genetic diversity in humans', *Selection*, 3: 115–25.

Wickham, C. (1991) 'Systactic structures: Social theory for historians', *Past and Present*, 132: 188–203.

Wilkins, J.S. (1998a) 'The evolutionary structure of scientific theories', *Biology and Philosophy*, 13: 479–504.

———— (1998b) 'What's in a meme? Reflections from the perspective of the history and philosophy of evolutionary biology', Available at: http://jom-emit.cfpm.org/1998/vol2/wilkins_js.html.

Wilson, E.O. (1975) *Sociobiology: The New Synthesis.* Cambridge, MA: Belknap Press of Harvard University.

———— (1978) *On Human Nature.* Cambridge, MA: Harvard University Press.

Wimsatt, W.C. (1999) 'Genes, memes and cultural heredity', *Biology and Philosophy*, 14: 279–310.

Witt, U. (2004) 'On the proper interpretation of "evolution" in economics and its implications for production theory', *Journal of Economic Methodology*, 11: 125–46.

Wuketits, F.M. (1990) *Evolutionary Epistemology and Its Implications for Humankind.* Albany, NY: SUNY Press.

Young, H.P. (1998) *Individual Strategy and Social Structure: An Evolutionary Theory of Institutions.* Princeton, NJ: Princeton University Press.

Ziman, J.M. (ed.) (2000) *Technological Innovation as an Evolutionary Process.* Cambridge: Cambridge University Press.

NOTES

1 A longer version of this chapter, incorporating at least brief discussions of the missing evolutionary fields, is available from the author on request.

2 See also note 25.

3 Another evolutionary anthropological approach (one which also overlaps with evolutionary psychology) is human behavioral ecology. For overviews, see Laland and Brown (2002: Chapter 4) and Cronk, Chagnon and Irons (2000). A further interesting and expanding approach is that of cultural phylogeny, or the construction of evolutionary trees of descent from cultural data (e.g., Mace and Holden, 2005). The evolutionary ecology approach is another new and noteworthy perspective in studies of cultural evolution (Blute, 2002).

4 There are two other important gene-culture coevolutionary approaches. One is advanced by Lumsden and Wilson (1981). It is often called a sociobiological approach (versus the population approach of Boyd and Richerson) and focuses on direct adaptations brought about by genes and

'culturgens', which are very like memes. Their account is not included in this section because it has been considerably less influential than the population-level approach (see Laland and Brown, 2002: Chapter 7). The other is William Durham's (1991). He investigates cultural variability using several categories of gene-culture interaction. For general overviews of contributions to gene-culture evolution, see Aoki (2001) or Laland (2003).

5 See Boyd and Richerson (2005) for discussion of the differences between their own approach and that of evolutionary psychology. A key element is the evolutionary psychological focus on *evoked* culture (from genes by the environment) versus Boyd and Richerson's on *epidemiological* or transmitted culture.

6 The most famous example is the ability to digest lactose that is associated with the culture of keeping dairy herds and consuming fresh milk (see Aoki, 2001).

7 See also Rendell and Whitehead (2001) in regard to social learning and gene-culture evolution in whales.

8 See Plotkin (1987) and Hardcastle (1993) for overviews of cognitive evolutionary epistemology.

9 Bradie divides evolutionary epistemology into the 'evolutionary epistemology of mechanisms' (EEM) and the 'evolutionary epistemology of theories' (EET).

10 Ernst Mach and Georg Simmel, both writing in the 1890s, are usually considered to be the earliest evolutionary epistemologists (Coleman, 2002).

11 See Skagestad (1981) for criticisms of their 'hypothetical realism'.

12 Hahlweg and Hooker call themselves evolutionary epistemologists but their version is derived from Piaget's anti-Darwinist developmental model of cognition or genetic epistemology.

13 See Jon Stone's phylogeny of shell models (1996).

14 See Vromen (2004c) for an informative discussion of conservative, moderate and radical evolutionary economists.

15 Veblen and Schumpeter are variously claimed as providing the basis of modern evolutionary economics. Veblen used a Darwinian framework; Schumpeter did not (Hodgson, 1997). There tends to be little crossover between these two lineages of new evolutionary economics (Fagerberg, 2003). Hayek (1978) is another source of evolutionary ideas. Earlier evolutionary economists from the 1950s (Alchian and Friedman, whose work is extended by Nelson and Winter's ideas) are not discussed in this section (see Vromen's overview, 2004c).

16 For synopses of the wide area and diversity of theoretical frameworks covered by evolutionary economics, see Vromen (2004c), Ruth (1996), Hodgson (1999: Chapter 6), and Saviotti and Metcalfe (1991).

17 This is how Nelson and Winter identify themselves, although Hodgson (1997) notes their congruence with Veblen's and Darwin's ideas.

18 Hodgson calls this strategy 'universal Darwinism', a term that comes from Dawkins (1983) and Campbell (1965). See the conclusion for further discussion.

19 See Knudsen (2002) for an account of Nelson and Winter's deficiencies in not distinguishing replicator and interactor.

20 In the other forms of evolutionary economics, 'a menagerie of models and studies sui generis' (Dopfer and Potts, 2004: 195) attempts to incorporate concepts of heterogeneous populations, bounded rationality, dynamic change, multiple equilibria, historical contingency and suboptimal outcomes into economic research (Vromen, 2004c). Neo-Schumpeterian evolutionary economics appears to have developed the widest range of these models and simulations, which Nelson and Winter (2002) divide into two kinds: those abstractly exploring the effects of economic sub-processes on economic evolution, and those that aim to explain specified empirical phenomena.

21 Specifically, George Price's mathematical formalization of selection and fitness.

22 There are, in fact, some attempts to construct evolutionary trees or phylogenies of economic phenomena (e.g., Kastelle, 2005), but these have little to do yet with theoretical evolutionary economics.

23 This chapter excludes Luhmann's and Habermas's 'evolutionary' work. See the longer version of this chapter (note 1) for a brief discussion of why.

24 Some of these criticisms are warranted; others not. See Holmwood and O'Malley (2003) for a discussion.

25 A number of large-scale evolutionary studies of social change have been done by anthropologists with an institutional and historical bent (e.g., Sanderson, 1995; Dodgshon, 1987; Chase-Dunn and Hall, 1994; Hallpike, 1987). Most of them reject any use of biological concepts, especially adaptation (Hallpike) and selection (Sanderson). A future comparative analysis of evolutionary sociology might want to compare their achievements with the Darwinian-influenced examples chosen in this chapter.

26 Power has always been just another environmental factor in theories of cultural evolution, says Runciman (2002: 14), because cultural evolutionists have not properly theorized societies.

27 See Endler (1986) for a list of appropriate approaches in evolutionary biology.

28 Turner acknowledges the similarity of these forces to those posited by Gerhard Lenski (1966; 1970), an earlier evolutionary sociologist who has recently reformulated his own work (2005).

29 Turner's evolutionary work is admittedly fairly recent, although some of his earlier publications were pointing towards such a formulation.

30 Turner does note decomplexification or the dedifferentiation of institutions, but rarely finds it in the historical cases he uses.

31 Reductionism, biologization, and conservatism are the other major complaints against evolutionary approaches, but as these are generally inaccurate and uninteresting criticisms, no further space will be given to them.

32 Adaptationism (or panadaptationism) is considered to be a common fault of simplistic evolutionary biology and consists of the practice of presuming adaptive value for *every* observable characteristic (in the way design is attributed to the famous 'spandrels' of the San Marco cathedral). Such strategies effectively rule out alternative non-adaptive explanations such as drift (Gould and Lewontin, 1979).

33 Universal Darwinism covers all the above social-scientific areas, as well as evolutionary linguistics, evolutionary computer science, immunology, evolutionary medicine, evolutionary psychiatry, evolutionary chemistry, evolutionary physics and several more (see Cziko, 1995; Aunger, 2000: 1; Plotkin, 1994: Chapter 3; for a much earlier version, see Collective Authors, 1925). There also exist some very general evolutionary systems theories, which encompass cosmological, physical, chemical, biological, ecological, psychological and social systems. They combine selectionism with non-equilibrium thermodynamics and chaos theory, and use computer simulation and mathematical modeling as their tools (e.g.: Laszlo, 1987; 1991; Csányi, 1989; Jantsch, 1981).

34 Thanks to Francesco Guala for these points.

Interpretation, Critique, and Postmodernity

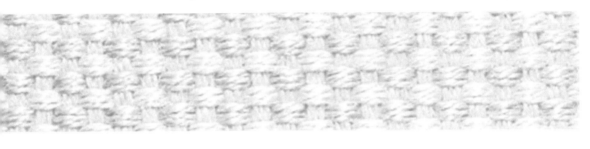

Introduction

William Outhwaite

The social sciences are confronted with the reality that their subject matter is carried out by or is the product of the activities of persons with their own understandings of what they do. These understandings are characteristically not particularly valuable with respect to the making of aggregate predictions. The consumers who decide that the price of strawberries is too high and refuse to purchase them will characteristically be able to give quite elaborate explanations of their assessment of the quality of the fruit, their sense of the usual prices, and the purposes for which they might have intended to buy the strawberries, but this material does not allow the analyst to answer such questions as what price will clear the market shelves of strawberries. However, understanding, particularly with respect to a deviant group, in different cultures, different sub-cultures, and both everyday activities and activities which are usually not reflected upon and understood, all seem to require understanding in their own right and understanding in the context of the social sciences. Even applied research—especially in such areas as nursing and in social problems-oriented interventions, or where the users of services are not well understood—in which decisions about policies and interventions relate to individual agents has invested heavily in qualitative research in order to produce better understanding.

This section of the book focuses on the primary alternative conceptions of the problem of understanding, as they relate to strategies of interpretative research, focusing especially on the contrast between the phenomenological tradition rooted in the analysis of consciousness and agency and the hermeneutic tradition rooted in the analysis of texts. Interpretive approaches, based on the opposition or reconciliation of 'explanation' and 'understanding', raise crucial issues of the relation between description and explanation in the social sciences. In positivist social science, description has traditionally been seen as a mere preliminary to explanation. Qualitative approaches have seen description (sometimes called perspicuous or, following the anthropologist Clifford Geertz (1973), 'thick description') as a valuable activity in its own right and even as substituting for explanation in the social sciences.

Interpretive approaches have a long history in social science, and in the later twentieth century, notably in the form of 'hermeneutic' and 'phenomenological' sociology, following

Alfred Schütz's classic work of 1932, republished in German in 1960 (the same year as Hans-Georg Gadamer's *Truth and Method*) and translated into English in 1967. The 'postmodern turn' in the 1970s recuperated and radicalized some of the themes of earlier interpretive sociology and anthropology and extended their influence to other areas of social science, in particular into the growing interdisciplinary field of cultural studies, in which the critical perspectives analyzed by Doug Kellner have been particularly prominent, as have many of the approaches discussed in the following two sections. Relativist and social constructionist approaches were already well established in the social sciences by the time of the publication in 1979 of Lyotard's *The Postmodern Condition* and of its English translation in 1984, but postmodernism provided a new vocabulary in which to present these approaches. Postmodern theory offered sociologists, human geographers, political scientists and others an attractive way of conceptualizing processes of fragmentation of work, family structures, political systems and even warfare. A more philosophically oriented variant of postmodernism restated skeptical views about the possibility of grounding knowledge of the natural and/or social world.

Grounded theory, discussed in the penultimate chapter of this section by Adele Clarke (author of *Situational Analysis: Grounded Theory after the Postmodern Turn* (2005)), remains identified with its two founders, Glaser and Strauss, but has also ramified in new directions as a research approach.

REFERENCES AND SELECT BIBLIOGRAPHY

Geertz, Clifford (1973) *The Interpretation of Cultures: Selected Essays.* New York: Basic Books.

Habermas, Jürgen (1981) *Theorie des kommunikativen Handelns.* Frankfurt: Suhrkamp.

——— (1984) *Theory of Communicative Action, vol. 1: Reason and the Rationalization of Society,* trans. Thomas McCarthy. Boston: Beacon Press.

Schwinn, Thomas (2001) *Differenzierung ohne Gesellschaft. Umstellung eines soziologischen Konzepts.* Weilerswist: Velbrück Wissenschaft.

Smith, Dennis (1991) *The Rise of Historical Sociology.* Cambridge: Polity.

Touraine, Alain (1973) *Production de la société.* Paris: Seuil.

——— (1977) *The Self-Production of Society,* trans. Derek Coltman. Chicago: The University of Chicago Press.

20

Understanding and Interpretation

H a n s - H e r b e r t   K ö g l e r

LANGUAGE, INTENTIONALITY, AND THE PROJECT OF GROUNDING SOCIAL SCIENCE

Taking our first cue from Dilthey's project of a 'Critique of Historical Reason', we might still conceive of the philosophy of social science as playing an epistemic, unifying and reflexive role. According to Dilthey, the first goal consists in grounding the epistemic claims made in all cultural disciplines, and thus justifying and guaranteeing their aspiration to be part of human or social science. The second goal is to use the epistemic grounding in order to synthesize the dispersed and fragmented knowledges of the social, historical and cultural sciences, and thus to erect a more coherent and unified understanding of the phenomena. And the third goal is to establish their relevance by addressing the relation between social–scientific knowledge and social reality, and to show how all social understanding remains reflexively tied to the social reality in which it is embedded (Dilthey [1910] 2004). Since some standard of truth and objectivity is indispensable if the claim to be a science is to be upheld, an analysis of the epistemic grounds of understanding human agency is still in order (Turner and Roth, 2003). Also, despite the widespread endorsement of methodological pluralism, issues such as the relation between social science and social theory, as well as the issue of a difference between natural and human sciences are still hotly debated and call for a more general conception of social–scientific understanding (Baert, 2006; Kögler and Stueber, 2000). Further, regarding the relation between social science and social reality, many claim that there is a uniquely reflexive relation between the social–scientific analysis and its social–cultural object domain, as the practical knowledge acquired in social science feeds back into a constantly transformed and renegotiated social life (Hacking, 2000).

As our reconstruction of the conceptual structure of understanding and interpretation will show, the grounds on which Dilthey attempts to erect his critique of historical and social knowledge cannot be sustained. But looking systematically at the discursive steps that lead from a psychological grounding toward a practical turn, and from there toward a linguistic grounding, helps clarify the foundation and unity of truth claims in the human sciences and establish how social science relates to social reality. In terms of a loosely understood construction of paradigmatic changes, we argue that the understanding of understanding and interpretation in the human and social sciences undergoes three ideal–typical phases.

First, we detect the project that all understanding is to be grounded psychologically, because *all phenomena are perceived and understood most directly by the individual mind*. Self-transparent introspection thus grounds epistemic claims to valid knowledge, and the ontological partner-thesis that human history is made by individual selves serves as a plausible realistic foundation. What needs to be shown here is how a first-person attitude of understanding is possible with regard to the thoughts of another historical or social agent. The problems associated with the issue of empathy and transpositional introspection lead, among other factors, to a turn toward a practical–historical understanding of understanding.

In this second phase, the *embeddedness of the individual agent in a prior network of significant relations and contexts* is emphasized. The replacement of the Cartesian self by a socially situated self paves the way toward an encompassing transformation of concepts such as meaning, purpose, action and intentionality in the human and social sciences. This, in turn, requires a new way of reconstructing the grounds for *explicit interpretation* in the human and social sciences. Instead of a quasi-immediate re-living of the other's thought and intentions, we now face the necessity of an interpretive reconstruction of the other's intentional acts in a reflexively appropriated background context. Hermeneutic understanding realizes that it must explicitly interpret the background understandings that the agent at stake takes for granted.

The attention thus paid to the process of explicating implicit meanings forces the focus on the process of interpretation itself and by doing so prepares the third reflexive step. In its wake, the turn toward *the linguistic mediation of all understanding, and social-scientific analysis and interpretation*, takes place. The prominence that language achieves in the philosophy of social science parallels the general linguistic turn in twentieth-century philosophy, but it is here uniquely motivated by the centrality of the linguistic articulation of meanings and actions situated in cultural practices.

This paradigmatic story overlaps with a continuous expansion of the hermeneutic discourse beyond its initial confines of an analysis of texts toward an inclusion of historical agency and social processes. The initial discussion of the grounds of human and social science is in 'hermeneutic philosophy', and here it moves from the psychological orientation in Schleiermacher and early Dilthey to the practical–cultural turn in late Dilthey, Heidegger and Merleau-Ponty (Grondin, 1994; Ormiston and Schrift, 1990). Building on this practical foundation, we witness a linguistic turn articulated most prominently in Gadamer's philosophical hermeneutics, but paralleled and prepared by the late Heidegger, late Merleau-Ponty, and Wittgenstein.

Wittgenstein's work provides the starting point for the second major development, as Peter Winch's influential work *The Idea of a Social Science and its Relation to Philosophy* leaves behind the hermeneutic focus on texts and history and addresses the issue of understanding with regard to culture and society (Gadamer, [1960] 1989; Habermas, [1969] 1988; Winch, [1958] 1991). In its wake, the contextual understanding of linguistically mediated meanings and reasons becomes the cornerstone of debates over the universality of rationality, truth and logic, and thus takes center stage in philosophy (Hollis and Lukes, 1982; Krausz, 1989; Wilson, 1971). The philosophy of social science thus directly communicates and challenges central disciplines in philosophy, such as the analytic philosophy of language and action theory, as it is in turn shaped by those discourses (Turner and Roth, 2003a). Yet, in an important third step, the discourse of general social theory takes on essential hermeneutic insights and turns them into basic building blocks for a theory of society. In the work of Habermas

([1981] 1984/87), Giddens (1984), Bourdieu (1990), and even Foucault (1977; 1976), intentional agency is understood as grounded in contextual practices, just as much as all explicit interpretation is grounded in an indispensable prior realm of practically and symbolically mediated background under-standings. Despite undeniable differences, what crystallizes in these social theories is a general conceptual frame of a situated and linguistically mediated intentional agency.

By reconstructing the conceptual motiva-tions behind these particular perspectives, we arrive at the sketch of an overall grounding, synthesizing and reflexive position based on the linguistic mediation of practical inten-tionality. In particular, the discourse on understanding and interpretation in the phi-losophy of social science articulates three basic claims:

1. All explicit understanding (i.e. the intentional interpretation of something as something) is grounded in some prior, implicit, practical, and contextual pre-understanding. This means that all scientific interpretation remains tied back to social and cultural contexts that set up a certain perspective and orientation vis-à-vis the object at stake.
2. The structure of understanding is essentially defined by intentional and value-laden concepts, such as meaning, norm, intention, purpose, value, etc. On the basis of this interrelated set of con-cepts, which are seen as indispensable for an adequate interpretation of social and cultural phenomena, the epistemological uniqueness of understanding in the social sciences is claimed.
3. Social–scientific interpretation, as it is epistemi-cally constrained by intentional or normative concepts, must then be conceived as the reflexive articulation of implicitly presupposed and cultur-ally situated meanings of agents-in-contexts. This argument for the reflexive articulation of inten-tional meanings is to remain in force even when the actual behavior of agents conflicts with the explicitly endorsed meanings and self-understandings. The need to account for meaning-constitution that transcends the *intentional understanding* of agents grounds a unique form of *action-explanation* that takes causal and struc-tural factors of the objective context into account.[1]

CARTESIAN PROMISES AND PITFALLS: THE PSYCHOLOGICAL GROUNDING OF THE HUMAN SCIENCES

From its inception as a general theory of human understanding, the hermeneutic perspective is internally defined by a twofold interest. On the one hand, the academic dis-ciplines dealing with human expressions and actions are supposed to achieve a level of rigor and objectivity that justifies their claim to be human *sciences*. The human and social sciences are seen in need of a grounding that shows how their theories and interpretations can make a rightful claim to be objective, valid, and adequate to the object. On the other hand, the hermeneutic paradigm is equally driven by the intuition that the way in which understanding occurs in the human sciences is essentially different from the natural sciences. Because here human beings understand other human beings, a different mode or process of arriving at valid explana-tions of the phenomena is at stake (Dilthey, [1910] 2004; Gadamer, [1960] 1989; Kögler and Stueber, 2000).

The trick is to reconcile the claim to scien-tific objectivity while equally maintaining that inter-human understanding differs in kind from an understanding of the natural and non-human world. And this trick is to be accomplished by an original and subtle com-bination of ontological and methodological claims, both being based on the fact that a specifically constituted human interpreter or scientist encounters a similarly constituted object of understanding. In other words, because of the *ontological nature* of the human scientist as a human, a *particular access* to the human–scientific object, which is itself human in nature, is possible and required. Yet, at the same time, this ontolog-ical grounding of the uniqueness of human understanding in a shared human nature is paired with a clear awareness that this ground implies and requires a methodologi-cal reflection on the mode of access toward human action and expression. Because humans are essentially defined as intentional and interpreting beings, the fact that an interpreter is human means that he or she can access the intentional interpretations found in the object, but it also means that this kind of access is essentially *required* to gain access to this human world of understanding. The hermeneutic paradigm thus builds a case for both scientific status and uniqueness by (a) suggesting that it is the shared human nature that grounds epistemic access, (b) conceiving the shared human nature as defined by the intentional interpretation of reality, and (c) claiming that an adequate understanding of acts and expressions by humans must take into account the intentional nature of their being and understanding. The fact that understanding in the intentional and interpretive mode is providing access to the actions and expressions of other human beings can then be taken as evidence that the human–scientific approach is both *scientifically successful* (the interpretations in the intentional mode allow us to disclose and reconstruct the cultural and social contexts of human agency) and *unique* (the epistemic access to such contexts and worlds is gained through a specifically first-person and value-based process) (Dilthey, [1910] 2004; Schütz, 1967; Weber, 1978).

It is in this vein of a combination of scientific objectivity and uniqueness that the attractiveness of the *early Cartesian grounding of human understanding* must be seen. Using the immediate access to one's own mind as a starting point seems to catch our two methodological birds with the same epistemic stone. The Cartesian self-transparency and self-givenness of one's own thoughts and feelings, if it can be shown to ground understanding of similarly constituted others, overcomes the apparent circularity implicit in the hermeneutic project. The circle arises since the uniqueness of intersubjective understanding is explained through the shared human nature, while that human nature is grounded in a unique way of understanding its expressions. But if we start with the Cartesian 'fact of phenomenality' (Dilthey, 1982), i.e., we assume that all experience is ultimately an

experience for me—as it is grounded in the self-given fact of being a *phenomenon* for my consciousness—an ultimate ground is reached. The givenness of the world in my experience, which as a phenomenon is itself beyond any possible doubt, further leaves no doubt about the uniqueness of this kind of experience. However, while I myself am given to myself in a unique and directly accessible way, the external world and other subjects are present to me only as inferred objects of my understanding. The Cartesian–psychological grounding thus avoids the problem of circularity, but is now in need of showing how an actual access to the object of understanding is possible—that is, *how the understanding of other minds is possible.*[2]

The early Dilthey's attempt at a psychological grounding of the human sciences (Dilthey, [1889] 1989) presents us with the most paradigmatic case of a Cartesian hermeneutics. The *Introduction to the Human Sciences* combines the aforementioned self-givenness of mental states with the ontological claim that history and culture emerge from the acts of individual subjects. Since individual agents are the 'basic cells' (*Urzellen*) of historical life, and since such life is given to me in my immediate self-understanding, psychology is destined to become the foundational discipline of all the human and social sciences. Inspired by J.S. Mill's similarly oriented work, Dilthey is, however, immediately confronted with two problems. On a *methodological plane*, he faces the fact that the self-givenness of psychological states in the subject presents the epistemologist with a culturally and historically formed 'state of mind'. Psychology is well taken as the grounding discipline, but the understanding of the psychological ground must itself grapple with the historical mediation of minds as shaped by their respective contexts and cultures. Thus, what we need is an approach that can filter out from the multifarious modes of mental life those forms that truly define the essential aspects of human understanding. On the more strictly *epistemological plane*, Dilthey recognizes that the standard philosophical conception of the Cartesian–Kantian mind is too thin to function as a basis for historical understanding: 'No real blood flows in the veins of the knowing subject construed by Locke, Hume, and Kant, but rather the diluted extract of reason as a mere activity of thought' (Dilthey, [1889] 1989: 50). Dilthey opposes the reduction of the subjective ground to a merely cognitive function and suggests a full-blooded embodied self, which encompasses cognitive, volitional and emotional aspects, as the epistemic foundation of the human sciences.

Yet the acknowledgement that the psychological ground has both to be drawn out from its historical–cultural expressions and be broadened to include emotional and volitional aspects besides purely cognitive functions undermines the promise of a Cartesian grounding of history (see Makreel, 2000). The reconstruction of the epistemological foundation, which is to establish the validity of possible statements about human acts and expressions, has already to assume the possibility of such statements to arrive at its material for reconstructing the essential forms of human understanding. Following the founding statement of his project in the *Introduction to the Human Sciences* ([1889] 1989), Dilthey laboriously attempts to unfold the projects of a descriptive as well as comparative psychology that could cash out the foundational promise, only to be haunted by the circle that hermeneutic understanding has already to be invested in such an enterprise if it is to succeed (Dilthey, 1982). The (supposedly psychological) grounds of understanding in truth depend on the (apparently historical) modes of interpretation, which turns upside down the initial epistemological perspective.

Now recall that the plausibility of methodological Cartesianism is for Dilthey grounded in the ontological assumption that history is made by human subjects, that 'analysis designates the life-unit, the psychophysical individual, as the element from which society and history are formed, and the study of these life-units constitutes the most fundamental group of the human

sciences' (Dilthey, [1889] 1989: 80).[3] Yet acknowledging that the Cartesian self-givenness of mental states cannot be directly cashed in since those states are culturally mediated means that ontological solipsism is equally thrown into doubt. The self now emerges as a '*Wirkungszusammenhang*', as a unit that is itself formed within a socio-historically defined context, and *for that reason* cannot, in its mental self-given states, be taken to provide direct access to some universal psychological grounding. The hermeneutic doubts about a Cartesian grounding thus foster doubts about the methodological individualism that in the first place supported the idea that psychology could establish a foundation of the human sciences.

What we now need to understand, instead of chasing the red herring of a purely psychological basis for historical understanding, is the grounds on which the unavoidable hermeneutic circle of human understanding unfolds. What are the grounds for gaining access to the historically and culturally mediated acts and expressions of human agents? How are our own modes of self-understanding constituted so as to allow the reconstructive understanding of human subjects in cultures, societies, and epochs both similar and dissimilar from our own? How can the hermeneutic circularity of understanding, instead of merely undermining the traditionally conceived concept of epistemic grounding, serve as a productive source of understanding?

DECONSTRUCTING CARTESIANISM AND RECONSTRUCTING UNDERSTANDING: THE PRACTICAL EMBEDDEDNESS OF INTERPRETATION

In early hermeneutics, alternatives to Dilthey's idea of a unique yet scientific understanding of human agency are so tied up with the psychological grounding that they have often been misinterpreted. Yet the Cartesian concept of empathy, suggesting the transposition of an immediately self-given mind into another similarly constituted self, is not the only or the most prominent model. Indeed, the psychological paradigm was early on intertwined with a sense of the linguistic and historical mediation of situated human agents, and the concept of an empathetic and first-person-based understanding must thus be reconstructed and interpreted in light of the full scope of the theories at stake. We can distinguish here the articulation of (a) the role of linguistic mediation (Schleiermacher), (b) the irreducibility of a shared objective meaning (Dilthey), and (c) the function of an existential background understanding (Heidegger) concerning individual agency, all of which constitute essential moves beyond a psychological hermeneutics.

Schleiermacher's project of a 'General Hermeneutics' (*Allgemeine Hermeneutik*) has long been the classic whipping boy for positions critical of empathetic understanding in the human sciences (Schleiermacher, [1819] 1957; Gadamer, [1960] 1989; Kögler and Stueber, 2000). This is because Schleiermacher distinguishes between two modes of human–scientific understanding: the *grammatical interpretation* of the linguistic context and general use of terms by an author or agent, and the *psychological interpretation* of the particular intentions and beliefs of an individual person. Schleiermacher is seen as delegating the linguistic understanding of the general context-meaning to a preliminary and secondary place, whereas the psychological transposition of the interpreter into the other individuality seemed to be the highest teleological endpoint of all interpretation. In this view, the ultimate understanding of another human agent comes about through an empathetic re-living and re-constructing of the other's beliefs and intentions, which are to be invoked exactly as intended by the other self. Interpretation as transposition thus seems to exist in a somewhat mysterious act of transforming oneself into the other, of becoming the other by oneself adopting, albeit hypothetically, the other's beliefs,

assumptions and values, and thus being able to reconstruct how the other agent constructed his or her point of view.[4]

Yet as Schleiermacher clearly states, understanding human agency is a *reconstruction* of the other's *constructed* beliefs and assumptions, and as such involves a reconstruction of the medium in which beliefs and assumptions can be articulated. Schleiermacher's dictum— 'Everything presupposed in hermeneutics is but language' (Gadamer, [1960] 1989: 381)— is crucial here, since it points to the essential intertwinement of subjective intentionality and linguistic expression. Schleiermacher compares hermeneutics with rhetoric: the latter gives tools to express one's thoughts, the former tools to understand such expressions. All thought is thus dependent on the linguistic medium for its articulation and understanding; without the symbolic medium, human agency and thought are inconceivable (Schleiermacher, [1819] 1957). Seen against this conception of a linguistically mediated subjectivity, the claim of a psychological interpretation building upon and extending a grammatical reading of the context appears in a new and systematically important light: it must now be understood as the intentional interpretation of human agents who are seen as situated in particular historical and cultural contexts, and whose intentions and actions are reconstructed by hypothetically adopting an *interpretive stance* toward their linguistically mediated contexts as seen by them. 'Grammatical' and 'psychological' interpretation thus become two sides of the same coin, since they are both grounded in the linguistic mediation of intentional agency.

In a similar vein, but without the emphasis on the role of language, does the late Dilthey reject his own earlier psychological grounding of human science (Dilthey, [1910] 2004). Instead of suggesting an emotionally and volitionally expanded Cartesian mind as the ultimate ground of understanding, Dilthey now enforces the idea that hermeneutic understanding goes all the way down, that the intentional self is a being that is fully situated in a pre-interpreted world of shared social meanings. There is no core-self at the ground of meaning, but rather something akin to Hegel's 'objective spirit', if such spirit is stripped of its teleological evolutionary role and now includes both objective and absolute spirit, that is, historical-political and cultural-symbolic meanings and practices. The crucial point is that the self is from the start 'dipped into' a shared realm of objective meanings, that every building, stone, word and emotional expression is pre-understood by subjects situated in the respectively shared context. Understanding meaning in the human sciences, which besides 'meaning' includes other essential concepts such as purpose, value, intention and significance, is made possible because, as a human subject, the interpreter is immersed in a similarly shared and structured realm of meanings, and thus capable of expanding or extrapolating from her own background contexts of significations to that of another differently situated human agent. Instead of an introspectively conceived mental self, the methodological triad of 'Experience, Expression and Understanding' (*Erlebnis, Ausdruck, und Verstehen*) thus constitutes the possible ground of human-scientific interpretation. In fact, understanding as the self-evident yet culturally mediated grasp of expressions of intentional agency thus takes the central role in this new, hermeneutic grounding of human science.[5]

Dilthey's discovery of the irreducibility of objective social meaning, as a presupposition both for hermeneutic understanding and for the self-understanding of the situated subjects, forces reflection upon the methodological and ontological relation between individual intentionality and shared social background meanings. It was up to Heidegger to find a promising way to solve this problem. Heidegger's solution defines in its own way the movement from Cartesianism to hermeneutics, since his conception of the existential function of shared understanding overcomes and contrasts sharply with the earlier phenomenological conception of a constituting consciousness in Husserl (Husserl, [1913] 1964; Heidegger, 1982; 1985; Kögler, 2006). Heidegger both inherits and redefines phenomenology by sticking to an intentional conception of human agency and similarly rejecting the methodological

limitation of carving out an eidetic space of pure ideal meanings (Heidegger, 1988). Instead, the method of an uncompromised and adequate description of 'phenomena' is now put to use for analyzing our everyday existence, starting with the taken-for-granted aspects and elements that define, or rather pre-define, how human beings encounter the world, other agents and themselves (Heidegger, 1962; Dreyfus, 1994). Heidegger's contribution can be made clear by distinguishing three steps.

In a first move, the intentional understanding of something as something is defined as an essential feature of all human agency, which is in turn seen as being grounded in a pre-predicative, practical and socially shared understanding of the world. The conscious and explicit intentionality of the earlier Cartesian phenomenology thus becomes *practical intentionality*, as its projection of phenomena as such-and-such is seen as pre-constituted by its social–practical Being-in-the-World (Dreyfus, 1994). Heidegger can show that explicit encounters with entities depend on a prior familiarity with whatever is at stake, and he analyzes this background context as an enabling general feature of human agency and meaning (Heidegger, 1962; also Searle, 1989).

In a second move, Heidegger spells out the relation between the pre-propositional background and an explicit and articulate understanding of entities as being defined by three dimensions of meaning.[6] Since all agency is always already engaged in practical activities, there is a skillful, coping manner of understanding that constitutes a holistic referential network of practical and embodied background understandings (the fore-having). Such a practical background context indicates always a certain perspective on the issue at stake, since it is practically situated and thus pre-projects how something is to be understood (the fore-sight). Finally, all understanding moves in the realm of a conceptual pre-understanding of whatever it seeks to comprehend, which indicates and directs what needs further understanding and interpretation, and provides the realm in which any explicit interpretation can articulate its results (the fore-conception). Taken together, a hermeneutic theory of meaning defines those aspects as the practically grounded projection of a perspectival conceptual scheme onto entities: 'Meaning is the "upon-which" of a projection in terms of which something becomes intelligible as something; it gets its structure from a fore-having, a fore-sight, and a fore-conception' (Heidegger, 1962: 193).

In a third move, Heidegger connects this concept of a *hermeneutic fore-structure of understanding* to the explicit and intentional conception of interpretation, which he labels the *as-structure of interpretation*. The idea is that anything that is simply understood as being what it is, that is taken to reveal itself in a direct or pure gaze of perception or understanding, is in fact pre-constituted in a prior hermeneutic act founded upon the practical, perspectival and conceptual background understanding of human agents:

> Whenever something is interpreted as something, the interpretation will be founded essentially upon fore-having, fore-sight, and fore-conception. An interpretation is never a presuppositionless apprehending of something presented to us . . . if one likes to appeal to what stands there, then one finds that what stands there in the first instance is nothing other than the obvious undiscussed assumption [*Vormeinung*] of the person who does the interpreting (Heidegger, 1962: 192).

From this derives a radical reconceptualization of the task and process of human–scientific interpretation, as the conception of the discovery of *meaning as object* now makes space for a *reflexively conceived process* in which the interpreter's preconceptions are continuously invested and challenged in the encounter of meaningful human expressions and acts.

The major impact of early Heidegger on hermeneutics and the philosophy of social science cannot be overestimated, even though it fell upon others to flesh out its implications. While Schleiermacher emphasizes the cultural–linguistic mediation of subjective thought, and late Dilthey discovers the irreducibly objective nature of social meaning, it was Heidegger's ontological

turn that determined the definite threshold beyond a Cartesian or psychologistic conception of understanding. The intrinsic connection between the culturally situated background understanding and explicit interpretive accounts paves the way for a restructuration of the self-understanding of social science and its methodological tools. For one, an account of empathy as the mind-based transposition into another, or else as the analogical construction of meaning-hypotheses based on one's own self, cannot be sustained in light of the essentially practical, social and conceptually mediated nature of the human agent (Kögler, 2000). As the individual self must now be seen as the intentional and reflexive reference-point of a socially situated context of meaning, subjective empathy between one mind and another loses its conceptual ground. Similarly, the concept of a pure 'object of understanding', the encounter or description of which is the task of the human sciences, has to be thrown overboard, since the construction of a possible hermeneutic object cannot be conceived apart from the situated and pre-interpretive nature of the human interpreter herself.

What now needs to be shown is how the practical, social and conceptual pre-understanding is to be invested and employed in the human and social sciences such that the connection between a practical background and a theoretically explicit account can be made fruitful for hermeneutic interpretation. And this task can only be fulfilled by reconstructing the systematic role of language in the process of human interpretation.[7]

THE LINGUISTIC GROUNDS OF SOCIAL–SCIENTIFIC UNDERSTANDING: HUMAN AGENCY AND DIALOGICAL INTERPRETATION

The ontological turn in hermeneutic theory places interpretation at the center of human existence. Any experience of something as something is seen as grounded in a practically situated pre-conceptualization. It is only a matter of time before the role of language in this process is fully understood and consequently promoted to become *the prime medium of interpretive understanding*.

There are at least three reasons why language, if conceptualized in an adequate way, is extremely attractive for the philosophy of social science after the hermeneutic–practical turn. To begin with, linguistic expressions and statements are always about something, they are directed toward a meaning or content that they intend to express, state, or refer to. Accordingly, the basic insight into the *intentional* structure of human agency, which had hitherto motivated a teleological conception of the human psyche as the ground of understanding, is preserved and saved in this linguistic turn (Searle, 2002). Second, we can capture the insight into the social and non-psychological nature of meaning—differently expressed by Schleiermacher, the late Dilthey and the early Heidegger—by focusing on the medium of language. Since intersubjective understanding and communication require the assumption of a shared medium or code of understanding, the turn to language provides the right starting point for reconstructing how meaning can exist *among* individual agents (Taylor, 1992; Lee, 1997). And third, since interpretation in the human and social sciences is connected in a special way to the practical background of interpreters, there is a need for a medium that can connect the everyday pre-understanding of the social scientists to their *articulated* theories and explanations. If the social background proves to be essentially mediated by language, one might have found just such a connecting medium, because the theories and accounts of social science are themselves articulated in linguistic form (Habermas, 1988).

Against this attractive background, the superficial fact that many objects of understanding are linguistic in nature is of minor importance. Indeed, the actual objects of human and social science consist of a wide variety of intentional and meaningful acts

and expressions besides texts and speech acts, including gestures, practices, pictures, events and observable regular patterns of behavior. Yet, the unique combination of an epistemological and an ontological argument concerning the social–scientific significance of language accounts for the central place that the linguistic turn acquires within our context of discussion. On the *epistemological* or subject-centered level, the general replacement of a philosophy of mind with language means that interpretive scientific acts are essentially mediated by the linguistic forms in which they are expressed. Higher cognitive articulations require a medium in which fine-grained conceptual distinctions can be made, and thus cannot be conceived without their linguistic ground (Searle, 2002; Gadamer, [1960] 1989). On the *ontological* or object-oriented level, language is equally clearly of prime importance. Language serves as the major medium of social interaction, and it provides situated agents with the resources to participate in and integrate into their cultural and social contexts. What is more, individual agents are dependent on the linguistic medium in order to develop their uniquely human, value-based and conceptually rich identities, which in turn ties them closely to the socially and thus symbolically mediated contexts of their existence (Herder/ Rousseau, 1966; Humboldt, 1988; Taylor, 1985).[8]

It is with regard to the linguistic mediation of experience that a complex argument concerning understanding, built by Peter Winch and Hans-Georg Gadamer, can be reconstructed. Indeed, it is remarkable how the background of the later Wittgenstein (Winch) and the late Heidegger (Gadamer) provide an overlapping, at times parallel and at other times supplementing perspective on the unique mode of social–scientific understanding. What in particular defines this approach, besides an emphasis on the unique nature of understanding in the human sciences, is the specific attitude toward language for such methodological reflection. Both Winch and Gadamer reject the 'underlaborer' conception of philosophy vis-à-vis the sciences oriented at a clarification of their internal rules and methods; what Winch and Gadamer are interested in is rather a reflective reassessment of our understanding of understanding, of the conceptual assumptions in the social and cultural disciplines. Instead of focusing on the correct usage of terms to eliminate linguistic confusions, the real issue is that 'our idea of what belongs to the realm of reality is given for us in the language that we use. The concepts we have settle for us the form of the experience we have of the world' (Winch, 1991: 15). This is echoed by Gadamer when he states 'that language and world are related in a fundamental way does not mean, then, that world becomes the object of language. Rather, the object of knowledge and statements is always already enclosed within the world horizon of language ... Whoever has language "has" world' (Gadamer, [1960]1989: 450, 453)[9]. Accordingly, the task is to inquire into the linguistically mediated core of our conceptual pre-assumptions with regard to the reality as constructed in the social sciences, and to thus provide the grounding for adequate scientific approaches and results therein.

Winch's Wittgensteinian argument includes the claim that social–scientific understanding is different in kind from the natural sciences, and accordingly involves some particular methodological maxims. It is based on a three-step movement that draws out implications from Wittgenstein's use-conception of language as an adequate conceptual ground for understanding human agency. In a first move, we are reminded of Wittgenstein's demonstration that the identification of something as an identical thing cannot be privately accomplished through pure observation or ostensive definition, but requires a shared social context of rule-following: 'It is only in terms of a given *rule* that we can attach a specific sense to the words "the same"' (Winch, 1991: 27). 'The use of the word "rule" and the use of the word "same" are interwoven' (Wittgenstein, 1953: 225). Thus, for something to count as the same, it must be identifiable beyond my own inner mental memory. A rule requires a social context in which it can be verified as being followed, since being a

rule implies that it must be possible to be correctly or incorrectly applied, which can only be checked against some external (i.e., socially established and recognized) standard.

In the second and decisive step, Winch takes the rule-based account of object identification to the scientific context and shows that we deal with two different processes in the natural and social sciences respectively. The premise is that any scientist necessarily relies on a medium of identifying something as the same, but for the natural scientist this medium constructs natural reality according to the standards of his scientific community, while in the social sciences the object of understanding itself is governed by the very same structure of rule-following, which means that the sociologist needs to take into account those context-specific rules in order to identify the object of understanding:

> For whereas in the case of the natural scientist we have to deal with only one set of rules, namely those governing the scientist's investigation itself, here what the sociologist is studying, as well as his study of it, is a human activity and is therefore carried on according to rules. And it is these rules, rather than those which govern the sociologist's investigation, which specify what is to count as "doing the same kind of thing" in relation to that kind of activity' (Winch, 1991: 87)

The rules of the social agents must count since we aim in our scientific account at an explanation of social action. And since social action is intrinsically oriented at some purpose, meaning or idea, the rules according to which such ideas or concepts are constructed are essential for the object-identification. Ignoring the internal ideas of the agents would amount to a misidentification of the very object of one's study.

On the basis of the Wittgensteinian concept of language games, which are grounded in practical forms of life so as to provide rules for shared meaning, Winch thirdly draws out his major methodological conclusions.[10] The rules of the social scientist's own context cannot be immediately and unreflectively applied to that of another context, since (a) every object or meaning has to be understood according to its own contextual customs and practices, and (b) it is impossible and illegitimate to abstract and generalize rules from any context such that they are universally applicable. For example, logic and scientific standards of objectivity and consistency are just one rule-context among others and cannot be taken to apply to, say, religious practices and interpretations of other cultures. Yet with this final step, Winch also creates a paradox, since he states that (a) the identification of another social practice is only possible because the social scientist is herself or himself a social agent, and thus has a sense of the issues and concepts at stake (such that without some sense of what religion is, for instance, the understanding of a religious practice would be impossible), and (b) the particular rules and concepts of the scientist's own context (or 'language game') cannot be applied to that of a differently situated social agent. The issue opened up—one that drives the philosophy of social science to this day—is how exactly the background assumptions of the interpreter relate to those of social agents in diverse cultural, social, and historical contexts.

Gadamer's dialogical hermeneutics picks it up from here, as it were. Based on a similar emphasis on the historical–cultural pre-understanding as necessary for epistemic access to meaning, Gadamer develops a phenomenology of the interpretive act that shows all linguistically mediated understanding to be intentionally structured by one's own background understanding (Gadamer, [1960] 1989). To disclose what a text—or an action, a gesture, a picture, a practice—is about, is to understand its subject matter, *die Sache selbst*. Yet grasping the subject matter requires investing one's own projective understanding of the issue at stake; this, in turn, requires one to draw on background assumptions that are further tested in the process of making sense of the object. Gadamer insists—in this respect similar to Donald Davidson's focus on truth sentences

as a necessary bridge to other meaning—that our own understanding of something is to be considered valid and true, so we project similar truth or reasonableness onto the other text or action. Yet at the same time such an 'anticipation of rational completeness' (Gadamer) is necessarily situated and contextual, which means that we will always understand coming from our own perspective. Taken together, we can best capture both conditions—the necessary investment of taken-to-be-true assumptions and their historical character—by conceiving of *interpretation as a truth-oriented dialogue*. We cannot but aim to understand truthfully, in the most plausible sense, what another has to say or reasonably intends to do, and yet we cannot do this except on the basis of concrete contextual pre-assumptions. The process of such a validity-based interpretation is expressed by the formula of a '*fusion of horizons*', as here my own background necessarily influences how the meaning is understood, and yet it must fuse into some plausible view that I can rethink if understanding is to occur at all.

Two conclusions follow. First, *all understanding is interpretation*, since the construction of the object is only possible based on the fore-conceptions (Heidegger) of one's own beliefs and assumptions. And second, *all understanding involves application*, since the context-indexicality means that whatever makes sense will refer back to one's social context. Most importantly, however, understanding the meaning (including intentional orientation, purpose or sense) of a text or action is now seen as a *constructive process* in which the *reality* of the other text or context is presupposed, and yet its *understanding* cannot be disentangled from the conceptual resources at the disposal of the social scientist. This grounding of a *reflexive social science*, one that takes into account its own conceptual construction of the object domain without giving up claims to objectivity and adequate understanding, marks the major contribution of hermeneutics to the philosophy of human and social science.

THE HERMENEUTIC GROUNDS OF SOCIAL SCIENCE: RATIONALITY-STANDARDS AND THE UNDERSTANDING–EXPLANATION DEBATE

However, Gadamer's focus on the fusion of truth-oriented assumptions in the process of understanding causes his version of dialogical interpretation to fail as a satisfying grounding for social science. In the human and social sciences, a wide multiplicity of texts, discourses and practices are analyzed, and the task cannot be premised on achieving shared truth, but must rather be a contextual reconstruction of the reasons and motivations involved in meaningful behavior. Furthermore, the shared achievement of truth assumes that rational understanding emerges from this encounter without external or causal forces that influence meaning and understanding. Yet such an idealistic assumption begs the question of the possible external influence on interpretive understanding, besides being contradicted by many findings of the critical social sciences. Finally, the social conception of truth as an ongoing re-negotiation of the background consensus of a tradition neglects the role that the individual agent plays within a socially shared context. Yet the relation between individual and background (or between agency and structure) has proven of major importance in the human and social sciences when the explanation of empirical social behavior is at stake (Turner, 1996).[11]

In order to rationally reconstruct what remains useful of Wittgensteinian and hermeneutic insights for social science, and what needs to be reassessed in light of their internal requirements, we now turn to a discussion of (1) the problem of shared rationality standards as a presupposition for understanding, and (2) the causal influence of external factors on intentional understanding. Our aim will be to show how those issues are dealt with on the methodological basis introduced by the hermeneutic perspective.

Rationality-Standards

With regard to the issue of rationality, the two assumptions of (a) having to start from one's background, and (b) assessing the other's meaning necessarily in intentional terms create the challenge of doing justice to the other's contextual 'standards of rationality'. On the one hand, the fact that we have to have a conceptual pre-understanding of the subject matter means that we necessarily have to introduce our own sense of rationality or truth when we render the other's actions and expressions intelligible. On the other hand, if the concepts and rules of intentional agents are to be understood as embedded and situated in irreducibly concrete and complex action-contexts, then imposing our standards onto the cultural and societal practices of another must appear deeply mistaken. The challenge between an assimilating ethnocentrism (in which we would make sense of the other *in our terms*) and a rampant cultural relativism (which would follow if contexts had *entirely distinct standards*) demands a solution that maintains that understanding and interpretation starts at home, and nonetheless allows us to acknowledge cultural diversity such that it balances the recognition of contextual difference with accounting for the possibility of the cross-cultural intelligibility of action. In other words, what is needed is a model that situates the value-orientations of intentional agents in cultural and social contexts and yet allows us to understand how meaning between such contexts can be bridged and exchanged.

In the stage-setting essay, Peter Winch (1964) argues that imposing the logical rules of a scientifically minded culture onto the belief-system of a 'primitive culture' is mistaken since the logical contradictions that emerge if certain assumptions are followed through can be practically avoided by the customs and practices of the culture at stake. Winch argues that a belief is to be understood and evaluated in light of its contextual and practical use—beliefs depend on *rules* that are grounded in *forms of life*—which means, for instance, that in the case of the Azande belief in witchcraft, talk about contradictions is misplaced since the practices are structured such that the issue of rational consistency never comes up. In the following debate, Popperians defend a universal standard of rational assessment while neo-Wittgensteinians stick to practical standards (such as aesthetic or social norms) as the ultimate arbiter of reason (Hollis and Lukes, 1982; Wilson, 1971).[12]

The issue at stake is the apparent incommensurability of different conceptual schemes, grounded in instrumental, moral or aesthetic rationalities, themselves grounded in different cultural and social contexts. In this debate, Donald Davidson's argument concerning the impossibility of incommensurable conceptual schemes has been taken to overcome the impasse created here (Davidson, 1984). Davidson shows how the meaning of any particular action or expression is necessarily derived from correlating it with one's own taken-for-granted and assumed-true beliefs and assumptions. Davidson's *principle of charity* responds critically to Quine's thesis of the indeterminacy of translation, which suggests that observable stimuli in a shared environment are insufficient grounds for determining the meaning of the sentences used to express them, since they could be rendered equally well in logically incompatible conceptual schemes (Quine, 1960).

Davidson holds that the idea of *incommensurable* conceptual schemes is contradictory, since a conceptual scheme must necessarily be expressed in linguistic form; yet the identification of something as a meaningful linguistic statement involves the *correlation* of my own true beliefs with that of another rational agent. This correlation thesis, which methodologically defines the principle of charity, follows since, in order to identify an expression as meaningful, I have to interpret it as the expression of a true belief, which means that I have to employ my own truth assumptions to render the other's supposed linguistic statements intelligible. Accordingly, only if I and the other agent share a large amount of true sentences can I assume to understand his language and

even make sense of certain disagreements. Yet if this is true, the idea that another speaker or agent (a) speaks a language that entails a conceptual scheme, and (b) speaks and thinks in a conceptual scheme that is incomprehensible to us yet true must be rejected. The principle of charity suggests that radical or absolute incommensurability between different cultural and social contexts is a methodological fiction, because the interpretive access of the social scientist to any possible context of social action is grounded in a background of true and rational beliefs.[13]

Yet the necessity of relating the meaning of another agent to one's own taken-to-be-true beliefs and assumptions does not rule out a *hermeneutically comprehensible difference of rationality standards*. This is so because even though the interpreter has to start from his or her own background, the bridging principle that allows entry into another context of meaning is but a first step, one that can subsequently be replaced by the adoption of the contextually significant rules and practices that define how a term, gesture, belief or practice is to be understood given alternative background assumptions (for Davidson, see Bohman and Kelly, 1996; for Gadamer, see Kögler, 1999). For instance, while a pre-understanding concerning God and Gods is required for interpreting religion, the hermeneutic immersion into either a mono- or a polytheistic context determines how the meaning of a plurality of Gods is to be understood and evaluated.[14] What Davidson—and Gadamer—show is that the 'incommensurability' of standards of evaluating facts and events is itself a hermeneutic phenomenon which is based on *understanding* standards, values, rationality-assumptions other than one's own (Valadez, 2001). What they succeed in ruling out is the epistemic ghost of a true yet incomprehensible world—but what they push to the fore is the problem how to distinguish between the plurality of internally intelligible yet different value-assumptions and those causally effective factors that require a switch from an interpretive understanding to explanatory mode of interpretation.

Understanding and Explanation

Hermeneutic discourse shows that understanding human agency draws on one's own sense of rules and background practices (Winch) and therefore necessarily projects intentional concepts onto the other's expressions and actions (Gadamer/Davidson). This seems to constrain all understanding to an interpretation of other agency in intentional concepts. But what if the other's acts resist making sense in such intentional terms, even after having applied the most charitable *and* pluralistic conception of contextual perspectives on meaning and truth? Is it not possible, then, and in the case of a *breakdown of hermeneutic intelligibility* even necessary, to switch from a first or second-person perspective (oriented at the other's self-understanding) to a third-person approach that *explains* the other based on objective causal theories?[15]

One needs to acknowledge that intentional interpretation cannot exhaust the epistemic potential of social science, since this would imply making an idealistic assumption. Intentional interpretation as the sole approach to meaning would assume that the constitution of meaning is fully grounded in self-transparent conscious acts. Yet the thesis of a contextual background itself suggests that the full scope of meaning is not accessible to the individual agent. If agency is grounded in a socially constituted context that provides a meaningful background for acts of understanding, it is plausible to inquire *how objective social contexts cause the construction of the meaning-resources of the background.* This seems especially the case where one has reason to believe that the agents have a distorted view of themselves and social or natural reality.

The methodological limits of hermeneutics are explored in the debate between Gadamer and Habermas (see Ormiston and Schrift, 1990: 147 ff.). Habermas challenges the hermeneutic claim to universality based on the ontological premise that all understanding is grounded in language. Accepting the importance of language as a medium of social experience as well as one of understanding social agency, Habermas nonetheless questions that all interpretation is a historically situated and truth-oriented dialogue. What is left unexplored here is the extent to which social and cultural perspectives are shaped implicitly by forces other than a world-disclosing experience of truth. Precisely because language is the medium of all experience, intentional agency and reason are now subject to an *empirical a priori*: the particular forms or language games within which situated agents think, perceive and act (Habermas, 1988; 1990). Such linguistic schemes are themselves shaped and structured by objective social forces such as labor and power. Taking into account the structuring powers of social practices, such as a modern capitalistic economy as well as a modern bureaucracy, Habermas argues that a full understanding of human agency must involve intentional interpretation as well as causal explanation (see also his later theory in Habermas, 1984/87).

In his response to the charge of linguistic idealism, Gadamer defends his theory on a modified basis, suggesting that the universality of hermeneutics does not extend as far as being the ultimate and all-encompassing grounds of all understanding and agency, since the influence of power relations and work or market conditions on modern selves can hardly be denied (Gadamer, 1990). But what is universal about the hermeneutic starting point is that all understanding, whether in intentional or explanatory terms, begins from a normatively infused and historically situated background, and thus cannot itself claim to transcend the context so as to objectively explain the other from an absolute position. Since understanding is situated, strong explanatory claims such as used in the natural sciences are inadequate here, because one perspective (or social group think) cannot simply put itself above the cultural and social self-understanding of another. The relation between therapist and patient that Habermas invokes to explain the relation between a critical social explanation and the situated agent is inadequate here since we deal with other situated and yet rational agents.[16] The challenge articulated by this debate consists in the possibility of asserting the situatedness of one's own reasoning, which allows for a plurality of value- and truth-perspectives, and to still claim that another agent's perspective might be systematically distorted and thus subject to an explanation of causal or structural influences upon her beliefs and assumptions.

However, two issues are intertwined and perhaps confused here: namely, the assessment of the other's action in terms of a universally shared standard of rationality (which poses the question from which perspective or on what grounds one can *judge* the other), and the extent of unconscious causal and structural influences on his or her explicit beliefs (which creates a distortion of beliefs if the true conditions of belief are not understood and if they contradict the agent's own standards). If both tasks are to be addressed, the challenge is to show how (a) a universal standard of assessment might be possible, given that all understanding begins from one's own contextual background understanding, and (b) how social-scientific interpretation can both detect and help undo the unconscious influence of social factors vis-à-vis the self-understanding of situated agents.

MEDIATING AGENCY AND STRUCTURE: THE METHODOLOGICAL PREMISES OF SOCIAL INTERPRETATION

Since all understanding must begin from home—i.e., from one's own use of language—the first task involves drawing out some universal norms or value orientations that are entailed in anyone's contextual use of language and communication. In this vein, speech act theory can be used as a backdrop for a theory of universal validity claims that can in turn ground a cross-cultural understanding of human interaction (Habermas, 1984/87).[17] Addressing the second task,

which involves explaining how causal or structural factors can influence intentional agents, poststructuralist theorists like Foucault (1990) and Derrida (1978) can be understood as providing methodologies designed to break the taken-for-granted-background understanding of intentional agents (Frank, 1989; Kögler, 1999). The purpose is to confront agents reflexively with unacknowledged background assumptions and practices.[18] The fact that the social scientist is situated in dialogical practices provides the resources to generalize formal features of rational agency. The same fact also provides the scientist with a particular outsider perspective vis-à-vis other social contexts that can be used for reconstructing hidden and unacknowledged assumptions and practices. Both aspects of a hermeneutically situated social interpretation must, however, assume that the individual social agent is capable of drawing out the universal as well as reflexively detaching resources of one's contextual background understanding. The relation between individual agency and social background thus acquires center stage.

Relating the acts and beliefs of individual agents to objective social and cultural structures, including those dynamics beyond the conscious grasp of individuals, has always constituted a major challenge to social science and theory. We saw that understanding human agency requires intentional concepts grounded in the agent's background, and yet unintended consequences and background contexts constitute social structures that transcend individual agency. It was precisely this that made a psychological grounding obsolete, and yet the reference to intentional agency cannot be given up. It is here that the intermediary model of a symbolically and practically structured background functions as a solution. Indeed, in a variety of social-theoretical projects, this very idea has been prominently explored and theorized. Whether rendered in terms of a *lifeworld* grounding communicative acts and relating to social systems (Habermas, 1984/87), a *practical knowledge* that entails rules and resources (Giddens, 1984), an *embodied habitus* that equips individual agents to participate in social fields (Bourdieu, 1977; 1990), or as the *discursive and social practices* that define reality and objectivity for situated individuals (Foucault, 1979; 1990; 1994), the idea of a holistically constituted background that shapes the intentional awareness of subjects by being connected to larger societal structures is articulated in different forms. One can see that an underlying hermeneutic shift has occurred in social theory.[19]

In order to make this move fruitful for a methodological grounding, we need to clarify how exactly the mediating 'hermeneutic' background is to be understood. The idea is that any intentional act is only comprehensible on the basis of a pre-understanding that is holistically structured and symbolically mediated. Intentional understanding, while intrinsically defined by conscious agency and related to reflexive and thus self-determining acts, points to a social background that is more encompassing than individual agency. Having thus brought into our purview the realm of social meanings, we can now analyze and describe how the background itself is structured, how it is internally organized. We thus arrive at a notion of social practices, fields, or systems—but must emphasize that those concepts still retain, ontologically speaking, their reference to an intentional agent. While we abstract from agency when we describe the logic of these processes, we similarly keep in mind that these processes emerge from the cooperation of individual agents who are themselves socialized in cultural settings. The abstraction of individual agency is thus a methodical move that never leads to a full-blown ontological abstraction of such processes from intersubjective understanding and communication. The advantage of this conceptualization of the relation between individual agency and social structure is that we avoid reducing social processes to individual acts without ignoring the existence of the processes themselves, yet neither do we disconnect them from the possible reflexive and causal influence of individual agency. Only if trans-individual structures are introduced as *background conditions for agency* can we make sense of the following methodological premises that follow from the intentionalist approach to social-scientific understanding.

The *first of those premises* has been with us from the start: the fact that human agency can only be identified if we employ a set of intentional concepts including meaning, purpose, intention, significance and norm. Such notions require reference to an intentional agent that can understand meanings, purposes and norms, and yet remains always embedded in contexts and structures that escape full and articulate self-understanding. The social scientist will devise conceptual schemes that reconstruct the logic and composition of the background contexts without forgetting their intrinsic relativity to agency.

The *second premise* constitutes the necessity to recognize the linguistically mediated self-understandings of the agents themselves. Winch and Gadamer both emphasize that the identification of meaning requires being hermeneutically sensitive to the object-identifications and rules of the other, as it is here that the 'object' of understanding is constituted. If social theory conceives of social reality in terms of an embedded agency drawing on larger background meanings in order to make sense, the need to take into account the other's own beliefs and assumptions, however mediated by one's own sense, is adequately reflected on the level of social reality. It is recognized that any so-called 'objective' or 'systemic' meaning refers back to the very agents that interpret themselves in the concepts and schemes provided by these backgrounds. Taking them into account will do justice to the way in which objective social practices provide meaning-constituting backgrounds for intentional agents.

The *third premise* addresses the relation between social science and social reality. We have seen that the linguistic mediation of social science and social reality allows us to understand the construction of social theories as the reflexive articulation of embedded meanings. Social science can claim to be a reflexive and critical tool for social agency only if we conceive of individual agency as practically embedded in social structures, such that the meaning-constituting holistic backgrounds can be thematized by the agents themselves. If we mediate agency and structure in this way, we can reclaim the core project of a critical theory of society, even if we leave the place of an articulated grid of rational concepts or a super-theory of social institutions unnamed for the time being. If we situate the project of an explication of hidden and unthematized structures of social reality in the reflexive potential built into the linguistically mediated self-understanding of agents, reflexive agency is more than an epistemic concept. Besides being the conceptual ground of the construction of meaning in the human and social sciences, reflexive agency is also the condition of possibility for the critique and transcendence of unacknowledged and unnecessary relations of power.

REFERENCES

Baert, Patrick (2006) 'Social science and social theory', in Gerard Delanty (ed.), Handbook of Contemporary European Social Theory. London/New York: Routledge.

Blackburn, Simon (2000) Ruling Passions: A Theory of Practical Reasoning. Oxford: Clarendon Press.

Bohman, James (1991) New Philosophy of Social Science. Cambridge, MA: The MIT Press.

Bohman, James and Kelly, Terrence (1996) 'Rationality, intelligibility, and comparison: The rationality debates revisited', Philosophy and Social Criticism, 22 (1): 181–200.

Bourdieu, Pierre (1984) Outline of a Theory of Practice. Cambridge: Cambridge University Press.

―――― (1990) The Logic of Practice. Stanford, CA: Stanford University Press.

Davidson, Donald ([1984] 2001) 'On the very idea of a conceptual scheme', in Inquiries into Truth and Interpretation. Oxford: Clarendon Press.

Delanty, Gerard (2006), Handbook of Contemporary European Social Theory. London/New York: Routledge.

Derrida, Jacques (1978) Writing and Difference. Chicago: University of Chicago Press.

Dilthey, Wilhelm ([1889] 1989) Introduction to the Human Sciences, Selected Works, Vol. I, Rudolf Makreel and Frithof Rodi (eds.) Princeton: Princeton University Press. (1st edn, Einleitung in die Geisteswissenschaften, 1889.)

―――― (1982), Die Geistige Welt, Ges. Schriften V. Stuttgart: Teubner.

―――― ([1910] 2004) The Construction of History in the Human Sciences. Princeton: Princeton University Press.

Dreyfus, Hubert (1980) 'Holism and hermeneutics', Review of Metaphysics 34(1): 3–24.

―――― (1993) Being-in-the-World: A Commentary on Heidegger's Being and Time. Cambridge, MA: The MIT Press.

Fay, Brian (2003) 'Phenomenology and social inquiry: From consciousness to culture and critique,' in Stephen Turner and Paul Roth (eds.), The Blackwell Guide to the Philosophy of the Social Sciences, Malden, MA/Oxford, UK: Blackwell, pp. 42–63.

Foucault, Michel ([1975] 1979) Discipline and Punish. New York: Pantheon Books.

―――― ([1966] 1990) The Order of Things. New York: Vintage Books.

―――― ([1976] 1994) History of Sexuality: An Introduction. New York: Vintage Books.

Frank, Manfred (1989) What is Neostructuralism? Minneapolis: University of Minnesota Press.

Gadamer, Hans-Georg ([1960] 1989) Truth and Method. New York: Crossroads.

―――― (1990) 'Reply to my critics', in Gayle Ormiston and Alan Schrift (eds.), The Hermeneutic Tradition: From Ast to Ricoeur. Albany: SUNY, pp. 273–97.

Giddens, Anthony (1984) The Constitution of Society. Berkeley and Los Angeles: University of California Press.

Grondin, Jean (1994) Introduction to Hermeneutics. New Haven, CT: Yale University Press.

Habermas, Jürgen (1971) Knowledge and Human Interests. Boston: Beacon Press.

―――― ([1981] 1984/87) Theory of Communicative Action, Vol. 1 and 2. Boston: Beacon Press

―――― (1987) The Philosophical Discourse of Modernity. Cambridge, MA: The MIT Press

―――― ([1969] 1988) On the Logic of the Social Sciences. Cambridge, MA: The MIT Press.

―――― (1990) 'The Hermeneutic Claim to Universality', in Gayle Ormiston and Alan Schrift (eds.), The Hermeneutic Tradition: From Ast to Ricoeur. Albany: SUNY, pp. 245–72.

―――― (1992) 'Toward a Critique of the Theory of Meaning', in Postmetaphysical Thinking, Cambridge, MA: The MIT Press, pp. 57–87.

Hacking, Ian (2000) *The Social Construction of What?* Cambridge, MA: Harvard University Press.

Heidegger, Martin ([1927] 1962) *Being and Time.* New York: Harper & Row.

——— (1971) *On the Way to Language.* San Francisco: HarperCollins Publishers.

——— (1977) *Basic Writings.* San Francisco: HarperCollins Publishers.

——— (1982) *The Basic Problems of Phenomenology.* Bloomington: Indiana University Press.

——— (1985) *History of the Concept of Time.* Bloomington: Indiana University Press.

Herder, Johann Gottfried and Jean-Jacques Rousseau (1966) *On the Origin of Language: Two Essays.* Chicago: University of Chicago Press.

Hollis, Martin and Lukes, Stephen (1982) *Rationality and Relativism.* Cambridge, MA: The MIT Press.

Humboldt, Wilhelm von (1988) *On Language: The Diversity of Human Language-Structure and its Influence on the Mental Development of Mankind.* Cambridge: Cambridge University Press.

Husserl, Edmund ([1913] 1962) *Ideas: General Introduction to Pure Phenomenology.* London: Collier Macmillan Publishers.

——— (1970) *Logical Investigations.* London: Routledge.

——— (1991) *Cartesian Meditations.* Dordrecht; Boston: Kluwer Academic Publishers.

Kögler, Hans-Herbert (1999) *The Power of Dialogue: Critical Hermeneutics after Gadamer and Foucault.* Cambridge, MA: The MIT Press.

——— (2000) 'Empathy, dialogical self, and reflexive interpretation: The symbolic source of simulation', in Hans-Herbert Kögler and Karsten Stueber (eds.), *Empathy and Agency: The Problem of Understanding in the Human Sciences.* Boulder, CO: Westview Press, pp. 194–221.

——— (2006) 'Hermeneutics, phenomenology, and philosophical anthropology', in Gerard Delanty (ed.), *Handbook of Contemporary European Social Theory.* London/New York: Routledge, pp. 203–26.

Kögler, Hans-Herbert and Stueber, Karsten (eds.) (2000) *Empathy and Agency: The Problem of Understanding in the Human Sciences.* Boulder, CO: Westview Press.

Krausz, Michael (ed.) (1989) *Relativism: Interpretation and Confrontation.* Notre Dame, IN: University of Notre Dame Press.

Lash, Scott (1998) *Another Modernity, A Different Rationality.* London: Blackwell Publishers.

Lee, Benjamin (1997) *Language, Metalanguage, and the Semiotics of Subjectivity.* Durham, NC/London: Duke University Press.

MacIntyre, Alasdair (1971) 'Is understanding religion compatible with believing?', in Bryan Wilson (ed.), *Rationality.* New York: Harper and Row, pp. 62–77.

Makreel, Rudolf (2000) 'From simulation to structural transposition: A Diltheyan critique of empathy and defense of *Verstehen*', in Hans-Herbert Kögler and Karsten Stueber (eds.), *Empathy and Agency: The Problem of Understanding in the Human Sciences.* Boulder, CO: Westview Press, pp. 181–93.

Mandair, Arvind and Zene, Cosimo (2005) 'Dialogue as the inscription of "the West"', *Social Identities,* 11(3): 171–75.

Mead, George Herbert (1934) *Mind, Self, and Society.* Chicago: University of Chicago Press.

Merleau-Ponty, Maurice (1964) *Signs.* Evanston, IL: Northwestern University Press.

——— (1973) *The Prose of the World.* Evanston, IL: Northwestern University Press.

McCarthy, Thomas (1989) 'Contra relativism: A thought experiment', in Michael Krausz (ed.), *Relativism: Interpretation and Confrontation.* Notre Dame, IN: University of Notre Dame Press, pp. 256–71.

Obeyeskere, Gananath (1997) *The Apotheosis of Captain Cook.* Princeton, NJ: Princeton University Press.

Outhwaite, William (2000) 'The Philosophy of Social Science', in Bryan Turner (ed.), *The Blackwell Companion to Social Theory.* Malden, MA/Oxford: Blackwell, pp. 47–70.

Ormiston, Gayle and Schrift, Alan (eds.) (1990) *The Hermeneutic Tradition: From Ast to Ricoeur.* Albany: SUNY.

Quine, Willard V. O. (1960) 'Translation and meaning', in *Word & Object,* Cambridge, MA: The MIT Press, pp. 26–79.

Ricoeur, Paul (1992) *Oneself as Another.* Chicago, IL: Chicago University Press.

Roth, Paul (2003) 'Beyond understanding: The career of the concept of understanding in the human sciences', in Stephen Turner and Paul Roth (eds.), *The Blackwell Guide to the Philosophy of the Social Sciences.* Malden, MA/Oxford, UK: Blackwell, pp. 311–33.

Sahlins, Marshall (1981) *Historical Metaphors and Mythical Realities.* Ann Arbor, MI: University of Michigan Press.

——— (1995) *How 'Natives' Think: About Captain Cook, For Example.* Chicago: University of Chicago Press.

Schleiermacher, Friedrich ([1819] 1957) *Hermeneutics: The Handwritten Manuscripts.* Atlanta, GA: Scholars Press for the American Academy of Religion.

Schütz, Alfred (1967) *The Phenomenology of the Social World.* Evanston, IL: Northwestern University Press.

Searle, John (1989) *Intentionality*. Cambridge: Cambridge University Press.

———— (1995) *The Construction of Social Reality*. New York: The Free Press.

———— (2002) *Consciousness and Language*. Cambridge: Cambridge University Press.

Stern, David (2003) 'The practical turn', in Stephen Turner and Paul Roth (eds.), *The Blackwell Guide to the Philosophy of the Social Sciences*. Malden, MA/Oxford, UK: Blackwell, pp.185–206.

Stueber, Karsten (2004) 'Agency and the objectivity of historical narratives', in William Sweet (ed.), *The Philosophy of History: A Reexamination*. Aldershot, UK: Ashgate Press, pp. 197–222.

Taylor, Charles (1985) *Human Agency and Language*. Cambridge: Cambridge University Press.

Taylor, Talbot (1992) *Mutual Misunderstanding*. Durham, NC/London: Duke University Press.

Turner, Stephen (1994) *The Social Theory of Practices: Tradition, Tacit Knowledge, and Presuppositions*. Chicago, IL: University of Chicago Press.

———— (2003) 'Cause, the persistence of teleology, and the origins of the philosophy of social science', in Stephen Turner and Paul Roth (eds.), *The Blackwell Guide to the Philosophy of the Social Sciences*. Malden, MA/Oxford, UK: Blackwell,. pp. 21–41.

Turner, Stephen and Roth, Paul (eds.) (2003) *The Blackwell Guide to the Philosophy of the Social Sciences*. Malden, MA/Oxford: Blackwell.

———— (2003a) 'Introduction. Ghosts and the machine: Issues of agency, rationality, and scientific methodology in contemporary philosophy of social science', in *The Blackwell Guide to the Philosophy of the Social Sciences*. Malden, MA/Oxford: Blackwell, pp. 1–17.

Ulin, Robert (1984) *Understanding Cultures*. Austin: University of Texas Press.

Valadez, Jorge (2001) *Deliberative Democracy, Political Legitimacy, and Self Determination in Multicultural Societies*. Boulder, CO: Westview Press.

Weber, Max (1978) 'Basic sociological terms', in Guenther Roth and Claus Wittich (eds.), *Economy and Society*. Berkeley/Los Angeles: University of California Press, pp. 3–62.

Wilson, Bryan (ed.) (1971) *Rationality*. New York: Harper and Row.

Winch, Peter ([1958] 1991) *The Idea of a Social Science and Its Relation to Philosophy*. London: Routledge.

———— (1964) 'Understanding a primitive society', in Bryan Wilson (ed.), *Rationality*. New York: Harper and Row, pp. 78–111.

Wittgenstein, Ludwig (1953) *Philosophical Investigations*. Cambridge: Cambridge University Press.

NOTES

1 The general formulation of the connection between a practical pre-understanding and an intentional interpretation will now be traced with a particular view toward the systematic core thesis of a practically grounded linguistic intentionality. If anything today, the relation between the practical background and the linguistically articulate intentional meaning comes closest to the promise of an epistemically coherent grounding of social science in its own social reality. For the state of the philosophy of social science, see Outhwaite (2000).

2 We will see that the process of articulating this issue on the basis of a psychological theory of mind unfolds an internal dialectic that ultimately pushes the hermeneutic theory of understanding beyond its Cartesian beginnings. The reconstruction of the conditions of possibility of a uniquely human and intersubjective interpretation undergoes a radical transformation of its own epistemological self-understanding, leading first to the discovery of the practical embeddedness of all human understanding, and secondly to a new appreciation of the role of language for constituting and in interpreting the intentional agency of humans.

3 This idea goes back at least to Giambattista Vico (for whom in history '*verum et factum convertuntur*') and is, among many others, also invoked by Marx.

4 For a critique of this model of empathy that nonetheless tries to save the intuition of an empathetic understanding of other agents, see Blackburn (2000) and Stueber (2004).

5 Since understanding is still defined with essential recourse to intentional expression, it makes sense for Dilthey to largely retain the quasi-psychologist language of defining interpretation as an empathic reconstruction or reliving (*Nacherleben*) of objective meanings (Dilthey, [1910] 2004). But the new discovery of the essential role of a socially shared background understanding—the objective spirit—now poses the problem of how exactly to conceive the process of making sense of these objective yet value-laden and first-person-based meaning-contexts. Dilthey opts here for an objectivistic solution, claiming that epochs are to be analyzed as self-centered meaning-units (*in sich selbst zentrierte Bedeutungszusammenhänge*). For a critique, see Gadamer (1989) and Habermas (1971). For a methodology that attempts to reconcile empathetic interpretation and objective explanation, see Weber (1978).

6 Those dimensions can be analytically distinguished and yet form a unitary phenomenon with regard to meaning constitution. For a discussion and different use of this idea, see Dreyfus (1980), Kögler (1999) and Stern (2003).

7 Heidegger's extreme emphasis on the practical and pre-predicative nature of existential

self-understanding, combined with his ultimate lack of interest in a grounding of the human sciences as such, left the task of developing a philosophy of hermeneutic understanding and interpretation to subsequent thinkers. Hubert Dreyfus's attempt, however, to build such a theory on the sole basis of Heidegger's 'practical holism' fails since it leaves under-theorized the articulation function of the linguistic medium. See Dreyfus (1980) and for discussion Stern (2003). For a critique of the theory of practices, see Turner (1994).

8 The appreciation of this theme emerges in different traditions of philosophy, which put together provide the background for extending the analysis of language fully into the philosophy of social science. In the late Heidegger, language is seen as a *holistic world-disclosure*, which wants to say that the encounter of entities or events in the world depends on a prior opening of our perspective and interest toward whatever is at stake—and this opening of our vision and understanding emerges through language. Language, in turn, cannot then be understood as a tool to represent pre-existing objects used by a pre-existing mind, nor does it simply come in handy for subjects to communicate: it is rather the background on the basis of which expression, reference and communication are possible (Heidegger, 1971; 1974). In a similar vein, the late Wittgenstein rejects his own earlier identification of language with logical rules that organize simple names representing basic objects, and suggests that the full phenomenon of language includes an endless variety of acts and expressions, all of which depend on a contextual familiarity of their use. The rigid structure of language as a representational system makes way for an *open-ended contextual medium* that is the ever-shifting yet insurmountable bedrock of meaning (Wittgenstein, 1953). And in the phenomenological tradition, it is the late Merleau-Ponty who discovers the significance of semiotics for human experience. The intractable problems of understanding other minds based on a Cartesian conception of mind and meaning can be surpassed if, with Saussure, the transcendental necessity of a *shared code of communication* is acknowledged. What remains to be worked out is how embodied subjectivity and intersubjective experience of the concrete other are constituted within such a symbolically mediated context (Merleau-Ponty, 1964; 1973).

9 The general line of this idea is expressed also in the famous Gadamerian slogan: 'Being that can be understood is language' (Gadamer, 1989: see esp. 383ff. and 438ff.). See also Ulin (1984).

10 Winch plays here ingeniously on the double meaning of Wittgenstein's term 'language game', which can mean (a) the particular 'rule of use' (*Gebrauchsregel*) of terms, or (b) the whole context of multiple modes and rules embedded in a form of life. It is in the second, more encompassing sense

that cultural practices, scientific paradigms, and social traditions have been identified as language games, as here particular speech acts are seen as relying on some socially shared and generally acknowledged normative background. See Stern (2003) for more discussion.

11 There is no doubt that the linguistic turn defines the background against which understanding and interpretation are to be conceived in the social sciences. The fact that all interpretation has to draw on some prior understanding of the issue or purpose at stake, that such an understanding is defined by intentional concepts, and that explicit accounts in the social sciences thus assume the role of reflexive articulations of taken-for-granted beliefs, assumptions and practices, points to the mediating function of language for all understanding. Indeed, the fact that intentional interpretation requires the medium language for its articulation—a medium which it shares with its object domain social agency—accounts both for the possibility of a unique form of understanding vis-à-vis human action *and* presents its own set of problems. Those problems relate to how exactly the language- or context-dependency of the social-scientific interpreter is to be invested and mediated with the symbolically mediated beliefs, assumptions and practices of the other agent. For the general new context of discussion, see Bohman (1991).

12 In a similar more recent debate, the anthropologists Marshall Sahlins (1981; 1995) and Gananath Obeyeskere (1997) argue whether the killing of Captain Cook by natives upon his return to Hawaii is to be understood as based on an instrumental model of reason or should rather be seen in light of the mythological worldview of the Hawaiians. While all parties involved agree that human agency requires an orientation of the reasons that motivate agents, the ultimate value orientations that underlie the reason-based actions are constructed along the lines of divergent models. This shows (against Roth, 2003) that a meaningful debate about what evidence counts for a particular model of rational agency always presupposes some intentional construction of the object of understanding, the final determination of which, as in all good science, then depends on the assessment of the concrete case at stake.

13 The principle of charity is similar in outcome to Gadamer's premise of an anticipation of rational completeness, which is hermeneutically grounded in the concept of a fusion of horizons as the unavoidable process of interpretive understanding. However, while both emphasize the need for shared assumptions to get interpretation going, Gadamer equally asserts the need to be open to alterity within the interpretive process.

14 The belief in a multiplicity of Gods is either an endorsed and positive part of a polytheistic universe or else must mean, in the context of a monotheistic worldview, the negatively evaluated existence of demons (see MacIntyre, 1971).

15 The uniqueness of such an account of causal or structural explanation versus the intentional hermeneutic interpretation consists, however, in the fact that the general perspective on agency remains based on an intentional understanding. We have seen that such an approach is necessary to identify human agency and to gain epistemic access to the meaning at stake. For the persistence of intentionality (or ' teleology'), see also Turner (2003); for a critique of universalizing the explanatory attitude toward all beliefs and assumptions, see McCarthy (1989).

16 While Gadamer is right to invoke caution with regard to assuming an explanatory position over and above the self-understanding of the other, the last point begs the question inasmuch as the socially caused distorting influence on the *rational* self-understanding of the agents is what is at stake. At the same time, Gadamer is certainly right that reference to a universal standpoint, similar to a God's-eye view, is impossible and ruled out if one has understood the hermeneutic point regarding background understanding (see Kögler, 1999).

17 Searle (1995) explores the implications of speech act theory for a general theory of social agency and social understanding.

18 Such a 'critical hermeneutics' of unmasking power-related and unacknowledged factors of one's traditional fore-understanding accepts the radical situatedness of all interpretation and thus remains firmly within the confines of an approach based on intentional understanding.

19 To bring out its methodological core might help us reconnect empirical studies of concrete phenomena to a theoretical understanding of social reality. The fact that the social scientist has to draw on his or her own background understanding is especially attractive here, because it shows that the ontological constitution of individual agency, which is itself mediated with the social structure by a holistic background, is akin to the methodological grounding of social-scientific interpretation. The argument that intentional agency understands intentional agency, and does so on the basis of a similar ontological–hermeneutic structure, thus comes full circle.

21

New Controversies in Phenomenology: Between Ethnography and Discourse

Mark J. Smith and Piya Pangsapa

INTRODUCTION

Phenomenology has so often been associated with the history of sociological theory, social research and ethnographic practice that at times it is easy to treat it as part of the barely noticed conceptual furniture of the way that social science is conducted. Whenever words like understanding, meaning, typifications and authenticity are used, they are often said with unacknowledged phenomenological assumptions embedded in the sentence deployed. In addition, insights from phenomenology are often synthesized with concepts and theories from other traditions, including structuralism, interactionism, neo-Marxism, poststructuralism and discourse analysis. As a result, it is often difficult to identify exactly where phenomenology has had an influence on contemporary research practice. Nevertheless, it is an important task to identify the ways that the phenomenological approach has been deployed. This chapter explores how phenomenology has informed the conduct of social science and still continues to do so. Moreover,

it considers the relevance of the *postulate of adequacy* in offering a solution to the problem of scientism in knowledge production as the character of research shifts from disciplinary to transdisciplinary fields of inquiry, offering an approach to research that is object-oriented rather than procedure-bound.

While phenomenology informs diverse fields within philosophy, bringing in, amongst others, Dilthey, Husserl, Heidegger, Merleau-Ponty and their poststructuralist progeny, in the social sciences there is distinctive contribution from both Schütz and Garfinkel, respectively portrayed as the originators of mundane phenomenology and ethnomethodology. In their own distinctive ways they attempt to make phenomenological insights 'intelligible' within contemporary social science, taking account of what is assumed to be unquestioned while at the same time systematically problematizing these assumptions, opening up gaps in the field, pointing to the vast repertoires of human experience that have been overlooked, and challenging both the ontological and epistemological assumptions of traditional explanatory social science while at the same time integrating sociological theories such as pragmatism and forms of neo-Kantian social theory. Following the diaspora after the rise of Nazi Germany, phenomenology entered into a creative dialogue with those kinds of social science that were compatible with the anti-scientistic sociological and political-economy approaches through which émigré theorists and researchers were able to assimilate into the discourses of the host communities they inhabited (Smith, 2000a).

As an approach to knowledge, phenomenology has been concerned with the interpretive techniques that understand meanings, often at the expense of generating general explanations (or at least that is the way that explanatory methods are understood by empiricist and even certain kinds of non-empiricist idealist epistemologies such as neo-Kantian and rational choice approaches). Explanatory methods seek to generalize from particular cases to all cases of the same type in order to establish their authenticity. However, phenomenological social research and those approaches informed by phenomenology start from the presumption that evidence about specific conditions of a particular time and place may not be open to generalization about all situations. The mundane phenomenology of Alfred Schütz draws together the three strands of Weberian neo-Kantianism, Bergson's intuitionism and Husserl's transcendental phenomenology as addressed in the next section.

BEYOND THE EGO – THE LEGACY OF A STRANGE ENCOUNTER

This was in large part a result of the peculiar conditions of the synthesis of the philosophical sensitivities of continental philosophy and the hard-nosed reliance on the authoritative discourses of empiricism by mid-twentieth century American social science. Before we address this, it is crucial to provide more context, in particular on the contribution of Edmund Husserl (1931, 1960, 1970) providing a significant extension (and what he believed to be a more rigorous analysis) of Cartesian thinking in developing phenomenology. The main purpose of this account was to demonstrate the fallacies and prejudices in objective and detached scientific inquiry, while at the same time challenging the separation of the objective world from subjectivity. For Husserl, it was crucial to move beyond the *ego–cogito* principle ('I think, therefore I exist') through which conscious reasoning enabled us to provide accounts of the external world, and instead proposed *ego–cogito–cogitatum*: that acts of thought involved intentionality or thinking about something and as such that the ego was intimately involved in the constitution of the objects of the external world. In addition, he developed the technique of the *transcendental epoche* (phenomenological reduction) or 'bracketing' of the objective—whereby phenomenologists suspend their belief in or abstain from judgment about the existence of the external world, so that conscious reflection is the sole focus. In terms of the Kantian tradition, since things are created through acts of consciousness, the distinction between phenomena and noumena can no longer be sustained.

For Husserl, this process led to a very specific problem: in a state of pure consciousness, how can the transcendental ego accept the existence of other egos, and as a result how do we understand the ways in which subjectivities are connected to each other? The problem of addressing precisely this issue is the source of the project of phenomenological or mundane sociology. Shortly after the original German publication of *The Phenomenology of the Social World* (1932/ 1967), Husserl recognized Schütz's talent in penetrating the core meaning of his project. In particular, Schütz transformed the problem identified by Husserl into its solution. For Schütz, it is the condition of 'intersubjectivity' through which actors are able to grasp each other's identities and at the same time construct their own lifeworld (*lebenswelt*)— i.e., that intentionality is a social product based on active engagements in everyday life. This approach synthesizes Husserl's account with critical insights on Max Weber's conception of ideal types (the deliberate simplification in order to make sense of complex situations) and Henri Bergson on intuition and the 'simultaneity of experience' (the shared time and space through which actors communicate) so that meaning and understanding can be located in the 'stream of consciousness'.

Once located in the US after 1939, Schütz incorporated the pragmatist thinking of John Dewey and William James to explore the simultaneous coexistence of the alter ego and through this elaborated his account of the use of typifications in intersubjective exchanges as a route to discover the taken-for-granted common-sense assumptions through which the social appeared orderly and predictable. Rather than a problem, the ability of actors to understand each other by grasping what is going on in each others' minds provides a route to knowledge of lived experience (Schütz 1932/1967: 112–3). Many of these insights were the product of methodological discussions in the *Miseskreis* 1928–30 in Vienna, where the chief concern was refocusing the central problem of economics from being about rationalist and utilitarian state planning (which Hayek later referred to as the 'fatal conceit') to the coordination of plans in a situation where knowledge is acknowledged as widely dispersed and unevenly distributed. Since phenomenology has been so associated with sociology and related areas of social-scientific practice, the original impetus in what is today described as the field of institutional economics and liberal political philosophy, whereby the social is understood as a the result of a spontaneous process of mutual exchange, is often overlooked. In addition, he saw all lifeworlds as constituted 'within the framework of the categories of familiarity and strangeness, of personality and type, of intimacy and anonymity. Furthermore, each of these worlds would be centered in the self of the person who lives and acts in it' (Schütz, 1943: 136).

It is crucial not to see the self as pregiven, fixed or even as a conclusive identity generated by childhood experiences (as outlined in the kinds of psychoanalysis emerging during Schütz's lifetime). The self is always underway and in process; moreover it is re-invented and open to transformation through exchanges with others. This insight operated in parallel with symbolic interactionism, where socialization is viewed as a lifelong process and where the institutional context of the research can be problematized, such as Goffman's concern with the way total institutions in a mental health context can lead to the 'mortification' and reconstruction of selves so that they can be rehabilitated in 'normal' society.

It is in this sense that Schütz sought to find an appropriate balance for researchers between detachment and involvement and between concepts that offered some means of generalizing while at the same time retaining the insights of understanding particular contexts. For example, he developed the metaphors of 'the stranger' (Schütz, 1943; 1944) and 'the homecomer' (Schütz, 1945) as a way of epitomizing particular types of relationships between the researcher and research subjects or physical environments. The stranger works somewhere between detached experts and indigenous natives by being detached enough to identify patterns and ways of thinking that are taken as tacit knowledge in the context in question. The homecomer captures the experience of moving from a place and returning, recognizing the key cartographic features and landmarks but feeling a sense of distance from the changes that have been wrought in the absence of the observer.

Mundane or Schützian phenomenology has had a significant impact on the conduct of social research since the mid-twentieth century, providing a persuasive epistemological standpoint (though not the only one) for understanding the meanings of everyday life. While this branch of phenomenology has often been portrayed as an antidote to empiricist and some forms of neo-Kantian idealist approaches to knowledge production (those concerned with constructing objective knowledge), it also provides an opportunity for reconciling the goals of explaining and understanding social relations and processes and in finding an appropriate balance between detachment and involvement. Schützian approaches also aid social-scientific practitioners in the difficult task of conceptual clarification, providing a manifesto for a more 'realistic' or 'practically adequate' social science. While phenomenology has found some disciplinary audiences more receptive (in particular, sociology) the adoption of this standpoint has been most explicitly welcomed in applied social science characterized by research in the context of application. Recently, phenomenology has been taken as a source of inspiration in mapping the emergence of 'transdisciplinary knowledge' (mode two knowledge production) in the 'new production of knowledge' debate. This chapter will assess the efficacy of mundane phenomenology in providing a map of the current state of socially distributed knowledge and its institutional context.

In the conclusion, we focus on the contemporary terrain of social science as increasingly object-oriented rather than procedure-bound. To aid us in the task of doing so, Schütz provides a principle and two postulates. The *principle of relevance* invokes the need for researchers to take account of the motives and intentions and the means and ends of the agents at work in any specific context that serves as the object of analysis. Two recommendations follow: the *postulate of subjective interpretation*, that social researchers should ask what type(s) of identity can be constructed and what typical thoughts and motives can be attributed in order to explain and understand the situation in question; and the *postulate of adequacy*, so that each term or concept used by the researcher should be constructed so that the social relations and processes described are intelligible to those being studied. As a result, the use of phenomenological insights is best characterized as a deployment of a set of ongoing practice where the outcomes are provisional. Indeed, as Hammersley and Atkinson's (1995: 229) response to Schütz's account of the 'stranger' highlights, meanings are grasped

retrospectively. For this reason the next two sections focus on the relationship between phenomenology with ethnography and discursive social science to convey how the basic principles or postulates have been translated into a set of methodological procedures and a substantive field within an academic discourse.

ETHNOGRAPHY AND PHENOMENOLOGY

Phenomenological methods have been more often incorporated into other social research traditions rather than operating as a distinctive set of research methods. The main starting point is to approach social relations as accomplishments and understand that these are shaped through intersubjective relations. As a result qualitative research techniques (in-depth interviews and participant and non-participant observation) are often preferred in order to understand the meanings and intentions of those involved. While quantitative sources are not excluded, they tend to play less of a leading role in phenomenological research and are approached in a different way. For example, a phenomenologist would be more interested in how secondary sources are constructed, the assumptions behind the selection and use of data, such as Jack Douglas's (1967) analysis of suicide statistics and the problematization of Durkheim's classic study on this issue for accepting coroners' decisions at face value and ignoring the common-sense assumptions and values that inform the classification of deaths. Ethnography has a more problematic history arising from anthropological research that often emphasized detachment and objectivity, imposing the assumptions of Western societies when interpreting the evidence gathered during fieldwork within other cultures (for example, assuming the normality and universality of particular kinds of family, kinship and community networks).

Even today, this remains an issue. For example, Chandra Mohanty (2003) has criticized both western feminist and 'Third

World' ethnographic researchers for writing about the other or their own cultures from a Western ethnocentric standpoint. As a useful corrective to this problem, Baca Zinn (2001) examines Chicano (Mexican-American) families in order to talk about the ethnographer as insider, offering her perspective as a minority researcher (sharing the same ethnic identity with the Chicano women) while at the same time being an outsider as a researcher, in order to consider marital power relations and the gender dimensions of conjugal roles within this culture. She concluded that being an insider contributed to the quality of her work; that it is less likely to prompt hostility and distrust from respondents; that as a researcher she had a better understanding of the nuances of the group and avoided the problems created by the self-protective strategies for dealing with outsiders—of 'being allowed to see only what people of color want them to see' (Baca Zinn, 2001: 160). In another example of a researcher doing similar work, Patricia Zavella (1996) found that, despite having the same gender, class and ethnic background of Chicano working mothers in the US, being a researcher and a feminist campaigner in the Chicano movement had changed her, creating a distance between her experiences and those of her respondents. Consequently, she was forced to recognize that she did not sufficiently question her own identity and that this hindered her work with the respondents. This demonstrates the complexities of managing the insider and outsider roles simultaneously, and that it can never be assumed and is always an accomplishment in qualitative research.

These examples show how contemporary ethnographic research now combines reflexivity when it comes to sense-making in the field as well as interpreting texts in the field and within the academy, with a stronger awareness of the role of the observer external to the group being investigated, primarily to avoid being a non-observing participant. This can go too far, since the belief in the independence of the observer may inhibit the researcher's awareness of the impact of their presence on the group's behavior and even how they understand their social context. The rhetoric of ethnography as a process of discovery of the respondents' lives by a neutral and independent inquirer can also mean that the researcher's interpretations of events are privileged over those of the respondents. Critical ethnography (explored in more detail below) adopts a position that deliberately embraces the values and norms of the researcher, deploying ethnographic research in pursuit of social and economic emancipation and aiming to produce accounts of the (often marginalized) groups under investigation that do more than just discover but can change the power relations in these contexts and prompt reassessment of the stigmatized and pathologized characterization of such groups. For example, Michael Burawoy (1991: 271), in responding to the critique of participant observation as 'incapable of generalization and therefore not a true science', develops the 'extended case method' to establish better connections between theory and research techniques and increased reflexivity. He urges researchers to document diverse forms of resistance or struggles that are taking place, in order to highlight the totalizing nature of the capitalist system. It is the recognition of the normativity of ethnographic research that leads us to consider how phenomenology can provide a useful guide for working through these issues.

In another example from the critical tradition, the importance of the postulate of adequacy comes into high relief. Ann Ferguson's study of the 'Holy Grains' workers' collective bakery in San Francisco focused on both the internal structure and external factors that contributed to the longevity of the collective. She felt obligated to provide the research outputs to the group studied: the conduct of meetings, the characters and how they resolved problems and crises; and the power relations between drivers, and baggers and bakers as work teams, which she labeled different 'castes' in the work setting. She portrayed the delivery drivers as the 'warrior caste' because they retained control over their wages and work conditions, in part as a result of their autonomy and having to respond to traffic delays and unpredictable difficulties in delivery. She 'wanted the group to validate my findings by recognizing themselves in the story she was telling' (Ferguson, 1991: 128), and consequently sent the paper to one of the respondents (a female baker), who then set up a meeting so that she could make an oral summary of her findings to the workers. In making herself intelligible to the group, she solicited feedback and responded to comments at the meeting, and also met individuals who had more detailed comments (including one respondent who claimed that no outsider can really capture the reality of the bakery and another providing six pages of single-spaced comments). For these reasons, we can see why Diane Wolf (1996) argues that feminist ethnographers view phenomenology (and associated approaches) as being a preferable starting point for revealing a women's standpoint in a way not captured in other epistemologies.

While Schütz originally stressed the importance of drawing upon first-order constructs to inform the second-order constructs of researchers and theorists in the 1940s and 1950s, the progressive political implications of this insight were developed later in these kinds of ethnographic research. It should be added that this association of phenomenology with progressive and radical thought is fairly recent, emerging during the cultural revolt of the 1960s. Indeed, Schütz is more accurately characterized as a liberal concerned to avoid social engineering and protect the liberties of individuals. While a part-time scholar for most of his life, Schütz was closely associated with the early emergence of neo-liberal associations, including key intellectuals in this movement, such as Ludwig von Mises and Friedrich von Hayek, and his initial work was more focused on the methodological problems of economics than on sociology (Schütz, 1932/1967). The association with classical liberal thinking, and the dangers of state power and intervention in the coordination of plans in the market, shaped Schütz's early writings as well as his affiliations with members of the Mont Pelerin Society (MPS) from the late 1940s (including acting as a recruitment sergeant for a business-member of the MPS). In a similar way to Hayek, he commented on how the attachment to detachment and preference for objective knowledge in empiricist and neo- Kantian philosophy had generated conceptual confusion in social science, highlighting six different ways in which the concept of rationality can be understood, the analysis of which was later extended by Garfinkel to fourteen kinds of rationalities (Garfinkel, 1960; Schütz, 1943, 1953; Smith, 1998, 2000a).

Garfinkel's approach takes Schützian phenomenology and applies it to the central problem of sociology: the problem of order, a preoccupation of Garfinkel's doctoral research, supervised by the functionalist Talcott Parsons. However, Garfinkel was not concerned with the integration of social (sub-)system nor interested in producing a grand theory to rival Durkheim's account of social solidarity. Instead, he sought to understand 'orderliness' in everyday social relations, processes, events and states of affairs. Order is thus portrayed as ordinary and indigenous to lived experience as well as self-organizing, not in the sense of an autopoietic system but rather as a 'spontaneous order' analogous to the notion of social order developed by Hayek (1960). When considering the relationship between the knowing subject and objects of analysis, Garfinkel recognizes the complicity between the researcher and the people studied. The ethnomethodologist is epistemologically presented as being in the same situation as those who participate in the situations serving as the focus of inquiry, recognizing that the identities of the researcher(s) are engaged in the activity flows of the context of application in the same way as respondents. It is in this sense that Garfinkel advocates the importance of understanding how 'practical reasoning' generates orderliness (or, as some put it, lived ordering) as part of the production of reality in specific social settings. In this sense, both phenomenology and ethnomethodology prompt lower-case theorizing in reconstructing the taken-for-granted common-sense knowledge that informs empirically observable actions and interactions. In this way both challenged the received view of the purposes of scientific accounts of 'the social' and, in particular, the assumption that social scientists can provide a detached account and authoritative knowledge of the institutions that regulate and administer human populations.

In some ways then, it may not be surprising that Schütz's legacy is so often associated with radical thought and social constructionism, especially their critique of how existing institutions reproduce power relations. When considering the humanist and libertarian direction of many currents of radical and socialist thinking after the 1950s, when Western Marxists were distancing themselves from the political oppression and economism of the Marxist-Leninist tradition (Anderson, 1976), social research focusing on the micropolitics of control, domination and classification of human behavior as deviant and the consequent challenges to 'normality' lends itself to this task. The focus on marginalized groups and the operation of power relations in research from the 1960s through to the 1980s demanded an account of subjectivity that could be harnessed by critical analysis concerned with economic exploitation, political domination and ideological mystification.

This is best summed up by Howard Becker's plea for research partisanship. In 'Whose side are we on?' (Becker, 1967), he wrote that researchers should recognize the plight of underdogs, stand in their shoes and provide a voice for those groups who lacked the capacity to speak on their own behalf. Schütz's appeal for research to draw from the everyday life of those studied, and at the same time produce knowledge outputs that would be intelligible to those groups, provided a unique contribution to emancipatory social science, even if that had not been his original intention. Critics of radical social science (who were themselves concerned to maintain the role of authoritative experts to speak on behalf of others) unkindly designated these attempts to represent the

marginalized as 'the sociology of nuts and sluts'. Of course, there are always problems of authenticity when researchers attempt to represent the experiences, values and beliefs of groups that lack a voice or are subject to the pathologizing practices of mainstream social science, practices that convey the status of the group as 'abnormal'. This is still an important issue in contemporary qualitative social science.

In critical ethnography, which explores the ways in which ethnographic research can contribute towards emancipatory praxis, these issues remain paramount. For example, Katherine Fox's study of AIDS and the politics of prevention among drug users involved the use of observation and interviews with outreach workers who were themselves former drug users. By comparing conventional drug rehabilitation and intervention with innovative outreach strategies, Fox notes the problems of stigmatization in public health discourses (based on biomedical assumptions) compared to ethnographic models which see drug subcultures as a social problem. In public health, rehabilitation involves falling into line with the expectations of treatment from relevant authoritative experts—that drug dependency is a personal difficulty rather than a social problem (Mills, 1959). However, the public health approach had clearly demonstrated its inadequacy in realizing the objectives of reducing dependency on narcotics.

The outreachers understood the drug subculture, using their distinct experiences to promote clean drug use. They developed ethnographic techniques to gather information through detailed observation. They were also able to develop a relationship based on a degree of trust with drug users—they were seen as credible in the street culture. The outreachers were, in effect, treading a fine line between insider and outsider (Hammersley and Atkinson, 1995). Fox discovered that while the outreachers were pessimistic of the effectiveness of the public-health model, describing it as exhausting and unrealistic, and that the ethnographic model helped to counter the despondence of the outreachers by dealing with hidden groups on their terms, this alternative approach was still not a panacea. While the ethnographic approach helped to normalize drug users and lessen the effects of stigma, and hoped that it can change and will change some behaviors when drug users are motivated to avoid consequences of ill-health, they worried about reinforcing drug use (for example, handing out needles and bleach to prostitutes as preventative measures for HIV infection).

In this case, ethnography contributed to a better understanding of drug subcultures and drew attention to the need to change the way that drug use is viewed by the Federal and State Agencies. Fox argued that a structural (sometimes referred to as 'macro-social world') perspective is necessary as well, as advocated by Burawoy (1991). There are always limits to the effectiveness of ethnographic research which depend on broader issues of power relations. For Fox herself, the experience was also transformative. On entering the field, she was influenced by an unhappy outreacher who described the public-health approach as 'bandages for the wounds of communities rather than cures for social problems' (Fox, 1991: 245). As a result she explored the tricky insider/outsider issue and highlighted the problems of ethnographic researchers having no personal affinity with the groups being studied. Fox valued the expertise of outreachers over her own and saw this as morally superior to current academic research on the issues in California. However, by the end of the research, she realized she had less in common with the outreachers (using ethnographic techniques themselves) than she presumed and concluded that she lacked the capacity to become an insider. According to her respondents, no amount of ethnographic training could ensure that her interpretations were 'correct'. While her disenchantment with research in academic sociology was reinforced, she found that she did not feel at home either within the academy or on the street. What was considered to be sociologically important was often not the case in the field; in fact, she felt guilty and ashamed at

being an ethnographer in this subculture, even potentially guilty of exploiting the outreachers for professional gain, feeling that it was like moving back and forth between two lifeworlds.

While the Fox study deals with a group that is criminalized and seen as a threat to the social order, research studies on other marginalized and powerless groups—e.g., homeless women—also raises issues of trust and access. While vagrancy remains a criminal offense in the UK and homeless people are pathologized in both the mass media and the academic research literature, the next case study highlights how the same issues arise for researchers studying a group that is not remorselessly policed for criminal intent. Annabel Tomas found that with this vulnerable and semi-literate group of respondents, who had a justifiable history of distrust with authoritative persons, many conventional research techniques were simply inappropriate and even alienated her respondents, and felt that she had to find a new way to gain their trust and build a clearer picture of their experiences and understandings. The visual life history interview technique developed by Tomas used visual representations that are constructed by the subjects in conjunction with the researcher, to re-establish forgotten knowledge and establish links between experiences of education, phases of housing instability and personal relationships. In the process, the homeless women in the study made sense of their lives and their relationships, and even erased memories of abusive and exploitative relationships in their past.

Two relevant aspects of this study can be highlighted here. First, Tomas found that her own understanding of the experiences of homeless women had transformed her as well. In this respect, the key point was joining homeless women on the street in Brighton (UK), in this instance actually sitting on the street where the homeless engage in begging, a place that she had previously regarded as one for walking, not sitting. It was not just a matter of developing an empathetic relationship with her respondents but seeing how the world was constructed for them, and examining the responses of others towards homeless women. Second, her interviews and visual life histories provided crucial insights into the meaning of 'home' for homeless women. For people who are not homeless, the meaning of home was a place, in a physical location or compared to some notion of 'ideal home', whereas for homeless women she came to understand that the meaning of home was relationships with other people, not with place. So, when researching subjects in action, asking why it is that they are doing it this way and why the subjects that researchers observe act in particular ways at different times, the aim is to establish how they adapt and change in the environment in question, at the same time as allowing the ethnographer to contextualize and make sense of their actions. In short, interventions such as these create the possibility that the ethnographer may change not just behavior but how the subjects view themselves, reflecting on their taken-for-granted common-sense assumptions while at the same time experiencing the same processes. This is the essence of ethnographic reflexivity.

While the examples provided so far focus on subcultures and groups that exist at a distance from mainstream culture, people with disabilities have also been subject to the detached expertise of those in authoritative positions within biomedical institutions. In particular, people with autism or Asperger's Syndrome have been subject to pathologizing practices in medicine and psychology, to the point that they were often classified as 'imbeciles' or 'sociopaths' and placed in institutional care. While it is increasingly recognized that autism is simply an exaggeration of a fundamentally human trait, the capacity for dealing with detail, attributions of blame for what was described as a 'disorder' have included 'cold mothers' as well as mercury poisoning and, most recently, childhood vaccinations. Medical diagnosis, which remains essential to the release of financial resources for educational support and disability benefits, often stereotypes people with autism as suffering from communication 'disorders', obsessional behaviors and the

inability to feel emotions such as shame and guilt (a classificatory practice that connotes the absence of conscience). Wendy Lawson, a researcher with Asperger's Syndrome, draws on her own experiences and those of other people with autism to challenge these medical classifications. Rather than accepting the implicit use of categories of normal and abnormal, she focuses on how autism is better understood as the inability to deal with change and the behaviors of 'neurotypicals'. For example, *monotropic* and repetitive behavior is reinterpreted as a way of imposing order on the world to make things predictable while *literality* inhibits the ability to interpret the use of analogy and metaphor in neurotypical communication. Lawson draws upon the first-order constructs of the emerging 'Aspie social movement' to reveal the inadequacies and misinterpretations of scientific research, which imposes classificatory systems and the values and assumptions of neurotypicals on a group of people that simply think differently, and at the same time prompt a re-evaluation of how people with intellectual impairments should be understood.

The marginalized and the powerless are not always groups classified as 'abnormal' but simply vulnerable and disposable. In the sweatshops of Southeast Asia, many of the manufactured goods available in the consumer economies of Western societies, ranging from T-shirts, leather goods and lingerie to jewelry and electrical products, are produced by women working at least 96 hours a week, 352 days a year in occupational settings without effective health, safety and labor regulations in place. The ethnographic research of Piya Pangsapa provides a vivid portrayal of these conditions, drawing on the experiences of women factory workers and how, against insuperable odds, they manage to organize in defense of their interests. Pangsapa went into this intensive research project assuming docility amongst workers at the end of the global supply chain as well as the effectiveness of factory discipline and wanted to find out why. As the research project unfolded, rather than seeing factory women as dominated and compliant with gender-specific norms, she discovered that they were adversarial, proactive, capable, hard-headed, outspoken and 'no nonsense' in their responses to their situation. In addition, her presence as an ethnographic researcher caused them to reflect on their own situation, becoming more independent and more conscious of their own assertiveness. In the case of the more militant women workers they also reassessed how they were making a difference by advising workers (including male workers) in other factories, joining NGOs and aligning themselves with other activist networks. Two workers, Pik and Nay, even became researchers for labor campaigns (often with inadequate resources from the sponsoring research institutes). They had distrusted the largely quantitative and technical methods of previous researchers (or perhaps the researchers' intentions), but the ethnographic research techniques of Pangsapa appeared as a 'genuine' attempt to hear their story, involving listening with interest.

As a result of the free flow of communication, Pangsapa put them at ease and the respondents were happy to share—i.e., she was seen not as extracting information just wanting to understand. As a researcher, Pangsapa makes remarks on the feelings of awe at such intimidating and articulate respondents who were able to bring the often dry and detached research literature to life. This project explored the variety of ways in which different groups of women subverted mechanisms of control. She also came to realize that research had to be adaptable, and that she had more in common with these women than she expected when considering differences of socio-economic background (i.e., a professional researcher working in the context of sweatshop production). In addition, Pangsapa discovered that humor can provide strategies against exploitation and hopelessness (that educated people from more privileged backgrounds can be uncivilized and childish) so that workers used imitation, ridicule and even pity to rise above the bad behavior of both female and male managers. The effects on the researcher included a crash-course in perseverance and sacrifice,

and subsequently her recent work has focused more on activist movements, seeking to make a concrete difference by highlighting how academic research should be relevant to the situation of respondents, although she continues to stress the importance of drawing on the *women's own voices* to convey their dignity and passion, and that justice has central place in research (Pangsapa, 2007).

These four studies highlight a crucial epistemological issue that illuminates how assumptions about knowledge construction both shape and are shaped by how researchers characterize the people, relations and processes they study. Researchers adopting a behaviorist approach assume that the actions of individuals are the result of direct stimulus-response relations. For example, behaviorism assumes that comments on intentions, purposes and motives are metaphysical speculation so that they only see the actual acts of respondents as relevant evidence. In contrast, phenomenology is interested in these intentions while at the same time recognizing that researchers have values, prejudices and purposes that should be acknowledged in research practice (i.e., that researchers and those people they study are reflexive agents that can alter or be transformed in the research process).

In assessing the contemporary role of phenomenology in the next section, this chapter also considers its potential contribution to the increasingly sterile debate between discursive approaches (often inappropriately and misleadingly characterized as 'social constructionism') and critical realism. Critical realists have attempted to appropriate insights from phenomenology on the role of tacit knowledge in order to address shortcomings (including the tendency to engage in pathologization), in an approach that tends to emphasize the 'pre-existence of social forms'. Critical realist traditions emerged from structuralist social science in the 1960s, in particular from Structuralist Marxism.

One of the difficulties faced by Marxist scholars was how to develop an adequate account of subjectivity to avoid the problems of determinism (especially economic varieties), at the same time as recognizing the formation of identities that have the potential of subverting or are conducive to the social reproduction of capitalism. Ethnographic and phenomenological insights and research experience provided the tools necessary for understanding the social reproduction of capitalist social relations. In what is now a classic study, *Learning to Labour* (1978), Paul Willis explored how the attitudes (including sexist and racist ones) and resistance strategies of working-class boys (described by respondents as 'having a laff') not only reinforced their sense of educational failure as being acceptable but actually led them to value manual work as the inevitable outcome for them as soon as they reached the minimum school-leaving age. Just as Willis explores how working class boys became working-class workers, so too Pangsapa demonstrates how the social relations between female factory workers and between workers and management are reproduced (sometimes in a modified way through intersubjective exchange)—that the 'structures in production' are reproduced, modified or even transformed through the agents in the process. This will be explored in more detail in the conclusion, but before we can approach that, the next section considers how phenomenology and ethnomethodology have been deployed in the emergence of discourse analysis.

DISCOURSE AND PHENOMENOLOGY

Discursive approaches have also drawn on phenomenology and ethnomethodology as part of their conception of data analysis as a craft-skill, although each appropriation is a partial one, taking elements of phenomenology alongside elements of symbolic interactionism and pragmatism, as well as approaches exploring the use of language and symbolic representation from social psychology, sociology and other social sciences. In the study of discourse as social interaction, whether in linguistics or sociology, it is the detailed analysis of written and printed representations of speech that often serve as the focus of study. Discursive approaches to research focus on three distinctive objects of analysis (social interaction; minds, self and sense-making; and culture and social relations) but it is also useful to consider *discourse* with a small 'd' and *Discourse* with a big 'D' (Yates, 2004: 233–45). *Discourses* can be understood as systems of knowledge that have a clear substantive organizing principle such as race, environmental degradation, justice, genetic science or neo-liberal politics. In these cases the organizing principle or key concept in the research provides the main focus for the researcher. In this context, *discourses* are those communicative exchanges that take place in a specific social situation where the focus of research could be communication in a school, hospital, clinic, university department or tutorial group. In short, the study of a *Discourse* will include the analysis of a variety of *discourses*, but it is also likely that research on a *discourse* in a specific situation will identify more than one *Discourse* as relevant.

For example, to study the *discourse* of genetic science, one might start by drawing upon the *discourses* of scientists (such as those involved in mapping the human genome, the application of genetic knowledge to animal cloning, and in medical practices such as genetic screening). In addition, in this example it is useful to explore the interventions of agents as diverse as concerned academics and researchers (such as Tom Shakespeare on the implications of genetic science for disabled people), policy communities (on health issues or, perhaps, the genetic modification of plants) and political organizations such as *Life* and animal rights groups (who articulate concern about the implications of genetic technologies for the unborn and non-human animals). In each case, it may be necessary to consider a range of texts from the formal publications of the scientists involved, seminars and workshops where scientists communicate with each other, or wider public forums such as public inquiries and television discussions, the interventions of concerned stakeholder groups (such as children with disabilities and their parents) and the varied forms of media reports on the issues involved. Both the primary sources of the varied dialogues on genetic science and a range of secondary sources will all be relevant.

If we start with *discourse* with a small 'd', for example by initiating a study involving discourse analysis of the attitudes and behavior of children and their interaction with teachers to understand differential educational attainment (why some children succeed or fail) in a specific set of classrooms, then the study may discover some of the reasons for the improved educational performance of female pupils as well as cast light on the reasons for gender differences between students from different ethnic backgrounds. In order to understand the complex relationships that exist in these classrooms, the researcher is likely to consider some aspects of *Discourses* of race/ethnicity, gender, social class, national culture, parental responsibility, juvenile delinquency and so on. Again the range of agents and textual sources are often diverse although selected according to the needs of the research project concerned. The onus is on the researcher to keep the focus clearly on the materials that address the rationale of the research. Discourse analysts with an interest in small scale face-to-face social interaction are more likely to be engaged in the study of *discourse*, while those with an interest in the regulation of the production of meaning with broader cultural and social relations are likely to focus on *Discourses*.

Turning to the first of the three substantive objects of inquiry, social researchers can provide insights into the everyday interactions of participants though this may be related to questions about identity and social organization (that are akin to *Discourse*) in some studies. Conversation analysis (CA) is concerned to use empirical evidence from direct observations of talk or transcripts of talk (in situations where the talk has been recorded on audio or video equipment). Drawing on Simmel and interactionist accounts, a clear distinction between form and content is assumed: between the specific content of each situation and the formal generalizations that could be made across a range of situations such as the concept of 'career' or 'total institution'. For example, Harvey Sacks is concerned with both the *content of talk* and the *structure of the interaction*—i.e., by specifying the structured features of talk, CA attempts to establish the *patterns* of communication (such as turn-taking in the roles of speakers and listeners). Of course it is difficult to predict specific outcomes in a conversation. Participants often speak simultaneously, introduce gaps or pauses in a dialogue, respond to earlier questions somewhat later in the sequence, redefine the questions asked so as to provide preferred answers, add different gestures and body language to statements so that the same words could have different meanings, and so on. Since conversations are notoriously unpredictable events, the best we can do is to try to map the tendencies that participants are likely to engage in. For example, it is possible to identify fairly common ways in which conversations are opened and closed, and there are grounds for seeing conversations as following sequences. Moreover, there are distinctive strategies for 'repairing' the damage of troublesome conversational interaction, such as veiled apologies, denials of received meaning, and changing the subject.

In practice, using previous studies by symbolic interactionists, such as those by Erving Goffman (1981), and ethnomethodologists (Garfinkel, 1967) as well as phenomenological insights and concepts identified above, this generates opportunities for a more practically adequate account of the meanings of those engaged in social interaction. In some cases, the focus is solely on the technicalities of interaction and sequences of talk, focusing on the 'surface meanings' that can be empirically identified in face-to-face exchanges. Others draw more on phenomenology and ethnomethodology in more detail, like Harvey Sacks, who sought to dig deeper into the tacit (taken-for-granted) knowledge of participants. By disrupting conventional exchanges, it is possible to shine a spotlight on where unspoken rules were violated and thus highlight the taken-for-granted rules of conduct in talking. Such studies also seek to establish the way that participants say one thing but mean another. Despite these differences, what they all agree on is that talk is not simply an unreflective action with utterances transferring meanings like containers moving goods. Instead they argue that participants are *actively doing talk*, seeking to accomplish goals by admonishing, rewarding, informing, persuading and cajoling (to name a few) as they talk.

If talk involves doing things, then special attention needs to be devoted to the context in which it takes place. The key issue is whether the context matters to the meanings of the talk. Yates (2004: 239) mentions a conversation about ballet at a football match: that if the conversation is solely about ballet the analyst may decide to ignore the context, but if, in the conduct of the conversation, the acrobatic skills and performances of players are compared, then contextual relevance has to be explored. Context for the discursive study of social interaction is therefore simply whether the surrounding environment has an impact on the content and structure of talk. While some researchers remain skeptical of the value of such research, some of the benefits of this kind of research include improving teacher–pupil or doctor–patient interactions or the 'ordinary' activities of air-traffic controllers. They also provide insights into the negotiations between different participants in an industrial dispute or the representatives of national governments engaged in resolving conflict and/or achieving a common international treaty for controlling the use of ozone-depleting chemicals or preventing deforestation (negotiations which have so far failed). When considering CA as research practice, in terms of providing careful and detailed empirical evidence of speech or talk, it is potentially classifiable as empiricist; however, it is not engaged in the search for empirical regularities (i.e., if x then y), for conversations are much more malleable and unpredictable. Moreover, it is assumed that the mental constructs aiding understanding of conversational interaction can be stated prior to empirical research (an

idealist assumption). In addition, in focusing on *talk as doing*, a focus on human intentions is explicit (as is the role of values), though there is also a stress on how this works in the social context in which the talk takes place. The links with those forms of idealism with a clear focus on intersubjective relations provide a clear and explicit link to the idea of doing empirical research without the assumptions of empiricism.

Discursive psychologists are concerned with *function*, *construction* and *variability* in discourse in order to challenge traditional psychological explanations of attitudes that treat the mind as independent from language (an assumption that features heavily in survey research that observes, measures and explains attitudes as a description of a pre-existing mental state). Discursive psychology uses CA-type methods but does so in the context of models of language, interaction and the mind that draw from psychology. Rather than seeing language function in a mechanical way, Potter and Wetherell (1994) are interested in the functions that can be identified by seeing linguistic interventions as speech acts produced in specific contexts for a purpose (similar to the emphasis on talking as doing in CA). As a result participants select and use linguistic resources to construct versions of 'the social', though not always necessarily in a conscious way (unlike the focus on conscious purposes in idealist approaches, such as that associated with Weber). The construction of 'versions' highlights that participants in communication describe the social in different ways in order to attempt to match their talk to the situation with which they are faced. In short, participants' descriptions exhibit *variation* as they perform different actions and it is this variation that can provide useful clues as to what is happening in talk.

If all forms of representation are acts produced in specific contexts for a purpose, then, Potter and Wetherell argue, the uses of numerical data in 'factual accounts' can be seen in the same way, as quantification practices that are themselves situated. Factual accounts based on statistical evidence are reinterpreted in this approach as a form of storytelling, as a set of 'procedures through which some part of reality is made to seem stable, neutral and objectively there' (see Potter and Wetherell, 1994: 47–64). In a similar way to phenomenologists and ethnomethodologists treating official statistics as a topic of research rather than as an unquestionable resource (for example, that crime statistics are the product of a series of decisions by people in authoritative positions in the criminal justice process), so too discursive psychologists are interested in *discourses as a topic of research as well as a resource for research*. Unlike other qualitative research, discursive psychology suggests that form and content cannot be separated, that we should instead investigate 'words as deeds' in the rhetorical and argumentative organization of talk and texts.

Potter and Wetherell highlight the selective and purposeful uses of quantitative data by all agents of knowledge production; they use this to reflect on what *data analysis* itself means in the study of discourse. In place of the application of a codified set of procedures (as implied by the positivist 'assembly line' approach to knowledge) that can be applied to research techniques such as experiments and surveys, they present a significant part of discourse 'analysis' as a craft-skill involving careful planning and considered judgment. As part of the process of moving from data to conclusions and in attributing adequacy to the knowledge produced, they highlight five interconnected kinds of analysis.

1. *Variation or variability* is an effect of seeing discourse as a performance by participants while also acknowledging the inconsistency of communicative acts: for example, the same participants offering very different versions of an event tailored to context and the repertoires upon which they draw. In addition, participants may say the same things but mean very different meanings. Even small variations indicate that work is being done in the text; so, by studying and comparing these different versions, researchers can gain insights into the repertoires involved and also functionality (asking questions like 'why is this version in this context' or 'what does this version

achieve?'). As a result, this *variation can be used as a lever* to unpack the small differences in expression and classify statements in texts according to the purposes of the participants and the product of the different intentions of those involved, including the use of numerical evidence as part of quantification practices.

2. *Reading the detail* follows from a concern with variation, given that many researchers tend to focus on explaining processes—say, in the economy or the mind. In qualitative research, events tend to acquire a greater importance, and in discourse analysis it is the detail that serves as the main focus. There is no simple formula for reading the detail, given the processes of academic training where the objective is to offer a unitary summary or thumbnail sketch that can be generalized. Discourse analysis explores how categories are used (that 'rare' could mean 'unusual' or 'atypical' depending on the use), and therefore much depends on the performances of the participants.

3. *Looking for rhetorical organization* is a key 'orientation' for discourse analysis. If variation is to be identified through careful reading and interpretation, then researchers have to be sensitive to the uses of argument and evidence to substantiate and demolish claims and assertions. For example, participants are concerned to make clear and strong points on the incidence, diagnosis and prognosis of a particular issue. Discourse analysis tries to identify not only how arguments and claims are deployed but also where attempts are made to undermine the arguments and claims of other participants. If the participants have motivations and intentions, then so do the researchers, suggesting that reflexive self-awareness is a feature of 'the social'.

4. *Looking for accountability* involves a focus on the justifications or excuses that accompany arguments in the discourses studied. The construction of arguments, as versions of 'the social', does not take place in a vacuum. Potter and Wetherell draw on ethnomethodological insights that all human conduct involves strategies for making our claims robust (i.e., difficult to undermine). For example, when considering texts such as television programs, discourse analysts are looking for the taken-for-granted assumptions, the rhetorical arguments of documentary film-makers, how they are conducted in a genre-specific way, and the associated assumptions of impartiality and balance. The adoption of a format that connotes impartiality lends itself to the generation of the

audience's trust in the arguments made, conveyed in a format that suggests truth, accuracy, precision, fruitfulness and consistency.

5. *Cross-referring discourse studies* link the research project in question to the corpus of knowledge in the field. It should come as no surprise that discourse analysis draws upon a common stock of knowledge that is based on past research practice. All approaches to research justify their professional integrity and make claims to provide a unique insight into the social, to analyze both subtle phenomena or complex institutional situations. However, given that this is a relatively new field, it should also be expected that innovation and flexibility (as a form of craftwork) is demanded in the study of the complex relationships between *Discourse* and *discourses*.

In this way, discursive psychology highlights the connections between performances generating conceptions of others and ourselves, within the context of wider systems of representation (interpretive repertoires enabling certain ways of talking but also constraining talk that is not permitted) through the day-to-day interaction of conversations and the various types of text produced. This links insights from phenomenology to Mulkay's (1991) conventionalist notion of an 'interpretative repertoire' (the resources scientists use in negotiating the acceptance of specialized knowledge claims) and to a more common use of discourse drawn from the study of rhetoric and conversation analysis.

In common with conversation analysis, for discursive psychology it is the performance of participants that is crucial. The use of speech act theory from John Austin on words and talk as deeds highlights how participants draw upon linguistic resources, their competences, in order to accomplish goals through the uses of language. By synthesizing these approaches, they have generated insightful analyses of the meanings and uses of concepts such as 'community', racist attitudes and identity formation. Like phenomenology they recognize the intentions of researchers, that this also involves 'deeds', and that psychology is an explicitly moral and political science.

It is possible to criticize the looser understanding of data analysis and point to the dangers of failing to distinguish between collection, analysis and writing-up. In their defense, Potter and Wetherell argue that their object of analysis and their research practices make this impossible, but they do acknowledge the importance of finding a way to generate trust in their findings. In the place of these traditional criteria for ensuring valid knowledge, they do emphasize the role of the replication of studies of new discourses to substantiate the claims made. In reply to such critics, we could also consider the argument developed by Potter and Wetherell on quantification practices, for it poses a challenge to the uncritical use of evidence drawn from survey methods and statistics.

Finally, some kinds of discourse analysis are concerned with *Discourses*, specifically the role of systems of knowledge or representation in regulating the production of meaning. These tend to view *discourses* as exemplars or illustrations of a specific *Discourse* (i.e., *discourses* only have a bit part to play in social research of this type). The kinds of analysis here include the problematization of foundational concepts such as 'being' or 'the subject', as well as oppositions such as 'same/other' and 'reason/unreason' that have proved to be influential in the narratives of social science research. They argue that meaning is produced through the intertextual relations between elements that can be defined and combined in different ways—that meaning is established through the relations between words but also that *Discourses* are also always in process and changing, except in rare cases where they acquire a more solid grounding in our institutional practices (such as in the study of crime and juvenile delinquency). In particular, they highlight the use of devices such as the 'march of progress narratives' or stories that feature in social-scientific knowledge, such as applied social studies stressing the humanitarian and altruistic motives of welfare systems.

Foucault provides an alternative vision of such narratives as part of power–knowledge relations, where *Discourses* construct 'subject positions' that are either endorsed by us or imposed upon us. We often aspire to the idea of 'the effective manager' or the 'respected researcher', but for some the subject positions of 'juvenile delinquent', 'hysterical woman' and 'emotionally disturbed child' are imposed on individuals or groups of people, translating them from active into docile bodies, as objects of surveillance and control. As social scientists producing knowledge in these networks we are complicit in the power relations involved. Ethnographic methods are often used in this poststructuralist approach, such as Salzinger's study of female factory workers on the Mexican–US border, the forms of factory surveillance and discipline at work, sexual objectification, and whether through the women's experiences of exploitation, new subject positions can emerge to replace those of 'docile daughters' and 'impoverished mothers' with all their associations with 'habitual docility' (Salzinger, 2003: 165). The factories studied, labeled Panoptimex, Particimex, Andromex and Anarchomex, each highlight the role of gendered *Discourses* and each results in distinctive forms of 'subject position' formation. While it is not appropriate to elaborate here, research on the uses of ethnography in poststructuralist and other critical traditions of research, sometimes bringing discursive and critical realist approaches together as Critical Discourse Analysis (Fairclough, 1992, 2001), is long overdue.

The main critical response to discourse analysis, critical realism, like critical ethnography, is an explicitly normative approach seeking to promote human emancipation, although this is seen more in terms of transforming social structures where power relations operate (from unwanted to wanted kinds of determination). For critical realists, such as Roy Bhaskar (1989a, 1989b) and Andrew Sayer (1992), researchers need a better understanding of the underlying structures of the social world. Bhaskar and Sayer would accept that social structures (for example, gender and age relations in the family or the relations that structure the relationship between employer and employee) are saturated with meanings and are reproduced or changed through meaningful human interactions. However, they want to hold on to the notion that social structures

enable and constrain the range of meaningful human interactions that are possible. For Foucault, 'social structures' and 'real causes' are discursively constituted (Foucault, 1980, 1982); for realists, social structures are seen as the condition and the outcome of social agency—so structures are, in a sense, beyond social practices and discursive meanings, even though they only exist because of them.

Both these approaches (the realist and Foucauldian) accept that the social world is produced out of social meanings and practices and that these meanings and practices constitute social structures or 'formations'. However, they each emphasize a different kind of analysis. Realists give priority to a pre-existing social materiality which they see as shaping and limiting discursive practices. In contrast, Foucauldians emphasize the power of discursive practices to produce that which they name, suggesting that discursive practices produce the social materiality prioritized by realists.

This chapter presents a case for mundane phenomenology as a pathway that avoids some of the pitfalls of realist and discursive accounts. First, it provides a basis for constructing a research program that can acknowledge the discursive complexities of representation. Second, it offers a practical research focus on the embedded tacit knowledge within material practices, rules of conduct and institutional conditions. In turn, the discursive analysis of 'subject positions' and 'power/knowledge' relations also provides a new conceptual vocabulary with which mundane phenomenology can engage in a constructive dialogue. This chapter will also argue that in applying the 'postulate of adequacy' as a normative practice, social researchers are able to sustain the critical analysis of the lived experiences of social agents while seeking also to ensure that the knowledge produced is intelligible to those studied. This aspiration (for it is not always realized despite our hardest efforts) is one that will seek to ensure that the typifications devised by social researchers are less often imposed upon evidence and more often drawn from the situated knowledge of lived-experience. In this respect, the conclusion of this chapter

Table 21.1　Modes of knowledge production

Mode of knowledge production	Mode 1	Mode 2
Problem solving	Problems are set and solved in an academic community.	Problems are set and solved in the context of application.
Knowledge base	Disciplinary	Transdisciplinary
Extent of organizational unity/diversity	Homogeneity	Heterogeneity
Organizational form	Hierarchical	Heterarchical and transient
Communication of knowledge	Dissemination through established institutional channels [peer review journals, conferences]	Diffusion through problem solving and in new contexts of application [communication networks]

Source: Smith (2005: 166)

will attempt to clarify the criteria for producing socially robust and practically adequate knowledge of 'the social', 'orderliness' and the 'vocation' of the social scientist.

CONCLUSION: BEYOND CRITICAL REALISM AND POSTSTRUCTURALISM

At the start of the chapter, the 'new production of knowledge' debate was highlighted as a significant opportunity for drawing these strands of phenomenological influences together. Research on the organization of research and the status of disciplines has led to a dialogue with phenomenology. Gibbons et al. (1994) as well as Jacob and Hellstrom (2000) highlight the interconnection between the knowledge produced by researchers and the institutional context of its emergence in the academy. They draw a sharp contrast between Mode 1 (disciplinary) and Mode 2 (transdisciplinary) forms of knowledge production (see Table 21.1) to highlight the emergent diversity in research practice and the increasingly competitive criteria by which we judge what is valued in academic output.

Mode 1 exists in hierarchically organized disciplinary science primarily located in the university system, whereby accountability is located in the academy through mechanisms such as peer review and a promotional system that works on patronage (with the researcher's subject position being 'the custodian'). It is a 'complex of ideas, methods, values, norms'

established to diffuse knowledge in an appropriate way, in this case based upon a model of scientific practice, whereby failure to adhere to these norms ensures exclusion from the academic community. Mode 2 is non-hierarchical, operating within a context of application, where, as is common in the approaches considered in this chapter, research problems are not set in the disciplinary matrix but arise from elsewhere. It is characterized by a transdisciplinary approach and heterogeneous organizational forms constructed for the purposes at hand. Mode 2 social science, because it involves collaboration on a localized problem, involves a range of actors with greater opportunities for accountability within and beyond the academy. Quality control and assurance tend, therefore, to use a wider range of criteria and, according to Gibbons et al., create better conditions for reflexivity and social accountability, changing our conception of science at the deepest levels. Rather than science and scientists, in Mode 2 we have knowledge and practitioners with:

1　knowledge intentionally useful in industry, government and a variety of wider audiences;
2. knowledge formed through a process of negotiation between different agents with different interests (contrary to the pretence of disinterested detachment in disciplinary knowledge);
3. institutional diversity—Mode 2 work takes place in departments and laboratories but also in think-tanks, institutes, research centers and consultancy networks;

4. variety of application, not just in the traditional sense of applied knowledge, since M2 knowledge production reaches the parts that disciplinary knowledge fails to touch.

The focus in M2 is problem solving, which can only be achieved in a transdisciplinary way, whereby practitioners develop temporary agreements in the context of application and are prompted into creativity to make it work (or fail in the attempt) so that the end result does not map on to disciplinary knowledge. Since transdisciplinary knowledge is explicitly motivated by interests, it actively violates the fact/value distinction that remains an important part of the rhetoric of knowledge production in science. In *Rethinking Science*, Nowotny et al. (2001) revisit these issues in a more cautious way. Transdisciplinarity is seen as a response to the loss of belief in the project for unified knowledge, seeking to address this without simply bolting disciplines to each other (as in multidisciplinary social science) nor simply seeking new research questions by looking over the territorial boundaries of disciplines before retreating back into Mode 1 knowledge production (as in interdisciplinary social science). They go further to suggest that transdisciplinary research involves a form of problem solving that involves a process of communication between knowledge producers and the multiple heterogeneous stakeholders bringing different forms of situated expertise into the process and creating the scope for various criteria to be relevant in assessing the knowledge produced, replacing the sole use of reliability with 'socially robust' knowledge.

At this point, we need to find bridges to bring together these new strands in the textures of social science (phenomenology provides some of the tools for building this bridge), but the hostility between these strands remains a problem. For example, the cultural theorist Stuart Hall once remarked that when considering representation and the formation of identities (as provisional and in process), the critical realists 'just don't get it' (Hall, 1997a). However, at the same time,

poststructuralists are so preoccupied with novelty and innovative social change that they often neglect the impact of the pre-existing social structures in regulating the production of meaning. Actually, Hall is aware of the significance of this, but treats it temporally, as if it is 'history creeping in through the back door' (Hall, 1997b). There are some situations where structures matter more, while in others agency or discourses provide the starting point. In addition to providing a research program that recognizes the unsynchronized character of the empirical, the actual, and the real or the deep, critical realism also offers a new way of thinking through the issues in structuration theory raised by Anthony Giddens and the transformational model of social action developed by Roy Bhaskar. While Giddens privileges 'agency' as logically prior to structure, Bhaskar highlights the significance of pre-existing social formations (i.e., structures) over agency (Bhaskar, 1983; Giddens, 1984; Smith, 2002).

However, each is searching for a 'one-size-fits-all' theoretical basis for research practice rather than accepting, as phenomenology does, that starting with a specific object demands that we have more flexible procedures and criteria depending on the context of application. The density of the social structures at work in a specific context and their effectiveness in reproducing themselves is an empirical question, not a theoretical one. Phenomenology, like critical realism, highlights how necessity is *post hoc*, while when approaching new objects and ongoing processes the social relations involved should be regarded as contingent.

To return to an example from critical ethnography elaborated earlier, Pangsapa (2007) focuses on the relationships and experiences of two factories. These factories, drawing on the descriptions of the women workers themselves, are described as *Thai-Jai-Dee* (pronounced 'ji-dee' and meaning kind, kind-hearted or nice) and *Thai-Jai-Rai* (pronounced 'ji-rye' and meaning mean, without kindness or even heartless). The controlling mechanisms at one factory fostered acquiescence and accommodation, while objective conditions at another provoked worker discontent and rebellion. At *Thai-Jai-Dee*, control was maintained by providing workers with fairly decent working conditions along with mutual and cordial relations between management and workers. Dependence on overtime work and pay and paternalistic work arrangements fostered loyalty and worker commitment, while enabling the factory to profit from maximum labor productivity. At *Thai-Jai-Rai*, on the other hand, poor work conditions and a harsh working environment eventually led to worker discontent. Hence two currents of worker consciousness can be identified from within these two different work settings. But worker consciousness started to transform and change following the 1997 'economic crisis', whereby worsening conditions of work and pay compounded with fear and economic hardship differentially affected workers at the two factories. At *Thai-Jai-Dee*, women started to question their conditions at the same time that the factory was up for inspection. At the other setting, the 'crisis' led to a diminished workforce and caused workers to become less outspoken, more reserved and more fearful in voicing their demands as they tried to hold on to their jobs.

The women workers had many things in common—the internalization of the monotonous rhythm of assembly work and adjusting their living conditions with low wages—but differed in their responses to how that work affected and shaped them. While both groups accepted factory work to earn a living, women at *Thai-Jai-Rai* chose not to accept the work conditions and fought to challenge the management. The processes that shape women workers' consciousness were contingent on the structure of the workplace environment, treatment by employers, women's differential experiences within and outside the factory, and the dynamics and social interactions developed among the women themselves.

At *Thai-Jai-Dee*, women worked in a stable and stress-free environment, which they perceived to be their 'second home'. For both factories, long working hours stand out as the most exploitative conditions of factory work, but it was the deplorable working conditions, rather than the long working hours, that prompted the women at *Thai-Jai-Rai* to organize. Despite some of the unlawful practices at *Thai-Jai-Dee*, workers there did not feel threatened or abused, unlike workers at *Thai-Jai-Rai*, where deplorable working conditions and a poor work environment were permanent fixtures that ultimately provoked reaction. In addition, *Thai-Jai-Rai* workers had the opportunity to meet and mingle with unionized women workers from adjacent factories during their lunch or dinner breaks, or on their way to work. At *Thai-Jai-Rai*, this led to the discovery of unlawful practices at non-unionized factories and gave women workers the opportunity to talk about their working conditions. As a result, *Thai-Jai-Rai* women workers made their unity, camaraderie and their solidarity their 'home' (a parallel with Tomas's account of homeless women investing the meaning of 'home' in relationships rather than place) in the struggle for justice in the workplace. This transformed the workplace into a hotbed of worker militancy, as they built strong alliances among themselves and with other workers in their commitment towards achieving common goals.

These kinds of insights highlight four things that signify the importance of dialogue between the various strands of research drawing on mundane phenomenology considered in this chapter. First, only qualitative research based on a relationship between researcher and respondents characterized by trust is likely to provide insights on the precise conditions involved. Second, these insights are not purely limited to specific contexts but have the capacity for formal generalization across cultures and in future empirical research (in the case of the object of analysis for Pangsapa and Salzinger, this would be new research on other factories at the end of the global supply chain). Third, research should seek not only to draw on the first-order constructs of those studied but also aim to make the knowledge produced (the second-order constructs) relevant and intelligible to those studied. This implies that the marginalized and powerless actually do not need researchers to speak for them as such but that they just need academic investigations to start and finish with respondents in mind. Finally, to think of the conduct of research as primarily concerned with what feminist epistemologist Sandra Harding (1986) describes as the 'context of justification'— the collection of evidence, testing of hypotheses, interpretation and evaluation of evidence—neglects the 'context of discovery' where research problems are identified and the values upon which research conduct is actually based are determined. So, as part of reinventing the meaning of 'discovery' in research (including ethnography), we need to acknowledge that all social research is normative and can be the basis for securing change in unjust conditions.

Since phenomenology is often associated with the terms of debate from the mid-twentieth century, we propose that it is more accurate to think of this approach as neophenomenology (a product of its articulation in divergent forms of social research practice): as a sensible pathway for crossing between analytical and continental philosophical traditions as well as structure-centered and agency-centered modes of social inquiry (although it is likely that it is not the only such pathway, since discursive psychology may provide an alternative). By bringing together insights from critical ethnography, critical realism and poststructuralism while at the same time addressing the deficiencies of each in failing to acknowledge tacit knowledge (the taken-for-granted assumptions of agents), neo-phenomenology provides a route-map for making social research more relevant and applicable to the practical contexts that qualitative researchers investigate.

REFERENCES AND SELECT BIBLIOGRAPHY

Anderson, P. (1976) *Considerations on Western Marxism.* London: NLB.

Baca Zinn, M. (2001) 'Insider field research in minority communities', in R.M. Emerson (ed.), *Contemporary Field Research: Perspectives and Formulations.* 2nd Edition. Prospect Heights, IL: Waveland Press, pp. 159–66.

Becker, H. (1967) 'Whose side are we on?', *Social Problems*, 14 (3): 239–47.

Bhaskar, R. (1983) 'Beef, structure and place: Notes from a critical naturalist perspective', *Journal for the Theory of Social Behavior*, 1: 85–95.

—————— ([1979] 1989a) *The Possibility of Naturalism: A Philosophical Critique of the Contemporary Human Sciences.* Hemel Hempstead: Harvester Wheatsheaf.

—————— (1989b) *Reclaiming Reality.* London: Verso.

Burawoy, Michael (ed.) (1991) *Ethnography Unbound: Power and Resistance in the Modern Metropolis.* Berkeley: University of California Press.

Douglas, J.D. (1967) *The Social Meanings of Suicide.* Princeton, NJ: Princeton University Press.

Emerson, R.M. (ed.) ([1983] 2001) *Contemporary Field Research: Perspectives and Formulations.* Prospect Heights, IL: Waveland Press.

Fairclough, N. (1992) *Discourse and Social Change.* Cambridge: Polity.

—————— (2001) 'The discourse of New Labour: Critical discourse analysis', in M. Wetherell, S. Taylor, and S.J. Yates (eds), *Discourse as Data: A Guide for Analysis.* London: Sage, pp. 229–66.

Ferguson, A.A. (1991) 'Managing without managers: Crisis and resolution in a collective bakery', in M. Burawoy (ed.), *Ethnography Unbound: Power and Resistance in the Modern Metropolis.* Berkeley: University of California Press, pp. 108–32.

Foucault, M. (1980) *Power/Knowledge: Selected Interviews and Other Writings 1972–1977.* Brighton: Harvester Press.

—————— (1982) 'The subject and power', in H.L. Dreyfus and P. Rabinow, *Michel Foucault: Beyond Structuralism and Hermeneutics.* Brighton: Harvester Press, pp. 208–26.

Fox, K.J. (1991) 'The politics of prevention: Ethnographers combat AIDS among drug users', in M. Burawoy (ed.), *Ethnography Unbound: Power and Resistance in the Modern Metropolis.* Berkeley: University of California Press.

Garfinkel, H. (1960) 'Rational properties of science and common sense activities', *Behavioral Science*, 5 (1): 72–82.

—————— (1967) *Studies in Ethnomethodology.* Engelwood Cliffs, NJ: Prentice-Hall.

Gibbons, M., Limoges C., Nowotny, H., Schwartzman, S., Scott, P. and Trow, M. (1994) *The New Production of Knowledge: The Dynamics of Science and Research in Contemporary Societies.* London: Sage.

Giddens, A. (1984) *The Constitution of Society.* Cambridge: Polity.

Goffman, E. (1981) *Forms of Talk*. Philadelphia: University of Pennsylvania Press.

Hall, S. (1997a) 'Conversation with Mark J. Smith', *The Stuart Hall Conference*, Pavis, Walton Hall, The Open University.

———— (1997b) 'Response to Angela McRobbie', *The Stuart Hall Conference*, Pavis, Walton Hall, The Open University.

Hammersley, M. and Atkinson, P. ([1983] 1995) *Ethnography: Principles in Practice*. London: Routledge.

Harding, S. (1986) *The Science Question in Feminism*. Milton Keynes: Open University Press.

Hayek, F. (1960) *The Constitution of Liberty*. London: Routledge.

Husserl, E. (1931) *Ideas: General Introduction to Pure Phenomenology*. London: Allen and Unwin.

———— (1960) *Cartesian Meditations*. The Hague: Martinus Nijhoff.

———— (1970) *The Crisis of European Sciences and Transcendental Phenomenology*. Evanston, IL: Northwestern University Press.

Jacob, M. and Hellstrom, T. (eds) (2000) *The Future of Knowledge Production in the Academy*. Buckingham: Society for Research into Higher Education/Open University Press.

Mills, C.W. (1959) *The Sociological Imagination*. New York: Oxford University Press.

Mohanty, C.T. (2003) *Feminism without Borders: Decolonizing Theory, Practicing Solidarity*. Durham, NC: Duke University Press.

Mulkay, M. (1991) *Sociology of Science: A Sociological Pilgrimage*. Buckingham: Open University Press.

Nowotny, H., Scott, P. and Gibbons, M. (2001) *Re-thinking Science: Knowledge and the Public in an Age of Uncertainty*. Cambridge: Polity.

Pangsapa, P. (2007) *Textures of Struggle: The Emergence of Resistance Among Garment Workers in Thailand*. Ithaca, NY: Cornell University Press.

Potter, J. and Wetherell, M. (1994) 'Analyzing discourse', in A. Bryman and R.G. Burgess (eds), *Analyzing Qualitative Data*. London: Routledge, pp. 47–66.

Salzinger, L. (2003) *Genders in Production: Making Workers in Mexico's Global Factories*. Berkeley: University of California Press.

Sayer, A. ([1984] 1992) *Method in Social Science: A Realist Approach*. London: Routledge.

———— (1999) 'Long live postdisciplinary studies!', The British Sociology Association Conference, April, Glasgow.

Schütz, A. ([1932] 1967) *The Phenomenology of the Social World*. Evanston, IL: Northwestern University Press.

———— (1943) 'The problem of rationality in the social world', *Economica*, X (May): 130–49.

———— (1944) 'The stranger. An essay in social psychology', *American Journal of Sociology*, 49 (6): 499–507.

———— (1945) 'The Homecomer', *American Journal of Sociology*, 50 (4): 363–76.

———— (1953) 'Common-sense and scientific interpretation of human action', *Philosophy and Phenomenological Research*, 14 (1): 1–38.

Smith, M.J. (1998) *Social Science in Question: Towards a Postdisciplinary Framework*. London: Sage.

———— (2000a) *Rethinking State Theory*. London: Routledge.

———— (2000b) *Culture: Reinventing the Social Sciences*. Buckingham: Open University Press.

———— (2002) 'Rethinking normality through postdisciplinary practices: Philosophies of pathology', in D. Hook and G. Eagle (eds), *Psychopathology and Social Prejudice*. Cape Town: University of Cape Town Press.

———— (2005) 'Territories of knowledge', *International Studies in Philosophy*, 37 (2): 159–80.

Tomas, A. (1998) 'Interview with Mark J. Smith', BBC/Open University

———— (2004) 'The visual, life history interview', in S. Yates (ed.), *Doing Social Science Research*. London: Sage: 141–6.

Willis, P. (1978), *Learning to Labour: How Working Class Kids Get Working Class Jobs*. Farnborough: Saxon House.

Wolf, D.L. (ed.) (1996) *Feminist Dilemmas in Fieldwork*. Boulder, CO: Westview Press.

Yates, S. (2004) *Doing Social Science Research*. London: Sage.

Zavella, P. (1996) 'Feminist insider dilemmas: Constructing ethnic identity with Chicano informants', in D.L. Wolf (ed.), *Feminist Dilemmas in Fieldwork*. Boulder, CO: Westview Press, pp. 138–59.

22

Liberal Humanism and the European Critical Tradition

Douglas Kellner and Tyson Lewis

The birth of the modern European critical tradition can be traced back to the Enlightenment and in particular to the philosopher Immanuel Kant's (1724–1804) critique of reason. Kant's revision of the liberal humanist tradition replaced metaphysics (speculation about external reality) with critique. For Kant, critique consisted of tracing the origins of experience back to the faculties of the mind. Stated simply, before Kant, science described the world passively, but after Kant, science was seen to write on to the world what human categories imposed upon it. For Kantians, science no longer extracted knowledge from the proverbial thing-in-itself (which remains fundamentally unknowable): rather, science produced knowledge of the phenomena of the world.

Kant's analysis of the human mind attempted to understand cognitive faculties in order to determine the proper usages and limits of reason; hence his critique of pure reason was boundary setting. His work built a structured architecture of the mind in order to address three important questions: What can I know? How can I act morally? What can I hope for? Broadly speaking, Kant divided the mind into three components or faculties. First, the faculty of sensibility organizes the raw and chaotic manifold of sense materials in accordance with the forms of sensibility: space and time. These forms are an *a priori* possession of the mind rather than observed phenomena. Understanding, the second faculty of the mind, takes these appearances and files them under categories (unity, cause, etc.) producing objects of cognition. Reason (the third faculty) occurs when the understanding no longer applies itself to appearances or sensory objects. The result of reason is the production of ideas in the noumenal realm. Because ideas cannot be experienced directly, they do not have causes and are positioned in the a-temporal or metaphysical dimension. As such, no one can properly know that ideas such as God, freedom, or immortality exist; they cannot be subject to understanding.

Thus, in the end, Kant's critique of metaphysics does in fact rehabilitate a super-sensible reality. Only now, universals exist within the interior of the human mind rather than in external, objective reality. These ideas are not simply flights of fancy or chimeras. Although we cannot experience them, they nevertheless follow logical rules of thought, and we can reasonably act as if they exist. For Kant, acting as if freedom were possible is not delusional. In fact, it makes us act morally to conceptualize and act upon the ideas of God or freedom.

Kant's humanistic side is most clearly articulated in his theory of freedom. For Kant, humans are not simply the aggregate of natural forces. Humans are distinctly unique because we freely give to ourselves an imperative to follow. To be moral is to act in accordance with a universal law. In Kant's writings there are essentially two versions of this categorical imperative: act according to a maxim which can be a universal principle, and act in such a way that you treat humanity as ends, not means. To be moral is to act beyond the contingency and particularity of everyday life and to act in unison with a transcendentally possible imperative. Society as a whole must be measured against this imperative to see if it is rationally and thus morally true. In the end, by using reason properly and not confusing the faculties of the mind, Kant believed that pre-Enlightenment superstition, cruelty, and ignorance would be replaced by both individual liberty and universal peace. Thus, as Kant writes in the influential essay 'An Answer to the Question: What is Enlightenment?' (originally published in 1784), enlightenment is the courage to use our individual understanding properly to critique the irrationality of the world.

While Kant's intentions were progressive for the time, the results of his liberal humanist tradition of critique are to be questioned. As liberal humanism became a dominant cultural logic of Western society, it became increasingly problematic. For many later critical theorists, liberal humanism led to elitist, colonialist and patriarchal ideologies. Thus many of the central figures we will discuss here are in some way responding to this crisis in Kant's universalizing position, either attempting to reconstruct reason or reject it completely.

HEGEL'S CRITICAL DIALECTIC

If Kant's philosophical project can be summarized as an attempt to define a-historical categories and their functions, G.W.F. Hegel's (1770–1831) work could be seen as the interjection of time and history into such a system, rendering Kant's systematic absolutism into a historical organization of concepts. Whereas Kant sees the categories as timeless, Hegel sees in them a dimension of temporal unfolding through a series of immanent negations. Thus reality is no longer static but, rather, dynamic and developmental. This dialectical process will become central to the future of western theories of criticism; hence we must explain what Hegel means by dialectical movement.

For Kant, contradictions formed a series of antinomies that were permanently irreconcilable. Yet, for Hegel, contradictions are not so much problems as the motor through which concepts become increasingly more determinant. Contradictions are in fact the internal development of concepts. As such, negation is not simply destruction but is productive, leading on to ever higher levels of reason and ever more generalized and universal knowledge. In short, thinking is not simply the manipulation of preformed concepts but a movement and a development in which what has come before is not simply abandoned to the dustbin of history but rather understood as necessary phases on the road to absolute knowledge itself.

Hegel's dialectic sought to overcome a gap that Kant initiated between the thing-in-itself as a radically unknowable external object and the knowing subject. Through negation, Hegel is able to state that the object that is not a subject is an object. Seemingly redundant, this dialectical formulation proposes that the subject is at its core mediated by the object and the object is mediated by the subject. In other words, the subject becomes objectified and the object becomes subjectified. Thus the object contains within itself its negation (subjectivity) and the subject contains within itself a negative movement towards the object, thus producing a conceptual space for critique.

Hegel's *Phenomenology of Spirit*, published in 1807, thus teaches us how absolute knowledge is arrived at through negation, mediation and synthesis in the necessary unfolding of contradictions of consciousness. His is a philosophy of overcoming dualisms, synthesizing and summing up. It is a retrospective exercise that results in a new way of connecting with the past. This relationship to what has come before must be, for Hegel, complete without omissions (thus incorporating contradictions as inherent rather than aberrant) and transparent (rationally organized in a series of immanent negations through which problems are solved and new problems produced). In this sense, what is more inclusive, more complete and more transparent becomes absolute knowledge; and what is not complete, transparent and inclusive is up for critique.

Although it is arguably true that Hegel's philosophy justified Prussian oppression as well as slavery and exploitation as necessary stages in historical development, his dialectical method is also a critical tool that opened many new paths for future philosophers and social theorists. Ideas and concepts emerge as historically conditioned, and thus never totally innocent, as constructs that are partial, subject to critique, and thus provisional.

GENEALOGY, POWER, AND CRITIQUE

Friedrich Nietzsche (1844–1900), like Hegel before him, historicized Kant's version of critique through a technique called genealogy. Nietzsche argued that Kant's a-priori universals are born from historical struggles between competing interests. A particular idea gains ascendancy not because it is universally valid, but rather because a particular will to power animates it. Thus Nietzsche's critical method attempts to uncover the hidden will to power behind necessary and absolute truth claims. Yet Nietzsche must be separated from Hegel on two important accounts. For Hegel, this process of historical development is a self-contained internal movement of reason towards absolute knowledge, but for Nietzsche such movement is linked with a will to power that constantly attacks status quo ideas, personalities and institutions. Second, Hegel values synthesis, and the 'truth' lies at the end of the

process of development, gazing back upon itself. For Nietzsche, on the other hand, 'truth' lies at the beginning where terms are pure, before they are corrupted and debased by certain historical struggles between the powerful and the weak. Thus the origin rather than the summation becomes the source and fundament of critique.

Nietzsche's radical skepticism and critical force are amply on display in *On the Genealogy of Morals* (originally published in 1887). Here Nietzsche traces the descent of moral ideals back to their rather questionable origins. For Kant, to know the self was to understand the structure of the mind, but for Nietzsche, to know the self is to understand the legacy of war and violence carried within seemingly neutral and self-evident concepts like morality. Thus Nietzsche poses a simple question that in the end has radical implications for our self-understanding: how were the concepts 'good' and 'bad' invented? In Nietzsche's historical analysis, those who are strong-willed, virile, healthy and noble created the words that we use to describe social relations and actions. Thus the nobility invented the term 'good' to describe themselves and their activities.

Opposed to the superior stood the common people. Because they were not noble, healthy or strong, the aristocracy called them 'bad'. Yet soon there was a radical inversion of these terms, and this inversion was the result of a third class between the nobility and the commoners: the priests. The priests were, according to Nietzsche, jealous of the aristocrats and identified with the common, suffering peasants. In an act of revenge, the priests appropriated the language of the nobility and labeled the good as bad and the bad as good. The result is a slave morality that values malice, sickness and vengefulness over health, vitality, and righteousness. For Nietzsche, the result of this inversion for human evolution is tragic. As the priests led a slave revolt against the masters, the world witnessed the rise of Christianity, which is a religion of physical and moral disease.

Overall, Nietzsche is not a complete relativist. It is not simply that he is critiquing all concepts, but rather that he is critiquing those ideas that generate cultural, moral and biological illness (such as asceticism and Christian morality). Through the act of critique, Nietzsche liberates himself from the constraints of limiting concepts and in the process increases his life power. By overcoming social constraints and taboos, Nietzsche strives to become the 'superman', a figure unbounded by conventions. The superman holds nothing above his or her freedom to invent, create, and cultivate great genius.

Perhaps the philosopher most widely recognized as carrying on Nietzsche's genealogical criticism is the French postmodernist Michel Foucault (1926–1984). Like Nietzsche, Foucault desires to disrupt enlightenment narratives of progress, teleology and monumental history. For both, history is not so much a linear process as it is a chaotic and violent war of positions, full of fissures, fault lines and radical breaks. Genealogy as a form of critique exposes these fault lines and focuses on contingency, rather than continuity and internal necessity. Whereas Nietzsche proclaimed the death of God, Foucault, in an equally dramatic flourish, proclaimed the death of 'man' as a historical category, which like all other ephemeral things will be washed away in the sand.

Also, like Nietzsche, Foucault takes a great interest in the concept of the body. For Nietzsche, the life force emanating from the body cannot be contained or controlled by slave morality, or else illness will ensue. For Foucault, the body is the primary site for the inscription of power relations and of resistance. Yet there are also radical differences separating the two theorists. Whereas Nietzsche is unabashedly elitist, Foucault sides with the dispossessed, the forgotten, the marginalized and the 'abnormal'. Whereas Nietzsche's will to power is biological and highly individual, Foucault's theory of power is social and relational. Thus Foucault is not simply appropriating Nietzsche's methodology. He is also critiquing and reworking many of Nietzsche's central ideas.

Foucault provides a compelling example of the genealogical critical method in *Discipline and Punish* (1979). Here Foucault examines the rise of disciplinary power as the dominant mode of power in the modern era. Emphasizing a break from feudal society and the spectacular might of the sovereign, Foucault outlines the mechanisms, instruments, institutions and discourses that collectively function to maintain a homogenized, pacified, normalized and docile population of workers/consumers. Rather than grand displays of awesome force, disciplinary power functions covertly, silently, and on the micro-level of common everyday reality. It is dispersed throughout society as a whole, functioning to train the body and the soul of individuated subjects. The perfect example of a disciplinary technology is Jeremy Bentham's panopticon. The panopticon was originally a plan for the ideal prison. In the panopticon, prisoners are subjected to the gaze of the guards who sit in a tower overlooking a circular cellblock. The prisoners themselves do not know if the guards are present in the tower or not. Thus over time, the prisoners, suspecting they are constantly under the watchful eyes of the guards, become self-regulating, internalizing the disciplinary gaze. According to Foucault, the panopticon became a generalizable principle organizing all of our major social institutions including schools and clinics.

Thus, Foucault's genealogy enables us to critique normalizing power relations and pinpoint their various instruments of application. He asks the question: how do institutions both subject us to discipline and through this subjection produce us as subjects? The next question, one which Foucault himself could not fully answer before his untimely death, is thus: what are forms of resistance that enable subjects to produce themselves according to their own pleasures and desires? On this level, Foucault and Nietzsche once again meet, for both advocated a strong sense of aesthetic creativity against a mass culture of conformity.

PSYCHOANALYSIS AND THE CRITIQUE OF CULTURE

Sigmund Freud (1856–1939) originally saw psychoanalysis as a clinical technique used for the treatment of hysteria in late nineteenth-century society. Yet as he developed his dynamic theory of the mind, the broad social and political implications of his analysis of the unconscious became more and more explicit. For Freud, there are essentially three fundamental tenets to psychoanalysis. First, Freud rejects the Kantian transcendental notion that the mind can fully and completely grasp its essence through critical self-reflection. Drawing inspiration from the Romantics, Freud viewed the mind as ultimately unknowable by the individual subject. Inside of the mind are active and dynamic forces resisting conscious realization of our motives or desires. While these motives may be analyzed through the analysis of slips in language, free association word games or dreams, the unconscious remains largely impenetrable.

Second, Freud's theory of the mind is located at the frontier between the body and the psyche. Neither simply biological nor purely mental, psychological drives are Freud's attempt to understand the relation between the somatic reality of the senses and language itself. Third, and perhaps most controversial, Freud argued that the origin of physical symptoms such as hysteria is to be found in childhood sexual development and the inadequate resolution of what Freud calls the Oedipal complex. With these fundamental assumptions, Freud expanded psychoanalysis out of the clinic and into the realm of social critique.

In 1929, Freud's book *Civilization and its Discontents* was an important foray into social and political analysis. As opposed to Kant's optimistic teleology that ends with perpetual peace and individual freedom, Freud argues that as civilization becomes increasingly complex, the pressures exerted on the individual psyche become increasingly difficult to bear. In exchange for perceived safety and security, the individual enters into a social contract, agreeing to renounce his or her instinctual satisfaction. Society fundamentally demands that limits be placed on our innate sexual desires (Eros) and aggressive tendencies (Thanatos). Sexuality is sublimated into productive work, which results in the perpetual deferral of gratification. By placing restrictions on

the externalization of our aggressive drives, Thanatos turns inward, producing self-destructive tendencies in the form of an overly punitive conscience. While this eternal struggle between individual happiness and the constraints of civilization cannot be fully resolved, Freud does suggest that civilization must begin to take into account the impact of its severe demands on our fragile psyches. As long as social demands ignore the reality of instinctual forces, civilization will inevitably produce neurotics and hysterics, as well as much unhappiness and misery. Thus Freud's work ends with a great warning, a warning that has yet to be adequately heeded.

While there have been many revisions of Freud's theories, Jacques Lacan's (1901–1981) return to Freud is compelling and important for the history of critique. In his many seminars, Lacan utilized structural linguistics to unlock the radical kernel at the heart of Freud's theory of the subject. This linguistic turn is most succinctly summarized in Lacan's famous aphorism: 'The unconscious is structured like a language.' Here we see an interesting rejection of one of Freud's fundamental tenets of psychoanalysis: that the human psyche is composed of a dynamic relation between the somatic and the linguistic. For Lacan, the pre-linguistic imago of the unconscious is replaced by the broader category of the signifier. With these significant revisions of Freudian theory, Lacan then turns to an analysis of social relations through what he terms 'the four discourses', which include the discourses of the hysteric, the university, the master and the analyst. These discourses articulate the structural relations between social agents and the 'other', revealing that below the conscious level of interaction there is always already operating a dimension that is repressed. Here critique amounts to the uncovering of this 'obscene' dimension below a constituted social fantasy.

Today Slavoj Žižek (1949–) is the most widely recognized proponent of Lacanian psychoanalysis. In his many books and articles, this Slovenian philosopher combines Lacanian theory with ideology critique (see below) to expose the fundamental phantasy supplying the support for many contemporary social and political debates. Žižek's goal is to traverse the underlying phantasy structure suturing social relations, thus opening up a space where subjects can 'act' in the world. The act for Žižek is a fundamental rupture, a decisive move beyond the logic of capitalism and its attending ideology of neoliberal democracy. Žižek's Lacanian theory of the act is meant to disrupt two notions of action prevalent in Western philosophy. Against Kant's notion of a fully conscious self who freely acts according to a universal imperative, Žižek argues that acts occur in a moment of miraculous surprise that does not support the idealist notion of a self-transparent gesture. Second, Žižek is firmly against what he labels as 'postmodern identity politics'. As opposed to Foucault whose resistance takes place within the preexisting networks of disciplinary power and normalizing discourses, Žižek calls for a radical revolutionary split that opens a new space of possibilities. It is Lacan's notion of traversing the fundamental phantasy that opens a space for rethinking politics beyond what has been labeled as Foucauldian forms of postmodern resistance.

If Lacan's reading of Freud is controversial, then *Anti-Oedipus* (originally published in 1979) by Gilles Deleuze (1925–1995) and Félix Guattari (1930–1992) is often viewed as a mad postmodern masterpiece. In this text, the authors argue that capitalism unleashes a massive flow of unbridled desire. Yet because desire is inherently revolutionary, capitalism must at the same time recode or reterritorialize these very same flows. According to Deleuze and Guattari, Freudian psychoanalysis is a technology that attempts to recode desire and control it by inextricably linking desire to the Oedipal complex and the guilt of incest. For these authors, Lacan is equally an agent of capitalist territorialization. Where Lacan sees desire as a lack in the signifying chain, Deleuze and Guattari argue that desire is always productive.

As opposed to psychoanalysis, Deleuze and Guattari propose schizoanalysis. Here the goal is to expose the discourses, social structures, institutions and practices that constrict desire and to open up fissures where desire can escape these recodifications. Schizoanalysis smashes the Freudian ego and de-Oedipalizes desire itself. Because Deleuze and Guattari reject notions of conformity, discipline and homogenization, they embrace the figure of the schizo or of nomadic tribes, both of which are unbound by striated society. Here the figure of the schizo recalls Nietzsche's concept of the superman, who is essentially an individual lacking the internal agent of the Oedipal complex: the punitive super-ego.

In these three cases, psychoanalysis provides many important tools of social, political and cultural critique. From the psychoanalytic perspective we begin to recognize the tensions between the individual and society, the problematic of desire, and the role of unconscious forces in determining our perception of the world. Whether Freudian, Lacanian or Deleuzian, psychoanalytic critique is an important tradition whose basic assumptions are constantly being revised and/or rejected by critical theorists in a variety of fields and disciplines.

MARXISM AND THE CRITIQUE OF CAPITALISM

Karl Marx's (1818–1883) critique of capitalism began with his rejection of German Idealist philosophy. The young Marx defined his project through a sustained criticism of Hegel's philosophy of the Spirit. As interpreted by Marx and his contemporaries, Hegel properly grasped human history as a process of continual development; yet for him labor was always mental labor. All struggles were simply mental struggles in the conscious unfolding of Spirit. Thus Hegel retreated into the idealist sphere of pure thought and denied the true motor of history: concrete, physical labor.

As opposed to Hegel's idealist philosophy, Marx adopted instead a historical-materialist view of social reality. Historical materialism is historical in the sense that all ideas are embedded in their social contexts, and it is materialist in the sense that such ideas are the result of the organization of the material relations of society. Thus different modes of economic ownership produce different social relations and different sets of ideas. Whereas Nietzsche traced morals, cultural norms and common-sense beliefs back to the hidden source of power animating them, Marx traced cultural manifestations back to their economic determinants. And unlike Freud, who saw consciousness as determined by unconscious, libidinal forces, Marx saw personal consciousness as a reflex of the individual's particular location within the relations of production.

History for Marx is a dynamic process precisely because of the continual conflict that emerges between forms of ownership and the mode of production. For instance, in capitalism there is a central contradiction between the individual ownership of the means of production by the capitalist class and the communal mode of production in the factories. Here, the unknowable thing-in-itself, which Kant's idealism could not adequately approach, is transformed by Marx's materialism into class struggle as the objective motor of history. In order to resolve this contradiction, the workers have to take over the means of production. Thus the truth of capitalist productivity and its promised wealth lies only with overcoming the limitations of the capitalist system with socialism.

As long as we live within a capitalist society, the class that controls the economic base also controls the production of ideas. Ideology articulates the ideas of the ruling class (individualism, profit, market logic and the entrepreneurial spirit), transforming class specific interests into common, social interests. Thus ideology acts to universalize and naturalize bourgeois ideas, and in the process conceals the fundamental and inescapable reality of class conflict. Because of its mystifying nature, ideology is conceived of as producing a false consciousness or a set of false ideas that merely act to reinforce the ruling class's dominance and ensure their position of power and prestige in society. Therefore ideology for Marx is almost always associated with negative or pejorative connotations. Ideology is imposed upon the subjugated working class as a form of domination, preventing the working class from consciously recognizing that their objective interests stand opposed to those of the bourgeoisie.

While the basic premises of historical materialism remain largely unchallenged within Marxist debates, the function of ideology is hotly contested. For the Italian Marxist Antonio Gramsci (1891–1937), military/economic domination by a single class is not enough to maintain its position of power within a society; instead the ruling class must *legitimate* this rule. In order to lead the people, the dominant class cannot simply impose upon them a set of distorting and oppressive, ideologically infused ideas. The answer for Gramsci is that ideology must become common sense and is constructed in a struggle over hegemony and control between social groups. Hegemony is thus a contested terrain, a negotiated space, and a relationship of social power over subordinate groups. As opposed to Marx's concept of ideology, hegemony is not simply a false consciousness imposed upon the masses by the ruling class, obliterating working-class values. In order to gain the consent of the subordinate class, hegemony attempts to take into account the needs, fears and hopes of the populace. Put another way, hegemony must contain rhetorical constructs that attempt to *persuade* and *convince*. As such, hegemony is never absolute domination of one class position over another. In summary, opposing class interests need to be addressed and rearticulated by a hegemonic political process. Hegemony thus incorporates subordinate groups into its coalition. The subordinate groups accept their inferior position without contestation, consenting to the domination of the ruling class. Put another way, they consent to be led by the ruling class. The important point here is that hegemonic power is not guaranteed simply by class position but must be won.

Struggles for hegemony take place in the realms of media culture and civil society. As

Gramsci states, the press is a most important weapon in constructing an 'ideological front'. Also, civil societies—churches, schools, clubs, and so on—are all sites of hegemonic struggle. In order to understand how a hegemonic coalition is being formed, Gramsci argued that media culture and civic institutions are politically charged fields of contestation. As such, Gramsci moved Marxian analysis beyond its focus on economic relations of production and into the sphere of media culture.

As we can see, Gramsci's view of hegemony is more dynamic than Marx's formulation of ideology in three very distinct ways:

1. The hegemonic social position is never absolute but must be continually constructed, maintained, and defended. Domination over ideas is never guaranteed by one's position in a system of economic production.
2. It is not purely false consciousness, but is a negotiation between a variety of voices that are stitched together into a dominant ideology that supports the ruling-class agenda, and that will take different forms in different historical contexts and eras.
3. The struggle over culture and politics takes precedence in Gramsci's theory as a necessary component for gaining economic power, and as such, analysis of civic institutions and media culture becomes paramount for understanding hegemonic struggles.

Another central figure in rethinking historical materialism is Louis Althusser's (1918–1990) version of structural Marxism. First, Althusser seriously complicates any reductive reading of the Marxian base–superstructure distinction. While insisting that the mode of production is determinant in the last instance, Althusser grants a certain relative autonomy to the superstructure. Here society exists in an always already complex totality from which an originary class struggle cannot be extracted. The various elements within the superstructure relate to one another in terms of a differentiated unity wherein all struggles are 'overdetermined' by a series of antagonisms (political, cultural, and of course, economic). Second, Althusser, in contradistinction to Marx's purely negative reading of ideology, argues that ideology is productive and necessary for the individual to imagine his or her relationship to the social totality. Ideology might be illusory but it is also an allusion to very real material conditions. Furthermore, ideology is, as opposed to both Marx and Gramsci, largely unconscious and embedded in our material practices. Finally, by reading Marx closely, Althusser theorizes a new method of critical analysis which he coins 'symptomatic reading'. Symptomatic reading is the philosophical equivalent to clinical psychoanalysis, both of which expose the latent content that causes contradictions and inconsistencies within the manifest text: class conflict. These innovations, while controversial, offer important syntheses of Marxism with two other strains of cultural critique: structuralism and Lacanian psychoanalysis respectively. Thus Althusser, more than any other French Marxist of his generation, explored the relationship between historical materialism, linguistics and theories of the subject, producing a powerful form of Marxist criticism.

While there have been many different lineages of critical thought derived from historical materialism and ideological critique, the following sections of this text will look in some detail at two of the most influential: Frankfurt School critical theory and British Cultural Studies.

FRANKFURT SCHOOL CRITICAL THEORY

The 'Frankfurt School' refers to a group of German American theorists who developed powerful analyses of the changes in Western capitalist societies that have occurred since the classical theory of Marx. Notably, the theorists loosely affiliated with the Frankfurt School shifted Marxism away from economic determinism towards a primary concern with the superstructure and with questions of culture and subjectivity. This radical shift in emphasis came about after failed revolutions in the early decades of the twentieth century, the subsequent disillusionment with classical Marxism, and the rise of advanced cultural institutions and media communications (all of which seemed to prevent mass movements from rebelling against capitalism).

Working at the *Institut für Sozialforschung* in Frankfurt, Germany in the late 1920s and early 1930s, theorists such as Max Horkheimer (1894–1972), T.W. Adorno (1903–1969), Herbert Marcuse (1898–1979), Leo Löwenthal (1900–1993), and Erich Fromm (1900–1980) produced some of the first accounts within critical social theory of the importance of mass culture and communication in social reproduction and domination (Kellner, 1989). The Frankfurt School also generated one of the first models of a critical cultural studies that analyzes the processes of cultural production and political economy, the politics of cultural texts, and audience reception and use of cultural artifacts.

Moving from Nazi Germany to the United States, the Frankfurt School experienced at first hand the rise of a media culture involving film, popular music, radio, television and other forms of mass culture. In the United States, where they found themselves in exile, media production was by and large a form of commercial entertainment controlled by big corporations. Two of the Frankfurt School's key theorists, Max Horkheimer and T.W. Adorno, developed an account of the 'culture industry' to call attention to the industrialization and commercialization of culture under capitalist relations of production. This situation was most marked in the United States where there was little state support of film or television industries, and where a highly commercial mass culture emerged that came to be a distinctive feature of capitalist societies and a focus of critical cultural studies. As we shall see, their critical cultural studies model drew on Max Weber's theory of rationalization, Marxist categories such as alienation and ideology, and, finally, Freudian notions of repression, projection and displacement.

During the 1930s, the Frankfurt School developed a critical and transdisciplinary approach to cultural and communications studies, combining political economy, textual analysis, and analysis of social and ideological effects of socio-cultural institutions and forms. They coined the term 'culture industry' to signify the process of the industrialization of mass-produced culture and the commercial imperatives that drove the system. The critical theorists analyzed all mass-mediated cultural artifacts within the context of industrial production, in which the commodities of the culture industries exhibited the same features as other products of mass production: commodification, standardization and massification. The culture industries had the specific function, however, of providing ideological legitimation of the existing capitalist societies and of integrating individuals into their way of life. Adorno's analyses of popular music, television and other phenomena ranging from astrology columns to fascist speeches, Löwenthal's studies of popular literature and magazines (1961) and the perspectives and critiques of mass culture developed in Horkheimer and Adorno's famous study of the culture industries provide many examples of the Frankfurt School approach. In their view, mass culture and communications stand in the center of leisure activity, are important agents of socialization and mediators of political reality, and should thus be seen as major institutions of contemporary societies with a variety of economic, political, cultural and social effects.

Furthermore, the critical theorists investigated the cultural industries in a political context as a form of the integration of the working class into capitalist societies. The Frankfurt School theorists were among the first neo-Marxian groups to examine the effects of mass culture and the rise of the consumer society on the working classes that were to be the instrument of revolution in the classical Marxian scenario. In particular, Horkheimer and Adorno turned to Freud rather than to Marx in order to explain the lack of revolution in the working class. Because the proletariat was 'repressed' or, to use Fromm's language, 'feared freedom', they could not easily be transformed into the revolutionary subjects that Marx hypothesized. As such, questions of subjectivity came to dominate Frankfurt analyses of radical opposition. Horkheimer and Adorno also utilized Freudian concepts such as projection in order to explain the role of racism in Nazi Germany.

As we can see, the project of the Frankfurt School required rethinking Marxian theory and produced many important contributions as well as some problematical positions. The Frankfurt School focused intently on technology and culture, indicating how technology was becoming both a major force of production and a formative mode of social organization and control. In a 1941 article, 'Some Social Implications of Modern Technology', Herbert Marcuse argued that technology in the contemporary era constitutes an entire 'mode of organizing and perpetuating (or changing) social relationships, a manifestation of prevalent thought and behavior patterns, an instrument for control and domination'. In the realm of culture, technology produced mass culture that habituated individuals to conform to the dominant patterns of thought and behavior, and thus provided powerful instruments of social control and domination.

Victims of European fascism, the Frankfurt School experienced first hand the ways that the Nazis used the instruments of mass culture to produce submission to fascist culture and society. While in exile in the United States, the members of the Frankfurt School came to believe that American 'popular culture' was also highly ideological and worked to promote the interests of American capitalism. Controlled by giant corporations, the culture industries were organized according to the strictures of mass production, churning out mass-produced products that generated a highly commercial system of culture, which in turn sold the values, lifestyles and institutions of 'the American way of life'. Thus, within liberal democracy the Frankfurt School witnessed the seeds of fascism, deconstructing tried and true dichotomies that at the time positioned American 'freedom' in opposition to German 'totalitarianism'.

Furthermore, both liberal democracy and fascism represented the dialectic of enlightenment whereby rationality turned against itself, becoming a mythology and a tool to promote ongoing domination of the self and of nature. Unlike Kant and Hegel who saw reason as an instrument of emancipation, members of the Frankfurt School, in particular Adorno, realized that reason itself contains within its own concept its negation. The germinal seeds of totalitarianism and domination inherent within reason were precisely the pre-conditions that enabled reason to be appropriated by capitalism in the name of labor exploitation and allowed science to divorce itself from ethical concerns and critical self-awareness. Thus, with the Frankfurt School, philosophical criticism of enlightenment projects intersects with political and economic analysis to create one of the most impressive and comprehensive forms of criticism within the Marxist tradition. The net result is a dialectical, totalizing social theory, which describes the contours, dynamics and tendencies of the philosophical, political, social and economic historical situation.

Max Horkheimer and T.W. Adorno developed this dialectical theory of critique in a highly influential analysis of the culture industry published in their book *Dialectic of Enlightenment*, which first appeared in 1948 and was translated into English in 1972. They argued that the system of cultural production dominated by film, radio broadcasting, newspapers and magazines was controlled by advertising and commercial imperatives, and served to create subservience to the system of consumer capitalism. While later critics pronounced their approach too manipulative, reductive and elitist, it provides an important corrective to more populist approaches to media culture that downplay the way the media industries exert power over audiences and help produce thought and behavior that conforms to the existing society.

The Frankfurt School also provided useful historical perspectives on the transition from traditional culture and modernism in the arts to a mass-produced media and consumer society. In his path-breaking book *The*

Structural Transformation of the Public Sphere, Jürgen Habermas (1929–) further historicizes Adorno and Horkheimer's analysis of the culture industry. Providing historical background to the triumph of the culture industry, Habermas notes how bourgeois society in the late eighteenth and nineteenth centuries was distinguished by the rise of a public sphere that stood between civil society and the state and which mediated between public and private interests. For the first time in history, individuals and groups could shape public opinion, giving direct expression to their needs and interests while influencing political practice. The bourgeois public sphere made it possible to form a realm of public opinion that opposed state power and the powerful interests that were coming to shape bourgeois society.

Habermas notes a transition from the liberal public sphere, which originated in the Enlightenment and the American and French Revolutions, to a media-dominated public sphere in the current stage of what he calls 'welfare state capitalism and mass democracy'. This historical transformation is grounded in Horkheimer and Adorno's analysis of the culture industry, in which giant corporations have taken over the public sphere and transformed it from a site of rational debate into one of manipulative consumption and passivity. In this transformation, 'public opinion' shifts from rational consensus emerging from debate, discussion and reflection to the manufactured opinion of polls or media experts. For Habermas, the interconnection between the sphere of public debate and individual participation has thus been fractured and transmuted into that of a realm of political manipulation and spectacle, in which citizen–consumers ingest and passively absorb entertainment and information. 'Citizens' thus become spectators of media presentations and discourse which arbitrate public discussion and reduce its audiences to objects of news, information and public affairs.

Habermas's critics contend, however, that he idealizes the earlier bourgeois public sphere by presenting it as a forum of rational discussion and debate, when in fact the proletariat, many social groups and most women were excluded (see the essays in Calhoun, 1992). These critics contend that Habermas neglects various oppositional working classes and plebeian and women's public spheres developed alongside the bourgeois public sphere to represent voices and interests excluded in this forum. Yet Habermas is right that in the period of the democratic revolutions a public sphere emerged in which for the first time in history ordinary citizens could participate in political discussion and debate, organize, and struggle against unjust authority. Habermas's critical theory, which focuses on communicative action, also points to the increasingly important role of the media in politics and everyday life and the ways that corporate interests have colonized this sphere, using the media and culture to promote their own interests.

The American literary critic and philosopher Fredric Jameson (1934–) is today one of the leading figures in the second generation of Frankfurt School theorists. His widely influential text *Postmodernism, or the Cultural Logic of Late Capitalism* (1991) utilizes Frankfurt School critical theory to analyze the 'postmodern condition' of late capitalism. Here Jameson argues for the centrality of meta-critique, periodization, and totalization as methodological principles necessary for grasping the crisis in representation which accompanies globalization and is figured in much of postmodern media culture. Central to Jameson's political project is his insistence on 'cognitive mapping' as a pre-condition for renewed revolutionary activism. Here cognitive mapping refers to the necessary yet impossible representation of the social, political and labor networks that structure relations between first and third worlds within the overall framework of transnational corporations and global economics. Without an adequate form of cognitive/aesthetic mapping, we remain disoriented and unable to effectively critique and combat new modes of capitalist oppression and exploitation. Thus Jameson reinvigorates the political thrust of Frankfurt School social theory in order to take into account the ever-changing and ever-expanding dimensions of capitalism.

BRITISH CULTURAL STUDIES AND THE BIRMINGHAM SCHOOL

The forms of culture described by the earliest phase of British cultural studies in the 1950s and early 1960s articulated conditions in an era in which there were still significant tensions in Britain and much of Europe between an older working-class-based culture and the newer mass-produced culture whose models and exemplars were the products of American culture industries. The initial project of cultural studies developed by Richard Hoggart (1918–), Raymond Williams (1921–1988), and E.P. Thompson (1924–1993) attempted to preserve working-class culture against onslaughts of mass culture produced by the culture industries. Thompson's historical inquiries into the history of British working-class institutions and struggles, the defenses of working-class culture by Hoggart (1958) and Williams (1961), and their attacks on mass culture were part of a socialist and working-class-oriented project that assumed that the industrial working class was a force of progressive social change and that it could be mobilized and organized to struggle against the inequalities of the existing capitalist societies and for a more egalitarian socialist one. Williams and Hoggart were deeply involved in projects of working-class education and oriented toward socialist working-class politics, seeing their form of cultural studies as an instrument of progressive social change.

The early critiques in the first wave of British cultural studies of Americanism and mass culture, in Hoggart, Williams and others, thus paralleled to some extent the earlier critique of the Frankfurt School, yet valorized a working class that the Frankfurt School saw as defeated in Germany and much of Europe during the era of fascism and which they never saw as a strong resource for emancipatory social change.

The early work of the Birmingham School was continuous with the radicalism of the first wave of British cultural studies (the Hoggart–Thompson–Williams 'culture and society' tradition) as well as, in important ways, with the Frankfurt School. Yet the Birmingham project also paved the way for a postmodern populist turn in cultural studies, which responds to a later stage of capitalism.

It has not yet been recognized that the second stage of the development of British cultural studies—starting with the founding of the University of Birmingham Centre for Contemporary Cultural Studies in 1963/64 by Hoggart and Stuart Hall—shared many key perspectives with the Frankfurt School. During this period, the Centre developed a variety of critical approaches for the analysis, interpretation, and criticism of cultural artifacts. Through a set of internal debates, and responding to social struggles and movements of the 1960s and the 1970s, the Birmingham group came to focus on the interplay of representations and ideologies of class, gender, race, ethnicity and nationality in cultural texts, including media culture. They were among the first to study the effects of newspapers, radio, television, film and other popular cultural forms on audiences. They also focused on how various audiences interpreted and used media culture in varied and different ways and contexts, analyzing the factors that made audiences respond in contrasting ways to media texts.

The now classical period of British cultural studies from the early 1960s to the early 1980s continued to adopt a Marxian approach to the study of culture, one especially influenced by Althusser and Gramsci. Yet although Hall (1980a), Bennett (1982), and others usually omit the Frankfurt School from this narrative, some of the work done by the Birmingham group replicated certain classical positions of the Frankfurt School in the social theory and methodological models for doing cultural studies as well as in the political perspectives and strategies. Like the Frankfurt School, British cultural studies observed the integration of the working class and its decline of revolutionary consciousness, and studied the conditions of this catastrophe for the Marxian project of revolution. Like the Frankfurt School, British cultural studies concluded that mass culture was playing an important role in integrating the working class into existing capitalist societies and that a new consumer and media culture was forming a new mode of capitalist hegemony. Both traditions focused on the intersections of culture and ideology and saw ideology critique as central to a critical cultural studies. Both saw culture as a mode of ideological reproduction and hegemony, in which cultural forms help to shape the modes of thought and behavior that induce individuals to adapt to the social conditions of capitalist societies. Both also saw culture as a form of resistance to capitalist society, and both the earlier forerunners of British cultural studies (especially Raymond Williams) and the theorists of the Frankfurt School see high culture as forces of resistance to capitalist modernity. Later, British cultural studies would valorize resistant moments in media culture and audience interpretations and use of media artifacts, while the Frankfurt School tended, with some exceptions, to see mass culture as a homogeneous and potent form of ideological domination—a difference that would seriously divide the two traditions.

From the beginning, British cultural studies was highly political in nature and focused on the potentials for social critique in oppositional subcultures, first valorizing the potential of working-class cultures and, then, youth subcultures to resist the hegemonic forms of capitalist domination. Unlike the classical Frankfurt School (but similar to Herbert Marcuse), British cultural studies turned to youth cultures as providing potentially new forms of opposition and social change. Through studies of youth subcultures, British cultural studies demonstrated how culture came to constitute distinct forms of identity and group membership, and appraised the oppositional potential of various youth subcultures (see, for instance, Hebdige, 1979). Cultural studies came to focus on how subcultural groups resist dominant forms of culture and identity, creating their own style and identities. Individuals who conform to dominant dress and fashion codes, behavior and political ideologies thus produce their identities within mainstream groups, as members of specific social groupings (such as white, middle-class conservative Americans).

But British cultural studies, unlike the Frankfurt School, has not adequately engaged modernist and avant-garde aesthetic movements, limiting its focus by and large to products of media culture and 'the popular', which has become an immense focus of its efforts. It appears that in its anxiety to legitimate study of the popular and to engage the artifacts of media culture, British cultural studies has turned away from so-called 'high' culture in favor of the popular. But such a turn sacrifices the possible insights into all forms of culture and replicates the bifurcation of the field of culture into a 'popular' and 'elite' (which merely inverts the positive/negative valorizations of the older high/low distinction).

Against academic formalism and separatism, cultural studies—like the metatheoretical framework of the Frankfurt School—insists that culture must be investigated within the social relations and system through which culture is produced and consumed, and that analysis of culture is thus intimately bound up with the study of society, politics and economics. Employing Gramsci's model of hegemony and counter-hegemony, it sought to analyze 'hegemonic', or ruling, social and cultural forces of domination and to seek 'counter-hegemonic' forces of resistance and struggle. The project was aimed at social transformation and attempted to specify forces of domination and resistance in order to aid the process of political struggle and emancipation from oppression and domination.

Some earlier authoritative presentations of British cultural studies stressed the importance of a transdisciplinary approach to the study of culture that analyzed its political economy, process of production and distribution, textual products, and reception by the audience—positions remarkably similar to the Frankfurt School. For instance, in his classical programmatic article, 'Encoding/ Decoding' (1980b), Stuart Hall began his analysis by using Marx's *Grundrisse* as a model to trace the articulations of 'a continuous circuit', encompassing 'production–distribution–consumption–production'. Hall concretizes this model with focus on how media institutions produce meanings, how they circulate, and how audiences use or decode the texts to produce meaning.

In more recent cultural studies, however, there has been a turn to what might be called a postmodern problematic which emphasizes pleasure, consumption and the individual construction of identities in terms of what Jim McGuigan (1992) has called a 'cultural populism'. Media culture from this perspective produces material for identities, pleasures and empowerment, and thus audiences constitute the 'popular' through their consumption of cultural products. During this phase—roughly from the mid-1980s to the present—cultural studies in Britain and North America (and then globally) turned from the socialist and revolutionary politics of the previous stages to postmodern forms of identity politics and less critical perspectives on media and consumer culture. Emphasis was placed more and more on the audience, consumption and reception, and displaced focus on production and distribution of texts and how texts were produced in media industries. Yet it could be argued that this form of postmodern cultural studies theorizes a shift from the stage of state monopoly capitalism, or Fordism, rooted in mass production and consumption, to a new regime of capital and social order described by Jameson as postmodern and characterizing a transnational and global capital that valorizes difference, multiplicity, eclecticism, populism and intensified consumerism in a new information/ entertainment society. As such, a postmodern cultural studies is a response to an emergent era of global capitalism, functioning both as a symptom and as a diagnostic tool.

During the current stage of cultural studies there is a widespread tendency to decenter, or even ignore completely, economics, history and politics in favor of emphasis on local pleasures, consumption and the construction of hybrid identities from the material of the popular. This cultural populism replicates the turn in postmodern theory away from Marxism and its alleged reductionism, master narratives of liberation and domination, and historical teleology. In fact, as McGuigan (1992) has documented, British cultural studies has had an unstable relationship with political economy from the beginning. Generally speaking, rather than take up Frankfurt School insights into industrial capitalism, Hall and other practitioners of British cultural studies (i.e., Bennett, Fiske, Hartley, et al.) either simply dismiss the Frankfurt School as a form of economic reductionism or simply ignore it. Yet this dismissal seriously misrepresents the dialectic strengths of the Frankfurt School's theory of capitalism and critically hinders the explanatory power of British Cultural Studies.

The emphasis in postmodernist cultural studies articulates experiences and phenomena within an emerging mode of social organization. The emphasis on active audiences, resistant readings, oppositional texts, utopian moments and the like describes an era in which individuals are trained to be more active media consumers, and in which they are given a much wider choice of cultural materials, corresponding to a developing global and transnational capitalism with a much broader array of consumer choices, products and services. In this regime, difference sells, and the differences, multiplicities and heterogeneity valorized in postmodern theory describe the proliferation of differences and multiplicity in a new social order predicated on proliferation of consumer desires and needs. The forms of hybrid culture and identities described by postmodern cultural studies correlate with a globalized capitalism with an intense flow of products, culture, people and identities, and with novel configurations of the global and local and new forms of struggles and resistance. Corresponding to the structure of a globalized and hybridized culture are proliferations of cultural studies, which, in order to regain their critical capacities, must combine with the more progressive elements in Frankfurt School social theory and thus produce a more synthetic and comprehensive analysis of cultural resistance and cultural homogenization within techno-capitalism.

SOCIAL MOVEMENTS, THE POLITICS OF REPRESENTATION, AND POSTCOLONIAL CRITIQUE

Following the poststructuralist moment of the late 1960s and 1970s, there was a proliferation of new critical theories that connected with new social movements, producing a proliferation of 'posts' and theory wars from the 1970s to the present. During the 1960s and 1970s, critical theories turned to a 'politics of representation' and identity politics that linked critique with social movements. This enterprise involved analysis of the ways that images, discourses and narratives of a wide range of cultural forms from philosophy and the sciences to the advertising and entertainment of media culture were embedded in texts and reproduced social domination and subordination. Critical theories thus developed within feminisms, critical race theory, gay and lesbian theory, and other groupings associated with new oppositional political movements. Feminists, for instance, demonstrated how gender bias infected disciplines from philosophy to literary study, and was embedded in texts ranging from classics of the canon to the mundane artifacts of popular culture. In similar ways, critical race theorists demonstrated how racial bias permeated cultural artifacts, while gay and lesbian theorists demonstrated sexual bias. Although each of these movements constitutes its own unique notion of critique, here we will focus on two trajectories: feminism and postcolonialism.

Although most often associated with the 1960s and the 1970s, feminism is far from a contemporary theoretical and political invention. Mary Wollstonecraft's (1759–1797) *A Vindication of the Rights of Woman*, first published in 1792, argued that Enlightenment freedom could not be fully achieved without equality of men and women. Thus Woll-stonecraft clearly recognized the centrality of gender in political and economic struggles against oppression. Developing a wide range of critical tools, feminism has, since Wollstonecraft, made a variety of important interventions into many of the critical traditions we have thus far discussed, including psychoanalysis, Marxism and critical theory, while at the same time forming unique projects for the liberation of women and society as such.

In relation to psychoanalysis, theorists such as Simone de Beauvoir (1908–1986) furthered the feminist theoretical project by famously arguing that women (and by extension, men) are made, not born. In 1952, in *The Second Sex*, she drew a critical distinction between sex and gender missed by Freud, wherein sex is biological and gender is constructed socially and politically. As such, gender becomes contingent, the product of a certain power relationship within cultural traditions.

Nancy Chodorow (1944–) has further exposed Freud's sexism by systematically criticizing his more patriarchal concepts and his normative reliance on male sexuality to define women as castrated and scarred. Emerging from such studies are two principal concepts in feminist criticisms of ideology: phallocentrism and patriarchy. Here phallocentrism refers to male dominance both in the collective imagination and in the history of production, reproduction and social formations. French psychoanalyst and philosopher Luce Irigary (1932–) has attempted to construct a theory of female sexual pleasure outside of such phallocentrism. In Irigary's comprehensive criticism of western phallocentrism, female sexuality has been systematically foreclosed. Thus patriarchy operates via the exclusion of the feminine, which returns as a silence or as an absent presence within male, heterosexual discourses. Irigary then proposes a series of psychoanalytic concepts which do not fall into the trap of phallocentrism, reorienting questions of sexual pleasure away from male genitals towards unique configurations of female sex organs and the resulting pleasures.

Others have utilized feminist critique to address serious lacks, oversights and gender biases in Marxian theory. Nancy Hartsock's (1943–) work provides some theoretical concepts needed to understand gendered relations of domination (Harding, 2004). Drawing on both Marx's historical materialism as well as Georg Lukács' standpoint theory, Hartsock argues that women's position in social relations generates positive knowledge of the social totality lost in more traditional, male-centered accounts of the proletariat. Women are in a privileged social position to understand the politics of phallocentrism embedded in the sexual division of labor, and thus reveal a level of oppression barely touched upon in classical Marxism. For Hartsock, feminist consciousness—predicated on human reproduction—reaches a level of social strata beneath class consciousness, which is located in the sphere of economic production alone. As such, Hartsock's Marxian-infused feminist standpoint theory opens up an important theoretical problematic: the relation between reproduction of life and the reproduction of labor power.

Judith Butler (1956–) offers a uniquely postmodern form of feminist criticism that calls upon a variety of traditions including psychoanalysis, deconstruction and queer theory, as well as Foucault's theory of power. Butler further complicates analysis of gender by arguing that the classical distinction between sex and gender ultimately deconstructs itself and that sex is always already gendered and as such socially constituted and performed. By limiting feminist scholarship to the sex/gender binary, feminism has become complicit with heteronormative values which ultimately maintain the concepts of 'man' and 'woman' as essentialized substances. Here heterosexuality becomes an exclusive domain of truth that excludes queer subjectivities from being incorporated into feminist thought, and as such feminism itself becomes a mode of oppression.

Patricia Hill Collins (1948–) and bell hooks (1952–) further feminist scholarship by introducing the dimension of racism and race relations. Hill Collins (Harding, 2004) in particular theorizes a black feminist epistemology which emphasizes the centrality of the African-American experiences as a source for producing new knowledge as well as powerful criticisms of the sexism and racism within a white, male-dominated patriarchal society. Most importantly, bell hooks critiques both male patriarchy as well as white feminism for marginalizing issues of race, racism and class. For hooks, class, race and gender are integral factors in the constitution of subjectivity and must be discussed together in order to have a more comprehensive notion of the critique of representation and of oppression. Other feminists such as Uma Narayan (1958–) (Harding, 2004) place feminism within a global sphere, offering a third-world critique of Eurocentric feminist epistemologies, methodologies and practices, and open up a 'third space' for the articulation of non-western women's voices, standpoints and epistemologies. Thus Narayan merges postcolonial theory and feminism, moving us on to the last topic in this review: postcolonial criticism.

Postcolonial criticism, in its broadest definition, concerns the analysis of colonization, neocolonization, and postcolonization within a global economic, political and social context. Emerging from multiple struggles to liberate the 'third world' from European colonial enterprises, postcolonial theory is most often associated with resistance movements against cultural appropriation/ misrepresentation ('orientalism') by the west as well as economic exploitation. Also of importance is the analysis of the subjectivity of both the colonizer and the colonized. In *Black Skins, White Masks* (1967), Franz Fanon (1925–1961) developed a psychoanalytic/ existential theory of psychological alienation which results from the colonial condition. According to Fanon, the colonized are forced to identify with and, in turn, internalize the image of the colonizer, thus becoming their own oppressors. The result is a form of psychological alienation which Fanon articulates using Marxist theories of alienation and psychoanalysis, as well as his own experiences as a black psychologist working during the Algerian War.

Third, postcolonial studies attempts to deconstruct Eurocentric representations of the cultural 'other'. Critics such as Edward Said (1935–2003) have demonstrated the imperialist assumptions at work within the western canon of literature and art. He exposes how racist images of the 'exoticized' east legitimated European and United States colonial occupations. Finally, Homi Bhabha (1949—) and Gayatri Spivak (1942–) search for forms of resistance in subversion and mimicry. These authors, heavily influenced by deconstruction, always foreground their analyses with an understanding that such resistance—far from the total revolution advocated by Fanon in 1961 in *The Wretched of the Earth* — is itself informed by and inscribed within the very matrix of the colonizer's views of freedom, liberty, democracy, and so on. As such hybridity (the constantly shifting and intersecting relationship between cultural, economic and political systems within colonization) becomes a central issue for postcolonial theorists interested in the question of national culture, identity politics and the deconstruction of reductive dichotomies that separate out the 'civilized' west from the 'primitive' east.

CONCLUSION

In conclusion we would advocate that critique must, as Hegel suggested, become familiar with its own historically conditioned past. Rather than support one theory over another, we would also argue that a 'multi-perspectival' approach to critique is necessary in order to account for all forms of political, economic, and social oppression, subjugation, and exploitation. Thus we must analyze each theory of critique in terms of its strength and weaknesses, progressive moments and conservative limitations, and work towards a more robust theory of criticism that is capable of cognitively mapping the vast system of global capitalism that

functions within and conditions a predominantly Eurocentric, patriarchal, white, heteronormative, male-dominated global economy and networked society.

REFERENCES AND SELECT BIBLIOGRAPHY

Adorno, T.W. (1991) *The Culture Industry*. London and New York: Routledge.

Althusser, Louis (2001) *Lenin and Philosophy and other Essays*. New York: Monthly Review Press.

Bennett, Tony (1982) 'Theories of the media, theories of society', in Michael Gurevitch (ed.), *Culture, Society, and the Media*. London: Macmillan.

Bhabha, Homi (1994) *The Location of Culture*. London: Routledge.

Bloch, Ernst (1986) *The Principle of Hope*. Cambridge, MA: MIT Press.

Butler, Judith (1999) *Gender Trouble: Feminism and the Subversion of Identity*. London: Routledge.

Calhoun, Craig (ed.) (1992) *Habermas and the Public Sphere*. Cambridge, MA: The MIT Press.

Chodorow, Nancy (1989) *The Reproduction of Mothering*. Berkeley: University of California Press.

de Beauvoir, S. ([1967]1989) *The Second Sex*. Harmondsworth, UK: Penguin.

Deleuze, Gilles and Guattari, Félix (2000) *Anti-Oedipus: Capitalism and Schizophrenia*. Minneapolis: University of Minnesota Press.

Fanon, Franz ([1967]1986) *Black Skin, White Masks*. London: Pluto.

———— (1966) *The Wretched of the Earth*. New York: Grove Press.

Foucault, Michel (1979) *Discipline and Punish: The Birth of the Prison System*. New York: Vintage Books.

Fromm, Erich (1941) *Escape from Freedom*. New York: Rinehart Winston.

Freud, Sigmund (1989) *Civilization and Its Discontents*. New York: W.W. Norton & Company.

Gramsci, Antonio (1971) *Selections from the Prison Notebooks*. New York: International.

Habermas, Jürgen (1989) *The Structural Transformation of the Public Sphere*. Cambridge, MA: The MIT Press.

Hall, Stuart (1980a) 'Cultural studies and the centre: Some problematics and problems', in Stuart Hall (ed.), *Culture, Media, Language: Working Papers in Cultural Studies, 1972–79*. London: Hutchinson, pp. 15–47.

———— (1980b) 'Encoding/decoding', in Stuart Hall (ed.), *Culture, Media, Language: Working Papers in Cultural Studies, 1972–79*. London: Hutchinson, pp.128–38.

——— (ed.) (1980). *Culture, Media, Language: Working Papers in Cultural Studies, 1972–79*. London: Hutchinson.

Harding, Sandra (2004) *The Feminist Standpoint Theory Reader: Intellectual and Political Controversies*. London: Routledge.

Hebdige, Dick (1979) *Subculture: The Meaning of Style*. London: Methuen.

Hegel, G.W.F (1977) *Phenomenology of Spirit*. Oxford: Oxford University Press.

Hilferding, Rudolph (1981) *Finance Capital*. London: Routledge and Kegan Paul.

Hoggart, Richard (1958) *The Uses of Literacy*. New York: Oxford University Press.

Hooks, Bell (1990) *Yearning: Race, Gender, and Cultural Politics*. Boston: South End Press.

Horkheimer, M. and Adorno, T.W. (1972) *Dialectic of Enlightenment*. New York: Herder and Herder.

Jameson, Fredric (1991) *Postmodernism, or the Cultural Logic of Late Capitalism*. Durham, N.C.: Duke University Press.

Irigary, Luce (1993) *An Ethics of Sexual Difference*. Ithaca: Cornell University Press.

Kant, Immanuel (2000). *Critique of Pure Reason*. Cambridge: Cambridge University Press.

——— (1983) *Perpetual Peace and other Essays*. Indianapolis: Hackett.

Kellner, Douglas (1989) *Critical Theory, Marxism, and Modernity*. Cambridge and Baltimore: Polity and John Hopkins University Press.

Kracauer, Siegfried (1995) *The Mass Ornament. Weimar Essays*. Cambridge, MA: Harvard University Press.

Lacan, Jacques (1981) *The Four Fundamental Concepts of Psychoanalysis: The Seminars of Jacques Lacan Book XI*. New York: W.W. Norton & Company.

Löwenthal, Leo (1961) *Literature, Popular Culture and Society*. Englewood Cliffs, New Jersey: Prentice-Hall.

Marcuse, Herbert (1941) Some Social Implications of Modern Technology', *Studies in Philosophy and Social Science*, 9 (1): 414–39.

Marx, Karl and Engels, Fredrich (1978) *The Marx–Engels Reader* (ed. R. Tucker). New York: W.W. Norton & Company.

McGuigan, Jim (1992) *Cultural Populism*. London and New York: Routledge.

Narayan, Uma (1989) *Gender/Body/Knowledge: Feminist Reconstructions of Being and Knowing*. New Brunswick, N.J.: Rutgers University Press.

Nietzsche, Friedrich (1969) *On the Genealogy of Morals* and *Ecce Homo*. New York: Vintage Books.

Said, Edward (1979) *Orientalism*. New York: Vintage Books.

Spivak, Gayatri (1990) *Postcolonial Critic: Interviews, Strategies, Dialogues*. London: Routledge.

Williams, Raymond (1961) *The Long Revolution*. London: Chatto and Windus.

Wollstonecraft, Mary (1988) *A Vindication of the Rights of Woman*. New York: W.W. Norton & Company.

Žižek, Slavoj (2001) *The Sublime Object of Ideology*. London: Verso.

23

Grounded Theory: Critiques, Debates, and Situational Analysis

Adele E. Clarke

INTRODUCTION

Since its development by Barney Glaser and Anselm Strauss (1967), grounded theory (hereafter GT) has become a leading method used in qualitative research globally,[1] not only in sociology (e.g., Strauss and Corbin, 1997) and nursing (e.g., Benoliel, 1996; Schreiber and Stern, 2001) where it was originally taught, but also in feminist studies (e.g., Clarke, 2006; Keddy, Sims, and Stern, 1996), organization and management studies (e.g., Locke, 2001), education (e.g., Cresswell, 2002), cultural studies (e.g., Gelder and Thornton, 1997), computer and information science (e.g., Bryant, 2002; Star and Strauss, 1998), social work (e.g., Riessman, 1994), science, technology and medicine studies (e.g., Clarke and Star, 2003, 2007), queer studies (e.g., Gamson, 2000), and beyond. GT has been, almost since its inception, exceptionally influential in the domains of qualitative research, perhaps most especially in terms of promoting empirically-based inductive (actually abductive, as discussed below) conceptual work (e.g., Atkinson et al., 2003:

148–52; Bryman and Burgess, 1994: 220). Writings by Strauss and Corbin on GT have been translated extensively, and books on GT by new authors have recently appeared in German (Strübing, 2004, 2007) and Polish (Konecki, 2000).[2] GT has also been quite well elaborated over the years by a number of scholars,[3] and I have very recently developed an extension of GT called situational analysis (hereafter SA) that takes it around the postmodern turn through the turn to discourse(s) (Clarke, 2003, 2005).[4]

Any method as popular as GT invites an array of critiques. In this chapter, I first lay out what I think GT is, and then turn to common critiques of the method itself and of research done using it. Next I turn to the major divergences and debates that have been increasingly expressed among grounded theorists and others since c. 1990, often described as a schism between the two founders, Glaser and Strauss, but actually much much more than that. Last, I offer my own critique of the conditional matrices used in the Strauss/Corbin versions of GT to situate the analysis, and lay out how SA may offer some fresh pathways for researchers that take a wide array of these critiques into some account.

WHAT IS GROUNDED THEORY?

'Social phenomena are complex. Thus they require complex grounded theory' (Strauss, 1987: 1).

GT is first and foremost a mode of *analysis* of largely qualitative research data. That is, it does not claim to offer a fully elaborated methodology from soup to nuts—from project design to data collection to final write-up. Many elements of a full-blown methodology are offered, but data analysis is the focus of most of the texts. GT is a deeply *empirical* approach to the study of social life. The very term 'grounded theory' means data-grounded theorizing. In the words of Atkinson et al. (2003: 150), 'Grounded theory is not a description of a kind of theory. Rather it represents a general way of generating theory (or, even more generically, a way of having ideas on the basis of empirical research).' The theorizing is generated by tacking back and forth between the nitty-gritty specificities of empirical data and more abstract ways of thinking about them. Philosophically, this tacking back and forth is called '"abductive" reasoning ... a sort of "third way" between the Scylla of inductive reasoning and the Charybdis of hypothetico deductive logic' (Atkinson et al., 2003: 149). 'Abduction is to move from a conception of something to a different, possibly more developed or deeper conception of it' (Dey, 2004: 91; Richardson and Kramer, 2006). Ideally, the theorizing offered downstream in research reports should comfortably 'handle' the data, be sufficient to address variation and change, and offer a fresh theoretical grasp of the phenomenon that has practical applications.

In the most common practices of using/ doing GT, the researcher/analyst initially generates a research question and tentatively decides what kinds of data would speak to that question in interesting and meaningful ways. Most GT research has been based on field research/participant observation and/or in-depth open-ended interviews, although this is now beginning to change. Appropriate institutional permissions would then be sought for pursuing human subjects-based research. In the US, this typically involves extensive research design, including specification of and permissions from sites for participant observation (if private), and interview guides (sometimes for the different categories of persons to be interviewed). Once permission is in hand, data collection begins. And in GT, so too do the analytic processes.

Typically, the researcher codes the qualitative data (open coding)—word by word, segment by segment—and gives temporary labels (codes) to particular phenomena. Over time, the analyst determines whether codes generated through one data source also appear elsewhere, and elaborates their properties. Memos are written on codes. Related codes that seem robust through the on-going coding process are then densified into more enduring and analytically ambitious 'categories'. Ambitious memos are written about each designated category: what it means; what are instances of it; what is the range of variation within it found in the data to date; what it does and does not seem to 'take into account'? Those categories that endure (over time some disappear from interest and others may collapse into one another) are ultimately integrated into a theoretical analysis of the substantive area that is the immediate focus of the current research project.

Thus a 'grounded theory' of a particular phenomenon of concern is composed of the analytic codes and categories generated abductively in the analysis and assessed in terms of their theoretical/analytic capabilities. Over time, the categories are explicitly integrated to form a theory of the substantive area that is the focus of the research project. In Straussian versions of GT, analytic diagramming is encouraged, placing the key forms of human action (basic social processes) at the center and key conditions for and consequences of that action arrayed somehow around them. Thus the analyst generates an empirically-based 'substantive theory' of x that is grounded in empirical work. Traditionally, over time, after the researcher(s) have generated multiple substantive theories of a particular broad area of interest through an array of empirical research projects—or so the argument went—more 'formal theory' could be developed (see esp. Strauss, 1995). Formal theory was used here in the modernist/enlightenment sense of social theory aiming at 'Truth' across time, space and circumstance, and I return to this point below.

What remains relatively unique and very special to this approach was, first, GT's requirement that analysis begin as soon as there are data. Coding begins immediately, and theorizing based on that coding does as well, however provisionally (Glaser, 1978). Second, if the data do not seem adequate to the goals of the project, data-gathering strategies may change and/or expand. In GT, what is known as 'sampling' is driven not necessarily (or not only) by attempts to be 'representative' of some social body or population or its heterogeneities, but especially and explicitly by *theoretical* concerns that have emerged in the provisional analysis to date. Such 'theoretical sampling' focuses on finding *new data sources* (persons or things—and *not* theories) that can best explicitly address specific theoretically interesting facets of the emergent analysis. For example, the researcher might seek out the person(s) they think would know most about x from a particular angle of vision that the researcher wants to understand. Or if a particular technology is part of the research scene, participant observation around that technology in actual use might be arranged. Theoretical sampling has been integral to GT from the outset, remains a fundamental strength of this analytic approach, and is also crucial for SA.[5]

In fact, it can be argued that in GT precisely what is to be studied *emerges* from the analytic process over time, rather than being designated a priori. I wholly agree with Atkinson et al.'s (2003: 163) summation that 'the true legacy of Glaser and Strauss is a collective awareness of the heuristic value of developmental research designs [through theoretical sampling] and exploratory data analytic strategies, not a "system" for conducting and analyzing research.' This can be a much more modest than arrogant approach to the production of new knowledge. It can take 'experience' into account in all its densities and complexities (Scott, 1992)—especially the experiences of the researcher with the project and their reflexivity about it.

Most research using GT has relied on fieldwork to generate interview and/or ethnographic data through which to analyze human action (e.g., Glaser, 1993; Strauss and Corbin, 1997). Conventional GT has focused on generating the 'basic social process' occurring in the data concerning the phenomenon of concern—the basic form of human action. Studies have been done, for example, on *living with* chronic illness (Charmaz, 1991), *disciplining* the scientific study of reproduction (Clarke, 1998) and pain medicine (Baszanger, 1998), *classifying* and its consequences (Bowker and Star, 1999), *making* CPR the main emergency response to sudden death (Timmermans, 1999), and *creating* a new social actor—the unborn patient—via fetal surgery (Casper, 1998).

In a traditional GT study, the key or basic social process is typically articulated in gerund form connoting ongoing action, and at an abstract level. Around this basic process, the analyst then constellates the particular and distinctive conditions, strategies, actions, and practices engaged in by human and non-human actors involved with/in the process and their consequences. For example, sub-processes of disciplining/making the reproductive sciences included *formalizing* a scientific discipline, *establishing* stable access to research materials, *gleaning* fiscal support for research, *producing* contraceptives and other techno-scientific products, and *handling* the social controversies the science provokes (e.g., regarding use of contraceptives) (Clarke, 1998). Excellent projects have been done using GT, and this action-centered approach continues to be fundamentally important analytically.[6]

CRITIQUES OF GROUNDED THEORY METHOD AND RESEARCH

Critiques have been mounted of both GT as a research method per se and of GT research in practice (i.e., how GT has actually been used by researchers). First, over the forty years of its existence, the wide array of critiques of GT as a method have largely fallen within the general critiques of qualitative research as not positivist (enough), reliant upon oral statements which can be lies, reliant upon researchers who are likely biased, etc. That is, GT as a method for qualitative research has been viewed by some as on the far side of the natural/social science/ interpretation divides, and I will not elaborate upon these critiques here (but see, e.g., Clarke, 2005: Chap. 1; Denzin and Lincoln, 1994; 2000; 2005).

Coming from those for whom qualitative research is legitimate, critiques of GT as method include the views that it is too esoteric and difficult to learn except via apprenticeship, which is not always possible; that there is slippage or 'method slurring' between grounded theory and phenomenology for example; and that in small studies the data may be over-theorized and/or over-generalized.[7] Atkinson et al. (2003: 148, 150) note that GT is often written about in an 'over-reverential way' and that 'a set of stultifying procedural orthodoxies' have become common, especially but not only since the Strauss and Corbin *The Basics of Qualitative Analysis* (1990) appeared. They also note that, contra some users' assumptions, GT is not a school of sociological theory.

Another critique emerges from some who prefer narrative and other individual voice-centered modes of research who take GT to task for 'fracturing' the data, for 'violating' the integrity of participants' narratives, for 'pulling apart' stories, etc. (e.g., Mattingly and Garro, 2000; Riessman, 1993). To me, analysis such as that offered by GT and various narrative projects of (re)representation are two deeply different qualitative research approaches. They do different work in the world and can themselves be viewed as

standpoints (G. Miller, 1997) or perspectives that privilege different facets of social life.[8] Both can produce valuable and useful contributions to knowledge.

From a quite different angle came (neo-) Marxist critiques of ethnography generally and of GT in particular, asserting since the 1960s that these approaches took neither power nor social structures seriously enough, and were too devoted to micro-level analytics.[9] This is a now quite old and tired debate. But let me note that, for Strauss, structure and power are always relentlessly processual (enacted and hence existing in and through actions/concrete practices); they are also relentlessly social, organizational and structural through the plastic/elastic forms of social worlds, arenas, discourses and negotiations at the meso level. At any given moment, there is some version in effect of a negotiated or processual ordering (Strauss, 1993)—ways of working, sets of operant if continually revised practices—close to what Foucault (1991: 75) called a 'regime of practices'. This is precisely what Strauss sought to operationalize in GT through the conditional matrices discussed below. In the 1990s, Denzin (1992: 63) declared: 'The problem of the astructural bias in symbolic interactionism is a dead issue.' Resurrecting it in the new millennium, Bourdieusians and others have re-animated such critiques of Chicago School/interactionist field research more generally (e.g., Burawoy, 2000; Wacquant, 2002), and interactionists have responded (Anderson, 2002; Dunier, 2002; and Newman, 2002). My personal response is that these critics have a woefully insufficient grasp of the range of work that uses GT, including at the meso level and explicitly including analyses of structure and power. As Anderson clearly stated, this is 'an ideologically driven critique' (2002: 1533).

Over the past forty years that GT has been used by researchers, a wide array of critiques has arisen of some of this work. While there are intellectually and theoretically inadequate users of all research methods, I must concur, after recent reviews, that GT does seem to suffer from this substantially, perhaps due to its popularity. Strauss lamented this frequently in his lifetime (he died in 1996). The main critiques include the views that GT researchers too often have:[10]

- too small a 'sample' or number of participants;
- generated thematic analyses rather than action analyses of the 'basic social processes' characteristic of the domain of inquiry;
- used the phrase 'using grounded theory' as a rhetorical gloss or *mantra* rather than as a statement of actual research practice;
- reflected a deeply inadequate grasp of theoretical sampling;
- reflected an inadequate grasp of the Meadian concept of perspective which undergirds GT, thereby problematizing researcher reflexivity;
- failed to move analytically from codes to categories;
- rarely offered analytic diagrams that lay out the basic forms of action/process in the substantive area studied and the conditions which affect them; and
- both reflected a deeply inadequate grasp of theoretical integration as a practice and failed to do it.

The greatest problem seems to be 'analysis lite', which is not enough. As Locke noted, the grounded theory label is used too often as a 'rhetoric of justification as opposed to a rhetoric of explication' (1996: 244).

What is to be done? Certainly researchers can be aware of and work against such risks and dangers, and Strauss and Corbin explicitly suggested strategies to do so (1990: 249–58; and 1998: 265–75). In addition, more constructivist grounded theorists encourage more modest claims-making. For example, what Charmaz calls 'interpretive sufficiency' (Charmaz, 2006) means both more explicitly situated analytic claims-making and the avoidance of over-generalization and over-abstraction (e.g., Van den Hoonaard, 1997). In Daly's words, the challenge for presenting a theoretical text today is to present theory 'not as objective truth but as a located and limited story … [T]o keep theory in play but to redefine theory in a way that keeps the theorist in play—all within the bounds of science' (1997: 360, 353). This may sound easier, but is actually more complex and demanding.

DIVERGENCES AND DEBATES *AMONG* GROUNDED THEORISTS

Within the multiple and heterogeneous social worlds where GT method is used, some serious rifts have occurred over the years, largely articulated since c. 1990. These can be described as occurring at least between Glaser/Glaserians and Strauss/Straussians, or Strauss and Corbin *Basics* advocates, and/or between those who pursue traditional/positivist (increasingly called 'classic') versions of GT and those for whom more constructivist/postmodernist versions are much preferred, and/or between those who are more theoretically functionalist (while claiming an atheoretical neutrality/objectivity) and those who are more or less explicitly symbolic interactionist/poststructuralist. There is much overlap but there are also many more than two positions on the various issues involved, and I seek to avoid over-simplification here.

Historical Background

Historically, Glaser and Strauss (1967), Glaser (1978) and Schatzman and Strauss (1973) argued that GT as a methodological approach could be effectively used by people from a variety of theoretical as well as disciplinary perspectives. That is, they initially took a 'mix and match' approach. Their challenge—which they ably met—was to articulate a new theoretically oriented methodology in the belly of the *haut* positivist quantitative sociological beast of the 1960s. They sought to do so through a *systematic* (rather than impressionistic) approach to analyzing mostly (but not only) qualitative research data.[11] Their emphases in the early works cited were on taking a *naturalistic* approach to research, having initially *modest* (read substantively focused) theoretical goals, and being *systematic* in what we might today call the interrogation of research data in order to work against what they and others then saw as the 'distorting subjectivities' or biases of the researcher in the concrete processes of interpretive analysis.

Strauss and Glaser sought to make theoretical sense within an increasingly quantitative and scientistically oriented discipline of sociology with increasingly mechanistic methods. They sought to do so by providing what was then most obviously missing from the disciplinary toolbox: a reasonable approach to collecting and analyzing qualitative data that seriously attempted to be faithful to the understandings, interpretations, intentions and perspectives of the people studied on their own terms, as expressed through their actions as well as their words. Another goal of Strauss and Glaser was for a method that could travel across some of the usual divides of the academy without violating core disciplinary and/or social science/humanities concerns. In these too they succeeded, perhaps beyond their wildest dreams.

In the 1970s, Glaser published his own 'take' on GT, emphasizing *Theoretical Sensitivity* (1978). Here we can see emerging the increasingly abstract version(s) of GT for which Glaser is known, perhaps most especially in his chart of the 'basic social processes' compared to social structural units (cf. Glaser, 1978: 109–13), declared adequate to address most projects. In the 1980s, Strauss published his vision of GT, *Qualitative Analysis for Social Scientists* (1987). In contrast, this was deeply grounded in the actual practices of doing GT research and analysis, through Strauss's use of transcripts of actual sessions of working analysis groups to illustrate how various problems could be addressed. He led such groups at UCSF until his death, emphasizing movement into analysis, coding, memoing, diagramming, theoretical integration, team meetings and the importance of generating a positive interactive culture for group data analysis. Engaged group work provokes layered reflexivities, as participants continuously bump into the perspectives of others on both their own and others' data, and must take these somehow into account.[12] Strauss built such provocations to reflexivity into his usual GT work processes. I see this as the fundamental site of difference between Glaser and Strauss.

Then, in 1990 Strauss published the first edition of *The Basics of Qualitative Analysis: Grounded Theory Procedures and Techniques*, co-authored with Juliet Corbin, a nurse-sociologist with whom he had collaborated on projects on chronic illness, and dedicated by both to Barney Glaser. Their goal was simultaneously to make GT more accessible, especially to researchers in applied fields, and to improve the quality of actual GT research (see back cover of *The Basics*). As this (too?) handily accessible version of GT was taken up around the world, most criticism centered on how *The Basics'* approaches to the tasks of GT were too formulaic (do *x*, then *y*, add *z* and stir). I myself and many other long-time grounded theorists generally shared in this criticism (ongoing personal communications: Kathy Charmaz, Susan Leigh Star, Carolyn Wiener), but kept on going, continuing to use the versions of GT we had constructed for ourselves from the earlier texts and work with Strauss and/or Glaser.[13] But the most extensive critique has come from Glaser, and it continues today.

In a nutshell, GT co-founder Barney Glaser (1992) accused Strauss of abandoning their original version of GT, and 'forcing data' through the procedures outlined in *Basics* rather than allowing 'emergence' and 'letting the data speak for themselves'. Other points of Glaser's critique include the importance of *abstract agency* over and against reflexivity/acknowledgement of the researcher in the research; avoidance of preconceived questions, frameworks and a priori categories; refusal of hypotheses; avoidance of the multiple kinds of coding (e.g., axial); and so on. In general, the basic procedures promoted by *Basics* were to be eschewed. For Glaser (1992: 43), 'categories emerge upon comparison and properties emerge upon more comparison. And that is all there is to it.' Glaser has often written unclearly, unhelpfully and contemptuously about individuals. With many others, I find Glaser's diatribes unprofessional at best.[14]

Strauss did not choose to respond to Glaser at length. He did, however, make some sharp if not barbed points about openness to change and ownership of intellectual property. To wit, the epigraph on the dedication pages of Strauss and Corbin's *Basics* of both 1990 and 1998 is a Deweyan commentary on the importance of change to creativity that I believe was addressed to Glaser: "'If the artist does not perfect new vision in his process of doing, he acts mechanically and repeats some old model fixed like a blueprint in his mind"—John Dewey, *Art as Experience*, 1934, p. 50.' Strauss and Corbin (1994: 283) also noted that 'no inventor has permanent possession of the invention—certainly not even of its name—and furthermore we would not wish to do so.'

Current Debates

Cutting across yet deeply imbricated in these more personalized and sometimes oddly personified debates, and muddying as well as clarifying them, are a much broader set of theoretical and methodological issues. At the same time that Strauss and Glaser were elaborating the method they had jointly produced and thousands were using it, a sea change was occurring across the social sciences and humanities—and in many ways across the entire academy. Beginning in the 1930s and cresting from the 1970s through the 1990s, the deepest questions of the sociology of knowledge were placed on the academic discussion table (e.g., McCarthy, 1996): Who produces what kinds of knowledge? For whom? Under what conditions? What other kinds are eclipsed in the process? Simultaneously, the social construction of reality (e.g., Berger and Luckmann, 1966), poststructuralisms and discourse studies more generally (e.g., Foucault, Deleuze and Guattari, Derrida) posed massive challenges to traditional positivist approaches to the making of knowledge. Cutting back across all these currents came waves of scholarship and theorizing from feminists, critical race theorists, and postcolonial and technoscience studies scholars (e.g., Spivak, Stuart Hall, Latour, etc.). Since at least 1980 in the US, all these challenges have been broadly taken up in qualitative methods in general (e.g., Denzin and Lincoln, 1994; 2000; 2005)

and in GT in particular (however inadequately, I subsume them under the rubric 'the postmodern turn' [cf. Clarke, 2005: xxiii–xxvii and *passim*]).

The Glaser/Strauss debates can thus be read as an instantiation of struggles around these fundamental paradigm shifts—known in some places as the culture wars or science wars (Ashman and Barringer, 2001). Glaser and Strauss can thus be viewed as representing some key positions in these paradigmatic battles of discourse and practice. The person who led off on the constructionist 'side' in bringing these issues explicitly into the GT debates is Kathy Charmaz, a former student of both Glaser and Strauss at UCSF who, aside from them, has likely written the most about GT over the years.[15] In 'Between Positivism and Postmodernism: Implications for Methods' (1995), Charmaz discussed how GT stood uneasily between positivism and postmodernism, asserting that both tendencies were pursued within the domain of GT, and delineating GT's roots in both Columbia-style functionalism (Glaser) and Chicago-style symbolic interactionism (Strauss). By 2000, Charmaz was noting how traditional GT generally tends to preserve tastes and flavors of 1950s' and 1960s' styles of American positivism and scientism, and that such tendencies were clearly present in the original works done by Glaser and Strauss themselves (Charmaz, 2000). Others soon echoed this viewpoint (Atkinson et al., 2003; Bryant, 2002; 2003; Locke, 2001). Manning and Cullum-Swan (1996) assert that this was utterly common in the 1960s, when Goffmanian and ethnomethodological approaches were considered radical.

Since 2000, then, an array of critics has expanded the critique of traditional or classic GT (e.g., Bryant 2002, 2003; Clarke 2003, 2005; Dey 1999, 2004; Locke 1996, 2001). They find that while many scholars working in the GT tradition have long since embraced some version of constructionism and truth with a small 't', a certain (sometimes) naive realism or 'bottom line-ism' lurks in positivist versions. This can be manifest in the following practices of which such grounded theorists may or may not be aware:

1. a lack of reflexivity about research processes and products including a naive notion of giving 'voice' to the unheard from 'their own' perspective, including the pretense that the researcher can and should be invisible;
2. oversimplifications such as emphases on commonalities and strains toward coherence;
3. oversimplifications such as analytic reduction to a single (rather than multiple) social process as characteristic of a particular phenomenon or situation;
4. interpretations of data variation as 'negative cases'; and
5. the search for 'purity' in grounded theory.

Here I will only discuss current debates about the search for 'purity' and 'objectivity' by more positivist grounded theorists, who tend to believe methodological (and perhaps other) purity is not only possible but desirable, contra more constructivist, postmodern, interactionist versions of GT (on points 1–4, see Clarke, 2005: 11–16).

To begin, over the last decade of his life, I saw Strauss as more and perhaps increasingly constructionist in how he used and understood GT in both his teaching and independent writing (Strauss 1987, 1993). Strauss was also clearly and deeply rooted in interactionism and commented on this as a difference between himself and Glaser (see esp. Corbin, 1998: 125–6). Much of Strauss's writing towards the end was exactly on interactionist theorists and their legacies (Blumer, Davis, and Hughes), writing that also served to situate his own work among that of these admired colleagues.[16] During these years, several of Strauss's students began asserting (in part through the sociology of knowledge and inflected through science and technology studies) that epistemology is not separable from ontology, and that grounded theory/ symbolic interactionism constitutes a theory/ methods package.[17] Star (1989) framed such packages as including a set of epistemological and ontological assumptions along with concrete practices through which a set of practitioners go about their work, including relating to/with one another and the various non-human entities involved in the situation. This concept of a theory–methods package

focuses on the non-fungibility of ontology and epistemology as co-constitutive. 'Method, then, is not the servant of theory: method actually grounds theory' (Jenks, 1995: 12).

In sharp and vivid contrast, for Glaser, grounded theory 'is not underlined by symbolic interaction nor constructed data. GT uses all as data, of which these are just one kind of data' (Glaser with Holton, 2004: Section 2, p. 7). I read this as constituting two distinct points. First, Glaser disavows symbolic interactionism as grounding (his version of) grounded theory. I agree with this, as his version is deeply positivist, most significantly eschews Mead, and even includes 'core variable' language. Second, and of great significance, Glaser demonstrates here (and *passim* in his recent work) that he does not understand social constructionism as an epistemological/ ontological position. He thinks *some* data are 'constructed' while *other* data are 'pure'. Constructionism asserts that *all* meanings of all kinds of things—material and non-materials—are constructed by people as they 'do' life; there is, therefore, no space outside/ beyond construction (e.g., Berger and Luckmann, 1966; Blumer, 1958).

Related to this point are several issues about researchers' reflexivity. The first concerns the role of the researcher. Locke attributes Glaser and Strauss's methodological disagreements to fundamental differences in perspective on the role/presence of the researcher in the research process:

Strauss locates agency for [grounded] theory development in human researchers, whereas Glaser confers agency on neutral methods and data ... Thus Strauss and Corbin's (1990) rewriting expresses a very active, even provocative, role in which researchers essentially interrogate the data they gather to arrive at conceptual categories ... Glaser [assumes] a one-way mirror through which the natural world might be revealed ... Clearly, in this tradition, the natural world is 'out there' ... This portrayal of researchers presented in Glaser's 1992 publication is consistent with the images scientists in the positivist tradition present of themselves ... [In contrast, Strauss and Corbin] view researchers as interpreters of the data they study who can build good complex theories by actively 'opening up' the data to discovery (Locke, 1996: 240–1).[18]

Glaser is clearly *not* animating data as the 'nonhuman actant' in some version of semiotic actor–network theory (Latour, 1987). Locke (1996: 241) notes that, *au contraire*, Glaser is using a rhetorical device named by Charles Bazerman and James Paradis (1991) as 'the active seeking of passive restraints'— attempting to use methods that will constrain the influence of the researcher. I find that Glaser goes beyond this to further claim that using such methods erases all traces of the researcher, and agree with Locke, Bryant (2002; Bryant, 2003), and many others that this is a conceptual and practical impossibility. Strauss himself also noted a lack of reflexivity on Glaser's part (Corbin, 1998).

On another point of serious concern, Glaser asserts that GT pertains only to social psychology (Glaser with Holton, 2004: Section 4). While much if not most research using GT does fall within social psychology and focus on making sense of individuals' lived experiences of *x*, *y* or *z*, I certainly see it as conceptually much broader. GT is not only fully sociological, but also fully capable of handling meso/organizational concerns, as it did for Strauss (e.g., 1987, 1993). It can also be relevant far beyond sociology. For example, an excellent article challenging traditional economic theory offers a sophisticated gendered reconceptualization of social indicators based on the use of GT with focus group data in Australia (Austen et al., 2003). Shim's (2005) work similarly deconstructs the epidemiological categories of race, class and gender, reflexively using the master's tools on the master's tools.

The last point of debate that I will address concerns the concept of 'context.' I frame it here through Glaser, Strauss and GT, but it goes far beyond them (e.g., Miller, 1997). According to Glaser, 'context must emerge as a relevant category or as a theoretical code like all other categories in a GT. *It cannot be assumed as relevant in advance*' (Glaser with Holton, 2004: Section 2, p. 8, emphasis added). Undergirding Glaser's refutation of context as to be taken into account is the assumption of the possibility of transcendent social theory. Glaser's position is that '... the

goal of GT is conceptual theory abstract of time, place and people' (Glaser with Holton, 2004: Section 2, p. 9); or, grounded theory can and should be transcendent. Neither history nor geography nor culture, much less gender, race, class, or ethnicity, necessarily matters in a Glaserian world. Glaser is claiming the meaningful 'voice from nowhere' that will guide us to some heavenly methodological redemption from messes, ambiguities, contingencies, embodied researchers and other materialities, multiplicities, etc. (Haraway, 1991, 1997). He explicitly seeks the 'god's-eye view' position (Haraway, 1991) from which to write up research while claiming to dwell in what Traweek (2000) has called 'the culture of no culture'—i.e., Western science. This is precisely the 'turn' that the sociology of knowledge per se refutes. *All knowledges and knowledge productions are situated and non-innocent.* Voices from nowhere are merely hidden claims-makers and, as Hughes (1971) argued, 'Things can always be otherwise.' Taking all this into account is part of the paradigm-rupturing transition, or turn from modern to postmodern, that Haraway (1991: 186) brilliantly calls 'a kind of epistemological electro-shock therapy'. Glaser has wholly refused this turn (e.g., Bryant, 2003). Strauss only partially did so.

Dey (2004: 92) has argued that if a goal of GT was to 'generate theory that is relevant and practical as well as analytic, ... [h]ad Glaser and Strauss accepted theory as context-bound rather than aspiring to make it context-free, they might have effected a happier reconciliation between these values'. Strauss's prolonged disagreement with Glaser on this point of the salience of context is demonstrated through his development of the conditional matrices, discussed next. In this emphasis, along with his reflexivity, Strauss moved partly, and I would say significantly, around the postmodern turn. Thus it is with Strauss that I have asked, 'How, then, can we meaningfully incorporate analysis of the precise ways in which particular contexts may matter into the processes of doing qualitative research?' I next use the conditional matrix as a platform from which to launch SA as one possible set of answers to such questions (however partial).

FROM CONTEXT TO THE CONDITIONAL MATRIX AND THE DEVELOPMENT OF SITUATIONAL ANALYSIS

Scientific theories begin with situations ... Theories are responses to the contingencies of these situations—courses of action articulated with yet more courses of action. The theories that scientists form about nature are the actions that both meet specific contingencies and frame future solutions (Star, 1989: 15–16, emphasis in original).

For interactionists, structural elements are the enduring, 'given' aspects or *conditions* of *situations*, the aspects which we can bet with relative assuredness will remain basically stable, 'in place' and predictable for some time. Structural elements are not unchanging; rather, they are just slower to change, more obdurate. Towards the end of his career, Strauss worked assiduously on framing and articulating ways to do GT research that included *specifying structural conditions*—literally making them visible in the analysis— along with the action. The brilliance of Strauss's interactionist sociology was rooted most of all in understanding action as situated activity (Hall, 1987; Katovich and Reese, 1993). Strauss's conditional matrices are thus means of enabling researchers to more easily and more fully capture the specific conditions under which the action occurs and which must be taken into sociological account. The main problem, as we shall see, was that the Straussian conditional matrix did not adequately address how researchers could explicate the structural conditions of situated action.

Strauss and Corbin developed several versions of the conditional matrix, intended to provide systematic paths for grounded theorists to follow. Figure 23.1 offers Strauss and Corbin's (1990: 163) Conditional Matrix. The matrices are generally organized into 'levels': international (economic, cultural, religious,

scientific, and environmental issues); national (political, governmental, cultural, economic, gender, age, ethnicity, race, particular national issues, etc.); and, depending upon where the research is undertaken, community, organizational, institutional, or local group and individual/(inter)actional setting. At the core is action—both strategic and routine.[19] Both macro-to-meso-to-micro and micro-to-meso-to-macro impacts can be significant.

To me, the conditional matrices do not do the conceptual analytic work Strauss wanted done in terms of GT method. Strauss gestured too abstractly toward the possible salience of the structural elements of situations rather than insisting upon their concrete and detailed empirical specification and clear explication as a requisite part of doing GT *analysis* in practice. There was an a priori and formulaic feeling about the matrix rather than good directions toward empirical work.

Instead I offer a Situational Matrix (see Figure 23.2). *Here, conditions of the situation are in the situation.* There is no such thing as 'context'. The conditional elements of the situation need to be specified in the analysis of the situation itself, as *they are constitutive of it*, not merely surrounding it or framing it or contributing to it. They *are* it. Regardless of whether some might construe them as local or global, internal or external, close in or far away, or whatever, the fundamental question is: '*How do these conditions appear—make themselves felt as consequential—inside the empirical situation under examination?*' At least some answers to that question can be found through doing situational analyses.

Ultimately, what structures and conditions any situation is an empirical question—or set of questions. Certainly there are expectable elements of any situation that we would consider in the abstract and seek out in their specificities in the concrete (i.e., in the empirical data). These are, I believe, what Strauss and Corbin were pointing toward with 'national', 'regional', 'community' and 'professional' analytic signposts. And many of the elements Strauss and Corbin included are also present in my Situational Matrix, an

Figure 23.1   Strauss & Corbin's Conditional Matrix

Source: Strauss and Corbin (1990:163)

interim diagram standing between the conditional matrices and situational analyses. The Situational Matrix frames situational analysis. In it we can see that the elements formerly arrayed *around* the action are now imaged as *in* the action, as actual *parts of* the situation of action. Where to next?

WHAT IS SITUATIONAL ANALYSIS?

Through SA, I seek to push GT more fully around the postmodern turn, through explicitly extending analysis to discursive data including narrative, historical and visual materials. Because *we and the people and things we choose to study* are all routinely both producing and awash in seas of discourses, analyzing only individual and collective human actors no longer suffices for many qualitative projects. Increasingly, historical, visual, narrative and other discourse materials and non-human material cultural objects of all kinds must be included as elements of our research and subjected to analysis because they are increasingly understood/interpreted as both constitutive of and consequential for the phenomena we study. The

Figure 23.2 Clarke's Situational Matrix

Source: Clarke (2005: 73)

trend toward multi-site research is thus supported. SA allows researchers to draw together studies of discourse and agency, action and structure, image, text and context, history and the present moment—to analyze complex situations of inquiry broadly conceived. Thus it can support researchers from heterogeneous backgrounds pursuing a wide array of projects.

SA has a radically different conceptual infrastructure or guiding metaphor from the action-centered 'basic social process' concept that undergirds traditional GT. In SA that is supplemented with Strauss's

situation-centered 'social worlds/arenas/ negotiations' framework.[20] Building upon and extending Strauss's work, SA offers three main cartographic approaches:

1. *Situational maps* that lay out the major human, non-human, discursive and other elements in the research situation of inquiry and provoke analysis of relations among them;
2. *Social worlds/arenas maps* that lay out the collective actors, key nonhuman elements, and the arena(s) of commitment and discourse within which they are engaged in ongoing negotiations—meso-level interpretations of the situation; and

Figure 23.3   Messy Abstract Situational Map

3. *Positional maps* that lay out the major positions taken, and *not* taken, in the data vis-à-vis particular axes of difference, concern and controversy around issues in the situation of inquiry.

All three kinds of maps are intended as analytic exercises, fresh ways into social science data that are especially well suited to contemporary studies from solely interview-based to multi-sited research projects. They are intended as supplemental approaches to traditional GT analyses that center on the framing of action—basic social processes. Thus, in addition to action, these maps elucidate the key elements, discourses, structures and conditions that characterize the situation of inquiry. Through mapping the data, the analyst constructs the situation of inquiry empirically. The

situation per se becomes the ultimate unit of analysis, and understanding its elements and their relations is the primary goal. Thus SA can deeply situate research projects themselves.

Here I will offer only one map to provide an introductory sense of SA. See Figure 23.3: Messy Abstract Situational Map. Obviously drawing deeply on Strauss and Corbin's conditional matrices as conceptual resources, I see a wide array of structural/conditional elements as potentially constitutive of situations in their ethnographic, discursive, non-human, technological and other specificities. The map as a whole *is* the situation of inquiry. Many kinds or genres of people and things can be in that situation and the labels are intended as generic, awaiting empirical specification by the researcher.

The fundamental assumption of this map—and of SA generally—is that everything in the situation *both constitutes and affects* most everything else in the situation in some way(s). Everything actually in the situation or understood to be so conditions the possibilities of action relationally. People and things, humans and non-humans, fields of practice, discourses, disciplinary and other regimes/formations, symbols, controversies, organizations and institutions—each and all can be present and mutually consequential. Here macro/meso/micro distinctions dissolve in the face of presence/absence and co-constitutiveness.

The first goal is to descriptively lay out as best one can all the most important human and non-human elements in the situation of concern of the research broadly conceived. In the Meadian sense, the questions are: Who and what are in this situation? Who and what matters in this situation? What elements 'make a difference' in this situation? The map should include all the analytically pertinent human and non-human, material and symbolic/discursive elements of a particular situation as framed by those in it and by the analyst.

The situational map can be used to design and execute multi-site projects in a flexible and iteratively responsive manner useful from preliminary thinking through the completion stages of research. That is, the situational map can be constructed *and reconstructed over time* to specify the major elements in the research situation of concern about which data need to be gathered, analyzed and written. The maps are intended to capture and discuss the messy complexities of the situation in their dense relations and permutations, and intentionally work *against* the usual simplifications so characteristic of scientific work. The situational maps are emergent, allowing the research to feature and background different elements without losing track of potentially important things/issues. The long-term research goal is to get a grip of some sort on most everything in the situation.

Thus SA supplements constructivist GT with alternative approaches to *both* data gathering and analysis/interpretation. It enhances our capacities to do incisive studies of differences of perspective, of highly complex situations of action and positionality, of the heterogeneous discourses in which we are all constantly awash, and of the situated knowledges of life itself thereby produced. It offers the possibility of simultaneously addressing voice and discourse, texts and the consequential materialities and symbolisms of the non-human, the dynamics of historical change and, last but far from least, power in both its more solid and fluid forms.

CONCLUSIONS

While scholars utilizing grounded theory have ranged from positivist to social constructivist over the decades, recent work is shifting toward more constructivist assumptions/epistemologies (Baszanger and Dodier, 2004; Bryant, 2003; Charmaz, 2000; Locke, 2001). SA is part of these shifts. I seek with Charmaz (2000: 510) to 'reclaim these tools from their positivist underpinnings to form a revised, more open-ended practice of grounded theory that stresses its emergent, constructivist elements', and to 'use grounded theory methods as flexible, heuristic strategies.' Charmaz emphasizes that a focus on meaning-making furthers interpretive, constructivist, and, I would add, relativist/perspectival understandings. Building on Straussian GT usually used with field data and/or in-depth interviews, SA explicitly extends analysis to discursive data including narrative, historical and visual materials. The important trend toward multi-site research in the social sciences and humanities is thus supported.

The groundedness of good grounded theorizing lies not only in the data per se but also in the seriousness and thoroughness of the analyst's representational practices. The commitment to representing *all* understandings, all knowledge(s) and action(s) of those studied—as well as the analyst's own—as perspectival is crucial to 'bring out the amazing complexity of what lies, in, behind, and beyond, those data' (e.g., Strauss, 1987: 110; 1993; 1995). More modest and partial but serious, useful and hopefully provocative grounded and situational analyses and theorizing are sufficient. Further, rather than focusing on commonalities, we can pursue directions and angles of vision that reveal difference(s) and complexities, heterogeneous positionings, including but not limited to differences in power in situations. The work of doing GT and SA should make thick description and thick interpretation possible, what Fosket (2002: 40) called 'thick analysis'. The possibility of analytic extension of theorizing into other parallel or related situations remains, but is here accomplished through making comparisons of the conditions in the different situations rather than through formalized abstraction of theory from history and circumstance.

As with other research methods, critiques and debates about GT have existed since its inception with more or less intensity. Far more than technical methods squabbles, these are manifestations of some of the most important intellectual and social shifts of the twentieth century, with extensive implications in the twenty-first. Glaser and others have devoted much energy to policing boundaries and promulgating methodological 'anti-miscegenation laws' intended to prevent change and innovation in this method. Careful readers will recognize my very deep appreciation for and usage of many facets of GT, yet I am in deep disagreement with many of Glaser's recent fundamental(ist) points, and turn instead to Strauss (esp. 1987, 1993). Those who pursue GT and SA today and in future will need to negotiate their own pathways through all the potent questions of the sociology of knowledge and the postmodern turn as they are engaged by GT and SA. I believe the effort is well worthwhile, and fresh guidance is available in *The Handbook of Grounded*

Theory (Bryant and Charmaz, 2007). I find myself with Lather (2007: viii) seeking 'a fertile space and ethical practice in asking how research based knowledge remains possible after so much questioning of the very ground of science … gesturing toward the science possible after the critique of science …'.

ACKNOWLEDGEMENTS

I would like to thank Kathy Charmaz, Leigh Star, Virginia Olesen, and Patti Lather for their invaluable comments on this paper. I have also benefited for decades from our conversations about research methods generally and grounded theory in particular.

REFERENCES AND SELECT BIBLIOGRAPHY

Anderson, E. (2002) 'The ideologically driven critique', *American Journal of Sociology*, 107 (6): 1533–50.

Annells, M. (1996) 'Grounded theory method: Philosophical perspectives, paradigm of inquiry and postmodernism', *Qualitative Health Research*, 6 (3): 379–93.

Ashman, K. and Barringer, P. (2001) *After the Science Wars*. London and New York: Routledge.

Atkinson, P., Coffey, A. and Delamont, S. (2003) *Key Themes in Qualitative Research: Continuities and Change*. Walnut Creek, CA: AltaMira Press.

Austen, S., Jefferson, T. and Thein, V. (2003) 'Gendered social indicators and grounded theory', *Feminist Economics*, 9 (1): 1–18.

Baker, C., Wuest, J. and Stern, P. (1992) 'Method slurring: The grounded theory, phenomenology example', *Journal of Advanced Nursing*, 17: 1355–60.

Baszanger, I. (1998) *Inventing Pain Medicine: From the Laboratory to the Clinic*. New Brunswick, NJ: Rutgers University Press.

Baszanger, I. and Dodier, N. (2004) 'Ethnography: Relating the part to the whole', in D. Silverman (ed.), *Qualitative Research: Theory, Method, and Practice*. 2nd edition. London: Sage, pp. 9–34.

Bazerman, C. and Paradis, J. (eds.) (1991) *Textual Dynamics of Professions: Historical and Contemporary Studies of Writing in Professional Communities*. Madison: University of Wisconsin Press.

Bell, S.E. (2000) 'Experiencing illness in/and narrative', in C.E. Bird, P. Conrad and A.M. Fremont (eds.), *Handbook of Medical Sociology*. Upper Saddle River, NJ: Prentice Hall, pp. 184–99.

Benoliel, J.Q. (1996) 'Grounded theory and nursing knowledge', *Qualitative Health Research*, 6 (3): 406–28.

Berger, P. and Luckmann, T. (1966) *The Social Construction of Reality: A Treatise in the Sociology of Knowledge*. Garden City, NJ: Doubleday.

Blumer, H. (1958) 'Race prejudice as a sense of group position', *Pacific Sociological Review*, 1: 3–8.

Bochner, A.P. and Ellis, C. (eds.) (2001) *Ethnographically Speaking: Autoethnography, Literature, and Aesthetics*. Walnut Creek, CA: AltaMira Press.

Bowker, G. and Star, S. Leigh (1999) *Sorting Things Out: Classification and Its Consequences*. Cambridge, MA: MIT Press.

Bryant, A. (2002) 'Re-grounding grounded theory', *Journal of Information Technology Theory and Application*, 4 (1): 25–42.

——— (2003) 'A Constructive/ist Reponse to Glaser', *FQS Forum: Qualitative Social Research*, 4 (1). Available at: www.qualitative-research.net.fqs.

Bryant, A. and Charmaz, K. (eds.) (2007) *The Handbook of Grounded Theory*. London: Sage.

Bryman, A. and Burgess, R.G. (1994) 'Reflections on qualitative data', in A. Bryman and R.G. Burgess (eds.), *Analyzing Qualitative Data*. London: Routledge, pp. 216–26.

Burawoy, M. (2000) 'Introduction', in M. Burawoy et al. (eds.), *Ethnography Unbound: Power and Resistance in the Modern Metropolis*. Berkeley: University of California Press, pp. 1–27.

Carey, J.W. (2002) 'Cultural studies and symbolic interactionism: Notes in critique and tribute to Norman Denzin', *Studies in Symbolic Interaction*, 25: 199–209.

Casper, M.J. (1998) *The Making of the Unborn Patient: A Social Anatomy of Fetal Surgery*. New Brunswick, NJ: Rutgers University Press.

Charmaz, K. (1991) *Good Days, Bad Days: The Self in Chronic Illness and Time*. New Brunswick, NJ: Rutgers University Press.

——— (1995) 'Between positivism and postmodernism: Implications for methods', *Studies in Symbolic Interaction*, 17: 43–72.

——— (2000) 'Grounded theory: Objectivist and constructivist methods', in N. Denzin and Y. Lincoln (eds.), *Handbook of Qualitative Research*. Thousand Oaks, CA: Sage, 2nd ed., pp. 509–36.

——— (2005) 'Grounded theory in the 21st Century: A qualitative method for advancing social justice research', in N. Denzin and Y. Lincoln (eds.), *Handbook of Qualitative Research*. Thousand Oaks, CA: Sage, 3rd ed., pp. 507–36.

——— (2006) *Constructing Grounded Theory*. London: Sage.

Charmaz, K. and Mitchell, R. (2001) 'Grounded theory in ethnography', in P. Atkinson, A. Coffey, S. Delamont, J. Lofland and L. Lofland (eds.), *Handbook of Ethnography*. London, Thousand Oaks, CA: Sage, pp. 160–74.

Clarke, A.E. (1991) 'Social worlds theory as organization theory', in D. Maines (ed.), *Social Organization and Social Process: Essays in Honor of Anselm Strauss*. Hawthorne, NY: Aldine de Gruyter, pp. 17–42.

——— (1998) *Disciplining Reproduction: Modernity, American Life Sciences and the 'Problem of Sex'*. Berkeley: University of California Press.

——— (2002) '*Neue Wege der Qualitativen Forschung und die* Grounded Theory' (New Directions in Qualitative Methods and Grounded Theory Analysis), in D. Schaeffer (ed.), *Qualitative Gesundheits- und Pflegeforschung (New Directions in Qualitative Health Research)*. Bern: Verlag Hans Huber.

——— (2003) 'Situational analyses: Grounded theory mapping after the postmodern turn', *Symbolic Interaction*, 26 (4): 553–76.

——— (2005) *Situational Analysis: Grounded Theory After the Postmodern Turn*. Thousand Oaks, CA: Sage Pubs.

——— (2006) 'Feminisms, Grounded Theory and Situational Analysis', in S. Hesse-Biber (ed.), *The Handbook of Feminist Research: Theory and Praxis*. Thousand Oaks, CA: Sage. pp. 345–70.

——— (forthcoming) 'Situational Analysis: A Haraway-Inspired Feminist Approach to Qualitative Research', in S. Ghamari-Tabrizi (ed.) *Thinking with Donna Haraway*. Cambridge, MA: MIT Press.

Clarke, A.E. and Friese, C. (2007) 'Situational Analysis: Going Beyond Traditional Grounded Theory', in K. Charmaz and A. Bryant (eds.), *Handbook of Grounded Theroy*. London: Sage, pp. 694–743.

Clarke, A.E. and Star, S.L. (2003) 'Symbolic interactionist studies of science, technology and medicine', in L. Reynolds and N. Herman (eds.), *Symbolic Interactionism*. Walnut Creek, CA: Alta Mira Press, pp. 539–74.

——— (2007) 'Social Worlds/Arenas A Theory/Methods Package', in M. Lynch, O. Amsterdamska, E.J. Hackett, and J. Wajcman (eds.), *The New Handbook of Science and Technology Studies*. Cambridge, MA: MIT Press. pp. 113–37.

Corbin, J. (1998) 'Comment: Alternative interpretations – valid or not?', *Theory and Psychology*, 8 (1): 121–8.

Cresswell, J.W. (2002) *Educational Research: Planning, Conducting, and Evaluating Quantitative and Qualitative Research*. Upper Saddle River, NJ: Merrill/Prentice Hall.

Daly, K. (1997) 'Replacing theory in ethnography: A postmodern view', *Qualitative Inquiry*, 3(3): 343–65.

Denzin, N. (1989) *Interpretive Interactionism*. Newbury Park, CA: Sage.

——— (1992) *Symbolic Interactionism and Cultural Studies: The Politics of Interpretation*. Oxford: Basil Blackwell.

Denzin, N. and Lincoln, Y.E. (eds.) (1994) *Handbook of Qualitative Research*. Thousand Oaks, CA: Sage, 1st ed.

——— (eds.) (2000) *Handbook of Qualitative Research*. Thousand Oaks, CA: Sage, 2nd ed.

——— (eds.) (2005) *Handbook of Qualitative Research*. Thousand Oaks, CA: Sage, 3rd ed.

Dey, I. (1999) *Grounding Grounded Theory: Guidelines for Qualitative Inquiry*. San Diego, CA: Academic Press.

——— (2004) 'Grounded theory', in C. Seale, G. Gobo, J. Gubrium and D. Silverman (eds.), *Qualitative Research Practice*. London: Sage, pp. 80–93.

Dingwall, R. (1999) 'On the nonnegotiable in sociological life', in B. Glasner and R. Hertz (eds.), *Qualitative Sociology and Everyday Life*. Thousand Oaks, CA: Sage, pp. 215–225.

Dunier, M. (2002) 'What kind of combat sport is sociology?' *American Journal of Sociology*, 107 (6): 1551–76.

Ellis, C. and Flaherty, M. (eds.) (1992) *Investigating Subjectivity: Research on Lived Experience*. Newbury Park, CA: Sage.

Fishman, J.R. (2004) 'Manufacturing desire: The commodification of female sexual dysfunction', *Social Studies of Science*, 34(2): 187–218.

Fosket, J.R. (2002) 'Breast cancer risk and the politics of prevention: Analysis of a clinical trial', Ph.D. dissertation, University of California, San Francisco.

——— (2004) 'Constructing "high risk" women: The development and standardization of a breast cancer risk assessment tool', *Science, Technology & Human Values*, 29 (3): 291–313.

——— (forthcoming) '"Situating knowledge": Analyzing a clinical trial', *Qualitative Inquiry*, in review.

Foucault, M. (1991) 'Questions of method', in G. Burchell, C. Gordon and P. Miller (eds.), *The Foucault Effect: Studies in Governmentality*. Chicago: University of Chicago Press, pp. 73–86.

Fujimura, J. (1992) 'Crafting science: Standardized packages, boundary objects and "translation"', in A. Pickering (ed.), *Science as Practice and Culture*. Chicago: University of Chicago Press, pp. 168–214.

Gamson, J. (2000) 'Sexualities, queer theory and qualitative research', in N. Denzin and Y.E. Lincoln (eds.), *Handbook of Qualitative Research*. Thousand Oaks, CA: Sage, 2nd ed., pp. 347–65.

Gelder, K. and Thornton, S. (1997) *The Subcultures Reader*. London and New York: Routledge.

Glaser, B.G. (1978) *Theoretical Sensitivity: Advances in the Methodology of Grounded Theory*. Mill Valley, CA: The Sociology Press.

——— (1992) *Emergence Versus Forcing: Basics of Grounded Theory Analysis*. Mill Valley, CA: The Sociology Press.

——— (2002a) 'Constructivist grounded theory?', *FQS Forum: Qualitative Social Research*, 3(3). Available at: http://www.qualitative-research.net/fqs.

——— (2002b) 'Grounded theory and gender relevance', *Health Care for Women International*, 23 (8): 786–93.

——— (ed.) (1993) *Examples of Grounded Theory: A Reader*. Mill Valley, CA: The Sociology Press.

Glaser, B.G. with the assistance of Holton, J. (2004) 'Remodeling grounded theory', *Forum for Qualitative Social Research*, 5 (2). Available at: http://www.qualitative-research.net/fqs-texte/2-04/2-04glaser-e.htm

Glaser, B.G. and Strauss, A.L. (1967) *The Discovery of Grounded Theory: Strategies for Qualitative Research*. Chicago and London: Aldine and Weidenfeld and Nicolson.

Hall, P.M. (1987) 'Interactionism and the study of social organization', *The Sociological Quarterly*, 28 (1): 1–22.

——— (1997) 'Meta-power, social organization, and the shaping of social action', *Symbolic Interaction*, 20 (4): 397–418.

Hall, P.M. and McGinty, P.J.W. (2002) 'Social organization across space and time: The policy process, mesodomain analysis, and breadth of perspective', in S.C. Chew and D. Knotterus (eds.), *Structure, Culture and History: Recent Issues in Social Theory*. Lanham MD: Rowman and Littlefield Publications, pp. 303–22.

Haraway, D. (1991) 'Situated knowledges: The science question in feminism and the privilege of partial perspective', in *Simians, Cyborgs, and Women: The Reinvention of Nature*. New York: Routledge, pp. 183–202.

——— (1997) 'Modest_Witness@Second_Millennium', in *Modest_Witness@Second_Millennium. Female Man©_Meets_OncoMouse™: Feminism and Technoscience*. New York: Routledge, pp. 23–45.

Hughes, E.C. (1971) *The Sociological Eye*. Chicago: Aldine Atherton.

Jenks, C. (1995) 'The centrality of the eye in western culture: An introduction', in *Visual Culture: An Introduction*. London and New York: Routledge, pp. 1–16.

Katovich, M.A. and Reese, W.A. (1993) 'Postmodern thought in symbolic interaction: Reconstructing social inquiry in light of late-modern concerns', *The Sociological Quarterly* 34 (3): 391–411.

Kearney, M.H. (1998) 'Ready to wear: discovering grounded formal theory', *Research in Nursing and Health,* 21: 179–86.

Kearney, M.H., Murphy, S. and Rosenbaum, M. (1994) 'Mothering on crack cocaine: A grounded theory analysis', *Social Science and Medicine*, 38(2): 351–61,

Kearney, M.H., Murphy, S., Irwin, K., and Rosenbaum, M. (1995) 'Salvaging Self: A Grounded Theory of Pregnancy on Crack Cocaine', *Nursing Research*, 44(4): 208–13.

Keddy, B., Sims, S. and Stern, P.N. (1996) 'Grounded theory and feminist research methodology', *Journal of Advanced Nursing*, 23: 448–53.

Konecki, K. (2000) *Studies in Qualitative Methodology: Grounded Theory* (in Polish). Warszawa, Poland: PWN.

Kools, S., McCarthy, M., Durham, R., and Robrecht, L. (1996) 'Dimensional analysis: Broadening the concept of grounded theory', *Qualitative Health Research*, 6 (3): 312–30.

Lather, P. (2007) *Getting Lost: Feminist Efforts Toward a Double(d) Science*. Albany, NY: SUNY Press.

Latour, B. (1987). *Science in Action: How to follow scientists and engineers through society*. Cambridge, MA: Harvard University Press.

Lessor, A. (2000) Using the Team Approach of Anselm Strauss in Action Research', *Sociological Perspectives*, 43 (4): S133–S147.

Locke, K. (1996) 'Rewriting the Discovery of Grounded Theory After 25 Years?', *Journal of Management Inquiry*, 5 (1): 239–245.

——— (2001) *Grounded Theory in Management Research*. Thousand Oaks, CA: Sage.

Maines, D.R. (1978) 'Structural Parameters and Negotiated Orders: Comment on Benson, and Day and Day', *The Sociological Quarterly*, 19: 491–496.

——— (1995) 'In search of mesostructure: Studies in the negotiated order', in N.J. Herman and L.J. Reynolds (eds.), *Symbolicl Interaction: An Introduction to Social Psychology*. New York: General Hall, Inc., pp. 277–86.

Mamo, L. (1999) 'Death and dying: Confluence of emotion and awareness', *Sociology of Health and Illness*, 21 (1): 13–26.

Manning, P.K. (2000) 'Semiotics, semantics and ethnography', in P.Atkinson (ed.), *Handbook of Ethnography*. London: Sage, pp. 145–59.

Manning, P.K. and Cullum-Swan, B. (1994) 'Narrative, Content and semiotic analysis' in N. Denzin and V. Lincoln (eds) *Handbook of Qualitative Research*, first edition. Thousand Oaks, CA: Sage, pp. 463–78.

Mattingly, C. and Garro, L.C. (eds.) (2000) *Narrative and the Cultural Construction of Illness and Healing*. Berkeley: University of California Press.

May, K. (1996) 'Diffusion, dilution or distillation? The case of grounded theory method', *Qualitative Health Research*, 6 (3): 309–11.

McCarthy, D. (1996) *Knowledge as Culture: The New Sociology of Knowledge*. New York: Routledge.

Melia, K.M. (1996) 'Rediscovering Glaser', *Qualitative Health Research*, 6(3): 368–78.

——— (1997) 'Producing "Plausible Stories": Interviewing Student Nurses', in G. Miller & R. Dingwall (eds.), *Context and Method in Qualitative Research*. London: Sage, pp. 26–36.

Meltzer, B.N., Petras, J.W., and Reynolds, L.T. (1975) *Symbolic Interactionism: Genesis, Varieties and Criticism*. Boston: Routledge and Kegan Paul.

Miller, G. (1997) 'Introduction: Context and method in qualitative research', in G. Miller and R. Dingwall (eds.), *Context and Method in Qualitative Research*. London: Sage, pp. 1–11.

Miller, S. (1996) 'Questioning, resisting, acquiescing, balancing: New mothers' career reentry strategies', *Health Care for Women International*, 17: 109–31.

Newman, K. (2002) 'No Shame: A View from the Left Bank', *American Journal of Sociology*, 107 (6): 1577–1599.

Prendergast, C. and Knotterus, J.D. (1993) 'The new studies in social organization: overcoming the astructural bias', in L. Reynolds (ed.), *Interactionism: Exposition and Critique*. Dix Hills, NY: General Hall, pp. 158–85.

Richardson, L. (1992) 'The consequences of poetic representation: Writing the other, writing the self', in C. Ellis & M. Flaherty (eds.), *Investigating Subjectivity: Research on Lived Experience*. Thousand Oaks, CA: Sage.

Riessman, C.K. (1993) *Narrative Analysis*. Newbury Park, CA: Sage.

——— (ed.) (1994) *Qualitative Studies in Social Work Research*. Thousand Oaks, CA: Sage.

Samik-Ibrahim, R.M. (2000) 'Grounded theory methodology as the research strategy for a developing country', *FQS - Online-Text*. Available at: http://www.qualitative-research.net/fqs/fqs-eng.htm.

Schatzman, L. and Strauss, A. (1973) *Field Research*. Englewood Cliffs, NJ: Prentice Hall.

Schreiber, R.S. and Stern, P.N (eds.) (2001) *Using Grounded Theory in Nursing*. New York: Springer Publication Company.

Scott, J.W. (1992) 'Experience', in Judith Butler and Joan W. Scott (eds.), *Feminists Theorize the Political*. New York: Routledge.

Shim, J.K. (2005) 'Constructing "race" across the science-lay divide: Racial projects in the epidemiology and experience of cardiovascular disease', *Social Studies of Science*, 35 (3): 405–36.

Shostak, S. (2005) The Emergence of Toxicogenomics: A Case Study of Molecularization', *Social Studies of Science*, 35 (3): 367–404.

Star, S.L. (1989). *Regions of the Mind: Brain Research and the Quest for Scientific Certainty*. Stanford: Stanford University Press.

Star, S.L. and Griesemer, J. (1989) 'Institutional ecology, "translations" and boundary objects: Amateurs and professionals in Berkeley's Museum of Vertebrate Zoology, 1907–1939', *Social Studies of Science*, 19: 387–42.

Star, S.L. and Strauss, A.L. (1998) 'Layers of silence, arenas of voice: The ecology of visible and invisible work', *Computer Supported Cooperative Work: The Journal of Collaborative Computing*, 8: 9–30.

Stern, P.N. (1994) 'Eroding grounded theory', in J. Morse (ed.), *Critical Issues in Qualitative Research Methods*. Thousand Oaks, CA: Sage, pp. 212–23.

Strauss, A. (1984) *Feldtheorie-Grundzüge der Grounded Theory*. Hagen: University of Hagen Press.

Strauss, A.L. (1987) *Qualitative Analysis for Social Scientists*. Cambridge: Cambridge University Press.

———— (1993) *Continual Permutation of Action*. New York: Aldine de Gruyter.

———— (1995) 'Notes on the nature and development of general theories', *Qualitative Inquiry*, 1 (1): 7–18.

Strauss, A.L. and Corbin, J. ([1990] 1998) *The Basics of Qualitative Analysis: Grounded Theory Procedures and Techniques*. Thousand Oaks, CA: Sage.

———— (1994) 'Grounded theory methodology: An overview', in N. Denzin and Y.E. Lincoln (eds.), *Handbook of Qualitative Research*. Newbury Park, CA: Sage, 1st. ed., pp. 273–85.

———— (eds.) (1997) *Grounded Theory in Practice*. Thousand Oaks, CA: Sage.

Strübing, J. (2004). *Grounded Theory. Zur sozialtheoretischen und epistemologischen Fundierung des Verfahrens der empirisch begründeten Theoriebildung. [Grounded Theory: On the Epistemological and Social Theoretical Roots of Empirically Grounded Theory-Building.]* Wiesbaden, Germany: VS Verlag für Sozialwissenschaften.

Strübing, J. (2007) *Anselm Strauss*. Konstanz, Germany: UVK Verlagsgesellschaft mbH.

Timmermans, S. (1994) 'Dying of awareness: the theory of awareness contexts revisited', *Sociology of Health and Illness*, 16 (3): 322–39.

———— (1999) *Sudden Death and the Myth of CPR*. Philadelphia: Temple University Press.

Traweek, S. (2000) 'Faultlines', in R. Reid and S. Traweek (eds.), *Doing Science and Culture*. New York: Routledge, pp. 21–48.

Van den Hoonaard, W.C. (1997) *Working with Sensitizing Concepts: Analytical Field Research*. London: Sage.

Wacquant, L. (2002) 'Scrutinizing the street: Poverty, morality, and the pitfalls of urban ethnography', *American Journal of Sociology*, 107: 1468–1532.

Wiener, C.L. (2000) *The elusive quest: Accountability in hospitals*. New York: Aldine de Gruyter.

Wilson, H.S. and S.A. Hutchinson (1996) 'Methodologic mistakes in grounded theory', *Nursing Research*, 45 (2): 122–24.

NOTES

1 Online searches performed on September 22, 2005 found the following: 94 books with GT in the title, and 95 books with GT as a keyword (*Melville* – the UC Systemwide Library); 1811 references in *ISI Web of Knowledge* – *Web of Science*; and in *Sociological Abstracts*, there were 861 listings in journals; 95 in conferences; and 16 websites. A *Current Contents* database search on GT done on May 25, 2004 found 1353 citations, 435 of which were after 2002. Samik-Ibrahim (2000) further views GT methodology as a key research strategy for developing countries (see http://www.qualitative-research.net/fqs/fqs-eng.htm). The original book did not limit the use of GT to qualitative research.

2 Strauss published a book on GT in German in 1984. In terms of translations, see http://www.ucsf.edu/anselmstrauss/pdf/translations.pdf. See also Clarke (2002).

3 See esp. Annells (1996); Charmaz (1995; 2000; 2005; 2006); Clarke (2003; 2005; forthcoming); Clarke and Friese (2007); Dey (1999; 2004); Glaser (1978; 1992; 2002a); and also Glaser with Holton (2004); Keddy et al. (1996); Kools et al. (1996); Locke (1996; 2001); Strauss (1987; 1993; 1995); Strauss and Corbin (1990; 1994; 1998).

4 There are several websites which should be seen as supplementing this chapter. On Strauss's work, including unpublished papers, see www.ucsf.edu/anselmstrauss/. On Glaser's, see www.groundedtheory.com and www.gtreview.com. On Clarke's, see www.situationalanalysis.com. Internationally, see www.qualitativesociologyreview.org.

5 On theoretical sampling, see Glaser and Strauss (1967: 45–77), Glaser (1978: 36–54), Strauss (1987: 38–9), and Strauss and Corbin (1998: 201–15).

6 For example, for publications offering wonderful analytic diagrams see Miller (1996), and Kearney (Kearney, 1998; Kearney et al., 1994; Kearney et al, 1995). For lovely elaboration upon early Glaser and Strauss work on awareness contexts, see Timmermans, (1994) and Mamo (1999). For more meso-level projects on collective action, see the several works on disciplinary emergence, Baszanger (1998), Casper (1998), Clarke (1998), Fishman (2004) and Shostak (2005); on racial formations in/and science, see Shim (2005), and on the organization of large-scale clinical trials, see Fosket (2004, forthcoming). GT has even been used in economics to generate new economic indicators (Austen et al., 2003).

7 See for example Baker, Wuest, and Stern (1992) Glaser (1978; 1992; Glaser with Holton, 2004); on "method sluriring," Wilson and Hutchinson (1996) on research mistakes, May (1996) on dilution, and Stern (1994) on preserving the earliest (Glaser & Strauss, 1967), most positivist version of grounded therory.

8 By rerepresentation, I mean attempting to successfully represent in another medium—such as oral interview into scholarly writing. See, for example, Denzin (1989), Ellis and Flaherty (1992), Bochner and Ellis (2001), Richardson (1992), and Bell (2000).

9 A summary to 1975 is in Meltzer, Petras and Reynolds (1975: 83–123). For key interactionist responses, see Dingwall (1999), Hall (1987; 1997), Hall and McGinty (2002), Maines (1978; 1995), Prendergast and Knotterus (1993).

10 These are common critiques. See, for example, Atkinson et al. (2003), Charmaz (2006), and Charmaz and Mitchell (2001). On 'liteness' and the absence of theory, see, for example, Atkinson et al. (2003), Bryant (2002), Bryman and Burgess (1994), Dey (1999; 2004), Glaser (1992), and Locke (2001).

11 See also Atkinson et al. (2003: 148–52). Glaser (1978; 2002a) and Glaser and Holton (2004) continue to argue that grounded theory could also be used with quantitative research.

12 See Lessor (2000) and http://www.ucsf.edu/anselmstrauss/pdf/rememb-charmaz.pdf.

13 Strauss often asserted that symbolic interactionism was like a banquet buffet: those who came took what they wanted and left the rest. Thus there are, of course, many symbolic interactionisms and many related interpretive empirical approaches, all situated and grounded somehow in contrast to most scientist positivisms. Carey (2002: 200) wrote, 'Wanting a tradition within which to work, I invented my own take on symbolic interactionism ...' and on grounded theory.

14 For extended comparisons of Glaserian and Straussian perspectives, see commentary by Atkinson et al. (2003: esp. 148–52), Bryant (2002; 2003), Charmaz (1995; 2000), Clarke (2005), Corbin (1998), Dey (1999; 2004), Locke (1996; 2001), and Melia (1996).

15 See Charmaz (2000) for an excellent discussion of the range of epistemologies associated with grounded theory past and present. See full citations to her work in my downloadable bibliography at www.situationalanalysis.com

16 See his curriculum vitae on http://www.ucsf.edu/anselmstrauss/cv.html.

17 On theory/methods packages, see Star (1989), Star and Griesemer (1989), and Fujimura (1992). On GT/SI as such a package, see Clarke (2005: 2–5) and Clarke and Star (2007).

18 See also Atkinson, Coffey and Delamont (2003: esp. 148–52), Corbin (1998), Charmaz and Mitchell (2001) and Melia (1997).

19 In the second edition of *The Basics,* published after Strauss's death (Strauss and Corbin, 1998: 184), Corbin replaced action in the center of the diagram with the individual, reifying an erroneous micro/macro framing. See also Clarke (2005: 65–73).

20 Strauss's work on social worlds/arenas/negotiations was undertaken over many years at the same time as he developed grounded theory. On Strauss's own work, see http://www.ucsf.edu/anselmstrauss/social-worlds.html. See about Strauss's work the English translation of Baszanger's 1992 essay, available at http://www.ucsf.edu/anselmstrauss/pdf/essays-baszanger.pdf . See also Clarke (1991, 2005: 37–52, 65–73).

24

Does Postmodernism Make You Mad? Or, Did You Flunk Statistics?

Ben Agger

Many social scientists really hate postmodernism! I once worked in a sociology department in which colleagues circulated a cartoon lampooning the wordplay of postmodernists. In another university, I found that same cartoon posted on a librarian's door; she was married to a guy in my department, who I knew didn't like postmodernism. I have, and had, colleagues who characterized me as a 'postmodernist,' even though I am not one, exactly, and even though they don't have the foggiest idea what one is. A good book on postmodernism that clarifies some of these misunderstandings is Charles Lemert's (2005) *Postmodernism is Not What You Think*. Like me, Lemert is sympathetic to many postmodern ideas, but, also like me, he uses non-postmodern ideas in his empirical discussions and theorizing. Even to write or talk about postmodernism earns the wrath of mainstream people.

In this chapter, I discuss various methods (or methodologies, as my empirical colleagues often call them) for conducting social research. I also discuss some of Derrida's key ideas in order to demystify postmodernism, which I interpret as a valid, if incomplete, research method. Every introductory social science textbook talks about the scientific method, including both quantitative and qualitative research. Here, I want to broaden this discussion by examining both empirical research and theory as sources of valid insight about the virtual self and postmodern capitalism. Indeed, I go beyond social-research methods proper to include literary, poetic and artistic methods for gaining social understanding. A good place to begin this discussion is the raging debate over postmodernism, which, as I will explain, is really a debate about science. I defend the idea that postmodernism is serious business and can even be used to enhance empirical social research, even though I don't consider myself a postmodernist in the sense of rejecting all 'big picture' views of the social world. In an ironic way, postmodernism may actually be more conducive to ground-level empirical research than it is to the broad-gauged social theorizing of Marx, Weber and the Frankfurt School.

I have known little that angers and agitates people as much as postmodernism. Even women's studies, African-American studies,

Marxism and critical theory don't arouse as much animosity. Queer theory (Butler, 1990; Seidman, 1997, 2002) gets some people steamed, especially when they think it is secretly postmodern. Foucault was gay and postmodern. Postmodernism has blended with all these perspectives; indeed, one of the things people dislike about postmodernism is its imperialist nature, the way it takes over all fields, or seems to. Postmodernism underlies many complaints people have about those of us who do it, or at least read it. What they really dislike are our postmodern points of view, but sometimes they don't say this because it would appear intolerant and parochial and so they say other things: He's not rigorous; he doesn't have data; he publishes in the wrong places. I once applied to be chair of the sociology department at a major Southern university, persuaded by a famous friend of mine there to do so. I was turned down, I was told, because certain members of the department there didn't like the fact that I said in my application letter that I played tennis; they viewed this as sarcasm or some such. What they were really saying is that they didn't want a postmodern or Marxist chairperson, but they couldn't bring themselves to say that and so they found something, anything, to complain about! I'm not special; we all suffer slights. My point is that mainstream people go to great lengths to disqualify postmodernism, even if they end up talking about tennis. (I could have this all wrong, perhaps because postmodernists are paranoid. Maybe saying I play tennis suggested I wasn't serious enough about my profession to be chair!)

Below, I list the things that I know people dislike about postmodernism. I then respond to each one of these frequent criticisms:

1. Postmodernism is difficult, wordy, abstruse, abstract and invents words! This is true about much of the work of Jacques Derrida, an Algerian who has played a major role in the development of postmodern theory. In this chapter, I briefly introduce four of Derrida's central contributions to postmodern theory: the concepts of undecidability, deferral, deconstruction and othering. His book *Of Grammatology*

(1976) is a very difficult read, requiring much philosophical and literary background; I rarely inflict it on my students. He invents words and uses existing words in new ways. But Derrida is trying to make a point about language, suggesting its inherent flexibility and ambiguity. He is demonstrating that clear language does not necessarily resolve philosophical quandaries. Indeed, language breeds more language, as people try to clarify, and clarify again. This is an infinitely long process because even definitions need to be defined.

Derrida terms this *undecidability*, the first of his four major concepts. What is 'undecidable' about every text is its meaning, which is ever elusive because it is only through language and writing that we can approach interpretive meaning—and interpretations thus beget new quandaries of meaning, ad infinitum. Derrida would probably say that the criticism of postmodernism as unclear and wordy implies that people have access to clearer, cleaner languages that do not involve themselves in the endless, infinite process of interpretation. But a Derridean believes that there are no such languages, even mathematics: There are no languages that perfectly mirror nature and don't need to be explicated, explained, defined, worried through. Positivism is the illusion that such languages exist. And it is a powerful illusion, posturing science and mathematics as royal roads to truth and suppressing philosophical investigation and interrogation as muddle-headed. Although I wish that Derrida would have been more systematic at times, he was a literary theorist who viewed the boundary between philosophy and literature as quite permeable. Philosophical language can be creative and metaphorical, suggesting insights by the way it writes and talks.

2. Postmodernists are relativists, denying truth. This is one of the most prevalent criticisms of postmodernism, and the least valid in my opinion. Postmodernism holds that there is no supreme vantage point, outside of history and beyond time and place, from which we can see and then write about the world in a totally objective way. The perspective or vantage point of the knower, seer, writer or scientist matters hugely to his or her conclusions about the world. Some weeks after the space shuttle Columbia exploded, two separate investigations were undertaken into the causes of the explosion. One was run by NASA, which sent up the space shuttle in the first place. The other was

conducted by an expert commission, headed by a former military officer, charged by the government to find the causes of the disaster. Why would there need to be two separate investigations, especially since NASA employs many space and aeronautical experts? The answer is to be found in Derrida, who recognized that what you know is relative to your vantage point; knowledge is perspectival. It is at least partly a matter of perspective, especially the perspective imbedded in language. Here, the independent commission was set up to investigate the accident because the government wanted to avoid the appearance of a possible cover-up by experts at NASA, who not only want to protect the shuttle program but also their own jobs. This is not to say that NASA experts will flat-out lie but rather that they may, consciously or unconsciously, minimize their own culpability for launching a craft that may have been unsafe, and that they suspected was unsafe. Experts are considering whether NASA's own expensive recent overhaul of the Columbia, the oldest ship in the shuttle fleet, may have unintentionally reduced rather than increased safety, especially where the suspicious left wing was concerned. Derrida and Foucault do not deny the existence of an objective truth; they would recognize that the space shuttle Columbia exploded for a reason, and that investigators can uncover the reason and then communicate it to the world. They don't deny science and its pursuit of truth. They simply make the point that all knowing, writing, observing, counting and teaching take place within contexts, including language itself, that necessarily taint their information. These don't introduce error so much as they introduce perspective, the way you see something, especially where basic assumptions are concerned.

Borrowing from Nietzsche, Derrida views language as a prison in which authorial meaning is incarcerated. Although we can approximate meaning, this is a circular process: defining words with definitions that must be defined in turn. Thus, writing is a process of *deferral*, endlessly pushing meaning into the future through interim interpretive and interpolative acts. Undecidability and deferral are clearly linked: the elusiveness of meaning makes endless interpretation necessary.

Let me take another, more social science example. Criminologists have hotly debated the efficacy and utility of the death penalty for years, especially since the US Supreme Court under President Reagan once again opened the door to legal execution of convicted murderers, deciding that the decision to execute murderers should be left up to individual states. My own state, Texas, executes felons at a much greater rate than any other state, with our local courts having little mercy for offenders, even where DNA testing now demonstrates that people convicted in the past may have been convicted wrongly. Anyway, academic criminologists have begun to examine the death penalty, and in particular the issue of whether capital punishment deters murder (see Cheatwood, 1993; Decker and Kohfeld, 1990; Radelet and Akers, 1996; Sorensen et al., 1999). Many criminologists decided that the issue of deterrence is best studied by examining homicide rates in contiguous states (states next to each other), one having the death penalty and the other without it. One could then test whether, within relatively homogeneous socio-economic and cultural environments, the existence of the death penalty actually served to reduce the homicide rate. The data collected in this way suggest that it doesn't. But why doesn't it, criminologists wonder? Because most homicides, more than two-thirds of them nationally, occur between intimates and constitute the proverbial crimes of passion, committed in the heat of the moment. Lovers' quarrels and domestic abuse might fall into this category. In these cases, there is little or no premeditation; that is, the person who acts murderously doesn't reflect carefully on what he is about to do, including estimating his chances for beating a murder rap and escaping the electric chair or death by lethal injection. But other criminologists, who are more disposed to favor the death penalty for either professional or personal reasons, argue that the question of deterrence is best answered by asking people whether knowing that their state has the death penalty would actually deter them from committing murder. Here, the vast majority of Americans answer that the death penalty would deter them.

Who is correct? Is there a 'truth' to be found about the death penalty? Derrida would notice that how you ask the question of the death penalty's possibly deterrent effect has much impact on your answer. If you take the contiguous-states route, the death penalty is not deterrent. If you poll citizens, the death penalty is deterrent. Just because the criminologist is working from perspective, a central Derridean idea also shared by phenomenology, does not mean that there is no truth. There is, but getting at it depends on what and whom you ask. Thus, according to postmodernists, less important than establishing the relationship between truth and method is stipulating the ways in which your method already depends on certain theoretical assumptions and perspectives. No method is value-free. Although there *is* a truth out there about whether capital punishment deters murder, there isn't a single correct method for discovering this truth.

3. Postmodernists sometimes seem to deny the existence of the real world altogether. This criticism of postmodernism is an extension of the criticism just discussed, about relativism. Foucault has done a great deal of work that could be called empirical social science. He has studied the history of punishment (Foucault, 1977) and the history of sexuality (Foucault, 1978), thus earning a place in the literatures of criminology and social-control theory and sexuality and gender. Lyotard (1984) has written on science. Baudrillard (1983) has addressed advertising and other aspects of consumer culture. All these approaches are empirical, examining the real world, even if they are non-quantitative. The incorrect impression that postmodernism ignores reality probably stems from postmodernism's denial that there is a single reality upon which everyone will agree, and which can be described using a single language, especially mathematics. Postmodernism's non-representational, non-positivist theory of knowledge is sometimes confused with an idealism that denies 'reality' altogether. Actually, postmodern theorists pay attention to the ways in which culture and discourse construct the world's meaning, thus requiring that culture and discourse receive critical attention. Culture and discourse are 'real', every bit as real as the World Trade Center towers. But the world is not simply a text, even though all texts are worlds—nucleic societies of readers and writers through which power is transacted.

4. Postmodernists oppose progress and are too cynical. This all depends on what we mean by 'progress'. To be sure, postmodernism, like the Frankfurt School's critical theory, stems from Nietzsche's unsparing critique of the Enlightenment, which sometimes gives the impression of nihilism (there are no values) or cynicism (all values are bad). Also, postmodernists, especially Lyotard and Foucault (but probably not Derrida), reject Marx's 'grand narrative' or large story of progress because they contend that no story, however large and all-encompassing, will capture every nuance. Marx's theory was secretly authoritarian, these postmodernists contend, because Marx, following Hegel, wrote a total theory of world history in which, as Hegel termed it, history is the slaughter bench of individuals, who are sacrificed to the cause of History as expedients. But postmodern theorists are generally sympathetic to progressive social movements, such as environmentalism, postcolonialism and gay and lesbian rights, precisely because such causes unite the 'margins': those who, as Other, have been left out of the white-male-heterosexual European narrative of progress. Whether contemporary Marxists can accommodate these sorts of difference and marginality is an open question. I would argue that postmodernism in general has been more attuned to marginal people and groups than has an orthodox Marxism that still invests its theoretical and political energy in the white-male proletariat, even where there is scant evidence that the traditional working class is likely to become a revolutionary actor in the near future.

5. Postmodernists take classical and contemporary works of culture and 'deconstruct' them into meaninglessness; this thwarts the traditional civilizing function of the liberal arts. Although Derrida first suggested deconstruction as a legitimate intellectual activity, he never embraced deconstruction-'*ism*', a methodology to be applied to any and all texts. For a wide-ranging discussion of deconstruction, see Jonathan Culler's (1982) *On Deconstruction*. Indeed, Derrida did not even intend deconstruction as something done 'to' texts, from the outside as it were. His third major concept, *deconstruction* is the tendency of all texts to unravel, to come apart at the seams as their glosses, inconsistencies, contradictions and deferrals of meaning eventually get the better of the seamless impression they try to create—including Derrida's own works, and certainly this work! Deconstruction isn't done 'to' the work, from the outside, but is the tendency of the work to dissolve when prodded and probed, an image remarkably similar to Marx's image in *The Communist Manifesto* of 'all that is solid melt[ing] into air', which he identified as a central tendency of capitalism.

Derrida wants to make the point that writing is a mistaken-ridden, partial and necessarily incomplete project that, in being read by strong-willed readers who supply their own sense to what they read, is necessarily transformed. This is the sense in which Derrida implies that reading is writing, a strong version in its own right. It must be, given that texts suppress and defer a variety of their internal problems, begging questions that can only be answered in new texts (and so on). Thus, there is no single correct reading of Shakespeare but only versions of him, indeed as many versions as he has had readers. This no more renders the text irrelevant than does postmodernism ignore social reality in favor of nihilism or solipsism (thinking that the world is a figment of one's imagination). Deconstructing literature draws attention to novels' tendencies to suppress tension and defer meaning.

Novelists such as Mark Twain intend to tell the whole story, even if they write sequels. The greatest works are full of inconsistencies and blind spots that cry out for elucidation. That may be why we consider them 'great'. This does not weaken their authority but reveals the human artifice behind them: they were written by people, and can be rewritten. Indeed, they are being rewritten every time that they are read (think of the Bible or Shakespeare), as readers resolve their quandaries of meaning in their own imaginative ways. Every text is undecidable; that is, according to Derrida, you cannot once and for all grasp its meaning, which can then be clearly communicated, in a book review or Cliff's Notes. Critics of deconstruction also indict deconstruction for supposedly reducing 'great books' to the level of ordinariness, treating them critically on the same level as television, journalism, comic books or pornography (Eagleton, 2003). That is exactly what cultural studies does, unashamedly!

Although there are many links between postmodernism and cultural studies, the critical analysis of culture industries does not necessarily require Derrida's deconstruction. Cultural studies makes the valid point that mass culture and media culture are worth studying by anyone interested in the politics of culture. Derrida would agree that every text, no matter how 'high' or 'low', is susceptible to being deconstructed, that is, to deconstructing itself, as readings probe its text or discourse for evasions, inconsistencies or deferrals. But Derrida did not introduce deconstruction in order to end civilization as we know it, or to 'deconstruct' Great Books curricula of the kind found at Columbia University and the University of Chicago. There is a tendency for people who drink deeply of postmodernism to broaden the canon of so-called great books to include marginal voices, as well as media productions, just as there is a tendency for people who do postmodern theory to be interested in cultural studies. But Derrida's thesis of texts' deconstructibility is not culturally nihilist. In fact, most of Derrida's own published deconstructions address very important works of Western philosophy, such as the writings of Hegel and Rousseau.

6. Postmodernism comes from Europe, especially France, and is un-American. Homegrown Midwestern empiricists of the kind who dominate many Ph.D.-granting US social science departments tend not to like theory of any kind, especially European theories, because they are somehow beside the point, which is getting at the facts, using mathematics and statistics. Americans often use the term 'pragmatic' as a positive thing. 'Useless' is its antonym, and that is what many people think postmodernism is. As a former quantitative colleague said to me, about social theory generally, 'So what?' The American rejection of postmodernism is frequently anti-intellectual as well as ethnocentric. I know that these are fighting words. But, after having worked in several primarily quantitative sociology departments, I am convinced that empirical social scientists, many of whom are men in plaid, dislike postmodernism because it is the most exotic of the already offensively exotic species of theory. It plays with words; it intellectualizes; it speculates beyond the data; it is political, supporting weird causes such as the rights of queer people. I had a colleague, who was very quantitative but only mildly productive in publishing his work, tell our whole department that postmodernism is 'speculative bullshit', exuding over-determined anger (anger that has many sources and manifestations) at European theory as a whole. To be sure, French postmodern theory makes an easy target for down-to-earth, number-crunching empiricists who would rather count than theorize.

7. Derrida and Foucault talk only about texts and not about 'reality', making them inadequate inspirations for sociology and social science. It is true that Derrida in particular is steeped in textual readings: of Hegel, Rousseau, Marx, even Shakespeare. He tends to view the whole world as a text, even though he of course knows better. We didn't get to see fully the political and social science side of Derrida until his (1994) *Specters of Marx*, in which he declares his Marxism and theorizes the Internet's impact on

society and culture. Foucault has always talked about 'reality', although he understands, as does Derrida, that reality is mediated through, and constituted by, texts, especially by what Foucault calls discourses (systematic habits of speech and figuration implanted in everyday life). His point, in his voluminous studies of madness, crime and punishment, and sexuality, is that professional and punitive discourses such as psychiatry and criminology exercise power over people in achieving social control. Foucault realizes, in a way paralleling the Frankfurt School, that it is no longer adequate to understand power and domination as simply 'done' to people but as now to some extent self-imposed, as external control and self-regulation are blended to the point of identity. But this doesn't mean that Foucault ignores 'hard', empirical social structures such as prisons, economies and families. He theorizes and studies the discursive practices that, to some extent, constitute these institutions. He contends that discourse constitutes selves, as much as it is constituted by them. In this respect, he blends the analyses of culture and power.

8. Postmodernism opposes science, and especially mathematics. Derrida, Foucault and Baudrillard have written little about science. Lyotard has delved further than the others into the philosophy of science. It is possible to apply deconstructive insights in the realm of the sociology of science, reading science much as a postmodern critic might read literature, film or advertising. As I have been saying, science is an authored project, not a photographic representation or mathematical machine. It is different from literature only in that it suppresses the author, covering over the literariness of its text, indeed denying that science is writing at all: it is secret writing, as I have suggested. 'Literariness' means 'having the qualities and appearance of literature'. So the appropriately deconstructive project is to *authorize* science, bringing to view its literary artifice, its having-been-written-from-a-certain-vantage and disgorging its subtle argument, its political rhetoric, for one state of affairs over others. This is not anti-science at all, but only anti-positivist, which, more than other scientific epistemology, suppresses the author so deep in the densely figured mathematical journal page that the page seems to be sheer representation, when in fact it is science fiction—the author's way of being human through chemistry or demography.

A postmodern and critical-theory version of science is eminently possible, as I have shown in my work, and as Marcuse (1955, 1969) has shown in his writings on new, gay or happy science, an image of non-positivist science that he develops in his blending of Freud and Marx. The reading of postmodernism as anti-science is an act of sheer projection—supposing that another person or theory will do something bad to you because, secretly, you want to do something bad to it. Blending Freud, Schiller and Marx, Marcuse suggests that science is a vital play impulse, a self-creating and productive mode of cognition that freely plays with concepts and data in order to envision the world. This is, as he tells it, a literary process, a practice of authorial artifice. He does not theorize this discursive component of free cognition, of science, because he was writing at a time (the 1950s) before French postmodern theorists had begun to develop their discursive perspectives on power and culture. The *Tel Quel* group, centered in Paris and including the founders of postmodernism such as Derrida and Foucault, did not form for another decade. There has remained a symptomatic silence between German and French theory, especially on the issues of science and culture, that has only recently begun to be bridged (see the work of Agger, 1989; 2000; Aronowitz, 1988; Huyssen, 1986; Kellner, 1995; Luke, 1989; Ryan, 1982).

9. Postmodernism, because it is amoral and relativist, leads to amoral and immoral activities, such as September 11. I would never have thought that anyone with intellectual credibility could blame postmodernism for that distressing day in September 2001. Although Dinesh D'Souza (1991) and Allan Bloom (1987) had already weighed in on the intellectual scandals of campus postmodernism in their twin diatribes composed during the Reagan years, these are not criticisms taken seriously by many in the academy, even though their books have sold briskly in the trade markets. But recently I came across a debate between a *New York Times* cultural correspondent (Rothstein, 2001) and the theorist Stanley Fish, who has done interesting work on the relevance of Derrida for literary criticism and legal studies. The cultural correspondent argued that the relativism of postmodernism has entered the culture, indeed the global culture, and that this relativism and amorality had led, at least indirectly, to the attack on Western icons such as the World Trade

Center Towers and the Pentagon. If I hadn't read this argument with my own eyes I wouldn't have believed it: it was too silly. But there it was, in the pages of the *Times*. Later came Fish's well-argued rebuttal in *Harper's* (2002), in which he exonerates Derrida for having caused the airplanes to be hijacked and their passengers flown to their deaths, and the subsequent deaths of thousands more.

It is one thing to call postmodernism relativist: that is wrong, but fairly innocent. It is quite another to blame postmodern epistemological relativism for a global climate of amorality and immorality, licensing wanton attacks on hallowed Western institutions and American citizens. Although Derrida and his student Gayatri Spivak (1999) have written on postcolonialism, as has the Arab theorist Edward Said (1994), these thinkers have not licensed or launched an intellectual *jihad* against the West but simply tried to understand the 'othering' of marginal groups, non-Western cultures, and gay and lesbian people as an outcome of a certain Enlightenment view of Europe, of European science, and of what lies beyond, both culturally and intellectually. '*Othering*', Derrida's fourth central concept, emerges from dualist thinking (e.g., man/woman) that, once probed deconstructively, reveals a secret hierarchy—man *over* woman (indeed, for Freud, women are defined by their lack of male properties). Derrida believes that dualities conceal hierarchies, with one polarity of the dichotomy achieving dominance over the other, which is inferiorized or 'othered'. I have already suggested the causal chain that takes us all the way from the Enlightenment, through the Holocaust, to the creation of Israel, to Bin Laden and September 11 in the concluding chapter of my (2002) *Postponing the Postmodern*. I argue that September 11 is bound up with hostility to Israel, which was created because European culture was deeply anti-Semitic.

It is not the Nietzschean-inspired critique of the Enlightenment and positivism developed by Derrida that led to various immoral acts and organized catastrophes during the twentieth and twenty-first centuries. It is positivism itself—a worldview that views nature and other people as things to be manipulated. Adorno and Horkheimer were the first to recognize that fascist authoritarianism redirects anger about authority figures against Jews, Slavs, Gypsies, queer people, who are 'othered' and then exterminated as mere objects, not also selves. Their critique is consistent with Derrida and Foucault's discussions of othering and otherness.

10. Postmodernism is not serious or rigorous, but merely wordplay, mastered by any fool. The notion that any amateur can master postmodernism is false on the evidence. No amateur, unacquainted with Western philosophy and literature, can begin to fathom Derrida's dense work. And yet Foucault praises the amateur and amateurism because he wants to disestablish official knowledges, which he regards as discourse/practices of power and control. In this respect, his healthy respect for amateurism, for grassroots knowledge, is similar to Garfinkel's own conception of practical reasoning found in his ethnomethodology (1967). The real amateur for Derrida and Foucault is the reader, who enters the text in a subordinate power position with respect to the writer, who may even be the recipient of royalty payments generated by the purchase of her book. But deconstruction quickly turns the tables as readers further enter the sense and sentience of texts that cry out for interpretation, and even correction, by readings that, as such, become writings. Pick any difficult and lengthy work of fiction: Tolstoy's *Anna Karenina*, Shakespeare's *Hamlet*, Thomas Pynchon's *V*. The literate but perhaps unpublished reader works her way into these texts, cracking the code and becoming immersed in the plot. Eventually the mind wanders, imagining the world of the main characters, the author's intention and sensibility, the relationship between the fictional characters and one's own life and times.

This interpretive intervention, done by amateurs, is called forth by the sheer indeterminacy of all writings that do not easily give up the key to understanding themselves, even if they possess glossaries of terms at the end. Even glossaries are fictions, requiring further elaboration, and perhaps glossaries of glossaries, definitions of definitions, endlessly. I have added glossaries to a few of my books, but I always intended the main text to be a kind of glossary, too, defining itself as well as terms I use in my official glossary. I say this because I want you, dear reader, to think theoretically about which is the 'real' glossary, and why! So there is a sense in which postmodernism praises the amateur in the figure of the reader, she who ventures forth into the thickets of novels and science with a compass, compassion and common sense and thereby begins to *transform* what she is reading into her own version—a reading of *Hamlet* appropriate to America in the early twenty-first century, perhaps drawing analogies between Shakespeare's protagonist and certain contemporary political figures, who author and experience their own tragedy. This transforming reading might notice that Shakespeare probably composed his tragedy in the year 1600, when the Enlightenment commenced, and tease out of this fact certain insights into the continuity (or discontinuity) between Shakespeare's life and times and our own. In any case, there is nothing wrong with amateurism if the amateur becomes an author in her own right, perhaps one day even breaking into print. It is liberating to know that anyone can do deconstructive detective work, auguring a world of literate public citizens who read a lot and proffer their own writings.

POSTMODERNIST INTOLERANCE

I have just presented the much-misunderstood side of postmodernism, which is viewed with contempt by cultural conservatives and quantitative methodologists alike. But this would be an incomplete portrait without discussing intolerance that flows the other way, from the Derridean humanities toward natural and social sciences that not only rigorously analyze the world but use numbers and statistics to do so. There are humanists galore who unreasonably despise not only positivism, the rather circumscribed *enfant terrible* opposed by critical theory and postmodernism, but all empiricism, which bases knowledge on direct observation, experiments, surveys and large data sets. It is worth remembering that the early Frankfurt School, in the 1920s, 1930s and 1940s, conducted many empirical social research projects. The Frankfurters wanted to support and enrich critical theory with empirical studies of prejudice, the family, authority, the working class, mass media. They found a world of difference between empiricism and positivism; they believed that one could develop empirical research methodologies, perhaps even using mathematics and statistics, that

did not hold to narrow positivist strictures about value freedom, perfect representation and the existence of social laws.

By the 1950s, the Frankfurt thinkers had largely given up empirical social research, convinced that even their non-positivist work risked being atheoretical. Instead, they began to write more systematic works of social theory, such as Marcuse's *Eros and Civilization* (1955) and Adorno's *Negative Dialectics* (1973). Although these books addressed the empirical world, they did not deploy data in the usual sense of responses to surveys or economic indicators. By the 1970s, when American sociology was becoming much more quantitative and statistical, there was a widening gulf between critical social theory and quantitative social science empiricism (see Agger, 2000; Turner and Turner, 1990). For their part, the French postmodern theorists never pretended to be either social scientists or empiricists. Their work was composed largely as commentary and critique of works of philosophy and literature, as I have already discussed with respect to Derrida. By the end of the twentieth century, many theorists and humanists took for granted not only differentiation between theory and empiricism but also opposition. Further, the distinction between empiricism and positivism (a value-free, law-seeking version of empiricism) had faded as theorists demonized empirical research, much as they were demonized by Midwestern empiricists as nihilist. Intolerance abounded on both sides.

All of this is quite contrary to the magisterial works of the original social theorists: Durkheim, Weber and Marx. These thinkers discussed the empirical world; they had little time to engage in metatheory—theory about other theories—although Marx began his career by putting distance between himself and Hegelian idealism. And yet their pages were not littered with the figures and gestures of mathematics; they were accessible to well-educated and even amateur readers interested in the division of labor, suicide, bureaucracy, religion, economic markets, the degradation of work and workers. This is not to suggest that Marx agreed with Durkheim and Weber on all issues, especially the weighty issue of what Hegel called the 'end of history'. For Durkheim and Weber, modernity would fulfill or complete itself with capitalism. For Marx, capitalism was the third-to-last stage of civilization's necessary development, to be followed by socialism and then communism.

There are differences in the substance of their theories of modernity, but great similarity in their intellectual methods: *They essay the world*, recognizing that their empiricism is theoretically framed, indeed collapsing those categories altogether. I seriously doubt that any of the three great theorists of modernity would have compartmentalized the empirical and the theoretical; they would have regarded their writings as totalities of sense, seamlessly unfolding the world as they knew it, and sometimes advocating a different, better one. Again, one should not oversimplify: Durkheim and Weber, although they essayed, believed that sociology should be a science and seek to describe social laws; in this, they were positivists. Marx believed that positivism, especially bourgeois economic science, was an ideology, promoting false consciousness among workers, who, upon reading about the inevitability of their social fate, would reproduce it in their everyday lives, going to work dutifully and refusing to commit the revolutionary deed. They differed, but they were similar in how they put pen to paper, making up the world as they went along. In particular, none of them relied on methodology, a rigorous protocol for conducting empirical research. And they didn't rely on quantitative methodologies, even though they dotted their pages with numbers, especially as they discussed wealth, the suicide rate and population growth.

Just as Marx, Durkheim and Weber essayed, so were they systematic, addressing typical patterns of social structure and social behavior, patterns that endure, but that can change. In Lyotard's famous term, they wrote grand narratives, big stories not just about France or England but about 'modernity', about a global society emerging first in the factories and families of western Europe and Great Britain. Whether or not they overemphasized the West is a fair question, but not the most important one here. More important is the scope of their theories, which was global, general, even total, to again borrow Hegel's word. They tried to explain 'everything', not just particular things like their home countries, the world between 1850 and 1865, industrialized nations. They sacrificed nuance for scope, a methodological decision at its most crucial. Methodologists call this a problem of the *level of analysis*: typically, within social science, distinguishing between individual-level and aggregate social phenomena—your household income versus the pattern of all household incomes, for example.

Postmodern theory tends to be intolerant of sweeping stories, including the classical nineteenth- and early twentieth-century theories of modernity. One of the characteristics of postmodernity, it is said, is that it resists global, total narratives but can only be captured in fragments, requiring local, individual-level, even intuitive methodologies. Some contend, with good reason, that the postmodern only discloses itself in architecture and art. Grand theories tend to become grandiose, beating the reader over the head with the author's perspective, which is necessarily selective. Postmodernists, thus, often counsel flying below the radar in order to capture nuance and local flavor.

This aversion to grand, global theory is curiously matched by the frequent postmodern aversion to mathematics, especially as deployed in the human sciences. Numbers are too abstracting, like grand theory sacrificing the particular and personal to the general. The notion that we cannot summarize human experience in either concepts or numbers runs deep among many humanists, including postmodernists. This is what makes the project of a postmodern science so important, retaining the possibility of counting things and people, keeping track of the economy, analyzing DNA, calculating the infant-mortality rate. Postmodernists are correct that counting and numbering are always already theoretical acts, rooted in certain assumptions about what will be counted. But because math and science are theory-laden, this does not mean that they are to be sacrificed to expressive narratives rich in experience but lacking concepts, structures, numbers, generalities. I am arguing here that one can do natural and social science, counting, graphing, summarizing, testing, as well as develop general theories disclosed in grand narratives *as long as one recognizes that methodological decisions are always already theoretical ones*, involving the author's philosophical and social assumptions about the nature of the world. The text of mathematics and science is never free of context; but that doesn't mean that we should abandon counting and analyzing as impure activities. All intellectual activities are impure in the sense that knowing helps constitute what is to be known; it constructs it. Text and context blur, just as all versions are deeply grounded in the body of the author, her world, her time, her gender, her race, her class. The postmodern aversion to science and mathematics because they are perspective-ridden is misguided, especially where deconstructive insights and techniques can bring these literary gestures to light, in effect theorizing them.

When I read science or math in sociology presentations, I attempt to authorize them, replacing figure and gesture with the concepts and theories that underlie them. I exhume their arguments, their rhetoric, their advocacy. One can decode science in this way, especially science clogged with methodology, technique and statistical operations. By the same token, one can translate theoretical constructs into empirical terms, not so much making them testable, whatever that might mean, but grounding them in examples. What are we otherwise to make of 'negative dialectics', 'total administration', 'undecidability'? In this sense, both science and theory can be read from the outside, translating them into terms of each other.

Methodology poses and solves intellectual problems, typically translating technical terminology into other languages that illuminate them, from the outside. In social science, there are already well-established quantitative and qualitative methods, involving surveys, testing, measurement, interviews, direct observation, experiments and narratives. One of the main problems of our discipline is that forays in method have overtaken forays in theory and conceptualization, substituting figure and number for concepts. 'How' we study problems, and analyze data, has gotten the better of 'what' we learn. Again, this is in large part because sociology, beginning in the 1970s, became a science-like discipline in order to impress deans and foundations. We need to undo this trend, albeit without dogmatically rejecting all mathematics and method, especially where we redefine methodology as a textual, theoretical practice, a process of opening up texts so that readers can see the machinery of argument and make their own arguments in turn.

My position is that there is nothing wrong with methodology if method is understood as a way of writing, composing an argument, intellectually engaging with the world, translating one's own language into others' and others' into one's own. We all use 'methods' in our intellectual work, some of them quantitative, qualitative, theoretical, intuitive, representational or non-representational. They are all legitimate 'versions', to use a Derridean word, in that they are all ways of expressing ourselves; they are literary postures that, at a profound level, reconfigure the experienced and observed world as *something other*, creating distance, which is frequently quite uncomfortable, between the reader or viewer and her comfortable conception of the order of things.

Adorno highly valued distance, as well as dissonance, as a source of liberating insight. The problem for him and for his close colleague Max Horkheimer (1974) is that in late capitalism people tend to become so immersed in the world that it is very difficult for them to see the forest for the trees, to grasp the big picture, and to tell large stories that help explain the totality. Critical theory could be described or defined as an intellectual methodology for *gaining distance*, for thinking about the world as something other, going beyond everyday appearances to understand its deepest structures and its most distant reaches. This is one way of talking about 'globality', which is an interesting theoretical term used both approvingly and disapprovingly. The critical theorists were noticing that our experiences of the world are framed by cultural discourses that position us in the world as consumers, citizens, family members, educators and the educated. This notion of being positioned by culture has become an explicit topic of French postmodern theorists such as Foucault, who approach the issue of distance and closeness in ways very similar to the Frankfurt School. This is no accident in the fact that Foucault studied Marcuse closely and learned from him.

MEANING, NOT METHOD

As I have said, every writer has a method— whether the method involves computers and data-analytic software packages or simply a pen—for writing fiction and theory (a certain kind of fiction!). My conception of social science, especially in a time when the self is struggling to assert her identity as a literary (reading and writing) subject, would de-emphasize methodology, without making it totally irrelevant. It can't be totally irrelevant because one needs to learn an intellectual style, or, preferably, styles. But method is more about how one composes oneself on the page than about truth, which, I contend, is less about intellectual techniques than about meaning. For every truth, there are many possible methods. I will go further: multiple methodologies enhance the search for truth, allowing us to view the world and ourselves from different angles, and with differing depths and dimensions.

As I write these words, I am a composing self, banging away on our new home computer. It is nearly 2006, and the US is at war in Iraq, for quite dubious reasons, I strongly feel. My kids and I made a lawn sign that said 'No War'. It was stolen off our lawn within a few hours, in plain daylight! A neighbor who witnessed this political statement (a protest of a protest) said that high-school kids tossed the sign into the local creek, and it sank. Enough about me. What is the problem here: the writing self? The war in Iraq? Wayward adolescents? The subject of methodology?— or maybe all of them! My writing could well be enriched by looking at the problem, or problems, from a different angle: Why is the US at war in Iraq? What geopolitical theory is President Bush using? What does he, and his military and intelligence teams, know that I don't?

Before I sat down to write this section of the chapter on methods, and after I helped my 15-year-old daughter with her homework—preparing for a test on World War II—she asked me 'What was the Holocaust?' We talked for a while, and I decided that I would do two things. I'd download some stuff from the Internet the next day at work (we don't have it at home, for reasons regarding the colonization of everyday life and the acceleration of childhood). Recently, my daughter, prodded by lunch-table banter among boys in her grade, looked up www. dildo.com on my wife's work computer. *That* initiated an interesting discussion! I also decided to give my daughter the harrowing but necessary *Eichmann in Jerusalem* by Hannah Arendt (1994) and Sartre's *Anti-Semite and Jew* (1948). I was going to lend the Eichmann book to an Israeli student who plays on our university tennis team, but he said that this transforming moment in Israeli history was so intensely troubling to him that he couldn't yet read the book; he is 25, and a pilot in the Israeli air force as well as an engineering student with nearly straight As. I will not yet show my daughter photographs of the inhuman bodies that the Allies found at the liberated camps. She has nightmares.

This is, of course, a discussion about methods. How to teach the Holocaust? Whether or not to have the Internet at home? How to compose a chapter on methodology? I can only conclude that multiple methods enrich single methods, but that all the methods in the world, a real cacophony of voices, don't get us to the truth without the difficult process of *just thinking it through*. Method doesn't solve intellectual problems but can quickly become a problem where we expend all of our energy refining our measurements and improving our experiments. At the end of the day, all methods are distractions from the real business of thought and reflection. You need a method—how to teach my daughter about the Holocaust—but these methods don't absolve us of thinking for ourselves. In the wrong hands, they become formulas for disaster.

Let me summarize my views of methodology:

1. There are lots of good methodologies—quantitative, qualitative, narrative, autobiographical, fictional, poetic, artistic, filmic. None is inherently superior to the others, and none avoids its own blind spots, its perspective-ridden nature. That is, every methodology tends to ignore certain problems by focusing on other ones. And some of the best methodologies are found outside of social science, in the humanities and in art.

2. Methodologies, especially quantitative ones, that pretend to be totally free of bias and perspective are not only deceiving themselves and their audience. They pretend to be free of bias in order to assert their own intellectual superiority, especially by comparison to 'soft' methods such as participant observation, ethnomethodology, sheer fiction.

3. Methodologies are really literary strategies; they are ways of making arguments. In this sense, methods *prove* what the scientist or sociologist knew all along. They are intellectual seals of approval that make their work seem legitimate and authoritative. Typically, researchers write their methodology sections of their papers and books last, cleaning them up and presenting them as if they solved intellectual problems. This is not to deny that methods—systematic ways of knowing—are important. Indeed, every literary strategy is a method, by definition. But people have high expectations of methodologies that they cannot meet; they are merely ways of writing up one's argument. As such, they are rhetorical devices, not inherently superior to arguments that don't have methodology sections, such as a poem or a film. Methods make the reader believe that she is reading science and not fiction; but it is all fiction anyway.

4. Since the 1970s, the burden of sociological argument has been shifted from theory to quantitative methods in order to reverse the decline of disciplinary prestige in the United States. Papers are evaluated by reviewers in terms of their methodological sophistication, not the sophistication or reasonableness of their theoretical arguments. Quantitative sociologists might deny this. But my study, *Public Sociology* (2000), for which I read hundreds of articles and reviews by specialists before the articles were published or rejected for publication, demonstrates that our discipline has become *methods-driven*, as I term it. This is reflected in the reviews I read, in the articles themselves, especially those published in high-prestige journals such as *American Sociological Review* and *Social Forces*, and in graduate-school sociology curricula, which are heavily weighted toward methods and statistics courses. US sociology is much more quantitative than thirty years ago, even though there are pockets of people who use qualitative and literary methods and who emphasize the importance of theory.

5. People who value quantitative methods tend to view non-quantitative methods as illegitimate—as non-science. They especially reject and resent interdisciplinary methods and theories, such as postmodernism, critical theory, cultural studies, feminist theory, queer studies. They place impermeable boundaries around the discipline of sociology, and also strong barriers, perhaps even a moat, between the empirical social sciences and the humanities.

6. By the same token, many theorists and qualitative methodologists reject counting, mathematics and statistics out of hand, returning to an intellectual position formerly known as neo-Kantianism. This position sharply distinguishes both the methods and substance of natural sciences and social sciences. This position rules out of court the analysis of large data sets, including census data. This prevents learning about shifts in household income by gender and race, unemployment figures, crime patterns, data about migration and immigration. There is mistrust and defensiveness flowing both ways, across the methodological divide separating quantitative and non-quantitative scholars. Along with this mistrust one finds basic differences in what, and how, people publish: Quantitative people tend to publish articles, as physicists and chemists do, whereas theoretical people tend to publish books. This reflects and leads to struggles within universities and departments about what constitutes 'real' research. Highly quantitative social scientists may view published books as

worthless or nearly worthless when they make hiring and tenuring decisions, whereas theory and qualitative people may devalue co- and multi-authored journal articles delving into the fine details of a particular research problem, about which one can spend a whole career writing. When I was a university dean, I found few scholars genuinely 'polyvocal' (capable of speaking, or learning, diverse methods).

I hope I have demystified methodology for you, at least a little! Your methodology won't rescue you from intellectual quagmires. You must think your way out of them, using insights and ideas, not algorithms or technical terminology. Hating other people's methods is parochial and ungenerous. Their methods correct your errors and enrich your perspective. The problem remains that positivism—a subset of all empiricisms—is imperialist and usurps all knowledge for itself. But we must resist the temptation to reject empiricism as we reject positivism. Empiricism—openness to the world as it is, and could be—is the engine of what Habermas calls the project of modernity, which, in these dismal times, is well worth defending.

REFERENCES

Adorno, Theodor W. (1973) *Negative Dialectics*. New York: Seabury.

Agger, Ben (1989) *Reading Science: A Literary, Political and Sociological Analysis*. Dix Hills, NY: General Hall.

——— (2000) *Public Sociology: From Social Facts to Literary Acts*. Boulder, CO: Rowman and Littlefield.

——— (2002) *Postponing the Postmodern: Sociological Practices, Selves and Theories*. Boulder, CO: Rowman and Littlefield.

Arendt, Hannah (1994) *Eichmann in Jerusalem: A Report on the Banality of Evil*. New York: Penguin.

Aronowitz, Stanley (1988) *Science as Power: Discourse and Ideology in Modern Society*. Minneapolis: University of Minnesota Press.

Baudrillard, Jean (1983) *Simulations*. New York: Semiotext(e)

Bloom, Allan (1987) *The Closing of the American Mind*. New York: Simon and Schuster.

Butler, Judith (1990) *Gender Trouble: Feminism and the Subversion of Identity*. New York: Routledge.

Cheatwood, Darrol (1993) 'Capital punishment and the deterrence of violent crime in comparable counties', *Criminal Justice Review*, 18: 165–79.

Culler, Jonathan (1982) *On Deconstruction*. Ithaca, NY: Cornell University Press.

Decker, Scott and Kohfeld, Carol W. (1990) 'The deterrent effect of capital punishment in the five most active execution states: A time series analysis', *Criminal Justice Review*, 15: 173–91.

Derrida, Jacques (1976) *Of Grammatology*. Baltimore, MD: Johns Hopkins University Press.

——— (1994) *Specters of Marx*. New York: Routledge.

D'Souza, Dinesh (1991) *Illiberal Education: The Politics of Race and Sex on Campus*. New York: Free Press.

Eagleton, Terry (2003) *After Theory*. New York: Allen Lane.

Fish, Stanley (2002) 'Postmodern warfare', *Harper's*, July-August, pp. 33–40.

Foucault, Michel (1977) *Discipline and Punish*. New York: Pantheon.

——— (1978) *The History of Sexuality*. New York: Pantheon.

Garfinkel, Harold (1967) *Studies in Ethnomethodology*. Englewood Cliffs, NJ: Prentice-Hall.

Horkheimer, Max (1974) *Eclipse of Reason*. New York: Seabury.

Huyssen, Andreas (1986) *After the Great Divide: Modernism, Mass Culture, Postmodernism*. Bloomington: Indiana University Press.

Kellner, Douglas (1995) *Media Culture: Cultural Studies, Identity and Politics Between the Modern and the Postmodern*. New York: Routledge.

Lemert, Charles ([1997] 2005) *Postmodernism is not What You Think*. Boulder, CO: Paradigm.

Luke, Timothy W. (1989) *Screens of Power: Ideology, Domination and Resistance in the Informational Society*. Evanston: University of Illinois Press.

Lyotard, Jean-Francois (1984) *The Postmodern Condition: A Report on Knowledge*. Minneapolis: University of Minnesota Press.

Marcuse, Herbert (1955) *Eros and Civilization*. New York: Vintage.

——— (1969) *An Essay on Liberation*. Boston: Beacon.

Radelet, Michael and Akers, Ronald (1996) 'Deterrence and the death penalty: The views of the experts', *Journal of Criminal Law and Criminology*, 87: 1–16.

Rothstein, Edward (2001) 'Attacks on US challenge postmodern true Believers', *New York Times*, September 22.

Ryan, Michael (1982) *Marxism and Deconstruction*. Baltimore, MD: Johns Hopkins University Press.

Said, Edward (1994) *Orientalism*. New York: Vintage.

Sartre, Jean-Paul (1948) *Anti-Semite and Jew: An Exploration of the Etiology of Hate*. New York: Schocken Books.

Seidman, Steven (1997) *Difference Troubles: Queering Social Theory and Sexual Politics*. New York: Cambridge University Press.

———— (2002) *Beyond the Closet: The Transformation of Gay and Lesbian Life*. New York: Routledge.

Sorensen, Jon, Wrinkle, Robert, Brewer, Victoria and Marquart, James (1999) 'Capital punishment and deterrence: Examining the effect of executions on murder in Texas', *Crime and Delinquency*, 45 (4): 481–93.

Spivak, Gayatri (1999) *A Critique of Postcolonial Reason: Toward a History of the Vanishing Present*. Cambridge, MA: Harvard University Press.

Turner, Stephen and Turner, Jonathan (1990) *The Impossible Science: An Institutional Analysis of American Sociology*. Newbury Park, CA: Sage.

Discourse Construction

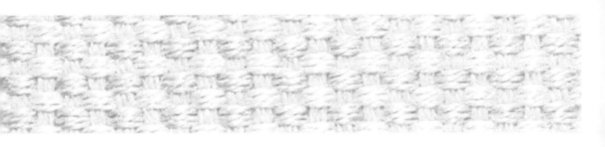

Introduction

Stephen P. Turner

'Facts' become facts that can be used either to justify claims or to establish other, higher truths, by a process of construction or writing in which certain conventions are followed. The scientific article or the social research report is a presentation of facts. But it is also a construction according to conventions: literary conventions, or rhetorical conventions. We ordinarily ignore these conventions in reading research reports, but their role is visible in the course of training. Learning how to write an article, how it is supposed to look, what is supposed to be included, how it is supposed to be expressed, and so on are a central, though usually not formal, part of training in social research.

Ken Gergen and Mary Gergen discuss one of the approaches to discursiveness: constructionism. They note that truth is something that is established within communal traditions: e.g., the traditions of physics. The problem, for constructivism, is to understand how this works and to create a way of talking about the ways in which communal practices enable the establishment of truth in that community. This emphasis on the conventional element in the background of all truth claims has political implications. Where some persons are disfavored by the 'facts', such as the results of a testing regime, there is an issue. Is the regime itself a means of oppression, which conceals its conventional character and parades its factual character, for example in the form of an 'objective' test score? And do these scores then enter into the construction of a self-identity in which the background or convention is further obscured?

Gergen and Gergen point out that such questions pose a deep dilemma for 'methodology'. It seems as though the alternatives are to accept any methodology as equally valid because equally conventional, or to dogmatically affirm one set of conventions as uniquely valid. But constructivist arguments point beyond this dilemma to some strategies, such as reflexivity, auto-ethnography (which openly acknowledges and embraces subjectivity), building multiple voices into the presentation of research, and becoming self-consciously 'literary' or self-consciously 'performative', that is to say, explicitly persuasive and presentation-oriented in one's relation to the audience. With these new or newly reconceived more self-conscious approaches have come new ways of thinking about validity and truth which are self-conscious about the constructed or conventional element itself.

One of the major elements in this new self-consciousness involves rhetoric. Understanding that all speech and writing is rhetorical, that is it functions by fulfilling conventional expectations, allows us to employ a pre-existing tradition of analysis going back to ancient Greece. Rhetorical analysis asks, as Ricca Edmondson says in her chapter, 'how do we carry out operations like "bringing people to see the world in a particular way," and moreover do it using methods we can reasonably defend?' The rhetorical tradition uses such notions as enthymeme (an unstated element necessary for an inference) and tropes (or terms which are similar but transform ordinary meanings, such as the term 'market' used metaphorically to describe both the place one buys groceries and any competitive quest to get people to choose in one's favor).

Rhetorical analysis does not denigrate. Rather it is concerned to replace the contest between different forms of persuasion by focusing on excellence within forms of argument. 'Discourse analysis', discussed by Michael Lynch, is a family of topics whose main feature is attention to the detail of writing, conversing, speaking, and their associated actions and gestures. Lynch focuses on situated language use as distinct from formal constructions of 'language', the idea that a language is similar to a scientific theory, with formal rules like principles, and specifiable, fixed, meanings. The study of situated language use, in contrast, requires ethnographic description at a level of detail beyond our ordinary level. This brings out commonplace events, such as one person finishing another person's sentence, that are absent from the standard model of language.

One of the examples given in Lynch's chapter is remembering. Many levels of claims, excuses, and denials are made on the basis of, or about, memory. What discourse analysis can do is to disentangle these many types of claims by showing how they have distinctive meaning in different kinds of interaction or setting.

Even science itself, as Lynch points out, has been subject to this kind of analysis, with revealing results. The analysis amounted to a shift in focus from using one's taken-for-granted knowledge about a given situation—such as a science lab—as the resource for understanding or a topic in its own right. Rather than taking scientists' shoptalk or gossip about their competitors at face value, we can see their usages as examples of typical discursive strategies. Explaining one's competitors' opinions as 'errors' that result from their background, limitations, or interests is a commonplace example of a kind of discourse that is central to establishing the authority and greater plausibility of one's own views, yet not one which will be found in a book on scientific methodology.

Like the other methods discussed here, discourse analysis is reflexive—it can be readily applied to its own forms of argument and description. As a consequence, these methodological approaches cannot become fixed or stabilized as invisible taken-for-granted ways of producing results. This feature makes these approaches seem to be something other than 'methods'. There are examples, or models, of analysis, and each approach has some standard terms associated with it. But the same kind of closure promised by such methods as experiment is not possible: the technique of making invisible conventions visible precludes its own conventions from becoming invisible.

25

Social Construction and Research Methodology

Kenneth J. Gergen and Mary M. Gergen

Social-science dialogues on the nature of research methods are more spirited today than perhaps ever before. To be sure, such dialogues are replete with critique and antagonism; at the same time they are suffused with enthusiasm and unparalleled creativity. As many believe, the social sciences are now moving through a period of dynamic revolution. In significant degree, the current dialogues have been incited by a wide range of intellectual developments often adumbrated by the term *social construction*. It is the purpose of the present chapter to explore in greater detail the relationship between social constructionist thought and contemporary issues in research methodology. To this end we shall first outline central elements in social constructionist scholarship relevant to our theme. This will set the stage for attending to some of the fractious cross-currents in the field of methodology, not with the aim of settling the disputes or of moving the field toward new foundations, but opening opportunities for generative dialogue. Approaching the issues from a social constructionist standpoint, we may treat these tumultuous

encounters as harboring opportunities from which richer potentials of social research can be realized than ever before.

ELEMENTS OF SOCIAL CONSTRUCTIONIST METATHEORY

The phrase *social construction* typically refers to a tradition of scholarship that traces the origin of knowledge, meaning or understanding to human relationships. The term *constructivism* is sometimes used interchangeably, but most scholarship associated with constructivism views processes inherent in the individual mind—as opposed to human relationships—as the origin of people's constructions of the world. Although one may trace certain roots of social constructionism to Vico, Nietzsche and Dewey, scholars often view Berger and Luckmann's, *The Social Construction of Reality* (1967) as the landmark volume. Yet, because of its lodgment in social phenomenology, this work has largely been eclipsed by more recent scholarly developments. One may locate the primary stimulants to the more recent development of social constructionist thought in at least three, quite independent movements. In effect, the convergence of these movements provides the basis for social constructionist inquiry today.

The first movement may be viewed as *critical*, and refers to the mounting ideological critique of all authoritative accounts of the world, including those of empirical science. Such critique can be traced at least to the Frankfurt School, but today is more fully embodied in the work of Foucault, and associated movements within feminist, black, gay and lesbian, and anti-psychiatry enclaves. The second significant movement, the *literary/ rhetorical*, originates in the fields of literary theory and rhetorical study. In both cases, inquiry demonstrates the extent to which scientific theories, explanations and descriptions of the world are not so much dependent upon the world in itself as on discursive conventions. Traditions of language use construct what we take to be the world. The third context of ferment, the *social*, may be traced to the collective scholarship in the history of science, the sociology of knowledge, and social studies of science. Here the major focus is on the social processes giving rise to knowledge, both scientific and otherwise.

Our aim here is not to review the emergence of these three movements. Not only are there numerous and detailed sources already available to the reader,[1] but various chapters in the present Handbook also treat these movements in considerable detail. Rather, in what follows we shall briefly outline a number of the most widely shared agreements to emerge from these various histories. To be sure, there is active disagreement both within and between participants in these various traditions. However, there are at least four major lines of argument that tend to link these traditions and to furnish the major bonds among those who identity with social constructionism. This discussion will prepare the way for a treatment of contemporary issues and developments in research methodology.

The Social Origins of Knowledge

Perhaps the most generative idea emerging from the constructionist dialogues is that which we take to be knowledge of the world and self finds its origins in human relationships. What we take to be true as opposed to false, objective as opposed to subjective, scientific as opposed to mythological, rational as opposed to irrational, moral as opposed to immoral, is brought into being through historically and culturally situated social processes. This view stands in dramatic contrast to two of the most important intellectual and cultural traditions of the West. First is the tradition of the individual knower, the rational, self-directing, morally centered and knowledgeable agent of action. Within the constructionist dialogues we find that it is not the individual mind in which knowledge, reason, emotion and morality reside, but in relationships.

The communal view of knowledge also represents a major challenge to the presumption of Truth, or the possibility that the accounts of scientists, or any other group, reveal or approach the objective truth about what is the case. In effect, propose the constructionists, no one arrangement of words is necessarily more objective or accurate in its depiction of the world than any other. To be sure, accuracy may be achieved within a given community or tradition—according to its rules and practices. Physics and chemistry generate useful truths from within their communal traditions, just as psychologists, sociologists and priests do from within theirs. But from these often competing traditions there is no means by which one can locate a transcendent truth, a 'truly true'. Any attempt to establish the superior account would itself be the product of a given community of agreement.

To be sure, these arguments have provoked antagonistic reactions among scientific communities. There remain substantial numbers in the scientific community, including the social sciences, who still cling to a vision of science as generating 'Truth beyond community'. In contrast, scientists who see themselves as generating pragmatic or instrumental truths find constructionist arguments quite congenial. Thus, for example, both would agree that while Western medical science does succeed in generating what might commonly be called 'cures' for that which is termed 'illness', these advances are dependent upon culturally and historically specific constructions of what constitutes an impairment, health and illness, life and death, the boundaries of the body, the nature of pain, and so on. When these assumptions are treated as universal—true for all cultures and times—alternative conceptions are undermined and destroyed. To understand death, for example, as merely the termination of biological functioning would be an enormous impoverishment of human existence. A more enriched perspective on the nature of life would be found among those who believe in reincarnation, the Christian doctrine of 'a life hereafter', or the Asian and African tribal views of living ancestor spirits. The constructionist does not abandon medical science, but attempts to understand it as a powerful cultural tradition.

The Centrality of Language

Central to the constructionist account of the social origins of knowledge is a concern with language. If accounts of the world are not demanded by what there is, then the traditional view of language as a mapping device ceases to be compelling. Rather, a Wittgensteinian view of language is invited, in which meaning is understood as a derivative of language use within relationships. And, given that games of language are essentially conducted in a rule-like fashion, accounts of the world are governed in significant degree by conventions of language use. Empirical research could not reveal, for example, that 'motives are oblong'. The utterance is grammatically correct, but there is no way one could empirically verify or falsify such a proposition. Rather, while it is perfectly satisfactory to speak of motives as varying in intensity or content, discursive conventions for constructing motivation in the twenty-first

century do not happen to include the adjective 'oblong'.

Social constructionists also tend to accept Wittgenstein's (1953) view of language games as embedded within broader 'forms of life'. Thus, for example, the language conventions for communicating about human motivation are linked to certain activities, objects and settings. For the empirical researcher there may be 'assessment devices' for motivation (e.g., questionnaires, thematic analysis of discourse, controlled observations of behavior), and statistical technologies to assess differences between groups. Given broad agreement within a field of study about 'the way the game is played', conclusions can be reached about the nature of human motivation. As constructionists also suggest, playing by the rules of a given community is enormously important to sustaining these relationships. Not only does conformity to the rules affirm the reality, rationality and values of the research community, but the very *raison d'être* of the profession itself is sustained. To abandon the discourse would render the accompanying practices unintelligible. Without conventions of construction, action loses value.

The Politics of Knowledge

As indicated above, social constructionism is closely allied with a pragmatic conception of knowledge. That is, traditional issues of truth and objectivity are replaced by concerns with that which research brings forth. It is not whether an account is true from a god's-eye view that matters, but rather, the implications for cultural life that follow from taking any truth claim seriously. This concern with consequences essentially eradicates the long-standing distinction between *fact* and *value*, between is and ought. The forms of life within any knowledge-making community represent and sustain the values of that community. In establishing 'what is the case', the research community also places value on their particular metatheory of knowledge, constructions of the world, and practices of research. When others embrace such knowledge they wittingly or unwittingly extend the reach of these values.

Thus, for example, the scientist may use the most rigorous methods of testing emotional intelligence, and amass tomes filled with data that indicate differences in such capacities. However, the presumptions that there is something called 'emotional intelligence', that a series of question and answer games reveal this capacity, and that some people are superior to others in this regard, are all specific to a given tradition or paradigm. Such concepts and measures are not required by 'the way the world is'. Most importantly, to accept the paradigm and extend its implications into organizational practices may be injurious to those people classified as inferior by its standards. For others who find it a useful mode of understanding managerial success, it may be beneficial.

This line of reasoning has had enormous repercussions in the academic community and beyond. This is so especially for scholars and practitioners concerned with social injustice, oppression, and the marginalization of minority groups in society. Drawing sustenance in particular from Foucault's power/knowledge formulations (1979, 1980), a strong critical movement has emerged across the social sciences, a movement that gives expression to the discontent and resistance shared within the broad spectrum of minorities (Marchand and Runyan, 2000). In what sense, it is often asked, do the taken-for-granted realities of the scientist sustain ideologies inimical to a particular group (e.g., women, people of color, gays and lesbians, the working class, environmentalists, communalists, the colonized) or to human well-being more generally? Traditional research methods have also fallen prey to such critique. For example, experimental research is taken to task not only for its manipulative character, but its obliteration of the concept of human agency.

From Self to Relationship

As earlier discussed, the constructionist dialogues shift attention from the individual actor to coordinated relationships. The drama here

is substantial. On the broadest level, constructionism represents an unsettling of the long-standing Western investment in the individual actor. One of the major outcomes of Enlightenment thought was its privileging of the reasoning powers of the individual. It is the individual's capacities for reason and observation that should be valued, cultivated, and given power of expression in society. It is the individual who is responsible for his/her actions, and serves as the fundamental atom of society. Such presumptions continue into the present, as represented, for example, by concerns within both scholarly and professional circles with bringing about optimal states of cognition, emotion, motivation, self-esteem, and the like. Yet, as the constructionist proposes, all that we take to be rational and real emerge from a process of coordination. These are not possessions of the individual, but of people acting together. In the same way, neither the distinction between 'me' and 'you', nor the vocabulary of individual minds is required by 'the way things are'. It is not individuals who come together to create relationships, but relationships that are responsible for the very conception of the individual. The constructionist dialogues thus serve to undermine three hundred years of accumulated belief, along with the instantiation of these beliefs in the major institutions of society.

That the conception of individual selves is constructed is not in itself a criticism. Many would agree that precious traditions of democracy, public education and protection under the law draw their rationale from the individualist tradition. However, to recognize the historical and cultural contingency of individualist beliefs does open the door to reflection. As many critics see it, there is a substantial dark side to constructing a world of individual agents. When a fundamental distinction between self and other is established, the social world is constituted by differences. The individual stands as an isolated entity, essentially alone and alienated. Further, there is a common prizing of autonomy—of becoming a 'self made man', who 'does it my way'. To be dependent is a sign of weakness and incapacity. To construct a world of separation in this way is also to court distrust; one can never be certain of the other's motives. And given distrust, it becomes reasonable to 'take care of number one'. Self-gain becomes an unquestionable motive, both within the sciences (such as economics and social psychology) and the culture at large. In this context, loyalty, commitment and community are all thrown into question, as all may potentially interfere with 'self-realization'. Such are the views that now circulate widely though the culture.[2] One may not wish to abandon the tradition of individual selves, but constructionism invites exploration into creative alternatives.

The most obvious alternative to the individualist account of human action is derived from constructionist metatheory itself. As the metatheory suggests, relationships may be viewed as the fundamental source of all intelligibility, including the intelligibility of all action in society. Thus, theorists from many different perspectives attempt to articulate a vision of a *relational self*. For example, as psychoanalytic theory has shifted toward 'object relations', therapists have become increasingly concerned with the complex relations between transference and countertransference (see, for example, Mitchell, 1995). No longer is it possible to view the therapist as providing 'evenly hovering attention', for the therapist's psychological functioning cannot be extricated from that of the client. From a separate quarter, many developmental theorists and educators are elaborating on the implications of Vygotsky's early view that everything within the mind is a reflection of the surrounding social sphere (Wertsch, 2006). From this perspective there are no strictly independent thought processes, as all such processes are fashioned within particular cultural settings. Stimulated by these developments, cultural psychologists now explore forms of thought and emotion indigenous to particular peoples (Bruner, 1990; Cole, 1996). Discursively oriented psychologists add further dimension to relational theory by relocating so-called 'mental phenomena' within patterns of discursive exchange. For example, rather than viewing

thought, memory, attitudes or repression as processes 'in the head' of the single individual, they are reconstituted as relational phenomena. Theory and research have come to articulate reason as a form of rhetoric, memory as communal, attitudes as positions within an argument, and emotion as performance within relationship.[3]

These four themes—centering on the social construction of the real and the good, the pivotal function of language in creating intelligible worlds, the political and pragmatic nature of discourse, and the significance of relational process as opposed to individual minds—have rippled across the academic disciplines and through many domains of human practice. To be sure, there has been substantial controversy, and the interested reader may wish to explore the various critiques and their rejoinders.[4] However, such ideas also possess enormous potential. They have the capacity to reduce orders of oppression, broaden the dialogues of human interchange, sharpen sensitivity to the limits of our traditions, and to incite the collaborative creation of more viable futures. Such is the case in research methodology as it is in the global context.

THE LIBERATION OF 'METHODOLOGY'

Given these major themes in social constructionist scholarship, what are the major implications for research methods in the social sciences? There are two broadly resounding challenges. First, no authoritative statement about 'the nature of things' stands on any foundation other than its own network of presumptions. All attempts to credit (or discredit) a given research practice rely on historically and culturally situated agreements within a given community. In terms of research methodology, nothing is required by 'the nature of things', because all methods are born out of presumptions about such matters. In effect, it is the presumptive base, generated within a given community, that makes demands on methodology. What is learned about the world through employment of a given method will necessarily construct the world in terms of the presumptive base. Thus, within the social sciences the subject–object dualism embedded within much logical empiricist metatheory is congenial with a narrative of persons as respondents to causal inputs (e.g., behaviorism). And both the metatheory and theoretical orientation give rise to methods of experimentation (Gergen, 1994). In contrast to this behaviorist orientation, the humanist assumption of personal agency is more congenial to phenomenological research methods. And, to presume that persons harbor unconscious motives, as in the psychoanalytic case, lends itself to practices of probing dreams and fantasies.

In effect, the constructionist dialogues serve a profound liberating function. They remove the privilege of any group to establish the 'necessary and desirable' in methods of research. In broader terms, they relinquish the grip of 'methodology' as the royal road to truth. Methods themselves do not provide guarantees of 'objective knowledge', so much as they attest to one's commitment to the realities of a particular community.

Yet, there is a second major outcome of constructionist argument for research methods. It is not simply the demise of authority that is hastened by constructionism, but, rather, the creation of an open field of possibility. For most constructionists, all voices may justifiably contribute to the dialogues on which our futures depend. Thus, to understand all knowledge claims as socially constructed is not to render them false or insignificant. Again, it is to recognize that each tradition, while limited, may offer us options for living together. In this way constructionism invites a posture of infinite curiosity, where new methodological amalgams stand ever open to development. In recognizing that the realities of today depend on the agreements of today, enormous possibilities are opened for methodological innovation.

These two outcomes of the constructionist dialogues have incited intense and broad-ranging controversy within the social sciences, and have added force to an enormous creative surge in research methods. At present there are myriad questions, dilemmas, and possible trajectories that remain open. In what follows we shall focus specifically on three sites of controversy in methodological inquiry: the crisis of validity, the rights of representation, and the place of the political in social research. We shall follow this discussion with several provocations to future methodological development.

VALIDITY AND BEYOND

The constructionist view of language leads to substantial skepticism concerning the epistemological foundations of scientific practices. The pursuit of universal or general laws; the capacity of science to produce accurate portrayals of its subject matter; the possibility of scientific progression toward objective truth; and the right to claims of scientific Truth are all undermined. In the context of methodology, it may be said that we confront what Denzin and Lincoln (2000) have called a 'crisis of validity'. If there is no means of correctly matching word to world, then the warrant for scientific validity is lost, and researchers are left to question the very role of methodology and how it might be evaluated. By what rationales, if any, are methods to be evaluated; how are standards to be set? How do we find a viable path between the chaos of 'anything goes', and building new 'prisons of necessity?'

These questions have simultaneously stimulated heated debate and bursts of creative energy. For many researchers critiques of validity resonate with long-standing resistance to nomothetically based research and its methodological penchant for converting all observation to numerical systems. Many such researchers turn to qualitative methods in the hope of generating richer and more finely nuanced accounts of human action. Within qualitative circles many argue that the empiricist emphasis on quantifiable behavior left out the crucial ingredient of human understanding, namely the private experiences of the agent. Both these views—that qualitative methods are more faithful to the social world than quantitative ones, and that individual human experiences are important—remain robust in today's qualitative community, with diverse proponents of grounded theory research (Strauss and Corbin, 1994; Bryant and Charmez, 2007), phenomenology (Georgi, 1994; Georgi and Georgi, 2003), and feminist standpoint theory (Miller and Stiver, 1997; Naples, 2007) among them.

Yet, as the validity critiques have played out, they bite the hands of the qualitative enthusiast that feed it. If the idea of language as a picture or map of the real is rejected, then there is no rationale by which qualitative researchers can claim that their methods are superior to the quantitative in terms of accuracy or sensitivity. A thousand-word description is no more valid as a 'picture of the person' than a single score on a standardized test. By the same token, the validity critiques challenge the presumption that language can adequately map individual experience (Bohan, 1993; Butler, 1990). When a person gives an account of his/her experience, in what sense are the words a map or a picture of an inner world? Accounts of 'experience' seem more adequately understood as the outcome of a particular textual/cultural history in which people learn to tell stories of their lives to themselves and others. Such narratives are embedded within the sense-making processes of historically and culturally situated communities (cf. Bruner, 1990; Sarbin, 1986).

Emerging Innovations in Methodology

Although social constructionist views are sometimes accused of no-exit nihilism, this skepticism has had enormous catalytic effects in the development of research methods. An effusive range of methodological contributions has resulted. Four of these innovations—reflexivity, multiple voicing, literary representation, and performance— deserve special attention. Their importance derives in part from the way in which they

challenge the traditional binary between research and representation—that is, between acts of observing or 'gathering data' and subsequent reports on this process. There is increasing recognition that because observation is inevitably saturated with interpretation, and research reports are essentially exercises in interpretation, research and representation are inextricably entwined (M. Gergen, Chrisler, & LoCicero, 1999). In effect, such explorations function as both a critique and an alternative to traditional demands for validity:

Reflexivity

Among the primary innovations have been those emphasizing reflexivity. Here investigators seek ways of demonstrating to their audiences their historical and geographic situatedness, their personal investments in the research, various biases they bring to the work, their surprises and 'undoings' in the process of the research endeavor, the ways in which their choice of literary tropes lends rhetorical force to the research report, and/or the ways in which they have avoided or suppressed certain points of view (cf. Kiesinger, 1998). In effect, there is an admission that the research report is a human construction. Such disclosures neither invalidate nor validate the research outcomes. They simply bring the reader into a consciousness of construction.

Such forms of self-exposure reach their extreme in the flourishing of autoethnography (Ellis and Bochner, 1996; Lockford, 2004). Here investigators treat themselves as ethnographic subjects, revealing their experiences as a bulimic, a mudfighter, a stripper, and so on. At the same time they are typically sensitive to the ways in which their personal history saturates the ethnographic inquiry. However, rather than giving the reader pause to consider the biases, the juxtaposition of self and subject matter is used to enrich the ethnographic report. The reader finds the subject/object binary deteriorating, and is informed of ways in which confronting the world from moment to moment is also confronting the self.

While a valuable addition to the vocabulary of research methodology, reflexivity does not fully subvert the concept of validity. Ultimately the act of reflexivity asks the reader to accept itself as authentic—that is, as a conscientious effort to 'tell the truth' about the making of the account. We thus approach the threshold of an infinite regress of reflections on reflection (Gergen and Davis, 2003).

Multiple Voicing

A second significant means of disclaiming validity is to remove the single voice of the omniscient researcher by including multiple voices within the research report. There are many variations on this theme. For example, research subjects or clients may be invited to speak on their own behalf—to describe, express or interpret within the research report itself (Lather and Smithies, 1997; Naples, 2003). In other cases the research may seek out respondents with wide-ranging perspectives on a given matter, and include the varying views without pressing them into coherence (Fox, 1996). Or, researchers may reflexively locate a range of conflicting interpretations that they find plausible, and thereby avoid reaching a single, integrative conclusion (Ellis et al., 1997). Some researchers also work collectively with their subjects so that their conclusions do not eradicate minority views (Fine and Weiss, 1998). Multiple voicing is especially promising in its capacity to recognize the problems of validity while simultaneously providing a potentially rich array of interpretations or perspectives (Hertz, 1997).

Yet, multiple voicing is not without its complexities. One of the most difficult questions is how the author/researcher should treat his/her own voice. Should it simply be one among many, or should it be granted special privileges by virtue of professional training? There is also the question of identifying who the author and the participants truly are; once we realize the possibility of multiple voicing it also becomes evident that each individual participant is polyvocal. Each possesses a multiplicity of ways to 'tell the story'. Which of these voices is speaking in the research and why; what voice is simultaneously suppressed? Finally, moves toward multiplicity are not always successful in giving all sides their due. Typically the investigator serves as the ultimate author of the work (or the coordinator of the voices), and thus serves as the ultimate arbiter of inclusion, emphasis, and integration. These rhetorical maneuvers are often invisible to the reader and possibly to the researcher as well (Gergen and Davis, 2003; Naples, 2003).

Literary Styling

A third important reaction to validity critique is the deployment of stylized representation, and particularly the replacement of traditional realist discourse with forms of writing cast in opposition to 'truth telling'. For example, the investigator's descriptions may take the form of fiction, poetry or autobiographical invention. The use of literary styling signals the reader that the account does not function as a map of the world, but as an interpretive activity addressed to a community of interlocutors. For many researchers, such writing is especially appealing because it offers a greater expressive range and an opportunity to reach audiences outside the academy (Richardson, 1997; Rinehart, 1998) and thus accomplishes significant political work.

While inviting opportunities for creative expression, such writing is vulnerable to the criticism of singularity of voice. The lone author commands the discursive domain in full rhetorical regalia. Again, however, critique gives way to innovation: literary styling may be combined with other methodologies to offset the criticism. For example, in her dissertation on relationships among African-Americans after the Million Man March, Deborah Austin joined with one of the participants in the March to co-create a narrative poem to illuminate the event (Austin, 1996). While certain pitfalls of traditional literary forms are avoided in these innovations, claims that they are not appropriate for scientific representations are prevalent. These critiques are even more pronounced with regard to performance.

Performance

Finally, to remove the thrall of objectivity while sustaining voice, an increasing number of scholars are moving toward performance as a mode of research/representation. This move is justified by the notion that if the distinction between fact and fiction is largely a matter of textual tradition, as the validity critiques suggest, then social scientists are not limited to traditional forms of scientific writing. While visual aids such as film and photography have long been accepted as a means of 'capturing reality', they have generally been viewed as auxiliary modes within written traditions. However, when it is realized that the communicative medium itself has a formative effect on what is taken to be the object of research, then the distinction between film as recording device as opposed to performance (e.g., 'a film for an audience') is blurred. And with this blurring, investigators are invited to consider the entire range of communicative expression in the arts and entertainment world—graphic arts, video, drama, dance, magic, multimedia, and so on—as forms of research and presentation. Again, in moving toward performance the investigator avoids the mystifying claims of truth, and simultaneously expands the range of communities in which the work can stimulate dialogue. Milestones in this developing form of research/representation include Carlson's *Performance, A Critical introduction* (1996), and Case et al.'s edited volume (1995), *Cruising the Performative*. Today such research occupies a significant place in the qualitative research arena.[5]

Enrichment or Erosion?

Yet, in spite of the bold and creative zest accompanying many of these ventures, there is also a growing unease with the drift away from conventional scientific standards. Epithets of excess—narcissistic, overly personal, navel-gazing, exhibitionistic—may be located. Some argue that the interpretive researcher should continue to engage in the long, hard work required to produce 'thick descriptions', and not let other intellectual fashions distract from

that duty (Marcus, 1998). Patricia Clough takes emotionally charged autoethnographic writing to task for its symbiotic relationship with television drama and for 'keeping theoretically motivated critical interventions at a distance' (1997: 101). Some feel that adventurous texts are little more than experiments with words. They see 'literary word-smithing' as too little concerned with actual social change. The methodological experiments lend themselves to an ethos of 'fun and games', and are not sufficiently sober about the world's pressing needs (Wilkinson, 1997).

Vistas of Validity

One might view such critique as numbing in consequence, possibly functioning as an enervating backlash, a return to the conventional, and the end to methodological experiments. It could also fragment the field, as researchers may simply terminate dialogue and go their separate ways. However, such outcomes would be both unfortunate and unwarranted. At the outset, it would be intellectually irresponsible simply to return to business as usual, as if the validity critiques had never occurred. At the same time, those engaged in the new endeavors can scarcely declare that the validity critiques are fully justified. By their own account there are no foundational rationalities from which such warrants could be derived. Further, few of any persuasion would welcome a unified field of inquiry, a rigid framework in which all methods were prescribed in advance. Thus, rather than a desert of nomadic and isolated tribes, it may be useful to invoke the metaphor of generative tension. If there are now on the floor a variety of voices, reasons and values, what new avenues are encouraged? What futures could be opened? Drawing from recent developments, the following would appear prominent:

Reframing Validity

In the conventional terms by which it has been formulated, the debate on validity has reached an impasse. On the one hand those pursuing their work as if their descriptions and explanations were transparent reflections of their subject matter lack any rationale for this posture. Yet, those who find fault with this position are, in the end, without means of grounding their alternatives. Thus, rather than either reinstantiating the modernist tradition of objective truth, or opening the throttle to anything goes, discussion opens on ways of reconceptualizing the issue. For example, McTaggart (1997) abandons concern with whether research 'tells the truth', in favor of inquiry into the effects of a research practice. He suggests that the concept might be reconceptualized in terms of the efficacy of research in changing relevant social practices. More radically, Patti Lather (1993) attempts to recast validity largely from a constructionist standpoint. If we accept the view that language is a chief means by which reality is constructed, what kinds of research could be accepted as valid? As she outlines, *ironic validity* would foreground the insufficiencies of language in 'capturing' the object; *paralogical validity* would be achieved through illuminating undecidables, limits, paradoxes, discontinuities, and complexities; *rhizomatic validity*, symbolized by the taproot metaphor, would be achieved when conventional procedures are undermined and new locally determined norms of understanding are generated; and *voluptuous validity*—'excessive', leaky', 'risky', and 'unbounded'—would illuminate the ways in which ethics and epistemology are entwined.

Situating Knowledge

Closely related to the revisioning of validity, but raising questions of its own, are explorations into situated knowledge. Employing a constructionist perspective, one may see all knowledge claims as situated, both culturally and historically. This does not invalidate knowledge claims so much as place them within particular contexts of use/value. As Donna Haraway (1988) and others have suggested, the concept typically serves an ameliorating function, reconciling constructionist and realist positions. Because few traditionalists

wish to argue that their interpretations uniquely 'capture' the character of their subject matter, and few constructionists would maintain that there is 'nothing outside of text', a space is opened for situated truth, that is, 'truth' located within particular communities at particular times, and used indexically to represent their condition. In this way people commonly speak as if the term 'sunset' maps the sinking sun in the evening sky, and astronomers can simultaneously agree that 'the sun does not set.' Descriptions and explanations can be valid so long as one does not mistake local conventions for universal truth.

Yet, while a useful beginning, further dialogues on the conceptual possibilities are needed. We border on the banal if our only stance is that everything can be valid for someone, sometime, somewhere. Such a conclusion closes off dialogue among diverse groups and leads to the result that no one can speak about another. Such an outcome would spell the end of social-science inquiry. Dialogue is invited, then, into how situated validity is achieved, maintained and subverted. Further, how do various methods function in this regard, and for whom? By what means do they variously achieve a sense of validity?

One important option is for the research community to develop practices through which situated knowledges can be brought into productive (as opposed to annihilative) relationships with each other. Frequently many methods of inquiry support (or 'empower') particular groups. This outcome contributes to the situated knowledge of the group, but also tends to diminish other realities. The question, then, is how methods of inquiry could be used to generate productive exchanges at the border of competing or clashing realities. Attention is increasingly directed to methods that would facilitate transversing realities (cf. Cooperrider and Dutton, 1998; Gergen, Gergen, and Barrett, 2004).

Rhetorical/Political Deliberation

Finally, contemporary debates on validity would be enriched by extending the process of rhetorical/political deliberation. That is, one might usefully bracket the question of validity as traditionally conceived in favor of a range of alternative queries into the ways various methods of research function within the culture. Given the impact of social science pursuits on cultural life, how do we estimate the comparative value of various methodological/representational forms? There is already an extensive sociopolitical critique of the patriarchal, colonialist, and hegemonic consequences of realist accounts of the world (Braidotti, 1995; hooks,1990; Said, 1978). While such work represents an important opening, there has been little exploration of what many would consider the positive functions of the realist orientation—both politically and in terms of rhetorical potential. For example, the language of statistics is but one form of rhetoric; however, it is a discourse that, for certain audiences and in certain circumstances, can be more compelling and more functional than a case study, poem or autoethnographic report. More significantly, we have yet to explore the various sociopolitical and rhetorical implications of the new developments discussed above. For example, do ventures into multi-voicing or fictional styling diminish or enhance audience interest or engagement? In a society where clear, no-nonsense answers to serious issues are often demanded, such offerings may seem too impractical, irrelevant, or playful.

And, it may be asked, what are the negative repercussions of self-reflexive and autoethnographic methods. Do they not privilege individual experience over social or communal construction? Can these orientations be faulted for their contribution to an ideology of self-contained individualism? In sum, broad-scale comparative analyses are needed of the various rhetorical/political assets and liabilities of the many emerging methodologies.

RIGHTS OF REPRESENTATION

Critical reflection on the empiricist program has provoked a second roiling of the methodological waters, in this case over issues of representation, its control, responsibilities and ramifications. Again it is Foucault's (1979; 1980) disquisitions on power/knowledge that have figured most centrally in these critiques. For Foucault, knowledge-generating disciplines—including the social sciences—function as sources of authority, and as their descriptions, explanations and diagnoses are disseminated through education and other practices, they enlarge the potential realm of subjugation. For example, as the concept of mental disorders and the diagnostic categories of the psychiatric profession are increasingly acknowledged by professionals and laypersons, so does the culture capitulate to the disciplining power of psychiatry. The implications of such arguments are sobering to the research community. Increasingly painful questions are confronted: to what extent does research convert the common sense, unexamined realities of the culture to disciplinary discourse; in what ways does research empower the discipline as opposed to those under study; when is the researcher exploiting his/her subjects for purposes of personal or institutional prestige; does research serve agencies of surveillance, increasing their capacities of control over the research subject?

Confrontation with such issues has been intensified by increasing resistance among those subjected to social-science inquiry. Feminists were among the first to issue complaints, both for omissions and commissions in regard to characterizations of women in the research literature (Bohan, 1992; Sherif, 1979). Minority-group members have become increasingly aware that the media's distortion or misrepresentation of their lives also prevails in human-science research. The psychiatric establishment was among the first professional group to be targeted, when it was forced by 1960s gay activists to withdraw homosexuality from the nosology of mental illness. It has also been the message delivered by African-Americans angered by a social science literature depicting them as unintelligent, irresponsible or criminal. Similarly, the elderly, AIDS victims, 'psychiatric survivors' and many others now join to question the rights of scientists to represent (appropriate) their experience, actions and/or traditions for their own purposes (Brown, 1989; Collins,1990; hooks, 1990). Given the problems of validity discussed above, these various critiques have troubling implications for future research. What right does any person or group have to represent (depict, explain) the lives of others?

Yet, such contentions are not without their limitations. When extended to their extreme they are as problematic as that which they challenge. In reply to Foucauldian critiques, human science research often functions in counter-hegemonic ways, bringing into critical focus institutions of governance, economic control, educational institutions, the media, and so on. In this sense such research can function as a force of resistance and social justice. Further, to suspend all 'study of the other' would be to terminate virtually all traditions—ethnic, religious, and otherwise—that depend on the capacity to 'name the world.' In addition, there are limits to the claims and critiques of interest groups as well. For one, claims to rights of self-representation exist alongside a host of competing claims made by human scientists—including rights to freedom of speech, to speak the truth from one's own perspective, to contribute to science, and to pursue one's moral ends. Self-representation may be a good, but it is not the only good.

It is also clear that the concept of self-representation is not itself unproblematic. If pressed to its conclusion, no one would have the right to speak for or describe anyone else. One might even question the possibility of individuals representing themselves, for to do so would require that they borrow the language of other persons. The solitary individual would have no private voice, no language of private experience. Without depending on the language of others, intelligibility could not be achieved.

Consistent with the central theme of this chapter, these various tensions within the research community have generative potential. They have, in fact, stimulated a range of significant methodological developments. Two of these deserve special attention:

Conjoint Representation

One methodological means of easing the problem of 'representing the other' is to join in generating outcomes with those who would otherwise be viewed as 'the subjects of the research'. In this way the line between researcher and subject is blurred, and control over representation increasingly shared. In early attempts of this sort, research participants were given a broader space in which to 'tell their own stories'. Often, however, the researcher's hand subtly, but strongly, shaped the voice through editing and interpretation. To compensate, some researchers have invited participants to join in writing the research account itself. For example, in their innovative research, Lather and Smithies (1997) worked in a support group composed of women with the AIDS virus. The resulting volume on these women's lives included the women's own narratives, along with anything they wished to share with the world about their conditions. Rather than obscuring their own positions, the investigators devoted special sections of the book to their own experiences and understandings. To compensate for the ways in which these various accounts were cut away from the discourses of medicine, economics and media, the authors supplemented with more formal academic and scientific materials. Finally, the entire volume was submitted to the participants for their comments. Blending these various modalities, however, 'complicated the question of ethnographic representation' (Lather, 2001).

Distributed Representation

Critiques of 'representing the other' are also countered with emerging methods of distributed representation—that is, attempts by the investigator to set in motion an array of differing voices in dialogic relationship. For example, in her research on child sexual abuse, Karen Fox (1996) carried out open-ended interviews with a victim of child sexual abuse, and then served as a participant-observer of a therapy session with the convicted sex offender. The research report was arranged in three columns, in which the quoted voices of the abuser and the victim occupy two columns, and Fox's own commentaries are carried in a third. The inclusion of the investigator's comments are especially pertinent in this case, as Fox was herself the victim of child sexual abuse. The flow of the text encourages the reader to consider the three different perspectives—separately and in relationship. Although the selection of quotes and textual arrangement was Fox's, each of the participants had the opportunity to read and comment on all the materials. Ultimately the arrangement facilitated a full expression of emotion: ambivalence, sorrow, rage and affection.

Another illustration of distributed representation is offered by a group of three researchers, who were also the objects of their mutual study (Ellis et al., 1997). For five months the trio met in various configurations in diverse settings to discuss the topic of bulimia. Two of the researchers had long histories of eating disorders. The culmination of their research was a jointly written and edited account, in which they described a dinner at an elegant restaurant. This setting was provocative for their particular involvements with food, and permitted complex relations to be treated. The text of their combined efforts also revealed the private reflections and active engagement of each within the relational narrative.

THE PLACE OF THE POLITICAL

A third site of controversy is closely related to issues of validity and representation, but raises issues of a distinct nature. The focal point in this case concerns the political or valuational investments of the researcher. Thirty years ago it was commonly argued that rigorous methods of research were politically or valuationally neutral. Ideological interests could properly determine the topic of research or the ways in which the results were used, but the methods should themselves be ideologically free. However, as the constructionist critiques have made clear, there is no simple means of separating method from ideology. Methods of

inquiry acquire their meaning and significance within broader networks of meaning—metaphysical, epistemological, ontological—which are themselves wedded to ideological and ethical traditions.

For example, to conduct psychological experiments on individuals presumes the centrality of individual mental functioning in the production of human affairs. Much the same privilege is granted by phenomenological methods attempting to tap individual experience. In this way, both methods implicitly support an ideology of individualism. Along similar lines, methods that presume a separation of the researcher from the object of study (a subject/object binary) favor an instrumentalist attitude toward the world and lend themselves to a sense of fundamental alienation between the researcher and the researched.

This expanding realization of the political has had a significant impact on the conception and uses of research methods. If inquiry is inevitably ideological, the major challenge is then to pursue that research which most deeply expresses one's political and valuational investments. To paraphrase, 'if social science is politics by other means, then we should pursue inquiry that most effectively achieves our political ends.' On the one hand, this has meant that many investigators select methods that are themselves ideologically preferred. Methods emphasizing polyvocality, performance and collaboration, as described above, are all employed not only to illuminate a subject matter but to instantiate political values. In addition, however, investigators may select any method that will enable them to generate findings that support a given political position.

At the same time, this realization of the political potentials of methodology has led to significant tension within the research community. We confront a range of highly partisan but quite separate commitments—to feminism, Marxism, lesbian and gay activism, ethnic consciousness raising, and anti-colonialism among them. Each group champions a particular vision of the good, and, by implication, those not participating in the effort are less than good and possibly obstructionist. Many also wish to see research become fully identified with a particular political position. For example, as Denzin and Lincoln propose, 'A poststructural social science project seeks its external grounding not in science ... but rather in a commitment to a post-Marxism and a feminism ... A good text is one that invokes these commitments. A good text exposes how race, class, and gender work their ways in the concrete lives of interacting individuals' (1994: 579). For others, however, such cementing of the political agenda threatens a new form of marginalization. There are many whose humane concerns turn toward other groups (e.g., the aged, the abused, mental patients, the handicapped), and still others who find much to value in using the long-standing positivist tradition to enlighten policy-makers, organizational leaders, and so on.

It is here, however, that the same logic inviting unabashed ideological commitment begins to turn reflexively and critically upon these very commitments. If the constructionist dialogues undermine validity claims, they simultaneously open a space for political or valuational investments; however, all arguments—rational, realist, ethical or political—serving to ground ideologically based research simultaneously lose transcendental legitimation. If one cannot lay claims to empirical truth, then accounts of class oppression, poverty, marginality and the like are similarly rendered rhetorical. Remove such forms of argument and evidence and you simultaneously remove the grounds from value critique. And, as this form of argument has become progressively articulated, so has it produced a new range of tensions (M. Gergen, 2001; Hepburn, 2000). The politically partisan turn on the constructionist arguments once favoring their causes and variously condemn them as 'relativist', 'conservative', or 'irrelevant' (see for example, Burman, 1990; Wilkinson, 1997).

Yet, when more fully elaborated, constructionist arguments do offer a means of conjoining both a consciousness of construction with political realism (K. Gergen, 2001).

There is nothing within constructionism that argues against political action; indeed, as we have seen, constructionism has been useful in opening the door to such expressions. Further, the discourse of political realism may be enormously useful as a means of inciting such action. All that constructionism removes from the committed activist is an ultimate ground for silencing all other voices. In eliminating the sense of foundation may lie humankind's best hope for a viable future.

In terms of methodological implications, there is much to be said for polyvocality. There is a pervasive tendency for scholars—at least in their public writings—to presume coherency of self. Informed by Enlightenment conceptions of the rational and morally informed mind, a premium is placed on logical coherence, conceptual integration, and clarity of purpose. The ideal scholar should know where he/she stands, and be responsible to his/her conception of the good. It is in this same sense that one may lay claim, for example, to 'being a Marxist', or 'a feminist', or 'gay'. Yet, as the constructionist dialogues have made clear, the conception of the singular or unified self is deeply problematic.

Thus, in terms of going beyond the political animosities pervading the methodological arena, polyvocal methodologies offer promise. Researchers are encouraged in this case to recognize, both within themselves and those they study, a multiplicity of competing and often contradictory values, political impulses or conceptions of the good (Banister, 1999). Researchers may each carry impulses toward Marxism, liberalism, anarchism and so on, along with potentials for those ideologies antagonistic to them. Feminist theorist Rosie Braidotti moves in this direction with her conception of 'nomadic subjectivity'. A nomadic consciousness 'entails a total dissolution of the notion of a center and consequently of originary sites of authentic identities of any kind' (1995: 5). Political theorist Chantal Mouffe suggests that a liberal socialist conception of citizenship 'allows for the multiplicity of identities that constitute an individual'

(1993: 94). However, the challenge of transforming pure partisanship to polyvocality is a radical one that would ultimately invite all parties to the research to give expression to their multiplicity—to the full complexity and range of contradictions that are typical of life in postindustrial society. There is movement in this direction, but we have scarcely crossed the threshold.

RESEARCH AS FUTURE MAKING

Thus far we have seen how dialogues on social construction have served as a catalyst not only for probing discussions of the limits, grounds, and potentials of various research methods but also for the development of a rich range of new practices. To conclude this discussion it is useful to consider these developments as presaging a possibly profound sea-change in the very conception of research. We are particularly struck by the emerging concern with the relationship of research to temporal change. Traditional research methodologies are wedded to a conception of a relatively fixed subject matter. The researcher may spend years in studying a topic within a given population or subculture; several years later the work may be published, with the hope that it will remain informative for the foreseeable future. The underlying presumption is that the phenomena of concern remain relatively fixed or stable, and will continue to be so.

Yet, a major premise of much social constructionist writing is that patterns of human action are highly contingent. With changes in the way people construct themselves and the world, there are likely to be alterations in action. And, given that constructions are largely discursive, changes in human behavior may occur with the rapidity of an emerging linguistic fashion. The good can become evil, and vice versa, with the speed of a well-turned phrase. Further, as constructionist thought has made clear, research is not so much a revelation of the real, as it is as an active insinuation into social life. Or as we have seen, research is inevitably political in

its implications, and as a result may alter the very phenomena it seeks to illuminate.

The slowly emerging implication is that research is ill-defined as exploration into *what is* the case. Rather, we may more properly view research as a means of fostering what *will become* the case. This unspoken assumption in many of the new methodologies becomes fully embraced in the domain of action-research methods (Greenwood and Levin, 1998; Reason and Bradbury, 2001). Here researchers offer their skills and resources in order to assist groups to develop projects of mutual interest (Fine et al., 2003; Lykes and Coquillon, 2007). Early work, often called participatory action research (McTaggart, 1997), has now given way to a wide range of change-oriented initiatives. Thus, for example, Baldwin (2001) has worked with teams of social workers to help them develop more sophisticated ways of handling the tensions between competing professional and bureaucratic standards; Hills (2001) has used a form of action research to transform the mode of evaluating nursing students in clinical practice; Whitmore and McKee (2001) have used action methods to help recreate an urban drop-in center for teens; and various practitioners of Appreciative Inquiry have worked with a range of organizations to create positive change (Cooperrider and Whitney, 1999; Barrett and Fry, 2005). The future of research methodology may be importantly linked to developments of this kind.

REFERENCES AND SELECT BIBLIOGRAPHY

Austin, D. (1996) 'Kaleidoscope: The same and different', in C. Ellis and A. Bochner (eds.), *Composing Ethnography: Alternative Forms of Qualitative Writing.* Walnut Creek, CA: AltaMira Press.

Baldwin, M. (2001) 'Working together, learning together: Co-operative inquiry in the development of complex practice by teams of social workers' in P. Reason and H. Bradbury (eds) *Handbook of Action Research: Participant Inquiry and Practice.* London/Thousand Oaks, CA: Sage. pp. 287–93.

Banister, E.M. (1999) 'Evolving reflexivity: Negotiating meaning of women's midlife experience', *Qualitative Inquiry*, 5: 3–23.

Barrett, F. J., and Fry, R. E. (2005). *Appreciative Inquiry: A Positive Approach to Building Cooperative Capacity.* Chagrin Falls, OH: Taos Institute Publications.

Bellah, R. N. et al. (1985). *Habits of the Heart.* Berkeley: University of California Press.

Berger, P.L. and Luckmann, T. (1967) *The Social Construction of Reality: A Treatise on the Sociology of Knowledge.* New York: Doubleday/Anchor.

Billig, M. ([1987] 1996) *Arguing and Thinking.* Cambridge: Cambridge University Press.

Bohan, J. (ed.) (1992) *Seldom Seen, Rarely Heard: Women's Place in Psychology.* Boulder, CO: Westview.

——— (1993) 'Regarding gender: Essentialism, constructionism, and feminist psychology', *Psychology of Women Quarterly*, 17: 5–21.

Braidotti, R. (1995) *Nomadic Subjects: Embodiment and Sexual Difference in Contemporary Feminist Theory.* New York: Columbia University Press.

Brown, L. (1989) 'New voices, new visions: Toward a lesbian/gay paradigm for psychology', *Psychology of Women Quarterly*, 13: 445–58.

Bruner, J. (1990) *Acts of Meaning.* Cambridge, MA: Harvard University Press.

Bryant, A., and Chamez, K. (eds.). (2007). *The Handbook of Grounded Theory.* London/Thousand Oaks, CA: Sage.

Butler, J. (1990) *Gender Trouble.* New York: Routledge.

Burman, E. (1990) 'Differing with deconstuction: A feminist critique', in I. Parker and J. Shotter (eds.), *Deconstructing Social Psychology.* London: Routledge. pp. 208–220

Carlson, M. (1996) *Performance, A Critical Introduction.* New York: Routledge.

Case, S., Brett, P., and Foster, S. (eds.) (1995) *Cruising the Performative: Interventions into the Representation of Ethnicity, Nationality, and Sexuality.* Bloomington: University of Indiana Press.

Clough, P.T. (1997) 'Autotelecommunication and autoethnography: A reading of Carolyn Ellis's Final Negotiations', *The Sociological Quarterly*, 38: 95–110.

Cole, M. (1998) *Cultural Psychology: A once and future discipline.* Cambridge, MA: Harvard University Press.

Collins, P.H. (1990) *Black Feminist Thought: Knowledge, Consciousness, and the Politics of Empowerment.* Boston: Unwin Hyman.

Cooperrider, D.L. and Dutton, J. (eds.) (1998) *No Limits to Cooperation: The Organization Dimensions of Global Change.* Thousand Oaks, CA: Sage.

Cooperrider, D.L. and Whitney, D. (1999) *Collaborating for Change: Appreciative Inquiry.* San Francisco, CA: Barrett-Koehler Communications.

Denzin, N.K., and Lincoln, Y.S. (eds.) ([1994] (2000) *Handbook of Qualitative Research.* Thousand Oaks, CA, London: Sage.

Ellis, C. and Bochner, A.P. (eds.) (1996) *Composing Ethnography: Alternative Forms of Qualitative Writing.* Thousand Oaks, CA: AltaMira Press.

Ellis, C., Kiesinger, C. and Tillmann-Healy, L. (1997) 'Interactive interviewing: Talking about emotional experience', in R. Hertz (ed.), *Reflexivity and Voice.* Thousand Oaks, CA: Sage, pp. 119–49.

Fine, M., and Weiss, L. (1998) *The Unknown City: The Lives of Poor and Working-Class Young Adults.* Boston: Beacon Press.

Fine, M. et al. (2003) 'Participatory action research: From within and beyond prison bars', in P. M. Camic, J. E. Rhodes, and L. Yardley (eds.). *Qualitative Research in Psychology: Expanding Perspectives in Methodology and Design.* Washington, DC: American Psychological Association. pp. 173–198.

Foucault, M. (1979) *Discipline and Punish.* New York: Vintage Books.

——— (1980) *Power/Knowledge.* New York: Pantheon.

Fox, K.V. (1996) 'Silent voices: A subversive reading of child sexual abuse', in C. Ellis and A. Bochner, (eds.), *Composing Ethnography: Alternative Forms of Qualitative Writing.* Walnut Creek, CA: Alta Mira Press.

Gamson, J. (2000) 'Sexualities, queer theory, and qualitative research', in N. Denzin and Y.S. Lincoln (eds.), *Handbook of Qualitative Research.* Thousand Oaks, CA: Sage. pp. 347–65.

Georgi, A. P.(1994) *Phenomenology and Psychological Research.* Pittsburgh, PA: Duquesne University Press.

Georgi, A. P. and Georgi, B. M. (2003). 'The descriptive phenomenological psychological method', in P. M. Camic, J. E. Rhodes, and L. Yardley (eds.). *Qualitative Research in Psychology: Expanding Perspectives in Methodology and Design.* Washington, DC: American Psychological Association. pp. 243–274.

Gergen, K.J. (1994) *Realities and Relationships, Soundings in Social Construction.* Cambridge, MA: Harvard University Press.

——— (1999) *An Invitation to Social Construction.* London: Sage.

——— (2001) *Social Construction in Context.* London: Sage.

Gergen, K.J., Gergen, M.M. and Barrett, F. (2004) 'Dialogue: Life and death of the organization', in D. Grant, C. Hardy, C. Oswick and L. Putnam (eds.), *Handbook of Organizational Discourse.* London: Sage. pp. 39–59.

Gergen, M. (1992) 'Life stories: Pieces of a dream', in G. Rosenwald and R. Ochberg (eds.), *Storied Lives.* New Haven, CT: Yale University Press. pp. 127–44.

Gergen, M. (2001). *Feminist Reconstructions in Psychology: Narrative, Gender & Performance*. London, Thousand Oaks, CA: Sage.

Gergen, M.M., Chrisler, J.C., and LoCicero, A. (1999) 'Innovative methods: Resources for research, teaching and publishing', *Psychology of Women Quarterly*, 23: 431–456.

Gergen, M. and Davis, S.N. (2003) 'Dialogic pedagogy: Developing narratives research perspectives through conversation', in R. Josselson, A. Lieblich, and D. McAdams (eds.), *Up Close and Personal: The Teaching and Learning of Narrative Research*. Washington, DC: APA Publications, pp. 239–58.

Greenwood, D. and Levin, M. (1998) *Introduction to Action Research: Social Research for Social Change*. Thousand Oaks, CA: Sage.

Hacking, I. (1999) *The Social Construction of What?* Cambridge, MA: Harvard University Press.

Haraway, D. (1988) 'Situated knowledges: The science question in feminism and the privilege of partial perspective', *Feminist Studies*, 14: 575–99.

Hepburn, A. (2000) 'On the alleged incompatibility between relativism and feminist psychology', *Feminism and Psychology*, 10: 91–106.

Hertz, R. (ed.) (1997) *Reflexivity and Voice*. Thousand Oaks, CA: Sage.

Hills, M. D. (2001) 'Using co-operative inquiry to transform evaluation of nursing students clinical practice' in P. Reason & H. Bradbury (eds), *Handbook of Action Research: Participant Inquiry and Practice*. London: Sage. pp. 340–351

hooks, b. (1990) *Yearning: Race, Gender, and Cultural Politics*. Boston: South End Press.

Kiesinger, C.E. (1998) 'From interview to story: Writing Abbie's life', *Qualitative Inquiry*, 4: 71–95.

Lasch, C. (1979). *The Culture of Narcissism*. New York: Norton.

Lather, P. (1993) 'Fertile obsession: Validity after poststructuralism', *Sociological Quarterly*, 34: 673–93.

Lather, P. and Smithies, C. (1997) *Troubling the Angels: Women Living with HIV/AIDS*. Boulder, CO: Westview Press.

Lather, P. (2001). 'Postbook: Working in the ruins of feminist ethnography', *Signs: Journal of Women in Culture and Society*, 27: 199–227.

Lockford, L. (2004) *Performing Femininity: Rewriting Gender Identity*. Walnut Creek, CA: AltaMira Press.

Lykes, M. B. and Coquillon, E. (2007). 'Participatory and action research and feminisms: Toward transformative praxis' in S. N. Hesse-Biber (ed.) *Handbook of Feminist Research: Theory and Praxis*. London, Thousand Oaks, CA: Sage. pp. 297–326.

Marchand, M. H. and Runyan, A. (eds.). (2000). *Gender and Global Restructuring: Sightings, Sites and Resistances*. New York: Routledge.

Marcus, G. (1998) *Ethnography through Thick and Thin: A New Research Imaginary for Anthropology's Changing Professional Culture*. Princeton, NJ: Princeton University Press.

McTaggart, R. (1997) *Participatory Action Research: International Contexts and Consequences*. Albany, NY: State University of New York Press.

Middleton, D. and Brown, S.D. (2005) *The Social Psychology of Experience, Studies in Remembering and Forgetting*. London: Sage.

Miller, J.B. and Stiver, I.P. (1997) *The Healing Connection: How Women form Relationships in Therapy and in Life*. Boston: Beacon Press.

Mitchell, S. (1995) *Hope and Dread in Psychoanalysis*. New York: Basic Books

Mouffe, C. (1993) 'Liberal socialism and pluralism: Which citizenship?', in J. Squires (ed.), *Principled Positions: Postmodernism and the Rediscovery of Value*. London: Lawrence and Wishart. pp. 85–104.

Nagel, T. (1997) *The Last Word*. New York: Oxford University Press.

Naples, N.A. (2003) *Feminism and Method: Ethnography, Discourse Analysis and Activist Research*. New York, London: Routledge.

Naples, N. A. (2007). 'Standpoint epistemology and beyond', in S. N. Hesse-Biber (ed.) *Handbook of Feminist Research: Theory and Praxis*. London, Thousand Oaks, CA: Sage. pp. 579–590.

Parker, I. (ed.) (1998) *Social Constructionism, Discourse and Realism*. London: Sage.

Reason, P. and Bradbury, H. (eds.) (2001) *Handbook of Action Research: Participative Inquiry and Practice*. London, Thousand Oaks, CA: Sage.

Richardson, L. (1997) *Fields of Play, Constructing an Academic Life*. New Brunswick, NJ: Rutgers University Press.

——— (1998) 'Meta-Jeopardy', *Qualitative Inquiry*, 4: 464–68.

Rinehart, R. (1998) 'Fictional methods in ethnography: Believability, specks of glass, and Chekhov', *Qualitative Inquiry*, 4: 200–24.

Said, E.W. (1978) *Orientalism*. New York: Pantheon Books.

Sandoval, C. (1991) 'U.S. third world feminism: The theory and method of oppositional conciousness in the postmodern world', *Genders*, 10: 1–24.

Sarbin, T. (ed.) (1986) *Narrative Psychology: The Storied Nature of Human Conduct*. New York: Praeger.

Sherif, C.W. (1979) 'Bias in psychology', in J. Sherman and E.T. Beck (eds.), *The Prism of Sex: Essays in the Sociology of Knowledge*. Madison, WI: University of Wisconsin Press. pp. 93–133.

Strauss, A. and Corbin, J. (1994) 'Grounded theory methodology: An overview', in N.K. Denzin and Y.S.

Lincoln (eds.), *Handbook of Qualitative Research.* Thousand Oaks, CA: Sage, pp. 273–85.

Wertsch, J.V. (2006) *Voices of the mind: A sociocultural approach to mediated action.* Cambridge, MA: Harvard University Press.

Whitmore, E. and McKee, C. (2001) 'Six street youth who could ...', in P. Reason and H. Bradbury (eds.), *Handbook of Action Research: Participative Inquiry and Practice.* London and Thousand Oaks, CA: Sage. pp. 396–402.

Wilkinson, S. (1997) 'Prioritizing the political: Feminist psychology', in T. Ibanez and L. Iniguez (eds.), *Critical Social Psychology.* London: Sage, pp. 178–194.

Wittgenstein, L. (1953) *Philosophical Investigations.* New York: Macmillan.

NOTES

1 See, for example, Gergen (1994; 1999); Hacking (1999).

2 See, for example, Bellah et al. (1985); Lasch (1979).

3 See, for example, Middleton and Brown (2005); Billig (1996).

4 See, for example, Nagel (1997); Parker (1998).

5 See, for example, the performance research list-serve: performsocsci@jiscmail.ac.uk.

26

Rhetorics of Social Science: Sociality in Writing and Inquiry

Ricca Edmondson

INTRODUCTION

Rhetoric is an approach to communication and argument which responds to the fact that they are social as well as reasoned: they operate between people, and make sense within the contexts of social and intellectual practices. This transforms how we perceive arguing, investigating and claiming, in the social sciences and elsewhere, and hence how we *do* them: what we see as legitimate or illegitimate, and the justifications we use. The first part of this chapter explores what this view of rhetorical communication entails, starting from the construction and ownership of arguments and highlighting the role of audiences, and then considering the nature of persuasive argument itself. The second part begins from the problem of hostility to rhetorical analysis, urging that this hostility be abandoned, which will help us better to understand what is going on in social-scientific argumentation. It is true that rhetorical analysis can expose textual manipulation and ideological bias, but this does not enable us to excise them altogether and attain complete neutrality. Arguments cannot be made from no point of view; we

shall see that 'quantitative' texts, sometimes envisaged as neutral in this way, are as rhetorical as those which are not. The third part of the chapter shows what a rhetorical approach can contribute to specific questions about social-scientific method, such as what stipulations we should make for ethnographic writing, what authors' and subjects' 'voices' entail, the demands of social-scientific 'reflexivity', and the implications of political and other forms of advocacy. This returns us to the question from which we begin: what to expect of 'good argument' in the social sciences.

Rhetoric, then, interrogates the practice of discourse as it is actually carried out—not least in a democratic context. In the social sciences, concern with citizens' participation in furthering the public good has been present from the start (Turner and Turner, 1990). But in the light of the various enthusiasms for professional and natural-scientific styles through which the social sciences have passed during their short history, this concern has sometimes seemed naïve. It has recurrently been assumed that social-scientific argument should be free of social and personal influences—even if it was often taken for granted that such objectivity would ultimately support some preferred political outcome. On this view, the boundaries between theories, methods and politics could seem relatively clear-cut. But since the work of Habermas in particular, it became more widely accepted that human knowledge cannot be understood independently of systems of sociopolitical practice. Knowledge inevitably has 'interests': underlying goals towards which it is directed and which govern its form. The fundamental rejection of any idea of social-scientific commitment has had to be revised, but debate continues on just what this implies. Postmodern responses accentuate a view of *choice* in commitment which locates the choice itself outside the parameters of systematic debate. But the tradition of rhetoric maintains that the entire process of building an argument—which includes espousing an ethical or political position, engaging with an interlocutor, and locating oneself vis-à-vis the public good—must be subject to reasonable evaluation.

Rhetoric is the theory and practice of producing arguments, notably in social and political affairs, which their producers make as convincing—and, in the best cases, as conducive to the common good—as the predicaments in question allow. A rhetorical approach thus resists some views about how linguistic communication works, which remained common, even dominant, during the twentieth century. It designates an approach to language which rejects rigid distinctions between communicators, recipients and 'information' transferred between them, stressing, instead, interaction and flow. From the beginning (contra Gaonkar, 1997), rhetoric has viewed argumentation as socially situated: it sees deliberation in the social and political world as inevitably affected by those reasoning and by those addressed (Ryan, 1984; Woerner, 1990). In the days of sociology's stress on 'natural-scientific' style, conjoining these issues appeared misguided. Now, it has begun to seem much more sophisticated.

A major reason for which rhetorical approaches to arguing may seem surprising is this explicit acknowledgement of social and even emotional components as parts of *reasoning*. This set of rhetorical concerns remains relatively underplayed in debate on social-scientific theory and method, despite acknowledgement in principle of the role of 'interests' in argument. Recognizing specifically human constituents in arguments is still often taken to imply *either* that they undermine those arguments' validity *or* that the idea of validity must be rejected altogether. Much social-scientific work has adopted the view, conventional in Western thought in the last two centuries, that thinking is an entirely cognitive operation (cf. Dixon, 2003). To the extent that social, characterological or emotional influences on deliberation are examined, in the sociology of knowledge and elsewhere, these influences are assumed, as Bauman (1978) points out, to be deleterious, operating in the interests of political forces which are generally viewed as objectionable. Rhetorical studies, by contrast, explore how deliberation involves more than cogitation, how it is social as well as individual, and how it can yet be reasonable. This stance usually rejects relativism. It does not imply freedom to choose what we believe, according to preferences which are themselves immune from evaluation. For Toulmin (2001), being reasonable is a 'calling'. Much about the human world remains opaque to us, but there are basic issues on which we can and must take a stand.

Thus the study of rhetoric highlights with unusual clarity both the closeness and the tensions between method and theory in the social sciences: how to do it depends on what you think you are trying to do. For this reason, much that has been written about rhetoric in the human sciences has focused on what these sciences are and what they should be aiming to achieve. The textbook assumption that social scientists first do research into what is going on—and then write it up as clearly as they can—is not shared by students of rhetoric. They see writing as only the most publicly apparent part of an entire process to be interrogated:

why is it done, where, when, with what means, and to whose benefit? Richard Harvey Brown has argued that acquiring new social-scientific views is a matter of 'conversion', poetical and creative. Like Alan Gross (1997), he sees change in any kind of scientific belief as entering into fresh combinations of perceptions and priorities, radically changing how we see the world. *Why* these new positions are adopted often looks different at the time of the conversion from the reasons proffered in retrospect, when the new paradigm has been worked out. Rhetorical analysis can trace how these changes, as they develop, are taken to be convincing by those concerned. Thus, for John Nelson (cf. Simons, 1990), rhetoric is the rhetoric of *enquiry*: it deals with reasoning itself, not just with writing, and its concerns make no distinction between sociology, politics or any of the human sciences. Rhetoric deals with groups of people, how they 'invent' what they say, how they address and convince each other, and how we can trace, engage in and assess these means. It does analyze specific techniques and their effects. But it does so in the light of the overall enterprises to which they belong, exploring and sometimes exposing them.

Social-scientific texts are inevitably argumentative in the sense of urging positions and changing, or endorsing, readers' viewpoints; some do this consciously. John Urry, in *Sociology Beyond Societies* (2000), overtly tries to get readers to form new perceptions about the social world; it is an integral part of his project to make impacts on his audience. He argues that sociology emerged in a world which promoted the conception of 'societies' as discrete national entities; but that remaining fixated on this image of the social arena yields a mechanical, distorted picture of how the world works—how it really works, as far as he can tell, given his awareness of the uncertainty of human insight. Urry's argument will not take effect unless he can *transfer our attention* from conventional within-nation phenomena to flows and movements, getting us to *shift perspective* away from the blocks and boundaries to which everyday social perceptions habituate us. This, in

rhetorical terms, adjusts the 'presence' accorded different aspects of the world. It is also where Brown (1987) would identify a conversion: we are to *reach a state of mind* in which we *experience* global flows, changing human/natural relations, as more interesting and salient than, say, local government regulations, themselves only part of a continuously evolving flux. There are, as Urry (2000: 210f.) acknowledges, overall thought styles which organize our imagination, and his arguments aim to move our allegiance to new ones, in the interests of global 'emancipatory interests'. Writing about society is a social activity, designed to convince others. To make sense, it must be able to function reasonably as a source of coherence, meaningfulness and appeal (Nelson, 1998). For social-scientific writing to make rhetorical sense, it needs not only to identify pressing areas for research and to relate narratives, making them intelligible, but also to help audiences appreciate the argumentation which makes this intelligibility work.

How do we carry out operations like 'bringing people to see the world in a particular way', and moreover do so using methods we can reasonably defend? Conventional logic and methodology do not account for these aspects of inquiry, referring—if at all—to vague attributions of 'effectiveness' in marshalling data, assumed to account sufficiently for changes of mind. In contrast, rhetorical analysis illuminates processes of inquiry in general (Nelson, 1998; cf. Booth, 2004). It deconstructs and reconstructs the interacting influences of paradigms, ideologies, fashions, schools, groups and individuals on the way the human sciences are practised (for writers like Gross, all sciences are human sciences). This goes beyond 'technique' in the senses of orderly data presentation or embellishing texts by inserting rhetorical figures. There are certainly textual techniques which can be analysed and learned (Sloane, 2001), but their use in composition is far from mechanical. In effect, rhetoric offers an extended demonstration of how sense-making between people is carried out.

PART 1: ARGUERS AND AUDIENCES IN THE RHETORICAL ANALYSIS OF ARGUING

An unparalleled impetus to observing major flows among interblended currents of argument remains Aristotle's *Rhetoric*. This observation is not intended to endorse a 'historical' approach to the subject; rather, it supports an approach to language which stresses its use by human agents in reasonable argumentation. Aristotle distinguishes between currents associated with author, audience and argument, and shows how they contribute to inference itself, via rhetorical (enthymematic) deduction and induction (Edmondson, 1984; Woerner, 1990). These are not intended as the sole analytical instruments offered by a rhetorical approach to social-scientific arguing (cf. Atkinson, 1990: 25). During the twentieth century, as Vickers (1988) complains (cf. Burke, 1945), attempts were made to reduce rhetoric's conceptual armory to small numbers, usually featuring metaphor and one or two others. In contrast, the Aristotelian distinctions do not obliterate other rhetorical patterns, but clarify the argumentative streams into which they fit. They expose arguments' phenomenological structures, guiding our perception of roles played within them by styles such as realism, or by tropes (terms substituting for or transforming conventional meanings) such as metonymy, synecdoche or metaphor.

This phenomenology of argument is both diagnostic and prescriptive. It shows how we argue as a matter of fact, and how to do it better. This diagnosis also stresses the constant *interaction* between major components of arguing. The 'argument itself', 'logos', is always informed by its social situatedness, for arguments are made by people to people. 'The argument itself' is a like an iceberg whose tip is visible, but which is based on a vast below-surface assemblage of styles and practices in reasoning. As Bazerman (1988: 23) remarks, the text does not end where the page does. But there are only some things that can effectively be said in a given situation to a given set of people; an argument is always constrained by the need to find 'the available means of persuasion' (Aristotle, *Rhetoric*: 1355b) in *these* circumstances. Though not explicitly a student of ideologies, Aristotle notes that particular political environments make particular arguments seem plausible and understandable, and rule out even the perception of others. We are forced to argue in different ways in democracies, oligarchies or monarchies. This observation is not intended to justify us in becoming sycophants but to alert us to the parameters of what can be communicated in a given setting.

Hence the salience of the other two components of the argumentative triad: 'ethos' is equivalent to 'the character of the speaker' as the argument shows it; 'pathos' relates to the ways in which an audience reacts (Ryan, 1984; Woerner, 1990). A speech addressed to a particular hearer can only sensibly be constructed in terms of the world of meaning that person inhabits: 'It is the hearer, that is the speech's end and object' (Aristotle, *Rhetoric*: 1358b 1). This does not imply that we are entitled to say whatever appeals to our listeners. It underlines that speakers, searching for arguments which both fit the case and make sense to recipients, draw on socially evolved pools of assumptions and inferential conventions which they share with listeners. Gaonkar (1997) complains that classical rhetoric naively privileges the intention-driven independence of speakers. Yet Aristotle says the opposite of this. A speech must adapt to those means of persuasion functioning in the world the *hearer* lives in, and the hearer's activity is needed to complete its meaning.

In the social and political world of argument, interpreting *what is said* usually takes account of *who is arguing*: 'ethos' and 'pathos' are crucial (cf. Garver, 1995). Perelman and Olbrechts-Tyteca (1969: 18) point out that, under normal circumstances, 'some quality is necessary in order to speak and be listened to at all.' Arguing 'does not take place in a social void' (Edmondson, 1984: 16). Analyses like Goffman's in *The Presentation of Self in Everyday Life* (1959) explore what makes people convincing to each other, like white coats and airs of authority for doctors. Ethnographic and political studies supply evidence of a vast, culturally highly variant, range of grounds on which people are prepared to take each other's views seriously: being (or not being) a woman or a priest; being (or not being) an acknowledged scientific expert. Such phenomena traditionally count as the rhetorical *use* of attitudes towards arguing, means of persuasion *external* to an argument itself. Aristotle confines 'ethos'—elements of argument connected with the speaker—to what the speaker actually says (or writes; for reasons of brevity, the two are treated as equivalent here). There are social phenomena which people happen to find impressive or otherwise, for good or bad reasons which require their own arguments; but to understand arguing itself we should distinguish between what arguers intend to claim, what they may count as claiming, and what some particular audience takes them to claim.

The words of an argument represent a small part of the network of reasoning making the case for the position concerned. Most of this network remains submerged, a complex mass of assumptions, priorities and connections at which the audience must guess, or, where the topic of debate is complex, cannot even guess. Nonetheless the audience must form an opinion whether the speaker knows as much about the topic as s/he claims, whether s/he is really a good judge of the matters at hand, whether s/he is arguing with integrity. Decisions of this sort lead us to rely on or reject each other's judgment all the time. This is not only inevitable but often also justified. This becomes clearer when we examine three components of ethos emphasized by Aristotle: circumspection and well-informedness in practical reasoning, human or ethical fitness for dealing with the issue at hand, and well-disposedness towards the audience. The last two concern not just whether a speaker is arguing honestly, but whether s/he has gone to lengths to understand the audience's position and offer the most comprehensive argument possible. If

so, it is reasonable to rely on the ethos of the speaker to give credence to the argument. Given that we can never know everything another speaker knows, it is sensible to try to estimate that person's overall qualities as shown in this particular argument (rather than, say, going on general acquaintance with the speaker's reputation). This is particularly urgent in human affairs, where exactitude is often impossible; we seldom know as much as we would ideally wish for to arrive at a conclusion. The more uncertainty such questions involve, the more crucially, and inevitably, we are influenced by what speakers convey of their qualities for deliberation (Aristotle, *Rhetoric*: 1356a 6ff). Hence ethos is particularly important in the human sciences. When situations are fluctuating and not fully understood, we depend especially strongly on the integrity and judgment of arguers. We rely on them not to conceal or distort the accounts they give and to be serious in their efforts to comprehend the issues at hand. These are unspoken preconditions for finding arguments in the human sphere convincing at all.

But it is *audiences* which play a key and active role in classical accounts of rhetoric. Arguments need to mean something to their recipients: the first role of an argument is to get someone else to grasp what is being said. The hearer functions as the *judge* of the speech, not its helpless victim. It would be self-contradictory to try to pervert hearers' judgments, like trying to measure with a crooked ruler. Only crude and manipulative speeches are intended simply to manipulate hearers' feelings. Nonetheless speakers need to understand human beings with their characters, feelings and values (Aristotle, *Rhetoric*: 1356a 22–5), because it is normal that these elements influence how we assess arguments. 'Our judgements when we are pleased and friendly are not the same as when we are pained and hostile' (Aristotle, *Rhetoric*: 1356a 15–16). In particular frames of mind, certain aspects of a situation seem to us important, others insignificant; this makes all the difference to what can convincingly be urged about them. Judging plausibilities is not a matter of logic alone but 'also a matter of proper psychological disposition' (Rehg, 1997: 372; cf. Leff, 1978). Frames of mind induced by an argument—'pathos'—encourage us to stress phenomena enabling us to take in what is being claimed, even if not to accept it. They embody judgments, and belong to legitimate argument.

Woodward (2003) quotes a story by a feminist activist, attending a protest march on a stormy night. A march monitor charitably offers advice should she not 'keep up' with the rest—which hits the activist hard. This phrase transforms her view of her whole political world. Formerly a problem for men because she is a woman, she is now a problem for women—because she is 65 years old. Previously insignificant aspects of her social world, people's ages, have suddenly shifted to center stage: she understands arguments about ageism in a way she had not before. Cases like this underline the connections between emotions and comprehension. For 'hearers in particular moods or with particular preconceptions, certain contentions are in an important sense *unintelligible*': actually understanding particular arguments 'involves sympathy and experience as well as intellect' (Edmondson, 1984: 19, emphasis in original). In the absence of such sympathy and experience, what the author writes will not even make sense to readers. Thus a major effect of operations connected with pathos can be to dismantle an audience's barriers against taking in what is argued. These operations aim to put audiences in a place from which they can 'see' what a writer means. Billig (1991: 206) contends that ancient rhetorical theory had a stronger sense than modern psychology of the capacities of individuals hearing a speech to react in lively and contrasting ways. The concept of pathos makes it legitimate to take this into account.

Classical rhetoric is highly conscious that arguments are situated in real-life circumstances which force us to make them with the material to hand. Greek and Roman authors were sufficiently comfortable with sociality in thought to recognize that arguing begins from shared resources in the community, not assuming that sociality makes an argument defective. Thus they assembled a vast collection of suggested starting points for argument under 'invention'—the first stage in composing an argument. Cicero (who *defines* rhetoric as 'speaking well') suggests that lawyers interrogating cases should examine 'witness statements, documents, contracts, agreements, examinations, parliamentary decisions, court judgements, administrative order, legal assessments' (Cicero, 2001 (*De Oratore* II.xxvii), 116).

These suggestions recall methodological guides for social-scientific researchers. Hammersley and Atkinson's (1994) recommendations for doing ethnography stress distinctions in time (is an emergency ward to be observed on Friday nights or Tuesday afternoons?) or place (what counts as 'part of' the hospital—does the car-park count?). The classical tradition lists considerations of this sort as 'commonplaces' for starting arguing, acknowledging socially-shared assumptions about what will make sense as a basis from which to begin. This applies too to the intellectual operations which follow. What relations have these states of affairs to persons concerned with them? Arguments about persons ('*loci a persona*') may concern their backgrounds, allegiances, family, nation, ages, education, status, and so on (Lanham, 1968). Further subdivisions to consider might involve cause, place, time, means: checklists in rhetorical handbooks were intended to ensure that no relevant argumentative avenue was left unexplored. Yet no argument could explore every single one. Consistently emphasising some at the expense of others—people, say, at the expense of places—conveys a particular worldview. The configurations of commonplaces from which arguments start offer instruments for tracking the argumentative influence of ideologies, paradigms and schools.

Conventional twentieth-century approaches to these intertwined elements of human reasoning were often fragmented, assuming the (sometimes conflicting) vantage points of several modern disciplines to address phenomena seen by the Greeks and Romans as interconnected. A rhetorical account attempts more holism, as in Edmondson's (1984) dissection of sociological texts to show that their arguments engage in a plethora of interpersonal, emotional, ethical and political processes. These extend into the heart of social-scientific inference: rhetorical (enthymematic) deduction and induction often fuse logos, ethos and pathos. Far from detracting from texts' reasonableness, this may demonstrate their strength. Hobbs' (1988) interpretation of criminal activities in London via the trope of 'entrepreneurship' induces readers to make new inferences by stimulating their imaginations. His cases offer humor, sarcasm and surprise, giving practice in a new perspective. Guard dogs pursue aspiring thieves to steal their ham sandwiches; the author becomes embroiled in infractions on his own account; he charts the disappointed pretensions of incompetent crooks and the startling respectability of competent ones. Only after an imaginative shift to envisaging practices and career structures which criminals share with businessmen can the reader infer the entrepreneurial motivations Hobbs describes. His argument is an exercise in rhetorical reasoning.

Everyday Rhetoric and Good Arguing

Rhetoric refused from the start to conceptualize communication as abstract. It stressed that argumentation, especially public argumentation about social and political affairs, takes place between human beings, in areas where everything going on is fluctuating, uncertain and incomplete. Taking this initial step of noticing how arguments are conducted *without denigrating them* can be the most difficult perceptual shift of all. In a twentieth-century context, recognizing the conventionality of human thought and the sociality of opinion seemed to undermine the idea of any such thing as a 'good' argument. Rhetoricians strenuously resist this. They uphold a tradition of understanding reasoning occluded during post-Baconian modernity,

which—as McCloskey (1997) underlines—retreated from regarding reasonable persuasion as a sensible, intellectually interesting option, preferring forms of natural-scientific proof as paradigms. In fact, argumentation about social, political and ethical affairs uses what technical evidence it can, but relies centrally on everyday forms of reasoning. Gadamer claims that rhetoric's greatest achievement is showing that such argument about human concerns can be reasonable and adequate; '...the theoretical tools of the art of interpretation (hermeneutics) have been to a large extent borrowed from rhetoric' (1997: 318).

Thus the social psychologist Michael Billig (1991: 41) vehemently opposes a model of 'thinking' as purely cognitive. He contends that models of thinking in terms of problem-solving, information-processing and rule-following produce an image which 'curiously demeans the nature of thought itself', pointedly excluding everything creative, critical and interpretive. Billig (1996) embraces a Protagorean model of argumentation and debate: any question always has at least two sides. Human relatedness to the world is essentially one of disputation, of dialogue between two or more stances. But this is exactly what some professional styles suppress. McCloskey (1986) points out that conceptualizing economics in natural-scientific terms has pushed the moral, political and social aspects of the discipline underground, prohibiting them from being adequately discussed. Richard Harvey Brown's conception of reason as a creative, intersubjective practice (1977) is intended to combat this reification of rationality and induce tolerance of the ways other people think—though not to discourage the constant search for better reasons. Bazerman in *Shaping Written Knowledge* (1988) or Nelson in *Tropes of Politics* (1998) object to the dominance of quasi-natural-scientific language in the human sciences, not only for encouraging us to forget that thinking is carried out by people but also for luring us to depend on inappropriate arguments and superficial conceptions of data. Political science, Nelson contends (1998: 79–80), tends to derive information from news headlines, and research questions from popular controversies. He wants to make researchers more vigorously aware that theories are *arguments* which must be tested, 'realistically and rigorously' (1998: 96). Rhetoric is not less demanding than conventional methods, but more.

Good arguing, therefore, relies on multifunctional textual elements. In social-scientific work, it is vital to be able to trust authors' judgments—not least when this work is resistant to direct replication or uses methods which, like those in higher statistical reaches, transcend many readers' competence. Methodological acknowledgements, such as listing long periods the author has spent carrying out *in situ* research, or consultations held with luminaries in the field, indicate that the author is conscientious; a person of standing whose genuineness can be relied upon. Detailing methods is a professional necessity, *and* one exhibiting writers' judgment and integrity, their ethos. But strategies for demonstrating ethos vary not only with authors' paradigms but also with those of readers. The palette of ethnographic styles investigated by Van Maanen emphasizes contrasting operations to establish authority on authors' parts. Where realism demands confident detachment, and confessionality the opposite, impressionistic accounts offer dramatic sequences of quotation, metaphor and 'the expansive recall of fieldwork experience' (Van Maanen, 1988: 102). Consequently, divergent audiences' expectations of arguers may be too stringent or too exclusive to be satisfied by the same author. Social-scientific arguing demands a variety of investigations and styles.

PART 2: ANTIPATHY TO RHETORIC, AND THE IDEA OF 'INVISIBLE' ARGUING

Three special aspects of rhetoric—its acknowledgement of the committed quality of human deliberation, of its interpersonal nature, and of its composition on a broader basis than cognition narrowly understood—have implications for social-scientific methods. In principle, they allow us to uncover more about how arguing works in human inquiry, and how to improve it, without assuming we are exposing double-dealing whenever we notice extra-'cognitive' elements in an author's work. But in practice, it is easiest to analyze the construction of arguments which strike us as wrong. Those we accept may appear the only genuine approaches—scarcely 'arguing' at all. Hence it remains common to see rhetoric as a source of 'error and deceit', dubiously allowable in entertainment or public oratory but best avoided in earnest attempts to speak truthfully (Locke, [1690] 1979: III.X.34).

Expressions like 'mere rhetoric' or 'empty rhetoric' suggest that there are two sorts of argument: biased, manipulative, 'rhetorical' ones on the one hand, and on the other objective findings which transcend argumentation altogether. This contrast, posited frequently (though not ubiquitously) between the sixteenth and the nineteenth centuries, is now less often seriously maintained than pressed into service as shorthand, to indicate arguments one dislikes but cannot take the time to dissect. Similarly, terms like 'left-wing rhetoric' or 'right-wing rhetoric' point to, or allege, argumentative stances deplored by the speaker: tendencies to ignore the political impact of individuals, perhaps, in the first case, or to exaggerate it in the second. Terms like these imply that important aspects of the world are ignored by the 'rhetorics' in question—that is, by their characteristic clusters of argument and style. People guilty of such arguments are said to be 'blinded by their own rhetoric': their argumentative responses, it is suggested, are so rigidly pre-set that they cannot perceive anything that puts them in doubt.

Accusations like these are often used without corroboration. Supporting them would involve demonstrating what groups of assumptions are fundamental to the argumentative stances under debate, which moves they legitimate and which they rule out. Thus, McCloskey (1986) shows that elevating the claims of the natural-science paradigm in economics eliminates discussion of human motivations and values. Feyerabend's (1975) account of Galileo shows how Galileo got people to believe his innovative claims by playing on what they already believed. Flyvbjerg (1998) explores how different political backings for arguments affect whether people accept them— as does official and economic support (Gorges, 1997). Bostdorff (2003) explores the 'covenant renewal' metaphors and allusions in Bush's speeches after September 11, 2001, with the aim of explaining not only his appeal to supporters but also some aspects of his foreign policy. Rhetorical analysis can be used in this way to diagnose patterns, perspectives and priorities used by arguers and audiences, dissecting their consensus on what makes sense in the social contexts they share. It can dismantle what we assume about social reality—for example, how descriptive accounts of the world are built up to seem reassuringly real to their exponents (Potter, 1996). Ideologies, paradigms and schools are all made up of evolving, multi-layered patterns and characteristic combinations of argument. Though far from entirely consistent in their views of the world (Freeden, 2003), they proffer linked expectations about what forms a convincing case to make. These expectations can be productively explored using rhetorical tools. But to suppose that 'rhetoric' is fundamentally distorting is no more justified than assuming that, because people sometimes tell lies, 'communication' is fundamentally deceptive.

'Rhetorics' are connected with ideologies, paradigms and schools by virtue of the fact that all favor characteristic selections of argumentative treatment. The differences between them include their scales of operation and their systematicity: the 'rhetoric of consumerism' is less systematic than, say, the human rights school of interpreting natural law, but more extensively used. Within these groupings, substantive arguments are inevitably colored by styles, since 'style' itself implies highlighting some types of

argument and avoiding others. Different social-scientific methodologies dictate, for instance, different stylistic conventions for establishing ethos. To take an interpretive instance, Fairhurst's (1990) work investigating procedures in a nursing home in England offers material on what she experienced in the home; it also shows her sensitivity to human predicaments and the fact that she is not afraid to admit discouragement in the field. This enhances her ethos as an ethnographic interpreter, who is her own research instrument: it is relevant to know that she can monitor her own reactions and react appropriately to moral issues. Demonstrating these qualities would not convey ethos if the author had been doing exclusively survey-based work. What shapes ethos also dictates what arguments to seek.

Styles of social-scientific procedure thus specify priorities in choosing objects of study, preferred methods, types of example counted as convincing, or conventions to be followed in reading implications into a work. Styles may be associated with favored metaphors: shorthands for the selection and interpretation of social phenomena to which they attribute priority. Turner and Turner (1990) comment on the pervasive influence on sociology of its Spencerian metaphors: evolutionism, organicism and functionalism, which have to this day not been despatched. Urry (2000: 22ff.) adds to this list the social-scientific metaphors of exchange, structure and vision or gaze; he urges replacing them by 'metaphors of network, flow and travel'. What arguments from metaphor do not explain, what they assume can be taken for granted, may be their most important premises—specifying the sorts of person and process they imagine in the world, which argumentative operations they value and which they prohibit.

Thus Bazerman (1988) traces the generation of social-scientific paradigms such as the APA style, showing that the natural-scientific conventions it imitates are less even-handed than it claims. He analyzes a well-known article from the history of behaviorism, Watson and Rayner's account of a boy conditioned to be afraid of rats (cf. Watson and Rayner, 1920). He shows how the article functions rhetorically to invite readers to choose between people, not just ideas—Watson or Freud? This process rests on readers' involvement in a textual process paralleling a short story, featuring 'narrative simplicity, clarity of argument, and broadness of issue' (Bazerman, 1988: 270). As here, the styles favored by some schools include pretending to have no style, which does not entail lack of rhetorical effect. Since these effects often seem more striking when one objects to them, they are often identified with critical intent—like the 'exoticism' described in Clifford's (1988) account of 'ethnographic surrealism' and its preoccupation with the bizarre in other people's behavior. Rosaldo examines the implications of 'distanced normalizing discourse' in ethnographic accounts, to which a taken-for-granted professional authority is attributed, although it makes members of other cultures appear less than human (Rosaldo, 1987: 95, 106). Adopting these stylistic conventions, Rosaldo (1987: 89) argues, militates against the overall aims of anthropology itself: appreciating the diversity of human possibility.

Rhetorical analysis may also be applied to the rhetorical *use* of texts or ideas. For example, the 'realist' school in international relations produces narratives in which nation-states take the place of persons as main actors. What nation-states 'do' takes up much space in realist accounts; 'their' activities and strategies are envisaged in considerable detail. But Beer and Boynton (1996: 380, 373) show how foreign policy speeches by US senators mix the 'minimalist parsimony' of the realist narrative with elements appealing to a more everyday imagination, embellishing realist 'tropes'—'buffer zones' and 'spheres of influence'—by endowing national agents 'with a thicker subjectivity: history and memory, morality and emotion'. Thus the putative academic prestige of a theory is pressed into political service to support a picture of how foreign 'nations' such as France or England might 'behave'—by analogy with how Americans might expect

individuals in stories to behave to each other, with emotions like jealousy or shame. To the extent that these implications feed off the original theory without argumentative legitimation, a school has been reconstructed in political debate to carry the overtones of an ideology.

Rhetoric and Quantification

The Lockean assumption that plain language is a-rhetorical has encouraged the view that quantified social science is a-rhetorical. This is vehemently denied by John (1992), who draws attention to 'quantification rhetoric' in psychology and elsewhere. Citing a quantity or measurement is often treated as if it had argumentative force in itself. Aspects of a debate amenable to quantification are routinely treated as more significant than aspects which are not. Statistical competence may be taken by some audiences to establish ethos in itself, irrespective of other capacities. But it is important to note that ethos in quantitative social science depends also on showing inventiveness in imagining and exhaustively testing possible explanations. In this process quantitative authors devote efforts to discussing the fallibility of their data and constraints on what can be inferred from it. They often pay more conscious attention to their readers than do qualitative writers, who seem reluctant to highlight why they might be wrong, even though their interests in social construction might in principle be expected to confer lively apprehensions of their own views' limitations. Critical social scientists sometimes maintain, for example, that professional life in late-capitalist societies grew chaotic and unpredictable, lacking the comfortable patterns of earlier times. Giving evidence that destandardization applies to families, but *not* professions, Brueckner and Mayer (2004: 49) claim themselves 'constantly baffled by the contrast between what ... data show ... and how contemporary commentators [have] interpreted the social conditions' – that is, with uncritical faith in their own intutions.

Part of the explanation for this contrast may lie in the structures of the argumentative strategies concerned. Quantitative writers are forced to defend a variety of measurement issues (for instance, whether like is being compared with like). To the extent that these defenses are imperfect, so are the writers' inferences from their data; it is crucial to show that everything possible in the circumstances has been taken into account. 'Ethos' and 'argument' coincide. Since interpretive accounts are more processual, it is less clear what starting points they should most urgently defend. But quantitative social scientists' attention to the point and impact of their work often also extends to using pathos for directly political ends. In some cases, authorial reticence has strong rhetorical effects—implying that computation alone demonstrates the tenability of political claims whose relevance readers will perceive. Clues are used to provoke moral and political responses, as in Breen's (2004) treatment of social mobility, which casts doubts on defenses of contemporary liberal capitalism which are no less compelling for occurring partly off the page. In contrast, Heath's approaches to social mobility (1981) or ethnic discrimination (Heath, 2006) are entirely frank in outlining the concern for fairness which motivates their investigations—and which readers are taken to share. This style, therefore, is far less ethically and politically non-committal than is sometimes claimed.

Rhetoricians like Alan Gross argue that the impact of sociality on the natural sciences themselves make them rhetorical enterprises (Gross, 1997) despite what Campbell (1989) terms attempts at rhetorical 'invisibility'. Gross does not mean that scientists write whatever they like, unconstrained by what exists: that the surface of the moon is someone's personal invention. Rather, natural-scientific claims are reached via human attempts to discover what is happening; and sociality cannot but impinge on the forms and conventions such enquiry adopts. Nelson (1998: 5) stresses that *all* fields of enquiry make cases and persuade. Rhetorical elements 'are so thoroughly engrained in scholarly research as to affect every step of the enterprise—how sources are used, how data are interpreted, how findings are communicated'

(Coughlin, 1984: 1). Precisely how any particular natural-scientific work is affected by its socially situated, suasive and addressed nature (Bitzer, 1968) must be explored in each case. Thus Prelli (1989) dissects an ethological dispute in terms of rival 'scientific virtues', Mertonian versus 'revolutionary' ones. This particular dispute is about gorillas' linguistic capacities; Kennedy's (1998) account of rhetoric extends it even to social animals.

PART 3: MULTIPLE HERMENEUTICS IN SOCIAL SCIENCE: TRANSLATION, ADVOCACY, REFLEXIVITY IN THE SEARCH FOR EXCELLENT ARGUING

Discussion of rhetoric as such highlights interactions between arguer, audience and subject. The social sciences complicate this triad: their *respondents* also have views, positions and (perhaps) even claims to appear in texts. A double, or multiple, hermeneutic arises from the tension between faithfulness to respondents' views and adapting to audiences' capacities to understand them. This issue may be addressed in quantitative traditions too: King et al. (2004) aspire to offering survey respondents arrays of choice rich enough to approximate their own communicative fields. But this is not only a question of meaning. Conveying respondents' positions carries *ethical* injunctions about the integrity of authors' relations with both respondents and readers. Lynch (2000) argues that respondents' ownership of textual accounts of themselves is a human-rights issue. This may not oblige authors to let their respondents' versions of events dominate the textual account, but it does oblige them to give excellent reasons if not. 'Interpretive' aspects of social science thus straddle worlds inhabited by respondents and those of readers, on whom writers are trying to make an impact. This links the rhetorical structure of a text with questions of translation: how does it mediate between its subjects' experiences and its audience's? Some authors evade this question not by increasing the distance between authors and respondents but by abolishing it. Both in co-authorship approaches and in social-scientific advocacy, authors' and respondents' voices overlap to become almost identical.

The idea of translation makes the author responsible for textual means of conveying aspects of respondents' worlds, and bringing readers to understand them. It is impossible to achieve this merely by quoting, since words often change their meanings when taken out of one context and inserted into another. Ethnographic authors are generally trying to convey not primarily other individuals' experiences, but what an entire social world is 'like', which they themselves might have spent years attempting to learn, however incompletely. They confront the alarming task of transforming their own extensive and often inchoate experiences into one relatively brief text. This translation takes place not just between languages but between 'modes of thought'. Its exponents must devise rhetorical operations which will put *readers* in a position to appreciate what people in another culture are doing—even though this may mean stretching their own language into 'unaccustomed forms' (Asad, 1986: 157). For Gadamer (1975), such intercultural hermeneutics have the rhetorical effect of changing readers' reactive repertoires, extending their horizons. One textual strategy with this effect involves presenting details sufficiently familiar to readers to engage their responses, yet which, combined, form an impact leading them to picture hitherto unexamined states of affairs. Hondanagneu-Sotelo's account of immigrant domestic workers in the US combines instances of coldness from employers, or exhaustion induced by demanding children, with a comparison between types of exploited labor: 'While leafy streets and suburban homes are easier on the eye than poorly lit sweatshops, it takes a lot of sweat to produce and maintain carefully groomed lawns, homes and children' (Hondanagneu-Sotelo 2001: 1). Readers may extend their sympathies and their comprehension to aspects of domestic work they have hitherto overlooked.

Interpretive social science cannot be conducted without rhetorical strategies of this kind, but their choice attracts some criticism. Pratt (1986) claims that ethnographers reproduce 'travel writing' conventions from their own social worlds to try to show what they have learned from their experiences—often unsuccessfully, she suggests. Asad (1986) rightly criticises 'self-confirming' elements in ethnographic accounts, which may develop into powerful published concoctions to which respondents are in no position to object. Ethnographic texts may indeed change their readers, but in misleading ways. But according to Geertz (1983: 120, 44), studying other peoples entails just this continuous, disputed dialectic, morally essential to human life: 'Life is translation, and we are all lost in it.'

Textual 'Voice' and Social-Scientific Advocacy

Addressing the rhetorical problems of drawing distinct audiences into interpretive efforts implies, as Richardson (1994: 523) indicates, directing new texts on the same material to each new audience. This accentuates the role of *time* in explicatory processes, depending on audiences' developing reactions. For Richardson it also requires heightening the sense of responsibility of the author, who must preserve his or her own integrity while addressing fresh audiences in appropriate ways. This entails continual adjustments between situations the text addresses, and what (in the author's view) helps readers comprehend them. 'Finding a voice' for an author is discovering how to debate a particular subject matter with a particular audience, maintaining precision, preserving loyalty to both respondents and readers, and dealing with conflicts this may entail. A 'voice' is a communicative style, a selection of starting points, emphases, priorities and tones. Developing an authorial voice in this sense has no 'magical' resonance with one's own personality (King, 1999), though it does denote responding to ethical and political problems. To ignore this, presenting an account as completely independent of its author and as following a linear development which makes its conclusions seem inevitable (as criticized by Gusfield, 1976), presents the voice of the researcher as competent and controlling, far beyond what can reasonably be justified (Richardson, 1990).

Gilligan's *In a Different Voice* (1993) approaches varieties of 'voice' used by *respondents*, disputing Kohlberg's equation of an 'advanced' grasp of ethics with a grasp of abstract rules. Gilligan's interviews with women about moral dilemmas in their lives reveal their higher priority for personal relations and expectations; discussing the morality of this position compels her to use a different voice from Kohlberg's, embracing phenomena he downplays. Gilligan reconstructs the viewpoints of people involved in moral decisions, allowing an attitude of sympathy and respect to govern interpretations of their moral reasoning. In the abstract, 'voices' which convince do so by virtue of qualities suggested by 'ethos': integrity, good argument and commitment to deliberative processes in the cause of justice (King, 1999: 235). Gilligan is concerned with *situated* voices, points of view arising from some shared social situation. In effect she is exploring what the qualities of ethos imply in *this* situation. For her, if we do not appreciate the experience of this social embeddedness, we fail to appreciate both a social phenomenon and the ethical contentions it generates.

Getting audiences to react like this is a rhetorical challenge. Brief textual descriptions rarely achieve 'the integrity Chekov demanded: "to describe a situation so truthfully ... that the reader can no longer evade it"' (King, 1999: 229). Failing this, the demands of pathos, bringing readers closer to positions whose relevance and force derive from experiences they may not share, can entail extensive learning processes, if it can be achieved by textual means at all. Yet this closeness need not entail approval. Hobbs' (1995: vii) anxiety to communicate the voices of the criminals he studies is aimed at inducing understanding of a social

milieu, not endorsing it, as his accounts of safe-blowing and drug-dealing show what Winch (1958) termed 'how to go on' in the contexts concerned. As authors' and audiences' conventions of reading and writing change with time, ethnographers dispute how to do this without unwanted implications. Geertz (1988: vi, 82), whose own rhetorical allegiance is to Kenneth Burke, rejects Malinowski's 'rhetorical tic': 'oscillation' between pilgrimage and cartography. Subsequently, Clifford repudiates Geertz's own alleged appearance of being 'in full control' of the ethnographic process (Pearce and Chen, 1989: 123). Using terms like 'poesis' to stress the createdness of ethnographic accounts, Clifford advises writing texts together with 'indigenous collaborators'. Their voices, not the author's, should address the reader.

Thus for some commentators, authorial conventions in themselves invoke rhetorics of superiority and control, producing both ethical and epistemological distortion in vulnerable cases. Cynthia Cockburn co-authors texts with her respondents, producing a special ethos accentuating commitment to authenticity. Cockburn's investigations touch on women's experience of civil strife and war; here, one can appreciate a reluctance to assume social scientists can communicate more effectively than their respondents. The collaborative style also affords public expression to people otherwise barred from it; and its 'knowledge-out-of-action together' offers rhetorical means to stimulate responses to cataclysmic events (Cockburn and Mulholland, 2000: 137). But such a method places unusual portions of the text's burden of proof on its authors' ethos. It uses more authors, some living permanently in the cultural settings concerned, but, in the very nature of sociality, individuals' experiences cannot encompass the entirety of events. There remains room for social scientists to make arguments about people's social worlds which these worlds' inhabitants would not advance. These should not occlude arguments the inhabitants do make, but surely this also applies the other way round.

Moreover, attention to communicative processes not only vis-à-vis respondents but within research teams generates its own conventions and indeed its own rhetoric—highlighting, for example, strategies relating to care and responsibility (Oakley, 1992; Byrne and Lentin, 2000)—and this rhetoric too demands investigation. Lastly, the collaborative approach does not overcome the need for translation. Author(s)-and-respondents must still evolve rhetorical modes which seem to them effective for reaching audiences they address.

Advocacy in Social Science

Social scientists are pictured as writing *about* settings; social-scientific advocacy combines this with speaking *from* the setting, or replaces it altogether. The point is not to achieve interpretive understanding, or not only this. It stems from realizing that political-policy decisions necessarily derive from values about how to live together (Fischer, 2003: 12). Policy advice should, therefore, include evaluative commitment, which may coincide with the values of some of the actors in a predicament. Thus, in environmental social science, interpretations may be used to endorse the reasonableness of a point of view, using professional knowledge to make people see the world differently (as science itself has always done, Yearley (1991) claims). Adrian Peace (1993: 203) analyses an Irish environmental dispute, taking account of 'the newly rhetorical discourses' embraced by each side but making clear his sympathy for 'ordinary folk' struggling within 'structured circumstances which consistently work to deny them any effective voice at all'. Such a stance is accentuated when social-scientific 'experts' work alongside citizens as advocates, putting their professional capacities at their service (Edelstein, 1998). Fischer (2003: 206) argues that citizen participation in knowledge-generation has potential to heighten democracy, particularly through incorporating local knowledge into debate. Shapiro (1987: 378) generalizes this position from a Foucauldian stance:

social scientists should 'provide ways of speaking (and therefore of thinking) that make it possible to resist power'. For Fuller (2003), rhetoric itself needs to function as advocacy, for its proper sphere is the public world, currently 'under assault'. This sphere needs, literally, to be recreated. Fuller offers the example of the Science Policy Forum which emanated from the American Association for the Rhetoric of Science and Technology, in order to create and sustain public debate on the theme of global warming. Fuller contends that here a public sphere was actually created where none had existed before—a step towards achieving the 'rhetorical reclamation' of science for public debate.

Rhetoric, Reflexive Sociology, and Arguing Well

Far from pursuing the manipulative aims popularly attributed to rhetoricians, the rhetorical writers surveyed in this chapter are committed to arguing *well*. Yet, within the social sciences, rival paradigms generate different sets of expectations about what arguing well implies. Heterogeneity in social-scientific theory and practice occurs on every rhetorical level: recurrent disagreements about admissible forms of argument construction highlight conflicting standards for ethos and pathos. Since the social sciences grapple with problems which have been central to understanding the human condition for three millennia, this should not seem surprising. Indeed it would be alarming were it not the case.

But this diversity can cause social scientists to become locked into schools with little mutual contact—despite the cogency of arguments favoring combining at least some of their positions (cf. Outhwaite, 1987). The rhetorical agreements needed for social-scientific writing are complex and demanding. Working within familiar landscapes of shared standards and procedures saves time and discord. Within methodological liaisons, roughly agreed parameters of style and tone establish accepted voices (though Platt (1996) shows that such accord is seldom unitary). From inside such territories, local rhetorical conventions make those who flout them seem ludicrously misguided, at the same time offering practitioners security in writing for audiences whose reactions they know. Though this spares them constant self-justification, these accepted conventions can become trite and their apparent ethos merely careerist. Colleagues may be tempted to write in ways persuading peers to approve of them; 'admissions' of political alignment often have this effect. Pre-empting criticism of the 'unauthorized' political commitments of one's work is equivalent to being authorized, for some audiences. Miller (1997) rightly insists that rhetorical situations inevitably involve power. As Brown (1987: 89) puts it, 'the superordinate rhetor typically seeks to restrict communication to the denotative content and forbid discussion of the terms of the relationship that she has imposed.' What begins as a methodological convenience ends in methodological bullying.

For solutions to such problems, we can turn to two allegedly general sources of good arguing: first, the 'reflexivity' which attempts to be ingenuous about social scientists' roles in creating their own texts, and then the argumentative ideals generated by the criteria of rhetoric itself. Reflexive social science stipulates that researchers should declare their biases and expose proclivities influencing their own outcomes. But our deepest interpretive biases are hidden from ourselves: the traditions which influence us are 'encompassing but unnoticed', 'transparent' (Bineham, 1995). We argue from what we think self-evident, such as that individuals are distinct from each other, or that they are not; our own rhetorical styles remain 'invisible' to ourselves, as we assume that any ordinary or reasonable person would reach similar conclusions. Under these circumstances, claiming to achieve reflexivity via self-examination can function rhetorically to seduce targeted readerships—for instance, by emphasizing texts' identification with oppressed groups. Even collaborating to interrogate methods as they progress can just result in orienting a text to colleagues rather

than a wider audience. We should be skeptical about claims to assuage bias by 'owning up'. Reflexivity can be sought by dissecting *arguments*, not their makers' souls.

Furthermore, not all an argument's rhetorical implications are consciously intended by its author, so not all can be confessed. A text's implications may be so numerous and extensive that no-one *could* intend them all at once. But Fuller (1997; 2003) interjects here that claiming on rhetorical grounds that particular implications 'could' be ascribed to a text fails to show that anyone else actually *has* read it like that—especially in view of all the extraneous reasons people have for reactions to what they read. What canonical texts are reputed to contain may surprise anyone who takes the trouble to attend to them (Edmondson, 1984; Nelson, 1998: 12f.). Fuller (1997: 290f.) rightly emphasizes 'invisible colleges' in which 'opinion leaders' with academic and financial power determine what view of given texts is taken in a discipline. So if we want to argue about what, instead, they 'really' say, we need to distinguish different types of implication and authorship.

Some interpretations read texts in the light of frameworks selected for the social and political insights they offer (e.g. Eagleton, 2004). Conversely, historical interpretations may try specifically to ascertain an author's intentions, but this (contra Gaonkar, 1997) is not standard in rhetoric. Here, interpretation is directed more to what makes a text *count* as bearing a certain meaning. Rhetorical accounts expect authors, readers and wider semantic and social fields to contribute to meaning-production. Toulmin's *The Uses of Argument* (1958) began to expose the warrants, backings and conditions for refutation implied by arguments' formal and informal logic, irrespective of authors' conscious intentions. But what texts are *in fact* counted as meaning may also be affected by local or temporal reading cultures. Certain commonly agreed meanings were attributed to the Bible before the Reformation, after which groups with new attitudes to texts began to perceive new implications in it. This fact of historical change leads some rhetoricians to attribute textual meaning entirely to encompassing hegemonic constructions. Carolyn Miller (1997: 159) exposes this wholesale abandonment of the author as exaggerated: rhetorical agency is both intended *and* governed by large-scale systems of meaning. People making and interpreting arguments are not as free to reach decisions as if they had no rhetorical contexts at all. But neither are they manipulated like ventriloquists' puppets. For Jasinski (1997: 214), 'Traditions enable and constrain practice but do not dictate or proscribe.' As King (1999) emphasizes (cf. Overingon, 1982), recognizing authors' responsibilities does not entail a view of texts exclusively as intended.

H.W. Johnstone (1959) observed that people repeatedly forget they are arguing a case. We become more sharply conscious of the terrain-bound nature of our own argumentative habits by being brought up against others' conventions: when we are forced to argue in a foreign language or an unfamiliar culture—or when we engage in comparative rhetoric. 'Rhetoric of inquiry examines the reasoning of scholars in research communities,' including 'their devices of inspiration, evidence, speculation, assumption, definition, inference, method, reporting, and criticism' (Nelson, 1998: xiii); these *differ* in different circles. Thus Kennedy's (1998) comparative rhetoric takes a global approach to discerning different means for accomplishing similar rhetorical ends. An intercultural social-scientific rhetoric would, *inter alia*, analyze rhetorical patterns used when people from different cultures interact. How, if at all, do they achieve understanding? Nelson's (1998: 25) injunction would apply specifically to intercultural contexts: 'Field by field, project by project, book by book, article by article, page by page, sentence by sentence: how does argument in fact proceed?'

These paths to rhetorical reflexivity are obstructed by the hostility which remains in Western cultures to conceptualizing thinking and arguing as social, and especially to acknowledging their evaluative dimensions (MacIntyre, 1981; Toulmin, 2001). Even Pearce and Chen (1989) are surprised by the ethical implications of Geertz's and Clifford's ethnographies, feeling the need to 'expose' them. The demands of both professionalization and bureaucratization have supported the image of 'thought' as distinct from sociality and contaminated by feeling. This produces accounts of rhetorical 'persuasion' which treat it, counterfactually, as attributing a consistent psychological motive to discourse. Rhetorical persuasion as a function of language is concerned with making cases, but also has the more general effects of getting communication to take effect and invigorating worldviews. Kennedy (1998) terms this an 'energy'. It is not an add-on *motive*, but part of the process. Rather than, like Ricoeur (1997), contrasting what they see as rhetorical persuasion with imaginative creativity, Perelman and Olbrechts-Tyteca (1969) more perceptively trace the argumentative roles of imagination itself. Such insights became obscured in the twentieth-century relegation of rhetoric to university departments of speech in America, and its near abandonment in Europe. It is the burden of McCloskey's (1997: 104) complaint that the closer a field is to democratic persuasion, the lower its academic prestige.

The sociality of rhetoric underlines the political dimensions of arguing *well*. Petrarch saw Cicero as carrying on Aristotle's tradition more effectively than its originator: by conveying knowledge in a way that makes us want to be good. A strong Ciceronian legacy connects the social sciences with social participation, from social improvement through critical sociology, culminating in the aspiration to emancipatory social-scientific research. King (1997: 299; cf. Jardine, 1998) takes rhetoric's context-dependence to its conclusion. He argues that it is impossible to have good political rhetoric without a genuine polis, which cannot exist under the domination of technicized science and big corporations. 'The dominant voice of our time is a corporate voice, international, unaccountable, and inescapable ...' (King, 1997: 314). For

Billig (1991: 196), if rhetoric is not just to support structures of power, 'at its core must be a moral vision, in which past and present can be criticized in terms of a future.' Billig (1991: 198) refers here to Benjamin's contrast between tradition and conformism: we are not unencumbered selves who make choices free of context, but we are still responsible for our actions in the public sphere.

Treatments of informal reasoning often highlight manipulation and deceit, but the tradition of rhetoric supports *constructive* informal reasoning. Richard Harvey Brown (1987) writes on excluding bad faith, and Gadamer (1975) on revising one's conceptual and evaluative habits so as to understand what another person is saying. Booth (1974: xiv) calls rhetoric 'the art of discovering good reasons, finding what really warrants assent'. Good reasoning has traditionally been interrogated under the term 'wisdom'. Inevitably, 'wisdom' too is contested. Garver (1987) interprets it in terms of the prudential reasoning he attributes to Machiavelli, while others revive Cicero's notions of decorum: the attempt to communicate about a subject matter in appropriate terms. Edmondson and Woerner (forthcoming; cf. Edmondson, 2005) trace multiple origins of Western traditions of wisdom and show how they can be reconstituted partly in terms of rhetorical practices such as those described here. For these approaches to wisdom, rhetoric is connected with the public life of a society, with discerning the common good. This reinforces an 'emancipatory' version of the social sciences, if, as Nelson (1998: 49) writes, 'The social sciences have inherited so many perspectives and questions from rhetoric that we might even describe them collectively as a continuation of the older discipline by other names and means.' As large-scale debates on matters such as the global environment demand systematic forms of combining evaluative with political and technical stances, rhetorical approaches to arguing will become more extensively acknowledged in social science in the future.

ACKNOWLEDGMENTS

The writing of this chapter was supported by research fellowships from the Irish Council for the Humanities and Social Sciences and the Institute for Advanced Studies in the Humanities at Edinburgh University.

REFERENCES AND SELECT BIBLIOGRAPHY

Aristotle (1946) *Rhetorica*, trans. W. Rhys Roberts. Oxford: Oxford University Press.

Asad, Talal (1986) 'The concept of cultural translation in British social anthropology', in James Clifford and George E. Marcus (eds), *Writing Culture: The Poetics and Politics of Ethnography*. Berkeley: University of California Press, pp.141–64.

Atkinson, Paul (1990) *The Ethnographic Imagination: Textual Constructions of Reality*. London: Routledge.

Bauman, Zygmunt (1978) *Hermeneutics and Social Science: Approaches to Understanding*. London: Hutchinson.

Bazerman, Charles (1988) *Shaping Written Knowledge*. Madison: University of Wisconsin Press.

Beer, Francis A. and Boynton, G.R. (1996) 'Realist rhetoric but not realism: A senatorial conversation on Cambodia', in Francis Beer and Robert Hariman (eds), *Post-Realism: The Rhetorical Turn in International Relations*. East Lansing: Michigan State University Press, pp. 369–83.

Billig, Michael (1991) *Ideology and Opinions: Studies in Rhetorical Psychology*. London: Sage.

——— (1996) *Arguing and Thinking: A Rhetorical Approach to Social Psychology*. 2nd edition. Cambridge: Cambridge University Press.

Bineham, J.L. (1995) 'The hermeneutic medium', *Philosophy and Rhetoric*, 28: 1–16.

Bitzer, Lloyd (1968) 'The rhetorical situation', *Philosophy and Rhetoric*, 1: 1–14.

Booth, Wayne (1974) *Modern Dogma and the Rhetoric of Assent*. Chicago: University of Chicago Press.

——— (2004) *The Rhetoric of Rhetoric: The Quest for Effective Communication*. Oxford: Blackwell.

Bostdorff, Denise (2003) 'George W. Bush's post-September 11 rhetoric of covenant renewal: Upholding the faith of the greatest generation', *Quarterly Journal of Speech* 89, 4: 293–319.

Breen, R. (ed.) (2004) *Social Mobility in Europe*. Oxford: Oxford University Press.

Brown, Richard Harvey (1977) *A Poetic for Sociology: Toward a Logic of Discovery for the Human Sciences*. Cambridge: Cambridge University Press.

———— (1987) *Society as Text: Essays on Rhetoric, Reason and Reality*. Chicago: University of Chicago Press.

Brueckner, Hannah and Mayer, K.-U. (2004) 'The de-standardization of the life-course: What it might mean? And if it means anything, whether it actually took place?', in Ross MacMillan (ed.), *The Structure of the Life Course: Standardized? Individualized? Differentiated? Advances in Life Course Research, vol. 9*. Amsterdam: Elsevier, pp. 27–53.

Burke, Kenneth (1945) *A Grammar of Motives*. Berkeley: University of California Press.

Byrne, Anne and Lentin, Ronit (eds) (2000) *(Re)Searching Women*. Dublin: Institute of Public Administration.

Cicero (2001) *Cicero on the Ideal Orator*, trans. James M. May, Jakob Wisse. New York: Oxford University Press.

Campbell, J.A. (1989) 'The invisible rhetorician: Charles Darwin's third party strategy', *Rhetorica*, 7: 55–85.

Clifford, James (1988) *Predicaments of Culture: Twentieth-Century Ethnography, Literature, Art*. Cambridge, MA: Harvard University Press.

Cockburn, Cynthia and Mulholland, Marie (2000) 'Analytical action, committed research: What does a feminist action research partnership mean in practice?', in Anne Byrne and Ronit Lentin (eds), *(Re)searching Women*. Dublin: Institute of Public Administration, pp. 119–39.

Coughlin, Ellen K. (1984) 'Finding the Message in the Medium: The Rhetoric of Scholarly Research', *Chronicle of Higher Education*, April 11, p. 18.

Dixon, Thomas (2003) *From Passions to Emotions: The Creation of a Secular Psychological Category*. Cambridge: Cambridge University Press.

Eagleton, Terry (2004) *The English Novel: An Introduction*. Oxford: Blackwell.

Edelstein, M.R. (1998) *Contaminated Communities*. Boulder, CO: Westview Press.

Edmondson, Ricca (1984) *Rhetoric in Sociology*. London: Macmillan.

———— (2005) 'Wisdom in Later Life: Ethnographic Approaches', *Ageing in Society*, 25: 339–56.

Edmondson, Ricca and Woerner, Markus H. (forthcoming) *Crises of Wisdom*.

Fairhurst, Eileen (1990) 'Doing ethnography in a geriatric unit', in Sheila Peace (ed.), *Researching Social Gerontology: Concepts, Methods and Issues*. London: Sage, pp.101–14.

Feyerabend, Paul (1975) *Against Method*. London: New Left Books.

Fischer, Frank (2003) *Reframing Public Policy: Discursive Politics and Deliberative Practices*. Oxford: Oxford University Press.

Flyvbjerg, Bent (1998) *Rationality and Power*. Chicago: University of Chicago Press.

Freeden, Michael (2003) *Ideology: A Very Short Introduction*. Oxford: Oxford University Press.

Fuller, Steve (1997) '"Rhetoric of Science": Double the Trouble!', in Alan Gross and William Keith (eds), *Rhetorical Hermeneutics: Invention and Interpretation in the Age of Science*. Albany: State University of New York Press, pp. 279–98.

———— (2003) 'The globalization of rhetoric and its discontents', *Poroi*, 2 (2) (November).

Gadamer, Hans-Georg (1975) *Truth and Method*. New York: Seabury Press.

———— (1997) 'Rhetoric, hermeneutics, ideology-critique', in Walter Jost and Michael J. Hyde (eds), *Rhetoric and Hermeneutics in our Time: A Reader*. New Haven: Yale University Press, pp. 313–34.

Gaonkar, Dilip (1997) 'The idea of rhetoric in the rhetoric of science', in Alan Gross and William Keith (eds), *Rhetorical Hermeneutics: Invention and Interpretation in the Age of Science*. Albany: State University of New York Press, pp. 25–85.

Garver, Eugene (1987) *Machiavelli and the History of Prudence*. Madison: University of Wisconsin Press.

———— (1995) *Aristotle's Rhetoric: An Art of Character*. Chicago: University of Chicago Press.

Geertz, Clifford (1983) *Local Knowledge: Further Essays in Interpretive Anthropology*. New York: Basic Books.

———— (1988) *Works and Lives: The Anthropologist as Author*. Stanford, CA: Stanford University Press.

Gilligan, Carol ([1982] 1993) *In a Different Voice: Psychological Theory and Women's Development*. Cambridge, MA: Harvard University Press.

Goffman, Erving (1959) *The Presentation of Self in Everyday Life*. Harmondsworth: Penguin.

Gorges, Irmela (1997) 'Technology and context: The impact of collective action on the development of knowledge', in Ricca Edmondson (ed.), *The Political Context of Collective Action: Power, Argumentation and Democracy*. London: Routledge, pp. 47–63.

Gross, Alan (1989) 'The rhetorical invention of scientific invention: The emergence and transformation of a social norm', in Herbert Simons (ed.), *Rhetoric in the Human Sciences*. London: Sage, pp. 89–107.

Gross, Alan (1997) 'What if we're not producing knowledge? Critical reflections on the rhetorical criticisms of science,' in Alan Gross and William Keith (eds) *Rhetorical Hermeneutics: Invention and Interpretation in the Age of Science*. Albany: State University of New York Press, pp. 138–55.

Gusfield, J. (1976) 'The literary rhetoric of science: Comedy and pathos in drinking driving rhetoric', *American Sociological Review*, 41: 16–34.

Hammersley, Martin and Atkinson, Paul (1994) *Ethnography: Principles in Practice*. London: Routledge.

Heath, Anthony (1981) *Social Mobility*. London: Fontana.

———— (2006) 'Conclusions', in Anthony Heath and S.Y. Cheung (eds), *Unequal Chances: Ethnic Minorities in Western Labour Markets*. Oxford: Oxford University Press for the British Academy.

Hobbs, Dick (1988) *Doing the Business: Entrepreneurship, Detectives and the Working Class in the East End of London*. Oxford: Clarendon Press.

———— (1995) *Bad Business: Professional Crime in Modern Britain*. Oxford: Clarendon Press.

Hondanagneu-Sotelo, Perrette (2001) *Doméstica: Immigrant Workers Cleaning and Caring in the Shadows of Affluence*. Berkeley: University of California Press.

Hoover, Kenneth (1984) *The Elements of Social-Scientific Thinking*. New York: St. Martin's Press.

Jardine, Murray (1998) *Speech and Political Practice: Recovering the Place of Human Responsibility*. Albany: State University of New York Press.

Jasinski, James (1997) 'Instrumentalism, Contextualism, and Interpretation in Rhetorical Criticism', in Alan Gross and William Keith (eds), *Rhetorical Hermeneutics: Invention and Interpretation in the Age of Science*. Albany: State University of New York Press, pp. 195–224.

John, I.D. (1992) 'Statistics as rhetoric in psychology', *Australian Psychologist*, 27: 144–9.

Johnstone, H.W. Jr. (1959) *Philosophy and Argument*. University Park, PA: Pennsylvania State University Press.

Kennedy, George A. (1998) *Comparative Rhetoric: An Historical and Cross-Cultural Introduction*. New York and Oxford: Oxford University Press.

King, Andrew (1997) 'The rhetorical critic and the invisible polis', in Alan Gross and William Keith (eds), *Rhetorical Hermeneutics: Invention and Interpretation in the Age of Science*. Albany: State University of New York Press, pp. 299–314.

King, G., Murray C.J.L., Salomon J.A. and Tandon, A. (2004) 'Enhancing the validity and cross-cultural comparability of measurement in survey research', *American Political Science Review*, 98: 191–207.

King, Robert L. (1999) 'Voice and the inevitability of ethos', in Christine Mason and Rebecca Sutcliffe (eds), *The Changing Tradition: Women in the History of Rhetoric*. Calgary: University of Calgary Press, pp. 225–36.

Lanham, Richard (1968) *A Handlist of Rhetorical Terms*. Berkeley: University of California Press.

Leff, Michael (1978) 'In search of Ariadne's thread: A review of the recent literature on rhetorical theory', *Central States Speech Journal*, 29: 73–91.

Locke, John (1690/1979) *An Essay Concerning Human Understanding*. Oxford: Clarendon Press.

Lynch, Kathleen (2000) 'The role of emancipatory research in the academy', in Anne Byrne and Ronit Lentin (eds), *(Re)searching Women*. Dublin: Institute of Public Administration, pp. 73–104.

McCloskey, D. (1986) *The Rhetoric of Economics*. Madison: University of Wisconsin Press.

———— (1997) 'Big rhetoric, little rhetoric: Gaonkar on the rhetoric of science', in Alan Gross and William Keith (eds), *Rhetorical Hermeneutics: Invention and Interpretation in the Age of Science*. Albany: State University of New York Press, pp. 101–112.

MacIntyre, Alasdair (1981) *After Virtue: A Study in Moral Theory*. London: Duckworth.

Miller, Carolyn (1997) 'Classical rhetoric without nostalgia: A response to Gaonkar', in Alan Gross and William Keith (eds), *Rhetorical Hermeneutics: Invention and Interpretation in the Age of Science*. Albany: State University of New York Press, pp. 156–71.

Nelson, John S. (1998) *Tropes of Politics: Science, Theory, Rhetoric, Action*. Madison: University of Wisconsin Press.

Oakley, Ann (1992) *Social Support and Motherhood*. Oxford: Blackwell.

Outhwaite, William (1987) *New Philosophies of Social Science: Realism, Hermeneutics and Critical Theory*. New York: St. Martin's Press.

Overington, Michael (1982) 'Responsibility and sociological discourse', *Qualitative Sociology*, 5 (2): 106–20.

Peace, Adrian (1993) 'Environmental protest, bureaucratic closure: The politics of discourse in rural Ireland', in Kay Milton (ed.), *Environmentalism: The View from Anthropology*. London: Routledge, pp. 189–204.

Pearce, W. Barnett and Chen, Victoria (1989) 'Ethnography as sermonic: The rhetorics of Clifford Geertz and James Clifford', in Herbert W. Simons (ed.), *Rhetoric in the Human Sciences*, London: Sage, pp. 119–31.

Perelman, Chaim and Olbrechts-Tyteca, L. (1969) *The New Rhetoric: A Treatise on Argumentation*. Notre Dame, IN: University of Notre Dame Press.

Platt, Jennifer (1996) *A History of Sociological Research Methods in America 1920–1960*. Cambridge: Cambridge University Press.

Potter, Jonathan (1996) *Representing Reality: Discourse, Rhetoric and Social Construction*. London: Sage.

Pratt, Mary Louise (1986) 'Fieldwork in common places', in James Clifford and George Marcus (eds), *Writing Culture: The Poetics and Politics of Ethnography*. Berkeley: University of California Press, pp. 27–50.

Prelli, Lawrence (1989) 'The rhetorical construction of scientific ethos', in Herbert W. Simons (ed.), *Rhetoric in the Human Sciences*. London: Sage, pp. 48–68.

Rehg, William (1997) 'Reason and rhetoric in Habermas's theory of argumentation', in Walter Jost and Michael J. Hyde (eds), *Rhetoric and Hermeneutics in our Time: A Reader*. New Haven: Yale University Press, pp. 358–77.

Richardson, Laurel (1990) 'Narrative and sociology', *Journal of Contemporary Ethnography*, 19: 116–35.

——— (1994) 'Writing as a method of inquiry', in Norman Denzin and Yvanna Lincoln (eds), *Handbook of Qualitative Research*. London: Sage, pp. 516–29.

Ricoeur, Paul (1997) 'Rhetoric – poetics – hermeneutics', in Walter Jost and Michael Hyde (eds), *Rhetoric and Hermeneutics in our Time: A Reader*. New Haven: Yale University Press, pp. 60–72.

Rosaldo, Renato (1987) 'Where objectivity lies: The rhetoric of anthropology', in John Nelson, Allan Megill, and Donald McCluskey (eds), *The Rhetoric of the Human Sciences: Language and Argument in Scholarship and Public Affairs*. Madison: University of Wisconsin Press, pp. 87–110.

Ryan, Eugene (1984) *Aristotle's Theory of Rhetorical Argumentation*. Montreal: Éditions Bellarmin.

Simons, Herbert (ed.) (1990) *The Rhetorical Turn*. Chicago: University of Chicago Press.

Shapiro, Michael J. (1987) 'The rhetoric of social science: The political responsibilities of the scholar', in John Nelson, Allan Megill, and Donald McCloskey (eds), *The Rhetoric of the Human Sciences: Language and Argument in Scholarship and Public Affairs*. Madison: University of Wisconsin Press, pp. 363–80.

Sloane, Thomas (2001) *Oxford Encyclopaedia of Rhetoric*. Oxford: Oxford University Press.

Toulmin, Stephen (1958) *The Uses of Argument*. Cambridge: University of Cambridge Press.

——— (2001) *Return to Reason*. Cambridge, MA: Harvard University Press.

Turner, Stephen Park and Turner, Jonathan (1990) *The Impossible Science: An Institutional Analysis of American Sociology*. Newbury Park, CA: Sage.

Urry, John (2000) *Sociology beyond Societies: Mobilities for the Twenty-First Century*. London: Routledge.

Van Maanen, J. (1988) *Tales of the Field: On Writing Ethnography*. Chicago: University of Chicago Press.

Vickers, Brian (1988) *In Defence of Rhetoric*. Oxford: Clarendon Press.

Watson, John B. and Rayner, Rosalie (1920) 'Conditioned Emotional Reactions', *Journal of Experimental Psychology*, 3 (1): 1–14.

Willard, Charles (1997) 'Rhetoric's lot', in Alan Gross and William Keith (eds), *Rhetorical Hermeneutics: Invention and Interpretation in the Age of Science*. Albany: State University of New York Press, pp. 172–91.

Winch, Peter (1958) *The Idea of a Social Science and Its Relation to Philosophy*. London: Routledge and Kegan Paul.

Woerner, Markus H. (1990) *Das Ethische in der Rhetorik des Aristoteles*. Freiburg: Alber.

Woodward, K. (2003) 'Against wisdom: the social politics of anger and aging', *Journal of Aging Studies*, 17 (1): 55–67.

Yearley, Steven (1991) *The Green Case: A Sociology of Environmental Issues, Arguments and Politics*. London: Harper Collins.

27

Discourse Analysis

Michael Lynch

The word 'discourse' is notoriously ambiguous, but a few things can be said about it that hold broadly if not universally. One is that discourse includes both spoken and written language, as well as various other communicative media. Another is that it refers to larger organizational units than the sentence: narratives, stories, and conversational exchanges. A third is that discourse is a matter of language-*use*: communicative action produced in 'naturally occurring' (non-experimental, observed or recorded in homes, offices, and public places) situations of social interaction.

Discourse analysis (DA) is a name for various social-scientific and literary methods associated with linguistic pragmatics, sociolinguistics, anthropology of language, semiotics, communication studies, literary deconstruction, critical theory, cultural studies, cognitive science, philosophy of language/linguistic philosophy, studies of social interaction, human-computer interaction, and many other fields and approaches. DA is not a single method, or even a continuous research field, and while it is possible to list and compare various approaches, many of them have very little to do with one another. DA covers a broad range of communicative phenomena, and different approaches are integrated with distinct lines of social theory and philosophy.

This chapter will not attempt to provide a comprehensive review of discourse analytic methods. Instead, it will focus on what, in my view, is most distinctive of (some) DA approaches to language use and social interaction, mind and cognition, and scientific practice. In a nutshell, these approaches identify structures of action with the contingencies of *inter*-action: the interrelated sensibilities of utterances in conversation; the involvements of 'mind' in the world; and the intertwining of things and signs in scientific practice. Given the ambiguity of the word 'discourse' and the arbitrariness of what to include under 'discourse analysis', a brief word may be in order about what I am not including.

Michel Foucault's (1972) *Archeology of Knowledge* arguably provides an 'analysis' of 'discourse', but one that is couched at a level of abstraction well beyond the approaches to natural language use and textual organization that I shall discuss. *The Archeology of Knowledge* is among Foucault's most abstruse writings, and he later abandoned the conceptions of discourse and discursive formation he developed in that book. What *is* clear (though less from *Archeology* than from some of his other writings) is that he endeavored to break with the history of ideas in order to encompass historical formations that integrated architectures, bodies and souls, technologies of power and self, and the administrative (human) sciences. Nevertheless, Foucault's grand 'statements' and 'formations', like Lyotard's 'master narratives', have at best a tenuous hold upon the specific instances of writing, conversing, speaking and acting that preoccupy the discourse analysts discussed in this chapter. Foucault does analyze specific texts, and delves into textual structures (most famously the author function), but he does so from such a 'high', distant and comprehensive vantage point that any effort to muck around in textual or conversational detail is likely to seem banal and insignificant. Foucault's 'statement' is not the sort of statement that a logician would compose or unpack, nor is it a linguist's analytical object or a conversation analyst's utterance. Though careful not to confuse discourse with ideology, Foucault allows it to fill the space vacated by ideology. It is not a perfect fit. Discourse spills over that space, and spills into others, and no longer becomes analytically distinct from built environments and the bodies that inhabit them.

Jürgen Habermas (1984; 1987), Foucault's philosophical rival and occasional interlocutor, also developed a (since abandoned) theoretical conception of discourse, or something like discourse—the 'ideal speech situation'. Habermas imagines this ideal to be something like a perpetual seminar in which all parties enter as equals and resolve their conflicts by participating in a conversation of reasons rather than by resorting to power plays and deceptions. It is possible to use the *ideal* speech situation as a foil for the *actual* speech situations discussed in empirical discourse analysis (see Bogen, 1999), but I see no compelling need to do that here.

For reasons having to do with my own interests and background as well as the practical limits of what can be contained in this chapter, I shall focus on studies of situated language use. Such studies have affinity with a philosophy of ordinary language that had

major influence on Anglo-American philosophy in the post-World War II period, prior to the ascendancy of the cognitivist and scientistic tendency that currently dominates analytical philosophy (Hacker, 1996). Many discourse analytical studies also draw eclectically from Continental philosophy (existential phenomenology and poststructuralist literary theory and deconstruction), and American Pragmatism.

LANGUAGE-USE IN SOCIAL INTERACTION

A conception of language-*use* that is key to any decent understanding of DA methodology derives from Wittgenstein's ([1953] 2001) later philosophy of language and the post-World War II ordinary language philosophy of J.L. Austin, Gilbert Ryle, Peter Winch and other, mostly English, philosophers. John Searle's (1969) speech act theory traces itself back to Austin's (1962) conception of performative utterances—words and phrases that, when uttered in the appropriate circumstances, perform actions such as christening ships and sentencing criminals—but Searle's theory tends to reinstate the very logical and linguistic formalism that the notion of language-use threatens (Derrida, 1977; Turner, 1970; Schegloff, 1992), and it has thus had limited value for the empirical and literary approaches to situated language use, social interaction and textual organization that flourished in sociology, social anthropology and other social science and literary fields in the past few decades.

One of the signal features of language-use that is emphasized in these approaches is what is sometimes called *reflexivity*. This contrasts to more familiar conceptions of reference—the capacity of signs to refer to some stable idea or independent thing—and it has little to do with Enlightenment notions of self-reflection. The reflexivity of natural language use does not mean that language is self-referential, but that its sense is tied to and reacts back upon the immediate circumstances of use. An implication of this idea is that the meaning and grammatical organization of words, gestures, utterances and stories is not inherent in the formal features of the linguistic 'objects' taken in isolation, but is a property of their production and reception as actions in context. Reflexivity in this sense subsumes the idea that meaning is 'intentional'—that words and utterances are directed toward referents, and oriented to audiences or recipients—but it is not limited to intentional actions, and it does not imply that meaning is a mental content somehow attached to forms of discourse. 'Unintentional' actions are no less meaningful, and their sense is no less reflexive to the context of their production. Classical semiotics handles situated language-use by first specifying a 'code' or 'grammar'—stable, context-free rules and components of language—and then describing how the code becomes appropriated and nuanced in the situated flow of speech. While the Saussurian distinction between *langue* and *parole* may facilitate analytical clarity, it tends to restrict the radical creativity of situated language-use, first by specifying stable analytical features in a separate space, and then by bringing them to bear on occasions of use. A more radical conception of reflexive language use suspends commitment to *any* pre-set code, and insists that the analytical elements of language are themselves locally produced in and through situated actions and interactions. In other words, the analysis of discourse is itself internal to the social production of discourse.[1]

Methodological Requirements

The fact that discourse analysis is a reflexive property of discourse production has profound methodological implications. One implication is that characterizations of discursive form are inseparable from characterizations of function and meaning. Another is that such characterizations are contingent, fallible and occasionally contested in 'actual' situations of conduct. And still another is that the methodology of discourse analysis is continuous with the very phenomena it seeks to analyze. The methodology of discourse

analysis is thus deeply ethnographic. One does not first outline the objective linguistic or behavioral elements and then examine how they are organized into larger pragmatic wholes. It is necessary to grasp the relevant context in which elements, no less than holistic actions, are situated.

A simple example is provided by Gilbert Ryle's contrast between a 'wink' and a 'blink', which he uses to exemplify his notion of 'thick description'. The contrast casts into relief the difference between a minor gesture that performs a communicative action and one that is, at least sometimes, simply an involuntary reaction.

> Two boys fairly swiftly contract the eyelids of their right eyes. In the first boy this is only an involuntary twitch; but the other is winking conspiratorially to an accomplice. At the lowest or the thinnest level of description the two contractions of the eyelids may be exactly alike. From a cinematograph-film of the two faces there might be no telling which contraction, if either, was a wink, or which, if either, were a mere twitch. Yet there remains the immense but unphotographable difference between a twitch and a wink. For to wink is to try to signal to someone in particular, without the cognisance of others, a definite message according to an already understood code. It has very complex success-*versus*-failure conditions. The wink is a failure if its intended recipient does not see it; or sees it but does not know or forgets the code; or misconstrues it; or disobeys or disbelieves it; or if any one else spots it. A mere twitch, on the other hand, is neither a failure nor a success; it has no intended recipient; it is not meant to be unwitnessed by anybody; it carries no message. It may be a symptom but it is not a signal. The winker could not *not* know that he was winking; but the victim of the twitch might be quite unaware of his twitch. The winker can tell what he was trying to do; the twitcher will deny that he was trying to do anything (Ryle, 1971).

One might object that Ryle privileges intentional communicative action, and by doing so limits his analysis to signs 'given' while ignoring the communicative import of signs 'given off' (Goffman, 1959: 2ff.). The latter include sometimes highly significant revelations that slip through a person's effort to manage impressions and are 'picked up' by alert others. In some circumstances, a startled blink may 'tell' its unintended recipient much more than a calculated wink. Such subtleties aside, Ryle's distinction helps us to grasp one of the methodological requirements of discourse analysis: that describing discourse requires more than a diligent realism that focuses on particles of speech and bodily motions arrayed in space-time. Ryle uses the term 'thin description' for a cinematic portrayal of an action that, despite its impressive detail, omits all reference to relevant context, whereas 'its thick description is a many-layered sandwich, of which only the bottom slice is catered for by the thinnest description.'

Clifford Geertz (1973) turned Ryle's 'thick description' into a trademarked anthropological method. Though not a method of discourse analysis per se, Geertz's 'thick description' requires a reflexive sensitivity to natural language-use in relevant cultural contexts and an awareness of the transformations brought about when discourse is quoted, cited, paraphrased, characterized, synthesized or otherwise reported upon in anthropological field notes and published reports. There is a difference worth exploring between Ryle's relatively casual examples of 'thick description' and Geertz's more methodical treatment in anthropological field research. Ryle is not recommending a social-science method, but is instead pointing to a difference between the natural accountability of a 'wink' and that of a 'blink'. It requires no special methodological training to see and describe the difference between the one and the other. A mastery of ordinary language is all that is needed, though Ryle leads us to appreciate that such mastery is quite impressive in its own right. There is, of course, a critical edge to what Ryle writes, which is that 'thin description' is the stock and trade of behaviorism, advanced in the name of science and hard-headed realism. He is not recommending 'thick description' as a wispy alternative, but is instead pointing to its necessity for adequately describing actions as well as for understanding what someone is doing. Accordingly, a 'thin description' of the spatio-temporal movements of eyes, face and bodily limbs for someone winking, leering,

ogling, staring intently, gazing longingly or glancing furtively (cf. Coulter and Parsons, 1991) would misleadingly describe the action, and thus be unrealistic.

By turning thick description into a methodology for anthropologists, Geertz systematizes its use and hardens the difference between the interpretative method he favors and the objectivist approaches he rejects. Thick description is no longer a name for an ordinary capacity to see and describe what someone is doing; a capacity that various professional regimes train out of us in the interest of objectivity. Instead, it is an alternative method, designed for descriptive adequacy, if not objectivity. It also requires training, and can be done well or poorly. This takes us to another key distinction, having to do with the word 'analysis'.

Analysis as Topic and Resource

In some DA approaches, the word *analysis* has a dual meaning. In common with other academic uses of the word, 'analysis' refers to a professional endeavor: a scholarly method involving laborious systematic work. Analysis in this sense requires theoretical understanding, skill and practice. Often some recording equipment is necessary (tape recorders, field notebooks, and sometimes fancier equipment), along with artful ways of rendering, encoding, decoding, decomposing, recombining, comparing, contrasting and synthesizing the recorded material. Members of the research communities involved in discourse analysis criticize each other's analyses, attune their sensibilities, and sort out adepts from novices. However, there is another, more distinctive, use of the word 'analysis', which is most closely identified with the field of 'conversation analysis'—a field that, depending upon where one draws the lines, can be viewed as a particular branch of discourse analysis or as a rival approach. As Harvey Sacks and his colleagues Emanuel Schegloff and Gail Jefferson repeatedly made clear in programmatic lectures and writings, the term 'analysis' not only refers to a professional method, it also refers to a constitutive property of concerted actions (Sacks, 1992; Sacks et al., 1974; Schegloff, 1968).

This conception of analysis derives from ethnomethodology (Garfinkel, 1967) and refers to an ordinary, recognizable and describable interactional 'methodology'—a native (constitutive) methodology (ethnomethodology). In this sense, the 'analysis' of a conversation comes with the territory—to respond to a greeting appropriately requires that you 'analyze' the token 'Hello' as a greeting directed to you for which a reply is appropriate. The minimal conversational exchange—A: 'Hello'; B: 'Hello'—is linked via B's displayed recognition of what A is *doing*. Such recognition involves contextual understandings involving unstated backgrounds as well as relevant details of a local situation. Analysis of discursive structures is not only a matter of dredging layers of interpretation from the context of the utterances. The structures of utterances themselves—sequentially, in time—are composed in, of, and as the expression of each speaker's reciprocal analysis of what the other is doing. Together, the co-participants in the exchange reciprocally produce an elementary social thing: a greeting.

Discourse Analysis and Linguistics

It is common to define discourse as a phenomenon of language, and to identify it with units of organization larger than the sentence. However, many approaches to discourse analysis do not simply map on to linguistics. For the most part, discourse analysis is neither a branch of linguistics nor an application of linguistics. It does not describe larger organizational units in terms of elementary phonetic, lexical and syntactic elements. Instead, the analysis extends all the way down to minor, seemingly trivial, utterances and gestures, and places them on a different organizational base: a shifting base of situated communicative actions rather than a stable base made up of linguistic rules and meanings stored in the head of a speaker. For studies of spoken discourse, silences, cut-off

words, inflections, bodily movements and postures, evident practical engagements and relevant ecologies can all be treated as interactionally significant actions and contextual features. Similarly, studies of written discourse treat unstated margins of authorship, implied audiences, political and cultural repertoires, organizational and historical conditions, and expansive semiotic networks as potentially relevant features of literary organization.

For conversation analysts, an *utterance* is not equivalent to a linguist's *sentence*. Emanuel Schegloff (1984: 31) observes, for example, that utterances can act as questions in conversation even when they do not take the syntactic form of questions. Schegloff (1984: 31) also notes the converse: that utterances that *do* take the syntactic form of question do not necessarily *act* as questions. By 'act as questions' he specifically does not mean 'act' in the way defined by speech act theory (Searle, 1969)—a theory that builds pragmatic functions of speech on to a base provided by sentence grammar. Instead, Schegloff treats the pragmatic import of the utterance (how it 'acts') as a property of how it functions as part of a local interactional sequence. Analytically, this requires a grasp, not only of the 'sense' of the words and phrases uttered, but of how the recipient treats that utterance in the relevant context(s) of interaction.

In addition to demonstrating that utterances in discourse are not identical with sentences taken in isolation, conversation analysts point to a deeper issue about how discourse (and its analysis) is not (or, at least, need not be) a simple extension of language as defined by linguistics. As Schegloff points out, 'question' is a vernacular category: a category that competent language users know and deploy. Although he goes on to recommend that such vernacular categories have limited technical value for professional conversation analysis, the very fact that such categories are known and used by masters of a natural language itself identifies an important property of language-use for ethnomethodologically inspired approaches to discourse: the *reflexivity* of natural language use (Garfinkel, 1967).

Examples of how pragmatic linguistic categories depend upon local, interactional and institutional contingencies are abundant in courtroom interrogations. Cross-examiners are enjoined to 'ask questions' and adversary attorneys frequently object when they do not (Heritage and Greatbatch, 1991). For example:

People v. Orenthal James Simpson (April 12, 1995):

Scheck:	Mr. Fung, I noticed that on direct examination, you were not asked whether Detective Fuhrman showed you four red stains on the bottom exterior of the Bronco door on the morning of June 13th.
Mr. Goldberg:	I object to that.
The Court:	Sustained. It's not a question, counsel. It's testifying. The jury is to disregard that last question. Ask a question Mr. Scheck.

Nevertheless, despite the rule, and the fact that it is invoked (and specifically formulated by the judge in this instance), quite often interrogators solicit 'answers' with utterances that are neither formed nor intoned as 'questions'. For example, in the following sequence, the cross-examiner follows the witness's affirmative answer to a question about Paul Ferrara with leading 'questions' that take the overt form of statements on behalf of what the witness knows:

People v. Orenthal James Simpson – ML transcript

Neufeld:	And are you familiar with another member of the committee, Paul Ferrara?
Cotton:	Yes.
Neufeld:	And you know that Paul Ferrara is the director of the Virginia Division of Forensic Sciences.
Cotton:	Yes, and he's also the director of the ASCLAD Lab Accreditation Group.
Neufeld:	And I take it that he is someone whose opinions you respect.
Cotton:	That's correct.

In this sequence there is no objection to the form of the interrogator's utterances. Whether syntactically phrased and intoned

as questions (And, do you know …?) or statements (And you know …) the interrogator's utterances solicit confirmation. It is possible to hear each of Neufeld's utterances in this sequence as elaborations of one continual question, interspersed by Cotton's confirmations, each of which functions to confirm phases of an ongoing line of interrogation. How one analytically 'hears' each utterance is not only a function of its formal features, but of institutional and interactional contingencies that arise in the course of the exchange. In a courtroom situation, 'questions' and 'answers' are normative as well as linguistic categories, and the coding of utterances as questions or answers is situated, and sometimes contested, within the very dialogues that are built up by series of 'questions' and 'answers'.[2]

Syntactic form is relevant but not dispositive for what counts as a 'question' or 'answer'. Interrogators frequently complain that a question has not been answered, even though the witness's utterance may take the form of an answer. For example:

Josiah Sutton case (Houston, 2003) p. 214

Mr. Herbert (Defense Attorney) :	So in spite of all of these precautions, after five years, your lab is still unaccredited; is that right?
Cristy Kim (Prosecution witness) :	Right, we have not been accredited because of the money issue.
Mr. Herbert:	Objection, Judge, nonresponsive.
The Court:	Overruled.

In this instance, the interrogator challenges the witness's answer for being 'nonresponsive'—apparently objecting to the way the witness gives a reason for *why* her lab was not accredited, rather than simply confirming *that* it was not. The judge overrules, allowing the answer to stand, as such. Often, a witness's counsel makes the reciprocal complaint that the witness already answered (sometimes many times over) the question on the floor. Such complaints imply that the witness has been honest and forthright, and that the interrogator is guilty of 'badgering'. Although there is much more to say about such complaints and their implications, such instances from courtrooms serve to show that *categorizing* as well as *producing* utterances as questions or answers is internal to the colloquy and consequential for the activity. 'Question' and 'answer' are not simply formal categories of 'speech act', because they have normative and substantive implications in particular dialogues.[3] Pragmatic form and epistemic content are deeply intertwined; a questioner's analysis of whether or not, and how, a witness is answering implicates *what* the witness says, and whether it is said relevantly and truthfully.

DISCOURSE AND MIND

The difference between discourse and language has ontological as well as methodological implications. The capacity to speak and the grammatical structures of language are often treated as psychological and, increasingly, biological matters. Though language continues to be defined as a communicative medium, and particular languages are recognized to be cultural legacies, long-standing efforts to map structures of language on to structures of the brain have been given a large boost by brain-imaging technologies that enable continuous neurological and metabolic processes in living subjects to be visualized.[4] Depending upon how one conceives of discourse, discourse analysis is not necessarily incompatible with the cognitive (and neurological) turn that has transformed psychology and psycholinguistics (van Dijk, 2006). However, for approaches to discourse that stress the interactional contingency of discursive structures, it simply cannot make sense even to *try* to trace such structures back to stable, internal mechanisms of mind, brain, or mind-brain (Button et al., 1995). When discourse is construed as dialogical, materially expressed, embodied in media (including the human body's verbal and gestural expressions), and interactionally and ecologically situated, it is localized in a public space *between* people. Though such a view of discourse is not currently popular in the sciences and philosophies of language, it offers a challenge that is not easily rebutted (though it is frequently ignored).

The structural phenomena described in conversation analysis and related approaches to discourse—openings and closings of conversations; turns at talk; adjacency pairs (question-and-answer, greeting-return greeting, invitation-acceptance/refusal, etc.); repair sequences; gaps and overlaps; 'rounds' of jokes and stories (Sacks and Schegloff, 1979; Sacks et al., 1974; Schegloff, 1968)—are organized in and through social interaction. Conversations—as well as organizationally specific activities such as courtroom hearings, meetings and debates—can be likened to material structures that are built up through a coordinated labor process involving a division of labor.[5] While the knowledge and capacities of the individuals who take part in the action cannot be ignored, the action unfolds as a material production in a public space. For the most part, the conversation analyst attempts to characterize the organizational structure of the building rather than the psychology of the builders. However, as discussed earlier in the case of 'questions', the material structures through which conversations are composed are structures of action with contingent features and identities. The beginning and end of a conversational *turn* may at times coincide with the beginning and end of a grammatical sentence, but it frequently happens that a speaker must make serial attempts to begin a turn, and, once underway, a turn (like a story) may project past a series of possible endings before another party speaks. Moreover, in a 'collaborative turn sequence' (Lerner, 1991), one speaker may finish a grammatical sentence begun by another.

In addition to insisting that discourse is a social organizational phenomenon that is irreducible to individual psychology, some discourse analysts attempt to respecify mental and cognitive phenomena as discursive constructs (Coulter, 1987; Edwards and Potter, 1992; Shotter and Gergen, 1989; Potter and

Wetherall, 1987). Again, Wittgenstein's later philosophy and the philosophy of ordinary language set the table for such treatments with arguments and examples that disrupt the Cartesian opposition between a private, inner state consisting of mental processes, and a public, objective domain of things as such. Contrary to the currently popular scientific tendency to explain 'mental processes' as though they were subject to the same order of causal principles that operate for physical or biological mechanisms, Wittgenstein, Ryle, and other philosophers of ordinary language elucidated how 'mental' predicates make sense in the contexts of everyday communicative situations. Discourse analysts build upon such insights by initiating systematic investigations, often using 'found examples' of written and spoken discourse which perspicuously exhibit activities such as categorization (Sacks, 1972), perception (Coulter and Parsons, 1991); remembering and forgetting (Coulter, 1985; Lynch and Bogen, 1996; Middleton and Edwards, 1990); following plans and instructions (Garfinkel, 2002; Suchman, 1987); and ad hoc numerical and geometrical reckoning (Lave, 1988).

A direct challenge to psychology was posed by a program of 'discursive psychology' started in the 1990s by a group of social scientists (mainly sociologists) at Loughborough University. A programmatic piece on discursive remembering in *The Psychologist* (Edwards et al., 1992a; 1992b) elicited numerous comments by psychologists, many of whom seemed baffled by the very idea that anything could be learnt about memory by examining overt discourse recorded in non-experimental contexts. Perhaps the most direct demonstration of the difference between a psychological approach to remembering and forgetting and a discursive analytic approach was a re-analysis of an article by psychologist Ulric Neisser on John Dean's testimony during the Watergate hearings. Neisser's treatment was by itself unusual for psychology, as he examined tape recorded discourse produced in a non-experimental setting. However, a fortuitous aspect of the Watergate investigation provided him with a

systematic basis of comparison. John Dean, who had been President Richard Nixon's legal counsel during a key period covered by the 1973 Senate investigation, was a key witness who broke ranks with the administration and testified about a concerted 'cover-up' effort. Neisser raised a question that many others who viewed the televised hearings also asked: how accurate was Dean's memory of the White House meetings he described in such great detail. It turned out that the meetings were themselves tape-recorded, and when, after a long struggle, the White House was ordered to release transcripts of the tapes, Neisser was able to compare Dean's testimony to the transcripts of particular meetings he described. In an insightful analysis, Neisser pointed out that Dean's allegedly photographic memory was inaccurate about many of the details he reported. Nevertheless, Neisser concluded, Dean's recollections were correct for the 'gist' of what transpired in particular meetings, and he accurately reported upon recurrent themes that ran through several meetings.

Edwards and Potter (1992) acknowledge Neisser's insightful analysis, but challenge his judgment that Dean's testimony was true for gist, albeit not correct for many details. They point out that the Senate Watergate hearings were a highly contested affair, and that Nixon's defenders on the committee (especially Senator Gorney, who actively interrogated Dean) were inclined to seize upon points of ambiguity and (possible) inaccuracy in Dean's testimony (Molotch and Boden, 1985). The senators had evidently not been privy to the White House tapes at the time of the hearings, and so they pursued (arguable) discrepancies within Dean's testimony, and between his testimony and that of other witnesses. In such a highly politicized situation, to excuse Dean of particular discrepancies and inaccuracies, and to accept the 'gist' or 'upshot' of his testimony was to treat him as a credible witness: the very issue in dispute. In such a politicized situation, it was unlikely that all parties would agree to a standard of how much discrepancy was excusable. Edwards and Potter were not accusing

Neisser of bias; instead, they suggested that, given the abundant discrepancies between Dean's testimony and the White House Tapes, *any* judgment of Dean's overall accuracy (or honesty) was likely to be disputed. Consequently, an assessment of Dean's recollections was bound up with an assessment of his credibility, and both were subjected to highly charged politicized readings. In other words, this was a concrete instance of what, in a different context, Ian Hacking (1994) has called 'memoro-politics'.

Discursive activities associated with memory—remembering, forgetting, recollecting, recounting, reminiscing, and so on—are not aspects of the same underlying mental process. Though it would be silly to deny the existence of the neurological mechanisms that afford such activities, when persons say they forget, or when they recount an episode, they are not simply giving voice to an underlying mental process. To again use a courtroom example,[6] consider the commonplace situation when a witness says that she *cannot recall* the answer to a question. Government witnesses failed so frequently to recall during the 1987 Iran-Contra hearings that a popular magazine called the phrase 'I do not recall' the 'Contra *mantra*': insinuating, of course, that the witnesses were being evasive.

However, under some circumstances, discursive 'failure to recall' neither implies that the person has *forgotten* the event in question, nor that they are feigning not to recall what they actually do remember. As Jeff Coulter (1985: 132ff.) points out, the vernacular expression 'I don't recall' differs significantly from 'I forget' or 'I forgot'. Avowals of forgetting make retrospective knowledge claims. Saying that one forgot something—for example, 'I forgot that today is our anniversary'—implies the existence of the object-complement (the event, occasion, identity or action in question).[7] *Something* had been forgotten, and one may admit to culpability for having forgotten it. Saying 'I don't recall' or 'I don't remember'—for example, 'I don't recall that we've met'—may or may not imply the prior existence of the event in question. By saying this, a speaker

can express a skeptical stance toward an event that he or she *would have* recalled had it happened. Alternatively, the speaker can let the matter stand as an equivocal possibility, perhaps to be resolved later. Such implications, as well as their strategic interactional uses, do not map neatly on to a mental substrate of memory processes. For one thing, they are interactional—what a speaker does, or gets away with, involves audience judgments about what a person 'like that' may actually remember or not; what they may be motivated to hide; and what possibly could have occurred in the past. What *can* be remembered is *implicated*, but not through direct correspondence (or lack of correspondence) with what is *said*.

Judgments about a variety of other matters are made, invoking the plausibility that a particular category of person would forget a particular object complement. For example, how likely is it that a person presenting himself as heir to a family fortune would be unable to recall the names of his brothers and sisters? Moreover, strong moral imperatives may be involved—a patient may forget an appointment with a doctor (perhaps at the cost of a fee), but a doctor had better not 'forget' the appointment (the doctor's staff is likely to be held responsible for such a 'mental' lapse).

Discursive psychology is a provocative idea, though it is doubtful that it is a matter of doing *psychology* by other means and with different materials. It does not simply redistribute 'cognition', because it opens up a different phenomenal field in which ostensibly psychological phenomena no longer have the coherence that psychology grants them. It is not as though psychologists could solve their problems by taking up the study of naturally occurring discourse. However, it is also not the case that 'memory talk' is a superficial layer of action that has an unknown relation to 'real memory'. Instead, how people talk of memory—or, rather, how they discursively *perform* remembering, forgetting, and so on—is ordered in its own right, and is investigable; it is not a chaos whose orderly basis awaits the results of controlled experiments.

SCIENCE

All literary and social-science methodologies make use of discourse, and all of them in one way or another analyze discourse. Indeed, all *scientific* methodologies make use of, and analyze, discourse. Criticisms of efforts by social scientists to stabilize vernacular language for purposes of developing conceptual schemes, conducting social surveys, and operationalizing ordinary words as variables and concepts, convinced some social scientists to turn away from the ambitions of objective social science and to focus instead on *situated* uses of discourse. C. Wright Mills's (1940) pithy account of the concept of motive provided an early recipe for how to turn a social science concept ('motive') into an investigable phenomenon ('vocabularies of motive' used in recurrent social situations of conduct, judgment, and justification) (see also Burke, 1950; Winch, 1958.) The transformation of resource (social-science concept) into empirical topic (discursive phenomenon) became an option for the minority of social scientists who sought empirical methods alternative to the dominant experimental and survey approaches. Implied in this transformation, though less obviously, was a way to understand what Harold Garfinkel has called 'constructive analysis'—the work of a social science through which vernacular discourse is turned into an instrument for collecting quantifiable data.

Garfinkel's (1967) account of research assistants' coding practices for rendering discursive interview responses into standard categories shifted attention away from the empirical adequacy of the code and toward the ad hoc practices the coders used to resolve ambiguities and make conceptual sense of the data. Social science methodology itself thus became a subject of ethnomethodological research. A general theme Garfinkel used to summarize a diversity of analytical problems for logicians, early artificial intelligence projects, and empirical sociologists was the translation of 'indexical' expressions into 'objective' expressions. Defined narrowly,

indexical expressions are words and statements whose meaning varies with the occasion of use, in contrast to objective expressions, which have stable, context-free meanings (Bar-Hillel, 1954). A classic example of an indexical expression is the utterance 'It's very hot'. What 'it' is, and what temperature counts as 'very hot' is relative to the situation (in some vernacular contexts, 'hot' can even refer to a quality of music, or an argument). The canonical objective statement is: 'Water boils at 100 degrees centigrade.' When indexicality is understood broadly, however, the concept applies to the objective statement as well, since, may it require further specification or correction (for altitude, purity of the water, and so forth), and in different circumstances of use, it can be read as a scientific fact, a phrase to be pronounced in a language lesson, or a philosopher's example (Garfinkel and Sacks, 1970).

Topic and Resource

Starting in the 1970s, sociologists and anthropologists began to explore the possibility that their colleagues in the natural sciences also swam in a sea of discourse, and also faced problems having to do with discursive translation and stabilization of language (Knorr, 1981; Latour and Woolgar, 1979; Lynch, 1985). Social constructionist (or, simply, constructionist) orientations began to proliferate in the sociology of science, as well as in many other fields. At roughly the same time, literary scholars began to analyze the organization of scientific writing (Bazerman, 1981).

One development within the broader constructionist movement explicitly declared itself to be 'discourse analysis' (Mulkay et al., 1983). Michael Mulkay was the leading figure in this group, and his students Steve Woolgar, Malcolm Ashmore, Nigel Gilbert, Steve Yearley and Jonathan Potter went on to develop lines of research which explored and experimented with 'reflexive' discourse in science studies (Ashmore, 1989; Woolgar, 1988), and challenged psychology with discursive psychology (as described above). The best-known, and arguably the best, exemplar of this species of discourse analysis was a book by Gilbert and Mulkay (1984), which was based on interviews and textual analyses focusing on a controversy over a metabolic process known as oxidative phosphorylation, a metabolic pathway of cellular respiration.

Gilbert and Mulkay borrowed some of the polemics and methods of ethnomethodology and conversation analysis, which they integrated with the skeptical orientation to science that had become characteristic of the sociology of scientific knowledge (SSK). In common with earlier sociological and social-historical work in SSK (Collins, 1975), they examined a scientific controversy without assuming that one side or the other had a correct grasp of natural reality. *Unlike* proponents of SSK, however, Gilbert and Mulkay, as well as others who took up similar lines of argument, insisted that skepticism about truth claims should also apply *reflexively* to substantive sociological claims made in analyses of controversy. Skepticism (in the sense of a suspension of belief) was an important methodological device, as it provided leverage for shifting analytical attention away from the truth or falsity of naturalistic claims and toward their grammatical and rhetorical forms (verbal, graphic and pictorial instruments through which scientists attempt to secure, enhance or undermine the credibility of their own and others' statements about nature). Another way to put this is that Gilbert and Mulkay reversed the classic social scientific effort to translate indexical expressions to objective expressions. Apparent objective expressions—'the energy available from oxidation-reduction reactions is used to drive the formation of the terminal covalent anhydride bond in ATP' (Gilbert and Mulkay, 1984: 41)—were shown to be indexical expressions in specific contexts of use—in this case, presented by a scientist as a 'long-held assumption' that recent research has challenged.

Mulkay, his students, and others who took up the DA banner, deployed a polemical distinction between 'topic' and 'resource', which had earlier been used by ethnomethodologists (Garfinkel and Sacks, 1970; Zimmerman and Pollner, 1970), to signal a shift from treating the organization of language-use as a tacit resource for social science research (for example, as a resource for designing questionnaire 'instruments') toward treating it as an explicit topic for analysis. (As noted earlier, this did not suggest that sociologists should become linguists, but that they should examine the contextual *uses* of language in various ordinary and professional settings of conduct.) One might say that DA insisted on a variant of the 'golden rule': that we should (analytically) do unto our own (social-science) discourse what we would do unto others' (natural-science) discourse.

The 'Sociology of Error' as Discourse

Aside from reflexively examining the way social-science writing constitutes its subject matter (a 'literary turn' that soon afterwards became even more prominent in anthropology (Clifford and Marcus, 1986; Marcus and Fischer, 1986)), discourse analysts in the sociology of science innovatively transformed a polemical conception—'the sociology of error'—which had previously been used in arguments supporting the 'Strong Programme' in the sociology of knowledge (Barnes, 1977; Bloor, 1976). 'Sociology of error' refers to a familiar interpretative approach in sociological studies of belief. If a sociologist assumes that a subject's (professed) belief is incorrect (or unverifiable), then social factors will be used to explain it. To use a current example, 'sociology of error' would explain adherence to Darwinian theory by citing the solid evidence for the theory, while explaining adherence to young-earth creationism by citing the closed nature of regional communities, religious indoctrination, economic and political exploitation of naïve constituents, and other social and cultural factors. The methodological move for which the Strong Programme became famous (or, in some circles, infamous) was to insist that social and cultural explanations should be used across the board, regardless of any preconception that the knowledge/belief[8] in question is true or false. Gilbert and Mulkay made a further move, which was to treat 'sociology of error' as an idiom or 'repertoire' that has a constitutive role in scientists' discourse. So, for example, when explaining away a prominent rival's theory of oxidative phosphorylation, a scientist interviewed by Gilbert and Mulkay (1984: 65) asserted that the rival was 'brought up with the chemical theory', and was friends with other prominent scientists associated with that theory. Gilbert and Mulkay identify such ad hoc 'social explanations'—with their mention of socialization, associations, interests, and the like—with the 'contingent repertoire', which they contrast with the 'empiricist repertoire'. The latter draws upon elements of a realist view of nature and a classic ideal type of the scientist as an objective and disinterested figure.

A key point about the contrast between empiricist and contingent repertoires is that both can be found in abundance in scientific writings, in interviews with scientists, and in the informal shoptalk of scientists. Often a single scientist will rapidly shift between an empiricist characterization of her own findings and a 'sociology of error' characterization of her rivals' 'beliefs'.[9] The point is not that particular scientists simultaneously hold two contradictory 'beliefs', 'epistemologies' or 'ideologies' in their heads; instead, it is that the repertoires are used in a way that supports the scientist's conviction about her findings. Of course, the rivals are likely to give the reverse account, again in a way that is consistent with their convictions.

A related ideal–typical schema is used by Latour (1987) to contrast characterizations (made by scientists as well as analysts of science) of 'ready-made science' and 'science-in-action'. The former overlaps with Gilbert and Mulkay's empiricist repertoire, and is promoted in 'official' and formal discourse, but it also includes a whole array of standard versions of scientific methodology, testimonies to the virtues of the scientific community, and so on. Science-in-action is

the science observed by ethnographers and described by scientists in more candid situations. Both ideal types feature prominently in scientific discourse, as they come into play in different contexts of action and publication.

Gradations and Exchanges

In analyses of day-to-day laboratory work and shoptalk, gross contrasts between 'repertoires' have limited value. The talk and action is far too variegated and subtle in its organization to resolve neatly into 'empiricist' and 'contingent' boxes. However, another type of schema proved influential in early work on scientists' discourse. This schema, best exemplified by Latour and Woolgar's (1979) series of 'statements' in which 'modalities' (qualifying words or phrases, situational markers) are added or subtracted to the basic form of an 'X is Y' proposition, presents a gradation rather than a simple Cartesian contrast between polar types. Latour and Woolgar (1979: 147) trace the history of a 'fact', which they equate with the statement, 'TRF is Pyro-Glu-His-Pro-NH2' (TRF is the acronym for a growth hormone, Thyrotropin Releasing Factor, and Pyro-Glu-His-Pro-NH2 is the chemical formula that was derived through a laborious project that Latour and Woolgar described). In a rather peculiar inversion of standard accounts of discovery, Latour and Woolgar treat this 'fact' as the outcome of work that successfully operated on *inscriptions* (rather than chemical substances) by removing 'modalities' ('is' replaces 'might be') and traces of authorship ('we think that') from prior forms of the statement.[10]

In a related treatment of observational accounts, Pinch (1985) identifies a series of linguistic formulations that variously refer to a physical object (neutrino) under investigation, and a graded series of mediating contingencies that lend a greater or lesser degree of 'externality' to that object (also see an early paper by Woolgar (1976) on pulsars). In different contexts of research and communication, investigators may refer to characteristics of 'data' ('splodges' or patterns on a screen), possible instrumental conditions producing those data, or alternative phenomena that can lead to similar traces. To pronounce publicly, and without qualification, that a 'neutrino' was observed, may risk ridicule, and so any account that is given is geared to an assessment of how it will be received in the community. Questions about evidential support are implicit in such formulations.

The most detailed analyses of scientists at work deployed audio and videotapes and made use of conversation-analytic transcription conventions (Garfinkel et al., 1981; Goodwin, 1995; Lynch, 1985; Ochs et al., 1994). The situations described, as well as the descriptions, are quite 'thick' and defy simple schematization. In each study, an attempt is made to examine how moment-to-moment exchanges among interacting parties are coordinate with, and further implicate, unfolding instrumentally mediated displays of the things at hand. Together with studies of the visualization of natural phenomena in laboratory and field science, these ethnomethodological and conversation-analytic studies elucidate how observations unfold over time, through work with instrumental displays that highlight, count, geometrize and mathematize the pictorial and graphic phenomena at hand.

Immutable Mobiles

Laboratory ethnographies initially contrasted formal versions of scientific practices, such as those found in texts, with the actual, situated, moment-to-moment production of science at the laboratory bench or field site. However, it did not take long for questions about the trans-situational stability of scientific discourse to be renewed in the face of the thick descriptions of scientific work. The most influential answer was provided by Latour's (1990) conception of 'immutable mobiles': texts, graphs, maps and other literary inscriptions that fixate situated knowledges and enable their reproduction and dissemination. Latour's immutable mobiles are not representations of 'objects out there',

but are themselves material things that afford manipulation, calculation and persuasion (also see Shapin, 1984). The principal challenge faced by Latour when he theorizes about immutable mobiles is to account for how stability of material and semiotic form secures stability of use and meaning in different places and times, and in relation to different projects. The promise, or hope, held out by the notion of immutable mobiles is that it will account for the global dissemination, coherence and stability of inscriptions without trading upon realist notions of the objectivity of the referent. As a number of critics have pointed out (Knorr-Cetina and Amann, 1990; Johns, 1998; Jordan and Lynch, 1992), the immutability of inscriptions is not guaranteed by any formal or material property of the inscription or the material it is inscribed upon. Indeed, the insights from laboratory studies (including Latour's) are that the things of the laboratory are no less indexical than the things of the marketplace or family dinner conversation: stable forms are undermined, transposed, decontextualized and re-appropriated in local practices, and divested of any alleged 'original' meaning (Latour, 1995). The best account that Latour gives in the face of such possibilities is to show how the fragile materials of science are woven into a continuous fabric of signs and things. There is never a complete gap between discourse and the world; instead, there are overlapping *chains* (with their localized gaps), composed of systematically varied combinations of 'original' specimens, material traces, residues, sketches, labels and other signs. Latour disavows an interest in *discourse* as such, and what he provides is less of an analysis than a collage, in which the things interact in surprising and contingent ways with the persons who attempt to set them in order.

CONCLUSION

As mentioned earlier, the reflexivity of natural language-use is the way discourse emerges from and reacts back upon its immediate occasion of use. In other words, discourse is action, even when frozen in texts (or other immutable mobiles)—it is active, reactive, and inter-active. Discourse analysis itself is discourse, reflexively bound to what it studies. This binding has at least two sides or vantage points. One is that analyzing discourse (academically, professionally) requires 'thick description'—not necessarily a grasp of intended meaning, but a grasp of situated intelligibility (intended meaning does not exhaust intelligibility). The other is that analysis is already 'contained' in the materials studied by (professional) discourse analysts. Such endogenous analysis may or may not be indifferent to the aims of a professional analyst, but the latter analyst cannot be indifferent to it.

'Analysis' is too limited a word to encompass all the possible ways in which discourse makes itself (and is found to be) sensible or intelligible. The main advantage of the word is that it closely identifies a methodological skill with the constitution of *what* it investigates. Especially when discourse is identified with concrete interaction, it is possible to appreciate the fact that sense or intelligibility is not contained within a thought bubble that accompanies the overt action, but that the actions are bound together in chains of contingency and relevancy, struggling towards the achievement of sense—not for the sake of detached contemplation, but as part of getting from one moment to another or completing a day's work. The methodological requirement is one of being there, of living with the achievement of sense. Interventions may be unavoidable, and are not limited to controlling sources of variation or attempting to facilitate desired outcomes.

The 'methodology' of discourse analysis is also its phenomenon, but this does not imply that an analysis of scientific discourse must itself be scientific. It does imply that in order to describe, for example, what some mathematicians are *saying* (or inscribing), one must have a first-hand grasp of what they are *doing* (Garfinkel, 2002: 175; Livingston, 1986). Otherwise,

> it is quite analogous to looking at a mathematical proposition as an ornament. It is of course an absolutely strict and correct conception; and the characteristic and difficult thing about it is that it looks at the object without any preconceived idea (as it were from a Martian point of view), or perhaps more correctly: it upsets the normal preconceived idea (runs athwart it) (Wittgenstein, 1970: sec. 711).

Does this imply that discourse analysis cannot be critical, or that it must eschew imaginative license? Not necessarily, but it does provide a challenge to familiar analytical gambits that project a theoretical scheme of relevancies on actions that otherwise appear to be indifferent (unconscious, falsely-conscious) of them (Schegloff, 1987). If, as is endlessly repeated in programmatic writings about situated action and interaction, the sense and relevancy of any discursive action is locally *contingent*—conditioned by what came before and what comes next; often set in surprising juxtapositions and exploited in an improvised way—then a pre-set scheme or theory is likely to itself become swamped by the surplus of relevancies with which it engages. The methodology of discourse analysis is, therefore, always on the verge of crisis.

REFERENCES

Ashmore, Malcolm (1989) *The Reflexive Thesis: Wrighting the Sociology of Scientific Knowledge.* Chicago: University of Chicago Press.

Austin, J.L. (1962) *How to do Things with Words.* Oxford: Clarendon.

Bar-Hillel, Yehuda (1954) 'Indexical expressions', *Mind*, 63: 359–79.

Barnes, S. Barry (1977) *Interests and the Growth of Knowledge.* London: Routledge and Kegan Paul.

Bazerman, Charles (1981) 'What written knowledge does: Three examples of academic discourse', *Philosophy of the Social Sciences*, 11(3): 361–88.

Beaulieu, A. (2001) 'Voxels in the Brain: Neuroscience, Informatics and Changing Notions of Objectivity', *Social Studies of Science*, 31 (5): 635–80.

Bloor, David (1976) *Knowledge and Social Imagery.* London: Routledge and Kegan Paul.

Bogen, David (1999) *Order without Rules: Critical Theory and the Logic of Conversation.* Albany, NY: SUNY Press.

Burke, Kenneth (1950) *A Rhetoric of Motives.* Berkeley: University of California Press.

Button, Graham, Coulter, Jeff, Lee, J.R.E. and Sharrock, W.W. (1995) *Computers, Minds and Conduct.* Oxford: Polity.

Clifford, James and Marcus, George E. (1986) *Writing Culture: The Poetics and Politics of Ethnography.* Berkeley: University of California Press.

Collins, H.M. (1975) 'The seven sexes: A study in the sociology of a phenomenon, or the replication of experiments in physics', *Sociology*, 9: 205–24.

Coulter, Jeff (1979) *The Social Construction of Mind: Studies in Ethnomethodology and Linguistic Philosophy.* London: Macmillan.

——— (1985) 'Two concepts of the mental', in K.J. Gergen and K.E. Davis (eds.), *The Social Construction of the Person.* New York: Springer-Verlag, pp. 129–44.

——— (1989) *Mind in Action.* Oxford: Polity Press.

Coulter, Jeff and Parsons, E.D. (1991) 'The praxiology of perception: Visual orientations and practical action', *Inquiry*, 33: 251–72.

Derrida, Jacques (1977) 'Limited inc. abc', *Glyph* 2: 162–254.

Drew, Paul (1992) 'Contested evidence in courtroom cross-examination: the case of a trial for rape', in P. Drew and J. Heritage (eds.), *Talk at Work: Interaction in Institutional Settings.* Cambridge: Cambridge University Press, pp. 470–520.

Dumit, Joseph (2004) *Picturing Personhood: Brain Scans and Biomedical Identity.* Princeton, NJ: Princeton University Press.

Edwards, Derek, Middleton, David and Potter, Jonathan (1992a) 'Toward a discursive psychology of remembering', *The Psychologist*, 5: 56–60.

——— (1992b) 'Remembering, reconstruction and rhetoric: A rejoinder', *The Psychologist*, 5: 7–9.

Edwards, Derek and Potter, Jonathan (1992) *Discursive Psychology.* London: Sage.

Foucault, Michel (1972) *The Archeology of Knowledge.* New York: Pantheon.

Garfinkel, Harold (1967) *Studies in Ethnomethodology.* Englewood Cliffs, NJ: Prentice Hall.

——— (2002) *Ethnomethodology's Program: Working out Durkheim's Aphorism.* Lanham, MD: Rowman and Littlefield.

Garfinkel, Harold, Lynch, Michael and Livingston, Eric (1981) 'The work of a discovering science construed with materials from the optically discovered pulsar', *Philosophy of the Social Sciences*, 11: 131–58.

Garfinkel, Harold and Sacks, Harvey (1970) 'On formal structures of practical actions', in J.C. McKinney and E.A. Tiryakian (eds.), *Theoretical Sociology: Perspectives and Development.* New York: Appleton-Century-Crofts, pp. 337–66.

Geertz, C. (1973) 'Thick Description: Toward an Interpretive Theory of Culture', in *The Interpretation of Cultures.* New York: Basic Books, pp. 3–30.

Gilbert, G. Nigel and Mulkay, Michael (1984) *Opening Pandora's Box: An Analysis of Scientists' Discourse.* Cambridge, UK: Cambridge University Press.

Goffman, Erving (1959) *The Presentation of Self in Everyday Life.* Garden City, NY: Doubleday Anchor.

Goodwin, Charles (1987) 'Forgetfulness as an interactive resource', *Social Psychology Quarterly* 50: 115–31.

——— (1995) 'Seeing in depth', *Social Studies of Science* 25 (2): 237–74.

Habermas, Jürgen (1984a) *The Theory of Communicative Action, Volume I. Reason and the Rationalization of Society*, trans. Thomas McCarthy. Boston: Beacon Press.

——— (1987) *The Theory of Communicative Action, Volume II. Lifeworld and System: A Critique of Functionalist Reason*, trans. Thomas McCarthy. Boston: Beacon Press.

Hacker, P.M.S. (1996) *Wittgenstein's Place in Twentieth-Century Analytic Philosophy.* Oxford: Basil Blackwell.

Hacking, Ian (1994) 'Memoro-politics, trauma, and the soul', *History of the Human Sciences*, 7 (2): 29–52.

Heritage, J. and Greatbatch, D. (1991) 'On the institutional character of institutional talk: the case of news interviews', in D. Boden and D.H. Zimmerman (eds.), *Talk and Social Structure: Studies in Ethnomethodology and Conversation Analysis.* Cambridge: Polity Press, pp. 93–137.

Hutchins, Edwin (1995) *Cognition in the Wild.* Cambridge, MA: MIT Press.

Johns, Adrian (1998) *The Nature of the Book: Print and Knowledge in the Making.* Chicago and London: University of Chicago Press.

Jordan, Kathleen and Lynch, Michael (1992) 'The sociology of a genetic engineering technique: Ritual and rationality in the performance of the plasmid prep', in A. Clarke and J. Fujimura (eds.), *The Right Tools For the Job: At Work in Twentieth-Century Life Science.* Princeton, NJ: Princeton University Press, pp. 77–114.

Knorr, Karin (1981) *The Manufacture of Knowledge.* Oxford: Pergamon.

Knorr-Cetina, Karin, and Amann, Klaus (1990) 'Image dissection in natural science inquiry', *Science, Technology & Human Values* 15 (2): 259–83.

Latour, Bruno (1987) *Science in Action.* Cambridge, MA: Harvard University Press.

——— (1995) 'The 'pédofil' of Boa Vista: A photo-philosophical montage', *Common Knowledge*, 4 (1): 144–87.

——— (1990) 'Drawing things together', in M. Lynch and S. Woolgar (eds.), *Representation in Scientific Practice.* Cambridge, MA: MIT Press, pp. 19–68.

Latour, Bruno and Woolgar, Steve (1979) *Laboratory Life: The Social Construction of Scientific Facts.* London: Sage.

Lave, Jean (1988) *Cognition in Practice.* Cambridge, UK: Cambridge University Press.

Lerner, Gene (1991) 'On the syntax of sentences-in-progress', *Language in Society*, 20: 441–58.

Livingston, Eric (1986) *The Ethnomethodological Foundations of Mathematics*. London: Routledge and Kegan Paul.

Lynch, Michael (1985) *Art and Artifact in Laboratory Science*. London: Routledge and Kegan Paul.

——— (1993) *Scientific Practice & Ordinary Action: Ethnomethodology and Social Studies of Science*. New York: Cambridge University Press.

Lynch, Michael and Bogen, David (1996) *The Spectacle of History: Speech, Text and Memory at the Iran-Contra Hearings*. Durham, NC: Duke University Press.

Marcus, George and Fischer, Michael M.J. (1986) *Anthropology as Cultural Critique: An Experimental Moment in the Human Sciences*. Chicago: University of Chicago Press.

Middleton, David and Edwards, Derek (1990) *Collective Remembering*. London: Sage.

Mills, C. Wright (1940) 'Situated actions and vocabularies of motive', *American Sociological Review*, 5: 904–13.

Molotch, Harvey and Boden, Deirdre, (1985) 'Talking social structure: Discourse, domination and the Watergate Hearings', *American Sociological Review*, 50: 273–88.

Mulkay, Michael, Potter, Jonathan and Yearley, Steven (1983) 'Why an analysis of scientific discourse is needed', in K. Knorr-Cetina and M. Mulkay (eds.), *Science Observed: Perspectives on the Social Study of Science*. London: Sage, pp. 171–203.

Neisser, Ulric (1981) 'John Dean's memory: A case study', *Cognition*, 9: 1–22.

Ochs, Elinor, Jacoby, Sally and Gonzales, Patrick (1994) 'Interpretive journeys: how physicists talk and travel through graphic space', *Configurations*, 2 (1): 151–71.

Pinch, Trevor J. (1985) 'Towards an analysis of scientific observation: The externality and evidential significance of observational reports in physics', *Social Studies of Science*, 15: 3–36.

Pollner, Melvin (1974) 'Mundane reasoning', *Philosophy of the Social Sciences*, 4: 35–54.

——— (1975) '"The very coinage of your brain": The anatomy of reality disjunctures', *Philosophy of the Social Sciences*, 5: 411–30.

Potter, J., and Wetherall, M. (1987) *Discourse and Social Psychology: Beyond Attitudes and Behaviour*. London: Sage.

Ryle, Gilbert (1971) 'The thinking of thoughts: What is "Le Penseur" doing?' Chapter 37 of Ryle, *Collected Papers: University Lectures, no. 18* (1968), available at http://lucy.ukc.ac.uk/CSACSIA/Vol14/Papers/ryle_1.html.

Sacks, Harvey (1972) 'An initial investigation of the usability of conversational data for doing sociology',

in D. Sudnow (ed.), *Studies in Social Interaction*. New York: Free Press, pp. 31–74.

——— (1984) 'Notes on methodology', in J.M. Atkinson and J. Heritage (eds.), *Structures of Social Action: Studies in Conversation Analysis*. Cambridge: Cambridge University Press, pp. 2–27.

——— (1992) *Lectures on Conversation*, Vols. 1 and 2. Ed. Gail Jefferson. Oxford: Blackwell.

Sacks, Harvey and Schegloff, Emanuel A. (1979) 'Two preferences in the organization of reference to persons in conversation and their interaction', in G. Psathas (ed.), *Everyday Language: Studies in Ethnomethodology*. New York: Irvington. pp. 15–21.

Sacks, Harvey, Schegloff, Emanuel A. and Jefferson, Gail (1974) 'A simplest systematics for the organization of turn-taking in conversation', *Language*, 50 (4): 696–735.

Schegloff, Emanuel A. (1968) 'Sequencing in conversational openings', *American Anthropologist*, 70: 1075–95.

——— (1984) 'On some questions and ambiguities in conversation', in J.M. Atkinson and J. Heritage (eds.), *Structures of Social Action: Studies in Conversation Analysis*. Cambridge, UK: Cambridge University Press, pp. 28–52.

——— (1987) 'Between micro and macro: Contexts and other connections', in J. Alexander, B. Giesen, R. Münch and N. Smelser (eds.), *The Micro-Macro Link*. Berkeley: University of California Press, pp. 207–234.

——— (1992) 'To Searle on conversation: A note in return', in J.R. Searle, Parret, Herman and Verschueren, Jef (eds.), *(On) Searle on Conversation*. Amsterdam and Philadelphia: John Benjamins, pp. 113–128.

Searle, J.R. (1969) *Speech Acts. An Essay in the Philosophy of Language*. Cambridge: Cambridge University Press.

Shapin, Steven (1984) 'Pump and circumstance: Robert Boyle's literary technology', *Social Studies of Science*, 14: 481–520.

Shotter, John and Gergen, Kenneth J. (eds.) (1989) *Texts of Identity*. London: Sage.

Suchman, Lucy (1987) *Plans and Situated Actions*. Cambridge: Cambridge University Press.

Turner, Roy (1970) 'Words, utterances and activities', in J.D. Douglas (ed.), *Understanding Everyday Life: Toward the Reconstruction of Sociological Knowledge*. Chicago, IL: Aldine Publishing Co., pp. 169–87.

Van Dijk, Teun (ed.) (2006) *Discourse, Interaction and Cognition*, Special Issue of *Discourse Studies*, 8(1).

Winch, Peter (1958) *The Idea of a Social Science and its Relation to Philosophy*. London: Routledge and Kegan Paul.

Wittgenstein, Ludwig (1970) *Zettel*. Trans. G.E.M. Anscombe. Berkeley: University of California Press.

———— ([1953] 2001) *Philosophical Investigations.* Tr. G.E.M. Anscombe. Oxford: Blackwell.

Woolgar, S.W. (1976) 'Writing an intellectual history of scientific development: The use of discovery accounts', *Social Studies of Science*, 6: 395–422.

Woolgar, Steve (ed.) (1988) *Knowledge and Reflexivity: New Frontiers in the Sociology of Knowledge.* London and Beverly Hills: Sage, pp. 14–34.

Zimmerman, Don H. and Pollner, Melvin (1970) 'The everyday world as a phenomenon', in J.D. Douglas (ed.), *Understanding Everyday Life: Toward the Reconstruction of Sociological Knowledge.* Chicago: Aldine Publishing Co., pp. 80–103.

NOTES

1 To avoid misunderstanding, it is important to consider 'analysis internal to discourse' not as a reflective moment requiring contemplation (like a thought bubble in the head of a cartoon character) but as a matter of instantaneous judgment of what to do next, which is visible in and through action (like a skilled outfielder 'judging' the path of a batted ball while moving rapidly to catch it). For a discussion on this point, see Sacks (1984).

2 Attorneys are adept at turning comments into questions, such as in the following excerpt (*People v. Simpson*):

Fung:	This was a minor thing in my mind. I didn't—I didn't—in my mind, I didn't place a lot of significance on it. It was a request she made of me and I performed the phenolphthalein test, and at a later time I said I've done it and that's all I thought about it.
Scheck:	A minor thing.
The Court:	Is that a question?
Scheck:	You thought it was a minor thing?
Fung:	I didn't—I didn't think it was—needed a report written at the time I did it.

3 'Dialogue' is a term of convenience here. Such exchanges can, of course, involve more than two parties.

4 See Beaulieu (2001) and Dumit (2004) for studies of how researchers attribute psychological and psychiatric states and processes to brain images.

5 The theme of 'distributed cognition' (Hutchins, 1995) is close to this conception of coordinated discursive activity, but it remains an open question as to what 'cognition' adds to the older concept of division of labor.

6 The choice of courtroom examples in this chapter is partly a matter of convenience (I have such examples at hand through my own studies of them), and also because they make very good illustrations due to the combination of their formality and familiarity.

7 For a study of a particular way in which 'forgotten' items can be implicated, and relationally organized, in conversation, see Goodwin (1987), and for further implications of not recalling in testimony see Drew (1992) and Lynch and Bogen (1996).

8 Coulter (1989) points out that the Strong Programme runs into conceptual difficulty when attempting to use ordinary concepts of 'knowledge' and 'belief' as equivalent terms. Later, it became commonplace in science studies to pluralize 'knowledges'.

9 A precursor for this treatment of contrasting repertoires of discourse is Pollner's (1974; 1975) analysis of 'mundane reason' and 'reality disjunctures' in courtroom situations.

10 For a more elaborate criticism of this analytic procedure of privileging statements and inscriptions, see Lynch (1993: 90ff.).

Evaluation, Engagement, and Collaborative Research

Introduction

Stephen P. Turner

In the very earliest days of the history of social research, questionnaires were open-ended and asked respondents to explain as well as describe features of their world related to the problems of interest to the researchers. The model soon changed. People were treated as possessing attributes and properties or statuses, such as 'married', as well as attitudes, which were understood on the same model, not as reasoned opinions that were part of a complex web of belief. These attributes were then turned into data points which could be correlated with other data points. Interpreting the results was the business of the expert researchers, not the subjects. There were always variants of this model, such as participant observation, in which the subjects had a larger role, and which allowed their own understandings to peek out from behind the facade of academic prose. Indeed, in its original usage, 'participant observation' meant the observations of a participant in a social-reform activity, partly removed but partly engaged in the activity itself. But even participant observation eventually came under the influence of what Michael Scriven, in his chapter on evaluation research, calls the value-free approach.

Evaluation research can be understood narrowly as a form of applied social science of this kind, one in which 'evaluation' consists entirely of collecting statistics on a relationship, such as the relationship between the inputs and outputs of a particular social intervention or program. Costs can be calculated in relation to effectiveness; programs can be continued or discontinued according to the numbers. But Scriven argues that this narrow conception is misguided by the value-free model itself. Evaluation, he suggests, necessarily involves the element of 'valuation' that the word is made out of. True evaluation research leads, he argues, from sound reasoning to an evaluative conclusion. Program evaluation is one type of evaluation, but no more than that. The big picture of evaluation research is this: it is concerned with making sound research-based judgments of worth. These are themselves value claims.

Methods courses, as he points out, do not teach the values part of evaluation. Yet a proper evaluation, even of a social program, will include legal, moral, ethical, and professional value codes, as well as assessments of needs, which is itself a valuative concept. Characteristically, issues over these kinds of evaluative considerations arise in connection with the side-effects of programs. The sophisticated evaluation researcher knows this, and is able to deal with it. But the evaluation research community is torn between dealing with these questions and hiding behind limited, 'applied social research' methods. The consequences of a narrow view of evaluation are serious: good programs which had significant positive side effects can get cancelled when the main intended effect cannot be measured. As Scriven points out, we as readers do not accept narrow notions of evaluation when we are ourselves evaluating alternative courses of action. We try to determine all the implications and to weigh them against one another. We accept that personal relations matter, and often matter more than 'effectiveness'. This, he suggests, is also the proper model for evaluation research.

This broadened conception of evaluation research points toward an even more radical change in the relations between researchers and subjects. AIDS patients rejected the model of medical research requiring double-blind testing. Poverty and development researchers, together with agricultural development experts, discussed the view that knowing what the 'subjects' knew was necessary to successfully implement or even devise programs. Some of the impetus for this change has come from feminist criticisms of the suppression of authentic women's voices resulting from the blinders imposed by masculine methods and assumptions. This model quickly spread to the representations of other suppressed standpoints. Out of this, a new model of collaborative research has developed, and older methods, such as the focus group, were rethought as means for giving voice to viewpoints that have been ignored.

Susan Hekman's chapter discusses the history of the key feminist ideas on method. In this literature the notion of giving voice to ignored viewpoints has been most fully developed, especially in connection with a critique of standard methods. The background to the feminist critique included the critique of scientific method, which led to such movements as constructivism. The feminist contribution

extended this by asking whether there was an alternative set of starting points for science that was distinctly feminine. There were many answers to, and formulations of, this basic question. Some feminists dismissed the 'scientific method' itself as masculine ideology; others saw the methods as sound, but saw eradicable biases in their use. 'Standpoint epistemology' sought to reclaim the notion of objectivity for feminism by claiming that critique from the standpoint of the experience of the oppressed produced a higher kind of objectivity than the biased kind of standard methods. This conflicted with 'postmodern' equalizations of standpoints.

Quantitative methods have traditionally been regarded as the paradigm path to 'objectivity'. For many feminist thinkers, however, qualitative methods are not only better suited to feminist ways of knowing, they are better means of allowing women's voices to be heard. And this fits with another feature feminists routinely accept: that researchers should be politically relevant and support the cause of women. Much subsequent writing on feminist methodology has been concerned with reconciling and dealing with the implications of these various commitments. What if women in some social groups reject the political actions and feminist voices of the women's movement as failing to represent them? Aren't these voices authentic? Has the commitment to social constructivism about knowledge and the analysis of language gone too far? Is the body, or materiality, a better focus?

Nancy Naples takes up some of these issues in the practical context of actual research. How, she asks, can we implant our insights or standpoints into the research projects? She gives a number of examples in which the complexities and conflicts between basic feminist ideas become apparent and need to be dealt with. One involves essentialism. If one of the main tasks of feminist analysis is the critique of ideological constructions of women, what if these critiques undermine the political strategies—especially of asserting claims about women's victimization—of the women's movement?

What if emancipation politics and solidarity require ideology, or at least simplifying representations? In any case, isn't this what research always does: represent in clearer form what is being studied? And this produces the usual dilemma of conflict between the representer and the represented. Whose voice really counts? As Naples's examples show, these painful dilemmas need to be worked through on a personal level, rather than by a formula.

Naples points to community-based research as one of the main methods of choice for feminist researchers, as it embodies the key preferred elements of representing viewpoints, qualitative techniques, and political activism. Michael Root discusses the issues with this strategy in greater detail, under its many labels, such as 'action research' and 'participatory research'. These projects challenge, and deviate from, the expert-based model in various ways, but power sharing is the most basic one. The researcher and the subjects are not only co-participants, but co-decision-makers. But the extent and nature of collaboration varies considerably. In some cases the collaboration is only in problem definition. In others it may include choosing methods and devising questionnaires, as well as communicating research findings. These arrangements may lead to decisions which raise questions about objectivity and the credibility of results, and thus undermine the effectiveness of the research in producing change. Yet, in some respects, there are values which participation supports, such as collective learning, that no pure 'expert' project could achieve.

Norman Denzin and Katherine E. Ryan discuss these issues in relation to another method, focus groups. They argue that focus groups, while originally conceived as a means of augmenting and correcting for some of the limitations of quantitative research for advertisers, proved to be a flexible and rich technique that social scientists belatedly discovered as a means of acknowledging different voices and as part of community mobilization. The format of the focus group, which encourages participants to articulate their own views on a topic, and to be stimulated and respond to the views of other participants, can, as Denzin and Ryan point out, become more than a method: namely a form of dialogue, which in turn can become the basis of a relation in which the researcher becomes an advocate for the participants.

These various attempts at committed, engaged, and politically effective collaborative research all presume that there is a more or less straight line from the research to the implementation of progressive reform. As John Law points out in the final chapter, matters are seldom so simple. He considers an actual piece of applied research in which he participated. The problem was typical of applied research. A hospital wished to know why its treatment of patients with alcoholic liver disease went so badly. The researchers formulated the problem in a classic way. They proposed working out the typical trajectory of a patient through the system.

As they soon learned, there was no such thing. The reality was not only more complex, it was messy: resistant to the kind of representation that researchers had imagined they could readily construct. Did they fail? In an obvious sense they did. They could not write the kind of helpful report with suggestions that they promised and expected to write. The world itself was messy in ways that would make any neat representation false. The right response, Law suggests, is to give up on the ideal of neat representation in such cases and be messy along with the messiness that the research represents.

28

Evaluation Research

Michael Scriven

DEFINITION OF EVALUATION

The definition of evaluation is still a bone of contention, even amongst evaluators, and is often completely caricatured by other social scientists. The consensus of the dictionaries defines it as the process of determining merit, worth or significance, which means that evaluation research is this process when done with the degree of skill and sophistication that we associate with research in contrast to amateur reflection. There seems to be no good reason to abandon the dictionaries, and thereby confuse students and clients by using the term in a way different from their own. Evaluators tend to think that the term should refer to whatever evaluators do, but that is like saying that the definition of 'research mathematician' should include teaching calculus since many of them do it. It is easier to go with the dictionaries, while allowing that a good deal of what evaluators do is just survey research or performance testing, etc., tasks for which many of them are very well-trained, but which are exactly the same as those done by any appropriately trained social scientist. That is clearly not what makes them evaluators, and therefore should not be in the definition.

What is distinctive about the aim and results of evaluation research is simple enough, and most self-styled evaluators do at least some of it. It is research that leads by sound reasoning from the results of skilled and systematic investigation to an evaluative conclusion—that is, a conclusion which asserts that the thing evaluated (for which we here use the term 'evaluand') has some degree of merit, worth or significance (here-after, m/w/s). Typical examples of evaluative conclusions: 'This approach is clearly a good way to teach Spanish', or 'worth what it cost', or 'a complete waste of public funds', or 'better than the only other one on the market', or (in product evaluation) 'It certainly needs some improvement in the design of the control panel', or 'It's a real break-through in portable computing', etc. That's the name of the professional game: establishing evaluative conclusions with a high degree of validity and objectivity. The evaluator won't settle for 'the students in the experimental group increased their score by 10 percent,' but wants the answer to the next question, usually the really important question: 'Is this the best we can do, with our resources?' or 'Is a 10 percent gain worth what it cost?' That is, as an unknown methodologist once put it, the evaluator will not settle for answering the question 'What is so?' but goes on to answer the question 'So what?'

Of course, the possibility of doing any such thing as establishing evaluative conclusions from scientifically supported premises was denied by proponents of the value-free doctrine. Not only were those arguments fallacious but also, as we will see, irrelevant. Evaluative conclusions can be reached only by using certain specific methods for handling carefully stated value premises, as discussed below. These can often be combined with quantitative empirical premises, or, on some occasions, by using largely or entirely qualitative methods throughout. The recent push for 'mixed-method' approaches shows that some of the sting has gone out of the contrast between the qualitative and quantitative approaches. But not all: in what follows, we will note one issue that shows the fight has metamorphosed but not stopped.

Evaluation research, after a small cloud of dust has settled (see next paragraph), is, then, the effort to deal with that set of evaluation questions which requires the special investigative efforts and techniques for which we reserve the term research. Or, conversely, you might—equally correctly—take it to be that slice of research that is concerned with determining the value of things. In terms of a geographical analogy, let us suppose that evaluation in general—including non-research evaluation—is represented by those Arctic regions that are covered with tundra or ice, circling the globe, and let us say that research is North America. Evaluation research is then the Canadian and Alaskan Arctic. The Nordic and Siberian Arctic is most of the rest of evaluation, which includes the vast areas of judgmental evaluation (formal or informal, by trained or untrained judges, demonstrable or mere opinion), occupied by such tribes as football and volleyball referees; Olympic judges of synchronized swimming, freestyle skating and diving; literary and drama critics; the buyers at livestock auctions, DeBeers diamond allocations and rug galleries; along with the crowds of citizens shopping at markets, malls and used car lots. Of course, one can do *research on evaluation*—for example, on its sociology, its economics or its politics—which we will

represent as the province of British Columbia, in our map analogy, since some of that research is itself evaluative while other parts are purely empirical. And there is also (systematic) *evaluation of research itself*—welcome to the North Slope of Alaska—a chilly climate indeed, where the evaluator can get shown lots of cold shoulders, since more than a dozen countries are now doing it at the national level and driving their allocation of state funds by the results; hence in that area both critical *and favorable* evaluations strike hard at someone's livelihood.

First, however, we need to explain the comment in the opening sentence of the last paragraph about 'dust settling'. That comment refers to the fact that there was a brief period in the recent epoch of resurgence in professional evaluation[1] during which a few writers attempted to give the term 'evaluation research' a special meaning. Unfortunately, the mother of all dictionaries, the *Oxford English Dictionary (OED)*, whose reaction time is measured in generations rather than years, took fifty years to realize that the term 'evaluation' does not just refer to the assessment of the value of real estate for taxation purposes (the definition in its first edition), and when it began to move towards enlightenment on that point—not yet achieved (even in the Oxford American version)—it picked up and listed some echo of this aberrant use. It defines 'evaluation research' to mean 'research on evaluation methods'.[2] I don't know anyone *in the profession* who uses—or ever used—that meaning, but it is mentioned since you might find references to it in older, or out-of-date though new books, including the dear old *OED*'s latest edition (including 1996 supplements).

THE TERRITORY OF EVALUATION RESEARCH

In the second quarter of the twentieth century, the phrase 'educational evaluation' in the title of an academic book commonly meant that it dealt with the testing of students. So these books did not deal with or even mention in passing any aspect of evaluating the teacher, or the course content, or the curriculum, or the administration; but they still felt entitled to call themselves books on educational evaluation. Thus the power elite protects itself from criticism by selective blindness.

Our insight has improved; that would not be acceptable today. But tunnel vision has not vanished: beginning in the third quarter of the twentieth century and too often since, when the more general term 'evaluation' is used in book titles, suggesting that the book covered the field, it now only refers to program evaluation. Hopefully, this kind of narrow-mindedness is beginning to look as absurd as history books that treat history as the story of men's achievements. Major long-lived self-styled divisions of evaluation, to many of which professional researchers have devoted their entire working lives, include, besides program evaluation, personnel evaluation, product evaluation, policy analysis, proposal evaluation, portfolio evaluation (in the stock market as well as in the hiring of commercial artists and faculty review), performance evaluation (here student testing/ scoring—like Olympic trial design and equivalencing for altitude differences in the test sites—are just two of a score of sub-divisions). And there are also huge stand-alone fields of evaluation that we do not normally realize are parts of the discipline because they are not so labeled: for example, medical diagnosis of the kind provided in the context of annual physicals (not differential diagnosis itself, which is taxonomy) since these are evaluations of the patient's health; or the jurisprudence of the appellate courts, which is entirely devoted to the evaluation of the reasoning of lower courts; or the large slice of critical thinking that is argument evaluation. In many of these areas, indeed, there are a number of sub-divisions that have occupied good researchers' entire careers— for example, within personnel evaluation, this is true of the evaluation of schoolteachers, or of high-level administrators of large organizations. So program evaluation is a small slice of the field, with no claim to generality. The field is immense, and every

branch of it has its own research needs, often enough in dire need of further work. The influence of the value-free doctrine led us to overlook this ubiquitous discipline that slept beneath us, and has recently begun to awake as a whole instead of in spots here and there.

As it does so, we begin to identify some of the sub-areas that are in particular need of serious further evaluation researchers, ranging from proposal evaluation, on which much of our professional life depends,[3] to portfolio evaluation outside the stock market context (where it has been massively analyzed because of the payoffs from doing it well),[4] and perhaps especially the evaluation of professional judges outside the courts, a.k.a. judgmental evaluators. Curiously enough, this was the area where one might argue that the first scientific work in evaluation began, astoundingly close to the emergence of the social sciences themselves, which were, not long after, to renounce all evaluation as impossible or inappropriate for scientific study.

It may be that Hughes's classic 1917 paper on 'what goes on in the corn judge's head' best marks the first major effort to use social science methodology to do evaluative research. But there are good arguments for earlier work. For example, Raymond Cattell's 1886 doctoral thesis under Wilhelm Wundt was good work on judgment by experts[5]—for its time, amazingly good work. These early workers have not received the appreciation they deserve in the histories of evaluation. And the scandalous results of virtually every serious later effort at the evaluation of judges' validity, reliability and objectivity—whether in wheat judges, soil judges, probate judges, criminologists or clinical psychologists—have not been major themes in introductory texts, perhaps just because they are examples of evaluation.

As a result, introductory courses are less exciting than they could be; adult citizens, courts, and the nation still waste vast resources on pseudo-experts; and science fails to move forward on fronts where great opportunities for research payoff have emerged. Note, for example, the importance of some of the secondary discoveries in this kind of evaluation research (in this case, it is evaluative research on evaluation)—e.g., the discovery that the success of experts in prediction tasks is not correlated with the extent of their experience (established in Meehl's [1954] meta-analysis and supported yet again by the recent research in which experienced detectives did no better at identifying lying by suspects than did rookies). Nor does success correlate with the judges' confidence level in their conclusions.

These highly evaluative and useful[6] results surfaced or matured during the reign of the value-free doctrine, which may partly explain the extent to which they were down-pedaled. They are widely unknown to graduates and graduate students outside the clinical field, even though the evaluative conclusion is very close to following by deduction, by virtue of the meaning of the words in it and the premises. If the judge is trying to predict something and we find that he, as a matter of fact, rarely gets it right—little if any better than we can do by tossing a coin—then it is pretty well a matter of the definition of 'bad judge' in that context which entitles you to conclude that he is a bad judge. Even the dogma of value-free science cannot overcome such obviously valid inferences. And perhaps that explains why medicine and engineering were able to proceed without blinking an eye of acknowledgment in the direction of the value-free doctrine: common sense demanded that you could legitimately go from the factual premise, 'You have terminal stomach cancer,' to the evaluative conclusion, 'You are seriously ill.' Well, evaluation thrives on such inferences, and can extend them by careful unpacking of the meaning of many evaluands (e.g., 'public health programs informing citizens about smoking and lung cancer'), so that evaluative conclusions often follow, almost by definition,[7] from empirical premises. We will just take a couple of paragraphs to expand this point before coming back to our territorial survey, to increase its legitimacy.

Evaluation research on the quality of evaluators—or for that matter the quality of evaluations—is called meta-evaluation, a term coined in 1969 (i.e., seven years before

'meta-analysis'), and it is one of two new types of evaluation research that have emerged into the floodlights of serious attention as the discipline has matured. To understand the other type we need to take a moment to look at the geography of the whole field. In the last few paragraphs, we have probably appeared more than a little imperialistic in claiming substantial areas of research as part of the general field of evaluation. But the case for this is strong: in all these areas, the conclusions drawn, by MDs, clinical psychologists, corn judges or Supreme Court judges are categorically different from the plain vanilla, factual/empirical, conclusions that one can get from value-free science. They involve a specific vocabulary of values and value-impregnated terms, and, by and large, you just cannot get those conclusions—which are the ones you often need in the practical world—from premises that contain no value claims. That means we have to have some value premises to get them, and that is just what the value-free doctrine forbade, mainly on the grounds that such premises could not be established scientifically. This was often expressed by saying that they were no more than mere expressions of opinion; or, sometimes, that they were not even real statements since they were not testable. Well, let us look at some of them.

- Children of this age need (i.e., should get, from the medical point of view) at least 200 units of vitamin C daily on average, computed every 5 days.
- OSHA safety regulations specifically stipulate that you must (i.e., it is legally obligatory to) have a fire extinguisher within 20' of the furnace control panel.
- Scoring below 500 on the GRE quantitative test makes an applicant at a good college in the US a very bad bet for a graduate major in statistics.
- It is completely irresponsible (i.e., obviously inconsistent with the profession's well-supported code of conduct) to attempt a cataract operation on a patient still using a daily standard dosage of Flomax up to the time of surgery.

These statements all make the kind of value claim that we have to think supportable in order to reach the kind of evaluative conclusion we are looking for, the ones that tell us which action to take out of the life-affecting choice that we face, whether it is about diet, immediate factory equipment upgrades, college admissions or medical procedures. Now, commonsensically speaking, is there any great difficulty in knowing how to establish the truth, or falsity, of any of these? Social scientists fought to avoid using them because they had accepted a bad philosophical analysis of the nature of value claims. They thought the paradigm of these was either (i) matters of taste or preference like 'I prefer white wines to red,' which is simply an expression of personal preference, with no claim to be generalizable to others; or (ii) irresolubly disputatious claims like 'I think the Republicans have a better platform this year.' These are very unlike the kind of value claim that is important to serious evaluation research, as illustrated by the examples above. Many practicing social scientists have long realized that they could perfectly well use such premises, plus the facts they dug up from hard work from surveys, observations and measurements, to generate evaluative conclusions. That is why the arguments that were put forward to support the value-free doctrine were largely irrelevant—they rested on assumptions about value judgments that were mere caricatures. If you use verifiable claims like those above, or the ones used by *Consumer Reports* to reach their conclusions, it is not hard to establish exactly the kind of conclusions we need to establish in order to improve our decision-making—for example, by generating a conclusion like: 'The "Success for All" beginning reading program appears, on the evidence we have obtained, to be the best of those available for use in this elementary school'.

Once that has become clear from examples, two conclusions follow: (1) we can often and quite easily establish evaluative conclusions from factual and evaluative premises established in the traditional way, by observation, testing, and inference; and (2) these premises are often quantitative and also often quite precise. Sometimes they need to be one or both of these things; but often even rough approximations in the premises will be adequate for establishing crucial evaluative conclusions, such as those about drugs or reading programs with substantial main and side-effects.

Back to the survey of territory. So far we have been talking about the named subdivisions of the field of evaluation (program and personnel evaluation, etc.) and a number of fields that are clearly evaluative, although not conventionally listed as such (medical and engineering topics related to health and safety, for example). And I mentioned one newly labeled field: meta-evaluation, the evaluation of evaluators and evaluations. There is another field of evaluation of great importance in understanding the extent of the 'sleeper discipline': we call it 'intradisciplinary evaluation', and it has some overlap with the previously identified subjects.

The professional activity of a social scientist includes a great deal of evaluative work, some of which is sufficiently serious to qualify as research, and all of which is sufficiently important to justify research on it. For example, s/he reviews proposals, reviews manuscripts submitted to journals, reviews theses, and assesses candidates for fellowships or departmental appointments or promotion or tenure. These are examples of evaluation within the purview of the discipline and are essential parts of the processes that keep the discipline operating at a high level; most of them fall under one or another of the sub-divisions of evaluation already listed. We have occasionally looked seriously at some of them: for example, in improving the process of reviewing manuscripts for journal publication, we have made some of the more obvious moves towards removing bias. This of course shows that there was something very schizophrenic about the attack on evaluation, since it was operating— and being improved—at the roots of the disciplines that were doing the attacking. People sometimes say that *this* kind of evaluation was not the kind the value-free doctrine was attacking. One only has to look at the arguments provided by the proponents of the doctrine to see that they are completely general; they allegedly make it impossible to give rational justifications for *any* evaluative conclusion. Moreover, if all that was intended was to exclude, say, political values, they were already excludable on the perfectly respectable grounds of irrelevance or undecidability. No, the value-free doctrine was after bigger game, and its proponents did not realize that their arguments inevitably required that they shoot themselves in the foot, in fact both feet.

Overall, the situation is much worse—the examples of intradisciplinary evaluation given so far come close to home; but evaluation comes much closer than that. Pick any article at random from an issue of a professional journal. It begins with a 'review of the literature', which is not of course a review of *all* the literature but only the important stuff, the significant material—an evaluative conclusion to start with. Then a research design is proposed and justified, an evaluative procedure. The investigation proceeds and the results are critically reviewed—in other words, evaluated—probably in terms of the quality of the data and the quality of the inferences from it. This process of scientific research is permeated with carefully orchestrated evaluation. In fact, the difference between good science and pseudo-science is itself an evaluative distinction. Science is a concept that is highly charged with careful evaluation. And *that* is why intradisciplinary evaluation is an important area; it is what we spend our time trying to teach graduate students how to do well. Work on chess masters' evaluation of board positions is an important part of the history of cognitive psychology; it could also have been work on psychologists' evaluation of research. (And, lately, some of it has been on that!) My conclusion is, of course, that the domain for further evaluation research comes very close to home for every social scientist, and we should expect to get some results from it that improve at least the teaching and perhaps also the practice of the social sciences.

Back to more conventional parts of the territory of evaluation research. It is useful at this point to introduce another graphical model, this time to describe particular efforts at evaluative research. Think of a conventional three-axis display, which we can refer to by thinking of ourselves as standing in the middle of a rectangular room, looking towards a corner of the floor, which we will think of as the origin point for all axes. On the wall to your left, which we'll call the Sub-Field Plane, imagine that we have drawn big ellipses to represent the various branches of evaluation we have discussed above: the seven Ps (program, personnel, product, performance, proposal, policy and portfolio), the two new areas (meta-evaluation and intradisciplinary evaluation), and the areas from applied fields that are essentially evaluative (health and safety areas in medicine and engineering, functional design issues in architecture and industrial design, for example). On the floor at your feet, there are big ellipses representing the application areas: health, social services, defense, education, business, international development, etc. This is the Application Plane. And the wall on your right is the Methods and Models Plane. The general idea is that any given evaluation research project will be represented by a volume within this room, defined by its properties in these three dimensions. To round this out, we need to turn now to look at the Models and Methods side of evaluation research.

MODELS AND METHODS

One of the most interesting aspects of the emergence of an autonomous profession of evaluation since the 1960s has been the variety and creativity of the 'models' for it that have emerged. These are sometimes methodological recommendations, sometimes epistemological or ontological platforms, and most often a mix of these. They range from the Jurisprudential Model (a recommendation for an advocate–adversary approach) to the Empowerment Model (get the program staff to evaluate themselves), the Evaluation Standards (two of them now accepted as ANSI (American National Standards Institute) standards), several checklists, the

Appreciative Inquiry approaches, and most recently the currently widespread Theory-Based or Logic Model School. My own favorite, though it is more a meta-model than a front line strategy, is the Transdisciplinary Model, according to which evaluation is one of the few ubiquitous disciplines that not only have and develop their own subject matter, but provide deep-rooted service to many or most other disciplines: logic, statistics, and design are other transdisciplines. It would take too long to review these critically, but several such reviews have been undertaken recently, of which Alkin (2004) is perhaps the most comprehensive. One way to use the right-hand wall would be to mark out areas representing each of these, with overlaps, as the third dimension. But we need that wall to do several jobs, so we are going to 'tab' it—that is, make it serve several purposes, each of which can be brought to bear by pressing on a thumb-tab listed on an overlay. So the first tab is marked 'Models'.

The next tab concerns 'Purposes', and there is a good deal of agreement that a four-way division of that plane will cover most of these. The most familiar of these divisions are 'formative' and 'summative', referring respectively to evaluations undertaken for (i) purposes of improvement, and (ii) for disposition decisions (i.e., decisions about termination/continuance, increased/reduced funding, etc.). There is considerable agreement that these need to be supplemented by a third category, referring to evaluations undertaken simply to increase our knowledge, as for example most evaluations done by historians, or by students for practice. And a case can be made that summative evaluation should be distinguished from evaluation for accountability purposes, so we will add that category as well. When the Purposes tab is pressed, the three-dimensional space allocated to a particular project—perhaps a formative evaluation of a new educational campaign to reduce the recreational use of methamphetamines—will highlight, occupying a quite different volume from that illuminated when the tab for Models is pressed.

The third tab refers to 'Logical Type', and is of great importance since almost entirely

different designs are required depending on the category selected here. The four major categories are: Ranking, Grading, Scoring and Apportioning, with the last referring to the evaluative procedure, familiar to every administrator, of distributing some valued resource across a set of candidates (projects, departments, personnel) in a way that is dependent on a combination of their merits, needs and demands, and the context of the evaluation. One result of methodological research here was the development of the procedure known as 'zero-based budgeting' introduced to the federal budget process by President Jimmy Carter. It is speculated that there is a way to reduce apportioning to ranking and grading, but this has not yet been proven. Of course, apportioning is the evaluative operation most closely tied to portfolio evaluation.

That completes a rather sketchy taxonomy of evaluation research; it is now time to show that it is useful in exposing some common misconceptions about the field. While still in the section on Methods, we can pick up the common misconception, still present in leading texts, that evaluation is essentially applied social science research. Of course, that is not true of evaluation overall, since huge fields of it are not even remotely dependent on social science methods: obvious cases are the greater part of so-called informal logic or critical thinking devoted to the evaluation of arguments, the part of jurisprudence concerned with the role of appellate courts in evaluating the decisions of lower courts, and the noble arts of the restaurateur and drama critic. Could we save the position by restricting it to program evaluation and perhaps personnel evaluation and policy analysis? No, because, like all branches of professional evaluation, a large slice—perhaps half—of their methodology is something taught in no social science classes: the techniques for dealing with the values part of evaluation. This deficiency is the cross that social science still carries from the value-free days, and it costs dear in dealing with serious program evaluation.

In order to evaluate a program one must first identify all relevant values—that is, all that may have a significant impact on the evaluative conclusion that we need to get (whether it is a ranking of alternative choices, a grading, etc.). These will almost always include legal, ethical, and professional value codes, and the result of professional-level needs assessments of the needs of the population impacted by the program, whether intentionally or not. But there are another 17 value types that need to be checked for relevance in the list published in one source (Scriven, 2006), so this is not a trivial task.

And it brings other demands with it: doing a valid needs assessment is a skill that needs considerable conceptual sophistication in providing objective distinctions between, for example, wants and needs and between needs and ideals, and some skill in using fault-tree analysis, for instance. The reference to 'intentionally or not' reminds the researcher that the issue here is not what the program meant to do but what it did. It is just as important to find every side-effect as it is to find every intended effect—they kill people just as dead, or help them just as valuably, as if they were intended. But there are no chapters on finding side-effects in the sociology texts I have seen: it is a tricky and arcane business. And it is one of the reasons for the inapplicability of the entire hypothesis-testing model of experimental design that so many social scientists are wedded to: after all, you can hardly formulate the hypothesis to include outcomes you haven't thought of yet—but nor can you leave them out of any half-competent evaluation.

Identifying relevant values will never be complete until the study is almost complete, because one will often find side-effects very late in the study, and will then have to recheck the list of values checked so far to see if it covers all that are relevant to the side-effects as well.

But identifying relevant values is only the first of five steps in the list of value competencies. The others steps require skills in specifying them in terms applicable to the present case (e.g., specifying what would count as a conflict of interest in this case); verifying them—establishing their legitimacy in this

context; measuring in qualitative or quantitative terms the extent of the impact here (e.g., minor, medium, major or 1 to 5); and balancing off the conflicts between the values, which often point in different directions. Even if the techniques of multiple-attribute utility technology worked here (they do not, because they assume a common scale), they cannot handle the interaction with or between ethical and legal considerations (because the difference is not captured by linear weighting). So one must have at least the rudiments of skill in ethical argumentation and/or orthogonal weighting (e.g., the difference between 'bars' and weights) to cope with these essential aspects of managing the values dimension of evaluation research.

These are massive omissions in the social scientist's methodological repertoire; in fact, they are often better found in good legal reasoning courses in law school, or in the best texts on moral reasoning or critical thinking, than in the sociology or psychology courses. But that is by no means the whole list. I think it is fair to say that cost analysis, especially the analysis of non-money costs, has not yet become a staple in the social science doctoral requirements, though it is essential in program evaluation; but I'll let that one go.

I will just mention one more example. It would take us into territory requiring more space than we have here to explore this example (which is of overwhelming importance), so I will just describe it. The training of social scientists today, with rare exceptions, not only leaves them unable to deal competently with the analysis of causation but severely handicaps them in dealing with it, as we can see by the number of first-rate social scientists who have declared allegiance to the RCT (randomly controlled trials) flag in the current 'causal wars'. It is impossible for someone familiar with the serious analysis of causation in the logic of science over the last fifty years not to see the proponents of RCTs as replaying the tragedy of the vast majority of social scientists who bought into the idea that statistical significance represented scientific significance, and crippled the development of their subjects for more than half a century. Perhaps even closer to home, it as well to remember the degree of credibility most social scientists afforded the arguments for the value-free doctrine, when in fact every social scientist was actively engaged in serious and systematic evaluation on every working day (and reading *Consumer Reports* on his holidays).

IMPLICATIONS

We have space here for only a few examples of how the uncovering and taming of 'the sleeper discipline' of evaluation is beginning to produce useful results, not just in its own 'named territory' (i.e., the areas with evaluation in their names—the seven Ps of program, personnel, ... evaluation) but across the whole range of its underpinning of all scientific research. In the named territories, perhaps the most pervasive impact of serious research on evaluation, although it is one not yet fully realized, is the destruction of the simple-minded idea that program evaluation consists in determining whether a program has met its goals. One still sees this assumption in both professional and public discussions, although it has long been obvious that an ill-aimed program—one that is not even pointed at the real needs—is just as much a waste of resources as an ill-functioning program. So a valid and current needs assessment is an essential part of good program evaluation, and, all too often, not to be found. Further, with the model of FDA's good work in finding drug side effects, and its well-publicized misses on that front, we also know that hitting the goals is not enough—you must also check for the side-effects. And then there are the cases where the goal is reached and there are no side-effects—but nobody checked to see whether there are other ways, better or cheaper or both, to get to the same goals. And more recently, there is the pathetic switching by United Way and what seems to be half the philanthropies in the country from the fallacy of process-based program evaluation to the fallacy of outcomes-based evaluation: just as foolish, just as likely to cause harm. It seems odd to have to remind philanthropies that the end does

not justify the means, but what do they think is different between that and outcomes-based evaluation without any check on process?[8]

In personnel evaluation, the hot approach to teacher evaluation for a while recently was the so-called 'research-based' approach which recommended using indicators of good teaching that had been shown in empirical studies to be positively correlated with better learning outcomes. Of course, this involves not only the fallacy just discussed but another one as well. Suppose we do a computer-based pattern recognition of golf swings and discover that the best golfers tend to display factors A, B and C significantly more often than weaker golfers. The 'research-based approach to golfer evaluation' would presumably argue that we could skip all that nonsense about traipsing around 72 holes on the PGA tour events in favor of the much faster and cheaper process of having the computer analyze the entrants' swings with a driver, a couple of irons, and a putter. Come to think of it, why not give degrees on the basis of SAT and GRE scores? Answer: because it is (1) unethical (the best players on the day won't get rewarded, but that is what you are supposed to be rewarding), and (2) it has very bad consequences: it reinforces the copying of secondary indicators instead of achieving the fundamental performance. Teachers have duties, mainly to bring about valuable learning, and that is all they can be held accountable for. They did not sign on to imitate the style of other teachers, even successful ones, unless they are *not* able to succeed by doing it their way. And until you have shown that they do fail in their chosen style, on the task they undertook, you cannot penalize them for not adopting the secondary characteristics of those who are a little more likely to succeed— maybe. This point was a major victory, still ignored at times, for the logic of evaluation over the logic of empirical indicators of merit as acceptable surrogates for direct measurement of merit.

Outside the named areas—in intradisciplinary evaluation, for example—can we really expect that the new-boy-in-town discipline of evaluation will come up with improvements in the techniques on which the disciplines themselves were founded and have developed their present great strengths? Two big hints about the answer are already visible: (1) the concealing the authorship of manuscripts sent out for review by journal editors, and (2) the evaluation of the validity of experts at predicting human behavior. These are cases of psychology being applied to psychology, but they are also of course the thin end of the wedge of standard evaluation methodology being implemented in standard scientific practices. There are many such cases, beginning with honing the edge on these. Present systems for blinding reviewers are amateurish and easily penetrated—for example, by using your brains or Google on the references list. The pathetic results of experts in predicting behavior should be applied to experts predicting the future performance of experts who are candidates for jobs as researchers. We are still treating this as part of the holy process of peer review, but in fact that icon only has a minor role in identifying the quality of 'within-paradigm' research. It does not have any validity in predicting the future production of high-quality within-paradigm research, let alone the importance (which means future impact) of new-paradigm research. These two prediction tasks fall under the Meehl results, and it is time to develop new indicators for that task.

Two of the above examples show that evaluation is often helpful in seeing what does not work (and there are plenty more of these, notably in the poor standards still common in the evaluation of international development efforts). But there are also plenty of examples of the conventional kind, where good evaluations have led evaluators to support programs that would otherwise have been neglected, which of course does not mean that the funding agencies supported the programs. An interesting example is the proven success of computer tutoring, probably the only possible solution for 'education for all', but up against a combination of fear of computers replacing people and thinking that computers would be better used to do other tasks in education that in fact they do badly or cost-ineffectively.

It may be appropriate to conclude this section with an example which illustrates a valuable lesson about the limits of evaluation in guiding decisions. This was a case where an evaluator was completely wrong in judging the utility of a routine evaluation. (I was the evaluator.) Working as an external evaluator for a community foundation some years ago, I evaluated a currently funded program that was up for review and that seemed an easy target: there was no evidence of need for it; it was expensive; and it didn't work. I confidently submitted the recommendation to stop its funding—after all, there were plenty of other programs and unmet needs in that community, where the money could be well spent. I was completely wrong, committing an error that evaluators often make: the error of thinking that merit (or cost-effectiveness) is the only legitimate basis for program support. It is not; there are other values that the Board of Directors should (and did) weigh against merit when making the disposition decision. In this case, those included legal, political and personal obligations that I was not privy to, and could not, for reasons of confidentiality, have been fully informed about, and should not have assumed had no relevance.

FUTURES

Evaluation research is the future of most useful research, since in the practical context merit or worth or significance are almost always at stake. The big questions are: how long will it take for this situation to become clear to social scientists, and how will they respond? Since we already have many social scientists who argue, wrongly, that evaluation is part of social science, I think it is likely they will try to salvage their view by adding what it takes to expand social science to include the basics of evaluation, as they have done with statistics and measurement in the past. That still will not make the discipline of evaluation part of social science—think of product evaluation and all the rest of evaluation within other disciplines—but it is a benefit to social science, so let us hope it happens. It will bring more expertise to bear on developing both the foundations and the applications of evaluation, which have so far only started to bud, not yet to bloom. And this increase in the workforce will bring about confrontation with other vital questions of which surely the most important is this: as much of ethics is concerned with the evaluation of human social behavior, is there any reason to suppose that it, too, cannot be tidied up a little and then regarded as part of social science? It seems to me that this is really an Emperor's-new-clothes kind of question. The fact is that at least nine branches of science and logic have crossed the border into the territory of providing scientific foundations for ethics[9] and it is just that no one has had the nerve to point out what has already been done (though not given its proper name). Perhaps evaluation can have the honor of bearing that banner in the crusade it will take to win that prize.

REFERENCES

Alkin, M.C. (ed.) (2004) *Evaluation Roots: Tracing Theorists' Views and Influences.* Thousand Oaks, CA: Sage Publications.

Hughes, H.D. (1917) 'An interesting corn seed experiment', *Iowa Agriculturalist*, 17: 424–5.

Meehl, P.E. (1954) *Clinical Vs. Statistical Prediction.* Minneapolis: University of Minnesota Press.

Scriven, M. (1993) 'Hard-won lessons in program evaluation', *New Directions for Program Evaluation*, 58: 1–107.

———— (2006) 'Key evaluation checklist', Western Michigan University, The Evaluation Center. Available at: http://www.wmich.edu/evalctr/checklists/kec_october05.pdf (accessed June 2, 2006).

Shanteau, J. (1999) 'Decision making by experts', in J. Shanteau, B.A. Mellers, and D.A. Schum (eds), *Decision Science and Technology: Reflections on the Contributions of Ward Edwards.* Boston: Kluwer.

NOTES

1 There was a profession of product evaluators in the heyday of the great Japanese sword-makers, nearly two thousand years ago, who would sign off on the tang of the blade after performing a suite of suitable tests on it.

2 Uncharacteristically, the examples it gives do not support this interpretation, but the one used here.

3 Most of the considerable extant wisdom about proposal evaluation reposes in the experience and skills of the big agency program officers who have been managing (and sometimes manipulating) review panels for decades.

4 Our professional lives depend on this, too, since the funding of graduate programs within graduate schools is an exercise in portfolio evaluation and the only book on it that gets much reference is basically disastrous.

5 There is an excellent historical review in J. Shanteau (1999).

6 Not only for defense attorneys, but for researchers looking for fields where more research and new methods are needed.

7 These 'almost by definition' inferences are sometimes called 'probative inferences'. They create a status for their conclusion that is called *prima facie* truth in the law, from which the term 'probative' also comes.

8 A long list of lessons learned about program evaluation can be found in Scriven (1993).

9 The more obvious candidates are: evolutionary ethics, the altruism gene discussion in genetics, decision theory, game theory with the solution to the Prisoner's Dilemma, political theory's discussion of the justification of democracy, evaluation with the logic of value management, probative inference in informal logic, community psychology and welfare economics as recently revived.

29

Feminist Methodology

Susan Hekman

Feminist social analysts and theorists have developed a distinctive approach to the methodology of the social sciences that constitutes a significant contribution to these disciplines. Feminists have exposed the masculinist bias that informs the methods and concepts of the social sciences, and developed alternative approaches. Feminist research has transformed social-scientific disciplines by revealing the boundaries imposed by the hegemonic concepts of those disciplines. As a counter they have developed concepts and methods that open up new avenues of research. Feminist methodology has broadened and redefined the parameters of the social sciences.

Like any other academic movement, however, feminist methodology did not develop in a vacuum. It is closely connected to a number of intellectual trends that shaped twentieth-century thought. Even though feminists have employed the ideas of twentieth-century philosophers and social theorists for their own purposes, it is nevertheless the case that the roots of feminist methodology can be traced to a series of developments in twentieth-century thought, trends that changed the direction of social theory and practice in this century.

As Anthony Giddens so famously put it, the social sciences were born in the shadow of the triumph of the natural sciences. The success of the natural sciences in understanding the natural world caused the budding social sciences to attempt to mimic their methods. What this entailed at the beginning of the twentieth century was that the social sciences embraced the philosophical approach of positivism. Positivism was thought to be the correct translation of the scientific method employed in the natural sciences into the social sciences. Positivism posited the separation of the knower from the object known, it relied exclusively on the abstract logical analysis of facts, and it defined objective, value-free knowledge as the goal of all scientific analysis. For social scientists, positivism was seen as the correct means of approaching the study of the social world. And, most importantly, it was seen as providing the scientific status that the social sciences wanted to achieve.

But from the very beginning there were critics of the use of positivism in the social sciences. The *Methodenstreit* that raged in Germany at the end of the nineteenth century pitted the positivists against the subjectivists who claimed that positivism was an inappropriate method for the social sciences. In the twentieth century this debate was revived with the advent of a range of approaches that called positivism into question.

Phenomenologists argued that the starting point of social-scientific analysis must be the social actors' concepts, not the 'objective facts' of positivism. Ordinary language analysts argued the same point from the perspective of a Wittgensteinian understanding of language. Critical theorists argued that it is impossible to remove the normative dimension from the social sciences because all knowledge has a normative intent.

None of these approaches were concerned with gender; none discussed feminist issues. But these critiques of positivism are relevant to the emergence of a feminist methodology for a number of key reasons. The focus of all of these accounts is value. The anti-positivists claimed that values are inseparable from the social sciences in several respects. They asserted that the values of the social-scientific researcher determine the object of study in the social sciences. They also argued that the object of study itself is constituted by the values and concepts of the social actors. These arguments would become the centerpiece of the feminist critique of the social sciences. Feminists claim that the social sciences are defined by the values of the social-scientific researchers, values that are inherently masculinist. As a consequence, the experiences of women are invisible in these disciplines because they are not conceptualized in the scientific discourse. Feminists also claim that looking at the experiences of women as they are conceptualized by women yields a very different picture of the social world, a picture missing in masculinist social science.

Another aspect of the value argument advanced by the anti-positivists is also relevant to the emerging feminist critique. If, as the anti-positivists argued, value is inseparable from the social sciences, then the criticism that feminists are bringing an inappropriate value dimension to their analyses is inapplicable. But feminists took this argument in a direction not envisioned by the anti-positivists. They argued that the values that define the social sciences are masculinist and, thus, that bringing feminist values into these sciences, far from violating the canons of scientific objectivity, is rather a necessary corrective to that bias.

Another development in twentieth-century thought, which, like the anti-positivist critiques, had no feminist element, also became influential in the development of a feminist methodology. A number of philosophers of science, most notably Thomas Kuhn, began to question the objectivity and value-freedom of the natural sciences themselves. Kuhn argued that the concepts of the natural scientists create the facts that they study and, consequently, as those concepts change, so does the world that they study. Kuhn questioned the progressive nature of science—moving from error to truth—and instead proposed that scientific truth is defined by the paradigm dominant in science at any given time.

Kuhn was not alone. Other philosophers of science advanced similar arguments. Mary Hesse (1980) argued that both the natural and the social sciences are hermeneutic, that is, that they are constituted by the meaning of the concepts of the science itself. One aspect of this argument became a central element of the feminist critique of science. If all science is hermeneutical, then it follows that the distinction between the natural and the social sciences is moribund. The work of Hans-Georg Gadamer (1975) reinforces this thesis. Gadamer attacks the privileging of the natural sciences over the social sciences by arguing that all knowledge is hermeneutic knowledge; this is the pattern of all human understanding. But Gadamer goes further and argues that the path to knowledge in the natural sciences, far from being the model of all knowledge, is instead an aberration. The abstraction that characterizes knowledge in the natural sciences, he argues, is not the paradigm of all knowing, but an exception to the pattern of human understanding. From a different but related perspective, Wittgenstein also cast doubt on the certainty of knowledge in the natural sciences and mathematics. Uniting all these perspectives is an interest in language and its constitutive function. What all these thinkers are arguing is that language gives us a world and that the constitutive function of language holds for both the natural and social world.

Although this perspective is certainly not without its critics, it has now become an established aspect of the philosophy of science. Social studies of knowledge abounded in the last decades of the twentieth century. Extending the sociology of knowledge to the natural sciences and mathematics, theorists such as David Bloor (1976) and Barry Barnes (1974) argued that all knowledge is socially constructed. Knowledge, for these theorists, is not constituted by the act of an individual knower observing natural phenomena, but, rather, is socially constructed through the concepts of the scientific community.

Once again, although these arguments were devoid of a feminist perspective, they were both useful and relevant to the emerging feminist critiques. Extending the critique of scientific method to include the natural as well as the social sciences strengthened the argument substantially. But from a feminist perspective, this move was significant in another sense. Attacking the privilege of the natural sciences was tantamount to attacking the bastion of masculinity. It was the ideal of abstraction and logical purity in the natural sciences that established this model as the paradigm of all knowledge. If this view of knowledge, as these thinkers were arguing, is an illusion, then the validity and dominance of the paradigm is called into question, and, significantly, so is the dominance of the masculinist values that inform this paradigm.

Both these intellectual movements formed the backdrop of the feminist critique of the natural and social sciences and the development of a feminist methodology for both branches of science. Feminists began their inquiry into the relationship between women and science by examining the obvious discrimination against women in science. It soon became clear, however, that a much more fundamental cause was at work in the exclusion of women from science. Feminist theorists turned to the beginnings of modern science in the seventeenth century and asked what it was about this activity that created a mindset so thoroughly antithetical to the feminine. They began to explore the fundamental assumptions guiding modern science in an effort to explain the exclusion of women from science.

What they found was very revealing. As Virginia Woolf (1984: 263) put it, 'Science, it would seem, is not sexless; she is a man, a father, and infected too.' From its inception modern science has been defined in terms that characterize it as a solely masculine activity that excludes women. Francis Bacon labeled modern science the 'Masculine Birth of Time'. Sexual metaphors pervade the descriptions of Bacon and other early scientists. These scientists describe their activity as stripping away the veil of nature to reveal her secrets. They speak of penetrating the recesses of nature and uncovering her mysteries. The relationship between the scientist and nature is characterized in terms that range from chaste marriage to gang rape. But in every case it is a sexual relationship, in which the male scientist dominates and subdues female nature (Hekman, 1990: 114–16).

Feminist research also revealed that the practice of science was rooted in masculinist values. Scientific practice is based on a competitive model that pits individual scientists against one another. Cooperation, an attitude associated with the feminine, is defined as dysfunctional. Further, scientific practice requires the abstraction of the scientist from the object known. The scientist is the subject of knowledge, the thing studied its object; subject and object are conceived in dichotomous terms. Relational thinking, also a feminine characteristic, is, again, proscribed. Finally, the goal of scientific practice is objective knowledge, knowledge that eschews bias and the influence of values. This is a particularly difficult belief to combat because it masks the masculinist bias that pervades the scientific ethos. Objectivity, feminists revealed, is male subjectivity. But it is difficult for feminists to convince their male colleagues of this fact because of the pervasiveness of masculinist values.

The feminist response to the realization that modern science is inherently and thoroughly masculinist has taken two directions. The first is epistemological, the attempt to formulate a feminist critique of science and to define a feminist position on scientific knowledge. The second is methodological, the attempt to outline the parameters of a feminist science. As with any issue in feminist thought, there is no unanimity among feminists on either of these issues. Furthermore, the positions articulated in the 1980s that initially defined the debate have been substantially reformulated in terms of issues that are now in the forefront of feminist theory.

In 1986 Sandra Harding summarized the central issues in the feminist critique of science, both natural and social, in *The Science Question in Feminism*. Harding articulated three epistemological positions on science that characterized most feminists' understanding of the relationship between women and science at the time. The first position is feminist empiricism. This position is the least radical of the three positions. Feminist empiricists do not reject the scientific method or positivism but, rather, aim to correct it. They argue that the sexism and androcentrism of science are correctable and the biases that produce these errors can be eradicated by stricter adherence to the existing methodological norms of scientific inquiry. In other words, feminist empiricists argue that sexist science is bad science, and that by eliminating sexist bias, good, feminist science can be produced.

The issue of whether the scientific method and/or positivism is inherently sexist is still in contention in feminists' discussions. Although Harding praises the studies of feminist empiricists, it is clear that she, like many feminists, would prefer a more radical stance on the scientific method. She even argues that feminist empiricism effectively subverts empiricism while claiming to espouse it. She asserts that feminist empiricists claim that women as a group are more likely to produce unbiased results than are men (Harding, 1986: 25). It is, however, doubtful that all feminist empiricists would accept Harding's assessment. Feminist empiricists claim that bias can and should be eliminated from science and that this goal is one that feminists should also pursue.

The second position, feminist standpoint epistemology, has been immensely influential in discussions of feminist science. Unlike feminist empiricism, feminist standpoint epistemology entails a wholesale rejection of positivism and the scientific method. This position has its roots in Hegel, Marx and Lukacs. It was adapted to feminism by Nancy Hartsock, Dorothy Smith and Harding herself. At root, standpoint epistemology claims that all knowledge is perspectival, that is, the social position of the knower determines the knowledge produced. It further asserts that some social positions produce 'partial and perverse' knowledge, while others produce an accurate understanding of social reality. Marx's concern was with the social positions of the bourgeoisie and the proletariat. He claimed that only the proletariat could achieve a true understanding of social reality; the dominant position of the bourgeoisie precluded such an understanding. Feminists, on the other hand, are concerned with the dominance of men. They assert that men's social dominance produces partial and perverse knowledge while woman's subjugated position provides the possibility for more complete and less perverse understandings.

Closely connected to the development of feminist standpoint epistemology is a theory of child development that became influential in feminist discussions in the 1980s: object relations theory. Object relations theorists claimed that women and men develop distinctively different psychological natures due to the different ways in which mothers raise girls and boys. The theory posits that mothers produce daughters with 'feminine' qualities of nurturing, relational skills and fear of autonomy. In contrast mothers produce sons who embrace autonomy and competition and lack relational skills. This psychological theory of gender differences dovetails neatly with feminist standpoint theory and the feminist critique of science that it generated. It offers an explanation for why men find the scientific ethos congenial and women do not. The autonomy and abstraction that define science match men's psychological inclinations and clash with that of women. Object relations theory is also useful in explaining the origin of the feminist standpoint. It pinpoints the source of the unique experiences of women that produce this standpoint.

Feminist standpoint theory had the advantage of providing a distinctive approach to scientific knowledge that constituted a radical departure from positivism. It provided a feminist critique of the natural and social sciences that was grounded in the universal features of women's experience understood from the perspective of feminism. But it was also clear from the outset that standpoint theory had disadvantages as well. The most central of these was the question of how it was possible to talk about the feminist standpoint when it was obvious that women's experiences vary widely. One way of answering this question is to claim that there is not one but many feminist standpoints. Patricia Hill Collins, for example, developed the black feminist standpoint partly as a counter to this objection (1990). But this development raised its own questions. If there are multiple feminist standpoints, is one more true than another? And, more fundamentally, if all knowledge is perspectival, how can we claim that one perspective is more true than another, the basic claim of standpoint theory?

One way of answering these questions is provided by the third position in the debate: feminist postmodernism. Unlike feminist standpoint theorists, feminist postmoderns rejected all claims to universal knowledge and stable identities. Following the work of postmodern thinkers such as Lyotard, Derrida and Foucault, feminist postmoderns argued that all knowledge, including scientific knowledge, is created by discourses that establish the rules for truth and falsity. Thus scientific knowledge is created by the discourses of science. It does not mirror the reality of nature, either natural or social, but, rather, reality is created through the deployment of its concepts.

Again, this position had advantages and disadvantages for the feminist critique of science. It is very useful in explaining how scientific concepts create a world in which it is 'true' that women are inferior to men. Donna Haraway's (1989) critique of the discourse of primatology is an excellent example of the strengths of feminist postmodernism. Haraway illustrates how the scientific discourse of primatology created the truth of women's inferiority, and how, as that discourse changed, so did that truth. But Haraway's analysis also reveals the liability of feminist postmodernism. What Haraway is proposing is that we replace the story of women's inferiority with the story of their equality. This is not a compelling argument. Postmodern epistemology entails giving up on the assertion of universal truth. But if we give up on universal truth then we must also give up on the truth of women's oppression and the necessity of liberation. If discourses are simply stories, then the feminist discourse of women's domination by men is also just a story.

These epistemological explorations set the stage for the second direction of feminist discussions of science: what would a feminist science look like? If, as both the feminist standpoint theorists and the feminist postmoderns claimed, we must fundamentally challenge the scientific method of positivism, how do we replace it? On a simplistic level, what feminists were calling for was the opposite of the epistemology they were challenging. Thus while positivism calls for the objectivity and abstraction of the scientific researcher, feminists are calling for connection and relation instead. An early example of this definition of feminist science is the work of Evelyn Fox Keller. In 1983 Keller published an analysis of the work of the biologist Barbara McClintock that held up her work as a model for feminist science. McClintock, although not explicitly a feminist herself, advocated an approach to science that embodied many feminist principles. She rejected the subject/object dichotomy that informs scientific method and instead tried to gain intimate knowledge of the plants she studied. She claimed that good science involves deep emotional investment, not value-free detachment. For McClintock something beyond reason is required in science: intuition that leads to understanding.

One of the major themes of the postmodern critique of science is that the concepts of the scientist create the reality that he (*sic*) studies. Feminist critiques of science, even those that had no connection to postmodernism, began to explore this perspective in the attempt to formulate a feminist approach to science. Feminist sociologists, for example, argued that the concepts employed in sociology ignore areas of social life that are central to women (Millman and Kantor, 1975). Private life, emotion, work inside the home, and other feminine spheres are not conceptualized in the discourse of sociology. As a consequence they are invisible, they do not exist in the reality created by the discourse. These spheres of social life are also rendered invisible by the reliance on empirical methodology. This methodology entails that only quantifiable data are subject to analysis. Many of the spheres of social life important to women's lives are not susceptible to quantification and are, thus, invisible.

Another major theme of the discussion of a feminist science, particularly in the social sciences, is breaking down the separation of the subject and object of research. Barbara McClintock attempted to do this with the plants that she studied by trying to get a 'feeling for the organism'. Breaking down this distinction is even more central to the feminist social-scientific researcher. Informing the hegemonic discourse of the social sciences is the dictum that the researcher must remove him/herself from the object studied. Feminist researchers reject this dictum, arguing instead that subject and object of knowledge should be located in the same critical plane. Feminist social analysts argue

that they are not, as researchers, removed from or superior to those they study. Rather, they argue that researcher and researched inhabit a social situation that is jointly constituted by both parties.

In her 1987 collection, *Feminism and Methodology*, Sandra Harding argues that feminists should not be preoccupied with method. Whether or not feminists have heeded Harding's admonition is an open question. Since 1987 there has been an outpouring of writings on feminist methodology. This outpouring, however, confirms a claim that Harding also makes in this collection: there is no single feminist method. In the 1992 collection, *Feminist Methods in Social Research*, for example, Shulamit Reinharz devotes each of her eleven chapters to a feminist research method. The list is extensive, including interviewing, ethnography, survey research and many others. Reinharz's message is clear: feminist research is varied and cannot be categorized under a single approach.

Despite this diversity, however, there are certain recurrent themes in feminist research. Pervading almost all feminist research is a focus on the distinctive experiences of women. This focus is the result of the convergence of several trends in feminist critiques of science. The revelation that the concepts of the social sciences made the experiences of women invisible has led many feminist researchers to create new concepts to examine those experiences. Feminist researchers have analyzed the unique experiences of women both at home and in the workforce. Explorations of domestic violence, sexual harassment, and the 'second shift' experiences that were ignored in mainstream social science have been major topics of feminist research.

Another impetus behind the focus on women's experience is the widespread feminist interest in defining the feminist standpoint. Dorothy Smith's work here has been definitive. Focusing on women's experiences and adopting the feminist standpoint, Smith argues, not only illuminates the hidden experiences of women, it also reveals the liabilities of the hegemonic discourse of sociology. The ethic of objectivity in sociology, Smith argues, is predicated on the separation of knower and known. Smith (1987: 91) asserts, 'Women's perspective, as I have analyzed it here, discredits sociology's claim to constitute objective knowledge independent of the sociologist's situation.' Smith calls for a 're-organization' of sociology that places the sociologist in her particular place and makes her direct experience of the everyday world the primary ground of her knowledge. Although Smith claims that this 're-organization' of sociology does not constitute a radical transformation of the discipline, it is hard not to come to this conclusion.

Another aspect of the focus on women's experiences is that in several disciplines it has opened up an entirely new dimension of the discipline that did not exist before the advent of feminist research. This is perhaps most evident in the discipline of history. Prior to the women's movement, the discipline of history had defined 'historical facts' as, with few exceptions, the activities of elite men in a narrowly defined political arena. The activities of women (and those men outside the political realm) were only rarely conceptualized; they did not qualify as 'historical facts' and were thus excluded from the discipline.

When feminist historians began to look at women's lives in history, and other social historians began to look at the lives of African-Americans or working-class white men, the concepts they developed to examine those lives transformed the discipline of history. The boundaries of the discipline were stretched to include a previously unconceptualized reality. It is significant, furthermore, that in bringing a new aspect of social reality into the discipline of history, feminist and social historians also developed new historical methods. As many critics of science have argued, methods are linked to theories and the facts they create. The traditional methods of history were inappropriate for the examination of women's history. These methods focused on sources such as congressional records, politicians' memoirs and legal enactments; women were not present in these sources. The new methods of 'social history'

had to be created in order to analyze a new category of facts. Feminist and social historians began to look at new sources: oral histories, diaries, census records, material culture, even fiction (Hekman, 1999: 81–2; Kelly-Gadol, 1987).

Another issue that pervades discussions of feminist methodology is the applicability of quantitative research. The issues raised in this discussion are complex. On one hand it seems clear that feminist methodology constitutes a challenge to the hegemonic methods of the social sciences and that quantitative research is the centerpiece of those methods. The social sciences, in their effort to mimic the natural sciences, have enthusiastically embraced quantification and placed it at the center of their methodology. A significant consequence of this is that aspects of social life that cannot be quantified are ignored by social-scientific researchers. Many feminists, in their attempt to study the experiences of women, have been led to reject quantitative methods out of hand. Feminists have argued that these methods not only obliterate the experiences of women but they also represent everything that is wrong with the hegemonic methodology of the social sciences.

But the issue of quantification is not quite so easily dismissed. Several mitigating factors have been raised by feminist researchers. First, feminists, despite their oppositional stance, want their research findings to be accepted and taken seriously. In most social-scientific disciplines this can only be accomplished by using quantitative methods. Second, some feminists have argued that there is nothing inherently wrong with quantitative methods but, rather, that it is their exclusive use that is the problem. They have further argued that, if feminists claim to be truly eclectic in their methodology, they should not exclude any method, even quantitative research (Jayaratne and Stewart, 1991). It is significant, furthermore, that with the advent of feminist history discussed above, feminist historians employed quantification specifically as an oppositional method. Traditional political history did not employ quantitative methods. But as feminist and social historians searched for methods to explore the new subject matter of women's history, they turned to quantitative methods to achieve their goal.

Another major theme of feminist methodology is a commitment to political change. Positivist methodology is predicated on the rejection of politics. Social-scientific research is defined as a value-free realm that necessarily excludes political elements. Feminist researchers oppose this by arguing that all feminist research has the goal of social change. Feminists employ research to change women's lives. The information they gather is not value-free but is, on the contrary, designed to promote the value of improving the lives of women. This issue is perhaps that which unites feminists more than any other. Most feminists would agree that if the point of feminist research is not to change women's lives then it is a meaningless activity.

The title of a 1991 collection edited by Mary Fonow and Judith Cook is *Beyond Methodology: Feminist Scholarship as Lived Research*. This title expresses a widely held belief of contemporary feminist methodologists: feminist methodology is, by definition, oppositional. Most feminist methodologists today would assert that feminist methodology goes beyond and constitutes a repudiation of the hegemonic methods of the social sciences. A central aspect of that repudiation is the political orientation of feminist scholarship. The issues raised in the articles in the collection revolve around the political goal of feminist research and the relationship between the researcher and the researched in feminist scholarship. These issues are at the heart of what constitutes feminist methods for most contemporary theorists and practitioners.

Feminist methodology has always been closely tied to feminist theory. It was the discovery that women and men understand the world in fundamentally different ways that led to the original feminist critique of science. The difference feminism of the 1980s informed the feminist methodology of that period, a methodology that focused on the unique experiences and perspectives of women. Likewise, the postmodern feminism of the 1990s produced a feminist methodology that focused on the creative powers of discourse and the linguistic creation of reality.

The situation of feminist methodology today is, likewise, informed by current trends in feminist theory. Two issues at the forefront of contemporary feminist theory are similarly at the forefront of discussions of feminist methodology. The first of these is the issue of differences. If the 1980s were the era of difference feminism, feminist theory has now moved into the era of differences. Beginning in the 1990s feminists began to criticize difference feminism from a number of perspectives. It became obvious that 'women's experience' is a widely varied phenomenon, not a singular experience. It also became obvious that the concept of 'woman' was both hierarchical and ethnocentric. Feminists came to the conclusion that focusing on 'woman' as a monolithic category resulted in the marginalization of 'different' women who did not fit the universal definition.

The emphasis on differences between women quite literally revolutionized feminist theory and practice. Universal 'woman' is no longer employed in feminist discussions. Rather, issues that focus on differences—of race, ethnicity, sexual orientation, age, etc.— are at the forefront of both theory and practice in feminist discussions. The movement to differences has had the effect of opening up new avenues of feminist research. Women's experiences are analyzed from multiple perspectives. Journals and anthologies of feminist research abound with articles about women in all areas of the world. They focus on the unique problems these women face; they analyze their situation from the particular context in which these women live.

The focus on differences has, however, also raised questions, particularly questions of method. Feminists have not yet developed what might be called a 'method for differences' (Hekman, 1999). It is clear that contemporary feminist researchers have abandoned universal categories and are focusing on differences between women. What is not clear, however, is how far differences extend. Ultimately, difference is a slippery slope: every woman is different from every other woman. The question is one of where we can legitimately draw lines between groups of women and for what purposes. Is it, for example, legitimate to analyze the situation of women factory workers in an Indian city, exploring the particular problems they face and the specific issues they confront? Or is it necessary to break down this category further, into, for example, married vs. unmarried workers? Feminist theorists and methodologists have not yet dealt with these difficult issues. Yet they must be confronted as feminism moves into the era of differences.

In the move toward differences much of the emphasis is on non-Western women. Second-wave feminism was an overwhelmingly Western phenomenon. The 'woman' this movement theorized did not include women outside the Western world. The realization of this led feminists to explore the condition of non-Western women. But this exploration turned out to be more difficult than anticipated. In an influential article, 'Under Western Eyes' (1984), Chandra Mohanty lays out the difficulties entailed in Western women studying non-Western women. Mohanty argues that feminist discourse creates a monolithic category, 'Third World Woman' that ignores the diversity of these women. In this discourse, Mohanty argues, the oppression of women in the Third World is homogenized and systematized. In her effort to analyze how this discourse is produced, Mohanty touches on all the key methodological problems facing feminist discourse. She asserts that the ethnocentric universalism of feminist discourse has three roots: the universal concept of 'woman', the methodological universalism produced by the empirical method of positivist social science, and the definition of power and struggle employed in the analysis.

Mohanty's counter-methodological proposals provide an outline of contemporary feminist methodology. First, she argues, 'woman' must always be placed historically, socially, culturally and ethnically. Universal woman no longer has any cogency in feminist methodology. Second, the use of empirical methods must be highly circumscribed if not rejected outright. Mohanty argues that it may be possible to gather quantitative data about a specifically defined group of women, but even this must be done carefully and with attention to differences within the group. Third, we must develop an alternative conception of power. The conception of power that informs Western social science, Mohanty argues, is monolithic. It characterizes power as emanating from a single source and producing a monolithic class of people— the powerless and oppressed. This definition of power creates the illusion of woman as a homogeneous and powerless group. Against this Mohanty proposes a Foucauldian definition of power that characterizes power as multiple, emanating from many different sources in society. This conception allows us to define women as resisting power in multiple ways.

The methodology that Mohanty (1984: 345) espouses, then, is 'careful, politically focused local analysis'. She asserts that no concepts can be used without specifying their local and historical context. Mohanty's methodology has become orthodoxy for a whole generation of feminist researchers. This approach, which some have labeled 'contextual methodology' (Wing, 2000), is particularly influential in analyses of what Mohanty calls 'Third World Women'. Adrienne Wing's recent collection, *Global Critical Race Feminism* (2004), exemplifies this approach. The articles included range across the globe. There is no universal 'woman' here, only women in particular social and historical contexts.

But Wing's collection also illustrates a problem that is emerging with this methodology, a problem that has also been widely discussed by contemporary feminist theorists: the tension between universal human rights and the cultural integrity of particular women. Part 4 of Wing's collection is entitled 'Human Rights Confronts Culture, Custom and Religion'. The articles in this section contrast the cultural integrity of women in traditional societies with the impetus for universal human rights. The question these articles address is whether feminists should respect the cultural integrity of women throughout the world or protest the subordination and even mutilation of women by appealing to universal human rights. Several prominent feminist theorists, most notably Martha Nussbaum (1999) and Susan Moller Okin (1999), have argued that we should not, on the grounds of cultural integrity, unquestioningly accept cultural traditions that are harmful to women. They assert that an appeal to universal human rights is necessary to combat the subordination of women in many cultures.

This is a difficult problem that has no easy solution. The contextual methodology of contemporary feminist researchers inclines them to accept cultural traditions without scrutiny. The result of this approach, however, is that it leaves in place traditions that subordinate and even harm women. This is a consequence that many feminists find unacceptable. Opposing these traditions, however, seems to entail a reversion to the ethnocentrism that contemporary feminist methodologists are seeking to avoid. At this point in the debate no one has proposed a solution to this problem that has gained wide acceptance.

The second question at the forefront of contemporary discussions in feminist methodology is the issue of the status of knowledge and truth claims. From the outset, feminist methodologists have defined their method as oppositional, challenging the hegemonic discourse of positivism. Central to this challenge was rejecting positivism's claim to objective, value-free knowledge. As Dale Spender (1985: 5) put it, 'At the core of feminist ideas is the crucial insight that there is no one truth, no one authority, no one objective method that leads to the production of pure knowledge.' With the advent of postmodernism, this rejection of objective knowledge became even more pronounced. Postmodern feminists argued, with Nietzsche, that truth is a metaphor, a production of the discourse in which it is located.

As feminist methodologists pursued their research, however, they found that challenging the hegemonic scientific conception of knowledge and truth, although opening up a new paradigm, also had negative consequences. The social sciences take objective truth seriously. For feminists to claim that there is no objective knowledge and, thus, that feminist research, like all research, does not produce valid truth effectively marginalizes feminist research within the social sciences. If feminists want their research to count, to be taken seriously by the communities in which they are located, then they must make some claim to produce valid knowledge. This situation creates a dilemma for feminist methodology and theory. Donna Haraway describes this dilemma through the metaphor of the greased pole. Doing feminist research, Haraway claims, is like trying to climb a greased pole while holding on to both ends at the same time. The point of climbing the pole is to achieve valid knowledge. But the commitment to science is understood in the context of the belief that knowledge is socially constituted. This knowledge prevents feminists from ascending the pole (Haraway, 1991: 188; Ramazanoglu and Holland, 2004).

Feminists have attempted to deal with this dilemma in a number of ways. Some have argued that there is nothing inherently wrong with empiricism. This is not a widely held position, however; the feminist opposition to empiricism is too deeply rooted. Other feminist theorists have attempted to redefine empiricism in a way more congenial to feminism (Hekman, 1999: 56–66). Helen Longino (1990), for example, argues that we should explore how—not whether—values play a role in scientific research. While not abandoning the goal of objectivity, Longino argues that it should be redefined as the practice of the community. The result is what she calls 'contextual empiricism'. Lorraine Code (1991) takes a similar position in *What Can She Know?* Code's thesis is that we should reject the objective/subjective dichotomy that grounds empiricism and replace it with a conception of knowledge that is perspectival and situated.

Lynn Hankinson Nelson is also concerned to save empiricism for feminist methodology.

In *Who Knows?* (1990) Nelson argues that, at root, we are all empiricists: we live in a commonsense world in which we expect events to occur in a regular way. Her thesis is that this commonsense world and the world of science are connected: the empiricism of science is not a foreign language divorced from the language of everyday life. Relying on the work of Quine, Nelson argues that although there is no pre-theoretical view of the world, the world 'matters': it is a factor in scientific analysis. Nelson argues for an understanding of knowledge as community-based rather than individual. This allows her to embrace an empiricism for feminist research that produces knowledge about a 'real' world.

Sandra Harding's (1991) attempt to redefine scientific truth and objectivity takes a different tack. Harding focuses her attention on the pillar of scientific knowledge: objectivity. Her thesis (Harding, 2004: 55) is that the objectivity of empiricism is too weak; it does not take account of the whole of the scientific situation. Specifically it ignores the historical values that shape scientific inquiry. As a counter Harding proposes what she calls 'strong objectivity'. Strong objectivity recognizes the social situatedness of all knowledge. It further recognizes that some social situations are capable of generating more objective accounts than others. Harding's thesis is that the socially situated grounds and subjects of standpoint epistemologies require us to generate stronger standards for objectivity than do those that fail to provide systemic methods for locating knowledge in history (Harding, 2004: 40). In sum, starting research from women's lives will generate more objective knowledge.

All these attempts to rescue some version of empiricism for feminist methodology can be characterized in terms of Haraway's greased pole. The problem is that once we acknowledge that knowledge is socially constituted, it appears that any claim to objective, true, knowledge is suspect. This is a problem not only for feminist methodology but for science studies in general. The literature on social studies of science is similarly concerned with the question of how, in Nelson's sense, to make the world matter. In the case of feminist methodology, however, there is another aspect to this problem that is unique to feminism. Feminist theorists have argued that if we go too far in the direction of the linguistic constitution of the world we will lose the real women in the world who are experiencing real pain. If everything is, as the postmoderns claim, discourse, then how can we talk about the pain that women experience, the pain that we, as feminists, seek to eradicate? There has been an intense debate between two prominent feminist theorists, Judith Butler (1993) and Susan Bordo (1993) on precisely this issue. Butler argues that looking to language can adequately assess the situation of women in the 'real' world. Bordo argues that we must keep our focus on women's bodies and their pain and that this entails that we look beyond the linguistic.

One of the most intriguing and promising attempts to 'make the world matter' is found in the work of a feminist physicist, Karen Barad. She argues that the loss of the material element implicit in postmodernism and poststructuralism is unacceptable for feminist theory and practice. She proposes as an alternative, which she calls 'agential realism', a position that gives an account of materiality as an active, productive factor in its own right (Barad, 2001: 77). Barad's thesis is that different theories give agency to different aspects of matter; matter becomes agential through theory. Her agential realism privileges neither the material nor the cultural but, rather, posits that the apparatus of bodily production is material-cultural and so is agential reality (Barad, 1996: 180). In other words, our constructed knowledge has real, material consequences. The realism that Barad proposes 'is not about representations of an independent reality, but about the real consequences, interventions, creative possibilities, and responsibilities of intra-acting within the world' (Barad, 1996: 188).

Barad's most striking example of agential realism is her discussion of the practice of analyzing fetuses with ultrasound devices (1998). Her point is that the ultrasound machine gives agency to the fetus at a very early point in its development. Before the development of ultrasound technology the fetus was not visible (agentic) at this point. Barad's agential realism leads her to the conclusion that aspects of matter, in this case the fetus, became agentic through the interaction of the material-discursive practices of the ultrasound machine. The profound material and legal consequences of this practice should be obvious. Barad's point is that this practice cannot be understood as purely material nor purely social/cultural but rather as a result of the complex interaction between the two forces. What Barad's theory leads us to is an understanding of knowledge as the interaction of the social/cultural and the material, not as one or the other.

The effort on the part of contemporary feminist theorists to 'bring the world back in' is significant. It constitutes a recognition that the direction of much contemporary feminist research requires a course correction. Feminist methodology has its roots in the critique of positivism, a critique grounded in the insight that knowledge is socially constructed. But this insight has led many feminists, along with those engaged in the social studies of science, to posit a dichotomy between socially constructed and valid/objective knowledge. This dichotomy has produced an either/or situation: either knowledge is socially constructed or it is objective and true. What theorists such as Longino, Code, Harding, Nelson and Barad are arguing is that this is a false dichotomy. Their thesis is that knowledge is the result of the complex interaction between the material and the cultural, which are not, in themselves, neatly separable. The way out of this dilemma is not to abandon the insight that knowledge is socially constructed. Rather, it is to explore the material/cultural interaction that produces knowledge—to, as Barad puts it, meet the universe halfway. The next wave of feminist methodology will explore this possibility.

REFERENCES

Barad, Karen (1996) 'Meeting the universe halfway', in Lynn Hankinson Nelson and Jack Nelson (eds), *Feminism, Science, and the Philosophy of Science*. Dordrecht: Kluwer, pp. 161–94.

——— (1998) 'Getting real: Technoscientific practices and the materializations of reality', *differences: A Journal of Feminist Cultural Studies*, 10 (2): 87–128.
——— (2001) 'Reconfiguring space, time, and matter', in Mariane Dekoven (ed.), *Feminist Locations: Global and Local, Theory and Practice*. New Brunswick, NJ: Rutgers University Press, pp. 75–109.
Barnes, Barry (1974) *Scientific Knowledge and Sociological Theory*. London: Routledge and Kegan Paul.
Bloor, David (1976) *Knowledge and Social Imagery*. London: Routledge and Kegan Paul.
Bordo, Susan (1993) *Unbearable Weight*. Berkeley: University of California Press.
Butler, Judith (1993) *Bodies That Matter*. New York: Routledge.
Code, Lorraine (1991) *What Can She Know? Feminist Theory and the Construction of Knowledge*. Ithaca, NY: Cornell University Press.
Collins, Patricia (1990) *Black Feminist Thought*. Boston: Unwin Hyman.
Fonow, Mary and Cook, Judith (eds) (1991) *Beyond Methodology: Feminist Scholarship as Lived Research*. Bloomington: Indiana University Press.
Gadamer, Hans-Georg (1975) *Truth and Method*. New York: Continuum.
Haraway, Donna (1989) *Primate Visions: Gender, Race, and Nature in the World of Modern Science*. New York: Routledge.
——— (1991) *Simians, Cyborgs, and Women: The Reinvention of Nature*. New York: Routledge.
Harding, Sandra (1986) *The Science Question in Feminism*. Ithaca, NY: Cornell University Press.
——— (ed.) (1987) *Feminism and Methodology*. Bloomington: Indiana University Press.
——— (1991) *Whose Science? Whose Knowledge? Thinking from Women's Lives*. Ithaca, NY: Cornell University Press.
——— (2004) 'Rethinking standpoint epistemology', in Sharlene Hesse-Biber and Michelle Yaiser (eds), *Feminist Perspectives on Social Research*. New York: Oxford, pp. 39–64.
Hekman, Susan (1990) *Gender and Knowledge*. Cambridge: Polity Press.
——— (1999) *The Future of Differences: Truth and Method in Feminist Theory*. Cambridge: Polity Press.
Hesse, Mary (1980) *Revolutions and Reconstructions in the Philosophy of Science*. Bloomington: Indiana University Press.
Jayaratne, Tody and Stewart, Abigail (1991) 'Quantitative and qualitative methods in the social sciences', in Mary Fonow and Judith Cook (eds), *Beyond Methodology*. Bloomington, IN: Indiana University Press, pp. 85–106.

Keller, Evelyn Fox (1983) *A Feeling for the Organism.* New York: W.H. Freeman.

Kelly-Gadol, Joan (1987) 'The social relation of the sexes: Methodological implications of women's history', in Sandra Harding (ed.), *Feminism and Methodology.* Bloomington: Indiana University Press, pp. 15–28.

Longino, Helen (1990) *Science as Social Knowledge.* Princeton, NJ: Princeton University Press.

Millman, Marcia and Kantor, Rosabeth Moss (eds) (1975) *Another Voice: Feminist Perspectives on Social Life and Social Science.* New York: Anchor Books.

Mohanty, Chandra (1984) 'Under western eyes: Feminist scholarship and colonial discourse', *Boundary 2,* 22 (3), 23(1): 333–58.

Nelson, Lynn Hankinson (1990) *Who Knows? From Quine to a Feminist Empiricism.* Philadelphia: Temple University Press.

Nussbaum, Martha (1999) *Sex and Social Justice.* New York: Oxford University Press.

Okin, Susan Moller (1999) *Is Multiculturalism Bad for Women?* Princeton, NJ: Princeton University Press.

Ramazanoglu, Caroline and Holland, Janet (2004) *Feminist Methodology: Challenges and Choices.* London: Sage.

Reinharz, Shulamit (1992) *Feminist Methods in Social Research.* New York: Oxford University Press.

Smith, Dorothy (1987) 'Women's perspective as a radical critique of sociology', in Sandra Harding (ed.), *Feminism and Methodology.* Bloomington, IN: Indiana University Press, pp. 84–96.

Spender, Dale (1985) *For the Record: The Meaning and Making of Feminist Knowledge.* London: Women's Press.

Wing, Adrien Katherine (ed.) (2000) *Global Critical Race Feminism: An International Reader.* New York: New York University Press.

Woolf, Virginia (1984) 'Three Guineas', in *A Room of One's Own and Three Guineas.* London: Chatto and Windus, pp. 107–310.

30

Feminist Methodology and Its Discontents[1]

Nancy A. Naples

INTRODUCTION

Over fifteen years ago, feminist philosopher Sandra Harding asked: 'Is There a Distinctive Feminist Method of Inquiry?' In answering the question, she distinguished between epistemology ('a theory of knowledge'), methodology ('a theory and analysis of how research does or should proceed') and method ('a technique for . . . gathering evidence') (Harding, 1987: 2–3). She pointed out the 'important connections between epistemologies, methodologies, and research methods' (Harding, 1987:3). Following Harding, I start with the assertion that the specific methods we choose and how we employ those methods are profoundly shaped by our epistemological stance. Our epistemological assumptions also influence how we define our roles as researchers, what we consider ethical research practices, and how we interpret and implement informed consent or ensure the confidentiality of our research subjects. The goal of this chapter is to highlight the ways in which different feminist epistemologies guide the choice of different methodologies and to illustrate how feminists implement particular methods. Due primarily to my own epistemological stance, I feature feminist standpoint, materialist feminist and postmodern epistemological approaches.

HISTORICAL BACKGROUND

Feminist methodology is the approach to research that has been developed in response to concerns by feminist scholars about the limits of traditional methodology in capturing the experiences of women and others who have been marginalized in academic research. Some of the earliest writing on feminist methodology emphasized the connection between 'feminist consciousness and feminist research', which is the sub-title of a 1983 edited collection by Liz Stanley and Sue Wise. Over the years, feminist methodology has developed a very broad vision of research practice that can be used to study a wide range of topics, to analyze both men and women's lives, and to explore both local and transnational or global processes.

Feminist methodology includes a wide range of methods, approaches and research strategies. Beginning in the early 1970s, feminist scholars critiqued positivist scientific methods that reduced lived experiences to a series of disconnected variables that did not do justice to the complexities of social life. Feminist sociologists like Dorothy Smith (1987) pointed out that the taken-for-granted research practices associated with positivism rendered invisible or domesticated women's work as well as their everyday lives. She argued for a sociology for women that would begin in their everyday lives.

Feminist philosopher Sandra Harding (1987; 1998) has also written extensively about the limits of positivism and argues for an approach to knowledge production that incorporates the point of view of feminist and postcolonial theoretical and political concerns. She stresses that traditional approaches to science fail to acknowledge how the social context and perspectives of those who generate the questions, conduct the research and interpret the findings shape what counts as knowledge and how data are interpreted. Instead, she argues for a holistic approach that includes greater attention to the knowledge production process and to the role of the researcher. Harding and Smith both critique the androcentric nature of academic knowledge production. They argue for the importance of starting analysis from the lived experiences and activities of women and others who have been left out of the knowledge-production process rather than starting inquiry with the abstract categories and a priori assumptions of traditional academic disciplines or dominant social institutions.

During the 1970s and 1980s feminists operating from different epistemological traditions, including liberal feminism, radical feminism, lesbian feminism, black and Latina feminisms, and Marxist and socialist feminisms, contributed to a diverse and expanding body of literature that challenged androcentric, classist and racist assumptions in fields as diverse as family studies, labor studies, politics and science. Feminists were among the first scholars to highlight the marginalization of women of color in academic research and to offer research strategies that would counter this trend within academia (Baca Zinn, 1979; Collins, 1990). More recently, feminist scholars have stressed the importance of intersectional analysis, an approach that highlights the intersection of race, class, gender and sexuality in examining women's lives (Crenshaw, 1993), and, influenced by the so-called postmodern turn in the academy, have pointed out the fluidity of gender identities and the importance of discourse for shaping constructions of masculinities, femininities and sexualities.

Following a comprehensive review of feminist research, Shulamit Reinharz (1992) identified ten features that appear in efforts by feminist scholars to distinguish how their research methods differ from traditional approaches. These include the following: (1) feminism is a point a view, not a particular method; (2) feminist methodology consists of multiple methods; (3) feminist researchers offer a self-reflexive understanding of their role in the research; and (4) a central goal of feminist research is to contribute to social changes that would improve women's lives. The themes of reflexivity and research for social change are two of the most important aspects of feminist methodology that distinguish it from other modes of research.

A year earlier, sociologists Mary Margaret Fonow and Judith A. Cook published a collection of essays in a book titled *Beyond Methodology: Feminist Scholarship as Lived Research* (1991), which illustrated how different methodological techniques could be used to capture the complexities of gender as it intersects with race, sexuality and class. The authors also explored the ethical dilemmas faced by feminist researchers: How does a researcher negotiate power imbalance between the researcher and researched? What responsibilities do researchers have to those they study? How does participatory research influence analytic choices during a research study? Feminist scholars have consistently raised such questions, suggesting that if researchers fail to explore how their personal, professional and structural positions frame social-scientific investigations, researchers inevitably reproduce dominant gender, race and class biases.

In 2005, Fonow and Cook revisited the themes that were prevalent when they wrote *Beyond Methodology* and highlighted the continuity and differences in the themes that dominate discussions of feminist methodology at the beginning of the twenty-first century. They found that the reflexivity of the researcher, transparency of the research process and women's empowerment remained central concerns in contemporary feminist methodology. They also point out the continuity in the multiple methods that are utilized by feminist researchers that include participatory research, ethnography, discourse analysis, comparative case study, cross-culture analysis, conversation analysis, oral history, participant observation and personal narrative. However, Fonow and Cook (2005) note, contemporary feminist researchers are more likely to use sophisticated quantitative methods than they were in the 1980s and 1990s.

THEORIZING FROM EXPERIENCE: STANDPOINT EPISTEMOLOGY AND FEMINIST METHODOLOGY

One of the most persistent and controversial approaches to feminist methodology is offered by feminist standpoint theorists who assert a link between the development of standpoint theory and feminist political goals of transformative social, political and economic change. From the perspective of feminist praxis, standpoint epistemology provides a methodological resource for explicating how relations of domination contour women's everyday lives. With this knowledge, women and others whose lives are shaped by systems of inequality can act to challenge these processes and systems (Weeks, 1998: 92).

Feminist standpoint theory developed in the context of third-world and postcolonial feminist challenges to the so-called dual systems of patriarchy and capitalism approach that was associated with socialist feminist theory. The dual systems approach was an attempt to merge feminist analyses of patriarchy and Marxist analyses of class to create a more complex socialist feminist theory of women's oppression. Critics of the dual systems approach pointed out the lack of attention paid by socialist feminist analyses to racism, white supremacy and colonialism. In contrast, feminist standpoint theory offers an intersectional analysis of gender, race, ethnicity, class and other social structural aspects of social life, without privileging one dimension or adopting an additive formulation (for example, gender plus race).

Broadly defined, feminist standpoint epistemology includes Nancy Hartsock's (1983) 'feminist historical materialist' perspective, Donna Haraway's (1988) analysis of 'situated knowledges', Patricia Hill Collins's (1990) 'black feminist thought', Chéla Sandoval's (2000) explication of third world feminists'[2] 'differential oppositional consciousness',[3] and Dorothy Smith's (1987, 1990a, 1990b) 'everyday world' sociology for women. Standpoint epistemology, especially as articulated by Hartsock (1983: 117), draws on Marxist historical materialism for the argument that 'epistemology grows in a complex and contradictory way from material life'. In reworking Marx's historical materialism from a feminist perspective, standpoint theorists' stated goal is to explicate how relations of domination are gendered in particular ways. Contemporary approaches to standpoint theory retain elements of Marxist historical materialism for their central premise, namely, that knowledge develops in a complicated and contradictory way from lived experiences and social historical context.

By arguing for the development of multiple standpoints that derive from what she terms the 'matrix of domination', Collins's approach to standpoint epistemology evokes Donna Haraway's notion of 'situated knowledges'. Collins reaffirms her standpoint analysis of Black feminist thought as follows:

In developing a Black feminist praxis, standpoint theory has provided one important source of analytical guidance and intellectual legitimation for African-American women. Standpoint theory argues that group location in hierarchical power relations produces shared challenges for individuals in those groups. These common challenges can foster similar angles of vision leading to a group knowledge or standpoint that in turn can influence the group's political action. Stated differently, group standpoints are situated in unjust power relations, reflect those power relations, and help shape them. (Collins, 1990: 201)

She also stresses the importance of *praxis*—the interaction of knowledge and experience—for Black feminist thought. Collins's work, in particular, has influenced Nancy Hartsock to revise her earlier formulation to account for 'multiple subjectivities', although critics like Katie King (1994: 87) continue to find that Hartsock's approach lacks an 'understanding of the shifting, tactical, and mobile character of subjectivities' found in work by Chéla Sandoval and others influenced by postmodern perspectives.

From the perspective of feminist praxis, standpoint epistemology provides a methodological resource for explicating 'how subjects are constituted by social systems' as well as 'how collective subjects are relatively autonomous from, and capable of acting to subvert, those same systems' (Weeks, 1998: 92). However, standpoint theorists utilize different constructions of 'standpoint'. From my review of the diverse approaches to feminist standpoint epistemology, I identified several major connections among them, as well as some important differences. One of the most salient themes that links the different perspectives on standpoint theorizing is the connection to the women's movement's method of consciousness raising. Consciousness Raising (CR) was a strategy of knowledge development designed during the late 1960s and early 1970s to help support and generate women's political activism. By sharing their individual-level experiences of oppression, women recognized that their experiences were shaped by social structural factors. The CR process assumed that problems associated with women's oppression needed political

solutions and that women acting collectively are able to identify and analyze these processes (Fisher, 2001). The CR group process enabled women to share their experiences, identify and analyze the social and political mechanisms by which women are oppressed, and develop strategies for social change.

The second significant theme is the assertion of a link between the development of standpoint theory and feminist political goals. In Harding's (1986: 26) formulation of this connection, 'feminism and the women's movement provide the theory and motivation for inquiry and political struggle that can transform the perspective of women into a "standpoint"—a morally and scientifically preferable grounding for our interpretations and explanations of nature and social life.'

A related theme that links different standpoint perspectives is the emphasis on the importance of experience for feminist theorizing and feminist research. Feminist ethnographers who begin analyses from women's diverse social locations have 'contributed significantly to reconceptualization of sociological categories—especially, "politics," "work," and "family"—typically used to analyze social life' (Naples, 1998a: 3). In my research with urban community workers hired by the War on Poverty, I analyzed the extent to which women's militancy has been masked by the traditional categories used to assess political action. Since much of the women's community activism occurred outside the formal political establishment, traditional measures of political participation would have underestimated their political work. My analysis of the community workers' oral histories revealed

a broad-based notion of "doing politics" that included any struggle to gain control over definitions of self and community, to augment personal and communal empowerment, to create alternative institutions and organizational processes, and to increase the power and resources of the community workers' defined community—although not all of these practices were viewed as "politics" in the community workers' terminology' (Naples, 1998b: 179).

I conceptualized their community work as 'activist mothering', which I defined as 'political activism as a central component of mothering and community caretaking of those who are not part of one's defined household or family' (1998b: 11). This analysis offered 'a new conceptualization of the interacting nature of labor, politics and mothering—three aspects of social life usually analyzed separately—from the point of view of women whose motherwork historically has been ignored or pathologized in sociological analyses' (Naples, 1998b: 112–13).

Mareena Wright also uses standpoint analysis of rural women's everyday experiences to reconceptualize models of work that are limited by the separation of unpaid household labor from paid labor. She develops a 'multidimensional continuum model of women's work' (Wright, 1995: 216) that 'contradicts old [dual spheres] notions that household work is somehow different or less significant to society than is waged work' (Wright, 1995: 232). By moving beyond the dual spheres model, Wright's multidimensional continuum model 'changes the way we perceive a number of issues' (Wright, 1995: 232) such as women's labor decision-making processes, women's life-course patterns, and our current social policies, especially those regarding the care of children and the elderly. Virginia Seitz also draws on standpoint theory for her examination of white, working-class Appalachian women's understanding and practice of class struggle. Seitz (1998: 213) examines how women from southwestern Virginia successfully 'challenged the coal company, the state, and, eventually working-class men' and therefore contested taken-for-granted constructions of gender and working class politics. As she emphasizes, however, 'sharing the same ... set of experiences does not necessarily translate into shared political analyses, organizational strategies, and leadership style' (Seitz, 1998: 213). In illuminating the 'powerful ways in which these women drew upon their gender, class, and racialized ethnicity as "Appalachians" to help wage a successful strike against the powerful Pittston Coal Company,' Seitz (1998: 213) illustrates the partiality of standpoints as they intersect in and through different women's political understandings and self-expression.

Feminist ethnographers emphasize the significance of locating and analyzing particular standpoints in differing contexts to explicate relations of domination embedded in communities and social institutions. Many studies of community development tend to rely on influential or powerful 'key informants'. Although community leaders provide particular insights, feminist standpoint ethnographers, following a feminist standpoint perspective, can deepen understanding of the problems of, as well as solutions to, a particular community's economic concerns by analyzing the perspectives and experiences of women and other marginalized groups. For example, Christina Gringeri (1994), in her examination of rural development from the diverse perspectives of women home-workers and rural development officials in two Midwestern communities, helps explain how rural development strategies are perceived differently by planners and by those who pay the costs of development (see also Naples, 1997).

Even when they do not directly evoke standpoint epistemology in their work, feminist ethnographers such as Lila Abu-Lughod (1993), Ruth Behar (1993), Sondra Hale (1991), Suad Joseph (1988), Dorrine Kondo (1990), Susan Krieger (1983) and Maria Mies (1982) demonstrate the value of *positionality* for developing strong self-reflexive research strategies as well as for ethnographic analysis. The concept of positionality foregrounds how women can strategically 'use their positional perspective as a place from where values are interpreted and constructed rather than as a locus of an already determined set of values' (Alcoff, 1988: 434). Reflexive practice informed by standpoint analyses of positionality encourages feminist scholars to examine how gendered and racialized assumptions influence which voices and experiences are privileged in ethnographic encounters. Since the conceptualization of 'standpoint' has multiple meanings, depending on which aspect of standpoint epistemology is referenced, I prefer the term positionality when referring to subjectivity and subjective knowledges. The notion of positionality provides a conceptual frame which allows one to 'say at one and the same time that gender is not natural, biological, universal, ahistorical, or essential and yet still claim that gender is relevant because we are taking gender as a position from which to act politically' (Alcoff, 1988: 433). The 'position' from which one acts politically is also subject to investigation. A sensitivity to positionality in feminist research requires reflexive practice. In the next section I discuss the processes of reflexivity and feminist approaches to objectivity.

REFLEXIVITY AND STRONG OBJECTIVITY

Reflexive practice includes an array of strategies that begin when one first considers conducting a research project. Reflexive practices can be employed throughout the research process and implemented on different levels, ranging from remaining sensitive to the perspectives of others and how we interact with them to a deeper recognition of the power dynamics that infuse ethnographic encounters. By adopting reflexive strategies, feminist researchers work to reveal the inequalities and processes of domination that shape the research process. Diane Wolf (1996) emphasizes that power is evident in the research process in three ways: first, the differences in power between the researcher and those she or he researches in terms of race, class and nationality, among other dimensions; second, the power to define the relationship and the potential to exploit those who are the subjects of the research; and third, the power to construct the written account and therefore shape how research subjects are represented in the text.

Feminist researchers argue that dynamics of power influence how problems are defined, which knowers are identified and given credibility, how interactions are interpreted, and how ethnographic narratives are constructed. Feminist researchers stress that if researchers fail to explore how their personal, professional and structural positions frame social scientific investigations, researchers inevitably reproduce dominant gender, race and class biases.

For example, while feminist researchers who draw on positive or interpretive[4] theoretical traditions might utilize a methodology that generates oral narratives or ethnographic data, what counts as data and how these data are interpreted and reported will vary significantly depending on the specific epistemological stance undergirding the research process. Since there are diverse feminist perspectives, it follows that there are different ways feminist researchers identify, analyze and report 'data'.

How one defines the nature of the relationship between researcher and researched also depends on one's epistemological stance. Of course, a researcher does not have complete autonomy in shaping relations with subjects of his or her research. Research subjects have the power to influence the direction of the research, resist researchers' efforts and interpretations, and add their own interpretations and insights. As Leslie Bloom (1998: 35) observes: 'The idea that the researcher has "The Power" over the participant [in a research study] is an authoritative, binary discourse that may function to disguise the ways that "the flow of power in multiple systems of domination is not always unidirectional" (Friedman, 1995: 18).' This point has been well established in the field of anthropology where over the last 20 years ethnographers have grappled with the intersection of representation, subjectivity and power in the practice of ethnography.[5]

Third-world and postcolonial feminist scholars call on scholars to reflect on their research and writing practices in light of political, moral and ethical questions that arise from the inherent power imbalances between many ethnographers and those they study. Feminist ethnographers have responded to these challenges by examining how certain cultural representations in ethnographic accounts contribute to colonialist practices and further marginalize the lives of third-world and other non-white peoples, even as they are brought to the center of analysis (see Hurtado, 1996). However, some of the strategies utilized by feminist ethnographers, such as attempting to develop more intimacy and egalitarian relationships between subjects of research and themselves, have led to the recognition of other dilemmas in fieldwork. Tamar El-Or, who is Lecturer of Sociology and Anthropology at the Hebrew University in Jerusalem, conducted research among those living in Gur Hassidim, a suburb of Tel Aviv close to her home. She describes how intimacy between researchers and informants can mask the objectification of the researched. Writing from a postmodern frame, El-Or (1997: 188) states:

> Intimacy thus offers a cozy environment for the ethnographic journey, but at the same time an illusive one. The ethnographer wants information, this information happens to be someone else's real life. The informant's willingness to cooperate with the ethnographer might arise from different motivations, but it usually ends when the informant feels that he/she has become an object for someone else's interests. So it seems that intimacy and working relationships (if not under force or fallacy) go in opposite directions.

She concludes her analysis with the following statement about her post-fieldwork relationship with Hanna, one of her key informants: 'We can't be friends because she was my object and we both know it' (El-Or, 1997: 188).

Sociologist Judith Stacey argues that the appearance of friendship with subjects in ethnographic research could result in greater exploitation than in other approaches: 'For no matter how welcome, even enjoyable, the field-worker's presence may appear to "natives," fieldwork represents an intrusion and intervention into a system of relationships, a system of relationships that the researcher is far freer than the researched to leave' (Stacey, 1991: 113). Stacey suggests that 'the postmodern ethnographic solution to the anthropologist's predicament is to acknowledge fully the limitations of ethnographic process and product and to reduce

their claims' (Stacey, 1991: 115). She draws on James Clifford's analysis to emphasize the limits of ethnographic research: 'Ethnographic truths are thus inherently *partial* — committed and incomplete' (Clifford, 1986: 7; quoted in Stacey, 1991: 116; emphasis is Clifford). She points out, however, that postmodern strategies cannot counter feminist concerns about the 'inherently unequal reciprocity with informants; nor can it resolve the feminist reporting quandaries' (Stacey, 1991: 117).

Feminist ethnography and feminist work with narratives are two of the methods in which feminist researchers have been the most concerned with processes of reflexivity. Susan Chase's (1995) approach to oral narratives includes attention to the way women narrate their stories. Rather than treat the narratives as 'evidence' in an unmediated sense of the term, Chase is interested in exploring the relationship between culture, experience and narrative. In her work on women school superintendents she examines how women use narrative strategies to make sense of their everyday life experiences as shaped by different cultural contexts. Leslie Bloom adopts a 'progressive-regressive method' derived from Sartre's notion of 'spirals' in a life to examine how the individual can overcome her or his social and cultural conditioning, 'thereby manifesting what Sartre calls "positive praxis"' (Bloom, 1998: 65).

Drawing on Dorothy Smith's institutional ethnographic method, Marjorie DeVault (1999) utilizes narratives she generates from ethnographic interviews to explore how 'relations of ruling' are woven into women's everyday lives such that they are hidden from the view of those whose lives are organized by these processes of domination. The institutional and political knowledges that DeVault uncovers illustrate the link between institutional ethnography and feminist activism. In the context of activist research, feminist analysts using Smith's approach explore the institutional forms and procedures, and informal organizational processes, as well as discursive frames used to construct the goals and targets of the work that the institution performs. This approach ensures that a commitment to the political goals of the women's movement remains central to feminist research by foregrounding how ruling relations work to organize everyday life. With a 'thick' understanding of 'how things are put together', it becomes possible to identify effective activist interventions.

One example of this point is found in Ellen Pence's (1996) work to create an assessment of how safe battered women remain after they report abuse to the police. Pence draws specifically on Smith's (1987: 1990a) institutional ethnographic approach[6] to shift the standpoint on the process of law enforcement to the women whom the law attempts to protect and to those who are charged with protecting them. Pence developed a safety audit to identify ways criminal justice and law enforcement policies and practices can be enhanced to ensure the safety of women and to ensure the accountability of the offender. Pence's safety audit has been used by police departments, criminal justice and probation departments, and family law clinics in diverse settings across the country. Pence asserts that her approach is not an evaluation of individual workers' performances but an examination of how the institution or system is set up to manage domestic violence cases.

Harding (1986), whose approach to standpoint analysis differs from Smith's, argues for a self-reflexive approach to theorizing in order to foreground how relations of power may be shaping the production of knowledge in different contexts. The point of view of all those involved in the knowledge-production process must be acknowledged and taken into account in order to produce what she terms 'strong objectivity', an approach to objectivity that contrasts with weaker and unreflexive positivist approaches. In this way, knowledge production should involve a collective process, rather than the individualistic, top-down and distanced approach that typifies the traditional scientific method. For Harding (1991), strong objectivity involves analysis of the relationship between the subject and object of inquiry. This approach contrasts with the traditional scientific method that either denies this relationship or seeks to

achieve control over it. However, as Harding and other feminist theorists point out, an approach to research that produces a more objective approach acknowledges the partial and situated nature of all knowledge production (also see Collins, 1990). Although not a complete solution to challenging inequalities in the research process, feminist researchers have used reflexive strategies effectively to become aware of, and diminish, the ways in which domination and repression are reproduced in the course of their research and in the products of their work. Furthermore, feminist researchers argue, sustained attention to these dynamics can enrich research accounts as well as improve the practice of social research (Naples, 2003).

A scholar who approaches the research process from the point of view of strong objectivity is interested in producing knowledge for use as well as for revealing the relations of power that are hidden in traditional knowledge-production processes. Strong objectivity acknowledges that the production of power is a political process and that greater attention paid to the context and social location of knowledge producers will contribute to a more ethical and transparent result. In fact, Harding (1991) argues that an approach to research and knowledge production that does not acknowledge the role that power and social location play in the knowledge production process must be understood as offering only a weak form of objectivity.

Another aspect of traditional approaches to science and knowledge production that contributes to a weak form of objectivity is found in the move to greater and greater generalization. As a result, material reality is replaced with abstractions that bear little resemblance to the phenomenon originally under examination. Smith (1987) explains that the traditional androcentric approach to sociology that privileges a white, middle-class and heterosexual point of view produces results that are both alienating and colonizing. Harding (1998) has been especially concerned with the role of colonization in marginalizing the situated knowledges of the targets of colonization. Western science has developed through the exploitation and silencing of colonial subjects. In this way, much useful knowledge has been lost or rendered suspect (see Sachs, 1996). Strong objectivity involves acknowledging the political, social, and historical aspects of all knowledge (Longino, 1990). The strongest approach to knowledge production is one that takes into account the most diverse set of experiences.

Postmodern critics of Harding's approach point out that the goal of producing a strong objectivity replicates the limitations of traditional scientific methods, namely, privileging one or more account as most 'accurate' or true (Hekman, 1997). Postmodern theorists stress that all social positions are fluid. Such fluidity makes it impossible to identify individual knowers who can represent any particular social group. Furthermore, they insist, the search for truth, even one that is partial, is fraught with the risk of marginalizing other accounts. However, those who adopt the stance of strong objectivity argue that it can avoid the 'arrogant aspirations of modernist epistemology' (Longino, 1993: 212). While feminist standpoint epistemologies offer powerful tools for exploring the relations of ruling in everyday life, the power of feminist standpoint methodology can be enhanced by incorporating insights from postmodern and postcolonial perspectives on power, subjectivity and language.

POSTMODERN AND POSTCOLONIAL CHALLENGES TO FEMINIST METHODOLOGY

Postmodern critiques of the practice of social-scientific research raise a number of dilemmas that challenge feminist researchers as they attempt to conduct research that makes self-evident the assumptions and politics involved in the process of knowledge production in order to avoid exploitative research practices (see, for example, Barrett and Phillips, 1992). Postmodern scholars emphasize the ways in which disciplinary discourses shape how researchers see the worlds they investigate. They point out that without recognition of disciplinary metanarratives, research operates to re-insert power relations rather than challenge them.

Many feminist researchers have grappled with the challenges posed by postmodern critics. D. Wolf (1996) explains that some feminist scholars' postmodern theories provide opportunities for innovation in research practices, particularly in the attention they pay to representation of research participants or research subjects and to the written products that are produced from a research study. However, many other feminist scholars are concerned that too much emphasis on the linguistic and textual constructions decenters those who are the subjects of our research and renders irrelevant the lives of women or others whom we study.

For example, rural sociologist Carolyn Sachs (1996: 19) fears that a postmodern emphasis on 'fractured identities' and 'the multitude of subjectivities' could lead to 'total relativism' that precludes political activism. Women's Studies scholars Jacqui Alexander and Chandra Mohanty express concern that

> postmodern theory, in its haste to dissociate itself from all forms of essentialism, has generated a series of epistemological confusions regarding the interconnections between location, identity, and the construction of knowledge. Thus, for instance, localized questions of experience, identity, culture, and history, which enable us to understand specific processes of domination and subordination, are often dismissed by postmodern theories as reiterations of cultural 'essence' or unified, stable identity. (Alexander and Mohanty, 1997: xvii)

Concerns about the depoliticizing consequences of postmodern theories are a consistent thread in feminist debates on the value of postmodernist theories for feminist praxis. For example, anthropologist Margery Wolf (1996: 215) is concerned that feminist ethnographers 'are letting interesting critical positions from outside feminism weaken our confidence in our work; perhaps we are taking too seriously the criticisms of our process by those who have never experienced it.'

Postmodern analyses of power have destabilized the practice of research, especially research that involves human subjects. If power infects every encounter and if discourse infuses all expressions of personal experience, what can the researcher do to counter such powerful forces? This dilemma is at the heart of a radical postmodern challenge to social-scientific practice in general, but has been taken up most seriously in feminist research. While postcolonial feminist scholars also point to the myriad ways in which relations of domination infuse feminist research, they offer some guidance for negotiating the power relations inherent in the practice of fieldwork. Mohanty (1991) calls for 'careful, politically focused, local analyses' to counter the trend in feminist scholarship to distance from or misrepresent third-world women's concerns.[7] She draws on Maria Mies's (1982) work on lace makers in Narsapur, India, to illustrate this ethnographic approach:

> Mies's analysis shows the effect of a certain historically and culturally specific mode of patriarchal organization, an organization constructed on the basis of the definition of the lace makers as 'nonworking housewives' at familial, local, regional, statewide, and international levels. The intricacies and the effects of particular power networks not only are emphasized, but they form the basis of Mies's analysis of how this particular group of women is situated at the center of a hegemonic, exploitative world market. (Mohanty, 1991: 65)

Furthermore, Mohanty (1991: 65) remarks, 'Narsapur women are not mere victims of the production process. Instead, they resist, challenge, and subvert the process at various junctures.' Despite the valuable efforts of ethnographic researchers such as Mies to produce more balanced accounts of third-world women, some postcolonial critics fear that 'a "non-colonialist" (and therefore non contaminated?) space remains a wish-fulfillment within postcolonial knowledge production' (Rajan, 1993: 8). Alexander and Mohanty (1997: xix) recommend 'grounding analyses in particular, local feminist praxis' as well as understanding 'the local in relation to larger, cross-national processes'.

Many feminist postmodernists who offer alternative research strategies center textual or discursive modes of analysis. For example, following an assessment of the limits and possibilities of feminist standpoint epistemologies for generating what she calls a 'global social analytic', literary analyst Rosemary Hennessy (1993) posits 'critique' as materialist feminist 'reading practice', a way to recognize how consciousness is an ideological production. She argues that in this way it is possible to effectively resist the charge of essentialism that has been leveled against standpoint epistemology. In revaluing feminist standpoint theory for her method, she reconceptualizes feminist standpoint as a 'critical discursive practice'. Hennessy's methodological alternative effectively renders other methodological strategies outside the frame of materialist feminist scholarship.

However, even poststructural critics of feminist standpoint epistemology within the social sciences conclude their analyses with calls for discursive strategies. For example, Clough (1994: 179) calls for shifting the starting point of sociological investigation from experience or social activity to a 'social criticism of textuality and discursivity, mass media, communication technologies and science itself'. In contrast, standpoint epistemologies, especially Smith's (1990a) approach, offer a place to begin inquiry that envisions subjects of investigation who can experience aspects of life outside discourse. Feminist standpoint theorists like Smith tie their understanding of experience to the collective conversations of the women's movement that gave rise to understandings about women's lives which had no prior discursive existence. In this way, despite some important theoretical challenges, standpoint theory continues to offer feminist analysts a theoretical and methodological strategy that links the goals of the women's movement to the knowledge-production enterprise.

My own strategy for negotiating these challenges has been one of praxis, namely, to generate a *materialist feminist standpoint epistemology* that speaks to the empirical world in which my research takes place. In their introduction to *Materialist Feminism: A Reader in Class, Difference, and Women's Lives*, Rosemary Hennessy and Chrys Ingraham (1997: 7) describe materialist feminism as 'the conjuncture of several discourses—historical materialism, Marxist and radical feminism, as well as postmodern and psychoanalytic theories of meaning and subjectivity'. Materialist feminists view agency 'as complex and often contradictory sites of representation and struggle over power and resources' (Hesford, 1999: 74). Materialist feminist epistemology, as I reconstruct its intellectual history, has its roots in socialist feminist theories and has been particularly influenced by the theoretical critiques by African-American, Chicana and third-world feminists, who in turn contributed to the development of diverse feminist standpoint epistemologies as discussed above. For example, in the Introduction to *This Bridge Called My Back*, Moraga passionately ties the political consciousness of women of color to the material experiences of their lives. This 'politics of the flesh' (Moraga, 1981: xviii) does not privilege one dimension and artificially set it apart from the context in which it is lived, experienced, felt and resisted. In fact, literary scholar Paula Moya (1997: 150) argues that Moraga's 'theory in the flesh' provides a powerful 'non-essentialist way to ground ... identities' for the purposes of resistance to domination.[8]

Contemporary formulations of materialist feminism are also informed by Michel Foucault's analysis of discourse. For example, Sandoval argues that 'the theory and method of oppositional and differential consciousness is aligned with Foucault's concept of power, which emphasizes the figure of the very *possibility* of positioning power itself' (Sandoval, 2000: 77, emphasis in original).[9] Foucault is an unlikely resource for feminist praxis given two features of his work: his neglect of the dynamics of gender in his analysis of power and his displacement of the subject as a central agent for social change. However, Hennessy finds that 'Foucault's project *has* opened up productive avenues for developing materialist feminist theory'

(Hennessy, 1990: 254, emphasis in original). Using a Foucauldian articulation of power, education theorist Jennifer Gore analyzes power 'as exercised, rather than as possessed' (1992: 59). This approach, she argues, requires more attention to the microdynamics of the operation of power as it is expressed in specific sites.

I have also found in Foucault's approach to discourse a powerful methodological tool for materialist feminist analysis of US welfare policy and policies associated with community control (Naples, 2003). In addition, I utilized a materialist feminist discourse analysis to explore the social and institutional locations from which survivor discourse is generated and how relations of ruling are woven in and through it.[10] I address the construction of the term 'survivor', which is often used to refer to those who have experienced some sort of crime or abuse and who have redefined their relationship to the experience from one of 'victim'.[11] This redefinition can occur as a consequence of personal reformulation, psychotherapy, or in discussions with others who define themselves as survivors. I argue for the importance of locating survivors' discourse in the material sites through which it is produced by survivors of childhood sexual abuse and others. Processes of dialogue and consciousness raising remain central to the establishment of alternatives to the totalizing and depoliticized medical/psychiatric and recovery discourse on treatment of adult survivors. While I acknowledge the limits of rational deliberation for 'emancipatory' goals,[12] engagement with others in struggle can provide a strong basis for understanding the personal, political and collective possibilities for progressive social action.

RESEARCH FOR SOCIAL CHANGE

A consistent goal expressed by those who adopt feminist methodology, regardless of their epistemological stance, is to create knowledge for social change purposes. The emphasis on social action has influenced the type of methods utilized by feminist researchers as well as the topics chosen for study. For example, feminists have utilized participatory action research to help empower subjects of research as well as to ensure that the research is responsive to the needs of specific communities or to social movements (Fonow and Cook, 2005; Naples, 1998b; Reinharz, 1992). This approach to research is also designed to diminish the power differentials between the researcher and those who are the subjects of the research. In an effort to democratize the research process, many activist researchers argue for adopting participatory strategies that involve community residents or other participants in the design, implementation and analysis of the research. Collaborative writing also broadens the perspectives represented in the final product.

A wide array of research strategies and cultural products can serve this goal. Yet such strategies and cultural products can be of more or less immediate use for specific activist agendas. For example, activist research includes chronicling the history of activists, activist art, diverse community actions, and social movements. Such analyses are often conducted after the completion of a specific struggle or examine a wide range of different campaigns and activist organizations. This form of research on activism is extremely important for feminists working toward a broadened political vision of women's activism and can help generate new strategies for coalition building. These studies may not answer specific questions activists have about the value of certain strategies for their particular political struggles. Yet these broad-based feminist historical and sociological analyses do shed new light on processes of politicization, diversity and continuity in political struggles over time.

On the one hand, many activists could be critical of these apparently more 'academic' constructions of activism, especially since the need for specific knowledges to support activist agendas frequently goes unmet. The texts in which such analyses appear are often not widely available and further create a division between feminists located within the academy and community-based activists. On the other hand, many activist scholars have developed linkages with activists and policy arenas in such a way as to effectively bridge the so-called activist/scholar divide. Ronnie Steinberg (1996) brought her sociological research skills to campaigns for comparable worth and pay equity. She reports on the moderate success of the movement for comparable worth and the significance of careful statistical analyses for supporting changes in pay and job classifications. As one highlight, she reports that in 1991 systematic standards for assessing job equity developed with her associate Lois Haignere were translated into guidelines for gender-neutral policies incorporated by the Ontario Pay Equity Tribunal. In another example of feminist activist research, Roberta Spalter-Roth and Heidi Hartmann (1996) testified before Congress and produced policy briefs as well as more detailed academic articles to disseminate their findings about low-income women's economic survival strategies. Measures of a rigid positivism are often used to undermine feminists' credibility in legal and legislative settings. Even more problematic, research generated for specific activist goals may be misappropriated to support anti-feminist aims by those who do not share feminist political perspectives. For example, proponents of 'workfare' programs for women on public assistance could also use Spalter-Roth and Hartmann's analysis of welfare recipients' income packaging strategies to further justify coercive 'welfare to work' measures.

Some feminist scholars working directly in local community actions have also brought their academic skills to bear on specific community problems or have trained community members to conduct feminist activist research. Terry Haywoode (1991) worked as an educator and community organizer alongside women in her Brooklyn community and helped establish National Congress of Neighborhood Women's (NCNW) college program, a unique community-based program in which local residents can earn a two-year Associate's degree in Neighborhood Studies. By promoting women's educational growth and development within an activist community organization, NCNW's college program helped enhance working-class women's political efficacy in struggles to improve their neighborhoods.

As with feminist work more broadly, the goal of community-based activist research is to produce an analysis that retains the integrity of political processes, specific events, diverse actors, and social context while revealing the broader processes at work that may not have been visible to the individual participants at the time they were engaged in the struggle, or even to the researchers when they conducted the research (Naples, 1998b). In an effort to democratize the research process, many feminist researchers argue for adopting participatory strategies that involve community residents or other participants in the design, implementation and analysis of the research.[13] This analytic process can be further deepened when dialogic reflexive strategies are adopted. This form of reflexive practice is a collective activity involving ongoing dialogue between and among participants and co-researchers.

In her activist research with parents from the predominantly African-American high school her daughter Sarah attended, sociologist Susan Stern (1998) demonstrated that conversational strategies can become an integral part of daily life, and of politicization and ethnographic analysis. In small groups or as conversation partners, participants in the conversational research project can assess findings and refocus research questions.[14] Stern pointed to the significance of friendship in providing grounds for more egalitarian conversation-based activist research. She showed how 'conversation-based research builds on ordinary friendship conversations in which exploration of the personal realm grows to include investigation of shared social conditions' (Stern, 1998: 110). Dialogue among participants in an activist

project helps in the development of grassroots analyses of personally experienced realities that are inevitably politically constituted.[15]

Analysis of community activism or the process of politicization can be deepened by making one's activist experiences and standpoint visible. Activist researchers have been ambivalent about writing themselves into the narrative record. On the one hand, this strategy can lead to a more honest account of the social movement activities or activist organization in which they participated. Incorporating one's activist experiences and positionality into the analysis can result in a deeper understanding of the political strategies chosen and the process of politicization (Naples, 1998a). On the other hand, such a strategy may be viewed as an attempt to create a more 'true' or 'authentic' depiction of the field encounter, thus once again privileging the researcher's voice over the voices of those whose lives are the subject of the inquiry. In addressing this dilemma, sociologists Kathy Charmaz and Richard Mitchell (1997: 194) find a middle ground between 'deference to subjects' views and audible authorship' and stress that they 'do not pretend that our stories report autonomous truths, but neither do we share the cynic's nihilism that ethnography is a biased irrelevancy.' They offer a strategy for writing an ethnographic account where 'the writer remains in the background and becomes embedded in the narrative rather than acting in the scene. The reader hears the writer's words, envisions the scenes, and attends to the story, not the story teller' (Charmaz and Mitchell, 1997: 214).

In addition to the value of reflexive practice and dialogic strategies for collective action and activist research, they can also enrich the practice of research more broadly. In order to render visible what is at stake in the knowledge-production process, reflexive practices provide valuable tools throughout the research and writing process. The goal of reflexive practice is 'to avoid creating new orthodoxies that are exclusionary and reifying' (Grewal and Kaplan, 1994: 18).

CONCLUSION

Feminist methodology was developed in the context of diverse struggles against hegemonic modes of knowledge production that render women's lives, and those of other marginal groups, invisible or dispensable. Within the social sciences, feminist researchers have raised questions about the separation of theory and method, the gendered biases inherent in positivism, and the hierarchies that limit who can be considered the most appropriate producers of theoretical knowledge. Feminist reconceptualizations of knowledge production processes have contributed to a shift in research practices in many disciplines, and require more diverse methodological and self-reflexive skills than traditional methodological approaches. Some feminist scholars question whether or not it is possible to develop a reflexive practice that can fully attend to all the different manifestations of power (Lather, 1992; also see Stacey, 1991). However, since feminist methodology is open to critique and responsive to the changing dynamics of power that shape women's lives and those of others who have been traditionally marginalized within academia, feminist researchers often act as innovators who are quick to develop new research approaches and frameworks.

REFERENCES

Abu-Lughod, Lila (1993) *Writing Women's Worlds: Bedouin Stories.* Berkeley: University of California Press.

Alcoff, Linda (1988) 'Cultural feminism versus post-structuralism: The identity crisis in feminist theory', *Signs: Journal of Women in Culture and Society,* 13 (3): 405–36.

Alexander, M. Jacqui and Mohanty, Chandra Talpade (1997) 'Introduction: Genealogies, legacies, movements', in *Feminist Genealogies, Colonial Legacies, Democratic Futures.* New York: Routledge, pp. xiii–xlii.

Anzaldúa, Gloria (1987) *Borderlands/La Frontera: The New Mestiza.* San Francisco: Spinsters/Aunt Lute.

Baca Zinn, Maxine (1979) 'Field research in minority communities: Ethical, methodological, and political observations by an insider', *Social Problems,* 27: 209–19.

Behar, Ruth (1993) *Translated Woman: Crossing the Border with Esperanza's Story.* Boston: Beacon Press.

Behar, Ruth and Gordon, Deborah A. (eds.) (1995) *Women Writing Culture.* Berkeley: University of California Press.

Barrett, Michelle and Phillips, Anne (eds.) (1992) *Destabilizing Theory: Contemporary Feminist Debates.* Stanford, CA: Stanford University Press.

Basu, Amrita (2000) 'MillerComm Lecture. Mapping transnational women's movements: Globalizing the local, localizing the global', in *UIUC Area Centers Joint Symposium: Gender and Globalization.* University of Illinois, Urbana-Champaign.

Bloom, Leslie Rebecca (1998) *Under the Sign of Hope: Feminist Methodology and Narrative Interpretation.* Albany: State University of New York Press.

Campbell, Marie L. and Manicom, Ann (1995) 'Introduction', in *Knowledge, Experience, and Ruling Relations: Studies in the Social Organization of Knowledge.* Toronto: University of Toronto Press, pp. 3–16.

Cancian, Francesca (1996) 'Participatory research and alternative strategies for activist sociology', in Heidi Gottfried (ed.), *Feminism and Social Change: Bridging Theory and Practice.* Urbana and Chicago: University of Illinois Press, pp. 187–205.

Charmaz, Kathy and Mitchell, Richard G. Jr. (1997) 'The myth of silent authorship: Self, substance and style in ethnographic writing', in Rosanna Hertz (ed.), *Reflexivity and Voice.* Thousand Oaks, CA: Sage, pp. 193–215.

Chase, Susan E. (1995) *Ambiguous Empowerment: The Work Narratives of Women School Superintendents.* Amherst: University of Massachusetts Press.

Chew, Judy (1998) *Women Survivors of Childhood Sexual Abuse: Healing Through Group Work Beyond Survival.* New York/London: The Haworth Press.

Chodorow, Nancy (1978) *The Reproduction of Mothering.* Berkeley: University of California Press.

Clifford, James (1986) 'Introduction: Partial truths', in J. Clifford and G. Marcus (eds.), *Writing Culture: The Poetics and Politics of Ethnography.* Berkeley: University of California Press, pp. 1–26.

Clifford, James and Marcus, George E. (1986) *Writing Culture: The Poetics and Politics of Ethnography.* Berkeley: University of California Press.

Clough, Patricia Ticiento (1994) *Feminist Thought.* Cambridge, MA: Blackwell.

Code, Lorraine (1991) *What Can She Know? Feminist Theory and the Construction of Knowledge.* Ithaca, NY: Cornell University Press.

Collins, Patricia Hill (1990) *Black Feminist Thought: Knowledge, Consciousness, and the Politics of Empowerment.* Boston: Unwin Hyman.

———— (1998) *Fighting Words; Black Women and the Search for Justice.* New York: Routledge.

Cotterill, Pamela (1992) 'Interviewing women: Issues of friendship, vulnerability, and power', *Women's Studies International Forum,* 15 (5): 593–606.

Crenshaw, Kimberly (1993) 'Mapping the margins: Intersectionality, identity politics, and violence against women of color', *Stanford Law Review,* 43: 1241–99.

DeVault, Marjorie (1999) *Liberating Method: Feminism and Social Research.* Philadelphia, PA: Temple University Press.

DeVault, Marjorie and McCoy, Liza (2001) 'Institutional ethnography: Using interviews to investigate ruling relations', in Jaber F. Gubrium and James A. Holstein (eds.), *Handbook of Interview Research: Context and Method.* Thousand Oaks, CA: Sage, pp. 751–76.

Diamond, Timothy (1992) *Making Gray Gold: Narratives of Nursing Home Care.* Chicago, IL: University of Chicago Press.

El-Or, Tamar (1997) 'Do You Really Know How They Make Love? The Limits on Intimacy with Ethnographic Informants', in R. Hertz (ed.), *Reflexivity & Voice.* Thousands Oaks, CA: Sage, pp. 169–89.

Ellsworth, Elizabeth (1992) 'Why Doesn't This Feel Empowering? Working Through the Repressive Myths of Critical Pedagogy', in C. Luke and J. Gore (eds.), *Feminisms and Critical Pedagogy.* New York: Routledge, pp. 90–119.

Ferguson, Ann (1991) *Sexual Democracy: Women, Oppression, and Revolution.* Boulder, CO: Westview.

Fine, Michelle (1992) *Disruptive Voices: The Possibilities of Feminist Research.* Ann Arbor: University of Michigan Press.

Fisher, Berenice Malka (2001) *No Angel in the Classroom.* Lanham, MD: Rowman and Littlefield Publishers.

Fonow, Mary Margaret and Cook, Judith A. (eds.) (1991) *Beyond Methodology: Feminist Scholarship as Lived Research.* Bloomington: Indiana University Press.

———— (2005) 'Feminist methodology: New applications in the academy and public policy', *Signs: Journal of Women in Culture and Society,* 30 (4): 221–36.

Foucault, Michel (1972) *The Archaeology of Knowledge and the Discourse on Language.* New York: Harper and Row.

Friedman, Susan Stanford (1995) 'Beyond White and Other: Relationality and narratives of race in feminist discourse', *Signs: Journal of Women in Culture and Society,* 20 (1): 1–49.

Gore, Jennifer M. (1992) 'What we can do for you! What can "we" do for "you"?: Struggling over empowerment in critical and feminist pedagogy', in Carmen Luke and Jennifer Gore (eds.), *Feminisms and Critical Pedagogy.* New York: Routledge, pp. 54–73.

Grewal, Inderpal and Kaplan, Caren (eds.) (1994) *Scattered Hegemonies: Postmodernity and Transnational Feminist Practices.* Minneapolis, MN: University of Minnesota Press.

Gringeri, Christina (1994) *Getting By: Women Homeworkers and Rural Economic Development.* Lawrence: University Press of Kansas.

Hale, Sondra (1991) 'Feminist method, process, and self-criticism: Interviewing Sudanese women', in Sherna Berger Gluck and Daphne Patai (eds.) *Women's Words,* New York: Routledge, pp. 121–136.

Hale, Sondra (1996) *Gender Politics in Sudan: Islamism, Socialism, and the State.* Boulder, CO: Westview.

Haraway, Donna (1988) 'Situated knowledges: The science question in feminism and the privilege of partial Perspective', *Feminis Studies,* 14 (3): 575–99.

Harding, Sandra (1986) *The Science Question in Feminism.* Ithaca, NY: Cornell University.

———— (1987) 'Is there a feminist method?', in Sandra Harding (ed.), *Feminism and Methodology.* Bloomington: Indiana University Press, pp. 1–14

———— (1991) *Whose Science? Whose Knowledge?* Ithaca, NY: Cornell University Press.

———— (1998) *Is Science Multicultural? Post-colonialisms, Feminisms, and Epistemologies.* Bloomington: Indiana University Press.

———— (2004) *The Feminist Standpoint Theory Reader: Intellectual and Political Controversies.* New York: Routledge.

Hartsock, Nancy (1983) *Money, Sex and Power: Toward a Feminist Historical Materialism.* New York: Longman.

———— (1987a) 'The feminist standpoint: Developing the ground for a specifically feminist historical materialism', in Sandra Harding (ed.), *Feminism and Methodology.* Bloomington: Indiana University Press, pp. 157–80.

———— (1987b) 'Rethinking modernism: Majority theories', *Cultural Critique,* 7: 187–206.

———— (1997) 'Comment on Hekman's "Truth and Method: Feminist Standpoint Theory Revisited": Truth or Justice?' *Signs: Journal of Women in Culture and Society,* 22(2): 367–63.

———— (1999a) *The Feminist Standpoint Revisited and Other Essays.* Boulder, CO: Westview.

———— (1999b) *Postmodernism and Political Change.* New York: Routledge.

Haywoode, Terry (1991) 'Working class feminism: Creating a politics of community, connection, and concern', Ph.D. dissertation, The City University of New York.

Hekman, Susan (1997) 'Truth and Method: Feminist Standpoint Theory Revisited', Signs: *Journal of Women in Culture and Society*, 22(2): 341–65.

Hennessy, Rosemary (1990) 'Materialist Feminism and Foucault: The Politics of Appropriation', *Rethinking Marxism*, 3(3–4): 252–274.

——— (1993) *Materialist Feminism and the Politics of Discourse*. New York: Routledge.

Hennessy, Rosemary and Ingraham, Chrys (eds.) (1997) *Materialist Feminism: A Reader in Class, Difference, and Women's Lives*. New York: Routledge.

Hesford, Wendy S. (1999) *Framing Identities: Autobiography and the Politics of Pedagogy*. Minneapolis: University of Minnesota Press.

Hurtado, Aída (1996) *The Color of Privilege: Three Blasphemies on Race and Feminism*. Ann Arbor: University of Michigan Press.

Joseph, Suad (1988) 'Feminism, familism, self, and politics: Research as a Mughtaribi', in Soraya Altorki and Camillia Fawzi El-Solh (eds.), *Arab Women in the Field: Studying Your Own Society*. Syracuse, NY: Syracuse University Press, pp. 25–47.

King, Katie (1994) *Theory in its Feminist Travels: Conversations in U.S. Women's Movements*. Bloomington: Indiana University Press.

Kondo, Dorinne K. (1990) *Crafting Selves: Power, Gender, and Discourses of Identity in a Japanese Workplace*. Chicago, IL: University of Chicago Press.

Krieger, Susan (1983) *Social Science and the Self: Personal Essays on an Art Form*. New Brunswick, NJ: Rutgers University Press.

Lather, Patti (1992) 'Post-critical pedagogies: A feminist reading', in Carmen Luke and Jennifer Gore (eds.), *Feminisms and Critical Pedagogy*. New York: Routledge, pp. 120–37.

Longino, Helen (1990) *Science as Social Knowledge*. Princeton, NJ: Princeton University Press.

Martinez, Jacqueline (2000) *Phenomenology of Chicana Experience and Identity: Communication and Transformation in Praxis*. Lanham, MD: Rowman and Littlefield.

Mies, Maria (1982) *The Lace Makers of Narsapur: Indian Housewives Produce for the World Market*. London: Zed Books.

——— (1991) 'Women's research or feminist research? The debate surrounding feminist science and methodology', in Mary Margaret Fonow and Judith A. Cook (eds.), *Beyond Methodology: Feminist Scholarship as Lived Research*. Bloomington: Indiana University Press, pp. 60–84.

Mitchell, Juliann, and Jill Morse (1998) *From Victims to Survivors: Reclaimed Voices of Women Sexually Abused in Childhood by Females*. Washington, DC: Accelerated Development, Taylor and Francis Group.

Mohanty, Chandra Talpade (1991) 'Under western eyes: Feminist scholarship and colonial discourses', in Chandra Talpade Mohanty, Ann Russo and Lourdes Torres (eds.), *Third World Women and the Politics of Feminism*. Bloomington and Indianapolis: Indiana University Press, pp. 51–80.

——— (1997) 'Women workers and capitalist scripts: Ideologies of domination, common interests, and the politics of solidarity', in M. Jacqui Alexander and Chandra Talpade Mohanty (eds.), *Feminist Genealogies, Colonial Legacies, Democratic Futures*. New York: Routledge, pp. 3–29.

Moraga, Cherríe (1981) 'Introduction', in Cherríe Moraga and Gloria Anzaldúa (eds.), *This Bridge Called My Back: Writings by Radical Women of Color*. Watertown, MA: Persephone Press, pp. xiii–xix.

Moya, Paula M.L. (1997) 'Postmodernism, "realism", and the politics of identity: Cherrie Morago and Chicana feminism', in M. Jacqui Alexander and Chandra Talpade Mohanty (eds.), *Feminist Genealogies, Colonial Legacies, Democratic Futures*. New York: Routledge, pp. 125–50.

Naples, Nancy A. (1997) 'Contested needs: Shifting the standpoint on rural economic development', *Feminist Economics*, 3 (2): 63–98.

——— (1998a) *Grassroots Warriors: Activist Mothering, Community Work, and the War on Poverty*. New York: Routledge.

——— (ed.) (1998b) *Community Activism and Feminist Politics: Organizing Across Race, Class, and Gender*. New York: Routledge.

——— (2003) *Feminism and Method: Ethnography, Discourse Analysis, and Activist Research*. New York: Routledge.

——— (2006) 'Future directions in feminist methodology: Standpoint theory and beyond', in Charlene Nagy Hesse-Biber (ed.), *Handbook of Feminist Research*. Thousand Oaks, CA: Sage.

Narayan, Uma (1997) *Dislocating Cultures: Identities, Traditions, and Third World Feminism*. New York: Routledge.

Pence, Ellen (1996) 'Safety for battered women in a textually mediated legal system', Ph.D. dissertation, University of Toronto.

Rajan, Rajeswari Sunder (1993) *Real and Imagined Women: Gender, Culture and Postcolonialism*. New York: Routledge.

Reinharz, Shulamit (1992) *Feminist Methods in Social Research*. New York: Oxford University Press.

Sachs, Carolyn (1983) *Invisible Farmers: Women in Agricultural Production*. Totowa, NJ: Rowman and Allanheld.

——— (1996) *Gendered Fields: Rural Women, Agriculture and Environment*. Boulder, CO: Westview.

Sandoval, Chéla (1991) 'U.S. Third world feminism: The theory and method of oppositional consciousness in the postmodern world', *Genders,* 10: 1–24.

———— (1993) 'Oppositional consciousness in the postmodern world: U.S. Third world feminism, semiotics, and the methodology of the oppressed', Ph.D. dissertation, University of California, Santa Cruz.

———— (2000) *Methodology of the Oppressed.* St.Paul, MN: University of Minnesota Press.

Seitz, Virginia R. (1998) 'Class, gender, and resistance in the Appalachian coalfields', in Nancy A. Naples (ed.), *Community Activism and Feminist Politics: Organizing across Race, Class, and Gender.* New York: Routledge, pp. 213–36.

Smith, Dorothy E. (1987) *The Everyday World as Problematic: A Feminist Sociology.* Toronto: University of Toronto Press.

———— (1990a) *Conceptual Practices of Power.* Boston: Northeastern University Press.

———— (1990b) *Texts, Facts, and Femininity: Exploring the Relations of Ruling.* New York: Routledge.

———— (1992) 'Sociology from women's experience: A reaffirmation', *Sociological Theory,* 10 (1): 88–98.

———— (1999) *Writing the Social: Critique, Theory, and Investigations.* Toronto: University of Toronto Press.

———— (2005) *Institutional Ethnography: A Sociology for People.* Lanham, MD: Alta Mira.

Spelman, Elizabeth V. (1988) *Inessential Woman: Problems of Exclusion in Feminist Thought.* Boston: Beacon Press.

Spalter-Roth, Roberta and Hartmann, Heidi (1996) 'Small happinesses: The feminist struggle to integrate social research with social activism', in Heidi Gottfried (ed.), *Feminism and Social Change: Bridging Theory and Practice.* Urbana and Chicago, Illinois: University of Illinois Press, pp. 206–24.

Stacey, Judith (1991) 'Can there be a feminist ethnography?', in Sherna B. Gluck and Daphne Patai (eds.), *Women's Words.* New York: Routledge, pp. 111–19.

Stanley, Liz and Wise, Sue (1983) *Breaking Out: Feminist Consciousness and Feminist Research.* London: Routledge and Kegan Paul.

Steinberg, Ronnie J. (1996) 'Advocacy research for feminist policy objectives: Experiences with comparable worth,' in Heidi Gottfried (ed.), *Feminism and Social Change: Bridging Theory and Practice.* Urbana and Chicago, Illinois: University of Illinois Press, pp. 225–55.

Stern, Susan (1994) 'Social science from below: Grassroots knowledge for science and emancipation', Ph.D. dissertation, City University of New York.

———— (1998) 'Conversation, research, and struggles over schooling in an African American community', in Nancy A. Naples (ed.), *Community Activism and*

Feminist Politics: Organizing across Race, Class, and Gender. New York: Routledge, pp. 107–27.

Tappan, Mark B. (2001) 'Interpretive psychology: Stories, circles, and understanding lived experience', in Deborah L. Tolman and Mary Brydon-Miller (eds.), *From Subjects to Subjectivities: A Handbook of Interpretive and Participatory Methods.* New York: New York University Press, pp. 45–56.

Visweswaran, Kamala (1994) *Fictions of Feminist Ethnography.* Minneapolis: University of Minnesota Press.

Weeks, Kathi (1998) *Constituting Feminist Subjects.* Ithaca, NY: Cornell University Press.

Wolf, Diane L. (1996) 'Situating feminist dilemmas in fieldwork', in Diane L. Wolf (ed.), *Feminist Dilemmas in Fieldwork.* Boulder, CO: Westview, pp. 1–55.

Wolf, Margery (1996) 'Afterword: Musing from an old gray wolf', in Diane L. Wolf (ed.), *Feminist Dilemmas in Fieldwork.* Boulder, CO: Westview, pp. 215–22.

Wright, Mareena McKinley (1995) "I never did any fieldwork, but I milked an awful lot of cows!' Using rural women's experience to reconceptualize models of work', *Gender & Society,* 9: 216–35.

NOTES

1. Portions of this chapter are excerpted from Naples (1998a; 1998b; 2003; 2006).

2. See, for example, Narayan (1997). Chicano studies scholar Chéla Sandoval defines third-world feminism as the coalition 'between a generation of US feminists of color who were separated by culture, race, class, sex or gender identifications but united through their similar responses to the experience of race oppression' (Sandoval, 1993: 53). She argues for 'a "coalitional consciousness" in cultural studies across racialized, sexualized, genderized theoretical domains: "white male poststructuralism," "hegemonic feminism," "third world feminism," "postcolonial discourse theory," and "queer theory"' (Sandoval, 1993: 79).

3. Sandoval's (1991: 2) analysis of 'oppositional consciousness' focuses on the development of third-world feminism 'as a model for the self-conscious production of political opposition'. In challenging the separation of different political approaches, Sandoval (1991: 3) demonstrates how political actors can function 'within yet beyond the demands of dominant ideology'. She emphasizes how 'differential [oppositional] consciousness makes more clearly visible the equal rights, revolutionary, supremacist and separatist, forms of oppositional consciousness, which when kaleidescoped together comprise a new paradigm for understanding oppositional activity in general' (Sandoval, 1991: 16; see also, Sandoval, 1993, 2000).

4. Education and human development scholar Mark Tappan (2001: 47) discusses 'interpretive' approaches to social and psychological research as linked to 'hermeneutics, the art and practice of textual exegesis or interpretation, [which] is the methodology most appropriate for understanding "recorded expressions" of human existence and experience.' Drawing on Wilhelm Dilthey's philosophy, Tappan (2001: 46) cautions that 'interpreters must be aware of the power that they hold to shape the understanding of others' lived experience'.

5. See, for example, Behar and Gordon (1995); Clifford (1986); Clifford and Marcus (1986).

6. Institutional ethnographers examine how ruling relations are woven into the production of texts used to organize people's activities in various locations such as schools or government agencies or professional offices (see Campbell and Manicom, 1995; DeVault and McCoy, 2001; Diamond, 1992; Smith, 2005).

7. Mohanty is critical of Western feminist constructions of third-world women as victims rather than as agents. By emphasizing these women's experiences of male violence, colonial processes, economic development and religious oppression, Western feminists construct a totalizing image of 'the' third world woman that masks the great diversity in such women's lives and their resistance to oppression. In addition, Mohanty argues, first-world feminists gain power by distancing themselves from third-world women's concerns and constructing themselves as liberated. See also Alexander and Mohanty (1997); Grewal and Kaplan (1994); and Narayan (1997).

8. Sandoval (2000: 7) asserts that Moraga's 'theory in the flesh' is 'a theory that allows survival and more, that allows practitioners to live with faith, hope, and moral vision in spite of all else.' Moraga's 'theory of the flesh' and Anzaldúa's (1987) construc-

tion of *la conciencia de la mestiza* are built from 'gut-wrenching struggle', as communication scholar Jacqueline Martinez explains (2000: 83). She cautions: 'The attention to the embodied flesh that is the substance and methodology of much of Chicano feminist theorizing must not be theorized away in abstract language that allows for a distanced and removed engagement' (Martinez, 2000: 84).

9. In *Methodology of the Oppressed*, Sandoval (2000: 77) defines her complex project as exploring 'the mobile interchange between the sovereign, Marxist, and postmodern conceptions of power' in order to explicate the development and political potential of 'differential consciousness'.

10. Dorothy Smith (1987: 2) defines 'relations of ruling' as a term 'that brings into view the intersection of the institutions organizing and regulating society with their gender subtext and their basis in a gender division of labor.' The term ruling is used to identify 'a complex of organized practices, including government, law, business and financial management, professional organization, and educational institutions as well as the discourse in texts that interpenetrate the multiple sites of power'.

11. See Chew (1998) and Mitchell and Morse (1998).

12. See Elizabeth Ellsworth (1992) for a fascinating discussion of the limits of 'empowerment' in critical educational practice.

13. See, for example, Cancian (1996); Fine (1992); Hale (1996); Reinharz (1992); M. Wolf (1996).

14. Mies (1991: 71) describes this process as 'reciprocal research'. Although she shared neither culture, class nor ethnic background with her 'conversation partners' (to use Stern's term), Mies found this process enriched her work with Indian women.

15. See also Code (1991); Hale (1996); Joseph (1988), for discussions of the complications associated with friendships with research subjects.

31

Community-Based Research

Michael Root

INTRODUCTION

Qualitative research contrasts with quantitative research and pure with applied, but what contrasts with community-based research in the social sciences? All social scientists study communities or their members and, as a result, could be said, in one sense, to be doing community-based research. As most social scientists use the term 'community-based', however, they mean doing research *with* and not simply *on* members of a community.[1] To be community-based, in any significant sense, a study has to be done in collaboration with members of a community rather than entirely by an outside expert. So understood, community-based research in the social sciences is an exception rather than the rule, for in most studies subjects have little if any say over how the research is to be conducted. A social scientist or expert chooses the words and writes the script, and, as a result, within the social sciences, a community-based study contrasts with one which is under the direction or control of an expert (Park et al., 1993).

When an expert studies members of a community, she decides what questions to ask and how they are to be answered. She collects the data, gathers the facts, tests the hypotheses and transmits the finding or results to a client or audience. Expert-based studies have been called 'vampire projects'; they extract information from the members of a vulnerable group or community and give them little (a pain in the neck?) in return.[2] They have also been likened to scientific expeditions into exotic lands; the expert takes away artifacts and seldom returns; the residents are poorer for his visit and distrustful of anyone else who, in the name of science, comes to peer into their tents or dig around their ruins.

Community-based studies are seen to be less acquisitive and more open-handed. Control over the agenda is shared. Power is distributed between the social scientist and her subjects. The subjects have a say over what is studied and how the study is carried out. Moreover, community-based studies are often part of a social movement undertaken by a group of people who have in the past had little public influence (such as the poor, an indigenous people, or a racial or ethnic minority), and the emphasis on community reflects a growing interest in public participation in the development of science and public policy. Community-based studies combine three activities that expert-based studies keep separate—research, education and activism—and offer an alternative to the more familiar, elitist or command-and-control models of research.

POWER-SHARING

There isn't one community-based approach to research in the social sciences but many, and they carry a variety of labels: for example, 'action research', 'participatory research', 'participatory action research', and 'community-based participatory research' (Reason and Bradbury, 2001). They differ in degree of collaboration, but all assume that a social scientist should not take more from her subjects than she gives back to them, and that she should teach or embolden and not simply observe, survey or probe the members of the community she has chosen to be the subjects of her research (Whyte, 1991).

Each variety of community-based research opposes at least one of the following assumptions on which conventional, expert-based research relies:

1. The role of a subject is to be a source of data for the expert.
2. Any accommodation to the interests of a subject should be limited to what is necessary to gain his consent or cooperation.
3. For the results to be reliable or valid, the attitudes of the expert towards her subjects, when conducting her study, must be detached and disinterested.
4. Since the expert has training in the social sciences and her subjects do not, she should control how the study is conducted, and they should not.
5. Experts rather than their subjects are the primary audience for the study.
6. An expert is better able to interpret or explain facts about her subjects or their community than they are.

7. A study should be designed to discover true generalizations about the members of a community based on data collected from a sample of the members.

Because they oppose one more of the assumptions, community-based studies are often said to be done with their subjects, while expert-based studies to be done on or to them.

Community-based research can be qualitative or quantitative, but the choice of method is not entirely the social scientist's to make (Creswell, 2003). While expert-based studies usually begin with a hypothesis to be tested, community-based studies often begin with a problem to be solved and employ whatever techniques promise a solution. Often these are qualitative, but they could be quantitative.

Community-based studies fall into one of three categories. First, some are designed to evaluate a community's current programs or policies (Judd et al., 2001). The aim here is to discover how a community can improve what members are already doing. Second, some are designed to increase the members' ability to identify problems and develop plans to solve them (Mies, 1983). Third, some are designed to make a case for a public policy favored by members of the community (Gaventa and Horton, 1981). Studies of the first and third kinds are likely to employ quantitative methods while research of the second is likely to employ qualitative methods. But often studies of each kind employ a mixture of both.

Experts often distrust the understanding their subjects have of their social situation or the causes of their problems. They assume that the causes are hidden from their subjects' view or that in order to understand the situation, special skills or tools are required that they possess but their subjects do not. As a result, they do not see a subject as someone with whom they might be able to collaborate; they assume that to be objective or scientific a study has to abide by the seven rules given above. So, for them, the only reason to grant a subject some control over the study is to win his informed consent or encourage him to participate.[3]

HISTORY OF COMMUNITY-BASED RESEARCH

In 1889, Jane Addams invited residents of the south side of Chicago to participate in a study of land use patterns in their neighborhood; her study became part of the social service mission of the Hull House and a model for the urban sociology developed by Robert Park and Ernest Burgess at the University of Chicago (Harkavy and Puckett, 1994). But many early examples of community-based research come from outside the United States, in particular from countries struggling to become independent or free of foreign control or influence. In those countries, the social sciences were often viewed with suspicion and seen as servants or vestiges of colonial rule. In response, social scientists working there began to cede control to their subjects and, in order to counter the subjects' suspicion and the legacies of colonialism, began to give them a say over how the research would be conducted (Hall et al., 1982).

Paolo Freire was a prominent proponent of participatory research among disadvantaged people in developing countries. The social scientist should, in his view, help members of an oppressed group to mobilize and act on behalf of their collective interest. Many members of the communities with whom he worked were illiterate, and a primary aim of his research was to teach them to read, raise their political consciousness and encourage them to become critical of their circumstances (Freire, 1998). Freire's 'pedagogy for the oppressed' encouraged other social scientists in the developing world to think of how their work could be redesigned to suit the situation and interests of the least well-off members of those communities.

In the United States, community-based research was a mission of Highlander Folk School in Tennessee. The School, founded in 1932 by Myles Horton, developed a model of adult education and collaborative research and brought grassroots leaders, community organizers, educators and social scientists together to address social, environmental and economic problems facing the region (Horton, 1989). In 1933, the School brought timber workers and their families together to study the logging industry and find a way to protect the forests and the workers from threats posed by the industry. Highlander continued to play an important role in social movements within the region, including the movement in the 1950s to racially integrate southern labor organizations and the public schools. At the present time, Highlander is a center for social activists and academics with an interest in collaborative research.[4]

Kurt Lewin, a social psychologist, studied how social interaction between members of a group influences the rate with which groups change (Lewin, 1948). He wrote about the industrial development movement in the United States in the 1940s and explained how a business organization could become more productive if a manager or expert shared control with workers on the production line. Lewin coined the term 'participatory research' and is credited with shifting the role of the social scientist from simply describing or explaining the actions of members of a group to working with members to increase their role in management.

Many prominent proponents of community-based research align themselves with Lewin and the industrial-democracy tradition.[5] They oppose top-down models of social organization and attempt to make the practice of research more democratic by allowing their subjects to decide what questions to ask and what tools to use to answer them.[6] They do not place any limits on those tools: focus groups, interviews, statistical analyses, ethnographies, life histories, tests, and controlled or naturalistic observation are allowable, as long as the subjects have some say over their use and the tools enable them to exercise more control over the social organization than they would be able to exercise without them (Greenwood and Levin, 1998).

CURRENT EXAMPLES

Today, community-based studies can be found within what has come to be called 'public sociology', a movement to take the work of professional sociology back to the community (American Sociological Association, 2004). Drawing on the work of Jane Addams and Myles Horton, public sociologists apply the tools of sociology to the solution of a public problem and look to members of a local community to assist them. Some public sociologists try to increase workplace democracy, as Lewin had years before. In 2000, for example, sociologists at the University of California established a multi-campus research program to work with labor activists to study labor and employment in the area (Minkin, 2004). Other public sociologists attempt to inform and promote public debate over class and racial inequalities, environmental risk and the causes and prevention of crime.

In 1970, the American Psychological Association established a group to carry out community-based research within the field of community psychology (Duffy and Wong, 2003). The psychologist looks at how social factors affect the attitudes of members of at-risk communities (teens at risk of pregnancy or drug use, for example) and ways to collaborate with the members to better understand or influence the risky behavior. According to the expert model, a social psychologist interested in studying teen pregnancy gathers data from a sample of teens, identifies the variables associated with unprotected sex and uses some statistical techniques to find the cause of their behavior.

Such a study, though scientific, is not collaborative. The subjects tell but don't ask; and while she listens, the psychologist doesn't intervene. In a community-based study of teen pregnancy, the psychologist counsels as well as interrogates. She questions teens about how often or in what circumstances they engage in unprotected sex but also talks to them about contraception and reasons to choose protected over unprotected sex.

In a collaborative study, a psychologist helps her subjects to reduce a risk rather than wait, as many experts would, for a change in public policy to do so. Whether a community-based or an expert-based study is more likely to reduce the rate of teen pregnancies in a given community is debatable, but proponents of community psychology offer evidence to show how, in a number of communities, the risk has been reduced by means of collaboration (Paine-Andrews et al., 2000).

Feminists, as a rule, favor community-based studies over expert-based studies in the social sciences.[7] Since they seek to improve the status of women, they usually share control over their studies with the women who agree to be their subjects (Gottfried, 1996). Sometimes they work with a woman to see a problem which is hidden from her view, and help her to see her situation more clearly or, to use a somewhat dated but still useful term, to raise her consciousness (Maguire, 1987).

A research project in Cologne, for example, grew out of an effort to draw attention to the abuse of women in the city (Mies, 1983). The research was part of a campaign to create a shelter for the victims of abuse. The campaign did not begin with an interest in research, but the need to document the seriousness and extent of the problem led women campaigning for the shelter to survey wife battering in Cologne. Such surveys were usually prepared by experts using standard interviewing techniques or official records, but, in this case, those in the campaign developed their own methods for proving the need for the shelter because of the cost of professional research, the absence of records and the women's desire to increase their own power and authority on questions concerning the safety of women.

The women established the need for a shelter by organizing street actions and conducting interviews with people attracted to them. The actions and interviews were reported in the press. The continuing publicity brought wives in search of shelter to leaders of the campaign, and the leaders sheltered some of them in their own homes. In using their own homes as shelters, they called more public attention to the problem of abuse and increased the pressure on municipal officials to act. The officials began to document cases of battering, and in time there were statistics to show that many women were in need of protection. Finally, the social welfare department was convinced or pressured into admitting that there was a problem and that the city should fund a shelter.

COLLEGES AND UNIVERSITIES

Many land-grant universities in the United States include community service as part of their mission (Strand et al., 2003). To assist farmers or farming industries, many schools established an extension service, or hired experts to work side by side with farmers and businessmen to improve the agricultural economy within the state. Universities with medical schools or programs in public health were often expected to set up clinics or offices in underserved communities and work with members to improve their health and reduce the rate of morbidity and mortality within the community. Colleges of law organized and funded legal clinics, and graduate programs in social work and public affairs undertook or sponsored studies designed to increase or improve the services available to communities with special needs.

While community-based studies have for a long time been part of what universities call 'outreach', at many schools, relations with members of a disadvantaged or at-risk community have been marked more by conflict or false promises than cooperation. As a result, when an expert reaches out, members, whose interests have often been overlooked or set aside, view her with suspicion; and when she sets up shop in their neighborhood, they see her work there as more in her than their own interest (Jackson, 1993).

Members have reasons to be suspicious, since a university's tenure and promotion decisions often rest on studies published in journals more likely to accept expert-based than community-based research, and the more members of the community have control over a study, the less credit the expert receives from her peers for a study's findings. As a result, a social scientist can be required to balance her own academic or professional advancement against the interests of her subjects, and her subjects can have a reason to wonder whose interests she is serving when she chooses to reach out to them or invite them to collaborate in her research.

Studies conducted at universities are usually addressed to experts, policy-makers or social service agencies. Often the findings are written in the language of experts and not available to members of the community who are the source of the study's data.[8] The findings might appear in the popular press but only if especially provocative or controversial.[9] As a result, popular reports of an academic study, though more readable than a paper in an academic journal, often add to a community's suspicion of research in the social sciences.

Community-based studies allow the subjects to choose the language in which the findings are written and the audience to whom they are to be addressed. Though the language might not appeal to the editors of an academic or professional journal, the words are familiar to the subjects and relevant to their interests. As a result, they are more likely to trust the findings and more inclined to use them when deciding how to solve a problem.

Most proponents of community-based research offer rules of thumb or suggestions for how to avoid or reduce the difficulties experts face in attempting to make their studies collaborative (Nyden et al., 1997). The rules call upon the social scientist to school herself in the culture of her subjects and be aware of differences in interests between members of the community she has chosen to work with, and they also call on the community to exercise caution or diligence in dealing with the expert (Suarez-Balcazar, 2003).[10] In short, the history of community-based research in colleges and universities is mixed. While community-based studies are conducted there, they often play second fiddle to studies based on the interests of experts.

INFORMED CONSENT

In the social and biomedical sciences, rules regulate how research with human subjects can be conducted; the rules are designed to respect the subjects' autonomy and protect their interests. In particular, the rules require a researcher to obtain the informed consent of her subjects before she is allowed to study them (Adair et al., 1985). However, as an unintended consequence, the rules can limit the degree to which she is able to collaborate or cede control to her subjects, since, according to the rules, before the expert is allowed to begin a study, she has to spell out in some detail how it will be conducted. As a result, in order to win approval from a review board, a social scientist has to have written some of the script herself before any of her subjects are allowed on the stage or permitted to begin to direct the performance.

Community-based research poses another problem for review boards. Informed consent is usually understood to apply to the individuals who are to be tested, observed, questioned or surveyed, and not to the social groups or communities to which they belong. But the subjects in community-based research are often entire groups or communities and not simply some one or more of the members. As result, when considering issues of harm or informed consent, a review board has reason (a) to consider not only the harm to individual members of the community but harm to the group or community as well, and (b) to want the community and not simply some individual members to say 'yes' or 'no' to the study, since the community (not simply the individuals who will most actively or directly participate) is the subject of the study.[11]

However, seeking consent from a group raises questions not raised when seeking consent from an individual member. In order for a social scientist to obtain community consent, she has to be able to turn to someone who is able to speak for the community. If a community is formally organized or has a widely recognized leader, she can look to the leader, but if a community is only loosely organized or is divided, there is no one voice for her to listen to. Though some of the communities with whom social scientists collaborate are formally organized, many are not, and when they are not, though a social scientist can turn to a few members for consent, she has reason to wonder who they are speaking for.

CATEGORIES

When describing or explaining some trait of her subjects or their community, a social scientist will assign her subjects to categories; she will classify them, for example, by age, gender, occupation, ethnicity, political affiliation, race, income, wealth or educational achievement. Often the categories she assigns them to are ones to which they assign themselves, but not always. To the extent that she is looking for patterns, e.g., a pattern in the distribution of income within a population, she will prefer categories that enter into true generalizations with respect to the trait, and if her subjects' categories are less likely than her own to reveal a pattern, then she will choose her categories over theirs to use in her study.

So, for example, a sociologist might employ a system of class categories even if her subjects do not use them, should she believe that there is a statistically significant correlation between the trait whose variation within the population she is studying—e.g., voting behavior or religious affiliation—and a member's class position. Should her research be designed to test a hypothesis about differences within the community in voter turnout, she has a reason to classify the members by class if, according to the hypothesis, turnout varies with class location, even if the members do not classify one another by class.

On the other hand, some of the categories her subjects use to classify themselves might not have much descriptive or explanatory power or correlate with any social or economic trait, and, as a result, the social scientist might choose not to use them in her research, even though her subjects use them when they talk about each other. In the US, for example, people classify each other by religion, but when stratifying the US population in order to study differences in the distribution of a social or economic trait, a social scientist has no reason to use the category unless the trait varies with a person's religious affiliation.

Whatever the theoretical virtues of using her own rather than her subjects' categories in her studies, her use of her own categories can place limits on the degree to which she is able to collaborate with her subjects. Should they not understand her class categories, they might be unwilling or unable to undertake a study that will identify members of their community by class or attribute differences in a political trait to differences in class. Given a say over how a study of differences within their community in voting behavior or party affiliation is to be conducted, her subjects might choose to employ categories that are part of their worldview rather than hers. Even if her class categories support generalizations true of how they vote, her subjects will have no reason to master or employ her categories unless they share her interest in discovering generalizations or explaining how or why a trait like voting behavior varies within the population.

A social scientist might want to replace her subjects' categories with her own because she believes that hers have more predictive or explanatory power than theirs do, or because hers have more critical or political power. Should she wish to study the sexual abuse of children in a community whose members would never describe their treatment of children in those terms, she would have to persuade the members to see their treatment as she does before they could collaborate with her in the study. She would have to raise their consciousness before they would be able to see the merits of such a study and before they would be able to help to conduct it.[12]

NEUTRALITY

Community-based research usually begins with a problem to be solved rather than a theory or hypothesis to be tested. Thus, the research rests on a judgment that a particular condition or practice is problematic. Since the word 'problematic' implies undesirable, community-based research does not claim or aspire to be value-neutral. Moreover, since the research is designed to change and not simply describe or explain a trait—e.g., a high rate of teen pregnancy—it doesn't simply say what is but also what ought to be. Expert-based research, in contrast, claims to be neutral.

Studies in the social sciences, according to the neutral ideal, should be a collection of truths, and stay clear of evaluations or statements of right and wrong (Root, 1993). A study of the distribution of a socioeconomic trait within a population should, according to many social scientists, be descriptive (positive) rather than prescriptive (normative). Community-based studies combine the two, since they include judgments of both what is and what ought to be.

Expert-based studies are often designed to inform public policy and, in particular, advise whether or how changing X (say, class size) would affect Y (graduation rates) in a population P (Minneapolis). A policymaker who accepts (1), in the following syllogism, would have a reason to accept (3) were the findings of an expert-based study to confirm (2).[13]

(1) An increase in Y is desirable within a population P.
(2) A decrease in X will cause Y to increase in P.
So, (3) Decrease X in P.

That is, expert-based studies are designed to test or establish the minor premise, viz. (2), in a policy syllogism. On the expert's view, (2) is policy-relevant though value-neutral, since (2) provides reasons for (3) given (1) but does not say whether increasing Y or decreasing X is desirable. Whether (2) is true is a policy-relevant scientific question, one that the expert designs her study to answer. Though the expert-based study is not designed to offer any benefit to any of the subjects who are tested or interviewed, they, like other members of P, could benefit if (3) were to become policy and (1) is true.

In a community-based study, in contrast, an expert would work with members of the community to increase the rates of graduation if members thought that an increase was desirable. Benefits to the members would not depend solely on whether officials decide to adopt (3). The study would be designed to directly benefit the community by providing members with skills and information they could use to change their schools even if the findings of the study did not lead to any change in public policy.

Community-based studies are not only less disinterested but more democratic than expert-based studies to the extent that their subjects help to decide what is to be studied and how the study is to be conducted. In community-based studies, the role of the expert can vary from principal investigator to teacher or willing assistant, but the subjects are given a say on what the expert's role will be, and the community decides which members will participate in the study and represent them. Moreover, the participants are not selected by the expert and need not be a random or stratified random sample of the population.

In some community-based studies, the expert acts as 'a friendly outsider', and while she always takes her subjects' opinions seriously, she offers her own expertise to members when they are in doubt over how to proceed.[14] As an outsider, she may be able to say what her subjects cannot say and prompt them to consider issues or changes they would otherwise ignore, and, should she be affiliated with a university, she might be able to draw on the school's resources to push the collaboration forward. But if her research is to be based in the community, she should not limit the role of the members, even if, in the eyes of other experts, her study is less scientific for her not having done so.

Community-based research often requires an expert—a social scientist from outside the community—to get the process going, but the expert is expected to identify with the politics or values of the community and, not, as with expert-based research, try to be impartial or disinterested. Since she is not a detached or disinterested observer, her study will, however, seem to many social scientists to be partisan or biased. Her attachment, in their eyes, will seem to oppose good, objective, reliable or valid science or scholarship.

CREDIBILITY

Terms like 'scientific', 'objective' and 'reliable' confer importance and credibility on a study's findings, and should the findings be viewed as unscientific, they are very likely to be ignored by academic or government elites.[15] As a result, a good deal has been written on whether research can be collaborative and at the same time objective or reliable (Conner and Hendricks, 1989). How much control can a social scientist cede to her subjects without losing her claim to be doing good science? The answer depends, in large part, on how broadly or narrowly we define 'science'.

Social scientists often rely on interviews to collect information about the members of a community (Richardson, 1965). Much of the interviewing is directive rather than non-directive. Directive interviews are taken to be more reliable, and, as a result, the data they collect are taken to be more scientific than the data collected by less structured or more open-ended forms of interviewing. In directive interviews, the social scientist determines the topic of the interview and the questions the respondents are asked. In addition, she limits the answers they are able to choose from.

Directive interviewing prescribes a unilateral relationship in which the interviewer elicits but does not give out information. He is required to question a respondent about her life but not permitted to answer questions about his own. In a collaborative relationship, it is customary for both parties to share in giving and taking information, while in a directive interview one party takes and the other gives (Oakley, 1981). According to most handbooks on how interviews should and should not be conducted, the interviewer can bias the responses, should he allow himself to be questioned by his respondents, as he will disclose his own view and values, and his disclosure can alter how his subjects answer the interview questions (Sjoberg and Nett, 1968).

Social scientists disagree, however, over whether data collected by non-directive interviews are in fact unreliable and whether non-directive methods are less scientific than directive methods. Some question the measures of reliability and objectivity on which the case for directive interviews depends, and others question whether to be scientific a study has to collect data at all or collect data according to a precisely defined protocol. But should a social scientist choose directive over non-directive interviews, she will limit the degree to which her study is collaborative or serves her subjects' interests rather than her own.

Some community-based researchers eschew textbook methods of collecting data in order to make their studies more directly relevant to the interests of their subjects. The textbooks, they argue, are dated and rely on a too narrow conception of science. The term 'science', they say, picks out a family of practices whose members do not share an essence and can include qualitative as well as quantitative techniques and rely on open-ended conversations (e.g., ethnographies) as well as directive interviews.

'Science' is an essentially contestable term (Gallie, 1956). That is, people use the term to promote what they approve of, and often disagree over what should count as scientific. While philosophers of science once looked for a principle of demarcation, a simple way to distinguish science from non-science, most have given up looking, and instead describe the ways one science (e.g., psychology) differs from another (e.g., economics), or how much the different fields within a science differ from one another in their methods or design (Gieryn, 1983).

John Dewey had a different conception of science than Karl Popper did, and if community-based studies rely on Dewey's conception and expert-based on Popper's, debates over which are more scientific are rhetorical. The interesting question is not whether a study is scientific but in whose eyes a study needs to be creditable in order to realize a given purpose (Jordan et al., 2005). A study designed to teach members of a community to read, write their own history, conduct surveys or organize has to be credible to them even if not to an expert in survey design or statistical inference. A study designed to test a generalization about all the members of a large population based on a small sample or explain variations within the population in a social or economic trait has to be creditable to the expert even if not to individuals in the sample who differ with respect to the trait.

Expert-based studies often attempt to test a causal hypothesis like (2)—the minor premise in the policy syllogism—or estimate the likelihood of a change in Y, given a change in X, within a population P. The expert, in such studies (a) measures X and Y in a large or representative sample of P, (b) establishes the degree of correlation between the two variables, and (c) using a statistical tool (e.g., regression analysis) attempts to determine whether the association between X and Y is causal or accidental. As long as the expert, in doing (a), (b) and (c), sticks to the handbook, her test of the hypothesis will be taken to be credible by experts even if not by her subjects.

Could a more collaborative study test the causal hypothesis as well as a less collaborative one? Could members of P be allowed to decide who will be measured and how the values of X (class size) and Y (graduation rate) will be determined? Might there be reasons to believe that a decrease in X would cause an increase in Y in P other than requiring (a), (b) and (c)?

A collaborative or community-based study could provide evidence of a causal connection between X (class size) and Y (graduation rate) in something like the following way. Representative members of P could be invited to discuss how X and Y are connected. Even if they are not able to agree on whether larger classes are a cause of high drop-out rates, the discussion could move the issue to the top of the community's list of concerns and prompt the members to step up their current efforts to keep their kids in school. As part of the study, parents could act as classroom assistants or tutors.[16] Should a higher percentage of kids remain in school following the increased presence of the parents in the classroom, then even if no one could say for sure whether their presence caused the increase in graduation rates, the study would give members of the community some reason to think that their presence was, at least in part, responsible.

The study would not show, as an expert-based study would be designed to, that if, in other communities, parents were to increase their presence, then graduation rates would increase in all likelihood as well. But the members of the community might not have any interest in extrapolating their findings beyond the doors of their own classrooms and, unlike the expert, no interest in testing a broad statistical generalization about class size and graduation rates.

The community-based study might not have tested the hypothesis in a textbook sense of 'test', but might have been more useful in relation to the interests of members of the community than a study that did. In many cases, community-based studies are not intended to identify evidence of causality or measure the strength of an association between an intervention and an outcome, and in other cases those who design the study do not assume, as many experts do, that the only way to identify such evidence is by randomization, matched communities, strict sampling procedures, a long study period or an experimental design (Judd et al., 2001).

To most experts, the findings of the community-based study might seem anecdotal, subject to chance or biased, but to a community-based researcher the success of a study is not simply a matter of how well the evidence

collected in the study supports a particular hypothesis—for example, (2)—but how much members of the community learned as a result of having participated in the study (Humphreys and Rappaport, 1994). As long as community- and expert-based studies are designed to serve different interests, most debates over which are more credible, more objective, more reliable or more scientific will continue.

A community could have control and choose standard quantitative methods (like (a), (b) and (c)) for use in a study; members might not want to use techniques which, in the eyes of experts, look like 'so-so science'. In order to make a case to officials who will only be convinced by research that meets an expert's standard of objectivity or reliable data, members might choose directive over non-directive interviews or a randomized control study over a more collaborative one (Jordan et al., 2005). As a result, a study can be community-based and use many of the methods taught in the expert's handbook.

CONCLUSION

With community-based research, a social scientist collaborates with her subjects, but collaboration comes in degrees and can occur at any of a number of stages in the research process: (1) identifying the issue, (2) constructing the research questions, (3) collecting the data, (4) interpreting or analyzing the information, (5) drawing conclusions, (6) reporting the findings, and (7) issuing recommendations. A goal is to transfer a skill from the expert to her subjects or allow her subjects to employ their skills in the service of their interests. As a result, community-based studies are often more about educating members of a community than predicting or explaining their behavior or more about changing than describing the situation in which they find themselves. However, the distinction between expert and community-based research is not sharp, and the fewer the number of stages subjects are able to control, the harder to see any contrast between expert and community-based research.

A number of Internet sites rehearse the virtues of community-based studies and offer advice on how best to conduct them. I have included the web addresses of some in my list of references at the end of this chapter, and recommend a visit to a few in order to discover the many ways an expert can share control over her studies with her subjects and the many reasons why that might be a good thing for her to do.

REFERENCES AND SELECT BIBLIOGRAPHY

Adair, J.G., Dushenko, T.W. and Lindsay, R.C.L. (1985) 'Ethical regulations and their impact on research practice', *American Psychologist*, 40: 59–72.

American Sociological Association (2004) *An Invitation to Public Sociology.* Washington DC: ASA.

Blumer, H. (1939) *Symbolic Interactionism.* Englewood Cliffs, NJ: Prentice-Hall.

Conner, R.F. and Hendricks, M. (eds) (1989) *International Innovations in Evaluation Methodology: New Directions in Program Evaluation.* San Francisco: Jossey-Bass.

Couto, R.A. (1987) 'Participatory research: Methods and critique', *Clinical Sociology Review*, 5: 83–90.

Creswell, J.W. (2003) *Research Design: Qualitative, Quantitiative and Mixed Approaches.* Thousand Oaks, CA: Sage.

Dewey, J. (1927) *The Public and Its Problems.* New York: H. Holt and Co.

——— (1915) *The School and Society.* Chicago: University of Chicago Press.

Duffy, K.G. and Wong, F.Y. ([1996] 2003) *Community Psychology.* Boston: Alyn and Bacon.

Elden, M. and Chisholm, R.F. (1993) 'Emerging varieties of action research: introduction to the special issue', *Human Relations*, 46:121–42.

Freire, P. (1998) 'Cultural action and conscientization', *Harvard Education Review*, 4: 499–521.

Gallie, W.B. (1956) 'Essentially contested concepts', *Proceedings of the Aristotelian Society*, 58: 167–98.

Gaventa, J. and Horton, B.D. (1981) 'A citizens' research project in Appalachia', *Convergence*, 14: 30–41.

Gieryn, T.F. (1983) 'Boundary work and the demarcation of science from non-science: Strains and interests in professional interests of scientists', *American Sociological Review*, 48: 781–95.

Gottfried, H. (ed.) (1996) *Feminism and Social Change: Bridging Theory and Practice.* Urbana: University of Illinois.

Greenwood, D.S. and Levin, M. (1998) *Introduction to Action Research: Social Research for Social Change.* Thousand Oaks, CA: Sage.

Hall, B., Gillette, A. and Tandon, R. (eds) (1982) *Creating Knowledge: A Monopoly.* New Delhi: Society for Participatory Research in Asia.

Harkavy, I. and Puckett, J.L. (1994) 'Lesson from Hull House for the contemporary urban university', *Social Service Review*, 68: 299–321.

Horton, A.I. (1989) *The Highlander Folk School: A History of its Major Programs.* Brooklyn: Carlson Pub.

Humphreys K. and Rappaport, J. (1994) 'Researching self-help/mutual aid groups and organizations: Many roads one journey', *Applied and Preventive Psychology*, 3: 217–31.

Jackson, T. (1993) 'A way of working: Participatory research and the aboriginal movement in Canada', in P. Park, M. Bryon-Miller, B. Hall, and T. Jackson (eds), *Voices of Change: Participatory Research in the United States and Canada.* Westport, Conn.: Bergin and Garvey.

Jasanoff, S. (2003) '(No?) accounting for expertise', *Science and Public Policy*, 30: 157–62.

Jason, L.A., Keys, C., Suarez-Balcazar, Y. and Taylor, R. (eds) (2003) *Participatory Community Research: Theories and Methods in Action.* Washington, DC: American Psychological Association Books.

Jordan, C., Gust, S. and Scheman, N. (2005) 'The trust-worthiness of research: The paradigm of community-based research', *Metropolitan Universities Journal*, 16: 39–57.

Judd , J., Franksh, C.J., and Moulton, G. (2001) 'Setting standards in the evaluation of community-based health promoting programs', *Health Promotion International*, 16: 367–80.

Laslett, B. and Rapoport, R. (1975) 'Collaborative inter-viewing and interactive research', *Journal of Marriage and the Family*, 37: 968–77.

Lewin, K. (1948) *Resolving Social Conflicts.* New York: Harper.

Maguire, P. (1987) *Doing Participatory Research: A Feminist Approach.* Amherst, Mass.: Center for International Education.

Mies, M. (1983) 'Towards a methodology for feminist research,' in G. Bowles and R.D. Klein (eds), *Theories of Women's Studies.* London: Routledge and Kegan Paul, pp. 117–36.

Minkin, S.A. (2004) 'Public sociology and UC's Institute on Labor and Employment', in *An Invitation to Public Sociology.* Washington, DC: ASA.

Moynihan, D.P. (1965) *The Negro Family: The case for national action.* US Department of Labor. Available at: http://www.dol.gov/asp/programs/history/webid-moynihan.htm.

Nyden, P.W., Figert, A., Shibley, M. and Burrows, D. (eds) (1997) *Building Community: Social Science in Action*. Thousand Oaks, CA: Pine Forge Press.

Oakley, A. (1981) 'Interviewing women: A contradiction in terms', in H. Roberts (ed.), *Doing Feminist Research*. London: Routledge and Kegan Paul, pp. 30–61.

Paine-Andrews, A., Fisher, J.L., Harris, K.J. and Lewis, R.K. (2000) 'Some experiential lessons in supporting and evaluating community-based initiatives for preventing adolescent pregnancy', *Health Promotion Practice*, 248–58.

Park, P., Bryon-Miller, M., Hall, B. and Jackson, T. (eds) (1993) *Voices of Change: Participatory Research in the United States and Canada*. Westport, Conn.: Bergin and Garvey.

Petra, E.M. and Porpora, D.V. (1993) 'Participatory research: Three models and an analysis', *The American Sociologist*, 107–26.

Reason, P. and Bradbury, H. (2001) *Handbook of Action Research: Participative Inquiry and Practice*. Thousand Oaks, CA: Sage.

Richardson, S.A. (1965) *Interviewing: Its Forms and Functions*. New York: Basic Books.

Root, M. (1993) *Philosophy of Social Science: The Methods, Ideals, and Politics of Social Inquiry*. Cambridge, Mass.: Blackwell, pp. 12–32.

Sjoberg, G. and Nett, R. (1968) *A Methodology of Social Research*. New York: Harper and Row.

Squires, Gregory D., and Willett, Dan (1997) 'The Fair Lending Coalition: Organizing Access to Capital in Milwaukee', in Philip Nyden, Anne Figert, Mark Shibley, and Darryl Burrows (eds), *Building Community: Social Science in Action*. Thousand Oaks, CA: Pine Forge Press, pp. 52–7.

Strand, K.J., Marullo, S., Cutforth, N., Stoecker, R. and Donohue, P. (2003) *Community Based Research in Higher Education*. San Francisco: Jossey-Bass.

Suarez-Balcazar, Y. (2003) 'University-community partnerships: A framework and an exemplar', in L.A. Jason, C.Keys, Y. Suarez-Balcazar, and R. Taylor (eds), *Participatory Community Research: Theories and Methods in Action*. Washington, DC: American Psychological Association.

Whyte, W.F. (ed.) (1991) *Participatory Action Research*. Thousand Oaks, CA: Sage.

INTERNET REFERENCES

Center for Urban Research and Learning www.luc.edu/curl

Comm-Org http://comm-org.utoledo.edu

Community-Campus Partnerships for Health http://depts.washington.edu/ccph

Institute for Community Research www.incommunityresearch.org

International Development Research Center http://web.idrc.ca/en/ev

LOKA Institute www.loka.org

PARnet: www.parnet.org

Praxis Project www.thepraxisproject.org

Society for Community Research and Action www.apa.org/divisions/div27

NOTES

1 The term 'community', as I use it here, refers to geographical communities (e.g., a neighborhood or region), as well as communities of interest (e.g., pregnant teens).

2 But, of course, the term 'vampire project' is not entirely apt, since a subject does not become an expert as a result of having had information extracted from her by one.

3 In other words, the expert is responsive to the interests of her subjects only to the extent necessary to enroll or retain them in the study. In a longitudinal study, when a subject has to allow herself to be observed, interviewed or tested over an extended period of time, an expert might have to turn some control over to her in order to win her continued participation, but the concession is self-serving, and, as a result, the study is more expert than community-based (see Laslett and Rapoport, 1975).

4 Highlander is now called 'Highlander Research Education Center.'

5 The writings of John Dewey also inspired the industrial democracy movement. See, for example, *The Public and Its Problems* (1927) and *The School and Society* (1915). According to Dewey, the good of an organization is advanced when members at all levels help to decide and implement important practices or policies. The proper role of education, on his view, is to provide everyone with the training or skills needed to contribute to those decisions and implement the policies.

6 Expert-based research, on their view, discourages citizen involvement in decisions that affect public life and limits the criticisms of research on which public policy rests. See Jasanoff (2003) for a discussion of opposition to public reliance on expert-based research.

7 Though feminists have conducted community-based research for many years, their work is often overlooked in books on action research or participatory research or in discussions of how studies in the social sciences can become more collaborative.

8 An aim of some community-based studies is to translate the findings of expert-based research so

that they can be understood and used by members of the community to achieve their own objectives. See, for example, Squires and Willett (1997); Nyden et al. (1997: 52–7).

9 Some of the findings of Daniel Patrick Moynihan's study of black families in 1965, for example, were reported in many papers, but the stories were limited to a list of ways black families, according to the study, were more dysfunctional than white families.

10 The trust on which collaborative research relies, according to Nyden et al. (1997: 5), 'is not something both sides sign off on in a contract, it is something that emerges as a working relationship develops ... and usually involve[s] a number of steps that start with smaller, limited projects to test the waters and then build into larger research projects.'

11 Expert-based studies can also cause harm to an entire community. However, many of the rules governing the use of human subjects in the social and biomedical sciences were designed with individuals rather than a community in mind and to protect an individual's rather than a group's rights or interests; as a result, the rules do not protect groups from harms, whether the study is directed by an expert or members of the group.

12 According to Herbert Blumer (1939: 39), for example, the task of the sociologist is to 'lift the veils that cover ... group life.' Members of a community, Blumer thought, often fail to see some social phenomena even when they are in front of them; as a result, an outside expert might be needed to see what they are not able to.

13 An expert-based study, on the policymaker's view, could confirm (2) but not (1), since (2) is a matter of fact, while (1) is a matter of value, and only matters of fact can be studied or confirmed scientifically, according to conventional wisdom.

14 Greenwood and Levin write, for example, 'Good professional action researchers achieve a balance of critique and support ... [they must] be expert at opening up lines of discussion ... [and making] evident the tacit knowledge that guides the local conduct' (Greenwood and Levin, 1998: 104–5).

15 Nyden, a prominent advocate of community-based research, writes that inattention 'to rigorous research methods can undermine the credibility of the research ...' and if the community wants to use its resources well, 'it is in its best interests to use solid research techniques' (Nyden et al., 1997: 10).

16 This would decrease class size as measured by the ratio of students to teachers in a classroom if a parent volunteer in the classroom was counted as another teacher.

32

Qualitative Methodology (Including Focus Groups)

Norman K. Denzin and Katherine E. Ryan

OVERVIEW

In this chapter we analyze recent developments and controversies in the uses and representation of qualitative research methodology. Resistances to qualitative inquiry will be reviewed. In this discussion we will privilege focus group methodology as a research style and as a strategy for gathering empirical materials that addresses many of these criticisms. Different styles of qualitative and quantitative research will also be discussed as will interpretive paradigms, strategies of inquiry, and methods of collecting and interpreting empirical materials

In North America qualitative research operates in a complex historical field which crosscuts seven historical moments. These seven moments overlap and simultaneously operate in the present. They can be defined as the *traditional (1900–1950)*, the *modernist or golden age (1950–1970)*, *blurred genres (1970–1986)*, the *crisis of representation or interpretive turn (1986–1990)*, including the narrative turn, and the *postmodern,* a period of experimental and new ethnographies *(1990–1995)*; *post-experimental inquiry (1995–2000)*; and

the *future (2000–)*, which is now. The future, the seventh moment, is concerned with moral discourse, and the use of qualitative research for social justice issues. The seventh moment asks that the social sciences and the humanities become sites for critical conversations about democracy, race, gender, class, nation, freedom and community.

Successive waves of epistemological theorizing move across these moments. The traditional period is associated with the positivist, foundational paradigm. The modernist or golden age and blurred genres moments are connected to the appearance of postpositivist arguments. At the same time a variety of new interpretive, qualitative perspectives were taken up, including hermeneutics, structuralism, semiotics, phenomenology, cultural studies and feminism.[1] In the blurred genre phase the humanities became central resources for critical, interpretive theory and the qualitative research project broadly conceived. The researcher became a *bricoleur* learning how to borrow from many different disciplines.

The blurred genres phase produced the next stage, the crisis of representation. Here researchers struggled with how to locate themselves and their subjects in reflexive texts. Humanists migrated to the social sciences, searching for new social theory, new ways to study popular culture and its local, ethnographic contexts. Social scientists turned to the humanities, hoping to learn how to do complex structural and poststructural readings of social texts. The line between a text and a context blurred. In the postmodern, experimental moment, researchers continued to move away from foundational and quasi-foundational criteria. Alternative evaluative criteria were sought, ones that were evocative, moral, critical and based on local understandings.

North Americans are not the only scholars struggling to create postcolonial, non-essentialist, feminist, dialogic, performance texts: texts informed by the rhetorical, narrative turn in the human disciplines (Delamont et al., 2000). This international work troubles the traditional distinctions between science, the humanities, rhetoric, literature, facts and fictions. As Atkinson and Hammersley (1994: 255), observe, this discourse recognizes 'the literary antecedents of the ethnographic text, and affirms the essential dialectic' underlying these aesthetic and humanistic moves.

Moreover, this literature is reflexively situated in multiple historical and national contexts. It is clear that America's history with qualitative inquiry cannot be generalized to the rest of the world (Atkinson et al., 2001). Nor do all researchers embrace a politicized cultural studies agenda which demands that interpretive texts advance issues surrounding social justice and racial equality.

Lopez (1998: 226) observes that 'there is a large-scale social movement of anticolonialist discourse' and this movement is evident in the emergence of African-American, Chicano, Native American and Maori standpoint theories. These theories question the epistemologies of Western science that are used to validate knowledge about indigenous peoples. Maori scholar Russell Bishop (1998) presents a participatory and participant perspective (Tillman, 1998: 221) that values an embodied and moral commitment to the research community one is working with. This research is characterized by the absence of a need to be in control (Bishop, 1998: 203; Heshusius, 1994). Such a commitment reflects a desire to be connected to and to be a part of moral community. The goal is compassionate understanding (Heshusius, 1994).

These understandings are beginning to blur the spaces between the hypens that join researchers and those studied.

Reading History

Several conclusions can be drawn from this brief history, which is, like all histories, somewhat arbitrary. First, each of the earlier historical moments is still operating in the present, either as legacy or as a set of practices that researchers continue to follow or argue against. The multiple and fractured histories of qualitative research now make it possible for any given researcher to attach a project to a canonical text from any of the above-mentioned historical moments. Multiple criteria of evaluation compete for attention in this field. Second, an embarrassment of choices now characterizes the field of qualitative research. There have never been so many paradigms, strategies of inquiry and methods of analysis to draw upon and utilize. Third, we are in a moment of discovery and rediscovery, as new ways of looking, interpreting, arguing and writing are debated and discussed. Fourth, the qualitiative research act can no longer be viewed from within a neutral or objective positivist perspective. Class, race, gender and ethnicity shape the process of inquiry, making research a multicultural process.

QUALITATIVE RESEARCH AS PROCESS

Any definition of qualitative research must work within this complex historical field. Qualitative research means different things in each of these moments. Nonetheless, an initial, generic definition can be offered.

Qualitative research is multi-method in focus, involving an interpretive, naturalistic approach to its subject matter. This means that qualitative researchers study things in their natural settings, attempting to make sense of or interpret these things in terms of the meanings people bring to them. Qualitative research involves the studied use and collection of a variety of empirical materials—case study, personal experience, introspection, life story, interview, and observational, historical, interactional and visual texts—which describe routine and problematic moments and meanings in individuals' lives.

Three interconnected, generic activities define the qualitative research process. They go by a variety of different labels, including theory, method, and analysis, ontology, epistemology and methodology. *Behind these three terms stands the personal biography of the gendered researcher who speaks from a particular class, racial, cultural, and ethnic community perspective.* The gendered, multi-culturally situated researcher approaches the world with a set of ideas, a framework (theory, ontology) which specifies a set of questions (epistemology) which are then examined (methodology, analysis) in specific ways. That is, empirical materials bearing on the question are collected and then analyzed and written about. Every researcher speaks from within a distinct interpretive community, which configures, in its special way, the multicultural, gendered components of the research act. This community has its own historical, research traditions which constitute a distinct point of view. This perspective leads the researcher to adopt particular views of the 'other' who is studied. At the same time, the politics and the ethics of research must also be considered, for these concerns permeate every phase of the research process.

RESISTANCES TO QUALITATIVE STUDIES

The academic and disciplinary resistances to qualitative research illustrate the politics embedded in this field of discourse. The challenges to qualitative research are many. Qualitative researchers are called journalists or soft scientists. Their work is termed unscientific, or only exploratory, or entirely personal and full of bias. It is called criticism and not theory, or it is interpreted politically, as a disguised version of Marxism or humanism (see Huber, 1995; for a review, see Denzin, 1997: 258–61).

These resistances reflect an uneasy awareness that its traditions commit one to a critique of the positivist or postpositivist project. But the positivist resistance to qualitative research goes beyond the 'ever-present desire to maintain a distinction between hard science and soft scholarship' (Carey, 1989: 99). The positive sciences (physics, chemistry, economics and psychology, for example) are often seen as the crowning achievements of Western civilization, and in their practices it is assumed that 'truth' can transcend opinion and personal bias (Carey, 1989: 99). Qualitative research is seen as an assault on this tradition, whose adherents often retreat into a 'value-free objectivist science' (Carey, 1989: 104) model to defend their position. They seldom attempt to make explicit, and critique, the 'moral and political commitments in their own contingent work' (Carey, 1989: 104).

Positivists further allege that the so-called new experimental qualitative researchers write fiction, not science, and have no way of verifying their truth statements. Ethnographic poetry and fiction signal the death of empirical science, and there is little to be gained by attempting to engage in moral criticism. These critics presume a stable, unchanging reality that can be studied with the empirical methods of objective social science. The province of qualitative research, accordingly, is the world of lived experience, for this is where individual belief and action intersect with culture. Under this model there is no preoccupation with discourse and method as material interpretive practices that constitute representation and description. Thus is the textual, narrative turn rejected by the positivists.

The opposition to positive science by the postpositivists and the poststructuralists is seen, then, as an attack on reason and truth. At the same time, the positive science attack on qualitative research is regarded as an attempt to legislate one version of truth over another.

Politics and Re-emergent Scientism

The scientifically based research movement (SBR) initiated by the National Research Council (NRC) has created a new and hostile political environment for qualitative research. Connected to the No Child Left Behind Act of 2001 (NCLB), SBR embodies a re-emergent scientism (Maxwell, 2004), a positivist, evidence-based epistemology. Researchers are encouraged to employ 'rigorous, systematic, and objective methodology to obtain reliable and valid knowledge' (Ryan and Hood, 2004: 80). The preferred methodology has well-defined causal models using independent and dependent variables. Causal models are examined in the context of randomized controlled experiments which allow replication and generalization (Ryan and Hood, 2004: 81).

Under this framework, qualitative research becomes suspect. There are no well-defined variables or causal models. Observations and measurements are not based on random assignment to experimental groups. Hard evidence is not generated by these methods. At best, case study, interview and ethnographic methods offer descriptive materials that can be tested with experimental methods. The epistemologies of critical race, queer, postcolonial, feminist and postmodern theories are rendered useless, relegated, at best, to the category of scholarship, not science (Ryan and Hood, 2004: 81; St. Pierre, 2004: 132).

Critics of the evidence movement are united on the following points. 'Bush Science' (Lather, 2004: 19), with its experimental, evidence-based methodologies, represents a racialized masculinist backlash to the proliferation of qualitative inquiry

methods over the last two decades (Lather, 2004). The movement endorses a narrow view of science (Maxwell, 2004), celebrating a 'neoclassical experimentalism that is a throwback to the Campbell-Stanley era and its dogmatic adherence to an exclusive reliance on quantitative methods' (Howe, 2004: 42). There is a 'nostalgia for a simple and ordered universe of science that never was' (Popkewitz, 2004: 62). With its emphasis on only one form of scientific rigor, the NRC ignores the need and value of complex historical, contextual and political criteria for evaluating inquiry (Bloch, 2004).

Neoclassical experimentalists extol evidence-based 'medical research as the model for educational research, particularly the random clinical trial' (Howe, 2004: 48). But the random clinical trial—dispensing a pill—is quite unlike 'dispensing a curriculum' (Howe, 2004: 48), nor can the 'effects' of the educational experiment be easily measured, unlike a '10-point reduction in diastolic blood pressure' (Howe, 2004: 48).

Qualitative researchers must learn to think outside the box, as they critique the NRC and its methodological guidelines (Atkinson, 2004). We must apply our critical imaginations to the meaning of such terms as randomized design, causal model, policy studies and public science (Cannella and Lincoln, 2004; Weinstein, 2004). More deeply we must resist conservative attempts to discredit qualitative inquiry by placing it back inside the box of positivism.

Mixed-Methods Experimentalism

Howe (2004) observes that the NRC finds a place for qualitative methods in mixed-methods experimental designs. In such designs qualitative methods may be 'employed either singly or in combination with quantitative methods, including the use of randomized experimental designs (Howe, 2004: 49). Mixed methods are direct descendants of classical experimentalism. They presume a methodological hierarchy, with quantitative methods at the top, relegating qualitative methods to 'a largely auxiliary role in pursuit of the *technocratic* aim of accumulating knowledge of "what works"' (Howe, 2004: 53–4).

The mixed-methods movement takes qualitative methods out of their natural home, which is within the critical, interpretive framework (Howe, 2004: 54; but see Teddlie and Tashakkori, 2003: 15). It divides inquiry into dichotomous categories: exploration versus confirmation. Qualitative work is assigned to the first category, quantitative research to the second (Teddlie and Tashakkori, 2003: 15). Like the classic experimental model, it excludes stakeholders from dialogue and active participation in the research process. This weakens its democratic and dialogical dimensions, and decreases the likelihood the previously silenced voices will be heard (Howe, 2004: 56–7).

The Pragmatic Criticisms of Anti-Foundationalism

Seale et al. (2004: 2) contest what they regard as the excesses of an anti-methodological, 'any thing goes' romantic postmodernism that is associated with the critical, interpretive qualitative tradition. They assert that too often the approach we value produces 'low quality qualitative research and research results that are quite stereotypical and close to common sense' (Seale et al., 2004: 2).

In contrast they propose a practice-based, pragmatic approach that places research practice at the center. Research involves an engagement 'with a variety of things and people: research materials ... social theories, philosophical debates, values, methods, tests ... research participants' (Seale et al., 2004: 2). (Actually this approach is quite close to our own, especially our view of the *bricoleur* and *bricolage*.) Situated methodology rejects the anti-foundational claim that there are only partial truths; that the dividing line between fact and fiction has broken down (Seale et al., 2004: 3). They believe that this dividing line has not collapsed, that we should not accept stories if they do not

accord with the best available facts (Seale et al., 2004: 6). Oddly, these pragmatic procedural arguments reproduce a variant of the evidence-based model and its criticisms of poststructural, performative sensibilities.

This complex political terrain defines the many traditions and strands of qualitative research: the British and its presence in other national contexts; the American pragmatic, naturalistic and interpretive traditions in sociology, anthropology, communications and education; the German and French phenomenological, hermeneutic, semiotic, Marxist, structural and poststructural perspectives; feminist studies, African-American studies, Latino studies, queer studies, and studies of indigenous and aboriginal cultures. The politics of qualitative research create a tension which informs each of the above traditions. This tension itself is constantly being re-examined and interrogated, as qualitative research confronts a changing historical world, new intellectual positions and its own institutional and academic conditions.

We turn now to a brief discussion of the major differences between qualitative and quantitative approaches to research.

QUALITATIVE VERSUS QUANTITATIVE RESEARCH

The word qualitative implies an emphasis on processes, and meanings which are not rigorously examined or measured (if measured at all) in terms of quantity, amount, intensity or frequency. Qualitative researchers stress the socially constructed nature of reality, the intimate relationship between the researcher and what is studied, and the situational constraints that shape inquiry. They deploy a variety of interpretive strategies, including participant observation; traditional, auto and on-line ethnography; case study; and visual and discourse analysis, as well as grounded theory strategies.

Such researchers emphasize the value-laden nature of inquiry. They seek answers to questions which stress *how* social experience is created and given meaning. In contrast, quantitative studies emphasize the measurement and analysis of causal relationships between variables, not processes. Proponents claim that their work is done from within a value-free framework.

Research Styles: Doing the Same Things Differently?

Of course, qualitative and quantitative researchers both 'think they know something about society worth telling to others, and they use a variety of forms, media and means to communicate their ideas and findings' (Becker, 1986: 122). Qualitative research differs from quantitative research in five significant ways (Becker, 1996). These points of difference turn on different ways of addressing the same set of issues.

Uses of Positivism and Postpositivism

First, both perspectives are shaped by the positivist and postpositivist traditions in the physical and social sciences. These two positive science traditions hold to, respectively, naive and critical realist positions concerning reality and its perception. In the positivist version it is contended that there is a reality out there to be studied, captured and understood, while the postpositivists argue that reality can never be fully apprehended, only approximated (Guba, 1990: 22). Postpositivism relies on multiple methods as a way of capturing as much of reality as possible. At the same time emphasis is placed on the discovery and verification of theories. Traditional evaluation criteria like internal and external validity are stressed, as are the use of qualitative procedures that lend themselves to structured (sometimes statistical) analysis.

Historically, qualitative research was defined within the positivist paradigm, where qualitative researchers attempted to do good positivist research with less rigorous methods and procedures. Some mid-century qualitative researchers (Becker et al., 1961) reported participant observations findings in terms of quasi-statistics. As recently as 1999 (Strauss and Corbin, 1999), two leaders of the grounded theory approach to qualitative research attempted to modify the usual canons of good [positivistic] science to fit their own postpositivist conception of rigorous research.

Flick (1998: 2–3) usefully summarizes the differences between these two approaches to inquiry. He observes that the quantitative approach has been used for purposes of isolating 'causes and effects ... operationalizing theoretical relations ... [and] measuring and ... quantifying phenomena ... allowing the generalization of finding' (Flick, 1998: 3). But today doubt is cast on such projects, 'Rapid social change and the resulting diversification of life worlds are increasingly confronting social researchers with new social contexts and perspectives ... traditional deductive methodologies ... are failing ... thus research is increasingly forced to make use of inductive strategies instead of starting from theories and testing them ... knowledge and practice are studied as local knowledge and practice' (Flick, 1998: 2).

Acceptance of Postmodern Sensibilities

The use of quantitative, positivist methods and assumptions has been rejected by a new generation of qualitative researchers who are attached to poststructural, postmodern sensibilities. These researchers argue that positivist methods are but one way of telling a story about society or the social world. They may be no better, or no worse, than any other method; they just tell a different kind of story.

This tolerant view is not shared by all. Many members of the critical theory, constructivist, poststructural and postmodern schools of thought reject positivist and postpositivist criteria when evaluating their own work. They see these criteria as being irrelevant to their work, and contend that they reproduce only a certain kind of science; a science which silences too many voices. These researchers seek alternative methods for evaluating their work, including verisimilitude, emotionality, personal responsibility, an ethic of caring, political praxis, multi-voiced texts, dialogues with subjects, and so on.

Capturing the Individual's Point of View

Both qualitative and quantitative researchers are concerned about the individual's point of view. However, qualitative investigators think they can get closer to the actor's perspective by detailed interviewing and observation. They argue that quantitative researchers are seldom able to capture the subject's perspective because they have to rely on more remote, inferential empirical materials.

Examining the Constraints of Everyday Life

Qualitative researchers are more likely to confront and come up against the constraints of the everyday social world. They see this world in action and embed their findings in it. Quantitative researchers abstract from this world and seldom study it directly. They seek a nomothetic or etic science based on probabilities derived from the study of large numbers of randomly selected cases. These kinds of statements stand above and outside the constraints of everyday life. Qualitative researchers, on the other hand, are committed to an emic, ideographic, case-based position which directs their attention to the specifics of particular cases.

Securing Thick Descriptions

Qualitative researchers believe that rich descriptions of the social world are valuable, while quantitative researchers, with their etic, nomothetic commitments, are less concerned with such detail. They are deliberately unconcerned with such descriptions because such detail interrupts the process of developing generalizations.

The five points of difference described above (uses of positivism, postmodernism, capturing the individual's point of view, examining the constraints of everyday life, securing thick descriptions) reflect commitments to different styles of research, different epistemologies and different forms of representation. Each work tradition is governed by a different set of genres; each has its own classics, its own preferred forms of representation, interpretation and textual evaluation. Qualitative researchers use ethnographic prose, historical narratives, first-person accounts, still photographs, life history, fictionalized facts, and biographical and autobiographical materials, among others. Quantitative researchers use mathematical models, statistical tables and graphs, and usually write in an impersonal, third-person prose.

The focus group is a methodology that effectively addresses these five issues.

THE FOCUS GROUP

Compared to other qualitative research methods like individual interviews and participant observation, the focus group is a relatively new method. Originally called the focused interview (Merton and Kendall, 1946), focus groups are a particular kind of group interview. Focus groups are distinguished from other types of group interviews because the researcher/interviewer asks a set of targeted questions designed to elicit *collective* views about a specific topic (Fontana and Frey, 2005; Merton et al., 1956).

The focus group as a research method was conceptualized and implemented by Robert Merton when he joined a project directed by Paul Lazarsfeld in the Bureau of Applied Social Research at Columbia University. Based on an experimental, quantitative approach to studying audiences' responses to wartime radio propaganda, a group of individuals ($N = 12$) pushed red and green buttons indicating a negative or positive response to what they listened to on the radio. To augment the quantitative studies, the focus group method was designed to provide a window into how the groups thought and talked about what they watched—a view of others' reality by asking them questions (an interview) about what they heard.

This early focus group example illustrates the flexibility and richness of this qualitative method. On the one hand, this method can be easily used to complement quantitative work

Table 32.1　Descriptive Typology for Comparing Focus Group Genres

	Adjunct to Quantitative Methods	Traditional Qualitative Method	Qualitative Interpretive Practice
Epistemology	PostPositivist	Postpositivist	Interpretive Turn
Purpose	Pre-test, hypothesis generating	Build theory, access to hard-to-reach populations or sensitive issues	Emancipation and knowledge construction
Setting	Lab	Natural or field setting	Natural setting or safe space
Researcher Stance	Scientific Neutrality	Empathic	Politically laden
Structure	Standardized, replicable, directive, predetermined	Mixed structure	Non-standardized, variant, emergent, spontaneous

by providing detailed descriptions about focus group participants' perspectives. Further, focus groups can be used to examine the meanings and group processes involved in participants' experiences and what is being studied (Bloor et al., 2001). Interestingly, while focus groups have been used consistently in consumer research since the 1950s, the focus group technique was largely absent in social science research until the 1980s (Bloor et al., 2001; Morgan, 2002).

The focus group method is ideal for illustrating the current tensions and controversies characterizing qualitative methodology. Table 32.1 presents a descriptive cataloging of what we identify as focus group genres present in qualitative methodology in the social sciences. Clearly, a table such as this fails to capture all the theoretical complexities and is an oversimplification. In addition, as this table demonstrates, while there are distinctions among these approaches, overlap is clearly evident. Nevertheless, there are notable distinctions in epistemology, purpose, stance, setting and structure among these genres. Below we elaborate these distinctions discussing how these genres evolved from a historical perspective.

As an Adjunct to Quantitative Methods

Focus groups re-emerged in social research in the 1980s about the time of the interpretive turn in the social sciences (see discussion on

p. 584). The contemporary interest in focus groups has been linked to a rising interest in qualitative methods and the acknowledgment of and efforts to understand diversity in society (Morgan, 2002). Large-scale social and educational program evaluation studies from the 1970s, using only experimental methods with no explanation for null findings, led to an increase in mixed-methods designs (Greene, 2000; House, 2005). While the quantitative methods within a quasi-experimental mixed design were perhaps more valued, the focus group provided information about how different groups (e.g., males and females) experienced a program or treatment (e.g., math instruction) (Morgan, 2002).

Survey researchers also used the focus group for pre-testing questionnaire wording or to examine how different groups (e.g., Blacks and Whites) interpreted items (Fontana and Frey, 2005). Further, at the intersection between political science and consumer research, focus groups were beginning to be used to understand public perceptions of political issues and candidates (Stewart and Shamdasani, 1990).

Initially, focus groups primarily gained acceptance in the social sciences in the 1980s within the postpositivist framework. These kinds of focus groups, like the original focused interview, would be held in a lab setting with some kind of randomized sample. While the generalizability of focus group findings is often questioned, there is a scientific orientation towards replication. The researcher maintains an objective stance by following a standardized interview protocol composed of structured questions. By maintaining this structure, the focus group was and continues to be a qualitative method that serves as an adjunct to quantitative methods (Bloor et al., 2001; Morgan, 2002).

As a Traditional Qualitative Method

Although qualitative researchers had often ignored or compared focus groups unfavorably to other qualitative methods (Agar and MacDonald, 1995; Morgan, 2002), by the early 1990s focus groups were beginning to be used as a self-contained method by qualitative researchers (Morgan, 1988). Focus groups were used as a standalone method in traditional qualitative investigations for studying sensitive topics (Zeller, 1993), as a research approach with hard-to-reach populations (e.g., low-income, minority females) (Jarrett, 1993), and as part of community mobilization (Plaut et al., 1993). Feminist qualitative researchers began to use the focus group for work with diverse groups of women (e.g., low-income, women of color) (Fine, 1994; Madriz, 1997, 2000).

As a more traditional qualitative method, the focus group structure is open to more variation. Researchers serve as facilitators of conversations using a structured or unstructured interview protocol (Jarrett, 1993; Madriz, 2000). Further, when conducting focus groups, the researcher stance may shift from scientific neutrality towards an empathetic stance (Fontana and Frey, 2005). There is considerable range in how an empathetic stance is conceptualized, including breaking down barriers between the researcher and researched to actual advocacy for participating groups. The empathetic stance is illustrated in Jarrett's work (1993), when she breaks down barriers between her (the researcher) and low-income women (the researched). For instance, she personally meets and asks each

potential focus group participant at the local Head Start where these women bring their children each day. Jarrett also visited their neighborhoods.

Feminist qualitative researchers began to use the focus group for work with diverse groups of women and continued to reconceptualize the focus group structure (Fine, 1994; Madriz, 1997; 2000). After critiquing individual interviews for reproducing the unequal power relationships between the researcher and researched subject, homogeneous focus groups (e.g., race, class, age or appropriate combinations of these) were proposed as an alternative (Madriz, 1997). Power relationships were rearranged with focus groups because the number of researched increased in relationship to the researcher. Such rearrangements were theorized to reduce the social isolation of these women as individuals setting the stage for them to empower each other and validate their own voices and experiences (Madriz, 2000).

As Qualitative Interpretive Practice

While Madriz (1997) used focus groups to build theory from the lived experiences of women—a defining characteristic of postpositivist qualitative research, this work is a turning point for focus groups (Kamberelis and Dimitriadis, 2005). By redefining the power relations, it was here that focus groups began to shift from a qualitative research method to a set of qualitative, interpretive research practices. Work by Lather and Smithies (1997) illustrates the focus group as qualitative research practice (Kamberelis and Dimitriadis, 2005) where they shift the boundaries between the researcher and researched in focus groups. In their work with women with HIV/AIDS, focus groups were reconstructed as a dialogue, with both researcher and researched each having unique domains of knowledge. It is through the dialogues in focus group interactions between and among the researcher and researched that new knowledge, including new descriptions, interpretations, and explanations, are co-constructed about the issues at hand (women and HIV/AIDS).

As a qualitative, interpretive research practice within the interpretive turn, the purpose is emancipatory while changing what counts as knowledge. The structure is changed substantially where focus groups may define or have the opportunity to prepare a list of issues for dialogue. The empathetic stance is politically laden, with the researcher defined as an explicit advocate. Researchers serve as advocates by using the results from this kind of work to contribute to improved social conditions for the particular groups participating in the focus group (Fontana and Frey, 2005).

WORKING THE HYPHEN – THE OTHER AS RESEARCH SUBJECT

From its turn of the century birth in modern, interpretive form, qualitative research has been haunted by a double-faced ghost. On the one hand, qualitative researchers have assumed that qualified, competent observers could with objectivity, clarity and precision report on their own observations of the social world, including the experiences of others. On the other, researchers have held to the belief in a real subject, or real individual, who is present in the world and able, in some form, to report on his or her experiences. So armed, researchers could blend their own observations with the self-reports provided by subjects through interviews, life story, personal experience, and case-study documents.

These two beliefs have led qualitative researchers across disciplines to seek a method that would allow them to record their own observations accurately while also uncovering the meanings their subjects brought to their life experiences. This method would rely upon the subjective verbal and written expressions of meaning given by the individuals studied, these expressions being windows into the inner life of the person. Since Dilthey (1900/1976), this search

for a method has led to a perennial focus in the human disciplines on qualitative, interpretive methods.

Recently, as noted above, this position and its beliefs have come under assault. Poststructuralists and postmodernists have contributed to the understanding that there is no clear window into the inner life of an individual. Any gaze is always filtered through the lenses of language, gender, social class, race and ethnicity. There are no objective observations, only observations socially situated in the worlds of the observer and the observed. Subjects, or individuals, are seldom able to give full explanations of their actions or intentions; all they can offer are accounts or stories about what they did and why. No single method can grasp the subtle variations in ongoing human experience. Consequently, qualitative researchers deploy a wide-range of interconnected interpretive methods, always seeking better ways to make more understandable the worlds of experience that have been studied.

Interpretive Paradigms

All qualitative researchers are philosophers in that 'universal sense in which all human beings ... are guided by highly abstract principles' (Bateson, 1972: 320). These principles combine beliefs about ontology (What kind of being is the human being? What is the nature of reality?), epistemology (What is the relationship between the inquirer and the known?), and methodology (How do we know the world, or gain knowledge of it?) (see Guba and Lincoln, 2000). These beliefs shape how the qualitative researcher sees the world and acts in it. The researcher is 'bound within a net of epistemological and ontological premises which—regardless of ultimate truth or falsity—become partially self-validating' (Bateson, 1972: 314).

The net that contains the researcher's epistemological, ontological and methodological premises may be termed a paradigm or interpretive framework, a 'basic set of beliefs that guides action' (Guba, 1990: 17). All research

Table 32.2   Interpretive Paradigms

Paradigm/Theory	Criteria	Form of Theory	Type of Narration
Posititivist–Postpositivist	Internal, external Validity	Logical-deductive, grounded	Scientific report
Constructivist	Trustworthiness, credibility, transferability, confirmability	Substantive–formal	Interpretive case studies, ethnographic fiction
Feminist	Afrocentric, lived experience, dialogue, caring, accountability, race, class, gender, reflexivity, praxis, emotion, concrete grounding	Critical, standpoint	Essays, stories, experimental writing
Ethnic	Afrocentric, lived experience, dialogue, caring, accountability, race, class, gender	Standpoint, critical, historical	Essays, fables, dramas
Marxist	Emancipatory theory, falsifiable, dialogical, race, class, gender	Critical, historical, economic	Historical, economic, sociocultural analyses
Cultural studies	Cultural practices, praxis, social texts, subjectivities	Social criticism	Cultural theory as criticism
Queer Theory	Reflexivity, deconstruction	Social criticism, historical analysis	Theory as criticism, autobiography

is interpretive and is guided by a set of beliefs and feelings about the world and how it should be understood and studied. Some of these beliefs may be taken for granted, only assumed, while others are highly problematic and controversial. Each interpretive paradigm makes particular demands on the researcher, including the questions that are asked, and the interpretations that are brought to them.

At the most general level, four major interpretive paradigms structure qualitative research: positivist and postpositivist, constructivist-interpretive, critical (Marxist, emancipatory), and feminist-poststructural. These four abstract paradigms become more complicated at the level of concrete specific interpretive communities. At this level it is possible to identify not only the constructivist but also multiple versions of feminism (Afrocentric and poststructural),[2] as well as specific ethnic, Marxist and cultural studies paradigms.

Table 32.2 presents these paradigms and their assumptions, including their criteria for evaluating research, and the typical form that an interpretive or theoretical statement assumes in the paradigm.[3]

The positivist and postpositive paradigms work from within a realist and critical realist ontology, objective epistemologies, and rely upon experimental, quasi-experimental, survey, and rigorously defined qualitative methodologies. The constructivist paradigm assumes a relativist ontology (there are multiple realities), a subjectivist epistemology (knower and subject create understandings), and a naturalistic (in the natural world) set of methodological procedures. Findings are usually presented in terms of the criteria of grounded theory. Terms like credibility, transferability, dependability and confirmability replace the usual positivist criteria of internal and external validity, reliability and objectivity.

Feminist, ethnic, Marxist, cultural studies and queer theory models privilege a materialist–realist ontology—that is, the real world makes a material difference in terms of race, class and gender. Subjectivist epistemologies and naturalistic methodologies (usually ethnographies) are also employed. Empirical materials and theoretical arguments are evaluated in terms of their emancipatory implications. Criteria from gender and racial communities (e.g. African-American) may be applied (emotionality and feeling, caring, personal accountability, dialogue). Poststructural feminist theories emphasize problems with the social text, its logic, and its inability to ever fully represent the world of lived experience. Positivist and postpositivist criteria of evaluation are replaced by other terms, including the reflexive, multi-voiced text that is grounded in the experiences of oppressed people.

The cultural studies and queer theory paradigms are multi-focused, with many different strands drawing from Marxism, feminism and the postmodern sensibility. There is a tension between a humanistic cultural studies which stresses lived experiences, and a more structural cultural studies project which stresses the structural and material determinants (race, class, gender) of experience. The cultural studies and queer theory paradigms use methods strategically, as resources for understanding and for producing resistances to local structures of domination. Such scholars may do close textual readings and discourse analysis of cultural texts, as well as local ethnographies, open-ended interviewing and participant observation. The focus is on how race, class and gender are produced and enacted in historically specific situations.

BRIDGING THE HISTORICAL MOMENTS: INTO THE PRESENT

Two theses have organized the discussion till this point. First, in its relationship to the field of sociological inquiry, the history of qualitative research is defined more by breaks and ruptures than by a clear evolutionary, progressive movement from one stage to the next. These breaks and ruptures move in cycles and phases, so that what is passé today may be in vogue a decade from now. Just as the postmodern, for example, reacts to the modern, some day there may well be a neo-modern phase which extols Malinowski and the Chicago school, and finds the current post-structural, postmodern moment abhorrent.

The second assumption builds on the tensions that now define qualitative sociological inquiry. There is an elusive center to this contradictory, tension-riddled enterprise, which seems to be moving further and further away from grand narratives and single overarching ontological, epistemological and methodological paradigms. This center lies in the humanistic commitment of the researcher to always study the world from the perspective of the interacting individual. From this simple commitment flow the liberal and radical politics of qualitative sociological social-problems research. Action, feminist, clinical, constructionist, ethnic, critical and cultural studies researchers are all united on this point. They all share the belief that a politics of liberation must always begin with the perspective, desires and dreams of those individuals and groups who have been oppressed by the larger ideological, economic and political forces of a society, or a historical moment.

This commitment defines an ever-present but always shifting center in the discourses of qualitative research. The center shifts and moves, as new, previously oppressed or silenced voices enter the discourse. Thus, for example, feminists and ethnic researchers have articulated their own relationship to the postpositivist and critical paradigms. These new articulations then refocus and redefine previous ontologies, epistemologies and methodologies, including positivism, and postpositivism.

These two theses suggest that only the broad outlines of the future can be predicted, as the field confronts and continues to define itself in the face of four fundamental issues.

The first and second issues are what we have called the crises of representation and legitimation. These two crises speak, respectively, to the Other and their representations in our texts, and to the authority we claim for our texts. Third, there is the continued emergence of a cacophony of voices speaking with varying agendas from specific gender, race, class and ethnic and third-world perspectives.

Fourth, throughout its history qualitative sociological research has been defined in terms of shifting scientific, moral, sacred and religious discourses. Since the Enlightenment, science and religion have been separated, but only at the ideological level, for in practice religion and the sacred have constantly informed science and the scientific project. The divisions between these two systems of meaning are becoming more and more blurred. Critics increasingly see science from within a magical, shamanistic framework (Rosaldo, 1989: 219). Others are moving science away from its empiricist foundations and closer to a critical, interpretive project which stresses morals and moral standards of evaluation (Clough, 1998: 136–7).

Three understandings shape the present moment:

- The qualitative sociological researcher is not an objective, authoritative, politically neutral observer standing outside and above the social world (Bruner, 1993: 1).
- The qualitative researcher is ' historically positioned and locally situated [as] an all-too-human [observer] of the human condition' (Bruner, 1993: 1);
- Meaning is 'radically plural, always open, and ... there is politics in every account' (Bruner, 1993: 1).

The problems of representation and legitimation flow from these three understandings.

THE CRISIS OF REPRESENTATION

As indicated, this crisis asks the questions, 'Who is The Other? Can we ever hope to speak authentically of the experience of The Other, or An Other? And if not, how do we create a social science which includes The Other?' The short answer to these questions is that we move to including The Other in the larger research processes which we have developed. For some, this means participatory, or collaborative, research and evaluation efforts. These activities can occur in a variety of institutional sites, including clinical, educational, and social welfare settings.

For still others, it means a form of liberatory investigation wherein The Others are trained, perhaps using focus groups, to engage in their own social and historical interrogative efforts, and are then assisted in devising answers to questions of historical and contemporary oppression which are rooted in the values and cultural artifacts which characterize their communities.

For still other social scientists, it means becoming co-authors in narrative adventures. And for still others, it means constructing what are called 'experimental' or 'messy' texts, where multiple voices speak, often in conflict, and where the reader is left to sort out which experiences speak to his or her personal life. For still others, it means presenting to the inquiry and policy community a series of auto-histories, personal narratives, lived experiences, poetic representations, and sometimes fictive and/or fictional texts, which allow The Other to speak for herself or himself. The inquirer or evaluator becomes merely the connection between the field text, the research text and the consuming community in making certain that such voices are heard. Sometimes, increasingly, it is The Institutionalized Other who speaks, especially as The Other gains access to the knowledge-producing corridors of power and achieves entry into the particular group of elites known as intellectuals and academics or faculty.

The point is that both The Other and more mainstream social scientists recognize that there is no such thing as unadulterated truth; that speaking from a faculty, an institution of higher education or a corporate perspective automatically means that one speaks from a privileged and powerful vantage point; and that this vantage point is one to which many do not have access, either by dint of social station or education.

The Author's Place in the Text

There are many ways to openly return the author to the qualitative research text. Fictional narratives of the self may be written. Performance texts can be produced. Dramatic readings can be given. Field interviews can be transformed into poetic texts, and poetry, as well as short stories and plays, can be written. The author can engage in a dialogue with those studied. The author may write through a narrator, 'directly as a character ... or through multiple characters, or one character may speak in many voices, or the writer may come in and then go out of the [text]' (Bruner, 1993: 6).

THE CRISIS OF LEGITIMATION

It is clear that critical race theory, queer theory and feminist arguments are moving farther and farther away from postpositivist models of validity and textual authority. This is the *crisis of legitimation* that follows the collapse of foundational epistemologies. This so-called crisis arose when anthropologists and other social scientists addressed the authority of the Text. By the authority of the Text we reference the claim any text makes to being accurate, true and complete. Is a text faithful to the context and the individuals it is supposed to represent? Does the text have the right to assert that it is a report to the larger world, which addresses not only the researcher's interests, but also the interests of those studied?

This is not an illegitimate set of questions, and it affects all of us and the work that we do. And while many social scientists might enter the question from different angles, these twin crises are confronted by everyone. A variety of new and old voices—critical theory, feminist and ethnic scholars—have also entered the present situation, offering solutions to the problems surrounding the crises of representation and legitimation. The move is toward pluralism, and many social scientists now recognize that no picture is ever complete; that what is needed is many perspectives, many voices, before we can achieve deep understandings of social phenomena, and before we can assert that a narrative is complete.

The modernist dream of a Grand or Master Narrative is now a dead project. The postmodern era is defined, in part, by the belief that there is no single umbrella in the history of the world which might incorporate and represent fairly the dreams, aspirations and experiences of all peoples.

BACK TO THE FUTURE

The need for a civic social science remains (Agger, 2000). We want a civic sociology— by which is meant fieldwork located not only in sociology, but rather an extended, enriched, cultivated social science embracing all the disciplines. Such a project characterizes a whole new generation of qualitative researchers: educationists, sociologists, political scientists, clinical practitioners in psychology and medicine, nurses, communications and media specialists, cultural studies workers, and a score of other assorted disciplines.

The moral imperatives of such work cannot be ignored. We have several generations of social science which has not only *not* solved serious human problems, but has many times only worsened the plight of those we studied. Beyond morality is something equally important: the mandates for such work come from our own sense of the human community. A detached social science frequently serves only those with the means, the social designation and the intellectual capital to keep themselves detached. We face a choice, in the seventh moment, of declaring ourselves committed to detachment or in solidarity with the human community. We come to know, and we come to exist meaningfully, only in community. We have the opportunity to rejoin that community as its resident intellectuals and change agents.

And as we do so, we move more deeply into emancipatory interpretive qualitative research practices, seeking new ways of using focus groups and other dialogical practices for purposes of social advocacy.

REFERENCES AND SELECT BIBLIOGRAPHY

Agar, M.H. and MacDonald, J. (1995) 'Focus groups and ethnography', *Human Organizations*, 54: 78–86.

Agger, B. (2000) *Public Sociology: From Social Facts to Literary Acts*. New York: Rowman and Littlefield.

Atkinson, E. (2004) 'Thinking outside the box: An exercise in heresy', *Qualitative Inquiry*, 10 (1): 111–29.

Atkinson, P., Coffey, A. and Delamont, S. (2001) 'Editorial: A debate about our canon', *Qualitative Research*, 1: 5–21.

Atkinson, P. and Hammersley, M. (1994) 'Ethnography and participant observation', in Norman K. Denzin and Yvonna S. Lincoln (eds), *Handbook of Qualitative Research*. Thousand Oaks: Sage, pp. 248–61.

Bateson, G. (1972) *Steps to an Ecology of Mind*. New York: Ballantine.

Becker, H.S., Geer,B., Hughes, E.C. and Strauss, A. (1961) *Boys in White*. Chicago: University of Chicago Press.

Becker, H.S. (1996) 'The Epistemology of qualitative research', in R. Jessor, A. Colby and R.A. Schweder (eds), *Ethnography and Human Development*. Chicago: University of Chicago Press, pp. 53–71.

———— (1986) *Doing Things Together*. Evanston, IL: Northwestern University Press.

———— (1970) 'The life history and the scientific mosaic', in *Sociological Work: Method and Substance*. Chicago: Aldine Publishing Company, pp. 63–74.

Bishop, R. (1998) 'Freeing ourselves from neo-colonial domination in research: A Maori approach to creating knowledge', *International Journal of Qualitative Studies in Education*, 11: 199–219.

Bloch, M. (2004) 'A discourse that disciplines, governs, and regulates: On scientific research in education', *Qualitative Inquiry*, 10 (1): 96–110.

Bloor, M., Frankland, J., Thomas, M. and Robson, K. (2001) *Focus Groups in Social Research*. London: Sage Publications.

Bruner, E. (1993) 'Introduction: The ethnographic self', in Paul Benson (ed.), *Anthropology and Literature*. Urbana: University of Illinois Press, pp. 1–26.

Cannella, G.S. and Lincoln, Y.S. (2004) 'Dangerous discourses II: Comprehending and countering the redeployment of discourses (and resources) in the generation of liberatory inquiry', *Qualitative Inquiry*, 10 (2): 165–74.

Carey, J.W. (1989) *Culture as Communication*. Boston: Unwin Hyman.

Clifford, J. and Marcus, G.E. (eds) (1986) *Writing Culture*. Berkeley: University of California Press.

Clough, P.T. ([1992] 1998) *The End(s) of Ethnography*, New York: Peter Lang.

Conrad, P. (1997) 'Presidential address: Public eyes and private genes: Historical frames, news constructions and social problems', *Social Problems*, 44: 139–54.

Delamont, S., Coffey, A. and Atkinson, P. (2000) 'The twilight years?', *International Journal of Qualitative Studies in Education*, 13: 223–38.

Denzin, N.K. (2003) *Performance Ethnography: Critical Pedagogy and the Politics of Culture*. Thousand Oaks, CA: Sage.

Denzin, N.K. ([1989] 2001) *Interpretive Interactionism*. Thousand Oaks, CA: Sage.

———— (1997) *Interpretive Ethnography*. Thousand Oaks, CA: Sage.

Denzin, N.K. and Lincoln, Y.S. ([1994] 2000a) 'Preface', in Norman K. Denzin and Y.S. Lincoln (eds), *Handbook of Qualitative Research*. Thousand Oaks, CA: Sage, pp. ix–xx.

———— (2000b) 'Introduction: The discipline and practice of qualitative research', in N.K. Denzin and Y.S. Lincoln (eds), *Handbook of Qualitative Research*. Thousand Oaks, CA: Sage, pp. 1–29.

———— (2005) 'Introduction: The discipline and practice of qualitative research', in N.K. Denzin and Y.S. Lincoln (eds), *Handbook of Qualitative Research*. Thousand Oaks, CA: Sage. pp. x–xxx.

Dilthey, W.L. ([1900] 1976) *Selected Writings*. Cambridge: Cambridge University Press.

Dunbar, C., Jr., Rodriguez, D. and Parker, L. (2002) 'Race, Subjectivity and the interview process', in J.F. Gubrium and J.A. Holstein (eds), *Handbook of Interview Research*. Thousand Oaks, CA: Sage, pp. 279–98.

Fine, M. (1994) 'Working the hyphens: Reinventing self and other in qualitative research', in N.K. Denzin and Y.S. Lincoln (eds), *Handbook of Qualitative Research*. Thousand Oaks, CA: Sage, pp. 70–82.

Flick, U. (1998) *An Introduction to Qualitative Research*. London: Sage.

Fontana, A. and Frey, J.H. (2005) 'The interview: From neutral stance to political involvement', in N.K. Denzin and Y.S. Lincoln, (eds), *The Sage Handbook of Qualitative Research*. Thousand Oaks, CA: Sage Publications, pp. 695–728.

Freire, P. (1998) *Pedagogy of Freedom*. New York: Rowman and Littlefield.

Glaser, B. and Strauss, A. (1967) *The Discovery of Grounded Theory*. Chicago: Aldine.

Greene, J. (2000) 'Understanding social programs through evaluation', in N.K. Denzin and Y.S. Lincoln, (eds), *The Handbook of Qualitative Research*. Thousand Oaks, CA: Sage Publications, pp. 981–1000.

Guba, E.G. (1990) 'The Alternative paradigm dialog', in E.G. Guba (ed.), *The Paradigm Dialog*. Newbury Park, CA: Sage, pp. 17–30.

Guba, E.G. and Lincoln, Y.S. (2000) 'Paradigmatic controversies, contradictions, and emerging confluences', in N.K. Denzin and Y.S. Lincoln, (eds), *The Handbook of Qualitative Research*. Thousand Oaks, CA: Sage, pp. 163–88.

Gubrium, J.F. and Holstein, J.A. (2002) From the individual interview to the interview society', in J.F. Gubrium and J.A. Holstein (eds), *Handbook of Interview Research*. Thousand Oaks: Sage, pp. 3–32.

Heshusius, L. (1994) 'Freeing ourselves from objectivity: Managing subjectivity or turning toward a participatory mode of consciousness', *Educational Researcher*, 23: 15–22.

Howe, K.R. (2004) 'A Critique of experimentalism', *Qualitative Inquiry*, 10 (1): 42–61.

House, E. (2005) 'Qualitative evaluation and changing social policy', in N.K. Denzin and Y.S. Lincoln, (eds), *The Handbook of Qualitative Research*. Thousand Oaks, CA: Sage Publications, pp. 1069–82.

Huber, J. (1995). Centennial essay: Institutional perspectives on sociology', *American Journal of Sociology*, 101: 194–216.

Jameson, F. (1991) *Postmodernism, or, the Cultural Logic of Late Capitalism*. Durham, NC: Duke University Press.

Jarrett, R. (1993) 'Focus group interviewing with low-income minority populations: A research experience', in D. Morgan (ed.), *Successful Focus Groups: Advancing the State of the Art*. Newbury Park, CA: Sage Publications, pp. 184–201.

Kamberelis, G. and Dimitriadis, G. (2005) "Focus groups: Strategic articulations of pedagogy, politics, and inquiry', in N.K. Denzin and Y.S. Lincoln, (eds), *The Handbook of Qualitative Research*. Thousand Oaks, CA: Sage Publications. pp. 887–908.

Kincheloe, J.L. and McLaren, P. (2000). Rethinking critical theory and qualitative research', in N.K. Denzin and Y.S. Lincoln, (eds), *The Handbook of Qualitative Research*. Thousand Oaks, CA: Sage, pp. 279–314.

Kong, T.S., Mahoney, D. and Plummer, K. (2002) 'Queering the interview', in J.F. Gubrium and J.A. Holstein (eds), *Handbook of Interview Research*. Thousand Oaks: Sage, pp. 239–58.

Ladson-Billings, G. (2000) 'Racialized discourses and ethnic epistemologies', in N.K. Denzin and Y.S. Lincoln (eds), *The Handbook of Qualitative Research*. Thousand Oaks, CA: Sage, pp. 257–76.

Lather, P. (2004). This *is* your father's paradigm: Government intrusion and the case of qualitative research in education', *Qualitative Inquiry*, 10 (1), 15–34.

Lather, P. and Smithies, C. (1997) *Troubling the Angels: Women living with HIV/AIDS*. Boulder CO: Westview Press.

Lemert, C. (1997). *Postmodernism Is Not What You Think*. Boston: Blackwell.

Lincoln, Y.S. and Denzin, N.K. (2000) 'The seventh moment: Out of the past', in N.K. Denzin and Y.S. Lincoln, (eds), *The Handbook of Qualitative Research*. Thousand Oaks, CA: Sage, pp. 1047–65.

———— (2005) 'The Eighth and Ninth Moments: Qualitative Research in/and the Fractured Future', in N.K. Denzin and Y.S. Lincoln, (eds), *The Handbook of*

Qualitative Research. Thousand Oaks, CA: Sage, pp. 1115–1126.

Lopez, G.R. (1998) 'Reflections on epistemology and standpoint theories: A response to a Maori approach to creating knowledge', *International Journal of Qualitative Studies in Education*, 11: 225–31.

Madriz, E. (2000) 'Focus groups in feminist research', in N.K. Denzin and Y.S. Lincoln, (eds), *The Handbook of Qualitative Research*. Thousand Oaks, CA: Sage Publications, pp. 835–50.

———— (1997) *Nothing Bad Happens to Good Girls: The Impact of Fear of Crime on Women's Lives*. Berkeley, CA: University of California Press.

Maxwell, J.A. (2004) 'Reemergent scientism, postmodernism, and dialogue across differences', *Qualitative Inquiry*, 10 (1): 35–41.

Merton, R. and Kendall, P. (1946) 'The focused interview', *American Journal of Sociology*, 51: 541–7.

Merton, R., Fiske, M. and Kendall, P. ([1956]1990) *The Focused Interview*. Glencoe, NY: The Free Press.

Mills, C.W. (l959) *The Sociological Imagination*. New York: Oxford University Press.

Morgan, D.L. (2002) 'Focus group interviewing', in J.F. Gubrium and J.A. Holstein (eds), *Handbook of Interview Research: Context and Method*. Thousand Oaks, CA: Sage Publications, pp. 141–60.

———— (1988) *Focus Groups as Qualitative Research*. Newbury Park, CA: Sage Publications.

Nichols, L.T. (2003) 'Rethinking constructionist agency: Claimsmakers as conditions, audiences, types and symbols', *Studies in Symbolic Interaction: A Research Annual*, 26: 269–84.

Olesen, V. (2000) 'Feminisms and qualitative research at and into the millennium', in N.K. Denzin and Y.S. Lincoln, (eds), *The Handbook of Qualitative Research*. Thousand Oaks, CA: Sage Publications, pp. 215–56.

Plaut, T., Landis, S. and Trevor, J. (1993) 'Focus groups and community mobilization: A case study from rural North Carolina', in D. Morgan (ed.), *Successful Focus Groups: Advancing the State of the Art*. Newbury Park, CA: Sage Publications, pp. 202–24.

Popkewitz, T.S. (2004) 'Is the National Research Council committee's report on scientific research in education scientific? On trusting the manifesto', *Qualitative Inquiry*, 10 (1): 62–78.

Richardson, L. (2000) 'Writing: A method of inquiry', in N.K. Denzin and Y.S. Lincoln, (eds), *The Handbook of Qualitative Research*. Thousand Oaks, CA: Sage Publications, pp. 923–48.

———— (1997) *Fields of Play*. New Brunswick, NJ: Rutgers University Press.

Rosaldo, R. (1989) *Culture and Truth*. Boston: Beacon.

Ryan, K.E. and Hood, L.K. (2004) 'Guarding the castle and opening the gates', *Qualitative Inquiry*, 10 (1): 79–95.

Schwandt, T.A. (2000) 'Three Epistemological stances for qualitative inquiry', in N.K. Denzin and Y.S. Lincoln, (eds), *The Handbook of Qualitative Research*. Thousand Oaks, CA: Sage Publications, pp. 189–213.

Seale, C., Gobo, G., Gubrium, J.F. and Silverman, D. (2004) 'Introduction: Inside qualitative research', in C. Seale, G. Gobo, J.F. Gubrium and David Silverman (eds), *Qualitative Research Practice*. London: Sage, pp. 1–11.

St. Pierre, E.A. (2004) 'Refusing Alternatives: A Science of Contestation', *Qualitative Inquiry*, 10(1): 130–90.

Stewart, D.W. and Shamdasani, P.N. (1990) *Focus Groups: Theory and Practice*. Newbury Park, CA: Sage Publications.

Strauss, A. and Corbin, J. (1999) *Basics of Qualitative Research*, 2nd edn. Thousand Oaks, CA: Sage.

Teddlie, C. and Tashakkori, A. (2003) 'Major issues and controversies in the use of mixed methods in the social and behavioral sciences', in A. Tashakkori and Charles Teddlie (eds), *Handbook of Mixed Methods in Social and Behavioral Research*. Thousand Oaks, CA: Sage, pp. 3–50.

Tillman, L.C. (1998) 'Culturally specific research practices: A response to Bishop', *International Journal of Qualitative Studies in Education*, 11: 221–4.

Weinstein, M. (2004) 'Randomized design and the myth of certain knowledge: Guinea pig narratives and cultural critique', *Qualitative Inquiry*, 10 (2): 246–60.

Zeller, R.A. (1993) 'Focus group research on sensitive topics: Setting the agenda without setting the agenda', in D. Morgan (ed.), *Successful Focus Groups: Advancing the State of the Art*. Newbury Park, CA: Sage Publications, pp. 167–83.

NOTES

1. **Definitions**

Structuralism: Any system is made up of a set of oppositional categories embedded in language.

Semiotics: The science of signs of or sign systems—a structuralist project.

Poststructuralism: Language is an unstable system of referents, making it impossible to ever completely capture the meaning of an action, text or intention.

Postmodernism: A contemporary sensibility, developing since World War II, which privileges no single authority, method or paradigm.

Hermeneutics: An approach to the analysis of texts which stresses how prior understandings and prejudices shape the interpretive process.

Phenomenology: A complex system of ideas associated with the works of Husserl, Heidegger, Sartre, Merleau-Ponty and Alfred Schütz.

Cultural Studies: A complex, interdisciplinary field which merges with critical theory, feminism and poststructuralism.

2. Olesen (2000) identifies three strands of feminist research: mainstream empirical; standpoint and cultural studies; and poststructural, postmodern; placing Afrocentric and other models of color under the cultural studies and postmodern categories.

3. These are, of course, my interpretations of these paradigms and interpretive styles.

33

Making a Mess with Method[1]

John Law

INTRODUCTION

The presenting symptom is easily shown. Look at the picture and then reflect on the caption: 'If this is an awful mess ... then would something less messy make a mess of describing it?' This is a leading question. I'm looking for your agreement. Simplicity, I'm asking you to say, won't help us to understand mess.

So my topic is mess, messy worlds. I'm interested in the politics of mess. I'm interested in the process of knowing mess. I'm interested, in particular, in methodologies for knowing mess. My intuition, to say it quickly, is that the world is largely messy. It is also that contemporary social science methods are hopelessly bad at knowing that mess. Indeed it is that dominant approaches to method work with some success to repress the very *possibility* of mess. They cannot know mess, except in their aporias, as they try to make the world clean and neat. So it is my concern to broaden method, to imagine it more imaginatively. To imagine what method—and its politics—might be if it were not caught in an obsession with clarity, with specificity, and with the definite.

The argument is open-ended. I don't know where it will lead. I don't know what kind of social science it implies, or what social science inquiry might look like, methodologically or indeed institutionally. Here too, then, I find that I am at odds with method as this is usually understood. This, it seems to me, is mostly about guarantees. Sometimes I think of it as a form of hygiene. Do your methods properly. Eat your epistemological greens. Wash your hands after mixing with the real world. Then you will lead the good research life. Your data will be clean. Your findings warrantable. The product you will produce will be pure. It will come with the guarantee of a long shelf-life.

So there are lots of books about intellectual hygiene, about methodological cleanliness. There are books that offer access to the methodological uplands of social science research. No doubt there is much that is good in these texts. No doubt it is useful, indeed, to know about statistical significance, or how to avoid interviewer bias. Tips for research are always handy. But to the extent they assume hygienic form they don't really work, at least for me. In practice research needs to be messy and heterogeneous. It needs to be

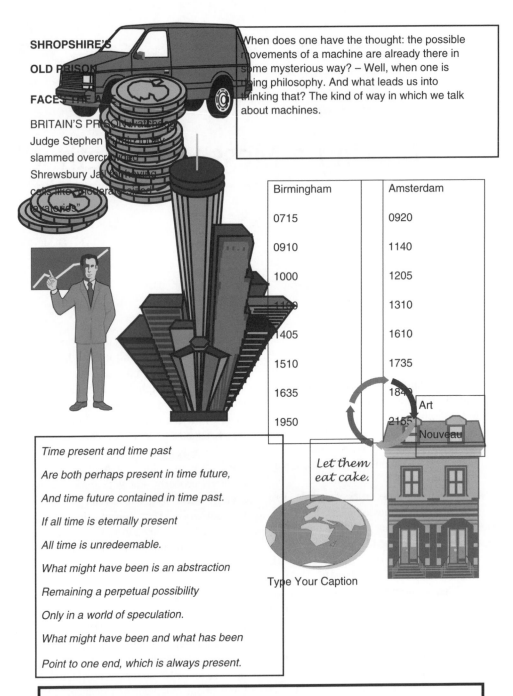

SHROPSHIRE'S

OLD PRISON

FACES THE AXE

BRITAIN'S PRISON watchdog Judge Stephen Tumim criticised slammed overcrowded Shrewsbury Jail with living cells like "moderate sized lavatories"

When does one have the thought: the possible movements of a machine are already there in some mysterious way? – Well, when one is doing philosophy. And what leads us into thinking that? The kind of way in which we talk about machines.

Birmingham	Amsterdam
0715	0920
0910	1140
1000	1205
1155	1310
1405	1610
1510	1735
1635	1845
1950	2155

Art Nouveau

Let them eat cake.

Type Your Caption

Time present and time past

Are both perhaps present in time future,

And time future contained in time past.

If all time is eternally present

All time is unredeemable.

What might have been is an abstraction

Remaining a perpetual possibility

Only in a world of speculation.

What might have been and what has been

Point to one end, which is always present.

**If this is an awful mess ...
then would something less messy make a
mess of describing it?**

messy and heterogeneous because that is the way it—research—actually is. And also, and more importantly, it needs to be messy because that is the way the largest part of the world is: messy, unknowable in a regular and routinized way. Unknowable, therefore, in ways that are definite or coherent. That is the point of the figure. Clarity doesn't help. Disciplined *lack* of clarity: now this may be what we need.

This is a big argument, and I can't make it properly in a short chapter.[2] Actually, since I live in a world without warranties, I can't make it at all, full-stop. What I can do, however, is pick at a few strands of the argument to try to give a sense of its flavor. So this is what I'll do:

- I'll start with a real research example of mess. I want to persuade you that this is a real problem, at least for me and some of my colleagues.
- Then I'll go philosophical on you, and talk a little about the common-sense realism of research and what I think this implies. What I'll try to do is to show that realism, at least in its conventional versions, has a highly prescriptive version of the nature of the real which rules that reality cannot be a mess. I beg to differ.
- Then I'll make a poststructuralist detour. I'll say that method may be understood as the simultaneous enactment of presence and absence. In poststructuralism (but also in common sense) presence by itself is impossible: presence *necessitates* absence. In research practice this suggests that some things (research findings and texts, for instance) are present but at the same time other things are being rendered absent. But what? The answer is: two *kinds* of things. First, whatever we are studying and describing, our object of research. And second, other absences that are hidden, indeed repressed. Othered.
- What does this imply for the common-sense realism of social science method? The answer, I'll suggest, is that method Others the possibility of mess. In which case the nice clear research findings which fill the journals rise from an Othered bed of confusion, paradox and imprecision. Perhaps this is fine: perhaps we *want* to Other mess. But perhaps it isn't (and this is my view). My interest, then, is in rehabilitating parts of the mess, of finding ways of living with and *knowing* confusion, and of imagining methods that live, as

Helen Verran puts it in a very different context, with disconcertment.[3]
- I'll conclude by hinting at what this might mean for research by returning to my original empirical example.

EMPIRICAL MESS

A few years ago Vicky Singleton and I were asked to investigate the way in which a local hospital trust handled patients suffering from alcoholic liver disease.[4] They thought that they weren't doing this very well, and as a part of this they were also worried about the drain on resources. In a phenomenon that they called 'the revolving door', the professionals described the way in which patients would be admitted, dried out, treated and released back into the community, only to turn up again very seriously ill in Accident and Emergency (A&E), a few weeks or months later.

We said we'd look into the organization of treatment within and beyond the hospital. Blithely, we told the consultant commissioning the research that we would map out the 'typical trajectories' of the patients as they moved through the health care system. How did they move in and out of the hospital? How did they move across the organizational divides between (for instance) the hospital trust, the community trust, general practice, and social services? When we said this we should have known that something was wrong: the ghost of a smile passed fleetingly across the consultant's face and he gently intimated that he wasn't sure that there was such a thing as a 'typical trajectory'. But we agreed to go ahead with the study on this basis anyway, and set off to interview some of the professionals: consultants, ward sisters, general practitioners, nurses and social workers.

The interviews were mostly fine, but in due course two problems began to take shape. First, it indeed proved difficult, indeed arguably more or less impossible, to map the trajectories of 'typical patients'. Often our interviewees were willing to play the game. They'd say that there was probably no such thing as a 'typical trajectory', but if there were it would, perhaps, look like this or that. But the real difficulty came when we came to try to map the different trajectories on to one another. It turned out that often they didn't, or they wouldn't. Trajectories offered by one interviewee didn't plug into trajectories suggested by another.

Here's an example. There was an alcohol advice center in the middle of the city. People were counseled there if they had an alcohol problem, and in some instances they were entered into alcoholism treatment programmes. But they could only go to the center with an appointment, and if they were sober. Some people in the hospital knew this but many didn't, imagining, for instance, that it was a drop-in center. Trajectories imagined and enacted in the hospital were inconsistent with those imagined and enacted in the advice center. There was, so to speak, no 'system'. Trajectories and movements were badly coordinated.

This is a small example (though not for those with an alcohol problem), but there were dozens of other similar instances. It is, of course, tempting to say that this is a case of bad organization, that the various bodies should simply have coordinated better. But if we look at it methodologically, another and parallel possibility emerges. This is that we were finding it impossible to map what was going on precisely because it *was* a mess. And, somewhat strangely in a way, our instinct was to ask reality to adjust itself so that it could indeed be properly mapped.

I said we encountered two problems. That was the first. The second, which dawned on us somewhat more slowly, was that we were trying to study something that was turning out to be a moving target. Actually it was becoming a shape-shifting target too. It was something like this. We had been commissioned to study the treatment of *alcoholic liver disease*: ALD as we called it. But it didn't take long before we found that we were talking about other phenomena that had something to do with ALD but weren't the same. For instance in some interviews we

found that we were talking about *liver disease* (in general, without the alcohol). Or we found that we were talking about *alcoholic cirrhosis*. Or, again, about *alcohol abuse*. Or (and this is not necessarily the same thing) about *alcoholism*. Or, indeed, sometimes about the overall *quality of life* in relation to substances including alcohol.

Here we had moments of concern that sometimes edged towards panic. What on earth, we wondered, was it that we were *actually* studying? Why couldn't we hold it still? Why did it keep on going out of focus? Why, when we were 'supposed' to be finding out about the treatment of ALD, did we end up talking about other things? These were related things perhaps, but nevertheless they were not what we were supposed to be talking about.

As you can tell from what I have just said, some of these questions were posed in a spirit of self-moralizing. Why were we such shoddy researchers? Why couldn't we get a properly focused set of interviews? Were we asking the wrong questions? Misleading the interviewees? Why did the interviewees want to talk about the wrong things? We certainly quite often felt that we were failing and weren't up to scratch. As time went on, however, we started to be kinder to ourselves. This is because it started to dawn on us that the object we were studying might be a shape-shifting reality. Textbooks are able distinguish nicely between (say) cirrhosis of the liver caused by alcohol and alcoholism 'in general', which includes a whole range of other symptoms (but, by the way, those who abuse alcohol do not necessarily suffer from cirrhosis). It is in theory—and sometimes in practice—possible to make distinctions between the various relevant entities, and then to relate them together. But maybe, we slowly came to believe, it wasn't actually like that in reality. Maybe we were dealing with a slippery phenomenon, one that changed its shape, and was fuzzy around the edges. Maybe we were dealing with something that wasn't definite and didn't have a single form. Perhaps it was a fluid object, or even one that was ephemeral in any given form, flipping from one configuration to another, dancing like a flame.[5]

To sum up, we'd made two discoveries. One was that there did not appear to be a way of mapping this part of the healthcare system in a consistent and coherent way. And the other was that it wasn't easy to pin down the object of study and make it unambiguous and clear. In addition, in the face of this vagueness, we'd also uncovered two possible responses. The first was methodological moralizing: that things *should* be clear, either because they needed to be put right, or because they really were clear all along and our methods weren't understanding them. And the second, which is where we ended up, was that things are at least sometimes vague and can only be known vaguely.

What to do about this? I'll put the question on hold while I talk a little about realism.

REALISM

I have neither the space nor the expertise to offer a well-developed critique of philosophical realism. My interest is much more pragmatic. I want to unearth what I take to be certain more or less common-sense realist assumptions that inform both a good deal (no doubt not all) of natural and social science research, and *talk* about natural and social science method by more or less professional methodologists. In particular, I want to be a little clearer about what it is that we are buying into when we think about 'reality' and talk about things 'out-there' in our research reports. I'm interested, in short, about what it is that counts as 'out-thereness': its form or forms.

In order to make progress quickly, I will offer a number of different versions of out-thereness in the form of a brief and more or less dogmatic list, and offer comments on each.[6]

1. I'm going to call the first version of out-thereness *primitive out-thereness*. Here the claim is very simple. In Euro-America, most research, and no doubt most of life, seems to be organized around the intimation that there is indeed a reality out-there and beyond ourselves. That is all. Nothing more. All I want to say about this (apart from noting that I buy into this myself both in research and in everyday life) is that this isn't saying very much. Certainly it isn't, by itself, very specific. This is the important point. It doesn't commit us to anything very definite about the character of out-thereness. So what might be added that would make it more definite? That would specify it? That actually specifies it in most research practice?

2. I think that most of the time Euro-American common-sense realism assumes that whatever is out-there is substantially *independent* of our actions and especially of our perceptions. (I say 'substantially' because it is, of course, also obvious that sometimes our actions and maybe even our perceptions make a difference, but right now I'm interested in the general case—what critical realists would call the 'intransitive'.) I will call this, then, a commitment to independence. Note that this is *not* the same as primitive out-thereness. In principle a reality might be out there, but not independent of our actions or our knowledge of it: parts of quantum mechanics certainly work on that assumption, as does poststructuralist metaphysics. Parts of social theory also note the performative character of parts of social science.

3. I also want to add what I will call *anteriority* to the list. This is the sense that whatever is real out-there in general precedes any attempt to know it. (Again one can think of exceptions.) Like independence, this is not entailed in a primitive commitment to out-thereness. It is a possible specification of it, yes, but one can be committed to primitive out-thereness without being committed to anteriority. No doubt this is the basis for some versions of philosophical idealism.

4. Then there is *definiteness*. Perhaps more than anything else, this is what we were wrestling with in our study of alcoholic liver disease. We thought we should be writing about something definite because we thought it was our duty to represent something that was indeed definite. But this is a specific metaphysical commitment rather than something that has to be so. It is certainly not entailed in primitive out-thereness. So it might, instead, be assumed that whatever is out-there is often (or always) vague, diffuse, uncertain, elusive and/or undecided. But the common-sense realism of social science doesn't readily entertain the possibility. If findings are vague then it isn't reality that is vague, but those doing the research. They've failed.

5. And finally I want to add what I will call *singularity*. Here the sense, the assumption and the commitment are that the world is a single reality that is more or less shared, held in common. This is a more or less standard plug-in in common-sense social science realism, but once again it is not implied in primitive realism. So it is possible to entertain the possibility that there are different and not necessarily consistent realities. I need to be clear about what is at stake here. This is not an argument that there are different *perspectives* on (a single) reality. We all know that this is possible. It is not, in other words, an argument about epistemology—about how to see (a single) reality. Instead it is about ontology, about what is real, what is out there. Most Euro-American metaphysics works on the assumption that there is a single reality. Different perspectives, but a single reality. I suspect that even the social worlds' literatures work that way. The assumption is that while we may live in multiple social worlds' we live in a single natural or material reality. But, as philosopher Annemarie Mol has shown in *The Body Multiple* (2002), it does not have to be that way.

Let's review the list. We've got five versions or possible features of a common-sense realist metaphysics of out-thereness (one could add more, but this will do): the *primitive* sense that there is something out-there; and then, more specifically, that whatever is out-there is *independent*, *prior*, *definite* and *singular*. My sense is that most of the time most of us work in practice around and through this metaphysics. I also think that this sets the conditions of possibility for most natural-and—more important in this context—social science research. Finally, it seems plausible to suggest that contemporary philosophical realism is a sophisticated expression of these sentiments in a reflexive and self-conscious world where it is a commonplace that uncontexted foundational knowledge is a will-o'-the-wisp, and social knowledge alters its objects of study. But that is by the way. Because the list also suggests

1. that we can be primitive realists without necessarily committing ourselves to the package deal. Contrary to our first instincts, realism doesn't have to come as a single tightly specified package.

2. that it could be very interesting, to put it no higher, to pick through the list and wonder when, where, why and whether any particular commitment is appropriate or useful.
3. that most of what we think of as 'research methods' in social science involve a commitment to the full package. In practice, research methods don't buy into realism à la carte. It is the full set menu, or nothing. And as you can tell, I think this ought to change.

THE POSTSTRUCTURALIST DETOUR

For me a poststructuralist detour is not a detour but an obligatory point of passage. This is because it helps us to think about the so-called 'metaphysics of presence'. I'm not going to follow Derrida closely here but I don't need to. What I need is an argument that is simple—indeed almost embarrassingly so, as are, indeed, its consequences for social science. The argument runs as follows:

As we seek to know the world not everything can be brought to presence. However much we want to be comprehensive, to know something fully, to document or to represent it, we *will* fail. This is not a matter of technical inadequacy. (There are always, of course, technical inadequacies.) Rather it is because bringing to presence is *necessarily* incomplete because if things are made present (representations of the world, for instance) then at the same time things *are also being made absent* (the world 'itself'). Necessarily. The two go together. It cannot be otherwise. Presence *implies* absence.

This is not a complaint: it is how it is. So what's the problem? One answer is that it's a problem when we *imagine* or *pretend* that everything can be made present and known by the all-knowing subject, the all-seeing eye, or the all-representing database. This can only be a pretence because, as I've just said, the knowable is dependent on, related to, and produced with the unknowable: that which is elsewhere and absent. So the problem does not have to do with the attempt to know. There are many reasons for trying to know in one way or another. Rather it lies in the failure (or refusal) to understand the logic, the character and the politics of the project of knowing. It lies in the failure to think through what is implied by the fact that knowing is constitutively incomplete.

There are three points I would like to tease out of this:

- First, in a metaphysics of presence, Othering, making absent, repressing and making unrepresentability are all *repressed* in what amounts to a politics of systematic exclusion. The problem is not exclusion as such. As I have just noted, Othering is always implied in making present. Rather it is about the *denial* of that exclusion. It is the refusal to acknowledge that this is going on, except perhaps in the most practical, technical sense. It is the refusal to recognize what is sometimes (though in a different register) called 'invisible work'.
- Second, and as an aspect of this, the fact that practice is *productive* also disappears. The productivity of practice is crucial to my argument. This is because the great representational trick of a metaphysics of presence, at least in the context of natural and social science, is to attribute its present representations to an absent reality that is *pre-given*. Reality determines representation. The common-sense realism of natural and social science assumes that its representations are warranted in one way or another by special reporting rights on that reality. Good method creates a reliable representational conduit from reality to depiction. It is a one-way street. Nature is made to speak for itself, end of story. But this is a sleight of hand. This is because *realities are being done alongside representations of realities.*[7] It follows that anteriority and independence do not hold. Instead realities are being *enacted* with more or less difficulty into being. Here, then, we have a version of the turn to performance.
- So then we get to the crucial question. *Which* realities? This is the crucial question because it is also *political* in character. Here is the opening. Realities are not fixed in concrete. It is not simply a matter of reporting them. Instead they might be otherwise. With difficulty, yes. No-one is saying they can be invented at whim. Nevertheless, we find ourselves with a new possibility, in the domain of an ontological politics.[8]

How does the poststructuralist critique of a metaphysics of presence fit with the various versions of realism? The answer is that it is entirely consistent with primitive realism. Actually, putting it this way is too weak. An argument about absence–presence is precisely a version of primitive realism. It is an articulation thereof. In this way of thinking, *of course* there is out-thereness as well as inhereness. If we are engaged in representation at all, then that is how it has to be. Presence implies absence. But what of the other parts of the common-sense realism package? The answer is: they don't fit very well. I'll repeat myself a little in order to make the list.

- Is out-thereness *independent*? The answer is: no, at least not in any simple way. If making present means making absent, then whatever is out-there is also being done, though not (I need to add again) arbitrarily. It may take a lot of effort. An absent 'hinterland' has to be crafted.[9] Some representations and realities may turn out to be undoable. But it *is* nevertheless being made.
- Is out-thereness *prior*? Again the answer is no, and for the same reasons. Not obviously. Particular realities-as-absences are made at the same time as representations-as-presences. (Scientific truths, let us remind ourselves, exist only in rarefied and rather special environments.)[10]
- Is out-thereness *definite*? The answer is: not necessarily. Perhaps it can be *made* definite—after all, some representational practices produce definiteness. But there is no particular reason to think that out-thereness is in general either definite or indefinite.
- Is out-thereness *singular*? Is there only one of it? Again, and finally, there is no particular reason to think so. Sometimes it is made singular in practice. But since there are many practices and many methods it is probably better to assume that there are multiple and more or less different out-therenesses. This is what Mol calls 'the problem of difference'. Note again that to say this is not to say that anything goes. It is *not* a relativist argument. No doubt the 'hinterlands' of different out-therenesses overlap and interfere with one another. No doubt they often have to be coordinated or held apart. No doubt (and we all experience this) making them is extremely hard work, particularly if we would like to make them differently.

In sum, if we take on board a poststructuralist critique of the metaphysics of presence, then we drive a coach-and-horses through the standard package of common-sense realism.

Realities *can* be made independent, prior, definite and singular, but that is because they are being *made* that way. It could be otherwise. Actually it is worse than that. If they are being made that way, then it is because the alternative—that they might be dependent, simultaneous, indefinite and/or multiple—is also being systematically Othered.

THINGS THAT DON'T QUITE FIT

If absence is made together with presence, then different forms of absence are made with different forms of presence. But now I want to distinguish two senses or versions of absence. Call these *manifest absence* and *Otherness. Manifest absence* would be what presence acknowledges or makes manifest. If Singleton and I describe the treatment of a patient with ALD in a ward—or a ward sister describes this to us—then that treatment is being made manifest. It is absent but explicit, a manifest absence. *Otherness* is absence that is not acknowledged. Here the list is endless. Indeed (the point is a logical one) Otherness cannot be brought to presence and listed. But we can hint, or we can look at other practices and notice out-therenesses that they don't acknowledge. Such, indeed, is the standard procedure of critical social science. It works to manifest what were Othernesses, and then to complain that they were inappropriately or unjustly Othered. What I am doing does not, of course, escape this logic.

Nevertheless we can imagine different styles of Othering:

- There is the *invisible work* that helps to make a research report.
- There is the *uninteresting:* everything that seems to be not worth telling.
- There is the *obvious*, things that everyone is taken to know.
- And then, to ratchet up the metaphor and what is at stake, there is everything that is for one reason or another being *repressed.*

Stick with repression. What is being repressed? Well, we don't know, do we? Not very well! But here is one suggestion. In much social science writing *everything that fails to fit the standard package of common-sense realism is being repressed*—everything that is not independent, prior, definite and singular.

We have reached the core of my argument. Predominantly, I want to say, our research methods work to Other that which does not fit a metaphysics of common-sense realism. It does this (a stronger claim still) *even as it depends on that Outhering.* The argument can be illustrated empirically, but it is also logical. Independence depends on lack of independence. Anteriority depends on simultaneity. The definite depends on the vague. And the singular depends on the multiple. Both are there. Both are always there. The only question is this: how do we choose to handle them?

Perhaps we can see it as a matter of policing, of how the border between the two forms of absence as manifest, and how absence as Otherness is or should be regulated. Here are two questions that arise:

- First step: do we *acknowledge* that there is a border: that inconsistent things are being Othered? Or do we prefer to police our methods to *repress* that possibility, to Other it? Common-sense realism tends to the latter. This is its version of the limits to the conditions of possibility.
- Second step: how do we *regulate* the traffic across the border? Do we do it knowingly or unknowingly? Let's be clear. We will always do the latter. This is built into the iron logic of Othering. Most of the policing will be unwitting. So the question is: what should or would we like to try to regulate more knowingly? What would we like to try to make manifest?

I think you can see where I am going. If I switch back to the alcoholic liver disease study, we can now see that we were floundering around about whether or not to police the border between the manifest and the Othered, using the assumptions of common-sense realism. If things seemed vague or multiple, perhaps this was bad research? That's the policing policy of common-sense realism and the larger part of social science method. Let's repress the mess: that is the policy. Let's

Other it. So in our study we tried quite hard to enact this policy, to work within the package of common-sense realism, and to police and re-enact the border. But we found it was just too difficult. We found we couldn't make a story of a clear clean single reality and actual reality match. A coherent object, a consistent set of trajectories, or a single condition? No! Our failing? Yes, if we buy into the standard package. No, if we don't. And in the end, as I've noted, we didn't. We stopped policing the borderlands of Otherness as defined in the standard realist package. We came to believe and argue instead that this was a reality that was multiple, slippery and fuzzy. Indefinite.

But, it turns out, this is not a very good research strategy in practice. Why? The answer is that the politics of research doesn't work that way. There is a lot at stake, a lot of investment, in holding the border between the manifest and the Othered steady, in re-enacting the Othering of the indefinite, the multiple, and all the rest. It is possible to make this argument by turning it into a critique of the institutions of social science. In my experience conference organizers, journal editors and referees, and grant-giving bodies all tend to buy into the full package of common-sense realism. They don't much care for the vague, the imprecise, the multiple. These become technical flaws and failings, signs of methodological inadequacy. But though we can complain about the institutions that Other research metaphysics that don't reproduce the common-sense realisms, more interesting is a larger question. What would it be to practice a research metaphysics that did not do so? How *would* one represent the vague, the multiple and all the rest? The interest in this question is in part that it doesn't offer a ready answer. But here are some thoughts.

Within the conventions of the academy, the moment we set pen to paper we are being caught up in arrangements that reproduce the metaphysics of the full realist package. As those who work with performance have argued, it is partly a matter of textuality. *Can* the ephemeral or the elusive be translated into and made present in textual form? Well,

possibly so, but possibly not. It's a matter for debate, isn't it? And the answer is bound to be: it depends.

But if it is a question of textuality *tout court*, then it is also a matter of the *forms* of textuality. As is obvious, the academic conventions of writing push us into reproducing versions of common-sense realism. Notwithstanding the aporias it is difficult to remake the real—whatever is out-there—in ways that do not re-enact its singularity, its anteriority, its independence and its definiteness. So where else to look? Straws in the wind. Poetry doesn't depend or produce a manifest out-thereness. There is no premium on singularity. Its warrant is different. So it is, too, with the novel. I guess that the realities these manifest—if indeed they may be said to do so at all—are 'imaginary'. So we read novels or poetry for other reasons, but not as reports about the state of the world, about out-thereness. So we might ask: should there be space for poetry within social science? Or novels, short stories? I don't know where I stand on this. Or, more to the point, I don't think it makes much sense to take a general stand at all. Sometimes. This surely is the most plausible answer if we want to nibble round the edges of common-sense realism. So let me end, instead, by suggesting that we might think more about the possibilities of allegory.

So what *is* allegory? Here's a quick and dirty set of suggestions. Allegory is the art of meaning something other than, or in addition to, what is being said. It is the art of decoding meaning, of reading between the literal lines, to understand something else or more. It is the craft of making several not necessarily very consistent things at once. It is the art of crafting multiplicities, indefinitenesses, undecidabilities. Of holding them together. Of relaxing the border controls that secure singularity[11].

Allegory might not come in the form of text. But then again, it might. Listen, then, to this:

Finding the door is difficult enough. In a terrace, between two cheap store-fronts in a run-down part of Sandside. The kind of street only three blocks from the big store that doesn't make it.

That doesn't make it at all. That smells of poverty. That speaks of hopelessness.

It is a nondescript door. Unwelcoming. A tiny spy glass. An inconspicuous notice. Nothing very obvious. Nothing very appealing. We are ringing the door-bell. Is anyone listening? Has anyone heard? Dimly we hear the sound of footsteps. We sense that we are being looked at through the spy glass. Checking us out. And then the door opens. And we're being welcomed through the door by a middle-aged woman. To find that there isn't a proper lobby. Instead, we're facing a flight of stairs. Carpeted, cheaply. Yes, shoddily.

So we've been admitted. We are, yes, Vicky Singleton and John Law from Lancaster University. And now, we're being led up a flight of stairs. And the building is starting to make an impression. An impression of make-do. Of scarce resources. Of inadequacy. For we're being told people have to come up all those flights of stairs. Some of them can hardly walk through drink. And some can hardly walk, full-stop. Up this long flight of stairs. For we're in the kind of Victorian building where the rooms on the ground floor are twelve feet high. Big fancy three-story houses. Built at a time of optimism. At a time of some kind of prosperity. Which, however, has now drained away.

So the clients need to negotiate these stairs, turn around the half landing, up a further short flight, and then they are on the first floor. Next to the room that is the general office, library, meeting room, leaflet dispensary, the place with the filing cabinets, the tables, the chairs. People are milling about. At the moment no clients, but a researcher who is smoking. Several social workers, the manager, community psychiatric nurses coming and going.

The leaflets and the papers are spilling over everything. Brown cardboard boxes. Half drunk mugs of coffee. New mugs of coffee for us. Clearing a bit of space. Not too much. There isn't too much space. Files and pamphlets are pushed to one side. Two more chairs. And the numbers in the room keep on changing as clients arrive, or people go out on call, or the phone rings. One client hasn't turned up. Relief at this. The pressure is so great. And then there's another with alcohol on his breath. A bad sign.

The staff are so keen to talk. Keen to tell us about their work. Keen to talk about its frustrations and its complexities.

What to make of this? Here is the suggestion (and I thank Vicky Singleton for letting me use our joint work here): that this building, and this account of it, can both be imagined as an allegory of health care for patients with alcoholic liver disease. What is happening? The answer, I think, is that organizational multiplicity (together with inadequate resources) are being brought to presence in this run-down building and the events within it. An alcohol advice center up a long flight of stairs? An incoherence. No meeting room? Another incoherence. The fact that those working here work for several different organizations with different charters and conditions of work? A not-very coherent multiplicity. The chaos of leaflets from twenty-plus sources? A further multiplicity enacting a criss-crossing plethora of locations, organizations, facilities and policies that don't quite fit together. The argument is that the building brings to presence an out-there that is multiple, vague, shifting and non-coherent. It may be read—it needs to be read—in different ways. These cannot be summed up, caught, or made neat and tidy.

Here then, both in the building and in our text, we are helping to make manifest a real that is not definite or singular. (Neither is it independent or anterior.) It *is* real, but it doesn't fit the package deal of common-sense realism. We could try to pretend that it does. But my conclusion, our conclusion, is that if we do so we are missing out. The argument, of course, is that it is better, instead, to find ways of enacting non-coherence. Notice this: it is not necessarily *in*coherence that's being done here either. Incoherence is a common-sense realist way of putting down something that doesn't fit the standard package. (This is the problem of talking about 'mess': as Lucy Suchman notes, this is a put-down used by those who are obsessed with making things tidy.) My preference, rather, is to relax the border controls, allow the non-coherences to make themselves manifest. Or rather, it is to start to think about ways in which we might go about this.

And the reason that I feel passionate about this is quite simple. It is not just a matter of the politics of research (though this is important). It is also a matter of the politics of reality. I've tried to argue that the making of what we know in-here goes along with the making of what there is out-there: that our methods are performative[12]. So it is, for me, a point that is simultaneously a matter to do with method, politics, ethics and inspiration. Realities are not flat. They are not consistent, coherent and definite. Our research methods necessarily fail. Aporias are ubiquitous. But it is time to move on from the long rearguard action which insists that reality is definite and singular. The long rearguard action was conducted in many locations including what counts as good social science method. 'There is more in heaven and earth, Horatio, than is dreamed of in your philosophy.' We need new philosophies, new disciplines of research. We need to understand that our methods are always more or less unruly assemblages.

REFERENCES

Barad, Karen (1999) 'Agential realism: Feminist interventions in understanding scientific practices', in Mario Biagioli (ed.), *The Science Studies Reader*. New York: Routledge.

Benjamin, Walter (1999) *The Arcades Project*, trans. Harry Zohn. Cambridge, MA/London: Harvard University Press.

Callon, Michel (ed.) (1998) *The Laws of the Markets*. Oxford: Blackwell and the Sociological Review.

de Laet, Marianne, and Mol, Annemarie (2000), 'The Zimbabwe bush pump: Mechanics of a fluid technology', *Social Studies of Science*, 30 (2): 225–63.

Hacking, Ian (1992) 'The self-vindication of the laboratory sciences', in Andrew Pickering (ed.), *Science as Practice and Culture*, Chicago and London: University of Chicago Press, pp. 29–64.

Haraway, Donna (1991a) 'A cyborg manifesto: Science, technology and socialist feminism in the late twentieth century', in Donna Haraway (ed.), *Simians, Cyborgs and Women: the Reinvention of Nature*. London: Free Association Books, pp. 149–81.

——— (1991b) 'Situated knowledges: The science question in feminism and the privilege of partial perspective', in Donna Haraway (ed.), *Simians, Cyborgs and Women: the Reinvention of Nature*. London: Free Association Books, pp. 183–201

——— (1997) *Modest_Witness@Second_Millennium. Female Man©_Meets_Oncomouse™: Feminism and Technoscience*. New York and London: Routledge.

Latour, Bruno (1987) *Science in Action: How to Follow Scientists and Engineers Through Society*. Cambridge, MA: Harvard University Press.

Latour, Bruno and Woolgar, Steve ([1979] 1986) *Laboratory Life: the Construction of Scientific Facts*. Princeton, NJ: Princeton University Press.

Law, John (1998) 'After Metanarrative: On Knowing in Tension', in Robert Chia (ed.) *Into the Realm of Organization: Essays for Robert Cooper*. London: Routledge.

——— (2002) *Aircraft Stories: Decentering the Object in Technoscience*. Durham, NC: Duke University Press.

——— (2004) *After Method: Mess in Social Science Research*. London: Routledge.

Law, John, and Mol, Annemarie (2001) 'Situating technoscience: An inquiry into spatialities', *Society and Space*, 19: 609–21.

Law, John, and Singleton, Vicky (2003) 'Allegory and its Others', in Davide Nicolini, Silvia Gherardi and Dvora Yanow (eds.), *Knowing in Organizations: A Practice Based Approach*. New York: M.E. Sharpe, pp. 225–54.

——— (2005) 'Object lessons', *Organization*, 12 (3): 331–55.

MacKenzie, Donald (2003) 'An equation and its worlds: Bricolage, exemplars, disunity and performativity in financial economics', *Social Studies of Science*, 33: 831–68.

Mol, Annemarie (1999) 'Ontological politics: A word and some questions', in John Law and John Hassard (eds.), *Actor Network Theory and After*. Oxford and Keele: Blackwell and the Sociological Review, pp. 74–89.

——— (2002) *The Body Multiple: Ontology in Medical Practice*. Durham, NC/London: Duke University Press.

Moser, Ingunn (2000) 'Against normalisation: Subverting norms of ability and disability', *Science as Culture*, 9 (2): 201–40.

Osborne, Thomas, and Rose, Nikolas (1999) 'Do the social sciences create phenomena?: The example of public opinion research', *British Journal of Sociology*, 50: 367–96.

Pickering, Andrew (1993) 'The mangle of practice: Agency and emergence in the sociology of science', *American Journal of Sociology*, 99: 559–89.

Porter, Theodore M. (1995) *Trust in Numbers: the Pursuit of Objectivity in Science and Public Life*. Princeton, NJ: Princeton University Press.

Singleton, Vicky (2005) 'The promise of public health: Vulnerable policy and lazy citizens', *Society and Space*, 23 (5): 771–86.

Verran, Helen (1998) 'Re-Imagining land ownership in Australia', *Postcolonial Studies*, 1 (2): 237–54.

——— (2001) *Science and an African Logic*. Chicago: University of Chicago Press.

NOTES

1 This paper arises out of conversations with Andrew Barry, Michel Callon, Kevin Hetherington, Annemarie Mol, Ingunn Moser, Vicky Singleton, Lucy Suchman, John Urry and Helen Verran. I am grateful

to them all, and in particular to Vicky Singleton for allowing me to use material from our joint work. I am also grateful to John Holm and Laura Watts for sharing some of the same obsessions in their Ph.D. work!

2 The argument is developed more extensively in Law (2004).

3 See Verran (2001).

4 Our findings are more fully explored in Law and Singleton (2003; 2005).

5 There is a small literature in the discipline of science, technology and society (STS), on topologically complex objects. See de Laet and Mol (2000); Law and Mol (2001); and Law and Singleton (2005).

6 Again this list is discussed more fully in Law (2004).

7 In STS the classic study which works this out is Latour and Woolgar (1986). It is developed in another version in the work of Donna Haraway. See Haraway (1991a; 1991b; 1997). The implications of this position for multiplicity and singularity are explored at length in Mol (2002). For related arguments in somewhat different idioms, see Hacking (1992); Pickering (1993); Verran (2001) and Barad (1999).

8 All the writers in note 7 work, in one way or other, in ontological politics. Perhaps this is clearest for Haraway, Mol and Verran. See in addition, Verran (1998); Mol (1999); Moser (2000); Law (2002) and Singleton (2005).

9 The notion of the hinterland is discussed in Law (2004: 27ff).

10 This is the point of some of the work in early versions of ANT (Actor-Network Society). See, for instance, Latour (1987).

11 This, to be sure, is a particular understanding of allegory, which, I am happy to see, is slowly being rehabilitated. Walter Benjamin is, surely, the most prominent social science allegorist. See Benjamin (1999). But I read much of Donna Haraway's writing with its talk about split vision as (her term, I think) ironic play, or allegory. And I have dabbled on knowing in tension, too. See Law (1998).

12 For the performativity of social science see, *inter alia*, Osborne and Rose (1999); Callon (1998); Porter (1995); and MacKenzie (2003).

Index